A History of Food

A History of Food

by

Maguelonne Toussaint-Samat

Translated from the French

by

Anthea Bell

6933

B

BLACKWELL
Reference

Original French text copyright © Bordas, 1987
English translation copyright © Basil Blackwell, 1992

French text first published 1987
English translation first published 1992
English translation first published in USA 1992

Blackwell Publishers
238 Main Street, Suite 501
Cambridge, MA 02142
USA

108 Cowley Road
Oxford OX4 1JF
UK

British Library Cataloguing in Publication Data
A CIP catalogue record for this book
is available from the British Library.

Library of Congress Cataloging-in-Publication Data
Toussaint-Samat, Maguelonne, 1926–
[Histoire naturelle & morale de la nourriture. English]
A history of food / by Maguelonne Toussaint-Samat; translated
from the French by Anthea Bell.
Translation of: Histoire naturelle & morale de la nourriture.
Includes bibliographical references and index.
ISBN 0–631–17741–8
1. Nutrition—Social aspects—History.   2. Food—History.   3. Food
supply—History.   I. Title.
TX353. T6413   1992
363.8'09—dc20   92–13999
                                                                    CIP

ISBN 0–631–17741–8

Typeset in 11/13pt Garamond
by Selwood Systems, Midsomer Norton
Printed in the United States of America by Maple-Vail Manufacturing Group

Tibi pauca meae...

The genius of love and the genius of hunger, those twin brothers, are the two moving forces behind all living things. All living things set themselves in motion to feed and to reproduce. Love and hunger share the same purpose. Life must never cease; life must be sustained and must create.

Turgenev, *Little poems in prose*, XXIII.

L'angoisse de la faim qui toujours hurle et gronde
Est le ressort puissant jouant au coeur du monde,
Et celui qui dévore est l'élu du destin.

[The fear of hunger, ever roaring and growling, is the powerful spring quivering at the heart of the world, and he who eats is the chosen one of Fate.]

Daniel Lesueur, *Poésies*, 'La lutte pour l'existence'.

'After thirty years of war and occupation, our dietary customs are the only tangible signs that we still exist as a people,' a Vietnamese has said.

The family meal, provided by the father and prepared by the mother, remains the essential bond, a bond in which the child sees the realization of those images of mother and father without which human beings have no internal stability, and a society ceases to build a civilization. The proud and ancient history of those craft industries which created our cheeses, wines and charcuterie must not be forgotten in the name of a sometimes dubious and vacillating science...

J. Trémolière, *Encyclopaedia Universalis*, vol. I.

Contents

CONTENTS

CONTENTS

CONTENTS

CONTENTS

CONTENTS

CONTENTS

Foreword

Turgenev invoked the genius of hunger.

From time immemorial, the human race has explored the world in search of food. Hunger has been the force behind its onward march. Hunger is still the source of mankind's energies, good or bad, the reason for its advance, the origin of its conflicts, the justification of its conscience and the currency of its labours.

Empires have done battle for food, civilizations have been built around it, crimes committed, laws made and knowledge exchanged.

The rest is only literature.

The practice of hunting and gathering, the consumption of salt and cereals, the discovery of stock-breeding and wine, the use of spices, sugar, potatoes, proteins, have all been stages along the way, each in turn shaking the known world to its foundations.

Acknowledgements

I would like to express my gratitude to all the people who have helped me with their advice, information, skills, and belief in this *History of Food*. In particular, I want to thank Professor Jean-Louis Flandrin, one of my directors of studies at the École des Hautes Études en Sciences Sociales, whose outstanding works on the evolution of culinary practices and taste in Europe have opened so many doors to me.

Rendering to Caesar the things which are Caesar's, I owe grateful thanks to my friends at the Séminaire Flandrin for their contributions and the information they provided from their own researches: Jeanne Cobbi with her expert knowledge of the pre-Renaissance gastronomy of Moorish Spain; Elisabeth Deshayes, who can conjure up the cookery of the seventeenth century; Mary and Philip Hyman, living archives of the culinary literature of the past; Bruno Laurioux, that great expert on spices, who so generously gave me access to the body of his work; Françoise Sabban, the most delightful of distinguished Sinologists, without whom Chinese dietary traditions would have been – not Greek, but Chinese to me. Nor of course must I forget Odile Redon of the CNRS, who as *maître assistant* at Paris VIII was my kind and skilful mentor in matters of medieval Italian cookery. Nor the patience and tolerance of Christiane Klappish, my director of studies at the EHESS, who was always an example to me.

Thanks too to my friend Monique Mosser of the CNRS, with whom I entered the garden of the Age of Enlightenment, and to Marie-Mechtilde Ilboudo, my sister among the Mossi people.

My thanks to Marie-Claude de Labbey, the efficient manager of the press department at the SOPEXA, to Guy Fauconneau, scientific director of the Industries Alimentaires et Agronomiques of the INRA; the Comité Interprofessionel de la Conchyliculture; Chantal Delanoë, press officer at the Maison du Miel; Didier Hadès, of France-Inter; Mme Ogino, of the Japanese Embassy in Paris; Mr Wilson, of the United States Embassy in Paris; Mr Defilhoux, agricultural officer at the

ACKNOWLEDGEMENTS

Australian Embassy in Paris; Christian Pétrossian; the Comité des Salines de France; Nicole Sourice of the Centre Interprofessionel de Documents et d'Informations Laitières; the Centre d'Études et de Documentation du Sucre; Marcel Paul-Emile of the FAO in Abidjan; the Comité Central des Pêches Maritimes; Jacques Cadoret, oyster farmer, of Riec-sur-Belon.

Thanks to my son, Thierry Alberny, whose inexhaustible memory was a great help in my search for quotations; thanks to Josiane Roy, the only person able to read my handwritten manuscript and type it both kindly and impeccably; thanks to Ruth Abergel for her help with logistics, and to Nysa, for all she meant to me during the long gestation of this book, and for helping me to bring order out of chaos...

Above all, so many of my thoughts go to my mother Renée Vally-Samat, my first reader, who criticized me (not enough) and encouraged me (so much) in this work of long scholarship, and did not close her eyes until I had written the last line.

But of course, more than ever, these pages are a little of myself for you, Ted, and in your memory.

M.T.-S.

List of Illustrations

LIST OF ILLUSTRATIONS

Introduction

Some 60 million years ago, at the beginning of the Tertiary period, a rather unimpressive tree-dwelling creature realized that it could feed itself more conveniently by using the ends of its front limbs to pick up anything that seemed edible and convey the food to its mouth. Thereafter this creature differed from other animals, which still plunged their muzzles into their food. It even ventured to take advantage of daylight to gather food more easily, instead of preferring the cover of darkness in its old way.

The subtlety of a mentally coordinated manipulation had come between the food to be eaten and the reflex of the open mouth. The animal, now able to adjust its gestures to the rhythm of its appetite, became aware of a chain of sensations: the stimulus of hunger, the excitement of gathering food, the satisfaction of appetite.

Eating, at first a purely visceral pleasure, became an intellectual process when the eyes, which had been laterally placed, moved towards the base of the forehead. Over the last few million years the forehead itself had been getting bigger, in line with the increased size of the skull. The brain, improving as it gained volume, was able to control vision in a larger, panoramic area, now seen in relief and in depth. Physically, the animal entered another dimension, and mentally too it stood erect. Its new possibilities of vision, together with the prehensile skill of its specialized hands, encouraged it to explore its environment more thoroughly in search of food.

The creature's memory had registered a large potential choice, but certain items turned out to taste better than others and give more pleasure. The pleasure was enjoyed and remembered. The creature wanted to experience it again. That unforgettable sensation stimulated curiosity and courage, impelled the creature to make further experiments, and eventually developed its intelligence, which itself was constantly being fed with new information.

The delightful sensation of satisfying hunger gave the biped such pleasure that

1

after several million more years or generations it was moved to express it in a cry. Not just any cry: a special one. Not a mere grunt either, but an articulated sound, a smacking of the satisfied lips and tongue, accompanied by a sigh. Pre-dating the concept of language, it came to mean a number of things in every idiom of the world: 'eat/drink'; 'the maternal breast'; 'mother'; 'survival'; 'life'; 'good'. The phoneme *mem* or *mam* was the first human discourse; the first word. Babies still utter it. Its message must of course be deciphered, having become weakened and modified as it echoed down the centuries. The phoneme *mem*, *ma*, becoming the root *bo* with its variations of pronunciation as *ouo*, *wo*, *pho*, *po*, *ba*, *pa*, *bi*, etc., implies not only the act of swallowing, eating or drinking, the sound of which is imitated by the smacking of the lips, but also the potential meanings of *food*, *plant*, and their corollary, *life*.

In the common heritage of the Indo-European languages, from which Sanskrit, the languages of India, Greek, the Germanic, Romance, Celtic, Slavonic and Iranian languages and their derivatives all arose, the ultimate sense of the vocable 'botany' is therefore 'those plants one must eat to live'.

A paleontologist can tell us what our ancestors of the Quaternary era ate from studying the traces of wear left by abrasive food particles on their dental enamel. The canines and incisors are very small by comparison with the large molars and premolars – the sign of adaptation to much mastication of vegetable matter which had to be well crushed before it was swallowed – and the traces of wear and tear on the teeth also show that vegetable fibres were eaten. However, atavistic and collective human memory, which we might usefully consult more often, itself tells us with all the clarity of language that plants were indeed our first food, the basic element of humanity: a memory, perhaps, of the abundant foliage of the primeval tree.

According to Heidegger's definition, it was in order to 'say' such things (*sagen*) that the ability to 'speak' (*sprechen*) was invented. The telling of the story of food had begun, in tones of gluttony.

Gluttony is a mutation: an aberration of a need which it ends up by controlling completely. We have to be very hungry indeed for all our conditioning to be negated by the sheer will to survive. Even the more highly evolved animals can be fussy over their food, and greedy, particularly when they are domesticated and have been corrupted by human company.

Scientific deductions, and methodical investigation of the debris left by our distant ancestors on their camp sites, have enabled us to discover by stages what they ate in as much detail as if they had invited us to dinner.

In pursuit of an increasingly carnivorous diet (consisting, in the interests of survival, of high-calorie animal proteins) humanity increased and multiplied, emigrated, and spread all over the world. Increasingly, it developed skills in order to acquire more and more such food, using methods which would help it to evolve towards civilization: weapons, tools, industry, social organization. As its diet became more varied, its intellectual capacity increased.

INTRODUCTION

As soon as the biped *Homo erectus*, now *Homo sapiens* by virtue of centuries of ingenuity exercised in search of his favourite foods, could use fire without fear he decided his food would be better cooked, especially as his intellectual growth meant that his digestive faculties had been modified and were now more restricted. His jaw, too, had lost some of its efficiency as his brain gained in power. Food was easier to digest cooked than raw. He also realized that his stocks of food could be better managed if he cooked them.

Organized civilization brought with it the idea of cookery: the intentional preparation of foods in the traditional manner of a particular social or ethnic group. Traditions derived both from local factors of climate, soil and fauna, and from religious taboos conveying ideas of cleanliness or of safeguarding the social structure.

As civilizations became more sophisticated all over the world, and commercial and cultural exchanges increased, the diet became ever more varied and complex. It has been said that civilization occurs when something we never missed before becomes a necessity. From now on food would be a social factor, sometimes even demonstrating social identity, as with the Lotophagi or lotus-eaters of Djerba in the tale of Odysseus. Tastes and culinary skills do in fact reflect a group mentality – 'Tell me what you eat and I will tell you what you are.' Despite progress, people with strict moral standards will tend to live on a sparse diet: examples are the famous black broth of Sparta, the frugal diet of even the richest Mormon communities in modern America, or the vigorous manner in which theologians tackled nutritional issues at the time of the Counter-Reformation.

While traditional recipes or festive rituals may relate to regional, national and religious characteristics, they also arise from a group's general liking for certain basic foods or certain aromatics. There are regions famous for wheat, rye, maize, potatoes, pasta, rice, wine, beer, oil, butter, dairy produce, garlic, onions, pork – tastes which have conditioned the local economy.

Curiously, the frontiers of these preferences generally coincide with dialectal frontiers. These cultural data fascinate ethnologists, particularly as such preferences are naturally more marked where a region has remained isolated. But deliberate choice sometimes seems to be involved too, and the local speciality is valued as an heirloom. There are also dietary aversions: if certain ethnic groups suffering from famine are given milk to drink, it will make them seriously ill.

It took the exploration, colonization and pollution of half the planet by the other half for a kind of nutritional standardization to be gradually imposed; in general, evolution has been in the direction of Western customs. (In those new African republics which have come to despise their local starchy foods, the new and expensive fashion is for white bread made with imported flour.) Invaders or emigrants have always brought their dietary customs with them, as if sentimentally importing a little soil from their native land. Conquered peoples, once they lose their own identity along with their desire to resist the invaders, end up adopting these new dietary standards, just as they accept new religious norms. Dietary adaptation is imposed on the entire population, from top to bottom of the social scale, as it evolves towards reflecting the image of the conquerors.

Diet, then, is a social signal. Since cannibalistic times, it has been associated with identification magic. The food of the strongest – like his religion, his spiritual food – is always regarded as the best. The strongest person is he who imposes his diet on others. 'Going native' in diet has usually been regarded as a lapse in a colonial – though sometimes as intellectual snobbery. On the other hand, the colonist always and unhesitatingly exports the exotic foodstuffs of the territories he has occupied. Some of these colonial products will become naturalized in the colonist's home country, either benefiting to a varying degree from people's curiosity or coming to satisfy real needs. They can then be exported to new colonies, where they become so commonplace that their original home is eventually forgotten. Such has been the fate in modern times of the tomato, the turkey, the potato and the cassava. However, we should not forget that most of the traditional fruits of Western orchards, such as the apple, the peach, the grape and the apricot, not to mention the fowls in our poultry yards, have followed the paths of human migration since ancient times.

The slow assimilation or progressive commercialization of foreign foods did not have much influence on the evolution (or evolutions) of humanity until the end of the Middle Ages. It was as the Renaissance dawned that things changed. The modern period was to be one of large-scale imports and exports, not just of food but also, for reasons connected with food, of human flesh: live human flesh, at least if it survived the voyage. Not, of course, to be eaten – the exporters and importers were good Christians, after all – but human flesh on foot, with strong arms for manual labour.

At the time of the conquest of the American continent, the ordinary people of Europe as a whole were in greater need of basic soup, with or without bacon, than the luxury of a more varied diet. But the new lands on the other side of the world had to be intensively cultivated and show a profit which would pay for the expense of conquering them. The large-scale agricultural exploitation of the colonies meant that their produce could infiltrate European markets quite cheaply, creating out of nowhere appetites which soon became necessities. Gluttony, as I suggested above, is a mutation or aberration of a need and ends up by controlling it.

Just as tea was involved in the independence of the United States, slavery marks an episode in the saga of the history of food, which is only another way of looking at the history of mankind. That saga extends over thousands of years and is played out against the background of the entire planet. Its episodes are so interesting in themselves that one risks forgetting the scientific disciplines which have gone into reconstructing them. The study of food relates to the human sciences (ethnology, ethnography, sociology, medicine, history), to environmental analysis (geography, climatology, botany, agronomics), and to the economy, where nutritional requirements are both an initial and a final stage (as in the markets for sugar and potatoes). Once we enter the realms of gastronomy, it also has elements of philo-

INTRODUCTION

sophy and art — 'the art and science of delicate eating', according to a dictionary definition.

Gastronomy can become a kind of religion, although the more Rabelaisian 'gastrolaters', in their over-enthusiastic devotion to the cause of gastrology, may find themselves in the consulting room of their near-homonym the gastro-enterologist, who specializes in curing the results of over-indulgence. But gastronomy has its own places of worship, at present given over to the rites of *nouvelle cuisine*, its pontiffs (such as Brillat-Savarin), its sacred scriptures (see the well-stocked cookery shelves of your local bookshop), choristers to sing its praises and merchants within its temple gates. In our own time new life-styles and technical advances (canning, freezing, freeze-drying), the standardization of exotic foods, and ecological fads have all contributed to a dietary revolution; there is no telling yet whether it will end in tablets taken twice a day, Chinese cuisine for all, black broth in the Spartan manner, or hydroponically grown cereals to be chewed 60 times before swallowing. All grist, one might say, to the internal mill.

As we become disillusioned with over-indulgence, our next major pleasure may be to fill the stomach scientifically. In an era of excess, there are some who pride themselves on adopting a new nutritional metaphysic: the fashionable diet. The conscientious consumption of diets as scientific as they are surprising gives psychological rather than physical satisfaction; people with access to too much good food eventually become obsessed with putting less and less on their plates.

We come, therefore, to a paradox: one part of the globe does not know what to do with its excess produce, but prices rise in proportion to surplus stocks, since so much has to be paid to a second part of the globe for the energy required to produce it. As for the remaining part of the globe, the Third World countries without either abundant harvests or oil, there is no saying yet whether its people will die of famine caused by drought, or because of bad luck, or through sheer incompetence. They urgently need help.

It would be sad if the history of food were to end with the word FAMINE.

PART I

During the Paleolithic age, hunger was satisfied by the methods of

COLLECTING
GATHERING
HUNTING

From Fire to the Pot

'There was a time', says a myth of the Chilouk people, 'when no one yet knew fire. People used to heat their food in the sun, and the men ate the upper part of the food, cooked in this way, while the women ate the underneath which was still uncooked.' The myth is not male chauvinism, but a kind of allegory of the sexual symbolism of fire.

Just as we do not know how, where or by whom fire was first domesticated, we cannot really tell anything about the way food was cooked in the most distant Paleolithic period. We can only base conjectures on the customs of existing primitive peoples. Bones and walnut or hazelnut shells have been found on excavated sites, but there is no means of knowing whether they are the remains of cooked meals, the debris of fires lit for heat, or even the remnants of incinerated raw waste matter. Professor Loon has studied the treatment of certain long bones cracked so that the marrow could be extracted, and believes they were sucked and gnawed raw. The Abbé Breuil and Dr Hulin are inclined to think the meat was roasted, from the evidence of Mousterian sites in Spain and the Dordogne. Similarly, we cannot be sure that the stones found around these hearths, some of them flat and some rounded, were really querns used for grinding grain. On the other hand, the discovery of organic ash in fossilized charcoal such as has been found at Hommersheim in Germany, together with the large number of cracked or broken bones in the immediate vicinity, does seem to constitute circumstantial evidence that these Aurignacian hearths were used for cooking food.

At any rate, the charred stones frequently found in the Dordogne appear to show that food was sometimes grilled. Again, the woolly mammoth tusks stuck, points down, on both sides of a Ukrainian hearth of the Upper Paleolithic period (the tenth millennium BC) clearly suggest roasting. The spit could have been green wood, as still used in Polynesia, or indeed in the West by Boy Scouts. Remains of a charred bird between two much reddened stones have been found in Ariège – a culinary method like the modern method of making waffles – the food in this case having been forgotten or burnt.

South American Indians still use hot stones for cooking. The ethnologist and prehistorian André Leroi-Gourhan succeeded in boiling water for two hours with hot stones, in an admittedly anachronistic rubber bucket. His aim was to support his theory that circular hollows around the fire on the Pincevent site may have held receptacles. The crucial question is: what were these receptacles made of? Wood hollowed out by fire, as in Amazonia? In fact, when we heat water for instant coffee with an electric mini-boiler in a hotel bedroom, we are using an age-old technique. The stilt-walking shepherds of the Landes area in France were still boiling sheep's milk with stones at the end of the last century.

The skin into which the Amazonians throw hot stones when making mead can also be put over the fire, so long as it is thick enough not to burst into flames. M. L. Ryder published an article in the journal *Antiquity* in 1966 entitled 'Can one cook in a skin?' It was illustrated by an engraving of 1581 showing a group of Irish people cooking soup in a 'pot' consisting of a sheepskin attached to three posts. Some texts suggest that Scottish soldiers were doing the same thing in 1327. M. L. Ryder tried the experiment (not in any very expert fashion).

However, suppose you had no sheepskin or other likely receptacle to hand, how could you cook a piece of meat except by roasting or grilling it? According to Herodotus, the Scythians had a method. 'If they have no cauldron, they cast all the flesh into the victim's stomach, adding water thereto, and make a fire beneath of the bones, which burn finely; the stomach easily holds the flesh when it is stripped from the bones; thus an ox serves to cook itself.'

The Indians of the northern United States and Canada were familiar with this method. The Mongols combine cooking in a skin and cooking with stones: they behead a goat and bone it neatly, extracting the inside parts through the neck. Then they cut the meat up small and put it back in the skin with white-hot stones. You wait two hours and then serve.

The Baloubas of Zaïre use the bark of trees for cooking *au plat*. Many tropical peoples, for instance the Malays, stuff hollow green bamboo canes with rice and cook them in the glowing embers.

If the first people to work clay did not instantly hit upon the idea of making fired pottery vessels, it must have been because they were getting on perfectly well without them. The people who lived in what is now Czechoslovakia some 27,000 years ago baked a number of items in the kiln discovered at the Dolné Vestonice site, but the fragments found are of ceramic votive objects: human or animal figurines. The first pottery vessels known to us were made by the Japanese in the thirteenth millennium, and it cannot be claimed that the art spread from them. When a need was felt, or chance took a hand, the idea could have occurred in a number of places. There is a theory which holds that, at a given time, ideas for certain inventions are in the air.

After the end of the last great Ice Age, about 12,000 years ago, climatic conditions favoured the spread of wild cereal plants. Mortars and mills hollowed out of the living rock at the entrances of inhabited caves have been found in Nubia and Egypt. But the communities who devoted themselves entirely to the practice of farming and depended on the cereals then cultivated did not take to pottery vessels until around the seventh millennium, when their culture was at its height. Vessels made of fired clay have been found at the Mureybet site in northern Syria. As in Czechoslovakia 12,000 years earlier, however, the oldest of the items excavated cannot have been for cooking; they are too small to be any use. They are modelled in the form of female figures, and seem to have been pots for make-up or sacred perfumes.

It may well be that the Neolithic people of Mureybet, who lived in curious round, hump-backed houses made of *unfired* bricks, derived the idea of the

Neolithic sandstone mill and grinder found in Algeria

possibilities of pottery from the sunken hearths in which they cooked their food. These ovens were just holes dug in the earth. If the soil was not naturally clayey, the sides were coated with smooth clay to make them more stable. Heaps of pebbles can still be seen at the bottom of such ovens, mingled with cinders; they are of great interest to scholars. The ovens were used to heat stones upon which food was then placed to grill (they still bear traces of their use for that purpose). The clay on the sides of the holes was baked at the same time. Such ovens are still used in the region for baking bread or mutton. The flat *naan* bread of northern India is cooked in a similar way, on the interior walls of clay ovens, although nowadays the ovens are portable.

Initially artistic or cultural, pottery did not become really utilitarian in that part of the world until the next millennium. But obviously the villagers of Mureybet, waiting for their soup to be cooked, perfected the original barbecue method as still practised from the Red Sea to the Caspian and through the whole of north Africa.

The Celts, particularly the Celts of Ireland, were cooking in holes in the ground 500 years before our own era, in the same way as the Mesopotamians. They used the method for boiling meat as well as spit-roasting it. The hole, lined with clay to make it watertight, was filled with water. Hot stones were plucked from a nearby fire with a bent stick of green wood and thrown into the water. It takes no more than half an hour to bring 454 litres of water to the boil by this method. The Irish

11

scholar Professor O'Kelly tried it, and found that a nine-pound joint of meat cooked to perfection in three and a half hours, just as well and as quickly as on a modern gas stove.

At the same time soups or stews – the ancestors of Irish stew – were being made in large metal cauldrons hung over the fire from chains attached to the roof rafters in Celtic houses of the period, which usually had a central hearth with a surrounding structure. Conical clay ovens were also in use, particularly for baking bread.

The pot-bellied cauldron full of delicious things simmering away has a prominent place in folk memory. It appears in a number of legends. In the myths of the Celts, who had hearty appetites, the cauldron of abundance magically provides both inexhaustible food and inexhaustible knowledge. Sinister concoctions, on the other hand, bubble in the cauldrons of witches or malevolent goddesses. In Chinese legend, the elixir of immortality is made in a tripod cauldron – reminiscent of the Irish sheepskin fixed to its three posts. Immortality is often the end to be achieved by drinking the boiled liquids of Greek myth. Medea boiled old King Pelias himself, claiming that he would be rejuvenated.

However, it is the image of the steaming pot on the table that has remained the symbol of tranquil family pleasures in the Paradise Lost of childhood. Supper,[1] the communal evening meal symbolized by the serving of soup, is seen as embodying the modest but stable pleasures and touchingly old-fashioned peasant virtues of the past. In France, a good mother who stays at home and is there when her family needs her is said to be 'pot-au-feu'.

> Quand on se gorge d'un potage
> Succulent comme un consommé
> Si notre corps en est charmé
> Notre âme l'est bien davantage ...

[When we fill ourselves with a soup as delicious as a consommé, it delights our bodies, and yet more our souls ...]

wrote Paul Scarron, cynic though he was.

Opposite: An open-air kitchen: engraving from *Dell'arte del cucinare, con il maestro di casa*, by Bartolomeo Scappi, Venice, 1570. The artist set out to show all the equipment necessary in a country kitchen (cauldrons, spits, covered pot, two-handled casserole, set of plates and bowls) as well as the two main methods of cooking food, by roasting (quarters of meat and poultry) and by boiling (soups and vegetables).

tenda

Cucina per Compagna

baston di ferro sostenato da doi spedere

caldari

boca
te

casse co piatti e mantili bianchi

pignato

hamicela   quatro piedi con un   caldaro sopra

Chapter 1

Collecting Honey

Honey in the Golden Age

> Next I come to the manna, the heavenly gift of honey ... A featherweight
> theme: but one that can load me with fame ...

writes Virgil in his own honeyed words, at the beginning of Book IV of the *Georgics*.

According to an Amazonian legend,[1] in the old days the animals were men who fed on nothing but the honey of bees. And indeed, from the dawn of time mankind has enjoyed honey, a food both miraculous and natural. After all, nature itself is a miracle. Though honey was not really the first food but only one of the first, collecting it was particularly gratifying, being very much a matter of luck and entailing just enough risk to stimulate the appetite. Delicious nourishment for travellers, hidden away like treasure, it has an element of reward about it. It was immediately associated with the most lofty and beneficent of symbolism, and I have chosen to open this history of food with honey.

> O Asvins, lords of brightness, anoint me with the honey of the bee,
> that I may speak forceful speech among men! (*Atharva Veda*, 91–258)

Fossilized 'bees' have been found in Baltic amber, trapped in resin of the Upper Eocene period some 50 million years ago, at the same time as the first primates were appearing in Africa and South America. However, this insect, *Electrapis* (the amber bee), differs less from bees of the present day than the primates of the Tertiary period do from ourselves. Many other fossil specimens descended from them tell the tale of their evolution to the modern *Apis mellifera* which, like so many other species around the world, seems to have originated in Asia. Coming by way of the Middle East, like almost everyone else, the various races of that social and industrious insect, the present-day bee, arrived in Europe and Africa to gather nectar from the flowers.

15

Tropical America also has social bees among its native hymenoptera. They can produce sufficient quantities of honey to provide man with a useful nutritional supplement. They are not, like the European honey-bee, Apidae but Meliponinae, and are known as *lambe olhos*, 'lick-eyes'. Although they lack stings and venom they have the unpleasant habit, as their name suggests, of attacking any two-legged or four-legged raider by trying to penetrate its mouth, eyes or ears to get at their secretions, which they find intoxicating. It is a very painful experience for their victims.

The American Meliponinae, who will feed on carrion as well as gathering honey (our own honey-bees also like meat juices), produce a runnier honey than their Old World counterparts. It is very dark and very sweet, and does not keep well unless it is boiled. It is seldom eaten straight, but is diluted in water, and is regarded as an aphrodisiac. The Indians enjoy it very much. 'O Indio e fanatico pelo mel de pau', Claude Lévi-Strauss quotes – 'wood-honey' because the bees' nests are usually found in trees – but the unclean habits of the worker bees can sometimes make it toxic.

In North America, a Cheyenne creation myth tells that 'the first men lived on honey and wild fruits and were never hungry.'[2] This may be considered a particularly apocryphal myth, although legends themselves are timeless, since tropical bees did not migrate north until quite a late date. According to Châteaubriand, the European bees now found in North America, whether they are domesticated or have reverted to the wild, were 'foreign to America, arriving in the wake of Columbus and his ships', and he adds that 'those peaceful conquerors have stolen from a New World of flowers only those treasures which the natives did not know how to use'. True enough, except that over the years the 'peaceful conquerors' have almost succeeded in annihilating their sisters, who may not have been actually natives but were certainly there first.

Le gouvernement admirable ou La république des abeilles, the 'admirable government or the republic of bees' (a title given to a treatise on apiculture by J. Simon in 1740), was thus socially and economically organized well before man had risen to his feet. The treasure stored by the provident insects was coveted by primates, and its appeal to bears is a byword. Both bears and primates will risk putting a greedy paw into a bees' nest when they smell its appetizing fragrance. Some monkeys, cleverer than others and tired of getting stung, have discovered how to stick a branch in and then suck the honey as we might suck it off a spoon.[3] Philippe Marcheray tells us that chimpanzees have been seen holding the palms of their large hands over their faces to protect themselves from the angry bees.

Spanish honey, which takes up quite a lot of space on the supermarket shelves of the European Community countries, being so reasonably priced, can claim what might be described as the oldest advertisement in the world, a rock painting in the Cave of the Spider near Valencia. The artist, working about 12,000 years ago, has made ingenious use of a cavity in the rock wall itself. A man clinging to creepers or ropes is putting one hand into the hole, and holding a basket to take the honey with the other. The bees are flying around him, determined not to lose their treasure. Similar rock paintings are found in South Africa and Zimbabwe. In one of them the honey hunter, decked with feathers in the Zulu manner, is perched on what looks like a ladder and holds a lighted torch up to the whirling cloud of insects as they fly away, in front of clearly depicted honeycombs.

Collecting honey: rock painting from the end of the Neolithic period, Pachamadhi, Central India

'So powerful is its gastronomic appeal that, were it too easily obtained, mankind would partake of it too freely until the supply was exhausted', says Lévi-Strauss of honey, with particular reference to the Indians, but the reflection is applicable to human behaviour in general. 'Through the medium of myth, honey is saying to man: "You would not find me, if you had not first looked for me."' Lévi-Strauss also recalls a creation myth of the Caduveo people: 'When the caracara (a species of falcon) saw the honey forming in the huge gourds where it was to be had for the taking, he said to Go-noeno-hodi the demiurge: "No, this is not right, this is not the way it should be, no! Put the honey in the middle of the tree so that men are forced to dig it out, otherwise the lazy creatures will not work."'

A Taste of Honey

Certain people famous for their wisdom are said to have been fed on honey in childhood, like the god Zeus, or at important turning points in their lives: they include Pythagoras and the first Celtic Christian mystic Erthne.

The poor of the past, like primitive peoples, regarded honey in its natural state as an occasional windfall, and were duly thankful. But as soon as cooking methods of any sophistication were developed – not that everyone could take advantage of them – honey featured as an important ingredient, and was to retain that importance throughout the Middle Ages. Besides having energy-giving properties, it was the only sweetener available in a pure and natural state, although the pulp of very sweet fruits such as figs or dates might sometimes be used if it was available.[4] Cane sugar, originally and logically enough known as 'reed honey', was to be a fabulous luxury for the Old World of the West until after the Crusades, as we shall see below.

Besides being primarily a sweetener, honey was an important condiment. Condiments were not solely substances with strong, sharp or very scented flavours, as they are today. From the days of classical antiquity to the height of the Renaissance – with some falling off in the late Middle Ages[5] – most foods had honey added to them, or later sugar, whether or not we would now classify them as sweet dishes or confectionery. Spices and salt were added at the same time and in the same proportions. Was this because of the sometimes dubious quality of the food? Or was it simply the taste of the times? It is a question that has often been asked, and Jean-Louis Flandrin comments:[6] 'In the dietary habits of peoples as in those of individuals, we have to distinguish between taste and necessity.'

There was and always will be a suggestion of luxury and of medicinal practices in the culinary use of honey, for in folk memory medicine derives from a kind of magic. Sweet things are perceived *a priori* as doing you good. This attitude of approval was passed on to sugar. Cooking with honey and then with sugar, a mark of privilege, was bound to be the best people's cookery. Herodotus, writing on Egypt, tells us that the beasts offered in sacrifice were stuffed before roasting with a mixture of flour, figs, raisins and aromatics mingled with honey – to enhance the pleasure of those taking part in the ceremony and feasting in the name of the gods.

The favourite honey stuffing of Greek banquets was indubitably *hyma*. It also contained chopped cheese, offal, vinegar, onions and small quantities of other ingredients, according to a recipe given by Epaenetes. Honey provided Democritus with a simpler satisfaction, in fact the final satisfaction in the life of the philosopher who advocated the pursuit of happiness through moderation in pleasure (he also invented the theory of the atom). The story goes that when the old man, who had always lived frugally, felt his end approaching after 109 well-spent years, he decided to omit some item from his diet every day. When there was nothing left to omit, the celebration of the festival of Demeter was in progress, and he did not want to commit the solecism of dying. He had a pot of honey brought to him, and absorbed only its fragrance by raising it to his nostrils. Once the festival was over, the pot of honey was taken away and he died.

The cook Erasistratus gave his guests a kind of honey pudding called *hyposphagma*. There is one delicious and very simple dish we can still make: curds with honey, or *hypotrides*. Boil milk and immediately add some slightly fermented honey. Stir to make the milk curdle. Pour it into a bowl to set, drain it and serve it with fruit. Another natural and authentic sweet dish comes from the Mohawks and the Algonquins of Canada. Since time immemorial, these tribes have baked small pumpkins in the embers of their fires, first removing the seeds and stuffing them with honey, cider and butter (in former times, with some form of vegetable fat or with beaver fat instead of butter). This dish, *ogwissiman*, was not their only recipe using honey.

Apicius' honey sauce for fish was a great Roman classic. The author of the *Ars Magirica* also gives the recipe for ham in a honey crust, quite a different dish from the famous honey-roast Virginia ham of the American pioneers. The North American Indians claim to have invented another early American dish, beans with honey, but others believe it came from the Chinese coolies who laid the railroad tracks of the American West.

Both the Greeks and the Romans also used honey as a cooking liquid. Julius Pollux, the Graeco-Egyptian rhetorician, evidently enjoyed stuffed leaves cooked in honey – not vine leaves but tender fig leaves. He gives the recipe in his second-century lexicographical work, the *Onomasticon*: make a stuffing of wheat flour, lard, eggs and brains. Divide it into small pieces and wrap in leaves. The stuffed leaves are first cooked in chicken or kid broth, then drained and cooked a second time in boiling honey. For centuries, until it disappeared from medieval hutches to return to the forests, a favourite way of eating the edible dormouse was preserved in a honey sauce or baked in honey. Guinea fowl with honey vinegar is still a speciality of the Périgord.

Honey was long used for preserving fruits, whole or as jam. *Oenanthe* was a preserve of wild vine flowers in honey. Even more delicious was rose petal paste. A similar exquisite paste was *miskwimin amo sisi bakwat*, strawberries crushed in pure honey, traditionally made in summer by the Amerindian tribes of Canada for their winter provisions. It is also delicious freshly made. In India, meat was kept from one year to the next coated in honey.

For the moment I will leave aside the pastries drenched in honey made by the people of the East and the Balkans and by the Arabs. Few if any innovations were made in the cookery of medieval Europe, but, as time passed and sugar gained ground, the use of honey was confined to sweetmeats and such delicacies, not forgetting its medicinal uses. Sweet and savoury dishes were more strictly segregated than before at this point. Today, nutritional ideas about natural foods and medical dietetics recommend the wider use of honey, but it is hardly used in cookery at all except for exotic effect. Since the 1970s, pollen and royal jelly have been highly regarded in nutritional laboratories and health food shops, much to the profit of beekeepers.

Honey in Legend

There is such a wealth of symbolism connected with honey that the facts of its story can hardly be told without mentioning all it represents in the human mind. Legendary traditions explain the customs which surround it and of which it is part.

The treatment of bees and the way in which their honey was collected and eaten had the character of religious ritual. We may almost have lost our sense of that significance, but we retain a certain respect for bees, as if they still fulfilled their initiatory and liturgical role. At both Ephesus and Eleusis, the priestesses were known as 'bees'.

The Hebrew for bee is *dbure*, from the root *dbr*, meaning 'word', whence the pretty first name Deborah, indicating the bee's mission to reveal the Divine Word, the Truth. Honey, miraculously made by the bees, signifies truth because it needs no treatment to transform it after it has been collected. It does not deteriorate, and until the discovery of sugar there was no substitute. What but the bee can actually create honey by settling on the centres of God's own flowers? Or the gods' own flowers; it came to the same thing.

This 'truth', a message from above, was thought to be passed on by bees in their honey so that the elect could express the truth in scholarship and poetry.[7] Accordingly, bees were supposed to have settled on the lips of Plato, Pindar and the well-named St Ambrose of Milan as children. Not every new-born baby can grow up to be a genius, but at least one hopes for its happiness: this is the idea of the women of the Ivory Coast and Senegal who still rub a baby's lips with honey as soon as it has uttered its first cry of fury at being born. Such a baptism of honey was part of ancient Achaean and Germanic custom, and came from the primordial steppes. There is still an Eastern custom whereby a spoonful of honey is poured into the palms of a newly married couple's hands. They must lick it off for each other as a sign that they will now take all their food together, and it is said to ensure that the husband will not lift his hand to his wife except to caress her, and none but loving words will spring to the wife's lips – not just during the aptly named honeymoon but for ever after. At the moment of initiation during the Eleusinian and Mithraic mysteries, the *mystes* (initiates) anointed their hands and tongues with honey. They were purifying themselves from evil, and the good was revealed to them. Philippe Marcheray adds that the Egyptians ate honey 'at the festival of Thoth, uttering the words "Sweet is the truth"'.

A perfect food, of the most sacred colour – golden yellow – honey features as a god in the Vedas, and as divine nourishment in the Graeco-Latin tradition. During the Golden Age, say the Orphic texts, honey ran from the oak trees and the Titan Kronos was sleeping, intoxicated with honey – the first sleep in the world – when his son Zeus chained him and took him away to the Islands of the Blest at the end of the world, where it was said that the ancient god and the Age of Gold could still be found. The implication is that honey, the first food, dates from the creation of the world, and existed even before the bees brought it to mankind.

This first food must obviously have been the food of the chief god. Greek legend situates the childhood of Zeus on Mount Lycaeus, or on Mount Ida, in Crete, where his mother Rhea hid him, and the bees supplemented the future god's diet of goat's milk with their honey. The Cretans claimed that his nurses Amalthea and Melissa were really princesses, daughters of King Melissus, who shared the care of the divine baby, Amalthea with the milk of her goat, Melissa with the honey of her bees; the name Melissa means 'she who makes honey'.

There is also a myth of a sacred cavern, a place of immortality where time did not exist, guarded by fiery bees. In the legend, Rhea gave birth to Zeus here, handing him over at once to the care of the insects. But four rash intruders wearing bronze armour for protection made their way into the cave to steal honey, which was still forbidden to humans. They were about to bear off their sacrilegious loot when the new-born child began to cry. Seeing him in his blood-stained swaddling clothes, the intruders were so frightened that their armour dropped off and the bees attacked them. But no one could die in that cave, particularly after touching the honey. To maintain the order of things, Zeus saved the robbers from the bees' venom by instantly changing them into birds which flew away. In gratitude to the bees for their devotion to duty, the god gave them bronze armour to hide their fiery nature in future, and having a good command of language for a new-born baby, he added that their courage would always remain a byword.

To turn to the legendary origin of bees themselves, in the *Popul Vuh*, the sacred tradition of the Maya Indians, the bee was born of the Universal Hive at the centre of the earth. Golden to the sight, burning to the touch, like the sparks of volcanoes, it was sent here to awaken man from apathy and ignorance; this is the general sense behind those rural Amazonian folk-tales which deal with honey and mead. Honey and bees are universally found associated with the generative, creative fire, and also with the cave, underground cavern, grotto or hollow tree which is part of the symbolism of the female principle in agrarian myths. Proserpina, the Roman goddess of spring, the season when the bees begin collecting honey from the flowers every year, was also Queen of the Underworld. Another of her titles was Mellita. The Romans offered sacrifices of honey to appease the god of the underworld so that he would not appear in the form of a fiery serpent, i.e., as volcanic lava. The people of Pompeii cannot have offered enough honey.

Ovid says that honey was a gift of the god of wine, Bacchus (Dionysus in Greek); on his way back from an expedition he was gambolling with his attendant satyrs, who struck their sistra to mark time. At the sound of the jingling instruments, a swarm of unknown insects flew out of the wood, and Bacchus guided them to a tree; they shut themselves up in it and filled it with honey.

The Greeks and Romans mingled wine and honey together in drinking bowls. A cousin of Dionysus was called Melicertes, 'he who mingles honey', by analogy with *melidraton*, water mingled with honey, the first stage in the fermentation of that other intoxicating drink, mead. Melicertes was drowned when his mother, the wine god's aunt and nurse, went mad and jumped into the sea with him. The ocean swallowed up his corpse, but he was resuscitated, riding a dolphin, as the sea god Palaemon, and thereafter, although properly a marine deity, formed part of the train of Dionysus with the satyrs and Sileni. The foaming waves suggest the foaming of mead fermenting in a vat or poured into cups. Possibly sailors took amphorae of mead with them to keep their courage up at sea.

The most famous myth about the origin of bees is the legend of Aristaeus. It concerns the (definitely mythical) spontaneous generation of bees, a notion that proved very tenacious, lasting into the seventeenth century. The spontaneous generation of bees was an article of faith in apicultural treatises, until the microscope revealed that the 'king' bee was actually a queen, in fact a queen mother whose sole function was to lay millions of eggs from which her young would hatch. But, to quote Virgil:[8]

> It is time to detail the famous invention of an Arcadian
> Bee-master, the process by which he often made
> A culture of bees from the putrid blood of slaughtered bullocks.

The Arcadian shepherd Aristaeus, son of Apollo and the nymph Cyrene, had pursued Eurydice with his attentions, and was guilty of her death; because he was also regarded as responsible for the death of her husband Orpheus, he was deprived of his beloved bees. On his mother's advice, he sacrificed to the shades of Orpheus and Eurydice: a poppy to Orpheus, to appease his anger, and to Eurydice 'four bulls of excellent body … and as many heifers'. When the ninth day has dawned:

> … a miracle sudden and strange to tell of
> They behold: from the oxen's bellies all over their rotting flesh
> Creatures are humming, swarming through the wreckage of their ribs –
> Huge and trailing clouds of bees, that now in the treetops
> Unite and hang like a bunch of grapes from the pliant branches.

The bees here are obviously seen as related to blowflies, whose maggots in fact have no connection with them at all.

The myth of Aristaeus also shows the tenacity of a sexual taboo which features in the beekeeping manuals of antiquity. The shepherd's first bees were taken from him because he had desired a woman, and someone else's woman at that; you had to abstain from carnal intercourse before trying to recover a swarm of bees (reputed to be virgins) or to collect honey (a pure substance).

22

Honey, like wax, was much used in ancient ritual. In funeral rites, the dead were given a supply of honey to enjoy in the afterlife, since honey denoted immortality. From Neolithic times onwards, the Aryans, Babylonians, Sumerians and Cretans buried their great men in honey. There are echoes of the custom in Herodotus and Strabo. Alexander the Great revived it when he was embalmed in honey on his own death, but there is no evidence to show that it was a common custom in the Balkans. Embalming was generally with wax, as in ancient Egypt, whence the word mummy, from Persian *mum*, wax. Finally, at the festival of the winter solstice, the Hopi Indians of Arizona symbolically buried the dead year, in a spirit similar to that of the Celtic celebration of Samhain, but with a communal meal consisting of honey and flour. The same foods are associated in the Russian Jewish celebrations of Rosh Hashanah, when the head of the household gives his children bread and honey as a good omen.

Honey in Nature and History

Nectar is a sweet substance, 75 per cent water with certain mineral elements, extracted from flowers by the bee as it flies from one to another. It has been called nature's bait for attracting insects, whose feet become laden with pollen as they work. Plant pollination is often necessary for fertilization and subsequent fruit. The more fragrance a flower has, the more it attracts visiting bees.

Bees fill their honey sacs with nectar, in which change begins to occur even on the way back to the hive, caused by the enzymes in the insect's saliva and gastric juices. The nectar becomes a mixture of invert sugars (glucose and laevulose). Back in the hive, the bees regurgitate this still very liquid honey and deposit it in the wax cells of the combs. To concentrate it further by inverting the proportions of sugar and water, the worker bees ingest and regurgitate it again, beating their wings to ventilate the atmosphere in the hive. After 20 minutes, when the process is completed, they seal the cell with a capping secreted from the abdominal glands of wax-making bees. As Philippe Marcheray points out, a kilo of honey represents a vast amount of labour; it takes the bees between 20,000 and 100,000 journeys to bring a single litre of nectar back to the hive, and five litres of nectar make one litre of honey.

The quality of the honey depends on the flowers visited by the bees, since it retains their fragrance and other properties, whether beneficial or (very rarely) toxic. The bee is particular in its choice of flowers, and a methodical worker. If it visits only a single species of flower in a day, it has to ingest nectar from 10,000 calices for a single drop of honey to be deposited in a cell. The beekeeper who wants to be selective in making his honey will therefore observe the main flowering seasons within range of his hives (bees have a range of several kilometres). He takes a

Engraving illustrating a sixteenth-century work on apiculture: the words *Non nobis* indicate that the bees themselves do not profit from the honey they make.

partial honey harvest at the end of each of these flowering seasons, so that he can offer honey derived from a single floral species, which is considered the best kind. If it comes from the nectar of several species of flower, the honey will be simply called 'floral' or 'country' honey.

From ancient times, migratory beekeeping has also been practised; the hives are 'moved with the seasons, sometimes over a great distance'.[9] In Scotland, bees were traditionally taken to the moorland heather in summer.

Honey may be thick or runny, clear or opaque. In France, the most usual sort is acacia honey, which is very sweet, liquid, and pale gold in colour. Sainfoin used to make the excellent white Gâtinais honey; this is still produced, but there is almost no sainfoin left. The thick, pale honey of Provence owes its intoxicating fragrance to lavender.

In Roman times, the ivory honey of Narbonne was the most famous honey in Gaul because of the rosemary which gives it its special flavour, as well as the plant's medicinal and in particular its digestive properties. Roman legions recruited in Tunisia are said to have started beekeeping in the Aude region as a spare-time hobby. At first, only consuls were allowed to eat the honey. Thyme honey, very dark and very strong, is made in Provence. But the occupying Roman forces liked Greek honey even better than the honey of Narbonne. This Greek honey was the famous honey of Mount Hymettus, beloved of the gods. In a way, it was divine honey, and was sold in the Via Sacra in Rome by shops stocking luxury foods. In spite of the many rules and regulations of the Eternal City, there were innumerable cases of fraud. Cunning beekeepers would place their hives in the thyme fields of the Iberian peninsula, or use concentrated infusions. Virgil, advocating this practice, recommended feeding the bees on plant decoctions in wine (*Georgics*, Book IV).

Brown, strong heather honey is produced in the Landes area of France. Buckwheat honey, another full-bodied variety, used to be made in Brittany, but is hardly ever found there now, since no more buckwheat is grown. This was the kind of honey that was formerly used in the traditional French spice-bread or gingerbread. Pine honey is unusual in that it is not entirely the work of bees. Bees, like ants and ladybirds, 'milk' the aphids which live on the sap of resinous trees, consuming so much that they regurgitate it in the form of *honeydew*. Honeydew can inundate oaks, elders, limes or cornfields in warm years when aphids abound. In 1976, for instance, the trees along the avenues of Paris and in the Bois de Boulogne dripped a kind of green syrup on car roofs and the heads of passers-by.

All the kinds of honey mentioned above, besides Spanish honey, Hungarian acacia honey and of course Greek honey, are subject to stringent legislation within the European Community.[10] As with wine, there are trade descriptions guaranteeing the quality of the product. A good honey is likely to be expensive. Its label should mention its floral origin and geographical provenance, and indicate the way in which it was harvested and the absence of any further treatment after extraction from the combs. Hives which have a natural environment, still rich in wild flowers and well away from industrial areas and busy main roads, will give honey of much better quality than the honey from plants grown with fertilizers and polluted by dust and petrol fumes.

Honey is taken in the summer months. The first harvest, which produces the finest honey, is taken between May and July, when the bees have had a chance to finish the nectar flow from the first flowering seasons. The second harvest is taken at the end of summer. The hives are opened when the sun is at its height; a particularly fine day will encourage the worker bees to go out to the fields, and 'sweet is their strange delight', as Virgil put it, adding:

> If rain threatens, be sure they'll not roam too far afield
> From their hives: they mistrust the sky, should an east wind be due.

Modern hives have movable frames hung inside the hive-box, to augment output and respect the timing of the bees' work. The lower part of the hive contains the

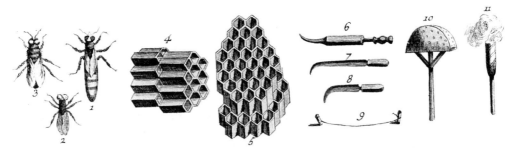

Engraving from a plate in Diderot's *Encyclopédie* devoted to bees: it shows different kinds of bees, the structure of their cells, and the instruments used for extracting honey.

larvae, or *brood*, and reserves of honey which must not be touched except to check that they are sufficient. This is the domain of the nurses who look after the young and the queen, the bees who make and repair the wax cells, and the bees who clean the hive; worker bees pass in and out. When honey is taken, the hive is fumigated through its entrance and removable top to make the bees inside lethargic and discourage angry workers returning with nectar. Modern beekeepers wear a kind of space suit with a helmet, veil and gloves, to protect themselves from stings. The bee knows its own hive, and there is no point in painting hives different colours, since bees can hardly distinguish colour at all.

The frames are carefully removed, one by one, and any bees still heroically clinging to them are brushed off. To save time, they are replaced by fresh frames already equipped with wax 'foundations' imprinted with hexagon shapes. This foundation makes it easier for the bees to reconstruct their combs. The beekeeper now checks to see that there is no brood in the cells of the frames which have been removed, and opens them with a large knife. Next, usually in a special shed, several combs at a time are placed vertically in a centrifugal extractor which removes the honey from the comb. The empty combs will be replaced later. In a good year, each can give two kilos of honey. To filter out any residue of wax or dead bees, the honey is strained into a tank with a spout from which it is poured into jars. Modern technology has made the whole process easier, but this in broad outline has been the method of taking honey for thousands of years. As a French proverb says, honey is one thing, the price of honey another.

Collecting wild honey is not for the lazy, and greed alone is no guarantee of success. Skill is also called for, and courage to face the bees' stings: in fact, the traditional qualities of the hunter. Consequently, collecting honey was regarded as a man's job relating to hunting, while the gathering or harvesting of vegetable crops was seen as women's work both culturally and in ritual. When honey-hunting became beekeeping it was still a masculine occupation, or so the naturalist Buffon evidently thought, expressing his opinion in verse: 'L'abeille est implacable en son inimitié/Attaque sans frayeur, se venge sans pitié/Sur l'ennemi blessé, s'élance avec furie/Et laisse dans la plaie et son dard et sa vie.'

[The bee is implacable in its hostility, attacks fearlessly, takes merciless revenge on the wounded enemy, hurls itself furiously forward, and leaves both its sting and its life in the wound.]

Taking honey becomes a battle with its established rules, man against the bee's weapon, its sting. (However, the Meliponinae of South America, although dangerous because they will infiltrate every orifice in the body, have no stings. The Indians therefore regard honey as a vegetable product – i.e., feminine – like the 'original sin' of gluttony.) Determined to view the central power of the hive as a worthy adversary, the entire Western world believed that the solitary mother insect, the queen bee, was really a king, until the discoveries of the Dutch doctor Jan Swammerdam set them right at the end of the seventeenth century. The queen bee is still described as the 'king' or 'father' of the bees in a number of rural European dialects.

Wild bees will make their nest in any cavity large enough for a colony which may contain 60,000 individuals: a hole in the rock, or most commonly a hollow tree, where they build their combs. It is interesting to read the Biblical account of an episode after a battle against the Philistines (I Samuel 14):

> 'And the men of Israel were distressed that day ... none of the people tasted any food. And all they of the land came to a wood: and there was honey upon the ground. And when the people were come into the wood, behold, the honey dropped. ... But Jonathan ... put forth the end of the rod that was in his hand, and dipped it in an honeycomb, and put his hand to his mouth; and his eyes were enlightened ... '

Had the swarm chosen a shelter low enough to form an angle with the ground, so that honey flowed out on it? Be that as it may, Saul's son Jonathan was instinctively using the technique employed by chimpanzees.

There is nothing surprising about the fact that the honey was found in a wood, since wild bees prefer woodland areas, where they can easily find flowers from which to take nectar and pollen, and buds to provide resin. They use the first two for provisions, turning the nectar into honey, their everyday food, while the pollen feeds their larvae. 'Bee glue' or propolis (Greek: *pro*, in front, and *polis*, city) is made from resin, and the bees use it to construct the stout defensive wall at the entrance to the hive, and for all repair work. Bees also secrete wax to make their combs, and royal jelly, the remarkable substance which enables a larva to reach sexual maturity when necessary and become the queen, the fertile mother of the colony.

Until our own times the only product of the hive which seemed to be of nutritional interest was honey. Today, particularly in alternative medicine, pollen and royal jelly are regarded as miraculous substances, elixirs of youth. Beeswax was and still is used for religious, domestic, cosmetic and medical purposes. Bee glue, besides its value in the making of a durable varnish,[11] has similar uses. We may note all these non-nutritional functions in passing.

The civilization of ancient Egypt was the first to exploit honey by breeding bees to make it. Although the Egyptians practised apiculture, as we can see from the frescoes in a Theban tomb of the seventh century BC, showing pottery hives similar to wine jars, a great deal of wild honey was still collected over the centuries. It is quite surprising that bees were not entirely wiped out, for they were ruthlessly plundered until medieval regulations intervened. Whole colonies were cheerfully slaughtered for a single harvest of their honey. But bees are resourceful insects, as their reproductive capacity proves. (The Japanese, moreover, have always liked eating the brood or larvae, a fashion which has spread to America today.)

The practice of smoking bees out, current as early as the date of the rock paintings, cannot have seemed to the Egyptians enough protection against the angry insects, even if the job was swiftly and efficiently done. Rameses III had his honey-gatherers escorted by archers (Philippe Marcheray). Presumably their arrows were supposed to ward off the bees' stings.

One of the first methods of setting up an apiary was simply to carry off the shelter in which wild bees had nested. If they had settled in a hollow tree, you merely had to chop off a suitable length of its trunk on both sides of the bees' entrance to get a hive ready to be taken away. You would first put the occupants to sleep, whether you did as Virgil suggests – 'release a smoke to chivvy them out' – or used an earthenware pot with a funnel containing a burning mixture of cow's dung (regarded as a courtesy to the insect), resinous substances and aromatic plants. A vessel of this kind has been found at Carthage. You then sawed off the tree trunk at suitable places, took the hive home, and as soon as they woke up the bees would go about their daily business to your own advantage. All you then had to do was empty the hive of its honey twice a year, in early and late summer, and you could go on taking honey for years.

The bees' favourite natural habitat of a hollow tree was an inspiration to beekeepers all over Southern Europe and Germany from the Middle Ages onwards. They burned out the insides of tree trunks, using red-hot iron for the purpose, to make homes for the swarms they took, and gave the bees rudimentary combs to help them settle in.

There have been hives made of cork oak, in imitation of tree trunks, in the south of France from Gaulish times to the present day; they are perfect for keeping the bees warm in winter and cool in summer. The French word *ruche* ('hive') is derived from this practice; it comes from Ligurian *rusca*, bark. The *chêne-rusc* is the cork oak of the Aude and eastern Pyrenees. (English *hive* comes from a probable Germanic root *húf-*, related to Latin *cupa*, a tub or cask, which gave rise to modern English 'cup'.) It is said that, for lack of trees and so as to transport their bees

Opposite: 'Various hives': engraving from *Le Portrait de la mouche à miel,* by Alexandre de Montfort-Luxembourg, Liège, 1646. The materials used and the shape of the hive differ depending on the severity of the climate.

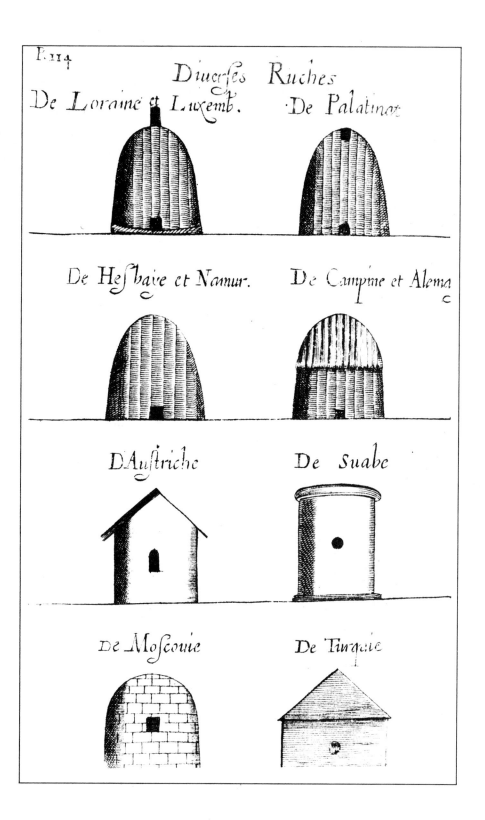

P.114

Diverses Ruches

De Loraine et Luxemb.   De Palatinat

De Hesbaye et Namur.   De Campine et Alema

D'Austriche   De Suabe

De Moscovie   De Turquie

more easily, the plaited wicker hive or skep was invented by the nomads of the steppes; it was then adopted by the Celts. The idea of fixing hives to the most sheltered wall of the house was subsequently introduced. Then came frame hives and hives in several readily accessible sections.

After the great invasions of the Dark Ages, apiculture, like many branches of agriculture, developed no further for some time. People made do with honey-hunting in the forests, usually thanking the bees for their pains by suffocating them to death. But Charlemagne, wishing to restore his lands to a state of organized prosperity, laid down regulations for beekeeping at the same time as he introduced a general policy of agrarian economy. Farms were obliged to keep bees and, most important of all, to pay the emperor dues in kind: two-thirds of all honey and one-third of all beeswax produced. As we shall see in the course of this history of food, Charlemagne was a great manager of general stores.

As early as the era of the Pharaohs, taxes were levied for the benefit not only of the sovereign but of the priests too. Even better, they alone had the right to the best quality honey and beeswax; the common people had to collect wild honey for themselves or make do with the left-over products of domestic bees. Another industrious civilization with an orderly system of government was that of the Maya Indians, who domesticated the native bees of Central America, the stingless Meliponinae, at about the same time as Charlemagne ruled in Europe. Here again, of course, the civil and religious authorities reaped most of the profits.

Still on the subject of religious authorities, abbeys all over Europe possessed great estates over a long period of time. The monks displayed great expertise in apiculture, as well as in making wine and cheese; this may have been the origin of the proverbial beekeeping skills of country clergymen.

Charlemagne died, but *abeillage*, 'bee dues', remained a duly regulated feudal right. Every vassal owed his sovereign a proportion of what his hives produced. Since forests belonged to the lord of the manor, any of the villagers who took a wild swarm nesting in a tree for his own use was regarded as a poacher and punished under the game laws. In France of the fourteenth and fifteenth centuries, there were sworn feudal officials, called *aviléors* or *bigres*, a kind of beekeeping gamekeepers, who alone had the right and duty to take swarms and settle them in clearings or on the outskirts of woods, in hives known as *bigreries* or *hostels aux mouches*, 'houses for the insects'. Laws also controlled beekeeping in various parts of the British Isles at the same time.

Similarly, the times when one might take honey were codified if not actually laid down by law. So were the amounts to be taken from the bees, to prevent any danger of starving them. These arrangements derived from empirical tradition as much as from apicultural treatises and the whole classical literature of natural science, from the Greek philosopher Aristotle to the Hispano-Roman Columella, and including works by Cato, Virgil and a number of others. Although these writers often incorrectly used mythological fables as scientific explanation, their works bear witness to genuine observation and have great literary charm. The Renaissance brought what may be regarded as serious apicultural treatises by Charles Estienne and Jean Liébault (*L'apiculture et la maison rustique*) and in particular the work of Olivier de Serres on the management of rural property, *Le théâtre d'agriculture et mesnage des champs*.

The ancient methods, however, displayed that common sense and wisdom which contact with nature was bound to arouse. In Greece, where every agricultural process was also a ritual, the first honey harvest formed part of a cycle of propitiatory ceremonies at the time when the figs ripened. This coincided with the fading of the wild flowers in late June and July. But, in addition, all the symbolism attached to honey made it even more precious. In ancient agrarian cults, the fig was regarded as a sacred tree by all Indo-European traditions of the Mediterranean area. It was universally associated with fertility rites and with rites of passage and initiation, just like honey.

The junior priests whose duty it was to 'reveal the fig' were known in Ancient Greece as *sykophantes*, the word for fig being *suke*. To 'reveal the fig' meant announcing the official date of its ripening and the picking season. At this fortunate time of year one might eat fruits and honey, sweet and long-coveted delicacies. The ritual opening of the season is not so far from the opening of the hunting and fishing seasons we still observe, or the opening of the vintage and coffee seasons in wine-growing and coffee-growing countries. In the time of Solon, who forbade the export of figs from Attica, people who denounced smugglers were derisively called 'sycophants', and thus the term came to denote all informers.

That is another story, but it does show how, in Philippe Marcheray's words, the bee, an 'insect omnipresent in human societies, is closely linked to human thought. The great number of folk names for the bee and its products shows how it has become part of man's daily life and those of the animal and vegetable kingdoms; it is situated at the meeting place of those three worlds.' I would be inclined, myself, to say four worlds, including the invisible world of the mind in which it was believed that, when our eyes and lips were rubbed with honey, what we saw and what we said would never be quite the same again.

Honey-Cakes, Spice-Bread, Gingerbread

In 1694, the first edition of the *Dictionnaire de l'Académie française* defined *pain d'épice*, 'spice-bread', a word now very frequently rendered into English as 'gingerbread', as 'a kind of cake made with rye flour, honey and spices'. An early English mention of a confection of this kind occurs in Chaucer: 'roial spicerye and Gyngebreed'.

People had been enjoying honey-cakes for centuries. The Chinese of the tenth century, under the T'ang dynasty which encouraged the arts, are thought to have invented the original recipe: their *mi-king* (honey bread) was a mixture of flour (wheat flour, since they did not grow rye) and honey. Aromatic plants were not essential. As a concentrated, energy-giving food, it was carried in the thirteenth-century saddlebags of Genghiz Khan's Mongol horsemen. The Mongols passed the taste on to the Turks and the Arabs. Pilgrims to the Holy Land enjoyed it, and Arnold of Lübeck reports that certain Crusaders who got lost in the Romanian marshes owed their survival to it.[12] The chronicler gives this valuable item of the wayfarer's diet a Latin name: *panis mellitus*. The *panis mellitus* of the Romans and the *melipecton* of the Greeks were both actually quite a different dish: a cake made of flour, usually sesame flour, which was not soaked in honey until after it had been cooked, and sometimes then sliced and fried. In the form of *panis nauticus*, this was sailors' biscuit.

We have to remember that all sweet dishes of the ancient world were made with honey, whether for domestic or sacrificial use. Thus the famous traditional birthday cakes of Rome, particularly for people reaching their fiftieth year, were made with honey, hence their name of *quinquagesima liba* (Varro, Cato, Martial). These *liba*, made of wheat flour, grated cheese, honey and olive oil, were eaten with *mulsum*, a honeyed wine, after the gods had been given their share on the family altar. A cup of honey, the 'libation', was also poured on the ground to rejoice the souls of dead ancestors. This custom is still practised in Romania when a dead friend is missing from the usual company of guests at a party.

The Middle Ages were not particularly inventive in their confectionery and sweet dishes, but in the thirteenth century we hear of a Flemish cake consisting simply of wheat flour and honey, like the Chinese *mi-king*. This cake is mentioned in the next century as a favourite food of Marguerite de Môle, wife of Philip the Bold, Duke of Burgundy. The people of Coutray therefore presented such a cake to the couple's grandson, Philip the Good, who was delighted and took both the cake and its maker to his city of Dijon with him.

A hundred years later, again in Dijon, we hear of *pain de gaulderye*. *Gaude* was a kind of traditional mush or gruel made with honey, and in this case was based on millet. To be made into a loaf, the *gaude* was put in a mould to solidify and cooked a second time in the oven or under the embers. This was a kind of Burgundian reincarnation of the Byzantine wheaten *grouta*. The *hassidat b'el âcel* of Tunisia, similarly, is a mixture of fine boiled semolina with the same volume of honey, and, if you are rich, with melted butter, chopped dates and raisins. It is not cooked again but chilled to make it set.

Pain de gaulderye was made in Dijon until the beginning of the reign of Louis XV. This was about the time when Bonnaventure Pellerin advertised himself as a 'seller of spice-bread and tavern-keeper'. Others followed his example, but it was not until the Empire that Dijon could claim a distinction boasted by the city of Reims since the time of the Hundred Years' War, when it began the commercial production of *pain d'espices* made to the recipe of a pastrycook of Bourges. He had invented it around the 1420s in honour of Charles VII, nicknamed 'the king of Bourges' because of his retreat to the region when hard-pressed by the English. The spice-bread consisted of black rye flour, dark, strong buckwheat honey from Brittany, and spices in the fashion of the times. The King's mistress Agnès Sorel, called la Dame de Beauté from the name of the estate he gave her, graciously let it be known that she could never tire of this spice-bread. A dish enjoyed at the best people's tables was savoury spice-bread cut into cubes and dipped in the sauce of meat dishes.

Spice-bread was also, of course, made in Paris, but it was not until 1596 that Henry of Navarre, a lover of good food, granted the Corporation of Spice-bread Makers its own statutes, making it a separate body from the Pastrycooks. To qualify as a Master Spice-bread Maker you had to produce a 'masterpiece ... the mixture weighing 200 pounds, flavoured with cinnamon, nutmeg and cloves, of which there shall be made three cakes each weighing 20 pounds ...' The corporation's coat of arms showed a large gilded spice-bread cake on an azure ground, accompanied by four wafers of the same placed in a cross (these spice wafers were very popular, and were sold in the streets of Paris until the First World War).

The Corporation of Spice-bread Makers of Reims had broken with the Pastrycooks (or Wafer Makers) in 1571, and its coat of arms remained innocent of wafers to mark the fact. The spice-bread makers of Dijon, whose products did not really become well known until the Napoleonic period, neither became a corporation nor had a coat of arms, but they successfully caught up with and even drew ahead of Reims in marketing their wares.

Ever since the time of Louis XIII, Reims could point to a flattering mention in the *Encyclopédie méthodique des arts et métiers*: 'The city of Rheims makes the best spice-bread, because of the care taken by the shopkeepers of that city in making their dough.' And indeed the Académie Française completed its definition of spice-bread with one brief and proud example: *pain d'épice de Rheims*.

At first spices were added with a heavy hand, typically for the time. Catherine de Medici is said to have added certain poisons of her own to rid herself of enemies, since the whole court had an attack of colic one day after eating spice-bread. With the Renaissance, a craze for sugar came in too. The only spices some modern recipes will allow are a dessert-spoon of aniseed or, in Alsace, where there is a considerable spice-bread tradition, a pinch of cinnamon. Lemon is another ingredient, green in the Reims tradition.

But part of the secret of traditional French spice-bread, in Dijon, Reims and Paris alike, was in its making. It consisted of letting the dough rest – like the Sleeping Beauty – for several months, a year, or several years for the very finest kind. The 'mother' dough, as it was called, was kept cool in wooden tubs, while the honey in it brought about a delicious fermentation. Until the end of the Second World War, all that was required for traditional French spice-bread was honey, from Brittany if possible, the same amount of flour (wheat flour in Dijon, rye flour in Reims), spices or a small amount of green lemon; the dough underwent an alchemical process in wooden tubs and was then cooked in wooden moulds, shaped either into slabs or into the figures of little pigs. But in this iconoclastic age, chemistry replaces alchemy: not only is baking powder now added to the ancient formulas to make the dough rise faster, but honey is replaced by golden syrup.

Some labels now specify that the product is *'pain d'épice au miel'*, which should be an entirely superfluous description, but is offered as a guarantee.

Up to about the seventeenth century, English gingerbread was very similar to the traditional French spice-bread, and consisted of equal quantities of breadcrumbs and honey, with colourings such as saffron for yellow or 'sanders', made from sandalwood, for red. Spice was also used for flavouring – not always or solely ginger; a fifteenth-century recipe for 'gingerbread' contains only pepper and cinnamon. This was the kind of stiff dough hardened in moulds and traditionally sold at fairs. ('An I had but one penny in the world, thou shouldst have it to buy gingerbread', says Costard in *Love's Labour's Lost*.) However, molasses or black treacle began to replace honey around the Restoration period, and gingerbread gradually became more like the ginger cake of today.

Mead and Sacramental Intoxication

The child of honey, the drink of the gods, mead was universal. It can be regarded as the ancestor of all fermented drinks, antedating the cultivation of the soil. In any case it is the simplest. Water was mixed with honey, was perhaps left standing and forgotten, and produced an alcoholic fermentation. The people of the tropical countries, as we have seen, seldom ate pure honey anyway, and an unfermented mixture of honey and water (hydromel) could have been common.

Claude Lévi-Strauss[13] makes out a good case for the invention of mead as a passage from 'nature to culture', a process defining human behaviour, as implied in the coded message at the end of the Amazonian myth of the origin of mead he cites; it reads like a kind of postscript, as if it belonged to some quite different story, but it is not there by chance. The most important part of a message may be contained in a postscript, and it is up to the audience to attend and draw conclusions.

The myth is told by the Matako people, who are still in the Stone Age period of cultural development. 'In ancient times there was no mead. An old man tried to make it with some honey. He mixed the honey with water and left the mixture to ferment for one night. The next day he tasted it and found it very good. The other people did not want to taste the drink, as they thought it might be poisonous. The old man said, "I will drink, because I am very old and if I died it would not matter." The old man drank much of the mixture, and he fell down as if dead. That night he awoke and told the people that the mead was not a poison. The men carved a larger trough and drank all the beer they made. It was a bird who carved the first drum, and he beat it all night, and at dawn he was changed into a man.' This mixture, the simplest of all, does not need cooking or fire, but it is still a culinary act, inviting us to praise the gods for the miracle of fermentation and the magic of intoxication induced by drinking the fermented liquor.

On this basis of water sweetened with honey – the *melikraton* of the Greeks, the *aquamulsa* of the Romans, which became the *meda* of medieval Prussia and the *tschemiga* of Russia – Columella, the Hispano-Roman naturalist, gives the classic recipe for mead in his *De re rustica*, an agricultural treatise written around AD 60. He recommends using perfectly pure demineralized or sterilized water. 'Take rainwater kept for several years, and mix a sextarius [about half a litre] of this water with a pound of honey. For a weaker mead, mix a sextarius of water with nine ounces [250 grams] of honey. The whole is exposed to the sun for 40 days, and then left on a shelf near the fire. If you have no rain water, then boil spring water.' Notice the 40 days: 40 is a number signifying a period of waiting and preparation, part of a cycle leading to resurrection or purification. The making of mead is a ritual act.

It is interesting, for several reasons, to look back at southern Brazil, where the Mocovi people make ritual use of mead as a 'sacred, shared beverage' at festivals and 'the natives lived in a constant state of intoxication'.[14] It was being made in this way in 1943, and the recipe – for there is only one recipe, and it goes back to the dawn of time – conforms to that of the Matako myth and to Columella's. No fire is needed, nor even in this case a wooden trough or a cooking pot, which shows that it predates any form of industry. 'The dried skin of a jaguar or deer was hung up by the corners to form a pouch, into which the honey was poured along with its wax, and then water was added. In the space of three or four days the mixture ferments naturally in the sun.'

The leather pouch, also used over a hearth by the Fuegians and Eskimos, is certainly the ancestor of the cauldron. It will not burn as quickly as wood, even the hardest wood, and here it is not even exposed to fire. When hot water is required for a more elaborate kind of mead, related to beer since it contains a decoction of plants, 'honey is poured into the water and the water is heated by hot stones'. The mixture is then left to ferment under a covering of bark. I shall return to the use of hot stones later.

The brewing of these liquors and its incidental aspects – cutting down trees to make troughs, flaying of animals, the laborious process of moving hot stones – make up the sequences of a communal, social act, like the sharing of the drink itself at a later stage. Hunting became a group activity when beating for game was introduced, but there is something more here than the fever of the chase and the satisfaction of hunger: an experience of shared intoxication which, in very many festivals, takes a group of people out of their normal state of mind, out of time, freeing them from the conditioning of the outside world. It is not far from this condition to the belief that one is in direct contact with the other world. Sacramental drunkenness – a communal experience which seals alliances – was part of the Celtic festivals of Samhain, the New Year which began on 1st November,[15] particularly in Ireland. The Irish are still great beer-drinkers, and James Joyce's *Ulysses* contains a paean in praise of drinking.

The rite, for such it is, of intoxication is linked to fertility, harvest, success, just as they are expressed in the symbolism of honey. Drunkenness was not condemned in the ancient world. It makes men feel like gods, and the Greeks, Romans, Celts, Germanic, Slav and Scandinavian peoples not only felt (like the Amerindians) that they were part of a group of friends and allies in that state, but also that mead was the drink of immortality. No god in any of their pantheons denied himself that liquor. In final homage to the fallen kings whom the ancient Irish sent to their fathers, they were drowned in a vat of mead and their palaces set alight. (If the Celtic mead-maker, particularly in Wales, was not really a seer and healer, he was credited with those powers. Healing, like fermentation, was a magical operation, both of them graciously granted by the gods to the specialists who mediated between them and mankind.)

The Bambaras of Mali regard mead in a much more serene light, although they too consider it divine. To them it is the drink of wisdom, knowledge and truth, by virtue of the honey and the bees who made that honey. Like the honeycomb itself, truth has neither a wrong side nor a right side, and is the sweetest thing in the world. Another curious fact is that, while the Koran condemns the consumption of fermented drinks, mead is quite kindly regarded by the very pious Muslims of Mali, although their version of Islam is much tinged by animism. It is true that they do not get drunk on it, or not very drunk – it is so hot in Mali that one might drink just a little too much so as to feel better. African mead also contains chilli as a stimulant. When two friends drink together, they use the same gourd, placing their lips side by side as a sign of shared friendship. The Bambaras descend from an ancient and noble civilization.

Here I should note that ethnographers and historians in the first half of this century, and the upright German scholars cited by Dr Maurizio,[16] claim that 'uncivilized' peoples did not have fermented drinks. Dr Maurizio, whose work is both important and fascinating in some respects, unequivocally stated that 'savages still at the gathering stage did not have alcoholic liquors ... [nor] did peoples still in the early stages of cultivation of the soil ... this coincides with the view of Hahn, who thought that alcoholic drinks dated from the first period of cultivation with the hoe. But it is my view that they appeared in the latter period of this stage of civilization, and perhaps not until the time of cultivation with the plough.'

The myth of the Golden Age and the Noble Savage was regarded as gospel truth by missionaries and ethnologists alike, and the idea that the invention of alcohol was linked to the widespread growing of cereals suitable for bread-making (not cereals suitable only for boiling, like millet) and grapes for wine requires correction. Later in this book, we shall see how the revolutionary progress from porridge to beer and bread was made. The pot of beer and the glass of wine have been so important in the daily life of Judaeo-Christian civilizations that we tend to overlook anything else, but before their day mead, still a part of Graeco-Roman mythology, had been around for thousands of years. It was then forgotten or at least neglected. 'It is true that we do not know of any savage people of the present day making a fermented drink with honey', said Dr Maurizio in 1927. But such examples are now coming to light, and are a source of great interest.

In the Middle Ages, the availability of beer and wine did not preclude the enjoyment of mead. Indeed, the three got on so well together for so long that no feast in the ancient world was complete without large amounts of honeyed wine, *oenomelites* or *mulsum*. Northern Germans partook of *Lantetrank*, and still added honey to their favourite barley beer or brewed a type of honey beer; from the sixteenth century onwards it was usual to add hops. The people of the Vosges had a special method of their own: they enriched their mead with mashed bees to obtain a *miessaude*, a good ferment. The addition of nitrogenous matter facilitated and accelerated fermentation, a process which requires impurities; very fresh and very pure honey, on the contrary, is almost antiseptic. Some kind of contamination is necessary for liquid to ferment, whether caused by contact or by atmospheric pollution.

Mead is even made with crushed fruits. The Indians of both North and South America brewed it from that base, and the Romans gave such drinks the charming name of *meloneli*. Milk meads have been made. Mead can be distilled, and will also make vinegar.

Practically no mead is brewed today; try looking for it in the off-licence or on the supermarket shelves. Despite some efforts by farmers to popularize it, it remains a small folk industry, perhaps drunk occasionally at an ecological gathering, or as a conscious celebration of the past, or out of amused curiosity. One enjoys it and then forgets it, which is a pity, when it used to signify so much that is also now forgotten. Perhaps the gods really are dead.

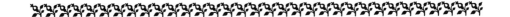

BOCHET

(This is a recipe given by the Ménagier de Paris, written about 1393. It is for a household mead rather similar to beer.)

To make six sesters of bochet, *take six pints of very soft honey, and set it in a cauldron on the fire, and boil it and stir it for as long as it goes on rising and as long as you see it throwing up liquid in little bubbles which burst and in bursting give off a little blackish steam; and then move it, and put in seven sesters of water and boil them until it is reduced to six sesters, always stirring. And then put it in a tub to cool until it be just warm, and then run it through a sieve, and afterwards put it in a cask and add half a pint of leaven of beer, for it is this which makes it piquant (and if you put in leaven of bread, it is as good for the taste, but the colour will be duller), and cover it warmly and well when you prepare it. And if you would make it very good, add thereto an ounce of ginger, long pepper, grain of Paradise and cloves, as much of the one as of the other, save that there shall be less of the cloves, and put them in a linen bag and cast them therein. And when it hath been therein for two or three days, and the* bochet *tastes enough of the spices and is sufficiently piquant, take out the bag and squeeze it, and put it in the other barrel you are making. And thus the powder will serve you well two or three times over.*

(Translated by Eileen Power, *The Goodman of Paris*)

Chapter 2

The History of Gathering

The Ancient Pulses

In the beginning there was gathering, the picking of plants. Starving people still instinctively put their hands out towards vegetation, like the baby with its eyes closed searching for the maternal breast.

Was it women who first gathered nutritious and sometimes medicinal plants in their wisdom – just as another and magical wisdom enabled them to grow children in their bellies to perpetuate the race? Is Nature herself to be seen as a Great Mother with a fertile womb, regular cycles and a capricious disposition? And if so many slow, secret creative processes depend on the female principle, is action a male prerogative by virtue of men's strength, speed and availability? For the hunters did not have to carry the future in their bellies or at their breasts, and were therefore available to hunt animals and make the gesture of sacrifice. Hunting implies danger, and can indeed be a risky business. Gathering denotes security, a modest but stable existence. Are we to regard meat-eating, with its connotations of heat and violence, as dependent on masculine skill, and fresh, soothing plant foods as the gift of feminine wisdom?[1] Simplified patterns of this kind are imprinted on our minds.

In fact there are no good grounds for supposing that the division of labour involved in getting food in the early days of the human race was inevitably along these gender-determined lines, other than by reference to various primitive societies of the present day. But do we know whether or not appearances of immutability are deceptive? Things may have changed. It is possible that such a dichotomy is the result of 'culture rather than nature, with the division of labour arising from a previously induced submissive attitude in women, not from supposedly distinct capabilities'.[2] Thus, if gathering food calls for the exploration of terrain extensive and rugged enough to conceal dangers, the whole group will have to be deployed

39

to do the work and keep watch. The animal kingdom provides countless examples of such arrangements.

The many kinds of plant food which are within easy reach of the gatherer's hand, and require no tree-climbing or digging with hands or sticks, include those extremely nourishing fruits which make up in number for their small size: seeds contained in pod-like structures. These seeds of small plants are less refreshing than tree fruits but a better substitute for meat than leaves. Chewed and swallowed, they give the stomach a sense of satisfaction and, best of all, they will keep in store for a long time.

The Romans gave the name of *legumen* 'to all edible seeds which form in pods and can be eaten as a porridge or made into a purée' (E. Benoist and H. Goëzler). The noun derives from the verb *lego*, to collect, gather, and also to choose or select, to take.

Until the eighteenth century, French *légume*, which has now come to mean vegetables of other kinds as well, was applied only to those plants we still call *leguminous*, the seeds of which were and still are often eaten dried. The word derives from *legumen*, by way of a form *léum*. In English, *legume* (in botanical rather than everyday use) still denotes solely 'the fruit or the edible portion of a leguminous plant, e.g., beans, peas, pulse', as the OED defines it. (*Pulse* is from Latin *puls*, a porridge made of meal or a similar substance.) 'As for legumes, they are seeds which abound in more varieties than any other vegetables: broad beans, peas, beans', wrote Olivier de Serres in 1600 in his *Théâtre d'agriculture et mesnage des champs*. Edible vegetables other than seeds are usually divided into *leaves* and *roots*. Leafy vegetables include lettuce, spinach, all the cabbages, etc., while root vegetables include turnip, radish and carrots. Leguminous vegetables are very nutritious because of the starch, proteins and mineral salts they contain, and have been described as 'the poor man's meat'.

If you go out for a country walk you may well come back with tendrils or hairy little seed-pods like flat matchsticks clinging tenaciously to your legs. The flowers of these plants, which look like little butterflies, belong to the botanical family of Papilionaceae. Only some of them, the most useful to us, have become cultivated plants.

Vetches, climbing plants found in hedgerows and as sweet peas in gardens, were probably the first to be gathered because of their natural abundance in the basin of the Eastern Mediterranean and in Eurasia. Often growing as weeds among cultivated cereal plants, they featured in the frugal diet of the poor until the eighteenth century, and even reappeared on the black market in the South of France during the Second World War; people will revert to such foods in times of hardship. Vetches had been considered fit only for pigs in previous years, and were not as good as lentils, but would do in the absence of anything better. St Bernard, in the famine of 1135, is said to have eaten bread made of vetch meal with his monks.

The broad bean, when picked in the wild state, as it was gathered tens of thousands of years ago in south-eastern Afghanistan, Central Asia and the Himalayan foothills, has seeds the size of a little fingernail. It was cultivated in Kashmir in very ancient times, and was quickly improved. Chester Gorman, a student from Hawaii, made a discovery in South-East Asia which may well reopen the whole question of the origins of farming. As early as the seventh millennium BC, a thousand years before any plants were domesticated in the Middle East, which is generally held to be the cradle of agriculture, the inhabitants of the 'Cave of the Spirit' in north-east Thailand were growing two kinds of broad bean which were already considerable improvements on the wild species, and also a variety of pea. And at about the same time as farming began in the Middle East, other cave-dwellers on the other side of the world, in the cave of Taumalipas in Mexico, were storing broad beans which had certainly been cultivated. The beans that have been found are seven thousand years old. Large seeds of gourds were discovered on the same site.

A happy accident of nature lent these first farmers a helping hand; something similar happened with corn, as we shall see. The wild broad bean like corn, has an extremely efficient reproductive system. When ripe the pod opens, rolls itself into a spiral and ejects its small seeds, which are scattered on the ground. But some abnormal pods never manage to open, and it was these that people picked to shell their seeds at home. Seeds collected in this way were sown to make it easier to gather beans from around the home camp-site. Accordingly, the plants they produced were the ancestors of cultivated broad beans which do not burst their pods. The 30 broad beans from a slightly earlier period found in a cave in northern Peru were harvested in their pods. Two of the pods have been retrieved – the pure, dry air of the Andes preserves substances very well – and it is possible to confirm that these pods, less fibrous than those of wild species, could not burst.

There is no reason to suppose that the same thing did not happen in other parts of the world. From the moment it began to be cultivated the broad bean, already remarkable among seeds for its size, improved even further, and improved quite fast. Its size and the nutritional value of the starch it contains soon made it one of the first foods to be stored. King Priam himself may have had sacks of broad beans among his treasures, like the cave-dwellers of Thailand and America; traces of such beans have been found on sites excavated at Troy.

The Greeks, who used broad beans as ballot papers in their election procedures, liked to eat them green, in their pods. Some people, incidentally, are extremely allergic to them. They are said to have caused the death of Pythagoras[3] at Metapontum – not by poisoning him, but because he so disliked broad beans either fresh or dried that he preferred capture and death at the hands of his enemies to escape across a beanfield. In fact there were philosophical and symbolic reasons behind the story of the sage's dislike of beans, although it seems to deal only with food. As a vegetarian, he would not let his followers eat them, apparently on the grounds that they were stimulating and indigestible.

The Romans, not being particularly Pythagorean,[4] used to make cakes of meal from dried beans, or *lomentum*, when there was a cereals shortage. The custom lived on at times of European crisis: Louis XV of France ate a roll of bean bread from a silver plate to show that he was sharing his subjects' privations.

From the time of Charlemagne and his collection of ordinances *De Villis*, making it compulsory for several rows to be grown in all gardens on his farms (the chick-peas described as Italian had to be grown as well), broad beans were very popular in the Middle Ages, particularly eaten early in the season, when they were called 'Lendict' beans in France, referring to the name of a fair held near Paris in June. They were sautéd with onions, saffron and a small piece of herring or porpoise.

Chick-peas, dear to the heart of Charlemagne, came from Western Asia. They soon became very popular from the Mediterranean to India, as the culinary traditions of those regions still show. The Phoenicians are said to have introduced them into Spain, where *garbanza* has been the poor man's staple dish ever since, but excavations of sites in Languedoc show that wild chick-peas were gathered in the seventh millennium, and were then followed by improved, cultivated chick-peas.

The word 'chick' has nothing to do with chickens, but derives from the plant's Latin name, *cicer*, whence modern Italian *cece* and French *chiche*. Roman vendors used to sell roast chick-peas at theatrical performances, just as peanuts or popcorn are sold today, and there are still fairground stalls in the South of France which sell enormous fritters known as *chichi fregi*, supposed to be made entirely of meal from chick-peas, like the *panisses* of Provence.

Grown in gardens, or spreading wild on the sunny hillsides of Mediterranean Europe and Asia Minor, lupins provide a magnificent show of pink, mauve and blue flowers, and a wealth of very nourishing seeds. They were simply gathered for a long time; the Greeks and Romans then took to cultivating them. They disappeared from culinary use around the time of the Renaissance. In modern times the Italians and some Eastern peoples preserve a kind of very large lupin seed in brine, using a recipe famous even in Byzantium, to be eaten as a cocktail snack like olives. The ancient Egyptians added lupin seeds to the barley from which they brewed beer, to give it a bitter flavour.

Lentils are another of the pulses of ancient tradition. Long before Esau came in from his fields so weary and hungry that he sold his twin brother his birthright for 'red pottage ... of lentiles', the Neolithic peoples of India, Egypt, the Middle East and Europe had begun sowing lentils, which grew wild in the Middle East and Central Asia, so that they could be harvested in quantity. The Greeks and Romans ate large amounts of lentils; they were the food of the poor, and the poor made up the majority of the population. The Egyptians were the main exporters of lentils in ancient times,[5] and, as the Romans imported them on a large scale, it is not altogether surprising that someone thought of making the little dried seeds into a useful packing material, one which would not be subsequently wasted. In the reign of the Emperor Caligula, the obelisk which now stands in St Peter's Square in the Vatican was brought by ship from the banks of the Nile, nestling among 120,000 measures of lentils. The Athenians made a fortifying lentil broth called a *ptisane*, and the lentil soup provided for the Roman legions by the consuls sustained their iron morale: dried lentils are rich in iron and phosphorus. Later, in the seventeenth century, people came to despise them, and eventually declared them fit only for horse fodder. It took the hard times of the French Revolution and the Continental blockade to bring them back from the stables to French saucepans, although Alexandre Dumas does not make much of them in his *Dictionnaire de cuisine*. Nowadays pickled pork and lentils is a trendy item on the menus of certain fashionable cafés. But, as far as I know, no wealthy Greek shipowner or oil-rich sheikh of our own time has emulated the Roman emperor Heliogabalus and mixed precious stones into his lentils.

Peas were a great standby of the Egyptians, Greeks and Romans, who grew them with some expertise. From the dawn of agriculture, constant selection improved the small round seeds, which were very common in the Mediterranean basin, the valley of the Nile and the mountainous regions of Asia. Peas have never lost their popularity since someone first gleaned and ate a handful. At l'Abeurador in the Hérault area of France, peas have been found among the debris left by the people who inhabited Languedoc in the seventh millennium, as well as chick-peas, vetches, broad beans and lentils improved enough to make it seem likely that they were cultivated. Such legumes may well have been the staple of these people's vegetarian diet, together with certain fruits. Alternatively, the place could have been occupied only seasonally, at the time for harvesting the seeds.

The Roman legions gathered peas from the sands around their camps in Numidia and Palestine to supplement the rations they received, consisting of flour, oil and salt meat, when not actually on service in the field. Our word *pea* is from Latin *pisum*, itself derived from Greek *pison*. The Old English term *pise*, becoming *pease* a little later, was misunderstood as a plural, and so the singular *pea* was coined.

Cultivated peas were mainly eaten dried in Roman and medieval times. Rabelais enjoyed dried peas cooked with a good piece of bacon – 'cum commentato' (with a gloss), as he explained. Split peas did not become part of the diet until the end of the nineteenth century, when the idea of rubbing off the indigestible skins occurred. The only dried peas now widely eaten in Western countries are split peas.

Green peas, or *petits pois*, made their entrance into French gastronomy some 60 years after the *mange-tout* or sugar pea, which had come from Dutch market gardens in the time of King Henri IV. In January 1660, on his return from Italy where he had been on a confidential mission (learning how to make liqueurs), the Sieur Audiger brought a hamper of green peas back from Genoa and presented it to Louis XIV in front of all his eminent courtiers. 'All declared with one voice', Audiger reported proudly, 'that nothing could be better or more of a novelty, and that nothing like them, in that season, had ever been seen in France before.'[6]

The Comte de Soissons (a name of good omen for leguminous vegetables, since the Soissons area is particularly famous for its French or haricot beans) shelled the peas, to universal acclaim. On the King's orders, Audiger entrusted the cooking of this wonderful new Italian vegetable in the French manner to the Sieur Baudoin, whose office it was to attend to such matters. 'There was a little dish of them for the Queen, another for the Cardinal, and the rest were shared between his Majesty and Monsieur' [the King's brother]. No sooner had news of the green peas spread than they became a positive craze: everyone wanted to eat them, at Versailles, in the outlying districts, in the worlds of finance and the Church. Mme de Sévigné hurried to her writing desk to tell her daughter all about them – while the King indulged himself in indigestion on a royal scale, and his head gardener, La Quintinie, worked miracles to raise young green peas in the glasshouses of Versailles.

But you can never please everyone, and in the next century *petits pois à la française* were accused of toxicity by Oliver Goldsmith in his letters.[7] The French way of cooking green peas, according to Goldsmith, made them practically inedible. Mere traveller's chauvinism, or a faithful reflection of contemporary British opinion? French cookery was a favourite target of English satirists, but it was still fashionable to have a French cook in London. The English method of cooking green peas flavoured only with mint leaves, instead of the onion and lettuce of the French tradition, is certainly delicious, perhaps because green peas are good enough to be eaten entirely on their own.

The French of the 1990s are not particularly fond of canned vegetables except – goodness knows why – for special occasions; they buy an annual 9 kilos of canned vegetables per head, as compared with the 38 kilos a head bought by Americans. However, canned peas, considered a rather superior sort of vegetable garnish, are the most popular in France, and indeed are preferred to fresh peas: three-quarters of the French pea crop goes straight to the canning factory. The British preference is for frozen peas. Peas are no longer picked by hand for either canning or freezing: the pea bines are reaped and the peas shelled in two almost simultaneous labour-saving operations.

Dried pulses left a special mark on Roman history: the famous names of several ancient Roman families proudly conveyed the information either (as one theory has it) that the founder of the *gens* was a man of those frugal habits on which the strength of Rome depended in the early days of the Republic, or (according to another theory) that he tilled the soil like Cato the Elder. Hence several Roman names referring to the chick-pea (*cicero*) the broad bean (*fabius*), the lentil (*lentulus*) and the pea (*pisolus*).

Finally, peas had the distinction of being used by the Austrian monk Gregor Mendel in his research when he laid the foundations of genetics. His experiments of 1865 enabled scientists to make great advances in botanical knowledge, and indeed, without Mendel and his peas genetics might not yet exist as a science at all.

The Symbolism of Beans

The traditional Twelfth Night cake contains a bean, often replaced by a small china fish or doll: these are allusions to classic Christian iconography. The parallel is not mere chance. Since time immemorial, the bean has been a symbol of the embryo and of growth in most societies.

The ancient Egyptians called the place in which the *Ka*, the souls of the dead, awaited reincarnation 'the beanfield'. In the sixth century BC, as we saw above, Pythagoras, the originator among other things of the word 'philosophy', who used various religious themes to illuminate his teachings, refused to escape his murderers by crossing a beanfield. He was acting in conformity with a major taboo. To his disciples, as to those who adhered to Orphic beliefs, eating beans denoted devouring one's own parents, and thus causing serious interruption in the cycle of reincarnation (whereas in many 'primitive' systems of thought the practice of cannibalism permitted assimilation, and was a kind of reincarnation).

Outside these communities of cult initiates, beans still symbolized the dead to the ancient Greeks and Romans, but they also saw them, being the first fruits of the soil, as representing blessings,[8] the bounty of those below the ground. Other seeds and cereals were viewed in the same way, but there was a deeper meaning to broad beans. Pliny, although dissociating himself from the Pythagoreans, conceded that there was indeed something of the souls of the dead in beans. When offered in sacrifice, they thus allowed communication with the invisible world, particularly at the spring and seedtime festivals. Spring itself can be seen as perpetual reincarnation. Beans were also a ritual offering in marriage ceremonies, each bean representing a male child in whom an ancestor would return to ensure the continuation of the family line.

The Etymology (and Entomology) of Haricot Beans

The Comte de Soissons figured briefly above, in connection with the arrival of green peas at the court of the Sun King, and so famous is Soissons for its haricot beans that it may seem strange I have not yet mentioned them. These New World beans, of the genus *Phaseolus*, are referred to in French as *haricots* whether they are eaten fresh, pods and all, or dried, whereas in English 'haricot' is usually reserved for the dried beans, and the fresh pods are known as French, kidney or green beans. You might have supposed I was saving them until last as a particular delicacy. The fact is that they did not reach Western tables until quite a late date. That date was 1528, when Canon Piero Valeriano was given some large, kidney-shaped beans

45

by Pope Clement VII. In a spirit of respectful curiosity, he sowed them in pots. The Pope himself had received them from the New World of the West Indies. The canon noted down the progress of germination as meticulously as Gregor Mendel later recorded the progress of his peas. He marvelled at their great fertility, and added that the dish prepared from his crop had been delicious. The seeds, known as *fagioli* by association with the traditional broad bean (*fava*) had soon conquered northern Italy.

At this time, Catherine de Medici, betrothed to the Dauphin of France, was packing before taking ship for Marseilles. Canon Valeriano, remembering that the way to a man's heart is through his stomach, persuaded the Medici family to add a bag of these *fagioli* to the future princess's dowry, tucked among the pearls and lace. Thus the famous bean dish of Languedoc, the cassoulet, originated in the landing of the haricot bean – not yet known by that name – on the shores of the Gulf of Lions.

The people of Provence, the first to eat these new beans, liked them very much and made them part of their *aïoli*. They featured in the Sunday version of the dish, the *grand aïoli*, since the new vegetable's price made it a luxury. Then it became less of a novelty, and once anyone could afford to get indigestion at a reasonable price from eating these *fayoun* (the Provençal name for the beans) the people of the Marseilles district, and elsewhere, realized that they were indeed inclined to cause flatulence. The jovial Provençals accordingly nicknamed them *gounflo-gus*, 'swell the poor man', and, with a play on words, 'swell the belly', since *gus*, related to standard French *gueux*, beggar, also meant 'stomach' (and a beggar may be seen as nothing but a stomach that needs filling). The *fayoun* or *fayot* made a good solid dish, and its reputation as a cheap stomach-filler guaranteed its popularity, although one voice was raised in dissent: that of Rabelais, speaking through the disrespectful mouth of Panurge, who accuses the *fazéolz* of making Lent even more disagreeable.

The French, kidney or haricot bean was thus first known in the Mediterranean countries by such names as *fagiolo*, *fayoun*, *fazéolz*, deriving from *fava*, the familiar broad bean. Then, suddenly, the word *haricot* surfaces in Oudin's dictionary of 1640, where it is defined as 'a kind of legume'. Eleven years later, Nicolas de Bonnefons felt able to mention 'the *fève de haricot* or *feverolle*'. Where did the word 'haricot' come from – a word which was to supersede all other names for these New World beans in French, and to be taken over in the English language to denote their dried seeds in particular? It was a word already familiar to every French ear and indeed stomach: the *haricot* or *héricoq*, recorded as early as the fourteenth century[9] (probably deriving from *harigoté* or *aligoté*, a word of Germanic origin meaning 'cut into pieces'), meant a stew or ragout of mutton and vegetables. The dish is still popular. But originally, and for very good reasons, there were none of the new beans at all in such ragouts. Instead, they contained root vegetables, particularly turnips. From the fourteenth century onwards, naturally, people were tempted to add haricot beans. But although Alexandre Dumas may cite Cyrano de Bergerac (the writer himself, not the character in Rostand's play) to support his theory, he is wrong in saying that a stew of mutton with haricot beans came first historically, and the beans were then 'dethroned by turnips'. The 'Revolutionary' (*sic*) ragout made with potatoes came in after the Empire period. This was to be the dish known as a *navarin*, somewhat confusingly, since the word may seem to suggest the *navets*, turnips, which it no longer contained. It is likely that the name refers to preparation of the ragout 'in the manner of Navarre' rather than to the battle of Navarin-Pylos fought in 1827.

The whole etymological puzzle, with its mistaken identities and coincidences, restored something like their original name to the foreign beans. For before anyone ever tilled the soil, the *ayacotl*, still a tiny bean, was gathered in Central America, south Mexico and Yucatan. A second centre of origin has been identified in the hot regions of Ecuador, Bolivia and Peru, where beans were found in Inca tombs. Confusingly, the large Lima bean comes not from Lima in Peru, but from Guatemala.

And that is not the whole story. As we shall see later in this chapter, the tropical regions of the American continent favoured root vegetables. *Phaseolus multiflorus* grows in Central America, a bean which not only is very prolific, as its scientific name indicates, but also has large, edible tubers. In fact it is a truly protean plant; the developing peoples of America and Africa (where New World beans have done very well indeed since being imported), more resourceful than Westerners who enjoy a superfluity of everything, eat the leaves as well, cooked like spinach.

By now it will be obvious why beans are second only to maize in importance in the Latin-American diet, from New Mexico to the Magellan Straits. The national dish of Brazil, the *feijoada completa*, is a kind of cassoulet, a baked bean stew which can be basic or grand depending on what else goes into it. Over a million hectares are given over to the cultivation of beans in Mexico, and they will even grow at an altitude of 3000 metres.

The 'French bean', as it is commonly known in the green state in English, had clearly acquired French nationality when some unknown person in the seventeenth century (perhaps Oudin himself) gave its name the Gallic form of *haricot*, but until early in the twentieth century reference books continued to profess ignorance of its origins. For instance, the delightful *Physiologie des substances alimentaires* published in 1853 'by the author', Stanislas Martin, a member of the Parisian Société de Pharmacie and of the 'Association of Inventive Artists', informs its readers: 'HARICOT (pron. A-RI-KO) = *Phaseolus vulgaris*. The haricot bean is a herbaceous plant native to Asia, and has been grown in Europe since time immemorial.' As witness the fact that a critic contemporary with Voltaire stated grandiloquently in a gazette:

> Jadis, d'un vain goût nos poètes esclaves
> N'entraient dans les jardins qu'embarrassés d'entraves;
> Phoebus ne nommait pas, sans un tour recherché,
> Le haricot grimpant à la rame attaché.

[Formerly, with futile tastefulness, our slavish poets entered gardens only hampered by impediments; Phoebus did not mention the climbing haricot attached to its beanstick without some elaborate turn of phrase.]

Like Martin, George Lindley, writing *A Guide to the Orchard and Kitchen Garden* in the early nineteenth century, informs us that '*Phaseolus vulgaris*, or Dwarf Kidney Bean, is the *Haricot* of the French. It is a half-hardy annual, a native of India ...'

It was not until 1901 that an entomologist's careful observation and a poet's meticulous scholarship between them restored its true identity to the haricot bean.

Jean-Henri Fabre was the author of a great ten-volume study of insects: *Les souvenirs entomologiques*. Like any southern Frenchman he enjoyed haricot beans, which he describes in moments of gastronomic emotion as *fèves*, the word which usually denotes broad beans, further describing the vegetable as 'blessed bean, consoler of the poor ... kindly bean'. But: 'Today', he writes, 'it is not my intention to extol your deserts. I want to ask you a question, simply out of curiosity. What is your country of origin? Did you come from Central Asia, with the horse bean and the pea? Did you belong to the collection of seeds which the first pioneers of husbandry landed to us from their garden patch? Were you known to antiquity?'

The answer to Fabre's question came not from the haricot bean itself but from a predatory insect, the weevil, more scientifically known as the bruchus, which is extremely fond of dried pulses. 'Here the insect, an impartial and well-informed witness, answers: "No, in our parts antiquity did not know the haricot. The precious legumen did not reach our country through the same road as the broad bean. It is a foreigner, introduced into the old continent at a later date."'

What proof of this assertion could the haricot weevil offer? The fact that it never eats haricot beans, but will gorge itself on other legumes, including much less appetizing varieties such as the lentil and the vetch, as soon as the seeds form. Why this chauvinistic prejudice?

> Apparently because this legumen is unknown to her. The others, whether natives or acclimatized foreigners from the East, have been familiar to her for centuries; she tests their excellence year by year and, relying on the lessons of the past, she bases her forethought for the future upon ancient custom. She suspects the haricot, as a newcomer whose merits she has still to learn. The insect tells us emphatically that the haricot is of recent date. It reached us from very far away, surely from the New World. Every edible thing attracts those whose business it is to make use of it. If the haricot had originated in the old continent, it would have its licensed consumers after the manner of the pea, the lentil and the others. ... This strange immunity can have but one explanation: like the potato, like maize, the haricot is a present from the New World. It arrived in Europe unaccompanied by the insect that battens on it regularly in its native land; it found in our fields other seed-eaters, which, because they did not know it, despised it. In the same way, the potato

48

and maize are respected over here, unless their American consumers are imported with them by accident.[10]

Fabre's reflections had reached this point when the invasion he feared in fact took place, starting in the Bouches-du-Rhône area and surely spreading from Marseilles, a seaport visited by many travellers, both official and unofficial. This particular illegal immigrant, reaching Maillane no one knows how, greedily attacked all the haricot beans it could find there, much to the astonishment of the people of Provence. Fabre was sent a 'bushel of haricots outrageously spoilt, riddled with holes, changed into a sort of sponge and swarming inside with innumerable Bruchi.' It was subsequently identified as an American species, and in the laboratory it refused to eat lentils, wheat, barley, rice or castor-oil seeds, none of them native to the New World.

Fabre had already been surprised to find the poet Virgil, in his *Georgics*, advising farmers to sow the *faselus*, translated in French dictionaries since the seventeenth century as 'haricot', in autumn, when every amateur gardener knows that it is a complete waste of time to sow French beans before Easter. Similarly, no naturalist of classical antiquity actually describes the kidney-shape of the seeds of the haricot bean, different from those of other leguminous plants, which are round and more or less flattened. 'They are quite silent on the subject of the sonorous bean. The word haricot itself sets us thinking. It is an outlandish term, related to none of our expressions. Its turn of language, which is alien to our combinations of sounds, suggests to the mind some West-Indian jargon, as do caoutchouc and cocoa.'

In fact the etymology which was puzzling Fabre before the American haricot weevil reached Maillane was explained by the great Parnassian poet José Maria de Heredia at the same time; one of those remarkable coincidences which do sometimes happen. Ideas are in the air, and several people seem to pluck them out all at once. Just as the American weevils were making their presence known, Fabre's eye fell on a magazine article, an interview with the author of *Les Trophées*. In it, the poet proclaims himself prouder of having discovered the etymology of the word *haricot* than of writing his famous sonnets, perhaps because of his own Cuban ancestry. José Maria de Heredia told the 'lady journalist' interviewing him:

> I found some particulars about haricots while searching through a fine sixteenth-century natural history, Hernandez' *De Historia plantarum novi orbis*. The word haricot was unknown in France until the seventeenth century; we used to say *fève* or *phaséol*; and in Mexican *ayacot*. Thirty varieties of haricot were cultivated in Mexico before the conquest. They are called *ayacot* to this day, especially the red haricot, with black or violet spots.

'How right I was', marvelled Fabre, 'to suspect that strange word haricot of being an American-Indian idiom! How truthful the insect was when it declared, in its own fashion, that the precious seed reached us from the New World!'

The story of the weevils is a reminder that tiny pests of this kind, not to mention innumerable rats, have been ransacking our granaries and silos for thousands of years. They might be held responsible for many famines if we estimated the thousands of millions of tonnes of food they have stolen from under our noses. Fabre remarked of the haricot weevil that a single couple of larvae – he describes the larva as 'a tiny white creature, with a red head' – scarcely visible to the naked eye, will reproduce at a rate of four generations a year. 'An isolated couple supplied me with a family of 80. … At the end of the year, the couples resulting from this source will therefore be represented by the fourth power of 40, reaching in terms of larvae the frightful total of over five million. What a heap of haricots such a legion would destroy!' Indeed, it seems miraculous that nature has not caused the world to disappear under a thick blanket of weevils and similar creatures.

Fabre optimistically concluded that 'with the aid of insecticides defence becomes relatively easy.' He could not know in 1901 that by the end of the century, when two world wars had provided the incentives for chemical research, DDT and other pesticides, while protecting crops and stored food, would also endanger the precarious ecological balance of everything from grass to the cow, from insects to birds. The problem does not seem near any solution yet. What is to be done? Should we take drastic pesticidal action after all? It is easy to think so in view of the wasted labour and empty stomachs found all over the world. And there is yet further cause for alarm in knowing that the great powers, running out of other ideas for methods of mutual destruction, have already drawn inspiration from the weevil. Nuclear bombs are out of fashion; introduce a few colonies of tiny larvae where required – voracious, prolific and tough because genetically 'improved' – and famine can quietly take over the world. This is not the scenario for some disaster movie, but a genuine threat by both sides, as the use of defoliants has already shown. There would then be nothing for the survivors to do but return to gathering, always supposing anything grew again to be gathered, in the shape of tiny, very tiny seeds. Gathering was the instinctive reaction of the starving, and we could yet see them make the same gesture again.

The Holy War of Cassoulet

Ever since the persecution of Protestants and the Albigensian Crusade in Languedoc, a holy war has been waged in that part of France, and it is nowhere near dying out. The various ways of making cassoulet are the issue at stake. For there is not just *one* cassoulet. The dish exists in several versions, each of which has its fanatical supporters, vehemently defending their faith. Every little local district proclaims that it alone practises the true rite – for rites rather than recipes are involved in the perfect preparation of this baked bean dish. People can discuss the matter for whole evenings on end as passionately as they will discuss sport. But all are in agreement on the following points:

– The dish's name derives from the *cassole* of Ussel, an earthenware pot which came from Ussel near Castelnaudary.

– Before the discovery of America and of New World haricot beans, cassoulet was made with broad beans, known as *favolles*. The best haricot bean to use is the *mounjete*, 'monk-bean', a bean of plump shape like a Capuchin friar, but the large, white, tender butter bean can be used if need be.

The beans must be cooked in two lots of water, the dish itself must be finished off in the oven, and its crust of breadcrumbs should be broken six times. The seventh crust (seven is a magical number) is the sign of the apotheosis of the dish.

In Toulouse, breast of mutton and the famous local sausage are essential ingredients.

In Carcassonne they preach the virtues of pork chops.

In Castelnaudary only preserved duck or goose is really acceptable, but a little garlic sausage may be tolerated.

Finally, it would be sacrilege to make cassoulet in Corbières without lightly salted pig's tail and ears.

Soya: the Most Widely Eaten Plant in the World

The dictionary defines cereal as 'a name given to those plants of the order *Graminaceae* or grasses which are cultivated for their seed as human food, commonly comprised under the name *corn* or *grain*', and although it adds, 'sometimes extended to cultivated leguminous plants', corn or grain is the generally accepted notion of cereal plants. The soya bean, however, should surely qualify.

Westerners have a rather vague idea of soya, familiar to us only in a few of its manifestations: bean-sprouts in allegedly Chinese cookery, the sauce which some people think is the juice of its fruits, and soya oil, valued mainly because it is cheap. It may be surprising to realize that the soya plant is eaten more widely than any other in the world – and as a food it comes in many other forms. The average Westerner might concede the likelihood that it is eaten more widely, since it comes from China and Japan, where there are so many mouths to feed. But having only a vague notion of botany as well as of geography, he might be hard put to it to say what the plant looks like.

Soya, then, is a legume like the pea, the haricot bean and the broad bean: a plant with papilionaceous flowers resembling broom, which grows to a height of 80 centimetres to a metre. Its flowers may be red, white or purple. As they develop they form hairy pods three to five centimetres long, each containing two or three seeds about the size of a pea or smaller, round or oval, and yellow, green, purple, brown, black or spotted in colour.

The scientific name of soya, *Glycine max*, also looks rather odd. 'Max' is not the diminutive of some botanist's first name, nor the abbreviation of 'maximum', but is a Portuguese transcription of the plant's Persian name. 'Soy' and 'soya' derive from the Japanese word *shoyu* for the sauce made from the salted beans. After acquiring the recipe from the Chinese in the tenth century, the Japanese manufactured it on a large scale. In China, it was called *jiangyou*. The Chinese and Japanese use the same ideogram in their written languages for the word which we render as soya; in Peking, however, it would be pronounced *dadon* and in Tokyo *dai-zu*.

Naturally there are legends about the discovery and popularization of soya. One tells the tale of two bandits or warlords, Yu Xi-ong and Gong Gang-shi, lost in the desert, who managed to survive on the beans of a hitherto unknown plant. According to an eighteenth-century Pekinese encyclopaedia, this happened 'very long ago'. Under the Ming emperors, in 1595, Li Shi-zhen devoted a section to soya in his treatise on botany and the medicinal properties of plants, the *Bencao gangmu* (Great Scheme of All Plants), but we have to go back to the sixth century BC to find the first written mention of soya in the court poems of the *Book of Odes*, a text full of information on many subjects. It states that the wild soya plant came from northern China, and began to be cultivated in the Chang period, around the fifteenth century BC.

The archaic ideogram *su* used to denote the plant is itself a lesson in agriculture. There is a row of little marks at the base of the character, said to represent the roots of the plant. Why go to all the trouble of showing them? Because the roots of the soya, even more than those of other leguminous plants, are able to feed the soil; the nodules they bear are storehouses of nitrogenous bacteria which disperse as the roots rot. Growing soya is therefore a way of replenishing soil impoverished by such greedy plants as wheat or maize, and it can be regarded as a green manure crop.

This useful property of soya, one that was recognized very early, is not its only virtue. In fact it could be described in the ornate Chinese fashion as a treasure-house of life. It contains, balanced in ideal proportions, all we need to sustain life: proteins, fats, carbohydrates, vitamins and mineral salts. It is easy, then, to appreciate its importance in the countries of the Far East, where there is so little cattle-rearing. Moreover, the people of those countries – perhaps by some genetic coincidence – often have a kind of hereditary allergy to milk, which they do not digest very well. One wonders if the reason is that they are traditionally unused to drinking milk once weaned from the breast. Be that as it may, nature has allowed the Asiatic peoples to make up for a serious dietary deficiency by providing a vegetable milk, soy-bean milk, a decoction of the dried beans, which is richer in protein than cow's milk. Bones of people who gathered wild millet, found on Paleolithic sites occupied before soya first appeared in their diet, have been found to bear clear signs that they suffered from rickets.

The Chinese Buddhist missionaries of the sixth century who reached Japan by way of Korea were well received there. They brought not only their religious message, but the miraculous plant which became a staple of the Japanese diet, in the same way as Buddhism merged with the native religion of Shinto. As the Shinto archives or *Kogiki* show, tithes levied on soya also fed the imperial treasury.

During the last war, the only survival rations carried by Japanese soldiers consisted of a bag of soya flour. Soya can be eaten in all kinds of ways: fresh, dried, plain, sprouting, ground, fermented, as curd, in soup, as a dessert or a drink. It is a curious fact that outside the Asiatic countries there has been so little interest in so versatile a plant. Until the second half of the twentieth century, Western countries have been particularly inclined to ignore it, while rice has been extremely popular in the Western diet ever since its first introduction, even though it has nothing like the same nutritional balance to offer.

Yet the Portuguese and Dutch sailors who traded with China and Japan from the end of the fifteenth century onwards were not unacquainted with soya. They mentioned it in their travel writings, always with indifference, at a time when Europe was experiencing periodic famines. In 1690 a German naturalist, Engelbert Kaempfer, published his *Geschichte und Beschreibung von Japan*, an account of his travels in Japan in which he mentions among other things that 'the Japanese use the *dad-fu*, or *daid* bean, which is almost the size of a Turkey pea,[11] as their daily food, and prize it second only to rice. They make a pulp of it, with which they prepare meat, as we use butter. And there is also *soeja*, a kind of *ammaba*, which they eat with their meals to stimulate appetite.'

The comparison with butter is applied to a paste of fermented, salted soya beans called *miso* by the Japanese. It is a thick and very savoury substance containing lactic bacilli and yeasts. It differs from region to region, and may also be made from crushed rice or barley, though the result is not so good. It is Chinese in origin; before soya became popular, and until the fifth century, the Chinese made a paste they called *jiang* using a fish purée.[12] At the time of the Han dynasty in the third century, soya paste became the standard ingredient of *jiang*, replacing a mixture first of fruits and then of cereals. Japanese development went through the same stages, but it was another three centuries before Japan acquired the soya recipe which by then was in use in Korea.

The famous *soshu miso*, from the Nagano region in the middle of the larger island of Japan, is said to have been created in the fifteenth century by a samurai named Takeda Shingu, a proud warrior and a gourmet, and *hatso miso*, dating from the same period, has been made by the same family for six centuries. Japan is a country of tenacious dynastic tradition. Various kinds of *miso* differ in colour and subtleties of flavour; they are all concentrates of vitamins and mineral salts, and no Japanese will willingly omit them from his diet. They are an essential part of the Japanese breakfast, a more fortifying meal than the Continental breakfast of Western Europe.

Engelbert Kaempfer's mention of *soeja* refers to what we now call soy or soya sauce. A contemporary of Kaempfer's, the Italian Gemelli Careri, following in the footsteps of Marco Polo, gives an account of meals consisting entirely of soya which he ate in the Peking area: 'They eat pieces of boiled paste, delicately sliced, and a soup of beans, called *tan-fou*, which is one of their most delicious dishes, for they dip their food into it. It is made of small, skinned white beans.'[13]

But Careri was no more able to interest the West in soya than any of his predecessors among travellers to the East. Even the fact that Asiatic peoples extracted a very useful oil from the plant excited no one's attention. The first soya crops grown in the Jardin des Plantes in Paris towards the 1700s and in the Botanical Garden in London were for private interest only. Certain dietary experiments were made, for instance at Étampes: the 'all-soya' meal served on 11 May 1911 by the Société Nationale d'Acclimatation aroused a passing interest in the press, but obviously none of these efforts went any further, for in spite of the subsequent food shortages of the First World War, still no one thought of exploiting the potential of soya.

It was not until after the Second World War that soya really took off, influenced not by Asia but by North America. The Americans were initially interested in its ability to regenerate the soil when grown in rotation with maize. Soya beans were used as animal feed, and in particular in the oil manufacturing industry. The Ford factories made plastics for car accessories from the residue of oilcake left after the oil had been pressed out. Suddenly American farmers reacted: soya growing began in the Central West of the United States, spread fast, and soon covered some 20 states. The USA, which had been the biggest importer of fats before 1940, now became their biggest exporter. There was a large concentration of soya fields on the banks of the Mississippi; the beans could easily be sent down the river on their way to seaports on the Gulf of Mexico. For some years now, the United States have been responsible for approximately two-thirds of world soya production, followed by China, Brazil and Argentina, which between them more or less account for remaining productivity.

Soya beans of a special variety grown solely for the extraction of oil and the production of the oilcake residue have several advantages over other oil-producing plants: they are very suitable for bulk transport, and they will easily stand up to long storage and travelling long distances. Harvesting the beans is very easy too: it can be done completely mechanically, whereas the fruits of the olive, palm or coconut trees have to be picked by hand. Moreover, thanks to a very short growth period (only 15 weeks from sowing to harvest), it is possible to adapt production easily to the demands of the world market. On the one hand, therefore, supply can be guaranteed, and on the other hand there is no risk of having to destroy a surplus.

Although originally a sub-tropical plant, soya is now grown up to latitudes of 52° north. The length of daytime hours is the principal factor affecting the crop's success. Each variety has its characteristic photo-period, the time when germination and seed development begin. Different varieties have thus been bred to adapt to different latitudes. In France, for instance, agricultural research has created hybrids suitable for growing in the Aquitaine area. However, it has not yet proved possible to grow soya successfully in Great Britain.

The beans are sown by heavy agricultural machinery in mid-May. They are harvested early in autumn by gigantic harvesters which cut a swathe of up to seven metres. At this point the soya fields look brown, since the leaves of the plant wither and drop before the beans mature, leaving only stalks and pods.

Besides the oil derived from a particular variety of soya bean, which as mentioned above is the principal market for soya in Western countries, various traditional soya-based foods adopted from Chinese gastronomy can be bought in health food shops or those specializing in exotic produce, or from the corresponding shelves of large supermarkets. The most common is bean-sprouts, used in salads or as a stir-fry vegetable; they are popular because they are so low in calories. In fact they are not usually the sprouts of soya beans, but of mung beans, which are similar but smaller. They are grown for the market in hothouses with warm sprinkler systems, and can also be raised at home on cotton wool in a warm place. Devotees of macrobiotic diets think highly of bean-sprouts, and of course they feature in Japanese and Chinese restaurant dishes, although the Japanese and Chinese themselves are not especially fond of them. As a vegetable they actually derive from a Vietnamese dish in which they are eaten only just cooked, to conserve vitamins. Bean-sprout salad is called *goi gia*.

Soya flour is now widely used in special diets to compensate for protein deficiency suffered by the very sick, old people and babies. Another excellent product to combat dietary deficiency is the soy-bean milk mentioned above. It is very good in liquid infant food and soups. It is sold in cartons, just like ordinary or protein-fortified milk, and its only drawback is that it is sometimes sweetened, in which case its usefulness is restricted. Soya pastes feature among exotic, vegetarian and macrobiotic foods, and as well as *miso* include *tofu*, Japanese soya bean curd, which may be either compressed or cream-like in consistency, and its Chinese counterpart *dou fu*. The arrival in the West of large influxes of refugees from the Far East has encouraged demand for green soya beans in specialist shops in some countries: they are eaten pods and all like mange-tout peas, and where available may be sold fresh, frozen or canned. The seeds are also sold as a dried vegetable, and are popular in Great Britain in vegetarian diets because of their protein content. Finally, soy sauce is used as a seasoning, sometimes to excess, in Chinese, Japanese or other Far Eastern dishes.

However, none of this is of anything but incidental gastronomic interest to Europeans, whereas the whole question of world famine remains extremely serious. Soya could help to overcome that terrible problem, not only as feed for the intensive rearing of animals bred for meat, or as a seasoning, but as what it originally represented to the Chinese and Japanese: a storehouse of nutritional riches.

Soya: Nutritional Facts and Figures

The human frame requires a minimum half-gram of protein per kilo of body weight daily. According to the optimum figures on a scale drawn up by the World Health Organization, this means, in grams per day:

baby:	minimum, 15	average, 20
child:	minimum, 45/50	average, 65/75
adult:	minimum, 35/45	average, 50/70

Alternative methods of supplying the daily protein requirements of an adult are:

soya flour:	140 grams	pasta:	585 grams
cheese:	280 grams	bread:	775 grams
fish:	280 grams	rice:	875 grams
meat:	410 grams	milk:	2330 grams
eggs:	540 grams	potatoes:	3500 grams

Moreover, soya protein contains all the amino acids necessary to the organism for the perfect synthesis of its requirements, and these amino acids are present in perfect equilibrium both of quantity and of type. They make soya a source of protein comparable to meat, milk, fish and eggs, all the so-called animal proteins. But unlike soya, meat lacks an important amino acid, methionine (while bread is deficient in lysine). Thus soya is a food with one of the best coefficients of digestive utilization, a figure of 82.

Soya has a high vitamin B content, including vitamin B1, higher than the vitamin B content of meat. It also contains vitamin E, calcium, phosphorus and iron. Finally, soya oil has a very high percentage of polyunsaturated fatty acids necessary to the human body, which cannot synthesize them itself, and this helps to lower blood cholesterol.

Soya flour and dried soya beans provide 392 calories per 100 grams.

Mushrooms and Fungi

Mushrooms are the plant *par excellence* for gathering. One hundred and twenty thousand species of mushrooms and fungi have so far been recorded throughout the world, and the 1841 species among them which are recognized as edible have surely been of interest to the human race ever since people began picking them. They offer a delicious food to be had for nothing but the trouble of bending down. However, the residues found in the course of archeological excavations provide no such evidence of mushroom feasts as can be relatively easily found when vegetable substances (like seeds and nuts) are protected by a cellulose envelope.

Cave drawings and paintings tell us hardly anything about the plants the cave-dwellers ate, and it is even rarer to find them showing mushrooms, which does not mean that the latter never featured on prehistoric menus. Residues identified prove that other vegetables were in fact eaten, even if few felt any urge to depict them on cave walls.

Moreover, if we look at the dietary customs of contemporary peoples who are still at the Paleolithic or Neolithic stage of development, there is plenty of evidence of an interest in mushrooms both edible and poisonous. The latter can be used in hunting, fishing, or indeed for homicidal purposes. Many tribes use the most dangerous cryptogamous plants in carefully calculated dosages for medication, or as hallucinatory or aphrodisiac drugs employed in certain religious practices. The empirical knowledge of the people who prepare these drugs is remarkable.

Mushrooms have been described as a vegetable meat. The term is something of an exaggeration, but they certainly have nutritional value. Besides their pleasing taste, which makes them a popular flavouring, they do indeed provide the organism with elements which we expect to find in meat and eggs: plenty of proteins and vitamins, mineral salts – and very few calories, a particularly appealing quality today.

As the scientific name of the common mushroom, *Agaricus campestris*, indicates, it is a field plant which grows in humus, the rotting vegetation found on damp soil. The English word *mushroom* derives from Old French *mousseron*, itself from late Latin *mussirio*. Certain species, however, have been cultivated since classical times, including *Agaricus hortensis*, known in France as the Paris mushroom. The ancient Egyptians and Romans greatly enjoyed mushrooms. Even today, the Papuans regard them as 'a food generating strength and courage'.[14] They grow in every latitude, in humid regions, although one species found on the shores of the Red Sea can remain more or less fossilized between the rare rainy seasons. This 'mushroom stone' was mentioned in the fourth century BC by Aristotle's pupil Theophrastus, but it does not look as if the Hebrews of the Book of Exodus thought much of it. The Bible, although full of references to food of many kinds, never mentions mushrooms, either in praise or otherwise. For reasons of hygiene or caution, they seem not to have been regarded as kosher.

The cultivated mushroom mentioned just now was grown on beds of horse manure. It was called the 'Paris' mushroom because the caves in the many stone quarries of the countryside around Paris have been used for nearly two centuries to grow it, in the dark and in particularly stable conditions of temperature and humidity. The hills of the Val de Marne and the Val d'Oise are riddled with mushroom caves, which can be located by their ventilation shafts above the ground. Mushrooms are also grown in the valleys of Maine-et-Loire and on the banks of the Gironde. In the United States, growing your own mushrooms is in fashion, and a corner of the family basement is reserved for them. Special cupboards, with boxes instead of shelves, enable the enthusiast for home-grown mushrooms to harvest a kilo of white mushrooms per square metre of mushroom compost, which is a mixture of humus and deodorized horse manure. The mycelium or spawn, consisting of branching filaments from which the mushrooms will sprout, is bought mail order, in compressed slabs. The United States is the biggest producer of mushrooms in the world, with France and Japan coming next.[15]

The Japanese grow the 'perfumed mushroom', *Tricholomopsis edodes* or shiitake, on a large scale. In the West, it has been available dried from the exotic food departments of stores and supermarkets, and recently European growers have also begun supplying it fresh. The spawn is introduced between the bark and wood of small chestnut or oak tree trunks, and the mushrooms grow on them.

So far as wild woodland and field mushrooms in general are concerned, interesting experiments in north Italy are opening up the distinct possibility of growing the boletus, chanterelle, parasol mushroom and species of *Psalliotus* for sale. The *Pleurotus*, or oyster mushroom, is already available commercially. In France, advertisements in agricultural and hunting journals offer the inducement of good profits to people who would like to grow cultivated morels in the gardens of their second homes.

But the supreme pioneers of mushroom cultivation must be the ants of equatorial America. In the same way as Western European ants rear aphids to milk them of honeydew, these tiny tropical farmer ants live exclusively on cultivated mushrooms. They carefully choose the right sort of soil, reduce the surface to a tilth with their feet, fertilize it by mixing it with a suitable compost of vegetable substances, and then add the spawn, tending it as it grows and matures exactly as the modern American tends the mushrooms in his basement. When they have to move house, they choose a new home in a place suitable for growing the spawn, first moving a relatively large piece which they then break up *in situ* to re-start the process. Even when food is in short supply they will never eat this sacred stock of spawn before it has reproduced; they will sooner eat their own eggs. When the spawn has started growing again they harvest the fungi judiciously, gathering the young mushrooms and taking care to leave enough of the basic stock in place. They had organized their mushroom-growing in this way long before man even evolved.

The mushroom, which may be either a delicious food or a deadly poison, was viewed very respectfully in classical times. There was something mysterious about its appearance after the rains and storms of autumn, as if it had been born of a thunderbolt, since it shows neither flower nor fruit. In fact the mushroom actually is a fruit, technically described as a carpophore in botanical terms. The Middle Ages, preoccupied as they were with sorcery, concluded that mushrooms were magic, and alchemists tried to discover the secret of creation from them: life regenerated by decay and death.

It is not surprising, therefore, that first Hippocrates in the fifth century BC, discussing the therapeutic virtues of certain mushrooms which unfortunately cannot now be identified, and then two other Greek doctors are our main sources of information about the contemporary cultivation of so valuable a plant, for doctors are always dealing with life and death. Nicander of Cleos, who was also a poet and grammarian,[16] explains in his *Theriaca* of the second century BC how mushrooms can be produced 'at will', in manure placed between the roots of fig trees. Dioscorides, a first-century physician, in his *Materia medica*, advocates sprinkling shredded poplar bark on compost to obtain the best mushrooms 'spontaneously', sown by the grace of the gods. And the grace of the gods was in great demand, so keen were his contemporaries on the boletus and other delicious field and woodland fungi. Dioscorides issues a warning about indigestion, to the effect that taken in excess 'even the best can do ill', and in such cases he recommends enemas of salt water as very efficacious.

However, the most prized mushroom of antiquity was the royal agaric, although the Empress Agrippina contrived to get rid of her unwanted husband the Emperor Claudius by serving him a dish of the fly agaric, similar in appearance but highly poisonous, and subsequently known as Caesar's mushroom. Fifty years later Horace (*Satires*, Book II, iv) thought that the sensible mushroom-lover would be wise not to risk such a fatal accident: 'Mushrooms from the meadows are best; others are not to be trusted.' If the sensible mushroom-lover disagreed with Horace's categorical statement, he could refer to the works of Pliny the Elder (AD 23–79), a contemporary of Agrippina and the unfortunate Claudius, who gives precise details of the appearance of various edible and poisonous species of fungi in his *Natural History*.

At the beginning of the fifth century, St Augustine denounced the dietary customs of the Manichaeans, vegetarian ascetics, 'who would think they sinned if they took a little bacon and cabbage with a few mouthfuls of pure wine, but will be served at three in the afternoon with every kind of vegetable, the most exquisite of mushrooms and truffles, flavoured with a wealth of spices.'

The famous Persian doctor and philosopher Ibn Sina, known to the Western world as Avicenna (930–1036), was particularly interested in poisonous mushrooms, as was Albertus Magnus, the thirteenth-century Dominican philosopher, who first gave its name of fly agaric to *Amanita muscaria*. He fed some flies with milk in which he had infused pieces of the fungus; not one of them survived. He then turned his attention to antidotes.

The first illustrated reference work on mushrooms, the *Corpus of Mushrooms*, was the work of a Siennese, Pietrandrea Mallioli (1500–77). The *Théâtre d'agriculture et mesnage des champs* of Olivier de Serres, published in 1600, contained useful advice on the cultivation in beds of the *mousseron* (as already mentioned, the source of the English word) which grows wild in woodland clearings and in pastures. Rabelais praised the Jew's Ear, *Auricularia auricula*, which grows on the trunks of old elder trees.

Morels preserved in salt were exported in the past by the people of the Narbonne and the papal state of the Comtat Venaissin. Louis XIII of France was very fond of them. He is said to have amused himself by threading them on strings for drying – in his own bedroom, because he liked their woodland scent so much –

and was occupied in this way on his deathbed. Cardinal Mazarin also praised the *mousseron* dear to the heart of Olivier de Serres. During the Frondist revolt, the daughter of Louis XIII's brother Gaston d'Orléans, known as la Grande Mademoiselle, glanced one day at the provisions destined for the royal family and the prime minister, against whom she was siding with Condé at the time, saw a basket of mushrooms and removed it, saying: 'These are too good. I do not want the Cardinal to eat them!' La Grande Mademoiselle had a reputation in some quarters for poisonous behaviour, but she was obviously no real-life poisoner, or she might have followed Agrippina's example and substituted other fungi.

Even though the dangerous species may be distributed over a much wider area than the edible mushrooms, it is a good idea to be able to tell them apart. The criteria for doing so were a matter of superstition as much as science in the popular mind for a very long time. In fact only the mycological knowledge of botanists can really be relied on. The members of the Société Mycologique de France include both eminent specialists and very knowledgeable amateurs, who themselves meet in a number of local societies. But outside exhibitions or guided walks, beginners are seldom able to say for sure whether a particular mushroom is edible or not.

Similarly, even the most detailed descriptions in books, colour plates, and the identification posters found in chemists' shops on the Continent of Europe, although useful, are not enough to provide positive identification of an individual specimen. The colour of a mushroom can vary in the course of the day. It must be smelt, felt and broken open as well as examined. Only experience and genuine knowledge are any guarantee of safety.

One should never, *never* take country lore and old wives' tales as a way of telling edible from poisonous wild mushrooms. If there is any doubt about it, consider the fungus poisonous. Purely for interest, I will mention a few of the tenacious popular beliefs still current, which have been responsible for some tragic postprandial accidents: that a silver coin or small silver spoon will turn black in contact with mushrooms being cooked only if they are poisonous, that onions or garlic (traditionally supposed to avert evil) will turn black in contact with a poisonous specimen, that slugs and ants will not attack dangerous species. There is no scientific foundation whatever for any of these beliefs.

However, part of the pleasure of gathering mushrooms is surely just walking in the woods or pastures in the pure morning air of late summer, when there has been warm weather followed by heavy showers. Every copse may reveal irresistible treasures, but they should never be eaten before an expert has been consulted. If you do not want to overload your basket, carefully lined with moss, however, you should never cut mushrooms (and they ought always to be respectfully cut, not pulled out of the ground) which have any of the three following features: scales under the cap, a ring, and a small sac at the base of the stem. All poisonous mushrooms show these three features, and if you leave fungi displaying them alone then at least you will be on the safe side: they may not be fatal but they will not be good to eat. Disregard the three warning signs of scales, ring and sac, and you could find yourself hurrying to the doctor for an antidote to something that seemed harmless.

Edible field mushrooms in Western Europe include those with pinkish caps, well rounded, and those with a cap like a Chinese coolie hat and a shell-like colour. Among the best of the woodland mushrooms are the yellow trumpets of chanterelles, ceps or boletus, with their large brown caps reminiscent of the Smurfs' houses; big parasol mushrooms with hollow stems which may grow 35 centimetres high and beige caps that may be 25 centimetres across, hollow morels with honeycombed caps looking like brown sponges on a white stem. (But beware of false morels, which resemble them. Eaten raw, they can be fatal. Dried and sold commercially, however, they are harmless.)

Dried substances looking like mushrooms and sold in the exotic food sections of stores and supermarkets are not really mushrooms at all if the packet bears the words *moq nhi*, but seaweed from the China Sea. The genuine black Chinese mushrooms are called *mu*, or in Japanese *kitinape*.

And finally, you do not need to have gathered a basketful of mushrooms to find yourself eating fungi. Moulds are fungi too. Most of them are not good to eat, particularly on fruit, but blue cheeses like Roquefort and Gorgonzola owe their delicious blue veining to a microscopic species of mould called *Penicillium roqueforti*. The velvety white rind of Camembert and similar cheeses is produced by *Penicillium camemberti*. Antibiotics were isolated from certain strains of *Penicillium*. Beer and wine yeasts are also fungi, the moulds of barley and of grape must respectively. Without these fungi, invisible to the naked eye, bread would not rise and champagne would not sparkle. Yeasts are a true food in their contribution to our intake of protein, vitamins and enzymes; we could not do without them.

I have not yet mentioned truffles, but I have not forgotten them; that would be unforgivable. Those 'black diamonds' will take their place in the section on charcuterie below, in the context of the traditions of Gaul and the Périgord area, for the truffle, like certain other luxury foods, did not achieve fame until the time of the Roman conquest.

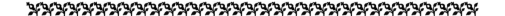

TEONANACATL, THE DIVINE MUSHROOM

OF THE AZTECS

*The first item to be served at banquets was a small black mushroom which
is intoxicating, and gives visions, and which also incites to lechery. They ate
it before daybreak, with honey, and when they began to feel heated, they started
dancing. Some sang, others wept, intoxicated as they were by these mushrooms,
while others did not sing but remained seated and pensive indoors. Some
foresaw that they would die, and wept; others imagined themselves devoured
by wild beasts, or yet again, becoming rich, or the masters of many slaves.
Others foresaw that they would be convicted of adultery, and their heads
crushed for that offence; others that they would commit theft, and be executed.
And there were many further visions too. When the intoxication caused by
these mushrooms had passed off, they spoke among themselves of the visions
they had seen.*

Fra Bernadino de Sahagún, *Historia general de Las Cosas de Nueva
España*

A LIBERTINE'S MENU OF MUSHROOMS

*We ate supper: and upon my word, I needed it. She served me morels, truffles
with a sauce made of ham, mushrooms* á la marseillaise ... *We hastened
straight from the table to bed ...*

Mirabeau, *Le libertin de qualité*

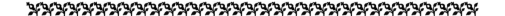

Roots

Many who were at primary school in the 1930s or 1940s may remember history lessons which imparted the information that 'in the Middle Ages the peasants lived a very wretched life. They were called villeins, and ate roots.' It all conjured up a picture in the child mind of a set of thin, villainous-looking people, their faces streaming with tears because they were so wretched, feverishly scratching in the ground for small, brown, earthy objects which they greedily devoured.

Such was the view of history presented. None of what we were told was actually wrong. The peasants of the Middle Ages did indeed have a hard life; they were called villeins, from Latin *villa*, a farm, and the word, though with a slight difference of spelling in English, is etymologically the same as 'villain'. And yes, they ate roots. So did the people of the towns. So do we today, at almost every meal. Roots have been part of man's diet throughout his history.

What exactly is a root? The dictionary defines it as 'That part of a plant or tree which is normally below the earth's surface ... serving to attach the plant to and convey nourishment from the soil to it ... the underground part of a plant used for eating or in medicine.' Besides being the plant's reserve and organ of nourishment, roots provide food for farm animals and for ourselves. Cooked or raw, roots such as radishes, turnips, salsify, beetroot, celeriac and carrots[17] appear on our tables daily.

A tuber, from Latin *tuber*, a hump or swelling, is defined as 'an underground structure consisting of a solid thickened portion or outgrowth of a stem or rhizome, of a more or less rounded form.' Tubers include potatoes, sweet potatoes and yams. The Amerindians eat dahlia tubers, and grew and gathered dahlias only for food. Rhizomes are swollen roots such as those of the garden iris. Of edible plants, the Jerusalem artichoke and the Chinese artichoke are tubers. Bulbs are plant organs formed from an underground swelling which produces many close-set leaves and stores food so that the parts of the plant above the ground can grow again every year. Bulbs include onions, leeks, garlic, Florence fennel, daffodils, tulips, etc.

'Root vegetables' are therefore those plants whose underground parts in particular are edible. Although he was certainly much richer than the peasants on his estates, the Duc d'Orléans gave a banquet consisting entirely of root vegetables on Good Friday of 1690, a meal that went down in the history of princely feasts.

The nutritional elements – starch, sugars, mineral salts, certain vitamins – which accumulate in roots, rhizomes, tubers and bulbs are very satisfying to the stomach, as the first gatherers of roots soon realized, even if they did not understand the reasons. The hotter and more humid a country, the better the underground parts of its plants thrive and the more useful they are. As the topsoil in such countries is often very thin there is hardly any need even to dig. Roots were a great blessing in such climates.

It was while searching for roots in the soil that the human race took the first step towards farming. The only tool you need to pick plants is the hand, but you had to scratch the earth to find its buried treasures. People soon began using pointed sticks or stones if the soil was dry and hard. The digging stick was the ancestor of the hoe and the plough. It may not be too far-fetched to suppose that if agriculture, the cultivation of the field (Latin *ager, agri*) first developed in the countries of the Middle East, it was because digging required a certain amount of effort in those parts.

In tropical zones, on the other hand, the soil is so swollen with water for most of the time that there is no difficulty in opening it up. Intensive agriculture developed much later in such regions than in temperate climates, and horticulture, the cultivation of the garden (Latin *hortus*), predominated. All you had to do in the gardens made in tropical clearings was scratch the surface of the humus or make a hole in it to plant cuttings or offsets of whatever grew best and most rapidly, including roots, tubers and bulbs dug up in the forest and now more readily available. Seed-sowing is always more risky because of the chances that seeds will rot or be eaten by pests.

If digging was the first step towards farming, it also proved to be one of the first agricultural methods. This was pure chance: where ground has been dug, the soil, which has been moved, aerated and mixed, becomes more fertile. The plant of the next generation will be more fruitful if something has been allowed to remain in the soil to reconstitute it. Gatherers observed this piece of agricultural wisdom. Similarly, hunters selected their game by allowing animals to go on reproducing. Ecology and respect for nature are lessons of the Paleolithic period.

Roots and tubers, gathered or cultivated, are the staple of the vegetable part of the diet in tropical zones, being easy and profitable to grow, but unfortunately they do not constitute a balanced diet, although they do provide plenty of energy: their high carbohydrate content is combined with a very small amount of proteins and vitamin C, which becomes even smaller after the removal of the large water content of the pulp, sometimes amounting to as much as two-thirds of it. The cooking necessary to make the starch digestible destroys any remaining vitamin C. Fortunately, people used to employ leaves in the cooking process, wrapping them round either the whole root or the pulp obtained by scraping or grating it.

The sacred flower of the Egyptians, the white lotus or water-lily, was represented over and over again by ancient Egyptian artists. Besides being used to perfume the hair, the table or the garden, it was also a providential foodstuff for the poor, who ate its seeds and rhizome either boiled, or dried and ground into flour. The Amerindians used marsh lotus of the New World, the pale yellow American lotus, in the same way. Since ancient times, the Sinhalese and Chinese have eaten the rhizome of their pink lotus, *lian-he*, dried or fresh and cut into serrated slices. Preserved, it has the delicious flavour of *marrons glacés*. This lotus, brought back by Alexander, was not introduced into Egypt until the Hellenistic era. The famous Lotus-eaters or Lotophagi of Djerba in fact ate ground jujube.[18] The botanical vocabulary is a jigsaw consisting of approximations and borrowings from antiquity, a time when confusions and approximations were frequent in any case. Many different plants were described as *lotus* or *lotos* in classical times, and Linnaeus accordingly gave the jujube tree the name of *Rhammus lotus*. In his *Travels in the Interior Districts of Africa*, of 1795, the Scottish explorer Mungo Park tells us that a bread made of the fruit of the lotus was eaten in Gambia and the Bambara district of Senegal-Mali. The lotus in question, he adds, was a tree growing wild in all the sandy sub-Sahelian regions. It can hardly have been a water-lily.

The sweet potato comes from the equatorial forests of America. A widely travelled tuber, it reached Polynesia two thousand years ago, and helps to clarify the problem of contacts between the Pacific islands and the north coast of South America. It is an additional proof that Melano-Polynesian migrations took place in ancient times. Until quite recently it was thought that the sweet potato was introduced into Africa at the beginning of the slave trade. We now have to put that date back several centuries, without knowing how or why it got there. Perhaps across the Pacific, as the intrepid Polynesian canoeists made their return journey from the coasts of Ecuador or Columbia to the archipelagos, then on either to Malaysia and South-East Asia or to East Africa by way of Madagascar. Maize,[19] groundnuts, peppers and cassava are thought to have accompanied the sweet potato. The coconut palm, the banana tree and the taro (a huge root known to the Romans) are also believed to have travelled in the canoes, together with agricultural techniques which are remarkably similar in all tropical regions (including hoeing, brush fires, terrace cultivation and long fallow periods), and which cast doubt on the sacrosanct belief that the Middle East was the 'cradle of agriculture', a title it appropriated without consulting the rest of the world.

The sweet potato, nutritionally richer than other giant roots (it contains vitamins, iron, calcium, sugar and carbohydrates) is a versatile tuber. It can be eaten boiled, roasted, mashed, stewed, ground into flour, preserved or in sweet tarts. The word potato comes from the Peruvian *batata*, designating any tuber, and the sweet potato has more right to it than the familiar everyday potato, which in English attracted the name by association.

When the potato and the sweet potato landed in Europe in a basket given to Queen Isabella by Columbus, the potato itself was not popular, and had to wait for the end of the eighteenth century before it came into its own. I shall therefore leave it until I am discussing nutritional developments of a later date. But the English of the Elizabethan era welcomed the sweet 'potatoe' with enthusiasm; at a time when sugar was so scarce and expensive, they liked its sweet flavour. The English colonists of North America made it one of their national dishes, following the example of the Indian tribes. When the potato itself came into fashion, therefore, it was regarded only as another 'potatoe', and the previously more popular sort had to be qualified by the addition of the adjective 'sweet'.

The people of the Antilles make a drink from the sweet potato, *ouycou*, from a Caribbean Indian recipe. The Empress Josephine tried to bring the sweet potato

65

back into fashion – Louis XV had been very fond of it – but its 'exotic' flavour put off the general public, who preferred the ordinary and more plebeian potato.

Jerusalem artichokes are not particularly popular today, although they are one of the ingredients of Algerian recipes for couscous. To the average Frenchman, they suggest the shortages of the Second World War, of which he will have heard even if he did not live through them, and they do not emerge particularly well from these memories, which in my view is a pity. (I cannot say as much for the swede, which I think was right to return to the mangers whence it came in wartime.) The Jerusalem artichoke crossed the Atlantic in the seventeenth century. It grew wild in the great prairies of the northern United States and southern Canada. The flowers resemble yellow daisies, and it is part of the sunflower family – hence, in English, its name, from French *girasol*, the sunflower which 'turns to the sun'. It has nothing to do with the city of Jerusalem at all. In his journal for 1603 Champlain, the founder of Quebec, mentions 'roots cultivated by the Indians, which have the flavour of the artichoke'; he meant the globe artichoke. The Jerusalem artichoke is almost the only food plant we get from North America, since in Europe the dahlia is grown only for its flowers.

The yam is as popular as the sweet potato in the West Indies. In the USA the name is sometimes applied to the sweet potato itself, but the real yam belongs to a different botanical family. The sweet potato is a climbing convolvulus, *Ipomoea batatas*. The yam is of the genus *Dioscorea*. It too is a climbing plant; however, the base of the stem does not form tubers but swells into a club-shaped rhizome. A single yam can provide a family with several meals, and specimens measuring half a metre in length and weighing up to 20 kilos are not uncommon. The yam grows naturally in clearings of tropical forests all over the world. It is not only very large but also relatively rich in protein. A purée of yam, cooked and allowed to cool and solidify into a flat bread called *foutou*, is the staple food of the people of the Ivory Coast; they eat it with whatever sauce is available.

Of all the giant tropical roots, the one most frequently eaten in Western Europe is the cassava. This may seem surprising until you know that tapioca is made from the tuber. Alexandre Dumas 'explains' the recipe in his *Dictionnaire de cuisine*, but incorrectly. The 'dried mixture' which Dumas, as a man of his times, describes as 'nourishment for the negroes in our colonies' is *gari* (or Antilles cassava), a favourite dish in the African regions around the Gulf of Benin.[20] The peeled and grated pulp is placed in cloth bags to drain and then to ferment slightly. It is then dried to produce a kind of acidulated semolina, used to thicken sauces on individual plates. The jellified appearance of tapioca is the result of warming the pulp until the starch changes to the consistency of an elastic dough, after which it is crushed and dried.

A Caribbean chief gave Christopher Columbus cassava at a feast on 26 December 1442. It is a remarkable plant, or rather shrub, which sometimes reaches a height of two or three metres. Its tender leaves are excellent cooked like spinach; older and tougher, they are used as wrappings around many foods to be grilled or steamed. The tuberous roots, arranged like the spokes of a wheel at the foot of the stem, can reach a weight of 25 kilos each. Parasites never touch cassava. Nature has ingeniously protected this tropical treasure with a skin containing poison (a kind of cyanide which the Indians use in hunting and fishing). The huge tuber has to be carefully and thickly peeled and then given a long soaking in water before it is crushed or grated and made into a dough or pottage, or cooked in flat cakes.

However, there is a variety of sweet cassava,[21] containing no prussic acid, and this is the variety which was brought from America to Africa and Madagascar at the time of the slave trade in payment for human beings. A very curious phenomenon occurs in Amazonia: though the Indians grow both varieties, they prefer bitter cassava in spite of all the complications of preparing it. It makes one wonder how the people who first came upon the dangerous wild cassava ever thought of eating it, since even a tiny quantity of the juice of the bitter cassava causes instant death. Was sweet cassava used first, and bitter cassava brought into the diet as a substitute at times of famine? That seems unlikely, since bitter cassava is gathered over a very wide area, sometimes where the sweet variety is unknown. Can a mutation in the plant have occurred after humans settled where it grew? No one knows.

In any case, the Amazonians, who grow this plant and no other in certain districts, know how to make good use of the bitter cassava, and waste none of it. The use of fire and a hatred of waste are typical features of Paleolithic cultures. The Kamyura Indians of the High Xingu rub pieces of the bitter tuber on stiff, finely perforated matting to extract the poisonous juice from the pulp. The juice falls into a waterproof basket or wooden trough, and is set out in the sun to dry. The hydrocyanic acid evaporates, and the jellified substance which remains can be safely used in cooking. The Caribbean peoples prepare cassava by peeling it, grating it on a board with thorns or pebbles stuck to it, and draining it through a wicker funnel. Again, the juice collected is put out to evaporate in the sun. 'Pepper-pot', the national dish of the Guyanese forests, is a stew made with evaporated cassava juice, fish, small game, crushed bones and peppers. It is kept simmering over the fire all the time, and as stew is taken out of the pot more ingredients are added, *ad infinitum*.

It is worth noting, with Jacques Barrau,[22] that over half of all wild food plants contain 'elements of an unattractive flavour which is more or less toxic'. And 'the wilder the plant, the more complex must be the method of preparation which makes it edible.'

These complex methods of preparation mean that those ingenious peoples we describe as 'under-developed' have made good use of utensils fashioned from objects we would hardly consider worth noticing: round stones or the jawbones of animals for crushing; flat stones or sticks covered with clay for grilling; chipped stones or sharpened bones for cutting; hollow stones, shells, nuts or gourds as containers; prickly leaves or small stones for grating; smooth leaves as wrapping material; sticks and woven fibres for many purposes; vessels made of leather pouches; wooden vessels hollowed out by fire. All this ingenuity makes the invention of pottery seem imminent, yet there are people like the Bushmen, the Negrillos, the Fuegians and the Samoans who feel no need for it.

And in final acknowledgement of those forest peoples who rendered so useful a tuber as the cassava innocuous, I must add that cassava flour was introduced into European bread during the First World War, though in much smaller proportions, of course, than in South America, where it is widely used. Some countries, such as Italy, a big importer of foreign wheat, went on making bread of mixed flours, the proportion of cassava flour being a modest 5 per cent. In most Western European countries, cassava consumption has shrunk to a very small amount. But the Africans, who already ate it as one of their everyday starches, can use it to make white bread like that of the 'developed' nations, which the inhabitants of their towns now crave, without spending too much precious currency.

Red August onion: engraving from the Vilmorin and Andrieux
catalogue of 1883, 'Les plantes potagères'.

One of the useful qualities of the onion, a bulb, is that it can be eaten raw. It grows wild from the Palestinian coast to the Gulf of Bengal, and quickly became a cultivated plant. Its powerful odour bears witness to its fortifying qualities. First the Chaldeans (2000 BC) and then the frugal Egyptian peasants adopted it to relieve the monotony of their staple diet of dates and fish. The Pharaoh Cheops paid for labour on the Great Pyramid in onions, garlic and parsley. Egyptian mummies set out for the afterlife with a stock of onions carefully wrapped in bandages, looking like another little mummy.

The onion is very rich in vitamin C, mineral salts, sulphur, and other trace elements. Empirical knowledge of its beneficial effects, understood as early as the building of the Pyramids, made it a part of the basic rations for sailors up to the last century. It helped to prevent scurvy during long voyages without fresh foods. Army quartermasters valued it for the same reasons. It was an essential part of the diet of the Greeks and the Phoenicians, great sailors themselves. Perhaps it was the onion that caused the Hebrews of Biblical times to weep 'throughout their families, every man in the door of his tent', for they lamented the lack of onions in their diet after the exodus from Egypt: 'We remember the fish, which we did eat in Egypt freely: the cucumbers, and the melons, and the leeks, and the onions, and the garlick: But now our soul is dried away: there is nothing at all, beside this manna, before our eyes' (Numbers 11, v).

Notorious for inducing tears, the onion obviously had the power to make people weep even by its absence. It is also supposed to be a meteorological vegetable: the thickness of its skin is said to forecast the weather of the coming winter. 'Quand oignon a trois pelures, hiver aura grande froidure', says a French proverb (when the onion has three skins winter will be very cold). It has been widely used over the centuries, as both a vegetable and a seasoning. The Romans were passionately fond of onions. Pliny listed all the different varieties and their provenances, providing a remarkable catalogue of flavours. Onions were pickled in honey and vinegar, a recipe of a kind still found in cookery books. One of its virtues was to stimulate thirst, so that Romans ate it throughout the meal. Later, the Franks adopted the same custom, and are said to have eaten onions as avidly as they drained tankards of beer.

It is sometimes thought, mistakenly, that onions are a particular feature of cooking in the south of France. In fact, in the same way as France divides into the country of the *langue d'oc* (the Provençal dialect which developed from Latin in that part of Gaul) and the country of the *langue d'oïl* (the dialect which became modern French), it is fair to say that garlic is the member of the onion family most popular in the *langue d'oc* regions of the south,[23] where cooking with olive oil also predominates. On the other side of the Loire, butter and onions rule. Onion tart and onion soup are typical dishes of northern France. Onion as an aromatic is not especially popular in Provence, except around Nice. Instead, it is eaten as a vegetable, and if Provençal cooks want to add a piquant ingredient to a dish at the browning stage, they prefer the white part of leeks.

There is even a religious sect of Worshippers of the Onion in Paris, duly registered with the authorities.

The *Allium* genus includes onions and leeks (very popular in the Middle Ages) as well as shallots, once thought to be a distinct species, *Allium ascalonicum*, which was brought to Western Europe during the Crusades. In fact shallots were known before that period, but they do not exist in the wild state; perhaps they are a mutation of the onion.

Garlic is thought to come from the desert of the Kirghiz people of Central Asia. A remarkably rich and ancient body of folklore surrounds it all over the world, just as its own odour surrounds the garlic-eater. This is largely due to its antiseptic and stimulating qualities. Did it reach America with the Asian hunters who made their way there, or were the seeds of its pretty star-shaped flower carried by the west wind? Be that as it may, garlic grows wild in the forests of Quebec, and the Amerindians of that province of Canada eat it a great deal.

Despite its well-attested virtues, garlic has its enemies. A number of people dislike it. The slaves who built the Pyramids will not have been asked for their opinion, but the priestesses of Cybele forbade entrance to their temple in Rome to anyone who had just been eating garlic (but there may have been magical reasons involved here). History does not say whether the ban applied to the Emperor Nero, who is held to have invented the garlic-flavoured sauce of *aïoli* in person. 'When they are seated around the divine *aïoli*, fragrant *aïoli*, deep in colour as a golden thread, where, tell me where, are those men who do not recognize that they are brothers?' inquired the Provençal poet Frédéric Mistral in the nineteenth century. But another poet, the Roman Horace, had declined to join that fraternity 2000 years before; it is true that he was suffering indigestion after eating a sheep's head with garlic on the day of his arrival in Rome. 'Should you taste such a dish, O sprightly Maecenas, may your mistress repulse your kisses with her hand and flee far from you!'

Horace was surely wrong; garlic is far from being a passion-killer. It contains sulphur of allyl, widely held to be an aphrodisiac. He could have advised his patron, 'sprightly Maecenas', to share a good *aïoli* with his mistress and then go to bed. Henri IV of France, said to have been baptised with a clove of garlic, was even more famous for his prowess as a lover than for the powerful odour he brought to his assignations.

The ancient Greeks were not particularly fond of garlic, but their heirs, the Byzantines, used it lavishly in their cooking, and would even eat it on its own when it was young and tender, roasted in the oven and then crushed with olive oil and salt, a delicious dish which turns up again in Spain. You have to be a garlic-lover to appreciate it, of course, but in fact it is not as strong as you might expect, and easy on the stomach, since the indigestible part of garlic is the germ. Was the Byzantine version of *aïoli*, *skoodaton*, the same as Nero's? It was enjoyed by all classes of Byzantine society, although if we are to believe one of the Emperor Alexis Comnenus's chroniclers, the Byzantines of the eleventh century were disgusted by the stinking breath of Raymond of Toulouse's crusaders. This may have been an expression of Greek annoyance at the insolence of the new arrivals, who behaved as if they were already in a conquered country..

King Alfonso of Castile, who disliked garlic as much as the priestesses of Cybele, would not have enjoyed this purée of crushed garlic, although his subjects must have eaten it to excess, for in 1330 the King issued a decree forbidding any knights who had eaten garlic or onions to appear at court, or to speak to other courtiers for four weeks.

Aillée was a very popular sauce in the twelfth to the fourteenth centuries in France, almost a soup, since slices of bread were dipped in it. It was made of garlic, almonds or walnuts depending on the region, and breadcrumbs, all pounded together and then added to meat or chicken broth. It was considered very healthful in winter, preventing colds and coughs.

There is a Provençal saying that garlic is the poor man's spice. It was also his medicine, and formed part of many diets and remedies to cure all manner of ills, not least the plague. When the plague was ravaging Marseilles in 1726, four thieves who were robbing corpses seemed to be miraculously and most unfairly immune. On being arrested and questioned, they told their secret; it was tried out on the grave-diggers who had been pressed into service, and the Chevalier Roze showed as much courage in taking the antiseptic preparation as in aiding his unfortunate fellow citizens. The remedy consisted of garlic steeped in vinegar, which was known as the 'Vinegar of the Four Thieves'. A pad inside a mask through which the wearer had to breathe was soaked in the mixture. Wearing a string of garlic around the neck at all times was also recommended; it stung the nose but spared the stomach.

This may be the reason why Alexandre Dumas, walking the streets of Marseilles while he was planning his novel *The Count of Monte Cristo*, says in his *Dictionnaire de cuisine* that 'The air of Provence is impregnated with a scent of garlic which makes it very healthy to breathe.'

Table 2.1   Vegetable Nutrition
(The use made of fruits, leaves, stems, pulp, roots, seeds)

Preparations	Parts used	Cooking method	Dishes
decoctions (90% water)	vatrious parts of plants, fresh or roasted (seeds)	in water	soup, broth
pottages, compotes (70% water)	seeds] crushed or fruits] whole roots pulps	in water	gruels, pastes, puddings, pasta, couscous, polenta, fruit pastes (10–5% water)
dishes of the *maza* type (50% water)	pulps fruits roots seeds true cereals } ground	in the embers, on stones, in ovens	pancakes, flat cakes, unleavened bread (4–5% water)
		braised in leaves, in water in water, then fermented	pasta sauerkraut
dough (30–45% water)	bread-making cereals + yeast, with or without flavouring (spices, honey) with or without fat (oil, butter)	in the embers, in ovens	bread, biscuits, cakes (10–30% water)

Source: A. Maurizio, *Die Geschichte unserer Pflanzennahrung von den Urzeiten bis zur Gegenwart*, Berlin, 1927.

Chapter 3

Hunting

The Great Days and the Decline of Game

Writers of novels set in prehistoric periods unhesitatingly use the word 'hunters' to mean men as distinct from women (who have no claim to be described by any particular term unless they happen to be 'mothers'). Homer called all the Greeks 'warriors' in much the same way. As we know not a word of the earliest vocabularies, 'hunter' must obviously be taken as a stylistic device, a convention which might seem to find some backing in the terms used of themselves in conversation by the last primitive peoples now living.[1] But although the people of the New Hebrides, the Mato Grosso or the Kalahari Desert may use such terminology to designate individual males able to provide the camp with game, there is no proof that things were the same in the Pleistocene era. During the 400 millennia in which *Homo erectus* developed into *Homo sapiens*, however, gathering did lose some of its importance, perhaps because of climatic conditions (the period concerned is 430,000 to 40,000 BC), only to recover it again when game became scarcer.

Man might not necessarily be a hunter by definition, but hunting, while not his sole purpose in life, was the only guarantee of existence for him and his family: it meant food from the meat of animals that had been caught or killed, a means of defence against dangerous or ferocious animal species, and the choice of companions for their strength, skill or cunning.

The whole economy of society could be summed up in a single word: game. Game provided almost everything necessary for survival over hundreds of thousands of years: the principal food, clothing, then instruments (tools made of bone were much easier to manipulate than stone tools), luxury items (such as the fat-burning lamps still used by Eskimos), ornaments, even aids to artistic creativity (carved bones, painted skins, etc.). It is easy to see why the first rock paintings showed

72

game and hunting scenes. Animals were depicted much more frequently than humans, especially in the earliest periods, for the animal was the whole point of the picture. Man is shown only about 20 out of 1000 times on the walls of French and Spanish caves. These rock paintings and engravings are fascinating for several reasons: first because of the beauty and precision of the works, then because they show almost all the local fauna from the beginning to the end of the Paleolithic period. I say 'almost' because there were certain small creatures which our ancestors saw no point in depicting even though they ate them (rodents, reptiles, molluscs and undoubtedly insects), as we can tell from fossils found around their hearths. Similarly, the vegetable kingdom was not shown. Small items of animal food were acquired as part of the gathering rather than the hunting process. One of the most remarkable of all the cave paintings, in the famous cave of Les Trois-Frères in Ariège, shows a man who is usually described as a sorcerer or witch-doctor – and why not? – wearing a complete skin, head and all, and dancing in the middle of a number of bison and deer. According to ethnologists, this is a magical dance shown not to create a work of art but to represent in almost concrete terms, rendering it timeless, the vision of an ideal hunt, with abundant and easily captured game.

The superb, almost photographic precision of the rock paintings arose from a keen faculty of observation: the hunter's eye and memory. Knowledge of the ways of animals, of the behaviour of the various kinds, their strength, their cunning, their number, their weaknesses, their tracks – all this went into the devising of as many methods of pursuing or catching them as there were creatures themselves. 'Hunting and the passion for hunting determined man's first relationship with the natural world', according to the preface of the catalogue of the World Exhibition of Hunting held in Budapest in 1971. The same could be said for the last peoples who were fundamentally hunters, and even for modern sportsmen whose hunting may be more than a mere pastime to them, almost a religion or a system of ethics.

Hunting led to technology. Man had to use cunning and ingenuity to compensate for his vulnerability and his inferiority to his prey in strength, number and sense of smell. It was to get game that he first made tools. Those tools became weapons, household and agricultural implements. It is easy to see the stick becoming the hunting spear, and that development can almost be seen leading on to the digging stick, the swing plough, the wheeled plough – and to the javelin, the gun, and all the way to the space rocket. Man dug pits on the paths customarily taken by game animals, traps like the efficient one shown in the Font-de-Gaume cave in Dordogne. There was a mechanism working this trap long before machinery was invented, for it caught a mammoth 50,000 years ago.

At the foot of the cliff of Solutré in the Saône-et-Loire region of France, a pile of wild horses' bones two and a half metres high is evidence that at least a hundred thousand horses threw themselves off the cliff in flight from their pursuers. It is easy to imagine the panic-stricken creatures, rounded up by the hunters in some kind of natural corral such as a valley with the exit blocked by trees, mounded earth or fire, and then driven the way the men wanted with yells, loud noises and

Earthenware stirrup pot, decorated with a warrior killing a deer: Peru, Middle Mochica artistic period (AD 200–800). The hunter's weapons are a kind of javelin; no doubt the function of the little dog seen at the foot of the deer was to bring the animal down.

flaming torches, much as Lapps drove the elk herds in the not so distant past, or as Buffalo Bill drove bison, using Indian tactics. The Lapps had used such methods since the dawn of the Neolithic era; rock engravings in their hunting grounds show them.

Hunting was not the only time when man followed the herds. The vegetation of the landscape altered during the climatic changes of the Middle Pleistocene period, when the ice sheets advanced from the extreme north of Europe until they

74

covered one-third of France, to retreat again at the end of the Upper Pleistocene. Before the steppes, suffering from drought because there was so little evaporation of the oceans and from violent winds, became tundra, they extended like a front line where animals fleeing from the rigours of the north took refuge. Herds of 'ancient' or 'southern' elephants,[2] woolly mammoths, the red deer of the steppes and forests, reindeer and elks were followed by hordes of hunters, themselves in retreat from the ice.

Faced with this abundance of big game, which they could not attack directly but must catch by cunning, the hunters used not only traps but missiles, which could be thrown from a safer distance. Even more efficient was the javelin-thrower, propelling a kind of harpoon. It has been found all over the world, and it is tempting to think it was spontaneously invented almost everywhere at the same time (like many other inventions, such as radio, but that is another story). In the same way bows and arrows, also found almost everywhere in the world, meant that man could strike down the fastest of herbivores, as well as birds. Many Mesolithic paintings found in Spain, the Sahara and Libya show archers fanning out after surrounding some deer-like creature or driving it out of cover, and attacking the bewildered animal with a rain of arrows.

At the beginning of the Quaternary period North Africa, protected by the waters of the Mediterranean, then an inland sea, was lucky enough to escape the ice which affected the greater part of Europe. The Sahara was naturally irrigated land, covered with forests full of animals.

In the Maghreb, near Algiers and Gafsa, the tools and weapons of a nomadic hunting people (they did not stay anywhere very long) have been found among the oldest stratifications of the Quaternary period. Pre-Chellean worked flints and pictures of game on cave walls – buffalo, antelopes, ostriches – mark out the area in which these hunters travelled through the centuries, as far as the mountain peaks bordering on a valley which was to become the valley of the Nile. It was a long time before they moved down from those heights, or at least before they actually settled lower down.

At about the time of the interglacial period in Europe the river basin of Central Africa, swollen with water from the vast amounts of local rainfall, finally found an outlet in the corridor of Upper and Lower Egypt, moving towards what would become the Nile delta but at this point still consisted of Pliocene lagoons and the beds of dried-up lakes. Marshes formed, rich in food plants with large roots, and in big and small game. The hordes were attracted to them, particularly because the progressive drying up of the Sahara was driving the fauna towards this plentiful stock of food. People came down from the mountains into the valley, saw how easy it was to find plenty of food, and stayed. Thousands of weapons made of chipped flint have been preserved from this period: hand axes, axes, arrow-heads, harpoons, spears. The many fossil bones of buffalo and elephants show that they ate well.

Between 4500 and 3500 BC, the clans expanded into territorial groupings with names generally referring to their totems and the fact that they owed their easy subsistence to the game they hunted. The clan totem alluded to an animal under whose protection, if only against hunger, that clan believed it stood. The allegory expressed gratitude which later became worship: cults of the falcon, fish, gazelle, jackal, plover, elephant or bull.

Over the centuries the protective fetishes of these proto-Egyptians became the gods of the *nomes*, the primitive social groups from which larger states emerged. Later on, after sporadic attempts at hegemony, these states became a federation. Representations of their totems, like coats of arms in heraldry, were still their emblems. Scenes engraved on schist plates can be seen in the Louvre and the British Museum. One such scene shows the Falcon clan setting out hunting. Finally the animal divinity of each *nome* became part of the solar and then the Osirian pantheon of gods, taking on human attributes as depicted by imaginative artists and in the legends and myths which grew up around them. Rites performed in temples assured the clan of security, prosperity and food, just as in the old days when the gods were still merely game.

Of course animal totems were not the only kind, and Egypt provides only one example of the sense of kinship between a people and the game it hunts. The phenomenon is found all over the world, with the Amerindians of North America the best known example.

However, taboos, including dietary prohibitions, could also be associated with the totem, which was perceived as the ancestor of the clan. Eating the totem animal then became a kind of cannibalism. In many places there were periodic ritual feasts when all members of the clan joined in eating it. Bonds of family or adoption were reinforced by complicity in the simulation of parricide, which also relieved the conscience of its vague wish to be rid of a troublesome father (or chief). According to Freud,[3] the subsequent 'festive feeling is produced by the liberty to do what is as a rule prohibited'. Eating the dead or captured enemies instead of game at actual cannibalistic feasts signified the assimilation of their virtues, strength and authority, which were thought to reside principally in the heart, loins, liver and marrow. Those parts were regarded as the choicest. Besides obvious remains of a hearth, the cave inhabited by *Sinanthropus*, Peking Man, found near that city, showed human bones which had been cooked and broken open so that the marrow could be eaten. When a powerful animal such as a bear, stag or boar had been roasted and was to be shared out at a normal meal, the choice morsels were given to the most honoured guests. In some areas, the custom has persisted. The Mossi people of Burkina Faso, formerly Upper Volta, will put the neck of a chicken on a male guest's plate, and the parson's nose on a woman's plate. Some ancient sexual connotation is evidently involved.

With the Ice Age drought that affected the northern half of the northern hemisphere, the scarcity of watering places gave rise to concentrations of small deer and goats. These were the first animals which man began to control, helping himself to them in judicious quantities, as analysis of the bones that remain has shown. When they were young, such animals could be caught in nets and brought to a convenient place near the camp site. People then had a supply of meat on the hoof which would keep fresh until slaughtered. Hunting became animal husbandry.

Man soon found an ally to help him pursue and catch game, and then to guard the captive livestock: the dog. It has long been thought that the first dogs developed from wolves domesticated by the Siberians of the late Upper Paleolithic era, but the latest archaeological evidence shows that marsh dogs, a kind of jackal, were being bred at Cäyönü in Turkey at almost the same time, around 9500 BC, and were probably used for hunting and as guard dogs rather than food. The first dog identified in Idaho in North America was barking around 9000 BC. Hounds were bred at Thebes in Egypt, and in Phoenicia. Many Babylonian bas-reliefs show mastiffs taking part in lion hunts. The lion was hunted either for sport or for safety, since it has never been considered very edible, any more than the dog. I shall look more closely at this prejudice against the meat of carnivores in the chapter on meat from farm animals.

Gazelles, fallow deer and antelopes were first kept in captivity in Sinai in the twenty-first millennium BC, a custom not adopted in Upper Egypt until the fourteenth millennium. Herds of reindeer were selectively exploited in Dordogne in the twelfth millennium – there are indications that rather more was done than simply controlling them, but we do not know what kind of supervision was involved.

Around 1500 BC great Egyptian nobles and members of the royal families, such as Queen Hatshepsut, might own several thousand gazelles, oryx and antelopes. The Queen even owned elephants. By now the practice of rearing game, as adopted by these owners, was well established. The Babylonians, such proficient huntsmen that their methods were used in Thebes, had supplied themselves with good, well-supervised stocks of game. The practice of preserving game for the royal hunt was to persist for centuries. In the twelfth century BC the last Chang emperor of China laid out a 400-hectare game park, almost a zoo, full of wild beasts, not just animals but birds and fish as well. His hunting schedules were impressive, and the deployment of dignitaries around their sovereign suggested a mixture of social ritual and army manoeuvre. Taking part in these hunts was the equivalent of doing military service as a reserve army officer in modern times. Indeed, the War Ministry was responsible for the organization of hunts in the Chinese empire; they were the guarantees of its security. Such hunts were forbidden to the common people on pain of death, for they symbolized power and were matched with an elaborate, almost religious ceremonial.

Today, private hunting of specially reared game has to be provided in Western European countries. Stocks of rabbits and hares have never really recovered from the myxomatosis epidemic. Hares in particular have almost vanished, their numbers reduced by civilization and the purchase of second homes as much as by the disease and hunting. Over the last few years more than 150,000 hares have been imported into France from Central Europe, where they are bred on an almost industrial scale, to replenish stocks. French-controlled breeding projects look promising; the main point is to maintain the quality of the hares by providing them with living conditions and food to suit their age-old habits. Game farms have also been started in the United States, where large numbers of gazelles are bred.

I am not going to make any pronouncements on the Buddhist tenet that all animal life should be respected, or Lao-Tsze's opinion of hunting as 'pernicious and a cause of trouble', or even the emotional reaction of the Emperor Caracalla when he wept at the slaughter of game, but it is fair to say that Nimrod, erroneously credited with the invention of hunting, was not a hunter in the sense which concerns us here. Nimrod, a great-grandson of Noah, described as 'a mighty hunter before the Lord' (Genesis, 10, ix), and the founder of Babylon, was merely a ritual slaughterer of wild animals, not a provider of food. As Erich Hobusch points out,[4] 'When the Tower of Babel was built in the time of Nebuchadnezzar II ... game between the Tigris and Euphrates had already been decimated and was reduced to a small stock.' In the same Old Testament context, we may note that the Lord declared a considerable amount of game unclean in the list he gave Moses (Leviticus, 11), including 'the coney, because he cheweth the cud ... and the hare, because he cheweth the cud', as well as a number of large birds and even snails, which may perhaps count as game (the French, after all, go hunting rather than gathering edible snails).

In Greek mythology, a Cretan hunter was the first lover of Demeter, the corn goddess; they lay together in a ploughed field, which sprouted wheat. Their child was Ploutos, Wealth. The idea was that, when hunters turned to agriculture, they grew rich. Stock-breeding of cattle began in Crete quite early, with indigenous species or those from the continent opposite being used at first, but the goats and sheep introduced into Crete from Asia Minor were wild game for some time before becoming farm animals. The Cretans liked hunting so much that before the dove, swan and wild duck were domesticated, they featured as Cretan ideograms. Even when stock-breeding became more widespread, hunting – which still goes on in the island today – meant a useful supplement to the meat supply.

The Cretans, who were experts in the training of fast, slender greyhounds with pointed ears, bred these animals especially to hunt the hares in which the countryside abounded. (A statue of a greyhound can be seen rubbing against the goddess Diana's legs in the Hermitage Museum in Leningrad.) They also hunted with the wild cat: the use of trained cats in hunting was brought to perfection later by the Touareg of Niger, who would carry a cheetah up behind them on horseback until a gazelle was driven from cover. Cretans ate all sorts of game, feathered as well as furred, for many migratory birds call in at the island. Capercaillies shared the long grass with goats; moorhens and ducks nested in the reeds. Wild boar, wolves and red deer lived in the forests, and on the mountain heights there were chamois and the *agrimi*, whose long, perfect horns made bows famous through the ancient world.

HUNTING

It is no surprise to find the huntsman of Zafer-Papoura depicted on his tomb with arrows and a long knife.

In the Peloponnese, the Mycenaeans of Agamemnon's time liked hunting large game animals; women took part in these hunts. It will be remembered that Apollo's twin sister, Artemis, was a huntress as well as goddess of the moon. She enters the Persian pantheon as Analita, and Scandinavian mythology as Tapo. The temple of Artemis at Ephesus was one of the seven wonders of the world. The frescoes of Tiryns on the plain of Argos show superb hunting scenes: two-horse chariots, a pack of hounds held in check by girls as slender as the dogs themselves, while men brandishing javelins hunt the hare or deer. A wild boar, harried by the hounds, is caught in a net to be finished off with a boar-spear.

The Greeks, heirs to Aegean civilization, added all the fine game so plentifully provided by the countryside to their menus: pheasant, partridge, pigeon, quail, wild guinea fowl and all kinds of small birds, including those we would leave alone, such as the robin, sparrow and oriole. Nocturnal birds of prey were also roasted with herbs, including various owl species, but not the little owl, associated with the goddess Athene. So as to avoid mistakes, therefore, and on the pretext of not offering competition to the city's butchers, hunting at night was forbidden on Athenian territory. Seagulls and pelicans were also eaten. Game animals included the wild boar and its young, especially the boar of Melos, the roe deer and the hare. Archestratus recommends eating hare plainly spit-roasted and still rare. 'The true gourmet is he who is not disgusted by an undercooked hare.' Rabbits had not yet reached Attica, but the fox, marten, mole and wild cat found their way onto the grill or into the casserole. Though they hardly counted as 'fur', and were certainly not 'feather', porcupines and hedgehogs caught in stony places were also regarded as game. The plump edible dormouse came to the end of its wild career in ancient Greece. Thereafter it was bred in hutches for 18 centuries. The Romans liked dormice so much that they kept them in jars, fattened them on walnuts, acorns and chestnuts, and finally cooked them in honey. The edible dormouse was considered a delicious titbit until the end of the Middle Ages.

As we shall see, once the noble austerity of the heroic age had passed, Romans were both gluttonous and anxious to have a good stock of provisions at the cook's command. Once Fulvius Lepinus had set the fashion for rearing game at Tarquinii, it became an established institution. Lucullus, Varro, Petronius and the rest had only to call on their well-stocked parks to be able to give lavish banquets where fallow deer, antelopes, gazelles and moufflons imported from overseas for breeding were served. Celsus, a doctor and a disciple of Hippocrates, recommended the red deer and roe deer as less exotic but 'more fortifying', especially for ladies. Galen was of the opposite opinion. The wild boar that devastated crops around Rome may have been so numerous and so bold because they were not popular food animals until the beginning of the Empire. After Cicero's time they came into fashion, and whole roast boar were served at the beginning of every smart banquet.

The meat of the hare was believed to preserve beauty, and the Emperor Alexander Severus ate it every day.

Great aviaries the size of houses were built for birds, to ensure that plenty were available. Lucullus had his private dining room set up inside an aviary, so that he could enjoying a roast thrush while its companions were flying above him. As Varro remarked, however, 'one must not forget the exhalations, which assail the nose'. Besides the small birds, sacrificial victims that included the nightingale (perhaps the enormity of the crime increased the pleasure), there were imported species such as cranes, whose eyes were put out before they were fattened, and parrots and bustards. Even ostriches were eaten, although they were so indigestible that at one banquet Heliogabalus served only the heads – 600 of them – and all the guests had to eat was the brains.

Reared in this way, game birds came to resemble plump poultry, and were eaten only by the privileged (who themselves were called *grassi*, 'fat people', by the Italians of the Middle Ages). Out in the country, only landowners and freemen might hunt. Roman law said that 'only that which is within my power may be mine'. As slaves had no power over anything, being nothing in themselves, they were forbidden to hunt, sometimes on pain of death if their master so pleased. The same legal ban was in force in Germania, for 'he who is authorized to bear arms may freely capture animals'. You had to be a free man to go hunting.

Venison was popular among the Gauls. Their reputation for gluttony amazed the Roman conquerors of the country, who regarded themselves as men of refined taste. The magnificent forests of Gaul were natural game reserves, and the marshes, adjoining rivers which were not yet managed in any way, harboured migratory birds in passing – birds such as geese, ducks and cranes, which tempted many archers. The Hercynian forest covered the mountains formed in the Tertiary era in eastern Gaul and Germania, from the Rhine to the Danube. It was swarming with large game animals eaten at convivial community banquets. Elks, which the Romans tried to domesticate, provided plenty of meat for the barbarian tribes. Julius Caesar has left us an account of them.

> There are also elks so-called. Their shape and dappled skin are like unto goats, but they are somewhat larger in size and have blunted horns. They have legs without nodes or joints, and they do not lie down to sleep, nor, if any shock has caused them to fall, can they raise or uplift themselves. Trees serve them as couches; they bear against them, and thus, leaning but a little, take their rest. When hunters have marked by their tracks the spot to which they are wont to betake themselves, they either undermine all the trees in that spot at the roots or cut them so far through as to leave them just standing to outward appearance. When the elks lean against them after their fashion, their weight bears down the weakened trees and they themselves fall along with them.[5]

Then, as now, the local inhabitants would obviously say anything that came into their heads to a reporter in search of copy who failed to check his sources. Pliny, in his *Natural History*, swallowed this story whole and passed it on as gospel truth. The elk (*alkê* to the Greeks, *eland* or *eluis* to the Balto-Germanic tribes, *Elch* or *Elen* in modern German) had already been almost exterminated in Western Europe when an edict of Otho the Great forbade elk-hunting in 843. The last surviving Central European elk was killed in Silesia in 1776. The elk still lives in North America, where it is known as the moose, and survives in Scandinavia and Siberia in the company of the reindeer (the prehistoric reindeer of Dordogne spent only the winter there, coming down from the north).

In the context of North America, where some of the larger species of deer took refuge, it is worth remembering that hares and rabbits, the Leporidae, first came from that continent, which was a New World only to the people of the old one. They emigrated between the Middle Pliocene and the Oligocene eras, taking a North Atlantic route before the continents separated. Making their way through Western Europe, they settled in North Africa before going back along the northern shore of the Mediterranean, which may be one reason for their absence from rock paintings. The rabbit did not reach France, from Spain, until the beginning of the Christian era. Later still, it was introduced into Great Britain from France in the time of the Norman Plantagenet kings.

The Greek naturalist Strabo placed the origin of the rabbit in the Balearic Islands, but it seems to have reached them from Morocco, where rabbits still live in great numbers, although there are none in Tunisia. However, Xenophon had described it in his *Cyropaedia*, calling it the 'little hare of the Greek islands', as being the size of a rat and deep russet in colour, resembling the rabbits still found in Madeira. In Latin, *cuniculus* (according to Pliny,[6] a word of Iberian origin) meant both the rabbit and its burrow – and by extension, any underground passage or canal. The old English word for a rabbit, 'cony' or 'coney', also derives from it; 'rabbit' itself seems to have been a word of Flemish origin, and was originally used only for the young animals.

Pliny writes: 'The animals in Spain called rabbits also belong to the genus hare; their fertility is beyond counting, and they bring famine to the Balearic Islands by ravaging the crops … the people of the Balearics petitioned the late lamented Augustus for military assistance against the spread of these animals …' He adds that Tarragona was entirely destroyed by rabbits. Pliny, like Caesar, is not averse to a tall story.

The rabbit was to be equally devastating in Australia, to which it was taken as a tame beast in the nineteenth century. Some of these tame rabbits escaped into the wild in the state of Victoria after a fire destroyed their quarters, and ten years later they had increased so prolifically, in a country without carnivorous animals to help maintain the ecological balance, that all possible measures had to be taken to exterminate them. But nothing worked – especially as once back in the wild they had learned to swim (extremely well) and to climb trees. Although 25 million rabbits were slaughtered in New South Wales in 1907, by 1925 there were several hundred million again. Rabbits are still a serious problem in Australia.

Introduced into France in the Middle Ages to top up stocks of game, and kept in warrens, the rabbit soon became acclimatized. Wild rabbits in France as in England (where they were originally escapees from warrens) came to be considered vermin, and to protect crops and please the peasants King Louis XVI gave permission for anyone to hunt them. In Great Britain too, the rabbit has never had quite the same status as other game animals, the hare included. In 1950 a French veterinary surgeon, exasperated by the damage done to his property by wild rabbits, injected some of them with myxomatosis. The virus, passed on by fleas, spread to such effect that two years later the rabbit population of France, both wild and tame, was practically exterminated and the hunting of rabbits was forbidden for several seasons. But by the latest reckoning the rabbit birth-rate is rising again. Much the same has happened to the rabbit population on the other side of the Channel.

The wild rabbit derives some of its succulence from the locality where it finds and eats the herbs which flavour its flesh. Louis XVIII of France had a well-earned reputation as the finest connoisseur of wild rabbits of his time. He could smell a rabbit fricassee and say that the animal had been killed in such and such a part of the country, and he was seldom wrong. He for one could not have been hoaxed 'in the less reputable restaurants of Paris, where they often serve fricassee of cat, pretending it is rabbit', as Stanislas Martin complains in his *Physiologie des substances alimentaires*, published in 1853. He hastens to assure his readers that 'there is no danger in the substitution'. Except to the cats of Paris at the time.

Until the timid half-measure taken by Louis XVI, and indeed up to the middle of the nineteenth century in most of Europe, game was out of reach to those who most needed it. Almost everywhere, the rich and powerful classes made hunting their jealously guarded monopoly. The history books tell us of the destruction of crops caused by great lords out hunting; they did as much damage as wild rabbits or wild boar, if not more. In 1520, Luther preached a sermon on private hunting which was one of the preludes to the revolt of the Black Forest peasants, who eventually attacked hunting lodges, hitting the landowning gentry of the day where it really hurt.

Game laws were not so much a relic of Roman or Germanic law as a social tradition which became a symptom of autocracy. One of the first laws passed after the time of the Roman Empire was a decree of the Merovingian King Dagobert in 648, regulating hunting in the royal forest of the Ardennes. It was thus that the word *forest* entered both French and, at a later date, English. It derives from medieval Latin *forestem* (*silvam*), which in turn comes from Latin *foris*, 'outside', and meant a place forbidden or protected by a barrier. The English word *foreign* is of the same derivation, denoting the stranger outside the royal territory, on the other side of the frontiers. The concept in general was of barriers around the territories reserved for royal hunts (and the felling of trees). The penalties for infringing game laws differed according to the legal code concerned. William the Conqueror had the poacher's eyes put out for the theft of a wild boar; under Charlemagne, taking a hare in a snare (this was before rabbits) meant a fine corresponding to the price of 60 cows. The peasants would not risk it unless they were absolutely desperate. On the other hand Charlemagne, in his *Inventaire des domaines*, distinguished for the first time between creatures to be regarded as game (so long as you had the right to hunt them) and those that might not be killed; the latter category included peacocks, pheasants, ducks, pigeons, partridges, turtle-doves, magpies, jackdaws and starlings. We still do not eat the last three. In recent times pigeons have invaded both town and country to such an extent that they have hardly been considered game birds at all, except in the last war.

The first Councils of the Church forbade 'all servants of God' to go hunting, but allowed them to eat game, and indeed water-fowl, like fish, were thought suitable food for fast days. The great prelates, who were often aristocrats – such as the late fifteenth-century Cardinal Ascanio Sforza, younger brother of the Duke of Milan and nicknamed the Nimrod of the Vatican – often preferred hunting and hawking to celebrating divine service. A Milanese chronicler mentions priests who said Mass booted for the hunt, their hounds tied up at the altar, their horses waiting outside the church door.

Small game (wild-fowl and water-fowl, hares, rabbits, partridges and quails, even rooks, crows and ravens, as well as small birds) might turn up on market stalls, so long as they had been legally taken and a fee paid for the licence to do so, or if they were being sold on behalf of the local lord of the manor. In Paris the game market was on the Quai des Augustins, in a place known as the Valley of Death because of the stink of tainted blood. Cookshop proprietors and poulterers sold such small game roasted or broiled. Quails, taken in a net, were profitably exported into England from France. But the 'noble' game, large beasts and such handsome birds as the pheasant and the capercaillie or even the peacock (which was reared, and was not really wild game), went straight from the lords' lands to their tables. Storks, herons, and their young were also eaten; the naturalist Pierre Belon, later murdered, hailed them in 1550 as 'royal meats, meats for great lords, exquisite among French delicacies'. When he had actually tasted these delicacies, to which should be added swans, cranes and bitterns, he thought them rather disagreeable, according to Dr Alfred Gottschalk,[7] who quotes another of his opinions: 'It is wonderful that the stomach of man can profit by all manner of birds, and yet there are some of them that even starving dogs would not eat.'

Birds such as these, admittedly, were old birds, neither plump nor tender – the Middle Ages did not appreciate young creatures – and in an advanced state of decay, inundated with spices and sometimes with sugar and verjuice. I shall return below to the ways of cooking game which sometimes made it harmful. The popularity of pies probably had some influence on the freshness and tenderness of the meats used. The Middle Ages loved pies. Even badgers and dormice went into them, and every region had its own recipes.

At great banquets, large joints of meat were also served in a crust, but it was

'Hunting stags with the bow: horse approaching the covert': miniature from Folio 30 v° of the *Livre du roi Modus et de la reine Ratio qui parle des déduis et de la pestilence*, by Henri de Ferrières, copied by Denis d'Horme (parchment of 1379). Notice that the rider of the horse carries no weapons; the archers concealed by the horse are to kill the deer.

usual to serve swans and peacocks, 'the meat of valiant knights', reconstituted into their living shapes, with a kind of ritual ceremony. The magnificent bird was flayed so that the feathers remained on the skin. It was then drawn, and stuffed with a highly seasoned forcemeat or with little birds (which were plucked in the usual way). Skewers fixed it in a natural pose. Generally the head was cut off and kept aside in all its glory. If not it was preserved from the fire during roasting by being sprinkled with cold water. Once the noble bird was cooked, its feet and beak were gilded, either with powdered gold or with a paste made of flour coloured with saffron, depending on the host's wealth. The plumage was put back on the bird and the head fixed in place. Wire kept the wings spread in an attitude of flight. A piece of lighted camphor in the bird's beak cast out sparks as it was carried to table on a silver dish, to the accompaniment of music. For great occasions, a company of ladies instead of the usual squires presented the dish to the knight who was guest of honour. Before the bird was carved, the hero of the feast had to make a vow. During the famous Banquet of the Pheasant held in 1453, Duke Philip the Good of Burgundy swore, on the pheasant concerned, to set out on a crusade and challenge the Sultan to single combat. The pheasant did not weigh heavy on anyone's stomach, and the solemn oath was quickly forgotten, the usual outcome of grand banquets serving political ambition rather than gastronomy: today as yesterday.

A great many interesting treatises on hunting were written in the Middle Ages and the Renaissance by experts who were often royal personages, but our concern here is with the game itself rather than the manner of hunting it.

In the seventeenth century, the better sort of game ceased for the first time to be the sole prerogative of princely tables, and was sold commercially. Agrarian crisis had followed agrarian crisis. Growing urbanization brought demand for more milk and more meat, town-dwellers' food, although less of both was being produced for want of enough farmers and enough pasture. As we shall see, cereal-growing was the obsession of the times. Consequently, pigs gradually encroached upon the mast of the forest floor, depriving the small game. Hunting became a profession, especially now that guns were used. Professional huntsmen served a long apprenticeship, and hunting became if not an industry at least a kind of business. Towns and working communities, particularly of miners, needed some meat in their diet as a change from salt pork, and the great landowners of the Continent became purveyors of venison. The Elector of Saxony set up smoke-curing establishments in Dresden which cured small predatory game such as hares, foxes and birds for the working people, and large beasts of prey such as the bear, lynx and wild cat for the upper classes and their town houses. The dichotomy whereby beasts of prey were meat for the gentry is revealing, and relates to the strength and cunning of the animals in question. 'Tell me what you eat, and I will tell you what you are.'

At the time of the French Revolution in 1789 the French peasants, not satisfied with Louis XVI's solitary concession of the wild rabbit, overturned the statutes containing game laws. Game in France was now indiscriminately slaughtered, and this highly profitable carnage hastened the passing of the new French law on hunting, to the effect that 'Every landowner or farmer may destroy game in his fields, using nets or other devices.' There were riots for universal game rights in Saxony in August 1790. In 1848, the Year of Revolution, the huge stocks of game in the Black Forest in Thuringia were reduced to almost nothing for a time. And had there been a revolution in Great Britain no doubt something similar would have happened, for the stringent game laws were much resented by the poor, and many poachers were transported to Australia in the late eighteenth and early nineteenth centuries.

Eventually, from the middle of the nineteenth century, hunting became accessible to almost everyone so long as a licence had been paid for. But game is still protected, and laws fix the dates of the open and close seasons of various species so that they can reproduce and preserve an ecological balance. Sometimes hunting or shooting certain creatures has to be banned for a while, and thus of course selling them and serving them in restaurants. There was such a ban in France in 1983 on a number of game birds including lapwings, woodcock, plovers and teal, to keep their numbers up. But poachers are always with us.

The importance of game in the carnivorous part of our diet has decreased as farmed meat has became ever more widely available. In the developed countries it is now a luxury, something out of the ordinary to be eaten on festive occasions during the hunting and shooting season. If you do not live in the country or have sportsmen friends who give you presents of game, of course you can get it from a poulterer or even a supermarket.

Game is expensive but, quite apart from the price, many people now hesitate to eat it for reasons of dietary principle which are not always properly understood. It is traditional to think of game as necessarily 'high'. People also forget that in many grand restaurant dishes it may not be the game itself which is indigestible or harmful, but the alcohol, spices and fats with which the sauce has been overloaded.

Nutritional Facts and Figures about Game

Tradition has it that game animals are not eaten on the same day as they are killed, when they will be too fresh. Indeed, the creature will have been frightened and tired before death, and so its organism, under stress, will have secreted large quantities of lactic acid to nourish its muscles. The muscles then reconstitute it as uric acid, a nitrogenous waste product caused by 'overheating'. The process affects venison in particular. When the meat has been hung, most of these substances evaporate, decreasing any risk of poisoning the consumer. However, the impact of a bullet may have perforated the internal organs or the bladder. All badly mauled or mangled animals should be thoroughly cleaned inside and eaten without delay.

However, smaller game, birds such as quails, partridge, wild duck or teal, can be eaten at once. The larger birds – woodcock, snipe, plover, capercaillie and pheasant – should be hung in a cool place for one or two days and protected from flies before preparation.

The pheasant is particularly associated with the idea of being 'high'. In fact, 'well hung' is not the same as 'high', since although the process of decomposition begins immediately after death it has not yet advanced very far in a bird well hung by modern standards. Game certainly used to be left hanging for a long time after it was killed, because the preference was for strong-tasting food, and the flesh would take on a very strong flavour as it putrefied. The term 'venery', the hunting of animals which thus became 'venison', was first used to denote that the beast must be made to run so that its flesh would be more tender. It had been realized that fatigue and fear changed the meat, although the effect of hormones was not yet understood. Incidentally, certain peoples of north Cameroon eat dogs, which are fed so poorly that they are obliged to scavenge for food like wild animals. The dog is then declared a 'thief', for the sake of the consumer's conscience, and has to be chained up and beaten for a day. It is not killed until it is thought to be panting enough, and they say there really is a difference in 'succulence' between a dog killed in a hurry and roasted at once and one well prepared in this way. This is one of the distasteful exceptions to the usual human taboo against eating the flesh of carnivorous animals. The death of the stag at bay is equally horrible. But to return to pheasants.

Brillat-Savarin (1755–1826) considered the pheasant at its best when decomposition was just beginning. 'At this time its aroma is developing in association with an oil which requires slight fermentation to be given off.' This was certainly an advance on the advice of Grimod de La Reynière (1758–1838) that 'a pheasant killed on Ash Wednesday should not be eaten until Easter'. It is hardly surprising that gout and the gravel were as much the mark of a gentleman as the gold watch-chain stretched across his waistcoat.

Hanging game, for a longer or shorter period, like 'venery' in its original sense, has the advantage of tenderizing a wild meat which has none of the softness and fat of farmed meat. A fat game animal is a sick animal, and should not be eaten.

Gastronomes preferred small birds such as woodcock not to be drawn. As soon as you returned from hunting, you hung them up by the feet until the insides, becoming deliquescent, dripped out through the beak and the feathers fell. They were then prepared, still often without being drawn.

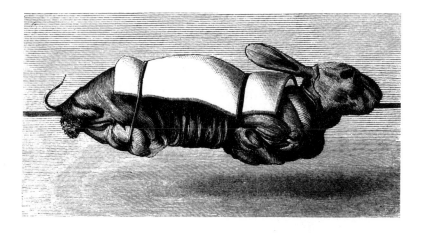

Hare on the spit: engraving from the *Livre de cuisine*, by Jules Gouffé, 1881

Marinades based on wine, spirits and aromatic herbs are also ways of tenderizing meat which might be tough, like that of the hare or wild boar, or large animals like the red deer, roe deer and fallow deer. They are put in a marinade as soon as they have been jointed, to prevent decomposition from setting in, and the marinade predigests, as it were, meat that is later casseroled or roasted. Young game needs no marinade at all, and after resting for a few hours can be roasted or baked, larded with bacon or other fat, since it is a lean, dry meat. Cooked like this, the natural flavour of game should satisfy the finest palate, and it will be perfectly digestible. Acid fruit accompaniments also aid digestion and assimilation. Wild boar, even when young, is usually marinaded anyway in the Continental European countries where it can be bought.

To tell if a bird is young, you take the lower part of the beak between your thumb and forefinger and let it hang. The beak of a young bird will break at the joint, because the cartilage has not yet ossified. A young partridge has pointed wings. Young game animals are small in size, their flesh is paler than that of older beasts, their teeth whiter and not worn down much.

Because game is lean meat, it has fewer calories than meat from farmed animals. For instance, 100 grams of farmyard duck contains 15 to 20 per cent lipids and 325 calories, while wild duck has 4 per cent lipids and 125 calories. The roe deer has only 3.6 per cent lipids compared with 25 per cent in mutton (a little less in lamb). The 2 per cent lipids in pheasant and its 108 calories are below the 145 calories of even the leanest chicken. But butter, bacon, stuffings, alcohol entirely cancel out the differences, and indeed may reverse these proportions.

Game animals contain plenty of mineral salts (phosphorus, magnesium and potassium) but game birds do not, which explains why game animals used to be considered a particularly stimulating, virile form of food.

Though venison is nutritionally valuable when prepared in a healthy way, being high in protein and low in fat – and of course it has a pleasing flavour too – the uric acid it contains, even in small quantities, and any possible germs that may be present, indicate that people should avoid it if they have digestive, cardiac, kidney or arthritic disorders, especially when it is served in sauces, marinated, or very high. Purin, a toxin present during decomposition, could set off allergic reactions even when the game seems fresh.

And finally – purely for the sake of anecdote – I will add that during the Middle Ages great medicinal virtues were ascribed to the blood of the hare, still part of the traditional recipe for jugged hare today.

PART II

*From the Neolithic period onwards, an agricultural and industrial
civilization employed methods of*

STOCK-BREEDING
ARABLE FARMING
MEAT
MILK
CEREALS

The Evidence of Occupied Sites

The last Ice Age, at the end of the period known as the Pleistocene,[1] lasted almost 100 centuries, from 20,000 to 10,000 BC. It was followed by a sudden warming and then, after several climatic oscillations, the temperature stabilized in the ninth millennium BC. The Holocene[2] period in which we are still living began.

Countering oceanic evaporation, and most important of all holding a great deal of water in the barrier ice and the glaciers which advanced over large areas, the great freeze of the Pleistocene was accompanied by a great drought. Coniferous forests thinned out, and the tundra invaded northern Europe. Southern Europe, the Near and Middle East became grassy steppes pushing the trees back to the foothills of the mountains. Finally, the progressive return to a succession of winter rains due to warming, the melting of the ice and the rise in sea levels allowed grasses which had adapted to the alternation of wet winters and very dry summers to spread around the Mediterranean and in the strip of land between the Black Sea and the Caspian Sea.

Nature thoughtfully provided these grasses with ears bearing rachides (the main axes of the separate spikelets) which were fragile enough to break under the weight of the seeds when they matured. These seeds or grains, larger than other seeds and ending in long awns, were dispersed by the wind and re-sowed themselves close or perhaps not so close to the parent plant, striking the soil like so many spears as they fell. The rubbing effect of stiff bristles at the base of the grains allowed them to dig themselves well in and away from predators. In this way the ancestors of the primitive wheats einkorn (*Triticum beoticum*) and emmer (*Triticum dicoccoides*) sowed themselves and became increasingly prolific year by year.

The hunter-gatherers, often disappointed by the decreasing amounts of game now available, did not fail to notice that these cereal plants provided a food which was filling and also kept well. In 1966 the American agronomist Jack Harlan carried out an experiment on the slopes of Mount Karacadag, a Turkish volcano, where these wheats still grow spontaneously, in abundance and remarkably true to type. He had only to bend down and gather the first part of his harvest with his bare hands, filling a bag with two and a half kilos of grain in an hour. Then, using a stone sickle, an archaeological relic of some nine thousand years ago, he increased his harvest to almost three kilos. Once it had been threshed and separated from its many husks, the grain weighed only two kilos, but it was of excellent quality. Analysis showed it to have an even higher content of proteins than the best American wheat. A Paleolithic tribe living in these parts, therefore, could have harvested enough grain in three weeks to keep them easily until the next summer.

Archeological sites almost everywhere which were successively occupied over a period extending from the twentieth to the seventh or sixth centuries BC provide evidence, in the shape of analysis of their sifted residues, that nutrition was

91

progressively evolving. Big game – Bovidae, Ungulata, Capridae – gave way to small game – Leporidae, rodents, birds, even snails (as in the pre-hunting period). Was this the result of climatic change, or of unthinking destruction of the wild fauna following on a growth in the number of consumers? Simultaneously, the proportion of berries, nuts and seeds eaten was growing. They seem to have become more than just a supplement to the diet.

Then came true cereals, deriving from one or two well-defined species such as einkorn and emmer. Their residues are found together with so many bones of herbivores of the same species that we seem to have evidence of the selection of animals to be kept as a captive stock over a long period, although it is probably still too early to speak of stock-breeding at this time.

Chapter 4

The History of Meat

The Birth of Stock-breeding and Society

Friedrich Engels, brought up in the comfortable bosom of the German bourgeoisie, remained very sensitive to the concept of family. In *The Origin of the Family* he wrote, of the Old World:

> Here the domestication of animals and the breeding of herds had developed a hitherto unsuspected source of wealth and created entirely new social relations.... Now, with their herds of horses, camels, asses, cattle, sheep, goats and pigs, the advancing pastoral peoples – the Semites on the Euphrates and the Tigris, and the Aryans in the Indian country of the Five Streams (Punjab), in the Ganges region, and in the steppes then much more abundantly watered of the Oxus and the Jaxartes – had acquired property which only needed supervision and the rudest care to reproduce itself in steadily increasing quantities and to supply the most abundant food in the form of milk and meat. All former means of procuring food now receded into the background; hunting, formerly a necessity, now became a luxury.

A little later Engels mentions the institution of slavery. 'More people were needed to look after [the herds] ...' And he concludes: 'According to the social custom of the time, the man[1] was also the owner of the new source of subsistence, the cattle.'

Besides reflecting the nineteenth century's state of knowledge and indeed its state of mind on the subject, these passages provide a very brief summary of a process of development which took tens of thousands of years, but then all books of Holy Writ, not excepting those of Marxism, tend towards the poetic compression of chronology and are inclined to regard their own part of the world as its centre. It is true, however, that stock-breeding constituted one of the first forms of communal or private property ownership (or theft from nature), which was a factor in the cementing and fermenting of those social organizations already beginning to form so that game could be tracked down or the vegetable resources of the environment exploited more efficiently.

Whereas a fertile mother goddess seemed to preside over the cultivation of the soil, the herding of animals, like everything else relating to them, proved to be an essentially male activity. Deriving as it did from hunting, it called for masculine protection, supervision and authority. Gratitude to the gods was thus in a state of equilibrium which conformed to the parental pattern. As in hunting, and for the same practical and cultural reasons described above, herbivores rather than carnivores were herded, tamed and then domesticated.

The ancient Egyptians, in fact, tried eating the hyenas that plagued their villages, but aversion to the idea was too strong to be overcome, and the hyena had the last laugh. The experiment was short-lived. I shall return to the pig, another scavenger, and banned from the diet by certain religions, in the section on pork and charcuterie below. Bacon, in the end, seemed a good deal more appetizing than the thin flanks of the carrion-eating hyena.

Learning to think ahead, such hunter-gatherers of the Upper Paleolithic as Cro-Magnon Man began on that process of economic development entailed by stock-breeding long before anyone thought of cultivating the soil. This seems logical in view of the fact that they already had the necessary 'stock in trade' at their disposal, but people still had to think of the idea.

They began thinking of it in the thirtieth millennium, at least in the region of what is now the Negev desert in the north of Sinai. Archeologists have discovered enclosures in which gazelles and fallow deer were kept, as large finds of bones in those areas indicate. Closer to our own time, between the twentieth and the tenth millennia, the cave-dwellers of North Africa herded the flocks of moufflons that inhabited the coastal plain; this wild species, with long hair around its neck and front legs, has been described as the ancestor of our present-day sheep, but in fact is only its uncle. Professor Saxon of Cambridge has been able to determine the criteria whereby animals were chosen for slaughter by analysis of teeth found in the heaps of fossilized bones left over from meals.

At the same period, but in Dordogne, where the rigours of the last Ice Age still prevailed, other cave-dwellers exploited reindeer in the natural corrals of the area, controlling the movements of the herds. Instead of capturing any animal at random, they slaughtered only males, leaving the females to ensure the survival of the stock. Evidence of the same technique at the same period has been found in Molodova in the Ukraine, where people seem to have specialized in herding reindeer. Still at this period, stags were exploited in a way developed in Italy, Switzerland, Great Britain and Denmark: judging by remains dating over a long period, the method ensured a constant supply of young male animals.

The exploitation of these herbivores – who went back to the wild when climatic change had driven the people who herded them away – took place over a period comparable with that which saw the appearance and then the herding of those species which have become our traditional farm animals. Tomb paintings show that gazelles (and even antelope) long constituted part of the wealth of great Egyptian landowners. The Romans were still herding elk imported from the north, to which the latter returned in modern times.

The ox (*Bos primigenius*) was first domesticated in the seventh millennium in Macedonia, Crete (as witness Minos) and Anatolia. Another bovine species was domesticated in North Africa towards the fifth millennium. Both breeds are now extinct.

So are those theories, so congenial to the Judaeo-Christian tradition, which held that stock-breeding came into existence almost of its own accord, if not by the grace of God, in the Fertile Crescent (those parts of Turkey and Iran bordering on northern Syria and Iraq). As we are always inclined to think that the world starts on our own doorstep, and as sheep, pigs, goats and oxen seem the only domestic animals suited to the diet of Westerners, who thereafter exported their own culture to the rest of the world, it was long assumed that stock-breeding, like agriculture, developed in the Middle East and spread from there; Engels was bound to echo this theory. The same prejudice exists in connection with horticultural food crops.

In fact it seems that dietary preference for the only seven categories of Middle Eastern livestock mentioned by Engels (sheep, goats, oxen, pigs, horses, donkeys and camels) can be ascribed to the cultural and economic influence of the fertile civilizations of those parts: the dominant civilizations of the planet, which will eventually devour all the others by making them eat in the same way.

Was this a matter of coincidence or infiltration? The Far East made the same choice with its own local variants of the species. Africa did not exploit its own fauna, but took to herding livestock introduced by various colonizers, thus accelerating the closing phases of a peaceable Neolithic culture. In the Americas, although the people of the Andes made good use of their few native ruminants, the inhabitants of the northern continent and the central isthmus had no turn for pastoralism, nor were the wild herds suited to it. It took the arrival of white men to make cattle-rearing a major industry in the United States and Argentina after the massacre of the bison. The same procedure occurred with sheep in Australia and New Zealand.

We do not really know why those species of sheep, cattle, goats, pigs and horses all over the world which are still proudly free kept or recovered their liberty. It may well be that the ancestors of our own domestic sheep, cattle, goats, pigs and horses, not forgetting the camel which no longer exists in a wild state at all, were particularly suited to the kind of symbiotic relationship which was established between them and us. Was it because of their gregarious disposition? Unlike those independent species which stayed in the forest or the bush, they followed in the footsteps of all the conquering races of mankind, infiltrating the world with them. We have used castration, of course, to curb their desire for freedom, but although

I shall be told that this is hardly a scientific conclusion, it does seem as if we were predestined for each other, or so at least the theory of Braidwood and Zenner[2] would make it appear.

The anthropologist V. Gordon Childe dates the beginning of this relationship from the end of the last Ice Age, when the climate of the Near East became very dry, and the Negev, where many gazelles roamed, became the desert we know today. She thinks that men and animals had to gather together around any water available in the oases, and their cohabitation led to close relationships which man used for his own ends.

Milking: detail from a limestone sarcophagus which contained the wooden coffin of Khaouit, the wife of an eleventh-dynasty king, Mentuhotep. Egyptian funerary iconography often showed the material goods that would be needed in the next world.

Table 4.1   Areas of Origin of the First Domestic Animals

	Places	First evidence of domestication
wild sheep	Middle East, Nepal, Tibet, Central Asia	Zawi Chemi Shanidar (Iraq)
wild goat	Middle East, from Turkey to Afghanistan	Ganj-Dareh (Iran)
wild cattle	the whole area between the 60th and 30th parallels north, from Western Europe to East Asia	Nea Nicomedia (Greece), Çatal Hüyük (Turkey)
wild pigs	the whole area between the 60th and 20th parallels north, except for Central Europe	Cayônü (Turkey)

ancestors	**differences**	**modern animals**
Bos primigenius or *urus* (primitive ox)	larger than	various breeds of cattle
Capra aegagrus (Bezoar goat)	spiral horns instead of the sabre-like horns of	goats
Ovis Ammon (wild sheep)	almost the same as our	sheep
Equus fossilis (fossil horse)	smaller than	horses
Sus scrofa (wild boar)	larger tusks than	pigs

Meat-Eating: Likes and Dislikes

Before the horse evolved into its present form and was domesticated it was frequently eaten, as we can tell from the remains left by the very first Americans, carbon-dated back to the twenty-second millennium, or those left by Peking Man in the Middle Pleistocene. At the famous Solutré site in Saône-et-Loire in France, fossil bones at the foot of the cliff allow us to estimate that more than 100,000 horses, undoubtedly driven by hunters, were forced to fling themselves over the edge for generation after generation. Why did such a perfect trap suddenly stop working? Had the horses been wiped out? We do not know.

Towards the end of the fourth millennium there was a whole magico-cultural system associated with the domestication of the horse, which gave mankind a genuinely new power – almost a new dimension. The animal was at the centre of complex symbolical meanings which would live on in race memory like fundamental archetypes, linking the forces of the underworld to the celestial powers. Psycho-analysts have seen the concept of the horse as the projection of our unconscious minds. Some brief remarks, therefore, are necessary here to explain how eating horse-meat could come to be seen as a kind of cannibalism, or as the ritual enactment of a crime, with all that its symbolism entailed.

However, the horsemen of Central Asia who brought us the horse – or were brought to us by it – and the barbarian Germanic tribesmen had enough common sense and frugality to eat the flesh of horses slaughtered at the end of their useful lives, or killed in battle. On the other hand, the noble steeds of chieftains were honoured with solemn funeral ceremonies.

Since ancient times, therefore, the horse has been bred mainly for riding and as a draught animal, although the latter duty has devolved more on its relatives, donkeys and mules, regarded as less prestigious mounts. Over the centuries eating horse-meat was to be a last resort, or at least a reluctantly adopted solution to economic need.

> Yet even that horse, when he weakens from illness or weight of years,
> You must pension off and spare no pity for age's failings,

advises Virgil, not caring to suggest an end in the cooking pot.

In Athens and Rome, as in Christian Europe, eating horse-meat was regarded with aversion, although it could fill famished bellies in times of disaster. The idea is repugnant to our own society, despite the dietetic recommendations of Geoffroy de Saint-Hilaire and his nineteenth-century colleagues who correctly noted the horse's resistance to tubercular infection and its nutritional value. But the pro-hibitions issued by Popes Gregory VII and Zachary I in Merovingian times were not to be so easily forgotten. Saint-Hilaire's banquet consisting of nothing but horse-meat was not a success.

However, the last Capet kings of France stopped posting guards around the knacker's yards of Montfaucon, preferring to see the poorest of their subjects survive even in a state of sin; without horse-meat they would have had only rats to eat. But it was still eaten with fear and revulsion, as Napoleon's surgeon Larrey discovered when he urged the soldiers of the Grande Armée during the siege of Genoa and the retreat from Moscow to eat their dead horses. The infantry had to lead the way.

Donkeys were still being eaten in Provence before the Second World War; it seems that that stubborn animal becomes increasingly tender with age – perhaps because it has been beaten all its industrious life? In any case, King Dagobert II, who once refused to dine on an ass's foal stuffed with small birds, eels and aromatic herbs, did so less for fear the meat would be tough than as an act of heroic mortification: he was about to free some prisoners jailed for debt, and wished to prepare for this charitable work with a clean soul and a light stomach.

The famous sausage of Arles owed its succulence to being made from a mixture of donkey meat and beef from the bulls of the Camargue. It was a favourite dish of the medieval Count René of Provence, titular king of Sicily and Naples.

Mules are still eaten in Spain, preferably dried fillets cut into paper-thin slices, like the dried meat of the Grisons.

The sheep was originally kept for its wool rather than its meat ('If wool-growing is your business, beware of barbed vegetation ... avoid too rich a grazing', Virgil advises), but mutton is a meat which adapts so well to hot, windy, dry or humid climates that it can be said to be eaten everywhere. It can store fat, like the camel (the meat of young camels is considered the best, and young camels' heels, enjoyed by Cleopatra, were a luxury dish in ancient times). The wild sheep of the Maghreb have fat tails which act as a food reserve when the sirocco has dried up the animal's grazing.

When the Romans decided to take a census in Palestine, 'when Cyrenius was governor of Syria', causing all the upheaval during which Jesus was born, the decree was not popular with the Jews, understandably when one knows that they had their own much more convenient methods of calculation: they counted the number of lambs killed ritually for the feast of Passover by the *cohens*, the rabbi butchers of the Temple, and multiplied it by ten. This, they no doubt reflected, was a logical process, since each roast lamb would feed ten people, no more and no less – they were economical but not mean – and they must have cursed the Governor.

The goat, the dominant farm animal of the Mediterranean, is even less choosy about its food than the sheep. Virgil remarks that goats 'blight the plants', and their ravages can be held partly responsible for the transformation of many Maghrebi and sub-Sahelian areas into desert. However, the poet also reminds his readers: 'These goats, too, we must guard with no lighter care [than sheep], and not less will be the profit', particularly from their milk and their fleece. They were not eaten as often as mutton, but the fine flavour of the kid was much liked. In the Middle Ages, the flesh of he-goats was salted and gave a strong flavour to thick soups.

Roasted sheep, goats, lambs and kids, and in some circumstances oxen, were the first sacrifices made to the gods. Whether in the Old Testament, Homer or Virgil, ancient literature is full of accounts of sacrifices, with the meat roasted over the fire,[3] its odour rising to heaven to please the deity, and its sizzling fat, mingled with aromatic herbs, anointing the altars.

> And he shall offer of it all the fat thereof: the rump, and the fat that covereth the inwards. And the two kidneys, and the fat that is on them, which is by the flanks, and the caul that is above the liver, with the kidneys, it shall he take away: And the priest shall burn them upon the altar for an offering made by fire unto the Lord.... And the Lord spake

unto Moses, saying, Speak unto the children of Israel, saying, Ye shall eat no manner of fat, of ox, or of sheep, or of goat. And the fat of the beast that dieth of itself, and the fat of that which is torn with beasts, may be used in any other use: but ye shall in no wise eat of it. For whosoever eateth the fat of the beast, of which men offer an offering made by fire unto the Lord, even the soul that eateth it shall be cut off from his people. (Leviticus 7)

We may add in parenthesis that the Chaldean, Greek and Roman priests read the future in the entrails and liver of sacrificial animals. African witch-doctors observe similar customs.

Around 1589 Father José de Acosta, back from the Americas, wrote his *Historia natural y moral de las Indias*, translated into English in 1604 as 'The Natural and Moral History of the Indies'. He finds himself in some difficulty when he has to ascribe the many and lavish sacrifices of Indian rituals to the Devil. The Old Testament was bound to come to mind. In fact it was the ceremonial which struck him as particularly pagan, rather than the system itself. Echoing St Paul's *Epistle to the Corinthians*, he writes: 'And as it is a fit thing and proper to religion to consume the substance of the creatures for the service and honour of the Creator, the which is by sacrifice, even so the father of lies hath invented the means to cause the creatures of God to be offered unto him, as to the Author and Lord thereof ...' Father de Acosta was a Jesuit. 'In like sort [to Biblical sacrifices] among some nations', he continues, 'he [Satan] hath been content to teach them to sacrifice of what they had; but, among others, he hath passed farre, giving them a multitude of customes and ceremonies upon sacrifices, and so many observances as they are wonderfull.' There might be human sacrifice on great occasions, but sacrifice was 'most commonly tallow burnt'.

The Indians often dressed their sacrificial animals in red, which particularly scandalized the missionary. All over the world, the colour red is connected with the symbolism of blood and animal fats, which are considered particularly valuable by races of hunters. Fire, also red, is fed by fat. Among the Tartars of the Altaï, says Uno Harva, the bridegroom's family place horse fat on the hearth while the bride's plaited hair is being loosened (this denotes opulence). The fact that the fat comes from a *horse* shows that this is an important ritual.

There has always been a kind of vague ambiguity in human attitudes towards the consumption of meat and its 'essence', fat, as if man were appropriating God's creatures, as Father de Acosta suggests, and must apologize, conciliating the deity with sacrifice. The early pages of the Bible mention the sacrifices made by Abel, who 'brought of the firstlings of his flock and of the fat thereof. And the Lord had respect unto Abel and to his offering.'

In all the myths of a lost Golden Age, or a state of grace to be recovered, vegetarianism, i.e., abstention from meat, has connotations of purity and virtue. Milk, which is permitted, is white and thus pure. It is represented as good in

Buddhism and Brahmanism, systems of thought to the forefront of Gandhi's mind, in the writings of Rousseau and Saint-Just, who hoped to feed the new generations of Republicans on bread, milk and water, and in 'cleansing' diets and popular therapies, and it also features in ritual fasts or those of initiation ceremonies.

The Church imposed fasting in Lent:[5] there were days when it was forbidden to eat meat or to engage in sexual intercourse (a certain ambiguity adhered to the word 'flesh'). In French these are known as *jours maigres*, literally 'lean days', as opposed to *jours gras*, literally 'fat days', on which meat could be eaten. 'Fat' implied the consumption of flesh, which was also felt to be 'hot'. Fish came to be regarded as suitable food for fast days because it came out of the water and was thus 'cold'. By extension, waterfowl was also suitable for fast days.

Although the most horrific permanent fasting diets were always the prerogative of mystics and certain religious communities with a particularly rigorous rule, throughout the Middle Ages and up to the end of the seventeenth century a holy, meticulous and implacable evangelical influence pervaded European kitchens. The dinner bell was set by the church bell. Every Friday, of course, was also a day of fasting in penitence for the death of Christ, and so were certain Saturdays. Meat-eating was forbidden on almost 180 days a year.

With the coming of the Counter-Reformation, religious folly reached such heights that the Church had to restrain the excesses of its most zealous servants in their renunciation of meat. The battle against gluttony could verge upon the commission of another mortal sin, the sin of pride: did not St Thomas recommend man to practise moderation, keeping his body in a state of equilibrium?

The guests at the great banquets of antiquity, Athenian and above all Roman, unimpeded by the idea of sin, were well able to face boards groaning with meat dishes: these tended to be mixed stews of unusual ingredients, exotic game, or especially suggestive offal such as the vulvas and teats of sows, or calves' testicles. The latter are still called *frivolités* (frivolities or trifles) in the Languedoc area of France.

Two Greek actors made a name for themselves as meat-eaters: one was a woman, Aglaïs, who could eat ten pounds of meat at a sitting, washed down with six jugs of wine. Her colleague Thangon astonished the Emperor Aurelian by consuming, before his eyes, a whole wild boar, sheep, pig and sucking pig, and drinking the contents of a cask of wine with them. The Emperor Maximinus, himself a colossus, kept up his strength by eating 40 pounds of meat a day.

Obviously the common people of Rome, who accounted for a good two-thirds of the city's inhabitants, almost a million individuals, knew about these banquets only by hearsay. They ate the staple gruel of classical times, supplemented by oil, the humbler vegetables and salt fish. Caesar gave the people a feast on the occasion of his Triumph, entertaining 260,000 *humiliores* as his guests. The menu, which was well lubricated, sounds very lavish today, comprising seafood, game, poultry and even asparagus, but there is no butcher's meat on it: butcher's meat meant the height of luxury in ancient Rome.

Juvenal[6] sighed for the good old days: 'For feast days, in olden times, they would keep a side of dried pork, hanging from an open rack, or put before the relations a flitch of birthday bacon, with the addition of some fresh meat, if there happened to be a sacrifice to supply it.' But when he invites his friend Persicus to supper, warning him that both the food and the service will be simple, he does not mention beef: 'Nor shall I have a carver to whom the whole carving-school must bow ... in whose school is cut up ... a magnificent feast of hares and sow's udders, of boars and antelopes, of Scythian fowls and tall flamingoes and Gaetulian gazelles. ... My raw youngster, untutored all his days, has never learnt how to filch a slice of kid or the wing of a guinea-fowl ...'

Horace, in praising frugality, does not mention beef either. It seems that eating beef was simply not a Roman custom, since it was a popular dish in Greece (home of the first domesticated cattle). In *The Frogs* of Aristophanes, Persephone, like a good housewife, is described as preparing for the arrival of Heracles with a little family supper which includes 'a prime ox' roasted whole, and lentils. If such things were mentioned on stage, we are dealing with the lower middle-class customs of the period.

In the time of Pericles (500 BC) Darius the Persian, a self-indulgent gourmet in a country where beef was seldom eaten, had whole oxen served at his own table at banquets, but behind screens which hid them from the eyes of his court.

The absence of beef from the Roman diet, therefore, seems to have been just a matter of taste.

Up to the end of the Middle Ages the butcher's meat which constitutes what we now think of as the main part of a meal – beef, veal, even mutton – was the exception rather than the rule. Pork (discussed below) provided daily fare, and in particular it added fat to the diet. When beef and other butcher's meat was obtainable, it often passed through the salting tub to preserve it. It was then eaten boiled, dressed with oil and vinegar. Salted or dried meat (pemmican) was a staple item in the mess bowls of soldiers and sailors over a long period.

The reading of medieval documents provides striking evidence of the popularity of offal, particularly in towns. Under that heading we may include the internal organs and tripe, the animal's feet and glands, and especially the tongue (salted). It may have been so popular for economic reasons: bullocks and calves consisted mainly of muscle rather than tripe and tongues, and we must remember that the prime joints had already found their way to the kitchens of the great.

In country areas cattle have always represented capital, as draught animals and for their milk. An animal was not slaughtered until it was fit for nothing else. Tough meat of this kind, still called *les vieilles marraines*, 'the old godmothers', in La Villette, added a gastronomic wealth of recipes for *daubes*, casseroles and *pot-au-feu* dishes to the country cooking of France, and in the eighteenth century many of them found their way across the Channel to England to join the indigenous British stews and boiled or braised beef recipes.

Veal is easier to come by, representing annual income rather than capital. It can be slaughtered as soon as the problem of weaning arises. The fatted calf which marked the return of the Prodigal Son – when 'they began to be merry' (Luke 15) – was one of the choicest dishes on the festive table. From the thirteenth century to the sixteenth, calves' eyes were considered the most exquisite delicacy of all. A story by the fourteenth-century Italian writer Sacchetti[7] depicts a boorish Florentine of the period appropriating the eyes from the trencher (the slice of bread which served as a plate) which he is sharing with his host, according to custom. The other guests are horrified, not by what appears to us a revolting choice, but by the greed and gluttony of the character.

Ever since Roman times the Italians have been very fond of *vitello*, veal, which is the basis of most of their meat dishes. The Spanish find the milk-fed veal on which the best prewar butchers of France prided themselves insipid. To the French palate, however, it was made even better by the raw eggs which the calves had been fed. It is hard to imagine such a state of affairs now, when calves are hobbled, battery-reared and stuffed with hormones. The veal they provide is still a pearly pink, but it usually owes that colour to artificial processes, and the Spanish – understandably enough these days – prefer the veal of a grazing calf which has just been weaned; escalopes from such an animal, which they fry in plenty of oil, are a very pale red colour.

Beef has always been a particular favourite in Great Britain, where 'the roast beef of Old England' is the proverbial national dish. The nickname 'Beefeaters' for the Yeomen of the Guard in the Tower of London derives from the term 'beefeater' used of a living-in servant fed on a good diet. Oxtail soup, however, regarded as very English, could have arrived in the country with French émigrés during the Revolution; Menon's *La cuisinière bourgeoise* of 1774 contains a recipe (p. 43) for *queue en hochepot*. Anglomania was rife in France at the time of this book's publication, and pages 31 and 53 are devoted to '*rôt de biffe*' – which in fact at the time in France meant mutton, the joint consisting of the saddle and hind legs of the animal which was called a *baron*, a term which may be from *bas rond* (round lower part). The word is applied in a culinary sense solely to 'a baron of beef' in English. The *rôt de biffe* was larded with bacon and spit-roasted.

Beefsteak has found its way into the French language as *bifteck*, and crossed the Channel after Waterloo when the English troops were encamped in the Tuileries gardens. Fried potato chips (see the chapter on fruit and vegetables below) took advantage of the advent of grilled or fried steak to become its regular companion in France and England alike. But with the new popularity of steak, the boiled beef of the middle classes took second place on the menus of French households, though it is still a favourite Sunday evening supper dish. The *ancien régime* chapter in the cookery books had closed.

To return for a moment to the days of that *ancien régime*, however, in 1757, during the Hanoverian campaign, Marshal Richelieu conceived the notion of giving the captured court of East Frisia a supper consisting entirely of beef 'before setting them free', as Alexandre Dumas tells us in his *Dictionnaire de cuisine*, adding, 'The country was devastated for 80 kilometres around'. Nothing could be found but a single bullock and 'some roots'. There must have been some other ingredients in reserve, for the Marshal, having wagered that he would serve 'the finest supper in the world', ordered the bullock to be made into 22 different dishes, savoury or sweet, with 'what I have left in the way of preserves. So to work, and no more doubts!' he concluded, sending his perplexed cooks off to their stoves. In the end they managed very well.

The Horse, the Spirit of Corn

The horse was seldom sacrificed in classical times. But the Romans, who dedicated their cavalry to the god Mars, used to sacrifice one of the horses that had survived the year's battles after harvest. On 15th October its head was decked with heavy ears of corn, in thanks for the harvest that had been safely gathered in, it was slaughtered, and the head was then nailed to the citadel gates until the following year.

While Mars protected agriculture from natural disasters as well as defending his worshippers from their enemies, the sacred symbolism of farming peoples represented the Mother Goddess in the incarnation of a mare. As she galloped she spread life-giving rain. The ancient Indians sent a sacred horse galloping across country to ensure the coming of the monsoon to fertilize their crops.

Flood waters can also fertilize the soil, and so do the rays of the sun. It is said that a horse, embodying both principles, is still sometimes cast into the river by the Garo people of Assam. In the time of the Tsars the Russian fishermen of the river Oka, south of Moscow, practised the same rite. The last of the year's foals is cherished with special care by the peasants of Lorraine in France and Franconia in Germany. They believe that the germination of the next year's harvest depends on its strength, and say that it bears 'the spirit of the corn' within it.

Twelfth-century Irish kings were married to a white mare in the course of their enthronement ceremonies. The mare was then slaughtered and boiled in an enormous cauldron. Only the king took no part in this communal feast, but he then had to bathe in the broth. This rite, both magical and an initiation ceremony, ensured good harvests for the kingdom.

Fat Oxen and Prosperous Butchers

Aleph, our A, the first letter of the Phoenician, Cretan, Greek and Latin alphabets, began life as a representation of the head of the ox, the foremost source of wealth. The pictorial element is easily recognized if one reverses the half-turn sideways imperceptibly imposed on it by scribes over the centuries. The ox's only real rival in the often drought-stricken countries where those alphabets were used was the camel, whose characteristic profile gave us gamal, gamma, our G, the third letter; the second letter was beta, a tent or house. In just three letters of the alphabet, the stock-breeder emerges as an established figure.

This could be taken as an indication of the respect cattle enjoyed from ancient times for the services they rendered, a respect still shown to the sacred cows of India (a country where many people are vegetarian). There is further past evidence for it in the winged bulls of Assyria and Babylon, the zoomorphic Egyptian gods Apis and Osiris, the sacred cow of the Argyens and the Chinese, the Gaulish god Tarvos-Triganos, Mithras and the bull-headed Minotaur. While the Athenians sacrificed a garlanded ox for the festival of the Bosphonia, according to Pliny and Hippias of Elis the Sophist (author of a work on animals) a certain Phyges was condemned to death for killing the ox that drew his plough. The ancient Germanic tribes thought so highly of their livestock that, according to Tacitus, a girl's dowry was paid in cattle rather than gold.

The custom of calculating a dowry in head of cattle is still current all over Africa, and the agricultural and planning departments of the new African republics have great difficulty in persuading pastoral tribes, particularly the Peuhls, not to let their four-footed capital stand idle, since cattle may be hoarded for nothing but the pleasure of counting them,[8] in countries where protein deficiency is endemic and there is little trade with the outside world. The giant Masai tribesmen of East Africa, rather than killing the long-horned cattle they inherited from the Egyptians, drink their blood, drawing it from the neck with a hollow dart or collecting it to be mixed with a porridge of cereals.

It is tempting to regard the custom of parading a fatted ox at carnival mid-Lent festivities in Western Europe, common from the twelfth century until the 1930s, as a revival of ancient cults. The ox was always decked with ribbons, flowers, rosettes, and sometimes even gilded. Such carnivals were a happy celebration of a brief respite from the abstinence of Lent, and were held right in the middle of the Lenten season, on the twentieth day before Easter. It has also been suggested that the word 'carnival' itself comes from an imaginary expression *'carne n'avale'* ('eat no flesh'), while Italian speakers have incorrectly connected it with *vale* ('farewell meat'), but in fact it is from Latin *caro, carnis*, flesh, and *levare*, to remove, as in the medieval Latin terms *carnelevarium, carnelevamen*, signifying 'the putting away of flesh'. In the Catalan language, the word for carnival was *carnes toetes* ('meat removed'), which became *carnistoltes*.

However, the fatted ox should be regarded simply as the living emblem of the corporation of butchers. At carnival time, a brief but glorious period of feasting, the providers of meat had a place of honour and took advantage of the general atmosphere of jollity to parade their masterpiece, the finest and fattest of oxen, by way of advertising. All records were beaten in Paris in 1846 by a vast animal named Dagobert and weighing almost two tonnes. The tradition of the parade of the fatted ox at carnival time in Western European countries is one of those rare folk customs which are solely urban.

In medieval Paris, the procession left the slaughter-houses outside the walls of the city (where they used to stand on the *quais* of the Right Bank) to visit the provosts, aldermen and chief magistrates of the city's *parlement* (judicial assembly). These officials awaited it in state, in all the glory of their red robes – red being the colour of blood and of power, and also, as it happens, the colour of the robes of the magistrates who performed the sacrificial rites of classical times. But leaving aside such coincidences, the significance of which had been entirely forgotten, the only sacred part of the custom was the visit paid by the animal in its finery to a church generally belonging to the local corporation. The bishops did not particularly appreciate the honour.

In Provence, in the village of Barjols in the Haut-Var, the feast of Les Tripettes is still celebrated in memory of the providential arrival of an ox (no doubt escaped from a monastery) on St Marcel's day during a thirteenth-century famine. Was this the same St Marcel, or Marceau, Bishop of Paris in the fourth century, who saved the capital from a mad bull and is the patron saint of forage merchants? The ox of Les Tripettes, a proud beast surrounded by cowherds from the Camargue, whence it has been brought with all due solemnity, attends Mass before being slaughtered. It is roasted outside the church, while the Provençal *farandole* is danced (the priest used to join the dancing himself), and then everyone falls to feasting. The animal's offal used to be distributed *is escoulau e à la paurido*, 'to the students [of Aix] and to the poor', who were often one and the same. In Paris a slice of the fatted carnival ox used to find its way to the King's plate, and closer to our own times to that of the head of state.

The trade of butchery, with access to meat supplies, has always been one of importance in society. The business of butchers – indeed, why not call it an art, as the medieval Italians did? – was organized and controlled from very ancient times, although we tend to think back no further than the Middle Ages, which provide the best or at least the most highly coloured illustration.

The Romans, whose society in general was highly organized, distinguished *boarii*, butchers, from *suarii*, pork butchers, and *pecuarii*, vendors of poultry and game. The ancient Egyptians, who also had a well-developed administrative system, did not leave the butchery trade to chance either. The Metropolitan Museum in New York has a remarkable polychrome terracotta model showing farming activities from the tomb of Maken-Kwetre, a rich dignitary of the Eleventh Dynasty, and dating from the second millennium BC. It was probably included because the dead man had interests in the meat trade. A great many other tombs contained frescoes showing butchers at work.

Still in connection with the cartouches of the Egyptian butchers' corporation – for they had formed themselves into a body – the name of some great lady, frequently a Queen Mother, is often found mentioned as 'guardian of the corporation'. Queen Hete-Phere, mother of Cheops, was so proud of the title that it was carved on her throne. And I must not forget the cuneiform tablet of the seventeenth century BC with the famous Code of the Amorite king Hammurabi II, regulating the sale of livestock, like everything else which was eaten or drunk in Babylon.

Even before that, no doubt there were laws of solidarity regulating the trade, and no less respected for not being written down. Among the oldest evidences of butchery – large-scale but methodical – are the elephant left partly dissected on the Tornabalba archeological site in Spain 300,000 years ago, and a mammoth which was stuck in the mud and cut up on the spot at Clovis in New Mexico in the eleventh millennium, on a day when no fasting was surely observed.

This was the work of amateurs, of course. The first master butcher whom we know to have made the business his trade remains anonymous, but he kept a small shop in Jordan 8500 years ago. At the Beddha site, shops were grouped in threes in a number of alcoves on the ground floor of houses built of stone blocks. One of these shops contained rough knives of dressed stone, and such a pile of bones, so expertly jointed, that archeologists think the owner of the place must have been a specialist. Until he was abruptly interrupted in his trade, he must have been cutting up meat for his fellow citizens: the meat of goats and sheep similar to those whose small hooves have left their marks on the mud paving of another village of the same period at Ganj Darah in Western Iran. Did that particular flock end up as chops? Very likely, but we shall never know just how, or who did the butchery. All we have is that brief but lasting record of swift movement from one unknown place to another.

The word *butcher*, like French *boucher*, from which the English version comes, and old Italian *beccaïo*, dates only from the thirteenth century as a term denoting the person who prepared and cut up any kind of meat. Previously it meant a specialist in goat's meat, often salted because it was tough; in modern jargon the goat might be said to have been restructured to meet market demand. This etymology for the word 'butcher' in itself shows how low the consumption of beef was in the Middle Ages. Previously the French word *maiselier*, *masselier* or *macellier*, from Italian *macellaïo*, a term which never came into English, was used for the person who slaughtered and cut up creatures of any species as required, and who often kept a kind of cheap tavern. Then the word disappeared, its function being divided between butchers on one hand and innkeepers on the other.

Each quarter of Paris had many large butcher's shops even before the time of Philippe II (who reigned 1180–1223, and under whom the capital expanded) and their owners were soon prominent in the *parlement* and the *prévôté* (provostry, a kind of police headquarters). They even had letters patent of nobility, so to speak, since Hugues Capet, first of the Capétien dynasty of French kings, was descended from Robert the Strong, a soldier of fortune who distinguished himself against the Normans and is thought to have come from a Saxon family of meat traders brought to Gaul by Charlemagne. The Le Gois family, who led the rioting mobs of Paris in the fifteenth century, were butchers in the parish of Sainte-Geneviève; in 1411 another prominent figure in those riots, Simon Caboche, was a skinner at the

Butcher's shop: slaughtering and cutting up animals in the Middle Ages: miniature
from the *Tacuinum sanitatis in medicina*, after the twelfth-century Arab doctor
Albucacis.

butchery of the Parvis (forecourt) of Notre-Dame, said to be the oldest in
Paris.

Aubry, after whom a Parisian street has been named since the beginning of the
fourteenth century – the rue Aubry-le-Boucher in the 4th arrondissement – did
nothing more remarkable than conduct his trade in that part of the city. None the

less, in 1844, when the fashion for all things medieval was at its height, Henry Marvaille and Paul Fauquemont wrote a very popular four-act drama entitled *Aubry le Boucher* which was produced at the Théâtre Beaumarchais. 'The action', states the text, 'takes place in Paris in 1418 (*sic*). For the music, apply to M. Osay, orchestral conductor at the theatre.' In the popular English oral tradition of ballad and folk song in the genuine late medieval period, butchers figure several times, usually as strong men and prosperous citizens.

Religious communities owned butcher's shops: among them were the Templars who owned one in the rue Braque in Paris from the twelfth century onwards. The abbey of Saint-Germain-Saint-Denis sold meat as well as its own wine from the time of its foundation. In 1274, the prior, Dom Gherardt, had 16 new shops built in the rue de la Boucherie, near the present-day place Saint-Michel.

The *Ménagier de Paris*, a treatise of morals and domestic economy written around 1393 by a well-to-do citizen of Paris for the edification of his young wife, contains a list of the city's butchers at the time and their delivery services. The notes added by the Ménagier's nineteenth-century French editor, Baron Jérôme Pichon, are also of great interest: he tells us that there were 19 butchers in the Grande Boucherie, which stood on the site of the present Théâtre du Châtelet, and that 'the origin of this establishment went back to the time of the Roman occupation. Ownership of the shops, and the right to become a master butcher[9] after the age of seven years and a day' (!) was the exclusive right of the male members of a small number of families. These 'male family members were bound to exercise their fathers' profession themselves, or at least to give the business financial support.'

In the sixteenth century many descendants of these old and industrious families had risen to quite elevated positions, and had given up the butcher's trade. However, the rich butchers of the fourteenth and fifteenth centuries would not have occupied themselves personally with every detail of their businesses. Many had employees responsible for the actual cutting up and selling of the meat, while the master butchers themselves merely dealt on a large scale and through brokers in the livestock trade destined to feed the people of Paris.

If we are to believe the Ménagier and his nineteenth-century French editor, 'the sum of all the butcheries of Paris weekly, without counting the households of the King and the Queen and our other lords of France' came to 3080 sheep, 514 oxen, 600 pigs and about 300 calves (there follow details of the tastes of the court, a subject of great interest to good citizens then as now). These figures are quite high when one considers that the average population of Paris for that period is assessed at 100,000. At Carpentras in Provence, a town which became and remained prosperous because of the unprecedented boom caused by the luxury of the papal court at Avignon next door, we know that consumption per head rose in 1473 to 26 kilos of butcher's meat, especially mutton – more than in the time of Mistral, the late nineteenth-century Provençal poet! And one must always bear in mind those fast days when no meat was eaten.

In 1637 Paris had half a million inhabitants. The annual provision of butcher's meat for a population which had increased fivefold during the three and a half centuries separating Molière's Monsieur Jourdain from the Ménagier of Paris was 368,000 sheep and lambs, 67,800 calves – and 40,000 oxen. Dietary habits had certainly changed, and fasting was not observed so strictly or over such long periods.

Although the common people were to see their purchasing power decline sharply between the reigns of François I and Louis XIV, 'meat, in ever greater demand, was to lead to great market tensions between limited supply and expanding demand.'[10] The consumption of butcher's meat was always an urban phenomenon. Country dwellers, whether day labourers, farmers or the minor gentry, could not afford to eat their livestock even if they owned it themselves. Edifying tales are full of poor people obliged to sell their cow or even their goat in times of need – and if the animal did end up in the cooking pot that meant it was not even saleable.

People of means, or at least those who wanted to give that impression, lived in towns. Like white bread, roast meat symbolized social success in the time of Louis XIV. 'To be fat and pot-bellied would be the mark of success for several centuries to come.'[11]

From the Middle Ages to the French Revolution, and in practice up to the Third Republic proclaimed in 1870, the great majority of the dominant classes of clergy (except for the clerics of the medieval abbeys, and they were not the real beneficiaries of the system), nobility and bourgeoisie lived in towns. If rich men did happen to own a flock or so in the country, they sold their livestock to butchers and bought meat ready cut up, unlike their own game, of which they were proud, and which was both easier to transport and not supposed to be eaten very fresh. In the Régence period (1715–23) these prosperous people made up only one-fifth of the entire population of France, but they accounted for a great part of the butchers' turnover. As for the lower classes of townspeople, when they left the country they adopted typically urban dietary habits. Whenever the countryside was depopulated on a large scale (through invasions, climatic disasters, epidemics, etc.) demand for meat in the towns rose (as well as demand for salt fish), inevitably leading to the paradoxical situation described above: limited supply and expanding demand.

On the eve of the French Revolution 'the rich cities of Paris and Geneva were devouring huge quantities of meat (meat consumption in those two cities reached modern heights: 60 to 80 kilos a year per person,[12] as against only 20 to 30 kilos a year for the average inhabitant of Caen) ... Caen saw the fat oxen of the Bessin region set off for Paris, and kept the tough and skinny beasts for itself.'[13] The bigger, more middle-class and more commercial the city, the larger were sales of meat. Yesterday as today, the middlemen were the people who really profited from supplying foodstuffs, as we shall see when we come to the black market.

The high officer of the Crown who supervised the royal kitchens of the King of France – a post held by the famous Guillaume Tirel, called Taillevent, author of the *Viandier* – had a right to 'take five sous from every person selling cooked or raw meat in the kingdom' at the beginning of each reign, not a ruinous tax on the butchers' corporations of that kingdom, who were already doing very well on the whole, although they were naturally inclined to complain. The probate on one of the butcher's shops by the gates of Paris in 1383 gives us a picture of riches to make crowned heads green with envy. As Baron Pichon points out in his notes to the *Ménagier de Paris*: 'In view of an inventory of wealth so vast for its time, is it surprising that all historians of the fifteenth century emphasize the powerful influence of these master butchers?'

This upper class of Paris butchers, prominent among whom was the famous Étienne Marcel (proprietor of what we would call a 'holding' in modern terms, combining the meat trade, goldsmith's work and banking), was not a unique phenomenon. Every city and large town had to reckon with its butchers' corporation. The Ghent corporation was one of the most prosperous, and some dynasties were in the business for 500 years. Also legendary was the buxom beauty of the Ghent butchers' women, from whose ranks the Emperor Charles V chose his favourites.

In certain towns, for instance Poitiers,[14] which had 23 butchers in the fifteenth century (more than it can boast now), there was no corporation, but a *métier juré*, or 'sworn trade': the butchers showed their solidarity by taking an oath in chorus before the local lord. 'Sworn guards' controlled the market, and no one could sell meat unless he was 'under oath to the butchery' of a butcher's family.

As a hygienic precaution – for animals were slaughtered on the premises and the refuse and scraps thrown straight out of doors, much to the benefit of stray pigs, flies and rats – butchers were originally banned from setting up 'within the city' because theirs was *inhonesta mercimonia* (a vile trade). But gradually they came inside the walls. Old town plans show us primitive suburbs marked with such names as rue de la Bucherie, or de la Boucherie. The expansion of town centres and the new lay-out of their precincts brought the butchers into the heart of urban areas without their even having to move house.

Every butcher had a single bench on which he offered his meat for sale 'from sunrise to sunset'; trading by torchlight or candlelight was forbidden for fear of fraudulent dealing.

In general, animals were procured in the immediate vicinity of a town, and certain people, taking their cue from the usurers, did not shrink from extortion or delaying payment until it suited them. There was also considerable trading at the big stock-breeding centres, following the annual rhythm of the big fairs such as the one held at Beaucaire.

The butchers owned grazing, privately or communally, where their beasts waited for the moment of slaughter. Some of the richest set up as entrepreneurs in the stock-breeding business on a large scale themselves, either near towns or in remote rural areas. Thus, towards the beginning of the fifteenth century, at a time of abundance and good demography, the people of Arles were still protesting against the scarcity and expense of butcher's meat. The *mazels* or butchers of the big Jewish communities were suspected of fixing the market with the complicity of the

Christian butchers who had come to an 'understanding' among themselves. The affair almost turned into a pogrom. In fact the big livestock dealers, members of those business families of Marseilles and Aix who would be ennobled later, such as the Forbins,[15] were taking the line of least resistance by making Jewish agents their intermediaries and above all their bankers in the markets of Arles, Carpentras and Manosque. Among them were Pierre d'Arles and Giraud Paul, already rich men of property. All this may have favoured kosher butchery to the detriment of the ordinary kind (in Poitou no excommunicated butcher was allowed 'to sell flesh': observe the sacred character of meat, and above all the influence of the Church).

Besides speculating in fresh and salted meat, leather, skins, wool and tallow, the Forbins and their colleagues, forming themselves into associations, owned shares in vast flocks of sheep which they entrusted to *nourrigiers*, middlemen whose business it was to employ shepherds to take the animals to the mountain pastures. The hiring of these pastures was also up to the *nourrigiers*. In winter thousands upon thousands of animals took up their quarters in the Crau region or on the banks of the Huveaune near Marseilles. But the meat of these sheep, whose seasonal journeys are reminiscent of episodes in the works of the French rural novelist Jean Giono, proved so profitable when exported to the north of France, even to Flanders and the Empire, that country people were sometimes reluctant to let their near neighbours living in the local towns have it. Particularly in summer, therefore, the butchers reared small flocks living permanently near the town fortifications, and this practice sometimes led to conflict with the *ourtoulaïers* or market gardeners. Nothing is ever simple. The people of Marseilles, as we can tell from the registers of tolls on goods to be consumed within the city, had to go as far as Saint-Flour for their provisions in 1498. Even today the supermarkets of Marseilles offer their customers frozen lamb from the Antipodes and beef from Argentina, items similarly found in the meat cabinets of British supermarkets alongside the native Scotch beef and Welsh and English lamb.

Chapter 5

The History of Dairy Produce

Cheese and Curds

Archeologists excavating lake dwellings on the banks of Lake Neuchâtel have found potsherds pierced with holes which date back to at least six thousand years BC. They conclude that these vessels could have been drainers for separating curds from whey. I would not wish to suggest that the archeologists were influenced by the making of this discovery on Swiss soil, but still, the idea gave much pleasure to the Swiss themselves, who saw it as yet another honour bestowed on their country as one of the world's major cheese-making areas.

What kind of milk might the ancient lake-dwellers have been processing in this way? It is an interesting question. Although domestication of goats and sheep was beginning to change the way of life of the Mediterranean peoples at this period, we do not yet know if they had reached the stage of milking the animals and making dairy produce to keep. Cows did not appear on the Alpine scene until after the Roman conquest of the Valais 53 centuries later, and their advent was a landmark in the subsequent glorious history of Swiss enterprise.

Many people think that the pottery strainer in question, when new, was more probably meant for extracting the juice from crushed wild berries. I shall return to this idea in the chapter on wine. Let us leave the matter of which theory is correct on one side, and turn instead to the Middle East.

Cheese does not figure very prominently in the earlier pages of the Bible. The unfortunate Abel is depicted as the first shepherd, but curds and butter get no mention until after the story of Noah and his excessive potations. Noah's descendant Abraham, 'very rich in cattle' presented to him by Pharaoh, gave 'butter, and milk, and the calf which he had dressed' to the three angels who came to visit him

113

(Genesis 18, viii). We can roughly situate the possible existence of the father of the Jewish nation in the second millennium BC.

If we go yet farther back to the time of the Sumerians, 20 centuries before Abraham, we encounter another stock-breeder. This one is anonymous, but his existence is well attested by the careful accounts he kept, beginning in the fortieth year of the reign of King Shoulgi. These accounts, engraved in cuneiform on clay tablets, are now in the State Museum of the Middle East in what was formerly East Berlin. They tell us that the breeder's herd of cattle increased fivefold within eight years, and production rose from 1.8 litres of butter and 8 litres of cheese a year to 42.5 litres of butter and 63.3 litres of cheese, obviously an excellent output.

A kind of strip cartoon depiction in a polychrome Sumerian fresco of 2500 BC, now in Baghdad Museum, gives some idea of the methods used. It shows cows with their calves, still not very far from the primitive aurochs cattle, being milked by peasants on both sides of the gates of a corral which would not shame Texas. The milk is put into large, carefully cleaned jars. Then the cream is poured from a small jar into a churn, and comes out as butter.

A seal of almost the same period, now in the Chicago Natural History Museum, comes from the kingdom of Elam and shows a goat offering her milk to the goatherd, under the benevolent gaze of a fertility goddess seated beside two milk-churns. Finally, in the seventeenth century BC, the Code of the Amorite king Hammurabi II regulates taxes (even at this early date) on the dairy produce for sale in the market of Babylon, in the same way as it lays down the law on the sale of meat.

Goats and sheep will adapt easily to any climate and browse on any kind of weed; goats will eat most prickly plants as well. They long supplied most of the milk that was drunk or made into butter and cheese. Cattle, worked to the bone as draught animals, provided hardly any. We may assume that the Babylonian cows gave milk only at calving time, when they were enjoying a respite from work. Virgil does not seem very keen on cow's milk; at least, he recommends its use only for rearing the calves:

> Don't follow our forbears' custom, whereby
> Mother-cows filled the snowy milk-pails: their young should have all
> The benefit of their udders.

The first cheeses, therefore, were made from goat's or sheep's milk, which was easier to come by.

Before the precious liquid could be stored or transported in jars like those of the Sumerians – that is, before pottery came into general use – shepherds and goatherds used containers, in the manner of the Touareg or the nomads of Central Asia, made from the bladders or stomachs of slaughtered animals. This was a refinement on the knotted skins still found in the present-day Stone Age culture of the Amazonian Indians, who use them in making mead. Obviously milk in such containers would soon turn to curds, either because of the heat or carelessness (leave a cup of milk out in the sun and you will see how quickly it 'turns'), or because of the coagulant effect of natural enzymes contained in the stomachs of young ruminants. The *tauhem* of Anatolia and the sheep's milk *leskem* of the Caucasus have been made like this for thousands of years.

The Hebrews obtained primitive curdled milk products in this way until Moses forbade mixing milk with young animal products: 'Thou shalt not seethe a kid in his mother's milk.' The ten cheeses David's father Jesse gave him to take to the captain of his brothers' thousand (I Samuel 17, xviii) and the 'cheese of kine' given to David himself when he 'was come to Mahanaim' (II Samuel 17, xxix) will have been made by the action of the coagulant properties of certain vegetable substances such as fig tree sap, still used in the Balearic Islands, or thistle buds. Today, ecologically minded breeders of goats in Corsica and the lower Alps are returning to such methods. The wild flower plant known as Our Lady's Bedstraw or Yellow Bedstraw (*Galium verum*), another of whose English common names, aptly, was Cheese Rennet, was used for a long time to give Cheshire and Gloucester cheeses their orange colouring, and could also curdle the milk.

There is evidence of the making of cream cheese[1] in the Renaissance period, in a curious and fanciful verse menu devised by a poet at the court of the Sforza family: 'E sugo di tetta vaccine! Blancho sopra le fusche in gelatina' (And the juice of the cow's udder, blanched into a jelly on straw).

Marco Polo states that the Mongols simply left skimmed milk, either unheated or boiled, to dry out in the sun, as they still do, and the same method is employed by the Bedouin of Sinai. Skimmed milk was the basic material of cheese for a long time, indeed up to the modern period, the cream having been skimmed off to be churned into butter. The buttermilk or skimmed milk was then reduced by boiling and made into cheese, a procedure still in use today.

Although Homer describes the Cyclops Polyphemus merely putting the milk he had curdled 'in wicker baskets' to drain (in the Middle Ages, a soft white cheese in France was called *jonchée*, from the word *jonc*, rush, because it was made in rush baskets), the operation is described in more detail by Columella in first-century Gaul. He calls the woven rush baskets *fiscinae*, while pierced wooden or ceramic vessels, reminiscent of the remains left by the lake-dwellers of Neuchâtel, are *fiscellae*. The cheese drainer is not a recent invention.

In Columella's time, someone had the idea of a press which could be screwed down to compress the drained curds instead of simply piling stones on a lid or plate over them. The compressed curds were then moulded in a basket or a wooden box (*phormos* in Greek, *forma* in Latin), and the result was what we would now regard as cheese. The medieval French word was *formage*, from the Latin *forma*, the mould in which it was made, whence modern French *fromage*, while English *cheese* comes ultimately from Latin *caseus*, the foodstuff itself.

Cream cheese, curd cheese and cottage cheese are the drained curds eaten fresh, unlike cheese properly so called, which has undergone some form of treatment –

salting, drying, smoking or maturing in a cellar (the ripening process either occurs naturally or is induced by yeasts) – and can thus be kept for some time. Both cream cheeses and matured cheeses were widely used by pastrycooks throughout the classical period, particularly when they were made from full-cream milk, or milk from which very little cream had been skimmed. There are still many recipes of this kind: Russian *pashka*, English and American cheesecake, Corsican *cacavellu*, *fidone* and *cherchiole*, and the true *cassata* of Sicily.

The drained cream cheese called *turos* by the ancient Greeks, and *tiri* by their modern descendants, which is sometimes dipped in brine, was particularly valued in antiquity because it became hard as it dried. There cannot be much difference between a modern Chavignol goat cheese or *crottin* and the cheese which Nestor, according to Homer, recommended to Machaon to help him recover from his wounds at the siege of Troy: Nestor's woman Hecamede 'mixed a potion ... with Pramnian wine, and on this she grated cheese of goat's milk'. She served an onion with it, 'a relish for their drink'.

And what could be more fortifying than cheese, a concentrated form of milk, the best food in the world? The Tibetans, unfamiliar with Homer, who drink tea instead of wine, thicken that beverage with a kind of butter so rancid that it is more like cheese; they thrive on it. According to Pliny the Elder, Zarathustra acquired eloquence only after living entirely on cheese for 20 years.

A Roman recipe inherited from the Greeks, *moritum*, must have been equally fortifying: it was a salad of salted and matured cheese, grated and well seasoned with garlic, spices and aromatic herbs. This must have been something like the *cervelle de canut* (literally, 'silk-weaver's brains') of Lyons (famous for its silk-weaving), which is made with cream cheese. The Romans also ate cream cheese prepared in the Greek fashion: *hypotrima*, to which dried fruits and wine of the aperitif type were added.

The Romans liked to smoke cheese, and it is still smoked in Central Italy today. Pliny, who seems to have been a well-informed cheese-lover, gives a considerable list of the local specialities of the Iberian peninsula and Cisalpine and Transalpine Gaul, among them 'Luni cheese from the borderland of Tuscany and Liguria', a large and very heavy wheel-shaped sheep's milk cheese. He speaks appreciatively of the cheeses of the Cevennes and the Auvergne, the ancestors of today's Roquefort and Cantal.

After the fall of the Roman Empire and the great invasions of the barbarians (who cannot have been so very barbarous, since cheese formed a large part of their daily diet), the monks of the Benedictine and Cistercian monasteries, thanks to whom the population did not starve to death entirely during the Dark Ages, were the pioneers of the new cheese-making industry of medieval times. If the chronicles of Eginhard, Charlemagne's biographer, are to be believed, it was in one of these monasteries – probably the abbey of Vabres near Roquefort – that the Emperor, another lover of cheese, was given a sheep's milk cheese veined with mould. Much to his surprise, he liked it. He made the prior promise to send two crates of this

116

cheese a year to Aix-la-Chapelle, thus nearly ruining the poor community. Charlemagne was equally enthusiastic about the cheese of Reuil in Brie. A man of discernment, he pronounced it 'one of the most marvellous of foods', and requisitioned two crates of this cheese as well, to round off his dinners at Aix.

The monks, who ensured the survival of European agriculture during this period, turned out excellent wine-growers as well as cheese-makers (which may explain why wine and cheese have always seemed to go so well together). Grimod de La Reynière described cheese as 'the iron rations of drunkards'. As with liqueurs, the names of abbeys of this period are often associated with the making of cheeses, which kept those names even when they were subsequently produced elsewhere. Port-Salut and Maroilles, for instance, originally came from the abbeys of those names. The consumer's unconscious mind has not forgotten the connection, and nor have modern manufacturers, who often put the picture of a monk on their labels.

However, the large cheeses sold cut into sections – cheeses of the Jura, such as Emmenthal, Comté, Gruyère and Beaufort, or of Italy, such as Parmesan – need so much milk, up to 1000 litres for a single large cheese, that ever since they were first made in the twelfth century they have been produced by village or regional cooperatives. Reblochon cheese owes its name to the fact that it was made secretly, from a second milking or *rebloche* not officially declared by the tenant farmers and shepherds of Savoy. It thus escaped the dues levied by their lords, either lay or religious.

There was not much cash in circulation during the Middle Ages, and, as we shall see repeatedly in the course of this study, tithes were often paid in kind. Farm accounts and inventories show that dairy produce, which was easy to transport, made up a considerable part of these dues. Pierre Charbonnier[2] tells us that the Seigneur de Murol, a country gentleman of modest means, received ten *quintaux* of cheese from his farmers in 1418, for the use of his household alone, i.e. a little over half a tonne in modern terms. The cheese *quintal* was a special Auvergnat measure of weight, equivalent to 115 pounds.

Up to the eighteenth century a great deal of cheese was eaten in Europe, and especially in France.[3] Then people of high rank developed a sweet tooth. Sweet desserts became so popular that the only kind of cheese considered elegant was cream cheese heavily sweetened and flavoured with perfumed oils. Rove sheep's milk cheese sprinkled with orange-flower water is still a speciality of Marseilles. Eaten in the evening, it is supposed to be an aid to slumber.

Fortunately, the nineteenth-century bourgeoisie brought cheese back into fashion. Brillat-Savarin wrote that 'a dessert course with no cheese is a beauty with only one eye.' The first industrial dairy in Normandy was opened in 1875 to meet demand.

The French, who now regard cheese as their national speciality – particularly Camembert, popularly visualized as being eaten, with French bread, by picturesque characters wearing berets – are rather inclined to think that the varieties produced in France itself (at least 365 of them) are the only cheeses in the world. And France is indeed the world's major cheese-making country, producing over a million tonnes a year. General de Gaulle used to deplore the difficulty of governing a country which made more than 300 varieties of cheese. Winston Churchill, however, another lover of cheese, said during the Second World War that a country with so many cheeses on its table could not perish.

The other main producers are the USA, where immigrants taught the secrets of European cheese-making as well as wine-growing, Denmark, Italy, Holland, West Germany, Switzerland and Great Britain. Even Japan, which excels in imitation of every kind, makes cheese.

However, if French cheeses are internationally famous – only 26 of them have the right to label themselves *appellation contrôlée*, like French wines of guaranteed vintage – there are a thousand names of other cheeses made all over our planet, in every latitude, and all of them are different. Even the imitations differ from the original product. Curds and cheese are made not only with cow's, sheep's and goat's milk, but with the milk of the buffalo introduced into Lombardy by the Sforzas to pull loads in convoy on the *naviglii*. Buffalo's milk produces mozzarella, without which pizza is just a tomato tart. The milk of mares, female zebras, reindeer (a favourite with the Romans), lamas and yaks can also be made into cheese.

However, so far as anyone knows, cheese has never been made with ass's milk. Three hundred donkeys a day had to be milked to produce the mere 30 litres required by Poppaea for her beauty treatment when she bathed in it.

Yoghurt: Fermented Milk

The Balkans, Bulgaria in particular, are very proud of their remarkable number of people who live to be 100 and over. It appears that they owe their unusual longevity to a frugal diet consisting mainly of yoghurt.

Yoghurt is not curdled milk, but milk fermented by the action of two lactic bacilli acting together. *Lactobacillus bulgaricus* acidifies the milk and causes the formation of lactic acid from lactose ('milk sugar'). This lactic acid makes casein coagulate. *Streptococcus thermophylus* gives a particular and characteristic aroma under the influence of the slight warmth in which, as its name indicates, it thrives. A 120-millilitre pot of commercial yoghurt containing 125 grams of the product consists of 5.20 g protein, 6.40 g lactose, 1 g lactic acid, and 1.4 g mineral salts of which 0.2 g is calcium. It has 57 calories, 36 per cent protids, 20 per cent lipids, say 1.25 g, and 44 per cent glucids (if sugar or jam is added, the amount of glucids rises in proportion to the additive).

In fact the reason why 'natural' yoghurt contains very few lipids is that it is made with partly skimmed milk. Eating yoghurt with '0 per cent fat', therefore, is a purely morale-building aid in low-calorie diets. So-called Bulgarian yoghurt is fermented in a special way and left to stand to acidulate further; it remains more liquid and contains more calories than natural yoghurt. Finally, the same amount of 'full-cream' yoghurt contains 90 calories. Cream, and even powdered skimmed milk, has been added to the basic skimmed milk. A pot of yoghurt equals a glass of milk.

Yoghurt, when commercially made, may be flavoured with fruits (either pieces of fruit or natural extracts). As the extracts have no colour, permitted colourings have to be used to answer the expectations of the consumer, particularly the young consumer. Coffee, chocolate, caramel and vanilla are not compatible with the principle of yoghurt-making, so products with these flavourings are sold not as yoghurt but as milk thickened with starch or gelatine. Yoghurt can be made at home with a yoghurt-maker, or simply by tipping the contents of a pot of yoghurt into a litre of warm milk. You leave it to stand at a mild temperature for 12 hours, just as the peoples of the Balkans and Asia have always done.

Lactic acid, if not absolutely guaranteed to make you a centenarian, is very good for the digestive system, except in a few rare cases of allergy to milk. It destroys the microbes causing putrefaction (which is not digestion but its opposite), which are present in intestinal infections and cannot live in an acid environment. Finally, the decalcifying effect of yoghurt is legendary.

Yoghurt has been naturalized as part of the Western diet, particularly since the last war, and is even to be found in the supermarkets of Spain and Africa. However, it was known in France as early as 1542, when François I was suffering from what would now be diagnosed as severe depression. The doctors could do nothing for his listlessness and neurasthenia until the Ambassador to the Sublime Porte disclosed that there was a Jewish doctor in Constantinople who made a brew of fermented sheep's milk of which people spoke in glowing terms, even at the Sultan's court. The King sent for the doctor, who refused to travel except on foot; he walked through the whole of southern Europe, followed by his flock. When he finally arrived before François I, the latter's apathy had given way to a certain impatience, but he still did not feel well. After several weeks of sheep's milk yoghurt, the King was cured. The sheep, however, had not recovered from their long walk and caught cold in the air of Paris. Every last one of them died, and the doctor left again, refusing to stay despite the King's offers. He went home, taking the secret of his brew with him. The health of François I continued to improve, which was the point of the exercise, and yoghurt was forgotten for nearly four centuries.

The *kefir* of the Balkans, Eastern Europe and the Caucasus is whey fermented by the addition of granules of a particular lactic bacterium and dried, powdered *kefir*, an ancient method going back to the dawn of time. It becomes a fizzy drink, both acid and slightly alcoholic, sometimes up to a strength of 1 per cent alcohol. Half its volume is carbonic gas. All this makes it hard for some people to digest.

The *koumis* of Central Europe is made from fermented mare's milk, but its origin lies in farthest Asia. The 'barbarian' Huns and Mongols brought it with them. In the past Western Europe made milk-based drinks which were not yoghurt, but were more like *kefir* or diluted and flavoured curds. Such drinks bear witness to the memory of ancient migrations: they are the beverages of people who did not grow vines and whose only wealth was the flocks they drove ahead of them. The Celts of northern Gaul, the British Isles and Ireland used to celebrate great events with brews of curdled milk. The first emigrants to America, many of whom were Catholics from Celtic areas of the British Isles, still made them when they could: curdled milk-beer, for less important occasions, was a carefully adjudged mixture of one-third milk, one-third cream, one-third beer and lime juice mixed with cinnamon. The old recipe used cider vinegar instead of lime juice. A *posset* made of curdled milk and hot wine, well seasoned with spices, was drunk to aid digestion after the great medieval banquets. 'Lait sur vin, venin', says a French proverb, 'milk on top of wine is poison'. But, it continues, 'vin avec lait, santé': 'wine with milk, good health'.

Butter: the Cream of the Milk

Marc Bloch[4] suggests: 'It may be that in the final reckoning we owe butter to the nomadic peoples of the Euro-Asiatic plains.' He mentions the Mongolian technique of churning cream horizontally in a leather flask suspended above the ground, after it had been skimmed off the milk. This is the most archaic way of butter-making, still practised by the people of the Atlas.

By the time invaders from Asia settled at Sumer around 3500 BC, they were shaking cream in a vertically designed churn, as shown in a bas-relief now in Baghdad Museum. The Celts and then the Vikings passed on a taste for butter to their descendants; they may have derived that taste partly from their origins, but also from the fact that cattle did so well in their various adoptive countries, always chosen for green pastures.

The Berlin Papyrus Number 1, translated by Maspero, contains among other fascinating material the memoirs of an Egyptian corsair who lived at the time of the 18th Theban dynasty (*c.* 1500 BC). The author, in flight, had taken refuge with a nomadic Bedouin chief from north-east Sinai somewhere near Eilat on the Gulf of Akaba, a region where stock-breeding seems to have flourished. 'Here they gave me every kind of butter and cheese.' There were plenty of animals, but Sanuhate the Egyptian does not say what kind they were. However, the climate would have favoured sheep and goats rather than cattle, which were more likely to be found in the Gaza plain and Lebanon. The butter and cheese he mentions, therefore, would have been made with goat's or sheep's milk, as it still is in the hot regions of the Middle East and the Maghreb. Arab sheep's milk butter, almost white and even richer than butter made from cow's milk, is preferred for making couscous, particularly when it is rancid and has a Roquefort-like flavour.

The ancient Greeks and Romans did not use butter much in their cooking. Whatever its origin, they called it *buturon* (in Greek) or *butyrum* (Latin), meaning literally cow's cheese. Pliny mentions it as a food of the barbarians, and Strabo says of the people of the Pyrenees that 'their butter serves them as oil'.

Graeco-Roman butter being 'cow's cheese', it would be interesting to compare it with a butter-making recipe given in a fourteenth-century Venetian cookery book, the *Libro di cucina*. Chapter X of this work explains that cream cheese must be pounded with hot water. The fat which rises to the top is skimmed off and then beaten to make butter.

At this period, judging by the other cookery books just beginning to appear, butter seems to have been almost unknown in Italy. Nor does it enter into more than 2 per cent of the recipes given in Taillevent's French book of around 1380, *Le viandier*. Butter was not really used much in Italy until the fifteenth century; in France, it features in a third of the recipes of the sixteenth-century *Livre fort excellent*. The use of butter for thickening sauces, in the classic manner, was slow to infiltrate the kitchen.

The influence of the example set by the Vikings and Normans when butter consumption began is obvious; in those parts of Western Europe which they later colonized, there is no mention of butter among the dues in kind collected by the officers of the Merovingian, Carolingian and even the first Capetian kings of France until the conquerors had really settled in. Not until the fourteenth century did the Church have anything to say about butter in its directives for fasting. Meanwhile the eating of butter spread from Normandy and the Loire valley to the Netherlands and Switzerland, where people also began to make it. In the twelfth century no one was sure whether, unlike lard, it could be considered suitable for fast days, a suggestion made by an abbot of Saint-Denis.

As Jean-Louis Flandrin[5] points out, butter consumption is a natural development in regions suitable for cattle-breeding. In such places, popular taste and the local economy had gone right over to butter as a cooking fat within 400 years.

Flandrin is speaking of the butter-eating areas of Europe in the fourteenth to seventeenth centuries, but things are much the same today: 'The area covered a whole or part of the Alps, half or the northern two-thirds of France, the Netherlands, Great Britain, and countries as far north as Iceland. The Bretons, Flemish and Icelanders were famous for their butter exports.' The Icelandic butter made by the descendants of the Vikings is mentioned in a book of 1607, the *Thrésor de santé*, as being 'pressed into wooden vessels 30 to 40 feet long.' But in Paris, over a long period, the butter made in Vanves was regarded as the finest and enjoyed the greatest reputation, particularly in the last decades of the seventeenth century, when it commanded a high price.

When it was recognized that indulging in a now well-established traditional food on fast days was a sin, the people of those parts of France which prefer butter to oil were not pleased to find themselves deprived of it for long and frequent periods of abstinence. It must be admitted that the people of those parts which prefer oil regarded butter with great suspicion. There are accounts of medieval Provençal or Catalan travellers, obliged to journey through foreign countries or even stay there, who took their own olive oil with them, believing that butter made you more vulnerable to leprosy.

René of Anjou, when he became Count of Provence, was presented with a welcoming gift of jars of virgin olive oil by his new subjects; it was a great luxury in Provence, not yet as well planted with olive trees as it is now, but the Count could not conceal his disgust, thus hurting the feelings of the good Provençals. He had cows brought from Angers and pastured on the banks of the Rhône, in a place which became known as the Pâtis (grazing ground), and being a good Christian, he planted walnut trees near Aix to provide walnut oil for fast days.

Those good Christians who had a liking for butter were soon able to buy dispensations. The bull of the Crusades, or *Cruzada*, allowed Spaniards to eat lard,[6] and the dispensation was still in force during the eighteenth century, long after the Crusades were over. The Church did not make a fortune out of that particular dispensation, since Spanish stock-breeders raised *toros bravos* in preference to dairy cows, and oil is more popular as a cooking fat in Spain. The Comtesse d'Aulnoye, of the famous *Fairy Tales*, boldly crossing Pyrenean borders which were soon to change in the year 1681, complained of the scarcity of the rancid butter which was all they could provide for her, and the strong smell of the oil-fried food so popular among the Spanish, from fried eggs to prime steaks of beef, made her feel ill.

In his own time, and for his personal use, King Charles V of France had obtained a bull from Pope Gregory XI allowing him to replace Vanves butter on fast days by *oleum lardinum*, a charming if euphemistic term for rendered bacon fat. Anne of Brittany received a wedding present from the Holy Father when she married the King of France: complete absolution for her own gluttony, then for that of her household, and finally for all Bretons, who were known to enjoy salted butter. In 1495 the same dispensation was granted, although this time for considerable sums of money, to Germany, Hungary, Bohemia, and then France.

Matters had not yet reached that point when François de Bourdeille, the father of the historian Brantôme, visited Rome with ideas of his own in mind. 'The Pope having asked him, "What do you want of me? You shall have it", he asked only for a licence and dispensation to eat butter on fast days, since he could eat neither olive nor walnut oil; this the Pope readily granted and had a Bull sent, for him and for his, which could long be seen among the treasures of our house.' And indeed, over a long period the Church, well knowing on which side its own bread was buttered, made money by selling dispensations to eat butter. The 'Butter Tower' at Rouen was actually financed by such payments. The city of Strasbourg obtained both guns and butter in the shape of the *Ankerbuchsen*, cannon founded with the blessing of Bishop Albert of Bavaria.

A contemporary of Brantôme's father, although not in anything like such favour with the Pope, was Luther, who was particularly scandalized by this trafficking in indulgences in 1520. In his tract *An den christlichen Adel deutscher Nation* he complains that, 'in Rome, they make a mockery fasting, while forcing us to eat an oil they themselves would not use to grease their slippers. Then they sell us the right to eat foods forbidden on fast days ... but they have stolen that same liberty from us with their ecclesiastical laws.... Eating butter, they say, is a greater sin than to lie, blaspheme, or indulge in impurity.'

Flandrin[7] remarks, in this connection, that those countries which use butter for cooking are almost identical with those which broke away from the Catholic Church in the sixteenth century (although in the case of England the polygamous leanings of the King were perhaps more involved than gastronomy). As for the Languedoc area of France, where people would think a good cassoulet worth excommunication, traditionally olive oil was eaten in the south, walnut oil in the north, and goose fat everywhere, so it could do without butter very well.[8] If Protestantism did make a certain amount of headway here, perhaps the goose fat had something to do with it.

However, we should bear in mind that those countries of northern Europe which became Protestant are countries with a tradition of dairy farming. An obligation to eat oil in Lent was as hard to digest as the foreign debts incurred by importing it unnecessarily. Nor could people stomach the sight of an important sector of economic expansion being threatened annually by a sudden fall in sales. Indeed, the arguments in favour of the Reformation made their way into that situation like the proverbial knife through butter.

To give some idea of world butter consumption, I may add that as a matter of cultural fact those white populations which subsequently settled in the Americas, Australia and Africa have preferred to eat the fats of the customary diets of their countries of origin. The real natives of the countries they colonized have either clung to their local ancestral customs, or else, in 'developing', have adopted the dominant mode of the Westerners who now share the land with them. The popularity of oil and butter roughly coincides with the official spoken language. People in English-speaking countries tend not to eat much oil. Hispanic countries consume a great deal of it. The French-speaking countries, like France itself, are half-and-half. In places where people like to eat butter, but it is not produced locally, it is imported. But the European Community is still faced annually with the problem of its butter mountain.

Finally, in recent years the trend towards skimmed milk has led to a fashion for half-fat butter, and butter substitutes which are known only by their brand names and are made from buttermilk or whey, lecithin and soya. They offer people obsessed by their cholesterol intake 'butter' with only 50 per cent fat matter. As you cannot cook with these fats, they are just right for spreading on toast to go with decaffeinated coffee. This is progress. Fasting is a thing of the past, so we have reinvented it.

The Symbolism of Butter

Butter, as a luxury food, naturally occupied a prominent place in ancient religious ceremonies, either as an ointment (this is the meaning of its Irish name *imb* and its Breton name *ammanb*) or as a sacred or magical food. Not for nothing did Little Red Riding Hood take her grandmother a little pot of butter.

Until quite recently the Bretons would place a pat of butter near a person suffering from cancer. The butter was supposed to absorb the disease, and it was buried after the sick person's death. The Indians of Vedic times invoked butter as a primordial deity: 'Tongue of the gods, navel of the Immortal. Let us praise the name of butter, let us maintain it with our sacrificial homage.... As a wild steed breaks through barriers, so does melting butter caress the flaming logs, and the fire, satisfied, accepts it', says the *Rig-Veda* (IV, 58). Indeed, butter thrown on a fire will make it crackle as it nourishes and regenerates the flames. It is regenerating life itself. The offering of butter is a form of prayer, a source of sacred energy such as might create a universe.[9]

The butter made from the milk of Indian sacred cows was intended for religious ceremonies; it was a purified, clarified, liquid butter. Indians still use the clarified butter called *ghi* for cooking. In Tibet butter is made from yak's milk. It is eaten when very rancid, almost like cheese, and mixed with tea, the sacred drink. It is also spread on temple statues. There are even butter sculptures, which keep quite well in the climate at such altitudes. The Chinese annexation of Tibet put an end to the ancient custom of simmering dead lamas in boiling butter before embalming them.

Butter with its sunny, golden colour is so closely associated with fire in folk memory that in Iceland, according to seventh-century texts from the monastery of St Gall, the farmers' wives of that time were still asking the smith god Gobhin to look after the butter they made. Whether in the rites described in the Vedas, or in magical Celtic practices, butter features as a substitute for those natural golden treasures, honey and virgin wax, which themselves have sometimes been called the butter of the bees.

Chapter 6

The History of Cereals

Cereals as Civilizers

The discovery and study of Paleolithic refuse heaps has been facilitated by the fact that the grains found there were preserved from the ravages of time by more or less complete carbonization. They had been parched, probably to get rid of a husk which was indigestible or hard to crush. Cereals of poor quality were still being parched in the Middle Ages before undergoing further preparation. This suggests that cooking (if that is the word for these rudimentary Stone Age procedures), soon involving the use first of tools and then of utensils, may have been quite important in inducing people to settle in an environment already chosen for its wealth of cereals.

Several factors changed their way of life: the need to supervise equipment and provisions (a major consideration), a rise in population on account of a certain degree of comfort – relative but infinitely preferable to the hazards of the nomadic life of either hunters or herdsmen – and a certain physical and mental security, particularly by comparison with the dangers of big game hunting, and also the result of a better diet. The name of the epoch, the Pleistocene, says it all. Such methods of birth control as infanticide must have been less stringently applied. Life expectancy increased. People could afford to keep the old and sick alive. Competition between men and women, the young and the old, must have become less intense. The presence of old people in a society is important. It implies notions of memory, tradition, experience and cultural roots. Not for nothing does the same word, *culture*, apply to both intellectual development and the tilling of the soil.

Evidence that people succumbed to the attraction of cereals even before they thought of growing such plants themselves, and lost the nomadic impulse, comes from the settlement sites of hunters at the transitional stage, for instance in the Taurus and Zagros area and in Turkey. 'Property is the foundation of a farming or trading society', said the Abbé Raynal.[1]

125

When the hunters of the Taurus and Zagros, Egypt and Nubia (of the Qadian culture) settled down for good in regions rich in Gramineae they did it thoroughly, hollowing out mills and mortars in the living rock of their caves in which to crush the grain gathered from the surrounding countryside. Residues which have been excavated and sifted show that their diet of fish and herbivorous animals (eaten in sufficient quantities and selectively enough for us to suspect that they were herding those animals) was supplemented by large quantities of wild cereals, including barley, which was well adapted to local conditions. This gathering suited them so well that they were still practising it around 5000 BC, whereas the peoples of the eastern shore of the Mediterranean, in Syria and Palestine, had been growing barley and wheat along the river-banks from 10,000 to 7000 BC. These cultivated grains were not much better than the wild varieties, but they were sown on the alluvial mud when the floods had gone down. Around 3000 BC, from the valley of the Nile to the foothills of the Zagros mountains and as far afield as the Indus, almost everyone mastered the technique of surface irrigation, and sometimes of underground irrigation too, although we cannot actually say they were tilling the land; they simply deposited the seed.

Evidence of cereals from the beginning of the post-glacial age has been found in Syria, on the banks of the Euphrates. These cereals were certainly cultivated: their abundance shows it, and so does their location in an area definitely not predestined to grow such plants and a long way from the natural habitat of the wild grains. However, the variety excavated is exactly the same as the corresponding wild variety, showing neither improvement nor selection. These grains were still of the brittle type, with a fragile rachis that shed the seed easily, and the same poor genetic inheritance.

However, an extraordinary discovery has been made at Jericho on the banks of the Jordan, not far from a part of the mountains of Judaea which still grows heavy crops of brittle wild wheat. Jericho began as a mere camp of hunter-gatherers. But in the tenth millennium BC a permanent village was built on the site. In excavations of the level corresponding to that period, fossil cereals have been found: barley and wheat which no longer shed their seeds with the ease so useful to the wild grasses. This was a new development. What had happened?

Obviously people must have deplored the sheer wastefulness of the brittle cereals. If they decided a field was still too green to be harvested and waited another day for it all to ripen, they generally risked finding the panicles empty and the seed scattered to the four winds. Only a few sturdy ears here and there might still contain their treasure because of a whim of nature: a mutation.

Modern wheat is descended from those sturdy, well-ripened ears which were gathered first by hand, then with stone sickles. One long-held theory suggests that the women who had the job of gathering plants – men being better suited to facing the dangers of hunting – noticed how grain from the ears which had not shed their seed spontaneously produced crops with the same characteristic. Such sowings must have been accidental at first: some of the grain may have been spilt on the path as it was carried home, or a ritual offering of grain may have germinated on the sacrificial spot, or plants may have grown from a rubbish heap. We do not know. And in any case, the specific role of women in proto-agriculture is a controversial subject at present, despite reference to the last surviving 'primitive' societies. From this point on, however, cults of mother goddesses presiding over the crops and harvest developed; they were associated with fertile femininity. We can see this as a memory of the women gatherers of ancient times, as well as being clearly related to the general symbolism associated with woman. Comparisons between the 'breast' of the earth and the maternal breast, or the cyclical permanence of plant life and the female physiology, must have risen naturally to the minds of the first farming peoples – especially as wheat sown in the autumn needs nine months to grow before harvest in summer.

In any case, 10,000 years ago the inhabitants of Jericho laid out fields of cereals where two varieties of primitive but true wheat grew by design, einkorn (*Triticum monococcum*) and emmer (*Triticum dicoccum*), as well as two-rowed barley (*Hordeum distichon*). These wheats and the barley grew well; because of the proximity of wadis or watering places, they were sown in muddy soil (a mixture of clay and sand), which could be irrigated without too much trouble if necessary. Wild barley (*Hordeum spontaneum*), found in the Near and Middle East, in Asia Minor and Central Asia, and on all the plateaux of North Africa, often associates naturally with wild 'wheat', or with cultivated wheat when the climate allows the latter to thrive. But there are centres in Central and East Asia where barley was grown to the exclusion of all other cereals. It is of greater antiquity here than wheat, an imported cereal crop. Barley, which is very hardy, adapts spontaneously to the rigours of continental climates.[2]

The relative opulence of Jericho as a result of its cultivation of cereals, lentils and peas meant that its people were able to build a village settlement covering four hectares, an exceptional size for the end of the Paleolithic. Over the following centuries long occupation of the site turned it into a mound growing larger and larger as successive generations of buildings were constructed on one another's ruins. This type of settlement, quite common in the Near and Middle East, was often given the Arabic name of *tell* or the Turkish name of *hoycik*. Any such place, called by one or other of these names, is an artificial hill concealing a series of villages fitted into each other. Each level is a chapter of history. At Jarno in Iraq 16 stages in the life of the city have been counted. The oldest level at Jarno contained two kinds of wheat grains and barley, as at Jericho. They are seven thousand years old, and must have escaped the process of gathering after threshing separated them from their husks. Similarly, the impression of these grains has been found in the straw used for the mud walls of the houses. Carbonized grains have also been found, spoilt in cooking or charred by granary fires.

At Tell Mureybet, in northern Syria, the oldest level contained no cultivated wheat at all, only a very poor brittle einkorn (8600 to 7800 BC). The excavations at Khirokita in Cyprus, a site dating from the end of the sixth millennium, show that the cultivation of *Triticum dicoccum* began there at the same time as the breeding of goats and sheep. These animals were not native to the island and were imported. Does this imply that cereal cultivation was another import? We find the same phenomenon in Crete, where the people of Knossos had long been accustomed to fishing for such deep-sea fish as tunny. Slowly, from the sixth millennium onwards, all parts of the Balkans except for the coastal zones, and the strip of land extending from Anatolia to the north of the Iranian plateau, achieved technical progress in the form of simple but effective irrigation which subsequently made dry areas outside the famous Fertile Crescent productive. In a parallel development, stock-breeding became general rather than sporadic, giving rise to the inter-relationship between fodder, draught animals and natural manure. Pottery-making and metal-working began at the same time and were instrumental in raising the standard of living. A system developed whereby urban centres of increasingly dense populations were connected by a network of trade routes.

The Symbolism of Wheat

The farmer puts grain into the ground, as if burying the dead, and it is reborn as a plant which itself bears grain. To the ancient world, this process represented both the mysteries of life and the permanent cycle of the seasons. But as creation and perpetuation were seen as the miraculous mission of women, nature had to be a mother: 'the earth which, alone, gives birth to all creatures and nourishes them, receiving their fertile seed again,' said Aeschylus. The germination of the seed, the birth and death of the plant, and its reappearance every time its fruit returns to the bosom of the earth all suggested resurrection, so that an ear of corn became one of the emblems of Osiris, the Egyptian agrarian god who was cast into the Nile and returned to life, like the wheat sown on ground previously flooded by the river. Whereas the primary aim of all human beings is to avoid dying of starvation, the great hope held out by religion is to triumph over death itself.

The symbolism of wheat thus goes beyond the natural sphere to signify a passing from darkness underground into sunlight, or vice versa, which is equivalent to the passage from the non-manifest to the manifest, from ignorance to revelation. One of the rites of Eleusis, a temple dedicated to Demeter, consisted of contemplating grains of wheat. Among all peoples the agrarian deities, particularly the gods associated with cereals, have been regarded as initiators as well as nurturers, providing food for both body and soul.

Every cereal plant grown in a field, promising nourishment and bringing vitality, must be received and then offered up as a blessing. Cereals are the gift, given over and over again since the beginning of time, of the benevolent divinities, usually represented as goddesses: Demeter (or Ceres) gave the Greeks and Romans barley and wheat; Chicomecoatl gave the Aztecs maize. The Egyptians worshipped Renenoulet, the harvest goddess, and Min, the god of cultivation and master of

Table 6.1 The Long March of Cereals

10,000 BC	Jericho (Jordan)	non-brittle wheat (einkorn, emmer), two-rowed barley
8600	Mureybet (Turkey)	brittle einkorn
8000	Dordogne (France)	wild Gramineae
7500	Haman-Suho/Hokkaido (Japan)	buckwheat, barley, various wild cereals
6500	Southern Carpathians (Romania)	various Gramineae
6000	Khirokitia (Crete)	emmer
	Mexico	maize
	Central Western Europe and Hungary	large-grained Gramineae
	Mauritania	wild millet
	Balkans	wild millet, einkorn and emmer
5000	Kyushu (Japan)	millet
	Southern Europe	einkorn
	Cova de Oro (Spain)	four wheats, two barleys
4500	Panp'o (North China)	millet, then sorghum
4000	Denmark	minor cereals
	Egypt	wheat
	Siberia	millet
	Southern China	rice
3000	India	millet, rice
	Babylonia	barley, millet, sesame, emmer
	Africa	millet (from East to West)
	Ethiopia	large 'kaffir' millet, barley and wheat
2000	Central Europe	rye
	Mauritania	cultivated millet
500	Persia	wheat
400	Italy, Greece	soft wheat, then durum wheat
300	Northern China	soft spring-sown wheat (from West to East)
	Japan	rice
AD 100	Khartoum (Sudan)	barley, sorghum
	Europe	rye (from East to West) and cultivated oats
	Sahel, Chad	finger millet
1400	Lombardy (Italy)	rice
1520	America	rice
	Europe	maize
1640	Camargue (France)	rice
c. 1800	Australia	wheat

the generative force, whose son Nepi, the spirit of wheat, was a life-giving principle. Similarly, the Greek and Roman priests sprinkled the heads of sacrificial victims with flour or decked them with ears of corn before immolating them. Egyptian funeral rites always included an offering of wheat, which the dead took with them into the afterlife as food for the journey, and also as a lucky charm.

It should not be forgotten that millet too is a staple cereal eaten by a great part of humanity. The survival of the dead (ensured by ritual sacrifices) as well as the existence of the living depended on it. 'Prince Millet' was the celestial ancestor of the first Chou emperors of China, and every living sovereign was regarded as the trustee of the natural order of things, most clearly expressed by the agricultural cycle. Sowing and harvesting millet periodically reactivated the relationship of the two universes of the celestial world and the world below, between which the human race lives.

The Dogon people of Mali believed that African millet had been stolen from the starry sky by their Great Blacksmith Ancestor. The Mossi of Volta say it was discovered by a woman maddened by famine who caught a bird which had insulted her and meant to cook it. It owed its life to the millet droppings it produced in its cage.

If gold is the colour of wheat ripened in the sun, then black (or in heraldic terms sable) represents the fertile land, the generative power of the soil. Black is also the colour of the steed ridden by the third horseman of the Apocalypse, with a pair of balances in his hand to measure out wheat, barley, oil and wine, so that they should be fairly distributed at a fair price, to avert famine: 'A measure of wheat for a penny, and three measures of barley for a penny; and see thou hurt not the oil and the wine' (Revelation 6, vi).

As we have seen, the horse was often associated with the fertility of harvest. In Northern Europe, particularly Scandinavia, threshing grounds were marked out by the skulls of horses disposed at the four points of the compass. These skulls were struck rhythmically in time to the beating of the flail. Horses' heads have been found on archeological digs in Brittany, in levels dating from the first millennium BC. These Celtic relics baffled explanation for some time. The cockerel, a creature of the sun, and the dog are also associated with harvest festivities. Harvest falls in the middle of the 'dog-days' of summer, under the sign of the constellation of Canis Minor, but the dog also denotes Cerberus, guardian of the underworld, and thus a patron of all that comes from beneath the ground.

Imperialist Cereals

From Macedonia, cereals, acting as it were in tandem with sheep-breeding, gradually made their way all over Central Europe up the Danube, Maritsa and Morava rivers. This wave of cereals and sheep reached western Greece, Yugoslavia, Italy, and the South of France. The dual phenomenon settled in islands – Corsica, Sardinia, Sicily – and on the shores of North Africa. The use of obsidian (natural glass) for vessels and for seals, as well as similarities in the so-called cardial decoration of pottery made by imprinting it with a shell pattern, are all evidence of cultural cross-currents parallel to those in agriculture. At this point the spread of cereal-growing provides information about the migration of the peoples who consumed it, because they took their nutritional customs with them. That development is never reversed. However, one cannot always discount local development, often synchronous but apparently independent when there is no proof of outside contacts.

Thousands of years ago, and in an area as rich in game as the Dordogne, the people of 8000 BC were already adding wild grasses to their diet; traces have been found around their hearths. Stone blades with notches at the base have also been found. The notches suggest that the knives might have been set into handles, or at least tied to them, but in any case they were certainly used to cut grass stalks, since they show the characteristic gloss which is a sign of wear caused by silicon conveyed in the sap of such plants in the green state, and deposited in tiny crystals on the surfaces of stems and leaves.

At the sites of Gazel in Languedoc and Châteauneuf-lès-Martigues in Provence, excavation of pre-Neolithic levels has revealed mortars, but in this case there is nothing about their condition to show that they were used to crush cereals rather than fruits.

Where true agricultural practices such as tilling the soil are concerned, the digging sticks of the Aude, of Spain, and even the ox-drawn swing-plough shown in a rock-painting from Mount Bégo near Nice are evidence that people did not always sit about waiting for revelation to dawn in the East. The many collections of sickles and harvesting knives found in Switzerland, Northern Italy and Spain may be signs of a fifth-millennium proto-agriculture in the course of rapid evolution, but they are not so clear and incontestable a proof as that of the Andalusian settlement of the Cova de Oro.

This is only a cavern under the rock, not a collection of buildings like the villages of the Near East which were contemporary with it, yet four different species of wheat and two of barley have been found in it. This discovery is of great interest for several reasons. First, because it tells us that cereal-growing at a well-advanced stage (six cereals in all) does not *necessarily* go hand in hand with the building of solid dwellings (although such dwellings could have disappeared entirely; fortified castles have been known to give way to stony ground). Secondly, it shows that the Andalusians of the fifth millennium were already familiar with a range of grains, and we must suppose that these cereals, perhaps of different origins, were cultivated together, as a mixed crop. The practice of growing such crops, called *maslin*, which eventually came to consist of wheat, oats and rye, provided a certain amount of insurance if one or other of them failed because of disease or bad weather. Maslin-growing lasted almost until modern times. The peasants kept it for their own consumption, while they, or rather their lords, sold the major corn crops to feed the towns. Finally, this Spanish discovery shows that the grains were roasted, or 'parched', before being stored. It has yet to be established whether the cereals found and the practices associated with them were native to the area. Were these wheats and barleys derived from wild forms found locally? The same question applies to the techniques employed in cultivating them, and in the present state of our knowledge it has not been fully answered. But at least we know that the two major cereals were wheat and barley, and they have been exploited longer than any others.

The term wheat (*Triticum*) is applied to two ancestral species: einkorn and emmer. Einkorn is thought to be the older, being hardier and less particular about where it grows. The same qualities testify to the ancient origins of barley.

Primitive einkorn, *Triticum boeoticum* or *algilopoides*, grew naturally, and still does, all over the eastern Mediterranean·area: in the Balkans, Greece, Bulgaria, Turkey, Syria, northern Iraq and the southern Caucasus. The agronomist N. I. Vavilov[3] believes that the transition from the wild to the cultivated form occurred a priori in that area, which extends from the Black Sea to the Caspian. D. Zohary,[4] however, is inclined to think it took place in Anatolia in the south-east of Turkey. Medicine is not the only field where Galen says nay if Hippocrates says yea. There is even a third school of thought, the theory of De Candolle, which upholds the claims of the Euphrates. Cultivated einkorn, *Triticum monococcum*, established itself in Europe in the early part of the Neolithic age (5000 BC). It was still being grown in the nineteenth century in mountainous and barren regions such as the Lower Alps, but its cultivation is only a memory now, although a few fields are grown for purposes of ecological nostalgia.

The history of emmer (*Triticum dicoccum*) was quite different. In its spontaneous form, *Triticum dicoccoides*, it was found, as we have seen, in chalky, semi-arid regions with sparse and irregular rainfall, and grew in an area covering north-east Turkey, the Caucasus, Georgia, northern Palestine, and Syria as far as western Iran. However, Zohary thinks that this brittle variety was never improved. In that case the non-brittle mutation would have descended from a related species native to the Golan area which then spread from Israel, Transjordan and southern Syria. It was welcomed from the dawn of Neolithic times, first in Egypt and Babylonia, then in Central and Eastern Europe from Denmark to Switzerland and from the Ruhr to Bohemia.

Gradually, emmer, which was hardy but not very productive, and unsuitable for bread-making, gave way to true soft bread wheats (*Triticum aestivum* or *vulgare*), and in South Asia to *T. compactum*, a beardless wheat. These species were less hardy but had a better yield. Soft wheats were the result of cross-breeding (whether by chance or design) between the improved, non-brittle varieties of emmer and einkorn – i.e., hybridization.

The simplest forms of wheat are described as diploids, and have only two pairs of seven chromosomes. Hybrids like the early bread wheats are tetraploids, with four pairs of chromosomes. At first they produced crops of 'hulled' grain, with the husk clinging to the grain (hence the necessity of parching it before it was ground to destroy that hard, indigestible envelope). But at the Neolithic site of Çatal Hüyük in Anatolia a new hybrid appears, this time with six pairs of chromosomes. In this case the grain was 'naked', separating easily from the husk of the glumes. It had another important quality: the axis of the ear was stronger, and now even high winds could not blow a single grain away. Modern wheat had come into being. However, it was to be another 20 centuries before the Greeks and Romans finally adopted it in preference to emmer.

We now distinguish between hard or durum wheats and soft wheats. The hard wheats, sown in autumn, are also known as 'winter wheat'. They are not used much in bread-making, and their main use is for pasta. They contain less starch but more proteins. The soft or spring wheats, generally grown in temperate climates, are not so rich in protein. They are particularly suitable for making bread, biscuits and cakes, and for fermentation to produce alcohol. Ninety per cent of world production is soft wheat. More than 30,000 varieties of wheat have been recorded worldwide, and almost every day botanists are creating new and even better varieties.

Egyptian Wheat: engraving from *L'Égypte*, by
Georges Ebers, 1880

Wheat can be said to have remained the property of the Old World until white men arrived in America, and even for a little while afterwards, since the Emperor Charles V did not send his colonists wheat until 1520. China became acquainted with it rather later than the West.

Chinese civilization, which arose in the north of the country, in the provinces of Ho-nan, Chan-si and Chen-si, was nourished over a long period by a grain native to the area, which was already being gathered in its wild state towards 7000 BC in another large habitat, Japan. This was millet. Rice, as we shall see, was a native of south China, and its arrival in the north turned a new page in the history of the Middle Kingdom. As early as around 4500 BC the 600 souls of the village of Pan-p'o were practising a very elaborate system of agriculture on loess (alluvial mud), with equipment which although made of stone was very plentiful. This culture, and its farming, thus pre-dated what has always been regarded as the great point of departure for Chinese civilization, the building of the extraordinary capital of the Chang dynasty, Ngan-yang (or An-yang) in the sixteenth century BC.

Millet, which is still popular in China, soon spread to India, and then to Africa and southern Europe where, as we shall see, it competed valiantly with the maize brought from America after the eighteenth century, but eventually lost the battle. Its tiny but numerous grains still feed one-third of the population of the globe; millet is not just bird-seed. Wheat, although better-flavoured and above all better for bread-making than millet, is a plant for dry soils, and one of the many remarkable feats of the Chinese people was their eventual success in growing it. Wheat came to China around the fourth century BC, undoubtedly by the same route as Alexander the Great, and neither north China, which is very cold, nor south China, which is very hot, seemed naturally suited to it. In the end the southern part of the country turned to rice.

The severe winter climate of north China and the humidity of its brief summers made it suitable only for soft, spring-sown wheat, a hybrid of the Graeco-Roman period. Chinese ingenuity soon solved the problem of sowing in soil still hard from the winter. The *Fan Sheng-Chih Su*, an agricultural treatise of the first century BC, recommends soaking the seed-corn overnight in a light mash made of peas and the excrement of silkworms before sowing it at dawn 'so that the gruel and the dew moisten the ground together'. For a long time to come quantities of millet were the standard measures of volume.

The oldest text to mention cereals is not an agricultural treatise; it does give certain instructions, but they are more concerned with legislation. This is the famous Code of Hammurabi, King of Babylonia, consisting chiefly of a list of taxes on various agricultural products. I shall return to it shortly, since it deals with beer, the price of which was linked to the price of barley. Three other sets of Babylonian clay tablets exist, recording supplies. The first mentions sacks of grain delivered in 2400 BC.

Perhaps the most eloquent documentation comes from Egyptian tomb paintings. One such painting, now in the Louvre, shows a harvest scene from the Eleythya tomb dating from the seventeenth dynasty, i.e., 1750 BC. The annual flooding of the Nile meant that wheat had already been cultivated in the Delta for two thousand years, which has led to an erroneous claim that one of the most ancient of the Egyptian populations, the Badarians, invented agriculture. That is not the case, nor is agriculture merely the cultivation of wheat. However, in the Fayyum, south-west of Cairo and below Giza, people were reaping barley and millet at this period, with curious saw-toothed stone sickles. Storage pits, also of curious design, were used to keep the grain; they were dug out of the ground and lined with straw mats.

The Eleythya tomb painting shows a manual wooden plough in use at the time of the pastoral Semite kings, the Hyksos, but the sixth-dynasty Ti tomb depicts a yoke of oxen. While we are on this subject, it should be said at once that the tale of the famous 'Osiris' wheat found intact in a Theban tomb and successfully sown after 50 centuries is one of those archeological hoaxes upon which much ink has been expended. A hard wheat with 28 chromosomes was certainly found in the tomb, but it never germinated, for the excellent reason that seeds lose all their ability to germinate after ten years.

The Egyptian murals show heavily bearded cereals on stalks which must have been nearly a metre high. In modern wheats and barleys the ear takes up so much of the plant that they are practically dwarf varieties. The maximum height of the stalk is now 50 centimetres. Straw has become a useless or almost useless by-product; our modern substitutes for draught animals consume petrol instead.

The wheats shown in medieval illuminations are as tall as their Egyptian ancestors. Early in the reign of Louis XI of France the height of the wheat covering the hills of Montlhéry helped the King to defend his throne against the rebel nobles at the battle of 16 July 1465. The Burgundian cavalry, opposing him, became hopelessly entangled in the wheat and could do nothing but charge in disorder towards the French archers, who were systematically shooting them down. Total confusion ensued, and both the rebels and the crop were massacred. As a matter of fact, battles were very seldom fought at harvest time; it was usual to wait until the corn was safely in before you declared war. Even in the late nineteenth and the twentieth centuries, the Franco-Prussian war began in July 1870, the First World War in August 1914 and the Second World War in September 1939. If the troops were to be followed by a commissariat, it was a good idea to have stocks of grain in reserve, and the young men free to fight.

For six thousand years the strength of nations depended on their stocks of wheat; the significance of the slang term 'bread' for money is obvious. Throughout the Bible, harvests and the flour supply were evidently among the major pre-occupations of the Israelite leaders. Reverence for wheat and bread bordered on the religious. 'And thou shalt observe the feast of weeks, of the firstfruits of the wheat harvest, and the feast of ingathering at the year's end' (Exodus 34, xxii). 'And when ye reap the harvest of your land, thou shalt not make clean riddance of the corners of thy field when thou reapest, neither shalt thou gather any gleaning of thy harvest: thou shalt leave them unto the poor, and to the stranger' (Leviticus, 23, xxii).

These gleaning rights are involved in the charming story of Ruth the Moabitess. 'In the beginning of barley harvest' Ruth, on her mother-in-law's advice, went to glean in the fields of the rich Boaz, who, as the story goes, fell asleep on the threshing floor, woke to find the wise and beautiful Ruth there with him, and married her. Their great-grandson was King David, the ancestor of Joseph, who married the Virgin Mary. Solomon, David's son and heir, lived on such a grand scale that the daily consumption of his household, among other provisions, was '30 measures of fine flour, and threescore measures of meal'. The measure was equivalent to 600 litres.

The Phoenicians, who also invented the alphabet, devised the notion of separating the grain from the harvested ears by laying the sheaves on a floor and making oxen tread it out. Grinding was still as primitive as in the time of the Babylonians, Egyptians and Israelites. When Samson, as a prisoner of the Philistines, was humiliated by being made to grind grain in the prison house, he would have been using a roller in a stone trough. Despite fanciful versions of the incident depicted by painters, his great strength was not put to turn a wheel: rotary mills had not yet been invented. Even the Greeks of archaic times did not have them. Crushing grain manually in stone querns was long considered work for slave women, who were thus doubly enslaved: that was the sense of the insult to the virile Samson.

The Aegeans used huge jars, or *pithoï*, for storage: they were set in the floors of warehouses where millet, barley and wheat were kept cool (the wheat was a bearded winter wheat called *sithoï*). Oats, which had now appeared on the scene, initially as weeds of wheat and despised by the Egyptians and the people of the Near East, were not used for bread-making but for the preparation of boiled porridge or gruels known as *ptisanes*.

The prosperity of mainland Greece depended on a dual economic current: the wheat-fields of Attica could scarcely feed more than 75,000 people, but olives did so well, while needing comparatively little labour, that plenty of oil was exported from 600 BC onwards. Accordingly, local industries and silver mines, foreign trading houses and banks were encouraged, so that imported corn could be paid for, and if necessary distributed after a profit had been taken. The import-export trade of Athens was largely in the hands of immigrants who were not Athenian citizens but resident aliens, *metics* ('those living with' [Athenians]).

When the glory of Athens was at its peak, corn supplies were a major concern of the government, and no subsequent government escaped that anxiety. Laws forbade Attic farmers to sell their corn except to Athens; the *epimeletes* of the *emporion* supervised its arrival at Piraeus and authorized no exports greater than one-third, calculated according to rates which were strictly checked to avoid excessive profit-making and illicit contracts. Officials called *sytophylaques* were in charge of what amounted to an exchange on which Boeotian grain, which was particularly heavy (like the wit of the Boeotians themselves, in the Athenian view), was much sought after. But most of the corn that arrived in Athens came from the Greek colonies of the Black Sea, in what is now Romania, and of Sicily, where harvests were very prolific. The army that fought Xerxes was entirely provisioned by Gelon, tyrant of Syracuse.

The yield of flour after grinding improved with the invention of a rotary mill consisting of two heavy discs of stone, although they were only two feet in diameter.

They turned on each other around a metal axis, and were worked by a handle manipulated by unfortunate women, often former prostitutes who were no longer in demand, or who had been practising their trade unregistered. However, people still used pestles and mortars, of a kind in use even today in Africa. Their abundance of flour made the Athenians great bakers, as we shall see below, and in Greek mythology the figure of Demeter, goddess of crops and harvest, was one of the best-loved and most respected deities, rather as if she were everyone's foster-mother.

Homer defined human beings as 'eaters of flour', referring to the cereals which were already the staple food of the Achaeans of the heroic age, and in *The Republic* Plato called for a return to that healthy diet: 'And for their nourishment [men] will provide meal from their barley and flour from their wheat, and roasting and kneading these they will serve noble cakes and loaves on some arrangement of reeds or clean leaves.'[5] It sounds as if Plato's republic would have suited the followers of those macrobiotic or Zen cereal-based diets which have become so fashionable since their introduction from the Far East. However, it is interesting to find the suggestion in this text that the flour rather than the grain was roasted; that would mean it could have been eaten simply mixed with liquid, without further cooking, and would be perfectly digestible, rather on the principle of today's instant baby cereals.

In Sparta, where Lycurgus decreed that meals should be eaten communally, the basis of the democratic menu was a kind of barley porridge eaten with the famous black broth, which the Athenians thought disgusting. The black broth itself was a kind of liquid stew of a goulash-like consistency, and to claim his share of it everyone had to provide the administration with a *medimne* (just over 50 litres) of barley flour a month. Perhaps this was why barley always retained connotations of austerity, even when lavishly served.

The same trade network which brought Athens food from Egypt, the Near East and Sicily also fed the Romans; Rome made the wheat question the motivating force of her imperial expansion, turning North Africa in particular into her private granary.

While the authorities encouraged people to grow olives, large Roman landowners were not particularly interested in cereal-growing, less profitable because it involved more labour and equipment. Imports of corn were the only way to feed the towns. Great families invested heavily in estates in North Africa and Sicily, but never felt called upon to set foot there themselves. The rich native landowners of the Eastern colonies, more anxious to make money out of oil and wine than cereal, took the same line. At the end of the first century there was such a famine in Central and Western Anatolia that the Emperor Domitian tried advising – rather than decreeing – a change of crops and clearing the land of vines and olive trees. People took this very ill, regarding it as contrary to the Roman government's usual policy of non-intervention, and sent a protest. Cargoes of Sicilian grain therefore had to be sent out from Rome, and more than once. Every year 17 million bushels of corn arrived at the port of Ostia from Africa, Egypt, Spain and above all Sicily, and continued the journey up the Tiber to Rome in flat-bottomed boats.

The great Roman estates of the North African coast prospered until the fifth century. Then the anarchy and chaos that were part of the decline of the Roman Empire gradually made themselves felt, and it was this, rather than the Arab invasions of the seventh and eighth centuries, that led to their ruin. North Africa, notably Tunisia, did not start growing cereals on any scale again until the beginning of the twentieth century.

The Myth of Demeter

'Da', or even earlier 'Ga', meant 'earth' in archaic Greek. Da-mater or Demeter,[6] the generative force of the earth, the Earth Mother, was the daughter of the Titan Cronos and Rhea, mother of the gods. Her own brothers, Poseidon and Zeus, entertained feelings for the tall, beautiful, fair-haired and well-formed goddess which were taken for granted by gods, though sinful among humans. One story has it that Demeter gave herself to a young man, a Cretan hunter, in a furrow of a thrice-ploughed field, and by this liaison the goddess had a child called Ploutos, wealth. The field was instantly covered with magnificent wheat to make the baby a cradle, and Demeter was thenceforward honoured as the goddess of corn and harvest. By her brother Zeus, king of the gods, who assumed the shape of a snake to seduce her, she bore the beautiful flower-faced Persephone. According to the devotees of Orphic cults she was also the mother of Dionysus, god of the vine, by her brother Poseidon the sea god, but this was a mystery of which they did not speak openly. Other Greek myths make either Rhea or Semele the mother of Dionysus.

Demeter was in Sicily, supposed to be a favourite place of hers, when Persephone, playing with her companions in the Nysaean fields, was carried off by Hades, god of the underworld. Zeus, who was happy to play a trick on the faithless Demeter, was in the plot with Hades. Hearing the girl's cries from far away Demeter, who loved her daughter above all else, took the diadem off her bright hair and veiled herself in dark robes. Wailing with despair and flying bird-like over the water, which grew rough beneath her, and over the land, which turned to desert, she set off in search of Persephone. She wandered thus for nine days, carrying two lighted torches, refusing to partake of nectar and ambrosia or to bathe in any water but her own tears until her beloved daughter should be restored to her. No rain fell from the heavy clouds that covered the earth, and no plants grew or ripened.

Exhausted with wandering, despair and fasting, Demeter was taken in by poor people living almost on a level with animals on the outskirts of a forest: Dysaules, his wife Baubo, and their three sons, half-wild herdsmen. They consoled her, and at last made her smile and agree to drink a decoction of barley and mint, which revived her. In thanks to these good people, the goddess gave them the ears of corn she was still holding before she retreated to the temple of Eleusis. The couple's youngest son, Triptolemus, determined to travel the world spreading this divine gift. Through him men ceased to be savages, eating the plants they gathered, and learned to cultivate grain. He is depicted driving a chariot with winged wheels and holding a sheaf of corn as a whip.

Since no one had anything to eat in Demeter's absence, no sacrifices or offerings were made to honour the gods. Iris, goddess of the rainbow, was sent to reason with the inconsolable mother, but in vain. One by one the immortals came to lavish wonderful gifts upon her, but all Demeter wanted was her beloved daughter. At last Zeus sent Hermes, messenger of the gods and patron of merchants, down to the underworld, and Hermes, who was noted for his cunning, persuaded Hades to release Persephone. The lord of the underworld allowed his mourning wife to go, but when she opened her mouth in a cry of joy he seized his chance to make her swallow a pomegranate seed. She had now broken the fast enjoined upon all in the underworld, and would have to return to begin it again.

Hermes led Persephone to the temple of Eleusis, where Demeter was waiting. As mother and daughter embraced, the furrows opened and shoots of corn came up in thick rows. The earth was covered with green leaves and flowers, and branches were laden with fruit. When the harvest had been brought in, Persephone had to submit to her fate. From then on she passed one-third of the year underground, returning in spring to spend the remaining two-thirds of the year with her mother and the other immortals. Since then nature has been unable to deck herself with flowers, ears of corn and fruits until the penance of winter is over.

There are many variants of this myth, and it delivers various messages depending on the hearer. It does not actually go into the initiation ceremonies of the ancient world, but it teaches us that barley antedates wheat as a cultivated plant, and that before agriculture in the true sense of the world began mankind, represented here by the family of Triptolemus, herded but did not yet rear animals. Crete seems to have tilled the soil and grown cereals before Attica, where men still hunted game. In its own way a myth can be as eloquent as a prehistoric site.

Everyday Cereals

Before the Horatii had wiped out the Curatii, the Etruscans satisfied their hunger with millet. For a while the Romans, almost as austere as the Spartans, preferred barley. At first this was a primitive two-rowed barley (the two rows were of the grains), followed by winter barley, which was eventually replaced by einkorn and then by wheats of better quality.

To keep the straw intact and untrampled by draught animals, the corn was reaped in two stages. Until the Roman conquest of Gaul, the ears were cut with a bronze sickle, and later an iron one. The Gauls were said to be the inventors of a harvesting and threshing device, but the Etruscans had already invented a kind of reaper with iron teeth, the *vallus*, which the harvester pushed ahead of him. However, it was claimed, with justice, that this device pulled the corn out of the ground and mangled instead of cutting it, so that the straw which was so valuable to the cavalry was spoilt. The Gaulish reaper was therefore a welcome innovation.

The crushing of grain with stones and then, still manually, with a pestle and mortar, led to a kind of mill worked by a handle and later by a hydraulic system. Only now could people change from eating porridge or *pulmentum* to making bread, first flat cakes, then genuine bread in the Gaulish manner. The actual work of milling was extremely unpleasant and indeed dangerous for the slaves who had to do the job, since the dust which rose from the mills obstructed their respiratory passages. While mechanical mills were still rudimentary, the grain was moistened to make it easier to crush. However, when a system with two millstones which were not parallel and between which the dry flour was progressively refined came into use, owners had to make their labour force wear cloth masks, a precaution taken not out of kindness but from a desire to keep them at work; later it was also used with animals, and the fact that it prevented captives from eating as they worked was another advantage to the owner of the mill.

Emmer and spelt, coarsely crushed, produced a meal called *far*. As milling became more sophisticated, the *far* was further refined. It was sieved to obtain three different grades: *grandissimum*, *secundarum* and *minimum*. With the coming of the rotary mill, *far* became *farina*. Offerings for prayer (*ad orendum*) had to be of the finest flour, known to the Greeks as *chondrite*. In Rome the word was *alica* or more commonly *ador*, related to the verb *adoro*, whence our word 'adore'.

Fine white *farina* was more expensive, as it was supposed to be scrupulously sifted. People fraudulently mixed it with Naples chalk. As we saw with honey, there was widespread adulteration of luxury products. Pure wheaten flour, obtained after two grindings of the grain – the first before the bran was removed – was greatly valued by the Hebrews and is frequently mentioned in the Bible. When the three angels came to visit Abraham he told his wife Sarah to prepare food for them: 'Make ready quickly three measures of fine meal, knead it, and make cakes upon the hearth.' (Genesis, 18, vi). Curiously, the Romans called fine wheaten flour *similia*, a word of Sanskrit origin, whence the modern 'semolina', by way of Italian *semola*. Semolina has two meanings: it can be either the fine flour of hard wheat used in making pasta, or wheat, rice or maize granules for making such dishes as milk puddings.

In his treatise on nutrition the famous doctor Aulus Cornelius Celsus, of the school of Hippocrates, said in the time of Augustus that cereals of 'good pith' and flour were more nourishing the better they had been bolted. Modern dieticians, while not necessarily being of the school of Galen, would nonetheless oppose Hippocrates' disciple on this point. White flour with an extraction rate of 75 per cent, i.e., with 25 per cent of the waste produced by abrasion of the husk remaining, has been deprived of the best nutritional elements concentrated in that outer casing:

75 per cent of mineral salts, 35 per cent of lipids, 10 per cent of proteins, 50 per cent of the vitamin E in the wheat-germ and 75 per cent of the vitamin B. It also loses 95 per cent of its bran, which obviously means that the flour – or the bread or porridge made from it – is more digestible, allowing 90 per cent assimilation.

But the amount of bran in flour with an extraction rate of 95 per cent merely favours passage through the intestine. It is now thought that white flour may be a factor in intestinal and colonic cancers, diseases almost unknown among peoples who eat whole cereals. The enemies of wholemeal bread, however, will say that on the contrary, bran acts as an irritant to the mucous membrane of the intestine and contains residues of insecticides and phytic acid. Phytic acid in combination with the mineral salts of wholemeal flour makes them difficult to assimilate and may even cause dangerous decalcification, they add, claiming that three slices of wholemeal bread a day is the maximum tolerable. .

As usual, the ideal is a compromise: flour with an extraction rate of 85 per cent, as in Germany, or well mixed with protein-rich millet, as in Burkina Faso. That would give wholemeal bread fanatics an incentive to put their convictions into practice, chewing thoroughly according to macrobiotic principles, and refraining from talking and eating at the same time, in the manner enjoined on monks and nuns of the old days.

Up to the end of the second century BC grinding was part of the routine work of a household, like the making of porridge or bread. Only when very pure and very fine *farina* became common did the era of the Greek master bakers begin. They established a tradition which, as it happened, was developed to a very high level by the Gauls incorporated into the Roman Empire.

As for the barley which the Romans, unlike the Greeks and in particular the Spartans, increasingly despised as their standards of living rose, it was reserved for military commissariats. Eventually barley porridge became a punishment inflicted on soldiers under arrest. In seventeenth-century monasteries, brothers who had committed some fault did penance on water and barley bread.

However, barley was much grown by the Gauls even after the Roman conquest, because of its use in beer-making. They added the stimulant of oats, a cereal regarded by the Greeks and Romans as animal fodder. Colonization, however, forced the Celts to start growing wheat on a large scale; once the wheat had been reaped and threshed the grain went to Rome.

Invasions and poor or failed harvests sent people back to wild cereals, while the monasteries of the Dark Ages did manage to bring in harvests to provide bread for their flock, at least if the flour was mixed with ground bark or sometimes even clay. Subsequently, when feudal times ushered in a period of relative peace again – allowing great lords to destroy crops in the pursuit of game, as the history books point out – people often replaced wheat by maslin on fields that had been exhausted or badly farmed, mixing their seed wheat with barley or rye. Maslin flour, considered by Taine[7] a sign of poverty, was not necessarily the product of crops grown together. Different ground grains might be mixed. In the farms around Paris, according to Olivier de Serres,[8] there were two flours: grey maslin for the masters (a little rye and plenty of wheat) and black maslin for the servants, with the proportions reversed. One advantage of growing maslin was that it provided excellent mixed straw for animal fodder.

From the Middle Ages onwards buckwheat may be added to this list of cereal crops. It was originally a native of Manchuria and not, as its French name of *sarrasin*, Saracen corn, suggests, of the Middle East (although medieval Western Europeans regarded the whole of the East as vaguely 'Saracen' land). The English name means 'beech wheat', because the grains are shaped a little like beechnuts. This hardy cereal, which is not a member of the Gramineae or grass family, throve in soil where wheat, barley and even rye would not grow. It was good only for making porridge or sturdy peasant pancakes of the kind that are still a Breton speciality. Rye, initially considered a weed of wheat-fields, was not grown in Western Europe until the beginning of the Christian era, although the Thracians, Macedonians and Slavs were growing it in Hellenistic times. The Greeks despised rye porridge, which was reputed to smell bad, and the Romans would tolerate it only mingled with spelt in maslin flour for the *humiliores*, the lower classes. The Middle Ages actually liked the smell of rye (resembling violets, said Antoine-Auguste Parmentier, whose name at a later date is for ever linked with potatoes). Rye flour was also an essential ingredient of genuine *pain d'épice* (see Chapter 1). Rye could be grown on land too poor for wheat, and in harsh climatic conditions. When standards of living rose, its brown flour disappeared from the Western European diet, but it held its place in the culinary traditions of Central Europe and Scandinavia. *Ségala*, 'rye land', is the word still used in the southern part of the Massif Central for regions of crystalline and siliceous rock as opposed to the chalky, bare Causses area. Maslin, rye, barley and buckwheat flours were food for country folk: the wheat they grew went off to the towns, in the same way as Gaulish wheat was sent to Rome.

It is impossible to describe here all the ways in which large towns obtained their grain supplies, but I will mention that in Paris the wholesale market was in the Place de Grève (now the Place de l'Hôtel-de-Ville), and was supervised by officers with authority to check measures. The grain was then sold retail by vendors in the Les Halles market. Such charitable Parisian organizations as the Hôtel-Dieu, which had its own bakery, needed enormous amounts of wheat or maslin flour, and also rye, for reasons of economy, to make porridge as well as bread. 'Bought of a huckster, a *mine* [about 78 litres] of flour at Les Halles in Paris, the XXVIIIth day of the month of August, to make porridge for the sick', reports an entry in an accounts book of 1430.[9] At times of crisis – which occurred frequently – this coarse flour was not even bolted, and the bran left in it helped to swell the daily rations. Oats and barley were also needed for the hospital's farms and its many draught animals.

A decree of 1388, reorganizing the royal household during the madness of King Charles VI of France, gave the officers who bore the title of *porte-chape* (the *chape* or *capa* being the King's personal bread-bin[10]) the job of buying the necessary grain, which had to be of the best quality. The grain of Artois was especially highly valued: it constituted a rich market, one of the subjects of the Homeric disputes between French princes of the blood which had much to do with the Hundred Years' War.

As the *Ménagier de Paris* says, 'there is nothing better than wheat'.[11] City folk bought cleaned wheat (i.e., with its husk of bran rubbed away) from grocers to make certain kinds of cakes and the gruel known as *fromentée* ('frumenty' in English, where the relationship to French *froment*, wheat, is obvious), but the finest wheaten flour was necessary for making fritters or coating food for frying.

In 630 the Merovingian King Dagobert had made the grinding of corn a feudal right; private persons (noblemen and members of religious communities excepted) and master bakers had to have their grain ground at the communal mill belonging to the lord of the manor. Communal mills attached to local manors were also the norm in early medieval England. A fee was demanded for the service of grinding grain, and the miller was the lord's employee. But the millers of Paris were regarded as owners of their mills, paying a tithe to the bishop. The lord of the manor, or rather his agents, had to keep a check on the miller to see that he dealt fairly with his customers as well as his employer. Thus the fourteenth-century charter of Beaumont-sur-Argonne, in Lorraine, stated that 'millers may not keep geese or goslings, hens or chicks, pigs or piglets, or any other animals that go about the mill, to the detriment of the public good as regards both the wheat and the flour.' Rather than showing a concern for hygiene, the idea of this stipulation was to stop poultry and other farm animals getting fat at the expense of the milling business.[12]

People went on eating various forms of porridge or gruel, often made of millet or even chestnuts, for a long time: one good reason was that it got around the need to spend money on the communal mills and then the communal ovens. If the mistress of the household crushed grain in a mortar and mixed it with water or milk to make a paste, either thick or thin, which could be eaten just as it was or cooked on the hearthstone, she could fill her family's bellies equally well, and without putting money into the pocket of the local authorities.

Cash was scarce in the Middle Ages, and in the country payment for grinding corn, like many other dues, was usually in kind: a certain amount of the grain ground was kept back as a fee. The feudal system depended on a variety of taxes paid partly in money and partly in non-perishable produce, with corn (wheat, oats, barley and rye) heading the list.

The oldest remains of watermills are probably those found on English sites. A mill has been excavated in Tamworth which dates from the eighth century and has a horizontal wheel. The mill at Windsor, with a vertical wheel, is from about a century later. Other remains of mills found in Ireland date from the eighth and ninth centuries. These watermills were used for fulling cloth as well as grinding grain.

The Crusaders appreciated the windmills or 'Turkish mills' they saw on their travels, particularly in the islands of Greece and Crete, which were under Arab rule until the eleventh century. Such windmills made their first appearance in Western Europe in the time of Philippe I of France, who reigned from 1060 to 1108. The watermills of Paris, which made use of the relatively placid current of the Seine, were installed on barges moored between the Grand Pont and the Petit Pont. After a disastrous flood they were set up on the bridges themselves, with the overshot wheel in the river. But although people had to have their grain ground at the mill, bread could be made at home – so long as you paid a tax, of course. I shall return to this point later.

In late fourteenth-century Florence, the correspondence of the Merchant of Prato (in the Datini archives) shows that bread, even for a gentleman's household, does not always seem to have been made of good quality fine white flour. Ser Francesco deplores the use of the coarse flour reserved for servants, and writes to his wife with advice for the next baking: 'Bid Nanni take a sack to the miller and say that it serves for making bread for *me* – wherefore he must grind it as fine as he can.'

Wheat-fields formed part of the property of prosperous medieval citizens, and, like Ser Francesco de Prato, the author of the *Ménagier* is lavish with his advice. He was anxious to exterminate rats in his barns, and he too wrote to his young wife: 'Bid master Jehan the Dispenser send or cause to be sent others to visit your barns, to move and dry your grains and your other stores; and if your household beareth word that the rats be harming your corn, bacon, cheese and other provisions, tell master Jehan that he may destroy them in 6 ways.'[13]

One of these six ways, of course, was 'by having good array of cats'. Wheat was not a crop with an enormous yield anyway, and precautions against mould and rats were a good idea, although in fact grain was not stored very carefully until the time of the Enlightenment, with the coming of many agricultural societies and a true science of agronomy. (With the aid of his microscope Tillet, of the French Academy of Sciences, found a fungal mould infecting wheat which greatly interested Louis XV. Voltaire wrote in 1750 that 'the nation ... begins to discuss corn'.) In the twelfth century, grain might still be stored in underground pits like those of the ancient Egyptians, or in wells or cellars, particularly in monasteries and manors. The risk of fire was thus decreased and the grain better hidden, an ancient instinct acquired during invasions. In these rather damp and badly ventilated places, fermentation could form a crust on the surface of the heaps of grain. The crust may in fact have been useful as a deterrent to rats, and was encouraged by the use of lime, which itself acted as an insecticide. But such practices did not improve the quality of grain already soiled in transit by draught animals or containing dust from threshing with a flail.

Today, as we enjoy rustic wholemeal breads, it is hard to imagine what the bread of country people used to be like – 'black and heavy, made of mixed flour'[14] – under the *ancien régime* and even in the nineteenth century (see, for instance, Eugène Le Roy's *Jacquou le Croquant*). More or less anything was often used as flour. Maslin flour, of course, was widespread, and other materials used to adulterate cereals included peas, vetches, chestnuts, beechnuts, and at times of famine all kinds of weeds; grain shortages were almost as much of an enemy to the generals of the French Republic at the end of the eighteenth century as their European opponents. The flour was bolted as little as possible, so as to retain volume, as at the Hôtel-Dieu, and ergot poisoning, which is caused by a fungus on rye or wild oats and can produce a kind of mass hysteria, still lives on in folk memory. Then there were flours from heaven knew where concocted by charlatans in seventeenth-century Italy at a time of terrible famines, and used to make 'wild bread', which was harmful and hallucinogenic.[15]

It is understandable, then, that people who could afford white flour, such as the Ménagier de Paris or the Merchant of Prato, kept a close eye on its quality. To quote Marc Bloch again, 'There has been no clearer criterion of social class over the centuries', for even within a household or a social institution there was a hierarchy which determined the colour of the bread eaten. And bolting the flour was not the miller's business; he delivered it exactly as it came from the mill. It was sifted at home if the householder chose to knead his own dough, which must then be taken to the communal oven. If he went to a baker instead, possibly providing him with the flour, the baker sifted the flour for that particular batch before making the bread. Until the end of the twelfth century, a French baker was called a *talmicier* or *talemellier*, a sifter of flour.

During the Dark Ages gleaning any flour which might still adhere to the bran was allowed. This practice engendered abuses, the national exchequer being the first to suffer. Bran, which did not figure among the dues to be paid, might be sent back to the mill by the baker and ground finely enough to be added to bread dough. This was formally forbidden in 1668.

Although bread sold in Paris after the eighteenth century could call itself wheaten bread, even if it was not entirely white, one should note, like Marc Bloch, that 'the coming of wheaten bread, or in some regions just bread, to rural French households dates only from the nineteenth century, and often from the latter part of it.'

Harvest Festivals

Of all the events in the agricultural calendar, harvest is dearest to the heart, and the harvest home, harvest festival, or in some parts of England the 'horkey', is the most universal of the many traditions associated with it.

Once the last sheaf had been carried home in triumph, the celebrations of harvest festival began with a lavish and well-earned meal. All over the world and through the centuries, every country has had such a festival. Even now, when social life in the country has been transformed by mechanization, the countryman has changed very little at heart, although in many parts of Europe the life of the farming community now takes the form of cooperatives centred on vast combine harvesters.

Territorial and family solidarity, which used to manifest itself as physical aid, is now more a matter of sharing quotas or good operating procedures – for an impulse to mutual aid still exists in the countryside. Harvest, despite mechanization, is still an occasion when friends and relations gather for a party. Modern methods mean that many old customs now live on only in the ethnographic records. But in many country areas young people, conscious of rural lore, try to keep the old celebrations alive: without them, farming life would end up no different from the concrete jungle of the city.

While an old-fashioned harvest home is a festival, it also means work. If you are going to hold one in the old style you have to prepare for it three or four days in advance, as our grandmothers did. There were chickens to be killed, cold meats to be cooked, mountains of vegetables to be peeled, plates and glasses to be borrowed from neighbours. All must be ready when evening comes and the combine stops. Then the festival begins, around long wooden tables. At some traditional harvest homes in rural France the men still sit while the women serve food and drink, following a custom thousands of years old. As people relax and become slightly merry, the party takes its traditional course without any conscious stage-management. Though the words of the comic songs sung in chorus have changed in the course of time, they are still concerned, as they always were, with love.

Harvest festivals, calling on all a farm's resources, were prepared in accordance with tradition by all the neighbourhood women. They were more or less luxurious, from region to region, but always lavish and perfect in their simplicity. In Touraine, perhaps the most typically French province in France (the local dialect is still a version of Old French), harvest festival would not have been harvest festival without the harvest goose, which was nine months old when killed (note the time-span), and must therefore be one of an autumn brood hatched at the season of ploughing and sowing. To the Celts, this was Samhain, the beginning of the new year. The Christmas goose had been hatched at Easter. These traditions, which are often still observed although their significance is forgotten, echo ancient agricultural rites designed to perpetuate the rhythm of the seasons, ensuring passage from one agricultural cycle to the next.

Lasagne is the traditional harvest and hay harvest dish of the French Alps and the Isère region: when you have finished your work in those parts you are said to have 'earned your lasagne'. From the Rhône to the Italian border, from Valence to the Mediterranean, the main dish served at the cheerful harvest festival supper where masters and labourers sit side by side is an enormous pot of *daube* or *adobo* accompanied by either macaroni or polenta. The latter was probably brought to France by Italian farm labourers from Piedmont. Polenta, that traditional rustic dish, was provided in tribute to their energy, and is a version of the archetypal porridge, now made of maize but earlier of millet, and known as *pollinta* in Low Latin. The Provençal word *brigadéu* reminds one that these labourers were employed as a 'brigade' or gang, going from farm to farm; the widespread practice of hiring

146

casual labourers for busy seasons such as harvest was common in the British Isles as well.

In Champagne harvest labourers were engaged in spring, the agreement being concluded with a slice of ham. When a man had eaten the ham he was engaged as formally as if ten signatures had been set to a legal document. In Brie, the bargain was sealed with a dish of eggs.

The harvest traditions of the ancient German tribes were so intricate, and basically so grim, that they do not survive today. In fact the Germanic peoples did not cultivate cereals much except to obtain oats for porridge and fodder, and barley for beer-making. Their mythology envisaged a violent universe, and they regarded ploughing and sowing as a sacrilegious but necessary rape of an element, earth, which was not theirs by right. They therefore had to demonstrate their courage and power to Wotan or Odin, lord of the gods, so that if a reckoning came between the Immortals on high and the warriors below, they would be respected. Before ploughing (a job usually done by their prisoners) horsemen galloped across the field yelling and cracking whips. Either a horse's skull (the horse being a symbol of fertility) or the skull of a famous enemy was buried at each side of the field. The plough was known as the 'boar', an animal that roots in the ground, and wild boar teeth were sown along with the seedcorn to avert the wrath of Nature.

Seed was sown on Thursday, the day of the thunder god Thor. Thereafter the field was left strictly alone, and became an alarming place subject to the whims of the weather, and to ghosts and witches whose presence was made known in summer by the rippling of ears of corn in the wind. Hot air trembling at noon, the hour when ghosts were abroad, was a sign of the fury of the sun and the breath of hell.

Finally, when harvest came it was the occasion for collective hysteria: an outburst of yells intended to put the avenging spirits to flight. The last sheaf was treated as a prisoner of war and was bound up to the accompaniment of jeering and mockery, Afterwards, the stubble was burnt.

Strategic Cereals

As soon as trading in cereals, particularly wheat, began they became commodities for speculation. One of the first ways to make your fortune was to build up stocks of grain, buying cheap at times of plenty and selling at a much higher price when there was a shortage. It was even possible to fix the timing of shortages, making them occur by hoarding the stocks you had surreptitiously acquired.

Cereals were an excellent means of augmenting the power not of the poor farmer who grew them, but of the person who had them at his disposal. Ever since the time of King Hammurabi governments have done their utmost to regulate the home market, aware that unusually good harvests could not increase consumption beyond a certain point, and that not to the profit of producers. 'Everything here is bursting with wheat, and I haven't a sou. ... I have 200,000 bushels to sell, and cry Famine sitting on a heap of wheat', lamented Mme de Sévigné.

The first imperative was to foresee times of famine which would bring the wolves out of the forests, foresight being an important part of government. The blockade of Venice by the Genoans in 1372 was bound to fail, since the Venetian shops were full of millet. Millet will keep much better than wheat, sometimes for 20 years, and in the sixteenth century Venice, ever prudent and believed to have enormous supplies of it, was able to further her own interests by intervening in Dalmatia and the Levant whenever a shortage threatened.[16] King Charles IX of France, in 1557, and King Henri III ten years later, ordered the French cities to build municipal granaries which would hold three months' supply calculated at the rate of a setier (30 kilos) per person a month. However, despite the existence of official granaries and the ban on exporting wheat, the cities, with Paris to the fore, lived more or less from hand to mouth.

Not much grain circulated from one province to another in any case during the seventeenth century, with the fear of such famines as that of 1590 ever present. Abundance in one region might exist side by side with shortages in another, and there could be great price differences between areas, or from year to year in the same area. This chaotic pricing system often paralysed trade, as the Marquise de Sévigné lamented. In 1623 Strasbourg was paying four times more than Paris for wheat. But, from 1650 to 1652 and from 1661 to 1663, the price of a hectolitre of Alsatian grain did not even rise above seven or eight francs while Parisians were paying 30, 35 or even 40 francs for the same amount of grain from Rosoy-en-Brie at the end of the season. The time came when no one could buy. When wheat became unobtainable the authorities, hoping to get it back on the market, summoned ships from the Baltic ready to set sail with cargoes of rye. But communications were still extremely slow, and the Parisians did not like rye anyway.

In 1739 the Marquis d'Argenson expressed himself in tones of indignation. 'As I write, with the country at peace, and the prospect of a reasonable if not abundant harvest, people are dying like flies all around us from poverty, and eating grass. The provinces of Maine, the Angoûmois, Touraine, Haut-Poitou, Périgord, the Orléanais, and Berri are the worst off. Recently the Duc d'Orléans brought a piece of bread made from bracken to the Council; he set it on the King's table, saying: "Sire, this is the bread your subjects are eating."'

The peasants of the wheat-exporting nations of the seventeenth and eighteenth centuries were the last people to eat their own grain: 'The Poles keep back so little of their wheat that you might think they harvest it only to send it abroad. ... It is no exaggeration to say that a single town in the other states of Europe eats more wheat than the whole kingdom of Poland.'[17] The wheat of the black fields of the Ukraine was sometimes so abundant that there was no knowing what to do with it, but it was not meant for the mujiks. Fernand Braudel[18] quotes the report of a

French spy in 1784 to the effect that wheat was so cheap, many landowners had given up growing it. It is possible that the 1500 shipments of 'Cyprus wheat' and the 1700 shipments of 'wheat of the Levant and Barbary' which were unloaded in the port of Marseilles between October 1780 and September 1781 actually went on board in a Black Sea port.[19] Ukrainian wheat was given the same sort of welcome by Italian farmers in 1803 as that accorded to Italian wine in the port of Sète in France in 1983: it went up in flames. But in the same way as Marseilles imported Eastern wheat only to sell it again (preferring local Provençal produce such as the wheat of Salon), Genoa did not eat the Levantine wheat, herself consuming only the expensive flour of the Romagna.

This conveyor belt of grain, with deals enriching the merchants of the cities and large ports perhaps even more than exotic produce did, provided white bread to feed and fortify the middle classes, who would be administrators of the world in another few generations. They had much more cunning and far more discretion than the aristocracy, to whom ordinary people grudged possession of the wheat-fields. (Only after their ennoblement did the Medici, great corn chandlers among other things, begin to decline.) When the Duc d'Orléans was accused of gambling on wheat, it was not what you might call a gratuitous insult; wheat itself was far from gratuitous.

From the end of the seventeenth century to the end of the eighteenth, which was also to be the end of the *ancien régime* in France, aristocratic capitalists as well as merchants indulged wholeheartedly in speculation on the wheat market, acquiring stocks here, halting convoys there, juggling with the rises and falls of the market. The fight against abuses meant that obstacles were placed in the way of free trade in corn. The edict drawn up by the famous economist and statesman Turgot, and signed in September 1774, brought in a kind of nationalization, both inflexible and expensive to the nation, and instead of making the situation healthier and indeed more equitable it placed a burden on King Louis XVI. The following May saw the bread riots known as the *guerre des farines*, the Flour War, with rioting at Versailles, in Paris and in several large provincial cities. The trouble was probably started by gangs in the pay of the monopolists and speculators whose interests had been attacked or destroyed.

Stocks of corn could be worth as much as a good army, particularly if you had good spies, but it was not perhaps wholly to the credit of Louis XIV to have great quantities of grain requisitioned in anticipation of his Netherlands campaign, a bad example followed by all monarchs with a claim to be great strategists, for stocking up with grain supplies was only a matter of strategy.

Agricultural strategy too has been brought to bear on wheat. When it is entirely successful a great battle will have been won in the campaign against famine, for despite the lure of profit the producer has to remember that wheat, the finest of cereals, is a greedy crop, exhausts the soil in which it is sown, and cannot be grown there two years running. To keep wheat happy and bring in a regular harvest annually, ensuring a proper return on the capital investment of grain, one needs twice or even three times the amount of land required to grow it. Rotation of crops maintains the fertility of the soil by alternating other crops with wheat. In Southern Europe, leguminous or cruciferous plants were grown every other year, while a three-course rotation was usual in Central Europe with the land lying fallow in the third year. A field left fallow, after ploughing to turn in the stubble which acts as natural manure, becomes a natural meadow of weeds. Flocks graze on the weeds, and pay for their meal with their dung. 'Leaving the ground at rest for this time, although cultivated enough for plants to grow, does not drain it of substance', says Olivier de Serres in his *Théâtre d'agriculture*.

For the peasant, however, or rather for his master, rotation of crops was a difficult choice to make, since it seemed so clear for so long that cereals were the most important crops grown and you should never stop producing them, while hoping not to find yourself with a mountain of unsold grain. But land which never rests and never has a different crop grows corn of very poor quality. On the other hand, every field turned into genuine pasture was one field fewer for cereal crops. Livestock tended to be underfed, but with access to fields lying fallow they could get some nourishment there and fertilize them in exchange.

The English agricultural revolution of the late eighteenth century was made necessary by a rise in population as the great epidemic diseases died out. All those new mouths had to be fed. As in France and the Netherlands, an agricultural system based on scientific principles was born. Charles, 2nd Viscount Townshend (1674–1738), a great landowner and brother-in-law of Sir Robert Walpole, retired from politics to become an eminent agronomist. He replaced the old three-course rotation by an experimental four-course rotation such as he had seen in Flanders. This system proved its worth, bringing immediate profit and enriching the land: the introduction of good quality fodder crops (lucerne and clover) and winter roots (turnips, etc.), alternating with cereals, made possible a rotation of wheat, clover, barley or oats, and roots. When 'Turnip' Townshend, as he became known, suggested to ordinary farmers that they should follow his example, they may well have reflected sceptically that only a lord could afford to sow lucerne, but his ideas carried conviction when it became clear that his clover and roots fattened livestock during the winter months, and when the time to sow wheat came round again it was three times better than wheat grown on other land. The theories of an equally eminent gentleman farmer of the next generation, Coke of Holkham, Earl of Leicester (1752–1842), also carried weight. Coke was very keen on mechanization and the manuring of crops. He improved land which had always been obstinately infertile to such an extent that people came from all over Europe to admire his crops of wheat.[20] The great success of maize when it was introduced into the Old World can be partly attributed to the fact that like the fodder crops, it fitted in well with rotation designed to improve wheat, and thus meant companionship rather than competition. Finally, in the nineteenth century, sugar beet too became an ally of wheat.

At the end of the nineteenth century, however, mechanized cereal-growing in

150

the new countries of the United States, Canada and Australia showed that the yield of European grains was poor, and production costs high. Mechanization, despite the investment involved, means a great economy of labour, although that did not immediately become obvious. A hectare of corn raised entirely by mechanical means calls for only one day of labour performed by one man per operation. From 1880 onwards the effects were felt in a crisis from which Europe emerged only with difficulty, having finally realized that its autonomy depended on machines and large-scale farming methods such as cooperatives. Japan is passing through a similar period of change, and indeed her whole way of life has altered since the last war. The traditional Japanese crop of rice is becoming less popular than wheat, symbolic of the Western life-style.

It was not until almost 400 years after the arrival of Christopher Columbus that wheat conquered the New World. The maize-growing tradition was strong. Then a large colony of Mennonite Russians, members of an Anabaptist sect founded by one Menno Simons in 1506, settled in Kansas in 1873–4. These devout emigrants had brought with them some sacks of a variety of wheat called Turkey Red which, when sown in American soil, proved superior to all other varieties previously cultivated. In 1890 Turkey Red spread beyond the community's own lands and became the ancestor of all the winter wheat subsequently sown between the Atlantic and Pacific Oceans. It is remarkable wheat in having a high protein content, like hard wheat, while it is still as rich in gluten as soft wheat.

The American cereals industry owes its entire present importance to the Mennonites' Turkey Red. Cereal exports financed the industrial development of the American desert, the great plains where the bison once roamed. Wheat rather than livestock, and almost as much as oil, made the fortune of the far West. No other crop could adapt so well to areas of such low rainfall. Cereal production in the United States has tripled since 1900. In 1944, in the middle of the war effort, American cereal farmers celebrated their billionth bushel.[21] In 1975, the tally reached two billion bushels. The only problem now was to dispose of this grain mountain, since in that same year national consumption reached its ceiling at a billion and a half bushels, about 16.1 million tonnes, and stocks were growing larger by the year.

The Americans' dream customer was the Soviet Union, whose five-year plans did not always make her independent of imports, in spite of the wheat grown in the Ukraine and neighbouring areas. Supplies of wheat proved almost as useful a weapon as nuclear arms in the Cold War. President Reagan's policy until the summer of 1983 was to freeze shipments. Then the farmers of Kansas, Illinois, Ohio and Indiana intimated that at the next election they would vote for an administration likely to maintain their prosperity. Presidents, whatever they may say, are more amenable to political than humanitarian arguments. The serious incident of the destruction of the Korean civil airliner in the autumn of 1983 may have made it seem, briefly, as if wheat supplies might be suspended again, but they were not. There was an American science fiction film postulating a nuclear war set off by a wheat boycott, a message of some forcefulness.

151

Another ideal outlet for the great cereal-producing countries is the Third World, which unfortunately lacks both grain crops and the money to pay for them. During its first 12 years, from 1954 to 1966, the United Nations food aid programme provided 18 milliard dollars' worth of wheat and maize for the starving. That official total was in fact well below the cost of the operation, since favourable tariffs were agreed, adjusted, perhaps partly for propaganda purposes, by donor governments anxious to lower the levels in their silos. America heads the list of these benefactors, together with Australia, where the cereals industry has become highly mechanized, allowing production to double from eight million tonnes in the 1960s to 16.1 million in the 1980s – and all this grain has to be disposed of.

It might be a better idea, both for the developing nations who are maintained in a subservient position by the distribution of cereals amid much publicity and for their benefactors, if programmes of technological aid were encouraged instead, to develop an agriculture which might suit their own nutritional customs better. On the other hand, might that not sow the seeds of future competition? It is fair to say that if cereal growing was the motivating force behind successive civilizations, it can also show the failure of an economic order no longer able to think of itself except on a planetary scale.

As Voltaire said of the bread riots of his time, 'Tremble lest the day of reason never comes.'

Rice in the East

At the beginning of this survey of the staple cereal of three-quarters of humanity, not only an agricultural crop but part of their Culture with a capital C, I shall start by gathering a few tares, and separating them from the rice as well as the wheat.

What exactly are the Biblical tares? The Greeks named a grass often found growing as a weed among bread-making cereals *zizania*, a word translated into English as tares. These tares were wild oats, which were reputed to cause mental or digestive troubles when they got into flour, and thus had to be separated from the wheat before it was ground.

Today we can buy a grain called 'wild rice', which has grown in North America since time immemorial, and is delicious. This is not in fact rice at all, but an aquatic oat, *Zizania aquatica*, called *tuskaro* by the Iroquois and *manomin* by the Ojibwa Indians. Its stalk may grow to a height of three metres, and ends in a panicle of several small ears which makes it look like a tall branched candlestick. This hardy aquatic grass grows in marshes and on river banks all over North America, and was a great resource of the American Indians in places where maize will not grow.

To harvest wild rice, the tribes navigated the marshes by canoe, using a curved strap to hold the stems over the boats and thresh the grain out of them. Alternatively sheaves were bound together, and then reaped whole. As Bernard Assiniwi, an Algonquin historian and a food critic on French Canadian television, points out, 'Wild rice is now very expensive, but it is much more nourishing than any ordinary polished rice. You have only to taste it once, and you feel you can't do without it.'[22] He is quite right, costly as wild rice may be.

The Indians ate it as a staple food, often depending on it to support life, and one can see why Chief Martin of the Ottawa Indians wrote to the British authorities in 1842: 'We have no objection to the white men's mines, to their cutting wood or building farms. But we claim our rights, without let or hindrance, to the bark of birch and cedar trees, the plants that give sugar and rice, and first rights over our hunting grounds.'

Many place-names in the central United States and along its border with Canada recall the various names of wild rice. For instance, there are names connected with the Menomini tribe, who for religious reasons could only reap *menon* and not sow it. In fact *Zizania aquatica* does not take to cultivation very well, and grows better wild. It was the cause of many disputes (thus living up to its French name of *zizanie* meaning both the plant, tares, and figurative discord) between the Dakota and Ojibwa Indians for the possession of the fertile marshland.

After reaping the grain was winnowed by being trodden out in a pit, or was partially roasted on frameworks built above fires that were kept going for 36 hours. In the old days it was ground between two stones to make flour; it was then made into soups, pilaffs and gruels or flat cakes.

Another species of wild grass, *Setaria* or *manna*, also known as 'German millet' in English, but as *riz allemand*, 'German rice', in French, was harvested in a similar way and not actually cultivated in Northern Europe from the Middle Ages until the end of the eighteenth century. Very popular with the Slavs and the Baltic peoples, *manna* flour not only held its place in the peasant and indeed the public economy (as one of the 25 grains from which dues had to be paid in sixteenth-century Poland), but was also the object of quite large-scale foreign trade.

There is another kind of *Zizania* which grows in China, but true rice, *Oryza sativa*, has reigned supreme in South and East Asia for 5000 years. Easily the majority of annual world rice production is Asian, but international trade is little affected, since people eat almost nothing else in the countries which grow it, and consumption is 100 to 200 kilos per person a year.

Rice was not the cereal initially grown by the Chinese, for China's first centres of agriculture were in the north of the country, where, despite a harsh climate, fields of wheat and millet were grown six thousand years ago in loess soils, the fertile mud of the river basins. The cultivation of these grains seems to have been imported from the Middle East. The evidence of certain cults associated with it backs up this theory: they are almost identical with the Mesopotamian customs of a slightly earlier period. The former dominance of millet over rice in Chinese civilization is also shown by the naming of archaic measures of volume according to the amount of millet they contained. Rice was much more expensive than millet in North China over a long period, and was thus an exotic luxury food.

Rice-growing began thousands of kilometres from Ho-nan and Szechuan – for China is a vast country – in the Yangtze delta, a region which may itself be described as exotic. Rice is not native to it in the true sense of the word, since it reached the marshes of the Yangtze from India, perhaps coming overland, carried by birds and winds, or by sea, with currents and on flotsam. Several species still grow in the local jungle, and are true kinds of rice which, although 'wild', are not the same as American wild rice. Archeological evidence of a cultivated species that grew near Shanghai 3000 years ago shows improvement of the wild strains after some 15 to 20 centuries of care and experimentation.

At the same time as rice-growing developed in these southern provinces of China and the grain began to be commercially distributed all over the country, 'the hourglass of Chinese life turned', in the words of Fernand Braudel,[23] who continues, 'The new south took over the dominance of the old north – especially as the north had the misfortune to open on the deserts and routes of central Asia and would later suffer invasions and devastation.'

The Yangtze delta, the deltas of the Ganges in India and the Mekong in Vietnam, like Bengal, the Philippines and Java, are rich in endemic types of rice, venerated in the Hindu religion. The cultivation of rice seems to have begun in these places very shortly before the Chinese experiments. There is an extraordinary diversity of varieties here. They can be counted in their thousands, and when other cultivated rices are taken into account the result is a list of more than 80,000 different rices worldwide. A knowledgeable person is easily able to recognize the origins of grains and their merits, almost as a wine expert recognizes the *cru* of a good wine.

All varieties of rice in semi-maritime South-East Asia are grown on flooded land, usually by primitive methods which have hardly changed in five thousand years, such as the hoe or a rudimentary plough drawn by buffaloes or even women.

> More than once it happened to us to see a plough drawn by a woman, while her husband walked behind, and guided it. Pitiable it is to see the poor things sticking their little feet into the ground as they go, and drawing them painfully out again, and so hopping from one end of the furrow to the other. One day we had the patience to wait a long while at the side of the road, to watch whether the poor labouring wife, who was drawing the plough, was allowed from time to time to rest herself, and we saw with pleasure that there was a cessation of work at the end of each furrow. The husband and wife then sat down in pastoral fashion, on a little hillock, under the shade of a mulberry tree, and refreshed themselves by smoking their pipes.

This scene was described by Father Huc, a Lazarist French missionary, in the middle of the nineteenth century,[24] but Chairman Mao did not change things so very much.

Terraced paddy fields on the slopes of Mount Ungaran in Java, Indonesia: this typical Javenese
landscape is the result of intensive deforestation followed by burning; the soil was then formed
into terraces consolidated by low stone walls. As the paddy fields have to be irrigated by flooding
for a period of two or three months, the surface of the soil is perfectly horizontal, even on the
mountain-side. The terraces were built so long ago that the landscape shows no sign of ever having
been forested.

Such meticulous agriculture calls for a considerable labour force, in line with the
great density of the Chinese population. As the paddy fields have to be irrigated
by flooding for two or three months, the soil has been made perfectly level, even

155

on hillsides. It has been like that so long that the original appearance of the landscape is quite forgotten. The land is divided up like a chessboard into a certain number of sections separated by mounded embankments a dozen or so centimetres high, arranged so that water, which comes in through sluices and must never remain stagnant, can circulate gently. Originally, rice seems to have been a plant of dry soils which became semi-aquatic by mutation. Its bushy roots need the oxygen provided by the slow, regular movement of the water. If the soil is not firm enough to bear the weight of a plough and whatever human or animal draws it, it is hoed, great care being taken not to injure the little retaining dykes.

The rice is sown broadcast in spring into fields flooded with water that is already luke-warm. Working in the water is an arduous business, not so glamorous as the neo-realist Italian cinema of the postwar period suggested when inviting admiration of Silvana Mangano's superb thighs in the famous film *Bitter Rice*. The sower is preceded by a draught animal or another peasant pulling a plank, which levels the soil even more, and most important of all stirs up the mud into a suspension in the water. When they have passed, the mud, settling again, will cover the grain. Two or three days after sowing the water is gradually drained away, to let the sun warm the grains, now firmly settled in place, and help them to germinate. Once the first leaves appear the fields are progressively flooded again until the water is 10 to 15 centimetres deep. If no continuous water current is available other devices must be used to maintain this level as far as possible, and the water is changed weekly. An unseasonable monsoon means disaster.

Rice-growing and Chinese ingenuity are so intertwined that it is impossible to say which of the two influenced the other. The *Teng Dzen Tou*, one of the fine illustrated agricultural treatises of the late Ming epoch of the seventeenth century – like the famous *Gong Kaï un* and the *Nongzheng quanshu* – has a picture of an irrigation pump worked by pedalling of a kind not yet obsolete, and which Father Huc admired in the last century.

> In irrigation also they display great industry, often carrying the water through bamboo tubes up the sides of mountains, which are cut into terraces, and cultivated to the very top. They have a thousand contrivances, in times of drought to spread the waters of rivulets and ponds over their fields, and enable them to flow off again when the inundation is too great. They make use chiefly of chain pumps, which they put in motion with their feet, and which send the water from one reservoir to another with great rapidity. Sometimes they fix at the edges of streams large wheels of extreme lightness, which a very slight current is sufficient to turn. These wheels are most ingeniously constructed, and surrounded with vessels that take up the water from the rivulets and pour it into large wooden tanks, whence it afterwards runs through little rills into the fields.[25]

As for manure, roadside public conveniences await the contribution of the passer

Harrowing the river: one of a series of early nineteenth-century Chinese
engravings showing rice-growing

by; it is still not unusual to see the old gentleman in charge of collecting hurry in, small basket in hand, as the traveller emerges, thanking him with the utmost politeness. Father Huc adds, in his account of China, that 'the Chinese have, indeed, such a passion for human manure of all kinds, that the barbers even save the croppings of beards and the cuttings of nails, and sell them to farmers to enrich the soil.' He concludes that this is the exploitation of man by man in the fullest sense of the term. Father Huc, who had seen so much, does not tell quite the whole story.

Rice was the making of Chinese civilization, which owed it, besides a meticulous cast of mind, that vast administrative apparatus that neither time nor revolution have changed. (Indeed, it has gained ground, and rice now carries political connotations.) All communal irrigation systems depend on riverside dwellers cooperating, and on firm social rules. In Provence, for instance, where liberalism is still second nature, the *aïgadier*, the man with the job of opening and closing the *roubino*, small irrigation channels, is one of the most important people in rural life.

Rice is a plant of hot climates, and the evaporation of water must be taken into account, since the shoots cannot remain dry for more than a few days. The fields are drained only for harvest, which comes after four months. The crop depends on the amount of water and the quality of irrigation even more than on the sun, and almost as much as on the goodwill of the gods. A hectare of paddy field needs about 10,000 cubic metres of water, but the technique of planting out 15-centimetre seedlings grown in nurseries allows rice farmers to economize on seed and water and get a better yield. In America the practice of sowing by plane in the same way as crop-spraying has been adopted. The more warmth and water the rice gets, the faster and better it will grow. More than one crop a year is usually obtained: three or four in Java and Surinam in the tropics, two in South Vietnam and South China, but only one in Kampuchea, France and Italy.

So-called mountain rice is grown in Indonesia, North Vietnam, such African countries as Kenya and on the slopes of Fouta-Djalon on the borders of the Ivory Coast and Guinea. It is sown broadcast on forest land cleared by fire and terraced, and thrives in the high rainfall of such areas. Its yield is not as high as that of rice grown in marshy conditions, but the unique flavour of its pinkish grains is preferred by connoisseurs. Another problem facing the grower of mountain rice is the necessity of a rotation of crops.

Rice-growing techniques, in short, will adapt to most local, geographical or climatic conditions so long as the essential requirement of water is present. Even more than other cereals, rice has profoundly influenced the societies which live on it – that is, so long as they have co-existed for centuries; the modern exploitation of land previously used for very different purposes, even if it was not under cultivation, is too artificial to condition society.

Traditional rice-growing calls for a large, patient labour force, but there is more to it than that: when rice is the staple food, the diet can influence the character and conduct of the people who eat it. This is not fanciful: many nutritionists are of that opinion. Perhaps because of the high vitamin B content of the husk, people in rice-growing countries are wise enough not to remove it. Eastern people do not 'polish' rice any more than they waste the bran of the glumellae and pericarp; the absence of the bran causes a severe deficiency disease, beriberi, and in fact the study of the disease led to the discovery of vitamins and the part they play in a balanced diet. Synthetic vitamin B1 is now added to refined white rice.

'It is said that the cookery of a people reflects its civilization', writes Le Thanh Koi in a preface to the *Chant du riz pilé*,[26] a collection of Vietnamese writings published in France in the 1970s. 'The material civilization of Vietnam was founded on rice-growing in the plains and fishing in the innumerable pools and watercourses along its three thousand kilometres of coast.... As rice provides enough to feed everyone, it is an offering made in pagodas and on the altar of the ancestors, along with incense, flowers, aloes wood, and wax candles ... the perfumed rice of Bac Minh deserves its name, and is a feast in itself ...'

The Chinese too regard rice so much as their staple food that other foods are always described simply as 'accompaniments' to it. Although it is a staple, rice is not, unfortunately, a complete food, and the missing elements have to be added to the diet. The poorest people make do with a few vegetables cooked (very sensibly) for the minimum time, and soy sauce or pickled fish sauce, which provide the salt rice lacks and the necessary amino acids and phosphorus.

However, in Japan, now a highly developed and industrialized country, the image of a population fed exclusively on rice and fish is no longer correct. Japan came to know rice much later than China, during the Ya Yoi epoch (300 BC to AD 300), although we do not know exactly when it was introduced. Japan and South Korea were then a single kingdom, and Chinese influence gradually penetrated the archipelago. However, the Chinese do not seem to have introduced rice directly in the same way as soya.

In 1960 starches made up 69 per cent of the 2290 calories eaten daily by the average Japanese. In 1976 the proportion fell to 52 per cent, and half the proteins in the diet were provided by vegetables such as soya beans. This development reflects both an improvement in the standard and quality of living, and a Westernization of dietary habits which was to proceed yet further during the years that followed. Traditional rice consumption has thus decreased to a marked extent during the twentieth century, falling from 115 kilos per head a year in 1960 to 85 kilos in 1976. The climate of Japan does not, of course, allow for growing all the species of cereals produced in other temperate zones which take the place of rice in the diet, and this development has had repercussions on the economic equilibrium of the country, although it does not seem to have upset the balance of the Japanese diet.

However, before Japan began its extraordinary expansion, rotation of crops was quite widely practised, rice alternating with other cereals such as wheat, barley and soya. This rotation modified the agricultural landscape, since the paddy fields were hardly ever flooded. Then, when Japan attained her present prosperity, small farmers suddenly decided to return to their old traditions, realizing that rice was more profitable than other cereals, which did not have so much protection through price controls. Curiously, therefore, traditional rice-growing became the dominant form of cereal farming again. The authorities found themselves facing a dual problem: the country was no longer self-sufficient in the bread-making cereals demanded by Westernized consumers, while the rice surplus was growing annually. Up to that point rice had always been of key value in Japan, amounting to 35 per cent of the total agricultural product in 1976, with the 27 per cent of the product made up by stock-rearing coming second to it.

At present Japan has storage problems: not enough warehouses, the expense of keeping them full and preserving the rice, and the deterioration of the quality of the grain in store. Various measures have been taken to dispose of at least a part of the surplus: new rice-based products have been created; rice has been converted into animal feed, for which demand is rising; it is sent in the name of aid to developing countries (not all of which welcome it); and paddy fields have been converted yet again.

This problem of the Japanese rice mountain ends up by becoming a political problem, and one which illustrates the gravity of a situation which could become chronic if nothing is done to resolve it. Too much, proverbially, is as bad as not enough. A surplus of a traditional product which suddenly loses popularity with home consumers can pose problems for the authorities of various countries. The modification of the dietary habits and mentality of the Japanese is bound to entail a profound modification of agricultural structures. An agricultural revolution can thus derive from a cultural revolution, for what we have here is a cultural revolution, though a bloodless one, with nothing overthrown but the rice bowl.

The poorer countries of Asia, however, have not solved the problems of under-production of rice. In India and Burma, 60 to 70 per cent of rice production does not reach urban markets: the peasant, in his need, sells his grain before harvest at the lowest price, in a chaotic system which is the despair of ministries of trade. The situation in India is particularly dramatic, since rice-growing there has never been as well ordered as in China and Vietnam. Irrigation is unreliable, and two crops a year are gathered from only one-fifth of the land that might be expected to bear them. In desperation, the authorities have even started growing jute in what used to be the vast paddy fields of Bengal, although jute is no longer in demand even by sack manufacturers, who prefer plastic yarns.

China is at least trying to feed herself with her production of five million tonnes, which might be increased with more mechanization. Rural communities, freed from the exorbitant dues demanded by the landowners of the past, may have enough to satisfy their hunger, but there is very little left over for foreign trade, let alone good works in Africa.

The situation of Burma, the seventh largest world rice producer, is unique and curious. The British made the country into a huge rice granary, so vast that neither revolutions nor attempts at partition have been able to empty it. And as the agricultural labour force of Burma is the cheapest in the world, the Rangoon authorities can sell excellent rice at prices which defy competition – and which make any technical improvements such as are found in Malayan or Japanese rice farming unrealistic. The Burmese peasants, therefore, cannot even hope for any amelioration of their living and working conditions.

Around the tenth century, Arab and Indian traders brought rice to Madagascar, where it acquired its letters patent of nobility: Madagascan rice was long regarded as among the best. Today, however, in the island's very difficult economic situation, even a modest self-sufficiency is impossible, and Madagascar has found it hard to pay China her price for the small amount of rice which the People's Republic is almost giving away.

In Africa the traditional crops of millet, sorghum, maize and starchy roots are still serious rivals of rice, slowing down the development and modernization of the paddy-fields. Except in Senegal, Gambia and the Ivory Coast (which has many rice-eating Senegalese immigrants), investment in rice-growing here has not yet shown much profit. Although the national dish of Senegal, *thieb diem* ('admirable rice with fish'), is popular among the Dioulas of the south of the country, they seem to take little interest in growing this food crop, a demanding task, although they have proved themselves very good at it. They now prefer to produce groundnuts, much easier to grow although there is not such a steady market for them. The various projects for mechanized exploitation which include the development of the river Niger in Mali, the Richard Toll dam, and projects in Nigeria may have been too ambitious or undertaken with too much enthusiasm; the rice yield does not balance these investments, so that, almost all over the continent, part of the rice eaten in Africa has to be imported, even though rice is a supplementary rather than a staple cereal, and that puts a strain on budgets already much stretched.

In South America, however, the gamble on modern technology seems to have paid off; rice is becoming an increasingly important foodstuff, in spite of an almost religious attachment to maize. The Portuguese and Spanish began introducing rice into their conquered territories from the beginning of the sixteenth century, but no really significant rice crops were grown until the early eighteenth century. The south of Brazil, which is very well irrigated, lower Peru and in particular Surinam (formerly Dutch Guiana) are now beginning to export a certain amount. The excellent long-grain rice of Surinam is much in demand on European retail markets, although American rice (from the southern United States) has the advantage of enormous and efficient advertising campaigns which more or less pay for themselves. American rice is distributed packaged under various brand names, and with plenty of publicity to sustain its market.

Carolina rice dates from the seventeenth century when a ship was wrecked on a beach in South Carolina, then a British colony. Once the vessel, which was from Madagascar, had been made seaworthy again, her grateful captain gave the local colonists several sacks of untreated rice, which they immediately planted. They harvested rice of a quality never before attained, much better even than that of the countries where long-grain rice originally grew. Rice is not grown in Carolina any more, but it has spread to other parts of the United States: Arkansas, California, Louisiana, Texas, Florida and in particular the Mississippi. In the early nineteenth century American rice was shipped to European ports for the first time, and Alexandre Dumas was thus able to say, in the entry on rice in his *Dictionnaire de cuisine*, that 'the rice we eat in France comes to us from Italy, Piedmont and Carolina'. He is echoing Stanislas Martin, pharmacist and inventor, author of the *Physiologie des substances alimentaires*, which appeared in 1853, and who adds that 'this last [Carolina rice] is the most esteemed'.

The United States has been the sixth largest world producer and the leading exporter of rice over the last 20 years, and if the rice-growing Europeans of the Mediterranean basin are to stay in competition they will have to modernize: such, at any rate, has been Italy's decision in the Piedmont district of Lombardy, and France's in the Camargue. Spain, justly proud of her *arroz a la valenciana* and *paella*, has had trouble in getting the rice-growers of the Ebro delta to abandon their now outmoded ideas of farming.

How did rice get to Western Europe from China? The Persians and Meso-potamians first encountered rice towards the fifth century BC, as a result of diplomatic and trading contacts between Darius and the Chinese and Indian states. Rice-growing reached Egypt and Syria during the next two centuries, and Theophrastus, the spiritual heir of Aristotle, mentions *oruzon* as an exotic plant around 300 BC. The great virtues of rice-water in digestive disorders were of interest to the Greek doctor Dioscorides Pedanius in the first century of our own era. He praised the decoction of rice known as *ptisana*, and its benefits were confirmed by Horace, Pliny and Columella. Southern Spain owed its first rice-fields to the Moors of Andalusia, but Portugal did not follow its neighbour's example until the fifteenth century. Several attempts were made to grow rice in Italy in the early Middle Ages. At the end of the thirteenth century the Visconti dukes of Milan, a very shrewd family, took a personal interest in the possibilities of rice-growing, but it was their successors, Galeazzo Sforza and his brother Ludovico Moro, who brought rice to the Po delta, and with it prosperity, in spite of the endemic malaria which plagued the agricultural labourers who had to live in the miasmic atmosphere.

According to Fra Salimbene's *Cronica*,[27] St Louis, on his way to Aigues-Mortes to embark on the Crusade, stopped at Sens where he dined well on rice with almonds, a dish similar to one long traditional in Provence. This rice must have been imported, for Merovingian attempts to grow it in the Camargue had not lasted long. Rice did not return to the Rhône delta until the time of Henri IV, when Sully tried to reclaim land which had been abandoned to the wild bulls and mosquitoes. He and his master were inspired by the example of the fifteenth-century Milanese who had made such intelligent and profitable use of the river Po's tendency to flood fields in Lombardy and Piedmont. Only three years after the assassination of the King by Ravaillac there was talk of a crop, but thereafter the government of the Regent, Henri's widow Marie de Medici, took no interest in the scheme. Such a new venture as rice-growing seemed too exotic and arduous to the Provençal peasants, who liked the look of the market gardening of the other bank of the Rhône more than the idea of mud and fever all the year round; they did not see that doing them any good.

Henri IV and his minister had also turned their attention to the propositions of Quiqueran de Beaujeu[28] in a work entitled *De laudibus Provinciae*, which appeared in 1555. Its author was already writing with amazement of the vicissitudes of rice-growing in the Camargue through the ages, and the lack of enthusiasm shown by growers and the authorities. If the King had lived longer, perhaps his would have been the successful experiment. Another such experiment was made in the nineteenth century, when 300 hectares were planted with rice; the number had risen to 1000 hectares in 1906. The primary aim was to desalinate the land. The operation failed between the world wars; it was as poorly carried out as its predecessors and, like them, was misunderstood by the cattle dealers of the Camargue. Malaria, regional committees, and the fears of potential growers about sales left rice-growing of no interest to anyone but archivists, who had four centuries of projects to study.

Then, in 1942, severe food shortages had to be faced. Indo-Chinese and Madagascan troops who had come to fight for a country not their own, and found themselves high and dry in Provence, were asked to turn their strength and talents to the growing of a cereal they knew. Camargue rice became a reality. 250 hectares were planted with rice in 1942; in the 1970s the figure was almost 16,000 hectares. Yield rose from four and a half tonnes to six tonnes a hectare, as compared with a maximum two and a half tonnes in the best tropical soils. Rice has now taken over those areas of the Camargue not occupied by campers, and has increased the mosquito population (which could ask for nothing better) or alternatively has brought insecticides and weedkillers to threaten the region's increasingly rare flora and fauna, while the mechanical harvesters terrify the last of the bulls, which have retreated to Fos-sur-Mer, where they encounter oil. Economists and ecologists are at loggerheads, on land that is already naturally unstable. From time to time choices have to be made.

The famous pink flamingos of the Camargue present another ecological problem to rice-growers. These beautiful birds almost devastated the fields in 1980. They are a protected species, and take no notice of scarecrows. The French Environment Minister set up a study group to consider ways of defending the rice from the pink flamingos of the Pont-du-Gaut zoological gardens, north of Les-Saintes-Maries-de-la-Mer. It is hoped that some kind of psychological persuasion will stop the birds trampling down the rice as it germinates. According to the latest reports the flamingoes have not yet learnt to read the notices telling them to keep out.

The eight thousand varieties of rice can be classified into three kinds, depending on the length of the grain:

Short-grain rice: the grains are almost as wide as they are long (about 4–5 mm long and 2.5 mm wide). They contain a lot of starch and tend to stick together after cooking. Consumption of short-grain rice is decreasing in European countries, and it is used mainly in soups and puddings, which indeed were almost the only Western ways of cooking rice until early in the twentieth century. Short-grain rice comes from the Camargue, Italy and Spain.

Medium-grain rice: the grains are slightly longer than in short-grain rice (5 to 6 mm). They too contain a good deal of starch, stick together after cooking and are best used in the same way as short-grain rice. These are cheap varieties.

Long-grain rice: the grains, 6mm or more in length, are very slender and contain a different type of starch from round-grain rice. The grains remain separate when properly cooked. Consumption of long-grain rice is increasing all the time, and it has many uses, particularly in savoury dishes. Long-grain rice is more expensive than medium-grain, and is more of a luxury. The main producers of long-grain rice are the United States, Thailand, Surinam, Madagascar and the Camargue in France.

There is also an Asiatic variety, sticky rice, *Oryza glutinosa*, very popular among Eastern peoples, who make noodles and cakes out of it. The main basis of the rice liquor called *sake* is mountain rice, which is very rich in nitrogen, or sticky rice. Yellow rice wine, the *mai koa-lo* of China, may be either flavoured with flowers or fruits or left unflavoured. It is not often drunk at meals, except on festive occasions, but is used in religious libations. It is rather similar to Jura wine in colour and flavour.

Rice is used to make dietary flours, starches and thickenings; either short-grain varieties or broken rice are employed. Rice flour does not rise and so will not make bread on its own.

Finally, rice also has its industrial uses, as a product from which oil can be extracted, in cosmetics such as powder, and in paper, plastics, straw and glue.

The Symbolism of Rice

Rice has much the same symbolical and ritual significance as the other major cereals of wheat and maize. As a gift of heaven, it shows the care of the gods for mankind, and is said to have grown of its own accord in ancient times, perpetually filling the granaries. While rice was inexhaustible, a Golden Age reigned. The difficulty of growing it now is generally felt to be a just punishment for human ingratitude or presumption.

Like bread in the Christian liturgy, rice is a ritual food in the Shinto religion, and during great ceremonials the Emperor of Japan is said to share rice with the sun goddess. The sun and its light, which ripen the rice, make it symbolic of enlightenment and knowledge. The people of the East also associate it with the colour red, the colour of the life principle, the soul and the heart, denoting eternal youth through regeneration. The multitude of its grains symbolizes happiness and abundance, so handfuls of rice are thrown at weddings. In the Western world this custom, initially adopted in America, was probably imitated from the example of Asian immigrants.

The primordial gourd of Thai mythology contained not only all human races and all sacred writings, but also, instead of seeds, all varieties of rice.

Maize in the West

On 12 October 1492, after spending over two months sailing from east to west across the Atlantic, Cristóbal Colón, or Christopher Columbus, made landfall at the island of Guanahani in the archipelago of the Bahamas; on 27 October 1492 he cast anchor off Cuba; part of the entry for 6 November 1492 in the journal his son brought home reads: 'The land is very fertile, and is cultivated with yams and several kinds of bean different from ours, as well as corn.'

Christopher Columbus had only just discovered America, but maize had ruled the New World for a very long time. It was known to the Zuni Indians of New Mexico; their word for maize, *tawa*, also means 'old'. In fact maize had been growing there long before the first hunters arrived by way of the Bering Strait. Fossil pollen dating back 80,000 years has been found in the sub-soil of Mexico. The oldest remains left from a meal of maize were found in a cave in a valley near Tehuacàn in the south of Mexico. The tiny ears – only two and a half centimetres long – had been gnawed some 7000 years ago. Maize is so much the archetypal American cereal that from north to south of the United States it is known simply as 'corn', the word used by English speakers on the other side of the Atlantic for the major Western cereals, particularly wheat.

Until 1954, when 19 tiny grains of pollen were found fossilized in a rock 60 metres beneath the roads of Mexico, maize was also the archetypal American mystery. Not a single wild plant has ever been found in either North or South America, or indeed anywhere else. One species, 'pod corn', every kernel of which has its own husk, seems to be the most archaic, but it is a cultivated plant. It was long thought that a related grass, *Tripsacum*, was the ancestor, but when the great enlargement allowed by the electron microscope enabled scientists to compare its pollen properly with modern maize pollen, the different appearance of the two showed them to be cousins, but certainly not parent and offspring.

Could the 7000-year-old ears from Tehuacàn, minus the kernels they once bore and no longer than a little finger bone, be evidence of the much-sought wild ancestor? Nature, as a good mother, lets wild plants reproduce very easily and very fast. It has been mankind's task to modify cultivated plants so that they do not disperse seed with every wind that blows before the crop can be harvested. We have seen that both archaic wheat and leguminous plants dispersed seed easily because of the latter's precarious hold around the ear or in the pod. The tiny ears of maize from Tehuacàn, loosely enclosed in a husk, also seem to have been meant to drop their seeds as soon as they reached maturity. As there is no surviving evidence of such a plant, however, the question of what became of the offspring of the dispersed seeds over the centuries still had to be asked. And a question properly asked is already half-way to being answered.

Wheat, from the oldest to the most modern varieties, keeps its flowers so closely confined that there is no way for escaping pollen to reach related species, and thus there is no crossing and no hybridization. Wheat is self-fertile, its flowers being bisexual. Artificial insemination does not work either; the intruding pollen is rejected. Wheat, clearly, is a virtuous plant. Maize, on the other hand, is promiscuous. The male pollen at the top of the flower flies with the slightest breath of wind; the female organs, at the base of the spike, willingly accept whatever fertilization comes their way, either from their own companions or from some other wandering pollen, of the same species or of a related plant.

The most common weed of Mexican maize fields is *teosinte*, a vigorous grass which reaches a height of three or four metres. The growers of ancient times regarded it as a sort of good luck charm. In fact, when a clump of teosinte grows near or in a field, the seed of the maize subsequently harvested is more abundant and the grains themselves larger. This phenomenon occurred on a spectacular scale

1500 years before our era. Suddenly, maize became a magnificent and prolific plant. As a happy consequence of such harvests, the demographic and cultural level of the peoples of Tehuacàn and the rest of Mexico also rose fast, helping them to achieve true civilization.

But modern scientists do not put much faith in the miraculous power of love, even vegetable love, and they are still less ready to take the concrete results of the Platonic kind on trust. Experiments were carried out to see if crosses between cultivated maize and teosinte would prove fertile. All species of maize found in the Americas were mated with the handsome seducer. The results showed that there was no hybridization with modern varieties of maize. But when the experiment was tried with hardy, archaic species from remote areas, the results were encouraging. Finally, when the least imposing suitor arrived, a grain from the shores of Lake Titicaca, all the experimenters had to do was to call the banns. Not only was the marriage happy, it produced a number of fine children: a fairy tale come true.

The history of the plant could now be reconstructed. Three thousand five hundred years ago wild maize, similar to that found at Tehuacàn, was fertilized by teosinte. It produced better grains. The Indian gatherers noticed this wonderful corn-cob. It was cultivated. Its pollen flew away on the wind and landed on other wild maizes. A new generation was born, with grains which were no longer shed so easily. This was a stroke of luck for the growers, who could harvest them at more leisure. Gradually, all wild maize was tamed in this way, until there were no wild varieties left at all, although it took at least two thousand years for the operation to be completed.

However – for there is a however – Richard MacNeish, the moving spirit behind the digs at Tehuacàn and an expert on maize, found primitive ears dating back some 4000 years in the farther reaches of the Peruvian Andes, thousands of kilometres south of Mexico. These ears too were at the back of a cave, but they differed from those of Tehuacàn. The scientists supposed that, since the maize of Lake Titicaca had willingly allied itself with teosinte, the origin of the modern hybrid with its firmly attached seeds would be somewhere in the Andes between Bolivia and Peru. Coming slowly north over a period of three or four thousand years, crossing mountains, virgin forest and deserts on the wind, and on the feet of the bees which were also migrating up the continent, this improved maize ended up quietly colonizing Mexico. Transforming all wild maize as it passed, it then spread across the United States, going north and east to the St Lawrence.[29] Next it crossed the Caribbean Sea and settled in the Antilles, where Columbus found its offspring. It has been possible to establish, from analysis of successive levels of archeological sites, that around 3000 BC the inhabitants of the Mexican frontier and New Mexico were growing a cereal which was as small as that of Lake Titicaca – and of which only fossil evidence remains – but which can properly be called maize; it had several dozen grains per ear, and was not yet protected by the husk which later became usual. Then, around 2000 BC, the plant suddenly improved, and with it the population's standard of living, as other evidence shows.

Ten centuries before our era the Anasazis, ancestors of the Hopi Indians, built their famous *pueblos*; a *pueblo* was a single vast building which constituted an entire settlement. Their fields grew a high-yielding variety of maize. They were already making dough for *tacos*, the cakes of maize flour traditionally eaten by the Hopi Indians, cooked on flat stones and then rolled up. The Adenas of the Ohio certainly came from Mexico, expelled by the Aztecs. Did they bring seed maize with them? Improved maize was found in the area after their arrival. They were tumulus builders without much of a gift for agriculture, but even they knew how to profit by the mutation of the cereal.

Stirrup spout pot in the shape of a human form covered with cobs of maize: Mochica pottery (AD 200–800) of the north coast of Peru. The head, with its bulging eyes, is crowned by a diadem which bears another head. The frequent use of maize as a decorative motif is evidence of the plant's economic importance in pre-Columbian civilizations.

Whereas Old World civilizations were fed by wheat and grew slowly, the fertility and rapid mutation of maize allowed the Amerindian civilizations to develop faster, relatively speaking. Whether those civilizations subsequently failed or simply stagnated is another question. But once they picked up the idea of hybridization, they became the most ingenious farming civilizations in the world of their time. Ten centuries before our era a long garden was already winding its way from Mexico to Peru, like a green ribbon marking the path of maize all along the mountainous backbone of the Americas. To the Amerindians, maize was both the source of life and the reason for living. It was a part of all their primordial myths and religious rites. They did not take maize lightly, and everywhere they celebrated its harvest with great festivities.

The *Popol Vuh*, the great book of the Mayas, said that 'The first man was made of clay, and was destroyed in a flood. The second man, made of wood, was swept away by a great rain. Only the third man survived. He was made of maize.' It is obvious why the people of Guatemala, described by Miguel Angel Asturias in his book *Les hommes de maïs*,[30] consider the cereal sacred. In their view it should be reserved for feeding mankind, not grown to enrich the multinational companies. 'Sown to be eaten, it is the sacred food of the man who was made of maize. Sown for profit, it means famine for the man who was made of maize ... the earth will spoil and the *maïcero* will go elsewhere, leaving only a poor little ear of discoloured maize.'

Western city-dwellers tend to think of maize – feed for poultry – as yellow. However, it can also be blue, red, white or black. Some ears are multi-coloured, and are used in the West for flower arrangements. White maize is the richest in carotene (containing vitamin A) and makes very fine flour. There is also 'sweetcorn', opaline in colour, with a high sugar content.

Why those colours, however? The Zuni Indians are never at a loss when asked about maize. They say that once the great ancestors, the Ashiwis, lived underground. Among them was a group of very beautiful young girls. But as there is no light underground, the Ashiwis knew nothing of the marvellous appearance of the girls. Then one day – we are not told why – the men emerged from underground and went about their business. The young girls emerged into daylight too, and two sorcerers met them. 'Who are you?' asked the sorcerers. 'We are the maidens of the maize.' 'Where are your ears?' 'We are looking for them, but we have lost them.' Thereupon the sorcerers struck the ground with their heels, and up sprang six wonderful plants, each bearing an ear of a different colour, corresponding to one of the six emblematic colours of the six regions of New Mexico. When the six girls had received their ears they began to dance. Ever since, if crops are bad, it is because the maidens of the maize have been offended.

Planting maize is very simple. There is no need to plough the land, and in any case there were no draught animals in the countries where it originally grew. Striking the ground with your heel is no longer necessary either, but a Hopi Indian will test the earth with his bare foot. If it does not feel cold he pokes a hole with a stick, as deep as his middle finger. He puts a seed at the bottom of this hole – or if he is Peruvian he leaves his wife to sow the seed, for ever since the time of the Incas and even before, women have had the power of guaranteeing the best crops, especially after the first wife of the Great Inca sprinkled *chicha*, beer made from germinating maize, on the fields as a sacrifice. The Indian then half-fills his hole with a mixture of earth and human excrement or guano, the droppings of birds or bats. The rest of the hole is to take the rain, which he remembers to invoke, crying: 'Ah, see wonders, see the clouds in flower!' Sioux Indians will dance, singing:

> I have made a print with my foot
>   It is holy
> I have made a print with my foot
>   The leaves come up ...

The ritual painting on the faces of the dancers, black and white stripes, will also work wonders.

In Inca times in Peru, a well-ordered country if there ever was one, each Indian was given a *tupa*, a field with a surface area sufficient to grow 150 kilos of grain. As the country is mountainous, maize was grown on terraces: the secret of the technique was known in the southern hemisphere. As a staple food, maize (*centli*) figured prominently in the religious ceremonies of the Aztecs of Mexico from the fourteenth to the sixteenth centuries, a period of great moment for the world as a whole.

The divine couple of maize gods were honoured for ten days in the fourth of the 18 Inca months, a period known as *Uey Tozoztli* (the Great Eve): they were the god Cintlvatl and the goddess Chicomecoatl, who was also the first woman who learned to cook. The festivities began with a distribution of flowers and food by the emperor, and then processions of young girls carried ears of maize to the temple of Chicomecoatl. The people danced and sang. The festival culminated in the sacrifice of a young woman representing Xclomen, the goddess of the young maize. Dressed in a magnificent embroidered robe and a tiara of multicoloured feathers, she appeared with her face painted yellow and red, laden with gold and turquoise jewellery, and joined the dancing, sharing in the general merriment and pretending not to know her fate, or perhaps showing her pride at being chosen.

At the end of the day the heroine of the festivities was beheaded with a golden-handled flint knife. Then she was flayed while her body was still warm, very skilfully, so that the high priest could get into the skin, over which he wore his magnificent liturgical vestments. He then danced through the town, with four attendants who represented the mountain gods of rain. The rejoicings were now at their height. People ate little maize-flour cakes; the priests ate similar cakes, but theirs were mixed with human blood. For a week of celebration the high priest wore the bloody skin of the sacrificial victim. On the last day it was taken off him and laid with the utmost respect on a bed of state, together with the victim's head, which had been carefully kept in the cool.

In the sixth month, *Etzalqualiztli*, or the month of the dish of maize – and of boiled haricot beans too – the end of the dry season came, and prayers were offered to Tlaloc, the serpent-faced rain god, so that the ears would grow as large as possible. The story went that, in the beginning of the world, maize fell as golden rain when the sun exploded. 'Oh lord, sorcerer prince, maize is truly yours', wailed the nation with one voice. Young mothers ran to the temple with babies on their backs for the sacrificial offering of children whose howls would attract the attention of the god throughout the day. Families stuffed themselves with huge dishes of *etzalli* made with maize, as the name of the month indicates, while the priests for once fasted. From the St Lawrence to the Rio Negro, maize was so sacred and so greatly respected that the Zuni Indians of New Mexico sprinkled Juan de Onate with maize flour when he visited them in 1598. Despite this honour, paid only to representatives of the gods, the conduct of the Spaniards was such that the Zunis still regret the waste of good maize.

Maize porridge was the staple food of ordinary Amerindians; it might be either thick or thin, sweetened with honey, spiced with peppers, supplemented by any available vegetables, meat or fish, or, for really rich Aztecs, flavoured with cacao. It was made into flour for flat cakes. At the time of the Spanish conquest the Quichna Indians of Peru drank phenomenal amounts of *chicha*, a fermented beer made from germinated maize. But we owe popcorn to the Iroquois, who heated sand in a receptacle and then, mixing maize with the hot sand, put it to cook slowly until the kernels burst. The Mayas used milk of lime.

Maize, the Indians' treasure, was not always their friend. The colonists could not have settled in so fast and efficiently if they had not found a means of getting their daily bread on the spot. Not only did a major cereal exist here, one that would grow on all soils and in all climates, but the white men also reaped the advantage of techniques perfected by the native people over generations. Hybridization and artificial fertilization were no secret to the Indians. Up in the mountains they knew how to combine maize with the growing of beans and gourds in a symbiotic relationship which recurred in Hungary, and in Bresse in France, when maize reached the Old World. This is rather surprising, since no instructions for use or Indian technical adviser ever accompanied the seeds across the ocean. However, the stalks of gourds cluster at the foot of maize plants, where they are sheltered from the wind and do well, and New World beans will cling to the maize stalks and climb as close as possible to the sun. In exchange for services rendered leguminous plants enrich the soil with their roots, which contain colonies of nutritious bacteria.[31] The Indians also grasped the technique of a three-course rotation of crops to preserve the qualities of the soil and enrich it instead of exhausting it. Finally, they invented a way of storing the crop in ventilated clamps similar to those still used in the European countryside for storing roots.

From 1605 onwards the colonists, fascinated by a cereal which produced a crop in three months, took good note of all these methods and improved them further, to their own profit. At first the Indians were friendly towards the invaders, and supplies provided by many North American tribes eased the harsh conditions the European settlers encountered. The Indians willingly shared what they had, so that the terrible famines of 1522 and 1623 did not claim too many victims. The whites

An American Indian community, depicted by an anonymous sixteenth-century artist: 1) the chief's house; 2) the place of prayer; 3) ritual dance; 4) banquet; 5) tobacco; 6 and 7) maize fields, with a watchman on guard; 8) field of gourds; 9) ritual fire. The artist clearly wanted to show the organization of the Indians' society as well as their technical and economic system.

of Virginia would have been decimated if, as the archives of the state said, the Lady Pocahontas had not provided them with maize. They gave thanks to her and to God for saving the colony from death, famine and other tribulations.

But unfortunately gratitude is not always what it should be, and once the French colonists had full bellies and fields of their own, they indulged in a frenzy of destruction aimed at their benefactors. The English colonists were as bad. Very often soldiers were sent out purely in order to burn the Indians' maize plantations. Indeed, in their eagerness to dispute possession of a land which belonged to neither of them, the French and the English agreed on only one point: the Indians were more vulnerable to the destruction of their maize stores than the destruction of their villages. However, the American Indians had their pride, and soon adopted a scorched-earth policy, burning their fields and storehouses themselves before retreating. The whole concept of maize remained firmly linked to the American territory that became the United States. Having subdued the Indians, the new masters of the country continued to feel, like them, that its honour and its future went hand in hand with maize-growing. George Washington always regarded himself as a planter first and foremost. He ate maize, and when he entertained European guests he had wheaten bread made for them, but never touched it himself. When he resigned his high office of state he returned, like Cincinnatus, to his beloved plantations on Mount Vernon.

The Spanish invaders of Mexico began by regarding maize as a symbol of the most appalling paganism, because of the bloodthirsty ceremonies associated with its cultivation. The Emperor Charles V, wishing to guarantee his colonists' welfare by ensuring that they had Christian food, offered a settlement grant to any who would take seed wheat with them, although the wheat did not do very well and, as one must eat, they fell back on the Indian cereal which the first planters of all, Andalusians of Moorish blood, had grown successfully as animal fodder.

The maize god revenged himself to some extent for the unthinking slaughter of his children. If you eat almost nothing but maize you are vulnerable to a disease caused by vitamin deficiency, pellagra.[32] Maize has a very low vitamin content, and the Indians, who were quite intelligent enough to notice this, supplemented their diet, as they still do, with vegetables added to their maize porridge. Christian colonists, however, despised this mixture. At the end of the eighteenth century pellagra spread from Spain to the rest of Europe in areas where nothing but maize was grown. People had taken up the novelty too enthusiastically.

For while the Emperor Charles V's wheat was on its way to Mexico, maize was arriving in the Old World; it began to be widely known 50 years after Columbus's first voyage. Its first introduction might have been expected to be in Spain or Portugal, where the caravels came to harbour, or perhaps Italy and the port of Genoa. Not so; it came by way of the eastern Mediterranean basin, as if all European foods must necessarily arrive from the Middle East. Who first took it there? We do not know. Perhaps it was the Venetians, exchanging Mexican grain for sugar cane. There is firm evidence that maize was grown on the Syrian and

Lebanese coasts, and in Egypt, between 1520 and 1530. At the same time the Portuguese, installed in their fortresses, brought it to Africa. The encyclopedist Ruellus wrote in 1540 that 'Maize was brought by our ancestors from Persia to France', while a German traveller tells us that 'the plains of the Euphrates are covered with fields of maize.' Persia was governed by the Turcomans; is this why one name for maize is 'Turkey wheat' in English, and there are similar terms for it in other European languages?

Within a hundred years it had spread beyond the Balkans to the Danube and Central Europe, where it became a great asset. It began here as a vegetable grown on their own patches by serfs who cultivated it with particular enthusiasm because, being new, it was not among the dues that had to be paid to feudal lords and the state. It was exempt from such taxes as tithes until the beginning of the eighteenth century, when the authorities, finally alerted by the example of Prince Sherban Cantacuzino, who introduced maize to Romania in 1650, realized it had arrived and decided to open their fields to it. Although maize is not called 'Turkish' either in Turkish itself or in Pontic Greek, there are many such variants of references to its supposed origin in the Slavonic languages. As it superseded millet, millet itself acquired various different names. In many French dialects derived from the *langue d'oc*, maize was believed, or people pretended to believe it, to be a new variety of millet: it is called *millette* in the Lauragais dialect, *milhoc* in the Chalosse dialect. Even the Portuguese called it *milho*. Porridges and flat bread cakes made of maize flour, baked in the oven or fried, were known in most countries of south-west Europe as *milhas, mihas, millias* or *millat*. There was also *mamaliga*, a Romanian porridge or polenta, which did not change its name when the Romanians began making it with maize instead of millet. Italian polenta, however, has been a national *pulsum* since the time of Romulus and Remus; the grain chosen to make it has nothing to do with the case.

However, there is another hypothesis which is becoming increasingly popular: that the Melanesians took American produce over the Pacific to southern and then western Asia. Supporters of this theory quote travellers who saw – and may have brought back – oriental maize before the time of Christopher Columbus. Be that as it may, maize has now gone all round the world, the ultimate gift of the murdered gods.

The United States owe a large part of their economic prosperity to it. The 'corn belt'[33] has proved to be a golden girdle. The headquarters of the world maize exchange is in Chicago, and determines rates worldwide.

Another major producer is China, where maize figures in the chronicles for the first time in 1555. The chronicles concerned are those of a district in west Ho-nan. Maize seems to have been grown in a small area for a quarter of a century before it was considered worthy of mention. The chronicler tells us that it was introduced into China around 1530, coming perhaps from India or Burma but in any case from 'barbarous Western regions'. It is almost certain, however, that the foreign cereal was brought to the Ming Emperor as tribute in the middle of the century, whence its Chinese name *yu mai* (imperial cereal, 'mai' meaning any kind of cereal). It is not certain that it was introduced by land. Could it have come by sea? A missionary, the monk Augustin Martino de Hereda, reports seeing it at Fou-tien in the south.[34] As early as 1573 Li Che-techen's magisterial and encyclopedic pharmacopoeia, the *Pen ts'ao kang mou* ('Grand Project of All Plants'), grants maize its Chinese visa, so to speak, by including it among the plants mentioned.

The present success of maize, with a sharp rise in production since the Second World War, is the result of a remarkable technological revolution: the breeding of very high-yielding varieties. Although the former surface area of the American corn belt has been halved, for other uses, maize production is now double what it used to be, so actual yield has been quadrupled.

In France a special department in the National Institute of Agronomic Research at Clermont-Ferrand is carrying out some interesting experiments, the results of which can be seen in the French countryside, in fields where notices indicate the experimental varieties being grown. A hundred or so new varieties are bred annually in Mexico, and all the maize-producing countries are in the race too. Maize may have more varieties than any other plant. Harvesting the crop, with corn pickers, is entirely mechanized; breeding for uniformity of stem size has facilitated the operation. In any case less agricultural labour, in proportion to yield, has always been required for maize than for wheat. With unemployment high, this may be deplored in some quarters, but there is also a risk of another problem in the disposal of stocks.

Maize provides food for humans and animals (the famous chickens of the Landes area and Bresse owe their excellence to a diet of the maize grown in those parts, and the yellow-fleshed birds are now sometimes exported to England). The stems can also be used as fodder, and the leaves as litter or even material for human bedding; they once stuffed mattresses supposed to give children straight backs. The plant is also used in manufacturing matting, plastics and gramophone records, and its germ goes into oil and margarine. It can be a basic material for beer and spirits, particularly bourbon whisky. The stems make those pipes made famous by General MacArthur on the battlefields of the Far East between 1942 and 1945. South Dakota, a great maize-growing state, has its amazing Corn Palace, a casino disguised as a mosque and thatched with maize. Maize has had a more serious influence on architecture too: tower blocks in the shape of cobs have been built in Chicago and Créteil. Maize is used to make dolls in Africa, China and Mexico. Finally, hanging ears of maize in your bedroom or kitchen is supposed to assure good luck and fertility.

As Navajo medicine men say in their incantations, sprinkling maize flour on the walls of the Sacred House of Santa Fé: 'Joy and beauty, may the sweet yellow maize accompany you to the ends of the earth.'

Why Maize is Called 'I Have No More Gumbo'

There was once a great famine in the Mossi country of Burkina Faso (an event which, unfortunately, has occurred a good deal more often than 'once'). The people looked hopelessly at their millet storehouses, which contained nothing but cobwebs and mouse droppings. They had even been obliged to go against the advice of the village elders and eat their seedcorn, so that even hope for the next rainy season was gone.

There was one man who went on tilling the bare, cracked earth of his field from force of habit, since he had nothing to sow in it. Every evening he went home to his wife and children, exhausted. One day he found them finishing up a stew of a few bean leaves and a little gumbo the wife had managed to get hold of. But she gave her husband a dish containing a few tough, wild plants which barely covered the bottom of it, telling the poor man crossly, 'Ka-mana – I have no more gumbo.'

Several days passed in this way. The man no longer had strength to use his *daba* (hoe), and sat on a stone and wept. Suddenly a slight noise made him raise his head, and through his tears he saw a tiny creature with long, straight red hair. It was one of the underground gnomes known as *kin-kissi*. This person, who was particularly odd in being alone, contrary to the habits of his kind, answered to the name of Kin-Kirgo. He asked the farmer kindly why he was in distress, and then took from a bag a handful of golden grains as big as pearls. 'Sow these', he said, 'and in six weeks' time, after the rain which will come soon, you will harvest ears which you must roast. I promise that they will save you from famine.' The man thanked him and dug as many little holes as he had been given grains. Then he went home to eat his soup of weeds.

The promised rain fell next day, and when the sun came out again it shone on the fields, which were barren except for the worthy farmer's field. Little tufts of green leaves were coming up all over it, and he was wise enough to leave them alone, for he trusted the word of Kin-Kirgo. At the end of six weeks the tufts of leaves had become stems, and bore strange spindle-shaped fruit ending in a tassel of hair exactly like the hair of the *kin-kissi*. The man cut the ears, roasted some, and feasted on them before returning home with his harvest wrapped in his loincloth. In his hand he held a bundle of stems of the plants, as stout as sticks.

'Blow up the fire', he told his wife, and he roasted some of the ears he had brought back in the embers. 'Eat', he told his children. 'What's this?' cried his wife. 'Ka-mana', he said, throwing the nasty broth she was offering him across the yard. 'Ka-mana, did you say? Well, here's ka-mana for you!' And he took the bundle of stems and gave the shrew a beating she would not forget in a hurry. As for the white men who give the miraculous golden grains the strange name of maize, they do not even know why the Mossi call them Ka-mana ('I have no more gumbo').

175

Why Corn-Cobs are Thin and Small
(Bororo myth)

There was once a spirit named Burékoïbo whose maize fields were incomparably fine. This spirit had four sons, and he entrusted the task of planting to one of them, Bopé-joku. The latter did his best, and every time the women came to gather maize, he would whistle 'fi, fi, fi', to express his pride and satisfaction. And indeed Burékoïbo's maize was very enviable, because of its heavy grain-loaded cobs.

One day, a woman was gathering maize, while Bopé-joku was whistling away gaily, as usual. She was doing the work rather roughly and she cut her hand on one of the cobs she was picking. Upset by the pain, she insulted Bopé-joku, and complained about his whistling. Immediately, the maize, the growth of which depended on the spirit's whistling, began to wither and dry on the stalk. Since that time, and because Bopé-joku took his revenge, maize no longer grows of its own accord, but men have to cultivate it by the sweat of their brows.

However, Burékoïbo promised them that he would grant a good harvest on condition that, at sowing time, they blew upwards in the direction of heaven, while uttering prayers to him. He also ordered his son to visit the Indians at this time and to ask them about their work. Any who replied rudely would have only a poor harvest. Bopé-joku set off and asked each farmer what he was doing. They replied, in turn: 'As you see, I am getting my field ready!' The last punched him in the ribs and insulted him. Because of this man's action, maize is not of as fine a quality as before. But any Indian who hopes to gather corn-cobs 'as big as the bunches of the fruit of the palm tree' always prays to Burékoïbo and offers the spirit the first fruits of his field.

Zuni Legend of Maize Flour

The Zuni are the Pueblo Indians of the Rio Grande, a branch of the Cochise people. They tell a tale of some young girls who one day passed the dwelling of the ocean goddess, younger sister of the moon. The deity thought them pretty and invited them in.

Then the immortal goddess took a slab of lava and carved the first *metate* out of it. Using a round stone of fine texture, she made a *mano*, with which she crushed grains of maize in this trough until she had a very fine powder. Chanting an explanatory song, she showed the girls how to do the same. Then she went to the mountains, picked long grasses and made a brush to sweep up the flour. As the girls played they spread a little of the powder on their faces and bodies, and it made them even prettier. Back in their own village they were so much admired that ever since then, women have learnt to paint their faces at the same time as they learn to make the flour for delicious maize cakes.

From Porridge to Beer

Cereals, roasted to make them digestible and then ground and moistened or diluted with water to make a paste, either thick or thin, did not become gruel or porridge until people had the idea and the means of cooking them. They may initially have been cooked by hot stones in receptacles of natural substances, and then in utensils which could go straight over the fire.

Soup, in fact, derives from 'sop' or 'sup', meaning the slice of bread on which broth was poured. Until bread was invented, the only kind of thick soup was a concoction of grains, or of plants or meat cooked in a pot. Gruel or porridge was thus a basic food, a staple form of nourishment, and long held that place in Western countries, for in practice bread was a luxury eaten only in towns. A thick porridge of some kind is still the staple food of many peoples, and it is not always made of cereals, but may consist of other starchy foods: legumes, chestnuts or root vegetables. In the eighteenth century gruel was not only for small children who had just been weaned, or porridge only for poor peasants: 'If it rained porridge', said Goethe, 'the poor peasants would have no spoon to eat it.' Madame de Montpensier, in her memoirs, tells a tale of Louis XIV and the Duc d'Orléans, his brother, throwing plates of porridge at each other one evening.

From the *maza* of classical times, a cooked cereal mush which became thicker and thicker until it was the consistency of traditional Scottish porridge, people progressed to making thick pancakes on hot stones or tiles slipped into the embers of the fire. These were the 'cakes' of ancient times mentioned in the Bible, and the soft paste mixed with milk eaten by the Etruscans and called *pulmentum*, a kind of pudding served at the end of a meal like the sweet course of today. Archeologists excavating Stone Age Swiss lake-side settlements have found well-preserved examples of cakes made of pure wheat, millet or barley. Maize was eaten in this way in the Americas, and the Masai of East Africa mix millet flour with the blood of their cattle. The Tibetans make a paste of rye, tea and yak butter, and the people of the South Sea Islands pound the starchy pith of certain palm trees into a kind of mush.

The cakes frequently mentioned in the Old Testament and eaten fresh, i.e., still warm, were unleavened, made without any raising agent, for ritual meals served to visitors and eaten on holy days. The custom pre-dates the Exodus and the unleavened bread eaten in memory of the hasty departure of the Jews who had no time to let their bread dough rise: 'unleavened bread, and cakes unleavened tempered with oil, and wafers unleavened anointed with oil: of wheaten flour shalt thou make them.' This is the *matzo*, the Passover bread, still eaten every year. If the children of Israel, in flight from Egypt, 'took their dough before it was leavened', it sounds as if raising agents were in use, and had been for some time. But unleavened cakes of bread, *azymes*, were being served on solemn occasions two thousand years before our era. Lot, Abraham's nephew, entertaining the angels who came to warn him of the destruction of Sodom and Gomorrah, 'made them a feast, and did bake unleavened bread' (Genesis, 19, iii).

However, the discovery of raised bread cannot be attributed to the Hebrews, certainly not the only race to eat both porridge and cakes of bread. Someone, somewhere, probably made a mixture of flour and water and then forgot it, or for some reason it had to wait a long time before being cooked. The Middle East is a hot and dusty place. Dust, perhaps on dirty hands, carrying with it minute fungi or yeasts, could have settled on the paste, which then fermented and swelled larger, to the delight of the forgetful person who set it aside. She may have cooked a little of the strange, swollen dough, so that it should not be entirely wasted, and found the result palatable. Perhaps she then tried mixing what remained with more flour, and found that the fresh batch of dough was just as good: light and well flavoured. Who knows? But we owe the unknown inventor of bread a great debt. In Spanish, yeast is called *madre*, mother.

The Egyptians believed that one day Osiris, god of agriculture, made a decoction of barley that had germinated with the sacred waters of the Nile, and then, distracted by other urgent business, left it out in the sun and forgot it. When he came back, the mixture had fermented. He drank it, and thought it so good that he let mankind profit by it. This was said to have been the origin of beer.

In fact clay tablets from the second half of the fourth millennium, the most ancient written texts in the world, were found in the ruins of Uruk in Lower Mesopotamia (now Iraq) at the end of the last century. They tell the story of Gilgamesh, the fifth king of the second Sumerian dynasty. The pastoral Sumerians, who came from somewhere in central Asia, had settled in Lower Mesopotamia between the Tigris and Euphrates, and became as good at farming as their contemporaries, the ancient Egyptians. The Sumerians claimed to have arrived in Mesopotamia after the Deluge; archeologists believe it was in the first years of the fifth millennium. The story of the Deluge is told to Gilgamesh by Utnapishtim, the Sumerian equivalent of Noah, and is very similar to the Old Testament version. When he had built his ark, Utnapishtim says, 'I gave the workmen ale and beer to drink, oil and wine as if they were river water.'[35]

Like wine, beer, mentioned in other parts of the Gilgamesh epic, had been in everyday use, if not since before the Flood – although why not? – in any case since before the time of the great Babylonian civilization that followed the Sumerians. This is important, for the Babylonians have left us the first true recipes for making beer brewed from barley, emmer wheat, or a mixture of the two. The recipes specify that the grains should be from the last harvest and so quite fresh; they are not to be husked or ground; they must be soaked in several changes of water and then left in the sun to germinate. Why was the grain not husked, as it usually was before being crushed or ground to be made into porridge or flat cakes? Obviously it had been realized that the germ of the grain was better protected if it was not treated, and the husk would help it to ferment. Barley, an easy plant to grow, was to prove the best grain for beer; even after threshing it retains its husks. Once the grain had germinated the Babylonians stewed it in the purest possible water (good water makes good beer). Then the infusion was left to ferment. The mash might be cooked in pots over the fire or by plunging hot stones into the vessel containing it. In Austria, only a hundred years ago, a reputedly delicious beer was still being made like this in the *Steinbierbrauereien*.

Babylonian beer was cloudy; indeed, the brewers of the time liked to thicken it with flour and let the mixture stand before fermenting it a second time, thus producing something which could be described as edible beer or alternatively drinkable bread. It might sometimes be cooked, and produced a raised cake or loaf. Once the malt had served its purpose in the first operation it was retrieved and eaten, for it contained valuable vitamins. A quick beer could be made from crushed, leavened barley bread that had been cooked in the embers. Pliny, in his *Natural History* (XVIII-26), comments that the Iberians and Gauls carried out the reverse operation, using beer yeast (the froth skimmed off the surface of the fermenting beer) to make bread rise without the help of sourdough from a previous batch. However, I shall be returning to the subject of bread below. In the African bush it is not unusual to find masticated grains used to produce yeast for millet or palm beer. The grain paste starts working with the action of enzymes contained in the saliva. The Amazonian Indians like to get their yeast from cassava masticated by old women with bad teeth. Fermentation appears to purify everything.

The Egyptians followed in the footsteps of the Babylonians, and using scientific methods they became such famous brewers that their exported beer (called *zythos*), especially the beer made at Pelusa, was very popular with the Athenians. The Greeks brought beer to Gaul, Spain and the east coast of the Adriatic through their trade. From Illyria to the heart of Germania, beer spread very fast and became very popular.

Was this the 'strong drink' other than wine that St John the Baptist was never to drink (Luke, 1, xv)? It seems likely, since the Hebrews must have known it, although the Bible never mentions ale or beer. The Gallo-Romans gave their frothy, golden drink the name of *cerevisia*, in honour of Ceres the harvest goddess, although the god of beer was Sucellus, a deity depicted with a cooper's mallet. The old French word *cervoise*, barley beer, came from *cerevisia*. The Iberians called their beer *ceria* or *celia*, meaning fermented wheat, and did not adopt *cerveza* until after 1482, just when the word *cervoise* in French was being replaced by *bière*. Curiously, the name given to classical *zythos* in Illyria, *sabaiu* or *sabaïum*, was to become the name of an Italian delicacy, a frothy cream of eggs and wine (perhaps beer was once used) called *sabayon* or *zabaglione*. But the Romans preferred wine. Forbidding viticulture in those parts of Gaul suitable for cereals, with a view to protecting the vineyards of the Iberian peninsula, the Emperor Domitian inadvertently did much to make beer popular among the Gauls who were the ancestors of the modern French.

Leaving mead mainly to the priestly class, Celtic warriors, particularly the Welsh and Irish, would compete to see who could drink most beer at the feast of Samhain

179

on 1 November, the beginning of their New Year. Beer drunk in this way was supposed to ensure their immortality.

Hitherto, like most people, I have used the word 'beer' to designate a brew made from germinated cereals, and like most people I have been committing a solecism. The drink as we know it (beer to the English, *bière* to the French) did not exist until the sixteenth century, and the brew known as *cervoise* in French corresponds to English ale; I shall now revert, therefore, to the older term.

Domitian's decree, dividing the Gaulish provinces into cereal-growing and wine-growing country, to some extent determined what the local beverages would be. It was logical to use your home-grown resources to make your drink. Although vines were grown in more areas in the Middle Ages than they are now, ale could be made in humbler circumstances, and might be called home-brewed, though dues had to be paid for making the mash in communal brew-houses. A ninth-century text specifies: *uxor conficit bracem* (the wife makes the mash). *Brace* was a word for both a cereal – wheat of the spelt type, or barley – and the process of making it into ale, and the French *brasserie*, brewing, derives from it. In 1600 Olivier de Serres[36] remarked that 'this operation is not restricted to certain seasons of the year, since there is always wheat or barley in the granary, whereas the successful making of wine depends on the grape, which cannot be stored from one season to another. All grains which will make bread will also make beer.'

However, except in those truly Mediterranean lands where everyone drank wine, good or bad according to their means, the choice of beverage from the Loire to the Baltic (local and therefore cheap beer, wine which might be either local or imported but was bound to be more expensive) had connotations of class about it. As Léo Moulin[37] points out, class is often associated with comparative wealth, so that 'noblemen drink wine, the common people drink beer.' Moulin goes on to quote a little thirteenth-century verse from the *Livre de vie et de mort*:

> Li povre vont à la cervoise
> Si elle bone, il i font grand noise
> Et li plus rike vont à vin
> U a mies ou a lewekin.

[The poor resort to ale; if it is good, they make much noise, and the richer folk resort to wine, or to *mies* or *lewequin*.]

Mies was a light and not very strong ale, while *lewekin* or *linequin* was strong and syrupy. As Olivier de Serres summed it up: 'Small folk drink *médon*.' *Médon* had similarities with both ale and mead, partaking of the poorer qualities of both.

The ale of these times was only slightly alcoholic, since fermentation was stopped quickly quite early in the process, in case the brew went out of control and spilled over. The pious King Louis IX of France considered it a suitable drink for fast days, and indeed drinking some of the humbler ales must have been quite a penance. St Louis also promulgated the brewers' statutes of 1269, giving them official sanction: the previous year Étienne Boileau had stated in the *Livre des méstiers* ['Book of Trades'] that 'no brewers of ale may make it with anything but water and grain: that is to say barley, maslin and *dragées*.' The *dragées* he mentions were a mixture of vetches, lentils and oats, and in fact as ale was not filtered after fermentation it could contain plenty of valuable protein. In any case, it lined the stomach in a satisfying way, as one Henricus Abricensis of London, writing in Latin (of a kind) in the reign of Henry III of England, put it:

> Nihil spissius illa dum libitur
> Nihil clarius est dum mingitur
> Unde constat quod multas feces
> In ventro reliquit

[Nothing is thicker when it is poured, nothing is clearer when one makes water, whence we see that much of the dregs remain in the belly.]

A beverage of this sort, then, was likely to be a necessary last resort at a time when there were good reasons not to drink water, and all things considered, since ale was sterilized by the boiling of the water used in the brewing process, it must at least have been a slight precaution against epidemic disease.

Such, indeed, was the claim to fame of St Arnulf, a Flemish Benedictine monk, Bishop of Soissons at the end of the fifteenth century, who became the patron saint of brewers. During an epidemic of cholera he realized that those who drank ale were less apt to get colic than those who drank water. To persuade the latter to change their ways, he brewed a vat of ale with his crozier and made the sign of the cross over it. Everyone drank the ale, and they all lived.

In those monasteries too poor or situated too far north to make their own wine, unlimited ale-drinking was tolerated. Salt meat and fish, the everyday diet of such establishments, provoked a thirst, and so did singing Mass at the top of your voice.[38] Every monk received the *libere*, a generous measure of ale to last him through the night. The Council of Aix-la-Chapelle granted four litres of ale to the canons who took part in it, and there were nunneries where the holy sisters allowed themselves seven litres a day. St Benedict of Aniane authorized rations of ale in his houses twice as large as the allowance of wine, and food for fast days was a little bread and salt 'cum aqua aut cervisia' (with water or ale); obviously it made no difference. Only a monk doing a very heavy penance would feel obliged to drink water and not ale: 'aquam bibat', as the rule of St Columba stipulates. There was a hierarchy of ales drunk in monasteries, corresponding to the social hierarchy. The *prima melior* drunk by the holy fathers was of course of the best quality, while the brothers contented themselves with *potio fortis*. As for *cervisia debilis*, small ale, it was for all and sundry, as the name suggests: novices, poor pilgrims and nuns.

Whether *debilis*, *fortis* or *maxima*, the ale did not keep well and soon went off. Aromatic herbs came to be added to improve its flavour and keeping qualities: marjoram, bay, myrtle, sage, horseradish, clover, pennyroyal, oak bark, mint, wormwood and honey, your choice depending on how you wanted to flavour your brew and whether you wanted it to be refreshing, strong or soft. However, the use of stimulants, including certain spices, and of toxic additives was forbidden to laymen and clerics alike.

An ale made at Anthisne near Liège, for instance, related to mead and flavoured with juniper, had such a reputation as an aphrodisiac in the thirteenth century that the ecclesiastical powers did their utmost to ban it. A parchment found by the recently revived Confrérie de la Cervoise de l'Avouerie d'Anthisne reveals that 'François of Anthisne lived well, and fathered ten children, thanks to partaking frequently but never to excess of this mixture, known here by the name of *cerviel*.'[39] The *avouerie* of Anthisne was the castle keep of the town, served both as fortress and brewery, and is one of the finest monuments to the art of the Meuse area.

The brewery of Anthisne, like most municipal breweries, processed the citizens' own ingredients, but Dom Philiber Schmitz[40] has pointed out that 'brewing was one of the leading monastic industries. Except in the south of France, almost all monasteries had breweries, called *cambae*, even, curiously enough, in cider-making areas.' Food-growing in the Middle Ages, it should be remembered, owed almost everything to the monasteries, which were large enough landowners to employ the rotation of crops necessary for constant cereal production, and were alone in farming their lands in a profitable and intelligent way, unlike the secular lords, whose interests were not in agriculture. The monks therefore tried to improve the quality and quantity of their ale, just as they did with cheese, wine and liqueurs. The ale made by the Benedictines of Orgeval was so good that on one occasion it revealed a vocation for the Church to some young men who tasted it – a tale said to be true, although Bernard of Clairvaux himself had blessed the ale that day.

The ale brewed by the monks, when made on a large, almost industrial scale, was a good source of income to their orders. The old charters of St Gall in Switzerland mention three breweries within the monastery's jurisdiction, only one of which provided drink for the community itself; these breweries had a hot room for malting and a cold room for fermentation. The study of Gregorian chant could easily be reconciled with business acumen and a grasp of technology. Other great brewing abbeys were St Trond, Westminster, and Corbie in Picardy; monks from Corbie had been sent to darkest Westphalia by Louis I of France, known as *le Débonnaire*, where they founded the abbey of Corvey in 817 and taught the art of brewing.

The monks knew a lot about medicinal herbs – added to the ale as part of various secret recipes – and they were very likely responsible for the use of hops as well as the technological advance of the double-bottomed vat, which allowed two successive infusions of the mash. Hops, which imparted a specific aroma and clarified the brew, made ale into true beer.

Léo Moulin lists many places where hops, after the late eighth century, 'were part of the quit-rent paid to the monasteries ... but there is no explicit statement that they were for making beer. However, they were provided in such quantities that it is difficult to imagine any other use for them.' As these monasteries were in Flanders or Germany, it may well be that the clear ale which results from the use of hops is really a Flemish or German invention, and the name of beer was bestowed on it to distinguish it from ordinary ale, which was thick and brownish.

Now although Charlemagne's *Capitulaire* is an index of all the vegetable, cereal and medicinal plants in use at his time, it says nothing about hops, even though the Romans ate hop shoots in the same way as asparagus (Pliny, *Natural History*, XXI–50). Hops were considered good for the health even in Neolithic times by the people who lived on the shores of the Baltic, and were grown in most physic gardens of the Frankish period from the North Sea to the Tyrol, for their aperitif and diuretic qualities ('quod urinam provocet', said the School of Salerno), and as an antiseptic and soporific – in fact they were supposed to have every imaginable good quality, including that of being an aphrodisiac. People therefore tried putting them in ale from the ninth century onwards, like the other plants mentioned above; there is evidence of this from Cobbe and Corbie in particular. Evidently it was soon seen that they improved the appearance of the ale and were a diuretic. But it also appears that their aphrodisiac reputation made them suspect, for it took hops a long time – four centuries – to make their mark. The bishops of Liège and Cologne fought a long battle to get them banned (in fact they themselves were selling ale flavoured with other, very secret ingredients, and did not like the idea of competition). King Charles V of France, a lover of good ale, finally reduced the tax on hop beer in Liège and Utrecht. Beer had won the day. In 1409, Jean sans Peur (John the Fearless), Duke of Burgundy, created the Order of the Hop, with its motto 'Ich Zuighe', meaning in Flemish 'I savour'.

If the bishops of Liège and Cologne had their secrets, so did all brewers, clerics and laymen alike. These secrets arose from careful and judicious observation. The pragmatism of their brewing is striking; the value of their empirical processes has been confirmed by modern microbiology. For instance, they fermented at a low temperature. 'But the great art, the real secret, was to pick the psychological moment for adding hops to the bubbling liquid. The brewer therefore liked to be alone ... and would tolerate no curious onlookers.'[41]

Others who had their secrets, or at least their clever dodges, were the *eswarts* or *coeuriers*, inspectors authorized to keep a check on both the brewing and the storage of beer (brewers turned to the cooper's trade of cask-making when the temperature meant brewing was too risky). They fixed prices and controlled the density of the beer. In Alsace, Lorraine and Bavaria they had an infallible system residing in the seat of their leather breeches. They would pour a little beer on a wooden bench and sit on it, placidly smoking pipes. An hour later they rose to their feet. If the bench stuck to their breeches, the beer conformed to regulations. If it did not it was small beer, too light, and must be sold cheaper. No one dared protest against their decree, and there was no appeal: to be 'on the bench', after all, lent them legal authority.

In the seventeenth century beer became the special province, almost the monopoly, of the Flemish and Dutch, since hops were widely grown in Flanders, northern and eastern France and Bavaria, where the climate suited them. Wool merchants had already brought it to England around 1542, but the English, faithful to their own ales, began by suspecting it, believing, as the Carthusian monk Andrew Boorde said in 1547, that beer was 'a naturall drynke, for a Dutche man'. They did eventually add hops to ale to help it keep and make it clearer, although they went on drinking beer at room temperature and not chilled, as it has always been preferred on the continent of Europe. Porter had twice the usual amount of hops, and was therefore more bitter; the name apparently derives from its originally being drunk by porters, a stalwart race of men. An Italian of the time said much the same about English beer as the Romans had said of ale centuries before, that it was a liquor 'suited to the British constitution', meaning the barbarian constitution. The Spanish, faithful to the ale-making tradition of *cerveza*, continued to brew excellent beers.

The beer revolution was complete when barley became the chief cereal used for brewing almost all over Europe, ousting other grains such as spelt. Millet and rice beers are still made in Africa and Asia, and cassava is used in South America; every race shows its own kind of ingenuity. Gambrinus or Cambrinus, a legendary Flemish character famous for both his capacity (he was credited with drinking 117 pints a day) and his talents as a brewer, was not in fact Duke Jan Primus (John I) of Brabant, nor a canonized monk, as some theories have it. Nor was he the inventor of beer, despite pious inscriptions on the walls of some Belgian and German breweries proclaiming, 'Let there be beer, and there was beer'. Gambrinus was in fact a pure myth, owing his name to *camb*, an old Dutch word for brewing, the *cambatum* being the tax on beer. Nonetheless, so many tankards have been raised to Gambrinus that he must surely have become immortal.

The Technique of Brewing Beer

There are 13 operations involved in brewing beer – a lucky rather than an unlucky number, in this case.

Storage of the grain over a long period, to complete ripening and cause an increase in the amylases which play an important part in germination.

Steeping, alternating with drying-out, 12 successive times during a period of 90 hours, swelling the grain with very pure water until it reaches saturation point.

Germination over a period of 30 hours in hoppers, in a warm and humid atmosphere, to make germs and even radicles develop as the grain bursts under the pressure of amylases 'digesting' the starch to transform it into sugar. Malt has now been obtained.

Desiccation or kilning to stop germination and the formation of sugars at a precise point, in a very hot, dry atmosphere, which eventually roasts the malt to a greater

Women in a kraal making beer, probably from millet: English print by F. G. Angas, 1849. Interestingly, the women are in charge of the brewing here.

or lesser degree depending on the type of beer required (brown or pale, mild or bitter).

Degerming fixes the flavour of the beer by eliminating bitterness due to the tannin in the germ.

Grinding reduces the malt to flour.

Mashing is the major operation: the malt is mixed and stirred either in an infusion with the water progressively heated to 75 degrees, or in a decoction with part of the malt being boiled and added to the infusion, so that the sugars are completely dissolved.

The first filtration eliminates waste matter and refines the thick wort.

Washing with very hot water rinses the wort well, and it is added to the filtrate of the first filtration.

185

Boiling caused sterilization of the amylases; at this point the hops are added to the wort, in three stages, to obtain a different quintessence each time.

Fermentation, after several more filtrations, in fermentation vessels, at either a 'high' rate, with cooling to a steady 15 degrees, or a 'low' rate at 6 degrees. 'High' fermentation lasts about five days. Eight to ten days are required for 'low' fermentation. The bubbles hiss as they form, as if the beer were boiling.

Yeast is added in diluted form, made from selected stocks of bacteria depending on the special requirements of the beer.

Final storage of the beer in oak hogsheads allows it to mature well away from unwanted microbes for two or three months. It is then put in barrels, casks or bottles after a final filtration to make it bright and clear.

Water has a vital part in brewing beer. The purity of the beer depends on the purity of the water. If it is hard water, containing lime, fermentation may not work properly, and if it has too much iron in it the beer will never be really clear and bright. In fact there is something about water from every different source which influences the colour and flavour of the brew, so that experienced beer drinkers can easily recognize different kinds.

Alcohol is liberated by fermentation. The farther the process goes, the higher the degree of alcohol. But the alcohol content of beer is not a criterion of its quality. Bavarian beers (from Munich) and Alsatian beers are light. The strongest beer is German, known as *Kulminator*. In the sixteenth century, in rivalry with the beers of Bremen and Hamburg, French brewers put a highly alcoholic beer on the market and called it *quente* or *cuyte*. This beer emigrated to Belgium, where it became the Brussels beer known as *kuyte*, which even has a street called after it.

The colour of the beer, from very pale to almost black, passing through shades of yellow, red, amber and brown, is caused by the kilning, rapid drying of the malt at high heat. The change from wet to dry liberates aromatic compounds and the colouring agents produced by caramelization. The darker the beer, the more aromatic and even syrupy it will taste.

The hops play an important and complex part in brewing. The parts of the plant used are the female flowers, which contain antiseptic resins that cause bitterness, and also essential oils which give the beer its 'bouquet' (mild, fruity or vinous). The bitterness should be tasted as the beer is swallowed and is followed by an after-taste a second or so later. This after-taste – fine, acrid or harsh – is the real test of the beer.

Pasteurization of most beers, both bottled and draught, can kill them even while it makes them hygienic and helps them to keep well. Beer-lovers prefer a fresh 'live' beer which has to be drunk quite young. Unfortunately some traditional or locally made beers do not travel well. The breweries are trying to make pasteurization unnecessary by insisting on cleanliness (already very strictly observed during brewing), a rapid turnover and good conditions at point of sale.

The head on beer in the glass develops the aroma of the beer beneath. It is an important test of the product's quality: its behaviour, fragrance and persistence are all criteria (the head on some big-bodied beers can cling to the inside of the glass for 15 minutes). And the way in which beer is poured to give a good head also shows true expertise.

The History of Pasta

The Italians are always surprised to be told that pasta may have been brought back from China by Marco Polo in the thirteenth century. Judging by the editorials that have appeared in even the most staid of Italian journals, they have a particular grudge against Betty Crooke, a food writer highly regarded in America. She believes that macaroni, which became popular after the Venetian had returned from his travels, owes its name to a banquet given for the Emperor Frederick III. To show how cultivated he was, the handsome Emperor is said to have described this plate of pasta as *makarios*, meaning 'happy' in Greek. The idea appals Giuseppe Presolini, a well-known Italian gastronomic author, who has pronounced that 'Questa storia passo anche in una cinematografia!' (the story is fit for the cinema).

In fact the tale of the Chinese origins of Italian pasta arises from a liberty taken by Ramusio, the first editor of the printed text of Marco Polo's *Book* describing his travels, at the end of the sixteenth century. In Book II, Chapter 16, Marco Polo tells of his visit to the country of Fanfu, where he was shown a bread tree, from the fruits of which the natives obtained a meal similar to barley flour. 'They make of this a paste which they eat, and which is excellent', according to Marco Polo, but he says no more about it, and although he did bring a sample back to Venice, it evidently did not prove popular.

He does not mention vermicelli, macaroni or spaghetti for the good reason that no such terms existed in his time, around 1300. However, a note in Ramusio's edition states that 'They use cleaned and ground flour, and make it into lasagne and several pasta dishes of which the said M. Polo ate several times. He brought some back to Venice, and it is like barley bread, with the same flavour.' The original manuscript of the *Book* written in French by Rusticiano of Pisa, Polo's fellow-prisoner in Genoa, is lost, and so is the first direct copy taken from it. The most faithful of the later copies is the manuscript of the Ambrosian Library of Milan. It says nothing about the bread tree except the little remark quoted above. Pasta in Italian means a paste or dough made from flour of any kind mixed with water, whether for porridge, gruel, pancakes or bread, or the types of pasta now regarded as specifically Italian dishes. The reference to lasagne, which was familiar in the sixteenth century, may perhaps have occurred to Ramusio, in an over-zealous moment, as a better comparison. To Marco Polo himself the surprising thing was that a flour which could be made into dough came from the fruit of a tree and not a cereal grain.

Chinese noodles, made of wheat, buckwheat, rice or soya, had existed long before Marco Polo arrived in China, and he must have eaten them. If he did not think them worth mentioning, it could have been because he knew such dishes already, and so saw nothing remarkable in them.

Chinese vermicelli or *fen*, also known in Japan, where they are called *harusame*, look like skeins of transparent silk threads, and are made from a paste of germinated mung beans, not a cereal. They are usually assumed to be made of soya, like certain types of noodles, but such is not the case. They are soaked in water before being boiled for a few minutes or fried.

The Koreans claim to have invented pasta, and say they taught the Japanese to make *soba* noodles around the twelfth century, using Chinese buckwheat introduced into the northern part of the main island of Hondo (where rice would not grow) by an Emperor of Japan around the year 700. *Soba*, which have a considerable body of symbolism associated with them, were the staple Japanese diet from the sixteenth century onwards. They are traditionally given as gifts of welcome. They are cooked in water, drained, and served in a bowl lifted close to the mouth. Etiquette decrees that the skein of noodles should be noisily sucked in and swallowed, untouched by the teeth. An interesting dietetic point is that the cooking liquid is drunk with the meal.

But if Marco Polo did not bring pasta to the West, who really invented it? And where, when and how? Was pasta traditionally Roman, as one might assume from the eighteenth-century Italian translations of Horace's *Satires* and Martial's *Epigrams*, which render the meaning of the word *pastilla* as 'little pastas', whereas all translations before the fourteenth century (the time of Marco Polo) give the proper meaning of 'small round cakes', the kind used for sacrificial offerings? Some translators even described them as 'croquettes'. Varro makes it quite clear in one of his encyclopedic works that a *pastillum* was a bread roll (*panis parvus*). Undeterred by that, De Cange, an erudite seventeenth-century Frenchman, defined *pastillum* as a pastry stuffed with meat, in fact a kind of ravioli (or 'rafiole'), a very popular dish at the time. As I mentioned above, similar references to contemporary life had Virgil's broad beans erroneously identified with haricots.

Of all the countries which claim to have invented and popularized pasta – China, Japan, Korea, Germany, France and Italy – Italy stakes her claim most vehemently; perhaps it is in the Italian nature to do so. There are many supposed proofs of the truth of the assertion – a truth which actually depends on legend, tradition and poetry. Similarly, all Italian towns make their own claims, particularly Naples and Bergamo: 'We are the folk of Naples and Bergamo / Each claims to be the home of Macaroni ... / We are neighbours, and readier to fight for Macaroni than for Tasso!'

Tasso, the author of *Gerusalemme liberata*, died suffering from persecution mania; megalomania seems closer to the attitude of Naples speaking through the comic

188

poet Lemene (1634–1704), author of the passage above. In fact, while the fourteenth-century Italian cookery books – the *Neapolitan*, the *Angevin* (known as 'Latin') and the *Tuscan* – mention macaroni as being in current use before the Emperor Frederick and his apocryphal witty remark, they all say it originated in the Romagna, and they also allude to a dish from Cagliari. The Neapolitan Benedetto Croce, a logical man and a disciple of Hegel, quotes evidence to the effect that his medieval ancestors were known as 'mangiatori de ortaglia e non di pasta asciutta' – eaters of vegetables, not of pasta.

However, the term macaroni (or in Italian *maccheroni*) is definitely Neapolitan dialect, and may be related to Mascherone, one of the oldest traditional characters of the Commedia dell'Arte; he wears a grotesque mask and is a great glutton. According to one theory the word is a pun: a Neapolitan prince with a fine palate encountered this form of pasta, with its hole in the middle, and thought it very good. On learning that the new pasta had to be made by a specialist paid according to his skill, he exclaimed, 'Si buoni ma caroni!' ('So good, but expensive!') In standard Italian, the word would be *caro*, in the plural *cari*. But these derivations are fanciful: according to the major dictionaries, the ultimate etymology of the word macaroni is obscure.

The sixty-first of Sacchetti's *Trecento Novelle*, written in 1397, takes macaroni as its subject. A lord of Florence reproaches his steward for eating macaroni with bread, a provocative action in the face of the common people's poverty. But Sacchetti says nothing about the origin of the dish. Was the macaroni home-made, bought, or imported? Thirty years earlier Boccaccio writes of macaroni as if it were a kind of frumenty, but he may not have been speaking from personal knowledge.

Be that as it may, the first production of pasta on any kind of industrial scale was indeed in Naples in the early fifteenth century. However, this pasta did not keep well, and it was not until 1800 that the process which would make it really *asciutta* (dry) was discovered. It involved natural drying alternately in hot and cold temperatures. Perfect conditions were found at Torre Annunziata, some kilometres south of Naples itself, where the climate changes four times a day, to a regular pattern. The macaroni of Torre Annunziata is the *ne plus ultra* of Italian pasta.

However, the increasing popularity of *pasta asciutta* after the fourteenth century, rather than being attributable to any one Italian city, was because of progress in one form of the culinary art which had been practised on a domestic scale in the Mediterranean basin since ancient times, although there is a recent theory that it originated in the Baltic regions of Lithuania and Estonia in the first millennium BC, reached southern shores by the same route as amber, and gradually found its fullest expression there. In studying food, as in studying technology, it is often difficult to say precisely which elements were suggested by the particular needs of a period and which were the legacy of older practices, either native or imported.

The great merit of pasta is that (at least in its simplest form) it is easily made; it also takes up little storage space, but swells when cooked. Cooking it is simple too, since it does not need an oven like bread, only a large pot generally filled with water, although a few traditional methods call for cooking in oil. Pasta is a considerable improvement on gruel and porridge dishes, but there is no risk of its fermenting, which suggests that it derives from unleavened bread cakes, themselves a transformation of gruel, porridge or polenta dishes which did not require any raising agent.

Very small cakes of pounded cereals and poppy seeds have been found in archeological excavations of lake-side dwellings in the Vosge. Examination under the microscope shows that their starch was liberated when the cells were cooked in water and burst. Some of these cakes also show evidence of carbonization, and may also have been grilled. They are the distant ancestors of pasta and of the *flaous* or 'flans' of the Middle Ages; the word, now usually applied to a filled tart, originally meant a cake made of unleavened dough, flattened with a rolling pin made of wood or stone, and then coarsely broken up before being thrown into boiling water, in which the dough swelled. The *farfels* of Russian Jewish cookery are made on the same principle. In France, these *flaous* became *échaudés*, a traditional treat sold at street corners and fairs; the dough was boiled, then wrapped in leaves and roasted in the embers of the hearth (*focus*). From *focus* comes the word *fouace*[42] for a kind of cake still eaten, and rather similar to an English girdle-cake, although a *fouace* is made of an enriched bread dough which used to be cooked in direct contact with the heat, and is now baked in the oven.

Various fine, long, unleavened bread cakes resembling Jewish *matzos* are also made in Armenia and the Caucasus. They are cooked quickly, at high heat, to stop any fermentation and make the starch in the flour digestible. They are then immediately cooled and dried, hung over strings so that they are folded in half. The cakes are stored and eaten as required from bowls, crushed and with hot water and oil poured over them to swell them: a very ancient practice.

Of the many kinds of dried dough not made as flat cakes, special mention should be made of *nieules* or *nioles*, a popular medieval French delicacy which was sold at fairs, like *échaudés*. They were twisted ribbons of hard, unleavened dough, cooked in boiling water with the ashes of vine shoots, which contain natural potash. They gave the dough a dark colour (Latin *nigellus*, blackish), whence their French name and their savoury, smoky flavour. The *nieules* were drained, cut up and dried in the oven. When the Edict of Nantes was revoked, the makers of *nieules*, almost all of whom, oddly enough, were Protestants, emigrated *en masse* to Germany. Here *nieules* became *Bretzeln*, and the potash was replaced by coarse rock salt. There is another theory that *nieule* meant twisted, rather than blackish, and applied to the shape of the dough, which still survives in *Bretzeln*, whence modern American pretzels. In French culinary slang, the term *nioleur* is still in pejorative use for a specialist pastrycook.

The present usual method of cooking pasta in water has not always been a *sine qua non*. Various recipes for various dishes both in ancient times and in the Middle Ages show that pasta might be either fried or boiled, depending on circumstances, just as such dishes might be sweetened, salted or spiced, sometimes all at once. In general plain boiled pasta was not especially popular, and seemed too frugal a dish. It was finished off by frying or grilling. The Jewish *frimsels* of Alsace are cooked half by boiling and half by frying; they are mixed together before serving, and taste delicious. Other Jewish pastas called *p'titim* are first fried with onion, then just covered with boiling water to swell and cook over a low heat.

Do fritters and pasta have the same origin? Nothing is particularly new under the sun, as witness the Greek *euchytes* of the time of Demosthenes, made of a ribbon of firm dough forced into hot oil through a funnel. The piped dough took on unexpected shapes as it cooked, and was much liked. Greek colonists took this recipe to Spain, where it is still known under the name of *churros*, sold in the streets early in the morning and eaten as a breakfast delicacy, accompanied by frothy hot chocolate. The same delicacy, under the name of *Trichterküchli*, turns up in German-speaking areas of Switzerland; one wonders just how the recipe got there.

There was another Greek recipe, for deep-fried green pasta, which is well worth trying; it was known as *artolaggeion*, or bread in the pot. 'Take lettuces, wash them and pound them well in a mortar, adding wine. Squeeze out the juice and mix it with fine flour. Let the dough rest, then pound it with pork lard and pepper. Roll it out flat. Cut into thin strips, throw them into hot oil, and drain them over a sieve when you take them out.' The centuries-old recipe is authentic and still tastes delicious.

The flat cakes which became, among other things, the *piada* of the Romagna and Neapolitan pizza, could also be made into small pasta shapes for soup. It was usual in the Romagna to use up oddments of raw pasta by rolling them out like a *flaou*. The scraps were cut up with the point of a knife and thrown into chicken or veal broth. Sometimes you did not go to the trouble of rolling the dough out and cutting into strips, but simply rolled it into small balls in the palm of your hand and cooked them in broth like *gnocchi*. This was a practice of medieval times and onwards; Le Grand d'Aussy,[43] writing in 1783, tells us they were eaten in Provence, which has a number of gastronomic similarities to the Romagna.

For a long time, in fact, Provence was part of the (Germanic) Holy Roman Empire. Perhaps there is an association here, in lieu of a common origin, with one of the delicacies of German cookery: dumplings or *Knödeln* – *kruffle* or *knoffle* in the Alsatian dialect, *quenape* in Yiddish.

We still tend to think of pasta as long and thin like spaghetti, or flat and ribbon-shaped like noodles and lasagne. However, it comes in all shapes and sizes; strictly speaking, croquettes, quenelles and gnocchi are also pasta when made of a cereal dough, not necessarily of wheat flour. The principal use for the semolina made from the hard or durum wheat which grows best in hot, dry Mediterranean climates after a winter sowing is to make the classic types of pasta; bread and cakes are best made from other wheats. High-yielding hard wheats progressively ousted emmer and soft wheats in the Mediterranean after the Graeco-Roman period.

The Chinese, Koreans and Japanese have always made dumplings and croquettes, as well as noodles, out of rice, barley and soya, cooking them by either frying,

191

Pasta: engraving from the *Livre de cuisine* by Jules Gouffé, 1881

boiling or steaming. In the high mountains of the Shansi range on the Sino-Mongolian border, at altitudes where oats are the only cereal which will grow, people have eaten *yu-mien-wo-wo* from time immemorial; this dish consists of oat porridge made into a dough, rolled out thinly, then cut into squares and curled around the finger. The cigar-shaped curls are placed on end, close together, and steamed in a wicker strainer over a pot of boiling water.

Couscous can also be classed as pasta. It is made of wheat, sorghum or, in black Africa, millet, the grain being crushed rather than ground into flour. This coarse semolina is steamed, with salted butter added in several stages. In the sixteenth century Rabelais mentioned 'coscoton à la moresque' (Moorish couscous), which he says was highly regarded in Provence; he cannot mean maize-flour polenta, which was of later date. There was a good deal of contact with the Berbers in Provence and along the Ligurian coast.

It was from Provence that Dr Maloin, subsequently commissioned by Louis XV of France to write *L'art du boulanger* ('The Baker's Art'), which appeared in 1767, summoned the Sieur Sap, a specialist in pasta, to teach Parisians how to make it in 1749. The makers of vermicelli had a corporation distinct from the bakers. This period saw the rapid spread of a dish previously unpopular outside Languedoc, although Alsace learned to like noodles from soldiers of Italian origin billeted there during the Thirty Years' War. The presence of noodles in Strasbourg under their modern name of *nudlen* is recorded in 1671, in a book by the Abbé Buchinger. *Spatzele*, wide, fresh home-made noodles, are related to lasagne. Nineteenth-century French dictionaries gave the word for noodles, *nouilles*, a German origin (cf. modern German *Nudeln*) long before France temporarily lost Alsace and Lorraine to

Germany in the Franco-Prussian war of 1870–71.

According to sixteenth-century Italian historians, we owe pasta stuffed with chopped meat or herbs, cheese or even fish to a peasant woman of Cernusco called Libista.[44] *Se non è vero è ben trovato!*

The ravioli of fourteenth-century cookery books were usually deep-fried, like fritters. The *Libro de arte coquinaria* of Maestro Martino, a native of Como and chef to the Patriarch of Aquileia in Rome around 1450, gives directions for cooking them in meat broth (Chapter II, 144: 'Ravioli in tempo di carne'). These 'raphioulles' reappeared in *L'ouverture de cuisine* by Maistre Lancelot de Casteau of Mons, chef in his time to three princes of Liège, which appeared with 'permission from his superiors' on 26 February 1604, and was 'for sale at the Sign of the Golden Fleece, near the Church of the Eleven Thousand Virgins'. The recipe may have been brought to Wallonia by Florentine bankers.

But in its early days *ravioli* generally meant a stuffing made of meat, cheese, eggs and herbs wrapped in dough, a dish like modern *canneloni*. I found a manuscript in the library of Châlons-sur-Marne copied by one Rhimboldus d'Argentina (perhaps Strasbourg) in 1481, from another manuscript a century older written by 'N', a doctor of Assisi. It contains one of the oldest recipes of the kind, for 'tortelli in the Assisi manner'. These 'tortelli' do not even use a dough wrapping for the stuffing; the instructions are simply to roll the chopped meat mixture in flour. This coating of flour, having absorbed the fat from the chopped meat, would have coagulated slightly in the hot broth into which the tortelli were put to be cooked.

A contemporary of Petrarch, Francesco di Marco Datini, the famous Merchant of Prato, who dealt wholesale in spices among other things and had supplied the Papal court at Avignon, gives several indications in his letters (in the Datini archives in Florence) about various kinds of pasta and their uses in the early years of the fifteenth century. His dinner began, as it would today, with a first course of *minestra asciutta*, a dish of lasagne, ravioli or risotto. The stuffing of the ravioli was made of pounded pork, eggs, cheese, parsley and a little sugar. On fast days the ravioli were stuffed only with herbs and cheese. A lasagne dish suitable for fast days still survives in Haute-Provence under the name of *crouzets*, traditionally eaten on Advent Eve: it consists of alternate layers of home-made lasagne and walnuts pounded with goat's milk cheese, and is sprinkled with oil. It symbolizes the swaddling clothes of the baby Jesus.

Ravioli were eaten at banquets too, and were clearly very popular in Prato. They were not served alone, but as a garnish to a *torta* made of several layers of pastry filled with chicken fried in oil, garlic sausage, ravioli stuffed with ham, almonds and dates. A pastry lid covered the whole *torta*, and it was cooked in the embers.

There is also a very curious kind of Armenian ravioli, the recipe for which, I have been told, goes back to the year 1000. These ravioli are called *topic*. The dough is made of flour or a purée of chick-peas spread on squares of muslin. The *topic* are filled with their stuffing and the corners are carefully folded, the muslin held carefully so as not to break the dough. The opposite corners of the square are tied together to make little bundles, and then the *topic* are dropped into boiling water, four at a time. They are cooled in the muslin and unwrapped before being served dusted with cinnamon, or sprinkled with olive oil and lemon juice. These little pasta bundles are slightly reminiscent in shape of Chinese *won-ton* dumplings, which are made from a dough of wheaten flour and eggs, and served in the clear soup in which they were cooked.

Apart from pastas which are national specialities of other countries, most pasta still goes under Italian names. There are innumerable kinds, fresh or dried. All commercial pasta is made mechanically, and so indeed is home-made pasta nowadays; every Italian housewife has her pasta-making machine, worked by turning a handle, and such machines are now easily obtainable outside Italy. Only a purist still cuts up the pale yellow dough into ribbons with a knife, in the way commemorated by the name of *tagliatelle* (from the verb *tagliare*, to cut up). The commercially made dough is now passed through a grid with holes allowing it to come out in all kinds of different shapes.

Fettucine are the same shape as *tagliatelle* but twice as wide. Large sheets of lasagne with wavy edges are produced in ribbons too. A dish of veal with lasagne featured on the verse menu for a Lombard gentleman around 1495, written by Antonio Camelli, court poet to the dukes of Milan, whose remarks about cream cheese were quoted above:

> Il figlio de la vacca venne in corte
> Grasso tra il brado e'l caso e la lasagne ...

[The son of the cow comes to court, fat with broth, cheese and lasagne ...]

Macaroni is made with a hole down the middle, contrary to claims by comedians that the hole is added afterwards. *Rigatoni* are short, fluted lengths of macaroni. There is also a whole range of soup pastas including the traditional vermicelli, 'little worms'. Among stuffed pastas, I will mention only the tubular *cannelloni*, like stuffed pancakes, and the ravioli already discussed above, made from two sheets of dough with little heaps of stuffing between them; *tortellini* are twisted shapes, *cappeletti* are shaped like little hats, and the semi-circular shape of *agnelotti* suggests a sleeping lamb, its nose between its paws.

French cookery used to look down on pasta except as *timbales de macaroni* garnished with quenelles, brains and white sauce. Served in any other way, pasta was considered common, or only good enough for children, although vermicelli might be allowed in the broth of the Sunday *pot-au-feu*. And in Britain, canned spaghetti in tomato sauce was the only pasta widely eaten for a number of years in the middle of the twentieth century. Now, however, Italian cooking is popular, and supermarkets stock a wide range of freshly made as well as dried pastas.

The History of Grain Spirits

Around the year 420, so the story goes, the Irish monk who was to be revered under the name of St Patrick set off to travel Europe and the Near East, spreading the Gospel. In Egypt he learned the process of distillation, already described by Aristotle, which was used to desalinate sea water. St Patrick brought an alembic (in Arabic, *al-'inbik*) back to Ireland with him, a still like the one in a fourth-century illustration of the manuscript of the great alchemist of Alexandria, Zosimus of Panopolis, which is now preserved at St Mark's in Venice.

Perhaps because of the mysterious Pyramids, Egypt has been regarded as one of the high places of arcane knowledge, including the arts of alchemy and chemistry. But the Persians were the first who taught the Graeco-Alexandrians and then the Arabs alchemy. They were supposed to have derived their knowledge from the Chaldeans. The works of Abu Bakr Muhammad ibn Zakarigya Rasi of Teheran (844–932), the physician and alchemist known as Rhazes, contain the first written mention of spirits obtained from the distillation of wine, said to have been a chance discovery made by Geber the Sufi, a prominent Arab of the previous century.

The word 'alcohol' itself, from the Arabic *al-kuhl*, originally meant a very fine powder of antimony, the *kohl* used as eye make-up. It conveyed ideas of something very fine and subtle, and the Arab alchemists therefore gave the name of *al-kuhl* to any impalpable powder obtained by sublimation (the direct transformation of a solid into vapour, or the reverse process), and thus to all volatile principles isolated by distillation.

Tradition has it that the still and the alcohol it made – which the Arabs did not drink because by then their religion forbade it – were brought back to Europe by the Crusaders, as by St Patrick in the earlier legend. We do know for certain, however, that the Moorish scientists of Andalusia, the best in the world of their time, had already been using stills in their work for nearly five centuries before the Crusades. At the time when the Arabs tried expanding into France, wormwood was distilled to make absinthe at Sainte in the Charente-Maritime, or rather a maceration of wormwood in wine, itself a popular drink among the Gallo-Romans, was thus distilled.

A French twelfth-century manuscript,[45] *Les clefs de la peinture*, marvels at the fact that 'by burning fine and very strong wine in vessels intended for that purpose, one may obtain an inflammable liquid which consumes itself without burning the material upon which it is deposited.' The Catalan doctor Raymond Lulle or Lully, known as the Doctor Illuminatus (1235–1313), who had close contacts with his Saracen colleagues in Andalusia, knew how to make *al-kuhl* and distilled many essences to which he gave the name of *al-iksir* (essence, in Arabic). These elixirs or essences were described by Arnaud de Villeneuve in his treatise *De conservanda juventute*, which appeared in 1309, as 'eau-de-vie', the water of life. 'This liquor, drawn from wine but having neither its nature, its colour nor its effects, deserves the name of water of life because it makes a man live long. It prolongs health, disperses superfluous humours, revives the heart and preserves youth: by itself or with some other suitable remedy, it cures hydropsy, colic, paralysis, the quartan fever, and other afflictions ...' As a man of Languedoc, Arnaud de Villeneuve clearly also had contacts in Catalonia.

This eau-de-vie, or 'spirit', as it was also called, was described as *alcool vini* by Paracelsus (1443–1541), who acknowledged his debt to his Arab precursors. He too was a physician, and spirits of this kind remained the preserve of the pharmacopoeia until the sixteenth century. Then in France, once the makers of vinegar had obtained a licence to distil from King Louis XII in 1514, a distinct corporation of distillers formed in the reign of François I, while in Italy the Jesuits began selling spirits flavoured and sweetened in various ways. The history of liqueurs had begun. These spirits were grape spirits, or *marc*, a word originally meaning the must of crushed grapes.

However, monks at the other end of Europe had already been using stills and making considerable profits from a distilled spirit based on cereal grains. While the idea that St Patrick taught the Irish distilling is too neat a story to be credible, there were stills at work in Ireland in the eleventh century, or perhaps even earlier, if the Irish themselves are to be believed.

The monasteries of the Emerald Isle had no vines – or very few – but they did make ale with the barley or oats from their fields. Someone – St Patrick, according to legend – thought of distilling a must not of grapes but of cereals, in the Egyptian manner, to produce a spirit to warm monastic hearts and sweeten voices singing their chilly Matins. It is impossible to say just when the experiment was first tried, and the monks probably kept the results to themselves for some time, but around the eleventh century they began circumspectly selling their product.

The Scots, no doubt, would claim that their clansmen went to Jerusalem long before the Crusades and learned the use of a still there. But there is no saying whether Irish whiskey or Scotch whisky really came first.

Originally the pale, strong spirit was called *uisge beatha* (blessed water) by the Gaelic-speaking Scots and *uisce beatha* in the Irish form of the Celtic language until 1170. The word entered English when Henry II invaded Ireland. Some of his men were lucky enough to find themselves billeted in an abbey that distilled whisky, and found some oak barrels which they made haste to broach. Once they had sampled its contents they felt decidedly elevated, and shared their discovery with their companions. The English tongue transformed *uisce beatha* into whisky, and grain alcohol entered European history under that name long before Arab and Mediterranean scholars began their own experiments with grape spirit. The Irish would add that whisky is by no means the same thing as whiskey, and some connoisseurs much prefer the Irish variety, among them, apparently, Queen Elizabeth I. Even Peter the Great of Russia, from the other end of Europe, said that 'of all wines, Irish spirit is the best.' A taste for distilled grain spirit brought the Russians to make vodka (to which I shall return below), and from the seventeenth century onwards other recipes for grain liquor developed all over Europe outside the Mediterranean.

Irish whiskey can boast of the oldest written records: after Henry II's campaign the invaders evidently taxed it, and in 1276 only large stills were licensed, so that it was easier to apply fiscal controls. The Old Bushmills brand dates from that year, and has been made ever since. Whatever Elizabeth I felt about Irish whiskey, she was less than tender towards Mary Queen of Scots, and the struggle of Scotland for independence has been translated into rivalry between drinkers of whisky and drinkers of beer. Although Burns said that 'Freedom and Whisky gang thegither!' the Scots suffered a crushing defeat at Culloden in 1746, and whisky itself may be said to have been annexed as one of the jewels in the British crown. James Buchanan, distiller of the Black and White brand, Scotsman though he was, was very proud to obtain a contract to supply whisky to the House of Commons at the end of the eighteenth century, and for some time the firm's bottles proudly bore the words 'House of Commons'.

At the same time, drinkers of whiskey with an 'e' were raising their glasses to legislative independence in Ireland, and of course everyone sees truth at the bottom of the glass. One should perhaps be a little wary of asking for a Scotch in a Dublin pub.

Whiskey – and whisky – are grain spirits made in a pot still. The pot is descended from the cauldron, a magical and evocative utensil to the Celtic ancestors of the Irish. One difference between the Scottish and Irish versions of the spirit is that whiskey has a mellowness on account of a longer ageing period, between seven and twelve years. To make both, the soaked barley is germinated before being dried, as in the initial stages of beer-making. Scotch malt is spread above turf fires which give it its characteristic smoky flavour, while Irish malt is dried in a closed oven. Afterwards the grain is crushed to make a mash which ferments and sweetens before it is distilled, twice for Scotch whisky, three times for Irish whiskey.

Both spirits mature and take on their colour in old oak barrels which previously contained sherry. Why sherry? Probably because, in a country lacking vineyards, the first barrels thus re-used were recovered from the wrecks of Spanish ships bringing cargoes of Xeres wine to England; in spite of all differences of foreign policy between Spain and England throughout history, the English have always been extremely fond of that wine, to the point of naturalizing its name as 'sherry'. When spirit aged in such casks proved to taste particularly good, their use became an essential part of the process.

After the requisite maturing period, blending begins. Spirits from the same distillery are used, and the grain is always barley, but their age, the casks and even the place in which they have matured may differ. The best Scotch is unblended and can call itself 'pure malt'. Blended Scotch whiskies may contain grain alcohol made from various grains (barley, wheat, oats, rye, maize).

There are some 60 different whiskies, their precise composition being a trade secret in each case. A good quality blended whisky contains at least 45 or 50 per cent of barley malt. A standard blend may contain only 10 to 15 per cent. The ageing period indicated on the bottle is always that of the youngest whisky in the blend: 30 years for Ballantine's, 21 years for Royal Salute. Ordinary Scotch is only three or four years old.

The Irish traditionally drink whiskey in a tall glass as a long drink, diluted with the same volume of still water, and at room temperature. There is a saying that you should never add water to another man's whiskey, so each drinker is given a separate carafe of water and mixes his own. The traditional remark as you raise your glass is 'Slainte', and toasts are supposed to be in verse, which is likely to become increasingly lyrical as the evening wears on.

Standard blended Scotch is good diluted with water and ice, although some prefer soda water (itself an Irish invention). The best blended Scotch should not have anything but an ice cube added to it, and pure malt is drunk devoutly after dinner, like cognac, without either water or ice, and in a proper silence. Whiskies contain between 40 and 50 degrees of alcohol, but the bottles bear a figure giving twice that number followed by the word 'proof'. A spirit of 80 (half-degrees) proof sounds better than '40 degrees'.

The Anglo-Saxon colonists set about distilling whisky as soon as they arrived in the Americas, using the cereals they found there. American whiskey is known as bourbon, from Bourbon County in Kentucky, where it was first made. It is now distilled from maize (51 per cent) and malted wheat. It is aged in barrels of oak with their interiors burned out, which gives it a very characteristic taste. American rye whiskey, as its name indicates, is made from that grain, and so, above all, is Canadian whiskey.

Wherever whiskies come from, and despite various claims, they have no vaso-dilating properties making them beneficial to sufferers from heart trouble. Drinking whisky in France, where it is not made, is a rather snobbish social affectation of modern times.

The berries of juniper, an excellent medicinal plant, are used to flavour gin, a clear spirit made from malted barley, and also flavoured with other aromatic herbs such as coriander, angelica, cardamom and ginger. The name itself derives from 'Geneva'. The *g'nief* of northern France is a juniper-flavoured spirit made from a highly malted grain: barley, wheat, rye or maize, and derives from French *genièvre*, juniper. The name of juniper itself is from a Celtic word, *jenupus*, meaning bitter: the spirit is bitter, strong and colourless like Scandinavian *aquavit* or *kvarit*.

According to the Poles, along with the Russians the main consumers of vodka, that spirit, made from maize or wheat, is 'the only beverage that goes with herring, a fish that makes beer taste insipid and wine metallic.'[46] It may be flavoured with herbs or lemon, or coloured and flavoured with paprika. Its warming qualities make it popular during the long northern winters, and when knocked back in one draught it helps the people of the countries where it is the national spirit to digest their traditional dishes of smoked and oily fish. It is served in small glasses to accompany caviare, salmon and eel.

In Vietnam a spirit is made from sticky rice or *nep*, and is fermented in jars in the sun. It is called *choum-choum*, is partly medicinal, is Chinese in origin, and the Vietnamese claim that it dates back to 2000 years before our era. It was also supposed to cure the biliousness of colonial administrators when Indochina was still under Western rule, and it contains a high proportion of aromatic and digestive plants. Another rice spirit (or rice wine; the Chinese make little distinction) is *hoang-tsieou*, drunk in China at the end of meals.

In South America maize is germinated to make *chicha*, known as early as the time of the Incas. But North America had no spirits before the white men came. Firewater killed more North American Indians than did the colonists' guns. It killed their souls as well. 'Eau-de-vie', Bachelard has written, 'is a liquid which burns the tongue and catches fire at the slightest spark. It does not confine itself to the work of dissolution and destruction, like "strong water", but vanishes along with that which it consumes.'

PART III

In and around ancient Greece, food had an important part to play in society

THE THREE SACRAMENTAL FOODS

OIL
BREAD
WINE

The Fundamental Trinity

Certain periods in history seem to be of particular importance: at such times, a concentration of forces brings about radical changes in the whole framework of life and thought. Everything is back in the melting pot, in both material and intellectual terms, while major events drive civilization on at a great pace; their synchronized consequences cannot be properly assessed until later. The ship in which humanity is sailing changes speed and course. Such conjunctions of circumstances have punctuated recorded history ever since it has been possible to study its cycles, from one half-millennium to the next. A mere glance at a chronological survey is enough to make one stop and think.

The fourth and fifth centuries BC saw the dawn of certain events which, although local in nature, proved to be of considerable importance worldwide. As if four lights were coming on in the four corners of the known world of the time, four men were born during this period whose ideas, since our thinking largely determines the way we live, were to mould human life for a very long time to come. The human race had been intelligent, *Homo sapiens*, since time immemorial, but from now on man would exercise his mind simply for the pleasure of it. These four men were K'ung Fou-tse (Confucius) in China, Gautama (Buddha) in India, Zoroaster (Zarathustra) in Persia, and Pythagoras in Greece: four gigantic minds but four modest men, whose habits we know to have been frugal, wisdom being inimical to all passion and excess.[1]

Food, for those who do not despise it, is a doubly divine gift: the gift of skill given to mankind, and brought to bear on the fruits provided by nature.

The fact that these four great minds emerged almost simultaneously at the beginning of a new cycle of events was not mere chance, but the revelation, in four different perspectives, of the best thinking of which man is capable. Remarkably, the philosophical systems of those four wise men were of so universal a nature that everyone can find something of value for himself in their teachings. Here we shall draw upon them in the context of dietary concerns, which are, after all, of considerable importance, since the whole world must go in pursuit of food.

The long, laborious and patient work of Neolithic people in domesticating plants and animals had provided them with riches which could now be enjoyed. Mankind had reached the Bronze and Iron Ages. The physical relief of satisfying hunger could now be allied to the intellectual pleasure of the enjoyment of food, which had not yet – fortunately – been denounced as a mortal sin. It was a pleasure which, like other pleasures, became a vice only when it got out of control.

However, even before the invention of the art of cooking, well defined by Jean-François Revel[2] as 'the perfecting of nutrition', the industrious people of the Neolithic age had transformed natural products already much improved by agriculture into provisions which were easily consumed and of better flavour than before. This was not wild food, gathered to satisfy a need, but nutrition devised and organized expressly to supply it.

Just as the plastic arts express the skill and sensitivity of a civilization, the culinary or gastronomic art which comprises skill in both cooking and appreciation, 'the perfecting of cookery itself',[3] saw the light of day in Greece. It consisted in the making, generation after generation, of simple but delicious products, the first manufactured foodstuffs: bread, oil and wine.

The Greek lords of the *Iliad*, descendants of the leaders of those Aryan pastoral people driven as far as Greece by hunger, were in fact just farmers – large farmers, perhaps, but living plainly on the humble resources of land whose chief blessing came from the sun. Homeric duels might consist of seeing who could plough the straightest furrow.

Bread and wine, 'those two pillars of consumption in Western civilization', to quote Jean-François Revel again, were joined by oil, which might be described as the light of that civilization. The gift of this trinity, fundamental to the prosperity of the state and the health of its people, was attributed to benevolent and peace-loving deities, who might not be the most feared but were always the most loved of the gods: Demeter, Dionysus and Athene. Of course, bread, wine and oil had existed before the Greeks, but no one before them spoke so eloquently on the subject. The Greeks were always ready to discuss it and to develop ways of making those commodities as good as possible. Another much-loved god was Hermes, a great talker and famous for his skill and cunning. According to legend, Hermes rescued the baby Dionysos, god of the vine and of wine, which could account for a good deal.

Perhaps it was easy to be a good talker if you began your day, like the Greeks of the fifth century BC, with a breakfast of bread dipped in wine (*acratodzomai*, from *acratos*: pure as wine). This meal was identical with the propitiatory offerings given to the gods, a kind of grace before meals. The reason why this breakfast wine had to be pure, *acratos*, was that it began a day which might, for one reason or another, be the most important of a man's life, and which in any case ought to be as profitable as bread, as stimulating as wine, and as smooth as oil.

'What is abundance? In a word, and no more, the wise are content with what is necessary', said the Greek playwright Euripides. And what could be more necessary than bread, oil and wine?

Chapter 7

The History of Oil

Olive Oil

Tablets bearing inscriptions dating from the reign of Nebuchadnezzar, found in the 'Vaulted Building' in the north-east part of the south palace in Babylon, list oil rations, one of which is allotted to a certain La-Ku-U-Ki-Ni, prince of La-Ku-Du; this was Jehoiachin, the young king of Judah, taken prisoner by the Babylonians in 597 BC.

What kind of oil featured in these ancient records? It must have been olive oil, since the history of the olive tree is closely linked with the history of agriculture and of the Mediterranean basin. Indeed, its story begins with the Flood itself. 'And the dove came in to him in the evening; and, lo, in her mouth was an olive leaf pluckt off: so Noah knew that the waters were abated from off the earth.' (Genesis, 8, xi).

However, it cannot be stated with certainty that the olive comes from the Near East, for there is a kind of wild olive, *Olea chrysophylla*, with russet rather than silvery foliage, which will grow in stony ground over a large area extending from the Canary and Balearic Islands to the Cape of Good Hope and from the foothills of the Himalayas to the Mascarene Islands. This surviving ancestor of the olive tree is not found at all in the New World.

Wherever it came from, the tree was already being cultivated and its fruits pressed to extract their oil 5000 years ago on the eastern shores of the Mediterranean. Oil crushers were quite common after the third millennium BC, although Herodotus says there were no olive trees in Babylonia, so that oil such as that allotted to Jehoiachin would have had to be imported.

After the ox Aleph, the house Beta, and the camel Gamma, the olive or *zai* was the symbol denoting the fourth letter of the most ancient alphabets. Flocks and herds, housing, transport and agriculture were the four poles of a thriving civilization. And out of all cultivated plants, the olive tree was chosen as symbol rather than

Olives: engraving from *Mémoire et journal d'observations et d'expériences sur les moyens de garantir les olives de la piqûre des insectes*, by M. Sieuvre, 1769

any of the cereals, which may well seem surprising. However, dealing in olive oil was the backbone of the import-export trade in the ancient world. Great merchants came from such oil-producing countries as Phoenicia, Crete and Egypt to the Mediterranean basin and even farther; from the sixth century BC onwards, the Scythians of the southern steppes of Russia came to stock up with oil at the prosperous Greek trading posts of the Black Sea which later became the spas of Romania. Depositories of oil jars such as those of Komo in Crete are evidence of the importance of this trade.

The expansion of olive groves and of the civilizations that took root around the Greek and Phoenician trading posts went hand in hand. Oil was pressed in Sicily, Italy, North Africa and Catalonia. In Provence, according to Strabo, olives were brought to Massilia, now Marseilles, by the Phocaeans along with the first vine stocks. 'The vine and the olive tree', says Gaston Rambert, 'are synonymous with civilization.' The Massilians introduced the olive tree to the appreciative Ligurians, who soon anticipated Virgil in discovering that:

Olives ... require no cultivation
And have no use for the sickle knife or the stiff-tooth rake
Once they've dug themselves in on the fields and stood up to winds.
Earth herself, by the crooked plough laid bare, provides
Moisture enough for the plants and a heavy crop from the ploughshare.
Thus shall you breed the rich olive, beloved of Peace.

There has been a wealth of symbolism attached to olive trees and olive oil ever since humanity turned them to its own advantage. But as they provided one of the essential elements of diet in the ancient world, it was great material wealth that they principally engendered. King David, who died 'full of days, riches and honour', evidently regarded oil as a particular treasure, choosing supervisors of his olive trees and their produce from among his picked men: 'And over the olive trees and the sycomore trees that were in the low plains was Baal-hanan the Gederite: and over the cellars of oil was Joash' (I Chronicles 27, xxviii). Solon, the sixth-century Athenian legislator, brought in laws to protect and regulate olive groves. Caesar issued edicts demanding the annual payment of three million litres of oil as tribute from Numidia, the Maghreb of modern times. Tacitus lays much emphasis on oil production: Tunisia, where many olive groves had been planted with the aim of inducing the turbulent nomads to settle down, provided most of the torrent of oil which lubricated the daily diet of the Roman Empire. (The Romans recognized only one kind of oil, *oleum*, from *oliva*, the olive, whence the modern word *oil* in its various European forms.) The finest palates preferred oil from Venafro, in the south of the peninsula, or, failing that, oil from Iberia or Dalmatia. Any citizen who planted a certain number of acres with olives was excused military service. Olive oil was liquid gold long before fuel oil came to be described as black gold.

At the time of the Renaissance, Spanish and Portuguese caravels exported olive saplings to the Americas. South Africa and Australia began growing olives when their own turn to be colonized came. Henceforward olives could be found growing anywhere between 25 and 45 degrees latitude in either hemisphere, but preferably near the sea, where the wild olive with its russet foliage has grown since time immemorial.

The Dietary History of Olive Oil

'The Mediterranean ends where the olive ceases to grow', said Georges Duhamel, and much the same is true of dietary custom. The idea of Mediterranean cookery immediately evokes the fragrance of olive oil. Jean-Louis Flandrin puts it well in his study of diet from the fourteenth to the seventeenth century:

> The dividing line between the areas where olive oil and butter are used for cooking obviously has a natural basis: people cooked with olive oil where olive trees grew, and where there were no olive trees they resorted to butter ... natural pressures, however, were affected or consolidated by religious regulations.

As we have seen, the use of butter and olive oil respectively was stoutly defended. The matter was, and still is, almost a cultural precept. Lenten fasting was a problem

Picking olives in Tunisia: drawing by E. Girardet, 1884. Growing olives, traditional in North Africa ever since the Roman conquest, was a family activity. The olive groves of Tunisia, originally planted to induce unruly nomads to settle down, provided the entire Roman Empire with its supplies for centuries.

to the supporters of butter, whereas even in ancient times doctors correctly enough 'attributed all kinds of virtues, for instance against chills, worms and poisons ... to virgin olive oil' (Jean-Louis Flandrin). The characteristic flavour of olive oil and its high price could deter people (such as King René) north of the Loire and the Alps from using it for frying, and frying was a favourite way of cooking in those times, although, like Ronsard, they would still be willing to go to the expense of virgin oil for salads of boiled meat or lettuces. The poet liked his raw salads dressed with Provençal oil, while Montaigne spoke of 'the excellence of Italian oil'.

English cookery books from the end of the Middle Ages to the late Renaissance seldom specified that the oil used in their recipes should be olive oil. That could be either because the use of olive oil was taken for granted, or because the writers dared not be explicit about the nature of the oil. There was a considerable risk in London, Paris or Bruges of encountering blends with nothing virgin about them but their name; they should have been described simply as frying oils, and subsequent regulations ensured that they were. These oils, extracted from olive oilcake or poppy seed and rechristened, probably lay behind an English saying of the time of the Hundred Years' War – 'as brown as oil'.

The oil from olive oilcake used in London came straight from Languedoc in goatskin bottles, which would have made it smell even stronger. An English traveller in the time of Henri IV of France, Thomas Platter, claims to have heard in Montpellier that this oil, from a third pressing, was expressly intended for export. The natives of its area of production kept the best oil for themselves, and no doubt enjoyed it, but the English distrust of oil in cooking may be laid partly at their door.

The merchants of Flanders, Alsace-Lorraine and Burgundy used to adulterate poppyseed oil or linseed oil from locally grown flax with oil of turpentine before labelling it 'olive oil'. It is obvious why the people of Northern Europe hoped at best for a colourless, flavourless and cheap oil to help their Lenten fare down. Such hopes were finally fulfilled in the twentieth century.

> If you wish to acquire a genuine taste for oil you must live in that vast forest of olive groves lying end to end which stretches from the north side of the Esterel and Les Maures to Vercors. There, and only there, can you learn how to appreciate it. People in towns are not used to excellence. Everything there is mediocre, and the best oil is accurately described as tasteless.

That was Jean Giono's opinion.

However, as Jean-Louis Flandrin also points out, medieval Europe ate less fat than we suppose. Indeed, very little at all was used in cooking, even by the rich who used spices lavishly. It must have been a matter of taste. The fact that production of both oil and butter seems to have been quite low in the south and north alike was not necessarily just the result of low yields from still elementary techniques, but was also because demand rose only in line with demographic growth between the dawn of the Renaissance and the early stages of the French Revolution.

The lack of demand for olive oil north of the Loire confirms if it does not entirely explain that observation. In any case olive oil was a luxury product because of the expense of manufacturing and transporting it. Nor was medieval Provence as thickly planted with olive groves as popular mythology would have us believe.

In Italy, on the other hand, the rich merchants of big cities fostered the brand image of their products, with the export trade in mind, and encouraged the planting of olives on their estates, although at first only in the proportion of one olive tree to every seven vines. The comparative profit from growing olives or vines evened out in the course of time, largely because the olive trees were very well cared for, and grew. An olive tree will not give a crop for seven years after planting. But gradually the quantity and quality of Italian olive groves rose. Fourteenth-century Tuscany was an example. Tuscans and bankers are often thought of in the same breath, and bankers will seek investments, long-term investments included.

Had olive-growing in Provence and the Mediterranean areas of the Languedoc declined since the Gallo-Roman epoch, or even since the heyday of the great monastic estates such as that of Saint-Victor at Marseilles? There are no statistics or studies such as exist in the history of wine-growing to prove it. But, in any case, arable land and vineyards seemed to promise a quicker profit, needing less effort and preparation before a harvest could be gathered. Similar problems crop up today.

On the other hand, after the second half of the Middle Ages people in towns took to eating more meat, and the large flocks of sheep and goats in the South of France damaged the olive trees, nibbling their trunks and lower branches. Tired of lodging fruitless complaints against careless shepherds, the growers gave up cultivating olives instead.

Olive oil did not recover its former liquid gold quality until the time of what Guy Fourquin has called the 'agricultural convalescence'[1] of France, between the late fifteenth and the late sixteenth centuries, when the South of France tended to lag behind the Parisian basin and the south-west.

The revival of olive-growing was reflected in 1500 and 1560 by successive doublings of the decimal rents collected in two parishes in the Narbonne area, Gruissan and Moussan.[2] Olive groves were planted on fallow land, which would then yield a profit, even a double profit, since wheat and barley would grow well and ripen fully in the light shade of the olives. The trees themselves benefit from the ploughing and fertilizing of the land. Provençals, who like to believe that all their traditions go back to time immemorial, are unwilling to accept this. However, medieval Provence, rich in olives only near the sea – even in 1878 Mistral mentions a strip extending only 25 leagues inland from Marseilles[3] – kept most of the oil it produced for national and international trade, and though it could not be called butter country it moderated its use of olive oil as far as possible.

Louis Stouffe,[4] who has studied administrative accounts of the fourteenth and fifteenth centuries, is sure that if there had been a great deal of olive oil made at the time he would have found it in the records. Researchers may sometimes be suspected of generalizing from particular cases, but Stouffe's economic study of those difficult times is very thorough, and would have disappointed the Provençal writers of the nineteenth century.

> Specialists tend to assume that olive oil has always been lavishly used in Provençal cooking. René Joubeau, in *La cuisine provençale de tradition populaire*, begins his work with what amounts to a hymn to the olive. However, what is true of the twentieth or nineteenth centuries is not necessarily so of the Middle Ages, when it seems that oil was used only for cooking eggs and fish and frying broad beans. Beyond these few dishes – for instance, in soup-making – fat salt pork was used. Pea, bean or cabbage soup with bacon was the staple food of the peasants, artisans and ordinary people of Provence, and indeed of most Europeans in the late Middle Ages.

All legends, however, contain a grain of truth, a truth residing in the subject itself, and while we value olive oil highly now, a few drops seemed enough for health and happiness in those hard times. As the Koran says of the olive tree – for the Arabs too are great lovers of olive oil – 'Its very oil would almost shine forth, though no fire touched it.' (Surah XXIV–35).

Olive Oil in Legend and Symbolism

All the ancient peoples of the Mediterranean claimed the discovery of the olive tree and its uses for their own gods. The olive had general connotations of good things: peace, fertility, strength, victory, glory, even purification and sanctity.

Six thousand years ago the ancient Egyptians believed that Isis, greatest of the goddesses and wife of Osiris, had taught mankind to grow and use olives. The Greeks claimed that honour for Pallas Athene. Although some scholars now regard Athene, the goddess of peace, as only an avatar of Isis, the Hellenes saw her as the representative of eternal wisdom, the patron of the sciences and the arts, springing fully armed from the brain of Zeus. (In Rome the olive tree was sacred to Minerva and Jupiter, the Roman equivalents of Athene and Zeus.) One day Pallas Athene and Poseidon, god of the sea, were contending for Attica in the assembly of the gods. We know that the first inhabitants of Greece clung to the coastal areas until Indo-European invaders infiltrated the country from the Balkans, imposing their agrarian and pastoral civilization. Poseidon, perhaps wishing to keep

211

up with the times, caused the horse to rise from the depths of the sea, 'handsome, strong, able to pull heavy carts and win battles'. But Athene made an olive tree grow from the rock behind the Erechtheum,[5] 'able to provide a flame giving light by night, to soothe wounds, and to generate a precious food, rich in flavour and full of energy.'

The immortals thought the tree which symbolized peace even more useful to mankind than the horse, the symbol of war. They granted the goddess sovereignty over Attica and the city founded by Cecrops and his father, which was thenceforth called Athens. The first olive tree was treasured for many years; olives live to a great age. The olive trees which now stand on the Acropolis are said to have grown from its fruits. The name of the hill itself, literally meaning 'upper town', calls to mind a legend that Acropos, the son of Cecrops, taught people the art of extracting olive oil. Olives cannot be forgotten on the Acropolis.

According to another legend, at the time of the Persian Wars, in 480 BC, the army of Xerxes took Athens and set fire to the Acropolis, where the divine trees burned like torches. When the Greeks came home after the victory of Salamis, they found only ruins, ashes and desolation. But Athena made the sacred tree of the Erechtheum grow again overnight to a cubit tall, signifying, as Aeschylus put it, that 'her people could reverse disasters in the vigour of their youth and genius'.

To be born under an olive tree was a sign of divine ancestry: the nymph Latona bore the twins Artemis and Apollo, the Moon and the Sun, conceived in her adulterous relationship with Zeus, the lord of Olympus, under an olive tree on the island of Delos, which the kindly Poseidon caused to rise opportunely from the waves complete with its fields and woods. Romulus and Remus, descended from the gods, were also born under an olive tree. According to the Romans, Hercules was charged with spreading the olive as he travelled around the Mediterranean to perform his 12 labours.

In the Book of Genesis, the dove sent out by Noah at the end of the Flood returned to the Ark with an olive branch in her beak, evidence that the divine wrath had abated. Jesus suffered his Passion in the Garden of Gethsemane on the Mount of Olives, praying, 'O my Father, if this cup may not pass away from me, except I drink it, thy will be done.' The cross itself was made of olive wood. A story in the Book of Judges tells how the trees one day decided to choose a king, and naturally enough turned first to the olive tree, old, wise and experienced. 'They said unto the olive tree, Reign thou over us. But the olive tree said unto them, Should I leave my fatness, wherewith by me they honour God and men, and go to be promoted over the trees?' (Judges 9, viii–ix).

Moses told the children of Israel, as directed by the Almighty, to make offerings of cakes of wheaten flour 'tempered with oil' (Exodus 29 and Leviticus 2), and during the Exodus Yahweh taught him to make an anointing oil of olive oil mixed with spices and aromatics for the consecration of Aaron and his sons, as priests, 'that they may minister unto me in the priest's office'. This oil or chrism, used to anoint the priest-kings of Israel and thus giving them authority, power and glory in the name of God and the Holy Spirit, gave rise to the word Christ, from Greek *khristos*, meaning, like the Hebrew word Messiah which it translates, 'the anointed one'. Christ was thus the Lord's anointed. Early Christianity practised baptism by anointing with oil (Tertullian, *De baptismo*, 7).

It is not surprising that the Franks, known to have adopted a number of oriental traditions by way of the Visigoths, instituted the ritual of anointing their kings with virgin olive oil, contained in the Sainte Ampoule or Holy Ampulla said to have been brought by a dove to the bishop of Saint-Denis when Clovis was baptised a Christian.

The Greeks, who would allow only virgins or men of pure life to tend and process olives, used to anoint the faces of the dead with oil. This was an Eleusinian rite of oriental origin, and the gesture symbolized light and purity, beneficial to the dead in the darkness of the underworld. The tradition was known among the early Christians: distant as its roots may seem, it denoted something of real and perennial significance. Pseudo-Dionysius explains extreme unction as a rite of passage to eternal peace, while the oil of baptism initiated the child into his daily battle with the Evil One.

Certain alchemists saw olive oil as one of the elements in a 'great work', along with wine and wheat: a bond and also a form of protection.

In North Africa, the ploughshare is oiled before it cuts the first furrow, offering the invisible powers a solar, 'hot' substance in a ritual rape to be made as gentle as possible in order to fertilize the Earth Mother. In the Japanese Shinto religion, the primordial waters were made of virgin oil: the oil in which new-born babies have been washed the world over before being dressed for the first time.

Not surprisingly, since Christmas festivities descend from the rites of the Solstice, the traditional Christmas pastries of Provence are made with olive oil, like the offerings of the Old Testament Hebrews.

> Le temps qui devient froid et la mer qui déferle
> Tout me dit que l'hiver est arrivé pour moi
> Et qu'il faut sans retard amassant mes olives
> En offrir l'huile vierge à l'autel du bon Dieu

[The weather growing cold, the surging sea, all tells me winter has come for me, and I must not delay in gathering my olives, to offer their virgin oil at the Lord God's altar].

Also from Provence, like these lines by the Provençal poet Mistral, comes a proverb: 'Marchand d'òli, marchand jôli' (an oil merchant is a happy merchant).

Making Olive Oil

Growing olive trees and extracting oil from their fruit is still a small-scale or family industry over almost the whole Mediterranean and Lusitanian area. Techniques which archeology has shown to be thousands of years old are still perpetuated. An amphora in the British Museum is decorated with a scene of three peasants gathering olives, one perched in the tree, the second wielding a long stick, the third holding a basket. It is a harvest scene of late autumn such as Mistral and his fellow Provençal writers might have celebrated. 'For the swell of the centuries, their storms and terrors, may mingle peoples and efface frontiers, but Nature, our Mother Earth, still suckles her sons with the same milk. Her hard breast still gives the olive tree fine oil.'[6]

Anselme Mathieu, another Provençal writer and an associate of Mistral's in the 'Félibrige' movement to revive the Provençal language, known as 'the poet of kisses', wrote a delightful celebration of the olive harvest.

> Mai quand soun arrivado
> li frésquis óulivado
> dóu mendre ventoulet
> lou gisclet
> vous tèn li man plégado
> E lou gaugnoun vióulet ...
> Amelenco, argentalo
> groussano e vermeialo
> plovon de si pecou;
> de pertout
> sèmble que l'or davalo
> E coule à gros degout
> ... l'aura de poumpo à l'òli,
> De bougneto e d'aiòli;
> l'aura de calendau
> D'un pan d'aut ...[7]

[But when the fresh olives are ripe, falling with the slightest breeze, your hands are cupped and your cheek purple ... Amygdalines, argentales, groussanes, vermeilles[8] drop from their stalks; everywhere gold seems to be falling, flowing in great drops ... there will be brioches made with oil, fritters and aïoli; there will be Christmas cakes long as a *pan*.]

(A *pan* is a Provençal measure of length.)

The olive harvest of St Andrew's Day used to be the occasion for great merrymaking in Provence. After the trees had been beaten with long sticks, to the singing of traditional songs, the day ended with a celebration of the olive

214

transformed, an enormous dish of aïoli, with day labourers, masters and neighbours all seated together around trestles set up with a proper sense of respect under the trees, which deserved their tribute. When the feasting was over, the people danced the *ouliveto*, the farandole, and sang around the oil crushers

'Au moulin d'òli
dou mas d'Escanin
manja l'aïoli touti li matin!'

[At the oil mill of the Escanin farm you can eat aïoli all morning.]

The *roustido* of Maussane and the *buscauda* of Les Maures were the ritual dishes that accompanied the pressing of the first oil in the Alpilles range of Provence and the maritime Var region. They consisted of a large slice of coarse country bread rubbed with garlic and toasted, then dipped still hot into the new oil and held over an olive-wood fire on the metal point of a cane. The bread was sprinkled with salt, and tasted delicious. Adolphe Thiers, the nineteenth-century statesman and historian from Marseilles and Aix-en-Provence, was very fond of this dish.

Bread or green vegetables dipped in hot oil will make any day a Sunday in Ligurian regions. From Marseilles to Nice, such a dish is called *bagna caudo*; from Nice to Genoa and on to Piedmont it is *bagna cauda*.

Although olives had been grown in Provence for centuries, however, many trees were destroyed at the end of the nineteenth century to be replaced by vines, until the wine from the vines in its own turn proved hard to sell. Today the surviving olive oil businesses again face acute problems of profitability in competition with other, cheaper oils, manufactured on an industrial scale. Lyrical feeling such as Anselme Mathieu's has had its day.

It is very difficult to pick olives mechanically rather than manually. The young twigs are delicate and the olives themselves fragile. Only fruit of the same size and degree of ripeness should be picked, which means the pickers must go back to the same tree several times. This increases the cost of producing the oil, especially as pickers must be experienced and skilful and are therefore expensive; it is increasingly difficult to find them, and no doubt there will soon be none left.

Green olives are picked unripe, for eating. Black olives, which ripen at the time of the first frosts, are those used for oil, although the Romans in their day liked 'green oil', pressed from olives still hard and bitter. When they have been knocked out of the trees and caught in cloths spread on the ground (plastic is used now) the olives are sorted by size, state and quality, depending on whether they are to be preserved or made into oil. For oil they are put to stand and get warm, but they must not ferment. They are washed and then crushed, stones and all. This olive paste is then stirred by paddles in tubs to mix it well and make it unctuous.

215

Making olive oil: engraving by P. Galle after Stradanus (1523–1603)

The oldest known technique of oil extraction was the stone mortar, spherical or conical, in which olives were crushed by foot. Later on they were crushed by hand, with a pestle. Then the job of crushing was done by a large millstone turning in an open tub into which the olives were tipped whole to come out as a paste. Depending on the oil manufacturer's wealth, these crushers were worked by slaves, a mule or a donkey – or even his wife. The *molea olearia*, the Roman oil mill, was of this type; pictures have been found on murals excavated in North Africa. It was still in use in Provence until a few years ago – but, as a woman of Provence myself, I can assure you that only mules or donkeys were set to working it.

Next the paste has to be pressed. To this end it is divided into small portions. The only satisfactory procedure over thousands of years has been to use the *scourtin*, or *escourtin* as it is called by the people of Provence and Languedoc: a kind of very shallow basket made of esparto grass, or nowadays of synthetic fibres. These containers are piled up in stacks of 25 or 50, with a thick layer of olive paste between each disc. The resulting sandwich is mechanically compressed.

A fresco in Pompeii shows a wedge press. Such presses still exist in the Berber country of the Aures mountains. In Europe it was ousted by a type of press using a winch with a vertical axis which continued in use until before the last war, and was then replaced by the hydraulic press. Some ecologically minded oil crushing plants have rescued the old winch or screw presses from antique shops or from

216

transformation into lamp-stands and brought them back into use for the edification of tourists visiting the south of France. The esparto grass *escourtins* – the best, if Mistral's *Calendal* is to be believed, were made by the people of Cassis – are very popular with tourists, who buy them to make floor coverings, and indeed they are now made only for that purpose. Similarly, oil jars from Aubagne or Vallauris end up as flower pots.

Virgin olive oil, called *quicho* by the Provençals, is oil from the first pressing. This is the kind used for the holy oil of Judaeo-Christian tradition. It has a wonderful flavour of olives, and is low in oleic acid. It must be eaten fresh and transported in cans, sheltered from the light, since it does not preserve its properties or keep as well as the refined oil of the second pressing, which is steam-deodorized and has few beneficial properties. 'Pure' oil, so called, is a mixture of virgin and refined oil. The residue of olive oilcake between the *scourtins* still contains a small amount of oil. It is soaked in hot water, pressed, the liquid is poured off and the oil is separated from the water. This oil, of the kind which used to be exported from Languedoc to England, is cheap. Poor countries such as Portugal and Algeria consume it themselves so that they can export the virgin oil they need to sell for hard currency. Cheap olive oil is not worth much.

Nutrition is not the only use to which precious olive oil is put; it is also used medicinally and in manufacturing cosmetics.

Other Oils

'**Oil**, *sb.* ... A substance ... liquid at ordinary temperatures, of a viscid consistence and characteristic smooth and sticky (unctuous) feel, lighter than water and insoluble in it, soluble in alcohol and ether, inflammable, chemically neutral ... In early use almost always = OLIVE-OIL'.
(Oxford English Dictionary)

Though olive oil still holds pride of place for culinary use, there are a number of other, humbler oils which are increasingly used in these economically difficult times, or are of regional importance to a greater or lesser degree.

Groundnut oil comes from the leguminous plant *Arachis hypogaea*, also known as the peanut or monkey-nut. It is of Mexican origin; the Aztecs were growing groundnuts, popular all over South America, long before the Spanish and Portuguese arrived there in the fifteenth century. The plant is curious. Its seeds, lodged in pairs in a fibrous pod, form underground after the flower has been pollinated; its stem then becomes elongated and droops to the ground. The grower encourages the process by mounding up soil around the base of the plant.

The groundnut: nineteenth-century botanical plate

The American Indians ate groundnuts fresh, as a vegetable, or roasted them and then crushed them into an oily and very nourishing paste, rich in protein (25 per cent of the nut's weight).

Groundnuts were introduced into those parts of the Old World where the environment suited them at quite an early date. They were first grown near Portuguese trading posts which imported the nuts from Brazil. The Africans liked this new food crop, and began using groundnut paste to thicken and enrich sauces.

The most primitive way of extracting the oil was to boil the paste obtained by crushing the nuts and then skim the oil off the water. In modern industry the oil is first extracted from the crushed nuts by heat treatment and then refined with solvents.

India is the biggest groundnut-producing country, with a crop of one-third total production (almost six million tonnes). The People's Republic of China and the

United States come next (ex-President Carter's family fortune was founded on the plant). Brazil and other Latin American countries compete with Ghana and Senegal to produce groundnuts. They are West Africa's chief agricultural export; unfortunately the groundnut, though it may seem to invite speculation, has its drawbacks, since it depletes the thin layer of arable soil of such countries, to the detriment of other food crops which it may supplant. This entails serious risk when a country's export trade is in crisis.

The residue of oilcake left after pressing makes excellent cattle fodder, but even in times of need it is difficult to persuade black African cattle breeders to change their methods. The dry haulm is also good fodder. The oil, which has no flavour of its own, is suitable for all culinary uses and can be heated to a high temperature.

Sunflower oil, made from the seeds of Van Gogh's favourite flowers, comes mostly from the Eastern European countries, including Russia, which itself accounts for three-quarters of world production. There are vast tracts of land covered with the enormous flowers in the United States, Argentina, Uruguay and Morocco. The sunflower (*Helianthus annuus*) is the big brother of the Jerusalem artichoke (*Helianthus tuberosus*). Like the artichoke, it comes from North America and is one of the few food plants to have originated there. The oil of its seeds is extracted by the same double method as groundnut oil: pressing and extraction, then refining with solvents. Sunflower oil, which has a pleasant hazelnut flavour, is very popular with dieticians because it is so light.

The Sioux, one of the first peoples to make use of the sunflower, never called it after the sun to which it is supposed to turn. They simply named it the 'seed for grinding'. The Dakota Indians called it *waticha zizi*, 'yellow flower'. The Mandau believed the yellow plants were jealous women changed into flowers, and it was forbidden to pull them up. Anyway, said the Indians, the yield would hardly be worth it – a somewhat sexist remark.

Corn oil has been extracted from maize germ since the 1960s. Quite a lot of the cereal is needed to make corn oil, since maize germ at a sufficiently developed stage makes up only 8 per cent of the weight of the grain, and only half of that amount is oil. This is good news for maize growers, since corn oil is recommended in slimming diets and diets to combat arteriosclerosis.

Rapeseed oil comes from the rape, a member of the turnip family, with bright yellow flowers highly visible in the countryside in June. Eastern Europe has traditionally consumed rapeseed oil, especially Poland. India, Japan and Canada both produce and consume it. In France, the oil was used first for lighting and then for lubricating machinery, and its nourishing oilcake residue was fed to cattle. Michelet mentions its being made in the Maine area as early as 1835. It came on the national food market of France in the 1960s, but then it turned out to be capable of causing changes in the cardiac muscle, at least of laboratory animals. The hearts of consumers' associations beat with some alarm, and the oil was banned. The manufacturers went into the question, and were soon claiming that the dangerous erucic and ganoleic fatty acids had been rendered harmless. To the disappointment of growers, however, consumers did not rush to buy. Time will tell who was right.

Palm oil, from the palm *Elaeis guineensis*, comes from West Africa, as the botanical name of the tree indicates. Its cultivation and production were introduced to tropical America, America and Indonesia from the sixteenth century onwards. Most palm oil is consumed where the palms are grown, and it is also used in making margarine. It comes from the pulp of the fruit clusters, while palm kernel oil is made from the kernels of the seeds or nuts contained inside the fruits. The first kernel-crushing mill in West Africa began operating in 1877. Then a method of extracting oil from the pulp was invented. Small African producers simply pound the fruits with a pestle, boil them, and skim off the red oil which floats to the surface.

The oil palm is periodically ravaged by diseases which spread like wildfire; equally periodically, the economies of palm-oil producing countries suffer.

Copra oil comes from the coconut, the fruit of the coconut palm *Cocos nucifera*, found in all countries of West and East Africa, Oceania, Asia and the Caribbean. The natives of these countries use boards studded with nails to grate the white 'meat' of the ripe nut. This is copra, which they then boil to extract the oil which makes up two-thirds of its weight; the oil solidifies and turns white when cold. It can be used as it is or as an ingredient in margarine.

Cotton has been cultivated since at least the first millennium BC in Egypt and the Indies for its fibre, valuable in textiles (and known in German as *Baumwolle*, literally 'tree-wool'). In our own time it been discovered that cotton seeds, hitherto despised, could have 20 per cent of their weight extracted in the form of an excellent edible oil. **Cottonseed oil** is widely used in the cotton-growing United States. In parts of Africa, where manufacturers have speculated on its clarity and low production price, there are so many small local industries growing cotton that it tends to replace other oils. China, the Soviet Union, Mexico and Brazil have also invested a good deal in the cottonseed oil venture.

Soya (*Glycine max*) comes from Asia and has been grown in China and Japan for more than four thousand years. **Soya oil** is extracted from the crushed seeds, which are 20 per cent oil. It is cheap, is popular in the United States, and is increasingly grown in the collective farms of Europe.

Sesame oil from *Sesamum indicum* has competed with olive oil in India and the Mediterranean basin since ancient times. It has an excellent flavour, rather like roasted hazelnuts. Sesame, a herbaceous plant, spread from the Nile to Japan, and Western philosophic-cum-vegetarian diets inspired by the Far East make much use of the oil extracted from its innumerable tiny seeds. Since time immemorial oriental pastrycooks have mixed sesame seeds with wheat flour. Sesame-growing was introduced into Africa during the First World War. The oil can be used in making margarine.

Walnut oil, widely used in Central France until the middle of the nineteenth century, is expensive and does not keep well, but it can still contribute to the economy of regions where many walnut trees grow, such as the Périgord and Dauphiné in France, or Piedmont and the mountainous regions of the Balkans. It has been popular since the Middle Ages with those such as René of Anjou who dislike olive oil. René had walnut trees planted near Aix, around his hunting lodge which still stands there. The doctor of King François I of France claimed that walnut oil was 'very hot and too caustic'; taking its tone from him, the medical profession up to the nineteenth century accused walnut oil of being indigestible. Expensive to produce because it is made on such a small scale, but with a delicious flavour, it is sold in small bottles and is now regarded as a delicacy. An imitation walnut oil is made by macerating walnuts in a flavourless oil. In Corsica the crushed walnuts themselves have been used for centuries.

To complete this survey, I should mention mustardseed oil from Eastern France and beechnut oil made in forest areas and officially recommended by one Couppé, member for the Oise district in the late nineteenth-century French National Convention, as 'a patriotic substitute for butter ... these fruits are no longer forbidden to the people and reserved for the wild boars.' Beechnut oil is said to have a good, buttery flavour. Poppyseed oil was once made in Flanders. Other oils were made in the past from the seeds of rocket (the leaves of which can be eaten as a salad), and from the seeds of camelina or gold-of-pleasure, like rape a member of the Cruciferae family, but these are only memories now. However, grapeseed oil is a new departure on the part of modern wine-growers.

Overseas, karite oil is extracted from a berry which grows in the West African savannahs; most of this is for local consumption. Oil from rice bran is found in South East Asia, argan oil from the argan, a prickly plant found in the Atlas mountains, is made in Morocco, and an oil is made from water-melon seeds in China.

Whale oil, like seal oil, is a liquid animal fat. The people of the Far North were its main consumers. Western Europeans tried whale oil in the Middle Ages, but did not persist with it. Today the last whales are being pursued by a very few nations, while ecologists are hot in pursuit of the whalers themselves at the United Nations; it is to be hoped that the friends of Moby Dick will win the day.

Margarine

In 1869 Napoleon III, who prided himself on his social conscience and subsidized trade unionists attending the meeting of the First Internationale, launched a competition to 'discover a product suitable to replace butter for the navy and the less prosperous classes of society. This product must be inexpensive to manufacture, and capable of being kept without turning rancid in flavour or smelling strong.'

Although the name of margarine which Mege-Mouriès gave to the product he invented means 'pearl-like' (Greek, *margaritas*), and thus suggests something precious, it did not find much favour with the top people of the time. In 1910 a new process was developed, and the wars of 1914–18 and 1939–45 contributed to popularizing the use of this butter substitute, an emulsion of various inexpensive fats in water (which of course comes free) and/or milk. Margarine thus contains 16 per cent aqueous matter. 'Emulsion' means the dispersion of the aqueous phase in the fatty phase in very small droplets by the action of emulsifying bodies, lecithins, which are rich in phosphorus[9] and stimulate the brain, and of monoglycenides and diglycenides. All of these occur in groundnut, rapeseed and especially soya oil.

Almost all edible oils can be used, including animal oils such as whale oil treated to remove its flavour. Margarine guaranteed to be of all-vegetable origin, of course, contains no such animal oils. The liquid oils used solidify after a chemical treatment, hydrogenation, an improvement introduced in 1910.

In France, artificial colours are forbidden, so the appearance of butter is given to margarine by red palm oil, which is also a source of Vitamin A. Great Britain, Belgium, Scandinavia and the Eastern European countries eat a good deal of margarine, more than the French – not exactly a case of casting pearls before swine, but the French do have expensive prejudices. However, that is all a part of their gastronomic reputation.

Chapter 8

The History Of Bread and Cakes

The Bread on the Board

The Greek gods received offerings of a ritual uncooked bread made of fine flour mingled with oil and wine. This sacrificial offering, known as *psadista*, thus united the three basic foodstuffs of bread, oil and wine.

Although mankind had been eating flour before the Greeks – a great deal of it, first as porridge or mush and then made into flat cakes – it was they who made a true art of baking. In the third century of our own era Athenaeus listed at least 72 different kinds of bread with an established tradition behind them. Aristophanes, Antiphanes and Plato praised the outstanding talents of a certain baker called Theanos.

The flat cakes of Middle Eastern peoples might be raised with a leaven of fermented dough left over from the previous day: Jewish *zymi* were made in this way. The dough was light and well flavoured, but the Jews considered it impure, because it had fermented, and thus unworthy of the Lord. Unleavened cakes of bread, *azymi*, symbolizing purity, were eaten in his honour on solemn occasions, and constituted the ritual offering. Cooked at home on the hearth, in the embers, on a griddle, or on a stone or tile covered with an earthenware bell, the thick pancake would swell to a certain extent, but assumed no definite shape, and perhaps looked all the more artistic a creation for that. This kind of bread was *maza*.

However, from the twenty-fifth century BC onwards, judging by the evidence of tomb paintings, the Egyptians began to evolve baking techniques with results that were both creative and predictable. The dough, made from sifted flour – wheat flour, at least for the rich – was kneaded in large earthenware tubs. Its consistency was liquid enough for it to be poured into moulds pre-heated by being stacked in

223

a kind of oven. The stack of moulds, getting larger towards the top, suggested the shape of an inverted pyramid. This Greek word, meaning 'cooked dough', was applied by analogy to the vast Egyptian tombs, although the original connection between the concept of the Great Pyramid and its like and the stacking of bread moulds is obscure. While the pyramids took their name from this baking process, the semi-oval ideograph showing a flat cake denoted the letter T in the hieroglyphic alphabet.

Once the dough had been poured into the hot mould it was covered with a slightly larger mould placed upside down on it, and returned to the oven. When baked, the bread was the shape of a twin truncated cone. The Assyrians made dough of mixed wheat and barley flour and placed it in large earthenware vessels heated to a high temperature with embers or hot stones. The vessels were then hermetically sealed with a lid and buried in the ground: the bread inside them was baked on the haybox principle.

The first Greek breads were also cooked in the embers or under a dome-shaped bell, but then the Greeks invented the true bread oven, which could be pre-heated and opened at the front. This was to be the general model for culinary use. In ancient times barley *maza* was the staple food. Solon, drawing up laws to regulate everything, even the bread in Athenian mouths, decreed that wheaten bread, *artos*, might be eaten only on feast days. It was made at home in the form of a round loaf. In the fifth century BC, however, at the time of Pericles, *artos* could be bought from a baker's shop. So could *maza*, which was cheaper and long remained the staple food of the poor.

Meals consisted of bread or *maza*, and accompaniments to bread called *opson*. Oddly enough this way of describing food recurs in Chinese cuisine, where food is divided into rice and the accompaniments to rice. *Opson* meant any food but bread: olives, garlic, onions, vegetables, cheese, meat, fish, fruit and sweetmeats. Later the word came to be used only for fish, *opson* in modern Greek, the king of foods. In towns *opson* was seldom meat, which was far too expensive for most people, but in the country you might eat your bread either with vegetable produce you had grown or gathered, or with animal foods you had reared, hunted or most commonly fished. The *opson* was usually placed on the flat bread or the *maza*, just as it is in the modern *pan-bagnat* of the Ligurian coast. The custom persists in the Italian Romagna: the *piada* dates back to a period before the expansion of Rome. A kind of pancake cooked on an earthenware platter, the dish crossed Italy and became *pizza* and *pissaladière*. It was originally a *maza* topped with pickled fish and onions.

From the time of Pericles onwards the art of the Greek bakers lay not only in the mixing of various kinds of bread dough, but above all in the different shapes of the loaves they made, often designed to be appropriate to some particular occasion.

While grinding was a task for slave women throughout antiquity, as it still is in some parts of Africa and the Americas, kneading also seems to have required a female labour force in the kitchen, though we do not know how large a one. The Louvre Museum has a Boeotian terracotta of the end of the eleventh century showing four women in caps shaping oblong loaves while a bearded man, perhaps the baker, plays the flute, no doubt to provide a rhythmic accompaniment for the work, which is done in a kneading trough divided into four sections by deep grooves, useful for catching flour or scraps of dough. The kneading women and their male companion all seem to be naked from the waist up, perhaps to make it easier to model them.

What kind of bread were these women making? Obviously not the *keibanitos* mentioned in a play by Aristophanes, nor Cappadocian milk bread, both of which were baked in a mould. *Boletus*, as its name indicates, was mushroom-shaped and had poppy seeds sprinkled on top. *Streptice* was a plaited loaf; *blosmilos* was marked out into squares. *Daraton*, an unleavened bread, was the shape of a flat cake. *Almogaeus*, a coarse rustic bread, was made in country areas. *Phaios* was a wholemeal bread, and again was for the common people. *Syncomiste*, a dark bread made of unbolted rye flour, had the same aperient effect as the bran bread of today. The loaves shown in the terracotta may be *agoraios*, bread of the market-place, *agora*, quantities of which were sold by retailers. (The Greeks distinguished between the bread-making factory or *artokopeion* and the bread depository or *artopoleion*.) *Chondrite*, made from spelt, and *semidalite*, made from fine wheat flour, were popular with more prosperous customers. Hard tack for sailors was made at Rhodes. *Hemiarton* was the bread of Ephesus, crescent-shaped in homage to Artemis the moon goddess.

The list had better stop here, since a catalogue of the cakes sold by master bakers or made at home in private kitchens would be even longer. There were at least 80 different kinds, including many regional specialities. Some 50 recipes are known, although Chrysippus of Tyana, in a treatise on bread-making, lists another 30 kinds without further description. The fact that this list is included in the treatise shows that bakers did not confine themselves to making bread. There were no specialist pastrycooks until the end of the Roman Empire. *Plakon*, usually translated simply as 'cake', was a plain cake made of oat flour, cream cheese and honey. All varieties other than *plakon* had their own names, while the term *artos*, bread, covers any subsequently specified type of loaf.

Plakon, like most small cakes and pastries, was made with cream cheese; butter was almost non-existent, and fresh or ripened full-fat cream cheese was used instead. Alternatively, oil or animal fat might be used. The mixture was sweetened with honey and spiced. Many of these cakes were made to be eaten on particular occasions: at the theatre (*stolytes* and *artocras*, cakes rich with fat), or during religious festivities. Cakes for such festivals were made in suggestive shapes which, like the false phalluses worn at the Dionysia, were not considered at all indecent. The *mulloi* of Syracuse, made of wheat flour, honey and sesame seeds, were a realistic representation of the female genitalia. They were offered to Demeter and her daughter Persephone during the festival of the Thesmophoria. Crescent-shaped *anietes* and *diakonon* offered to Artemis were placed between small lighted torches. *Kiribanes*, shaped like the breasts of Aphrodite, had no purpose but to give pleasure. The *empetas* was a humorous creation shaped like a shoe and filled with cheese *plakos*.

There were also cheesecakes such as *euchylous* (containing dried fruit) and *bazyma* (made from flour, honey, dried figs and walnuts), but pride of place went to the type called *nastos*. The Greeks also made a multitude of fritters, cooked either in oil, such as *ekkrides* and *taggemides*, or in honey, such as the spirally shaped *streptes*, or in both, such as *epychites*. A kind of early boiled pudding called *thryon* is described by the grammarian and gastronome Pollux: lard, brains, eggs and cream cheese were beaten together, the mixture was wrapped in fig leaves (in the same way as puddings were tied in a cloth later) and boiled in chicken or kid broth, then untied and given a final cooking in boiling honey. At symposiums a sweetmeat called *bachylis* was eaten, dipped in wine, and it was an Argive custom for a bride to give her bridegroom a wedding cake.

Despite their close links with the Greeks, the Romans took little interest in baking until the eighth or seventh century BC. The people never actually demanded *panem et circenses* from Nero or anyone else; the famous phrase comes from a savage and contemptuous attack by Juvenal (*Satires*, X-81) on the decadent Romans of his time, 'the mob of Remus', a rabble with its mind solely on its stomach and the frequent availability of free entertainment: 'Duas tantum res anxius optat, panem et circenses' [It longs eagerly for just two things – bread and games]. However, the bread was often free, since emperors and careerists made large-scale distributions to ease their consciences or avert popular riots.

Having begun as a porridge of parched cereals before becoming the thicker *maza*, Roman bread was originally made at home, and the new-fangled foodstuff incurred the disapproval of conservatives such as Cato. Throughout the centuries purists forbade the offering of bread as a sacrifice in the practice of Roman religion, echoing the Jewish concept of the impurity of fermented dough. The sacrificial cake recommended by Cato was the *libum*, made with cheese and eggs (a pound of flour to two pounds of cheese and an egg).

When bread replaced *maza* the wealthier classes kept slave bakers; very grand people made these slaves wear gloves to knead the dough and masks to protect it from undesirable drops of perspiration and the breath of a common person. The baking of the raised dough evolved through the usual stages: in the embers, on a griddle, under a bell, and finally in a brick oven.

In 168 BC there was a considerable influx of craftsmen bakers (*pistores*) of Greek origin into Rome. They were also millers and baked bread to order, producing much better loaves than the slaves. The Greeks had established colonies on the Mediterranean shores of Gaul before the Romans did. Several clues – the workmanship of a wine-cup found in the Drôme district, other items found in various places – suggest considerable Greek penetration farther inland. The druidic alphabet, the notation of figures and the coinage of Gaul were all Greek. Fond as they were of good bread, the Greeks had trained native bakers to provide for the requirements of their trading posts, and the Gauls, showing talent that was to persist in their modern French descendants, soon became very good at the job. The high reputation of French bread from Japan to America is nothing new. The Gauls, who had already been introduced to beer by the Greeks, soon conceived the idea of using beer yeast as a raising agent: this was the *spuma concreta* or froth formed on the surface of the liquid by fermentation, and the Egyptians had already discovered its uses. Beer yeast made very light, well-risen bread, which was rightly considered delicious.

Around 30 BC, during the reign of Augustus, there were 329 bakeries in Rome, run by Greeks with Gaulish assistants. Although these immigrant workers had been granted permission to form a *collegium* – a guild or professional association – they were subject to Draconian regulations, perhaps as a consequence of nationalist feeling, although it has been suggested that there were economic reasons. This baker's 'college' ended up as exclusive a caste as any in India. A baker's son became a baker and could not follow any other profession, even if he married outside. One famous baker, Vergilius Eurysaces, had a monument of almost royal magnificence raised to him after his death, and it stands to this day, but his son was not allowed to enter the priesthood, the law or even the army. A baker had to save the Republic or the Empire before he was granted the right to sit in the Senate, in which case he would resign from the college and cede all his possessions to it.

However, resignations were not common in the college of *pistores*, since like other such guilds it paid suitable homage to the tutelary god who had granted the requisite talents. It was mainly a professional organization, of course, but there were certain initiatory rites, and it guaranteed the professional and moral probity of its members. Besides the religious ritual of college meetings, there was a sign language known only to the initiates: tokens and passwords which protected trade secrets. Great solidarity united the members of the *collegium*, and one can see the restriction of bakers to their own social group as simply the price of an honour ratifying the dignity of their trade, 700 years after the first *collegia* had been set up by the legendary King Numa Pompilius.

Eurysaces' monument has a frieze showing all the stages of bread-making, after the manner of a strip cartoon. For its time, the process seems remarkably modern, from the delivery of the wheat to the sale of the bread. The grain is shown being ground in a stone mill not unlike a huge vegetable mill of the kind found in kitchens today. The stone turning inside the mill and crushing the grain against the sides is worked by a horse, not by slaves. The frieze shows round loaves being shaped after kneading in a kind of mixer, also worked by a horse. They were then cooked in a brick bakehouse. The tomb of this enlightened entrepreneur provides a good deal of information, and two features are especially striking: first, the evidence of a form of mechanization, with the energy provided by horses, and second, the fact that the customers in the shop are all men, either slaves or free, but in any case of the supposedly stronger sex. This apparent sexism is not a personal statement by the architect of the monument, but reflects custom. As we shall see, women did not do the shopping, particularly not women who belonged, in the literal sense of the word, to families prosperous enough to buy their bread from Eurysaces. In contrast to the Greek custom, women never made bread either, except among the very lowest classes (and only the very lowest of the low did not keep one or two slaves as wretched as their masters). There were no women members of the *collegium*, although women were found in the colleges of greengrocers, vendors of clothing, and even tavern-keepers. Bread was a masculine business.

Roman bread was usually round, the tops of the loaves being shaped in many different ways, just as there were many different kinds of dough. A batch of loaves abandoned when the volcano erupted is one of the more touching discoveries at Pompeii. The loaves, weighing a pound each and shaped like eight-petalled flowers, in the same way as some modern Sicilian loaves, had been carbonized in their hermetically sealed oven. While the *siligineus*, made of fine wheaten flour, had a soft crumb which was much liked by patricians, loaves described as *plebeius* or *sordidus* and made of coarse mixed flour that had hardly been bolted at all filled more plebeian stomachs. *Ostrearius*, oyster bread, was eaten with oysters at banquets. Picenum bread, which contained dried fruit, was cooked in earthenware moulds designed to be used once only and broken to get the bread out. It was eaten soaked in milk sweetened with honey.

Roman cakes included a confection of flaky pastry of the modern Arab kind. It was stretched out thin in separate sheets and contained cheese and honey. Being intended to please – *placenda est* – it soon acquired the name of *placenta*. In modern times the word placenta has a different meaning, deriving from the shape of this flat cake. The dough of the *placenta* was also used to make cakes called *scriblita*, *spira* and *spherita*, shaped in ways corresponding to their names. Fritters were even more popular than in Athens.

The wedding cake, which we have already encountered in ancient Greece, was not made by the bride's own fair hands in Rome. Called a *confarreatio*, it was presented by the bridal couple as a pair, and was a cake of spelt wheat flour solemnly offered to Jupiter Capitoline in the presence of the Grand Pontiff and the priest serving the god, the *flamen dialis* who tended the flame on which the cake burned. The sacrifice marked the fact that the woman was placed under the *manus* (jurisdiction) of the man, and was evidence that the marriage was legal and sacred, like the declarations of willingness to cohabit made by bride and groom as 'Gaia' and 'Gaius'. Under Tiberius the custom of burning the cake lapsed, and the formalities and nuptial rites were changed. But eventually, and particularly after the eighteenth century, the wedding cake, now as a very fancy confection, became a part of European marriage customs again, no longer burned but shared among the wedding party. We shall be tasting traditional cakes later.

The Gauls of Roman times had proved skilful bakers; the Gallo-Romans of a slightly later date usually made bread at home, in an oven or in the embers. Bread was the basis of a meal in the cereal-growing land of Gaul, even more than in Greece. The high-quality flour from spelt (*arinca* in the Celtic language) made a round and very soft white loaf. However, texts or carved inscriptions relating to bread-making of this period are very rare: there is just one funerary stele at Narbonne. A hollow stone mould for baking cakes has been found at Sens, with engraved ornamentation on the inside including an inscription which some people think was the pastrycook's trademark. Otherwise we have only some representations of vendors (rather than bakers) offering their customers round cakes, sometimes with their tops marked out in diamonds or circles, and strung on a cord. One such scene, now in Dijon Museum, shows a vendor of pastries offering small items of some kind made into garlands for sale. These may be sweetmeats, but it is impossible to identify them, or be sure just what the customer is choosing from one of the six dishes shown.

In the early days of Christianity barley bread seems to have been considered a food suitable for religious penance or legal punishment. St Patroclus, a third-century French saint from Troyes, subsisted on barley bread dipped in water and sprinkled with salt. He was anticipating the soup which was to become a staple item of the European diet from the Dark Ages onwards: a slice of bread at the bottom of a bowl, with broth or soup made in a pot poured on to it. The word *suppa*, from Frankish, was used in Low Latin and has kept its original sense in Dutch *sopen*, to soak, cognate with English 'sop'. Soup poured over pieces of bread is popular in France: *garbure*, made of cabbage, bacon and preserved goose is one such example, so is French onion soup and the cabbage soup immortalized by René Fallet.

Bread soon became part of the standard table setting. From the Dark Ages to the Renaissance a thick slice of bread, known as a trencher and sometimes laid on a kind of wooden plate which could also be called a trencher, was the base upon which pieces of meat and their accompanying sauce were placed. One trencher served two people, who thus became literally 'companions', sharers of bread. The wealthier classes in the Middle Ages did not actually eat the trencher bread, even though it was soaked in good sauce, but threw it to the numerous dogs that roamed the room or the equally numerous crowd of poor people waiting outside the door. They received the trenchers as a windfall, for they were much tastier than the hunk of bread the peasant took out to the field in the day (his hot dinner, eaten in the evening, would be porridge). Gregory of Tours describes such scenes, and young workmen waking to breakfast on bread soaked in bad wine.[1] Joan of Arc is known to have liked eating such 'sops' of bread dipped in wine, although modern dieticians would not recommend the practice, which makes both the bread and the wine very indigestible.[2]

The Symbolism of Bread and Cakes

Bread, the staff of life, has become the prime symbol of nourishment. We speak of 'earning our bread'; we fear having 'the bread taken out of our mouths'. Bread demands respect, and is regarded as genuinely sacred, provided by the grace of God as addressed in the Lord's Prayer: 'Give us this day our daily bread.' Until quite recently French peasants of the old school would make the sign of the cross over bread before they cut or broke it. Bread placed the wrong way up is sometimes thought to be bad luck, but once, long before Christianity, it was an offering to the dead, even if inadvertently made: when presented with the top of the loaf turned towards the powers of the underworld, it drew them thence, for there was no eating there.

Eucharistic wafer stamp from Epirus in Greece: these wooden stamps, looking like large seals, were carved with symbolic patterns referring to Christ and the instruments of the Passion—a stylized tomb, the spear and sponge of the Crucifixion. There is an inscription repeated three times at the centre, consisting of Greek or Cyrillic characters which would be transcribed into the Roman alphabet as IS XS NI KA, meaning 'Jesus Christ victorious'—in Greek 'IesouS XristoS NIKA'.

The Eucharistic Host, a pure, unleavened bread, is regarded as the bread of life, but in this case spiritual life. St Martin recommended that the communicant receiving it should meditate on the three concepts suggested by its threefold symbolism: affliction and privation (both material and spiritual), preparation for purification (since it is unleavened) and the memory of our origins ('In the sweat of thy face shalt thou eat bread').

230

The place-name Bethlehem means 'house of bread', and it is significant that Jesus was born there.

A distinction should be drawn, in the Church's various rituals concerned with distributing bread, between consecrated bread and the sacrificial offering of the Eucharistic Host, deriving from the shewbread of the Jews. The bread which featured so prominently in payments made in kind in antiquity and the Middle Ages not only helped to compensate for the shortage of actual cash available at the time, but made such transactions more sacred than the materialist payment of money. Payments in kind, sometimes providing a community of canons or monks with all the provisions they needed, safeguarded the recipients' dignity and their vow of poverty.

Special kinds of bread for Christmas, Lent and Easter, and for harvest and the wine harvest, were ritual tokens of acceptance into the various different grades of rural society or even the right to pursue a trade. Such bread was accompanied by wine, and both might be shared with a man's master or his peers during initiation ceremonies. In Central Europe bread and salt were the tokens of welcome.

Sharing bread in the course of ceremonies or simply at ordinary meals forges bonds which, in principle, will never be loosed or forgotten. Your companions, as we have seen, are those with whom you have shared bread; the word is derived from Latin *com-*, 'together', and *panis*, 'bread'.

A bread poultice used to be used medically for skin disorders. It had its practical uses, but was probably also employed with the idea that there was a certain magic about bread.

In fairy tales, cakes are often magical or enchanted objects. They arouse the interest of an audience that likes to eat cake and can thus enjoy it vicariously, but their primary function, because they are a suitable sacrificial offering, is to convey a message. The cake in Little Red Riding Hood's basket, like the butter, shows her respect and love for her grandmother better than any words can do. The cake in Perrault's story of Peau d'Âne, a version of the Cinderella motif, has the princess's ring inside it, and acts rather like a bottle containing a message cast into the sea: the significance of the cake is that it is delicious, since it was made by a girl with virtues like its own, and the ring within it is the symbol of the marriage for which the girl hopes.

In nineteenth-century Provence girls of marriageable age made Advent cakes. They were put in a basket and then auctioned to the young men of the neighbourhood, who had of course had the name of the maker of the cake they should buy whispered in their ears. It was up to the lover to raise the bidding as high as possible, amidst much knowing laughter. The cake itself need not be particularly good so long as the young man admired its baker.

In Gascony, aniseed cakes used to be distributed after midnight Mass at Christmas. And indeed there are traditional cakes made and eaten almost everywhere in Western Europe between Christmas and early January. They include the Twelfth Night cake, which is in direct line of descent from the Roman cakes of Janus, after whom January is named. Janus, god of the double gate – the gate that opens and the gate that shuts – had two faces and a double mission: to look back at the past, the Old Year, and forward to the future, the New Year.

In all the folk rituals where gifts are solicited, from Roman times on, cakes have been given to children, who represent both our past and our future. These cakes are often anthropomorphic in appearance.

Cakes, as we have seen, were part of the ancient Greek wedding ceremony, and a joint offering by the Roman bridal pair. In Lorraine, tradition demands that the first officially sanctioned kiss between the newly married couple be exchanged across a dish piled with waffles. In Brittany, a proposal of marriage was made by the sending of a cake (*couign' ar c'houlennadec*). If the proposal was refused, an identical cake was sent to the suitor, but his own was not returned to him. If he was accepted and the wedding took place, the wedding cake had to be as big as possible, sometimes as much as a metre and a half in diameter. The people of Limousin served very hard flat cakes instead of a wedding cake; the bridegroom's attendants had to break these cakes with their fists.

Cakes were also shared at funerals in country areas, and were the only concession to luxury at a meagre meal without wine. In northern France, each mourner was sometimes given a cake not to eat there and then but to be taken away, or pieces of the cake might be distributed to neighbours and taken to people who had been unable to attend.

Cakes, in fact, are associated with all rites of passage. In Roman Catholic countries, besides the birthday cake and the christening cake there is a cake for a child's first communion, once a very important occasion. French army conscripts were given brioches … but if I were to enumerate all ritual and traditional cakes we should find ourselves going all around the world, and there is often more than one possible explanation of a traditional cake's origin.

Four Stages in the Development of Bread-Making

Pounded grains: the grain is eaten, from the hand, just as it is, either whole, cracked or crushed, either raw or parched.

Decoction, mash or porridge: the raw or parched grains are ground into a flour, either finer or coarser as the case may be. Water is added to make a dough which will be raw or, if the grain was parched, pre-cooked. Depending on the amount of liquid, the mixture is either eaten or drunk.

Maza: a thicker dough is mixed and then shaped into a flat or mounded cake, baked on hot stones or a girdle, in the embers, under a bell-shaped dome, or in a pre-heated oven.

Bread: only cereals suitable for bread-making are used: spelt, wheat, barley, oats, rye, buckwheat, maize. Leaven (sourdough from a previous baking) is added to the dough and the dough is left to rise. It may or may not be put into a tin or mould before it is cooked under a bell-shaped dome or in a pre-heated oven.

The Taste of Bread

Craftsmen bakers reappeared in the big cities of Europe from the sixth century onwards. Charlemagne, aware of their future economic importance and anxious to ensure that there were enough of them and that they ran hygienic establishments, decreed: 'Let the number of bakers be always complete, and the place where they work always kept neat and clean.'

Bakeries did not yet have their own bakehouses. As medieval houses were usually made of wood or wattle and daub, any fire could rapidly prove disastrous. Bread ovens were built well away from inhabited areas, usually near a river, with water available to put out flames that got out of control and to work the mills; windmills were not introduced until after the Crusades. In France, mills and bakeries were not separated until the early fifteenth century, when running the two in tandem seems to have led to too many abuses and cases of fraud and speculation.

The baker sifted or bolted the flour, and although he did not necessarily carry out all the operations involved in bread-making himself he did have the loaves baked to his requirements in the communal oven maintained by the local lord, secular or religious. The oven was not always near the baker's workshop and often served several bakers. But bread might also be made to order with flour brought to the baker by the customer himself, or by his servant if he were a prosperous man. These customs were common to all Western Europe. The lord's own bread was baked in his manor house. However, for a long time ovens for family cooking in ordinary private houses, and used for roasting meat or baking cakes, were too small to take the large loaves of the period, and the dimensions of these ovens were laid down by law.

If the baker had five pounds of flour brought to him, he had to deliver seven pounds of bread. A German edict of the seventeenth century, quoted by Maurizio, specifies that 100 pounds of unbolted flour will produce ten pounds of bran when bolted for ordinary bread and 15 pounds when bolted for white bread. A baker would often provide poor people with bread on credit, making sure that he was repaid (sometimes with interest) at the next harvest. The extremely complicated calculations involved allowed plenty of scope for fraud, since the customer might hardly understand them. Of all tradesmen the baker was the one who always gave most credit, bread being the last food people could dispense with. Literature and folk memory are full of stories of the tallies kept in pairs in a customer's name, one for the customer himself and the other for the baker. When you bought bread you presented your wooden tally and the baker produced his own. He set them face to face so that he could notch them with a single stroke of the knife, a notch for each loaf, leaving the same number of notches on both tallies. If any objections were raised the tallies were cut short.

When urban housing began to be built of more durable materials, there was less and less justification for keeping bakers' ovens well away from them, and Philippe II of France, known as Philippe-Auguste (1180–1223), realizing that the Carolingian safety regulations were now out of date, allowed bakers to have ovens attached to their shops; like the butchers' shops, these bakeries were confined to the outskirts of towns and situated close to the town walls, because of rats. A decree of Charles VI stipulated that there should be a space between the bakers' ovens and the adjoining party walls, for safety's sake, a practice which remained in force. The space was known as the 'tour du chat'.

St Louis gave town dwellers a dispensation from the obligation to use communal ovens and pay dues for that use. However, that obligation continued in force in rural areas until the end of the *ancien régime*, for the greater good of the lord of the manor's finances. The Paris region too retained communal ovens belonging to parishes, abbeys or the diocese. Instead of owning an oven, a baker might rent one, sharing it with his colleagues. Although there was not such strict regulation of the use of ovens now, there were still strict quality controls on the flour and the baking process. Hubert Collin[3] quotes a charter of Beaumont in Argonne specifying penalties in 1350:

> The baker who bakes bread must do it properly, and it shall be of marketable quality, well baked and made in accordance with the legal standard, which states that it shall be made of the best wheat on the market or within two deniers of that price. And if, on the contrary, it is found to be poorly baked, or too small in size, the baker shall pay a fine of 5 sols and the bread be given to the poor. And if it is found that he has failed to have bread baked every 24 hours he shall pay the same fine. ... And if it is the fault of the man who tends the oven that the people's loaves were not properly or sufficiently baked, then he shall repay the value of ten loaves.

The man who tended the oven was not the baker himself: his job was to maintain the oven, heat it and supervise the baking.

As the staple food, one that was both 'of the greatest economic value' and 'viewed with mystical respect',[4] bread in France was under the control of the most important man in the entire kingdom, the King himself. However, the task of regulating the bakery trade was entrusted, in the King's name, to the Grand Provost of Paris. In his own turn, he delegated the responsibility to the provost of every town. Étienne Boileau, Grand Provost in the time of Louis IX and author of the *Livre de métiers* (Book of Trades), included the corporation of bakers in his account, although it was not one of the 'six merchant bodies' which constituted the trade aristocracy. Both trade and craftsmanship were involved in the making of bread,

'The baker's cart,' by Jean Michelin, 1656: at first bakeries were confined to the outskirts of towns, for fear of fire, and for a long time bread was taken round the streets by itinerant salesmen.

and the bakers were prosperous enough to pay for the magnificent stained glass window depicting the Life of Christ in Chartres cathedral. They were proverbially held to make good money: not as much as the big butchers, but more than the smaller ones.

The master baker had to obtain a certificate of his skill before he could set himself up in a bakehouse and a shop. In Provence during the Second Empire, and even in the early days of the Third Republic, the master baker was still actually called *maître*, a distinction he shared with the master fisherman, that other provider of a noble food. The certificate was supposed to be acquired by the production of a 'masterpiece', the merits of which were judged by the candidate's peers, although

235

in point of fact it was bought from the royal, communal or manorial exchequer, and payment of an annual due called the *hauban* still had to be made.

The master baker was assisted by servants known as *valets*, or in Toulouse *massips*. They were also sometimes called *valets soudoyés*, 'paid servants'. They corresponded to the journeymen of other corporations, and could not act independently of their master. At the bottom of the hierarchy came the apprentices who were learning the trade and whose duty it was to keep their mouths shut, although like all apprentices they led a very hard life, heaving sacks of flour, feeding the wood-burning fire in the bakehouse and clearing out the ashes, which their master sold to make lye for washing clothes and making dyes. They did all the menial labour around the shop and the bakehouse, chasing rats away and preparing the food. The rest of their time was spent laboriously kneading dough, sometimes with their feet tied in sacking. The journeymen or *valets* then shaped the dough into loaves. The apprentices were not paid, although they had to buy their apprenticeships, but they did get board and lodging, and heating their accommodation was no problem, except in summer when the heat of the bakeries became intolerable. These apprentices were called *geindres* or *gindres*, from Latin *juniores*, 'the younger ones' (they had to be 14). The word in French sounds confusingly like *gendre*, 'son-in-law', but denoted no relationship with the master baker, although apprentices might indeed be inclined to court the daughters of the house, considering the prospects of promotion such a marriage would entail.

The bakery: anonymous late eighteenth-century engraving, from the *Almanach des maîtres boulangers*

In the case of a master baker's son wishing to succeed his father in the business, or the son-in-law of a baker with no male heir, the 'masterpiece' was often a mere

236

formality: some very easy task such as making three setiers of flour (about 156 litres) into various kinds of doughs and differently shaped loaves, the number and weight of which were supposed to be known only to initiates. After two or three years of apprenticeship the aspiring journeyman took an oath on the holy relics or the picture of the patron saint of the bakers' corporation. This patron saint was first St Peter, then St Lazarus, and finally St Honoré, who still holds the post. The journeyman promised to conform to the statutes of the community of which he was becoming a member, and swore that his health was good. He then had the right to train an apprentice. Journeymen or *valets* were not allowed to carry swords, or to wear breeches over their underwear in case they were tempted to go out. They might not wear hoods either.

Standing in for the King in his relationship to the Provost of Paris, the officer known as the 'Grand Panetier' (Grand Pantler) presided over the *Maîtrise* (a kind of committee) of the bakers' corporation. His official post at court, entailing responsibility for providing the royal bread, allowed him to pursue a number of other profitable activities. The post of Grand Panetier continued in existence until 1719. The bakers' corporation, like other corporations, was abolished by the French Revolution.

The first genuine treatises on bread-making in French were written by Malouin, *L'art du meunier, du boulanger et du vermicellier* (1775), and Parmentier, popularizer of the potato, *Le parfait boulanger* (1778). Parmentier and Cadet de Vaux opened a School of Bakery, which was closed by the Convention.

As mentioned above in the discussion of cereals, bread can be made only with a suitable flour which contains enough diastatic force to let dough ferment and rise, and enough gluten for it to increase in volume. As Maurizio writes: 'Like porridge, flat cakes and pasta can be made from a wide variety of fruits and seeds, but our bread-eating civilization has gradually limited the number of cereals used to those which will make the raised bread we like.' Except in times of famine and hardship, when bread has been made with anything available, its composition has been strictly regulated by the authorities, to preserve quality and prevent fraud, and to avoid wasting so precious a commodity as flour.

Most flour has been made of wheat since the twelfth century. The price of wheaten bread set the standard of prices for other breads made of barley or rye flour, oatmeal or maslin, which had of necessity to be cheaper. And wheaten bread, except by specific request, has been of remarkably similar quality everywhere – although not surprisingly the weight of a loaf varied according to the price of wheat, though the price of the loaf itself might remain the same. There were many contentious three-way disputes between the authorities, the bakers' corporation and consumers, none of which was ever able to obtain the support of either of the other parties. In 1594 the bakers of France were obliged to mark their loaves for purposes of identification if they were distrained to be checked. The French law controlling the price of bread dated right back to the reign of the seventh-century Merovingian King Dagobert, and was not abrogated until 1981. The price of the salt used in the dough also had to be included in the price of bread. A tax known as the *gabelle* was paid on salt, and bakers economized with it as much as possible. Bruyerin-Champier[5] tells us that only luxury breads were salted in the sixteenth century. Oliver de Serres confirms that statement in 1600, but it seems that the omission or inclusion of salt varied from region to region, for Montaigne, a native of Bordeaux, explains in his *Essays* that while he had his own bread made without salt by his private baker, this did not seem to be the custom of the country. It was generally incumbent on bakers to salt their bread. The Swiss obeyed the *Plaict général* of 1368 which made it a legal obligation, although an Englishman – the English, like the Swiss, being law-abiding citizens – was surprised to find that the French in the time of Louis XI salted their food and particularly their bread so lightly. Other travellers to France made the same comment in the time of Louis XIV. At the time of the Revolution, when the price of salt dropped from 14 sous to 1 sou, bakers were able to indulge their liking for both salt and liberty.

Around 1630 someone had the idea of making a luxury (and therefore salted) bread with milk, made even lighter and softer by the addition of beer yeast, a method of raising dough that had been almost forgotten. Marie de Medici, renowned for her greed, liked it so much that it was called *Pain à la Reine*, after her. Fifty years later the medical faculty frowned upon this bread, but the fashionable *précieuses* of the time would not give it up: their breakfast coffee or chocolate would not have tasted so good without it. Soft bread of this kind was banned under Louis XV: affairs of state were going badly and the people, obliged to eat hard bread, were discontented. As Necker said later: 'The people will never listen to reason on the price of bread.'

After 1650 bakers had almost stopped bolting their own flour. They now bought flour of varying degrees of whiteness from mills. But white wheaten bread took another two centuries to become common fare, and in particular to replace the porridge or mush that could be made of other cereals. The *Encyclopédie*, edited by Diderot, undertook the nutritional education of the masses and informed them that, 'As porridge is not fermented, it is indigestible.'

The Technique of Bread-Making

Technically speaking, the bread that appears on our tables daily is made by the following process.

Bread consists of a cooked dough made of wheat flour (and various additives, those permitted in France being 2 per cent bean flour, 0.5 per cent ascorbic acid, 2 per cent soya lecithin, 2 per cent salt, 60 per cent water) which has been fermented by the action of yeast (1 to 2 per cent).

Water is added to the flour and additives to swell the insoluble substances and dissolve the soluble ones.

The dough is kneaded to obtain a smooth, homogeneous consistency. The kneading used to be done by hand, but electric beaters are now employed. They incorporate more air into the dough and make it whiter.

The glucose contained in the flour ferments, producing bubbles of carbonic gas which raise the dough and swell it as they escape. The raising agent used to be leaven, a sourdough from the previous baking. Today compressed industrial yeasts are used; they belong to the family of beer yeast or *Saccharomyces cerevisiae*, are more active and work faster.

The fermented dough is divided into pieces which will be the finished loaves. They are then put to rise a second time at a temperature and for a length of time determined by the urgency or otherwise of the baking. This operation is called proving.

The loaves are baked in the oven at a temperature of 250°C. In the heat the bubbles of carbonic gas which result from fermentation swell again, and the bread increases in volume until the starch, turned to dextrin by the heat, caramelizes on the surface of the loaf, forming a firm crust once the evaporation of the water in the dough stops.

French *pain de campagne*, country bread, is made by the traditional sourdough method. Viennese bread is made of a particularly fine flour, with malt and powdered milk included. Bran bread has bran added to the usual bread flour. Gluten bread is enriched with gluten and contains 20 per cent of protids compared with the 7 per cent in ordinary bread. Unsalted bread is enriched with starch, and is not really completely saltless, since the flour itself contains some mineral salt. The proper term is 'hyposodic bread'. It does not rise as easily as ordinary bread. Wholemeal bread is made of unbolted flour, with nothing removed. Enriched breads may be sweetened and are cooked in tins.

Our Daily Bread

The traditional image of the average Frenchman is of a character wearing a beret, carrying a litre of red wine in a string bag, and with a baguette stuck under his arm. It may come as a surprise to the British, used to believing that French bread is in every way superior to the standard white sliced loaf of United Kingdom supermarkets (where, however, many alternatives are now available), to learn that our average Frenchman is no longer happy with his baguette. An opinion poll taken for a commission set up by the governing body of the bakery trade in 1982 found that 75 per cent of consumers complained of the quality of their bread. The bakery trade was already worried: whereas daily bread consumption was 600 grams of bread per head in 1880, it had sunk to 300 grams in 1950, and was barely 180 grams in 1977.

Of course it was not unknown for people to complain of the poor quality and flavour of their bread in the past. In 1895 the famous Dr Gallippe said that 'today's white bread is not as good as the coarse brown bread our fathers ate.' A hundred years before, the Abbé Jacquin, author of a work on *La santé*, described bread of the time of Louis XVI as 'a pitiful thing', while 'the ignorance and knavery of the bakers exposed the health and life of the people to every danger. Bread is the staple food, the most universal food in Europe, and the most essential; it is surprising, therefore, that in a kingdom such as France there should be so little control over the quality, weight and price of bread.'

In 1958 Professor Terroine, speaking to the Medical Association of the Paris Hospitals, seemed to believe that the consumers rather than the bread itself had changed: 'So far as the regret expressed by certain consumers for the disappearance of bread made with traditional leaven is concerned, I cannot say that I attach much importance to it when people of my own generation claim that they cannot digest today's bread as well as the old kind. I don't dispute what they say, but I think the fault is in them rather than the bread.'[6]

If modern bread does no harm, might it do too much good? Western civilization is obsessed with weight, and as our standard of living rises we tend to eat more meat, charcuterie and out-of-season vegetables and fruit. We may be eating less bread than before to keep our figures. Professor Trémollières, an authority on nutrition, says that 'bread must be regarded as the staple of our diet. There is no reason to reduce bread consumption, and eaten sensibly it will not mean weight gain.'

Shall we, perhaps, find ourselves eating bread out of a sense of duty rather than for pleasure, in order to stay healthy? For it cannot be said, despite pronouncements by the medical profession, that the three-quarters of French people who complain of their bread are wrong. Shall we find ourselves abandoning the ancient prayer, 'Give us this day our daily bread', for an indignant request to have our appetizing bread returned to us?

What exactly do people dislike about modern bread, the cheapest of our foodstuffs? Quite a number of things: its consistency, its flavour, its poor keeping quality. The national baguette of France is gradually giving way to so-called speciality breads, which although they look good and, despite being industrially produced, have rustic names, are often just one more trap for the unwary in the attempt to exploit people's feelings.

However, there are still excellent bakeries where 'old-fashioned' bread is produced, and where the bakers themselves make a fortune, which proves that good bread and profit are not incompatible. The bread may not look quite as pretty as supermarket baguettes, but it is very much better to eat. Really good bread makes you feel happy just to smell it, look at it, bite, chew and swallow it. It is worth going across town to find it. It is worth more than its slightly higher price. A baguette made with good traditional yeast should be golden, smelling of wheat, creamy inside and full of irregular holes, and with a nutty flavour. It can be savoured slowly, as it used to be, when the consumption of bread was almost a religious act. The other types of loaves made by these old-fashioned bakeries – round loaves, brown loaves, cobs, sourdough bread – leave a pleasingly acidulated flavour in the mouth, and can still be enjoyed the day after baking, when they are not quite so fresh but by no means stale – mature like a ripe fruit.

So who is to blame for the poor quality of modern bread? First, of course, the consumer, who has regarded the low price of bread as something sacred since the time of Dagobert, little as he now feels called to exercise self-denial in the face of the petrol pump or the cigarette packet. The baker is guilty too: he is a small industrialist nowadays rather than a craftsman, and his chief source of pride is usually the neon sign on his shop-front. Nobody wants to knead the dough by hand in a wooden trough for an hour, although it is possible that the perspiration of the human hand is part of the magic that brings the dough to life. However, even if you do believe in magic, kneading by electricity is no sin so long as the rate of mixing is 40 strokes a minute. The mixers tend to go faster, however – and 'faster, faster' is the cry of our times – kneading at twice that rate, 80 strokes a minute. Not only is this mad rush not the way to make good dough, it actually injures the cells. Much the same thing happens in mashing potatoes, and it explains the difference between mashed potato put through a vegetable mill or sieve by hand and mashed potato made with an electric mixer, when the pulp of the potato becomes a sticky, malodorous glue because of the way the starch in it has altered. Of course the bread rises faster and faster when electrically kneaded. In fact it ferments too much and starts digesting itself, hence the lack of flavour. Additives also obliterate or falsify the proper flavour of bread, and can cause wind: they include 0.30 per cent of malted flour and 2 per cent of bean flour (and this at a time when we are desperately trying to dispose of a European grain mountain). Ascorbic acid, soya lecithin, propionate of calcium, pesticides, preservatives and bleaching agents are also found in bread flour.

The baker says, 'Today's flour is often of poor quality and difficult to make into bread without additives. It's the farmer's fault.'

The farmer says, 'I have to sow the most profitable wheat, high-yielding varieties such as the English Mary Huntmans or the Dutch Clément. They provide an increase of 10 to 25 per cent in production from the same arable area. At last I can pay my debts and buy new equipment.'

The baker says, 'This high-yielding wheat does not make good French bread. It is all right for the soft breads they make in the Scandinavian countries but not for our baguettes.'

You might think someone would point out that increased production means grain surpluses. If there is too much wheat, what are we doing with it? And there must be far too much wheat, since we are eating less and less bread. Echoing the Abbé Jacquin in the time of Louis XVI, two centuries ago, a baker from Brive recently asked the press,

> Do the consumers know that bread is the only widely eaten food product not protected by any law? Society today seems to think more of animals

than human beings: meal for animal feed is protected and controlled, but there are no checks or protection for bread flours. The state has no control over the varieties of wheat sown, their treatment while they are grown and stored, the way they are made into flour or the baking of bread. We are unable to make good bread because we cannot know the quality of the flour we are using, and you cannot make good bread without good flour, any more than you can make good wine from poor grapes.

Laurent Vielmont of Brive waxes bitter:

We once knew what our basic material was like, but today we do not know the exact composition of the flour delivered to us. The millers are allowed to make a profit from bad flour, at the expense of flours of better quality. 'Pilot bakeries' hold demonstrations faking up bread-making to try to persuade us that acid-based products sold as pastilles or powders and christened 'improvers' for the occasion can be a substitute for high standards of baking and the quality of the flour.

We seem to be on the way towards a synthetic conveyor-belt bread made by robots in computer-programmed industrial bakeries. Most of the Anglo-Saxon and Scandinavian countries have very few independent bakeries run by true master bakers left. Perhaps the day will come when the last such bakeries are classified as protected historical monuments to be visited. As Samuel Wesley said of the monument erected to one Butler, 'He asked for bread and they gave him this stone.'

Special Cakes for Sundays

The bakers of France made cakes too until one day in 1440 when a specialist corporation, the corporation of pastrycooks, deprived them of the right to do so. The pastrycooks had begun by making pies – meat pies, fish pies. Their *pasté de poyres* (pear tart) had a layer of *crème patissière* under the fruit. They also sold wine. Some of their creations are still in existence, such as almond *craquelins* or cracknels, marzipan turnovers, cream cheese tartlets, and cream *darioles*. They also made biscuits, including the famous Reims biscuits; the word in French is used both for biscuits in the English sense and for a type of plain sponge cake, but in any case these biscuits were *bis cuit* 'twice cooked' – hence the name in both French and English. Even flaky pastry, the invention of which has been attributed to a cook employed by Catherine de Medici, already existed in the fifteenth century. The

Romans had known how to make a kind of flaky pastry sheet by sheet, like modern filo pastry, but the new method of adding butter, folding and rolling meant that the pastry would rise and form sheets as it did so. Louis XI's favourite marzipan turnovers were made with flaky pastry. Fritters could be bought from pastrycooks or made at home, like the rather similar *échaudés* and *gimblettes*, a kind of jumble. *Oublies* started as a sort of wafer, like the wafers used for the Host (their name comes from *panes oblationis*) and then became thicker like waffles, cooked between two irons. The waffle-makers broke away from the pastrycooks and formed a separate corporation. *Oublies* were sold in the streets.

With Arnaud de Villeneuve and his 'healthy' recipes, the late Middle Ages saw a craze for almond cakes such as *pignoulat*, allegedly an aphrodisiac. Many such delicacies came to France with Catherine de Medici; they included Italian delicacies such as macaroons and *frangipane* (flaky pastry filled with almond cream, invented by a member of the Frangipane family of Rome).

From the sixteenth century onwards convents made biscuits and fritters to be sold in aid of good works. One convent at Nancy was famous just after the Revolution for its macaroons. Missionary nuns took their talents as pastrycooks to the French colonies. The nuns of Lima had a great reputation after the sixteenth century, and chocolate owes a great deal to the convents. The puff pastries called *feuillantines* were first made in the seventeenth century in a convent of that name whose inmates offered the pastries to their guests.

Sugar and chocolate had now arrived on the scene; from the time of Louis XIV onwards those delicacies became extremely popular, as we shall see later. Butter, in widespread use at least in the northern half of France, was the secret of making *brioches*; the most famous were sold at Flechner's on the corner of the rue Saint-Antoine and the rue Saint-Paul in Paris. *Croissants* came from Vienna at the same times as ices. Their crescent shape was supposed to celebrate the defeat of the Turks in the siege of 1683. It was said that a baker going to bake a batch of bread had raised the alarm.

The Twelfth Night cake, eaten in France and England alike and containing a bean, started in France as the *gorenflot*, a cake very popular at Court in the sixteenth century. It was invented by a monk of that name who made cakes at the Louvre palace when not busy hearing the confessions of King Henri III's favourites. Its dough was of the savarin type, raised either with beer yeast or baker's yeast, of the same kind as the Alsatian *kugelhopf*, which the monk must have known. The guests attending a gathering were divided by seven, and a *gorenflot* was made for each set, in an octagonal mould so that there would be a slice left for God each time. The bakers, despite the rift between them and the pastrycooks, clung to their right to make Twelfth Night cakes. The corporation sent one to the King of France every year, thus bitterly offending the pastrycooks, who took the matter to law and in 1718 obtained a legal ruling that no one who was not a pastrycook might use butter, eggs and sugar in making cakes for sale. But there were such food shortages in 1740 that no Twelfth Night cakes were allowed to be made, even by pastrycooks.

Wedding cakes were now architectural masterpieces of the pastrycook's art, fashioned out of intricately assembled sweetmeats. It became fashionable in the seventeenth century to celebrate christenings with wonderful cakes as well. But simpler, homely cakes were regional specialities of the French provinces, while tarts were a family treat, their pastry cases filled with fruit in season or with *crème patissière*.

The *kugelhopf* was made in Lorraine before it became an Alsatian speciality, and came from Poland with the early eighteenth-century King Stanislas, who abdicated his crown in 1736 and received the duchies of Lorraine and Bar. Sweetened yeast cakes of this kind were common in Austria, Poland and Silesia. Legend has it that the King splashed his *kugelhopf* generously with rum and Malaga-flavoured syrup intending to flamber it for fun, and called this invention by the name of Ali Baba, being very fond of that hero of the *Thousand and One Nights*, his bedside reading. After his death, his pastrycook went to Paris and exploited his royal master's invention commercially. The *baba au rhum* soon became known simply as a *baba*.

There were many yeast cakes and buns and fruit breads in the British Isles as well; these were generally regional specialities, made of an enriched dough that might contain butter, milk, sugar and dried fruit, spices or other flavourings. They included the Scotch bun, various spice cakes and saffron cakes, Sally Lunn (the name may be a corruption of French *soleil lune*, a sun and moon cake), Chelsea and Bath buns, and hot cross buns traditionally eaten on Good Friday.

Gastronomy flourished in the nineteenth century, when the Genoese sponge cake was first invented. Known as *pain de Gênes* in France, it should not be confused with the *génoise* which is a kind of almond topping. Its name celebrates the siege of the city of Genoa by Masséna in 1800. A rather grisly detail is that the cake is flavoured with almonds because all the besieged citizens had to eat before they surrendered was 50 tonnes of almonds. Madeleines, made with a basic batter of the pound-cake type, are thought to have come from Commercy, and to have been invented by a cook called Madeleine Paumier, not, as is sometimes claimed, by Talleyrand's chef Avice. Fauvel, a chef working for the famous pastrycook Chiboust, invented the Genoese sponge and also had a hand in the creation of the *gâteau saint-honoré*, so called in honour of the patron saint of pastrycooks. It is garnished with choux pastry puffs, and choux pastry is also used in making éclairs and *choux à la crème*, and a kind of chocolate éclair known as a *religieuse* (nun), though no one knows why.

The art of the pastrycook has embraced various new introductions, such as glucose, cornflour, and icing sugar, and biscuit-making has now become a considerable industry.

THE RITUAL OF BECOMING A MASTER BAKER

The new baker, after four years of practice, had to go with all the other bakers and the 'maître-valet' ... to the house of the master of the bakers, with a new earthenware jar filled with walnuts and waffles, and utter the following words: 'Master, I have served and completed my four years.' When the assistants had confirmed the truth of his statement, the master gave him back his jar, which he was to throw against the wall of the house, and then all entered. They were given 'fire and wine', and each of them paid the master one denier in return.

A relic of this custom is found in the decrees promulgated by Louis XIII. During the first three years of their training, new master bakers paid the Grand Panetier, as head of the master bakers' corporation, 52 deniers, and at the end of the three years they brought him 'a new earthenware or stoneware pot, containing a plant of rosemary with its root, its branches being hung with comfits, oranges and other suitable fruits in season, the said pot being filled up with sugared almonds'. Later on the fee of the pot of rosemary was commuted to a louis d'or.

The Grand Panetier, we are told in L'État de la France *for 1749, was paid a salary of only 800 francs, and normally officiated only at great ceremonies and festivities. On such occasions, when the King left his bedchamber to go to Mass, the server of water cried three times from the top of a balcony or staircase, 'Messire ..., Grand Panetier of France, set the King's table!'*

In the Middle Ages the post had been more important and better paid. The Grand Panetier's office was one of the departments of the king's 'goblet', and its staff consisted of the Grand Pantler himself, with a salary of 1600 francs, 12 butlers, four assistants, one man to supervise the crockery, two porters and a launderer. This staff had to set the King's table, and subsequently to wash and put away everything used: plates, dishes, cups, linen and left-over bread.

A. Dubarry, *Histoire anecdotique des aliments*, Paulin, Paris, 1880

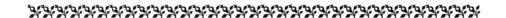

ALMOND TARTLETS

Poised on steady legs
First your poet begs
Several eggs.
Froth them to a mousse,
And then introduce
Lemon juice.
Shimmering like silk,
Aromatic milk
Of almonds will
come next, and next prepare
Pastry light as air
To coat with care
Each pretty pastry mould.
Which sweetly will enfold
The liquid gold.
Smile, a father, fond,
Wave your fiery wand,
Bake till blond.
Melting mouths and hearts,
Mmmmmm, saliva starts –
Almond tarts.

Edmond Rostand (1868–1918) *Cyrano de Bergerac*, Act II (translated by Anthony Burgess)

Chapter 9

The History of Wine

From the Vine to Wine

> Aujourd'hui, l'espace est splendide.
> Sans mors, sans éperon, sans bride,
> Partons à cheval sur le vin,
> Pour un ciel féerique et divin.[1]

[Space is magnificent today. Riding without bit, spur or bridle, mounted on wine, let us set out for a magical and divine heaven.]

The Greeks did not actually invent wine. They did even better: in making the god Dionysus its patron, they immortalized it.

We do not know the precise geographical origin of the grapevine, *Vitis vinifera*, 'the vine that bears wine', or rather bears the grapes from which wine can be made. It is generally thought to have come from the southern Caucasus, situated between Turkey, Armenia and Iran. This is more or less where Noah, famous as the first of all drunkards, is supposed to have landed his ark after the Flood: a pleasing coincidence. If the findings of Soviet scientists are to be believed, the bases of some jars of considerable diameter containing fossilized wine lees have been found in the Mount Ararat region near traces of wood – acacia wood, not wood from the cedars of Lebanon – which may once have been part of a large ship.

However, the grapevine was already growing in Western Europe during the Miocene, the third epoch of the Tertiary period, when monkeys first made their appearance in Africa. The impression of vine leaves has been found in the tufa rock near Montpellier, much to the satisfaction of the wine-growers of the Hérault area. The pips of grapes of a pre-*vinifera* vine have been found on many Mesolithic sites such as that at Castiona outside Parma. Vines in their wild state grew all over the central part of the northern hemisphere, a temperate zone which was divided when the continents drifted apart. The vines that continued growing in America evolved towards the species *labrusca*, or fox grape, the fruits of which have a taste, or rather an odour, of fox. This wild, phylloxera-resistant vine was to be used as a grafting stock in the late nineteenth century. In America, Europe and Asia alike, the wild vine is a robust creeper which clambers up trees.

The grapevine was domesticated when the wild pre-*vinifera* species was propagated by cuttings. Selection over the centuries helped a number of different varieties to emerge. They included Pinot Noir and Chardonnay, the main grape varieties of Burgundy; Riesling, the grape variety of the wines of Alsace and the Rhineland; Cabernet, the Bordeaux grape; Kardaka, from which the wines of Hungary and Romania are made; Nebbiolo, the grape of such North Italian wines as Barolo and Gattinara; Grenache, the variety used in the making of many wines of the South of France and of California; Groslot, which makes the wines of the Loire; etc. Clones or cuttings of hybrid vine-stocks raised from seed could also have been taken. The practice of grafting dates back to the Roman era.

But the soil – the cradle in which the vine lay, surrounded by fairy godmothers, each bringing her own blessing – was also extremely important. 'A secret alchemy brings out every least virtue of the soil, composing a matchless elixir', said Maurice Constantin-Weyer[2] in one of the best books ever written on the subject of wine – and there is no shortage of wine books. Other gifts to the vine, as well as the nature of the soil and the climate, are the slope of the vineyard, its altitude (never above 300 metres) and the amount of sunshine it gets, and those gifts are generously returned. 'The majesty of the setting sun fills wines with purple and gold, as if entrusting to them the task of describing it', Constantin-Weyer continues, going on to say that 'the influences which rule the vine are so subtle that the slopes of Vosne-Romanée, Chambolle-Musigny and Clos Vougeot, planted with the same Pinot grape, produce wines of such distinct personality that no gourmet … could mistake one for the other. The Cabernet grape gives both Médoc and red Graves.'

Grapes are also eaten as a fresh fruit. Those which make the best wine are not necessarily good dessert grapes; it all depends on the characteristics of different grape varieties. Wine grapes need to produce close-packed, juicy bunches, giving a must of good quality. The best dessert grapes grow in looser bunches, with an intensely fresh, juicy flavour to caress the throat. According to a Greek myth, Dionysus transformed himself into a bunch of grapes to seduce Erigone. She later hanged herself beside the tomb of her father Icarius, the first person in Attica to welcome the new god and introduce the drinking of wine. The people of Attica drank too much, became intoxicated, thought they had been poisoned, and killed the unfortunate Icarius. Such episodes were regrettable, but the dual theme of bloodshed – human blood exchanged for the blood of the vine – recurred regularly. The wise Plato was the first to condemn such violence:

> Moreover, as to wine, the account given by other people apparently is
> that it was bestowed on us men as a punishment, to make us mad; but

our own account, on the contrary, declares that it is a medicine given for the purpose of securing modesty of soul and health and strength of body.[3]

Besides giving wine a god of its own, the Greeks invented philosophy: it was surely no coincidence.

Who, then, did invent wine? The answer seems to be everyone and no one who lived between the Black Sea and the Persian Gulf. Initially, grapes would have been crushed with a stone or a wooden club to extract their juice, in the same way as other fruits were crushed. Cherries were being crushed in this way in Turkey in the sixth millennium BC. However, grapes are much juicier than cherries, and some of the abundant juice – perhaps left to stand by mistake, in the same way as a liquid cereal mush may have been forgotten and turned beery – fermented and had an extraordinary effect on the beverage. That effect was the result of alcohol, present in stronger concentration in wine than in beer.

As various populations abandoned the nomadic life, took up agriculture and settled down – that is to say, from the end of the sixth millennium to the middle of the fourth – the cultivation and exploitation of the vine came down through Asia Minor and into Egypt. Cuneiform texts from Mesopotamia mention trade treaties around the third millennium. The vine and wine reached Crete, no doubt crossing from Egypt to the southern shores of the island or reaching its eastern coastline from Phoenicia, at the time when the first trade contacts were being established between Mediterranean peoples. From Crete, the vine moved on to Greece, from Greece to Sicily, southern Italy, and Libya. The coasts of Provence and Spain owe their viticultural traditions to Greeks of Asia Minor, such as the Phocaeans. During the Bronze Age the vine and wine spread on in several directions, reaching India by way of Persia, and coming to Britain along the amber and tin trade routes. The Romans planted vineyards in their occupied territories wherever possible, until eventually it was made plain to them that Italian wine growers no longer approved of that policy. However, vineyards were planted again in Western and Central Europe in the twelfth century AD, in zones up to 55 degrees latitude north. Vine-growing in Normandy, Flanders, northern Germany and the Baltic countries dates from that period, or no earlier than the two preceding centuries. The acclimatization of vines in Norway (under glass) dates from the eighteenth century. However, in the last hundred years the area covered by vineyards has shrunk again. They have not proved profitable enough commercially. 'Under those skies where the summers were not sunny enough', wrote Jean-Marc Bloch, of medieval vines, 'there is no doubt that their yield was unpredictable, and at best was a thin, sour brew. But at least the lord of the manor and the prosperous peasant could be sure of having a little wine to drink, and, most important of all, the priest could celebrate Mass. For Christianity, a Mediterranean religion, had made the juice of grapes an essential part of its mysteries. Wherever it was not absolutely impossible, the Church went hand in hand with viticulture.' Today vines grow everywhere in France and south of the Parisian basin, in West Germany, Switzerland, and all the Mediterranean countries. There are also vineyards in the Balkans, southern Russia and North Africa. Norman vines were planted in England after the invasions of William the Conqueror, and recently wine-growing has been revived in the United Kingdom; vineyards covering 275 hectares in Somerset produce nine white wines, a rosé and a red which are not bad at all, although some people detect a slight menthol flavour to the last-named, a Pinot. The most northerly English vineyard is at Remshaw Hall, occupying a hectare of land just outside Sheffield, 53 degrees and 18 minutes latitude north; the vines of Latira in the Soviet Union grow at almost the same latitude. Depending on the vagaries of the weather, the yield at Remshaw has varied from 946 bottles in 1976 to nine in the following year. Twenty-five kilometres farther south the Riesling made by Major Rook near Nottingham, called Lincoln Imperial, is the heir, at least in traditional terms, of the vines planted by Roman legionaries to provide for the feasts held by their leader Julius Agricola.

Vines grow in China too. According to texts containing legends about the dynasty of the Model Emperors, around the third millennium BC, vines reached the Chinese Empire from the Caspian along the caravan route.

A Viking expedition led by Leif Eriksson found vines growing in America around the year AD 1000. The place may have been in what is now Massachusetts; Leif called it Vinland. Growing vines there would be impossible now, but the climate was favourable at the time. Subsequently, the Spanish colonists brought vines with them. From the sixteenth century onwards missionaries (demonstrating the close links which exist between wine and religion) encouraged the making of those Californian wines which today prevent Europe from exporting as much of its own wine to the United States as it would like. Some counties of California produce wine very like a claret, and, although French viticulturalists may resent the use of certain French names, Californian wines are often very good. Argentina too produces considerable quantities of wine; again, the vine was introduced by Spanish missions. In recent years the wine-making industry of Australia and New Zealand has also expanded.

Of course each of the great civilizations that arose in the Mediterranean areas of the Near East claimed to have invented wine itself, attributing the discovery either to one of its great heroes or to a major agrarian divinity.

Almost all mythologies (and not only in those parts of the world) include a legend of the Deluge. In the Babylonian text of the Gilgamesh epic, the captain of the ark is Utnapishtim; in the Book of Genesis, he is Noah. Both traditions make these figures contemporaneous with the first mentions of wine. Utnapishtim says, 'I gave the workmen ale and beer to drink, oil and wine as if they were river water.' The workmen concerned were the men building his ark, and they were taken on board for their pains, while Noah of the Biblical ark took only his immediate family aboard. When the waters subsided at the end of the Flood and

The story of Noah: thirteenth-century Byzantine mosaic

all the rest of the human race was dead, 'Noah began to be an husbandman, and he planted a vineyard: and he drank of the wine, and was drunken.'

The Bible does not mention vines or wine before Noah. Vines would presumably have been growing before the Flood, but was any antediluvian wine made? The events giving rise to legends of the Flood (or floods, for we have evidence of a period of tidal waves) took place around the beginning of the fourth millennium BC. If we take the two related myths literally, then the invention of wine was known to the Mesopotamians *before* the Flood, but to the Hebrews *after* the Flood.

It is a curious fact that the major legends about the invention of wine follow on from tales of great floods of water. Perhaps we are being told that water should always be mixed with wine, which itself is mainly made of water – the purest water in the world, the essential liquid passing through the sap of the plant's stem into the juice of its fruit. The ancient Greeks never agreed on anything except that wine should be mixed with water, and there they were unanimous. The wine they made was so strong and sweet and thick that taken neat it would have been rather like

251

drinking jam. There is yet another legendary coincidence here: in Greek mythology, Amphictyon taught people to mix water with their wine. (The inhabitants of Attica before him, as mentioned above, had failed to take that precaution, thought they were ill, and revenged themselves on Icarius by murdering him.) Amphictyon himself was one of the sons of Deucalion, the Greek Noah.

The legend of Deucalion was brought from Asia by the Hellenes, the pastoral people who invaded Greece and settled there. They were the first wave of Achaean tribes that came from the steppes by way of Thessaly, leaving the last of their pastures, which had been turned into swamps by torrential rains.[4] Their descendants combined the legend of Deucalion with the myth of Dionysus – and no doubt there were moments at which they had drunk enough not to be sure any longer which was which.

In Babylonia, Syria and Palestine, the festival of the New Year, annually celebrating renewal after the Flood, entailed generous libations in honour of the Sailor of New Wine, Dercos-Haleius, whose name foreshadows Deucalion. The Babylonian/Mesopotamian deluge was the work of the local Mother Goddess, Ishtar (Pyrrha in Cretan), whose name in both languages means the Very Red; the colour red is a primary and ritual characteristic of wine. Pyrrha was also the name of Deucalion's wife. Very ancient traditions added that Deucalion had a white dog, a bitch (the moon goddess Hecate, Selene or Hellene, 'godmother' of the Hellenes). This dog, no doubt upset by the voyage of the ark, gave birth not to puppies but to a piece of wood that was thereupon planted by one Orestheus, King of the Ozoles, younger son of Deucalion and brother of Amphictyon. A vine stock (*ozoi*) grew from it. It was to the wine made from this vine that Amphictyon added water after he had been visited by Dionysus. Finally, Dionysus himself sailed on a ship shaped like a crescent moon, as was Deucalion's ark. The moon herself, therefore, in the form of the dog, helped to bring vines into the world.

The moon and the sea are important to viticulturalists – the sea is of particular importance to the wines of coastal regions. As Maurice Constantin-Weyer points out:

> Wine-growers have long noticed that the phases of the moon have a considerable influence on bottling. They will not risk a really good cask by bottling its contents at the time of a capricious new moon. They wait until the moon, now older and wiser, is in her last quarter, and always choose as dry a day as possible for the operation. First they assess the wind: if it is coming in off the sea, bringing heavy rain-clouds, they will not bottle the wine.

Utnapishtim, Noah and Orestheus were well advised to wait until after the Flood to become viticulturalists. In fact the relationship between wine and the moon really is a strange one, and not solely a matter of legend, although the Egyptians too thought that Hathor, the gentle mother goddess who was crowned with the horns of the moon and the afterlife, midwife and consort of the old primordial god of heaven, Horus the nocturnal Eye of Ra, was also the frenzied mistress of intoxication and wine.

Offerings of wine and propitiatory libations at the great festival of intoxication were especially important to the Egyptians of the Delta. This festival took place on a particular day at the time of the New Moon, a day known as 'She has returned'. Herodotus records that 'more wine of the grape is drunk at that festival than during all the rest of the year'. Another well-lubricated Egyptian festival was that of the Full Moon, when beer flowed as freely as wine. Indeed wine, a luxury reserved for priests and nobles, was drunk by the common people only on great occasions. However, the Egyptians ascribed the invention of wine to Osiris, father of Horus and god of agriculture. Osiris did not himself feature in a legend of the Flood, but water and storms are part of his myth: he was cut into pieces by his brother Set and thrown into the Nile, but his sister-wife Isis retrieved the fragments of his body and put them together again. Osiris was also a power of the underworld, like Hathor, and Dionysus, his Greek avatar, had power in the underworld too.

Before wine was supposed to have been revealed by Dionysus in Crete (the Greek word for wine, *oïnos*, is from the Cretan dialect) and then in Attica and the Peloponnese, it had been known to the Akkadians, Sumerians, Hittites, Assyrians, Hebrews and Egyptians, who all understood its effects. The land of Canaan was founded by the son of Ham, cursed by his father Noah for tactlessness over the paternal drunkenness. In the future Promised Land, the Feast of Tabernacles was celebrated by orgies, a universal feature in such festivals: ritual intoxication was initially induced by beer, and wine made its mark only later. Beer came before wine everywhere, and it is sometimes claimed that Dionysus became the god of wine only after reigning as Sabazios, the archaic god of beer. He would thus have changed his name along with the area over which he ruled. The famous orgies of Thrace and Phrygia used beer before wine, and when they did take to wine instead they scandalized the Greeks by drinking it neat.

In fact the ancient world did not see intoxication, whether induced by mead, beer or diluted wine, as reprehensible. To some extent it was regarded as an act of religion in the literal sense of the word, creating a bond between man and God, like the use of drugs by Amerindians and some oriental sects to liberate the divinity hidden within every human soul in ecstasy. Given a good head, you could feel the god within you. The Greek term for ritual intoxication was *enthousiasmos*, divine possession. The veneration of Dionysus went hand in hand with a slyly indulgent attitude towards the acts of folly at the heart of his legend.

The Bible, though not especially indulgent towards folly, does not explicitly condemn the vine or wine, which are mentioned a great many times, although the author of the Book of Proverbs (23, xxxi–xxxv) warns against the effects of drinking. 'Look not thou upon the wine when it is red, when it giveth his colour in the cup, when it moveth itself aright. At the last it biteth like a serpent, and stingeth like an adder. ... They have stricken me, shalt thou say, and I was not sick: they have beaten me, and I felt it not.' However, the writer concludes: 'When

'The messengers sent by Moses to the land of Canaan returning with bunches of grapes': woodcut from *La Bible historice*, translated by Guyard des Moulins from the Latin of Pierre Comestor for Antoine Verard, Paris, *c.* 1498

shall I awake? I will seek it yet again.' What the Bible unequivocally does deplore is the conduct of Ham in seeing his father's nakedness and telling the tale to his brothers; Noah himself is not condemned for drinking. After seeing so much water fall he had surely earned his wine. The main target of Biblical criticism is indulgence in debauchery and orgies, and libations to idols are forbidden. St Paul echoes this in Chapter 10 of the First Epistle to the Corinthians: 'But I say, that the things which the Gentiles sacrifice, they sacrifice to devils, and not to God: and I would not that ye should have fellowship with devils. Ye cannot drink the cup of the Lord, and the cup of devils ...' He adds: 'Whether therefore ye eat, or drink, or whatsoever ye do, do all to the glory of God. Give none offence, neither to the Jews, nor to the Gentiles, nor to the church of God.' You may drink, he is saying, but create no uproar after drinking.

The worst insult, because unjustified, was that Christ had been 'vorax et potator vini', 'a gluttonous man and a winebibber'. The Jews had anticipated the Angevin proverb that 'wine is a necessary thing, and God does not forbid it, for if he had he would have made the vintage bitter.'

'Have we not power to eat and to drink? ... Who planteth a vineyard, and eateth not of the fruit thereof?' asks St Paul (I Corinthians 10, iv, vii). He may have had in mind Ecclesiastes 9, vii: 'Go thy way, eat thy bread with joy, and drink thy wine with a merry heart: for God now accepteth thy works.' Wine, then, like meat and bread, was offered in sacrifice to the Almighty, who rejoiced in it. The Last Supper, at which Jesus said, 'Drink, this is my blood', re-enacting the sacrifices of Melchisedek and Abraham, was the inspiration behind one of the great sacraments of the Christian Church.

The vine could serve as a symbol. 'I am the true vine, and my Father is the husbandman', said Jesus, who did not hesitate to change water into wine at the Wedding of Cana. St Paul, suspicious as he was of women, at least believed in the virtues of the grape. He advises his disciple, 'Drink no longer water, but use a little wine for thy stomach's sake and thine often infirmities' (I Timothy 5, xxiii).

Altogether, there are a great many references to wine in both Old and New Testaments, just as there are countless references to flour or bread, and to oil. As we have seen, bread, oil and wine make up the basic trinity of the diet.

Dessert Grapes

The two oldest dessert grape varieties in France are the Chasselas of Fontainebleau, long regarded as the best, and the Chasselas of Moissac. Chasselas is a village in the Saône-et-Loire area.

The improvement of dessert grapes began in the Renaissance, under King François I of France. Around 1532 the King had vines from Cahors and Mireval planted at Thomery, near Fontainebleau. From these vines came the Chasselas of Fontainebleau and of the 'Treille du Roi', 'the King's Vine', as well as the Chasselas of Thomery. However, grapes were seldom eaten fresh at this time. Wine-making was their main purpose.

The growing of grapes especially for the table developed gradually from problems peculiar to the viticultural industry. Until the beginning of the twentieth century dessert grapes were often grown only for the viticulturalists' own consumption. The various crises in the wine-growing industry, however, led to expansion in an attempt to create new markets.

The growing of dessert grapes has too often been seen only in association with the growing of grapes for wine, and it still is. As types of produce, however, they are very different: dessert grapes are grown and marketed like any other fresh fruit, while wine grapes are subjected to an industrial process of transformation.

All the same, grapes withdrawn from sale as fresh fruit are generally sent for wine-making or the manufacture of grape juice or concentrates. The grapes are picked ripe. Once cut, a bunch will not ripen any more.

Chasselas, white or golden, is the main dessert grape variety, and the earliest. Its bunches are long and plump. It represents about 57 per cent of current dessert grape production in south-western France, and ripens from August to early November.

Alphonse Lavallée, a black grape, is the most recent of the French varieties, and grows only in Mediterranean areas. Its growth is vigorous, and it ripens from late August to early November.

Black Hamburg makes up 7 per cent of total dessert grape production in France. It is grown in the Vaucluse, Var and Aude areas and in the valley of the Garonne.

Cardinal, the earliest of black dessert grapes, ripens at the end of July. The grapes are round, plump, purple in colour with sweet golden juice, and the variety is grown in the south-east of France. It ripens from August to early September.

Gros Vert is a late white grape, with yellowish-green round fruits and thick flesh. It is crisp and a good traveller. It represents about 15 per cent of French dessert grape production and is grown particularly in the Vaucluse and Bouches-du-Rhône areas. It ripens from October to early November.

Alphonse Lavallée, Chasselas and Black Hamburg between them make up three-quarters of French production of dessert grapes.

Italy also grows many dessert grapes, especially the white Dattier grape which keeps well for winter use. France imports over 85,000 tonnes of this variety a year from Italy.

These or related varieties are now also grown on the American continent, and imported to Europe. Seedless grapes, bred originally from the small seedless varieties of the Mediterranean but now often almost the size of a normal grape, have become popular in recent years.

The average consumption of dessert grapes in France is 3.4 kilos a head per year, i.e., 10 per cent of all fresh fruit consumption excluding citrus fruits and bananas. At the time of writing, this figure has been stable for five years, but with a slight rise in the consumption of black grapes. There are regional differences, black grapes being preferred in the north of France and white grapes in the south. Households of young people provide the main market for dessert grapes, which are generally served at the end of meals, or perhaps nibbled by all the family between meals.

Grapes can provide the body with some of the water, sugars, vitamins and mineral salts it needs daily. They have been a part of special diets for centuries, as a detoxifying and refreshing fruit. Their skins, well washed in cold water, are rich in pectins and yeasts and have a laxative effect. Black grapes contain a colouring substance called nocyanosis which has tonic properties.

The Technique of Wine-Making

How did people learn to make wine? No doubt by trial and error – or perhaps by accident, as one legend suggests.

How did grape juice first become wine? Certain yeasts called saccharomycetes, which dust grape skins with the powder we call the bloom, will multiply very fast in a confined vessel, causing an alcoholic fermentation of the crushed grapes which derives its energy from the sugar in the juice. This fermentation, taking place more or less rapidly and, lasting between five days to five weeks, removes colour from the grape skins to a varying extent, colouring the wine instead and extracting the tannin which carries the bouquet. The grape stalks provide the acidity necessary to counter excessive alcoholization. However, they may be entirely or partially removed, since they give a 'grapey' flavour which is not always wanted. This operation is performed either manually or with a tool – or nowadays by a machine.

The bunches of grapes are pressed or crushed to extract their juice. In ancient times the wine-growers used to remove the grape stalks and crush the fruit with a piece of wood. Later they crushed the grapes by treading them in a tub or vat, to the rhythm of ritual chanting: a kind of dance that could still be seen in Burgundy and Provence until the Second World War. The Emperor Charlemagne tried to impose the use of the screw press, a kind of rolling mill originally worked by hand and in our own time mechanically. If white wine from white grapes is wanted, more pressure has to be applied because of the viscosity of white grapes, but they are pressed immediately. This is why most ancient Roman wines were white. If red grapes are used for white wine then the residue of stalks and pips known as *marc* is removed, and can be distilled to make the grape spirit known as *alcool de marc* or simply *marc*. Alternatively, oil may be extracted from the residue, or the *marc* can be made into oilcake, fertilizer or plastic.

Rosé wine is not a mixture of red and white wine, but is made from black grapes; the skins are left to macerate with the juice for a few hours before they are extracted. This process is known as *cuvaison courte*, 'short fermentation in the vat'.

It is possible to add sugar to the must if there is not enough natural sugar in the grapes, sometimes because they are not ripe enough. This procedure is called *chaptalization*, and its application is strictly controlled by law or sometimes even forbidden, since it increases the alcoholic strength of the wine. It was invented in the Napoleonic period by the French chemist Jean-Antoine Chaptal. Other operations designed to clarify the wine, such as plastering or colouring, are similarly either controlled or banned in France. The agricultural organizations of the European Community are trying to standardize these regulations.

Fermentation changes the sugar of the grape juice into alcohol by the action of yeasts. Secondary reactions produce glycerine and succinic acid. Fermentation is in vats of wood, cement or even brick, open at the top. Vats made of synthetic materials have recently been perfected. Tuns can also be used – huge casks laid on their sides. Vats and tuns have to be descaled annually. In certain conditions a must made with selected grapes and cultured with selected yeasts can influence the course of fermentation: this is an American procedure.

The escape of carbonic gas shows that fermentation is taking place. It is described as 'tumultuous'. A head forms, consisting of the stalks, skins and pips. This head must not actually float on top of the liquid: if it does it is pushed down and held by grids to prevent the development of an acetic fermentation which could turn the wine to vinegar. Fermentation stops of its own accord when all the sugar has been transformed and the strength of the wine is at least 14 or 15 degrees. Today fermentation is not left to chance, as it used to be, but is carefully monitored, with constant checks on the temperature of the fermenting must. Some white wines are fermented under pressure in reinforced fibreglass vats. For making champagne or Burgundy, the fermentation rooms are often heated, but in the normal way they are kept at a temperature of less than 37 degrees centigrade. Sometimes, for instance in making port, fermentation is stopped by the addition of brandy to the vats.

The fermented wine is then 'racked', separated from the *marc* by pressing. Next it is put into barrels in the wine-makers' cellars to start the secondary fermentation which is the final stage of the process. The racking entails drawing the wine off from one container to another, to separate it from its sediment and lees. Fining, a favourite process with the ancient Romans, is the addition of products to clarify the wine yet further by inducing the progressive depositing of sediment. The products used have hardly changed since Caesar's time. They include clay, egg white, isinglass, veal gelatine and pig's blood. Today such practices are strictly regulated. The Germans and Americans use chemicals. Salt is still sometimes used in the manner of the ancient world: surprising as it may seem, its advantage is that it does not, like plaster, add alum to the wine.

The vats must always be absolutely full to prevent the development of *fleur de vin*, 'flower of wine', a mould caused by the layer of air at the top of the barrel. Any lowering of the level that may be caused by evaporation is frequently monitored. This operation is called *ullaging*, from Latin *ad oculum* (*oculus* = 'eye', referring to the bung-hole of the cask).

Finally the wine is bottled and left to age for a longer or shorter period. Sometimes this bottling is done only after the wine has been aged in casks. There is an enormous difference between wine aged in bottles and wine aged in casks, even when the wines themselves were originally identical. *Old* wine has aged in bottle only. The process of bottling, performed at the château in the case of the great Bordeaux wines and the *domaine* in the case of Burgundies, Côtes-du-Rhône, Loire wines, etc., is a guarantee mentioned on the label. The phrases *mise d'origine*, *mise dans nos chais* or *dans nos caves*, meaning bottled at the vineyard itself or at a specified place, are indications, not guarantees. As for the English wording, 'produced and bottled by ...', if it appears on a French wine that wine should not be bought as a matter of principle.

The Symbolism of Wine

Like bread and meat, wine carries a heavy load of symbolism. It used to figure prominently in sacrifices and oblations – perhaps even more so than bread and meat, since it promoted spirituality, its alcoholic content inducing in the consumer a state of euphoria which might be beneficial, but seemed to border on madness if it led to intoxication. In ancient times such madness was regarded as divine possession. St Clement of Alexandria says that 'wine is to bread what the contemplative life and gnosis are to the active life and everyday faith.'

Nor is it only in the traditions of antiquity that wine has been seen as a symbol and tool of knowledge and initiation. Its usual red colour suggests an association with blood; it is regarded as the blood of the vine. Like blood, it is a symbol of life, and is therefore forbidden to the powers of the underworld. Eternal life is the prerogative of the immortal gods: drinking wine makes man temporarily their equal.

Wine has always played an important part in celebrations and initiation ceremonies, both sacred and secular. Such sacred mysteries or social occasions include
ceremonies of reception into a group, the paying of homage, memorial ceremonies,
the taking of oaths. Wine is associated with love, and one of the characteristics of
Dionysus, the Greek god of wine, may be described as love of humanity. He gave
mankind wine to make men happier, not at first including himself. The legends
about him, like his successive mythological avatars as viticulture made its way
through the ancient world, suggest tales of popular rogues, archetypal figures
redressing wrongs and frustrating the joyless who would forbid merriment. The
punitive, purifying deluges which preceded his advent spared the just, who were
then charged with helping to reveal the blessing of wine. The symbolism of love
contained in wine makes it a ritual or magical drink, either in a state of communal
trance or with connotations of peace regained, while vine-growing and wine-making
are work in tune with Nature, peaceful and humble, in spite of the skill they
demand. We pay tribute to workers in the vineyard and makers of wine by enjoying
what they have produced. We are also paying tribute to Nature.

Muslims (though not all of them) eventually forbade the drinking of wine; we
may see in this ban a fear of the danger its uncontrolled consumption means to a
dogma which must not be discussed or questioned by those not equipped to judge.
But some Muslim mystics, for instance Nabulsi, make it the drink of divine love.
Suf'ists such as Ibn Arabi called wine the 'symbol of the knowledge of spiritual
states', echoing the Biblical tradition which does not condemn intoxication, for
similar reasons. A Chinese proverb says that wine does not intoxicate; it is man
who becomes intoxicated. Man is weak.

In Hebrew the characters denoting wine (*yaim*) and mystery (*sâd*) have the same
numerical value of 70, or universality, the interpretation of the numbers being the
key to knowledge. In Persian the word *dem* meant three things: 'wine', 'the vital
breath', and 'time'.

Wine, the vine and grapes were mentioned in Christ's teaching, particularly as
reported in the Gospel of St John, which contains the stories of the Wedding of
Cana, and the Last Supper at which Jesus said of the wine, 'This is my blood'. The
vine often denotes the kingdom of God. Such symbolism deriving from viticulture
may be not unconnected with the interest and care that monks have always devoted
to vine-growing.

Even unbelievers (or those who think themselves unbelievers) and materialists
respect wine. Those who revere it do not joke about it, although one of its
functions is to induce happiness. Indeed, they make what is almost a religion in
the literal sense of the word, a bond, of its proper use and all that surrounds it.
There is a whole language of wine to describe and appreciate it: the jargon of the
wine expert, metaphorical and ornate, full of comparisons with shapes, tactile
sensations or human qualities, a vocabulary which is often incantatory and not
always clear to the layman outside the charmed circle. It has also been said that
the choice of wine is an extension of the consumer's character: gentle men and

259

women will prefer a mellow wine, while forceful personalities with no time to waste over the long period of reflection which should properly follow each mouthful will choose a drier wine. The ritual of consumption is as important as the value of the vintage itself. A royal cup-bearer was always one of the most important of courtiers.

There are fraternities of wine, not always meant to be taken seriously, but partaking of the nature of secret societies, drawing on the Middle Ages or the Renaissance for costumes and accessories reminiscent of the legendary days of wine. Modern marketing has cunningly caught on to such ideas. Some people even go beyond mere consumption by collecting precious old wines which in view of their price and rarity are never to be drunk. In such cases wine ceases to be a drink at all, becoming a pure symbol – although of what? At this point an intellectual deviation, even an aberration, takes over from the pleasure of taste.

The Legend of Dionysus

Different traditions ascribe different mothers to Dionysus, the son of Zeus. Some legends make him the son of Persephone, the spring, with whom the lord of Olympus lay in the form of a snake, although one version tells that at the moment when the act was about to be consummated Demeter took her daughter's place, thus preserving Persephone's virginity. In this tradition, Dionysus, born with a crown of snakes on his head, is Demeter's son. All the traditional legends say that Hera, the deceived wife of Zeus, tried to do away with the child. He is also said to have been the son of Lethe, oblivion, or of Dione, the oak, a tree over which the wild vine frequently clambers.

The most common myth, however, is that Zeus lay with Semele, priestess of the Moon and daughter of Cadmus, the founder of Thebes. The jealous Hera, disguised as an old woman, advised Semele to ask Zeus for proof that he really was a god. Semele had already conceived Dionysus when she asked her lover this question. He incautiously appeared to her armed with his thunderbolts, and Semele perished in the lightning, but Zeus had time to snatch the premature baby from the ashes, and with the assistance of Hermes hid the child in his thigh. When the baby came to term Hermes delivered him; Dionysus was thus twice-born. Then Hermes, fleet-footed in his winged sandals, carried the child away to Mount Nysa, where beautiful nymphs lived in a deep and marvellous cave. On the arrival of Hermes and his precious burden the Moon in her glory illuminated the sky and a star appeared on the mountain peak. The nymphs laid the newborn baby in a golden cradle, fed him on honey, and gave him bunches of grapes from the vine growing around the cave to play with. They crowned him with ivy and taught him to play the cymbals. Some legends say that Hermes turned Dionysus into a goat to convey him to this safe place, and thereafter the animal was sacred to the god, who kept its horns.

Dionysus had tamed two lion cubs, which drew his chariot when they were fully grown as he set out to conquer the world. He achieved his aim when he pressed the juice of grapes into a golden cup and offered the purple nectar to the nymphs, satyrs and Sileni, who felt such joy as they had never known before. Wishing to dispel the cares and griefs of mortal men, and make them feel briefly the equals of the gods, Dionysus set out across the world followed by his intoxicated train. One legend says that Hera, taking her revenge for his beauty, turned him and his followers half mad. Altogether, there is a wide variety of legends – appropriately enough, since wine loosens tongues.

Dionysus next took ship on a vessel shaped like the crescent moon. The first man he met was Icarius of Attica; as thanks for his welcome he gave him the gift of wine. Unfortunately the people of Attica, having tried it and drunk too much, thought they had been poisoned and killed Icarius. Lycurgus, king of Thrace, was jealous of Dionysus and tried to lure him into an ambush, but he killed his own son under the delusion that he was cutting down vines. Dionysus had escaped by throwing himself into the sea, while the Bacchantes and Maenads of his train tore their enemy to pieces. The god was picked up by pirates who held him prisoner. Thereupon he made a vine grow around the mast of their ship, and turned the rigging into snakes and himself into a lion. At a sign from him the wind played music in the sails, which sprouted flowers. The pirates went mad, jumped overboard, and were turned into dolphins.

The ship carrying the god set sail for Naxos, where Ariadne, abandoned by the faithless Theseus, was lamenting. He married her, and in the joyful festivities of the wedding, celebrated by the Bacchantes, Sileni and satyrs, he flung the bride's crown so high into the sky that it became the constellation of the Corona Borealis, the Northern Crown. The couple lived happily ever after and had six children.

Having conquered the whole world as far as Libya, India and beyond, to the sound of flutes, pan-pipes, tambourines and cymbals, Dionysus wished to take his ease at the table of the gods. But he would not stay there while his mother was still held captive in the Underworld, and he bought her freedom from Persephone with a bunch of myrtle. While Semele was recovering in the temple of Artemis he asked her to change her name, to avoid trouble with any of the Olympian gods who were about to welcome him into their company. She became Thyone, 'the vexed queen', and hand in hand, mother and son ascended to the heavens. Hera was not pleased, but said no more about it.

The Proper Use of Wine

Wine, said the Greeks, is a civilized drink, and few would disagree today. Civilized drinking, to them, meant diluting wine with water. Greek wine, like all the wines of the ancient world, was undrinkable neat, and tasted even worse when medicinal herbs were added to it. Moreover the Greeks, even more than the Egyptians who had been the first real growers and makers of wine, were in the habit of cooking the grape-juice after fermentation, usually several times, to prevent deterioration. The process was a kind of early pasteurization. Wine was often thickened with honey or – an extravagant luxury, this – with cane sugar imported from Asia Minor. By now it was practically a medicine, and it was taken like medicine, in very small doses.

As the cask had not yet been invented, the concentrated wine was stored and transported in terracotta jars or amphoras, which might be as much as three metres high. The interiors of these heavy vessels were daubed with pitch to prevent excessive evaporation through the porous earthenware. This glutinous substance, obtained from the pine, gave the wine that resinous flavour which modern Greeks still like. Contrary to popular belief, however, the wine of ancient Greece did not actually contain resin; it already tasted quite strongly enough of turpentine. Wine for daily use was kept in goatskin bottles or pigs' bladders, which gave it their own flavour. However, it must be remembered that most people led very simple lives at the time, so that wine – however much it was diluted – was a drink for special occasions. Only the upper class drank it daily. The common people refreshed themselves with *ptisane*, a decoction of barley with or without herbs, or with small beer.

The Egyptians, who crushed grapes in large canvas bags, twisting them with sticks, made careful notes on their jars of the date when the wine inside had been made, its type and colour, and the names of the vineyard and the wine-grower. Sealed wines have been found in tombs which are equally carefully dated – to the great delight of later archeologists – and some of these wines were over two centuries old when they were put in the tombs; the dead took samples of the best of their household goods with them. They themselves were washed with wine on the outside after death, and on the inside after evisceration. Wine featured in Greek funeral rites only as a libation, strictly regulated in accordance with the sumptuary laws: a measure equivalent to just under ten litres of wine to three litres of oil. Libations were offered on the tomb. There would have been further libations at the funeral feast when the mourners fell to drinking. Marks found on amphoras which were bought and sold in the normal way, rather than being buried in tombs, obeyed legal regulations. Their handles bear the wine merchant's stamp and even the seal of the local magistrate whose job it was to check the jars.

Regulations safeguarding the ideal of communal life ruled by good laws (*eunomia*: 'good order') were very strict, as we have seen in the case of imported grain. Wine sold abroad was also exporting the fame of the Greek city states. In fact the respect paid to the drink of Dionysus amply justified the strict regulations. The taxes on wine were the result of protectionist measures, as at Thamos. The export of such sophisticated products of Greek agriculture as wine or oil brought a little air into a widespread and stifling system of self-sufficiency to which wheat, wood and metal were the only exceptions. Greek wine, grown on small estates, helped to maintain the fortunes of shipowners and banks in a trading economy that was entirely maritime, on account of the almost total lack of roads suitable for the carriage of goods in the ancient world.

Directly after the vintage season the Greeks began drinking the new wine, much as we drink Beaujolais Nouveau today. It had barely fermented and was almost like grape juice, but very mellow in flavour because the sun had given the grapes such a high sugar content. Unlike the Egyptians, the Greeks did not ferment wine in vats, and consequently they had problems with keeping it. To stop the wine turning sour and keep it palatable – at least to Greek tastes – they therefore had to institute a careful process of fermentation and blending. Success depended largely on the competence of the individual wine merchant. The wines of Zacynthus and Leucadia were fermented with the addition of plaster to clarify them, and seawater was added to the thick wines of Rhodes and Cos. Blending different vintages improved the wine of Icaria – the first ever known, according to the legend. It was mixed with the requisite amount of Lorcyran wine. The wine of Chios, which was considered rather bland, was strengthened by the addition of Lesbian and Erythnean wine. The muscats of Naxos and Thasos, when added to the naturally harsh Corinthian wine, made liquid velvet of it. In spite of this blending, however, wine experts claimed that the wine of Corinth was good for nothing but making criminals confess. Mendaean wine, which was unblended, was said to be able 'to make the gods themselves piss on their soft carpets'.

Wines drunk at Greek tables did not always come from Greece itself. The wine snobbery of the time extolled the merits of wines from the slopes of Mount Lebanon, from Palestine, Egypt and Magna Graecia – Greater Greece, i.e., southern Italy. The ten litres a day drunk by the famous wrestler Milo of Croton was a wine famous in Calabria, where Milo lived; this wine, Ciro, is still made.

Greek wines, so lovingly tended by their growers and makers, were much appreciated by the Romans. 'They are as numerous as the sands of the sea', Virgil marvelled. Later on the rich Italians of the Renaissance had Greek wines in their cellars. The Dukes of Milan were particularly well supplied with them. Lorenzo de Medici regarded Malmsey as a panacea for all ills; the description Malmsey, or Malvasia, is from Monemvasia, a town in the Peloponnese, which gave its name to a grape variety and the wine made from it, notably in medieval Crete. Lorenzo described wine and hunting as his two great joys in a miscellany which he called his *Symposium*[5] (1466), at a time of general enthusiasm for the ancient world.

The word *symposion*, often translated as 'banquet', really means a drinking party. At these parties, where the guests reclined on couches, crowned with flowers and with slaves to wash their feet, ideas as well as toasts were exchanged. Today the term *symposium* (really a barbarism: a hybridized Latinate version) is most usually applied in English to 'a meeting or conference for discussion of some subject; hence, a collection of opinions delivered, or a series of articles contributed, by a number of persons on some special topic' (OED).

Greek banquets had two stages: the first was devoted to gastronomic satisfaction, while the second, the *symposion* proper, lasted much longer. Beer and mead were drunk as frequently as wine. With the aid of these beverages and wine mixed with water, the guests held forth, making witty conversation, often at the expense of absent friends – unless they had decided to talk philosophy, as at Plato's party. Sometimes the games played were not all verbal. Alternatively, there might be an entertainment – dancing or music – a poetry recital, or a rehearsal of a political speech to be delivered next day, not much of which would be left intact after everyone had interrupted. Little snacks were served to stimulate thirst. They were called *tragemata*: beans, chick-peas, toasted grains, fresh or dried fruits, very sweet cakes. The guests seem to have had room to nibble these *tragemata* and continue drinking even after the meal they had just eaten, itself accompanied by beverages.

In ancient Greece the master of the house would open the festivity known as an *agape* (meaning literally 'love' in the sense of friendship) by pouring a libation of wine. For once, the wine was served neat, without water, and very little of it was drunk. Before any of the guests raised it to their lips the host emptied a cup of wine on the sacred family hearth, as the share for the gods, those of the hearth and the others. Then everyone sang a hymn to Dionysus. At a later date the host, not anxious to deplete his cellar further, would merely raise a cup symbolically to the domestic deities, but the praise of Dionysus was still sung.

Once these propitiatory offerings had been made with fervour – I will avoid saying *enthusiasm*, which indicates possession by a god, and if the god were Dionysus, drunkenness; it was a little too early for that – a kind of aperitif was served: wine flavoured with aromatics, served in an enormous drinking cup which passed from lip to lip. This cup, the *psycter*, was the one to which Alcibiades refers in Plato's *Symposium* on arriving at the party, and he was ready to drink its contents by himself.

> 'Let them bring a big cup, Agathon, if you've got one. No, never mind, bring that wine-cooler', he went on, seeing one that held more than half a gallon. He had this filled, and first of all drained it himself, and then told them to fill it again for Socrates, adding as he did so: 'Not that my scheming will have the slightest effect on Socrates, my friends. He will drink any quantity that he is bid, and never be drunk all the same.' The servant refilled the vessel for Socrates, and he drank.[6]

The last cup Socrates drank, of course, was of hemlock, and thereafter he certainly never risked intoxication again.

The lord of the feast, the *symposiarch*, personally supervised the dilution of wine to be drunk at his table. Achilles, receiving the ambassadors of Agamemnon at dinner, told Patroclus: 'Set forth a larger bowl, thou son of Menoetius; mingle stronger drink, and prepare each man a cup' (*Iliad*, IX, 202–3). In Plato's time, however, it was usual for the symposiarch to order slaves to pour wine and water into the *crater*, a huge bronze mixing bowl, in the exact proportions of two-fifths wine to three-fifths water. The heaviness of Greek wine explains the generous amount of water. The end product still had its effect on the guests. Neat wine, before it was mixed in the *crater*, was called *acratos*.

Throughout the meal and the symposium that followed, slaves dipped special long ladles into the mixing bowl and refilled the wine cups, which were made of terracotta or rarely of metal, and must never be left empty. Additional guests often turned up at the symposium: these were the 'parasites' (*parasitos*, one who sits at another's table). The word had no pejorative meaning at first, but came to mean one who sponged on others, paying for their entertainment in their own fashion by accepting mockery with a smile. They were often made drunk by force. The symposiarch of this second stage of the party might be chosen from among the new arrivals. Alcibiades, already rather merry on joining the party, enquires,

> 'Will you welcome into your company a man who is already drunk? ...
> Will you drink with me or not?' There was a unanimous cry that he
> should come in ... he ... made a wreath for Socrates, and lay back. As
> soon as he had done so he exclaimed: 'Come, sirs, you seem to me to
> be quite sober; this can't be allowed; you must drink; it's part of our
> agreement. So as master of the revels, until you are in adequate drinking
> order, I appoint – myself.'

Plato's *Symposium* contains some vivid slices of life, including this one. Xenophon's work of the same name records speeches rather less measured than Plato's, which read as if they were drawn from life. Plato himself – he died at the age of 81 – was a sober, refined and fastidious character who preferred nibbling olives to carousing.

Once the master of the revels had decided on the number of cups each guest should drink, a health was drunk to each man present. The formula was repeated as many times as there were guests, each returning the courtesy of the others. Those who gave up had to pay a forfeit: recite a poem, dance naked, walk on their hands, or carry around the room the girl flute-player who was a constant feature of such feasts. This girl was the only woman allowed at these all-male banquets. Women were formally excluded from any participation in social or political life. Aspasia, the mistress of Pericles, created a scandal by attending the statesman's banquets, because of her sex rather than her unmarried status. From that time on, however, around 500 BC, women artists, courtesans and hetaerae joined the flute-player. They came in at the end of the banquet, when heads had been sufficiently fuddled and philosophical discussion confused by wine. Banquets and symposia were not necessarily always given by the man who acted as host; men might decide to meet at a certain person's house bringing their own share of food and drink with them, but the ritual remained the same.

Plato's *Symposium* (385 BC), sometimes called *On Love*, is a series of speeches supposed to have been made during a symposium organized by the poet Agathon, winner of a prize for tragedy. The device was used by Xenophon in his work of the same name, for it was indeed a fact that the guests at these parties liked setting the world to rights, and wine inspired philosophy. Pasteur once wrote: 'There is more philosophy in a bottle of wine than in all the books.' Nor should it be forgotten that the tragic drama originated with Dionysus and wine. Initially a god of vegetation, Dionysus was an agrarian deity almost from the time the Greeks colonized their country, becoming god of the vine and wine at the end of the archaic period. It was at this point that dramatic representations began to form part of his worship. During the festivals of the Dionysia there were processions and dances of a more or less grotesque and obscene nature, and choruses singing hymns of praise to the god, called *dithyrambs*. The singers and participants in the processions, who were masked, wore goatskins (the goat was sacred to Dionysus) and displayed huge artificial genitalia, to the great amusement of the family audience. The Greek word *tragos* means 'goat'; *tragoidia*, tragedy, means literally 'goat-song'. In the sixth century BC there was a poet called Thespis who came from the town of Icaria, the home of the legendary Icarius credited with introducing wine to the Greeks. He had the idea of livening up the rather tedious choral chanting with dialogue. The new art form rapidly became popular, expanding until it was a real play. Thespis went from town to town with his company in a chariot; hence the literary expression 'the car of Thespis' and the description of actors as Thespians. His first play, the first play in the world, was performed at Athens under Peisistratus in 534 BC. We therefore owe the drama to wine.

However, not all the Greeks liked making merry: the Spartans did not need to attend their communal meals wearing the metal headband of the symposia, which was supposed to delay intoxication. The state provided them with their monthly ration of wine, probably not a very generous one, to the dismay of the Lacedaemonians when the Spartans occupied their territory; they revolted against Lycurgus, who bore the same name as the Thracian king of the legend of Dionysus, the god's personal enemy.

Cato the Elder or the Censor (234–149 BC), almost as austere in character as the Spartans, was one of the few men in the Roman world who drank only water. This in itself might have made him famous. The Roman name for Dionysus was Bacchus. 'Sine Baccho friget Venus', said Terence (149–159 BC), 'without Bacchus, Venus is cold'. For a long time, therefore, women were strictly forbidden to drink wine on pain of death. 'Should you find your wife drinking wine, kill her', advised Cato. At the beginning of the Empire, a period when women exercised considerable political power, aristocratic matrons began attending banquets or even giving them. But at home ladies still drank *passum*, a decoction of raisins.

Why was wine so explicitly forbidden to women? There were several reasons. Symbolically, as the legends show, wine was equated with blood; it was known as the blood of the vine. Women, regarded as being essentially mothers, were figuratively committing adultery by drinking strange blood, even though it was actually of vegetable origin; no civilized people, not even the Egyptians, has ever been as animist as the Romans. Furthermore, wine was thought to be an abortifacient: one kind of blood expelled the other. The four sacrificial, and thus magical, liquids were milk, blood, water and wine. Women, still suspected of having secret magic powers, even if they were only the powers of procreation, did not need the additional magic of intoxication. You may begin by drinking a little wine, but will you be able to stop at that if, of your very nature, you lack that *virtus* which is the essence of the masculine spirit? So thought the Romans who believed themselves experts on the subject, despite their own *virtus* (a word which denoted virility before it came to mean virtue in the modern sense). Intoxication causes a form of delirium which may be prophetic: it was better for a pretty woman to be seen and not heard. Delirium, especially the delirium of drunkenness, denoted possession – divine rather than demoniac possession at this period. However, possession implies violation, and a violated woman could never be regarded as chaste and pure again. There was another fear: who knew if such possession might not lead to the birth of a monstrous child whose father could be some licentious mythical creature, not the worthy *paterfamilias*? Theogenies were full of such tales. Wine, therefore, was regarded as a dangerous drug from which the weaker sex should be protected, and thereby the family was simultaneously protected from distress and dishonour. The Romans apparently introduced the custom of a man's kissing his wife on the mouth when he came home, so that he could tell from her breath if she had gone astray.

Among the peasantry, who still lived the simple life of early Roman days, even men hardly drank wine, which was too expensive, and refreshed themselves with vinegar and water; the Latin peoples do not like beer.

In his treatise *De agri cultura* Cato gives a very full account of the domestic rural economy, along with much other interesting information. He describes the drink rations allowed to farm labourers. At the time of harvest and the vintage they had three-quarters of a litre of the most ordinary sort of wine. Between vintage and the beginning of winter, wine was replaced by the sort of thin drink later called *piquette* in France: a fermented decoction of the new must from the crushed grapes. The labourer could have as much of this as he wanted. From December to the end of March, he was allowed the new wine, but only a quarter of a litre a day. From spring until harvest came round again, the master's generosity ran to half a litre a day. Slaves in chains, for punishment or because their manner was surly – 'vicious', was Cato's description – were not deprived of wine so long as they worked; their rations were in proportion to their output. Add to this the national or local religious festivals, when the labourer was entitled to a measure of wine of nearly half a litre, and the men working Cato's model farm of 100 *jugera* (about 25 hectares) drank some 200 litres a year. Cato writes in a spirit of some austerity, since Rome at his period was seeing an expansion of the Dionysiac (or to the Romans Bacchic) cult spreading northwards from Greater Greece in the south of Italy. A proliferation of secret societies indulged in orgiastic practices or initiation ceremonies which, it was feared, might put ideas into the heads of slaves: ideas which Christianity, in its different way, was subsequently to bring them. That seemed more dangerous to the patricians than excessive drinking. The Senate had taken many steps in the matter, along the lines approved by Cato the Censor, even at one time imposing the death penalty on those who joined in the rites of Bacchus. The army itself, which had to be very strictly disciplined because of its extremely heterogeneous composition, was given vinegar to make its drinking water wholesome: this was the vinegar that a Roman soldier gave Christ at Golgotha.

It was not until after 121 BC, Year 622 from the foundation of Rome, that Italian vineyards really made their mark. That particular year was so hot that the grapes shrivelled on the vines. Pliny, 200 years later, was to 'drink' some of this devoutly treasured wine: by then it was a rough but honeyed paste. Earlier, the texts speak chiefly of Greek wines, which helps to explain why the Romans considered the drink foreign, expensive, exotic and therefore suspect. But now Bacchus came to the Italian peninsula, and it would take many pages to list all the Italian wines catalogued, with comments, by Athenaeus, the third-century Graeco-Egyptian author of the *Deipnosophisti* ('men learned in the arts of the banquet'). The Romans preferred white wines. To satisfy demand, so-called black (i.e. red) wines were bleached with sulphur fumes. These wines were called black because they were as thick as their Greek counterparts. 'White' wine was actually the colour of amber, since it was aged for 15 years in the case of the wines of Alba, and as long as 25 years for Surrentinum, described by the Emperor Tiberius as *generosum acetum* – vinegar, but magnificent and well-sweetened vinegar! The Romans also, although to a lesser extent than the Greeks, cooked their wine and flavoured it with aromatics, thus obtaining *defrutum, caraenum* and *sagra*, wines reduced by half or two-thirds. The wine was sweetened with honey; *mulsum* for aperitifs called for 10 litres of honey to 13 litres of wine, and the mixture was then matured for another month before it was drunk, according to the recipes given by Columella, Pliny and Palladius. Tar might also be added!

Wines flavoured with medicinal herbs, such as *nectaulis*, flavoured with elecampane, or *murtidanum*, flavoured with myrtle, were taken as drugs, particularly the latter. Despite his distrust of wine and his misogyny, Cato recommended women to drink it, although only if they were suffering from colic or gynaecological disorders.

As well as all these wines, of course, Greek wines were drunk, and so were wines from Asia Minor, Egypt, Spain and Provence (Athenaeus deplores the small number of Provençal wines available), Narbonne and Aquitaine. Petronius said that Rome had laid hands on the world, and it also stored the world, so to speak, in its cellars.

The Romans proved as thorough in viticulture as in everything they did. They used grafting – said to have been invented by the Etruscans – with the vine 'married to the elm', as Virgil put it, or to the poplar, for it was still grown as a climbing plant. Libations of wine from a vine that had not been 'dressed' – pruned, trained and properly cultivated – were sacrilege, and so were libations of blended Greek wines. Wine must be pure and unmixed for religious purposes, like the sacramental wine of the Christian Mass at a later date. The pruning hook used for the vine was first dipped in bear's blood. The bear is a symbol of the moon and the underworld, and here the old Graeco-Egyptian symbolism recurs. The blade was wiped with beaver skin, but the reasons behind this custom remain obscure.

As soon as the grapes had been crushed by the well-washed feet of slaves, who fasted and were thus pure while they worked, the juice from the first pressing was drawn off. This was reserved for the aperitif *mulsum*. The remaining juice, filtered through wicker baskets, was fermented in jars (*dolia*); the barrel still awaited invention and export by the Gauls. Ashes, clay or plaster were added to clarify the wine, as in Greece, and sea water was sometimes added; it could be 'glued' with fish glue, gelatine, blood or pitch, so that particles would be deposited in suspension. Unlike the Greeks, however, the Romans never blended their wine.

Roman wine was aged for at least two or three years, and then stored in amphoras coated inside with pitch, their mouths stopped with plaster in the Greek fashion. The use of glass bottles spread at the end of the first century BC. Glass had been in existence for 4000 years – as it happens, it was a Mediterranean invention – but there are very few remains of glass drinking cups. Those of which we do have shards were usually cups for oblations. A small specimen of the third century BC, described as Roman but in fact of Syrian or Persian manufacture, was thus able to fetch the huge sum of 5,375,000 French francs at a sale in 1979. The cups used by the richest patricians were made of engraved and ornately fashioned metal, set with precious stones. There were also drinking cups of Baltic amber or of cornelian, such as the beautiful seventh-century Byzantine cup from the collection of Lorenzo the Magnificent.[7] The fabulous myrrhine glass cups from which the great patricians of the Empire drank were made from a kind of crystal and had nothing in common with the aromatic resin myrrh except its high price. The fragility of glass made it even more expensive. 'It seemed a poor thing to have a vessel proof against shocks', remarks Seneca. As for the common people, they drank straight from jugs or wineskins, or if they were slightly better off from cups made of earthenware, wood or metal.

With the bottle came the cork stopper, sealed with pitch. A *pittacium* (inscription) on an amphora indicated the place of origin of its contents (for as we have seen, the Romans distrusted blended wines) and the year the wine was made. The amphoras were not kept in cellars, an idea that was to occur to the monks living several centuries later, who first hid their wine underground simply for safety's sake in troubled periods of invasion. The Romans put their heavy amphoras on the top storey of their houses, in the *apotheca* or store-room, near the smoke pipes, like the Greeks. Contact at a luke-warm temperature with these porous earthenware pipes gave the wine a smoky flavour much liked at the time. According to Columella, the best smoke came from the pipes that carried it away from the bathhouse.

The ritual of wine-drinking at banquets was much the same as in Greece, beginning with an oblation offered to Jupiter. The *symposion* became a *comissatio*, a literal translation of the Greek term into Latin. We cannot generalize on the amount of heavy drinking that went on at such parties, any more than we can about the Greek symposia. The dinner given by the Syrian freedman Trimalchio, as described by Petronius, is a work of fiction, although it may reflect the excesses habitually practised by the imperial court. Ordinary plebeian gatherings, whether of family and friends, political allies or corporations, and most of the suppers given by honourable patricians such as Juvenal, Pliny and Martial, observed both decent behaviour and the sumptuary laws. The Emperor Trajan, in his villa at Centumscellae (modern Civitavecchia) held private dinners at which his friends, men of good character, peacefully spent cultural and relaxing evenings. Jérôme Carcopino[8] cites the banquet of the undertakers' *collegium* of Lanuvium in 133 BC. The *magister cenae*, master of the feast, gave each guest a loaf, four sardines and a small amphora of warm wine. A fine – in hard cash rather than the obligation to stand a round of drinks – was levied for any failure of conduct or civility.

Banquets were held in the evening, at dinner time. The *cena* began with a libation to Jupiter at about the eighth hour (four in the afternoon) and ended quite early in the evening, but in exceptional circumstances might go on until midnight, as Nero's banquet did. In the night life of Trimalchio's world men such as Petronius and Lucullus sat up drinking until the small hours, and might end the evening in a brothel. Juvenal did not approve of such late hours: 'It is the time when the morning star rises, the moment when generals call for the standards to advance and strike camp.' The revellers, however, would end up so drunk that they had to be carried home by their slaves, even if they had taken the precaution of inducing vomiting by tickling their throats with a feather once or several times during the banquet: 'Vomunt ut edant, edant ut voment,' said Seneca disapprovingly: 'they vomit to eat and eat to vomit'.

While these sprigs of fashion vomited up the surplus food and wine of which they had partaken, belching at table was a mark of politeness, as it became among the Arabs at a later date. According to Suetonius, the Emperor Claudius proposed to 'legitimize the breaking of wind at table, either silently or noisily ['flatum crepitumque ventris in convivio'] – after hearing about a man who was so modest that he endangered his health by an attempt to restrain himself.' At Trimalchio's banquet the orchestra gave the signal to break wind by playing appropriate music. According to Martial, some gastronomes had an attendant slave to help guests use the urinals in public when their heads became fuddled. Wine was valued as a diuretic, and considering the Roman diet that must have been a useful quality.

Guests might have to drink even more if the *magister cenae* had cunningly chosen his assistant for the night because of the number of letters in his three names. For instance, Caius Julius Caesar is 17 letters; you would therefore have to drink his health in 17 cups of wine, and the capacity of a cup might be from 1 to 11 *cyathi* (0.45 of a litre), depending on the capacity of the *cyathus*, the ladle or dipper. According to Suetonius, the proverbial sobriety of Augustus allowed him only three cups of wine a meal, which was not bad going if it meant about a litre and a quarter. To reward Pomponius Flaccus and Lucius Piso for drinking with him non-stop for two days and a night, Tiberius made the former governor of Syria and the latter prefect of Rome. Throughout his relatively short life the Emperor Claudius

270

was very fond of eating and drinking, and might have died of alcoholism if his wife had not poisoned him first.

Finally, failing philosophy which, after all, had already been invented by the Greeks, wine inspired the Romans to coin many a memorable phrase. On learning of the death of Cleopatra the poet Horace (64 BC–AD 8) commented 'Nunc est bibendum',[9] 'now is the time for drinking'. He had already written 'Nunc vino pellite curas' elsewhere, but the wine may excuse this repetition. Ovid (43 BC–AD 18) says that 'Bacchus, lord of the vine, is the enemy of art'.[10] Congratulating his friend Ariston on choosing a grown man rather than a youth as companion, Seneca concludes: 'A good bottle was a harsh, unpleasing wine in its youth, and a wine which is pleasing as soon as made is not a wine for keeping.' There is also Pliny's remark concerning wine: 'If anybody cares to consider the matter more carefully, there is no department of man's life on which more labour is spent – as if nature had not given us the most healthy of beverages to drink, water, which all other animals make use of.'[11]

'Copo, c[on]ditu[m] habes? – Est. – Reple, da!' ['Tavern keeper, have you any wine? – I have. – Fill up, give it to me!'] This inscription can be deciphered on a Gaulish flask of a curious ring-shaped form found during excavations below Paris when the Métro was being built. Many mottos and inscriptions on drinking cups or vessels bear witness to the cheerfulness imparted to the Gauls by wine. The pleasure they felt was one in which philosophical discussion and the refinement of the senses gave way to the wisdom of such later Frenchmen as Molière's Monsieur Jourdain. 'You will be unhappier if you drink little. You will be happier if you drink a lot', says another inscription.

Five hundred years before our own era the Phocaeans founded a colony at Massilia, modern Marseilles, and brought the first cultivated vine-stocks to Gaulish soil. It is almost certain that the first vineyards in France were on the hillsides of Palette, sheltered from the mistral by Mont Sainte-Victoire near Aix, and out of reach of the arrows of the Salii tribesmen of Entremont. The Palette vineyards still make a delicious rosé, but many parts of the region claim the honour of having the oldest wine-growing tradition of all, notably Bandol. There is no need to decide between their various claims.

However, higher up the valley of the Rhône in La Pègue, a small village in the Drôme area between Nyons and Dieulefit, shards of pottery cups of the Ionian type going back to the sixth century BC have been found. What wine did the people of La Pègue drink from them at the time? We do not know. Indeed, we do not know that they were for wine. While the vessels were certainly made locally their conical shape is Ionian, which at least proves that before the Phocaeans landed there had been some kind of Greek penetration into the territory of the Salii. As the original vessel is unlikely to have fallen from the sky, like the bottle of Coca Cola which falls among Bushmen in a famous film, the original model may have made a long journey before ending up in the hands of the Neolithic inhabitants of what is now La Pègue, who liked it and copied it. It is an entertaining coincidence to find the key to a mystery at the bottom of a wine cup: *in vino veritas*.

Wine from the Phocaean vines was destined for Greeks at home. The colonists settled near Massilia for good business reasons, though no doubt they themselves drank with the proverbial gravity and moderation in all things shown by the local high society, an attitude which was to remain typical of the local upper middle class. For the time being, however, the native Gauls preferred ale or mead – when they were not, as the ill-intentioned claimed was the case, drinking the blood of their enemies from the said enemies' skulls.

It was not until the end of the second century BC that Roman expansion brought the spread of the vine through Provence. Of course the native producer did not enjoy the fruits of his labours, or very few of them. As before, Gaulish wines found their way to the tables of the occupying power, and became very popular with the patricians of Rome. The Gauls received only small amounts of thin *piquette* and new wine, on the model of those Italian agricultural practices described by Cato. According to Cicero,[12] the regulations here were more strictly observed, with the approval of the Senate.

The Greeks had introduced viticulture into Mediterranean Gaul; the Romans regulated it. The Gauls themselves provided the ingenuity and talent. Soon they were going into the forest to find wild vines and transplant them. These early grapevines could not be grown north of Gaillac, and even then they needed a sheltered plain. Then, in the first century, the Allobroges of what is now the Dauphiné succeeded in breeding a new vine variety, robust and frost-resistant, which Pliny calls Allobrogica.[13] The chieftains of the Allobroges cashed in on this discovery to get Roman citizenship. The honour may have been worth less than the right it gave them to grow vines on their own account in future, like any free Roman family in Italy. The Bituriges Viliscii of Bordeaux followed this example, breeding a vine variety which would make the fortune of the humid and windblown soil of Aquitaine and the arid, pebbly Graves area ('Grave solum coelumque', Tacitus was to remark; both soil and climate were oppressive). Then Burgundy, Alsace, the Moselle and Beaujolais regions, the Auvergne, Savoy, the area around what is now Paris, even Normandy and Brittany began growing vines in a number of different ways: staked, on pergolas, or low-growing, depending on the local climate.

Gaulish wine-growing led to the opening of taverns where ordinary customers could buy wine on the spot. A Gallo-Roman bas-relief of the late second century, now in the Archaeological Museum of Dijon, gives a lively picture of a scene from daily life: out on the paved road, a customer wearing boots and a cloak is reaching a jug with a handle over to the man selling wine, who is about to fill it from a small pot. The tavern-keeper is perched behind a tall counter to the left of which stand stemmed cups, ladles and two bowls. Jugs hang in descending order of size over the front of the tavern. The cups suggest that customers could drink on the spot, but the Frankish laws later introduced, which remained in force until the beginning of the eighteenth century, forbade tavern-keepers to give customers wine if they wanted to come in and drink it; they could sell only wine to take away, and only the proprietors of public houses and then the innkeepers could sell liquor to be drunk on the premises. The call 'Ho there, taverner!', in the mouth of a seventeenth-century musketeer calling for a drink, the kind of thing to be found in French melodrama, may sound good on stage, but is a complete anachronism.

As Claude Royer comments, the Gallo-Roman tavern-keeper was already observing the requirements of medieval edicts. 'He sits at a half-door, his pot upside down. Only the upper part of the door is open. However, he can still pour the contents of a pot into the vessel held out by the customer in the street.' There is also a funerary stele showing the late tavern-keeper Voscius Crescens holding a cup in one hand and a pipette for drawing off wine with the other. Almost until the French Revolution, the tavern-keeper was either in business in a small way on his own account, or the employee of a big businessman. The great lords of France, of both Church and State, the religious houses, even the King himself, owned taverns. This trade, 'which could retain an aristocratic character only if it was not a profitable business, was one way of getting rid of surplus wine made by the seller on his own land.' The practice paid off, since taverns were exempt from the taxes imposed on wine-shops.

Taverniculae, 'little shops', started out as free-standing huts, but the one on the Gallo-Roman bas-relief at Dijon is in a row of other shops opening on the street. The barrel shown on the left obviously belongs to the shopkeeper next door. He may be selling salted provisions; what look like sausages hang from the front of his shop.

The barrel itself is a Gaulish invention of which their French descendants are particularly proud. (The mattress is another Gaulish invention, made by the people of what is now Cahors, and comes in useful after a drinking session.) The French word for barrel, *tonneau*, cognate with English *tun*, is of Celtic origin. Its Latinized form is from the Low Latin period. However, cooperage, the craft of barrel-making, was first associated with beer-drinking. There are many carvings and funerary inscriptions providing evidence of barrels made of chestnut or oak. They occur more frequently in the north of Gaul, beer-drinking country, than in the south, which was to prefer wine, and constitute further evidence of the association between beer and barrels. In the south, amphoras went on being used for wine for quite a long time; barrels were reserved for beer or for transporting goods. The Phocaeans of Massilia had the secret of making amphoras of micaceous earthenware which was hardly porous at all, so that they did not need any coating on the inside which might affect the flavour of the wine. These amphoras are found all over Languedoc. Nîmes, Béziers, Agde, Ansérune and Minerve are full of fragments and even complete specimens, sometimes retrieved from the sea, for the Tectosages tribesmen soon became skilful viticulturists, a tradition that was to continue among the people of Languedoc. Muscat from Béziers fetched a high price in Rome. The pines of the Landes area provided a plentiful supply of pitch, and cork stoppers came from the forests of Cerdagne and Corsica.

Hauling a boat along the Rhône in the Gallo-Roman period: the Gauls invented the cask and exported it, along with its precious contents. The Roman occupying power, however, was in control of the Gaulish vineyards.

Huge barrels were made at this time, barrels that could hold a complete chariot or one-third of a ship. Iron hoops were a late introduction, replacing hoops of soaked and bent chestnut saplings. Sucellus, Gaulish god of the underworld and father of mankind, was traditionally represented holding a mallet and with a small barrel at his feet. One of his attributes was to assure a good life in this world by means of liquor, first beer and then wine. He gave the dead the mystic beer of the afterlife. Like Dionysus, he was a vegetation god, one of those responsible for the cycle of the seasons. However, he was not regarded as the god of wine or wine-growers; wine had reached Gaul too late for that.

Curiously, the trade of a cooper was one of the few that lepers were allowed to practise in France up to the end of the Middle Ages. Wine purifies everything. The coopers, an important part of the labour force, were a major medieval corporation. Once a new master had produced his masterpiece in the sixteenth century and was received into the guild, he gave his colleagues a large loaf and as much as they wanted to drink.[14] Those in the trade were fond of lifting the elbow, but the biggest thirsts belonged to the stackers of barrels, men of disreputable reputation who often had connections with bands of thieves and ruffians. Their work consisted of rolling and stacking the barrels, rinsing them, and racking the wine. For the medieval cooper not only made and repaired barrels, he also bottled the wine, although he was not allowed to sell it. However, he did sell bottles and second-hand casks.

To the Gallo-Romans, wine meant neat wine improved in cask and not diluted with water: it was called *merum*. For table use it had pitch added (*picatum*) and was flavoured, or made bitter, by the addition of aloes juice. Cicero's expression of distaste, however, was not for the bitter wine but conveyed scorn when he remarked that 'They are afraid of poisoning themselves by mixing water with wine!' Not that Gaulish water was bad; far from it. No other country has so many natural springs of fresh, pure and often therapeutic water as France. But water is one thing, and wine another.

In any case, the Graeco-Romans thought poorly of native Gaulish banquets. French tradition has it that before the Roman conquest the Gauls ate seated, voraciously, noisily and cheerfully, never interrupting their feasting to discuss deep philosophical questions. To wind up the banquet they would enjoy a good fight, and weapons were kept within arm's reach along with the wine cups and wine bowls. However, the Gauls also drank from silver-bound horns, filled by the guests' own children, from skulls which might be those of a revered ancestor, or even from a bowl passed from hand to hand. They drank only a little at a time, but they drank often, and indeed continuously.

Glasses came later, when rich Gallo-Romans wished to imitate and even surpass the luxury of Roman patricians. The flasks made by Gaulish glass-makers, bottles shaped like the human form and twin hourglass-shaped vessels, are both attractive and expressive. A famous artist named Frontinus had several workshops in sandy regions; his products are found in both the Rhineland and in Normandy. He invented a small glass cask in imitation of the wooden barrel; examples are frequently found in tombs. Its function may have been to provide drink for the next world.

As mentioned above, glasses for table use appeared later, but their fragility made them a luxury until the beginning of the twentieth century. The gesture of clinking glasses when a toast is drunk by two or more people in company has its origin in the opacity of the old vessels. The original idea was not to make the glasses chink against each other – a risky business with fragile crystal – but to present the cups or mugs as if in a gesture of offering. It was a social ritual. As well as being a symbolic offering, it should be seen as a courtesy: the opacity of cups, mugs or drinking horns prevented other people from seeing what was in them. In presenting your cup when a health was drunk, you were showing that you really were drinking, and also that all guests were treated equally where refills were concerned. No one was better or worse served than the next man, regardless of rank or merits. The clinking of the glasses which is first noted by Rabelais in 1552 is an amusing little flourish added later. (We never clink china teacups.) It was sometimes the custom to raise your wine-cup to the level of your face or heart. The Scandinavians drank linking arms and looking one another straight in the eye.

The good wines made in Gaul called for a poet to celebrate them. They found one in the fourth century in the person of Ausonius, one of the Bituriges of Bazos in Aquitaine, the son of a doctor of the Iberian Emperor Valentinian. Himself first tutor to the Emperor Gratian, and then consul, Ausonius was a man of refinement and certainly a Christian. He first sang the praises of the wine of his native region, and then, posted to the Moselle valley, he dipped his pen in the local wine and wrote much fine poetry on the subject. His Saint-Émilion estate, the name of which has always been preserved, passed to his grandson Paulin, who was reorganizing its cultivation when the barbarians arrived. After the disaster, Paulin went to plant vines near Marseilles, which had escaped the barbarian ravages.

Once they had settled down, the barbarians themselves developed a taste for certain wines that had survived, but they were not very sophisticated drinkers. Their descendant Chilperic died at the white hands of Queen Radegonde, poisoned by a cup of wine flavoured so strongly with wormwood and honey that the taste of the venom was masked. Not all the uses of wine are proper.

Cooking with Wine

Wine has been used in cooking since ancient times. Athenaeus mentions cooked wine as one of the main condiments available to the Greek or Roman cook. Horace gave a recipe for the Roman sauce called 'single'. It consisted of oil mixed with wine and brine. If you boiled it with herbs and saffron you had 'a double sauce'. This became the *civum conditum* of the Byzantines, who were lavish in their ways and also added pepper, cloves, cinnamon and spikenard. Their porridge made of spelt, spiced and sweetened with honey, was seasoned with aromatic wines.

Wine sauces receive a blessing in the tenth century in the long list of dishes contained in the *Benedictiones ad mensam*, from the monastery of St Gall in Switzerland. Most medieval recipes, for instance those given in Taillevent's *Viandier* and by the *Ménagier de Paris*, contain wine: to make 'red *dodine*' (*dodine* was a kind of smooth, thick sauce made of various ingredients, usually white but in this case red), 'Take white bread and toast it until it is brown, then soak it in strong red wine'. The dish of *anguille renversée*, 'eel reversed', was boiled in red wine. Joan of Arc liked sops in wine, i.e., soaked bread; she 'had wine put in a silver cup, into which she put only half the amount of water, and five or six sops, which she ate, and she ate nothing else.' In the thirteenth century herrings were cooked in white wine, an early instance of the association of white wine with fish.

White wine is used in the seventeenth-century *Cuisinier françois*[15] for several dishes, including one called *Oeufs Filez*, 'spun eggs': 'Take a cup of white wine with a piece of sugar, boil them well together, then break in the eggs.' Meat jellies were made with wine. Among the great wine sauces, Alexandre Dumas mentions one *à la genevoise*, of which he remarks that the people of Geneva did not, as they claimed, use a mixture of Bordeaux and champagne to make the well-reduced fish matelote in the recipe concerned, but only boasted about it. 'We warn all travellers not to be taken in by this recipe, which is used in Geneva only to tell to foreigners. When a Genevan makes up his mind to treat himself to two bottles of champagne of Bordeaux, it is to drink them in company, never to pour them into a fish kettle.'[16]

The Swiss have a point. Cooking with wine does not call for a fine wine of a great year. A good wine will do, if it is young and has well-marked characteristics

THE HISTORY OF WINE

which will stand up to prolonged simmering. That does not mean that one should use up a collection of odds and ends of various bottles which may be stale or sour.

Using a young but respectable wine for cooking will cost less than using a wine from the same region but of a better year, of a famous *cru* and served at just the right time; such a wine may be drunk with the dish. As everyone knows, regional dishes should always be both made and drunk with the wine of their region. The flavours will harmonize, whether the wine is white or red, dry, very dry, or fruity.

What part does wine play in the preparation of a dish? Apart from its gastronomic qualities of flavour, wine puts all its nutritional virtues at the service of the cooking and digestion of food. Wine contains glycerine, so it helps to bind sauces, and less fat can be used. Wine is well flavoured, and allows the cook to go easy on salt or omit it altogether. Wine contains tannin, particularly when it has been cooked, and stimulates digestion. Wine contains alcohol, but very little of it indeed once it has evaporated in being cooked. It stimulates the tastebuds, and thus the appetite. It brings out the flavour of food and helps the system to digest fat. And it is very good for morale.

Finally, Alexandre Dumas has said perhaps all that needs to be said about wine and food in a couple of brief sentences: 'Wine is the intellectual part of a meal. Meats are merely the material part.' Choose food to go with the wine, not wine to go with the food. The food is only a foil.

Wine and God

'God only made water, but man made wine.' We may supplement that reflection of Victor Hugo's by adding that, without men of God, wine could never have achieved its present distinction.

After the unhappy period of the barbarian invasions there was a time, from the sixth to the ninth centuries, when monasteries flourished amid miraculous vineyards. The patient, methodical and hard-working monks proved themselves enlightened viticulturalists and masters of the art of making wine. Their talents were wasted at first, since the invading Frankish barbarians had neither palate nor manners. But the monks had an eye to the future. A monastery is a moment of eternity made manifest. The monks' prayers and chanting, their monastic habits and their labours are outside ordinary time which, like the vine, belongs to God. Making wine was a way of spreading the Gospel message.

In the first centres of monasticism, the monasteries of fourth-century Egypt where men lived alone (Greek *monos*), they went on growing vines just as people had grown them there for thousands of years. The aim was to ensure the community's modest subsistence by trade, and refresh and show courtesy to any visitors who passed by. In the chaos accompanying the destruction of the Roman

Monks making wine at Saint-Germain-des-Prés: detail from a fifteenth-century miniature. After the barbarian invasions had destroyed a great many Gaulish vineyards the monks reorganized wine-growing. They had hidden their wine from the invaders in cellars, which turned out to provide the best conditions for good wine.

Empire in the West, the European monks, growing corn and wine on their little estates, managed to preserve enough security to do their work, both spiritual and on the land. Was the hand of God at work? In France, the barbarians often dared not attack the monasteries, and turned away from walls marked with the Cross. Tortula the Ostrogoth shrank from the mere glance of St Benedict. Italy, perhaps contaminated by the infection of the decaying Roman Empire, was not so lucky, and the Lombards sacked Monte Cassino. In the next century the monastery was rebuilt to house both the vintage and the monks' prayers.

The necessity of hiding provisions from marauders produced that happy accident whereby barrels were locked away in underground rooms, and wine at last found its ideal home: the cellar. This was a revolutionary discovery, and from now on wine would never be the same again. Being stored in attics had done it no good at all.

Although literature, for instance in Rabelais and the *Ingoldsby Legends*, happily lampooned the brotherhoods of the Divine Bottle and Horace Walpole's comfortably slumbering 'purple abbots', apart from a few exceptions such accepted notions are unfounded and unjust. As Desmond Seward says, 'One of monasticism's greatest services to Western civilization has been its contribution to wine-growing and to the distillation of strong waters'.[17] Viticulture was to be one of the great driving forces of the international economy.

All over Europe monastic orders might now be found crushing grapes and filling vats: Benedictines on the banks of the Rhine, Cistercians in the Moselle valley, Provence and Languedoc. The monastery bell meant vines in Austria, Hungary, Switzerland, Italy and Spain alike. Calvin and Henry VIII put a stop to viticulture in Switzerland and England respectively when they introduced Protestant reforms, but monks continued making wine in Hungary until the communists came to power, the monasteries became collectives, and the wine of God became the people's wine.

Everywhere, wine labels bear words of monastic origin: *clos*, *Kloster*, *hermitage*, St So-and-So, *abbaye*, abbey, *prieuré* and *commanderie*. For we must not forget the wines made by the soldier monks and the Knights Hospitallers. The number of *crus* for which monastic orders were responsible adds up to 109 in France, 45 in Germany, 27 in Austria, 17 in Italy, 12 in Switzerland, 9 in Portugal, 4 in Great Britain, and about 10 in the United States, not forgetting Israel, Lebanon, Algeria, East Africa, Australia and New Zealand, and Argentina and Chile where missionaries piously – in the true sense of the word – acclimatized European vines and assured the survival of an art they had perfected. Sometimes the nomenclature of monastic wines can be a little misleading, for instance, the 'Sauternes' made by American Benedictines, but if it is a lie it is a white one.

It would take a book, and there are many already, to describe all these monastic vineyards and pay proper tribute to every order responsible for them. At the height of the Middle Ages they were found wherever Mass was sung. Every monastery that lived by its own resources, even those which did not sell their surplus wine or were situated in beer-making areas, had its little *clos*, its enclosed vineyard, for making Communion wine and if possible enough extra to safeguard the monks' health. This explains the expansion of monastic wine-growing northwards after the first half of the Middle Ages. St Benedict, in Chapter XL of his *Rule*, allocates every brother a *hemina* of wine (0.27 of a litre) per meal, explaining: 'Better to take a little wine of necessity than a great deal of water with greed.'

The wines of France (the Parisian region), the Loire and Burgundy, wines of the *langue d'oïl* area, were the most highly regarded in the kingdom, but the abbeys of Saint-Denis and Saint-Germain, not content with quenching Parisian thirsts, were keen to get their wine loaded aboard the barges that went down the Seine towards the Channel and England. Even before the Hundred Years' War, however, rich Englishmen preferred the wines of Aquitaine; perhaps that fact helps to account for the war itself. The English are still traditionally lovers of Bordeaux, even retaining for it the name of claret, anglicized from French *clairet*, meaning 'clear wine'. The monks of the south-west of France had taken generations to revive vineyards destroyed by the Moors in the eighth century; they then turned to draining the marshes of the Médoc. The Cluniac monastery of Moissac owed its fortune and its magnificence to the custom of Jean sans terre. Altogether, the inheritance of Eleanor of Aquitaine was very dear to the hearts of her sons.

Whether because of a long period of bad weather and the depredations of the Hundred Years' War we cannot tell, but no red wine made at that period, not even Burgundy, was really much good. Apart from a little red wine made at Mareuil in Périgord, only Bordeaux produced that 'carbuncle-coloured wine' praised by Erasmus; so, leaving the light red wines of the time to the English, the French took to drinking white wine. Until the eighteenth century the wine most usually drunk by the people was *clairet* – light-coloured – or *piquette*, the thin wine made from a second pressing. A proverb said that he who drank a pint of the wine of Montmartre would piss four. This thin *piquette*, called *guinget*, 'acid', was drunk in the public houses on the banks of the Seine, which thus became known as *guinguettes*. The Fair of Saint-Denis near Paris held on 9th October, the oldest fair in France, was at first mainly viticultural, for selling the abbey's surplus production. References to grapes and vines abound in the decoration of the basilica of Saint-Denis; these were Dionysian allusions, called forth by the erudition of the master builders, and they did not shock the monks of the abbey. They were also a reminder of its principal resource.

If the wine of the Paris area was the everyday wine of the time, of the producers of the best vintages of Burgundy Clos-Vougeot was the most successful. The priory of Clos-de-Vougeot, now the headquarters of the famous fraternity of Tastevins, was built in 1110 by the Cistercians among vines donated to them by the Seigneur de Chamballe. According to Petrarch, Pope Urban V was reluctant to return to Rome for fear of being deprived of this nectar ('he who drinks good wine sees God' is the local motto). Since the Revolution, tradition requires every soldier passing its walls to salute.

When St Bernard was serving his novitiate he dug, pruned and fumigated the vines like the other brothers in the Romanée estate donated by Alix de Vergy, Duchess of Burgundy. The Cistercians, a well-organized community, had different individual timetables for lay brothers and monks of the choir: either six or three hours of daily labour in the vineyards. All the brothers made their various contributions of work and prayer.

Medieval monks preached by example. With the prosperity won by their labours, they 'contributed to the well-being of society as a whole ... they provided the age's social and cultural services; dispensing charity, keeping the only hospitals and schools'.[18] An abbey, particularly a wine-growing abbey, could thus be considered as creating employment – Saint-Martin-de-Tours employed 20,000 people – but it also acted as social security and an education service. The name of an abbey guaranteed its products, and that image has remained with us. The abbey of Saint-Wandrille, however, had the peculiar distinction of being famous for making wine that was very nasty indeed; today it has gone over to keeping bees and producing beeswax. The local climate, better for growing grass and apple trees than vines, was more to blame than any lack of zeal or knowledge on the part of the brothers.

Nunneries were not far behind in their contribution to viticulture. We owe Gigondas to the Benedictine nuns of Saint-André in Provence, and the yellow wine or *vin de paille* ('straw wine') of the Jura (the grapes finish ripening on straw) to the nuns of the Abbey of Château-Châlon, the least of whom could display a family tree with no fewer than 14 quarters of nobility. The nuns of Remiremont in Lorraine, one of the richest landed properties of the time, owned the best vineyards in Alsace and a transport system to arouse envy in the hearts of the men in Flemish monasteries receiving their wine from Franconia. The smaller women's convents sent the sisters out to work in the vineyards, while the larger ones employed paid labourers.

The first of these devout viticulturalists, reputedly at least, and in any case a great pioneer, was St Martin. Were they already making wine at Ligugé near Poitiers when he first settled there? No one knows, but the abbey, which still exists, makes a very good red wine. In 1096 Pope Urban II found a vine said to have been planted by the saint himself at Marmoutiers, the second house he founded and one that bears his name (*Mar* = Martin; Moutier = *monastère*, monastery). One wonders if it could still have been bearing after six centuries, but at least the vineyard surrounding this holy relic was superb, and yielding very well. Martin is known to have encouraged the improvement of a local species of wild vine found in the nearby forest, and the successive grafting operations which led to the famous Chenin Blanc grape, incorrectly called the Pineau of the Loire, not to be confused with Italian Pinot Blanc. It ripens late, and easily takes the 'noble rot', *Botrytis cinerea*, which produced the Sauternes of the mid-nineteenth century. The presence of this fungus causes a reaction whereby sugar is concentrated under the affected grape-skins, accentuating the quality of the wine. Noble rot gives no flavour of mouldiness at all.

The Pineau grape, ancestor of the great growths of Touraine and Anjou, makes Saumur and Vouvray. It is said to have originated with St Martin. There is a legend that the saint was so absorbed in tending this vine that he forgot about his donkey, and the hungry animal nibbled the surrounding vine-stocks down to the wood. The monks were shedding tears for their loss when they saw unexpected regrowth. When they tasted that year's wine, they wept again, but tears of joy this time: it was the best they had ever produced. The method of hard pruning practised in the Loire had just been invented.

St Martin is regarded as the patron of wine-growers only in certain areas, particularly the Moselle. However, in the Middle Ages his feast day – Martinmas – was the day for payment of tithes in kind, i.e., barrels of wine. At least 30 saints are associated with wine-growing and locally revered. There is a preference for martyrs, because of the analogy between wine and spilt blood. The roll of honour is headed by St Vincent, who is also the patron of wine merchants, vinegar merchants – and the inspectors of indirect taxes on liquor. His name contains the word 'vin' and has been widely used on French pub signs (Ô Vincent ô = *au vin sans eau*, which translates roughly into English as 'The Sign of Neat Wine'). As he was a Spaniard, perhaps his popularity increased with that of Spanish wines. His relics are in the Parisian church of Saint-Germain-des-Prés, originally Saint-Vincent-hors-les-Murs. In the eleventh century, Saint-Germain-des-Prés produced more than 500 hectolitres of wine a year.

Whichever saint is invoked as the patron of wine in France or indeed elsewhere (in Bulgaria the patron saint, greatly respected even in the face of Marxist materialism, is St Truphon), his feast day always coincides with some particular activity associated with the vine. This fact has given rise to blessings, processions, and all kinds of rituals which are not necessarily or wholly Christian, and have elements of magic and boisterous folk customs about them. Claude Royer tells us that some of these saints, or at least their effigies, are beaten to punish them for the frosts they failed to prevent, or thrown into the river (an ancient ritual in magic involving water, although its significance has been forgotten). In Burgundy at the end of the last century, there were two simultaneous processions to celebrate the feast of St Vincent: the procession of the parish priest, with sprinkling of holy water and the singing of *Ave Marias*, and the procession of the Republican Left, with a tricolour flag and the *Marseillaise*. And there actually was a St Bacchus (a German named Bach) whose feast, coincidentally, often seems to reflect the revival of ancient cults not always erased from folk memory. His feast is celebrated on the eve of the feast of St Denis. St Bacchus, honoured at Suresnes, was ritually beaten at the celebration of the vintage on the slopes of Mont Valérien. This vineyard, like the hundred or so vine-stocks of Montmartre, has been re-created in an urban area on a site covering about 7000 square metres, and the grape harvest gives the local tourist bureau a chance to show what it can do. The wine is said to be very good – 'strong, perfumed, long in the mouth' (I quote). St Bacchus was also honoured on his home ground in Alsace, where another beating was inflicted on the loser in a drinking contest.

However, the most popular wine in the world, the best known, and most frequently imitated, is the wine of Champagne. Before it became the liquid laughter we know today, the golden nectar of wild nights and ceremonial occasions, the wine of Champagne was still, and was known as the wine of Aÿ. Next door to Aÿ, in the Seine-et-Marne region, the village of Vindey stands on the side of a gently sloping hill between the valleys of the Grand Morin and Petit Morin rivers, not very far from the Aube, which carried flat barges taking cargoes of *clairet* wine to Lutetia, later Paris, along the Marne and the Seine. Before the wine of Aÿ was drunk, people drank the wine of Vindey: *vinum dei*, the wine of God.

Close to Vindey, in the Tertiary tufa of Sézanne, a fossil wild vine has been found dating from the same period as the fossil vine that the Hérault can boast. The existence of this fossil is evidence that the soil was naturally favourable to vines, benefiting from a microclimate with adequate sun and drainage. It is the most northerly wild vine ever discovered. At the end of the Roman period the first vineyard outside Lutetia, which constituted the frontier between the Gaulish Parisi and the area occupied by the Franks, belonged to Vindey. It is said to have been planted by the Roman legions. Natural caves, once used as living quarters, were adapted to act as barns and then as wine cellars with an ideal mean temperature.

Vindey, *vinum Dei*, the wine of God, *vin d'Aÿ*, began as a wine for communion and for giving to guests in the convents and châteaux of the region: for the sake of reputation and to the greater glory of God, it was served as the best wine available. When King Wenceslas II of Bohemia came to Reims in 1397 to meet the King of France, or at least his suite, the wine of Aÿ flowed freely. The Bohemian king liked it so much that he ended up under the table, and was extracted to sign a treaty which, as a shrewd diplomat in the usual way, he was to regret once he had sobered up. The wine of Aÿ added greatly to the cheerfulness of those royal rites celebrated at Reims, and became part of the family gastronomic traditions of the Kings of France. François I, who was very fond of the wine, introduced it to Henry VIII, the Emperor Charles V, and even the Medici Pope Leo X. Of course the noble and magnificent wines of Burgundy outshone the wine of Aÿ on great occasions, but the cheerful feelings it induced seem to have made it particularly popular. Saint-Simon tells us that Louis XIV wished to drink no other, and dipped so many biscuits in it that he eventually got the gout. Fagon, the King's physician, tried to persuade his royal patient to drink Beaune instead, believing that the cause of his disorder was something to do with the colour of the wine of Champagne. And indeed the wine of Champagne, once red, was becoming more of a rosé, of the pinkish colour described as *gris*, and often the pale ruby known as *oeil-de-perdrix*, 'partridge-eye'. Louis XIV and his court preferred their champagne to be *gris*.

It so happens that a baby was born to a prosperous family at Sainte-Menehould in 1638, the same year as Louis XIV. This baby, whose family name was Pérignon, was christened Pierre, and was to make the favourite royal beverage of Champagne the greatest wine in the world. At the age of 20 he took vows in the Benedictine monastery of Verdun, where he was noted for his learning and his scientific, methodical mind. He studied so hard that his naturally weak eyesight soon failed. But his memory, as remarkable as his brain, was so good that blindness did not prevent him becoming steward or administrator of the monastery of Hautvillers, near Épernay.

Hautvillers was one of the principal abbeys in the north of the kingdom. Founded in 650, it owned an inestimable relic, the body of St Helena, mother of the Emperor Constantine. A priest of Reims had stolen it in Rome in 841. The saint evidently bore no malice, and had worked many miracles since she was installed in the crypt of Hautvillers. In particular, she sent rain when the wine-growers prayed for it. The abbey became so prosperous because of the crowds of pilgrims it attracted and all their gifts that it soon added to its estates, acquiring 40 hectares of excellent vineyards, to the revenues from which were added tithes paid in wine from the surrounding area. With wine from Champagne so fashionable at the Sun King's court, it was Dom Pérignon's job to administer this handsome property. He was soon obtaining the best possible yield from the vineyards, with the assistance of one Brother Philippe, his right-hand man and no doubt his eyes too. In 1694 the wine of Hautvillers was in such demand and fetched such a high price that they inscribed the sum on the wood of the wine-press.

The fashion was for white and 'grey' wines. Dom Pérignon, aware that he could not maintain his profits if he did not continue to provide such wine, was vexed by the fact that the wine turned out perfect only if the summer was sunny enough – i.e., not very often. The white, dry, fruity wine was made from white grapes: it was *blanc de blancs*. Dom Pérignon therefore tried to make a white wine from black grapes which would still have the quality of the *blanc de blancs*. In the old days the Romans had removed the colour from wine when it became red from contact with the skins, or must. The ideal would be to prevent its taking on that colour, but still retain the benefits of contact with the must. By pressing in a certain way, and letting the must macerate for only a short period, he finally obtained a perfect white wine from red grapes: a *blanc de rouges*. The finances of the abbey throve in spite of bad summers, for red grapes are less susceptible than white to the whims of the weather.

Besides his exceptional memory, Dom Pérignon had a superb palate and sense of smell. He only needed to taste grapes picked the previous day before his breakfast to know what kind of wine they would make. His biographer, Dom Groussard, tells us that 'he could tell at once what grapes came from which vineyards, and that the wine of one could be mixed with the wine of another, and he was never mistaken.'

Now the white wine of Aÿ, the wine of Champagne, had a peculiar characteristic: sometimes, in spring-time, it would become effervescent with a second, short-lived fermentation. The wine, imperfectly clarified, still contained yeasts which remained dormant in cold weather. Under the influence of the warmth of spring, when the sap begins its mysterious work in the vine, these yeasts wake and proliferate, and there is as much fermentation as the sugar present in the wine will produce. Ever since Carolingian times France has produced a natural sparkling and medium sweet wine, *blanquette de Limoux*, the oldest of its kind in the world. It was protected by a royal decree of 931.

However, Dom Pérignon sought to induce this second, accidental fermentation of the wine of Champagne at a given time, regulate it and keep its effervescence in the wine. When he was 60, he finally produced true champagne as we know it today. He owed the achievement in part to his revival of the use of cork stoppers, which had been practically forgotten since Roman times, but above all to a flash of that genius which always combines well with pragmatism. 'Christopher Columbus thought of breaking his egg', writes Maurice Constantin-Weyer. 'The monk broke all the known rules. Instead of laying the bottle on its side, he turned it upside down.'[19]

To make champagne, a very small amount of sugar is added to the wine in cask to feed it and start the second fermentation. Then it is bottled. The bottles are left stacked for months or years. When fermentation occurs a sediment of yeasts collects along the lower side of the bottle. To remove this sediment without letting the gas escape the bottles are not in fact turned upside down – Constantin-Weyer's enthusiasm leads him astray here – but on the diagonal. Every day for a season each bottle is gently shaken by hand in the technique of *remuage*, so that the sediment will slip towards the neck, whence it will be expelled by the process of *dégorgement*, now performed at a very low temperature which freezes the deposit. The frozen sediment shoots out when the bottle is very briefly opened.

Champagne, therefore, is an absolutely natural wine. Before the final corking with a special mushroom-shaped cork and wiring, what is called *liqueur d'expédition* may be added: a syrup of crystallized sugar, old wine and a little eau-de-vie. The dryness of the wine depends on the dosage: the champagne is *brut* if the dosage is 0 to less than 1.5 per cent, *sec* if it is 2 to 4 per cent, and *doux* if it is 8 to 12 per cent. At first the fashion was for the sweeter *champagne doux*.

Champagne was wildly successful. The Duc d'Orléans, Regent of France, drank it during his nights of revelry, and Madame de Pompadour said it was the only wine a woman could drink without looking ugly. Dom Pérignon died happy in 1715. He was buried among his vines. His tomb and the church of Hautvillers are all that now remains of the abbey, which was destroyed in the Revolution. There was never a vine-growing monastery in Champagne again. Moët et Chandon, the firm which bought the walls and vineyards of Hautvillers in 1794, gave the name of *Dom Pérignon* to their best wine. He was the only monk who could have said with perfect propriety, in Baudelaire's words, 'I will light up the eyes of your delighted wife.'

Champagne is known as champagne in every language in the world.

A Wine of Revolution

In memory of Pierre Alberny, of Capestang in the Hérault, cask descaler, communard, deported to Algeria, one of the 87 of the Argeliers march.

Over-simplification is to be avoided. The wine-growing abbeys, like the other capitalist landowners of the *ancien régime*, did not always live in idyllic harmony with the peasants. Hautvillers, for instance, wishing to retain the monopoly of white wine made from Pinot Rouge grapes at the period when modern champagne was being launched, insisted on taking its wine tithes 'at the stock of the vine' and refused to accept them in grapes any longer, claiming that once they had been picked the bunches could not be safely left out in the open waiting for the tithe collectors. The wine-growers liable to pay such dues therefore had to instal presses on the spot. Their equipment was inadequate, so the red must remained in contact with the white juice too long and coloured it. Claude Royer quotes an extract from their catalogue of complaints, made with dignity and good sense, and expressing the discontent this practice caused in village communities, since, they said, it

> deprives the owners of liberty to dispose of their property and make wine as they please. It is harmful to trade, in that it is impossible to make white wine. It is harmful to the State, in that as white wine is the most valuable and the most expensive, it is the wine which pays the highest dues. It is harmful to quality, in that when grapes are pressed at the foot of the vine, far from the grape-baskets, the wine evaporates and necessarily loses in quality.

As the wine had thus been rendered *ordinaire*, not only did it rid the abbey of competition, it also provided the monks with everyday wine for their own consumption, so that they need not make inroads into their own produce. However, less was needed than in the Middle Ages, when *vin ordinaire* was part of the salaries or allowances to domestic staff or persons performing statutory services.

A song from Burgundy runs: 'Grand guieu, qué métier d'galère que d'et' vigneron ...' – a wine-grower's lot is not a happy one. Given the economic importance of wine, which was almost a form of currency, the government, coming down even harder on wine-growers than the abbeys, put the common good before the good of growers in any given region, or alternatively allowed free rein to speculators or profiteers which it needed in some other capacity. On the whole no one took any notice of private interests except when they united to make enough fuss – or affray, as it was put in the Middle Ages – to give warning of possible social unrest, something as dangerous as poorly controlled fermentation in a vat; you had to be careful it did not spill over.

As early as the Roman Empire, itself a kind of EC, the citizens of Rome who grew vines in Italy and the province of Narbonne made it known in high places that the talents of their Gaulish colleagues, in particular the Allobroges and the Bituriges, were damaging their own export trade and even home consumption. Two thousand years on, the recent hostile reactions of French wine-growers to Italian and Spanish wines are the obverse of the same problem, and in the nature of deferred retaliation. Gaulish wines, plentiful because they could now be produced in cold or windy climates, although at the cost of quality, had plenty of buyers among the less prosperous Roman citizens because of their price. In our own days Italian, Spanish and even Algerian wines compete with modern French production, which is also threatened by the practice of blending with such wines for table use because of their higher degree of alcohol.

In the reign of the Emperor Domitian the cereals issue became even more acute in Rome than usual. Wheat was urgently needed. In AD 91, therefore, Domitian ordered the uprooting of mediocre vines occupying land that could be ploughed and was better suited to corn crops than wine-growing. It is all rather like the deliberations of today's EC powers-that-be in Brussels, with such considerations as agricultural specialization, the preference given to quality produce and the necessity of maintaining prices. But there is always someone who has to pay the costs of reorganization. The Gaulish wine-growers took their sacrifice with a very bad grace, and the legions had to be brought in to enforce obedience. For reasons that are still rather obscure, the vineyards of Bordeaux survived this holocaust without suffering too much damage. Six hundred years later, when the invading Arabs from Spain came up through France as far as Poitiers before being halted by Charles Martel, they made up for it.

At a period earlier than Domitian's edict, Minervois wine-growers in the southwest of the province of Gallia Narbonensis, although in a privileged position, were already complaining of the pressure put on them (even more than on their grapes) by the proconsul of Narbonne. This official, Fonteius, was illicitly imposing dues on the Minervois wines shipped from his quays. The wines then had to be sold below their proper price to remain competitive. Fonteius used the stolen money to pay for the services of a famous lawyer, none other than Cicero, who made one of his famous defence speeches on his behalf.

Two hundred years after Domitian, the Emperor Probus reauthorized the growing of vines all over Gaul. His aim was to keep the tribes on the Frankish borders loyal to Rome and to bolster a provincial economy which had become very important.

The economic importance of wine, mentioned above, has always justified a legislative and fiscal apparatus of controls and barriers around its production and consumption. It is an apparatus demanded by some (in the cause of protectionism) and opposed by others (in the cause of free trade). No other article of diet has been subject to so many regulations. Officially the reason is its alcohol content, but the many cultural connotations of wine must also have played their part.

Before and during the Hundred Years' War, the English, who owned the *crus* of Bordeaux, used taxation to restrict the free movement of the wines of the Périgord, Tarn and Quercy and keep them from the rich importers of the north. The Burgundians were not going to do any favours to the wines of the South of France, Languedoc and Provence, dismissing them as being 'of low quality, lacking both customers and principles'. Nor was the option of finding outlets in the already saturated Mediterranean countries open to these southern French wines. Over-production, a recurrent scourge, was the root cause of brandy production in the west of France: the wine was distilled to dispose of stocks and find a market in Northern Europe for a concentrated and less expensive product. Despite this solution – and the stock-piling of spirits is not unknown today – vineyards sometimes had to be destroyed: a drastic measure, adopted to safeguard quality. After the Middle Ages local assemblies of the big proprietors rather than lords from outside the area regulated that quality. They were little help to small wine-growers who had nothing to keep them but a vineyard of modest size. Indeed, monoculture is the great disadvantage of wine-growing.

The small grower was not, of course, blind to the fact that keeping an eye on quality is always the best course, but logical thought is difficult if you have no funds at your disposal and you are 'impeded by the structures of an oppressive social and political regime'[20] in any case.

One of the many impediments in the way of such growers was the use of communal wine-presses. A fee was charged for their use, which was usually compulsory, but there were not enough presses to cope with the simultaneous demands made on them when the signal for vintage was given. Moreover, that signal might be given before all the grapes were perfectly ripe, or alternatively not until they were past their best, to the delight of the birds. Just as there were always conflicts between wine-growers and the authorities, there was constant strife between labourers and owners. It has been said that 'the tendency towards individualism always emerges sooner and more strongly among wine-growers than farmers.'[21] And if no other food production process has ever been so strictly controlled and regulated as wine-making, none has ever caused so much uproar either. According to the research of Claude Royer, the French word *tintamarre*, for 'noise, racket', and uproar in the figurative sense as well, derives from the noise made by the angry wine-growers of the Blois region striking their *marres*, or spades, with a stone as a signal from estate to estate that they were going on strike. Strikes are not just a modern phenomenon. The perishability of the ripe grapes, and the urgency of the work on which the health of the vines and the quality of future wine depends, constitute an excellent means of applying pressure to owners. Cereal-growing does not, in practice, demand such a skilled labour force or such constant attention to the crop.

Viticultural agitation reached a peak at the end of the *ancien régime*, darkening the last years of the reign of Louis XV: it was one of the most striking symptoms of general discontent, not an isolated phenomenon in a catastrophic economic context. The period as a whole saw bankruptcies, high grain prices and a slump in wines, with prices oscillating between the prohibitive, when bad weather struck, and the cheap at times of over-production. Dues on wine-growing had multiplied by six in 1782, putting many small producers out of business. A strike against such taxes, begun by the syndics of Burgundy, soon turned to political agitation. Positions hardened on both sides, that of the lords and that of the wine-growers. People harvested grapes before the official proclamation of vintage so as to avoid controls.

These were the sour grapes that had kept so many generations of vine-growers malnourished and would set the teeth of the revolutionaries on edge.

The golden age of the wines of the South of France came at last, during the Second Empire. Morale was high in Languedoc and Provence at the time. A certain rise in the general standard of living made the French lower-middle classes good consumers of everyday table wine. Railway transport was a practical and orderly way of coping with over-production. In fact over-production was natural to the region, but the demagogy of a sovereign who wanted to appear enlightened did nothing to halt it, and the result was inflation. Investment – a reckless gamble on the future – looked even more likely than rising wages to usher in catastrophe.

But when catastrophe did strike it was from a completely unexpected quarter. Parasites are so small. *Oidium*, a fungus disease, had already wiped out over a quarter of French vineyards in 1852. Luckily the remedy was soon found, and dressing the vines with copper sulphate became customary thereafter. But in 1871, with Napoleon III overthrown and the South of France hardly recovered from the difficult period of the communes, the phylloxera beetle attacked the wine-growing *départements*, devastating them, particularly Provence, where almost all the vineyards were destroyed. In 1885, '61 *départements* had been affected ... millions of people saw their lives ruined. The invasion of the phylloxera beetle was the worst disaster French agriculture has ever known' (Claude Royer).

Sulphate was little use here, and the flooding practised in the Aude did not help much either. Frantic and desperate, wine-growers rooted out their vines as if pulling out their own hearts, under the supervision of official commissions and the police. The land was replanted with American stocks onto which the magnificent French vines were grafted, but it took several years to build up the vineyards again, and the operation had been so ill-considered that in 1890 over-production once again led to a slump in prices.

During the years of poverty, wine merchants had not hesitated to concoct an adulterated 'wine', or even better, artificial wine which was much cheaper than wine made from grape-juice. They used colouring powders, tartaric and sulphuric acid, sugar, and practically anything else. In debt, discouraged, hungry and scorned by northerners, the wine-growers of the South of France touched rock bottom. They were paid hardly anything by middlemen for the little wine they were able to sell. Families of great dignity sometimes had only one pair of shoes, which the children wore to school in turn. 'Beggars today, insurgents tomorrow', proclaimed the posters held aloft by the 250,000 people who met at Carcassonne on 27 May 1907 for a demonstration uniting the wine-growers of every village in the Pyrénées-Orientales, the Aude and the Hérault.

The demonstrators were led by a man known as 'the Apostle', and sometimes 'the Saviour'. He was a man of humble origin from Argeliers, a café proprietor and wine-grower called Marcellin Albert. Beside him walked the socialist Mayor of Narbonne, Dr Ernest Ferroul, who called upon Clemenceau's government to take steps. The demonstration at Béziers on 9th June numbered 500,000. Clemenceau's only response was to send in the troops. The 100th Infantry Regiment of Narbonne, which was made up of local conscripts, mutinied. On 18th June orders to appear before the authorities were issued against Dr Ferroul, Marcellin Albert and the people of Argeliers. Next day Narbonne was a scene of rioting, with the barricades up, firing, and five demonstrators killed. Perpignan and Béziers were in a state of confusion. The 17th Line Regiment, quartered at Agde, was called out. Its men were the sons and brothers of the wine-growers; once out of their barracks they went over to their own people. Never again, thanks to wine, have French conscripts been stationed in their region of origin.

On 29th June the *parlement*, which had been sitting non-stop for three weeks, finally brought in a law giving some satisfaction to the wine-growers of the south: the wine market was to be properly organized, and fraud would be prosecuted. Some years later, there were to be further riots in the Aube and the Marne, where champagne was being made with cheaper wine from other parts. In the end the wine-growers obtained satisfaction, but by now they were tired of protesting and seeing the cavalry sent out against them.

The fiery little Apostle, Marcellin Albert, had gone by train to meet Clemenceau, and then did not know what to say to him, for he spoke only the Languedoc dialect. Muzzled by Paris, he returned to obscurity, betrayed by the politicians who had made use of him. In the words of Guy Buchtel, '1907 left a deep scar on rural Languedoc. The great wave of protest still moves hearts.'

Wine represents not just the blood of the vine, but the blood and sometimes the tears of the wine-growers.

PART IV

The economic role of food under the Roman Empire

THE ECONOMY OF THE MARKETS

The Centre of the City

Before the city of Rome existed at all, there was first an encampment and then a market on a mound rising above the marshes on the left bank of the river Tiber, between the Capitol and the Palatine. Caravans bringing salt from the beaches of Ostia to central Italy and Etruria stopped here. There was a kind of caravanserai, which acquired a guard of an Etruscan garrison quartered on the hill-tops. The place was flanked by a village of huts. Legend has it that the herdsman Faustulus, foster-father of Romulus and Remus, lived in one of these huts, and the mud walls and thatched roof supposed to have sheltered the twins in childhood were still being venerated in Cicero's time. Archeology has gone some way towards validating the legend by showing that the most ancient extant Roman remains do indeed date from the middle of the eighth century BC.

The market, which progressively expanded with the draining of the marshes, attracted the covetous notice of emigrants (according to tradition, the Sabines and Latins were 'invited' to Rome by Romulus). In the reign of one of the first historical kings it became necessary to protect the territory of the growing settlement with a rampart thrown around the oppidum: the Servian Wall, called after King Servius Tullius. But there was no need to give material form to the bounds of the City itself, the City of Rome with a capital letter, the *Urbs*. The *pomerium* around Rome was an imaginary wall, symbolic, almost magical, marked only by occasional small columns or *cippi*. Rome was the navel of the world, and its boundaries, the scar of the furrow once traced around it by Romulus, might not be crossed without permission. 'So shall all who pass my walls perish in future', Romulus was reputed to have said when he killed his brother for jumping over the foundations of those walls in jest. Not everyone could become a Roman citizen. There was the *pomerium* (from *post murum*), and there was the rest of the world. The *pomerium* expanded to absorb successive suburbs as the Roman Empire itself extended its bounds. This synchronization of the growth of City and Empire accounts for the way in which the entire state was called by the name of the mother city, its soul. It was as if the whole entity lived and grew on energy emanating from Rome. In fact it grew so much that eventually it burst.

> Terrarum dea gentiumque, Roma
> cui par est nihil et nihil secundum.[1]

The centre of the City, the centre of the world governed by Rome, became a venerable monument. This was the Curia at the foot of the Capitol: the *Curia Hostilia*, so called because it was built by King Tullus Hostilius. It accommodated the Senate consisting of the *patres conscripti*, descendants of the chieftains once gathered together by Romulus. In front of the Capitol lay the Forum, or rather a succession of forums. The first was said to have been built by Tarquin the Elder to accommodate the early Etruscan market. The shops here, *tabernulae*, belonged to the state, which rented them out to shopkeepers. They faced away from the sun. This sensible arrangement allowed butchers to set up shop, although they later moved to the north of the Forum and the *tabernae novae*, the new shops, leaving the older site to money changers. The heart of Rome, if opened, would have proved to be a strongbox full of gold.

The fish market originally stood near the Temple of the Penates, in a hall, the *macellum*, which was burned down during the Second Punic War, around 120 BC. The vegetable market, or *Forum Holitorium*, stood on the other side of the great Forum, at the foot of the Capitol.

Julius Caesar, Augustus and Domitian all had their names associated with forums. And when the City had over a million and a half inhabitants (the majority of whom were not actually Roman citizens) Trajan's Forum was built. Constructed in the years AD 109–113, it was to remain a masterpiece. It was designed by a brilliant architect, the Syrian Greek Apollodorus of Damascus, and financed by treasure pillaged from the Dacians: *e manubiis*, 'built from the proceeds of booty'.

Apollodorus' ideas came back into fashion two thousand years later. His forum reflects the approach of modern city planners: it was the brain, heart, lungs and belly of the city, with life breathed into the whole by the ruling factor of money. Under the eye of the Imperial treasurers, *arcarii caesariani*, who ran the equivalent of a modern finance ministry here, and separated by esplanades and colonnades, the place comprised a legal centre, with open-air law courts so that everyone would know what was going on in them, an intellectual centre with libraries and academies or *scholae*, and a commercial centre occupying a five-storey building with terraces which united the functions of stock exchange, big department store, galleries of specialist shops and warehousing, and which even had ponds for the sale of live fish. Imagine a modern complex in which the administrative offices of a finance ministry, a large cultural centre with museums, libraries and art galleries, a big shopping centre and a food market are all combined into a practical and harmonious whole. Trajan's Forum had everything, including restaurants. Unlike the Greeks, who looked down on their *oinopeles* as disreputable dens, the Roman public eagerly frequented *thermopolia*, where hot drinks were sold. The fast-food merchants of the time offered cooked dishes for sale, to eat on the spot or to take away.

To construct this forum with its squares and buildings, Trajan and Apollodorus expropriated all the sites between the old Forum and the foot of the Quirinal before levelling them. The depth of excavation to make this forum, 38 metres, was the same as the height of the huge column which stood in the middle of the great central esplanade. Trajan's Column has ornamented St Peter's Square in the Vatican since the time of Pope Sixtus V (1588), with the equestrian statue of the emperor himself replaced by the figure of St Peter.

Trajan's Forum and its annexes are the legacy of the Greek *agora*, in the Mediterranean tradition of public places where people can buy or sell merchandise or opinions, talk to their acquaintances, see and be seen, all under the aegis of the civil and religious institutions. The architectural scheme as a whole is admirable; however, our present concern is with the part of the complex devoted to food.

Besides displaying produce from the Italian peninsula itself, the foodstuffs on sale here came from Rome's conquered peoples and her trading partners. Overseas produce and bulky goods from the south of Italy came by way of the port of Ostia, Rome's window on the sea, controlled by the *annona*, the office regulating food supplies. A temple dedicated to the imperial provisions, the Annona Augusti, stood in the middle of the forum of the corporations of Ostia. One can see the point of deifying an economic and social administration which could provide food every day for 150,000 people in need of it: the unemployed, army veterans, or simply resourceful layabouts who never had enough, like the city which had spawned them. 'The conquering Roman now held the whole world, sea and land and the course of sun and moon. But he was not satisfied.'[2]

Chapter 10

The History of Fish

The Fish of the Ancient World

The shops, or rather stalls, on the ground floor of the elegant brick semi-circle of the great Roman market halls opened straight on to the street. They sold the seasonable vegetables, fruit and flowers of the ancient world as well as early produce. Displays spilled from shallow loggias and out into the street, itself already crowded with shoppers, idlers, pickpockets and people pushing handcarts.

On the first floor, where a gallery of arcades let the daylight into a succession of vaulted rooms, jars carefully labelled and ranged in order held wines and oils from all over the world. There were also smaller rooms where the wholesalers' bookkeepers did their work.

Flights of stairs led up to the second and third floors, which were fragrant with spices both familiar and rare, worth a fortune and requiring armed guards to protect them day and night. Since the great building was set into the slope of the hill, these enchanted chambers could also be reached by a winding road, the *Via Piperatica*. This 'pepper road' still existed in the Middle Ages, when the great market halls had been reduced to heaps of rubble and the winds of history had blown the perfumes of Arabia away. By then it was known as the *Via Biberatica*.

The fourth floor was busy with the administrative staff of scribes working on the files which were as dear to the Roman heart as the sacks of pepper. This part of the building accommodated the offices of the *annona*, the social security organization which distributed grain to the poor either free or at subsidized prices. The tax inspectors and security services also had their headquarters here; the watchmen on every floor of the building were responsible to the latter. Inspectors of weights and measures, brokers, traders and banking agents also went about their business on the fourth floor.

Mali fishermen on the Niger: the river is progressively drying up, and fewer and fewer of them now pursue this traditional activity.

Whereas the butchers' shops of Rome, as in Greece and Palestine, stood near the temples, conveniently placed for sacrifices, this other great temple to the god of the Belly[1] culminated in the holy of holies at the top: the fish market.

Its stalls were piled high with every imaginable fish: fish from the Mediterranean and from more distant shores, fish from the rivers and lakes of Italy, fish from all over Europe. There were vast fishponds into which fishmongers dipped on demand. These aquatic treasures had been brought to market in tanker ships or carts carrying tanks of water, in wet sacks or packed in seaweed and ice – for the Romans knew how to keep ice. The fishponds were fed by pipes from the aqueducts supplying the city. Looking quite at home, sea fish swam calmly round and round their special tanks, filled with seawater from Ostia. Other tanks teemed with Atlantic crawfish, Red Sea turtles, Corsican lobsters. Oysters gaped 'with corrugated valves',[2] and there were mussels from the pools and lagoons of Provence, Narbonne and even Aquitaine. The Roman frugality of the Horatii and Curiatii was a thing of the past. You could even buy the 'succulent crayfish of Aterno' in the Roman fish market.

Fond of fish as the Romans were, however, they may well have been simply imitating the Greeks.

Fishing has provided mankind with one of its principal sources of food from the dawn of time. The sea contains far more species of living creatures than land areas do; there are 20,000 species of fish, most of them edible. Man quickly realized that fish was a good way to satisfy his need for protein. It is likely that the first fishermen caught the more sluggish fish of rivers and shallows by hand, or picked up those stranded on the sea shore by the tide. Then they may have started gathering shellfish, and later progressed to fishing with spears and harpoons once they had those weapons.

Rock paintings all over the world show pictures of fish. They appear on cave walls, and on the implements used in fishing. However, scenes showing fishing actually in progress are very rare, unlike hunting scenes. Perhaps fishing seemed to require less magic. The most famous of these few pictures shows salmon being caught with a line, and is engraved on a stone found in the cave of Beaume-Bonne at Quinson, in the Basses-Alpes. A trout is carved into the floor of the cave of Niaux. The cave known as the Abri du Poisson derives its name from a magnificent salmon one metre long and shown in detail, internal organs and all.

There are innumerable remains of fossilized fish to show that people were catching fish during the Lower Paleolithic, over 100,000 years ago. The oldest known find of sea fish, at Terra Amata, is 380,000 years old.

The many paintings and the waste matter found give us a clear idea of what fish our distant ancestors liked and what they could get. Salmon was top of the list. Salmon must have been extraordinarily abundant, as indeed they still were in the Middle Ages, and until pollution banished them from European rivers.[3] Next came trout, pike, perch, eels and burbot. Curiously enough, sea fish also seem to have been known in areas a long way from the sea. So do shellfish, their remains clearly predating subsequent marine deposits. There is a carving of a sole at Lespuge in the Haute-Garonne, and the carved tooth of a sperm whale has been found at the Mas-d'Azil, in Ariège. Admittedly a tooth could be passed from hand to hand, as an amulet or for use as a bradawl, but it is hard to see how a sole could have come from the Atlantic or the Mediterranean to the Haute-Garonne and still have arrived in a fresh enough state to be so faithfully depicted: the mystery must remain unsolved.

The Mesolithic site of La Baume de Montclus, in the Gard, had an installation for drying and smoking fish, impregnated with residues that can easily be analysed. The drying and smoking of meat and fish, practised all over our planet, goes back to the time when men first learned to use fire. Salting implies the proximity of a source of salt, either sea salt or mineral salt, or of trading posts along the salt routes. Fish preserved by drying, smoking or salting still constitutes a large part of the African diet, and some of the techniques employed have not changed for thousands of years. The people of India in Vedic times also liked preserved fish. Top of the league for the consumption of fish in all these forms, however, were the Japanese, as they still are. The sea has always fed them. Five thousand years ago the Babylonians derived a considerable proportion of their proteins from a concentrated paste made of dried fish which they crumbled into pottages. A similar foodstuff helped the Amerindians to balance their diet of maize.

The tomb of Kha, one of the architects of Pharaonic Thebes, contained many different kinds of provisions, including baskets of salt fish from that generous river the Nile. The dietary prohibitions of the Jews, going back to the exodus from Egypt, forbid them to eat certain fish, perhaps because of some confusion with snakes. In Mosaic law the only fish regarded as kosher, pure, have been 'whatsoever have fins and scales in the waters, in the seas, and in the rivers ... and all that have not fins and scales in the seas, and in the rivers ... they shall be an abomination unto you.'[4] Eels and conger eels were unclean.

The first pre-Hellenic Greek, or rather Cretan, civilization was that of a race of sailors. In the middle of the second millennium BC it derived a major part of its resources from the sea, but after the fall of Aegean power the Achaean invaders who settled in continental Greece seem to have betrayed their pastoral and nomadic origins by showing a positive aversion to the sea and everything in it, over quite a long period.

This archaic Greece was an essentially rural society, and great lords such as Odysseus, who were really no more than large farmers even if they farmed whole islands, were not above guiding the plough, but fishing was regarded as very much the last resort. 'A wretched food, the last resource of shipwrecked sailors', is Homer's description. Plato agrees, although myths were his only authority for his statement that 'Fishing, at this time, was an occupation unworthy of a man of good birth, for it takes more skill than strength.' Which makes one wonder how the Greeks acquired their reputation for cleverness.

Around the fifth century BC they were certainly clever enough to realize that their coastline, the most extensive in the known world of the time in relation to the land area (and indeed of the world today, with the possible exceptions of Japan and Indonesia, both of them fishing countries), lay next door to an inexhaustible food supply. Until the coming of oil tankers, the warm waters of the Mediterranean teemed with fish. The Greeks learned to catch them, with lines, nets, the harpoon, trident, *lamparo* and madrague. The word madrague means literally 'enclosure for catching tuna' and is from the Arabic *al mazraba*. It denotes a large area on the shore laid out like a labyrinth of nets staked down, towards which the fishermen drove the tuna shoals. Oppian, writing in the second century, gives us much useful information (in verse) about hunting and fishing. His descriptions of tuna fishing are as immortal as the sea itself.

The sheer size of the tuna means that a single fish will provide a great deal of flesh (sometimes as much as 900 kilos). Before the Second World War the fishwives of Martigues used to wheel their tuna out in barrows to sell it in the streets. The Greeks ate a lot of tuna salted and marinated in oil (tuna in oil is not a modern invention). Once the people of the Mediterranean began to appreciate fish they took all its treasures to their hearts: sea bream, grey mullet, red mullet, conger eels, turbot, moray, groupers. The fry, or shoals of young fish, were a choice dish when fried much as the people of Provence make their *sartanado* today; the recipe goes back to the Phocaean colonists of southern Gaul. Fishermen were ready to tackle swordfish and electric rays, and sturgeon from the Black Sea trading posts fetched a good price in the market. In fact the sturgeon was about the only freshwater fish to feature on ancient Greek menus (and then only on special occasions), since there are not many fish in the rivers of Greece. Other popular favourites were octopus, cuttlefish and squid.

The famous recipes of Archestratus – cook, gastronome, poet, philosopher and traveller – (as reported by Athenaeus) included a great many for fish. Archestratus of Syracuse, a contemporary of Aristotle in the fourth century BC, was a fellow-student of the son of Pericles. He was also notorious for his thin frame, and died of debility caused by a stomach ulcer. Modern *nouvelle cuisine*, with its emphasis on fish which is barely cooked, has rediscovered his precepts. The recipe Athenaeus gives for bonito wrapped in fig leaves and cooked in the embers is simple and good. The talents of the great chefs of the Hellenistic period were assessed by their way with fish. Of the six famous cooks who lived at the beginning of the third century BC, the first to be mentioned were always Algis of Rhodes, whose roast fish was a masterpiece, and Nereus of Chios, creator of a delicious broth of conger eels. Another culinary poet by the name of Anaxagoras, who followed Alexander's army in the capacity of a chronicler, cooked conger eels with such loving care that he was mocked one day by the Macedonian general Antigonus. 'O Anaxagoras, do you think Homer would have sung the deeds of Agamemnon so well if he had spent his time boiling fish?' 'Ah', replied the poet with his pot of fish, 'and do you think Agamemnon could have done so many great deeds if he had spent his time lounging around the camps watching other people cook conger eels?'

A Who's Who of Sea Fish

Out of the 20,000 or so recorded species of sea fish, European nations catch and consume only about 40 edible species.

Ask someone to draw a fish, and the picture will always show a long, tapering creature. However, fish come in plenty of other shapes. Some are flat (sole, turbot, ray). Some, such as common and conger eels, are snake-like in form. Others again, for instance the angler-fish (or monkfish) and the John Dory, have heads bigger than their bodies. Regardless of shape, however, fish are placed by zoologists in one of two groups, depending on the nature of their skeletons. Selachians – non-bony or cartilaginous fish – are the most ancient of surviving vertebrates. They have denticles instead of scales, small projections such as those which come off the rough skin of the thornback ray. Among these fish are the rays or skates and the dogfish (also known in French as *saumonette* because of the colour of its flesh, and sometimes similarly described by English fishmongers as 'rock salmon', a term also applied to other fish). The dogfish, which is really a small shark, is sold beheaded and skinned.

Teleosts, or bony fish, are more common, and can be identified by their flat scales, either large or small, which overlap like tiles on a roof. They comprise a number of orders and families:

The Gadidae family have long bodies, large heads and pointed teeth, sometimes in several rows. The scales are small and round. They have three dorsal and two ventral fins. They include cod, pout, haddock, ling, coley, pollack and whiting. The hake, another member of this family, has only two dorsal fins.

The Clupeidae family have long, rounded bodies covered with large, thin, supple, silvery scales. They have a single short dorsal fin, centrally placed. The tail fin is forked. They include herring, sardine and sprat. The anchovy, also a member of the order Clupeiformes, belongs to the family Engraulidae.

The Scombridae family have tapering bodies of varying thickness, covered with small scales. Small spines are situated behind or round their dorsal fins, which may be one or two in number. The broad tail is deeply forked. These are the characteristics of mackerel and tuna (the bluefin tuna, which can weigh up to 900 kilos, is the tuna of the Mediterranean; the smaller long-fin tuna swims the waters of the Atlantic. When it weighs less than five kilos it is called a bonito.)

The Carangidae family have two dorsal fins and a long abdominal fin. The tail fin is finely forked. This family includes the scad or horse mackerel.

The Sparidae family are thick-set, with a dorsal fin running from the head to the wide, forked tail. They include the red sea-bream, found chiefly in the Atlantic, and the silvery-gold sea-bream found chiefly in the Mediterranean. The gilt-head bream of the Mediterranean has a golden crescent on its forehead; according to legend this commemorates the guidance the fish gave to the ark of Deucalion, the Greek Noah.

Other fish families include the Congridae, to which the conger eel belongs. The Mullidae include the red mullet or surmullet, not to be confused (as it sometimes is) with the red gurnard, a member of the Triglidae family. The voracious sea bass, which belongs to the Percichthyidae family, is known in French as *bar* but also, in Provence, as *loup*, meaning 'wolf', and similarly as *loubine* in the Vendée.

The monkfish or angler-fish, a member of the Lophiidae family, has an ugly head (its enormous mouth will not close, according to legend as a punishment for greed). Because of its appearance it is sold headless, as monkfish tail or monkfish fillet. In English, 'monkfish' is also a name for the angel fish, a member of the Squatinidae family, but recently it has been far more usually applied to *Lophius piscatorius*, angler-fish, the equivalent of French *lotte*. The John Dory, one of the Zeidae family, is not visually very attractive either. Its French name is Saint-Pierre, St Peter, and according to legend the black spots on its sides are the fingerprints left by the saint while he was still plying his trade as a fisherman under the name of Simon. On catching the fish he was so startled by its ugliness that he let it sink to the bottom of the sea again. Here the saint was mistaken, for he was depriving himself of a particularly delicious fish. (Moreover, the 'sea' in which Simon fished was the Sea of Galilee, otherwise known as the Lake of Tiberias, and he certainly would not have caught any John Dory there.)

Flatfish, of the order Pleuronectiformes, live lying on one side in shallow waters; their undersides have thus become colourless and blind. The eyes are both on the other side of the head; in dextral flatfish they are on the creature's right side, in sinistral flatfish on its left side. Sinistral flatfish include turbot, brill, and megrim or sail-fluke; dextral flatfish include the dab, the lemon sole, the Dover sole, and the plaice.

These are the main sea fish likely to be found on European fishmongers' slabs.

The Salmonidae: a family of aristocrats

In many parts of Europe, France and England included, native salmon is now little more than a legend. If you catch a salmon in the Loire or the Adour, or in the rivers of southern England, the event gets into the local papers. However, an energetic campaign is being conducted to restock the rivers of the Basque country, and there are hopes that the Thames may eventually be sufficiently free of pollution for salmon to swim there again.

Luckily for gourmets – if they are not also anglers lucky enough to go salmon-fishing regularly in Ireland or Scotland – modern technology means that fresh chilled or frozen salmon can be bought in towns at a very reasonable price, and it retains the true salmon-pink colour which is a pleasure in itself. Most frozen salmon comes from North America, but Norwegian and Scottish salmon is also available. Irish salmon is seldom frozen; it is kept for salmon fishermen. Scottish salmon is also of the highest quality, but at the end of the 1970s an epidemic severely depleted the stocks in Scottish rivers.

The best salmon is the Atlantic fish, *Salmo salar*. This is the species found in Scotland and Ireland and farmed in Norway. Two reasons why the wild fish has become rarer are the pollution of rivers, which discourages the fish from returning there to spawn, and the building of dams which they cannot leap. Today some dams, particularly in Canada, provide them with 'salmon ladders'. But first and foremost, the Atlantic salmon has suffered from severe over-fishing at sea. Some years ago cod fishermen found the salmon's feeding grounds in the cold waters of the Davis Strait, between Greenland and Baffin Island, and systematically set about looting them.

Despite intensive fishing, Pacific salmon is still very plentiful. Its quality is slightly inferior to that of its Atlantic brothers. The chinook salmon, *Oncorhynchus tchawytscha*, is the giant of the family; it can weigh as much as 60 kilos, a fact which at present saves it from commercialization. It is fished for sport in lakes and the sea, and is only found fresh in shops. Silver or coho salmon, *Onchorynchus kisutch*, is the Canadian salmon *par excellence*, despite its relatively small numbers (10 per cent of the annual catch). It is spawned in the springs of northern California and swims downstream as far as Alaska, but it is also found in the Great Lakes of Canada and the rivers that flow into the Atlantic. It is fished only with rod and line, or 'trolled', which preserves its quality, since a net would bruise the flesh of the fish. Catching one of these salmon is a considerable feat, for it may grow to a metre in length and weigh six or seven kilos. It passes half of its four years of life in the sea. The high fat content of the flesh makes it one of the best kinds for smoked salmon, and it is also frozen. Finally, there is the sockeye salmon, *Oncorhynchus nerka*, which has very dark red flesh. Unlike other salmon, it can spawn only in lakes which discharge their waters into the sea along a fluvial network. It spends the greater part of its life at sea, returning to its native lake to reproduce after two or three years, when it weighs about three kilos. The colour of its flesh makes it ideal for canning. Pink salmon, *Oncorhynchus gorbuscha*, is the smallest of the family at a weight of 1.5 to two kilos, and also the greatest traveller. It goes on a great journey from California to the Bering Sea. It is caught before it begins preparing to spawn, and thus before its flesh is affected by biological change. Finally, the most democratic and least expensive of salmon, because the most readily available, is dog salmon, *Oncorhynchus keta*, a handsome fish which can reach a weight of 15 kilos but does not have such an attractive colour. It is also the least oily of the salmon, and is better for canning than smoking. Although it travels from Alaska to the Bering Sea in summer, it takes its time swimming down the rivers, and it must be caught before it reaches the river mouth to ensure that it shows no signs of exhaustion, which would detract from its quality. There is also a white salmon which swims in the Caspian Sea. It is extremely rare – only two tonnes a year are caught – and tastes delicious.

The life of the salmon is a perpetual journey. What makes it travel? Its story begins in autumn, some time between September and January. The female needs a stream of clear water with a moderate current and a gravel bed. Exhausted from her journey and starving, for she has not eaten since leaving the sea, she deposits her eggs on this spawning ground, and the equally exhausted male fertilizes them. Depending on the temperature of the water, the eggs hatch into tiny salmon between five and 21 weeks later. At this stage they are called alevins. They stay among the pebbles on the bed of the stream for one or two months. Then they become bigger and bolder, swim around in the stream and are known as parr. The parr stay in the fresh water for from one to five years, depending on species. When they are ready to leave and return to the sea, they are known as smolts, and their skin takes on a uniform silvery colour. The smolts linger for a while in the brackish waters they find in the river estuary, acclimatizing themselves to salt water. Then they enter the sea. They live there for up to six years before nature calls them again, and they turn and swim back to their native rivers – they are never mistaken –

to spawn. A fish which returns after one year is called a grilse; a fish which comes back later is a fully adult salmon. Leaping waterfalls on its way upstream, the salmon goes on its way to spawn and perpetuate an extraordinary life cycle.

That cycle is interrupted by salmon fishermen, who may use three techniques depending on location and species. The gill-net is stretched across the water near the mouth of the river, and the salmon, impelled by the instinct bringing it back to the river where it was spawned, becomes entangled in the net before it is worn out by fasting on the journey upstream. The seine is another kind of net and will surround a shoal of the fish. It encircles them and is closed by a cord drawn tight to form a pocket. The whole thing is hauled aboard fishing vessels and emptied straight into their freezers. Labrador dogs used to be trained to retrieve the two ends of the net as they swam. Line fishing or trolling offers the salmon a bait, usually herring, of which it is very fond, on the end of two or three hooks. This method is for sportsmen pursuing their expensive hobby.

Smoked salmon is usually made from top quality fish, not too fat and not too thin, since the flesh must have quite a high fat content if it is to remain tender. The fish is opened, gutted, boned and flattened into its two halves or sides. It is salted, then rinsed, and exposed to the smoke of a wood fire carefully composed to give a certain aroma. The temperature must not rise above 30 degrees centigrade. This process is cold smoking, which leaves the fish raw but gives it a unique flavour and a beautiful amber colour.

Although it is an oily fish, salmon contains no more lipids than lean meat: about 10 grams per 100 grams. It has 16 grams of protids and 155 calories, 300 milligrams of phosphorus, 60 milligrams of chlorine, 60 milligrams of sodium, and vitamins A and D. Its extra-cellular protein (i.e., contained in conjunctive tissue) makes it slightly indigestible, since the digestive juices are slow to break it down. The acidity of lemon squeezed over a slice of smoked salmon aids digestion, and drinking a dry white wine with it serves the same purpose, as does the vodka with which Russians accompany the fish.

However, it would be disingenuous to suggest that all the fresh, chilled, frozen, smoked and canned salmon we see on our tables is wild salmon, particularly when it is relatively inexpensive. Modern methods of aquaculture, as we shall see, have given rise to many salmon farms, especially in Scotland, Canada and Scandinavia, and their products constitute a large part of sales to the public. Salmon farming is certainly not a bad thing in itself, since the democratization of this delicious fish gives people who cannot afford the high price of wild salmon a chance to satisfy perfectly legitimate appetites. Obviously farmed salmon have never seen the sea, although the water in which they swim as adults is salt and well oxygenated, but the looting of the salmon's feeding grounds at sea may well mean that some day the opportunity of eating wild salmon will be confined to practical experiments in historical ethnography. For the time being, however, prosperous gourmets claim that there is as much difference between wild and farmed salmon as between a partridge and a battery chicken. Food snobbery has been with us since Roman times. We can at least be certain that farmed fish are a good species – usually Atlantic salmon – are well reared, and are prepared with as much care as expensive wild salmon.

To enforce a distinction, in fact, we should need legislation, which is usually a rather slow process, making it obligatory to specify whether a salmon is wild or farmed, whether slices of smoked salmon are ventral – the fatter and therefore more tender part – or dorsal, whether the fish has been smoked traditionally or industrially (sometimes using asepticizing gases), whether it was smoked in its country of origin or not, and finally whether fresh or frozen salmon was used. At the moment price remains both the best indication and the only guarantee of origin.

Trout is the salmon's smaller cousin. Today most trout too is farmed, although the icy waters of mountain streams still contain excellent wild fish. Spanish trout from the province of Leon used to be famous for their size, abundance and excellence. There is now strict legislation in force, in an attempt to preserve them.

In the British Isles, wild trout are still found in Scotland, Ireland, Wales and the Lake District of England; many streams in other parts of the country have been stocked with trout for anglers. On the continent of Europe, Alsace and Lorraine have always been traditional fish-breeding regions. Indeed, the oldest of contemporary fish farms is at Huningue, in the Haut-Rhin area of Alsace. The trout of Alsace and Lorraine are still considered excellent, and great care is taken in rearing them. Trout-farming is a small-scale industry uniting traditional techniques with modern efficiency. In these parts of France it has the environmental advantage of exceptionally pure water which brings out the best in this delicate fish. Forty or so fish farms, many of them small family businesses, produce about 1200 tonnes of trout a year, out of total French production of 25,000 tonnes. Unusually, by comparison with other major fish-farming areas, the fish are mostly sold retail.

Kaiser Wilhelm II of Germany, while staying in Haut-Koenigsbourg, enjoyed these famous trout, which have featured in a great many French counting-out rhymes and proverbs ever since the sixteenth century. One proverb tells us that 'A trout is worth a herring, but it is not worth bothering the police about.'

Sea trout, so-called, which can grow to 75 centimetres or more, live in the rivers flowing into the English Channel. They come down to the sea when the waters grow warm and return to the rivers to spawn like salmon.

Fishing in Legend

Greek tradition gave women a monopoly of fishing in the first place. Water and the sea were regarded as feminine. In Homer, Amphitrite meant simply the sea, the third element.

The nymph Amphitrite agreed to marry Poseidon, Zeus's younger brother, who had received the oceans as his share of the world. Their marriage denoted both the end of the matriarchy (Herodotus tells us that 'the Athenians ceased to take their mothers' names') and the fact that the priests had succeeded in depriving women of their fishing rights. To the Achaeans, fishing became a masculine and therefore a noble and dignified activity. Mythology, we should remember, was one of the first forms of history and a vehicle of its earliest (coded) records.

Poseidon in fact became god of the sea at quite a late stage. His name meant 'he who gives drink in the wooded mountain'. Like his elder brother Zeus, he originally carried a thunderbolt, which became a trident after his marriage to the sea nymph. The trident, a typically Mediterranean fishing device, is still used for catching sea bass and mullet.

Extravagance and Economy in Eating Fish

The Roman fish market, well stocked and handsomely laid out as it was, gives us only a faint idea of the Romans' passion for fish. Men with a reputation as great gourmets loved it. Lucullus had a channel bored through a hill-side to supply water to his private fishpond. Everyone owned a fishpond. Tradesmen used them to make money, the prosperous spent fortunes on them; large industrial fishponds, as well laid out as those of the *piscinarii* (private fishpond owners) contained large fish which were fed on small fry caught by an army of fishermen, but the wealthy Sergius, known as 'The Gilt-head Bream' *Orata*, reared bream from Lake Lucrino which were fed entirely on the best oysters, opened for them day and night. It should be added that Orata, Catiline's grandfather, was also a keen oyster farmer who owned extensive oyster beds, and the sale of the surplus made his fortune.

Just as there were famous vineyards in antiquity, there were places famous for their fish. To be worth eating, tuna had to come from Byzantium and be caught between the rising of the Pleiades and the setting of Arcturus. A gourmet could always tell. It would take a whole book to describe their individual tastes, with such strange recipes as the mad emperor Heliogabalus's sky-blue sauce, or octopus coloured with nitre, recipes besides which Alexandre Dumas' recipe for anchovies is merely a pleasing fancy. Squid and cuttlefish stuffed with brains were eaten with sauces so highly seasoned that the dishes themselves must have owed their reputation for being both aphrodisiac and indigestible to their accompaniments.

We do not know what sauce was served with a famous red mullet weighing four and a half pounds auctioned by Tiberius. There was competitive bidding for it between Apicius and another gastronome. The latter acquired the fish for 5000 sestertii, a huge amount of money (around £4000 in late twentieth-century terms). But this was small beer compared with three other red mullet mentioned by Suetonius, which fetched 30,000 sestertii, admittedly as a single lot. The red mullet seems to have been regarded as the last word in fish, and the pleasure of buying the most expensive variety on the market was as nothing to the pleasure of cooking it. In fact it was cooked by the simplest method, in water, but on the gourmet's table, in a crystal vessel which was heated very slowly – not to keep the crystal from breaking but so that the guests could enjoy the sight of the unfortunate fish's dying agonies, in the course of which it gradually changed colour, as dusk follows sunset.

A top quality red mullet, clearly, was supposed to be as large as possible, which now seems strange, since we consider that smaller ones have a better flavour. The red mullet is known in Provence as the woodcock of the seas, and is not gutted before cooking. *O tempora, o mores!* Domitian's famous turbot was so huge that it became an affair of state. Not only was a special cooking pot made to accommodate it, but the Senate was convened to deliberate on the best way to serve it (with a piquant sauce, they decided). When a really huge fish appeared in the market, no one dared buy it for fear of incurring the emperor's displeasure. We hear of such fears again in the fifteenth century, in one of Sacchetti's *Trecento Novelle*; the story tells of a courtier of one of the more ferocious Dukes of Milan who succumbed to imprudent impulse, and then presented the object of the crime to his master so diplomatically that his fortune was made – but it was a close shave.

When Caesar celebrated his triumph, the dishes served at the victory banquet included 6000 moray eels reared by Caius Hirrus, a famous *piscinarius* with an excellent head for business. However, the rumour that the really rich fed the eels on slaves is entirely unfounded. Pliny established the truth: at a banquet in honour of Augustus, his supporter the statesman Asinius Pollio proposed punishing a clumsy slave in this way, but the horrified emperor at once freed the slave, and had all the glassware Asinius owned broken and tipped into his fishponds.

Shellfish were extremely popular, and the Romans also ate the sea anemones enjoyed later by the people of Provence before oil refineries came to their coastline. The favourite soup of the Byzantines was a highly seasoned one made of fish and vegetables, not unlike modern Mediterranean fish soups except that it was also sweetened lavishly with honey.

The many rivers and streams in Gaul had always provided excellent fish. The shores of the Mediterranean abounded with grey mullet and tuna. Pliny tells us that dolphins stationed at the entrance to the saltwater lagoon of Berre behaved like beaters of game, rounding up the fish, and dolphins could still be seen leaping in the water at Berre-l'Etang before the Second World War, although it was a long time since anyone had seen them 'beating' fish. Where did they go? Dolphins themselves have almost never been eaten in the course of recorded history; they have been regarded as sacred, and of course are not fish but mammals.

From Port-Vendres to Genoa, the coastline of the Mediterranean has been a succession of fisheries since the days when the Greeks first colonized it, and salmon from the Atlantic and the rivers that flow into it have been profitably exported since the Roman Conquest. The ancient Gauls liked fishing in rivers with rod and line, and angling is still a favourite leisure pursuit in France. Ausonius, when posted to the Moselle, gives a fascinating account of angling at his time.

The fasts ordained by the Church on 166 days in the year, including the 40 days of rigorous fasting during Lent, made fish a major resource in the Middle Ages.

Charlemagne shrewdly decreed, in his capitulary *De Villis*, that his farms were to have fishponds for the rearing of pike, eels and tench. The farm managers sold the fish to swell the coffers of the imperial treasury.

Carp may have come from the East at the time of the Crusades; it was unknown in Europe until the twelfth century. In 1768 a carp of impressive size was shown in the royal aquaria at Strasbourg. Might the fish itself have been hatched during the Crusades? The large, golden carp lives to a very great age. There are fish in the pools of the Jardin du Luxembourg said to be centuries old, and to have eaten bread from the hand of Catherine de Medici. According to Grimod de La Reynière, the Strasbourg carp was a great traveller, going to Paris and back three times; its keeper wanted 225 louis for it, and no buyer could be found in the capital. Considering that the tongue and cheeks of the carp were still regarded as the choicest morsels in the eighteenth century, one can see why gourmets held back. The follies of the Roman Empire were long gone. But until the age of the railways, which brought fresh fish right to the gates of inland towns, far more freshwater fish was eaten in continental Europe than is consumed now. The lakes and ponds of feudal domains (both lay and monastic) were usually thriving concerns. The tenants who reared and sold fish, protecting them against their natural predators such as otters, against poachers and bad weather, had to pay their dues to the feudal lord partly in kind and partly in money, an unusual stipulation at the time, and one that shows what good profits were made from freshwater fish. Paul Charbonnier[5] quotes the dues payable from Lake Chambon, part of the Murols estate: 'Two hundred perch and four bream a year, as well as rent in money.' Curiously, the payment in kind remained fixed throughout the fifteenth century, while the cash rent varied considerably. Perhaps the market price of fish varied too.

Fish for sale was taken by cart to the nearest town, usually by a professional carrier. To ensure that it remained fresh the journey was not to be more than 25 to 30 leagues, about a day's journey by rapid stages. The *Roman de Renart* tells us of several tricks played on carriers of fish whose brains apparently went round more slowly than their cartwheels. One day, feeling hungry as usual, 'for the last ham had long since been eaten', Reynard the Fox is lying in wait, behind a hedge, for any windfall that may come his way. Before anything actually comes into sight, a strong smell of fish informs him that the cart carrying it is about to pass by. 'It is only a bowshot away.' The cunning fox shams dead in the middle of the road, the carriers pick him up, and Reynard is flung into the cart among all the baskets, where he starts feasting. 'He ate them raw, with neither salt, herbs nor mustard.' Having emptied the first basket, he starts on a second, and pulls out half a dozen eels threaded through the gills on a willow withy tied into a ring. Reynard puts his head through the circle of the withy and wears the eels like a necklace. Then he jumps to the ground, calling, 'Goodbye, and good luck on your way!' The fishmongers expecting the cart are naturally furious.

The stories of Reynard also illustrate the way the villeins fished in hard winters, breaking a hole in the ice on ponds. Reynard takes Isengrin the wolf to the ice, explaining that he has only to hang down his tail with a bucket tied to it. Master Wolf is soon caught in a trap, and has to leave behind his magnificent tail, cut off by a watchman's sword.

Indeed, fishing rights in ponds and lakes, whether frozen or not, were privileges subject to strict regulations, both to avoid the reckless depletion of stocks and to preserve the interests of the fishmongers. In Lorraine, for instance, 'any man found fishing in the lord's ditches or in his pool or in his fishpond shall be at the mercy of the lord's pleasure, both he and his goods.'[6] And the lord's pleasure might not be particularly merciful. James IV of Scotland passed a law against illegal salmon fishing making a second offence a capital crime.

Fish caught legally had to be of regulation size. 'The pike must be eight inches in length between head and tail. A man found to have taken a smaller pike shall pay a fine of five sous', specifies the charter of Beaumont-sur-Argonne. Fishing methods themselves were designed to protect the fry and very small fish. The same charter enumerates the various types of nets and other devices which might be used 'to preserve the fish of the river for the King'.

On the other hand, as rivers were more or less public property, certain charters granted fishing permits quite freely, although not to the lower classes: 'The burghers of Sathenay are granted the right to fish in the Meuse from the mill at Chorey to Monzay, with line and nets and sticks. And if any burgher have water running behind his house, he may set fishing pots in it.' Poor people, reduced to guile as usual, caught the small fry found in streams, or tickled fish from the millponds of the local communal mills.

The pools of feudal estates, like the reservoirs fed by rivers, were in the care of keepers who regularly saw that they were restocked. Certain pools and basins were kept for rearing fish fry, which sold for a good price. Rather than catching the adult fish in the normal way, given the quantity involved, the water was drained out through sluices and the fish shovelled up. They were then taken alive in tanks to the smaller fishponds belonging to manor houses or fishmongers. Alternatively, they might be smoked or salted at once. Bohemian fish farming set an example to the rest of Europe.

Fish supplies on a large scale were called for to satisfy the enormous demand. Sea fish (in France usually described as *marée*, the same as the word for 'tide', while *poisson* was reserved for freshwater fish) might arrive in towns still relatively fresh in winter, sometimes despite spending two days on the way, but transport in high summer presented serious problems.

However – in the case of France – the royal court and the households of great lords had special contracts with the fish carriers of the Channel ports. These laid down that fish must arrive alive, in regulation baskets. In 1670 the Duc d'Orléans made it known that dead fish, even if it was still fresh, would be paid for at only one-fifth its live value. The retail trade, strictly controlled itself, was even more particular in its requirements. It is easy to understand the vogue for fish pâtés, for which the *Ménagier de Paris*, like many other books, gives recipes. During the Renais-

'Fishing in a stream': painting from the fifteenth-century *Fables de Bidpaï.*
The castle glimpsed in the background reminds us that in the Middle Ages
feudal streams, rivers, lakes and fishponds were leased out against
payment of dues in money and in kind.

sance there was a whole range of fish 'charcuterie' which used almost anything,
even seals. Bruyerin-Champier, who ate some at the court of François I, thought he
was eating white pudding made from pork. Sturgeon pâté was the most highly prized.
Unlikely as it may seem today, sturgeon were very common in the Middle Ages. Those
caught in the river Rhône and in the Gironde cost no more than a sou a pound.

As a gesture to mark the New Year of 1775, Louis XVI, hoping to raise the
standard of living of the poor a little, made considerable reductions in the taxes

on the fish trade, taxes which were passed on to customers in the retail prices, explaining that it was 'one of the most useful branches of industry in our kingdom'. He was particularly keen to make salt fish readily available to everyone as a suitable food for fast days, for the observance of Lent was becoming rather lax. Then the dues levied on fish were abolished altogether except for a minimum levy payable to the Crown. However, the fishwives of Paris showed King Louis no particular gratitude when the Revolution came in 1789.

Louis XV had already offered a prize of 9000 francs to anyone who could discover a way to bring a fresh sea bream to Paris. Sad to say, no one won it. He may have been inspired by the memory of the unfortunate steward Vatel who committed suicide at Chantilly on the morning of 24 April 1671, believing the fish he had ordered for the dinner the Prince de Condé was giving the Sun King was not going to arrive in time. In fact the fish, driven at breakneck speed from the Channel, was unloaded from its carts only quarter of an hour after the death of the conscientious steward; not a fishy story, as one might think, but perfectly true.

The Symbolism of Fish

The fish cannot be dissociated from the water in which it lives, and the symbols of the two are often either linked or interchangeable. At a very early date, the remarkable fecundity of the fish and the swift regeneration of its shoals evoked the idea of rebirth and the perpetuation of natural cycles. It is not just chance that the double sign of Pisces (the male principle plus the female principle, hence procreation) is first in the springtime trio of the signs of the Zodiac, coming just before the equinox.

In Arab tradition, to dream of fish is a very good omen. Fish-shaped amulets, sometimes of a stylized pattern, have been good-luck charms since the days of ancient Egypt. The fish brings prosperity and passes on its own fertility. In Central America it is the visible manifestation of the god of maize, possibly by association with the shape of an ear of corn. But it is also a phallic symbol, found for instance among the Dogon people of West Africa, where circumcision is described as 'cutting the fish'. The literal translation of the name of the god of love in Sanskrit is 'he who has the fish for his symbol'. The love goddesses of the Hittites held a fish as their attribute and adornment.

From the spiritual viewpoint the fish has been used symbolically in several interpretations which are not so very far from these early concepts of fecundity and regeneration. As we see fish only when they touch the surface of the water, rising from the mysterious depths below, the fish in ancient India became an instrument of the revelation which allows spiritual rebirth into another, richer and more fruitful life. As an avatar of Vishnu, a fish saved Manu, father and legislator of the people of his time, from the deluge, and Vishnu gave him the sacred texts of the Vedas.

Christ is often compared with a fisherman, and Christians are represented as fish because they have received revelation and redemption by water at their baptism. The ideogram of the fish (Greek *iktus*) was the emblem of the early Church, its

'The fishwife' (1672), by Adriaen van Ostade (1610–85): small tunny fish, plaice and a crab can be identified on her stall, and there is a piece of salmon in the background.

five letters being the initials of the five Greek words describing the Saviour: Iesus Khristos Theou Uios Soter (Jesus the Anointed, Son of God, Redeemer). When Jesus reappeared to the apostles after the Resurrection, 'he said unto them, Have ye here any meat? And they gave him a piece of a broiled fish, and of an honeycomb' (Luke 24, xli–xlii). Like honey, signifying the revealed Word, fish was the appropriate first food for the resurrected Christ: it rises from the depths as he had risen again from the next world. Fish became one of the symbols of the Eucharistic meal, and features in many iconographies.

The Book of Leviticus, like almost all the religions of the ancient world, proscribed the sacrifice of fish, perhaps because of its connotations: it would be presumptuous to offer revelation and immortality to gods who already possess it. The Jewish people were allowed to eat fish, but not other aquatic creatures. To avoid any confusion or substitution, however, they could eat only species with scales and which did not resemble snakes. Similarly, while the common people of Egypt ate plenty of fish (which has been found among the provisions buried in a number of tombs), neither the priests nor the Pharaohs (i.e. no sanctified persons) were allowed to partake of it.

Why exactly was fish regarded as suitable Lenten fare for all classes, aristocrats and the poor alike, from the Middle Ages onwards? People had to eat something, obviously, but why fish? Because of its associations with the Eucharist? There was more to it than that: as we have seen, meat and fat were regarded as red, rich, hot food. They were therefore likely to induce euphoria or even excitement. Fish, by association with water, was cold, and was white, lean fare, sober and soothing, and in any case pure. The Church ordained Lent to make everyone do penance between Ash Wednesday and Easter, bringing home by imitation the significance of the fast Christ observed before he began his apostolic ministry. At the same time it was a mortification of the flesh, ideally leading to asceticism, and a sacrifice made once a year in reparation for sins committed.

On the other hand, it has been suggested that dietetic considerations were already finding expression, at a period when the extremely carnivorous diet of the prosperous called for occasional relief. And the moral aspect of abstinence was in line with Church thinking: we are all equal before God. If only for 40 days, a highly symbolic period always associated with a cycle of purification and regeneration (and fish symbolized regeneration), everyone would eat the same kind of food – meat, the cheerful sign of wealth, being replaced by the melancholy and humble fish, so that differences of status between high and low on the social ladder were erased. That did not in fact prevent the rich from enjoying luxurious Lenten fare such as roast pike, while the poor fasted on salt herring, as many stories show us. Massimo Montanari[7] makes the point well:

> To the members of the military aristocracy, eating meat did not just answer a need for sustenance. It was also a symbol of power, the dietary image of a violence inherent in their culture, a daily display of their

313

customs and attitudes. They felt it intolerable to be deprived of meat, so it is easy to see that a prohibition on eating it might seem a heavy penance. ... Obligatory abstinence from meat must also have been of symbolic value for the powerful, as the tangible sign of more or less temporary exclusion from the society of the strong ..., the image of a society in which food and dietary behaviour carried a strong emotional and communicatory charge.

Where the English have an April Fool tradition, the French equivalent is the *poisson d'avril*, the April fish. It first arose because until the reign of Charles IX of France, the year began on 1st April. In 1564, however, the king decided it should start on 1st January. This upset the calendar (nine years later, the Church brought in the Gregorian calendar and gave the new scheme its stamp of approval) and also the custom of giving New Year gifts in the same way as Christmas boxes in more recent times. From force of habit, people at first went on giving little presents on 1st April; then they gave presents designed to cause amusement, and to heighten the joke they started playing practical tricks. One of the most popular was to send a gullible person off to buy fresh fish, assuring him that the law had been changed and there was no longer a close season for freshwater fish from the day when the sun left the sign of Pisces on 20th March, the first day of spring, and entered the sign of Aries the Ram. (The fish spawned during this close season.) The victim would set off for the fish market, blissfully unaware that he had a paper fish pinned to his back so that everyone could see he had been fooled. Only a very stupid person would expect to buy 'April fish', and the joke ended with merry cries of 'Poisson d'avril!'

Uses for Less Profitable Fish

There will probably be seven billion people on Earth by the end of the twentieth century, and the problem of finding enough sources of protein to feed them all will be a pressing one. If we put our minds to it, intelligent exploitation of the seas and oceans, the 'sixth continent' of the world, could save humanity.

The Earth itself has cultivable humus to a depth of only a few centimetres, and that over an area which does not make up even half the land area of the continents which emerged from the seas. Covering a larger area than all those continents together, and not counting the deep waters of the oceanic abyss, the sea has 'active' layers to a thickness of several hundred metres.

Fishing today (100 million tonnes) accounts for only 12 per cent of animal protein needs supplied worldwide (dairy produce accounts for 43 per cent, butcher's meat for 35 per cent). If it were well managed, the exploitation (not extermination) of the fauna and even the flora of the seas could supply 25 per cent or more of those needs, i.e., some two billion tonnes a year.

For reasons of quick profit, combined with political short-sightedness on the part of the authorities all over the world, only the more easily saleable species are fished. There is damage done to the primary organic matter necessary to nourish marine fauna (for instance, it takes ten tonnes of primary matter to produce one kilo of tuna). Further damage is done by the intensive destruction of the fry when its natural habitat is affected by, for instance, pollution and bottom-trawling.

Among the 15,000 species of edible sea fish, only about 40, as we have seen, are sold in the developed and wasteful societies of Europe. Small fish and shellfish which are perfectly edible, not being in the least toxic, are thrown back into the sea dead to feed the gulls, or are turned into catfood. Accidentally caught fish with a great many bones or an unattractive appearance also go into canned catfood.

Professor Richet has written that 'the muscle of fish builds up human muscle'. He could have added 'and human brains', since fish is very rich in phosphorus. The Japanese, a remarkably clever people, eat more fish than anyone else in the world: 40 kilos per head a year, as against the French figure of 12.5 kilos per head. It is true that Western Europeans have a more varied diet available, but what will it consist of tomorrow? We also urgently need to think of the people of the Third World, who have the least protein in their diets. Japanese research into fish-farming and diet has pointed out a path it would be wise to pursue. We should not even be venturing into unknown territory, since the industrious people of the Middle Ages had a good notion of the way to turn the less choice species of fish into excellent products such as pâtés and sausages. Why make pâté out of monkfish and salmon when we could use the despised smaller fish instead?

Another future source of protein could be algae and seaweed; the Japanese and Chinese have long been eating various kinds of seaweed, which we vaguely take for fungi when we see them on the shelves of exotic food stores. In Europe the exploitation of seaweed is almost entirely confined to the extraction of its polysaccharides (agar-agar) for use as gelatine in the food industry; 1400 tonnes a year are produced in France. Seaweed is also used as fertilizer and animal feed. But interest has been shown recently in the biologically active substances present in it: their anti-bacterial, anti-fungal and above all anti-tumoral qualities. Their biomass could also provide appreciable quantities of methane.

At the Oceanological Centre in Brittany, broths of synthetic unicellular algae are used to feed farmed herbivorous fish and microscopic molluscs which themselves are the food of carnivorous fish fry. The process is still expensive, but may be regarded as a research investment. The day will come sooner than we expect when algae and seaweed make a direct contribution to the human diet, over and beyond providing a setting agent for our desserts. A centre for algological research has been set up at Pleuviau in the Côtes-du-Nord to draw up programmes for exploiting the prairies of the sea. Japanese algocultural techniques were introduced at Thau on the Mediterranean coast of France in 1982. We should neglect no possibilities and waste no resources.

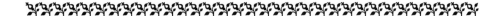

THE BRIMING OF THE HERRING

On Midsummer Night (the night of 24th to 25th June), five minutes after midnight, the great herring-fishing season opens in the northern seas. Flashing phosphorescence undulates and dances on the waves. 'There goes the briming of the herring!' is the traditional cry heard on all the boats. A whole living world has just risen from the depths to the surface, following the call of warmth, desire and the light. The timid fish like the pale and gentle light of the moon, the reassuring lantern which encourages them to celebrate their festival of love. They all come up together; not one remains behind. Sociability is the law of the herring race, and they are never seen alone. They live together, hidden in the twilight deeps; they rise together in the spring for their small share of universal happiness, to see the light of day, take their pleasure and die. Crowding in serried ranks, they can never be close enough to each other; they swim in dense shoals. 'It is as if the dunes set sail', the Flemish used to say. It looks as though a vast island has risen from the sea somewhere between Scotland, Holland and Norway, and a continent is about to emerge. An eastern section detaches itself and swims into the Sound, filling up the entry to the Baltic. In certain narrow straits it is impossible to row; the sea is solid with herring. Millions of millions of them, billions upon billions. Who would venture to guess the number of those legions? There is a tale that in the old days, near Le Havre, a single fisherman took 800,000 herring in his nets one morning. At one Scottish port they fill 11,000 barrels with herring in a night.

They advance like some blind, fateful element, and no destruction discourages them. Men and fish all fall upon them, but still they come, still they swim on ...

Jules Michelet (1798–1874), *La mer*

The Providential Nature of Salt Fish

It was usually necessary to smoke, dry or salt deliveries of fish when providing food for remote inland areas. Few fresh Mediterranean products are mentioned in the victualling records of the medieval Parisian courts, but a great deal of Mediterranean fish preserved in one way or another was eaten, whereas the converse was true of fish from the Channel and the Atlantic. The south of Spain, the Portuguese Algarve, Catalonia, Provence, Sicily, the Greek archipelagos, the Bosphorus and even North Africa sent cargoes of salted tuna and dried octopus and barrels of sardines and anchovies.

In his *Histoire du sel*,[8] Jean-François Bergier tells us that the Saint-Maurice customs post on the St Bernard Pass was imbued with the stench of the sacks of salt fish travelling over the pass in both directions. Storing sardines, anchovies and above all herring in bond was then forbidden.

The herring reigned supreme during medieval Lents. Although Latin texts of the period call the herring *alecum* or *alexium* (from Greek *als*, salt), the ancient world itself knew nothing of this fish from the cold northern seas. But the people of northern Gaul had long been relying on the abundant food it offered them. Vessels were sailing from the Baltic and the North Sea to catch herring, 'the wheat of the sea', before the year 1000. Then climatic change caused a perceptible drop in water temperature, and the shoals turned for preference to the Dogger Bank region of the North Sea, familiar to most of us from the shipping forecast.

The herring is an abdominal malacopterygian (soft-finned fish) of the Clupeidae family. Its gills are very large, its teeth pointed, its sides flattened, and its head narrow with a pointed nose. It is dark in colour, almost black on the back and silvery on the stomach. It can grow to a length of 25 centimetres. Today many people are familiar with it mainly in the form of marinated herring fillets, as rollmops (rolled up round a gherkin), or smoked, when it becomes a red herring, bloater or kipper. Usually it lives on the sea bed, but around the month of March the shoals rise to spawn near the coast, as described more poetically in Michelet's account. The herring is a great traveller and can swim thousands of kilometres to find its spawning grounds, which have not changed for millions of years, no one knows why. If sharks or other predators bar their way, the shoals will go around them (much to the annoyance of fishing vessels expecting them) but will always reach their original destination in good time.

This highly social fish seldom appears on our tables in solitary state. The discovery of a way to pack herring in barrels is ascribed to one Wilhem Beuckelszon, a Dutchman, in around 1350. A master fisherman, born in Biervliet in Zeeland, he is said to have had the brilliant idea of gutting the fish as soon as it was caught and using brine instead of salt to preserve it without, obviously, drying it. In honour of Beuckelszon's memory, but principally to please the Dutch and so further his political ends, the Emperor Charles V himself and his sister the Queen of Hungary came to visit the tomb of this benefactor of humanity in 1506. The Emperor's pilgrimage and the speech he made did not have the desired effect, but that is another story.

Charles V may not have sounded entirely sincere, for he probably knew that there was nothing new or original about the process. All the countries that fish for herring claim it as their own: Iceland, Sweden, Norway, England and France. Documents dating from 1080 (England), 1163 (Flanders), 1030 (Dieppe), 1083 (Fécamp) and 1170 (Le Tréport), the last three all French, tell us that the technique Beuckelszon is supposed to have invented was in existence well before his day. It could, of course, have been forgotten again, but, however that may be, Holland derived such profits from herring from the fourteenth century onwards, and her sailors became such masters of the seas, still barely explored at the time, that she developed into one of the greatest economic and seafaring powers in the world. The citizens of Amsterdam said proudly that their city was built on herring bones. As Jules Michelet put it, 'the herring fishers transmuted their stinking cargoes into gold.'

Packing herring in barrels was a good commercial business. Processing the fish on the spot meant avoiding expensive journeys, especially as the season was a short one, and loss of time meant considerable loss of profits. Previously, herring, a very oily fish, had been quick to decay if it was not processed the moment it was landed. The new or at least the rediscovered procedure meant that the price of an already inexpensive food could be lowered yet further, and the consumer took advantage of the fact. In the fifteenth century Dieppe was already packing 400 tonnes of herring in barrels a year. Soon France imposed prohibitive duties on Dutch cod to protect the barrelled herring industry. Quarrels over fishing grounds did not begin with the European Community: since the sixteenth century treaties have had to be concluded even when countries were at war, if only to feed their armies.

When France taxed cod from the Netherlands to discourage its import, she did so because the Dutch method with herring was soon being applied to cod, and proved even more spectacularly successful. The large cod is a member of the order Gadiformes and of the Gadidae family. It is a subbrachian malacopterygian, i.e., a fish with a bony skeleton and ventral fins beneath the pectoral fins. 'The cod alone has created colonies and founded trading stations and towns', adds Michelet.

The cod has large eyes, but is practically blind because of a thick opaque film over them. This does not prevent it from being an efficient and very greedy hunter. It swallows anything that comes into its ever-open mouth, which has several rows of sharp teeth. Its greed is its downfall, and brings it straight to our tables. It is caught with multiple lines from boats which go out among the shoals from the larger cod fishery vessels, and the cod take the hooks so greedily that the fisherman does not always save his line.

The cod is as prolific as it is greedy. Every female lays just under ten million eggs. If most of them were not eaten, as well as most of the fry which do manage to hatch, there would soon be too many cod for the seas to hold them all.

Fresh cod is an everyday fish to be found on the fishmonger's slab at a reasonable price. It was seldom eaten fresh until the sixteenth century, when it featured on the menu at dinners for special occasions. Until the nineteenth century it was more usually sold salted and dried.

Cod can be described as a universal food. The poorer countries of Europe, America, the Antilles and Africa eat it as a staple dietary item, especially Portugal, where *bacalaó* is the national dish. Despite its extraordinary fertility, modern methods of fishing it have proved so efficient that stocks are beginning to run out. It is also possible that naval sonar equipment disturbs the migration necessary for the fish to spawn. Long regarded as a cheap fish, the cod is becoming increasingly expensive, particularly in its traditional salt form. The modern method of selling cod steaks or fillets (either fresh, or smoked like haddock) is more convenient for the housewife and the fish trade, but the flavour the whole fish used to have seems to be missing. That may be because today cod is often frozen at sea before undergoing any further treatment.

The cod 'banks' of Newfoundland were discovered by Basque whalers around the year 1000. At spawning time cod approach coasts rich in plankton – the coasts of Norway, Denmark, the north of Scotland, Iceland and above all Newfoundland – to lay their eggs. Venturing as far as Newfoundland in pursuit of whales, which were widely eaten in the Middle Ages, the Basque seamen noticed the extraordinary abundance of cod making for the St Lawrence estuary. Incidentally, the same Basques may be credited with setting eyes on the New World some time before Leif Eriksson or Christopher Columbus, although it must be admitted that they kept prudently quiet about the precise geographical location of their source of profit. When Jacques Cartier 'discovered' the St Lawrence early in the sixteenth century, more than 1000 Basque fishing boats were assembled in the Gulf. The secret had finally become a persistent rumour, and King François I of France had sent the explorer to take possession of those prolific shores. Their waters, now territorial, became liquid gold.

The arms of the town of Biarritz show the hunting of a whale. The Gulf of Gascony was one of the places whales used to visit frequently. The whale itself, as everyone knows, is a mammal,[9] although described in medieval English law as a 'royal fish', and the specimens that were sometimes stranded on shore were regarded as great windfalls from prehistoric times onwards. Whales were still very numerous in the Middle Ages, and from the September equinox onwards watchmen would keep a lookout from towers, one of which still stands in the port of Biarritz, to announce the approach of the spouting whales with smoke signals and cries of 'Souffle! Souffle!' – 'There she blows!' Immediately boats full of harpooners would put out all along the coast.

Whales, huge as they are, can eat nothing but the tiny crustaceans known as krill which move around Arctic and Antarctic waters in vast shoals (their average size has been estimated at a weight of some hundred million tonnes). This thick protein purée seething in the cold seas has attracted the attention of Russian and Japanese scientists in view of its potential for the human diet, now that its natural predators have been decimated. Once, however, the whales used to move around in great schools in pursuit of their food, and in flight from the grip of the ice.

With the Basque seamen chasing the whales that chased the krill, hunting grounds soon expanded, for whales provided a number of different and very desirable products, still sought after by the Russians and Japanese, the last nations to exploit the whale. Those products included blubber, smoked whalemeat (known as lard, bacon or *craspois*), spermaceti, whalebone and whale hide.[10] A doggerel verse chanted by the seller of *craspois* figures among the *Cris de Paris*, the street cries of Paris:

> Lard à pois, lard à pois, baleine!
> De crier, je suis hors d'haleine
> C'est viande de caresme;
> Elle est bonne à gens qui l'aiment.

[Smoked whalemeat with peas, whale! I'm breathless with crying my whale. It is food for Lent, and good for those who like it.]

Whaling methods and technology were greatly improved during the whole of the twentieth century, with the result that today the several giant species of these marine mammals are almost exterminated. Under pressure from ecological action groups, international conventions have regulated the hunting of the last survivors, although it is difficult to make some countries implement the regulations.

Up to the Renaissance, however, whaling was a hard life but ensured the prosperity of the Basques. Then the great cetaceans gradually deserted the places that had proved so unwelcoming. The whale caught by the people of Biarritz in 1686 was the last of its kind to have occasion to realize, too late, it should have spouted somewhere else. If the individual whale was out of luck, so thereafter was the Chapter of Bayonne, whose privilege it was to receive the vast animals' tongues. Whale tongue is said to be delicious grilled and served with peas, like the smoked whalemeat, although Ambroise Paré, sixteenth-century surgeon and man of letters, does not seem to have thought much of it: 'Their flesh is little esteemed, but as the tongue is tender and delicious, they salt it likewise, and distribute it in a number of provinces; they keep the fat of the whale to rub it on their boats; this fat, once melted, never freezes.'

Despite the absence of whales, the Basques remained faithful to Newfoundland, where they long fished cod (one of the principal towns of the island is Port-aux-Basques). Some became corsairs, and had such a reputation for courage that they were granted the right to keep their hats on before Louis XIV, although the cod fishers might have deserved that honour quite as much as the corsairs.

Although climatic conditions have not changed, the life of a cod fisherman is still hard and poorly paid. Today the fishing boats described by Pierre Loti in *Pêcheurs d'Islande* have been replaced by large trawlers with freezing plants on board.

The fishing season in the Arctic waters of Greenland, Labrador, Newfoundland and even the south-east Atlantic lasts for nine months of the year, and the vessels go out three times. With vessels well equipped with radio and radar, infirmaries, cinemas, and sometimes helicopters, large modern fisheries need far fewer boats; the cod-fishing industry of France at present has only 17 trawlers, on which the fish is frozen as soon as it comes out of the water. The cod is then salted in factories when it comes ashore. In the eighteenth century a thousand cod-fishing boats left French ports for Newfoundland every spring, taking tonnes of salt with them. Today there is only a single French vessel that does nothing but salt cod on the spot. Fresh cod is still fished with multiple lines running out from smaller boats. As soon as they come on board the main vessel the fish are gutted, beheaded, and usually filleted before any further processing.

Cod salted on board the fishing vessels is known in French as *morue verte*, 'green' cod, not because of its colour, which remains very pale, but because it is naturally treated. In the past the cod-fishing boats which produced this 'green' cod did not always use all the salt they had brought (200 barrels for 5000 hundredweight of cod) and had to take it back to the home port, to the annoyance of the officials administering the salt tax.[11] Today cod to be salted is delivered to the factory 'green' or frozen. It is left whole, complete with the skin and bones which contribute to the flavour of good salt cod. At the factory it is scrubbed and then salted again. This is salt cod of the traditional type. Filleted cod is also scrubbed at the factory and then boned and filleted. It is packed in boxes, each holding a weight of 350 grams.

The simple method of drying cod has a very ancient tradition behind it. Fishermen used to process the cod themselves on the Newfoundland coast: then they buried it under turves and picked it up next season. The wintry climate of Newfoundland froze it and then progressively defrosted it again, so that it was gradually dehydrated. Today the 'green' cod is carefully scrubbed and placed in ventilated ovens. In some Hispanic-speaking countries of the west coast of Africa and the West Indies, salt cod of this kind is baked without preliminary soaking to rehydrate it and remove excess salt. It is strong-flavoured and feels hard.

Stockfish is cod intensively dried on stones until it becomes as hard as wood, 'stock' being from the Dutch *stok*, meaning a stock or block of wood, related to other Germanic words such as 'stake' and 'stick'. Stockfish has been a Scandinavian speciality since Viking times. It is mentioned by the *Ménagier de Paris* in the fourteenth century, under the name of *stofix*.

> Cod is not called 'morue' at Tournay unless it is salt, for the fresh fish is called 'cableaux'. It is eaten and cooked as follows. Item, when it is taken in the far seas and it is desired to keep it for 10 or 12 years, it is gutted and its head removed and it is dried in the air and sun and in no wise by a fire, or smoked; and when this is done it is called stockfish. And when it hath been kept a long time, and it is desired to eat it, it behoves to beat it with a wooden hammer for a full hour, and then set

> it to soak in warm water for a full 12 hours or more, then cook and
> skim it very well like beef. ... Fresh cod is prepared and cooked like
> gurnard with white wine. ... If the salt fish is too little soaked it tastes
> too salt, and if too much it is not good; wherefore whoever is buying
> it ought to taste it, by eating a little.

Until the First World War, stockfish or *estocafida* was a part of the usual family diet in Provence. The best sort was yellow as old ivory.

Like the herring, the cod has been the object of 'wars' of a more or less diplomatic nature between the great fishing nations as they dispute rights of access to territorial waters (cod, like herring, assembles near coasts to spawn). The Icelanders, who have very few other natural resources, are very touchy on the subject. In 1973 there was a memorable 'cod war' between Britain and Iceland, less violent than Britain's later Falklands War, but conducted with much ill feeling, considering the amount of money and the number of jobs involved.

In the Middle Ages, commercial interests in fishing rights went hand in hand with commercial interests in the salt necessary for the preservation of fish. Salt was state property in France. French salt was also imported to England at this period and known as 'Bay salt', after the salt produced in the Bay of Bourgneuf, and it was widely used for curing fish. Salt was a pressing need of the Scandinavian peoples, who could not market their large catches of fish without it. Salt-producing and salt-consuming countries therefore exercised a kind of mutual blackmail. An embargo by the former, or refusal to purchase by the latter, had dire economic consequences. Indeed, the whole trade was an economic network linking nations in alliances or competition and involving fisheries, salt, transport, taxes and the seizure of ports. Paradoxically, after the Reformation the northern countries which were no longer bound to observe Lent themselves went on making their living out of it, since their customers in the Catholic countries ate salt fish during the Lenten fast.

I have not mentioned the sardine, a member of the Clupeidae family like its cousin the herring, because I shall be discussing it at greater length in the chapter on canning: most sardines end up in cans. Always fished in abundance in the sea off Brittany and in the Mediterranean, along the Moroccan coast south of Portugal, sardines were salted and pressed all over the continent of Europe. In the eighteenth century people began preserving them in vinegar, in oil, or most frequently in melted butter. Brittany is butter country, and sardines brought a good income to a region sadly in need of it. The town of Port-Louis in the Morbihan area alone exported 40 million sardines a year, packed in casks.

The canning of sardines began quite early in the nineteenth century, but then Brittany unfortunately lost its sardines – known as Celtic sardines – in the early 1960s. We do not know whether a change of course by the current was to blame, or they disappeared because the sea become colder or because of unrestricted trawling. In any case, the sardine shoals now have to be caught farther away, on the coasts of Africa. Stocks of the large adult sardines or pilchards which used to be

'Dolphins preying on sardines': from
Le Petit Journal, illustrated supplement
of 30 March 1913. The dolphin is
both sociable and voracious. It is
very fond of sardines, either caught
in the open sea or already taken
in nets, and fishermen had to
defend their catch.

caught off the Cornish coast have also declined. Mediterranean sardines still exist, and seem to have adjusted to the open sewer which that sea now resembles, which must be a relief to the fishermen of Sète and Marseilles. A decline in stocks of anchovies has been observed at Collioures. There is a hoary old joke in France about the sardine that once blocked the port of Marseilles; everyone knows it was actually a ship called the Sardine which lost her rudder, but it is still good for a smile.

Just as the king's Grand Panetier was in charge of the corporation of bakers in the Middle Ages, another officer of the royal table, the Premier Queu (First Cook) appointed the officials who regulated the fish trade of Paris, which was divided into two corporations: the 'herring-mongers' or 'merchants of sea fish' (further divided by Louis IX and Étienne Boileau into two sections, for fresh fish and salt fish), and the 'freshwater fishmongers', for the sale of fish from rivers and lakes.

Drying, Salting and Smoking Fish; an Age-Old Procedure

People all over the world have always tried to store fish. Although such an excellent food, it will not keep long, for it changes even faster than meat, particularly freshwater fish. As sea fish are more plentiful, however, they have been the main subject of preserving methods because of considerations of price.

The flesh of fish has a high water content, one and a half times as much as that of meat, and people were quick to notice that if as much as possible of this water was removed (to be restored if necessary in preparation or cooking) it could safely remain edible for longer. Another advantage is that when fish has lost sometimes as much as 66 per cent of its weight in being dried, it is easier to store and transport it. Most important of all, however, its nutritional value increases considerably, despite the loss of certain vitamins which can be compensated for in the accompaniments to dishes made with it. Finally, it is as digestible as fresh fish, always provided, of course, that the preservation has been done properly.

Table 10.1, taken from the *Dictionnaire pratique de diététique et de nutrition*,[12] edited by Professor Apfelbaum, gives a comparison of the nutritional values of the most common dried, salted or smoked fish in relation to the consumption of the same species fresh.

Table 10.1 The Nutritional Values of Fish

constituents		fresh cod	stockfish (dried cod)	ordinary salt dried cod	fresh herring	kipper (smoked, salt herring)	smoked haddock
water	(%)	80.5	14.20	39	66.1	6.2	77
fat		0.3	1.4	1	15.8	13.4	0.4
protein		18.1	78.5	37.8	16.44	21.1	23
calcium	(mg)	20	160	60	40	140	3.1
phosphorus		200	950	300	320	380	
iron		0.6	2.5	1.6	0.6	0.75	
iodine		0.5	1.2	0	0.05	0.10	
vit. B1	(IU)	50	0	0	40	0	
B2		110	240	230	300	370	
B5		50	0	0	40	0	
B12		0.8	10	3.6	14	1.5	
calories (units)		70	325	160	205	205	103

Natural drying in the open air, or by exposure to the heat of the sun, is the oldest method used in all latitudes. Exposure to the heat of a fire makes the water contained in the cells of the fish evaporate more intensively and faster. From there it was a natural step to smoking, an especially common method in Northern Europe and North America, and in the forested zones of Africa. Smoking calls for a lot of wood, particularly from conifers. The gutted or flattened and salted fish[13] is impregnated with hydrocarbons (3–4 benzopyrene) which are given off in the form of smoke from a hot fire to which the fish is exposed at a suitable distance. Eating too much smoked meat and fish is known to be one factor in causing stomach cancers. Red herrings have been smoked for 48 hours. Today people prefer the less salty and more mildly smoked kipper. Other fish frequently smoked are haddock, sprats, trout, salmon, eel and cod's roe. Octopus, squid and cuttlefish used to be smoked, but the habit has died out. The process of both salting and drying fish calls for good salt supplies either locally available or provided through commercial channels. Either sea salt or rock salt is used. The fish is salted first, to induce partial dehydration, and the process is completed by natural or artificial drying near a source of heat. Small fish such as anchovies, sardines, mackerel and herring are salted whole, but tuna from the Mediterranean basin used to be sliced first. Cod was given a preliminary salting before the salting and drying process, which thus needed only about three-quarters the usual amount of salt. Brine for pickling is either a mixture of salt and water, or seawater concentrated by evaporation. It may have aromatics, saltpetre or even sugar added to it. Pickling dries the fish out less than salting.

Salted, dried and smoked fish cannot be stored in a warm, humid place or it will very soon go bad.

Aquaculture and Pisciculture: Fish Farming

Aquaculture is the breeding of marine species – not necessarily just fish – in a closed environment in order to return them to their natural element, where their life cycle will be completed, possibly ending when they are caught at the right point in their development. It could be described as the artificial fertilization or re-seeding of the ocean. However, aquaculture is a term also used for breeding sea fish and crustaceans in artificial basins until they are put on sale. The farming of shellfish is a form of aquaculture divided into two sections: oyster breeding and mussel breeding. A start is now being made on the farming of scallops and of clams; a taste for the latter is reaching Europe from the United States.

Pisciculture, a term which is properly speaking applied only to freshwater fish, was, as we have seen, very popular among the ancient Romans. Charlemagne brought the pursuit back into fashion, and most of the freshwater fish so useful in the Lenten diet from the Middle Ages to the Renaissance was reared in accordance with the technical and scientific facilities of the time.

On the other hand there was nothing scientific about the exploitation of the sea for a couple of decades in the middle of the twentieth century. Between the end of the Second World War and the beginning of the 1970s, the concepts of aquaculture, the restocking of the sea and fish farming would have appeared merely fanciful, particularly in France, which tends to lag behind the rest of Europe in such developments. In fact a war on fish had begun without anyone's noticing. Throughout the hostilities, from 1939 to 1945, fishing along French coasts was greatly reduced, while rivers and estuaries were spared further pollution. Accordingly the country saw a period of miraculous catches from the liberation of France to 1950. After this era of abundance, fish began to be less plentiful, but the technique of catching them using such methods as artificial light, bottom-trawling and sonic depth-finders had been so highly developed that the 1970s saw the threat of imminent catastrophe: great quantities of fish were caught without a thought for what should be left to ensure normal regeneration of the marine fauna. Add to that the pollution from oil slicks, radioactive waste, civil engineering undertaken without adequate precautions, the dumping off crowded resort beaches of raw sewage, faecal matter and detergent scum, and it will be clear that my remarks are not confined to France alone.

One of the first tasks of the aquaculture that began in the 1970s was to restore to the sea what 20 years of depredations and thoughtless wastefulness had destroyed, whether directly or indirectly. For instance, the native seaweeds of Mediterranean shores had been progressively replaced by a sterile and unpleasant kind of slime.

It takes a tonne of plankton to feed 100 kilos of zooplankton, which will feed ten kilos of fish fry, which in their turn will feed one kilo of large fish. In the course of the natural cycle it is estimated that about 20 per cent of fish and crustacean eggs are fertilized. The brood that hatches from these eggs is mostly eaten by predators if it does not die a natural death. It takes a million eggs to produce a single fish. Nature, with this fact in mind, has endowed the female fish with an impressive capacity for laying eggs.

Another project entails placing breeding females, caught at sea in nets and chosen from the best of the catch, in pools of seawater. They are then given company in the shape of fine male fish on the point of releasing their milt. Once the eggs have been laid – fertilization is generally 80 per cent – the parents are instantly removed, since they will be the first to prey upon their offspring if they are all left together in a confined space. Currents gently keep the eggs moving to complete the fertilization process, and they are then tipped into well-oxygenated 'incubators'. The larvae eat plankton made from algae and a supplementary organic nutrient. The yield is far greater than could ever occur in the best of natural conditions: 60 per cent of the eggs produce fish. Some of these fish, the fry of the most profitable species, are reared to their maximum size for the market. They are well fed and develop much faster than they would in the wild. The rest go back to the sea to live out their lives there, usually ending up in the belly of a stronger predatory species, and that predator itself may end in the fisherman's net.

Of course these experiments – for they are still at the experimental stage – have attracted criticism beyond the suspicions and anxieties of fishermen who do not have all the facts. Such criticism is directed at the considerable resources involved and their expense (i.e., the cost price of each unit of protein obtained), and the difficulty of situating aquacultural centres near unpolluted areas. However, putting a man on the moon must have seemed an equally fantastic project. The Japanese, who are known for their business sense, are pioneers of aquaculture. Interestingly, the late Emperor Hirohito was a notable marine biologist.

The disillusionment expressed in Venice at a congress of experts of World Mariculture in 1981 was thus of a kind inevitable when new techniques are just emerging, and should be seen as the price to be paid for the enthusiasm necessary to create them. The fact remains that, suitably fed and tended, and spared the exhausting business of swimming back upstream, salmon can produce a yield of 300 tonnes of flesh per hectare, which in economic terms is 15 times better than the yield of beef cattle. Pessimists may issue warnings about counting chickens before they are hatched, but, if optimism and the capacity to dream were not also human qualities, mankind would still be gathering primitive wheats and sucking wild honey from the combs.

I mentioned salmon because it might be described, mixing metaphors, as the warhorse of aquaculture. The most spectacular successes have been achieved with young salmon at the smolt stage, caught as they prepare to swim into the sea and grow to adulthood there. Instead, they finish growing in preserves cordoned off in various bays, and can be caught to order. The idea of their confinement may seem rather sad, but there is a great difference between these stretches of natural water and the stinking conditions under which battery hens live. The method has been successfully used in France in the Landes area, and has also been applied to the sea trout bred by the Oceanological Centre of Brittany. Swimming freely in basins of seawater, the smaller fish comes to think itself as good as its cousin, the lordly salmon. It grows as large as a fine sea bream, its flesh turns pink, and its flavour is improved by the sea air. Sea trout is so popular with Belgian restaurateurs that they have what is practically a monopoly of French production of the fish.

As the newspaper *Libération* wrote on 10 September 1980, 'this is the proof that Albert Vaillant (of the Oceanological Centre) and his team have not been working in vain these last ten years.' The reporter, Françoise Monier, concludes: 'Big companies wait for smaller firms to try a new project out before entering the fray themselves. Several American multinationals such as Raston Purina, the giant animal feed group, and Coca Cola, have now begun to move their pieces on the board.'

France-Aquaculture has sold the patent of a hatchery producing 200 million baby prawns a year to the southern United States; the secret of successful aquaculture also depends on water temperature. It takes 32 months in seawater varying from 5 to 20 degrees Centigrade (winter and summer temperatures) for a sea bass to grow to a weight of 250 grams. With water at a constant 24 degrees, the time taken to rear the same fish falls to 14 months. At the time of writing French aquaculture confines itself mainly to producing larvae in such conditions. Very soon, however, we shall be able to rear fish in warm water until they reach adulthood, as the Egyptians have done in a 1000 hectare basin installed by the French and financed by the World Bank. Experiments in the eel-rearing basins at Cadarache show that, when the water was kept at 20 degrees, the warmth being provided by the nuclear power station, the average weight of fish rose from 90 to 200 grams in a very short space of time.

Rearing eels is really pisciculture, since it is done in fresh water. Canada has had excellent results rearing trout near the Picketing power station. The farming of prawns at Gravelines and carp at Saint-Laurent-des-Eaux makes use of the heat from the water used to cool the reactors, which would otherwise be wasted.

In another project, at Mèze near the pool of Thau in the Hérault area, water from the sewers is purified as it runs through a system of basins: water, air and sun are the only agents used in the process. The result is very clean water, rich in the plankton used to feed carp and tilapias (or 'African' carp, the fish of Christ's miraculous catch).

Carp is king of the fish in Central Europe, where Christmas or Easter would be unthinkable without it. Even in the Middle Ages southern Bohemia had an international reputation for its well-organized carp breeding. More recently Hungary has combined the rearing of carp with that of rabbits and ducks or geese. Those fowls, reared near the ponds containing the carp, enrich the water with their droppings, and the fish grow to enormous size before they are caught. In fact the ponds are emptied of fish and drained every two or three years, and are then used to grow a cereal crop with a very high yield. In Central Africa pigs are raised together with ducks and tilapias. The Ivory Coast follows the same method, and dries its carp, which are much prized on the home market for their size.

But China is still carp country *par excellence*. The Chinese, who invented this method of mixed stock-rearing, began breeding carp 3000 years ago, and the fish has been their favourite for 30 centuries, a testimonial in itself. The Chinese name of the carp is *li*, which is also as common a surname as Dubois in France or Smith in England. The first piscicultural treatise in the world was written by a Chinese in 473 BC; the author's name was Fan Li. (Dare I suggest that he must have been a great carp fan?) That common patronymic was the name of a number of emperors of the famous T'ang dynasty. It appeared inappropriate to eat so sacred a totem, and so the carp respectfully disappeared from menus for three centuries. Gourmets must have breathed a sigh of relief when a new dynasty came to power.

However, Chinese fish farmers had branched out into other specialities, no doubt praying that no future sovereign would be called after the pike, roach or eel. Their piscicultural revolution was beneficial to fish breeding in general, introducing more variety. Today the Chinese have achieved the considerable production level of 800,000 tonnes of freshwater fish a year. Adding the fish caught in lakes and rivers – not to mention the paddy fields, which become fishponds when flooded, since no source of profit must be neglected – the figure comes to over a million tonnes, outstripping French sea fisheries, which produced only 732,000 tonnes a year. Chinese sea fishing, the third largest in the world after the fishing industries of Japan and the USSR, produces over four million tonnes. It is true that there are a lot of Chinese to feed, and a lot of fishermen to catch fish.

The Chinese have also created a kind of genetically engineered carp. They inject fish of both sexes with added hormones to stimulate egg-laying and fertilization; the operation is carefully carried out by breeders going from basin to basin. A single carp will then lay between 600,000 and a million eggs, depending on its variety. As the fry are well protected, it is easy to see that the yield is huge, especially as there is rivalry between rural communes to achieve the best results.

So far as the food economy is concerned, the trick is turning the pools into sewage farms, almost municipal dumps. Nutritional waste matter for the fish to feed on is thus obtained free. Pigs and ducks are also allowed to wallow or paddle in the mud on the banks of the pools, where they are very happy and do their own bit towards raising the nutritional level of the water. If there are not enough pigs, human manure is used, as in all Chinese cultivation. And even that is not all: the Chinese have herbivorous carp which, raised among the others, enrich the water of the basins yet further with their digestive products. A Chinese proverb says that 'One herbivorous carp will feed three black carp'. All this may not sound very appetizing, but the carp taste delicious when cooked. Sauces for fish are very important in China, as indeed they are elsewhere; the most popular Chinese sauce is sweet-sour.

Perhaps the oldest recipe in the world is for a Chinese fish salad (*yukai*) which appears in the 'Correct Principles of Eating and Drinking' (*Yinshan zhengyao*) by the imperial dietitian Hu Sihui. The work was written in 1330 bc, and is mentioned in texts going back to the Chou dynasty, which flourished in the eleventh century bc.[14] The salad consisted of slices of raw carp, marinated in a mixture of radish, ginger, chives, basil and peppered knot grass. The eating of raw fish – greatly enjoyed by the Polynesians over a very long period – is not really the invention of modern *nouvelle cuisine*.

Blue Europe or the Common Fish Market

Once regarded as 'a space free and open to all', apart from the narrow strip of territorial waters along coastlines, the sea, 'that grand idea', as the nineteenth-century writer Barbey d'Aurevilly put it, has become a more valuable prize than ever. Here nationalism and imperialism are basically expressions of a major economic concern, the issue of survival. Not only do states need the sea to feed them, they depend on it a little more every day for their energy, industry, scientific research, the primary matter of the nodules resting on the seabed, and of course in commercial and strategic concerns. But I shall confine myself to discussing fishing here.

For centuries, tradition has defined territorial waters, those directly subject to the jurisdiction of maritime nations, as a distance all along coasts equivalent to the range of a cannon ball, three nautical miles or about 3.6 kilometres. It was a case of the argument of the strongest. The seas and oceans as a whole, the hydrosphere, cover 361 million square kilometres, against only 150 million square kilometres of land. Territorial waters made up only 73 million of those square kilometres. They were not all particularly profitable, and landlocked states such as Luxembourg and Austria were completely excluded from them.

Two successive United Nations conferences on the Law of the Sea, held in 1958 and 1960, were unable to agree on a new and wider definition of territorial waters or on provisions governing sea space. In April 1983 the extension of territorial waters requested by the larger maritime states was ratified by a third conference. The extent of territorial waters was now 12 nautical miles from the coast, and furthermore – this was the crucial point – the maritime countries were to control an 'exclusive economic zone' of 200 nautical miles. In all, these provisions amounted to 35 per cent of the hydrosphere, calculated on a basis of all coastal waters, from those surrounding the smallest island to the seas around the Antipodes; the implications help to account for the Falklands War. Almost all areas abundant in fish thus came within the jurisdiction of the great maritime countries, to the dismay of the Third World and countries with no access to the sea.

In fact nearly all fish caught in the sea live on the continental shelf, the shallow area surrounding continents. In the Atlantic, that shelf never extends further than 200 miles from land. Hardly any edible fish are found beyond these limits, for lack of their own food, apart from big migratory fish such as tuna or cod while they are on the move.

With 3000 kilometres of coastline (including her overseas territories) France thus acquired rights to over ten million square kilometres, coming third after the United States and Great Britain (including the Falklands). The Soviet Union was fourth.

In the European context, where nothing is ever simple, the next task was to organize a Common Market of fisheries, or rather what was called a common fisheries policy. This 'blue Europe' was created in January 1983, just before the United Nations conference on maritime law. But after an incubation period of 12 years it had an even harder time hatching than its elder, green sister of the European agricultural policy, which is saying a lot, and it looked like having a difficult childhood. Fishermen are even touchier, prouder and more nationalistic than farmers, as grave incidents involving Danish and British fishermen have shown. Although the sector comprises only 200,000 jobs in the Community, as against the 8,500,000 in agriculture, it is at the centre of an industry of major importance in coastal regions which have no other advantages and are often underdeveloped, such as Brittany. As the paper *Le Marin* wrote on 28 January 1983:

> It may be thought that 12 years of effort have not been too much if a common policy can be found which will cover the 33-metre Breton, German or Irish trawler fishing for cod in the open sea off Norway or the St Lawrence, the 8-metre Sicilian sardine boat operating close to the island's coasts, the Danish, French or Dutch seiner with her catch of North Sea herring, the Danish 50-metre industrial vessel operating on an industrial scale for the fishmeal factories, and the Breton fleet at sea off Senegal which brings home several hundred tonnes of tuna every season. Without being a miracle cure, the common fisheries policy consists of a series of sensible regulations, financial provisions and agreements with the Third World which will guarantee all these fishermen the chance to make a living.

The extension of fishing limits had been closely related to the decline in fish stocks perceptible from the beginning of the 1970s. All countries tried to enlarge and protect their own preserves and manage them better. The question was particularly important in Europe, where fishing vessels, now often barred from waters which although a long way off were abundant in fish, found themselves trying to compete in areas to which they were not always adapted. The situation was aggravated by technical progress which, if it is not well regulated, increases the risk of over-exploitation. Herring fishing, for instance, had to be almost entirely halted between 1971 and 1981 in the Community area, and mackerel stocks are in danger of exhaustion.

The fishing industry has always had to face certain problems linked with the traditional characteristics of the sector: the diversity of fish available, fluctuations in production, the perishability of fish, inflexible demand, etc. Today, if fishermen are to be guaranteed employment and security, the sector has to adapt its structures to the modification of fishing grounds and the necessity of protecting the biological inheritance: in the long term, only such protection can ensure abundant catches at reasonable cost. At the same time, the fishing industry has to face a rise in production costs and the consequences of imports from non-Community countries. In fact such imports are sometimes favoured by competitive advantages, the development of the fish trade towards frozen and processed products, and finally by the tariff reductions granted to Scandinavian, Mediterranean and African countries which are linked to the Community by various agreements.

The common fisheries policy thus aims to help the sector to meet these challenges. It bears on four principal areas: access to stocks of fish, their conservation and management; the organization of markets; structural problems; and international relations.

In the field of fisheries the principle of non-discrimination between member states and the nationals of those states, based on the Treaty of Rome, means free access to all Community waters. However, within the economic 200-mile limit, which in principle is open to all European fishing vessels, member states are allowed to extend the fishing limits reserved for their own vessels and those of other member countries which have traditionally operated in those areas to 12 miles. A catalogue of such traditional operations has attempted to determine historical rights. Outside the 12-mile limit, however, the fishing of biologically endangered species is subject to a system of Community licences. The area concerned is north of the United Kingdom, in the sea off the Orkneys and Shetlands, where fishing is limited to a certain number of British, French, German and Belgian vessels. All these measures, applicable for a 20-year period, may be revised at the end of the tenth year after they came into force, i.e., in 1993.

The protection and management of Atlantic and North Sea resources are ensured by the fixing of quotas for the total authorized catch. The Council of Ministers of the Community fixes these quotas annually for species in danger of being over-fished, and they are shared out between the interested member states. The final allocation adopted on 25 January 1983 was to serve as a reference in subsequent years. It aimed to ensure the relative stability of the fishing operations of all countries involved on the basis of the following criteria: traditional fishing operations, the particular needs of those areas most dependent on fishing, and the loss of catches in the waters of other countries because of their extension of their own fishing limits.

It was envisaged that the Community would continue to develop conservation measures in the light of scientific opinion, with particular reference to restrictions on fishing in certain areas, the standardization of fishing equipment, and the fixing of minimum sizes for the catching of certain protected species. Complementary non-discriminatory national measures are not banned, but the Commission must be notified of them, and may request their modification or suppression.

Control of the application of these various measures is entrusted to the member states under the supervision of the European Commission, which employs a body of European inspectors for the purpose. It should be noted that all the foregoing applies, obviously, only to the community zone of the Atlantic in the wider sense (i.e., including the North Sea and its extension into the Baltic). The principle of the 200-mile economic zone was not in force in the Mediterranean at the time of writing.

The common organization of markets, set in 1970, was revised at the end of 1981. Its aims are to allow the sensible development of fisheries, ensure an equitable standard of living to those employed in the sector, stabilize markets and guarantee the security of supplies to consumers at a reasonable price. Standards have been fixed to this end: fish and shellfish offered for sale must conform to certain strictly controlled specifications affecting quality, size, weight, and presentation or packing.

In order to restructure, modernize and develop its fisheries and aquaculture, the Community aims to support national programmes for the building and modernization of fishing vessels (giving priority to investment in replacement and to those coastal areas with particularly strong fishing interests). It also intends to increase its aid to aquaculture (giving priority to projects involving innovation) and to support the building of artificial reefs to encourage restocking of the coastal zones of the Mediterranean. Grants in aid of scientific research are also envisaged.

Finally, the Community has signed agreements of a different kind with certain developing countries. In exchange for permission to fish in their waters, the Community is granting these countries aid for their own fishing industries in the form of money to be invested in those industries, contributions to scientific projects, and grants for study and for the training of local fishermen. Such agreements have been made with Senegal, Guinea and Guinea-Bissau. Others are being negotiated with Mauritania and Equatorial Guinea, and the Commission is pursuing its contacts with the African states on the shores of the Atlantic and the Indian Ocean, with a view to negotiating new agreements.

And once all this is achieved, the European Community will hardly need to go fishing for compliments.

From Fishing to Our Plates

Thanks to modern techniques the quantity of sea fish caught is growing annually, although there are fewer job opportunities in the fishing industry. In France, there were 60,000 fishermen in 1960 and only 30,000 in 1980. If the price of a fishing boat, even a small one, is a big investment, every voyage it makes incurs further expense because of rises in energy costs. It takes from one to five tonnes of oil to catch a tonne of fish, depending on species and fishing grounds.

On the eve of the United Nations conference on fishing rights, on 27 January 1983, the journal *La Croix* published the figures shown in table 10.2:

Table 10.2   The Economic and Social Potential of a Common
Fishing Zone of 1,240,000 sq km

	% of GNP from fishing in 1980	no. of fishing vessels in 1982	no. of fishermen	imports of fish products*	exports of fish products*
France	0.158	11,090	22,548	805	234
Denmark	0.717	3,396	14,909	234	573
Great Britain	0.102	6,879	23,289	579	255
W. Germany	0.020	697	5,133	579	185
Belgium	0.058	208	894	271	50
Holland	0.155	930	3,677	218	374
Ireland	0.423	1,616	8,824	25	59
Italy	0.193	22,492	40,000	570	77
Greece	0.488	892	46,500	44	11
Total EC	0.13	47,308		3,281	1,807

*In millions of ecus

From the administrative viewpoint sea fishing is subdivided into inshore fishery (vessels going out for a period of between 24 and 96 hours), deep-sea fishery (vessels usually leaving port for a voyage of over 96 hours), and high-sea fishery (vessels of 1000 tonnes or over, usually staying away from their home port or the port where they last put in for supplies for longer than 20 days).

Coastal fishery is on a small scale, and is much practised along French coasts, with their considerable total length of 3200 kilometres. The vessels used are of less than 25 tonnes, and they remain at sea for two or three days, not far from the shore, catching sedentary fish. Some 10,000 boats are employed in coastal fishing in France.

Deep-sea fishery seeks migratory fish and banks deeper than those near the shore. Vessels usually go out for 10 to 12 days. They are of over 25 tonnes, and fish the seas of the European continental shelf, Iceland, the Bay of Biscay and even the waters off African coasts. This is industrial fishery calling for well-equipped vessels belonging to large companies. As soon as the fish is caught it is sorted, often gutted and beheaded, and put into cold store on board until it is disembarked. Deep-sea fishery also needs ports organized for the dispatch or canning of fresh fish.

High-sea fishery is practised much farther away than deep-sea fishery, in the Arctic seas of Greenland, Labrador and Newfoundland, and French vessels even fish in the seas off the Kerguelen Islands. They go out for three months at a time. France has a dozen trawlers for high-sea fishery, on which the fish is frozen as soon as it is caught with a view to a long storage period. High-sea fishery is firmly oriented towards the future; its equipment means that we can buy a fish filleted and frozen far out at sea which will bear comparison with fish caught and prepared by rival fishing nations.

Mention should also be made of off-shore fishery, from small boats very close to land, and fishing on foot from the parts of the shore uncovered at low tide, or from the edge of the beach. Yields are negligible.

DISTRIBUTION Once caught, the fish is prepared to be marketed, i.e., it is usually sorted, graded, chilled and sometimes gutted. It may also be put in crates of a predetermined weight. As soon as it is disembarked, usually from midnight onwards, one or other of the commercial systems of distribution comes into play.

The traditional French distribution circuit is relatively long. It comprises several stages, and several intermediaries are involved:

Sales by auction are held in the morning for all fish brought ashore during the night. This method has developed considerably, gaining in hygiene and efficiency what it has lost in the way of picturesque charm. There is little in common between the quayside auctions of the past and the 'fish exchanges' of today.

The specialist fish wholesaler with his business headquarters at the ports is the first stage in the traditional circuit. Fish wholesalers today distribute 85 per cent of the fish landed. The profession, reorganized in France by a decree of 1967, has both a commercial and a technical side to it, the latter aspect dealing with the sorting, cleaning, beheading and above all the filleting of fish. The fish wholesaler regulates demand and supply. He ensures that supplies reach groups of purchasers, distribution chains, other wholesalers, collective organizations and retailers.

The wholesale trade of Paris is well organized, with wholesalers and groups of producers concentrated at the national market at Rungis. In the provinces, apart from certain large centres such as Bordeaux, Toulouse, Lyon, Rennes, Rouen and Caen, organization is not always so good.

The short distribution circuit, a system well established in Great Britain and Sweden, has not had much success in France. Its principle (sale by the producer direct to the retailer without intermediaries) is difficult to reconcile with the wide dispersal both of French production (see above) and of the French retail trade. In the United Kingdom, however, it works well.

Abbreviated distribution circuits involve only one wholesale stage: the inland wholesaler buys from the producer, or more often the fish wholesaler sells straight to retailers. Transport is by road, rail, or sometimes air. Road transport seems to be the most adapatable and popular method.

Paris and the surrounding area has a great many busy markets. In large cities, more people go to traditional fishmongers for their fish. In country areas, mobile fishmongers' vans are common.

The French law of 8 July 1965 and the decree of 31 March 1967 regulated control of animal products, creating a body of veterinary inspectors and specialist sanitary officers. The decree of 31 July 1971 completed these arrangements. From landing of the fish to the point of sale, these specialist inspectors control its quality: its freshness, condition and odour, the hygiene of the premises and the use of cold storage. The purchaser can usually check all these factors again at the point of sale.

ASPECTS OF CONSUMPTION Various food industries: factories for canning and freezing fish and making fishmeal are directly linked to sea fishing.

Regional variation: more fish is eaten in the west of France, the Paris region and the Mediterranean region than in the south-west, north and above all the east and eastern central parts of the country.

Variation depending on the degree of urbanization: most consumption is in the Greater Paris area.

Variation according to socio-professional categories: fish consumption increases in both value and amount as one rises in the social scale. Consumption is above average among high-salaried managerial staff and members of the liberal professions. It is below average among clerical and blue-collar workers and lower-salaried staff.

The French consumer has little imagination, and prefers to buy familiar fillets of cod, sole and whiting. Fish consumption is still linked to the now outdated tradition of fasting by eating fish on Fridays. An enquiry showed that Friday was still fish day among 70 per cent of those interviewed. However, over half the participants also ate fish on another day of the week. In any event, there is a definite rise in the consumption of fresh fish.

These findings, together with increasing urbanization and new ways of presenting fish (particularly boneless fillets) have led the French National Institute of Statistics and Economic Studies to predict an annual growth in fresh fish consumption per head of about 1 per cent.

Chapter 11

The History of Poultry

Facts About Poultry

The Romans are credited with inventing the capon. When the Lex Faunia of 162 BC forbade them to eat fattened hens, so as to save grain, Roman chicken breeders found a neat way around this sumptuary law, observing it to the letter but not the spirit. They castrated cockerels, which thus grew to twice their normal size and put on a lot of weight, as eunuchs do. Similarly, a fattened pullet is a spayed hen.

The gastronomic literature of the past dealt only with fattened pullets and capons.[1] The Abbé Delille, a late eighteenth-century poet and gastronome, 'reports' the dialogue of a pullet and a cockerel consoling each other for their mutilation: 'Alas, my poor pullet, it is done to fatten us and make our flesh more delicate.'[2]

The invention of the incubator is also attributed to the Romans, who hatched out eggs in quantity in chambers kept warm by hot vapour: they were fully conversant with the mysteries of central heating and plumbing. However, the Egyptians had already had 'ovens for hatching chicks', although you can practically fry an egg on the stones of the Pyramids in the hot August sun. The Chinese too had applied the technique to the eggs of their favourite domestic fowl, the duck, at much the same period.

The Romans did not rear chickens solely for direct consumption. They were often sacrificed to the gods, and poulterers, like butchers, tended to site their shops near temples. There were also sacred chickens used for auguries, which depended on the way they pecked up grain or the pattern they observed in doing so, a method of divination still found in certain countries, for instance in parts of West Africa. On learning that the sacred chickens would not eat at all when he wanted their guidance on the conduct of the Second Punic War, the general Claudius Marcellus cried, 'Then let them drink!' and had them thrown into the sea. His death in battle against Hannibal, prematurely cutting short his career, was put down to this impious action.

The chicken reached the Western world at quite a late date. It eventually arrived in Greece around the fifth century BC. A descendant of the russet-coloured megapode or mound-bird of Malaysia, it was first domesticated in the valley of the Indus and went to Persia when commercial contacts began. It reached Greece by way of Lydia, the country of King Croesus, famed for his wealth.

With the solitary exception of the turkey, which made its official appearance in Europe after the discovery of America, all the domestic fowls we eat today were found on Roman tables. Indeed, the Romans ate a rather greater variety than we do: certain birds, such as the swan, were dropped from the menu after the eighteenth century. Others, such as the stork and the bittern, have reverted to the life of wildfowl in the fields and marshes. Birds other than the usual species of domestic fowl, even if they are intensively reared in large sheds, are not now regarded as poultry.

The duck may be called the veteran of the henhouse, which might more properly be called the duckhouse, since poultry yards were first organized around that fowl. The Chinese domesticated it 4000 years ago, by taming captured wild species or hatching eggs. Duck dishes are still the pride of Chinese cuisine, after centuries of almost ritual practices to perfect them. The pleasures of taste are intensified by the poetic and symbolic associations of the duck (for instance, it stands for conjugal fidelity). The Egyptians too caught some of the ducks that paddled among the reeds of the Nile and kept them in captivity at quite an early date. The stela of the magistrate Sehetep-Ab and his wife Sedar-Sat (seventeenth dynasty, i.e. 1600 BC) shows the couple sitting at a table laid with a lavish meal which included both duck and goose. The only parts of the goose that the richer citizens of Rome ate were the head and the breast. Modern gourmets value only the *magrets*, lean fillets of duck breast, which can sometimes command a price almost as high as that of a whole bird.

The domestication of the goose goes back almost as far as that of the duck. Interestingly, archeological remains show that the Scandinavian and Slav peoples began eating that large migratory fowl at the same time as the Egyptians. The eating of goose on such ritual occasions as cyclical or seasonal feast-days comes to Western Europe direct from the Celts and the Germanic peoples, but it is common to many races. Captured geese fed the first English colonists of Virginia, who followed the example of the Powhattan Indians when they found themselves destitute. However, while the Indians had culled the geese sensibly, it was so easy to fill salting tubs and smokehouses when firearms were available that the ancient customs of the nomadic tribes were obliterated. The Powhattans disappeared entirely, and the geese stopped coming. Since the passing of laws to protect migratory fauna they have reappeared – a magnificent sight – though unfortunately in much smaller numbers than before, in what is now a Federal reserve, returning to a staging post on their journey whose precise location had never been erased from the memory of the species.

The Bible has little to say about domestic fowls. However, a sacrifice of pigeons or turtle-doves is mentioned in Leviticus as the offering to be made by a woman after childbirth. Were these birds wild or domesticated? We do know that domestic pigeons were already being reared in ancient Egypt and pre-Hellenic Greece.

The guinea-fowl, popular with the Egyptians, is of African origin. Its flesh retains a subtle flavour of the savannahs. It is still hunted in the African bush. *Mattye*, one of the most exquisite and delicious of Greek dishes, was made from a guinea-fowl killed by having a knife thrust into its beak; it was then cooked in broth with aromatic herbs – and its own chicks. It was served with a grape sauce. Guinea-fowl with grapes, still a classic way of cooking the bird, is thus a very ancient recipe. Today we pot-roast guinea-fowl larded with bacon, and without its young.

The Greeks classed the pheasant as poultry; they believed that it came from the river Phasis in Asia Minor, hence its Greek name *phasianos*. In fact it is a Chinese immigrant. The peacock, a cousin of the pheasant, was also considered poultry in Athens. It came by way of India and arrived in Crete, we do not know how, around the fifteenth century BC. It then took ten centuries to cross the Aegean Sea, whether voluntarily or otherwise, and was something of a sensation when it appeared in Athens in the fifth century. In their heyday the Cretans had invested the district of Argolis, of which Argos was the capital, in the north-east of the Peloponnese, and there could be some connection with the legend attached to the related peacock. Argos, a prince of the city of the same name, had 100 eyes, 50 of which were always open. The goddess Hera set him to guard Io, one of Zeus's many conquests, whom she had changed into a cow. However, Hermes managed to put the watchman's 100 eyes all to sleep at once, lulling him with the sound of his flute, and then cut off his head. Hera took the eyes to deck the tail of the peacock (*argos* in Greek, *argus* in Latin). Thereafter the bird was sacred to her.

Naturally the patricians of the Roman Empire, who valued anything beautiful and rare, ate peacock at their banquets. Each peacock cost at least 50 denarii, almost twice the price Judas Iscariot was paid for his betrayal. A shrewd character called Cresco made a fortune from rearing the birds, as great a fortune as he could have made from pisciculture, but with no need to bother about supplying water. The poet Horace disapproved of eating peacock. 'You are led astray by the vain appearance, because the rare bird costs gold and makes a brave show with the picture of its outspread tail. ... Do you eat the feathers you so admire? ... Yet, though in their meat they [i.e., a peacock and a pullet] are on a par, to think that you crave the one rather than the other, duped by the difference in appearance!' (*Satires*, II, ii, 20). It was all a piece of gastronomic pretension, but the peacock's tough, insipid flesh, always decked out in the magnificent feathers, was a fashionable dish on grand tables until the seventeenth century. In fact it was quite usual simply to admire the dish and eat none of it, perhaps a wise move. The *maître d'hôtel* could thus make money by re-selling the dish to another banquet. Consequently the plucked peacock was cooked in aromatic resinous substances which in effect mummified it.

Apart from the peacock, the poultry reared by the Romans was excellent. The way in which they were fattened, from the new moon to its last quarter, does not seem especially alien today, although it may strike us as distasteful for other reasons; Roman hearts were no more sensitive than their stomachs. Battery farming was a method they also used for pigeons, first breaking their legs. In his *Satires* (II, iv), Horace, so outspoken on the subject of roast peacock, gives a number of culinary tips including the following: 'If a friend suddenly drops in upon you of an evening, and you fear that a tough fowl may answer ill to his taste, you will be wise to plunge it alive into diluted Falernian: this will make it tender.' He does not actually say if the diluted wine was also used to cook the fowl, nor whether the unfortunate bird was plucked alive before immersion, or dead after cooking (in which case perhaps the guest was the one who deserved commiseration).

Geese, fattened by force-feeding since the time of the Greeks, came to Rome from Gaul, particularly from 'Morinie' (Picardy), and they came on foot, as Pliny tells us (*Natural History*, X-53). Useful watchdogs, like the peacock of the legend, and like that peacock associated with the goddess Juno or Hera, the famous sacred geese in her temple on the Capitol may actually have been uttering cries of joy rather than cackling a warning when their human compatriots from Gaul tried to take the citadel one night in the year 390 BC. Leaving the Romans, then, to enjoy the plump if not especially grateful birds, we will leave *foie gras* until we visit Gaul itself in the next chapter, pausing only to mention that Caesar (*Gallic War*, V, 12) says the ancient Britons did not eat goose: 'They account it wrong to eat of hare, fowl and goose; but these they keep for pastime or pleasure.' The 'pastime' may have been cock-fighting.

During the Dark Ages the goose was to maintain its place as the most prized domestic fowl, and it held that position until the Middle Ages, perhaps rivalled by the wild goose at feudal banquets. An engraving from the *Livre des proufists champestres* of Pierre de Crescens (1486) shows an idealized poultry yard with a goose enthroned at the centre, surrounded by a hen and her family of chicks, a cock, other birds that may be guinea-fowl, a peacock – and a stork. Pigeons fly up from a dovecote. For a long time pigeon-breeding was a noble privilege.[3] It is possible that the birds in the picture may be turtle-doves; these tender birds, the image of conjugal love, were regarded as especially choice eating at the time. They are mentioned quite often in the Merchant of Prato's account books. In Florence, the turtle-dove was believed to have 'the singular virtue of strengthening the memory and the emotions' – a kind of homeopathic food. Symbolism has always helped to season our diet.

The turtle-dove's close relative the pigeon, sacred to Venus in antiquity, was also considered the pattern of conjugal love, an idea echoed by La Fontaine. The Abbé Delille (1738–1813) wrote of the bird:

> Le père vole au loin, cherchant dans la campagne
> Des vivres qu'il rapporte à sa tendre compagne;
> Et la tranquille mère, attendant son secours,
> Échauffe en son sein le fruit de leurs amours.

[The father flies far afield, searching the countryside for food which he brings back to his tender companion, and the placid mother, awaiting his succour, warms the fruit of their loves in her breast.]

Obviously the meat of the pigeon was likely to be as tender as its feelings. King James I of Castile founded an Order of the Pigeon in 1379. It held banquets at which the appropriate fowl was served, roasted, but it survived only a year – not for want of pigeons' to roast, but for lack of enough faithful husbands to be members. It may have been the pigeon's amorous reputation that led nutritionists of the past to forbid persons of a 'dry and irritable' temperament to eat it, although one might have thought it would be good therapy rather than the contrary. Mohammed, whether 'dry and irritable' or not, never ate pigeon, but he trained a live one to come and peck his ear. It was through this intermediary that he claimed to receive divine messages.

The amount of poultry eaten by medieval people was considerable compared with their consumption of butcher's meat, but if pictures of banquets almost always show birds and not meat on the table the reason was purely aesthetic: a roast chicken is more decorative and easier to identify than a slice of meat or a plate of stew.

All kinds of roast fowls were offered for sale on the stalls of medieval 'poulterers', who did not belong to any particular merchant corporation or craft guild. These poulterers sold the birds ready cooked, and in Paris, from the Middle Ages to the Revolution, they operated in the rue de la Huchette, taking their spits and braziers out of service only during Lent. The fact suggests, as Alexandre Dumas too inferred, that Lent had a real part to play in maintaining an economic and nutritional equilibrium. If we are to believe the *Ménagier de Paris* – and why not? – the royal palace, the 'ostel du Roy', alone consumed daily '600 pullets, 200 brace of pigeons, 50 goslings'. For 'the Queen and the royal children, who have a separate establishment: 300 pullets, 150 brace of pigeons, 36 goslings'.

Jean Favier[4] gives us figures for the population of the Hôtel Saint-Pol in the time of Philippe le Bel, the early fourteenth century: from two to 300 people at the end of his reign, with a smaller staff for the Queen and the princes. By the *Ménagier*'s time, at the end of the century, the royal household had increased by perhaps half, or not much more. As Favier says, 'meal-times are the times for counting heads.' When the cry of 'Au queu!' ('To the cook!') was heard (today, in humbler circumstances, one would simply say that dinner was ready), no one might enter the palace to be fed at the King's expense. 'It was not sufficient for a courtier or member of the household to find that he happened to be with the King at dinner time to be sure of being fed by him.' Nonetheless, judging by the lists of provisions coming in, including the figures for poultry, the food was lavish. In the time of Louis XIV, Louis XV and Louis XVI, thousands of people ate well at Versailles; their royal pensions allowed them to claim free board and lodging.

Poultry featured on the menus of the clergy as well as the secular middle classes,

'Cook-shop proprietor's costume': engraving by Nicolas de Larmessin (1640–1725), from the book
of 'grotesques' in which he represented various characters dressed in the attributes
of their trades

popular malice crediting monks with a weakness for capons. The fattened pullet, out of fashion since Roman times, reappeared in the fourteenth century. The *minestra* of a dinner given by the Merchant of Prato to a dozen friends was to be a rich one: 'Broth thickened with cheese, grated almonds, a little cinnamon, cloves and sugar requires no less than six fat capons.' The fattened pullets which Rabelais several times mentions as his favourite fowls came from Le Mans, where they were fattened on maslin with aromatic herbs to give their flesh an even better flavour. This custom continued until the eighteenth century. As for the *poule au pot* which Henri IV wished every home in his kingdom to enjoy, it was the stuff of French dreams, even more than liberty, equality and fraternity.

The guinea-fowl was re-introduced into Europe not long before the turkey arrived, and is mentioned (as 'guynette') in Book IV, Chapter LIX, of *Pantagruel*. As we have seen, it was known in ancient times, and the Portuguese now brought it into Europe from Africa (or 'Guinea'). The Merchant of Prato provides evidence that it was thought especially good for invalids: he writes to a servant who is ill: 'I sent you three couple of guinea-fowl yesterday, and look to it, that you eat them, for you could eat naught better or more wholesome, and I will go on providing them for you.' Oddly enough the same fortifying qualities are also ascribed to the guinea-fowl in Africa itself, in Burkina Faso, where *bim*, guinea-fowl simmered in a very little water, almost braised as if for a *chaud-froid de volaille*, is the dish always given to women directly after childbirth to help them build up their strength.

The advent of the turkey is something of a mystery. It is usually said that what Brillat-Savarin described as 'the best gift of the New World to the Old' was brought home from his travels by Cortez, who had feasted on turkey in the 'West Indies' during the sixteenth century. But Dr Gottschalk, citing the accounts book of one Annot Arnaud, finds that roast turkey was served on 12 November 1385 at a banquet given by the luxury-loving Philippe of Burgundy. This event was almost two centuries before the wedding of Charles IX of France in 1570, at which the turkey is officially supposed to have made its first appearance in France. Birds of the time were apparently bred in Artois, as geese had been in the past.

However, there is another question to be asked. In French, the turkey is called *dinde*, the word deriving from a contraction of the phrase *coq* (or *poulletz*) *d'Inde*, (cock or hen of India). Rabelais uses the word in Book IV, Chapter LIX, of *Pantagruel*, in the 1548 Grenoble second edition, which is still well before the wedding of Charles IX (the passage does not occur in the Lyons first edition). In English, however, the word is 'turkey', which, to add to the confusion, was originally applied to the guinea-fowl. But why turkey anyway?

One tradition is that the first turkey to find its way into a British stomach was eaten in Cadiz by merchants on their way home from a business trip to Turkey. They encountered it at the house of a friend who knew the explorers of the West Indies: perhaps he was a Jesuit, since 'Jesuit' was the disrespectful French nickname for the bird for quite a long time. The merchants' host gave them some live birds which they brought back to England. This may or may not be true, but then why

Turkey rather than Spain? And anyway, were the merchants of the time to be believed? Marco Polo is witness to the fact that they guarded the secret of their merchandise's origin jealously. Asking a question properly is often half-way to answering it, so we may recall here that another word for maize, also from the West Indies, was and still is Indian corn; like the word 'Indian' for the American peoples, it perpetuates the misunderstanding of early explorers who thought they had found a new route to India. Yet another name for maize, however, was Turkey corn. The official arrival of maize in Europe coincides with the advent of the French *dinde*, 'Indian fowl', and English turkey. Turkeys are often fed on maize. It is strange to note that the turkey, 'that voracious fowl ... which eats as much as a mule',[5] arrived on our shores at about the same time as its food. Incidentally, that remark, from the sixteenth-century writer Charles Estienne, antedates King Charles IX's wedding feast by six years.

As we saw in the chapter on cereals, there is a good deal of evidence that maize gradually conquered Europe by way of the Balkans, the gateway to Turkey. This in turn reminds one that some products which were certainly native to Central America went round the world on their way to Europe, but in the opposite direction to Columbus and his expedition, and long before they were next exported. Did the turkey go to sea in a Maori dugout along with yams and maize? We do not know.

We do know, however, that like the wild geese of Virginia they turned up in time to feed the starving colonists from the *Mayflower*, just arrived in Massachusetts, on the last Thursday of November 1620. Ever since then Americans have devoutly celebrated the anniversary of the occasion as Thanksgiving Day.

Whereas the wild turkeys of America, some of which still exist in Florida, lived in flocks in the woods, climbing trees to roost there overnight, the birds bred at the palace of Versailles were luxuriously accommodated in the menagerie next to the Grand Canal. Louis XIV was very solicitous about those haughty fowls, which he himself rather resembled in later life. The keeper of the royal turkeys was a person of some importance, and bore the title of Captain of the Royal Turkeys. Ridicule was clearly not feared in France.

Choosing Poultry

Once upon a time fowls were reared almost at liberty on farms, pecking for food in the farmyard, on the muck heap, and on the outskirts of fields when the rain brought out the slugs. The farmer would supplement their diet with a few handfuls of grain, and scraps of food for which the poultry and pigs competed. Only fowls surplus to the farm's own requirements were sold in the local market or collected by vendors from towns.

These conditions were picturesque but unhygienic, and did not provide the fowls with enough food. Mortality rates in the poultry yard were high, and even higher because inbreeding meant that where any particular breed did exist it degenerated. Insanitary conditions of slaughter and transport impaired the freshness of the meat. Really good, fresh, healthy poultry thus sold at a price which made it a luxury: a Sunday roast to which only the minority could aspire. As the normal hatching season is spring, fowls only had the summer to reach a size when the best birds for roasting could be selected. Plenty of chickens were eaten at harvest homes, of course, a tradition echoing the solar symbolism associated with the cock and the goose.

The male birds were the ones most usually slaughtered; females were left to ensure reproduction and the egg supply. As the year wore on the birds grew older, which explains the household cookery tradition of a progression from roast chicken in summer to boiled chicken and chicken casseroles in winter, Nature being so well adjusted as to provide for our needs at the right time and in the right form.

Free-range farmyard birds can still be found if you know where to go for them. If you are lucky enough to find a good source, they are a real feast. With proper supplementary feeding and modern standards of hygiene, the free-range birds of today have a much lower mortality rate. However, rearing poultry in the old way calls for great application if it is to be a business proposition, and it is wise to approach such a venture in that spirit, even though it entails expense. Profitable poultry-farming cannot be run as a cottage industry.

Since the Second World War poultry has become a regular part of most people's diet. Three-quarters of French people interviewed for an opinion poll in 1981 said they ate poultry on any day of the week, particularly chicken, easily obtainable in supermarkets at a price no higher than butcher's meat. They considered duck and guinea-fowl more of a treat, more expensive, and more complicated to cook. Turkey and goose are still kept mainly for Christmas, but are also eaten when sold in joints and other ready-prepared forms; in fact, thanks to a vigorous marketing strategy, turkey is now rather cheaper than veal. However, the opinion poll also found that people thought poultry was 'not what it used to be'. Did the interviewees know how to choose it? Most people do not even feel they need to know. There is almost an impression that it would be bad form to show expertise.

What are the criteria for choosing a bird which will make any day of the week on which it is eaten a special day, redolent of the pleasures of Sundays of the past? First is the appearance of the bird, its size and its weight. Price is not always a guarantee, although it may strike the consumer as the most important piece of information on the labels, which should be read, understood and compared. When you know what they are actually telling you about the time taken to rear the bird, the method employed, the quality of its life and its food, you can decide on the best way to cook it. You also need to feel it and judge the weight of it in your hand. A young bird, neither too big nor too fat, is the one for roasting. Its beak and breast-bone should be flexible. If they are rigid and seem brittle they show that the bird is getting on. The skin of a young bird is smooth and fine-grained. Tell-tale signs of age are a thick, pitted skin, showing flecks of fat or stringy fibres in it; such birds should be boiled or casseroled. Pre-packed poultry is closely covered with plastic which smooths out the signs of age. The appearance of the feet is important too. Pre-packed poultry never shows its feet; it would be ashamed of them. The feet should be slender, shiny, covered with thin scales, and have supple nails that do not look badly worn. A battery chicken has no nails at all, or if it has they are atrophied, and sometimes the toes themselves are reduced to mere stumps; you will not get to see them at all.

Apart from these general criteria, each species has its own standards of comparison. The chicken is the most widely eaten domestic fowl, accounting for over 90 per cent of sales. There is now a wide variety of chicken on the market, to satisfy different needs and tastes. However, buying wisely does not necessarily mean buying what seems cheapest at the cash desk. The chicken with the golden eggs, or at least the most succulent flesh, is worth tracking down at the poulterer's. Incidentally, children who may refuse to eat ordinary minced beef or cooked ham tend to like chicken, so it deserves careful cooking. It has to be said that the supermarket chicken of the 1960s often left much to be desired, and must have risked putting some people off it for good.

For some time, the wish for good profits led chicken farmers to choose a feed with a basis of fishmeal, which made the bird taste of stale herring. This was during the years when more fish was being caught than people wanted. Then the chickens were given hormones or arsenical compounds. This type of chemical castration may have made the birds grow faster, but it also left them fat, flabby and decalcified – not to mention the possible risks to the consumer. French law now forbids hormones. On the other hand tiny doses of antibiotics, growth elements and prophylactics to prevent infection are still legal, amounting to one gram per 100 kilos of complete chicken feed, say 45 milligrams in all ingested by the bird in the course of its life, and metabolized so that none of it is left in the flesh: the medication stops some time before slaughter. Of course there are cases of fraud, but these are more likely in chickens without enough information on the label, sold at a 'bargain' price.

Thanks to new rearing techniques, a chicken takes only nine weeks to reach a size large enough to feed five people, about 1.7 kilos. Before the Second World War it took at least 20 weeks. As a result the bird is younger, more tender, less fat, and with a finer skin (although that means it is more liable to tear during cooking, especially if it has been damaged by mechanical plucking; then the juices escape and the meat is dry). The chicken should be roasted fast at first so that surface caramelization keeps the juices in.

Cheap chickens are sold even younger: these are battery fowls, or, as they are sometimes more elegantly called in France, 'industrial' chickens. They reach the counter at the tender age – in both senses of the word – of six to eight weeks. The battery itself is a huge shed where thousands of bewildered birds are literally stacked on shelves, each confined in a tiny space with nothing to do but eat and drink, to fatten them up. To make them eat and drink more, artificial light keeps them from sleeping. There is supposed to be air-conditioning, but it is not always in operation. It is difficult to get an idea of the scene without actually visiting one of these chicken factories, great ships turned upside down and lined to a height of eight metres with cackling, agitated birds. There is an incessant, chaotic noise, rather like a hailstorm, made by thousands of beaks frantically pecking at the grain which passes never-endingly on a conveyor belt, and the nauseating smell hits you before you even get inside the place.

Slaughtering, like feeding, is a conveyor-belt job done under veterinary super-vision. As soon as they are plucked and drawn, the dead birds are placed in well-ventilated drying chambers at a temperature of 0 degrees centigrade, and are chilled to a temperature of 4 degrees all through within a few hours. This fast chilling helps the birds to keep better and prevents the proliferation of bacteria. Once the carcases are chilled they are dispatched to various other parts of the plant to be jointed, packed or processed. The temperature in these areas is kept at around 7 degrees.

Once packed, the products are placed in stockrooms or dispatch rooms where the temperature is 0 degrees. They stay there as short a time as possible, and are dispatched to the point of sale within a few hours. The chickens leave the abattoir in refrigerated lorries. Those killed in the morning are delivered to the retailers on the afternoon of the next day, and go into in cold store or refrigerated displays until they are sold. The process is known as the 'cold chain'.

The sell-by date, specified on the packaging, is generally seven or eight days ahead for whole birds and five days for chicken portions. The time they will keep after purchase depends on the bacterial state of the packed birds, the conditions in which they are stored, and the maintenance of the cold chain. These battery chickens are sold in their plastic wrapping, ready to cook. They are no great gastronomic treat, but are at least a healthy, nutritious and economical food.

In France, about one-sixth of production bears the 'label rouge' – Red Label. The Ministry of Agriculture introduced this method of labelling in 1965 for birds of better quality, and of course more expensive, than ordinary battery fowls. The aim was to restore the reputation of industrial chicken farming, which had suffered badly during the period when hormones and fishmeal were fed to the birds.

An ordinary Red Label or Class A bird (Class B is never actually specified on the label) is simply a battery chicken, but 12 weeks instead of eight weeks old. It will have spent its last week in a slightly less confined space, to allow it to develop some muscles. Veterinary checks are stricter and more frequent. The statement of its place of origin, not always obligatory, may be an inducement to buy from the advertising viewpoint, but does not really imply any local flavour, since the poor creatures have never seen anything but concrete on their horizon.

Label rouge fermier, i.e. farm or free-range chicken, is not actually as authentic as the term may suggest. It obviously denotes a quality better than ordinary Red Label, so that when you eat it, it is easier to accept the exaggerated description than the proper use of language would allow. Advertising loves anything rustic. By way of farmyard, these chickens have grassy channels where every blade of grass provides its vitamin content, and they are fed on cereals for 13 or 14 weeks during which they get a certain amount of exercise. They are finally fattened up on skim milk (a useful way of lowering the level of the milk lake). The various 'breeds' thus reared have attractive names: they include the yellow Landes chickens (supposed to be maize-fed, hence the colour of their flesh, but if they have been the fact must be stated on the label) and the black chickens of south-west France, 'black' referring to their plumage – despite the name, their flesh is white. These black chickens come from Loué, Challans, Périgord and Mayenne. The bird is sold whole, complete with its handsome head and feet, but drawn to get rid of the intestines, a potential breeding ground for microbes. In France, a chicken which claims to be free-range but is pre-packed is not to be trusted; however, pre-packed free-range chickens coming up to the requisite standard for such birds are readily available in the United Kingdom.

The best French chickens are labelled with their place of origin, like wine and cheese. Their quality is strictly controlled, and they should be tagged with a ring bearing the number of the breeder. Their origin is plainly stated at the point of sale. They include Bresse chickens, which has always had a high reputation, and those from Bourbonnais and Le Mans. These birds are genuinely free-range, and have spent their four months of life in green spaces, well fed on the best cereals, before a final fortnight's fattening on a diet of skim milk, oats and maize.

Finally there is the most luxurious French chicken of all, *poulet au torchon*, i.e., chicken in a cloth, sold wrapped in a cloth which has to be white (a check cloth will not do); it has been fattened for 40 days, and it too is ringed to show its origin.

'Chickens' are young birds, four months at the most, either male or female. A *coquelet* is a young cockerel rather larger than a poussin or spring chicken, a month and a half old at the most, sold in France unlabelled but drawn and with head and feet intact, like the farmyard fowls mentioned above; this is to conform to French regulations, although the term 'coquelet' is not legally registered, and restaurants abuse it. In fact these birds, which do not have much flavour and will hardly feed more than one person, are little use except spatchcocked for frying or grilling. A capon castrated young is fed cereals to fatten it. A choice and expensive dish, it is not always to be found at a poulterer's, and should be ordered in advance. Its weight is between 3 and 3.5 kilos, and it should be sold drawn, with head and feet on. Its counterpart the fattened pullet, smaller in size at two kilos, was an ordinary pullet before her ovaries were removed. A fattened pullet is a luxury to be cooked with care, and deserves the supreme tribute of truffles to flavour it. A fully-grown cock can weigh up to five kilos at the age of 18 months. It is not a roasting bird and is best cooked jointed. There are no special labels guaranteeing its quality, which must be assessed from its good appearance and strong thighs. One of

Catherine de Medici's passions was for cock's kidneys and combs fried with artichoke bottoms. 'She ate so much of them at the wedding of Mademoiselle de Martigues that she thought she would die of it', the chronicler Pierre de l'Estoile tells us in his journal. Like the fully grown cock, the adult hen cannot bear the equivalent of a Red Label in France; such birds may be quite elderly, and are then extremely tough. They are often sold undrawn, and the strings of partly formed eggs inside them (which must be thrown away) can give a misleading impression of the real weight. A hen usually ends her maternal career in the pot, fulfilling the wishes of King Henri IV.

A boiling fowl is smaller than a cock, weighing only two kilos, and should not be either thin or over-fat, but nice and plump. The pot itself used to be as important as the fowl that went into it, preferably stuffed. A fowl cooked in a pressure cooker is not a proper *poule au pot*. Nothing will ever replace the genuine traditional earthenware pot, perfectly designed for its purpose, usually glazed inside but left plain and unglazed on the outside. The material of which they were made gave the dish its unique flavour. Shapes varied according to region, including the *toupi* or *toupin* of the Languedoc, which had three feet on which it stood in the embers. Another shape was narrow, and the fowl was placed upright inside it, with the cooking liquid up to its neck. It had a long, gentle simmering, while the flames, licking around the earthenware of the pot, worked a slow process of alchemy transforming the broth, with its herbs, chicken juices and a judicious amount of aromatics, into a wonderful nectar, and the superannuated boiling fowl into a dish fit for a king.

Weight for weight, ducks provide less meat than chickens. The duck has a heavier carcase, a thicker skin and, unless one chooses carefully too much fat, especially as it gets older. It should have a supple beak to show its youth. Before it is two months old it is called a duckling, and is best roasted. The adult duck has two small glands on its rump designed to waterproof its feathers. They must be removed, or they will give the bird an unpleasant flavour.

Barbary ducks are sold from September to February. Despite their name, they are European. They are larger, not so fat, and perhaps better flavoured than other ducks such as those of Nantes, which come on the market in the spring and have short legs and long, succulent breast fillets. These fillets, sometimes sold as *magrets*, are very popular, either fresh or frozen, and fetch a good price; they can be grilled, fried or smoked like salmon. In fact the Nantes duck really comes from Challans in the Vendée, a great poultry-farming area. It is a fairly new breed, and is regularly crossed with wild duck every year. As the crates containing deliveries from Challans to the wholesale market of Paris are labelled 'Gare de Nantes', their destination, this half-breed duck has come to be known as Nantes.

Rouen duck is famous, and is also the speciality of a famous Parisian restaurant. It is strangled so as to preserve all its blood, which gives the flesh a unique flavour. Ducks in general are killed only when they are almost about to be cooked, for they do not keep well. The classic English bird is the Aylesbury duckling.

There are people who prefer duck liver to goose liver, and duck also makes very good pâtés and terrines. The dish called a *dodine* is a boned, plump duck, stuffed with pieces of another plump duck. Gourmets prefer their duck only just cooked, whether it appears on the table as roast duck, duck breasts, or in any other form. One does not know just what the Chinese would think of this; next to carp, their favourite food is duck. As Françoise Sabban says, of Chinese cuisine: 'Cooking is entirely the business of the chefs. It would be ridiculous to ask a Chinese if he wants his meat rare, medium rare or well done. The dish is made according to certain intrinsic criteria, not to the customer's order.'[6]

However, the Chinese consumer finds pieces of the best ducks in the world on his plate, cooked to perfection and elegantly served. (It is still considered very vulgar in China to cut up a dish at table. In any case, the table setting includes no knives or forks, and just try cutting a duck with chopsticks!) The famous dish of lacquered duck is one of the few Chinese recipes where a large piece of meat is roasted whole, but it is jointed and prepared in the kitchen as artistically as it has been cooked; the cooking is almost a ritual. Alain Chapel, a well-known modern French chef, remembers how it fascinated him.

> We were in China, on a sight-seeing tour; in Peking, we went out for a full-scale banquet. We were amazed by the professional skill of a chef standing at his stove cooking lacquered duck. He was using a fire of fruitwood, which smelled delicious, whatever kind it was: peach, pear, apricot, jujube or vine shoots. The fire was glowing but not too fierce, the juices flowing out did not catch alight, the colour of the duck remained very pale and we felt extremely hungry. None of us said much.[7]

The Germanic tradition was to serve roast goose at Christmas, which is the Christian version of the winter solstice festival, and the goose is a solar bird. This is convenient, since the goose, a large bird, hatches in spring and is in its prime at eight or nine months old. Any older and it will not be a success roasted; it is better braised or casseroled. Fruit stuffings and accompaniments, popular in German cuisine, help to counteract the fatness of the flesh with their acidity and make it more digestible.

In Alsace it used to be customary to eat the *Martinsgans* on St Martin's Day, 11th November, to celebrate the riches of the harvest that had been gathered in during the autumn. The goose was also sometimes associated with Martinmas in Great Britain, but most often with Michaelmas, St Michael's Day, a couple of weeks earlier on 29th September. In more prosperous farming families the Michaelmas goose, killed when the first geese seemed fat enough for eating, was a kind of test of the quality of the poultry which would be consumed during the winter. Every housewife used the opportunity to improve on her own recipe with a view to Christmas dinner. The goose was generally served surrounded by choucroute, another source of the acidity whose usefulness with rich, fat dishes has long been appreciated. Up to the Renaissance, storks, caught before they flew south, were also eaten in Alsace at Michaelmas. After that time, fortunately, eating storks was regarded as sacrilege.

Geese, which need a large oven, were nearly always taken to the baker's for roasting – in Alsace, Italy, France, the Netherlands and Great Britain alike. It was a very long time before kitchens in town dwellings had ovens big enough to take such a bird, in fact not until the advent of coal and then gas stoves early in the twentieth century. In Dickens's *A Christmas Carol*,[8] when Scrooge is visited by the Ghost of Christmas Present, the Cratchit children 'boy and girl, came tearing in, screaming that outside the baker's they had smelt the goose, and known it for their own'.

For centuries the goose has provided many delicacies: they include not only goose liver, but stuffed neck of goose, boned stuffed *dodines* similar to the dish made with duck, pâtés, rillettes, and preserved goose gently cooked in its own fat. A cassoulet without a wing or thigh of preserved goose is hardly a cassoulet at all. In the South of France, goose fat is as important as butter in Normandy or olive oil in Provence. It is more than just a cooking fat; it is an article of faith.

Goose was the big roast served on special occasions until the turkey came to Europe. It arrived too late to acquire any genuine folklore. However, the splendid bird's weight and succulent flesh have made it the ideal dish for large, cheerful gatherings. It is more of an urban and middle-class, even aristocratic festive dish than the rustic goose, and is just right for a feast. Dom Balaguère,[9] the central character of Alphonse Daudet's story *Trois messes basses*, set at the end of the Renaissance, is clearly committing the sin of gluttony when the devil, in the shape of Garrigou the sacristan, makes him wild with appetite before divine service: '"Did you say two truffled turkeys, Garrigou?" "Yes, your reverence, two magnificent turkeys crammed with truffles. And I should know, seeing I helped to stuff them. You'd have said their skin would crack in the roasting, so tender as they were."'

Such rich and elaborate accompaniments to turkey are responsible for its reputation for heaviness. Goose has remained a simpler, more rustic dish, perhaps because of the antiquity of its tradition. In fact turkey is perfectly digestible, and sometimes even rather dry, since its flesh lacks the marbling of fat which keeps goose moist.

Small turkeys of up to 15 weeks old weigh no more than five kilos; the most popular weight for such birds is about 3.5 kilos. However, it is possible, especially in the United States, to buy real monsters of 15 kilos or more. These giants are seldom cooked and served whole; they are suitable for cutting up like butcher's meat to provide breast fillets, roasts, rolled joints, etc. Turkey breast makes escalopes which are not quite as meltingly tender but not quite as expensive as veal escalopes. The only trouble with jointed turkey is that it does not keep well, a disadvantage common to all poultry of whatever size. It cannot be kept for more than two days in the refrigerator without deteriorating.

The guinea-fowl is smaller than chicken, and has attractive amber flesh with a slightly gamy taste suggesting its ancestral African savannahs. Unlike the duck, which has a solid skeleton, the guinea-fowl has very slight bones, and is thus a 'good buy'. But you cannot expect to feed more than four people with a single bird. Our grandparents emphasized its gaminess by hanging it after its neck had been wrung so as to leave all the blood in it. It ripened slightly, like a wild game bird. However, as I have mentioned above, the blood which accumulates in the flesh of a fowl is an ideal breeding-ground for toxins and bacteria. It is better to cook the bird with herbs and aromatics, perhaps flambéd with alcohol, to bring out the best of its flavour.

Guinea-fowl too are industrially reared these days, with one square metre allotted to some eight to ten descendants of birds that once had the freedom of the African bush. Recently there has been a great increase in guinea-fowl farming by repatriated Algerians in the south-west of France. Even when kept in confinement, the flesh of guinea-fowls still tends to be dry, a disadvantage which can be quite easily counteracted with a soft cheese stuffing, or even better by inserting butter flavoured with pistachio or hazel nuts, anchovies or truffles, under the loosened skin of the bird. Like chickens, guinea-fowl have special labelling in France when they meet the requisite standards. Indeed, the 'Red Label' borne by the yellow guinea-fowl of the south-east of France indicates a quality superior to that of Red Label chickens: they have been reared out of doors, with only one or two birds per square metre, which is not exactly the African bush, but adequate for the 13 weeks of life they spend eating maize.

The flesh of domestic pigeons does not have the same flavour or colour as that of the wild species (including the pigeons which haunt public buildings in towns, and were frequently caught by hungry citizens during the Second World War). It is paler and tastes less musky. Only young pigeons are eaten, and they will only be tender up to the age of five weeks, when their necks are wrung so that none of the blood is lost. The high purine content of this lean meat thus means that people suffering from uraemia or gout should not eat it. In fact it was that stimulating nitrogenous content which gave the pigeon its former reputation as an aphrodisiac. Finally, pigeons were once put to a use which had nothing to do with gastronomy, although it was for seductive purposes: Lucrezia Borgia's beauty-care routine included the application to her face, like a mask, of the pulsating bodies of live pigeons cut in two, and she smeared their blood on her beautiful breast.

The Symbolism of Poultry

With the exception of the chicken, a descendant of a bird from the Malaysian jungle, and the guinea-fowl, which comes from the African bush, all domestic fowls are descended from wild migratory birds. Eating them is therefore associated in many ways with the observance of the solar and agricultural calendars. The

351

symbolism connected with them also refers to their faithful and regular return, and they were respected for their supposed value in divination or intercession.

The mystery of the migration of birds is still not fully explained: it involves such factors as a sense of the changing seasons whether they are normal or not, a sense of direction, faithful adherence to certain routes and places of departure and arrival. Ducks, geese and swans leave the northerly part of the northern hemisphere in autumn and fly to the tropics, or even to the south of the southern hemisphere, returning punctually next year; the journey of these honking birds in a V-shaped formation, like the point of an arrow indicating a goal to be reached under the guidance of a leader, always seemed magical. The wild wood pigeon is also a migrant, and the amazing sight of up to two million wild pigeons migrating from end to end of the American continent can still be seen. Trainers of carrier pigeons exploit their instinct for travel.

When wild ducks, geese or pigeons are caught, or even if they have been raised from a clutch of eggs, it is noticeable that from the moment birds of the same species leave their behaviour becomes agitated, even if they have not actually seen a single wild bird take flight. Farmyard geese and ducks, domesticated for thousands of years, seem to have forgotten the migratory instinct, but if they are returned to the wild memory returns to them after a few generations.

The naturalist Konrad Lorenz, who worked so closely with his geese that they adopted, or rather co-opted, him as one of themselves, mastered their language, for geese make conversation. Their constant cackling is an organized discourse in which Lorenz was eventually able to join. The noise we hear as wild geese pass overhead is a bulletin of travel news, containing information about speed, direction, regrouping and changes of position. In the poultry yard 'it is rather comic to hear the white domestic goose, who cannot fly, insist emphatically that she has no intention of doing so. However, she has inherited from her wild ancestors a language which has persisted longer than her aptitude for flight.'[10] All of which, perhaps, is something to bear in mind as one sits down to eat *foie gras*.

Almost all civilizations of the world which encountered geese regarded them as intermediaries between heaven and earth. The deified Pharaoh was the incarnation and personification of the sun. His soul left his earthly body in the form of a goose, for it was in that form that the sun first hatched from the primordial egg. Every time a new Pharaoh ascended the throne, geese were set free to fly to the four points of the compass.

A sacrifice of geese at the turn from one season to another was a universal custom in Europe, Central Asia, among the North American Indians and the Berbers of the Atlas. These sacrifices were of course followed by the consumption of the birds in a magical and ritual repast.

The goose at the ritual feast of the winter solstice, which became our Christmas, originally signified a claim laid to the sun, represented by the bird, for you could never be quite sure that the sun would really return as the days grew longer. At Midsummer, the summer solstice, no particular ritual meal is recorded either historically or regionally. As Van Gennep remarks, 'the number of ceremonial dishes in the cycle is very limited.'[11]

The spring equinox, of course, is marked by the eating of the Pascal lamb, and 23rd September, when duck was eaten in Romania, was a very important gastronomic occasion. As a migratory bird duck had the same significance as goose. At Forli in Emilia, fat, appetizing ducks were killed one or two days before the festival, preferably on a Saturday, and hung in the window, on display to the neighbours. They were cooked in the oven, on the spit, or in a casserole, and lavishly washed down with Sangiovese wine, while the day ended with games, cock-fighting and processions.

The Martinmas or Michaelmas roast goose is actually the perpetuation of the ceremonies of Celtic Samhain or Hallowe'en and Germanic Yule, originally the first day of the New Year, now our 1st November. Van Gennep, writing on French folklore, reminds us that it was a good occasion for feasting on tender geese that had just been fattened. Originally the roast goose was a thank-offering for the harvest that had been gathered in, the *Erntedankfest* or harvest home, a sacrifice first to the spirit of vegetation, then to the gods Odin or Thor. The goose, ritually eaten, magically ensured the regeneration in the months to come of nature as she went underground for the winter, precisely parallel to the Greek myth of the abduction of Persephone by the lord of the underworld. The dead too are underground. In all societies funerals are a ceremony of their separation from the living, a solemn farewell, but also an observance of their entry into the world of the dead, a rite of passage. Despite the farewell, a link remains between the two worlds, since the dead are the seed from which future generations grow, or their leaven. Whereas All Saints' is the Christian commemoration of the martyrs whose sacrifice assured the advent of Christianity, the next day, All Souls' Day, is a universal rite which used to coincide with the last hours of the Old Year and the first hours of the New. The Christian appropriation of these solemn rites, even the turning of Samhain into All Saints', dates from the early ninth century. The ritual reached Rome from Ireland in 835, and then, as conversions spread, came to the Frankish empire, the most active missionaries being Irishmen. (However, the old German name for the month of November, *Schlachtmonat*, the month of slaughter, has nothing to do with memories of the dead, but was the signal for the general slaughter of geese, cattle and pigs to be salted, smoked or preserved in fat, and provide food for the winter.)

The great feasts of Samhain-All Saints' and St Martin's Day on 11th November were thus rituals uniting the assembled company of the living with the spirits of the dead, or even with the gods in a ceremony of 'eating the god'. During the Renaissance the tradition of eating goose on All Saints' Day was still widely observed, especially in Lombardy and Tuscany. There are references to the custom in Sacchetti's *Trecento novelle*, Nos. 8 and 76.

In France, however, there was another custom which is supposed to have ceased at the time of the 1914–18 war, although it seems it is still sometimes practised.

Geese taken from the poultry yard at carnival time were not always destined for a quick and uneventful death leading them to the baker's oven. The rather unpleasant ceremony of tilting at the goose came first. A goose was hung alive by the neck, and had to be beheaded with a stroke of sword or stick. The 'players' in this game might or might not be blindfolded, and the winner had a free meal at the banquet that followed. Sometimes, as in Aunis, the goose was replaced by a cockerel (another solar symbol) made drunk and plucked alive, or by clusters of pigeons. The game is reminiscent of tilting at the quintain, with birds taking the place of the dummy, and may indeed have preceded the use of the dummy.

However, in regions where many geese were bred, including the whole south and south-west of France, there was no celebration of Martinmas with roast goose, or martyring of geese at carnival (force-feeding being martyrdom enough). Here the fowl was respected for its contribution to regional prosperity. Moreover, the goose may have retained a benevolent magical character in these areas, which were once occupied by the Visigoths, an echo of the beliefs of the distant steppes, where it was long seen as a messenger between the other world and our own, transporting the shamans of Central Asia on their visits to the kingdom of the dead. One theory about the old children's board game of Goose (mentioned by Goldsmith in *The Deserted Village* as being played in the alehouse, 'the royal game of goose'), interprets it as a ritual labyrinth; similarly, esoteric meaning has been traced by some folklorists in the Mother Goose tales. La reine Pédauque, 'Queen Web-foot', the depiction of a woman with webbed feet found over doorways of buildings in medieval France, was said to have been a great personage in the parts of Aquitaine occupied by the Visigoths. According to Caesar, as we have seen, the goose was so greatly respected in Britain before the Roman conquest that there was a taboo on eating it.

The turkey-cock was the symbol of virile power to the North American Indians, and the turkey-hen represented maternal fecundity. Why, however, did the cock become the emblem of France – for its sexual prowess, or its pride? In fact the reason lies in a pun on Latin *gallus*, the cock, and *gallus*, Gaulish. Personifying the sun in India, the cock is associated with the solar body everywhere. The Greeks consecrated it to both the solar and the lunar deities. The Chinese character *Ki*, denoting the cock, is homophonous with the adjective meaning 'of good omen'. When a cock is eaten in Vietnam the feet are boiled separately to be used for divination. The Peuhls of Africa and the Pueblo Indians of New Mexico, who associate the bird with maize, the solar cereal, also use it for purposes of divination.

The Greeks associated the cock, as a symbol of vigilance and herald of the mystic light of resurrection, with the divine messenger Hermes. In alchemy, it was therefore associated with mercury. It was also regarded as a suitable sacrifice to Asclepius, god of medicine and son of Phoebus Apollo, the sun. Such sacrifices might bring about a cure. When the patient died instead, the ancient Germanic tribes used the cock for funeral rites and in the funeral meal. A cockerel is still tied to a dying person's bed in Central Asia.

Finally, as a symbol of Christ the Redeemer, the cock keeps watch on church towers. When a real cock crows outside the usual morning hours, Muslims say that an angel has passed by, and they salute it.

The cock does not feature in the pantheon or legends of ancient Egypt, for the simple reason that they had no chickens.

Eggs: their Uses and Customs

Which came first, the chicken or the egg? The argument has gone on for generations, and has never been settled. However, the answer is to be found nesting in the history of food: the egg was first, for the very good reason that the chicken, as the latest addition to the poultry yards of Greece and Italy in the fifth century BC, found geese, ducks and guinea-fowl already installed, laying eggs and hatching them. Those eggs, which undoubtedly preceded the chicken, were seldom eaten. Eggs were not really part of the diet until poultry-farming became common, and, when they did, those most usually consumed were hen's eggs.

Was there some taboo, then, on eating the eggs of the earlier domestic fowls? It depends on the sense in which the term is used. Not necessarily a religious taboo, but more of an economic interdiction, since 'the egg is in the chicken, and the chicken is in the egg'. The Mossi of Burkina Faso in Africa have never troubled themselves with such philosophical reflections, but simply employ common sense. They will not let their children eat eggs for fear they will become thieves. The idea is not that, as a French proverb has it, 'qui vole un oeuf, vole un boeuf' – he who steals an egg will steal an ox – but because he who steals an egg is stealing a chicken. Poultry lives at large in the villages of Africa, laying eggs anywhere. Children must therefore be prevented from eating future broods, which would be community property, out of naughtiness or thoughtlessness, for these little Africans are spoilt by their parents and do not go hungry – I mean in normal times, of course. An egg unnecessarily stolen and eaten will never become a chicken, and thus a single person can deprive the community of far more nourishment than the stolen egg provides. Moreover, and even more seriously, the spirits will be offended, for all the poultry the Mossi eat has first been sacrificed to the local tutelary spirits. And an egg which does not hatch out interrupts a biological cycle, disturbing the order of things.

The Mossi are a special example. All over the world, from the dawn of time, eggs have been collected from birds' nests in times of need: those eggs, that is, large enough to be worth collecting. However, a respect for wild life led the people of antiquity to exercise restraint in their culling of eggs, even when it was unintentional. Similar scruples are expressed in a delightful moral tale which used to make French children of the Edwardian era shed tears: *En famille*, a story by Hector Malot, which is less remembered now than his *Sans famille*, a classic of

French children's literature. In *En famille* a little orphan girl, obliged to live in the woods, has nothing to eat, but finds a wild duck's nest on the river bank. 'There were eleven eggs there now instead of ten, which showed that, as the mother duck had not finished laying, she was not yet sitting on her eggs. This was a great piece of luck, first because the eggs would be fresh, and second because the duck, who could not count, would notice nothing.'

Farming the prolific chicken has allowed us to make eggs a part of our diet without harming its reproductive cycle. However, the very few ancient Greek recipes to mention eggs date from after the time of Pericles, when the chicken was introduced into Attica. It took some time for the habit of using eggs in cooking to catch on. We do hear of *thagomata*, made from egg whites, and various stuffings using egg yolks.

On the other hand the classic cake offered as a sacrifice by the Romans, the *libum*, called for one egg to a pound of flour. In the Roman period pastrycooks made much use of eggs for desserts as well as cakes. Apicius (25 BC) invented baked custard: milk, honey and eggs beaten and cooked in an earthenware dish on gentle heat. Eggs really made their way into the kitchen with Apicius, who mentions them frequently in the *Ars Magirica*. Beaten eggs were used as a thickening to bind sauces and ragoûts; hardboiled eggs became an ingredient of various dishes, sometimes with cheese, but there is no evidence that eggs were eaten just as they were, as a dish in themselves. That does not mean that they were *not* so eaten; it could simply indicate that they were not thought interesting enough for special mention. The poet Horace, usually very sensible when he writes about food, falls victim to prejudice in specifying the best shape of eggs to choose. 'Give good heed to serve eggs of a long shape, for they have a better flavour and are whiter than the round; they are firm and enclose a male yolk.'[12] Male chauvinism among the eggs? Even today, however, Europeans prefer brown eggs (regardless of what sex of chicken they would produce), although the colour of the shell has no connection at all with the nutritional value of its contents. It is just that anything dark in colour seems stronger and more nourishing, as we saw with meat.

Such doctors of the school of Hippocrates of Cos as Celsus recommended lightly cooked eggs as the most nourishing. This was to be one of the precepts of the Salerno School of the sixteenth century: 'Si sumas ovum, molle sit atque novum', 'if you take an egg, let it be soft and fresh'. Clovis, the barbarian crowned king of the Franks some centuries after the Roman Empire began to decline, knew nothing about dietetics, and suffered from such chronic indigestion that he consulted a Byzantine doctor recommended by Theodoric. The doctor tried (in vain) to persuade him not to eat so many hardboiled eggs.

One of the high spots of Trimalchio's banquet was an enormous carving of a wooden hen sitting on eggs – peahen's eggs, more elegant than the ordinary variety. The whole meal was accompanied by a string of jokes on the likelihood of the food being spoiled, and accordingly 'Trimalchio turned towards this fine sight and said, "I gave orders, my friends, that peahen's eggs should be put under a common hen. And upon my oath I am afraid they are addled by now. But we will try whether they are still fresh enough to eat."' The guests are alarmed, but the eggs do not contain peacock chicks after all. They are imitation eggs, their pastry crusts enclosing little fig-pecker birds, which themselves are stuffed with spiced yolk of egg.

Charlemagne, not a man for jokes, gave orders that each of his farms should have at least 100 hens and 30 geese, and calculated that in the end there would be more eggs than needed for reproduction. 'If there are surplus eggs or hens, let them be sold' – surplus, that is, after regular deliveries had been made to the court at Aix-la-Chapelle.

Lenten fasting became law at the Council of Aix in 837. Charlemagne was determined to see that it was observed, by force if necessary. Any baptized Lombard or Saxon chieftain who failed to do proper penance had his head cut off, an uninviting prospect which considerably slowed down the rate of conversions to Christianity. As an animal product, like meat and cheese, eggs were off the menu in Lent. They were kept for eating later or were put under a broody hen at Easter time, to provide tender roast fowls at harvest. This ban on eggs, classified as the meat which they only potentially contained, had appeared centuries before in the teachings of Pythagoras, a vegetarian. However, there was considerable confusion about eggs in the emergent Catholic tradition. The Premonstrants, and certain canons of St Victor, fasted from 15th September until Easter on meals consisting alternately of eggs and fish. The Augustinians ate eggs three times a week. Ordinary people could make very little of such canonical quibbles.

The lavish coronation feast of Pope Clement VI was held at the Dominican convent of Avignon on 19 May 1344, two months after the end of Lent. There must have been several thousand guests eating well on that occasion: since eggs are our concern here, I will mention only that 3250 dozen eggs were required to make the 50,000 tarts served. One wonders if the Lenten fasting of the poor had to be extended to provide so many.

Eggs were part of the modest everyday fare of ordinary people all over Europe. 'Eggs', says Braudel, 'were a cheap commodity, and their price accurately followed the fluctuations of the economic situation. A statistician can reconstruct the movement of the cost of living in the sixteenth century from a few eggs sold in Florence.' But what price would he have set on the eggs carried in his underwear by a pious monk called Lauro Bossi, who cannot have felt there was anything very comic about his situation as he cautiously scaled the interior ramp of the Castell Sant'Angelo in Rome in May 1501. The woman to whom Bossi was taking them signed an IOU for 400 gold ducats – not as the market value of the gift, but in return for his devotion, and indeed as the price of her own life: she was Caterina Sforza, daughter of the Duke of Milan, held prisoner in Rome and almost starving to death. She had suffered a year's imprisonment by the Borgias, who were giving her 'as little to eat as possible', and that little was liable to be poisoned. The one food that could not be poisoned at the time, before the advent of the hypodermic

'The egg seller' (1632), by H. Bloemart (*c.* 1601–1672): the woman is holding an egg up to the light to examine it for freshness.

syringe, was the egg. Thanks to a few eggs a week, Marie de Medici's grandmother survived her enforced fast until the French freed her.

Chapter LX of Book IV of *Pantagruel*, not of course a true story but a work of comic literature, mentions among the dishes for fast days those eggs which 'the Gastrolaters sacrifice to their Ventripotent God ... eggs fried, beaten, buttered, poached, hardened, boiled, broiled, stewed, sliced, roasted in the embers, tossed in the chimney, etc.' According to the *Ménagier de Paris*, there are two ways of making the 'eggs beaten' of Rabelais' list: 'Break the shell and throw yolks and whites on the fire or on hot embers, and then stir and eat them.' Alternatively, one might make a sweet *allumelle*, an omelette, accompanied by poached eggs, a dish anticipating Ali-Bab's 'oeufs dans tous les états', eggs cooked in all ways.[13] The eggs 'roasted in the embers' or 'tossed in the chimney' were put to cook whole in the glowing embers. As Nicolas de Bonnefons advises in his *Délices de la campagne*, they must be cracked first at the thicker end 'for fear they may explode'.

The old word *moieulx*, for the yolk of an egg, makes one wonder if it might be the real etymology behind 'mayonnaise', usually explained as referring to the taking of Port-Mahon in 1756. Could mayonnaise have begun life as *moieulnaise* since it is made only with the yolks of eggs? It might seem likely, except that the uncooked sauce itself is not described in any culinary texts until the beginning of the fourteenth century.

The etymology of the word 'omelette' ('homelaicte' in Rabelais) is also very obscure, although the dish itself goes back as far as the Romans. It is thought to derive ultimately from *lamella*, 'a thin plate', referring to the long, flat shape of the omelette, and to represent a gradual corruption of *allumelle* first to *allumelette*, then to *alomelette*. *Le cuisiner françois* of 1651 has *aumelette*. Jean-Jacques Rousseau, a dab hand with omelettes, had the dexterity and precision required to turn his beaten eggs by tossing them in the air, like a pancake. The Prince de Condé tried his duellist's wrist at the same trick, and his omelette finished up in the fire.

The *Cuisine bourgeoise* of 1784 uses the modern form of the word, *omelette*, carefully distinguishing between it and scrambled eggs, a new recipe of the time. It also mentions boiled eggs 'which the bourgeois like best: to cook them to perfection, when the water bubbles boil them for two minutes. Take them off the fire and cover the pan for a moment, to let the whites set, and then serve them in a napkin: cooked in this way they will be just right.'

Louis XIV was very fond of meringues made of egg white and sugar, a royal rather than a bourgeois dish, but Louis XV ate boiled eggs every Sunday, leaving his ancestor's unlikely *poule au pot* to his people. Parisians came in whole families to admire their sovereign's dexterity with an egg. In an almost religious hush, he would knock the small end off the egg with a single stroke of his fork, while an officer of the table called for attention, announcing, 'The King is about to eat his egg!' Perhaps to ensure that the item at the centre of this Sunday show was fresh, and in emulation of Louis XIV's rearing of turkeys beside the Grand Canal, Louis XV and Mme de Pompadour took to breeding chickens themselves. Laying hens were installed in the attics of the palace of Versailles, and the best layers accompanied the court on its travels. This was all that was needed to make artificial incubation fashionable, and everyone took an interest. Réaumur, the inventor of the thermometer, published two treatises in 1749 and 1751 on *L'art et la pratique de faire éclore en toutes saisons des oiseaux domestiques de toutes espèces*, 'the art and practice of hatching out domestic fowls of every kind at any season'. His incubator produced artistically soft-boiled eggs.

The food shortages of the Revolution saw eggs almost disappear; ration coupons were required for them, as also for butter, oil, salt, soap and candles. Eggs did still exist, but one needed plenty of money to get them. The police were in luck when an informer denounced the Parisian pastrycook Dubois, and they seized no less than 3000 eggs keeping cool in his cellars on 17 May 1794. It was the pastrycook's turn to do time underground.

Twenty years earlier Menon, author of the *Cuisine bourgeoise*, wrote of the egg: 'It is an excellent and nourishing food enjoyed by the sick and the healthy, the rich and the poor alike.' Eggs must be fresh, he insists, and like his predecessors since antiquity he suggests the usual methods of testing for freshness: holding them up to the light or putting them in water to see if they float.

In the Far East the egg is not so important an item of diet as in Europe, for reasons of reproduction rather similar to those of the people of Burkina Faso. It is a luxury for the rich, with all the symbolic and philosophical connotations that might be expected. The idea of the famous Chinese 100-year-old eggs (sometimes called 1000-year-old eggs) amazes and horrifies the European consumer, but the eggs are nothing like as old as that; the figures have no literal significance in a country where it is only polite to wish someone 10,000 years of happiness. The eggs have been kept for a few months buried in a mixture of paddy, tea leaves, lime, saltpetre, clay and aromatics. The shells turn a beautiful marbled black, and the inside comes to look like a hardboiled egg, but veined with jade green. They are perfectly safe to eat, and have a unique flavour.

The dyed or painted egg, decorated with a paintbrush, batik, or even set in gold, is an Easter tradition of the Christian West which has proved particularly tenacious in Central Europe, defying Marxist materialism. Fabergé, goldsmith to the imperial court of Russia, made some wonderful pieces in the Edwardian era which are greatly sought after by collectors.

When eggs were forbidden in Lent, from the time of Charlemagne until 1784 (five years before the French Revolution), all the eggs collected from the henhouse had to be kept either for hatching or to be eaten at Easter. For the latter purpose they were usually dipped into melted mutton fat or wax. Then they were decorated to make them more attractive. Most folklorists agree with Van Gennep that giving these pretty eggs to children was an elegant and agreeable way of getting rid of the surplus. A pretty egg tastes better.

It was also customary for the King of France to be given baskets of painted, gilded eggs after High Mass on Easter Day. He then distributed them to his courtiers. The painters of these eggs, pensioners of the Louvre, sometimes made them into delightful miniature works of art. Fabergé's eggs, even more sumptuous and given in the Tsar's family, were presents along the same lines. In France the biggest egg laid in Holy Week was the sovereign's by right. It was presented in the splendour of its nakedness, decorated only with a handsome ribbon, preferably red, a colour signifying good luck and glory in European cultures. The chocolate egg of later times still wears a ribbon.

The tradition of Easter eggs coincides, like many folk customs, with a self-explanatory universal symbol, in this case of creation, rebirth and spring. However, it is not a survival from classical antiquity or the ancient Celtic and Germanic worlds. The only possible ancient parallel is the soup with hardboiled eggs of the Jewish Passover, served after the Seder ceremony. There are no texts or documents earlier than the fifteenth century which mention the distribution of eggs at Easter, apart from a very local custom of the Coptic Christians of Egypt around the eleventh century. The first extant records of Easter eggs mention egg-hunts in the Palatinate in 1490. There are also accounts of Italian banquets where single enormous omelettes were served, and that is about all, with the possible exception of an Easter *Benedictio ovorum* in the church ritual of the twelfth century, possibly to celebrate the reappearance of eggs on the menu after Lent.

From the sixteenth century there are plenty of references, such as an Alsatian allusion to gifts of eggs dyed red (1553), taken up independently in references by various authors, including the German translator of Rabelais. In 1624 such eggs were dyed various colours: green, red, black and blue. According to the *Satire Ménippée* of 1594 they were banned from being sold in the streets of Paris. The authors of that satirical pamphlet against the Ligue employ the prohibition to back their argument, but rather than being an infringement of the people's rights, the reason may well have been the risk of poisoning by toxic dyes. The custom of giving painted eggs spread from the Rhineland areas to the French provinces of the east and the centre. Godmothers gave them to children. In other areas young people went to look for hidden eggs, singing as they searched.

A tradition that eggs are brought by the Easter hare is found in Alsace and many parts of Germany, but it goes no farther back than the seventeenth century. The Easter hare was even the subject of a medical dissertation at Heidelberg in 1682, where it was announced as a novelty. In some parts of Germany, instead of a hare, a bird or a fox brings eggs, or eggs may fall from the sky, together with church bells returning from a trip to Rome to be blessed. This started as a popular rather than a genuine folk custom of the South of France in the mid-nineteenth century, and was encouraged if not actually suggested by the clergy in an effort to make Easter celebrations more religious. Confectioners have spread the idea to all other countries, eggs and bells being an excellent way to market chocolate.

Decorated eggs are not by any means all meant to be kept; most are eaten. However, in Romania and the Ukraine the shells are saved to be thrown into the river (an ancient gesture with various different kinds of significance). The shells go down into the other world to tell the dead to be of good cheer: Christ is risen, and all at home are rejoicing. The gypsies 'write' eggs for the dead, ornamenting them with sinuous or broken lines which only the departed can decipher. The eggs are taken to graves, and the departed can thus still share in family joys. In Greece, on the afternoon of Easter Day, people go to the graveyard to eat eggs, taking a plate with the share of the dead on it. But the finest egg of all stays at home, standing next to the icon, as protection against lightning. The idea that eggs counteract fire is also found in the south-west of France: if you throw an egg laid on Good Friday into a fire it will go out at once. In Metz, such an egg given to a sorcerer will unmask him. In the Hautes-Alpes it is a specific against colic, and in Franche-Comté it will protect you from a dangerous fall. Almost all over Europe an egg laid on Good Friday or Easter Day, buried in your field or your garden, will keep away hail and protect the beehives. The shell of an egg laid at Easter is buried in a field when it is ploughed at the beginning of the opposite, autumn cycle. Sometimes a piece of pork is added. In any case, the future harvest will be good. This custom, very widespread in Greece, is echoed in the Dordogne, where carnival eggs are used, carefully emptied at Carnival time so that the shells remain whole, and stored in grain.

Like every time of festival, Easter is the occasion for amusements in which some have claimed to detect echoes of the springtime festivals of the Eleusinian, Orphic, Dionysian or even Zoroastrian rites. Eggs do enter into many popular games, but purely for fun; such games include egg races, egg-rolling, egg-throwing, and above all egg fights, the most famous and oldest being that of the chapter of Chester Cathedral in the Middle Ages. Before entering the cathedral, the bishop and the dean armed themselves with eggs, and at certain points in the Easter service threw them at the choristers, who were well provided with ammunition too! Afterwards everyone went to wash, before dining together on eggs.

The popular mind does, thus, retain something like a memory of the universal symbolism of the egg, one of the stages in the great life cycle. However, Van Gennep emphasizes that 'beliefs relating to eggs … are on several different mental planes, and do not seem to be a survival of any distinct magical and religious system.'

THE OPINIONS OF
M. JÉROME COIGNARD CONCERNING
EASTER EGGS

M Nicolas Cerise looked at my good master, a twinkle in his eye, and said, with a small smile:

'Monsieur l'Abbé Coignard, these eggs, the shells of which, dyed with beetroot, litter the floor at our feet, are not in fact as Christian and Catholic as you like to believe. On the contrary, Easter eggs are of pagan origin, recalling the mysterious birth of life at the time of the spring equinox. They are an old symbol which the Christian religion has retained.'

'One can just as reasonably argue', said my good master, 'that they are a symbol of the resurrection of Christ. Myself, I have no taste for cluttering religion up with symbolical subtleties, so I am quite ready to believe that the pleasure of eating eggs, which we have missed during Lent, is the only reason why they occupy a place of honour on our tables today, clothed in royal purple.'

Anatole France (1844–1924) *Les opinions de Jérôme Coignard*

PART V

Gaul, the beginnings of the food industry, and

LUXURY FOODS

The Revels of the Gauls

Let me celebrate the memory of my mother's father, Arborius, who derived his name from a line of Aeduan ancestors, uniting the blood of many a noble house, both of the province of Lyons, and of that land where the Aedui hold sway ... but trouble, all too jealous of lineage and proud wealth, weighed heavy upon him; for my grandfather and his father were proscribed when Victorinus was holding sway as prince, and when the supreme power passed into the hands of the two Tetrici. Then, while in exile in the lands through which the Adour breaks forth to the sea, and where wild ocean rages on the shore of Tarbellae, though still he feared the arrows of Fortune, who so long had sought his life, he was united in marriage with penniless Aemilia. In time a scanty sum gathered with great pains furnished his wearied age with some relief, though not with wealth. You – though you cloaked your pursuits – had skill in the measures of the heavens and in the stars which keep the secret of man's destiny. Not unknown to you was the outline of my life, which you had hidden in a secret tablet, and never betrayed; but my mother's forward care revealed that which the care of my shy grandfather sought to conceal. ... Now that you join in the assemblies of souls that are gone before, surely you have knowledge of your grandson's fortunes: you feel that a quaestor, that a prefect, and likewise a consul am I who now commemorate you with a tribute in your honour.

The distinguished grandson was the Gaulish poet Ausonius (310–396). He describes himself in a speech which he puts into his father's mouth. 'Our elder son rose to the highest pinnacle of dignity, as prefect of all Gaul, Libya and Latium; calm and kindly, gentle of glance and speech and mien, in bearing towards his father he was still a boy in mind and heart.' A few years later, he could add the post of tutor to two emperors and prefect of the Moselle to his *curriculum vitae*. Ausonius' father was a doctor in Bordeaux – 'of no mean repute in the art of healing; nay ... the foremost' – and a senator, perhaps an honorary post because, again in the words Ausonius gives him, 'For Latin I never had a ready tongue; but the speech of Athens supplied my need with words of choice eloquence.'[1]

Ausonius' father and his grandfather Arborius, both of whom died at the age of 90, were educated, indeed erudite men (cultivated Gauls long preferred speaking Greek to speaking Latin; the former language had been in everyday use since the time of Greek penetration into Gaul, well before the Roman conquest). Some scholars have thought that Arborius was possibly a druid and certainly a member of the resistance to the occupying Romans, which would explain his banishment by the Aedui, who were wholehearted collaborators. With the historian Régine Pernoud,[2] we may deplore what she generously calls a 'misunderstanding' that has taken firm root in the minds of French historians and writers ever since the seventeenth century. (Rabelais, one might add, was perhaps the last to feel truly Gaulish in every sense of the term.) 'Research could have been greatly simplified if proper consideration had been given to conditions in Gaul before the Romans arrived', says Régine Pernoud; her specific reference is to art, but her comment holds good for all aspects of the historical ethnography of Gaul. For far too long, the Gauls were regarded as a disorganized rabble, excitable, ignorant and materialistic, gluttonous and ill-educated, who achieved dignity and developed a well-ordered, fruitful culture only thanks to the Romans, who graciously went to the trouble of civilizing them.

Such was certainly the Roman view. As late as the 1940s, however, school textbooks in France still made generations of French schoolchildren (and children in the French-ruled African colonies!) learn the following edifying formula by heart: 'Our ancestors the Gauls lived much like the primitive peoples of today ...'

'This highly ingenious race', as Caesar himself, an expert on the subject, described it, was in fact 'a collection of peoples' (Régine Pernoud) of different kinds, although they were all branches of the great Celtic family tree, and they made a lasting mark: France is still a country of great diversity. One needs a careful balance of ingredients to make a good sauce.

A bare 60 generations separate these 'ancestral' Gauls from their modern descendants. French people still live in places, whether in town or country, once inhabited by the Gauls. We classify French as a Romance language, one of those derived from Latin, but it absorbed a considerable number of words from the Celtic language of the Gauls – such as *chat, lotion, brasserie, mouton, bracelet* – and a number of those words were used in England by the local Celtic people, becoming 'cat', 'lotion', 'mutton', etc.

We also have the Gauls to thank for many inventions making life more comfortable and food more palatable, including mattresses, bells, tin plate, silver plate, soap, hooded cloaks, reaping machines, good bread, *foie gras*, barrels, black pudding and white pudding, tripe, Roquefort cheese, a great many medicaments, the caulking of boats, adzes, brioches – and I could go on a great deal longer. Clearly they were an energetic race.

The word 'barbarian' was invented by the Romans, who applied it to anyone but themselves: the Gaulish 'barbarians', however, were not uncivilized. How does one define civilization, anyway? The ability to raise an army? The Gauls were well able to do that. They also had machinery, philosophy, religion, laws and social institutions. As for education, Ausonius' family was far from being exceptional. Even before the Romans arrived there were almost as many people in Gaul who could read and write as there were in France under Louis XIV. Of course they were the same sort of people, members of rich and noble families, but it was still a considerable number. At the time of the Roman conquest censuses, for which the Romans had a passion, showed that there were over 20 million Gauls; the country was thus more densely populated than in the time of the Sun King, and there was less poverty and disease.

It must have been a pleasant enough life, since among the best legacies the Gauls left to their descendants (along with *foie gras*) were a sense of humour, resourcefulness, and a liking for pottering about doing odd jobs. The Gauls might indeed be accused of a number of failings, much the same as those that make the French so very French today, but a modern Frenchman would hardly feel out of place if he could go back in time, visit them and eat at their tables, for the Gauls were extremely hospitable. All they asked of a guest passing through was that he should pay for his entertainment by telling the story of his life. Stories were very popular in Gaul, and it was only polite to your future audience to make sure that your life was eventful. In the absence of any genuinely exciting memories, you said anything that came into your head, and that was even better received.

Over the centuries, and taking Caesar's word for it, we have subscribed to the misapprehension that, before he arrived, Gaul was nothing but a collection of unwashed barbarians. However, the Celts themselves, arriving in successive waves over almost a thousand years in the country that became Gaul, found a society there which already contained all the germs of the civilization they would build together. Its memory would persist, enriched by contributions from the Romans, Visigoths and Franks, not to mention other invaders.

The classic caricature of the roistering Gaul was actually inspired by the habits of the Arvernii, ancestors of the people of the present-day Auvergne, who regarded Gaul as their own property for a century or more. They were quite a contrast to their descendants who, on discovering that they did not own Gaul after all, became sober, unassuming, peaceful people. The Arvernii of old used to gather around a hereditary ruler: the kind they liked was a chieftain with a taste for pomp and ceremony, the leader of uproarious tribes, and with every successive reign they made a great impression on their contemporaries – so great an impression, in fact, that it was applied to the Gauls in general.

Of these Arvernii rulers, Luern the Fox and his son Bituit the Everlasting really did conform to the Roman idea of the Gauls. The function of the king, in peace as in war, seemed to centre entirely upon magnificent and grandiose show. When he received envoys of other nations, Luern had a vast area of land enclosed, and enough provisions and huge vats of wine, beer and mead were accumulated for a banquet lasting several days. Everyone, from the humblest to the most powerful, was invited to eat and drink his fill. 'I want all peoples to rejoice and become intoxicated at the mere mention of my name', said Luern. He himself had a gargantuan appetite, and despised anyone who could not match it. He drew nourishment from words as well as plentiful roast meat: songs celebrated his glory as king of the Arvernii. Noblemen kept personal bards, appointed to speak for them in formal boasting contests with an energy that reflected their rates of pay. The bards of Luern and Bituit were generally considered incomparable, and the two kings appreciated these verbal ornaments to their banquets. When they appeared to take their seats, the bards instantly began praising the glory of the Arvernii at the tops of their voices, to the accompaniment of the lyre; it must have been hard to hear oneself eat.

A hundred years later, the Gallo-Romans were still enjoying their food so much that they did not like to think of the dead going without. Funerary carvings are full of representations of 'the feast of the dead', so realistic in their depiction of the domestic background that we can reconstruct every detail of the table setting and the menu. These scenes always depict *cena*, dinner in the evening, when the guests sat down to eat as their ancestors did, unless they had adopted the Roman fashion for reclining on couches. You did not bother to sit down to linger over your breakfast, *pentaculum*, or mid-day lunch, *prandium*.

In one of his poems Ausonius runs rapidly through the evolution of the Gaulish diet:

> I will speak also of our food, such as we have customarily eaten; of its seasoning of sea salt; of the acorn, a food once common to man and beast before ears of corn grew in the fields. Then came wheat, and with wheat gruel, the porridge that used to stand on the tables of the Roman people, their food and also their drink when mingled with water. Among plants, cumin is as sharp as pepper; the lentil is flat or round; a double casing protects the five kinds of nut; and honey, made by the busy labour of the bees, is pleasant both to eat and to drink ...

These lines obviously seek to evoke simplicity, in accordance with Ausonius' Aeduan character, and in contrast to the Arvernian taste for excess. In his works the prefect-poet frequently mentions the many products of Gaulish agriculture and industry which graced his table. A great connoisseur and true gastronome, he feasted a second time in describing the food he had eaten, and the letters he sends to his friends thanking them for presents of food combine object lessons, culinary history and superb sketches of everyday life. Naturally there were many social events in the life of a man of his quality. He describes a wedding:

> The looked-for day was come, and at the noble bridal, matrons and men, with youths under their parents' eyes, gather together and recline on coverlets of purple. Servants bring water for their hands, load in baskets the gifts of hard-won Ceres, and bear the roasted flesh of fat game. Most ample the list of their dainties: all kinds of fowl and flesh with wanton goat are present there, and sheep and playful kids, the watery tribe, and does, and timid stags: before their gaze and in their hands are mellow fruits.[3]

Before their gaze and in their hands fruit and even pieces of meat often disappeared in the folds of the *mappa*, the napkin every guest brought with him. No one thought this bad manners, and indeed menus were planned to provide for such extended hospitality. Had things been otherwise the hosts would have felt ashamed. Curiously, the same custom is found today in West Africa, particularly among the Baoule people of the Ivory Coast, where one must sometimes travel a long way to visit friends. Tradition demands that after the meal, or when the guest leaves, he is given a bundle of food; he himself, of course, did not arrive empty-handed.

The gastronomic and social customs described by Ausonius are obviously those of a refined society, but they already seem to show the moderation which was to be the strength of the French bourgeoisie. There is a greater distance between the serenity of Ausonius and the extravagances of the Arvernii than there is, for instance, between Ausonius and Courtine. Here is the prefect going down to visit his kitchen and see what the chef Sosias is cooking: 'Taste and make sure – for they often play you false – that the seasoned dishes are well soused and taste appetizingly. Turn your bubbling pots in your hands and shake them up: quick, dip your fingers in the hot gravy and let your moist tongue lick them as it darts in and out.'[4] Not very hygienic, but at least the master of the house of that period showed that he knew what went on in the kitchen. Later, in his *Directions to Servants*, Swift made similar recommendations, but satirically.

Depending on the household, the many plates and dishes were made of wood or most usually of pottery, copied from Italian models and quite as good as the originals. Richer houses might have the luxury of glass, and fine earthenware dishes. Pots and pans for cooking utensils, of which there was also a comprehensive selection, included terracotta vessels and the heavy iron or bronze cauldrons so popular with the Celts. In some ways the *batterie de cuisine* anticipated the cooking utensils of the South of France at a later date. Similarly, Gaulish cooking was done with loving care on the hearth; many specimens of superb bronze, iron and even pottery fire-dogs have been found. As Camille Jullian has remarked, not without humour, 'At the bottom of a Gallo-Roman ruin you will find a heap of crockery.'

If the Gauls knew how to eat well they also knew how to look after themselves. Gaulish doctors had been famous since the time of Crinas of Phocaea, great-grandson of the great explorer Pytheas (*c.* 150 BC), whose only methods of treatment were with the plants of the Mediterranean and a judicious diet. A contemporary of Ausonius, Marcellus, wrote a dictionary of phytotherapy which is both wise and knowledgeable.

One last word on the thermal waters of Gaul: the abundance and excellence of the Gaulish springs, which were always under the patronage of some benevolent god or other, made hydrotherapy a popular form of treatment. Two thousand years later the same springs are still functioning, although now under the patronage of the French health service, the Sécurité Sociale. Cicero's scornful comment, to the effect that the Gauls 'thought they would poison themselves by mixing their wine with water', may be seen as the gallophobia of a lawyer who had no qualms about defending the prefect of Narbonne on charges of trafficking in wine at the expense of those he governed. Wherever it came from, the water in Gaul was so good that the young Julian, proclaimed Emperor while he was in Lutetia ('my dear Lutetia', he called it), was sorry to leave a place where you could live so well and 'where the river water is pleasing to the sight and excellent to drink'. In those happy days the waters of the Seine were a crystalline liquid as clear as the elegant glasses of Frontinus that can still be admired in the glass cases of the Saint-Germain Museum.

And finally, as we imagine the pleasure of sitting down to dinner with the Gauls, let us recall a note on St Anthony by Henri Queffélec,[5] who comments on the Gallic enthusiasm for that hermit saint, the patron saint of swineherds (the smallest pig in the litter is known in English folklore too as St Anthony's pig, or 'the tantony pig').

> In the literature of the desert fathers, there is a tale of a Gaulish monk[6] who spoke warmly of his countrymen's achievements in the dietary field. 'As usual', said he to another monk, 'you never miss an opportunity of accusing us of being great eaters. However, it would be cruel to make us Gauls live as the angels live (and indeed I am convinced that the angels themselves eat, for the sheer pleasure of eating).'

Chapter 12

Treasures from the Sea

The History of Garum

Garum shared responsibility for the Roman conquest of Gaul, since its manufacture and marketing made an appreciable contribution to the prosperity of the trading posts which proliferated, from the time when Greek colonists first landed on the shores of Gaul, until a whole chain of them existed along the Ligurian (Provençal), Volcaean (Languedocian) and Iberian (Spanish) coastlines.

It should be said that the Greeks were already using *garon* when Rome was still nothing but a caravanserai. But garum was one of the great gastronomic passions of Rome, the basic seasoning used in its cookery, the supreme condiment. In fact the Romans had a mania for it. Scarcely a Roman recipe fails to mention garum. Amphoras recovered from shipwrecks all around the Gulf of Lions – at Ansérune and Agde, for instance – contain crystallized deposits of the sauce and bear manufacturers' seals showing that there was a trade in garum as early as the fifth century BC. Phocaean Massilia was an import-export centre of that trade. And in connection with the Romanization of Gaul, we may recall that it was the people of Massilia who invited the Romans into Provence in 181 BC, opening up their way into the whole country.

Each port had its own secret recipe for its special brand of garum, but the kind considered the best from the early days of the Empire, *garum sociorum*, 'garum of the allies', came from Carthagena and Gades (Cadiz) in Spain. Garum was a sauce made of the intestines of mackerel or anchovies, macerated in salt and then left out in the sun until the mixture had completely decomposed, or rather had digested itself by the action of the fish's own intestinal microbes. Carefully calculated amounts of concentrated decoctions of aromatic herbs were added. Then a very fine strainer was plunged into the vessel containing the mixture to collect the syrupy, strongly flavoured liquid. The garum was ladled out and left to mature. The residue or *alec*, an animal equivalent of the *marc* or residue of grapes pressed for wine, was not thrown away. Poor people used it to season and enrich their cereal porridges.

Garum could command fantastic prices; the price of caviare is nothing by comparison. The only possible parallel is with the essences used in perfume-making. In Caesar's time a *congius* (about three and a quarter litres) of garum cost 500 sestertii, something like £4000 in modern terms. I should add that only a few drops were enough to transform the flavour of the most insipid broth or gruel. 'Sanguine garum', which some people preferred, was made similarly from the intestines and blood of tuna. It was even stronger in flavour than ordinary garum. The freshwater sheatfish or catfish found in marshes, never considered good eating because of its bones and thick skin, could at least be pounded and turned into a kind of garum called *muria*. Garum diluted with water, *hydrogarum*, improved the daily diet of Roman soldiers; garum diluted with wine might be used to make the popular Byzantine sauce called *oenogarum*. Diluted with oil, it became *oleogarum*, and diluted with vinegar it was *oxygarum*.

The aroma was not the essential quality of this condiment: it was a concentration of the amino acids called lysines, and its richness in nitrogen and mineral salts made it a powerful tonic. The modern *nuoc-man* of South-East Asia is a kind of garum, and although it is made from putrefying fish there are no records of bacterial infection caused by eating it. Indeed, a few drops of *nuoc-man* are put into Laotian babies' bottles. Garum can hardly have been harmful either, or how could one explain its popularity over several centuries of intensive consumption?

Garum made the fortunes of the first Greek and Roman trading stations of southern Gaul and Iberia. On the Ligurian coast, it was the ancestor of the famous Provençal dish of *pissaladière* and in practice it continued to feature in the modest diet of coastal Provençals until the early twentieth century. *Peis-salat*, known as *pissara* in the Var and *pissala* in Nice, was a preserve made of very small, whole, salted fish – gobies, the small fry of sardines, anchovies not good enough to be sold, whitebait – to which soft roes, embryo crustaceans, and fish debris in general might be added.

The method was to place a layer of coarse sea salt in a small cask or stoneware jar, then a layer of mixed aromatic herbs, then a layer of fish, another layer of salt, and so on. As each new addition was made, it finished with a top layer of herbs. But the crucial thing was to fill the jar within a few days, and then keep it in a cool place with a flat stone on top to press the mixture down. When all the salt had dissolved the contents of the jar were turned into a sieve, reduced to a purée, and put back in the jar under a layer of salt.

This *peis-salat*, according to Mistral in *Le trésor du félibrige*, was eaten on a *pompe*, the traditional flat cake of bread. Ligurian *pissaladière* added onions and olives, and tomatoes when they became common in France, after the First Empire. *Pissaladière* and pizza are of very ancient origin indeed, evidence of the unbroken tradition of Mediterranean civilizations.

The History of Caviare

Once upon a time ... it seems appropriate to begin the story of caviare with that fairy-tale opening. Caviare is the last legendary food of modern times, and indeed is more than just a food, is hardly a food at all. As the son of one of the men who gave it its present status readily admits, caviare represents a dream.

There can be no doubt at all that the Gauls would have liked caviare if they had ever tasted it. Jean Markale[1] comments on the general Celtic fondness for words and disregard of historical facts. 'They dream their history, rather than living it.' All that was required of a guest, as I mentioned above, was to tell his life story before the company rose from table, and he might well dream one up instead. After all, what is truth: unpalatable reality or attractive dream?

So since this chapter began with the Gauls, let us dream in the Gaulish manner: a banquet of words, in the felicitous phrase used by Jean-François Revel[2] in the title of his book *Un festin en paroles*. Think of a banquet. Asked to do that, the man or woman in the street, 60 generations away from the time of the ancient Gauls, will close the eyes momentarily to facilitate dreaming, and then reply with this list of the ideal, 'paradisiacal' menu, which does not flow from Revel's pen by chance: 'Salmon, *foie gras*, caviare, truffles, crayfish, i.e., foods that are rare, unusual or unobtainable in the countries where they are thought of as luxuries.'[3] The dream banquet serves such foods, which seem to us as magical as did the ambrosia of the gods to the Greeks. Everyman and Everywoman, reverently eating modern ambrosia in the form of caviare, can identify as they indulge in the mad extravagance of swallowing it – even if they do not happen to like it, perhaps especially if they do not happen to like it – with what they see as the last incarnation of the Immortals, the international jet-set: mythical, billionaire beings with public relations officers as their Mercury, gossip columnists as their Homer, La Croisette, Marbella or Saint-Moritz as their Olympia, and complicated love-lives to suit the image. Caviare is the stylish food of important people. Here is the worthy Deume family, in Albert Cohen's book *Belle du Seigneur*, sparing no expense to entertain the Under-Secretary General of the League of Nations: 'Caviare is the *ne plus ultra* of foods, and the most expensive.'[4]

So what exactly is caviare, the *ne plus ultra* of foods, and the most expensive? Alexandre Dumas, who is sometimes wildly inaccurate, adds to the ignorance of his time out of vanity, recording in his *Dictionnaire de cuisine*: 'Caviare (a kind of sturgeon). I spent a month observing the caviare fisheries on the shores of the Caspian Sea ... the flesh of the caviare has a delicate flavour, rare among cartilaginous fish.' Clearly Dumas was dreaming in a very Gaulish manner.

Turning from the fantasies of Dumas, I will state at once that caviare consists of the eggs of the sturgeon. The word 'caviare' comes from a word of Turkish origin, *khavia*, meaning not just any fish's eggs, but those of the sturgeon. Thus the roes of mullet, cod, salmon and lumpfish are not caviare, not even poor man's caviare, not even substitute caviare: they are just mullet, cod, salmon or lumpfish roe. Despite American terminology, either something is caviare or it is not, and these roes are not. When you eat them you are not dreaming, you are pretending, which is not the same thing. Bad marks to the several major dictionaries which define caviare as 'the roe of sturgeon or other kinds of fish'.

The consumption of caviare dates back to antiquity, but for a long time the only people who ate it were poor fishermen who removed the roe of the sturgeon so that they could sell the fish containing it. The sturgeon itself was regarded as the finest fish in the world at the time of the Roman Empire. The Emperor Severus had it served up on a bed of roses, to the sound of flutes and drums. Ovid, in his *Metamorphoses*, described the sturgeon as 'pilgrim of the most illustrious waves', a ringing phrase of little gastronomic utility. Those recipes of Apicius which have come down to us do not mention sturgeon, but it may have featured in the complete manuscript. Apuleius mentions Sorrento sturgeon in his *Apologia*.

In fact, sturgeon (from a Germanic root giving rise to a Frankish word, *sturgo*) could have been caught by Noah before he boarded the Ark, for it is a truly antediluvian fish. The Acipenseridae family, ganoid cartilaginous fish, probably appeared at the beginning of the Mesozoic era. The sturgeon of the Caspian Sea, which produces the only caviare worthy of that name, was trapped in that gigantic inland sea after the waters receded in the Tertiary period of the Cenozoic era. It is a migratory fish (hence Ovid's pretty 'pilgrim' metaphor), like the salmon, with which it shares its home, and it too swims up the fresh water of rivers to spawn at the time of the autumn and spring equinoxes. In the Caspian, it has a certain preference for the multiple mouths of the Volga near Astrakhan, and the forked mouth of the Ural at Gourjev. There are few river mouths along the Iranian coast of the Caspian Sea.

With the bony plates along its back, its often impressive length, and its head which sometimes ends in a long, pointed snout, the sturgeon looks like a monster from another age, and could have inspired the artist who provided illustrations for Jules Verne's *Nautilus*, unless it was from Leonardo da Vinci that he drew his ideas. In fact there is more than one kind of sturgeon. Three are found in the Caspian: Beluga, a short-nosed sturgeon which can easily live to be 100, may be four metres long, and can weigh from 800 kilos to a tonne. The Osetr sturgeon has a long snout, can weigh up to 300 kilos, and is two metres long. The Sevruga sturgeon also has a long snout, but weighs only 60 kilos and is a metre and a half long. The caviare found in the females of all three may be 10 to 12 per cent of their body weight.

In the chapter on fish above, I mentioned the sturgeon of the Gironde and the Bouches-du-Rhône; were these the fish that provided the *caviat* mentioned by Rabelais at the head of his list of dishes for 'interlarded fast-days'? Or the caviare which Shakespeare's Hamlet equates with pearls cast before swine – 'twas caviare to the general'? Perhaps, but it is not impossible that these writers were speaking of exported Russian caviare. There are records of the accounts of caravans mentioning the carriage of caviare all across Russia, and even in the time of Charlemagne exotic foodstuffs might travel yet farther and reach Western Europe.

At any rate, however, it seems that the medieval Provençals were the only people in France to appreciate caviare. They also liked *poutargue*, dried, salted and pressed mullet roe such as is used to make Sardinian *butarga* and Greek *tarama*, crushed with olive oil and lemon. Rabelais must have eaten *poutargue* in passing through Montpellier, for his character Grandgousier liked it, and had 'a supply of botargos'.[5] It is true that this 'good jester ... had quite a liking for salt meat', to give him a better thirst for drinking. Bishop Quiqueran de Beaujeu,[6] less of a jester, was not likely to forget the *poutargue* he ate neat, in the manner of the fishermen of Martigues: 'Having tasted of that dish one day, feeling my stomach charged with humours, and nevertheless in robust health enough, I partook of it so freely that such a change for the worse came over me as obliged me, after long resistance, to moderate that medicament with water.' There is a suggestion of military duty and scientific probity about the Bishop's heroic consumption of *poutargue*.

Louis XV proved less heroic. However, he was only a child, although already crowned King, when Tsar Peter the Great's ambassador ceremoniously offered him a spoonful of precious caviare and he promptly spat it out, nauseated, on the carpet of Versailles. The ambassador was deeply offended, not by this want of etiquette – worse was known in Moscow – but by the royal retching. To Russians, the sturgeon and its caviare deserved the utmost respect, an almost mystical respect, even from kings. They are still revered by every Soviet fisherman, no doubt because their roe is now one of the most expensive foods in the world; they are like living gold. The first sturgeon caught, and the first caviare pressed, used to be the Tsar's by right. Regardless of the real colour of this king among fish, Russians did not visualize it in its usual pale greyish hue. In Russia, the sturgeon was the Red Fish, with capital letters: red like Glory, Fortune and Power. Banknotes of large denominations were red in Tsarist Russia. (The same association of ideas occurs in Madagascar, where gold and what we call silver, money or cash are described as *vola*, red.)

At the period when the Tsar sent caviare, Russian *ikra*, to the King of France, it would have been salted by the fishermen who removed it from the fish, and then rolled in a cloth. The cloth-wrapped packets were buried in the ground. Although no one knew just why, the soil along the coasts of the Caspian Sea had remarkable preservative powers. The same phenomenon, as we have seen, led fishermen of the past to bury their salt cod under the turf of Newfoundland. In fact the miraculous power of the soil in these areas is nothing but the chemical action of borax, which is found there in high concentration. Prewar campers used to keep their butter in borated water: the practice has now been abandoned, partly because of the availability of portable refrigerating devices, but also because borax has been condemned by the Food and Drug Administration. In a very high dosage, say for instance if one ate a kilo of caviare every day of one's life, it is not eliminated from the system. Today caviare is still salted but no longer buried, and usually it has a very small amount of borax added; the substance also has the advantage of improving the flavour of the caviare even more. But caviare destined for America is not borated, and so it is sometimes more highly salted than would suit European palates.

Caviare of the old style can be sampled if you eat the pressed caviare of which the Russians are still very fond. In Tsarist times no well-born Russian would have travelled without his stock of caviare in an isothermic container, hoping that he could replenish his supplies at the places he meant to visit.

That fact may have been in the minds of two well-bred young Russo-Armenians who escaped to Paris after the Bolshevik Revolution. The modern fairy-tale of caviare begins with them. They appear in the character of magicians, with the telephone as their magic wand. Let us return to that age-old formula 'Once upon a time'.

Once upon a time, then, there were two brothers called Melkom and Mougcheg, whose family was prosperously involved in fisheries and oil at Baku, near Kura. Then one day the Revolution came. The brothers went to France to study – one medicine, the other law – and found themselves in a Paris where all the gilded youth of Europe longed to be. It was the Gay Paree of the postwar period, of Montparnasse, the Charleston, champagne. But to the brothers' great surprise, there was no caviare. Caviare had not been so much as mentioned when Tsar Alexander III visited the city early in the twentieth century. The Tsar, the Little Father of All the Russias, would hardly have wished to see President Loubet repeat the unfortunate performance of Louis XV. Such episodes are not forgotten, even after nearly two centuries. Accordingly, the Tsar was well entertained, but caviare did not feature on the menu.

The two young Petrossians were stunned. A party without caviare was not a party at all. Once they had recovered from their surprise, the brothers made up their minds that such a state of affairs could not continue. They would import caviare. Where from? Russia. But there was no Russia now, only a Union of Socialist Soviet Republics. There was no Tsar; the people ruled. There were not even any diplomatic relations with Western capitals.[7] In this post-revolutionary chaos, the only thing still working normally was the telephone – at least, if you were lucky. Melkom and Mougcheg were lucky. 'Hello, who is that calling?' 'The Petrossian brothers, from Paris.' 'Paris?' '*Da.*' 'And – er – who did you want to speak to?' 'The Minister of Foreign Trade. I suppose there *is* a Minister of Foreign Trade?' '*Da.* But we have nothing to sell abroad.' 'Well, the fact is, we wanted to buy –' 'What? Hold the line!' 'We wanted to buy caviare. *Da*?' '*Da*!'

The switchboard operator who took the call in Moscow could hardly believe her ears. Long afterwards, she remembered it vividly, for the Petrossians' caviare decided her own fate. A second generation of caviare-buying Petrossians found her ensconced as the highly respected secretary of the chairman of the trade organization which supplied them. For the Petrossian brothers succeeded in getting caviare for their party, and some to spare. Indeed, quite a lot to spare. The Russians at the other end of the line could have wept for joy. Of course there was caviare! No one knew what to do with the stuff. You cannot feed millions of people in a starving country on caviare; agricultural production was already down by a half, and only one-third of that was being issued. The country urgently needed to export and acquire funds to buy wheat. It could reap a good harvest from caviare, paid for in advance, in hard currency. Yes, the caviare would indeed be paid for in advance, in hard currency. Then the Petrossians could consider it already on its way. But wait a moment – the Petrossians wanted just one more thing: priority rights to the importation of caviare. They were still getting them, to the tune of 63 per cent, 60 years later. Similarly, they were the only importers with the right to go direct to the source of supply and choose the caviare themselves, before sending it out of Russia by air; in the course of time a positive airlift of caviare was established. The *ne plus ultra* and most expensive of foods requires the *ne plus ultra* and most expensive form of transport.

When the caviare arrived in France in 1920, travelling by sea and land, it appealed to snobs because of its high price. But selling the bulk of the product on a wider market was a different matter. The mass market is not so fond of novelties, even if they are actually given away, as happened in the case of potatoes (see chapter 23). Think, then, of the resistance to buying a foreign product at a ridiculous price. When the economic crisis of the period between the World Wars set in, things became even worse. At the Gastronomic Exhibition in the Grand Palais the Petrossians had to have spittoons installed around their stand, since most people reacted like Louis XV. Tasting was free, and anything free finds takers. Husbands would recommend wives to take advantage of it. Husband and wife alike would spit the stuff out again, with expressions of distaste. But the tables were soon turned on those who mocked the idea of selling caviare. People of experience and good taste liked it, and by the time the exhibition closed it was a success. The venture had paid off.

At the first Foire de Paris under the Mitterrand government, 60 years later, it was thought unseemly to exhibit something that had become so fabulously expensive, and caviare was shown only in facsimile. However, lorries loaded with tins of genuine caviare had to be sent for as a matter of urgency, and the public eagerly bought them at the standard price, all the taxes on luxury goods included. For the price of a sizeable bet at the races, after all, you could briefly imagine yourself a Getty, a Princess Caroline of Monaco, a Julio Iglesias, and suggest to your wife that it's not bad on toast.

But to be serious, and caviare is a serious business: there are people who know how to appreciate it, and indeed their numbers are increasing. However, they will never be the majority: in the nature of things that fabulous food caviare must be a rarity, or it does not fulfil its function. As with breakfast at Tiffany's, 'it is desire that creates the desirable, and the plan that determines the aim', according to Simone de Beauvoir.[8] Corneille too made a comment to the effect that the desire our minds are always fixing upon some object is, in moderation, the guarantee of good health and the driving force of our ambitions. A creature without desire is sick, autistic like Gregory of Tours's monster, 'who lived from birth in this world of toil, his fists clenched and unsuited for work ... his knees drawn up to his belly, his hands close to his chest, his eyes shut. He was more like a monster than a human being.' The Stoic ideal is an apathetic ideal, and a society without desires is sterile. So we might as well avoid Stoicism and admit to natural if inessential desires, including the wish to eat choice foods. That was the true message of Epicurus. King Henri IV's *poule au pot* on Sundays was the forerunner of caviare.

And supposing the caviare of your desires does materialize some day, it should be appreciated properly if you are to relish it to the full, not wasting either the caviare, your money, or indeed the memory of the occasion. Caviare must be savoured for its own sake, as it deserves. The divinity of caviare, of course, has its religion, and the Petrossians are still its prophets, but it has its heresies too, the worst being the American way of serving it with onion, hard-boiled egg and piquant sauce. Caviare needs nothing, particularly not lemon juice, which is a great sin. Give it simply a thin slice of good bread, lightly toasted and buttered, and a small spoon. Hold the mouthful of caviare under the roof of the mouth for a moment, crushing it with your tongue, not chewing it. That is the way to taste it at its best.

Blinis and fresh or soured cream, for the sake of local colour, are typical of the trap of anachronism which always lies in wait for ignorant people who want to look knowledgeable. That was a good way to eat caviare in the days when the only caviare exported was either pressed or inexpertly preserved.

Nature in her wisdom ordained that the national drink of Russia, the home of caviare, should be vodka, a grain spirit. Vodka is the best thing of all to accompany caviare: they are made for each other. It should be a genuine white Russian vodka such as Moskovskaya or Stolichnoya, and well chilled.

And what wine do you drink to wash it down? Not Pouilly Fuissé. Not Chablis. Not any kind of Alsace wine. Champagne, *brut*, is the thing to drink. Only perfection should be called upon to celebrate sublimity.

A Who's Who of Caviare

To the true gourmet, the salted eggs of sturgeon from the estuaries of Canada, America, Romania and the Gironde in France (20 kilos a year of the latter are produced) cannot compare in perfection with caviare from the Caspian. This is basically to do with the saline quality of the water, with the plankton, and with the geographical situation of the Caspian Sea, landlocked and therefore unaffected by oceanic currents.

However, Caspian caviare may come from either Russia or Iran. Russian caviare has a tradition as old as Russia itself. Iranian caviare has been commercialized relatively recently, but it comes from the same species of sturgeon. The one

Making caviare in Russia (*c.* 1920)

drawback of the Iranian coast, so far as the fish is concerned, is its shortage of river mouths, which means sturgeon must be caught out at sea, while the north of the Caspian has many river deltas with abundant cold waters. At the time of writing only these Russian estuaries are regularly maintained by dredging; the ayatollahs of Iran have other concerns on their minds.

Since Islamic law, like the Book of Leviticus, forbids the faithful to eat fish without scales, and the eggs of such fish, Persia was not interested in its caviare until Rezah Pahlevi, father of the last Shah, seized power and modernized the country. Agreements were drawn up in 1927 granting the Russians two-thirds of Iranian caviare and sturgeon production in exchange for technical aid and a modern infrastructure. In 1953, at the same time as he was giving the Empress Soraya sables, Stalin handed the fisheries back to Mossadegh, who nationalized them. But it was only natural for Soviet technicians to continue running the industries that processed caviare and restocked the waters. Russia also retained rights to the biggest quota of Iranian caviare at the lowest price. It was given the superior treatment accorded to Russian caviare, from which it could not then be distinguished.

The supposedly famous white Iranian caviare is a snare and a delusion. It is actually the roe of albino sturgeon, and such fish have degenerated. Because of its colour, or rather absence of colour, it was sent to the Shah in the manner of all rarities presented to monarchs. The Shah, who had a good palate, swiftly passed it on to members of his entourage, who used to supplement their salaries by selling it to the gullible.

At present the Iranian government has neither the means nor the expertise to manage its fisheries. The Russians left the country hastily, and the Iranians found their access to the salt of Lake Ladoga was cut off. Ladoga salt contributes a good deal to the quality of Russian caviare. The Americans – when international tension is not too great – are alone, or almost alone, in buying Iranian caviare, in which salt has been supplemented by additives and pasteurization, while the 2000 tonnes a year of best quality Russian caviare from Astrakhan and the Ural, processed by the state-run Caspriba organization, supplies the Petrossian quotas.

All caviare exported from Russia is of high quality, since the market holds its value only by dint of its prestige; 63 per cent of the caviare sold on this market passes through France under the auspices of the Petrossian firm, who redistribute it. The caviare eaten in Russia itself, 1800 tonnes of it, is sometimes of second-best quality but is still extremely good; the caviare sold to tourists on the black market or in the street carries no guarantee at all, as many a tourist who thought he had a bargain has discovered. Caviare sold for hard currency in the duty-free Intourist shops bears the French label.

The serious purchaser can choose between three kinds of caviare, bearing the names of the three strains of sturgeon from which the roes come. Beluga is the rarest, the largest-grained (30 eggs per gram) and the most expensive. Its colour varies from pale to dark grey. It makes up 20 per cent of catches and sales. Osetr has a characteristic, slightly iodine flavour, and its grains are smaller than in Beluga caviare (50 to the gram). It is slightly less expensive. Its grey colour is tinged with gold here and there. It accounts for 30 per cent of catches and sales. Sevruga, though less expensive, is equally good. Its price reflects the fact that it is the most usual sort. It has small grains (70 to the gram) which are a very dark grey, almost black. It makes up 50 per cent of catches and sales.

The pressed caviare of Russian tradition should not be forgotten. It is the customary way of using over-ripe or under-ripe eggs. They are pressed until they lose three-quarters of their volume along with their liquid. The market price of pressed caviare is about half that of Beluga, and many people prefer it.

Finally, although few have ever encountered it, there is a very fine-grained caviare in which the grains are like sand. It comes from a small species of Caspian sturgeon, the sterlet, highly esteemed for its flesh. The fish is not common, and although its caviare used to be reserved for the Tsar, even he did not get it every year.

How to Keep Caviare Happy

The season is early spring or early autumn. The female sturgeon, feeling ready to lay the enormous quantity of eggs which makes up at least 10 per cent of her present weight, makes for the mouth of a river up which she hopes to swim, with her suitors in attendance, to spawn in fresh, cool, clear water.

For several days, factory ships have been waiting for flat-bottomed fishing boats to drive the shoals of these great fish towards them. The fish are easily driven, having just one idea in their tiny brains: swimming upstream. Even for a fish, the sturgeon is thought to be remarkably stupid. The females are also in the dull-witted state of their late pregnancy. But the sturgeon, although ignorant, is worth its weight in gold. Ignorance, one might say, is bliss. And curiously enough the immensely valuable eggs it carries will remain alive only as long as the fish is happy. Hurt it or frighten it, and stress will liberate adrenalin which kills the eggs, giving them an unpleasant acidity and odour. Perfect caviare must be made from perfect eggs: alive and happy.

Accordingly Russian fishermen, who anyway feel a deep respect for the fish that is such a gold-mine, take their catch with the utmost care. The sturgeon is hauled on board gently, almost lovingly. Men in white coats and caps, looking rather like a surgical team, surround the placid creature as it lies on a conveyor belt gasping for breath. The belt immediately starts moving towards a trapdoor giving access to a kind of operating theatre, where the same immaculate cleanliness reigns. The fish does not even have time to suffocate, but is stunned and anaesthetized by a well-aimed blow on the most vulnerable spot on its armour-plated head. Instantly, with one slash of a short, broad, razor-sharp blade, the great sac of eggs is liberated by Caesarean operation. The large clusters, held together by a membrane, are extracted with the opened hand as delicately as if a baby were being born. The sturgeon has died knowing nothing, blissful in her ignorance, and the eggs are perfect.

After this operation – in both senses of the word – the roes are turned into a tank of pure, chilled water, and rinsed. They are then spread on a *lekta*, a kind of very fine hopper against which the eggs are rolled to separate them from the membranes, very carefully, so as not to crush them. This process is supervised by a 'master', the English word being adopted into Russian for the function. His expertise is equal to that of a master wine-maker. Simply by touching and feeling the brown mass of eggs, with its faint iodized fragrance, he can tell what kind of caviare it should become: natural, with only the minimum of salt, 3 or 5 per cent depending on the maturity; borated or not, depending on whether it is destined for America. If the eggs are not all absolutely perfect it is better to pasteurize them, but they will not do for the French market. A slightly over-ripe sac of eggs will make pressed caviare.

The eggs are weighed and salted at once, hand-stirred, the amount of salt being decided by the master. Then the caviare is delicately put into cans with a spatula: blue cans with shiny interiors. These are large, two-kilo cans. When the caviare reaches Paris it will be reconditioned. The cans must be adequately filled but not over-filled, so that when the lid goes on they will be air-tight, but the grains will not be crushed. A tight rubber band round it, and the can goes into a cold chamber at below 2 degrees centigrade. This temperature has to be maintained as the caviare travels from the Russian factory ship lying off the Astrakhan marshes all the way to Le Bourget airport, and thence to the chilled display counters before which people are happy, let us hope, to stand and dream for a few moments.

The History of Shellfish and Crustaceans

Long before the Romans were getting oysters, their favourite shellfish, from the shores of Gaul in particular, the gathering of such creatures had preceded hunting or fishing. They provided basic protein in the diet of peoples who lived on sea coasts or beside lakes.

Extraordinary mounds formed by quantities of empty shells, accumulated over prehistoric millennia, are found all over the world. Many date back to the Upper Paleolithic. In the Scandinavian countries, and all down the west coast of the Americas – from north to south, from the Bering Strait (once an isthmus) off Alaska to British Columbia, California, Mexico, Peru and Chile – the beaches are littered with heaps of shells. The most spectacular site is probably at the Ilhas das Rosas in the Bay of Parangua, where a number of dressed stones have also been found in the mounds. Farther north, in Puget Sound near Seattle in the United States, the first Amerindians gathered giant clams weighing up to three kilos at every high tide. They might have neither the wish nor the means to fish for salmon, halibut or sturgeon out at sea, but they could feed their families simply by taking a walk on the beach.

After the last Ice Age, the Würm–Weichsel–Wisconsin glaciation of 10,000 years ago, the level of the seas, swelled by melting glaciers, rose several dozen metres, and most of the oldest deposits were submerged, but they emerged again when the waters went down in the sixth millennium BC. Huge mounds of freshwater shells have also been found, for instance in Kentucky and Tennessee in the United States, showing that large groups of humans had been settled there for a very long time. Some hills of shells are still being built. In Senegal, for instance, on the coast south of Dakar, there is a place called Fadiouth which is actually an archipelago consisting of the debris of billions of mangrove oysters. One of the three islands of Faboura a kilometre from Joal, President Senghor's native village, covers no less than seven hectares, reaching a height of ten metres. A village on stilts stands on this hill, rising higher generation by generation. The second island is used as a storehouse and the third as a cemetery. The people get from one island to another by canoe, paddling across a lagoon paved with oysters. Nor is this surrealist landscape devoid of vegetation, for baobab trees, greedy feeders on calcium, grow larger here than anywhere else, their thin shade covering the ground, which sparkles in the sun and grates underfoot. There is an acrid odour in the air, and the local villagers are happy and healthy. They have eaten oysters at every meal for centuries upon centuries, and never tire of them.

From the Upper Paleolithic onwards, shellfish have been used in trade all over the world, either for their contents as nourishment, or for their empty shells, which were the first coinage, the first jewels and the first implements used by man. Cowries, tiny porcelain-shells, still have monetary value in Africa. Around the Mediterranean basin, one of the first decorative motifs used on ceramics was made by pressing a small shell, the cardial, on damp clay. The cardial pattern, found on a number of archeological sites, is evidence of a ceramics industry. Quite early, then, man had uses for shells that went beyond their original consumption as food. They have been found a very long way from the sea: a magnificent scallop shell, for instance, dug up in the cave of Les Trois-Frères in Ariège. Archeologists who have examined shells from several sites which bear traces of exterior charring have concluded that they were used as cooking vessels.

Since the climate of the southern and eastern Mediterranean makes it dangerous to eat shellfish and crustaceans unless they have only just been caught, they were not consumed by either the Egyptians or the Jews, who inherited some of the dietary principles of ancient Egypt. The Hebrews classed them among unclean foods, as water creatures without fins or scales; shellfish soon go bad, and crustaceans are scavengers and eat carrion.

The Greeks of the archaic and then the classical period, however, ate and enjoyed a wide variety of seafood: oysters, mussels, sea urchins, crabs, all of them found in abundance on the jagged and rocky coastlines of Greece. The delightful poetic menu by the dithyrambic poet Philoxenus of Cythera, describing a dinner served at the court of Dionysius, tyrant of Syracuse, mentions various dishes including shellfish set on the table 'open, golden and still sizzling as they emerge from the oil in which they have been fried'. They sound very like the *mithia tighanita* or fried mussels served today in little restaurants in Piraeus. The Greeks also liked crawfish, oysters, shrimps and prawns – and sea urchins, which they cooked in honey, with parsley and mint.

Among other non-alimentary uses for shells, purple dye was made from murex shells, and conch shells were used as musical instruments. Shells even served political ends. As we have seen, the Greeks, inventors of both democracy and philosophy, loved to vote. They sometimes used broad beans in their ballots, but they might instead take a flat oyster shell, an *ostrakon*, and write on it the names of persons considered undesirable and suitable candidates for exile. The custom, established by Clisthenes in 487 BC, facilitated the exercise of the popular will. After a while the *ostrakones* became clay discs, which were easier to write on than shells. The Greek general Aristeides, known as 'the Just' for his integrity, was an early victim of ostracism, at a period when the original oyster shells were probably still in use. Even though he was such an upright character, he eventually antagonized the people, and Themistocles encouraged them to banish him. However, Aristeides was a man of such probity that when an honest but illiterate citizen, not recognizing him, asked him to write his own name on the shell he meant to use for voting he complied. First, however, Aristeides asked the man if the general had ever done him any harm. 'No', replied the peasant, 'but I am tired of always hearing him called "the Just".' Excavations in the Agora have produced over 1600 shells or potsherds bearing some 60 different names of people known to have been ostracized from Aristeides onwards, including Themistocles himself, Cimon and Thucydides. At least this ordeal by oyster is evidence of the degree of education and public spirit found among the Athenian people.

But enough of politics; let us get back to the stove. Athenaeus mentions his ancestors' partiality for crustaceans, but like all classical writers, he fails to distinguish between crawfish or spiny lobster and the freshwater crayfish, calling both *astacos* and to some extent confusing them with *karabos* – not some bad fairy of the sea, as the word might suggest, but the crab. Incidentally, the title of Carabas given by Perrault to his Marquis was initially the word for a heavy carriage, deriving from an earlier form, *carabe*, a sedan chair which was so heavy to carry that the footmen holding its stretchers had to proceed crabwise.

The provenance of the recipe for crawfish or lobster *à l'américaine* – Alexandre Dumas gives an excellent version in his *Dictionnaire de cuisine* – is vociferously disputed by the Bretons, who hold that it is really *à l'armoricaine*, in spite of the spices and alcohol used in the sauce, not at all in keeping with Breton cookery. In fact it is a Creole dish, hailing from such Hispanic areas as Cuba, Florida and Louisiana. Curiously, one of Apicius' recipes resembles it closely. Perhaps we might dismiss both the American and the Armorican claims and rechristen the dish *à la romaine*. The true lobster, a crustacean found only in cold seas, was unknown to the ancient Mediterranean and its people. They encountered it only in the Middle Ages, like herring – though at the other end of the seafood price range.

For his crawfish recipe, Apicius recommends chopping the live crustaceans into pieces just before putting them in oil, to keep the flesh firm. The dish, as I have said, sounds very like ours, even across the centuries: it was made with pounded pepper and lovage, dried mint, plenty of cumin, honey, vinegar and garum. Herbs such as nard or bitter valerian might also be added as flavourings.

Apicius himself liked nothing better than squills, also called flat or slipper lobsters, a kind of large crawfish without the big pincers. Learning one day that specimens larger than a man's hand might be found in Tunisia (and they are still found there today), Apicius chartered a ship and set sail, despite stormy weather, for the coast of Africa. In sight of Carthage, he saw a fishing boat. The fishermen came on board, offering a single basket of magnificent squills, but no more. The furious Apicius set sail again at once, hardly giving the fishermen time to leave his vessel, his disappointment even fiercer than the stormy wind blowing between Charybdis and Scylla (from which mythical monster the crustacean's Latin name of *Scyllarus arctus* derives).

However, the Romans' great passion was for oysters. An experienced connoisseur and a real expert on the subject called Mucianus, whom Pliny quotes, distinguished and compared the flavours of oysters of different provenance offered for sale in the Forum market: there were some ten different kinds, from the Sea of Marmora to the Armorican coast, and including Tripolitan, Aeolian, Istrian, Latian and Asturian oysters. As we have seen, the proconsul Sergius Orata, 'the Gilthead Bream', Catiline's grandfather, was famous among *piscinarii*. He had laid out artificial oyster beds to feed his favourite fish, and the surplus made him a nice profit. The oysters he bred in Lake Lucrino came from Tarentum or Brindisi.

Very soon after the conquest of Gaul, oyster-farming became one of the country's major resources. Natural oyster beds all along the Gaulish coasts provided excellent specimens. Around 7 BC the Greek writer Strabo, in his invaluable *Geography*,[9] praises oysters from the Étang de Berre, not far from Marseilles. No one walking there today can fail to be amazed by the layers of oyster beds, superimposed on each other since the dawn of time and clinging close-packed to the rocks which form the hill on which the town of Istres stands. You can see billions of them, fossilized in clearly visible strata. The name Istres itself, incidentally, means simply 'oyster'.

Pliny[10] mentions the oysters of the Médoc, and in the fourth century our old friend Ausonius[11] provides much information on Gaulish oysters and their culture. After four centuries of Romanization, it seems to have reached a remarkable degree of perfection and technical expertise. The Gaulish oyster-farming tradition was eventually swept away not by the sea, but by that unexpected tidal wave which arrived in the shape of the barbarian invasions.

Whereas Caesar divided Gaul into three nations – 'Gallia est omnis divisa in partes tres, quarum unam incolunt Belgae …' – Ausonius divides Gaul geographically, and rather whimsically, according to the quality of its oysters. First come the oysters of the Médoc, the writer's own country, although his family was of Aeduan origin and came from Lyons; next are the oysters of Provence, including Marseilles, the Étang de Berre and Port-Vendres, which he considers comparable to the oysters of Baiae near Naples and Lake Lucrino. He returns to Gaul, however, to include in this second category the abundant oyster beds of the Saintonge and Calvados areas. The third group comprises the oysters of Armorica, the country of the Picts (La Vendée), and Scotland, not forgetting Byzantium, which come a long way after the others, in terms of both distance and flavour. What, you may wonder, caused Ausonius to draw up this comparative list of the merits of Gaulish oysters? Posted to Trier, the prefect-poet, who happily combined his two callings, had been sent a small hamper of Médoc oysters and of mussels. The distance they had travelled does not seem to have done them any harm, since Ausonius, having feasted on the shellfish, writes a letter of thanks in verse, including his catalogue of oysters, from Gaul and other parts:

> Those oysters, rivalling the oysters of Baiae, fattened in the pools of the Médoc by the tides and easily counted [Theon had sent only 30] ... for me, the choicest above all are those bred in the Ocean of the Meduli, which, named after Burdigala,[12] high esteem hath raised even to Caesar's board, no less renowned than are our famous wines. These amongst all have pride of place, the rest lagging far behind: these be of substance both full fat and snowy white, and with their sweet juice most delicately mingle some flavour of the sea touched with a fine taste of salt. Next, though next at distance of long interval, are the oysters of Massilia. ... There are, too, such as praise the oysters of the Armoric deep, and those which shoremen gather on Pictonic coasts, and which the tide sometimes leaves bare for the wondering Caledonian ...

The exiled poet enjoyed the mussels as much as the oysters. For luncheon, Ausonius ate a dish of seafood which gave him both gastronomic and sentimental pleasure, much the same thing, perhaps, for a Gaul. 'The mussel, not without mud-haunting oysters, makes up a dish for early luncheon – a food delightful to the taste of lords and cheap enough for poor folks' tables ... it is hidden in the cavern of a double shell which, warmed by the steam of boiling water, reveals the milk-white substance within.' Mussels may be white or yellow-fleshed, depending on the plankton they have eaten.

All that was missing from Ausonius' feast was crustaceans, which he does not mention, but of which we have much evidence in the shape of decorative motifs on vases and mosaics. According to the bishop and poet Sidonius Apollinaris (430–489), the Gulf of Gascony was teeming with crawfish and crabs at this period.[13] Freshwater crayfish, which would begin disappearing from our polluted rivers early in the twentieth century, were once abundant in all water-courses, particularly on the outskirts of towns, where they found plenty of nourishment. Gargantua, in the company of his mentor Ponocrates, caught crayfish in the Seine at Gentilly, Boulogne, Montrouge, Vanves and Saint-Cloud. The Seine and the Oise still contain crayfish, very tiny and smelling strongly of oil. It takes courage to eat them. Edible crayfish today, at least those found for sale, are nearly all farmed. The majority come from Central Europe – by air.

The *écrevisse de mer*, 'sea crayfish', mentioned by the *Ménagier de Paris* and the *Viandier*, was the true lobster which acquired its French name of *homard* in the sixteenth century. The Latin name is *Homarus*, and the cognate German *Hummer* and related words in Scandinavian languages, even in Polish and Russian, show where most of these crustaceans came from: the North Sea and the Baltic, where lobster is a famous delicacy. Then, as now, it was a rare luxury for the tables of the rich. (The English 'lobster' is the odd word out, deriving from a corruption of Latin *locusta*, crustacean or locust.)

Oysters, on the other hand, seem to have invaded Paris in the seventeenth century; even if we believe only half of what Saint-Evremont tells us,[14] there would have been at least 2000 oyster sellers in the capital at the time of Louis XIV. The most prized oysters were still those of the Médoc – gratifying, no doubt, to the shade of Ausonius. The *vertes* or green oysters of Marennes were also known, and had been for some time, and although we cannot actually speak of oyster-farming at this date they were already being refined in the special basins called *claires*. Henri IV, in his day, got indigestion from eating oysters. Marshal Junot seems to have been the champion oyster eater of the early nineteenth century. Indeed, one may wonder whether he was showing the first signs of the insanity which eventually killed him: every morning he used to eat 300 oysters, never fewer, to keep himself fit.

Ausonius tells us only about the preparation of mussels, and even then his remarks are very brief indications of the fact that they were cooked. We have no information about the way the Gauls prepared their seafood when they were not following Roman customs. All we do know is that fisheries pickled oysters in barrels, particularly in the Pictish country, and the Roman military commissariat bought them to feed its garrisons.

Today France and the United Kingdom are the only oyster-producing countries which prefer to eat those shellfish raw, with a little lemon juice or shallot-flavoured vinegar. The art of gastronomy is to respect perfection. Alexandre Dumas' recommendation should be put down to his credit, making up for some of his odder culinary suggestions: he wrote that 'the true connoisseurs, however, swallow [the oyster] without lemon, vinegar, pepper or anything else.' This was a brave statement when Dumas was writing.

Until the early twentieth century oysters were eaten either cooked or raw, although mussels were seldom eaten raw, any more than they are today. The naturalist Pierre Belon, father of comparative anatomy, said in the sixteenth century that 'mussels are good for dropsy, for the purging of women, for gout and for jaundice'. Today jaundice, viral hepatitis, is often ascribed to the unwise consumption of bad raw mussels.

The oyster has always been included in the recipes for many grand dishes. Chicken or turkey with oyster sauce, a great favourite in the southern states of the

USA, and known as chicken (or turkey) Rockefeller, was a recipe known to Apicius, and to Menon at the end of the eighteenth century. The USA and Quebec have recipes for cooked oysters which must have come down from the family traditions of the first colonists; they were very popular in the Middle Ages and the Renaissance. In the United Kingdom, oysters were added to steak and kidney pie or pudding, and pickled oysters were also popular. Oysters were so plentiful in Victorian Britain that they were regarded as poor people's food.

One can only marvel at the sheer variety of shellfish, molluscs and crustaceans which the fish-carts brought to medieval towns, where they offered strong competition to freshwater crustaceans such as crayfish. As far inland as the wealthy city of Geneva, the shells that have been found when foundations for new buildings were dug bear witness to the quantities purchased.

If we look at cookery books from the fourteenth century to the eighteenth, we find that the earlier ones contain nothing about raw oysters, nor even any indication of the way to dress them; perhaps transport systems still left something to be desired. The usual way was to cook them as 'civey of oysters', meatless stews. The author of the *Viandier* recommends that they should 'always be very well washed and scalded'. Similar directions are given by the *Ménagier de Paris*.

L'ouverture de cuisine, published in 1604, has a recipe for the filling of an 'oyster pie', in which the first step is to wash the flesh of the shellfish in a little white wine; the recipe would be excellent if it included anything to thicken the sauce a little. These oysters must have come from the North Sea, since the book was published in Liège. Sixty years later, in 1664, *Le cuisinier françois* gives another excellent recipe for an oyster stew of the kind we would now call a *marinière*. There are further recipes for 'oyster fritters' and 'roasted oysters', and then, for the first time, a mention of the way to eat fresh raw oysters: 'You must open them, and choose the best, leaving them in their shells to eat them fresh.' This was still unusual at the time, since *Le cusinier françois* continues, 'And when you find any that are a little tainted, add to them a little fresh butter and some breadcrumbs and a little nutmeg, and put them on the gridiron; when they are cooked, heat the fire-shovel until it is red-hot and pass it over them until they take colour; make sure you do it in such a way that they are not too dry, and then serve them.' There is quite a modern ring to this recipe, but for the fact that we would discard 'any that are a little tainted'.

Opposite: 'The oyster luncheon', picture by Jean-François de Troy (1679–1752): this painting shows how greatly oysters were esteemed in the high society of the time. It was because of some baskets of oysters dispatched from the coast, which arrived rather late, that the Prince de Condé's steward Vatel committed suicide with his sword at Chantilly. Notice the wine cooler and bottles in the foreground.

Menon, author of *La cuisinière bourgeoise*, published in the next century (1774), begins his remarks on oysters by saying that 'they are usually eaten raw, with pepper.' He adds:

> They may also be served in their shells, cooked on the gridiron, with the fire below them and the red-hot shovel above them, and when they begin to open of their own accord they are done. They are called soused oysters. ... Oysters also serve to make ragoûts to eat with various kinds of meat, such as chickens, fattened pullets, pigeons, wild duck, etc. ... For this purpose, blanch them in their liquid over very gentle heat; make sure they do not boil, for that would toughen them. Next put them into cold water; take them out and drain them well on a sieve; you will now have a good rich broth, without salt; add two chopped anchovies and the oysters; heat them without boiling them and serve them with whatever you think suitable.

They sound good. The people of Louisiana were often French immigrants, whose cooks would have read Menon.

While the transatlantic recipe for lobster or crawfish *à l'américaine* delighted Dumas, who describes the sauce for it in his *Dictionnaire de cuisine*, he does not seem to have had much time for crawfish or spiny lobster in general, describing it as 'not so fine in flavour [as the lobster] and not so highly prized'. In his day crawfish were bought alive and taken to specialist crawfish boilers, who had stalls in the market of Les Halles, with stoves on which large pots of a plain court-bouillon were always standing. For 20 centimes they tied a numbered tag to the claw of your crustacean, plunged it into the liquid and handed it back, cooked to a nice red.

Before the invention of quick-freezing, which brought overseas crawfish and lobster at quite reasonable prices within ordinary people's reach, to be prepared as they liked, canning offered a relatively inexpensive chance of feasting on them from the middle of the nineteenth century onwards. Canned crawfish tails came from Canada, Japan, and especially South Africa. And then there was the sad story of the forgotten crawfish canners. The South African species, *Jasus lalaudii*, occurs not only around the Cape of Good Hope, but also in large colonies near the islands of Saint-Paul and Nouvelle-Amsterdam, tiny French possessions on the 40th parallel exactly half-way between Australia and South Africa. Two brothers, the Boissières, set up a flourishing crawfish business there in 1928. A number of Breton fishermen and their families came to join them, and they recruited Malagasy fishermen too. A well-equipped factory was built, and Saint-Paul acquired its first radio transmitting station. From October to April, the islanders went fishing, removed the crawfish tails and canned them. When they sent out a radio signal, a steamer came from La Réunion, 4000 kilometres away, to collect the cans and leave provisions. One day, however, the radio equipment broke down. No steamer came. Months passed. Two years passed. At last someone in the world outside thought it might be a good idea to go and see what had happened. The poor islanders, not so lucky as Robinson Crusoe, were in a very bad way. Those who were not dead were suffering from scurvy, beri-beri and despair. They had eaten nothing for 24 months but crawfish, which they ended up by loathing. The survivors were repatriated and the business abandoned.

Today the Japanese fish these extraordinary banks of crustaceans. They sell crawfish to Europe at a very reasonable price, but now it is frozen, not canned.

Facts about Crustaceans

Crustaceans are articulated creatures which spend most of their time in water, breathing through gills. Those usually found on the fishmonger's slab include crabs, shrimps and prawns, crayfish, Dublin Bay prawns, crawfish and lobsters. The woodlouse is a crustacean too.

The bodies of crustaceans are usually protected by a shell impregnated with lime from the seawater and sand they absorb. They shed it periodically as it becomes too small. This is known as moulting. The only time they are full of dense, well-flavoured meat is at the end of the period between moultings.

The true lobster (*Homarus gammarus*) is not closely related to the crawfish, or spiny or rock lobster (*Palinurus vulgaris*), but belongs to a different genus. It lives in cold waters, and although it is a solitary creature sometimes shares its burrow with the female conger eel. It is thought that they associate because each hopes to eat the other. The lobster is waiting for the conger to lay her eggs, and the conger is on the lookout for the moment when the lobster, shedding its shell, will be at its most vulnerable. They will fight pitilessly.

Once lobsters were fished all along the coasts of Brittany, but they began gradually emigrating northwards, to Jersey, Ireland, Scotland and Norway, where, however, they are now becoming increasingly rare. Much Western European lobster consumption is supplied by Canada, especially Quebec and Labrador. Lobster-fishing is a small-scale trade, for lobsters are never plentiful.

The lobster swims backwards, but can turn to face its enemies, which include the octopus as well as the conger eel. It is a very belligerent creature, and lobster fishermen cut the tendons of its strong pincers as soon as they take it out of the water; otherwise, whether kept in baskets or in tanks, the lobsters would eat each other alive.

Live lobsters do not have the familiar red colour we see in a boiled lobster. The different kinds can be told apart only before they are cooked: deep blue specimens are the small European lobsters, once the pride of Camaret in Finistère, although most of them now come from Scotland and Norway. The flavour of the European lobster is superb. Chestnut-brown lobsters are Canadian, less well flavoured, and their shells are not always as full of meat. However, they are only one-third the price of European lobsters. When you buy a cooked lobster, for instance in a restaurant, it is very likely to be Canadian, particularly if its place of origin is not mentioned. Ordinary freezing does not suit the lobster very well; it shrinks inside its shell.

Crawfish, which do not have the true lobster's powerful claws, have long feelers instead. They are peaceable and eminently social creatures, living in great crowds, preferably in warm seas or the warm currents of colder seas, for instance the Gulf Stream. The warmer the water the less fine is their flavour. Great quantities of green and yellow crawfish are fished at certain times in the Gulf of Mexico and the Caribbean, and it has recently been realized that these times coincide with migratory journeys, although it had previously been thought that crawfish were sedentary. Picture thousands and thousands of crawfish in single file, converging from all directions, moving like living rivers on the ocean bed, clinging to one another and assembling in swarming streams which finally join up somewhere in the middle of the Gulf of Mexico. Commander Cousteau's exploration ship *Calypso* brought back some astonishing pictures of the scene.

This kind of crawfish, the Cuban crawfish, reaches Europe frozen and usually pre-cooked. It has nothing like the succulence of the red, white-spotted crawfish from Brittany, Ireland, the United Kingdom, Martinique and Portugal, which fetch the highest prices. The Canary Islands crawfish are a pale pink and their flesh has much less flavour. The brown crawfish comes from South Africa and the Indian Ocean, and is nothing to write home about. Finally, there is the garnet-red crawfish of Madagascar, very cheap by comparison because of its poor flavour and rubbery flesh. The green crawfish of Mauritania are much the same. If you are buying fresh crustaceans they are at their cheapest in the middle of the fishing season, in summer. The females of lobsters and crawfish often have more meat than the males, which can be identified by their wider caudal fans. The females sometimes contain 'coral', their roes. The coral should be well hidden away inside, not visible. If the eggs can be seen between a female lobster's claws, she has just spawned, and will be thin and poorly flavoured.

A detail not for the squeamish: the rules of gastronomy usually insist that crustaceans should be cooked alive after being chopped into sections or cut in half lengthwise.

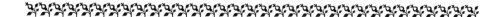

CIVEY OF OYSTERS

Scald and wash the oysters very well, cook them in a broth and drain them, and fry them with onion cooked in oil; then take grated bread or coarse breadcrumbs, and put to soak in a purée of peas or in the boiled liquid of the oysters and some plain wine, and strain it; then take cinnamon, cloves, long pepper, grain of Paradise and saffron for colour, bray them and moisten with verjuice and vinegar and set aside; then bray your grated bread or breadcrumbs with the purée or the liquid of the oysters, and add the oysters, for they will not yet have been cooked enough.

Le Ménagier de Paris (c. 1393).

The History of Shellfish-Farming

Oyster-farming is only one branch of shellfish-farming in general, which covers the culture of all edible shellfish. This is definitely farming rather than fishing; shellfish farmers are the peasants of the sea.

From the dawn of time to the middle of the nineteenth century, the coasts of France had an almost uninterrupted succession of natural oyster beds; you had only to gather what you wanted. At the time of the Roman occupation the oyster culture so well described by Ausonius in the fourth century had reached a degree of technical perfection almost the equal of today's. Then, with the barbarian invasions, both Atlantic and Mediterranean oyster farming ceased. Gastronomic history remains silent on the oyster for 1000 years, but the natural beds provided part of the everyday diet of coast-dwelling people. In large inland cities shellfish, difficult and expensive to bring to market fresh, were the prerogative of the rich from the fourteenth century onwards. Pickled oysters were not to be despised, though; they were a tradition begun by Gaulish fishermen, for instance at Saint-Michel-de-l'Herm in the Marais of Poitou. In the Middle Ages oysters were still being pickled there, and a hill 14 metres high, consisting of the accumulation of empty shells, contains a whole range of archeological finds from top to bottom: pottery, bones and coins dating from Caesar to medieval times.

Whether as a result of thoughtless plundering of the beds (100 million oysters a year were gathered at Tréguier and Cancale around 1775), or of a series of destructive storms, around 1850 even diligent searching could produce only 83,000 dozen oysters.

In 1852 Monsieur de Bon, the naval paymaster of Saint-Servan, had the idea of re-seeding the oyster beds in his sector by trying to collect the oyster spawn, or 'spat', with makeshift catchers. He succeeded, and set up new oyster beds on the emerging reefs.

Then a mason in the Île de Ré called Hyacinthe Boeuf decided to try artificial oyster farming, starting with small oysters bought cheap from such areas as the north of Brittany, where they seemed to be still freely available. He obtained the rights to a part of the coast which the tide uncovered twice a day, so that it was easy to get at it, and built a low wall to make a reservoir and, most important of all, break the strength of the current. He was going to Brittany to buy his stock when he realized that his wall was already covered with spat which had spontaneously come in from sea: 2000 baby oysters per square metre. The first oyster farm of the Île de Ré had just come into existence.

This truly empirical experiment came to the ears of Jacques-Marie Costes, a professor at the Collège de France and a great enthusiast for pisciculture. He knew that oysters had been reared in Lake Fusaro near Naples since classical times, and leaning on these ancient traditions he drew up a scheme in which he managed to interest the French government. In 1858 two sloops, the *Ariel* and the *Antilope*, seeded the Bay of Saint-Brieuc. They scattered some three million tiny oysters, picked up trawling in the open sea, on a bed of branches and shells. The venture was a success at first, but after a few years it failed because of bad weather, epizootic disease, inexperience and the haste of novice oyster farmers, who themselves had proliferated much too fast. The only French oyster known at the time, the European or flat oyster, *Ostrea edulis*, seemed much less hardy than its relative the Portuguese oyster, abundant in the estuary of the Tagus. It is true that the European oyster is very susceptible to parasites. *Martelia* attacked again in 1968, wiping out almost all European oyster beds. Ten years later, in 1978, when production had risen to 10,000 tonnes again, another parasite, *Bonamia*, struck, and the yield dropped to 4000 tonnes in 1980, 2500 in 1981 and 1000 in 1983.

Portuguese oysters, which are more robust, had been imported accidentally from India to the mouth of the Tagus in the fifteenth century by Portuguese merchant vessels, whose hulls had acted as natural collectors. After the hulls had been cleaned in dock, the molluscs scraped off them were thrown back into the water, where they throve and prospered.

In 1859, Costes had prepared the Bay of Arcachon for restocking with European oysters. With Emperor Napoleon III as his patron, he planned to have a floating pontoon above a bed of mother oysters, protected from the rain by a roof of Roman tiles. The spat which came in on the tide happily fastened upon those tiles, in such quantities that Napoleon III had imperial oyster basins installed in the bay. But in the same way as elsewhere, the European oysters fell sick after a few years. The people of Arcachon ordered stocks of Portuguese oysters. In 1868 the *Morlaisien*, with a full cargo of oysters, had to take refuge from a storm in the estuary of the Gironde. The storm went on and on; eventually the cargo began to spoil and had to be thrown overboard near Le Verdon. However, some of the Portuguese oysters were still alive. They liked their new environment so much that they reproduced fast. The larval oysters set off to invade the Charentais coast, and as the years passed by reached the Loire, proving so prolific that the oyster farmers of northern Brittany, who wanted to protect the native European oysters, obtained a decree in 1923 forbidding the farming of Portuguese oysters north of La Vilaine. In 1971, however, even the usually robust Portuguese oysters fell prey to a disease from Asia, and spat of the related species *Crassostrea gigas* had to be imported from Japan. These Giant or Pacific oysters proved highly resistant to the virus and have acclimatized very well, particularly in the Bay of Arcachon.

The art of the oyster farmer lies first in trapping the spat and then in recovering and rearing the tiny oysters. In 1859 Costes discovered that the babies seemed to prefer his Roman tiles as their cradles. At a slightly later stage, however, the small shellfish still had to be dislodged without coming to harm. A mason called Michelet from La Teste, near Arcachon, had the bright idea of coating the tiles with lime and sand before use. The collectors are then placed, convex side on top, in 12 alternate rows inside long wooden cages erected on the bottom. The spat which clings to the tiles is invisible to the naked eye at first. It takes eight months to grow to a size of three or four centimetres. The young oysters then have to be delicately dislodged. The tiles are removed from the cages and brought in. To dislodge (*détroquer*) the oysters mechanically is fast but means considerable losses, since the young shells are very fragile. It is better done manually with a round-ended knife. The tile is brushed down with lime first. The little oysters removed from it are put into small nursery basins or 'parks' for the first stage of rearing, *demi-élevage*. They have every comfort in these parks: relatively calm water, although it must not be too still, or it will not be properly oxygenated, and wire netting fences to keep them from being swept out to sea or preyed upon. The frames of their parks are mounted above the sea bottom so that they will not be silted up. They stay there for 18 months.

The next stage, the true *élevage*, known as *pousse* in French oyster-farming, differs according to the nature of the shoreline. The oysters may be placed in wire netting bags on the bottom, so long as it is firm enough for them not to silt up; this is the method in the Bay of Paimpol, where the oysters of Saint-Brieuc are boarded out for a while. They may go into oyster parks in deep waters, or be placed in cases on tables where there is a strong tide, or on vertical posts in the Mediterranean, where there is little or no tide. In any case, the waters where they live must be invigorating and rich in plankton. They are turned periodically to develop a good shape: deep and regular in the case of Portuguese oysters, round and flat for European oysters.

The final fattening and refining of the oysters is done in basins where the water is richer in plankton but not as salty as in the 'parks' where they were raised. European oysters take longer to fatten than Portuguese oysters. Every year, at the beginning of December, the containers of oysters are brought up and their contents sorted. Small specimens go back to the oyster beds. Adult shellfish (the Portuguese oyster is adult at three years and the European oyster at four years old) go off to be sold, graded by size and quality. This is the usual way of farming oysters.

In France, however, it is becoming increasingly usual to refine the oysters *en claire*, in basins usually converted from former salt marshes, in shallow water which is constantly changed and kept at the same level. The water is less salty than in the 'parks', but richer in mineral salts, and the plankton is different, giving such oysters a characteristic nutty flavour. Most important of all, however, a tiny seaweed organism gives these oysters a beautiful green tinge. This green tinge occurs only in the *vertes* of the Marennes-Oléron region. It can truly be said that oysters have their own local flavours, caused by climate, the salinity of the water, the nature of the seabed and of the plankton, and indeed by the way in which they have been reared. Similarly, British oysters are named according to region, and include Whitstable, Helford and Colchester oysters. 'Natives', as the word indicates, are of stock native to British waters, while the others may have been reared from French spat.

The European oysters known in France as *plates* are from Brittany, and most of their parks are found mainly in the Gulf of Morbihan, where the shellfish are placed directly on the sea bottom, which has been consolidated with sand or gravel near the shore. The first refining of these *plates* takes place at Belon, so they are called Belon oysters. They are the most expensive, fragile, iodized and best flavoured of all. They will also do well in deep waters, and are reared at a depth of three to 15 centimetres from the bottom in the Bay of Saint-Brieuc, on the Channel, and in the roadsteads of Brest. Buoys mark out the boundaries of these parks, which of course are invisible otherwise. Considerable investment is necessary for farming oysters out at sea: specially equipped dredger vessels, large land-based plants, a big staff, mechanization, fuel costs, etc. However, the superb quality of such oysters means that unless there is some unforeseen accident, the venture soon shows a profit. The *plates*, whether raised near the shore or farther out to sea, account for the majority of French exports. The *bouzigue* is a European oyster reared in shallow waters, of Breton origin, although it has been taken to Languedoc. Breton spat is raised on vertical bars in the Étang de Thau. Production is restricted, and the flavour delicious. Portuguese oysters are also raised at Thau, again on vertical posts of mangrove wood called 'cordes'.

Before they go for sale the oysters have to spend 24, 48 or 60 hours in basins which are not subject to the tides, to rid themselves of sand and small algae. They also get used to doing without the pull of the tide and staying closed; this enables them to survive transport and distribution better. This stage is known as *trompage*. Just before they set off by rail, road or air, they are washed down fast with jets of very pure sea-water from powerful pumps, to improve their appearance and give them a good smell of the sea to take with them.

Distribution and sale are subject to strict hygiene checks; every consignment of oysters must bring its certificate of health with it. Unfortunately the French fishmonger almost always conceals this label from customers, goodness knows why. However, the fishmonger might legitimately say that his customers hardly seem to care about anything but the price.

Oysters will keep in their packing for several days, crammed close together so that they will not open and lose their liquid. In fact they are best stored upside down, with the upper shell underneath, and they should be kept cool but not below freezing. Freezing kills them, so they must be eaten as soon as they defrost.

As far as freezing is concerned there is a clever method of opening oysters, a job which alarms many people. If you are afraid of cutting yourself with an oyster knife you can put oysters in the freezer for three hours, the right way up this time (however, this is not something you mention to the purist who simply waits in front of his plate). Three hours before you want to eat the oysters, you take them out of the freezer again. The low temperature will have made the flat shell gape; you only have to slip a short, strong knife into the gap, and your oyster opens as if by magic. You give your oysters just over two hours to return to normal temperature, and they will be as delicious as when they came out of the water — and perfectly free from bits of shell.

A considerable number of sea creatures will happily eat oysters, from the spat stage until they reach saleable size. These predators show great ingenuity in the pursuit of their prey, using methods which would sometimes be almost comic if they did not portend disaster for the oysters.

Starfish, far from being the placid, decorative forms of marine life they may appear, have some highly ingenious methods of breaking and entering. Not content with their ability to open the shells of bivalves by pulling opposite ways on the two halves of the shell with their feet, they can inject a paralysing liquid which prevents the shellfish from closing again. They then extrude their stomachs through their mouths, to be introduced into the shells and to feast *in situ*. They particularly like mussels. A whole army of them has been seen off Le Morbihan, 140 starfish to the square metre, extending over several kilometres. When they have passed by they leave nothing behind them but empty shells.

Among fish, the gilthead bream and eagle ray have muscular jaws and teeth that nothing can resist. The ray's seven rows of crushing teeth can reduce shells to powder. The bream has only five rows of molars above and three or four below, but it too can crush anything it comes across, like some extraterrestrial machine.

Winkles are cunning little creatures. Armed with a structure called a radula which acts as a kind of drill, they perforate the shells of fine adult oysters and mussels. The hermit crab is a greedy predator on mussel spawn. Octopuses will dislodge oysters, breaking the shells with their fearsome horny beaks and piling up great heaps of the ravaged remains around their burrows. Crabs will clean out the contents of collectors set to catch spat, and are ready to tackle larger specimens too. Sea urchins pierce oyster shells and suck out the flesh. Mussels at the larval stage will fasten parasitically on oysters, eating any available plankton and soiling their hosts with their evacuations.

Herring gulls are the worst scourge of all. In 1975 the 60,000 pairs of herring gulls in northern Brittany devoured over 80 tonnes of mussel spawn in a single season, according to the calculations of the environmental authorities, which have been trying desperately since then to find some permanent solution satisfactory to both ecologists and shellfish farmers. Various European and American countries have already adopted measures of controlled sterilization of herring gulls, which also threaten to swamp all other seabird species.

Further problems are posed for the shellfish farmer by pollution, both latent and accidental, by tidal waves, and indeed by seaside visitors in the summer; it is difficult to keep everyone happy.

All the same, the problem of over-production of oysters is appearing on the horizon. With new generations of oysters proving both prolific and disease-resistant, and the improvement of oyster-farming techniques, well over 120,000 tonnes have been sold by French oyster farmers since the beginning of the 1980s, and unfortunately home consumption is not rising to keep pace with production. Of course the cost of living is on the rise, and the traditional French household still regards oysters, which are not cheap, as a luxury food, certainly not a necessity and also rather ostentatious, in spite of their excellent nutritional value.

Moreover, oysters offered for sale and not bought immediately are thrown away, which is a terrible waste. The oyster farmers of southern Brittany are trying to find new outlets for their product, processing oysters and preparing them in the American or Japanese manner. The supermarkets of the United States and Japan contain frozen oysters which need no opening, a thankless task for the unskilled consumer who does not know the freezer trick. The delicious smoked oyster can also be bought there. This may be the future of French oyster farming. In the past oysters were sold pickled, in barrels; tomorrow they will be sold canned, smoked or frozen. The future of the mussel may be similar.

Natural mussel beds are still quite common along French and English coasts, but wild mussels are not very fat or well flavoured, and have often been tainted or polluted by oil. Mussels are extremely prolific, and sometimes block up the cooling pipes of thermal power stations despite the speed at which water is pumped through them.

Traditional mussel-farming means gathering mussels in their natural surroundings and placing them in the right conditions to ensure their growth and fattening. Mussel 'parks' have to be adapted to the character of the location. There are three ways of farming mussels in such parks or basins: on the sea bed, raised on stakes known as *bouchots*, or on ropes hanging in the water. In France, mussels may be sold, for instance, as *moules de bouchots*, but this description refers only to the method of farming them; they are all the same species.

The method of farming mussels in parks on the sea bed is supposed to have originated in the Croisic area, where the other ways present problems. This method is feasible only when the sea bed is firm, is not subject to very strong swells, and is not uncovered at low tide. But mussels stir up a lot of mud, and the disadvantage of the method is that the sea bed must be periodically cleaned if it is to be maintained in a good state and at the right level. This method is used in the Netherlands, in the estuary of the Aven in Brittany, and off Boulogne-sur-Mer and Cherbourg.

Mussel-farming on the rows of stakes called *bouchots* is the oldest method used in France, and is said to have been invented by an Irishman called Walton, who was shipwrecked near La Rochelle in the Baie de l'Aiguillon, and never left France again. He found that the nets attached to tall stakes driven into the seabed, which he had set to catch birds, were covered with mussels which were developing remarkably well, and the system proved very successful.

A classic *bouchot* area is 50 to 100 metres long. It consists of two rows of stakes, four to six metres tall, planted far enough apart to let a boat pass between them. In the Baie de l'Aiguillon the total length of the *bouchots*, if they were set end to end, would be over 600 kilometres. This method of mussel-farming is practised mainly from La Rochelle to Noirmoutier, and in Normandy.

Mussels are farmed on ropes in seas with very slight tides, such as the Mediterranean. The method is used in lagoons such as the Étang de Thau, but it also occurs in areas where there are considerable tides (such as the Spanish *rias*) and where depth rules out any other way of mussel farming. The young mussels are fixed to ropes hanging down into the water and attached to crossbeams mounted either on floating rafts or fixed structures, the *tables d'élevage* typical of Mediterranean French lagoons.

As well as those reared in such parks, mussels from two other sources may be found. Mussels from natural banks may be fished from the sea, and then well soaked, sorted and washed in installations subject to strict hygienic regulations. Or they may be fished from beds which are naturally clean; in France these are chiefly found out to sea off the Cotentin peninsula.

Mussels must not be sold loose in France. Before they reach the consumer they undergo various treatments, and stringent controls are enforced. At the point of production, the French Institut Scientifique et Technique des Pêches Maritimes (Scientific and Technical Institute of Sea Fisheries) supervises the various parks and undertakes research to improve rearing conditions. The Réseau National d'Observation de la Qualité du Milieu Marin (National Network for Observation of the Quality of the Marine Environment) now merged with the CNEXO – Centre National pour l'Exploitation des Océans – checks the water in which the mussels are raised to ensure that it is clean and healthy: the standards were set out in a departmental order of 12 October 1976.

The processing plants involved in the treatment and distribution of mussels have to be on a register listing all the recognized installations. Everything has to come up to certain very precise standards: the layout of the plant, the nature of the equipment, aeration, washing machinery, etc. Only then can the dispatcher put a label on his pack of mussels signifying that it is wholesome, the *étiquette de salubrité*. This label, a guarantee for the consumer, has to stay put until the mussels are sold to the public. It bears the number of the registered installation which packed them and the date of dispatch. Mussels farmed in all the ways described above and those fished at sea and then soaked and washed bear labels describing them simply as *moules*, mussels; mussels from natural banks (i.e., those fished at sea which do not need the soaking treatment) are described as coming from a *gisement naturel coquillier*, a natural shellfish bank. Three official bodies may check mussels at the point of sale, and can take samples away for inspection.

Shellfish-farming is not confined to oysters and mussels. Other shellfish such as clams, carpet shells, etc., are raised from their spawn. Some are fished from the sea and then put in parks to be fattened, when they are subject to the same checks on hygiene as oysters and mussels, and in France are sold with a similar label, with a yellow band on it. A label with a red anchor denotes shellfish straight from natural banks.

Scallops, unlike most molluscs, move around a great deal. They do so by snapping their upper valves firmly shut and thus expelling water. Their mantles – the outer folds of skin around their internal organs – are suitably modified for travelling.

Queen scallops, Iceland scallops and Bay scallops are smaller than the Great

Scallop or *coquille Saint-Jacques*. The queen scallop has a shell consisting of two convex valves with small radiating folds in them. Iceland and Bay scallops are very popular in North America, and are practically a national dish in Quebec.

The carpet-shell lives in sand or mud at a depth of one to five centimetres; an adult can be up to 12 centimetres deep. Two small holes in the sand at low tide reveal their presence. These are the openings of two small outlets, one for breathing, one for evacuation. They are farmed in Brittany, at Noirmoutier, off the Île de Ré and in Normandy, where the parks are filled with small carpet-shells fished from the sea, or spawn from hatcheries.

Clams are the very widespread North American cousins of carpet-shells. Clam farming began in France in 1914 in the Seudre estuary, in the traditional Marennes oyster-farming area.

Warty Venuses, also close relatives of the carpet-shell, bury themselves in the sand. Some shellfish farmers in Brittany and the central west coast of the Île de Ré fish them from the sea and rear them in parks, where they do very well, swiftly gaining in size and flavour.

Cockles, also bivalves, are very common in sandy and muddy estuaries on European coasts. They are always plentiful and therefore cheap.

Winkles and whelks are gasteropods with spiral shells of a greenish black colour. In some seaside places – in France, particularly in Brittany – winkles crowd thickly on seaweed-covered rocks. They too are very cheap. Along with cockles, whelks and shrimps, they are traditional British seaside food, often sold from stalls on the sea front.

Sea urchins are echinoderms. Their hemispherical shells bristle with 100 or so spines. Tentacles between these spines allow the urchins to move about quite fast. Their mouths have five beak-like teeth shaped like a parrot's. Sea urchins used to be widely eaten, especially in the Mediterranean, but now they are increasingly rare and also increasingly expensive, and they often prove to be empty.

The dog cockle has a circular shell and a hinge containing some 20 tiny teeth. Its favourite haunt is a sandy sea bed.

The ormer, abalone or ear-shell, with its beautiful perforated and nacreous shell (which is often made into an ashtray), had practically disappeared from French coasts until the Oceanological Centre in Brittany made it possible to rear these shellfish in the early 1970s. They have now reappeared on the market. No one has ever found ormer spawn out at sea; the smallest specimens fished measure at least 18 millimetres and are a year old. However, male and female ormers have been successfully mated in laboratory conditions, and their unions have been very fruitful. Scientific equipment was certainly needed to confirm that fertilization had occurred: the egg itself measures 200 microns (a micron is a millionth of a metre) and hatches into a larva measuring 220 microns after two weeks. The ormer is one of the few vegetarian molluscs, and its favourite algae measure no more than five microns.

The people of the Atlantic coasts of France like ormers very much in vinaigrette sauce or fried in butter. City dwellers may not appreciate them – although they are now being produced in increasingly large quantities – but France can always sell its ormers to Japan, which does not produce enough of its own (only 8000 tonnes a year) and also imports them from California, Mexico and Australia. The Chinese too like them very much. Ormers may be found canned in exotic food shops, usually labelled 'abalone'.

The Biology of the Oyster

West European oyster farming concentrates on two species: the European oyster, *Ostrea edulis*, more or less round, and the Portuguese oyster, *Crassostrea angulata*. However, there are 100 or more oyster species in the world, living in salt, fresh or brackish water.

The bivalved shells of oysters grow annually, and are extended with crystallizations of calcium carbonate extracted from seawater, calcite or aragonite. The flat or right-hand valve of the shell, and the deep or left-hand shell, containing the body of the oyster, are joined by a very strong ligament which forms a hinge and are sealed by an adductor muscle. This muscle allows the top shell to open or close, and when the creature is dead the two valves stay open. As it opens and closes its valves the oyster takes in a certain volume of water from which it extracts the nutritional content. It can process four to 20 litres of water an hour in this way. When danger threatens, the oyster perceives it by vibrations in the water and stays closed, as it does when it is out in the air. The body of the oyster is covered in very fine conjunctive tissue, the 'mantle', which when charged with glycogen gives the fattened oyster its meaty, milky appearance. The lobes of the mantle are bordered by three parallel swellings which seem to have different functions. The outer swellings contain the structural material of the valves, the middle ones contain the sensory organs, and the interior ones consist of a cavity separated by the gills into inhalant and exhalant chambers, through which the water enters and leaves. The oyster has digestive organs: a liver, stomach, intestine, mouth and anus. The liver swells with glycogen when the creature is well fattened; it is the most nutritional part of the body and has the best flavour. The heart, which can be seen near the adductor muscle, circulates colourless blood. Two kidneys filter the waste collected during the circulation of the blood through the tissues of the various organs. For digestive purposes, the oyster's stomach contains a kind of crystalline probe which processes the food collected from the water. This structure is reabsorbed as digestive juices are freed, and does not show at all when the oyster is fasting.

The oyster's sexuality and reproduction are unusual. First, the creature is alternately female and male. This successive hermaphroditism follows different rhythms in European and Portuguese oysters. The European oyster changes sex each time the genital products have been shed. The Portuguese oyster changes sex only once a season. Summer – the months without an R, when oysters are not eaten – is the oyster's reproductive period. It lays eggs three times during June and

July. Another characteristic of the oyster is that the European species is viviparous; that is, the eggs it lays in its female phase are concentrated in the inhalant chamber, about a million of them, waiting for the male sperm. This sperm may come from the oyster which produced the eggs or from a neighbouring oyster, since when the creatures are in the male phase they shed their sperm into the marine environment. It spreads into the current of water carrying oxygen and nutrition to the oyster and is carried into the inhalant chamber to fertilize the eggs. The oyster, both father and mother, completes its parental task by carrying the fertilized eggs for a dozen days until they reach the larval stage and are expelled. Nature, like a good mother, has provided these larvae or spat with minute devices like sails, made of vibratile cilia. The larval oysters have two weeks' freedom in which to find some place upon which to fix and settle. During this time they swim or follow the currents, unless they come to a premature end eaten by marine predators, carried away by a violent stormy current, chilled by a cold one, or polluted by an oil slick.

The fate of the Portuguese oyster's offspring is even more distressing. For one thing, the Portuguese oyster in its female phase has no maternal feeling at all. The unfertilized eggs move straight from the inhalant chamber to the exhalant chamber, are expelled to a distance of some centimetres from the valves and left to the mercies of the sea. They will be fertilized by spermatozoa passing nearby, either from the oyster itself or from its neighbours. The chances of eggs and sperm meeting at all are slim. The oyster lays 20 to 100 billion eggs, of which only a few dozen will grow to adulthood.

In fact the spat used in oyster farming, the tiny larval creatures measuring one-tenth or two-tenths of a millimetre, come from the natural beds of wild oysters which cling to rocks, ledges or reefs that are sometimes uncovered at low tide. In the past these beds were the only source of supply, and the oysters from them had a strong taste of the sea. Gradually, however, the beds have disappeared and have had to be built up again by oyster farmers. Tourists are forbidden to fish in those waters or gather the mother oysters: without their fecundity, the oyster parks could not be filled, particularly now that ever-increasing pollution is doing its best to wipe out whole colonies.

Although oyster farmers describe the appearance of larval oysters in the water as 'spawning', therefore, the term is inaccurate. The periods when the spat appears are logged in France by the Institut Scientifique et Technique des Pêches Maritimes. On D-Day (no one date is ever fixed, for meteorological reasons) the alert is given, and oyster farmers make haste to instal their collectors so that the larvae will fasten on them. If they do it too early the devices will be covered with mud or weed and the larva could not get a proper hold: too late and the larvae will be lying dead on the beach, a barely visible jelly being dissolved into the sand by the tides.

Tropical mangrove swamps offer good support to oysters, which can reach extraordinary sizes clinging to the trunks, branches, uncovered roots and even leaves of the mangrove trees which act as collectors.

An oyster that is not eaten or accidentally killed can live to be 50 years old. But oysters lose the best of their flavour after the age of five.

The Biology of the Mussel

Mussels have shells made of two equal valves, not, as is sometimes incorrectly said, two shells. Coloured blue-black, brown or yellowish, this shell is made, like the oyster's, of crystallizations of calcium carbonate.

The body of the mussel is contained in a double membrane, the mantle. Although it plays a part in circulating water through the gills, the main function of the mantle is to form the shell. The two adductor muscles, one at the pointed rear, one at the rounded front end of the shell, close it by contracting; they contract intermittently when the mussel is in the water or for a longer period when the mussel is out of it. Dead mussels stay open. The foot is a muscular projection of the mantle, and has mobility. It contains the byssogenous gland, the function of which is to emit the byssus or beard, a bunch of filaments ending in suction pads and enabling the mussel to fasten itself to its support. Unlike the oyster, which dies where it has settled, unless it is gathered first, the mussel can move around. When it does so it breaks the threads of the byssus and moves on, using its foot as the means of propulsion, to find some other resting place.

Like the oyster, the mussel breathes through gills. Two pairs of gills also circulate the water that feeds it (it filters three litres of water an hour). Also like the oyster, it has a crystalline probe as part of its digestive system, a kind of mixer turned by the stomach cilia to sort out the plankton and then digest the nutritional broth it has absorbed. Over-large particles of food are rejected, coated with mucus.

The sex life of the mussel is less eccentric than the oyster's. Mussels are either male or female in the usual way. Each sex lets its eggs or sperm float into the marine environment, where the movement of the current fertilizes the eggs. There are several spawnings during the season, producing a million eggs each time, of which only a few will reach adulthood.

Natural beds of mussels are still quite common in Western Europe, in spite of the oil slicks. But the mussels they produce are getting smaller and smaller, and there is no real guarantee that they will be wholesome and well flavoured. In fact, the mussel tends to get buried in mud which chokes and taints it. The Mediterranean mussel, *Mytilus galloprovincialis*, is quite large and quasi-rectangular in shape. The mussels of the Atlantic or the North Sea, more conical in shape, are *Mytilus edulis*. Other species are the bearded mussel, *Modiolus barbatus*, and the date shell, *Lithodomus lithophagus*, which is almost cylindrical. The Pacific shores of North America, the coasts of the Philippines, Australia, New Zealand and India have other related species, well known locally and widely eaten. About 70 species of mussels have been recorded in cold seas.

Chapter 13

The Treasure of the Forests

The History of Pork and Charcuterie

When the stormy sea threatened to shipwreck the Norwegian merchants who had carried off young Tristan in the legend of Tristan and Iseult, they changed their minds and put him ashore on the Cornish coast. 'With great difficulty he climbed the cliff and saw deserted moorland, with an endless forest stretching into the distance beyond it.' A party of huntsmen take the young man in, and they travel on inland, to countryside where 'he was surrounded by meadows and orchards, with springs of water, fishponds, and ploughed fields ...'[1]

The barbarian invasions had to some extent slowed down the progress of civilization, and the countryside had not changed so much in ten or so centuries that we cannot recognize the ancient Gaulish environment in this medieval description of King Mark's lands: a vast expanse of forest with occasional stretches of uncultivated moorland or fertile clearings[2] with villages standing in them. 'Those bright, green, cultivated fields, set among darker woodland, gave the impression of a rich, fortunate and well-tended domain, where the depths of the soil provided constant abundance. Not a clod of earth was idle, said one of the Ancients, and the forest itself was at work.'[3]

It was a sacred forest, a vast natural temple where every tree was the home of a god and where communities of druids lived; a sheltering forest, which hid peasants and their flocks fleeing from the invading Romans.[4] Centres of passive resistance were established in it. It contained 'the best game in the Western world. Gaulish hunting, a kind of rustic war, skilfully waged and with a quasi-religious element in it ... was the natural complement of agriculture, a means of exploiting land and beasts that had remained wild.'[5] For the forest also provided wood, the bark of trees, ashes, fruit and honey; it was *silva melliflua*, a forest flowing with honey, where

407

pigs not much tamer than the related wild boars – and none of them the products of stock-breeding – fed on acorns, wandering almost at liberty under the nominal supervision of swineherds who were hardly more civilized than their charges; swineherds were serfs on the very lowest rank of the social ladder.

Those forest-dwelling pigs were to make a considerable contribution to one of the glories of Gaulish and later French gastronomy. Where did they come from? The Suidae family to which the pig belongs appeared on earth during the first period of the Tertiary era; at the time when mammals began to diversify, a creature that may be described as a pig (*Sus*) was found in the northern Mediterranean area, in what is now Spain, France and Greece, and it also occurred farther east, in Persia. Longer in the leg and much smaller than the modern pig, it spread through Italy and Algeria during the Pliocene. In the Quaternary era it roamed the Maghrebi, Tripolitan and Saharan regions, which were not yet desert. By that time the wild boar (*Sus scrofa*) and the warthog were already roaming almost the whole of Africa and Europe. They reached the Asiatic shores of the Indian and Pacific Oceans and their islands, but they never reached America or the West Indies, to which the domestic pig was introduced by the Western conquerors: 'This species, although abundant and widespread in Europe, Africa and Asia, was not found in the New World', reported the great naturalist Buffon, 'but was brought there by the Spanish, who took black pigs to the American continent and almost all the large islands of America, where they multiplied, becoming wild in many places. They resemble our wild boar.'[6]

Although naturalists of the old school such as Cuvier and Geoffroy Saint-Hilaire believed that the domestic pig was descended from the wild boar, they are now thought to be cousins: one cannot be said to pre-date the other. The domestic pig, as Buffon remarks, easily reverts to the feral state if it is left at liberty, even changing its appearance.

When the hordes of nomadic hunters settled down to devote themselves to agriculture and stock-breeding, forest pigs soon came to sniff around their fields and middens. No doubt they were easily caught, and although they were still small, lean animals they would have provided a large quantity of instantly available meat. However, pastoral people who kept sheep and oxen cannot have thought much of this scavenging animal, which sometimes ate humans and nearly always carried parasites. The ancient Egyptians thought it transmitted leprosy, and forbade their very few swineherds, who in any case were the lowest of the low, to enter temples. Pigs are never shown in Egyptian tomb paintings.

That attitude could be at the root of the Jewish and Muslim prohibition of pig meat. Moses, brought up at Pharaoh's court, declared the animal unclean (Leviticus XI, vii) – so unclean that it should not even be touched. According to Buffon, this taboo slowed down Islamic expansion into China, for the Chinese love pork as much as carp and ducks. Whether correct or not, such was his opinion. Today a certain amount of pig meat eaten in Europe, particularly ham, actually comes from China, to the annoyance of European pig farmers. However, as a result of some rather complicated trade agreements, certain countries such as Romania pay for Western goods with their own pigs, keeping the Chinese animals for home consumption: they are cheaper, and have a certain diplomatic after-taste which does not go down too well in the West.

According to a tradition mentioned by Athenaeus, a sow had the honour of feeding the infant god Zeus with her milk. Sows have a great many nipples, usually 12. The third son of the peasants who entertained the goddess Demeter when she was wandering the world in search of her daughter was Eubulus, a swineherd. One version of the legend recounts that Eubulus saw his pigs swallowed up by the gulf into which Persephone had disappeared, and was thus able to tell the goddess what had happened to the girl. According to other Greek legends, the enchantress Circe turned the men who courted her into swine, and the pig was one of the many shapes taken by Proteus, a minor sea god. Proteus, who was skilled in magic, foretold the future to Menelaus. Homer, from whom the tale derives, frequently mentions swineherds, applying many laudatory epithets to Eumaeus, the faithful servant of Odysseus and one of the few in Ithaca to stand by him on his return.

It is interesting to notice the Homeric description of boiled pork (while his beef is always roasted): 'The pot boils while the pork melts in its juice.' Was the pork (*koiros*) that the Greeks ate fresh or salt? It probably depended on circumstances, but it seems that smoking meat, a method of preserving it invented by the people of central and northern Europe where there were plenty of forests, was popular only with the Romans. When eating pork as a meat, the Greeks cooked it quite simply, but it was prepared in ways which already suggest modern charcuterie by the *allantaupoles*, a specialist not to be confused with the *kreaupoles*, or ordinary butcher. *Koiridion*, a sucking-pig stuffed with herbs and roasted, was a dish for special occasions; the piglet was fattened on the must of grapes. Pig's liver 'cooked between two dishes' is mentioned by Aristophanes in the *Thesmophoriazusae*. It could also be roasted whole, wrapped in a caul, and appeared on menus under the name of 'Bashful Liver', perhaps because it hid in its wrappings. In general the average Greek liked pig's offal, particularly the tongue and the head. Aristophanes implies that such dishes were not sophisticated gastronomy but good food for the common man.

The pig was also popular with the Romans. According to Galen, its flesh tasted like human flesh, and it was to be discovered later that the cannibals of the South Sea Islands thought explorers were even better than pork. Such comments on 'long pig' all seem to agree, though I do not know that anyone has gone to the trouble of checking them.

But the real delicacy of patrician Roman banquets was a dish made from sows' vulvas and teats. No account of such festivities omits to mention them. Pliny goes so far as to claim that the vulva of a sow who had aborted her first litter was the best of all, while other writers of the time preferred the virgin sow. Comparisons were also drawn between the teats of a sterile sow and of one who had just given birth and was about to suckle her young. Apparently the deranged Emperor

Heliogabalus was capable of eating this dish ten days running. Asterix the Gaul was not too far out in claiming that 'These Romans are crazy!'

Although the Gauls are sometimes said to have invented ham, it does not actually seem to have been a speciality that originated in what is now France. The forests of Westphalia contained herds of pigs which roamed almost free, and were famous for the flavour of their flesh. Westphalian ham, dry-salted and then smoked as it still is today, was very popular with the Romans and was making the fortunes of Germanic tribesmen 2000 years ago. The poet Martial was one of the many who liked it. Cato recommends treating hams from Italian pigs in the same way, or at least giving them a slight barbarian flavour by brushing them with olive oil before and after smoking them and then steeping them in vinegar. But forest acorns were the real secret of the excellence of pigs from Gaul – particularly Sequania – the German forests and Iberia, and nothing could replace them. Indeed, acorns are still the secret of the well-flavoured charcuterie of Corsica. Pompeiopolis (now Pamplona) made a fortune exporting hams at the time of the Roman Empire. There is a legend still told in the Pyrenees about the origin of ham: a pig fell into a stream running from a salt spring near Salies-de-Béarn, drowned, and was fished out by herdsmen some time later. Its salted meat tasted delicious, particularly the hams, and the incident inspired the local people with the idea of the procedure. Marguerite of Navarre, in her *Heptameron*, mentions the fine flavour of Basque hams.

Another ham greatly prized at the time of the Roman Empire was the ham of the Rhineland. Its reputation was to survive the centuries. Rabelais refers to it, and so does Boileau in *Le repas ridicule*:

> Sur ce point, un jambon d'assez maigre apparence
> Arrive sous le nom de jambon de Mayence.

[And here a ham of rather lean appearance comes in under the name of Mainz ham.]

According to Athenaeus, when ham was served (as it always was) at Gaulish banquets, 'the bravest man was given the upper part of it, and if any other man disputed his right to it, the two of them fought to the death in single combat.'

Other Gaulish specialities besides ham were widely bought from Roman charcutiers, whose own national products were excellent. It may fairly be said that the sausage-making tradition has survived uninterrupted for 2000 years in both Rome and France, and the sausages themselves have remained much the same. Roman sausages included *circelli*, *tomacinae* and *incisia*, small sausages, *pendulus*, a large slicing sausage using the end of the large intestine, or caecum, as the skin, and *hilla*, a very thin sausage filled into the small intestine and rather like the dry mountain sausages of today. *Tucetta*, a speciality of Cisalpine Gaul, were large sausages of mixed pork and beef fillets. There was a Faliscan sausage resembling modern mortadella. Chitterling sausages like today's *andouillettes* might be smoked, and the

Gauls made a very good black pudding with milk and blood. This delicacy was a speciality of the *canabae*, the settlements of Aeduan charcutiers who set up shop near Roman settlements.

It is hardly surprising that the Lingones (the Gaulish tribe of the Langres plateau) used Moccus, a Celtic word for pig, as one of the epithets for Mercury, a favourite deity among the Gauls. Excavations of rustic shrines have found votive tablets praising pig-farming and its profitability. There is evidence of the activities of the *lardarius*, the Gaulish charcutier, in a number of bas-reliefs and inscriptions found at Narbonne, Bordeaux and Cologne, and at Rheims, where a bas-relief shows two of these specialists at work. One is gutting a pork carcase laid on a chopping block, while the other is preparing the next pig for slaughter. All the items of charcuterie shown in the relief are easily identifiable: black puddings, strings of sausages, joints of pork, pig's heads. The pig's head seems to have been a popular dish; it figures enthroned on a large platter in the middle of a table laid with a lavish meal. Another bas-relief seems to show a wild boar's head. Tripe or *omasum*, a dish of purely Celtic invention, although not particularly suitable for artistic representation, was still very famous; it was made with the garlic and onions of which Gaul exported large quantities. It is difficult to assess the price of these foods, but we do know that in first-century Cisalpine Gaul a piglet cost five denarii, five times the price of a litre of wine. Prices fell towards the end of the third century, when the prosperity of Roman Gaul was at its height.

During the period of the barbarian invasions, herds of cattle and flocks of sheep suffered severely from the misfortunes of agriculture in general, but it was easy for pigs to take refuge in the forests. Another advantage of the pig was its fecundity: a sow can easily have up to 12 piglets in a single litter. Pork and venison were thus the most readily available sources of meat, and both featured prominently on the tables of great lords and common people alike, particularly as the new masters of what had once been Roman Gaul were very fond of pork. At about the same time as the synod of Mâcon was meeting to resolve the important question of whether women have souls or not, Queen Fredegond, wishing to rid herself of Bishop Nectarius, accused him, man of God though he was, of stealing a ham from King Chilperic's kitchen. In fact religious communities were about the only people able to rear pigs properly at the time; the postscripts to the pastoral letters of an archbishop of Rheims show that the market price of ham ranked quite high among his preoccupations.

The people of the Middle Ages continued to eat a great deal of pork, both as fresh meat and as charcuterie. The Salic Law devotes no less than 16 of its articles to the subject. The *Ménagier de Paris* gives figures of pork consumption in the capital as impressive as those for other forms of butcher's meat mentioned above: 30,794 pigs a year were sold in a special market in a hall at the corner of the rue de la Ferronnerie and the rue des Déchargeurs. But as the author of the *Ménagier* explains to his young wife, prosperous citizens owned country properties where pigs were reared: 'It is said that the males should be killed in the month of November, and the females in December; and such is their season, as for example we speak of "a shrovetide hen".' The thirteenth-century medallions of the seasons in Amiens Cathedral show this December task: a villein, legs wide apart, is strangling a piglet wedged between his knees. He has already killed another animal which hangs beside him, head down, over a tub set to catch the blood for black puddings.

South of the Loire, however, pigs were and still are killed later, before carnival, so that they would be even bigger. The date of slaughter also made it possible to celebrate carnival with fresh meat. 'At St Anthony's tide, salt your pork and put away your oil', says a proverb of the Languedoc, obviously of Protestant origin, since it ignores Lent, which would soon have been beginning. St Anthony, whose day was 17th January, is the patron saint of charcutiers. In pictures, he is often shown with a pig, the animal chiefly associated with him, although it was really meant to represent the Devil and symbolize the lewd thoughts which tormented the hermit saint in the desert; real pigs are few and far between in the sands of Egypt.

The people of the Morbihan region of Brittany preferred to revere St Gildas; the local processional pilgrimage in his honour on 29th January was the signal to kill the pig, and a piece of salt or even fresh pork was offered to his statue. The sacrifices of the ancient world were a long time dying out. The Burgundians killed and salted their pigs just before Shrove Tuesday, so that they could take the meat out of the brine tub on the Wednesday morning of Holy Week.

From the south of the Auvergne to the Pyrenees, the pig was sacrosanct among farm animals: 'Sent Pourqui / Atan que s'apère, en parlau per respect.' [Saint Porker, wherever he is found, is spoken of with respect.] However, as Henriette Dussourt points out in *Les secrets des fermes au coeur de la France*, which also contains some excellent recipes, Saint Porker was not thought of so highly in the cattle country of central France: 'When a peasant mentioned his pig in front of someone towards whom he wished to show respect, he would always follow the word "pig" with an apologetic phrase such as "saving your presence". The pig, while alive, did not play much part in everyday life.'[7] Dead, it was a different matter: for centuries even the poorest of French peasant families managed to fatten their annual pig, thus ensuring that they had basic provisions of salted or preserved meat and fat, lard and bacon, not to mention rustic charcuterie.

Killing the pig was a great occasion in the French provinces until before the Second World War. In the Aude the whole process of slaughtering the animal and salting, pickling and in general preparing its meat for the household was called 'tiring out the pig', although if old people's memories are to be believed the farmers' wives must have felt more tired than anyone else at the end of this exhausting period.

Everywhere, the day of the slaughter was an important social occasion. A request for help from family and neighbours might be couched, in the Auvergne, in the polite terms of an invitation 'to dinner'. House after house, the village was in a state of bustling activity for two or three weeks when every morning was ushered in by the heartrending squeals of that day's protagonist.

A good fire was alight from dawn in the farmyard, heating pots of water to scald the slaughtered animal, which always, like the Duc de Guise, seemed bigger dead than alive. In the evening the *mija* was put to cook: this was the court-bouillon for the black puddings. After the pig was bled, women stirred the blood slowly in a huge cauldron – often a communal one in Périgord – watched with interest by the dogs who shared the general excitement of the household. The children, let off school for the day, were inclined to fool about and get slapped, though they might be allowed to cook bits of pork crackling over wisps of straw. Not so many of them would volunteer to go down to the river and wash out the pig's intestines.

Good manners required neighbours to exchange puddings and cooked meats, so that a little later on you could not be quite sure if the charcuterie you ate was from your own pig or another. 'No part of the pig was wasted, everything was carved up, chopped, prepared and pickled on the very day of the pig-killing, from the best to the less good parts of the animal. Even the bladder, inflated and dried, was used to keep tobacco in.'[8] The pig's generosity in this respect, whatever rude remarks townspeople may make about it, finds humorous expression in one of the last traditional charcutiers' shops of the Parisian area, in Champagne-sur-Oise, where the charcutier has painted a magnificent pink pig on the blank wall of his house, with a speech bubble boasting: 'I'm delicious all over, from head to tail.'

In the Périgord even the water in which the puddings were boiled, the *bougras*, brought luck to the farm animals. A little of this good soup was kept back for the stable, pigsty and henhouse so that the beasts and fowls would show their gratitude for such kindness by their fecundity through the coming year. The kitchen garden was not forgotten either; the last spoonfuls were emptied on the midden, making the dung more fertile than ever.

It was satisfying, when the pig-killing season was over, to think of all the good things tidily stored away: meat and bacon in the brine tub, rillettes and preserved pork in pots of fat, sausages and hams hanging from nails – but not just any nails, says Henriette Dussourt, or not in the Allier region:

> Care was taken to hang the hams well away from places where people sat, and certainly never above the table and the benches around it. I knew of a case in which a ham committed homicide. An old grandfather on a farm had placed his armchair underneath the hams, and one of them fell on him; the old gentleman died of a fractured skull. The locals concluded that it was the pig's revenge.

The recipes for charcuterie given by the *Ménagier de Paris* as early as the fourteenth century are excellent, clearly explained, and even now do not sound outdated: 'To make puddings [with onions, herbs and aromatics], to make a pudding of offal [with the lights]: *Note*, that good puddings may be made of the blood of a goose, but let it be lean, for the intestines of the lean goose are larger than those of the fat goose …' '*Quaeritur*, how the intestines shall be reversed to wash them; *responsio*; by a linen thread and a brass wire as long as a gauger's rod …' To make chitterling sausages:

> Item, make sausages of the paunch chopped into thin slices; item, of the meat which is below the ribs. … To de-salt hams, first boil them in water and wine, and throw away this first liquid, then cook them in fresh water. … Here follow all the names of those parts of a pig which are sold at the tripe merchant's for seven *blancs*.[9] *primo*, when the pig is cut open, the blood and the intestines come out first, and you may make them into puddings if you wish. Item, to those parts called the *froissure* [heart, liver, lights and tongue, not quite the same as modern French *fressure*, pluck] there belong 1) the fat; 2) the *haste-menue* [the spleen and kidneys]; 3) the *chaudun* [the duodenum and small intestine] …

The fat of the pig, or *sain*, became known as *saindoux*, sweet fat, in French because it was melted down and not salted like bacon; *saindoux* is the modern French word for lard (and somewhat confusingly, English 'lard' is the French word for bacon). The word *sain* was a modification of the Frankish *saïm*, which translated Latin *sagina*, fat food. *Sain* on its own was retained as the name for the fat of the wild boar in hunting terminology. In the Aude, the pig-killer who went from farm to farm slaughtering the animals was known as the *sainaire*, but in this case the word derived from *saigneur*, the man who bled the pigs. A famous medieval remedy for toothache consisted of an ointment of the lard from a boar pig and cooked goose droppings. Goose or chicken fat was known as *auve*, from Latin *avis*, a bird.

Medieval tripe merchants, as the author of the *Ménagier* indicates, sold the offal of pigs, cattle or sheep, and in towns fresh pork was bought from butchers. The 'chaircuitiers' who prepared the *chair cuite*, the cooked meat, were not allowed to slaughter pigs themselves, and they too bought their raw material from butchers. The Foire aux Jambons (Ham Fair) was held on first the Thursday and then the Tuesday of Holy Week, outside Notre-Dame de Paris, replacing a traditional meal for the cathedral chapter provided by the tithes of *bacon* or fat pork. The word 'bacon' is no longer French, although it is retained in English; it was originally an Old French word coming from Frankish *bako*, ham.

The charcutiers of the capital did not win recognition as specialists in the pork trade until 1705, after centuries of disputes with the butchers. Later, in 1741, they were granted the sole right to cure hams; the butchers had already lost the sole right to sell tripe. The reverse of the coin was that the charcutiers could no longer buy their pork direct from the provinces. For reasons of hygiene the markets of Paris, Poissy and Seaux were now the only authorized sources of supply, and they were strictly regulated.

The first *arrondissement* of Paris contains a street rather improbably called rue de la Cossonnerie; *cochonnerie* has come, from meaning pigwash, to mean in modern French rubbish or obscenity. The street was not so called because it ever contained a group of charcuterie shops, but took its name from an inn that stood there in the late sixteenth century, called *La truie qui file* – 'The Running Sow'. At mid-Lent carnival time young people used to resort to it, and there was a tradition of hoisting up a boy and a girl to kiss the sow on the inn sign. Then they had to spit in each other's faces. Should the couple seize their chance to exchange a kiss they were stripped from the waist down and publicly whipped. The street therefore takes its name from this rather broad joke.

For a long period, however, town streets really did belong to the pigs, who at least acted as scavengers in the absence of anything like a public cleansing department. Several kings of France, from Louis IX to François I, tried in vain to ban pigs from wandering at large in big cities. There were countless trials, in which sentence was passed not on the owners of the animals, who usually could not be found, but on the pigs themselves for the damage and accidents they caused. Pigs sometimes went into houses and ate babies. For a long time the public executioner was authorized to seize any pigs he found (apart from those belonging to the Antonine monks, which enjoyed the protection of St Anthony) and take them to a designated spot, where he could cut their throats if their owners did not ransom them for five silver sous a head. In Orléans, there was a kind of pig-hunt to drive all pigs outside the city walls before dark.

St Anthony's errant pigs were found in abundance in most European cities, a very tempting prey to anyone who did not keep pigs of his own out in the country. Sacchetti, in several of his *Trecento novelle*, describes the way in which Florentine rogues of the fifteenth century tried to acquire animals who were generally determined not to be captured. In one of these tales a pig makes its way into the house of a gouty and bedridden man who gets his terrified servant lad to slaughter this providential windfall. A scene of carnage ensues, with the boy, pursued through the bedroom by the bleeding pig, making more noise than anyone. As a story of clandestine pig-killing arousing the whole neighbourhood, it suggests the similar misadventure which befell the designer Jean Effel during the Occupation five centuries later. To 'squeal like a stuck pig' is not just a figure of speech, and undercover pigs tend to be the most vociferous of all.

These scavenging, muddy pigs, eating tainted food, splashing through the filthy gutters and consuming the contents of emptied chamber pots, usually made very unhealthy eating; their meat was likely to carry tapeworm infections and trichinosis at the very least. The Romans had kept very careful checks on the wholesomeness of their meat, and when the corporations were established in France in the reign of Louis IX such checks became the responsibility of the syndics of the butchers' corporation. A 'letter' of Charles V stipulates that 'two citizens shall inspect and visit the butchers' shops to see if anything of bad or defective quality is displayed there.' Under Louis XI 'no butcher may sell or cause to be sold in his shop pork from a pig that was fed in a barber's shop, or by a measly person, and if he has done so, the flesh shall be thrown into the river.' This can hardly have been good for the river, since barber-surgeons were in the habit of fattening their pigs on the pus and matter from dressings, the blood they took from their patients at a time when bleeding was a popular remedy, the debris left over after operations and even the product of purging. A 'measly person' meant a leper. The decree cannot have been good for the townsfolk either, since the poor would come after dark and fish this tainted meat out of the river, either to eat it or to sell it to others a little better off than themselves. Georges Chaudieu, describing such practices, adds that today meat not fit for consumption is treated so that it is impossible to eat it.

At the end of the Middle Ages the *langueyeurs*, inspectors of pigs' tongues, had to keep checks on pigs. They marked the ear of any beast suspected of having 'measles', and its meat might not be eaten. Porcine measles, thought by classical writers to be leprosy, is actually the result of tapeworm cysts which cause ulcerations of the pig's tongue. The *langueyeurs* therefore inspected the tongue of every pig offered for sale. But perhaps because of economic problems, two judgments in the Parlement court, of 1607 and 1667, allowed such meat to be made into charcuterie after a period of time in the brine tub, minus the tongue. Such food had to be sold separately, in designated places, but unfortunately there was no lack of customers for it.

Even if the meat looked wholesome, the way in which the pigs had fed could still betray itself after cooking. Henri III issued a mandate forbidding pigs to be fed 'on fish or on hemp seed, because of the particular flavour those substances give the meat' – a principle forgotten by battery chicken-farmers after the Second World War. In the nineteenth century pig farmers and pork butchers were hazy about the line to be drawn between liberty and public danger, and it was some time before proper meat inspection became established in France. Charcuterie could camouflage many anomalies. At the beginning of the twentieth century the unfortunate privates of the French army received meat that was little better than tainted carrion in their rations; there was a serious scandal in 1907, and the minister Chéron finally made supervision of meat and charcuterie compulsory. Today France has a national inspection service for animal foods, under the Ministry of Agriculture, uniting all the earlier municipal services. There are regulations controlling the various stages of production, slaughter, transport and distribution, and the entry into France of carcases from abroad.

The EC pig-farming crisis, affecting all the member countries, often gives rise to incidents, sometimes serious, sometimes less so, when pork carcases or hams cross frontiers which are supposed not to exist. One way of keeping out foreign carcases, quite often employed, is to query the wholesomeness of the meat. But pig wars are nothing new. In the late nineteenth century pig-farming in Serbia, later one of the republics in the Yugoslav federation, was a very prosperous business. Indeed, it was Serbia's chief asset, and its natural commercial outlet was the Austro-Hungarian Empire. Vienna accordingly played it as a trump card in its policy of oppression of the government in Belgrade. Every time Serbia was suspected of some attempt to emancipate itself from its powerful neighbour's political and economic domination, new regulations, both arbitrary and confused, were imposed on the quality, price and presentation of pig meat and paralysed sales. Serbia had to surrender. Unfortunately the pig war between Serbia and Austria-Hungary was followed by those far more serious events which set all Europe alight. Politics, as we might put it today, is a pig of a business.

About Ham

In French law, genuine ham comes only from the upper thigh and haunch of the pig (or, in those European countries where they still exist and are hunted as game, of wild boar or bear). Shoulder ham, meat from the shoulder cured in the same way, is not strictly speaking ham at all, and ought to be sold boned and rolled with a label identifying it correctly. But in actual fact ham, which we might expect to be the most straightforward kind of charcuterie, is a prime example of the traps that lie in wait for the consumer, who should beware and read the labels carefully, always supposing there are any: the absence of certain terms is a confession of some legal or gastronomic omission. If you do read the label you are less likely to find yourself with 'ham' which deserves no better than those inverted commas, enticing as the price may be.

There are two kinds of ham: cooked ham (boiled, and called *blanc* in France): Paris, York and Prague ham; and uncooked ham (dried or smoked): Bayonne, Savoy, Auvergne, Brittany and Lyons ham. These terms do not necessarily denote the ham's place of origin; they may simply imply that it has been cured in the manner of ham from those places. But labels with the wording Lacaune, Corsica, Parma or Westphalia ham guarantee that the ham actually came from those places.

COOKED HAMS Jambon braisé, braised or baked ham, is a snare and a delusion nine times out of ten, an ordinary ham in disguise, its outside browned with a quick burst of heat from a burner after it has been brushed or injected with artificial colourings and smoke-flavoured oil. However, genuine braised ham is delicious: very expensive and worth it.

In the past hams for baking were salted in the traditional way, with the ingredients of the cure rubbed in several times at intervals. Then it was dried and sometimes subsequently smoked. This procedure is still essential for dry-salted hams of top quality. 'White' hams are salted fresh, by injections.

Jambon de Paris, Paris ham, is a *jambon blanc*. Ham at the top end of the scale, sold in France 'au torchon', in a cloth, or 'au bouillon', cooked in bouillon, is the best, the most genuine, the hardest to find and the most expensive. It is made with fresh meat, and only the top of the pig's thigh and the haunch are used. This ham is salted by injections of brine into the venous system. The brine is not just very salty water: saltpetre or potassium nitrate and natural aromatics to taste are added to the solution of salt, which may or may not be nitrated. The ham is then steeped in this brine for three or four days before being drained, wrapped in a cloth, the 'torchon', and cooked in a court-bouillon as carefully composed as a good household stock. When it has cooled it is skinned and a certain amount of the fat is removed. Then it is boned; keeping the bone in during cooking improves the flavour and enriches the meat with calcium. Some hams, described as 'au foin', hay-cooked, are gastronomic delicacies; they are cooked wrapped in hay (dried sainfoin and clover), and making them is a small-scale rural craft. Imitations produced on a semi-industrial scale should be avoided. They do not necessarily use only natural products.

Jambon supérieur, superior ham, is frankly an industrial product. It is boned and skinned and has its fat removed before cooking, so that much of the flavour and the mineral salts are lost. It moves along a conveyor belt between two surfaces studded with hundreds of hollow needles, and brine is injected into the whole thing, not just the venous system. Then it goes into the brine tub, like the hams made by the traditional method. Next it is put into a mould, trimmed to give it the classic ham shape, and placed in an oven to be steam-cooked for three to five hours. This ham, a straightforward enough product, is 'superior' only to the following kinds.

Jambon 'surchoix', supposedly finest quality ham, may consist of an assortment of trimmings cut from the previous ham before it was put into the mould, with shoulder ham added. The whole thing is pressed in a mould, as you can easily see when it is sliced from the different colours and grains visible across the cut surface. In France, however, the Red Label on this ham does at least guarantee that the meat is of good quality. It is not a delicacy, but is a good enough buy.

Jambon 'premier choix', prime ham, hardly lives up to its name. An industrial product, it uses up any trimmings whatever left over from the hams mentioned above. They are very finely chopped and churned in a machine not unlike a concrete mixer. Polyphosphates (2 per cent) are added to the brine, as well as soluble sugars to fix the water in the meat (up to 74 per cent of total liquid content), thus increasing weight by 10 per cent. It is coloured pink.

Jambon, plain ham, is sold in France without any other description because no one likes to admit that it is a mixture of frozen meats of unspecified quality, with a higher percentage of polyphosphates (3 per cent), and with casein or lacto-protein and gluten added to bind the whole thing together. There is nothing the matter with these additives in themselves, except that the meat to which they are added is then sold as ham. It contains a great deal of water and is sold, cut to size, in plastic packs. Being cheap, it is the ham commonly used in canteens and for cheap sandwiches. In France it is usually imported, since French producers consider it beneath them. The amount of additives and liquid it contains mean that care must be taken to observe the sell-by date on the packet. It must also be kept cold, or it could ferment. The consumer should be on the alert for any suspicious smell when the packet is opened.

York ham is not boned, nor does it necessarily come from York or even from England. It may be produced on a quasi-industrial scale.

Prague ham is lightly smoked after it has been cooked, and is not imported from Czechoslovakia. It is of very good quality.

Labelling on the last two hams really indicates that they are prepared in the manner of Prague or York ham, not that they actually come from those places.

UNCOOKED HAMS Dry-cured hams are not injected with brine but are rubbed with a salting mixture in the traditional way.

The descriptions 'Bayonne' and 'Montagne' have no legal significance except to indicate the manner in which the ham is prepared, and imported ham may be used, though the difference in flavour is considerable compared with hams from animals which were genuinely reared in the locality suggested. However, that does not impair the basic high quality of such hams. In the absence of any precise indication of the place of origin, price is a good guide. Thus:

Bayonne ham which does not carry a label saying it was actually produced in the Bayonne region, and/or giving the manufacturer's address, may have been made anywhere in France with meat from any country. True Bayonne ham is made from pigs reared and fed in a carefully controlled manner. It is selected, then rubbed with a dry-salting mixture consisting of Salies-de-Béarn salt, saltpetre, sugar, pepper and natural aromatics. It is dried for five or six months in ventilated drying chambers.

Lacaune, Savoy and *Lyon hams*, if their place of origin is guaranteed, have very characteristic flavours, each according to its own locality, and they are excellent.

Corsican ham or *Prisuttu* is not often seen for sale. If it is, it too should be of guaranteed origin. It is made from pigs which wander almost at liberty, eating chestnuts, especially in the Castagniccia area, ranging the perfumed *maquis* of Corsica. Their meat has an unforgettable flavour. It is leaner than Continental hams. These Corsican hams spend about 40 days in the brine tub after being washed, skinned (but not de-fatted) and rubbed with pepper. They may also be smoked for three or four days in the traditional manner, but they should be left to mature for several months, like good wine, before they are eaten.

Parma ham comes exclusively from around Parma in Italy and is made from pigs guaranteed to be from that region. It is very fine and very well flavoured, and has been matured for eight to ten months before it is boned to make it easier to slice for sale. It has been famous for over 1000 years.

Westphalia ham really does come from Westphalia in the Federal Republic of Germany. It is expensive. It is dry-salted and then smoked for a week with special regional woods.

Boned hams are re-shaped by pressure. They do not keep as long as ham on the bone. Dried hams sold sliced in plastic packs come into this category. When the label on the pack mentions the additive E 450, it means that the contents have been injected with polyphosphates and not dry-salted. Ham of this kind contains a good deal of moisture, and you should make sure it has not been in the shop too long. It should be eaten soon after purchase.

Jambon persillé, 'parsleyed ham', is a delicious dish from Burgundy. It is made in many other places too, but when it is sold in France with a guarantee of Burgundian origin you can taste the difference. It consists of cured raw ham poached in a cloth in a court-bouillon containing wine. It is then chopped, put into a terrine, and topped up with the reduced cooking liquid, to which plenty of chopped parsley has been added, so that it sets to a natural jelly. Cheap *jambon persillé* is made from scraps of the ends of hams, set with gelatine.

Additives: by law additives must be mentioned on the label, but you still need a translation.

Preservatives:	E 250	=	sodium nitrite
	E 251	=	sodium nitrate
	E 252	=	potassium nitrate
	E 300	=	ascorbic acid
Colourants:	E 160	=	carotenoids
	E 100	=	curcumin
	E 120	=	cochineal, etc.
Gelling and softening agents:	E 450	=	sodium and potassium polyphosphates

Fat: in the past it was vital to have a diet rich in lipids to generate calories, particularly in winter. The fatness of meat from the pig was therefore an advantage. Meat in general was regarded as rich, fat food and thus good for you.

Today we lead a more sedentary life in over-heated, poorly ventilated buildings, and as we do not burn up so many of the calories in our food we resort to a kind of voluntary fasting: we diet. Moreover, animal fats are bad for the arteries and the heart, already strained by the stress of modern living and the effects of alcohol. In recent years we have come to require different qualities in pigs. They are bred to give more lean meat and less fat. Just as fat bacon is less in demand for cooking today, people do not want the fat that surrounds ham, and charcutiers sell what their customers want to buy: de-fatted ham cut to shape. This is heresy, as anyone who really understands food will know.

Ham fat is full of B vitamins, and unless one is actually ill there is no need to reject it so sternly when we accept fat in other kinds of charcuterie. In fact the cheaper those products are the more fat they contain, particularly sausages and pâtés. Rillettes are 50 per cent fat. Children do not like fat, but all the same a certain amount in the diet is good for the skin, the hair and the temper, although of course we should not overdo it; all excess is a mistake.

> 'This is what the common proverb says', broke in Panurge:
> 'While round a fat ham we drink together,
> The storms pass off, and give way to good weather'.
>
> (Rabelais, *Pantagruel*, Book IV)

Sausages

Sausages, both large and small, consist of meat chopped or minced, either finely or more coarsely, and stuffed into skins, which may be synthetic. Incidentally, China is the biggest exporter of natural sausage skins made from animal intestines, so there is a touch of *chinoiserie* about many sausages and black and white puddings from Europe. This kind of charcuterie is not necessarily made of pure pork; sausages can be a mixture of meats, or may be all beef, or even, in Arab and Jewish charcuterie, all mutton or lamb.

Saucisson sec, dry or keeping sausage, is best when it is made on a small scale. It can be identified by its coarse-grained appearance: raw meat and bacon are chopped with a knife and stuffed by hand into sausage skins usually made from the large intestine. These sausages also contain salt and peppercorns, which may be green. Some have olives or mushrooms added.

Most people who like sausages prefer the flavour of pork, but it is of no greater nutritional value than sausages made of a mixture of pork and beef.

Ordinary sausages may use meat of good quality, with all kinds of additions. Dry sausage of this kind sliced and sold loose does not say what is in it, but the ingredients must be stated on the packaging when it is sold pre-packed. It may contain various preservative salts (nitrites and nitrates), additives E 250 and E 252, sugar, colourants, anti-oxidants, monosodium glutamate as a flavour improver, E 450 (polyphosphates as a gelling agent), lacto-fermentation agents, and quite a number more.

Skins of these large keeping sausages, brushed with a gelling substance, may be covered with so-called Provençal herbs, crushed pepper, or even ashes. All this is reflected in the price.

Saucisson de ménage, household sausage, is of medium size. It should be made of pure pork, coarsely chopped with a knife if possible, rather than minced. It is eaten while still not too dry.

Rosette is a large sausage, tied with string, which should be made of coarsely chopped pure pork.

Jésus is a sausage with a very wide diameter; its skin comes from the end of the large intestine, or caecum. It is usually made of finely chopped pure pork, and may be covered with pepper, although this is not traditional.

Saucisson d'Arles, Arles sausage, is of medium size and is a mixture of beef and very fat pork. It was once made with donkey meat and beef, and sausages of this traditional mixture were still being sold in Provence until the Second World War.

Chasseur is the same as Arles sausage, but thinner.

Salami in principle is of Italian origin. It is a large sausage of very finely chopped pork and beef, coloured and smoked. It is seldom of very good quality.

Saucisson de montagne, mountain sausage, is a name meaning nothing in particular, applied to ordinary *saucisson de ménage* sold at a slightly higher price.

Saucisse sèche, dry sausage, often called Auvergne sausage, is very thin and is stuffed into skins made from the small intestine. It is extremely dry, and bent into a hairpin shape. The meat should be coarsely chopped by hand, and should be all pork.

Saucisson de Lyon, Lyon sausage, should not be confused with *cervelas de Lyon*, which needs cooking. It is large, like *rosette*, and is made not of pork but of finely chopped or minced beef mixed with diced bacon.

Corsican *lonzo* (called *lonzu* in Corsica itself) is a sausage made in small quantities, often as a cottage industry. It consists of fillets of pork, not minced or chopped, salted for a week, then smoked and stuffed into large skins.

Saucisson cuit, cooked sausage, or *saucisson à l'ail*, garlic sausage, is a mixture of very finely minced pork and beef, lightly smoked, with added starch, cooked with garlic. The 'skin' is often synthetic.

There are also sausages sold as:

Cervelas, cervelat or saveloy. In the time of Rabelais this was a cooked Milanese sausage with a basis of meat and pig's brains very finely chopped. Now it is made of pork and beef, coloured red with cochineal, finely minced and with added starch, stuffed into synthetic skins which are also artificially coloured. It is eaten with salad dressing.

Cervelas de Lyon should not be confused with ordinary saveloys. It is sold uncooked, and must be boiled before it is eaten. It contains nothing but very finely minced pork, and has either truffles or pistachios in it.

Mortadella, in Rabelais' day, was an Italian sausage stuffed with a mixture containing myrtle leaves (*morta* in Italian dialect). Still an Italian speciality, mortadella is now sold in a very large and wide synthetic or plastic skin. The filling, very fine, highly flavoured and coloured, contains pork, veal, and a great deal of powdered milk and starch, with coarsely diced bacon and sometimes pistachios.

There are a great many kinds of small sausage. Every region of Europe has its own speciality, not necessarily pure pork. Jewish and Arab sausages use beef and veal, and Arab sausages are often lamb or mutton.

Like large sausages, the smaller ones are made of minced or chopped meat. In France, the standard and indeed classic type of sausage-meat is entirely natural and made of pork containing 40 per cent fat. In general the more finely minced the meat, the more additives of the same kind as those used in the large sausages are put into it. Ascorbic acid prevents the colour from turning greyish. The large sausages described above are dried; the small ones are fresh.

There follows a list of the most usual sausages for grilling, frying or boiling in France:

Crépinette, sausage-meat, which may be flavoured with herbs, truffles or olives, is wrapped in a '*crépine*', a piece of caul, the membrane of the peritoneum. It is flattish. In the thirteenth century French 'chaircuitiers' gave their imagination such free rein that the authorities had to forbid the addition to these sausages of anything but 'salt, fennel, and other good spices'.

Chipolata sausages are thin, in synthetic skins which should melt away during cooking and which contain the same mixture as the larger *crépinettes*. Italian in origin, these sausages used to be made with onion, *cipolla*.

Saucisse de Toulouse, Toulouse sausage, is large, and the meat should be finely chopped with a knife.

Breton, *Savoie* and *Montbéliard* sausages contain the same mixture as Toulouse sausage, but saltier. They are dried slightly and then smoked.

Morteau is traditionally fastened with a sliver of wood. The best is flavoured with cumin. It is not fried or grilled, but gently simmered.

Strasbourg and *Frankfurter* sausages are often partly preserved, and are made of a fine, raw mixture of beef and pork. Frankfurters are slightly smoked. They are filled into thin synthetic skins. Strasbourg sausages have red colouring added, Frankfurters are yellowish, and both are sold in pairs. Apart from a few very exceptional specimens, they represent the triumph of additives, the most acceptable added ingredients being starch, soya protein and powdered milk. Their pork content may be nothing but almost pulverized rind.

Chorizo is a Spanish speciality, highly flavoured with paprika, which also gives it its red colour, and cayenne. It may be made of pure pork or pork and beef. It is fried, or if slightly dried may be eaten uncooked.

Gendarme sausage is square in section, and is made from pressed, finely minced beef, highly smoked, very peppery, and sometimes further seasoned with smoke-flavoured oil.

Merguez, a North African speciality, in principle contains only beef, or beef and fat mutton, seasoned with plenty of cayenne and paprika. It is a kosher sausage.

Figatelli are a Corsican speciality (*ficatellu* in Corsica itself). Their basic filling is pork liver, highly seasoned with salt and pepper, finely minced and filled into a thin skin from the small intestine. They are smoked for four or five days and then hung up in a well-ventilated place. *Figatelli* are eaten after a week, fried, baked or grilled. If they are kept for a month they can be eaten uncooked, but they will not keep very much longer, and may ferment.

The Symbolism of the Pig

Except in China and Vietnam, where the pig is a symbol of prosperity and abundance because of its plumpness and fecundity, the poor creature has a rather unfortunate reputation, even though it provides so much nourishment. First and foremost, it represents gluttony; we say someone who overeats is 'making a pig of himself'. Besides suggesting greed by its readiness to swallow almost anything, it also evokes other tendencies which our education teaches us to suppress: lust, egotism and ignorance. The Biblical parable of pearls cast before swine conveys the idea of a true message wasted because it is addressed to people unable and unworthy to profit by it.

The proverbial dirty habits of the pig (again, we say someone is 'a dirty pig', or is 'pigging it') go some way towards accounting for the Jewish distaste for it.

Finally, pork was the meat most commonly eaten by ordinary people from classical times to the nineteenth century, and was a fat meat. To have meat in your diet at all meant it was regarded as a rich one, and all carnivorous (i.e., rich, fat) food was banned during Lent. Ash Wednesday was thus a day of much busy scouring for the housewives of the Languedoc, who had to remove the slightest traces of fat from the insides of their frying pans, saucepans and casseroles; they used to gather on the river bank to scrub their cooking pans out with sand. In Picardy it was a considerable hardship for people to give up lard for cooking in Lent and use oil instead, and they sang a little song to cheer themselves up:

> Saint Panchard n'a point soupé
> Donne-z-y eune crout' d'pâté
> Taillez haut, taillez bas
> Ch'est a son cul qu'ch'tient l'plus gras.

[St Piggy has not dined today, so give him a piece of pie; cut it high, cut it low, it's fattest on his rump.]

The History of Foie Gras

If caviare is in the nature of a gastronomic dream, the thought of *foie gras* could be said to induce a kind of voluptuously mingled sense of greed and bliss. Indeed, *foie gras* exemplifies greed twice over, being the result of fatty enlargement of the liver of geese and ducks induced by cramming, i.e., the over-feeding to which the chosen fowls are subjected.

The goose itself invented cramming. The ancient Egyptians were the first to notice the phenomenon: at the season when wild geese are about to migrate, and must travel thousands of kilometres without any chance of feeding, they eat such large quantities of food that reserves of energy are stored in their livers as fat. Geese trapped by the Egyptians just before the great migration provided a real feast. Someone had the idea of cramming the domestic ducks and geese which, as we have seen, were descended from captured wild species.

The official whose title was The-Pharaoh's-One-Friend-Chief-of-his-Master's-Secrets-in-All-his-Dwellings-Chief-of-the-Royal-Works-Steward-of-the-Pyramids-of-Neferikare-and-Neontsere,[11] or to name him more briefly, the illustrious Ti, who lived at the end of the Fifth Dynasty and was buried at Saqqara, was so fond of *foie gras* that the painted bas-reliefs in his funerary apartments provide a graphic account of the cramming methods in use at the time. The series of scenes, rather like a strip cartoon, is now in the Louvre Museum. Poultry file past, watched by the deceased and his son – they are geese and ducks, since chickens were not yet farmyard fowls. The next image shows the cramming of these ducks and geese, and even of cranes: seated on the ground, two servants, or perhaps slaves, are mixing a dough in a round-bottomed pot set on a tripod. One of the young men holds a funnel, whether for force-feeding the birds or blowing up the fire is not certain. His companion is rolling the dough between his hands, making it into little regular sausage shapes. Moving on to another picture, we see the sausages of dough neatly arranged in a cup so that they only have to be picked out one by one and put into a bird's greedy beak. The bird is being helped to swallow it by pressure of the fingers around its neck, as if it were being massaged. Beside the crammers are vessels containing liquid, possibly oil to make the food slip down better. A whole flock of geese and ducks a little way off seem to be awaiting this feast impatiently. Some are already craning their necks, others are beating their wings, while others again, obviously satiated, are drinking.

Several other depictions of this subject, and representations of baskets full of fat geese, all dating from the Fifth Dynasty, show that the cramming of geese was a usual practice from the third millennium BC onwards.[12] According to Athenaeus, writing in the third century, fat geese were sent from Egypt as a present to Agesilaus, king of Sparta, around 400 BC. But we do not know exactly how the Egyptians cooked and ate the *foie gras* of their geese and ducks. Athenaeus simply repeats, in his *Deipnosophistai*, a remark said to have been made by the famous cook Archestratus: 'But now, Ulpian, you who ask us questions about everything that appears on the table, you will not refuse to tell us what text of the Ancients makes mention of these magnificent goose livers.' A little later he has the fine phrase, 'A liver, or rather the soul of a goose'.

The Greeks, still according to Athenaeus, were expert at fattening geese 'with wheat pounded in water'. The practice became common among the Romans, who were anxious to serve anything magnificent, enormous, of generous size, unique or monstrous on their tables. Cato, in the second century BC, explains how 'To cram hens or geese: shut up young hens beginning to lay, make pellets of moist flour or barley-meal, soak in water, and put into the mouth … cram twice a day, and give water at noon, but do not place water before them for more than one hour. Feed a goose the same way, except that you let it drink first, and give food and water twice a day.'[13] Columella,[14] in the first century, repeats Cato's advice verbatim and gives a description of the cramming of geese which would not be inaccurate in the French countryside of today. Palladius,[15] in the fourth century, says that geese should be fed on a vegetarian diet until they are fat enough, in 'a dark, warm place … but if you want their livers to be tender, you must roll pounded dried figs soaked in water into little balls, and give this to them at the end of 30 days of fattening, and continue to do so for 20 consecutive days.'

Pliny[16] gives no details about the cramming of geese, but he agrees that the Romans liked their tender liver, *foie gras*, the liver of the Gaulish geese that came 'on foot all the way to Rome from the Morini [Picardy] in Gaul: the geese that get tired are advanced to the front rank, and so all the rest drive them on by instinctively pressing forward in their rear.' After resting from their journey, no doubt these geese were crammed, and we may assume that their succulent flesh would be eaten too, despite Pliny's statement that, 'Our countrymen are wiser, who know the goose by the excellence of its liver. Stuffing the bird with food makes the liver grow to a great size, and also when it has been removed it is made larger by being soaked in milk sweetened with honey.' This 'enormous liver', as Juvenal called it,[17] was even better if it came, as Horace specifies, from 'a white female goose'.[18] The idea of soaking it in milk is not as odd as it may sound; today pork liver steeped in milk, although without honey, loses its bitter flavour and becomes more tender.

The dried and very sweet figs the Romans used for cramming geese would have made the geese even sicker than they already were – for *foie gras* is actually the liver of a severely diabetic bird. But *iecur ficatum*, 'fig liver', was regarded as so superior to all other *foie gras* that the Gauls forgot to go on calling it *iecur*, liver, and retained only the descriptive *ficatum*. This became the eighth-century word *figido*, and then *fedie* and *feie* in the twelfth century, ending up as *foie*. In modern French, therefore, all liver has a suggestion of *foie gras* about it – much as the word 'caviare' is optimistically applied to fish eggs other than those of sturgeon, all in line with the Gaulish dream.

Curiously, Apicius, the famous gastronome who is sometimes claimed to have invented the use of figs for fattening, has not a word about *foie gras* in his *Ars Magirica*, whatever Buffon says about it. It is true that we do not have a full text of anything definitely by Apicius; the *Ars Magirica* is a collection of recipes from two manuscripts dating from a couple of centuries after the gourmet's death, and indeed there were three epicures called Apicius, so even his identity is in doubt. The one interesting comment Apicius does provide is that sow's liver can be improved by feeding the animal milk sweetened with honey – no doubt, again, inducing diabetes.

How did the Romans eat the *foie gras* of their geese? If Juvenal is to be believed, it was served hot. 'Before the master is put a huge goose's liver, a capon as big as a goose, and a boar, piping hot.' Incredible as it may seem, the maddest of all the Roman emperors, the young Syrian Heliogabalus, fed his dogs on *foie gras* throughout the four years of his chaotic reign (AD 218–222). He died assassinated in the latrines with 'the sponge the Romans used to wipe themselves' across his throat, according to Montaigne, and one is tempted to say it served him right.

Alaric II, king of the Visigoths (484–507) showed more sense, and apparently ate *foie gras* regularly: though a byword for a barbarian chieftain, perhaps he was not so barbarian after all. It would be pleasant to think that he chose to occupy the south-east of France, a great centre of the production of *foie gras*, because of his gastronomic tastes. Brother Bernard, a character in Rabelais, invokes St Ferréol, 'he who fattens the geese', born at Limoges just north of the Corrèze border of *foie gras* country.

Henri IV of France, like his mother Jeanne d'Albret, liked fat salt geese, and had them delivered direct from Béarn, but few texts from his time mention *foie gras*. However, goose liver was distinguished from other kinds; Robert Estienne's Latin–French dictionary mentions liver in the definition of 'goose' and goose in the definition of 'liver'. Estienne's brother Charles, author of *La maison rustique*, offers advice on the fattening of geese without making it clear if he is speaking of forcible cramming: 'Wheat fattens them and makes their livers large. And they may be fed fresh or dried figs with leaven ... and even have their eyes put out to fatten them the better.' Modern science has shown that nervous depression is a major cause of obesity. ·

This liver 'which is to be steeped in cold water as soon as it is drawn from the bird' (*Le thrésor de santé*, Lyon, 1607) is served 'fresh' and hot. 'I have roasted the liver of a goose fattened by the Jews of Bohemia which weighed more than three pounds. It may also be made into a purée', says Humboldt's *Kochbuch*, published in Frankfurt in 1581. This is interesting, for it not only shows that geese were being crammed in Bohemia – a craft that gypsies continued to practise after the expulsion of Jewish communities – but mentions a purée of *foie gras* in 1581, obviously a forerunner of the famous pâté.

1651 saw the appearance of *Le cuisinier françois*, a revolutionary book which showed French cuisine branching out into new directions as it broke away from the superabundance of flavours of medieval cookery and the orgies of sugar that were typical of the Renaissance. '*Foie gras* cooked in the embers' does not specify that the *foie gras* should be goose liver; was that taken for granted, or was the liver 'fat' only because it was larded with bacon? In any case, the recipe sounds delicious, and would still be good today: 'It must be larded with bacon, and well seasoned with salt, pepper, pounded cloves, and a very small bouquet garni, then wrap it in four or five sheets of paper and bake it in the embers, as you would bake a quince. When it is cooked, be sure to pour off the sauce, stirring it, remove the top sheets of paper and serve on the bottom sheets, if you so wish, or on a plate.'

A few centuries later Valmont de Bomare's *Dictionnaire d'histoire naturelle* explains in the article on 'goose' that 'the liver of that fowl was considered an exquisite delicacy by the Romans'. Are we to infer that people no longer thought it so exquisite in 1768, or is this just reticence on the author's part? For by the end of the eighteenth century new editions of *Le cuisinier françois* and a number of works by eminent master chefs were in print: *Le cuisinier instruit*, *Le cuisinier royal et bourgeois*, the *Don de Comus*, and so on, and although Menon's *La cuisinière bourgeoise* of 1774 says nothing about *foie gras* and the way to serve it, these other works all give recipes for hot dishes prepared with *foie gras*: ragoûts, *crépines*, brochettes, liver cooked in the embers, *à la dauphine*, even made into stuffings for patties (*Le cuisinier instruit*). *Le cuisinier gascon*, published in Amsterdam in 1747, is possibly the first to suggest *foie gras* in a pastry crust, the filling for which is very like what we now know as *bloc de foie gras*.

The pâté of Périgueux mentioned in the *Dictionnaire portatif de cuisine* of 1767 is a recipe which sounds quite modern although very lavish, calling for 12 *foies gras*, two pounds of truffles, mushrooms and chives. This is highly suggestive of the modern tendency to confuse extreme richness with gastronomy. Perhaps the mention of Périgueux was a tribute to the fame of the truffles of that region. Pâté of Périgord had already been mentioned without any further explanation of the term by the *Mercure de France* in its issue of April 1718: a pâté *'maison'* possibly made of game, but without any *foie gras* or truffles. It was given by the Marquise de Lanmary to the Princesse de Bourbon, wrapped in a poem to which Princess Louise-Adélaïde replied in kind, and which the *Mercure* prints.

Woman in the Périgord cramming a goose

Périgord had long been noted for the excellence of its truffled pâtés, but they were made from the meat of the red-legged partridges shown on terrine dishes which are now museum pieces. Curnonsky traces their origin back to one Marie Rolet, a male chef of the sixteenth century. A lot of nonsense has been talked about the 'sacred alliance of truffles and *foie gras*', and there is a fanciful legend to the effect that the pâtés of Nérac which Henri IV liked consisted of *foie gras* and truffles. This is an invention of food writers.

The Charente is also famous for its pâtés and its *foie gras*. Casanova struck up a friendship with M Noël, 'the unique and greatly treasured cook' of Frederick the

Great of Prussia. He visited the chef's father in 1791; Noël senior was himself exercising his 'prodigious talents in the matter of pâtés' in Angoulême. The son's pâtés were equally prodigious, and Frederick's philosophic physician, Dr La Mettrie, died of indigestion after eating one; perhaps his philosophy was of the epicurean variety. The father's pâtés were exported as far afield as the Americas. 'With the exception of those lost in shipwrecks, they all arrived in perfect condition.' Casanova adds: 'His pâtés were mostly made of turkeys, young partridges, and hares, with truffles, but he made them also of *Foie Gras* [Casanova uses capital letters!], of larks, and of thrushes, according to the season.' Finally Toulouse, the former fief of Alaric II, must not be forgotten: according to Le Grand d'Aussy and his *Histoire de la vie privée des Français*, that city was one of the main centres of the making of *pâté de foie gras* in 1787.

At this point Alsace enters the picture. In 1788 Marshal de Contades, governor of Alsace, and Louis XVI exchanged a *pâté de foie gras*, in a pastry crust but without truffles, for a piece of land in Picardy. This pâté was the work, indeed the masterpiece, of the Marshal's chef Jean-Pierre Clause, a genius from Lorraine, although some claim he was of Norman origin. He received a reward of 20 pistoles from the royal hands. With this money he bought a trunk to hold his belongings, married, and opened a shop at no. 18 rue de la Mésange in Strasbourg, where he died 40 years later full of years and glory.

Clause's pâté is the earliest *pâté de foie gras* to have been officially promoted so impressively, but, as we have seen, such pâtés did not originally contain truffles. Alsace is not truffle country. However, the Revolution was to change many things, among them *pâté de foie gras*, the one, true, genuine article. You might call this a case of little oaks growing from mighty acorns, but gastronomy is a serious matter. The Constituent Assembly of 1789 ruined the fortunes of the presiding judge of the Bordeaux *parlement* and thus of his master chef, one Nicolas Doyen, who went travelling around France in search of work. On arriving in Strasbourg he met Clause, and suggested to him the use of the truffle, an essential flavouring in the south-east of France, where he came from. Clause added truffles to his *pâté à la Contades*, and Doyen opened a shop of his own, where he sold an identical *pâté de foie gras*. The competition did no one any harm, and indeed demand was such that it became necessary to have both of them supplying it. Some decades later, perhaps with some injustice towards Périgord, Alexandre Dumas said that, 'As everyone knows, the *foie gras* of Strasbourg is reputed to be the king of pâtés.'

Today *pâté de foie gras* has yielded first place in the gastronomic hierarchy to plain *foie gras entier*, enthroned in simple majesty. But although the two great *foie gras* regions, south-eastern France (the Dordogne, Gers, Lot, Landes, the Pyrénées-Atlantiques, the Haute-Garonne) and Alsace (the Haut-Rhin and the Bas-Rhin), still share production between them, epicures are divided into two camps: those who prefer the *foie gras* of Alsace, and those who claim supremacy for *foie gras* from the south-east.

In Alsace *foie gras* is cooked with an assortment of some 15 spices. Alcohol is added in the south-west. Certain purists in both camps, however, prefer to leave the liver exactly as it is, adding only a little salt. The different methods of cooking produce Alsatian *foie gras*, highly flavoured, slightly grey in colour, and south-eastern *foie gras*, plainer, with a sweet, nutty flavour, and pink as a baby's bottom. Finally, there has been a fashion in recent years for duck *foie gras*, which now accounts for 20 per cent of sales. It is a little cheaper, and is more rustic in character, with a slight bitter after-taste varying according to the locality.

Duck *foie gras* may also benefit by encouraging the blatant chauvinism situated in the pit of the stomach of every French gourmet. The fact is, though one hardly likes to admit it – but truth will out – that goose *foie gras* supposed to be from the Périgord, Gers, Alsace, etc., may now come from almost anywhere: Hungary, Czechoslovakia, Austria, Poland, Israel. Why? Because more and more of it is being eaten. In 1980 the French alone ate 500,000 kilos; 300,000 kilos were exported – and all this with national production amounting to just 400,000 kilos! It is easy to work out that in 1980 half of this French *foie gras* was not actually of French origin at all, and in 1984 two out of three allegedly French goose livers were foreign.

Indignation is misplaced; the law of the market-place prevails. Originally *foie gras* was a seasonal food eaten on festive occasions at the end of the agricultural year. Geese were hatched in spring and crammed in autumn. Today there is demand for *foie gras* all the year round. And as a representative of a group of manufacturers has pointed out, gastronomic juries find it very difficult to tell the difference between French and foreign goose livers, since there *is* no difference. A *foie gras* is equally good whether the bird it came from was reared in Bergerac or Tel Aviv. The vital secret is to cook it in the French way – and sell it under a French label. If the French do not buy the raw material for it outside France, other countries can make *foie gras* and sell it instead: this is a phenomenon beginning to be seen in Eastern Europe, for instance. Ducks are easier to rear than geese, they resist disease better, and are more amenable to cramming, so less labour is required. Although their livers contains more fat than goose livers – 50 per cent instead of 30 per cent – French production of *foie gras* from Barbary ducks and mallards is almost enough to provide for home consumption of duck *foie gras*; production of goose *foie gras* is another matter.

Some manufacturers, however, insist that their top-of-the-range *foie gras* (sold as *foie gras entier*) comes entirely from French fowls. They guarantee provenance with a label: red for geese, green for ducks. However, there is no legal compulsion to observe this practice, which is purely for advertising purposes; legal standards simply oblige the producer to state where the *foie gras* was cooked and packed. In the next kind down on the scale (*bloc de foie gras*), the chunks of whole liver visible in the purée may be mentioned in advertising as coming from French geese if the manufacturer wants to make a selling point of it (and of course if his claim is true), but there is no law obliging him to do so. Of course if the liver really is French, no manufacturer will fail to proclaim the fact in large lettering. These pieces of liver, 50 per cent of total weight in the finished product in the goose *foie gras*, 35 per cent in the duck *foie gras*, are set in a forcemeat of puréed *foie gras* which is definitely of foreign and therefore unspecified origin. Does their fear of losing sales really prevent manufacturers from being clear, precise and frank about the whole thing? Even allowing for the necessity of safeguarding a prestigious economic sector, surely the consumer would surely like to know the provenance of something he is buying at a price which in itself is no joke. No one would insist on knowing the proportions of the forcemeat surrounding the chunks of liver: 25 per cent of its ingredients are veal, pork or poultry (i.e., turkey). The forcemeat is simply described as 'traditional', 'farmhouse', or just *farce*, 'forcemeat', without any further literary flourishes, which hardly tells the consumer much more. What is the point of advising people to read the labels of their purchases when the labels themselves are uninformative? There is no point, as I have said, in waxing indignant about it, but nonetheless there is no need for all this mystery.

A future prospect may please lovers of *foie gras*, deriving from work done in the laboratories of INRA, the Institut National de la Recherche Agronomique, at its experimental station at Artiguères in the Landes area. Electric cramming has already become increasingly common, to facilitate the rearing and feeding of the geese (manual cramming takes a lot of time and labour), and now the scientists have succeeded in making the geese bulimic. The trick is simply to destroy the brain centres regulating appetite, situated in the hypothalamus. The goose is anaesthetized, trepanned, and an electrode is inserted into the base of the brain. A very brief electric shock of a few milli-ampères destroys the carefully located zone in the hypothalamus. For a week the goose will eat and eat, under artificial light; it is hallucinating. Then its frantic behaviour gradually decreases as the cells grow again. The treatment can be repeated if necessary, and within a few days the goose achieves a weight it would reach only after a month of manual cramming. An injection of chemical substances into the bird's brain can be substituted for the electric shock. Results are even more spectacular, and the bird greatly exceeds normal weight.

At the moment this research is purely a matter of scientific experiment, and French farmers, anxious about their customers, do not seem very enthusiastic. The question is, will farmers in other countries feel the same? The *foie gras* obtained as a result of such experiments is as normal as any other liver, if normal is the right word, given their unnatural size. However, although we may happily eat what is, when all is said and done, a diabetic liver, what about schizophrenic liver? Might we end up as mad as the Romans ourselves?

To return to our feast of *foie gras*, another important question arises: to add truffles or not to add truffles? Until 1981 *foie gras* without truffles was described as *naturel*, plain. This is no longer a legal description in France. However, if truffles are added, the fact must be stated. The amount of truffle is 3 per cent of total weight in the very best *foie gras*, *foie gras entier*, and 1 per cent in pâtés, purées and mousses. If there are no truffles in the *foie gras*, the label says nothing.

The fact is, *foie gras* is to be savoured for itself, and so are truffles. Their

431

association is not gastronomically obligatory. Indeed, purists hold that adding truffles to *foie gras* detracts from its unique quality. Rather than pay a high price for a few tiny particles of truffle which are supposed to make the pâté particularly choice, but which some people push carefully to the side of the plate, it would be more discerning and even creative to invest the difference in price between *foie gras* with truffles and *foie gras* without by buying a fine whole truffle, fresh, raw, to be lovingly cooked in a gentle oven for about 15 minutes larded with a very thin slice of bacon seasoned with salt and pepper, and wrapped in real paper, not aluminium foil. This delicacy could then be cut into very thin slices and placed on slices of *foie gras* for who those like to combine the two. That would be true gastronomy.

Another point of gastronomy is to serve *foie gras* correctly: chilled, but not over-chilled, as a first course or as a second course after some *hors-d'oeuvres*. The can or terrine should be put on the middle shelf of the refrigerator the night before the pâté is to be eaten. It is opened an hour before serving and left in a cool place for the flavours to 'breathe' and develop, like the bouquet of a good wine. Regular slices are cut with a knife, the blade being dipped in hot water between each slice, or if the pâté is in a terrine you spoon the wonderful stuff out: again, dipping the spoon in hot water. In neither case should salad be served with it; the acidity of a vinaigrette dressing would kill the flavour. Those who are particularly fond of *foie gras* eat it with a fork, but it can also be enjoyed on very lightly toasted fresh bread, without butter. Never with rye bread, *pain de campagne* or biscuits, which would be a sin.

The right thing to drink with *foie gras* is also the subject of much discussion. Tastes vary from region to region of France. In the south-west a Sauternes or a venerable Jurançon is chosen; a Meursault will also do very well. Pineau des Charentes is drunk in Angoulême. All these wines should be very well chilled. Port has its adherents, though some people think it too strong. The same applies to Madeira and sherry. The people of Bordeaux swear by Saint-Émilion. In Gascony, the rustic but magnificent duck liver pâté is accompanied by a powerful Madiran red. The Alsatians claim that their own Riesling, Sylvaner and Gewürztraminer wines were made for their own *foie gras*, or the other way round. As usual, most people will agree to drink champagne. But whatever wine you choose, only a very fine one will do.

Facts about Foie Gras

French law allows the description *foie gras* to be applied to any product containing only – and at least – 20 per cent of *foie gras* of goose or duck. *Foie gras entier*, goose or duck, is 100 per cent liver: one lobe, several lobes or part of a lobe, depending on the amount sold. It may come in a terrine, a can or a roll. Truffled *foie gras entier* contains at least 3 per cent of its weight in truffles.

The simple description *foie gras* denotes pieces of goose or duck liver surrounded with forcemeat (meat and liver of pork, veal, and/or poultry) or larded with a thin slice of bacon. Depending on price, the proportion of goose or duck liver may vary from 20 to 50 per cent. It will be indicated on the label. The proportion of truffle, if included, must be at least 3 per cent, as with the *entier* kind described above.

Bloc de foie gras, goose or duck, must contain at least 50 per cent of whole goose liver or 35 per cent of whole duck liver, visible when it is cut. The pieces are bound with a purée of *foie gras* and surrounded by the same forcemeat as the *foie gras* above, or by a thin slice of bacon, and if truffles are included the proportion is still 3 per cent.

Parfait de foie gras, goose or duck, consists of small pieces of liver mashed and moulded, surrounded by the same forcemeat and/or a thin slice of bacon, and if truffle is added the proportion is 3 per cent.

Pâté de foie gras, of goose or duck liver, contains a minimum 50 per cent of *foie gras* at the centre, consisting of mashed pieces as used in the *parfait*, surrounded by the classic forcemeat or a special forcemeat recipe, and sometimes by a thin slice of bacon. The word *truffé* implies the presence of only 1 per cent of the pâté's total weight in truffles.

Galantine de foie gras, of goose or duck, is a mixture of pieces of *foie gras* and of forcemeat, with at least 35 per cent of the pieces of liver distributed through it showing. It is said to be truffled if it contains 1 per cent of its total weight in truffles.

Purée or *mousse de foie gras*, of goose or duck or both, is made of 50 per cent of *foie gras* and 50 per cent forcemeat, crushed and mixed together. It is said to be truffled if it contains 1 per cent of its total weight in truffles.

The truffles used for the top-of-the-range *foie gras* are usually whole, and the manufacturers make sure you know it. Cheaper kinds use truffle peelings.

Foie gras described as *mi-cuit*, half-cooked, has been cooked at a temperature below 100 degrees centigrade, is only partially preserved, and should be kept at a temperature of 2 degrees and eaten within six months.

Foie gras described as *de conserve*, preserved, has been sterilized, and should be kept at a temperature of 10 to 15 degrees. It is best left to mature for a year before it is eaten.

The date of manufacture should be fully and clearly shown on all labels.

The Symbolism of Liver

According to the Roman poet Horace, the liver is the seat of the passions, particularly sensual love and anger. According to Suetonius, it is the centre of the intelligence and the mind. Since the *foie gras* we eat comes from geese, it need not present us with any metaphysical problems – the stupidity of a 'silly goose', after all, is proverbial – but it is true that consuming it provides a sensual, almost voluptuous pleasure.

The liver is traditionally linked to connotations of gall or bile. In the *Sou-wen*, the basis of all Chinese medicine, eating liver is supposed to engender strength and courage. In fact liver is very rich in iron. In the various related Chinese languages, the same word is used to express the concepts of the liver, bile and courage. The Chinese of very ancient times used to eat the livers of their enemies, thus both paying tribute to their courage even in defeat, and ensuring that there was nothing more to fear from them. The enemies were guaranteed to be dead, and the victors assimilated their courage along with their livers.

Examination of the livers of sacrificed animals was a method used by Roman soothsayers to predict the future. Later, tablets of terracotta were made representing livers, engraved with mysterious signs which were so many instruments of divination.

The History of Truffles

In his Fifth Satire, Juvenal describes a social climber called Virro, amusing himself by humiliating his guests of humble origin – his 'clients' in the Latin sense of the word – by serving them a menu as poor as themselves, while he himself feasts ostentatiously before their eyes on sumptuous dishes. 'Before the master is put a huge goose's liver, a capon as big as a goose, and a boar, piping hot, worthy of yellow-haired Meleager's steel. Then will come truffles, if it be spring-time and the longed-for thunder have enlarged our dinners. "Keep your corn to yourself, O Libya!" says Alledius; "unyoke your oxen, if only you send us truffles!"'

Lucullus, a true epicure and a well-educated man, also gave truffles a place of honour on his table. No recorded mention of truffles is found until the fifth century BC, when we are told that a metic, or resident alien in Athens, received the rights of citizenship in return for a dish of truffles prepared in an original manner. In the *Symposium* of Philoxenus of Leucadia, a work which has nothing in common with Plato's *Symposium* but its name, being a poem of purely gastronomic content, we are told that truffles baked in the embers are conducive to amorous play. This widespread belief would go far to account for the high esteem in which truffles have always been held were it not for the fact that they are also absolutely delicious. According to Brantôme the *dames galantes* of the sixteenth century, the amorous ladies of the French court, thought highly of truffles: 'And I have heard say that some ladies often consume pies made of the testicles of young cockerels, and artichoke bottoms, and truffles, and other delicacies, which they eat hot.' The cockerel's testicles were supposed to have a stimulating effect, like artichokes and truffles.

The truffle adds the attraction of mystery to its magical fragrance and supposedly aphrodisiac qualities. Speculation about its origin persisted over a long period and the explanations provided by classical writers on scientific subjects did little to solve the riddle. Theophrastus, Aristotle's disciple and successor, is content to report that 'It is said they are born of autumn rains, and if there is no rain or claps of thunder, being more plentiful in the latter case, for a flash of lightning is the principal cause of them.'

The Greeks and Romans did not even agree on the nature of truffles. Nicander, 100 years after Theophrastus, was inclined to think they were silt modified 'by internal heat'. Another century and a half finds Plutarch believing that they were mud cooked by lightning. Apicius was interested only in methods of preparing them. Martial lets them speak for themselves in one of his *Epigrams* (Book XIII, 1): 'We truffles that burst through the nurturing soil with our soft heads are of earth's apples second to mushrooms.' Finally, Galen prescribed truffles to his patients – it is true that they included the emperors Marcus Aurelius and Commodus – 'for the truffle is very nourishing, and causes general excitation, conducive to sensual pleasure.' Perhaps prudently, nature has made the truffle very rare.

However, it appears that the truffles of antiquity were not the same as ours. Martial describes them as bursting through the soil. Juvenal says they are gathered in spring. According to Pliny, they were reddish, black or white and no larger than a quince;[19] reddish yellow, says Dioscorides. The nouns *udnon* in Greek and *tuber* in Latin have been translated as 'truffle', but *tuber* defines any lump or excrescence. *Terrae tuber*, excrescence of the earth, has also been translated as the morel mushroom. The *tuber* of antiquity, with a few exceptions, was more probably what is now called *terfas*, mushrooms of tubercular shape which come up from underground and are common in marly soils all around the Mediterranean; they have a powerful flavour.

However, genuine truffles were served at the wedding feast of Charles VI of France and Isabeau of Bavaria in 1385. The luxury-loving duc Jean de Berry, of the *Très riches heures*, had introduced his brother to them. His household accounts record frequent payments for truffles in autumn. A trusted servant of the duchess brought them to Paris (Jeanne of Armagnac lived in Berry and made gastronomic purchases there on her husband's behalf).[20] The evidence of the account books is that the truffles came from Berry.

> ... À la cour souveraine
> Ou plusieurs sont par ce fruit attendant
> De pis avoir que d'accès de Tierçayne.

[... at the royal court, where several persons, by waiting for this fruit, are in worse case than if they had a tertian fever.]

If these lines of Eustache Deschamps[21] are to be believed, it would seem that the King of France's courtiers had also acquired a taste for truffles. Deschamps, born at Vertus in Champagne about 1346, soldier or diplomat as circumstances required under both Charles V and Charles VI, was a solemn bore who set up as a satirical poet in his spare time, if outright ill will deserves to be called satire. His *Miroir du mariage* is an attack on women, and the *Ballade contre la trufle* expresses his contempt for the 'black diamonds'. The whole poem, from which the three lines above come, would not be unworthy of Savonarola. Take this verse:

> C'est racine d'orrible vision
> Que l'on feret bien à fondre contrefaire
> Noire est dehors mais sa décohection
> Eschauffe trop, le goût en put et flaire.
> Celui qui, premièrement,
> La desterra fut cause de tourment.
> Par la bouche se met l'erbe vilaine
> J'en ai mangé dont mon las cueur se sent
> De pis avoir que d'accès de Tierçayne.

[It is a root of horrible appearance, which one would do well to disguise. It is black outside, but in decoction it overheats, and the flavour stinks and smells of that. He who first dug it up was the cause of trouble. This unpleasant plant is taken by mouth. I have eaten of it, and it left my weary heart in worse case than if I had a tertian fever.]

Doubt has been cast on the identification of these truffles from Berry with the classic Périgord truffle (*Tuber melanosporum*). The term 'Périgord truffle' is a botanical description, in the same way as we speak of Brussels sprouts or Savoy cabbage without any particular reference to the region where the vegetables were actually grown. It just so happens that the Périgord is an area preferred by *Tuber melanosporum*. Deschamps describes the truffles he despises as black on the outside. It has been thought that this implies the inside of the truffle was a different colour. The black-skinned white truffle – *Tuber aestivum*, the cook's truffle, and the only kind found in the United Kingdom – is gathered in May, confirming Juvenal's comment. The truffle Deschamps disliked was an autumn truffle, as the account books of the Hôtel de Berry confirm. It is therefore more logical to take his statement about its black exterior as meaning simply that its general appearance was black.

Périgord truffles are found not only in the Dordogne but in Aunis, Saintonge and indeed in Berry; they are also found in Savoie and particularly in the Vaucluse (the comtat Venaissan) and the Alpes de Haute-Provence. The Périgord legend claims that they were brought there by Pope John XXII in the early fourteenth century; he was a canon at Saint-Front de Périgueux and archpriest of Sarlat. If the legend were true it would, as we shall see, be little short of miraculous.

The Périgordins also claim that Provençal truffles are 'degenerate' and the only Périgord truffle worthy of the name is found in the Dordogne and a small part of the Quercy area. However, the truffle-lovers of the Haute-Vienne will have nothing to do with such notions. I have even met Provençals who are genuinely surprised to hear that truffles may be found outside the Luberon and 'their' Alps. Altogether, the truffle is clearly something about which its producers feel very sensitive. It may be small, but it is worth its weight in diamonds. Outside France and the provinces mentioned above, two other European nations claim to be the principal truffle producers in the world, and the fact is that France, Spain and Italy are the three major producers, with almost equal quantities of truffles depending on the year. And they are almost the only producers. Taking one year with another, their annual production is 50 tonnes each. For purposes of comparison, worldwide annual production of gold is 1,561.9 tonnes and of platinum 85 tonnes. Over a period of 20 centuries, 230 tonnes of diamonds have been found.

None of these three countries will take the other two major truffle producers seriously. Italy believes French truffles to be mere rumour and Spanish truffles a bad joke. Spain knows only one truffle, the Spanish sort. France simply dismisses the truffles of the other two countries as impossible.

In fact, in the absence of climatic disasters, production of the Spanish Périgord truffle is a few kilos ahead of French truffle production. When the French run out of their own truffles – and that means every year – they are quite happy enough to get them from the other side of the Pyrenees. In 1980 France imported 30 tonnes of Spanish truffles and gave them the prestigious description 'French'. Italy slipped France 20 tonnes while no one was looking. Portugal produces truffles too; Switzerland, Germany, Austria, Czechoslovakia and Yugoslavia also produce the few kilos which the French find they need to round up their figures. The French truffle market has orders amounting to 400 tonnes a year: 200 tonnes of fresh and 200 tonnes of canned truffles. The same problem arises as with *foie gras*, and even more acutely: France itself can produce only 10 per cent of the truffles it sells.

Brillat-Savarin called the truffle the 'black diamond' of cuisine, and, like diamonds, it is never, or hardly ever, to be found when and where it is wanted. The truffle is a vegetable, but it cannot be cultivated.

Truffles appear, if they feel like it, near a host plant (for instance, the oak called the *truffier* or truffle oak, certain hazels, and certain Austrian pines). They exist in a kind of symbiotic relationship with this host plant, by virtue of mixed organs or mycorrhizae (from Greek *mukes*, mushroom, and *rhiza*, root). Appearing no one knows how or why, these mycorrhizae cover the rootlets of the tree with dense tufts of filaments, measuring some two millimetres long by one thick, and are yellow to brown in colour. They convey mineral nourishment from the surrounding soil to the tree, which provides organic matter in return.

It has long been known that the truffle fly, which rejoices in the charming name of *Helomyza tuberivora*, burrows into the ground to lay its eggs where truffles are found. It used to be thought that the fly penetrated the roots of the oak and produced an excrescence similar to a nut gall, which became a truffle. In fact the truffle fly seeks out the truffles themselves, to lay its eggs there. The larvae which hatch out can then feast on the spot, and who can blame them?

The truffle is a fungus which reproduces by means of spores. As in all such fungi, the dissemination and germination of these spores produces mycelium, a substance stretching over an area of 20 centimetres below ground, in filaments called hyphae. These hyphae are simply non-differentiated cells. The mycelium may take a month, a year or several years before coming into contact with the rootlets of the tree in its life. Where it does, the mycorrhizae which produce the truffles form. The boletus mushroom reproduces in the same way, and it is interesting to note that the boletus is the mushroom referred to by Martial in connection with truffles.

There are several kinds of true truffles (*Tuber*). Périgord truffles are black both inside and out. Others, black outside and white inside, the 'cook's truffles' mentioned above, are *Tuber aestivum*. Others again are entirely white: these are the white truffles of Alba, the pride of Piedmont. Their faintly garlicky flavour is different from that of the black truffle. As I have said, the French refuse to recognize the white truffle; the Piedmontese recognize no other. It is inaccurately called *Tuber magnatum*, the enormous truffle. The weight of a truffle, either black or white, may vary by a few grams, but most of them weigh between 20 and 200 grams.

Black or white, the truffle is well hidden. Around their chosen trees, however, there is a circle five to ten metres in diameter where grass does not grow and the earth looks as if it had been scorched, proof of the voracity of the mycelium which draws nutrients from the soil. The oak itself does not look very healthy, and indeed the symbiosis is greatly in the truffle's favour: it is an underground vandal. However, in exceptional cases it does observe the terms of its contract. One of these cases is the holm oak of the Jardin des Arènes in Périgueux, a venerable and vigorous tree; the municipal gardeners busy around it with their spades in November are not employed solely in collecting dead leaves.

Truffles are gathered in October and November. In May, a small protuberance of the mycelium appears not far from a mycorrhiza. This is the truffle. By August it is the size of a hazelnut, but approaching the critical stage for truffles. Summer rains may rot it. In wet years the harvest is very poor: only a few kilos. If the summer is particularly dry, however, the truffles are dehydrated and disappear again, unless the tree, identified and well pruned, offers enough shade to prevent evaporation. What the black diamond prefers is violent summer storms, as the classical writers noticed. A French proverb says that 'if rain pours down on St Bartholomew's Day, there will be truffles in plenty'. The correct humidity can be maintained if the truffle beds, known or suspected, are lightly covered with branches. It has also been found that a sprinkling of phosphoric acid helps the development of truffles.

You do not harvest truffles, you hunt them. The truffle hunter – known as a *caveur* or *rabassier* in France – needs good legs, patience, and a close understanding of nature. The criterion of the truffle's maturity is not only its colour – black as coal – but its incomparable fragrance. Since truffles are buried underground, anyone who tells you his sense of smell leads him to it is having you on. The fact is that truffle beds can be recognized by the 'scorched earth' around them. Digging into the truffle bed at random is a sure way to destroy the mycelium. Truffles are not potatoes. The truffle hunter therefore uses his natural allies to lead him straight to the spot. The most obliging tracker of truffles is the fly mentioned above, *Helomyza tuberivora*, and it provides its services free. Around the middle of a misty day, or even better, when there is a slight drizzle to bring out the odours of the ground, the heavy insect appears, not whirling in the air as is sometimes claimed, but apparently just happening to pass that way. Without showing much enthusiasm, it comes down on the area, explores it, smells and recognizes the truffles. If the truffle bed is a rich one, or the truffles seem to be very fine, more flies will soon turn up, again as if by chance. The first comer then defends its territory, and there may even be a fight. The truffle hunter, coming up quietly, sweeps the soil to remove a fine layer of earth: the fly, heavy with eggs, will not be impatient when it wants to strike a good vein of truffles. It flies lazily away and comes back to settle several times in succession at the same spot. There will certainly be a truffle there. The truffle hunter picks up a handful of earth and smells it for the typical odour. Then, flat on his stomach, he gently excavates with his iron-tipped stick. If a small red beetle, *Liodes annamonea*, is found indignantly scrabbling in the soil, which suddenly seems much moister, or if a cigar-coloured earthworm wriggles away, he has hit the jackpot. Using his stick and his fingers, the truffle hunter continues digging until he finds his treasure.

The truffle must not be broken as he carefully extracts it from the surrounding matter. It may be a black diamond, but it is more fragile than glass. He slips his fingers under it, gently twisting to aid the 'birth' of his treasure, and then lifts it to his nostrils. He may be going to sell the truffle, but its fragrance rewards him. Finally, he carefully fills in the hole again.

Hunting with the aid of truffle flies is not an option for everyone, since it calls for a particular skill. The classic method is to use a pig or a dog. Foxes and badgers have also been used to hunt, and rabbit-hunters use ferrets.[22]

The truffle-hunting pig is usually a sow. At other seasons she produces her annual litter of a dozen piglets. Sows are better at the job than hogs or castrated pigs; they are gentler and less capricious. A truffle-hunting sow will have been trained from the age of a few weeks by being occasionally fed poor quality truffles, which she loves. However, she may sometimes develop a perverse taste for their poor quality, and then she ignores the best truffles and makes straight for rotting tubers. There is nothing to be done about that: the sow digs up truffles for her own pleasure and not as a kindness to her master. Her sense of smell detects the truffles from very far off. Once she has identified the spot, a well-trained sow will turn aside at once to ask for her reward of a handful of maize. While she eats it the truffle hunter swiftly extracts the truffle from the earth surrounding it. But sometimes the sow misbehaves and snaps up the black treasure she was supposed to find, not to eat. Then a tap on the snout from the truffle hunter's iron-tipped stick makes her drop the object of the crime. In the Périgord countryside, around All Saints' Day, some curious teams can be seen: truffle hunters in small cars with

A truffle hunter: anonymous engraving of 1891

trailers in which their sows are lolling at their ease. You do not need a lorry to bring the harvest home. In good years 25 kilos a day may be found, a magnificent haul.

In Provence truffle-hunters use dogs; over the last two centuries the Provençals have forgotten that they once had a special liking for pork. German shepherds, spaniels, fox terriers, poodles and even dachshunds make excellent truffle hounds. Unlike the sow, dogs do not care for truffles. All they are interested in is the reward they have been trained to recognize as associated with the truffle odour. Police dogs are trained in the same way. The sow digs with her snout; the dog instinctively scrapes at the soil with its paws, and must be prevented, both to avoid damage and because the dog's paws themselves are relatively fragile. Both sows and dogs, learning cunning from humans, may be untruthful and pretend to have made a discovery in order to get the reward.

So far all that would-be truffle growers have been able to do is maintain or improve natural truffle beds. Attempts have been made to create beds by planting selected trees or sowing acorns from truffle oaks in suitable places, where other crops cannot be cultivated. But planned truffle cultivation is still a dream. Although it has long been possible to make the spores of truffles grow in laboratory conditions, the result of outdoor sowing has never been successful. Attempts have also been made to raise oaks from the acorns of truffle-bearing trees, in humus from a truffle bed, and then replant them to create new beds. When the project does succeed, however, it may be because the terrain chosen was suitable anyway. In fact no attempt to grow truffles by the direct culture of laboratory-produced mycelium near roots susceptible to mycorrhization has yet produced results. The 'seed truffles' advertised for sale in the French press are pure deception.

And should industrial truffle cultivation become feasible some day, might that not make the truffles less interesting and detract from their value and prestige? Gold, diamonds and truffles can none of them really be manufactured.

The truffle fairs of Périguex, Sarlat, Thiviers and Forcalquier, and the similar fair of Alba in Piedmont, are remarkable occasions. Big commercial fairs are all to do with groups of businessmen who take no real interest in them, but the individual stocks of truffle hunters can more often be weighed in hectograms than kilograms. Nor are the truffles actually on display. You can smell them, and you know they are there because the whole area is bathed in their fragrance.

The truffle hunters of Périgord carry small baskets covered with cloths, in which the truffles lie, traditionally nestling in coffee filters, while the Piedmontese truffle hunter gravely paces around the hall in Alba, one hand in his pocket, the other Napoleonically tucked into his waistcoat. He keeps himself to himself, and does not look directly at anyone. A customer approaches: the truffle hunter turns, raising one shoulder slightly. This is not a ritual gesture, but indicates that he is taking a newspaper-wrapped packet out from between his jacket and his shirt. He undoes it furtively as he turns, holding the offering in his open left hand right under the customer's nose. Prices are mentioned, like an exchange of passwords. Agreement is reached or not, as the case may be. By midday everything has been sold and the truffles have gone. All that is left is a wonderful fragrance wafting through the streets of the town.

PART VI

The Middle Ages, a time of profitable trading in various specific foods, were

THE ERA OF THE MERCHANTS

Making a Good Profit

If we could travel back in history in a time machine, and it could stop and hover so that we could look down on medieval Europe, we should get the impression of observing an ant-heap. Not because the population of the period was so large – far from it – but because of all the activity, the busy coming and going of traffic between one town and another by road, river and sea. This was also the age of pilgrimages and crusades, and those who had faith, or simply a spirit of adventure, were not deterred by distance, bad weather or brigands.

> D'aqui se part lo bon Blondin
> E va ss'en par l'estrech camin;
>   E intra s'en per lo boscage
> Com bon cavallier de parage.
>   Apertatment el va sercar
>   Ventura, si porria trobar.

[Then Blandin leaves that place and takes to the narrow road. Deep into the forest he goes, like an honourable knight. He hopes to see if he can find adventure without further delay.][1]

Bearing in mind the physical difficulties of going on any journey at the time, one can only marvel at these enthusiastic, indefatigable, ever-curious travellers. They included merchants, long known by the nickname of *pieds poudreux*, dusty feet – the phrase became 'piepowders' in English – even when they were wealthy enough to ride mules or drive vehicles. They went from castle to castle, town to town, country to country, and they took with them news, ideas, knowledge, progress.

The planet was far more sparsely populated than today, when it has something like four billion inhabitants. However, no accurate assessment of the medieval population can be made in terms of actual figures, frustrating as the fact is to statisticians and the historians they serve. The Romans had a passion for censuses and accounts, but after the fall of the Roman Empire and in the chaos that followed the barbarian invasions no one was counting heads. In England, the Domesday Book, the survey of the country begun on the orders of William the Conqueror in 1085, gave details of the ownership of land and stock and some account of the numbers of peasants on various estates; it was compiled chiefly to give the king an estimate of the value of his lands, and for taxation purposes. In France, no assessment can be made until a census of the kingdom was taken around 1250, and any figures drawn from that are vague and incomplete, like the reckoning in the Domesday Book. The French census had two purposes: it was intended as an inventory of mouths to be fed, so that the necessary provisions could be calculated in advance, but most important, again like Domesday, it was an aid to fixing taxation. The principal tax, the *queste*, depended on the concept of the *feu*, literally the 'fire', the hearth or family home. But modern historians have been unable to determine in what relation the real hearth stood to the fiscal hearth, which involved the concept of solvency. For the population figures to have any meaning they would need to cover not just the solvent but those who, although also solvent, were exempt from taxation – the nobility and the clergy – not to mention all the people who managed to elude those agents of the king or the feudal lords who visited their homes. Then again, one must take into account the demographic fluctuations caused over five centuries by war, epidemic disease and famine.

At a rough reckoning, Fernand Braudel thinks an average of 69 million inhabitants is likely for medieval Europe. England, for which most references are available, had a population of about 3,757,500 in 1348, before the Black Death, which left the country with only 2,073,279 in the next generation in 1377. Another generation on, in 1400, the population had risen to 2,100,000, and was to be the same 30 years later. It is estimated that the Black Death killed over one-fifth of the people of Europe in 1350. The Italian plagues were even more disastrous.

As a whole Europe, and indeed the planet, was almost entirely populated by peasants; the rural peasantry made up 80 to 90 per cent of the population. Nonetheless, there were a great many towns, almost as many as exist now, despite periods of decline. Food supplies in general, those natural fruits of the earth which were not then subject to any industrial processing, except sometimes on a very small scale in home industries, were extremely sensitive to shortages. It was a vicious circle: the causes or effects of demographic depression – epidemics, wars, famines – also decimated the agricultural labour force and the livestock, and ruined harvests when disastrous weather had not already done so. Shortages drove the rural population out of the country, which no longer provided either security or food, and into the towns. When danger threatens, instinct always impels people to form groups and unite against it. Moreover, towns pursued the policy of the provident ant, and unlike rural areas kept some food stocks in reserve. As we saw in the chapter on cereals, governments have always encouraged the building of granaries. (In the two world wars of the twentieth century, particularly the 1939–45 war, the situation was reversed and the black market flourished; the peasants had learnt their lesson.)

As Braudel cogently puts it, 'all demographic tension involves … nutritional choices (affecting meat and bread in particular), and either agricultural change or widespread recourse to immigration.' The brief Ice Age of the fourteenth century thus hindered the Vikings in their expansion towards Greenland and, by delaying the European seizure of the Americas for two centuries, encouraged the initiative of the Hispano-Portuguese conquistadores of the early sixteenth century at a time when the change of climate, putting an end to deep-sea fishing of herring, cod and whale, had greatly changed the way of life of northern Europe, its farming activities and its whole economy.

Rising again from the Gallo-Roman urban structures destroyed by the barbarians, and inhabited by only about 10 per cent of the population, the towns were to become masters of the economic game from the eleventh century onwards. The town, born of the division of labour, does not produce food but represents what are called the 'tertiary industries'; it consumes and processes food. According to the theory of Georges Dumézil, it is the material embodiment of the three Indo-European power functions: religious, economic and political. Although it would be interesting to look at the first function in connection with the third, I shall consider only the second and third here. It may fairly be said, with Georges Duby, that the economic function was typical of the medieval town, however small it was. That function created it, or rather fertilized the ashes from which it sprang. And economic expansion capable of extending beyond the narrow regional context depended on the expansion of the towns. Urban topography – squares, market places, town halls – was determined by the town's economic function. The town became the magnet attracting all who, whether they liked it or not, no longer had a place in rural society, and not only them: the shelter it offered to owners of property, its lighted streets, its security and comfort also attracted those whose business it was to sell things.

Before the tenth century spices, like all valuable and exotic merchandise such as silk and cotton textiles, jewellery, curios, oil, precious stones and perfumes, were offered to the very select group of customers rich enough to buy them by travelling Levantine or Jewish merchants who formed into groups for reasons of security, moving in convoys along the bad roads and navigable waterways of Europe. These caravans were often joined by companies of entertainers.

After the year 1000, however, the Western world entered upon a period of great commercial expansion, initially condemned by the Church, which saw it as likely to encourage usury and the making of easy profits. This commercial expansion took concrete shape in the great fairs, succeeding local markets, where merchants met at certain fixed dates. Surplus produce from the estates of both the Church and, to a lesser extent, the secular feudal lords, was sold there, or sometimes bartered, for cash was a rare commodity. The fairs lasted several weeks, and closed on the eve of some religious festival. One such was the 'Lendit' fair held at Saint-Denis near Paris under the aegis of the abbey of that name, between the feasts of St Barnabas (11th June) and St John (24th June). The Fair of Saint-Germain, set up by Louis XI, lasted from Candlemas until Passion Sunday and was held in the vicinity of Saint-Germain-des-Prés; the monks themselves took charge of the renting and administration of sites for stalls at these fairs and made a good profit out of it. The best-known English fair was Bartholomew Fair, held annually in London for seven centuries, which opened on St Bartholomew's Day. Merchants came to these fairs bringing silks, furs and exotic foods from eastern European fairs such as Novgorod, goods which had come in caravans from Central Asia or Asia Minor and on up the Russian rivers. First and foremost, the fairs were wholesale markets where retailers bought their stocks.

When Europe became urbanized, from Carolingian times onwards, towns set themselves entirely apart from the countryside. The walls that began to arise around them showed that they were separate. Within these walls, originally stout palisades propped up by earthworks, a citadel was established (a borough, *bourg*, *Burg*, *portus* or *vik*, depending on its whereabouts in Europe), where the citizens carried out activities which were chiefly concerned with consumption. This borough was in a way the umbilical cord between the countryside that provided food and the people living in the shelter of the town. As we saw earlier, it was soon realized that some of their activities were likely to endanger the town buildings, perhaps by fire (the bakeries) or by the disease and bad smells they might cause (butchers' shops). Other activities, such as milling, needed water. All these were banished outside the walls into 'faux-bourgs', false boroughs, whence modern French *faubourg*, suburb. Records of the surrounding enclosures show that initially trades connected with the food supply were moved out towards the perimeter; then the attempt to do so was gradually abandoned, and they were taken into the heart of the city again, often in specialized quarters.

The spice trade, however, although it was no longer the nomadic affair of the past, still dealt in luxury products for the richest citizens of the towns, and required protection because of the value of the stocks the merchants held. They thus found themselves immediately situated in a place of honour and security at the city centre, conveniently close to the central market (*marché*, *mercato*, *mercado*, *Markt*, etc.). Being bourgeois in the old sense of the word, since they were burgesses, citizens of the borough, and also in the modern sense, since they were socially superior to other provisions merchants, the spice merchants carried enough weight to take part in civic administration. 'From the first', writes Robert Delors, 'the merchants, along with certain administrators and landed proprietors, constituted the most dynamic element in the new town.'[3] Nor are we speaking here of those great magnates of the spice trade who became bankers because of the requirements of international commerce.

All the medieval trading towns, large or small, worked like cogs in a vast machine, the movement of one involving the movement of the others in a system of exchanges and interlocking associations. The towns themselves were governed by administrators who, though they might not produce anything directly, initiated and encouraged food production in the surrounding countryside (whether the land there was owned by citizens or by feudal lords who themselves traded with the surplus of their feudal revenues), and in the suburbs supervised food processing and preservation and the first beginnings of industry that went beyond the craft stage. The towns also attracted, as if by some magnetic force, commercial products from farther afield: spices, grain and wine, not to mention manufactured goods, leather and skins, metal and fuels – although we are not concerned with such items here. Merchandise was not necessarily purchased in the place where it arrived; it could be sent on elsewhere.

Commercial exchange of this kind, between one town and another along the civic communications network, required a suitable climate to work well: it needed liberty. The civic authorities had a single aim in mind: if they were to trade freely, they must escape the authority of the local prince, sacred or secular. Florence, conversely, lost much of its credibility and dynamism when the Medici merchants made themselves dukes; Amsterdam, on the other hand, derived advantage from the energy of the new Dutch Republic. The free town attracted both capital and profiteers as a dog attracts fleas.

In 1187 and 1190 Marseilles, which had made itself a kind of republic administered by consuls and was the model of a Mediterranean port, having provided food, ships and troops for the Crusades, received thanks in the shape of commercial and judicial freedom, along with the Lebanese and Syrian ports which had fallen into Frankish hands. For the record, the citizens met to discuss important political or commercial affairs in the Accoules cemetery.

In the Old Port of Marseilles, quite a new port at the time, many ships from other Mediterranean ports landed spices from the Levant, leather and slaves from the African coast opposite, grain from Sicily, oil from Catalonia, etc. All these cargoes were swiftly exchanged for Flanders cloth which had come down from the fairs of Champagne by river. Soon Norman, Portuguese and Flemish ships were casting anchor off Marseilles as well. Strange as it may seem, the city became one of the chief centres of the Atlantic cod trade; the fish was distributed inland and enriched Marseilles even more than fish from the local deep-water creeks. This state of affairs continued for a long time. The Marseilles year-book of 1782 records an 'abstract of the manifests of the 1500 cargo vessels that came in during that period', listing 560 quintals (a quintal was about a hundredweight) of fresh cod and 288 barrels of salt cod from north Germany, 216 casks of cod oil and 8955 quintals of cod from England, and 260 packages of stockfish and 146 casks of whale oil from Spain, to mention only a few of the items.

Auxerre was another notable centre of Continental trade. Fra Salimbene commented in 1245 that 'The people of that country do not sow seed, or bring in the harvest, or gather their crops into granaries. All they need do is send their wine to Paris down the nearest river flowing to the city, and the sale of the wine there makes them a good profit which pays for all their food and clothing.'

While the freedom of towns might seem to provide ideal conditions for economic prosperity, trade between them also had to be conducted smoothly. In many places, however, the feudal lords were a thorn in the flesh of the merchants, who had to pay tolls on all the roads they used. The burgesses made many representations to their sovereigns, protesting against this practice. To take only the example of France, Philippe Auguste (Philippe II, who reigned from 1180 to 1223) was well aware that it was in his interests not to let the commercial life of the kingdom be strangled, and those lords who abused their position soon learned to fear his wrath. Eudes de Déols, son of a great seigneur in Berry who was accused of fleecing merchants on the roads, was summoned to appear in court, and in 1216 the Comte de Beaumont was forced to revise his tariff of tolls and dues payable on goods coming down the river Oise or crossing its bridges.

Tolls were a major source of revenue on many great feudal estates. The right to levy them could be ceded as a fief or an outright gift by the lords to whom they belonged. Hugues de Lusignan, who founded the abbey of Valence in 1230, granted it the rights to the local tolls and to the taxes on the fair which was held near the abbey over three days at the festival of St Denis. Sometimes the proceeds of tolls levied in this way were set aside to maintain a certain number of the sick in a hospice or a monastery, or to help support the monks – the money was often spent on their shoes.

Tolls, like other feudal dues arbitrarily levied by the lords, might include some bizarre conditions. Drivers of carts or drovers of livestock often had to discharge the toll by giving the lord's stewards one of the items they were transporting. Several of the king's officers acquired rights to fees in kind in this way, or to the payment of a sum of money for merchandise passing through Paris by either road or river.

In some places the tolls were not as heavy a burden as in Paris. Around 1093, Robert III, Comte de Meulan, known as 'Le Preud'homme', granted the abbey of Préaux remission of the taxes due to him on wines in the town of Mantes. The abbey had already obtained a similar remission in Meulan, granted by Comte Hugues II (d. 1079). Robert made one not very costly condition: the men steering the boats carrying the wine were to play the flageolet as they passed under the windows of the Comtesse de Meulan's apartments.

The charter listing the tolls due to the barons of Lescun was no less curious, and includes these provisions:

> A horse with four white feet is free of toll.
>
> A cart loaded with fish shall pay four sous and two deniers, and a carp and a pike of those carried by the merchant to whom the fish belongs, to be chosen from one of the casks in the said cart at the pleasure of the lord of Lescun or his tax farmer.
>
> A man carrying a load of glasses, and going on his way, and having bottles with him, shall pay two deniers, and if he then displays his wares in the lands of the said baron, he owes the second glass at the pleasure of the said lord of Lescun, and the said lord baron will give the merchant the glass full of wine.

The cherries which the people of Groslay in the Val d'Oise brought to Saint-Denis were exempt from road tolls after a woman of Groslay, who had taken her fruit to sell it at the fair, was detained there because she could not pay. While she was gone the baby she had left at home almost died of hunger, and the lady Richilde de Groslay, moved by this sad story, gave the abbey certain properties in return for the remission of the toll so that no such thing should happen again.

Throughout France, even the keenest toll collectors did not insist on seeing the merchandise unpacked; they were satisfied with the merchant's declaration on oath of the amount and value of his goods. Such was the respect for a sworn oath, even among humble folk and pedlars, that lies were never told.

However, the tolls had proliferated to such an extent and with a few exceptions were so heavy a burden that they were a great obstacle to trade. A highly significant fifteenth-century document is evidence of the importance of trade in Orléans at this period, and of the difficulties that faced merchants travelling along the Loire. The demands of the local lords were a severe inconvenience to them. They put up with it until the fifteenth century, when the merchants of Orléans formed themselves into an 'assembly of deputies of the merchants of the city who navigate and frequent the river Loire' for their mutual protection. Its headquarters was the Hôtel de l'Autruche. Delegations from almost all the trading towns between the Seine and the Loire soon gathered there. Three resolutions of the city of Nantes concerning elections are like three small municipal monuments to the place. The deputies were salaried officials, and had their own bursar and clerks, and their treasurer to collect the levy the King had allowed merchants of towns to impose on themselves. They also had lawyers at the presidial court of Orléans and the *parlement* or high court in Paris.

This confederation of merchants progressively enfranchised the river Loire. In 1429, the Seigneur de Fromentières tried to take more than was his due as set out in his tariff of tolls at Saint-Michau; a legal officer instantly served him notice from the king commanding him to cease his extortions, and when he refused he was taken to court. In 1451 the Sire de Ronignac, seigneur of Meance-sur-l'Allier, seized the cargo of a vessel that had been wrecked in the river Allier. He too was brought to court, for the merchants' association was anxious to protect navigation on the tributaries of the Loire as well as the main river. It lost no time in bringing charges, the merchants' case was laid before the court, and the Seigneur de Meance had to return the goods and pay expenses. After 1498 the association, which had already successfully resisted extortionate demands by the feudal lords, found itself facing the excessive zeal of the toll inspectors. It applied to the Court of Aids (roughly equivalent to a modern Board of Customs and Excise), which issued several decrees, sternly warning the inspectors:

> You are in future to visit the vessels of salt merchants only when they land to sell their cargoes. You are not, gluttons that you are, to cause yourselves to be invited to dinner. And when the vessels of the merchants shall be navigating in the middle of the river, go out in a boat to collect the toll. And if you do not wish to go to them, do not force them to come to you so long as, in passing by, they cast you the money inside a turnip, an apple or a cleft stick.

Victorious over the feudal system for a second time, most notably as represented by the widow of the Seigneur de Montjean, née Princesse de Bourbon, and Juvénal des Ursins, whose family, citing penance as a pretext, was levying excessive quantities of dues from the cargoes of figs and raisins carried by ships passing beneath their towers, the association next attacked the clergy, and obtained further injunctions. One was issued against the Chapter of Saint-Martin of Tours in 1525, another against the Chapter of Saint-Aubin of Angers in 1529. Nor was that all: the association also took on municipal councils such as the town council of Decize, which was levying a toll on ships to pay for the building of a bridge. In 1606 charges were brought against Decize in the King's Council, and once again the merchants won their case. However, under Louis XIV's reforming finance minister Colbert, the association had nothing to do but see that the dykes and hydraulic engineering of the Loire were kept in good order.

This confederation of the merchants of the Loire was not the only body to organize itself in such a way. On the Seine the issue of the free circulation of goods loomed even larger because it concerned the capital. Merchants came from Paris to Auxerre, as mentioned above, to sell salt and buy wine. In 1200 the Comte d'Auxerre, Pierre de Courtenai, decided to contest their right. As one man, the burgesses of Auxerre and of Paris appealed to the king, and the count had to issue a statement solemnly recognizing that he had committed an *excessum*, an abuse of power. Philippe Auguste was extremely supportive of merchants transporting their goods by water. Those of them based in Paris united in a kind of corporation called a *hanse*[4] (from a Middle High German word meaning 'company', particularly well known through the Hansa or Hanseatic League of German towns).

They had various disagreements over their spheres of influence with the *hanses* of other river ports along the Seine and its tributaries. The Normans of Rouen, for instance, wanted to sell their salt, either Atlantic sea salt or the 'boiled salt' made in England directly, without intermediaries. The king intervened personally in the negotiations, and in 1210 he made the merchants of Paris and Rouen swear an oath of mutual fidelity. The Rouen merchants might sell their salt freely, but under the authority of a sworn official licensed by the Paris *hanse*. This was rather in the nature of a judgement of Solomon, and did not go down well with the Normans, who complained, not without some justice, that after three centuries they were still regarded as foreigners. Rouen encountered yet another display of xenophobia when its merchants were forbidden to bring wines of Aquitaine and Anjou which had come up the Atlantic coast into the country by water from the mouth of the Seine, while the Paris *hanse* was freely allowed to send wines of 'France' and Burgundy down the river. In fact the chief concern was to protect those two wines and promote sales of them to England and northern Europe, for the wines of 'France' were difficult to export.[5]

There was another constant threat to trade: at this period foreign merchants were held jointly liable for debts incurred or extortion committed by their countrymen. The times were very troubled, and this code of solidarity, although customary, was invoked at the slightest occasion and greatly complicated the merchants' lives with the various risks they ran of having their goods confiscated. However, in 1185, when Philippe Auguste was at war with the Count of Flanders –

a circumstance which itself aggravated the situation of 'proxy' debtors – the Flemish merchants of the Ponthieu and Vermondois areas were granted freedom, protection and remission, so that they were able to attend the Lenten fair in Compiègne, where their brilliant commercial success was eventually likely to benefit the finances of the whole kingdom. In 1199, Philippe Auguste extended this favour to all merchants travelling in the north of France: 'Whosoever lays hands on them attacks our person.'

The fairs of Champagne were the crossroads where all Europe met. A 'Hansa of the Seventeen Towns' had been formed in the Low Countries to participate in them. The king found Italian merchants worth cultivating too. The Italians made their appearance in Champagne in the closing years of the century, and met the Flemish merchants there, so that each party travelled only half the distance. The meeting could equally well have been at Lyons, where many major roads and waterways met, but the counts of Champagne were particularly far-sighted for people of their time and their background. They organized, protected and in general rendered assistance to the series of six fairs in Champagne in an exemplary manner, providing the merchants with safe conduct, policing the fairs, and operating a system of jurisdiction which was to become the standard in all fairs of the known world even in the depths of Russia. Contracts were drawn up under this system. In England the special courts of justice at the fairs were known as Piepowder Courts, from the corruption of *pieds poudreux* (see above).

The Italians then created resident consulships for the fairs of Champagne, and the Catalans imitated them. The consul at first represented only a kind of *hanse*, an association of the merchants of some particular town (the Siennese set the ball rolling). He then came to represent the government of that town. Rather like the 'godfather' of a Mafia of Italian merchants, the consul settled differences between his own nationals or between them and the French, advanced loans and acted as a banker through a system of clearing agreements, ran a remarkably efficient postal service – and had a considerable body of secret agents firmly bound to him by credit. At the end of the fifteenth century this Italian espionage network was to be one of the foundation stones of Florentine banking, and the Medicis in particular made expert use of it until Louis XI of France lost patience and had the banks and their 'factors' and directors seized, or at least those of the latter who did not run fast enough in the direction of the Alps. This was the reason behind the imprisonment of Cardinal de La Balue, one of King Louis's ministers, for conspiring with Charles the Bold of Burgundy.

Initially there were about 15 consuls for the six fairs of Champagne; then all the Italians grouped themselves under one *capitano* who was even empowered to negotiate with the King of France on behalf of his principals. But when Philippe le Bel became Comte de Champagne, excessive taxation in the form of discriminatory measures against Jews and Lombards (and Florentines and Genoese as well) heralded the decline of the fairs of Champagne, at a time when the fairs of Lagny and Saint-Denis were making Paris increasingly important in any case.

It was at this period that the papacy was moved to Avignon and what amounted to a shipping line, to which we shall return in a moment, came into existence. It served Venice, Genoa, Marseilles, Lisbon, Southampton and Bruges, diverting a considerable amount of traffic from the Mediterranean to Flanders along this new route. Another land route also came into use, running along the right bank of the Rhône, which belonged to the German Holy Roman Empire; it started in Italy and passed through Avignon, Switzerland and along the Rhine on its way to the Low Countries.

Finally, the Low Countries themselves and Italy may be regarded as the two poles between which the economic currents of medieval Europe moved. For geographical reasons, however, the Mediterranean Sea remained the preserve of the Mediterranean peoples, particularly as regarded the spice market, which was bitterly disputed by the Genoese and the Venetians. Northerners might not enter Mediterranean waters except on sufferance, and they had to pay for the privilege.

It was when they looked east, where Marco Polo, in his day, was intoxicated by the spice-laden fragrance of the warehouses, that the trading and maritime cities of the Middle Ages found prosperity like that once enjoyed by Carthage to the great displeasure of Rome. Venice, Genoa, Marseilles, the ports of the Hanseatic League and of Flanders fought with or against Constantinople for their share of the markets. One of the real reasons for the Crusades was to secure the Lebanese shores where caravan routes ended and Frankish ships put in. It was essential for the Bosphorus, the only passage to the Black Sea and the Central Asian trade route, to remain open to Christian traffic; religion was brought into it only for conscience's sake.

In the long battle for control of the spice market in Europe, the Italians and particularly the Venetians proved the winners, and not just by virtue of their business acumen. As cunning as all their competitors and customers combined, they were to use or abuse their local advantages to ensure that they had a finger in every pie: business, diplomacy (if what to some extent was extortion and duplicity may be called diplomacy), even ship-building.

Venice was the first Italian state to help itself to the market. Its geographical situation and a combination of historical events gave it the advantage. From the time of its emergence as a separate power, in theory around the year 1000, it had been protected by its patron Byzantium, on which it originally depended and in whose shade it grew quietly while no one noticed that its teeth had been growing too. At the same time as Venice came to the end of its apprenticeship, the Mediterranean was seeing a revival of the naval activity which had stagnated during the centuries of insecurity and improvisation that followed the slow death agony of the Roman Empire of the West.

Strategically situated between the Black Sea and the Mediterranean, an intermediary in every sense of the word between the Slav world in the process of construction, the Arab world in the process of expansion, and the Latin world that was sleeping with one eye open, Byzantium had never given up its own maritime activities, and we owe the uninterrupted evolution of ship-building to Byzantium. The vessels the Venetians built, and their expert handling of mercantile diplomacy, were both Byzantine legacies. So were Greek relations with Turkey, of which they were to take bold advantage.

Besides good relations, a swift, easily manoeuvrable fleet, able to defend itself if necessary, was a useful asset to merchants. They did not need enormous ships to carry merchandise as small in volume as it was profitable: spices. The new light ships, carracks[6] and caravels which appeared at the end of the fourteenth century had a stern rudder far more easily manipulated than the older kind, and square sails that could be set to suit the prevailing wind. Above all, they had primitive artillery: they carried Greek fire, something that inspired great respect.

When the Venetian Republic liberated itself from Byzantium, it also liberated the large islands of the central Mediterranean from Turkish rule and set up banking houses there, or placed any already in existence under its own control. It next recovered the Ionian archipelagos and Rhodes and set about procuring exotic merchandise from Tyre and Sidon, and also from the Nile delta where foods and spices from India and the East Indies ended their journey, coming in by way of the Red Sea. The Venetians set up depositories all around the Black Sea, at the gates of Russia itself. Their vessels never arrived empty, for in the west they took on board any cargo requiring rapid transport, such as slaves or the pilgrims who would often end up as slaves too. And finally, Marco Polo was a son of Venice.

On the west coast of the Italian peninsula Genoa, with a history going back to the fifth century BC, was an insignificant port by comparison with Naples and Ostia until the year 1000 (although in its day Carthage had thought it worth destroying). It began making its name by allying itself with Pisa to drive the Arabs out of Sardinia and Corsica. Intervening even in Spain, it continued cleaning up in the western Mediterranean until it was unchallenged master of those shores, for Marseilles was not anxious to take on the tedious burden of rule. Taking advantage of the disputes between Venice and its former protector Byzantium, even lending its fleet to Emperor Michael VIII Palaeologus to fight the Venetians, Genoa in its own turn obtained considerable privileges in the east, uniting with Marseilles to make a clean sweep of merchandise from the famous fair of Saint-Gilles in Arles. Despite the pontifical interdiction after the fall of Acre, the *mahones*, family companies of the typically Genoese stamp, continued to do business with the infidel. After the war which finally pitted them against the Venetians and ended with the compromise of 1381, Genoa gradually had to abandon the Near East, and turned towards the Atlantic trade, passing through the straits of Gibraltar.

Two great families of *mahones*, counting among their ranks many Genoese Doges, the Boccanegras and Zaccarias, provided vessels with Spanish Basque crews and plied between Flanders and England, in convoys of ten merchant vessels escorted by galleys carrying cargoes to the amount of 8000 tonnes burden in a single annual voyage. (In the middle of the fourteenth century England had no proper fleet or navy, and foreign merchants – Flemish, Iberian and Italian – could take advantage of the fact that it had not yet fully understood it was an island.) From then on passengers and merchants from the northern countries preferred travelling these long distances by sea rather than using the tedious and tiring roads where so many tolls had to be paid. Finally, as everyone knows, the Genoese explorer Christopher Columbus crossed the Atlantic and opened the door to a New World.

In this brief survey of the Middle Ages, it will have been obvious that international trade remained principally the prerogative of the free towns. Despite the efforts of Philippe Auguste, and perhaps because of the policies of Philippe le Bel, the commercial cities of France were eventually to be centralized. France as a whole suffered from that change, and over a long period. Of course the whole world was changing at the same time, taking on new dimensions, but France, still the direct route between the Mediterranean and Northern Europe, with rivers that might have been placed there for that very purpose, was now circumvented by new trade routes: west across the Atlantic, east through Germany. An equally serious drawback was the fact that the authorities could not tolerate private enterprise for long. Jacques Coeur, the famous fifteenth-century French merchant and financier who tried to take control of the spice market away from the Venetians and Genoese, was disowned by his royal patron Charles VII and only just saved from the disgrace of bankruptcy by the obvious injustice he had suffered. But France had missed her big chance on the stage of international trade, and in future would play only a minor part there.

Should the French deplore that fact? At least they could say that they, and they alone, came out of the business with reasonably clean hands.

Chapter 14

An Essential Food

The History of Salt

A metallic compound described by chemists as sodium chloride or NaCl, salt is not just the first among seasonings, as Ausonius described it, or even the first among preservatives: it is essential to the human organism. As early as the sixth century, Isidore of Seville stated that 'Nothing is more necessary than salt and sun.' It is as absolute a necessity as water. The essential function of salt is to maintain the equilibrium of the liquids or serum in the body; it must remain constant. We are in even more imminent danger of dehydration without salt than we are without water to drink.

This phenomenon was not discovered by scientists until the end of the nineteenth century, but people have always known that salt is indispensable to life. Animal instinct tells them so. Farm animals, for instance, need more salt than we do because of their greater weight, and they are so greedy for it, particularly in summer, that they can be seen licking walls to make up for any deficiency.

The average daily needs of an average adult are met by six to eight grams of salt a day, ten grams in very hot weather or when hard physical labour induces heavy water loss through sweating: if you lick the area above your upper lip with your tongue at such times you can taste the saltiness of your skin. This essential quantity of salt is naturally present in the food we eat. But in fact we eat more than we need, over 15 grams a day: salt is added to food in cooking, for its qualities as a condiment – it enhances flavour – and for its value as a preservative, in charcuterie and cured or pickled foods.[1] We also eat the hidden salt that helps the bread-making process and is found in fizzy drinks, cakes, cheese, even medicines.

According to Plutarch, who described it as 'the noblest of foods, the finest condiment of all', salt is a delicacy, in the sense that we take no pleasure or satisfaction in eating food which contains only the small amount of salt occurring in it naturally (seafood, however, contains a great deal). 'Can that which is unsavoury

457

be eaten without salt? or is there any taste in the white of an egg?' inquired Job (6, vi). The habit of adding salt at table, frequently acquired in childhood from parents with a passion for it, is a bad one. We are greedy for salt, just as we are greedy for sugar and fat; we are greedy for all consumer goods, but we need stimulation to enjoy them. This systematic excess encourages the ills of modern civilization: obesity, nephritis, arteriosclerosis and hypertension.

The 'developing' peoples generally eat much more sensibly than we do, an elementary fact that nutritionists never tire of stating, and that most of us never tire of denying by our way of life. The Eskimo people, for instance, add no salt to speak of to their traditional diet. They do not feel the need for it, since the food they eat, mainly meat, contains enough already, and the cold climate in which they live is the best of preservatives.[2] I should say they *used* not to add salt to their food, since civilization has brought them our bad habits and the disorders that go with them. To be fair, however, it must also be said that people living on a vegetarian diet, as they do, for instance, in many parts of India, suffer from a salt deficiency which is particularly obvious in very hot weather.

Jean-François Bergier,[3] in his *Une histoire du sel*, says that cannibalism has been put down to a need for salt, which is quite possible, since many magical or religious dietary practices have nutritional reasons behind them.

Jesus called his apostles 'the salt of the earth', and salt is found all over the world: properly used, it is necessary to protect life and avert corruption, exactly what might be expected on the spiritual level of any religious faith.

Acquiring salt, now universally obtainable in almost every country of the world in sufficient quantities for its own needs (both nutritional and industrial; salt has many uses in the chemicals industry), was a major preoccupation of humanity over a very long period. First, because not all its potential sources were known, and people were not very good at extracting it, and much was wasted. Second, because of the difficult logistical problem of transporting it.

> Salt has been the subject of intensive trading, the cause of speculation by producers and anxiety to consumers who could seldom be sure of sufficient supplies for long. It has been the reason behind commercial and political strategy, has enriched some and has impoverished others. In short, for dozens of generations salt held a position similar to that of oil in our own time.

Jean-François Bergier's comment may fairly be emended to 'hundreds of generations'. The history of salt preceded the history of mankind.

Where is salt found? Most people's first answer to that question will be: in the sea. On reflection, they will add: in salt mines. Gold and gems are other substances mined from the earth, and salt has sometimes been given the nickname of 'white gold'. It has earned the name.

Salt occurs everywhere, in the sea and in the soil. Its great abundance is a curious natural phenomenon. The oceans and certain lakes contain an average 30 to 35 grams of salt per litre of water. Warm seas, which evaporate more rapidly, are saltier than cold seas.[4] There are at least seven million square kilometres of sea salt on the planet. It is more difficult to estimate the total amount of deposits of rock salt or halite, but Bergier thinks there may be as much as 100,000 square kilometres in Germany alone. Such an estimate may be correct, but can hardly be applied on a global scale. The quantity and quality of salt present in a given area vary, depending on geographical, geological and climatic conditions, and even on the basins where the salt once formed and whether they were of a primary or tributary nature.

We do not know if the sea was salt from the first, and if so why (in that case water and salt would have a common origin), or whether it became salt over the millennia, fed by the waters flowing into it. No satisfactory explanation for the first hypothesis has yet been advanced. To the second, one may object that the rivers which feed the seas are not salt themselves. Although there are places where salt springs spout from the earth and seem to be leaching large deposits at varying depths, the magmatic rocks of the surface itself contain very little salt except in some isolated cases. Despite the rivers that have run into them for thousands upon thousands of years, the seas have never become any less salty, not even that residual, landlocked sea the Caspian. It would appear, therefore, that the seas have been salt since their formation, although we cannot say why. Subterranean salt deposits, which may be up to 5000 or 6000 metres thick, consist of a sediment with a crust on top: such former sea basins, of great antiquity and very often situated near oil fields, are hydrocarbons resulting from the transformation of other organic deposits, as in Texas, the Sahara and Romania. Under the mud and sand, the bed of the Mediterranean is covered with a layer of salt up to 1000 metres thick. These regions may once have been a torrid area on either side of a former equator that existed from the Cambrian to the Tertiary geological periods, in which case they indicate a certain shift in the earth's axis.

Rock salt also occurs on the earth's surface in the form of salt mountains such as Mount Slanic-Praborva in Romania; a massive salt deposit imprisoned underground has been forced into a domed shape by the pressure of the upper sedimentary layers and has gradually risen above its surroundings at the rate of one or two millimetres a year. Salt mountains never stop growing.

Table salt is made either by pulverizing blocks extracted from rock salt mines, or by dehydrating brine made from a solution of rock salt, or by the evaporation of sea water in salt-pans. There is no difference between sea salt and rock salt when they are both pure, but they seldom are, particularly sea salt, which occurs in its natural state accompanied by potassium and magnesium chloride and calcium and magnesium sulphates, all of them dissolved in the water of the sea. Sea salt also contains iodine (the iodine content may be increased in the salt-making process) and organic micro-particles. Rock salt is a mixture of sodium chlorate and a double

A hall in the mineral salt mine of Wieliczka in Poland, near Cracow, one of the largest mineral salt mines in the world. 'Four hundred metres down, over two hundred leagues long and over forty wide, the place is one huge block of salt. The galleries carved out of the salt are sometimes twice as high as the vault of a church. These vast galleries lead to great squares, chapels, houses, sheds and stables all made of salt. Many of the workers in this underground town are born, grow up, grow old and die there ...' (G. Jost and V. Humbert, 1912).

sulphate of sodium and calcium called *sllott*. Sea salt is made on shores offering certain facilities: a flat terrain, a sea warm enough for an adequate degree of salinity, a climate with plenty of sun and moderate, constant winds. Such conditions occur on a few Mediterranean coasts, on the Atlantic coast between Brittany and Ghana, the shores of the China Sea and Madagascar, and a number of coastal areas in the southern United States and Central and South America. But many countries are not so favoured; they discovered, very long ago, how to extract salt artificially: necessity is indeed the mother of invention.

Installations for collecting the salt in sea water are usually called salt-pans. The word salt-works is used here for works producing terrestrial salt – either rock salt or salt from brine springs – although it may be found applied to any kind of salt-manufacturing plant. In Europe suitable deposits of terrestrial salt are found over a rather homogeneous geographical area: eastern France, including Franche-Comté and Lorraine, the Lüneburg area of northern Germany, the Austrian Alps and the Carpathians. In Africa the subsoil and sometimes the surface soil of the Sahara shows that there was once a large sea there, and salt is also found in Ethiopia and Katanga. China is well off for salt deposits too. North America has some famous salt lakes and even a salt desert, where the Indians used to gather salt, unaware of the potential of the salt marshes until the colonists of the sixteenth century arrived.

The salt mines of continental Europe encouraged prehistoric peoples to settle down. The most famous example is Hallstatt in the Austrian Salzkammergut, a name that speaks for itself and a very prosperous place from the early period of the Bronze Age. Whenever Neolithic people settled down, abandoning hunting in favour of agriculture and reducing the amount of meat in their very carnivorous diet (although that was a gradual process), it was a great blessing to have a salt supply in the vicinity.

If you did not have such easy access to rock salt or sea salt, and you could not get it by purchase or barter, you obtained it from vegetal ash, green plants, even wood, or for obvious reasons seaweed. Someone must have tasted it one day and had a brilliant idea. However, salt derived from vegetable sources is more potassium than sodium chloride. The Canadian Indians continue to prefer salt from coltsfoot leaves or, lacking that, sea salt. Bernard Assiniwi, their Brillat-Savarin, says that 'rock salt kills the flavour of Indian foods'. Coltsfoot, which also makes a good infusion for chest complaints, is one of a group of plants described as halophilous or halophytic: they like salt, and their roots absorb sodium from the soil rather than potassium, like most plants. The saltwort or marsh samphire grazed by the bulls of the Camargue and Andalusia is a halophilous plant, and so are the grasses of the salt meadows of Normandy, which are flooded at the spring tides: that accounts for the succulence of the sheep which graze those pastures. The Masai, who drink blood from the veins of their oxen, as we saw above, find it is a way of ensuring that they get their daily ration of salt – for they are certainly not vegetarians, and may even in an emergency drink their livestock's urine.

Salt market at Mopti in Mali: the salt sold here is not pure, but still contains sodium and calcium sulphates which will be removed by further refining.

Salt left stranded on shore by the evaporation of sea water is highly visible because of its brilliance on the rocks and sands which are covered and uncovered again at high and low tide. At first it was scraped off; then someone thought of obtaining more by taking a thicker layer of sand, putting it in vessels and running fresh water through it, then boiling that water until it had completely evaporated. Pliny reported that 'the Gauls evaporate salt water over wood fires', and hundreds of years later, in the eighteenth century, the French again resorted to this method of winning salt to escape paying the salt tax. But it can hardly have been a solely Gaulish invention, since the Africans, Chinese and Polynesians all devised the same method, showing that when an idea is a good one it will be found in many parts of the world even though people have not communicated it to each other. This technique of boiling the brackish waters obtained by leaching the salt from sand was also employed, and much improved, by the people of Scandinavia, Great Britain and Ireland, until it became cheaper for them to buy imported salt at the

462

end of the Middle Ages because of the expenditure of energy involved and the question of fuel. Whole forests were burned to make this boiled salt.

In the Libyan Sahara, the 'salt culture' of Fezzan, of the third century BC to the sixth century of the present era, used to boil crusted salt taken from the bed of a former lake and refined by successive precipitations until an almost pure salt was obtained. While still hot the salt was pressed into a block; the same method is still employed in Niger today. These blocks of salt, curiously phallic in form, are wrapped in matting and transported by camel. Salt is still used as currency in the Sahelian and sub-Sahelian regions.

The Hallstatt mines, at an altitude of over 1000 metres above sea level in the heart of the Austrian Alps, were already being worked by the Celts of the tenth century BC. These people had a salt culture of their own, living for and by salt. They were highly skilled at digging galleries and shoring them up, and selling the salt they mined. The richness of the 2000 tombs around the site shows that they were extremely prosperous, owning jewels and other goods from all over Europe and the Middle East. Notwithstanding our notions of the primitive people of the times, the salt trade was already international big business. The many archeological finds, preserved in perfect condition by the salt, include the corpses of buried miners, picks, knapsacks to carry the blocks of salt, torches, and earthenware pots for evaporation and moulding the salt into slabs. All these things, besides the techniques used to support the galleries, are striking evidence that not all the people of those times were the primitive savages of the popular imagination.

In other places, at around the same period, water to wash down the seams of salt was conveyed along conduits of hollowed-out wood which have also been well preserved by the salt. The water thus acquired was boiled until it evaporated; the forests provided all the fuel the salt-makers needed. We can only imagine the intense activity, skill and business dealings of these workmen; we have no actual records, for they have left us no literature or works of art, although a skill expertly developed is a work of art in itself.

The appropriately named town of Salins is in Franche-Comté, an area rich in salt, and so are the famous salt-works at Arc-et-Senans, built by Louis XV's architect. Claude-Nicolas Ledoux built what amounted to an industrial complex, a fine semi-circular building (the sun falls directly on every part of it), combining monumental symbolism with practicality. For centuries before him, the site had a complex system of pipes conveying spring water, by means of chain pumps worked by horses, to make a brine which was evaporated by boiling. A sixteenth-century Flemish tapestry exhibited in the Louvre Museum gives a perfect picture of the heavy plant involved. Arc-et-Senans and Hallstatt show how a food as essential as salt can be a means of expression to mankind's many-sided genius, ranging from empirical ingenuity to visionary aesthetics. The isolation of Ledoux' monument and the defensive system surrounding it also betray some of the less pleasing aspects of mankind's concern with salt — something so necessary that it can easily be unscrupulously used as an instrument of power. There was more hypocrisy involved with wheat. Cereals and wine had their tutelary gods; salt had none. The legend of the nymph Salacia 'reported' by the French translator of Camoëns in his *Remarques sur la Lusiade* (Canto VI) should be regarded as an elegant fabrication of the kind men of letters did not hesitate to construct. He writes, 'The Harpies are sometimes taken for the wind personified, and, as is well known, wind increases the sound of the waves; we may say as much of the nymph Salacia, who personifies the salt of the sea; now salt gives the waves weight and solidity, which as they clash one against another or break upon the rocks makes them roar more loudly than if they were fresh water.' One would need further proof of that!

Salt was used only in food and diet, including its function as a preservative, until the discovery of chlorine by the Swedish physician Scheele[5] in 1774 and of soda by the surgeon of the Duc d'Orléans, Nicolas Leblanc, in 1791.[6] Previously, soda had been obtained by burning halophilous vegetation (this was the natron of Roman times). The chemist Liebig wrote: 'The manufacturing of soda by means of common salt may be regarded as the cause and principle of the great progress made in every field by modern industry.'

From the nineteenth century onwards, therefore, there were other uses for salt. Most salt production is now for industrial use. It goes into over 14,000 different products, while nutritional science and technology have enabled preservation by salting to be replaced by bottling and canning, freezing, freeze-drying and vacuum packing, methods which seem likely to be joined by irradiation. Similarly, the value and prestige of spices have dropped with the Renaissance. Tastes have changed since those days, and we are not so fond of very salty food, especially as the medical profession frequently condemns salt. In his day, Pliny praised salt as a panacea for all ills, but in modern medicine it has been replaced by chemical products derived from it, such as bicarbonate of soda and sodium sulphate.

The people of the ancient world, as I have mentioned, ate very salty food, particularly the Romans, who did nothing by halves. The Emperor Claudius, on entering the Senate one day, is said to have asked the senators whether a man could live without salt meat. That grave assembly no doubt thought as he did, for salt helped those in power to plan the economy of the national diet and avoid waste of food, making it easier to distribute provisions when seasonal or unexpected circumstances meant there was little access to fresh food.

Along the *Via Salaria*, the salt road, caravans of salt merchants came up to the Etrurian plains from the marshes of Ostia, which were enjoying the benefits of the general lowering of the sea level at the time. They stopped on the banks of the Tiber at the staging post which later became Rome, and where the local people came to exchange their own few products for the precious salt crystals. A market was set up, and it may truly be said that the Eternal City was born from salt.

Salt was also one reason for the Roman conquest of Gaul. The prosperity of the Phoenician trading posts of the western Mediterranean had already been built on salt. The Phoenicians were great producers of pickled food and garum, and Rome could not ignore such prosperity once she was powerful enough to make it her own. The most succulent of Gaulish charcuterie came from areas with salt-pans or salt-works: the Béarn, Franche-Comté and Bouches-du-Rhône, as we saw in the chapter on pork. However, the Germanic barbarians, who were stock-breeders rather than farmers, needed salt too. Tacitus describes the wars they waged with each other over the saline springs. There were saline springs and salt mines almost under the nose of the Helvetian chief Ariovistus in Gaulish Sequania; they were among the main reasons which impelled him to cross the frontier into Gaul. In 58 BC Divitiacus, speaking for the Aedui and Sequanii, appealed to Caesar to halt the invasion and defend Gaul against Ariovistus, saying in a gathering of the chiefs: 'In a few years all the natives will have been driven forth from the borders of Gaul, and all the Germans will have crossed the Rhine, for there can be no comparison between the Gallic and the German territory ...'[7]

Several times, as we shall see, salt may not actually have made history but did considerably influence its course. It is perhaps not too fanciful to recall that the salt of the Dead Sea was one reason for the interest the Romans took in Palestine; if they had not colonized that country the story of Christ and Christianity would have been quite different, and so might the face of the whole world.

Almost until the fourteenth century, then, huge quantities of meat, fish and vegetables were salted. Cheese was salted more than it is now, and so was bread, to make it rise and keep better (today it contains 12 grams of salt to a kilo of flour). Salt was also added to wine and beer. The Egyptians used earthenware jars as salting tubs – they can be seen on tomb paintings – while the Gauls progressed to using barrels and those wooden chests dear to peasant tradition, the kind from which St Nicholas in the legend revived the three little boys. Frugal as they were in general, the people of ancient times did add a little salt to their meals, and salt was the only seasoning St Patroclus allowed himself with his bread and water. In the early days of Rome its soldiers were given a handful of salt a day. The salt ration was subsequently replaced by a sum of money allowing each man to buy his own, and relieving the commissariat of the trouble of transporting it. The sum was a very small one because salt, necessary as it was and unlike spices, was never very expensive. (It became expensive only towards the thirteenth century when it was used as a means of taxation and people went without, a fact not unconnected with the famines and deficiencies that afflicted so many generations.) The money received by the Roman soldiers was their salt money, their *salarium* or salary. In medieval France the soldier's *sol*, the coin which was his pay, was known as his *solde*, still the modern French word for a soldier's or sailor's pay. The word gave rise to *soldat*; English 'soldier' comes from Middle English *souder*, deriving from Old French *soudier*, *soldier*, in the same way. A 'salary' then became the term for the payment of civilians.

For a long time salt was sold as large crystals, grey in the case of sea salt, whiter when it was rock salt. Regular household tasks included crushing it or refining it into the form in which it appeared on the tables of the rich, in the magnificent salt cellars or 'salts' created by great goldsmiths. The salt cellar of François I of

France, made by Benvenuto Cellini, is one of the finest surviving examples. In the fourteenth century the *Viandier de Paris* tells us how

> to make salt white: take one pint of coarse salt, and three pints of water, and put them on the fire until they are all melted together, then run it all through a cloth, towelling or worsted, then put it on the fire and boil it very hard, skimming it; and let it boil so long that it is almost dry, and the little bubbles which appeared on the water are not seen, then take the salt out of the pan and set it on a cloth in the sun to dry.

Precious because so vital, salt was bound to be a temptation to those who lacked it and an instrument of blackmail in the hands of those who did not. Even more serious was the fact that the possession of salt endangered its owner if he could not make sure of his own safety. In a society which depended on power relationships, the exploitation of salt (manufacturing, storing, transporting and distributing it) required the patronage and protection of the powerful. Moreover, salt was a very ancient symbol, a substance partaking of all four elements: earth, air, fire and water – 'fire freed from the waters of the earth by evaporation', according to the alchemists. Even though salt had no god as its guardian, the Greeks had thought it a divine gift. The vacant position of guardian passed to the civil power, the only authority capable of assuming it.

Royalty too was a divine gift, a divine right, and so, as monarchies succeeded the Roman empire, salt became the prince's prerogative. Most important of all, it was his right to control it. The first royal document we have concerning legislation relating to salt is an edict of the Lombard King Liutprand issued in 715. It regulates dealings in salt and imposes two taxes, one to be paid by salt merchants and the other by their customers.

Up to the end of the twelfth century the authority of most sovereigns was moral rather than real. Moreover, salt-pans and salt-works on the great feudal estates, both of secular lords and in particular of the Church, made up a large part of their revenues. In the same way as the monasteries ran the rural economy after the barbarian invasions, they efficiently managed salt-making operations over a long period. They had most of the skilled labour force at their disposal: to work for the monks was, in a way, like working for God. As with wheat and wine, the abbeys and monasteries provided most of the salt supplies of Europe.

Legacies and donations were always adding to the monasteries' property, though not necessarily in immediate proximity to the mother house. As with agricultural produce again, the monks had salt brought from outside – sometimes from 100 leagues away – to the monastery, which distributed it to its people for their daily domestic needs and to help them lay up stored provisions. They sent the surplus (which was the larger part) on to ports or to towns where agents sold it for them. The monks had also made themselves ship-owners. Those of St Victor of Marseilles, a monastery founded when Chilperic made it a gift of the salt-pans of Marseilles in 528, made salt at Hyères and then exported it. At the other end of Europe, the Chapter of Viborg took a valuable tithe from a Danish island at the entrance to the Baltic where the people extracted salt by boiling it, for no salt-pans could be laid out so far north.[8] Organization and procedures were much the same in Ireland and England. But the tolls levied on salt merchants passing through the estates where the monks maintained the roads and bridges in good condition provided a far higher yield, economizing on the responsibility, labour and skill involved in direct exploitation. Such merchants did not necessarily travel in convoys; the salt pedlar in the *Miracle de Saint-Germain* went from fair to fair on his donkey by himself.

The continental salt-works, manufacturing rock salt, which had usually been the property of the religious houses, gradually passed into the hands of laymen, the great lords or the civic associations. The mines of Lorraine in Franche-Comté, for instance, became joint-stock companies in the fifteenth century. Halle in Saxony and Lüneburg near Hamburg, the only Northern European source of rock salt, were in a similar position. The Polish salt-works, always in the hands of laymen, were leased out to foreign businessmen by the King of Poland in the fifteenth century. These businessmen included Jews, and so the country's large Jewish community was attracted to it. The Wieliczka mines, huge workings containing monuments carved into the salt, were leased to Jews until 1772. The Nazis, with a gruesome feeling for coincidence, made them into one of the worst Jewish concentration camps of the Second World War.

The history of the salt-pans of Provence, producing sea salt, is of great significance, because it is to them that the origin of the *gabelle* has been traced, the salt tax which was to darken the lives of French people all through the *ancien régime*. Between the twelfth and thirteenth centuries, the abbeys began to lose their monopoly of the food supply. The feudal system, having survived its own growing pains and the Crusades, began to feel like interesting itself in its own estates. The monasteries lost prestige and saw the numbers of their communities fall. This is one of the reasons for a certain change in their preoccupations, which henceforth became almost entirely spiritual: the Middle Ages saw the Provençal monasteries and the great dioceses of Arles, Marseilles, Agde, Béziers and Maguelonne cede their rights to or exploitation of salt-works to the local barons, who became salt lords, *domini salis*. The Baron of Fos, who already owned a port which competed with Marseilles and brought him profitable customs duties, acquired the salt-marshes of Fos, Saint-Mitre and Istres around the Étang de Berre. The Vicomte des Baux secured control of Martigues. Free towns such as Arles, Toulon and Hyères also became the owners of salt-works.

The whole of that area was subject to an overlord, the Comte de Provence, who at this period was himself a vassal not of the King of France but of the Emperor. Even in the nineteenth century, when the Rhône was still the best natural route for traffic between Arles and Lyons, as witness Alphonse Daudet's *Le petit chose*, watermen on the river used the word *empèri* (empire) for the left bank on the Alps side, and *rèiaume* (kingdom), for the right bank on the Ardèche side.

Charles of Anjou, St Louis's brother, who had acquired Provence as his appanage by his marriage with the daughter of Raimond Béranger, needed money at the height of his political ambitions to win control of the kingdom of Naples. With the blessing of the Emperor Frederick Barbarossa, he exercised the ancient royal right and made a compulsory purchase of the whole of his vassals' salt production at a price fixed by himself so as to sell it again at a profit, particularly in the area east of the Rhône: the Provençal Alps are stock-breeding and cheese-making country, the Ligurian coast lives by fishing. Charles enlisted the aid of such distributors of goods in the area as the Genoese, and made a fortune. However, after the fourteenth century this salt from Provence came into competition with salt from the 'kingdom', from the shores of Languedoc belonging to the King of France. The salt-pans of Peccais near Aigues-Mortes had been bought from the monks of Psalmody and the lords of Uzès by Philippe le Bel in 1290 and were mostly leased out to the Italian rivals of the Genoese, notably the Florentines of the Papal court in Avignon, men such as the Merchant of Prato, whose correspondence is quoted several times above. Then, in 1481, the whole of Provence except the Comtat Venaissin was joined to the kingdom of France again.

After 1286 Philippe realized that the monopoly system of the counts of Provence was exactly what he needed himself, short of money as he always was despite successive devaluations (he confiscated the money of the Jews and 'Lombards', and is also notorious for his destruction of the Order of the Temple). Even the name of the salt tax suggested a programme of coercion and the application of the law of the strongest: *gabelle* derives from a German word meaning 'tribute'. No tax was ever levied more arbitrarily, brought with it so many abuses, or aroused so much anger and rebellion. The peasants were the first to suffer from it, in view of their needs, particularly as some of the central provinces which were a long way from any coast or saline spring, and were said to be subject to the *grande gabelle*; they not only paid more for their salt but were obliged to buy it in arbitrarily fixed quantities. Of course the nobles, clergy and prominent citizens of the towns known as *franc-salé*, free of the salt tax, benefited by immunity. This tax was one of the chief causes of the French Revolution, and when the *États généraux* met all three Estates were at one in demanding its abolition, the more privileged citing all the trouble it caused as a reason. In a greatly diminished and modified form, however, a salt tax remained in existence until 1945.

Louis X, le Hutin (the Headstrong), set up a corps of royal officers to replace the salt merchants who had found the answer to the salt tax in innumerable forged and fraudulent documents. In 1331 Philippe VI went further and set up salt warehouses, each with its own local area of jurisdiction and the right to fix the official quota that had to be bought. The price of salt was subject to the decree of the king and his delegates, and rose according to the sovereign's needs, which meant all the time. Accordingly when a ransom had to be paid for Jean le Bon, held prisoner in England during the Hundred Years' War, the tax rose to six deniers. From being set at 8 sous under Charles V and 12 under Louis XI, it rose to 21 livres per *muid* (274 litres) in the time of François I and his Italian wars, since he too had to pay a ransom.

In 1553 Henri II replaced some of the particularly venal royal officers by farming out the sale of salt. Urgent needs led him to sell some provinces exemption from the tax for cash down. They passed the expense on to the people under their jurisdiction; the provinces concerned were Poitou, Aunis, Saintonge, Angoumois, Périgord and Limousin. The Béarn, with a great many salt springs which could not be checked, paid nothing, and Brittany escaped payment until 1675.

The tax, then, varied from province to province and even from town to town. The 'free' provinces paid from two to nine francs per 100 pounds of salt, others paid 20 francs, others again 33 or even 62, depending on the tax farmers-general. These differences were bound to create a contraband industry, and that entailed constant supervision of the system by a large staff. In the seventeenth century there were 25,000 *gabelle* collectors. And if the tax did not bring in enough for the king's funds, the farmer-general's profit and the customs men's salaries, then the 'salt duty', i.e., the amount to be bought per head (a minimum 3.6 kilos), was simply raised, whether the consumer needed that amount of salt or not, and so was the price. Fraud increased and multiplied. It was a desperate situation, and a nightmare for ordinary people who, to make matters worse, were expressly forbidden to sell their surplus. The tax farmers administering the *gabelle* made profits even more scandalously high than the king's. A grand house called the Hôtel Salé still stands in the Marais quarter of Paris; it was built by a tax farmer of the time of Louis XIV, and now houses the Picasso Museum. The monopoly was protected by the entire judiciary apparatus: the jurisdiction of the salt warehouses, the provosts' courts, the high courts, and so on and so forth. Furthermore, to ensure that magistrates were committed to the pursuit of lawbreakers, their salaries were calculated on a basis of the provincial yield of the *gabelle*. An informer received one-third of the *corpus delicti*.

Those who contravened the *gabelle* were treated as forgers. They were *faux sauniers*, dealers in clandestine salt, and the clandestine salt itself was described as 'false salt'. The only *real* salt belonged to the king. Dealing in clandestine salt was a crime and was severely punished. The famous and popular eighteenth-century 'brigand' Louis Mandrin was in fact no more than a dealer in clandestine salt. In 1780, according to Necker's *Traité de l'administration des finances de la France*, there were 3700 seizures of contraband salt and 2300 men were arrested on the roads. So were 1800 women and 6000 children. 1100 horses and 50 carts were confiscated. 2000 people were given prison sentences, and 300 were sent to the galleys for life. To check the contraband trade, Montesquieu protested, the authorities had resorted to the kind of severe penalties that were imposed on the worst of crimes. At the time of the Revolution there were dozens of children aged 12 to 15 among the 1800 persons convicted of dealing in contraband salt by the courts of Louis XVI, that good family man. Receipts from the *gabelle* doubled in his reign.

The people of France, their tempers wearing thin, frequently rebelled against the hated salt tax, which they reviled as the worst of calamities. Protests did no good, and every attempt at an uprising provoked ferocious massacres. There was rioting in Rheims, Dijon and Rouen in the fifteenth century; it was savagely put down. In 1548, after the edict of Châtellerault extending the *gabelle* to all the western provinces, what amounted to civil war broke out in Guyenne, and the royal troops were unable to cope with the 40,000 peasants who gathered around Cognac and Châteauneuf. The peasants, frenzied with rage, routed the soldiers and then seized Saintes and looted it. The entire countryside between Poitiers and Blaye was laid waste. The people of Bordeaux were the next to rise. The head of the administration, Tristan de Monneins, was cut to pieces and salted like a piglet. The Constable de Montmorency was sent to suppress the rebellion (Brantôme described him as 'that vulture who never says his prayers on campaign without ordering some hanging or other, the massacre of prisoners, and the burning of the countryside for a quarter of a league all around').

This pious man set up gallows all over Guyenne, marched into Bordeaux like a knife going through butter, disarmed the people and confiscated all the church bells. After fining the city 200,000 livres, he suspended its *parlement* for a year, picked 125 of the more prominent citizens to go and dig up what remained of the body of Monneins with their bare hands, and then had them hung or sent to the galleys. In 1549 the King annulled the *gabelle* of the western provinces in exchange for an 'indemnity' of 450,000 livres.

Colbert reorganized the *gabelle* with his ordinance of May 1680, but he did not suppress any of the abuses; far from it. He divided France into areas of the *grande gabelle* where salt was sold at 20 times its cost price, and of the *petite gabelle*, and he set up 17 boards with all their attendant tribunals, chairmen, procurators and controllers, not to mention countless parasites growing fat on the percentage they took from seizures.

In 1675, when Brittany, previously exempt from the *gabelle*, rose in its turn to back a league of 14 parishes, the parishes in question drew up their statutes, which became known as the 'Peasant's Code'. One article in this code laid down that 'It is forbidden, on pain of passing under the yoke, to entertain the *gabelle* or its children, or to furnish them with food or any other commodity. On the contrary, it is right to shoot at the *gabelle* as you would shoot a mad dog.' Paris had sent 6000 men against Concarneau, Douarnenez and Audierne. The country was laid waste, and those of the Breton fishermen of Newfoundland who were not hung found themselves back at the oars, but this time rowing the Sun King's galleys. In 1698 the man whose name was reviled by convicts behind the walls of the fortresses he had built for over two centuries, the great military engineer and marshal of France Sébastien Le Prestre de Vauban, became disgusted by the exactions of the *gabelle* and wrote a *Projet d'une dixme royale*, not published until 1707, when it was instantly seized by the police. He did not shrink from stating that 'salt is a kind of manna with which God has blessed the human race, and upon which, consequently, it would seem that no taxes should have been imposed.'

The *gabelle* was abolished in 1790, but Napoleon put a tax of two centimes a kilo on it in 1804, and that duty was maintained until 1945. It is still forbidden in French law for anyone to take so much as a litre of sea water without the permission of the Ministry of Finance. Today French salt-pans and salt-works (whether they are large companies or private enterprises) are all subject to the general taxation laws, and the only tax directly affecting salt is VAT.

However, the *gabelle* was not an exclusively French phenomenon. Some claim that both its name and its nature derive from Arab countries (*al quabala*). Be that as it may, the Normans of Sicily levied it in a form inherited from their Muslim predecessors as rulers of the island. In very early times, according to Pliny, the rulers of China and India derived more profit from their salt taxes than their gold mines. All states at all times, up to the end of the twentieth century in which I write, have applied taxation of some kind to salt. England, having forced its American colonists to use only duly taxed European salt, succeeded in making an even greater profit from its Indian Empire. But the abuses and general incoherence of the French *gabelle* make it the best example – or perhaps the worst – of its kind.

The economic, financial and indeed fiscal importance of salt can be understood only in the light of its significance in commercial trends, both national and international. It would take too long, and the subject has been discussed above, to go into the ancient world's entire economy of exchange at this point. But from the tenth century onwards, salt was a catalyst in the energetic activity distinguishing the economic flowering of the Middle Ages on which this chapter concentrates. The term 'catalyst', incidentally, is employed in chemistry in connection with salt, as it once was in alchemy. Symbolically as well as scientifically, salt is an intermediary.

Salt from Provence and Languedoc, setting out from the Mediterranean ports, 'that fringe of contact between Latin Christianity and the Islamic and Byzantine worlds' (Georges Duby), was distributed by sea, and some of it went back inland. 'Besides the "human livestock" destined for the Muslims of Spain', writes Guy Fourquin, 'and the oriental foods going to the Lower Rhône and Provence, there was a trade in regional produce which seems to have been maintained on a regular commercial basis in several cities. This was the trade in salt, which was taken to towns near the seaboard before going on inland. Salt from the salt-pans of Fos and Istres went to Arles. Narbonne was another crossroads of the trade.'[9] Guy Fourquin is writing of Provence, but the same thing was going on in Italy and the Iberian peninsula; in the case of northern Germany and the Lüneburg salt-works, and the salt-works of Poland, traffic went the other way, from the interior towards the coast. There was commercial activity anywhere that salt was made and distributed, which meant almost everywhere. And it would be inaccurate to think of the salt trade as purely regional. In the exchanges of salt between north and south it was usually coupled with the fish trade, for fish urgently needed salt so that it could be preserved and sent on to other markets. The Mediterranean and Atlantic coasts, from the Loire estuary to Gibraltar, had salt and/or fish to hand, but north of Brittany, as we have seen, salt-winning by evaporation had to be replaced by the boiling process, which was very tedious and impracticable for large quantities. Salt merchants, therefore, were welcome: to buy in southern parts of Europe, to sell farther north.

These merchants were not necessarily southerners themselves. Some were Vikings. Contrary to the popular notion, piracy was only one of the activities the Vikings pursued: the speciality of a few, so to speak. The fish trade brought in a regular income and would help them maintain their families at home, particularly as population increase and the requirements of fasting imposed by the Church kept the European market very open. The Vikings – also known as Norsemen and Normans – were already welcome in Northern Europe and Russia, from the Gulf of Finland to the Black Sea, venturing along even the most dangerous of river routes. Now they slowly but surely infiltrated the more southerly parts of Europe. Unrefined salt thus went north to return to Rouen, packed around Baltic and North Sea fish or salting Irish butter; it travelled along the Seine to the great fairs of the Parisian basin, the fairs of Saint-Denis, Provins and Champagne, from which the merchants came away with wine and wheat. At some point or other in their travels they might well also be carrying striped Flanders cloth (*pallia frisonica*), slaves, furs, metals or spices.

Fish was not the only frequent companion of salt. A combination of the salt and wine trades was also common along the Atlantic coast: not just Bordeaux wine but also wine from Charente, where salt-pans had been in use since Roman times. After the right to replant vines was granted to the whole of Gaul by Probus, the vineyard of Saintonge continued developing, and salt was to be a good advertising agent for it in more northerly countries from the ninth century onwards. Until the French Revolution, ships from northern Europe (with cargoes of wood and cereals from Prussia and Lithuania) and from England came down to Charente to load their vessels up again with salt, and casks of the local wine for ballast.

Salt from the Bay of Bourgneuf was not in fact of very good quality, because it had not been well refined. Consequently, it was cheap. Sold for cash down in northern ports, it fetched only half the price of the fine German rock salt of Lüneburg. It had another value, though; there was a political savour to this salt.

Until the fourteenth century England provided its own salt supplies by boiling sea water, even supplying its neighbours across the water in the Low Countries, Flanders, Frisia, Norway and Sweden. Then there was a small industrial revolution in the country as the cloth trade began to boom. Neither the masters nor their men had any more incentive to boil salt, particularly as their foreign customers were beginning to find it expensive by comparison with the sea salt of Lower Brittany. As they could hardly raise their prices higher still, the English almost entirely stopped producing their own salt and, following the example of other countries, they bought supplies in the 'Bay' (between Brittany and Poitou), thus economizing on financial outlay, labour, fuel and worries. One might expect the Hundred Years' War, then at its height, to have been an obstacle to this trade, but

France alone was at war with England, and Brittany was not yet part of France. Its dukes prudently remained neutral.

A tiny and even more neutral territory, a genuine no man's land, the Bay of Bourgneuf marked the border between Brittany and Poitou. More than a century before, a treaty between those two seigneuries had made it common ground, a kind of free zone. However, the actual owners of the Bay of Bourgneuf and its almost deserted coastline were all great nobles, abbeys or the citizens of towns, and all of those owed allegiance to the Duke of Brittany. Always a poor area, Brittany knew that the profitable salt trade at its gates had to be well guarded and fostered. As long as the province remained independent, i.e., until 1532, its dukes did all they could for the physical, moral and fiscal good of the salt manufacturers. The Kings of France continued that tradition quite closely. Lightly taxed, Bay salt was cheap to buy, and supply could never meet demand. It was a perfect example of the way to stimulate an economic revival by light taxation, an idea which has always appealed to economists and alarmed governments.

After the Hundred Years' War all Atlantic salt, whether from Brouage, Oléron, Ré or Bayonne, was known simply as Bay salt. Even Portuguese salt was included in that description. When the salt cod industry was at its most flourishing whole fleets came farther and farther south in search of salt. In line with the vicissitudes of international trade, there were small naval wars, acts of piracy which might be less picturesque than the boarding of caravels carrying heavy cargoes of valuable goods from the West Indies, but certainly gave the pirates good practice. Bay salt enabled the Scandinavians to consolidate the fisheries boom and their economy in general. They were no longer the poor relations of a Europe obsessed by lands at the other end of the world.

The Portuguese salt made at Setubal had a political role too. It was of very fine quality, very cheap despite the distance it had to travel (low payment of the Portuguese proletariat is not of recent date), and it attracted the attention of Danish and Dutch merchants when the Hundred Years' War assumed proportions which made the export of Bourgneuf salt by the Straits of Dover difficult. They accordingly obtained exclusive rights to Portuguese salt.

This agreement was initially good for Portugal's foreign trade, but it became a source of vexation to diplomats when, as we shall see in the chapter on spices below, the Dutch and the Portuguese became involved in a bitter dispute over the lands of the East Indies and Brazil where cloves and nutmegs grew. In 1669 Portugal paid the Dutch with Setubal salt to leave Brazil, and the Dutch made for Guiana instead.

Naturally those great spice merchants the Venetians had a salt trade too. When the Normans, formerly pirates and salt and fish merchants, now vassals of the King of France, were installed in Sicily, Calabria and the Balkans under Robert Guiscard, his brothers, nephews and cousins, they entered into competition with that other people who had found salt a good way into a commanding position in international trade, the people of Venice.

473

The south of Sardinia, which like the Balearic Islands belonged to Aragon, eastern Sicily, now in Norman hands, and Cyprus, held by the Crusaders, all produced a good deal of salt. The Venetians soon took to loading their ships with cargoes of salt either coming or going on their trading voyages. This infuriated the Genoese and thwarted the grasping Norman newcomers; it also brought good profits without any worries about production, since the Venetians much preferred to negotiate for foreign salt than to win their own from the sea around them – not the only paradoxical feature of the city of lagoons.

Venice had come into existence at the time of the eighth-century Lombard invasion, when the descendants of the old people of the Veneto who once lived on the coast had fled to the islands in the lagoon. They were fishermen and coastal traders, and until the end of the ninth century they were under the domination of Byzantium. Being very poor, they bartered their only produce, salt and fish, for consumer goods from the Continent – meat, wheat and cloth. Towards the year 800, however, this modest trade (and their willingness to serve the Greeks as mercenaries) had made them rich enough to fill the lagoon with the fine merchant vessels they built so well. A century later their fleet was of some consequence in the Mediterranean. They soon added the spice trade to their commerce in salt and fish and, most profitable of all, the trade in slaves bought or captured in Dalmatia. Now independent of Byzantium, Venice colonized the coasts of what were later to be Yugoslavia and Albania, both for the slaves and for the salt-pans on the Eastern shores of the Adriatic. (Marco Polo was descended from a Dalmatian family which had settled on the Grand Canal in 900.) Salt reached the French Alps and the Valais by the good offices of the Venetians. As Bergier says: 'Producing it themselves, but preferring to trade in salt made by others, the Venetians left their mark on the salt trade of the Mediterranean until the period of their city's sad decline.'

But for salt, incidentally, Venice would not have had St Mark. In 828 some Venetian merchants trading at Alexandria realized the dream of one of their number by stealing the saint's body from his coffin and hiding it in a cargo of salt. It is said that the Evangelist himself helped them to flee, unleashing a storm which drove them back to the Lido. On that day, Venice's fortune was made – and history is there to prove it.

The Symbolism of Salt

The whole symbolical value of salt, and all the ritual meanings attached to it, can be explained in the light of its origin and its practical uses. It purifies and protects food from corruption and putrefaction, which seems natural enough, since it comes from the sea, the primordial source of all life. In the symbolism of freemasonry, it represents life, the mother, the woman: the creative female principle as opposed to the destructive male principle personified by sulphur. As creator and thus regenerator, it accompanies the initiate towards the resurrection of a new life granted by the light. Similarly, in the Roman Catholic baptismal service, salt completes the purification of the holy water and destroys the soiling of corruption left by the traces of original sin. As a redemptive element it allows the soul thus purified to attain wisdom, the light of the faith. Even before Christianity, the Romans gave salt, and with it wisdom, to a newborn baby. The sacrificial victims of the Jews and Romans were purified with salt to make them acceptable to the Deity, and everyone knows that the Devil will offer you a saltless meal. If you feel suspicious, and ask for salt, his evil influence will be broken in the same way as the sign of the cross destroys it. A handful of salt is thrown into the fire on the hearth to keep away the demons who might be attracted to it. Salt is used in the exorcism rites of most religions.

Salt, the gift of God, is sacred. In the language of Malagasy the same word denotes the ideas of salt and sanctity: *fanasina* (the 's' is pronounced 'sh'). Hospitality, one of the most sacred and beautiful gestures in the world, was always closely associated with salt in the Eastern Mediterranean and Japan, and by the ancient Greeks. Hospitality is also connected with the sharing of bread and salt and the implied promise that no harm will be done to the guest. Like salt, a true bond of fraternity, a promise may not be corrupted or destroyed. Nothing can take the savour from salt. It never spoils or goes stale.

Spilt salt, therefore, means the breaking of that bond and the lapsing of protection from on high. The risk must be instantly averted by throwing a pinch of salt three times over your left shoulder, towards the evil spirits lurking in wait behind you. In Leonardo da Vinci's great painting of the Last Supper, he shows a spilt salt cellar under Judas's elbow.

The Marquis de Montrevel, a marshal of France famous for his courage on a score of battlefields, including the field of Fleurus, died of fright on 10 October 1716 when a clumsy person spilled the contents of a salt cellar over him. It was death by suggestion, and the poor man is cruelly mocked in Saint-Simon's *Memoirs*.

Spilt salt was so unlucky a sign that the Romans threw it on the ground of cities they had taken to make that ground sterile. So did the Hebrews – 'And Abimelech ... took the city, and slew the people that was therein, and beat down the city, and sowed it with salt' (Judges 9, xlv). We all know what happened to Lot's wife.

A little salt on food, then, makes it appetizing and wholesome, too much makes it inedible – and our superstitions, of course, are to be taken with a pinch of salt.

The Technique of Winning Salt

Sea water contains a solution of various salts, compound substances which may be described as deriving from an acid by the substitution of one or more atoms of metal for a chemically equivalent number of hydrogen atoms: $NaCl$, or sodium chlorate (70 per cent), $MgCl_2$ or magnesium chlorate (10.8%), $MgSO_4$ or magnesium sulphate (4.7 per cent), $CaSO_4$ or calcium sulphate (3.6%), K_2SO_4 or potassium sulphate (3.5%), etc. These salts may be regarded as electrolytes.

Electrolytes are substances (acids, bases and salts) which allow an electric current to pass through their aqueous solutions. Thus the molecule of NaCl, sodium chlorate, is electrolytically separated into two ions, atoms carrying an electrical charge: a positive iron or *cation* (sodium) and a negative ion or *anion* (chlorate). This explains why, among the elements dissolved by sea water, sodium and chlorate, the most abundantly present simple substances, can combine naturally and as it were completely when their concentration is increased by evaporation, thus producing sodium chlorate or common salt.

The salt extracted from sea water, saline springs or mines of rock salt is called *salt of first intention*, being a natural product which has not been submitted to any processing. Production techniques are of three kinds.

The agricultural technique: this description sounds odd if we think of agriculture as purely the growing of plants and the breeding of livestock. However, winning salt is an agricultural activity in that the salt is 'harvested' in the open air after various operations resembling cultivation. The agricultural technique is used solely for the salt-marshes or salt-pans to which sea water is conveyed in order to evaporate by the natural action of sun and wind. Climatic conditions have to be favourable. (To take France as an example, the salt-marshes of the Mediterranean coast cover a considerable surface area of some 10,000 hectares, producing about a million tonnes of salt a year.)

There are three stages to the operation: Water is brought from the sea and pumped into basins called *partènements*. It circulates from one basin to another until a concentration and saturation of 280 grams of salt per litre is achieved. This strong brine is then run into 'crystallizers' occupying, in the case of the salt-pans mentioned above, 770 hectares. Salt is deposited in these rectangular basins during the three sunniest months of the summer, between May and August, forming a layer ten centimetres thick. In September the salt is 'harvested'. Before the Second World War it was raked up by hand, but today the process is entirely mechanized. With excavators, it takes only a day to lift 30,000 tonnes of salt from a surface of ten hectares. The salt is piled up in storage areas; the heaps are called *camelles*, camels, perhaps because they look like a series of humps. They are covered with tiles for protection.

The salt-pans of the Atlantic coast use a system of three kinds of natural basins connecting with the ocean (and here, of course, the tidal phenomenon is involved). A large channel conveys water to the pans, which it enters through a wooden or cement conduit. The first basin contains sea water in the process of separation from the mud it contains. From there, the water goes on to the second basin through a *comladure*, a plank pierced with holes which the salter can shutter off to regulate the flow. The water is concentrated in these basins before moving on into the third kind of basin, the *saline*, where it is taken through sluices to the central compartments, the *oeillets* (eyelets). Gradually evaporating as it circulates in a spiral

Aerial view of the sea-salt depot at Salins de Giraud: mounds of salt piled up in this way can be over ten metres tall.

through the peripheral compartments, the water is very dense by the time it arrives at the centre. The salt deposited in these central compartments is raked out daily during summer, and continues draining on small platforms or *ladures* on the ramps between the *oeillets*. Finally the whole harvest is stored in a single heap called the *mulon* in the highest part of the salt-works, with a tarpaulin over it to protect it from the southerly winds that might blow it away, or the wind off the sea which would humidify it.

The mining technique, the ancient method used at Hallstatt in Austria in Neolithic times, consists of mining underground or surface seams of rock salt or halite resulting from the evaporation of ancient seas, and covered to a greater or lesser depth by other sediments. Tectonic movements mean that the seams do not necessarily lie horizontally; they have often been shaped into domes by the pressure of the neighbouring rocks.

For a seam to be worth mining today it must have a pure salt content of at least 90 per cent, be sufficiently extensive and contain no faults or basins of underground water, but it must also be near springs that can supply water to be piped to it. The only rock salt mine of any importance left in France is the mine at Saint-Nicolas near Nancy. The shaft giving access to it, leading directly down to a depth of 160 metres, was sunk a century ago. Salt-mine galleries are dug and separated by cavities where columns of salt are left standing; their dimensions have been calculated by the mining engineers to guarantee the stability of the surface and of the galleries. The ventilation system of the mine must also protect it from fire-damp, concentrations of carbonic gas. The salt is hacked out in blocks and brought to the surface. Horses used to be kept at the bottom of salt mines to transport it; today they have been replaced by tip trucks, and the whole mine is electrically equipped, with blowing engines to ventilate it.

In Romania the old salt mines have been turned into sanatoria for people with respiratory troubles; they are said to be very beneficial.

The industrial technique: this means dissolving rock salt or halite *in situ* by the artificial injection of water under pressure, or by natural leaching from salt springs running through the seams and found by drilling. The water, once collected, is filtered and then evaporated by boiling. Water injected into a drilled hole under pressure dissolves the salt and then rises through a system of double-walled pipes. Improvements have been made to the old procedure of boiling the brine in vats by direct heat, and a steam thermocompression process has been introduced, producing *ignigenous salt* with regular crystals and a fine texture.

THE SALT MARCH OF MAHATMA GANDHI

5 APRIL 1930

Gandhi ... was released and allowed to recuperate in Juhu, just outside Bombay. Immediately Congress leaders flocked to see him, to discuss how the campaign should be reactivated. Gandhi's reply was typical. He had been convicted for six years and, had it not been for his illness and the compassion of the British authorities, he would still have been in prison. He would therefore take no part whatsoever in any action which could prove detrimental to the British until the entire six-year period had come to an end. When it did, however, there took place probably the most famous of all his massive campaigns of protest. Seventy-eight ashramites left the Sarbamati ashram outside Ahmedabad and marched some two hundred and forty miles to the beach at Dandi. There, the Mahatma, as he was now known, ritually broke the law by picking up a handful of salt crystallised by the evaporation of sea water. It was illegal to manufacture or sell salt except under licence from the British. By this symbolic march and simple act, Gandhi exhorted all fellow Indians to follow his example and break the law. The result was extraordinary. The British authorities were totally incapable of dealing with the scale of the protest. The whole salt campaign, culminating in the huge protest at the Darasana Salt Works, resulted in the Viceroy, Lord Irwin, summoning Gandi to Viceregal Lodge to be informed of the setting up of the 1931 conference to which he, Gandhi, was to be invited as the representative of the Indian Congress Party.

Richard Attenborough, *In Search of Gandhi*

Chapter 15

Spice at Any Price

About Spices

Perhaps more nonsense has been written about spices than any other food product. A participant in a French radio quiz show contrived to win 500 francs for ascribing the invention of pepper (*poivre*) to Pierre Poivre, governor of the Mascarene Islands,[1] in the eighteenth century. The magazine *Elle* claimed that 'Marco Polo was the first to bring spices into Europe', adding a list of the places where what it described as the classic spices came from: 'saffron from Greece or Spain, nutmeg from the West Indies, etc.'

It is true that the world of spices, aromatics and condiments is not an easy one to explore, particularly when viewed from a great height. Such a symphony of scents rises from it that the head soon swims, and it is difficult to pick out the separate notes in the fragrance.

Dictionaries are not much help. *Littré* defines 'spice' as 'any aromatic or piquant drug used for seasoning', and 'aromatic' as 'any substance of vegetable origin giving off a penetrating and pleasant odour'. (But there are also aromatics of animal origin such as ambergris and musk, and these were once used in food as well.) The *Oxford English Dictionary* defines 'spice' as 'one or other of various strongly flavoured or aromatic substances of vegetable origin ... commonly used as condiments or employment for other purposes on account of their fragrance and preservative qualities', and 'aromatic' as 'a substance or plant emitting a spicy odour; a fragrant drug; a spice'. *Littré* again, forgetting how to count, calls *quatre-épices*, literally 'four spices', 'a mixture of cloves, nutmeg, black pepper, cinnamon and ginger'. *Larousse* does no better, defining it as 'the common name of the cultivated nigella'. It is actually the sweet Jamaica 'pepper', *Pimenta dioica*, whose unripe berries, dried and crushed, are called allspice in English because, according to the OED, they were 'supposed to combine the flavour of cinnamon, nutmeg and cloves'.

To *Larousse*, a condiment (from Latin *condimentum*) is 'a seasoning, such as pepper, salt and garlic'; to the OED, 'anything of a pronounced flavour used to season or give relish to food, or to stimulate the appetite'. We might as well leave the lexicographers to their rather vague terminology and search for enlightenment in the past – for, contrary to the remarks in *Elle*, spices were already used in European cookery when the Polo family, which dealt in them, set off through Asia on a business trip.

Classical Latin uses the words *aroma* and *aromata* (in Apuleius, for instance, where they translate, depending on the context, as spices, odours or aromatics). Around the year 600, Isidore of Seville, in his *Libri differentiarum sive de proprietate sermonum*,[2] writes that 'Aromatics are those perfumed odours sent to us by India, the Arabian regions, and other places besides. And aromatics seem to derive their name either from their use on the altars of the gods, or because we see that they spread forth and mingle with the air. Indeed, their odour is carried by the air.'

In Chapter VIII of his encyclopedic work, in the section *de rebus rusticis*, Isidore classifies the following as aromatic trees (*de arboribus aromaticis*): myrrh, pepper, cinnamon, amomum (perhaps cardamom) and cassia. In Chapter IX he classifies as aromatic herbs (*de herbis aromaticis*): nard, saffron, cardamom, thyme, aloes, rose, violet, lily, gentian, wormwood, fennel and a number of others.

In the second century the Emperor Hadrian, a contemporary of Apuleius, used the neuter plural adjective *aromatica* in a substantive sense, meaning aromatics, while Apicius[3] has the following terms: *condimenta montaria* (a mixture of ground spices), followed by a list of the spices in it, and *condimenta viridia*, green plants which might be described as condiments. The manuscript that has survived is a fifth-century copy; Apicius himself, or at least one of the several gourmets who bore the name of Apicius, lived in the first century. The general tone of the language in this copy has been recognized as post-dating the fourth century. We cannot really tell whether the copyist was scrupulously rendering terms in use in the first century, or perhaps revising the entire text to suit the taste of his own day. The recipes of Apicius are followed by another text, *Excerpta* (extracts), by Vinidarius, described as 'an illustrious man'. The *Excerpta* include a list of the 'spices' necessary in a household to provide for the requisite seasonings. This appendix to the work generally referred to simply as 'Apicius' is much later than the first part; some experts have dated it as late as the eighth century.

However, the list itself, the *Brevis pimentorum*, is interesting on several counts. First, it applies the term *pimentum* to substances which we would regard as spices, whereas its earlier meaning was of 'pigment' or colouring, and it denoted only such spices as saffron. In this list saffron stands side by side with pepper, ginger, myrtle, cloves, cardamom, spikenard, etc. The list goes on to mention seeds (*de seminibus hoc*), including rue, bay, dill, celery, fennel, coriander, cumin, aniseed, parsley, caraway and sesame; 'dry substances' (*de siccis hoc*), including wild carrot, mint, sage, cypress, marjoram, juniper, onion, 'berries' of thyme, coriander, feverfew and citron leaves, parsnip, onion of Escalon,[4] dill, pennyroyal, garlic, dried vegetables, marjoram, elecampane, silphium and cardamom.

481

This list tells us what spices were used in the Merovingian period, and what aromatics as we would now define them. Silphium, an umbelliferous Mediterranean plant very popular with the Romans, must have been dying out at this time; it no longer grows in the Mediterranean area, and has been forgotten.

The new term *pimentum*, which thenceforward denoted any kind of spice, was applied by the Spanish to pepper (*pimienta*). In a similar manner, *poivre* was used in France for some time to mean any kind of spice. The Spanish, encountering the capsicums of America, the chillies and sweet peppers we know today, called them *pimiento*. In the twelfth century *Chanson de Roland*, before the heroes who died in the pass of Roncevaux were buried, 'ben sunt lavez de piment et de vin' ('they were well washed with *piment* and with wine'). In Old French, *pyment*, *piement* or *piument* was a spiced wine sweetened with honey which could be used, as required, as a tonic or to embalm the dead (presumably if its tonic properties had failed to revive them).

The word spice, in modern French *épice*, earlier *espesse* or *espice*, and one of the many words connected with food that England took from the Norman invaders, also made its appearance around 1150 in *Le roman de la Rose*, later translated into English by Chaucer (or a contemporary) as *The Romaunt of the Rose*:

> And many a spice delitable
> To eten whan men rise fro table.

Aldebrandin of Sienna's treatise on hygiene, the *Régime des corps*,[5] written in French in the late thirteenth century, devotes a very interesting chapter to the 'qualities of all spices'.

The Latin word *species*, which at first meant appearances in general, whether concrete or imaginary, and then objects, came to be used for merchandise, especially foodstuffs of particular value (in the Justinian Code, *species publicae* meant food sold on behalf of the state). It was thus applied to products which were indeed 'special'. In the sixth century Gregory of Tours classed all the fruits of the earth, grain, oil and wine, as *species* when they were the subject of commercial transactions. However, the word seems to have clung mainly to the most desirable kind of merchandise, exotic and expensive fine foods, unique of their kind. Macrobius, the fifth-century philosopher and politician, was the first writer to describe aromatics and spices as *species*, and he set the tone. Spice became the word for a particularly luxurious and fine substance used in food. Native European aromatics such as cumin (mentioned by Ausonius), dill and saffron were less highly esteemed than foreign produce and did not count as 'spices', since they were of no importance in trade, and were far too familiar to have any dream-like aura about them, something that may have meant more in the enjoyment of food than the actual odour of the spices.

Chinese thinking had anticipated European gastronomy and philology in this respect. Françoise Sabban, in her study of fourteenth-century Chinese cookery,[6] comments that the term *liaowu* (material, substance) had long been used to denote what Europeans called 'spices' from the height of the Middle Ages onwards.

Nor are these all the amazing revelations to be encountered along the road to the wonderful land of spices. The ancestor of all cookery books, the *Ars Magirica* of Apicius, as I mentioned above, uses the terms *condita* and *condimenta* for spices. Curiously enough the cookery books which appeared at the end of the thirteenth century, such as the *Liber de coquina* and the *Tractatus de modo preparandi*, edited in our own time by Marianne Mulon,[7] the book from Assisi found at Châlons-sur-Marne which I have edited myself, and the first edition of Platina's *De Honesta Voluptate*, all of them written in medieval Latin, express their authors' idea of spices not by *aromata* as in the day of Caesar or even Hadrian, not by *condimenta* like Apicius, but by *species*. It is certainly not classical Latin, but it is very revealing. Besides English spice and French *épice*, the word became *spezie* in Italian, *especia* in Spanish, and *Spezerei* in German (the last-named word, once very widespread, now in dialectal use). The recipe for *tortelli* in the Assisi manner, for instance, in the book I was lucky enough to discover at Châlons-sur-Marne, concludes: 'Et coque cum amygdalis mundis et specibus de super' ('and cook them with blanched almonds and spices on them').

If we do not count the legend of the 5000-year-old herbal of Chen-Nong, Emperor of China, the first recorded evidence of aromatic plants and products is found in Egyptian papyri of 2800 BC, and Sumerian tablets of 2200 BC. The ancient Egyptians seem to have made considerable use of such fragrant plants as marjoram, mint, juniper and styrax, of gum resins (such as *sontjer* or terebinth, *ânty* or frankincense, myrrh, *iber* or cyst-laudanum), and of spices as we would understand them today (such as cinnamon and cassia). Almost all these substances, reserved for the Pharaoh, the princes and the priests, had therapeutic, cosmetic and above all ritual uses; it is not easy to draw clear dividing lines. They were made under the supervision of the priests, but we know very little about their dietary use except that they were often thought to purify food offered to the gods. Garlic and onions were the only flavourings the common people had in their diet. Aromatics and precious ointments, of course, were also used in the embalming of persons of high rank.

The Bible contains many precepts about the obligatory use of aromatics in preparing food for sacrifices. The smoke and odour of roast meat was as pleasing to Jehovah as to the Greek gods, and the custom of employing aromatic smoke in ritual lingered on in many forms of worship, including the Roman Catholic liturgy. 'Take thou also unto thee principal spices, of pure myrrh 500 shekels, and of sweet cinnamon half so much ... and of sweet calamus two hundred and fifty shekels' (Exodus 30, xxiv). One wonders if the reed described as 'sweet calamus' was sugar-cane. After the ritual, 'all the meat offering that is baken in the oven, and all that is dressed in the fryingpan, and in the pan, shall be the priest's that offereth it' (Leviticus 7, ix), so in the end the aromatics would be put to nutritional use. Towards 950 BC, when the Queen of Sheba visited Solomon, she came with 'a very great company, and camels that bare spices ... and of spices great abundance, and precious stones: neither was there any such spice as the queen of Sheba gave king Solomon' (II Chronicles 9, i, ix). These aromatics would have perfumed the burnt offerings made by the priest-king, and camels also brought him 'algum trees' (probably sandalwood) of which he made 'terraces to the house of the Lord, and to the king's palace' (II Chronicles 9, xi). Sandalwood was to remain a perfume and never had any culinary use.

From the second millennium BC, as Herodotus and Pliny tell us, caravans laden with spices, aromatics and other precious merchandise made their slow way from southern Arabia, in particular from the port of Berenice, where the valuable produce arrived by sea. It had come from centralized collecting points in India and was bound for Egypt and the prosperous trading cities of Tyre and Sidon on the Phoenician seaboard. But Egypt too was a considerable naval power. Twenty centuries before our own era the Egyptians established commercial relations with the mysterious lands of Ophir and Pontus (Somalia and Aden), to acquire spices, rare woods, precious stones and gold, in the same way as King Solomon. The inscriptions in the temple of Deir-el-Bahari commemorate the famous expedition of the woman Pharaoh Hatshepsut in 1515 BC and the foods she caused to be brought back. Alexandria was a great spice-trading centre before it became the intellectual capital of the world. The Phoenicians distributed spices around the Mediterranean and even sailed round Spain to take them up the Atlantic shores, where they were exchanged for tin or amber. They could take an additional cargo of salt on board and offload it on the way, for spices were valuable merchandise but not heavy; ships carrying them were light and had space aboard to spare. Other Western Europeans took the same goods to more northerly countries by land; it is often forgotten that the Vikings, travelling by sea and river, were merchants (or sometimes pirates) involved in the spice trade. They might go as far as Palestine or Constantinople, where they had agents. When the Normans joined the Crusades, therefore, they had a good knowledge of the land and its people.

The Secrets of Spices

The first definite mention of a particular spice is of cinnamon in the Bible and the Egyptian papyri, as we saw above. *Kynnamomon*, its Greek name, can thus claim seniority among the well-known spices. The word may be related to one of Malay origin, *kaimanis*. Cassia, also known as bastard cinnamon or Chinese cinnamon, is a tree which has bark similar to that of cinnamon but with a rather pungent odour; the Indians obtained cassia from China. The writers of antiquity did not confuse the two. Cinnamon now grows in Egypt. In fact the trees now naturalized in the ancient land of the Pharaohs are all descended from two cinnamon saplings sent from the hothouses of the Jardin des Plantes in Paris in the nineteenth century.

A spice shop in the covered market of Calcutta, India: in tropical climates and
poor countries, spices are used as much to add necessary vitamins as to make
the flavour of rice more interesting.

The Indians have always used cinnamon lavishly, but the Greeks and Romans
did not really introduce it into their cooking until the final period of the Roman
Empire, around the third and fourth centuries. They valued it at first as a medicine,
a cordial and an aphrodisiac. In the Middle Kingdom, Chinese cinnamon or cassia
had the highest possible reputation: it was supposed to confer immortality – or
almost. To the Taoists it was the food of the immortals, a kind of ambrosia. The
hare of the moon climbed down a giant cassia tree to earth, nibbled the bark of
the tree and prepared the elixir, which also gave the body the divine colour, golden
yellow, and the power of *yang*. Carried on the person in a kind of pomander, a

485

piece of cinnamon was supposed to avert disease; it must certainly have helped the sensitive nostrils of the prosperous people who wore it to endure the stench of the towns of the time.

A fine inscription tells us that Antiochus and his son Seleucus, kings in Asia Minor where the caravan routes converged, gave generous gifts of cinnamon and cassia to the temple of Apollo at Miletus. Nero killed his wife Poppaea by kicking her when she was pregnant, but then made her funeral a very sumptuous occasion, burning all the cinnamon in Rome on her pyre. But for this distressing incident, those stocks of cinnamon would have been bought as usual from the *seplasarii*, the perfumiers and apothecaries who sold their wares at the foot of the Capitol. Capua too was famous for its *seplasarii*. According to Galen, all the Roman emperors had cinnamon in their treasuries. The Empress Livia had a temple built on the Palatine hill in honour of her husband Augustus around a huge piece of cinnamon laid in a golden vessel.

Whether the monastery of Corbie also regarded its cinnamon as something to be treasured, not used, or whether the brothers put it into mulled wine when they had colds and chills we cannot tell, but an official document mentions the gift by the Frankish king Chilperic II of five pounds (1.6 kilograms) of the precious spice to the monastery: clearly so magnificent a gift was deemed worthy of record.

Medieval people did not always have a very clear idea of the origin of cinnamon, a fact which raised both its prestige and its price. They still viewed certain authors of the first and second centuries as authorities, including the naturalist Pliny,[8] the Graeco-Roman botanist and doctor Dioscorides[9] and the Graeco-Egyptian geographer Ptolemy. Citing Herodotus, these all agreed that cinnamon was brought from the Egyptian trading posts on the Red Sea and came either from Ethiopia or from the Arab coast opposite, as it had in the time of the Pharaohs. The Via Serica, the Silk Road, had been in use since at least the third century BC, as Ptolemy confirms. It ran from China through Iran and Iraq to Tyre (and then, in Roman times, to Antioch, the city founded by those kings who offered cinnamon to Apollo). It had replaced a more northerly route following the Russian shores of the Caspian and Black Seas, and its existence demonstrates the importance of the Lebanese and Syrian ports where the Crusaders settled as soon as they could, with a view to taking part in the trade that passed along it.

But all such matters must have seemed very perilous and very far away to the people of Western Europe who stayed at home. Joinville, who surely had happy memories of the rice with milk and almonds, sprinkled with 'much cinnamon', served by the monks of Sens to Crusaders on their way from Paris to Aigues-Mortes (see the section on rice, chapter 6), accompanied his king to Alexandria, the centre of the cinnamon trade, in 1248. He firmly believed everything he was told in the souks: for instance, that cinnamon was fished up in nets at the sources of the Nile, on the very edge of the great flat platter of the earth, and opposite Paradise.

The members of the Polo family, who were more astute, knew where cinnamon came from, and may indeed have known more about the spice than their Venetian colleagues in trade who took delivery of it in Syria and Constantinople. But they were careful not to say so. Marco cautiously – and not by chance – omitted to mention in his *Book* that Seilan (Ceylon) was the main source of precious cinnamon bark, even though he called it 'the finest island in the world'. He said a good deal about the much less exquisite cassia or Chinese cinnamon 'from the province of Tebet [Tibet] ... cinnamon grows there in great abundance.' He also mentions cloves: 'a small tree with leaves like a laurel, but somewhat longer and narrower; it bears little white flowers, like our cloves.'[10] As the Venetian monopoly had to be preserved, he avoids being very precise, but whets his readers' appetites with his account of the Egyptian connection of his day. 'In the kingdom of Melibar [Malabar] ... there are also plenty of good spices. Other spices there are too ... and you must know that ships come here from many points, and the merchants likewise distribute what they purchase here over many countries. The wares taken to Aden are then carried on to Alexandria.'

Cinnamon

Cinnamomum verum or *zeylanicum*, true or Ceylon cinnamon, is a white-flowered shrub. The bark is the part used as a spice. The paler cinnamon is, the better its quality; pale bark comes from the young shoots, and the strips or 'quills' should be thin and delicate. Ground cinnamon soon goes stale, so it should be bought in small quantities.

Half a coffee-spoon of ground cinnamon in a cup of tea is an excellent remedy for diarrhoea.

It was in November 1271 that the Polo brothers and Marco, son of one and nephew of the other, left the town of Layas near Alexandretta, now Iskenderum, a port in South-East Turkey north of Antioch. 'On the sea-shore, there is a city called Layas, which is a great centre of trade; for you must know in sooth that all spices, and cloths of silk and gold, and all manner of precious goods of the interior are brought thither; and the merchants of Venice, and Genoa, and other countries flock there, and buy them and distribute them all over the world.' The Polos hoped to get to Ormuz by a complicated land route, and then find a ship to take them to China. 'On the shore there is a city called Ormuz, which possesses a harbour. You must know that here arrive the traders from India with their ships, bringing all kinds of spices, precious stones, gold and silk cloths.' However, the voyage was never made, because of plague and 'tempests', and the Polos took to the road again. 'It is a matter of no little peril to sail in those ships. I assure you that many are lost, for violent storms are frequent in the Sea of India.' Clearly Marco Polo was not anxious to encourage competitors.

During the thirteenth and fourteenth centuries, using networks of agents along the interior routes and down the maritime line, the Venetians had what amounted to a monopoly of the cinnamon trade. They fixed the prices, almost as exorbitant as in the time of Nero. But cinnamon had become a necessity; the cookery of the late Middle Ages could not do without it.

Panurge, through whom Rabelais speaks, drank hippocras, a cordial of wine flavoured with cinnamon, as did various of Chaucer's characters. It was used in innumerable dishes and sauces. Bruno Laurioux[11] has calculated that it occurs in 67 per cent of French recipes of the time, with other spices, of course, and always the same other spices. Cinnamon was an essential part of such casserole or ragoût dishes as 'civeys, *boussac* of hare, *trissolette* of partridge, *hochepot*' (a rich stew of meat and vegetables), to name only these medieval classics. The habit of adding cinnamon has persisted in Italy (for instance in *minestra de fagiole*), in Spain (with chocolate), in Catalonia (in *mouclade*, chicken and minced meat dishes)[12] and in the countries of the Maghreb and the East (in *pastilla, tajines*, etc.)

The French gradually dropped the cinnamon habit except in such comforting, homely dishes as apple compote and rice pudding. However, the French Canadians of Quebec remained faithful to it. Their cuisine, which is almost a gastronomic time capsule of France in the old days, still makes much use of cinnamon. They may perhaps, subconsciously, be stating the difference between themselves and English-speaking Canada, for the medieval English used cinnamon with moderation (in only 8 per cent of recipes, according to Bruno Laurioux), although as we shall see, they made up for it with their lavish use of ginger and pepper. However, England was to win the cinnamon war which really flared up in the sixteenth century and continued for some ten generations.

La Fontaine's fable of the robbers and the donkey proves its point in the great events of history as well as the small incidents of everyday life. First, all the trading nations of the Mediterranean, who were engaged in disputes and mutual betrayal to assert their authority overseas,[13] were taken by surprise by Portugal. Then, in the words of the fable:

> Arrive un troisième larron
> Qui saisit maître Aliboron.

['Along comes a third robber who seizes Master Ass.']
In this case the third robber was Holland, and there was even a fourth and unexpected contender – unexpected because England had ostensibly reduced her fleet. Portugal and Holland suffered the fate they had inflicted on others, and from being the robbers became the robbed. However, I am anticipating events here.

In the early years of the sixteenth century the Portuguese, in the wake of Vasco da Gama who had opened up the route to India around the Cape of Good Hope, fell greedily upon Ceylon (its secret had become known after all). They were totally obsessed with cinnamon. A year after their arrival in 1505, over 11 tons of the bark took ship for Lisbon. This was some consolation to the Portuguese for the 400 quintals, extorted from the Indians after the savage bombardment of Calcutta, which had been lost at sea in the shipwreck of Alvarez Cabral's vessel. It is tempting, but inaccurate, to say that no good comes of ill-gotten gains. For the sake of Ceylon cinnamon, the Portuguese imposed a 50-year reign of terror from Oman to Goa, which they held for centuries; the Sinhalese were enslaved, Arab or Malabar dhows were sunk on sight, and any Alexandrian, Genoese or Venetian agents hanged out of hand. For extra security the Portuguese devastated Mozambique on the African coast, and then settled there themselves to guard the route around the Cape.

When the Dutch arrived, half the world breathed a sigh of relief, only to find that they now had two masters instead of one, which was even worse. Finally, in 1656, the Netherlands obtained exclusive rights to the cinnamon trade, and subsequently transferred this concession to the Dutch East India Company.[14]

Of course these colonial ventures were subsidized by merchants and bankers, who were often the same. They made quick profits, while the glory went to the monarchs who patronized the fleets. A Frankfurt banker, famous for his ostentation, which greatly surpassed that of the Medici in their own day, invested his money very shrewdly in financing the Emperor Charles V's colonial adventures, and one day made the magnificent gesture of setting fire to a bundle of cinnamon bark with the document acknowledging the Emperor's receipt of a colossal overseas loan.

At this period only the wild cinnamon trees of the jungle were exploited. Under the Dutch of the East India Company, who were as methodical as they were ruthless, the forest, systematically stripped of bark by natives obliged to meet very high quotas, looked as if it would soon be exhausted. Strict supervision of the exploitation of wild cinnamon was imposed. A century after their arrival in Ceylon, the Dutch were sending 270 tons of cinnamon a year to Europe. Prices had fallen considerably since the Middle Ages, but unlike other spices, cinnamon was increasingly popular. The Netherlands were beginning to wonder whether they would be able to continue supplying demand when a colonist called De Coke suggested cultivating cinnamon trees. No one had tried before (for one thing, it was thought to be impossible).

It takes eight years for a tree to grow large enough for a crop to be harvested. Eight years after De Coke's happy notion, there was such over-production that the market looked like collapsing. As was to happen with coffee, the Dutch burned stocks or delayed the arrival of their ships so as to maintain prices. It was a curious form of speculation, with no competition in sight. But in any case the Dutch cinnamon empire collapsed when the English landed in Ceylon in 1796. Holland had left her political coalition with England to join the French, and London no longer had any official scruples. With Ceylon, Pitt the Younger restored economic health to a country that had lost her American colonies and had no access to the Mediterranean. The British behaved in an almost gentlemanly manner in Ceylon, and it brought them luck. Given the acceptability of a slightly lower quality – the market for cinnamon was larger and more democratic than before – production reached a thousand tons a year in the middle of the nineteenth century. But cinnamon was now being grown all over the lands of the Indian Ocean: in India, Malaysia, Java, Madagascar, Mauritius and the Seychelles. Cinnamon trees were also planted in the West Indies, Brazil and Guiana. The art of distilling unsaleable waste bark to obtain cinnamon essence had been known for 200 years; this important essential oil, with its high phenol content, is used for flavouring food or in cosmetics and is also a powerful bactericide. Cinnamon oil, therefore, has brought the spice back to one of its first uses as a medicinal substance.

Pepper

Piper nigrum belongs to the Piperaceae family and is a tropical climbing vine. In the wild state, it may grow to a height of six metres, and clambers as a parasite over forest trees. Grown on a trellis as a cultivated plant, it is never allowed to reach more than half that height. Its large, thick leaves, shaped like the ace of clubs, have a curious pattern of parallel nerves. The small white flowers, borne in spikes, grow on the stem, opposite the leaves, and produce bunches of densely packed berries which turn from green to red as they ripen.

Black pepper: engraving from Chenu's *Encyclopédie d'histoire naturelle* of 1873

If the berries are picked before they mature and dried in the sun, they wrinkle and turn very dark brown; this is black pepper. Alternatively, the berries can be left to finish ripening; they are then picked and soaked and the outer skins are rubbed off, leaving only the pale seed, which is dried to give white pepper. Green pepper, a fashionable condiment today, consists of the fresh berries soaked in brine, vinegar or their own juices, and is usually sold in cans or jars.

Once it has been ground, pepper goes stale very quickly, so it is best to buy peppercorns and grind them as required. Black pepper is the strongest, most natural-tasting kind; white pepper is less powerful. Green pepper has a piquant flavour. It

490

is best to add pepper to food at the end of cooking or just before it is served, or it will lose its flavour and become bitter.

As several Sanskrit texts show, the use of pepper by the peoples of India goes farther back than that of any other spice. The various forms of its name in the European languages, apart from Spanish (Greek *peperi*, Latin *piper*, Italian *pepe*, German *Pfeffer*, French *poivre*, English *pepper*), are from an Aryan vocable, *pippeli*, originating in the valley of the Ganges. The Aryans were the first exporters of wild pepper from the tropical forests of the Indian subcontinent.

Unlike cinnamon and indeed all other spices, pepper was used in foods in Europe as soon as it was introduced, around the sixth or fifth century BC, although Hippocrates, the first European writer to describe it, mentions it as a medicament rather than a culinary ingredient. It replaced myrtle berries, although they did not disappear from Mediterranean cooking entirely; as we saw above, they were contained in medieval Italian mortadella, to name only one dish. Like all spices, pepper was credited with health-giving properties, especially as a digestive, an aperient, to induce sneezing, and – most important of all – as an aphrodisiac.

Its rapid rise to favour is unprecedented among spices. Pliny expresses his surprise at the fact six centuries later in Book XII of his *Natural History*; its 'only pleasing quality is its pungency', it is 'bought by weight like gold or silver', although it consists of the seeds of wild trees. 'Who was the first person who was willing to try it on his viands, or in his greed for an appetite was not content merely to be hungry?' Moreover, he adds, pepper is adulterated with juniper berries which take on its flavour. Fraud is always with us, and today ground pepper that seems very cheap is probably the dust from the bottom of a sack.

The pepper the Romans liked so much was 'long pepper', whereas we now use round pepper, which became popular in the twelfth century and had replaced long pepper by the fourteenth. The classical writers knew both kinds. Three hundred years before our own era Theophrastus, the disciple of Aristotle and Plato, wrote his *Inquiry into Plants*, the first true European botanical treatise, naming those plants of Asiatic origin which had reached Europe in the aftermath of Alexander's conquests. He explains the difference between the two peppers. One is a round seed, resembling the bayberry. The other, preferred in classical times, is a long seed, and has a stronger flavour. That flavour, which is in fact rather bitter, may explain the Romans' preference; their palates were not nearly as refined as they liked to think. Theophrastus says that the main use of pepper is as an antidote.

In the first century AD, Dioscorides, Galen and Pliny make several mentions of black pepper and white pepper, showing that they know the pale colour of white pepper is due to the way the seed has been processed. But Pliny becomes a little confused. 'Those pods, when plucked before they open and dried in the sun, produce what is called long pepper, but if left to open gradually, when ripe they disclose white pepper, which if afterwards dried in the sun changes colour and wrinkles up.' He seems to be equating black pepper with long pepper.

Long pepper, a compact cluster of berries and not, as Pliny thought, a pod, was generally used whole and the peppercorns were not detached; they stick to each other and are smaller than those of round pepper. This custom ceased during the Middle Ages, and Philippe and Mary Hyman[15] have shown that the American chilli pepper, called *pimiento* by the Spanish from their own word for pepper, made a natural substitute for the long pepper of the Renaissance, both in flavour and in its similarity of shape when dried. When it first came into use it was called American long pepper.

Theophrastus, Dioscorides, Galen and Pliny had never seen the actual plant that produced this queen of spices, and it was not until the sixth century that travellers, itinerant monks and scholarly Arabs finally discovered pepper to be a vine that clambers up tall jungle trees in much the same way as wild vines and ivy. It was always known that it came from India. The only question was, where exactly *was* India, apart from being somewhere to the east?

Pepper therefore travelled the same road as cinnamon, and features as an Indian product in the records of taxes levied in Alexandria from the time of Marcus Aurelius onwards, under first the Roman and then the Byzantine Empires, and up to the time of the Muslim conquest. Duty was levied on it at the rate of 25 per cent.

Pepper has more of a flavour than an odour. It thus appeals to physical rather than mental sensations, and did not need the legendary aura surrounding cinnamon. Regarded as indispensable in Roman gastronomy, this foreign spice was very expensive, particularly for most of the population, whose standard of living was modest, to say the least. Around AD 390 Diocletian, in one of his edicts, fixed the price of whole long pepper in the Roman Empire at 15 denarii a pound (about £40), and 'shelled pepper' – round pepper? – at four denarii (about £14), while white pepper cost seven denarii (about £24). Since pepper was used lavishly, such prices represented great expense except for patricians with enormous fortunes, who did not, as it is too often forgotten, constitute the majority. The *honestiores*, persons who needed no aid from the state social services, certified to the *municipia* (the civic authorities) that they had capital of 5000 sestertii. Jérôme Carcopino[16] has calculated that the minimum sum necessary for a middle-class family man with a reasonable number of slaves to live on was around 20,000 sestertii a year.[17] With pepper so expensive, one can see why. The Roman weight of a pound, or *libra*, was about three-quarters of a pound in modern terms, just over 300 grams.

The foreign monarchs who owed allegiance to the Imperial City gave pepper to Roman consuls, senators, generals and indeed all figures of authority. The process was reversed with the decline of the Roman Empire. When Alaric, king of the Visigoths, entered Rome victorious in 408, he demanded payment of 5000 pounds of gold, 30,000 pounds of silver – and 3000 pounds of pepper. A large bale of pepper was among the presents sent to Attila by the Emperor Theodosius III.

At this point a question arises. What on earth was all this pepper used for? Even if the Roman patricians flavoured their food with it very lavishly indeed, including the *dulcia* or sweet dishes (and Apicius adds it freely even to his more subtle recipes), it seems hardly likely that Alaric's 3000 pounds of pepper were all used in his kitchens, even to feed a large court. The fact was, as we shall see in discussing the use of spices, there was a dimension to the possession of pepper which transcended its gastronomic importance, for once a certain amount of the spice is exceeded the food becomes inedible. Pepper more than any other spice, being stronger and more abundant than the others, came to be seen as a symbol of power and virility, qualities reflected in its powerful and aggressive flavour. The symbolic factor rated high, since such huge amounts, which could hardly all have been consumed, would have been bound to go stale.

In the same way, pepper, described as a 'useful' rent or due, was included among the spices presented to overlords in the Middle Ages, but it was generally specified separately, as a true determinant of the worth of the act of vassalage. A French proverb says that something is *cher comme poivre*, expensive as pepper. Pepper was often mentioned in dowries and as a part of ransoms and fines. These symbolical meanings meet in the pepper in the Christmas 'tax' imposed by Archbishops Bertrand and Rostaing de Noves on the 'perfidious Jews' of Aix-en-Provence. Their perfidy lay in their failure to accept the Christian faith, and they had to pay the tax if they wanted to keep their own cemeteries and their free schools.

When Clotaire III, the son of Clovis, founded the monastery of Corbie in 670, 30 pounds of pepper were among the various revenues he demanded from the demesne for the monks. Vicomte Roger was killed in 1107 in a rebellion of the citizens of Béziers; when the rebels had been suppressed by force of arms, one of the penalties his son imposed on them was a payment of three pounds of pepper a year by each family. Prior Geoffroy of the Vigeois in Auvergne, wishing to extol the magnificence of Guillaume, Comte de Limoges, tells us that the Count owned great quantities of pepper 'heaped up like acorns for pigs'. One day, when his cup-bearer came to get some for the Count's sauces, the officer who watched over this treasury took a shovel to it and gave him a basketful. An Abbé of Saint-Gilles, asking a favour of Louis VII, accompanied his request with several bags of cinnamon and pepper, a move which cannot have done his cause any harm.

Pepper was always more involved in trade than any other spice. In France, those merchants whose speciality was the pepper trade, the *pébriers* or *poivriers*, at first formed a corporation distinct from that of the grocers and apothecaries, but were subsequently absorbed by them. In medieval England the guild of Pepperers, later the Grocers, organized the spice trade; its existence is first recorded in 1180.

From the time of Marco Polo the people of the west coast of India had been cultivating peppers, supporting the vines on props like grape vines. 'There is abundance of pepper ... it is gathered in the months of May, June and July', says Marco Polo. 'You are to understand that the trees that produce pepper are planted and watered – they are not wild.' The cultivated pepper vines allowed more exports to satisfy European demand, but prices remained high until 1522, when the Dutch took over the sea route the Portuguese had obligingly opened up for them. Sailing direct from Antwerp to India and back round the Cape of Good Hope, they could supply the Northern European countries which were henceforward the chief consumers of pepper.

Harvesting pepper in the kingdom of Quilon (on the coast of Malabar in Kerala, India): miniature from the early fifteenth-century manuscript of Marco Polo's *Book* illustrated by the Maître de Boucicaut and the Maître de Bedford

The Portuguese themselves had to beat down prices to keep their monopoly; the pepper-growing regions were more or less their own preserve, and they had good stable relations with the Chinese, in some ways their allies and in others their rivals. The Venetians, who were on very bad terms with the Berbers, no longer seemed able to compete in the great race, but Lisbon had plenty of good Basque seamen, mostly out-of-work whalers.

The Chinese were already consuming much greater quantities of pepper than the people of Europe. Their merchants flocked to the north coast of Java when the port of Bantam became the world centre of the pepper trade. From now on the best pepper came from the Sunda Islands. The Bantam pepper market, almost a pepper exchange, and a city within the city, was soon in the hands of the Chinese. They used every trick in the trade to manipulate rates, freeze stocks, fleece the natives who produced the pepper, and have themselves appointed agents (at a very high rate) so that all the Dutch or Portuguese vessels had to do was load a cargo ordered on a previous trip, without any waiting about.

Wishing to avoid this early kind of Mafia, the French planted pepper vines on

494

their possessions in the Indian Ocean, the islands of Bourbon (later La Réunion) and the Île de France (Mauritius). Pepper-growing was also tried in the West Indies and Guiana, but the results were not very good. Pepper does not grow well in the Americas or Africa.

Guinea pepper, or Guinea grains, was (or were) another matter. When European trading stations began to proliferate all along the west coast of Africa (for dealing in slaves as well as other merchandise), black Eastern pepper found itself with a rival spice on the tables of the European home countries. In fact this spice was making a second appearance in Europe: it was Guinea pepper, mentioned by Pliny[18] as 'African pepper', and also known as Malaguetta pepper or grains of Paradise. Grains of Paradise had been very popular in the thirteenth century and again in the sixteenth; its popularity may have been due to the brilliant name thought up for it by some advertising genius born before his time. The author or the *Ménagier de Paris* recommends using it to improve wine 'which smells stale'. Muskier, less pungent and more aromatic than pepper, lacking that special bite which is characteristic of true pepper, medieval grains of Paradise were brought from the Gulf of Guinea to North Africa, and were taken on to Sicily and Italy. A series of Dioula, Haussa, Mandingo and Moorish caravans were involved. The Renaissance and the seventeenth century saw this spice decline in popularity, like many others, always excepting black pepper. It then made a comeback for a while in the eighteenth century.

The Africans liked Guinea pepper, and still do. Before they ever encountered the chilli pepper, which they called *pili-pili* and which came to them from America, they used Guinea pepper to season a particularly fiery soup, roasting it highly to increase its strength. This soup, dark in colour, may be made of game, fish or poultry and herbs, and is the national dish of the people of Guinea. Known as *pépé* soup, it is popular from Gambia to Lagos, and is sometimes jokingly called Touré soup, from the name of the late head of state of Guinea.

Guinea pepper would be of purely anecdotal or folk interest but for the fact that the French imported as much of the spice as possible from West Africa during the Second World War, to make up for the lack of imported Eastern foods. Guinea pepper helped the dismal wartime diet of swedes to go down better.

Ginger

Zingiber officinale, of the Zingiberaceae family, the tropical ginger plant, is about a metre tall with large lanceolate leaves and spikes bearing curious fleshy yellow, red-rimmed flowers. The part used as a spice is its knobbly, irregular rhizome. Ginger is sold fresh, dried, grated, ground, preserved in syrup or vinegar, and crystallized.

It was long thought that ginger took its name from Gingi, near Pondicherry in southern India, an area where it is believed to have originated. In fact the Greeks called it *dziggibris*, their version of Persian *dzungebir*, from Sanskrit *srngaveram*, 'of horned appearance' (referring to its shape). The word entered Latin as *zingiber*, giving French *gingibre* in the twelfth century and *gingembre* in the fourteenth. Italian *gengiovo* became *zinzebro*,[19] Old English *gingiber* became *ginger*, and in German the word passed from such forms as *ingewer, ingeber* to modern *Ingwer*.

The Persian trade missions Darius sent to India in the fifth century BC brought back ginger. The Indians used it lavishly, but it had only a limited success in Greece and Rome. Apicius scarcely mentions it in his first-century recipes, or at least not in the texts we have. Dioscorides and Galen thought it was the root of the pepper plant, but Pliny describes ginger as 'a small plant with a white root. The plant is liable to decay very quickly.' It sounds as if he may have tried to grow it. He adds in passing that ginger was sold for six denarii a pound (something over £20 per 300 grams). He says that it comes from the fabled land of the Troglodytes or cave-dwellers, which was supposed to be somewhere in South-East Egypt, Ethiopia or Somalia. Yet again we have a connection with India running by way of Egypt to Alexandria.

Bruno Laurioux, a modern scholar, describes ginger as 'the Proteus of medieval cookery. It featured in various forms in the kitchen and in the imagination of master cooks, whole or powdered, and the rhizome being described sometimes according to its colour (white ginger), sometimes according to its appearance (peeled, trimmed), sometimes according to its fineness (*mesche* or *columbin*).' The botanical name of ginger, *Zingiber officinale*, is evidence that it was credited with great medicinal virtues in the Middle Ages, when it was extremely popular.

We are told that the Frankish king Thierry I asked his colleague the Emperor of Byzantium to recommend him a good Greek doctor. The practitioner recommended was Anthimus. He maintained his patients' good health, or hoped to maintain it, by diet and nutrition, and obviously the best way to promote nutritional principles is to provide appetizing recipes showing their application, as bookshop window displays tell us. His *De observatore ciborum*,[20] accordingly, is a collection of recipes. ('Dietetics is probably one of the paths along which spices passed from the medical to the culinary sphere', as Laurioux puts it.) Since ginger facilitates digestion it is an ingredient in most of the dishes Anthimus prescribed; his influence was to be felt widely in medieval cookery.

A faculty of medicine founded in Salerno by four legendary physicians, a Greek, a Roman, a Jew and an Arab, prospered during the Middle Ages. Following the same line of thought as Anthimus, it produced a collection of precepts of hygiene and diet in Latin verse known as the *Regimen Sanitatis Salerno*. The Salerno school speaks highly of ginger (modern translation):

> Within the stomach, loins, and in the lung
> Praise of hot ginger rightly may be sung.
> It quenches thirst, revives, excites the brain
> And in old age awakes young love again.

More than anything else, the alleged aphrodisiac qualities of ginger ensured its success in the kitchen. Boileau remarked, of another spice, 'Do you like nutmeg? It is put into everything', and with the substitution of ginger for nutmeg the same could be said of medieval cookery.

Even in Paradise, those virtuous Muslims who, though dead, are still able to appreciate sensual pleasure will find ginger to honour the houris. 'They shall be served with ... silver goblets which they themselves shall measure, and cups brim-full with ginger-flavoured water from the fount of Selsabil', says the Koran (Sura LXXVI), adding: 'They shall be attended by boys graced with eternal youth, who to the beholder's eyes will seem like sprinkled pearls.' What more could one wish for? Even on earth ginger tea, called *omondji* by the people of Mali, *embourgui* by the Mossi (who add chilli pepper to it!) and *loumou roudji* by the Baoule people, is a favourite beverage of African men anxious to provide themselves with the best, most natural form of insurance for their old age by siring a great many children.

Ginger came to the coasts of Africa a very long time ago. It was very profitably exported from Sierra Leone and Guinea. The Portuguese, who naturalized the rhizome there, are said to have relied on ginger to maintain a high birth-rate on their slave stud farms – a rather gruesome detail. It may be mere coincidence, but the Japanese add ginger to a traditional dish which was once reserved for samurai and is now eaten on 15th May, which is Children's Day and no doubt Virility Day as well.

Ginger water 'to make sovereign Hippocras wine' is one of the recipes given by Nostradamus.[21] 'If you taste of it you will find that it takes all its strength from ginger. And you may add to it cinnamon, which will give it a flavour not to be scorned.' As Bruno Laurioux has remarked, the combination of cinnamon and ginger was a major theme in medieval cookery, particularly that of France.

Ginger also reached Europe preserved by the Arabs in the sugar they knew how to make, as we shall see in the next section. This delicacy was known as *gingembrat*, crystallized ginger. It has remained a great delicacy enjoyed, for certain ulterior motives, by the people of the East and the Far East. All shops specializing in Asian products display small pot-bellied ginger jars on their shelves, now mass-produced in their millions and filled with crystallized ginger or ginger in syrup, but once collectors' items.

In 1553 ginger was still very expensive, and Nostradamus suggests a substitute for preserved ginger which would convey the flavour but not bankrupt the consumer. His recipe employs roots which cost nothing at all, the roots of the sea-holly that grows on sand dunes (*Eryngium*), flavoured with a small piece of genuine ginger to impart its aroma to the whole preserve.

> To make a preserve of the roots of eryngo, which shall have all the virtues, goodness and qualities of green ginger, shall be smoother in flavour and exactly like green ginger: take the root of sea holly, which is called in our tongue [Provençal] *panicaut*, in the French tongue *hyringe*.

> ... thus you have a kind of green ginger which is scarcely different from
> *mecquin*. You will find that it has a pleasanter flavour, and more virtue
> ... it is not so much trouble to make, or so expensive.

Candied eringoes, like the ginger they imitated, were supposed to be aphrodisiac, and Falstaff mentions them in *The Merry Wives of Windsor*: 'Let it ... hail kissing-comfits, and snow eringoes.'

The fact that this preserve was not so fiery as genuine preserved ginger was clearly a recommendation. The period of Nostradamus was beginning to reject medieval extravagances, and sugar was ousting spice. 'Mecquin' meant the whole, dried ginger, described by the author of the *Ménagier de Paris* in 1392 as *mesche*: 'Note that there be three differences between ginger of mesche and columbine ginger. For the ginger of mesche has a browner skin, and is the softer to cut with a knife, and whiter within than the other; item, it is better and always more expensive.'

What was this *mecquin* or *mesche* ginger? Nostradamus tells us, giving a recipe for ginger preserved in honey: 'To make the preserve of green ginger which, although it be called green ginger, is of a ginger called Mecquin, and is from Mecca where Mahomet is buried.' In fact only the Arab traders who imported ginger from South India and Malaysia had anything to do with Mecca; the ginger itself never grew there.

Ginger has gone out of fashion in France; the culinary revolution of the Renaissance rejected such strong flavours. However, the Anglo-Saxon, Germanic, Flemish and Scandinavian countries are still faithful to it, and have been from the time of the Norman expansion. They all consume a great deal more than the French now do, mostly in sweet dishes, but in some savoury dishes as well. There is even a ginger-flavoured chewing gum. Ginger ale is a favourite soft drink, and so is ginger beer, which is fermented and so may be slightly alcoholic. Ginger wine is a cordial drunk at Christmas time. Jean Suyeux tells us that in Alsace, up to the time of the Second World War, turkeys were made drunk with ginger wine before slaughter, so that they would then marinate from inside, as it were.

Ginger has been naturalized very successfully in Madagascar and mainland Africa, and in the Americas. Oddly enough, though, no one has ever found a single root of wild ginger growing spontaneously,[22] even in its native area where it was first cultivated for the spice trade. A domesticated plant *par excellence*, ginger is also particularly sociable. It likes to be grown together with its cousin turmeric, which is another of the basic spices used in curry powder.

Curry springs to mind as soon as one thinks of Indian cookery. Is it a dish or a spice? In fact 'curry' is from the Tamil word *kari*, meaning a stew. Tamil is one of the most widely spoken languages of the whole vast Indian subcontinent. An Indian curry is indeed made rather like a stew. It may be of meat, fish or vegetables, and herbs and spices are added; they are mixed together and ground to a powder which itself eventually became known as 'curry'.

Originally every region and every family had its own secret formula. At the end of the nineteenth century, however, ready-prepared curry powder could be found for sale in Indian towns. Then, so the tale goes, an Englishman named Sharwood was dining with the Maharajah of Madras, who mentioned to him the shop kept by a famous master maker of curry powder called Vencatachellum. The Englishman visited it and obtained the secret of Madras curry powder, a mixture of Chittagong saffron, turmeric, cumin, Kerala coriander and a selection of Orissa chillies (Orissa is also the source of the word *harissa* for the hot red pepper seasoning used by the Arabs in couscous). The spices were first roasted and then ground to a powder. Many other less common spices might be added to the basic mixture, varying from region to region.

A few years before, Sharwood had also enjoyed a condiment of Bombay called *catni*, which has been anglicized as 'chutney', a sweet-sour pickle of fruits, sugar, ginger, chillis and vinegar. When he returned to London he had with him a licence to import these two Indian specialities. Initially sold only in the best English grocers' shops, curry and chutney soon conquered Europe, and in 1889, at the time of the World Exhibition in Paris, the French Colonial Ministry fixed the legal composition of curry powder sold in France.

For a really authentic curry, whether made of chicken, meat or fish, of course you would need to concoct the spice mixture yourself, but good curry powder is readily available in grocers' shops and shops selling exotic delicacies. The best, naturally, is the most expensive. It is a good idea to use very fresh powder and buy it in very small quantities, so that the spices still have their original aroma.

Turmeric and Cardamom

Curcuma longa, turmeric, one of the Zingiberaceae family, also called curcuma and Indian saffron, is a rhizomatous plant like ginger. The roots are bright orange, with a thin brownish skin. The large leaves and spikes of yellow flowers are of no importance; this popular spice comes from the rhizomes. They are dug up after the plant has flowered, then boiled, peeled, dried and ground to a powder. If ground turmeric is kept for any length of time its colour, flavour and aroma will soon go stale.

Elettaria cardamomum is also a member of the Zingiberaceae family and another rhizomatous plant, but in this case its dried fruits are the parts used. The plant has long, lanceolate leaves unfurling around a stem which may grow to a height of three metres. The flowers, borne not in terminal spikes but close to the stem, are yellow and blue, and produce fruits in the form of rounded capsules full of small black seeds. The fruits are picked before they ripen, and dried; the capsules should not be opened until the spice is required, and are best kept out of the light in an airtight container.

Turmeric originated in India, like ginger, but in France it is sometimes known as

'Bourbon saffron' when it comes from the islands of La Réunion (once the Île de Bourbon) or Mauritius. In fact it has nothing in common with saffron but its golden yellow colour. Buddhist monks used it to dye their robes. The colour comes from the rhizome, not, as in the case of saffron, from flower stamens. Dioscorides knew that the plant was related to ginger, so he must have seen a piece of a whole root before it was pounded, since the spice is used powdered. He mentions its Indian origin, its bitter flavour, and its rather surprising usefulness as a depilatory.

Turmeric was never particularly popular in Western Europe. However, the Arabs and Persians were very fond of it and, looking no further than its brilliant colour, took it for another form of saffron and called it *kourkoum*. The Spanish, almost the only people in medieval Europe who really liked it, turned this word to *curcuma*. The English *turmeric*, *tarmaret* in the sixteenth century, may be from a late Latin expression of unknown origin, *terra merita*, meaning 'deserving' or 'deserved earth'. Today the British are the main European consumers of turmeric, perhaps out of nostalgia for the Indian Empire.

Throughout Asia, turmeric is regarded as a magical plant because of its colour. It is associated with most agricultural and social rituals. A clump of turmeric is planted in the middle of the paddy fields to bring luck, and just as Arab women dye the palms of their hands and the soles of their feet with henna for festive occasions, Indian Tamil women colour theirs with turmeric for weddings.

Its pronounced aroma, peppery flavour and bright colour make turmeric one of the most popular spices added to South-East Asian cookery. Millions of people automatically add it to fish and shellfish dishes, and plain boiled rice seems less insipid if it is flavoured and coloured with turmeric. It also has distinct therapeutic virtues, particularly for liver infections. It was once used by both Asian and European apothecaries in accordance with the theory of 'signatures' or characteristics favoured by Paracelsus: its yellow colour seemed to indicate its suitability for curing jaundice and bilious fevers, a phenomenon which has actually been confirmed by modern herbal therapists. Turmeric from southern China and Bengal is still regarded as the best. The plant has been naturalized in Peru and the West Indies, and turmeric has entered Creole cookery.

Although it has a rhizome like ginger and turmeric, cardamom (also known as amomum, particularly in the Middle Ages), the third essential ingredient in curry powder, is grown only for the seeds inside its fruit capsules. Virgil said that 'Assyrium volgo nascetur amomum', 'Assyrian cardamom shall spring up on every soil', for long before the Europeans had ever heard of curry cardamom was being sold in the markets of Babylon, Thebes, Athens and Rome. Theophrastus mentions it, and Dioscorides classes it among medicaments in his *Materia Medica* of AD 65.

Amomon, a word deriving from the ancient Semitic languages used by the first foreigners who encountered and liked this South-East Asian spice, may be translated as 'very spicy, very strong'. The root of the word occurs again in Greek *kardamon*, cress; *karadra* means the bed of the stream where spicily flavoured watercress is gathered.

In the third century AD, Athenaeus[23] wrote of the classical Greek period: 'The following seasonings are listed by Antiphanes: grape juice, salt, cooked wine, silphium, cheese, thyme, sesame, natron, cumin, pomegranate, honey, marjoram, fine herbs, vinegar, olives, green stuff for sauce, capers, eggs, salt fish, cress, garlic, juice.' (Antiphanes was a comic writer who died in 306 BC.) The word Athenaeus uses is *kardamon*, cress, not, as has sometimes been supposed from too cursory a reading of this passage, *kardamomum*, cardamom, which was not yet in dietary use.

The Latin authors were unsure of the botanical description of cardamom. Pliny calls it the seed of a vine, which would have been the correct description of pepper, although he was not very accurate about pepper either.

The first use of cardamom, because of its exquisite aroma, was as a suitable burnt offering to propitiate the gods. The Greeks and Romans then mixed it with wax to make solid perfumes. They put these perfumes into shells worn gypsy fashion in the hair or pinned to the clothing. St Jerome, in the fourth century, is still denouncing Christian priests of refined habits who followed this fashion. Cardamom was also used as a dentifrice, since if it is chewed after a meal it will neutralize the taste of garlic. It soothed and disinfected sore throats, was good for a cough, and expelled intestinal worms. Naturally enough, then, it found its way into sauces for food.

The mind balks, however, at one recipe given by Apicius where cardamom is used to season truffles in combination with oil and garum. The cardamom seeds preferred at the time were still green and slightly soft. The darker, dried seeds were a little cheaper. Chicken in white sauce with a purée of leeks was flavoured with cardamom; this dish was a favourite with the young and deranged Emperor Heliogabalus, who may have been greedy but was not, as has been claimed, himself an amateur cook. The recipe for chicken with cardamom would sound delicious if it did not also contain rue, an insecticidal herb greatly liked in all kinds of dishes at the time.

As we saw above, Isidore of Seville twice mentions cardamom in his list of indispensable spices in the sixth century AD: once among the products of trees, as amomum, and again among aromatic herbs, as cardamom.

Eight centuries later there is no mention of the spice at all in Taillevent's *Viandier*, although it was coming into Europe by way of Acre or Rhodes at the time. At the same period, in 1359 and 1360, France was bleeding herself dry to pay the ransom (not to mention the board and lodging) of King Jean le Bon, who had been defeated at Poitiers by the Black Prince and taken to England as a prisoner. In fact he was not suffering any very harsh conditions, and even if he was not free to leave was comfortably installed with his English cousins; the account of his household expenses makes interesting reading. Among the spices which formed part of his prison diet, including all those in use in France and England at the time, were cardamom and sugar, ginger, mace, cinnamon and flower of cinnamon, cloves, nutmeg, white pepper, long pepper, and so forth.

Charles le Bel's widow Jeanne d'Évreux ate no cardamom if we go by the inventory of her household drawn up in 1372, but that may have been just a question of personal or national taste, since the French were never so fond of cardamom as the English. It is possible that Jean le Bon first met the spice in England. The Scandinavian countries, however, still import it in large quantities. Sweden today accounts for a quarter of all Indian cardamom production, often using the spice to flavour spirits, of which the Swedes also consume a considerable amount.

The Arabs often flavour coffee with cardamom, either adding a few seeds to the beans before they are ground, or sometimes, as an added refinement, opening a capsule full of seeds and wedging it into the spout of the coffee pot. As the coffee is poured it is filtered for a second time, through the cardamom, which imparts a delicious flavour. Since it became trendy for Westerners to travel to Kathmandu and India, cardamom-flavoured tea has also been popular. The idea came from Pakistan. Cocoa with cardamom, sold by luxury food shops, is another delicious beverage.

Cardamom is not only used in curry powder, like turmeric, but on its own as a flavouring for special Indian, Pakistani, Balinese and Bengali dishes.

Depending on its place of origin – Malabar, Sri Lanka, Indochina, Cambodia or Thailand – the quality and the price of the seeds vary. Cardamom from Cambodia has even given a name to the mountains on whose slopes the seeds are gathered: the Cardamon Mountains. It is the speciality, and indeed the sole economic resource, of a curious and interesting Khmer race, the Pohls, descended from freed royal slaves. The appalling Pol Pot who all but exterminated his fellow countrymen in the 1970s was one of them; perhaps the two facts help to explain each other. The Pohls gather cardamom wild from the forest or cultivate it on a small scale. Their whole life is lived for cardamom, and the timing of their religious festivals depends on its phases of growth. They sell the spice to dealers at a very low price, which rises to a very high one as it goes along the usual commercial channels.

Cloves

Eugenia caryophyllus or *aromatica*, of the Myrtaceae family, is a tropical tree that grows near coasts and may reach a height of ten metres or so. The leaves are very like laurel. The yellow-petalled flowers surrounding a group of stamens are rarely seen, for they are picked while still at the bright pink bud stage. These buds, dried in the sun, become cloves. The clove owes its aroma to an essential oil which oozes under gentle pressure. Powdered cloves have lost this oil; it has evaporated during the grinding of the spice, so although they are more expensive whole cloves should always be chosen.

The remarkable history of cloves, the most popular of all spices, contains all the ingredients of a best-selling novel or a screen spectacular. It has everything: mystery, exoticism, intrigues, fights, assassinations, wicked villains and virtuous heroes, great sailing ships and small traders.

The first episode opens at the court of a magnificent Chinese emperor of the Han dynasty, in the second century BC. A eunuch is leading officers of state to the throne-room to report to the Son of Heaven. Before the silken curtains open a slave offers a porcelain cup, from which each takes a dark brown object rather resembling a nail, places it in his mouth and chews thoroughly. The spice called *hi-sho-hiang*, 'bird's tongue', is nothing of the kind, but the dried bud of a highly aromatic plant. The courtier must sweeten his breath before prostrating himself and addressing the delicate person of his sovereign, who will then surely accede to his request.

The Chinese obtained their *hi-sho-hiang* from a neighbouring empire, the state of Mogada in the Ganges basin of East India, where people have been flavouring their food with the spice since time immemorial. It was known as *luvunga* in Sanskrit. *Luvunga* was not a native plant of Mogada, but originally came from islands to the south-east, many months' journey away by sail across the ocean.

The centuries pass, and now we see Arab dhows sailing down the coasts of the Sea of Oman, the Gulf of Bengal and the China Sea. They like the flavour imparted by the spice *luvunga* or *hi-sho-hiang* and buy it, recording its name in their bills of lading as *qarumfel*. They supply it to Lebanese and Syrian traders along the usual spice route. However, although Pliny mentions a spice called *caryophyllon*, a Greek word meaning literally 'petal of the nut tree', it is not certain that he meant the cloves we know today; there are too many inaccuracies in his description. Dioscorides, Theophrastus and the gastronomic writers of their period say nothing on the subject.

The second episode opens, like the first, amidst the luxury of an imperial court. This time we are in Rome. Three hundred and thirty-five years have passed since the Crucifixion. The Emperor is now a Christian, a recent convert but full of zeal. Having moved the imperial capital to Byzantium, now called Constantinopolis, the Emperor Constantine the Great, anxious to establish the principle of the divine right of the monarchy, wishes to show his deep respect for the Church of Rome. He gives Pope Sylvester the most magnificent present possible: 150 pounds (45 kilos) of *caryophyllon* sealed in vessels worthy of such a treasure. As we have seen with pepper, the importance of a spice did not reside solely in its commercial value.

This *caryophyllon* is described by Paul of Aegina around the year 650 as a valuable remedy, and, in the *Excerpta* which follow the recipes of Apicius, *carifolu* is mentioned among the spices essential to good households. *Carifolu* becomes *garofano* in Italian, and is likewise applied to the pink, a flower which also came from Syria and which resembles it. The word appears as *girofre* in France in the twelfth century: 'E gengibre et girofre a puignées mangert' – 'ginger and cloves in handfuls' – (*La vie de Saint Thomas martyr*). Next come the forms *giroufle*, *gérofle*, *giroffle* and *girofle*: the last-named is the spelling used in the *Viandier*'s recipe for *cameline*, a sauce containing 'ginger, cinnamon and plenty of cloves'. For the soup called *Menjoire*, a broth made from various birds, 'you need a little cloves'. The *Ménagier* reports the list of spices used by Master Helye for a wedding feast. He calls cloves simply 'clous', literally 'nails': 'A quarter of cloves and grains of Paradise, six sous'. The English word 'clove' comes from *clou*; in full, the French expression was *clou de girofle*, and in English the spice was originally called 'clove-gillyflower'. This full name was then reserved for the clove-scented pink, sometimes further corrupted to 'July-flower'.

Baron Pichon, the editor of the *Ménagier*, points out that all the spices used by Master Helye feature in royal decrees of February 1349 relating to the duties levied on various foods as they entered Paris. These documents show that pepper, sugar, cinnamon, rice, aniseed and cloves came in by the bale. Cloves are typically associated with grains of Paradise in medieval recipes, since the two spices complemented each other according to the taste of the time, and one wonders whether the 'quarter of cloves and grains of Paradise' was bought ready mixed. Baron Pichon thinks not, believing it unlikely in the Middle Ages, when the authorities were far too punctilious to. sanction the sale of mixed products in proportions that would be difficult to control. And cloves were infinitely more expensive than grains of Paradise, which were not exactly cheap themselves. For *bochet* (spiced mead): 'If you would make it very good, add thereto an ounce of ginger, long pepper, grains of Paradise and cloves, as much of the one as of the other, save that there shall be less of the cloves.'

To make a powder of spices for flavouring fruit compotes, the *Ménagier* recommends: 'Take three-quarters of stem of gillyflower, called stick of gilly-flower ...' Were these 'stems' or 'sticks', which feature on the list of the Italian merchant Pegolotti's *Pratica della Mercatura*, small twigs from the clove tree or the stems of the cloves themselves? The natives of the fabled spice islands where cloves grew used the fresh leaves as herbs to flavour their cooking. Since the early years of the twentieth century essence of cloves has been obtained by the distillation of leafy twigs.

As for the cloves themselves in their various forms – widely used in medieval cookery[24] and administered medicinally as a panacea by the pharmacopoeia on which the Salerno School, Paracelsus and Fioravanti based their thinking, and regarded as an 'anodine specific' against the plague, impotence and catarrh – the Arabs and the Chinese who were now supplying the Italians did not really know exactly where they came from, or if they did they kept the secret well. In his notes to the *Lusiad* of Camoëns, 'an epic poem on the discovery of the East Indies', tracing the tale of Vasco da Gama, the French translator of 1735, Duperron de Castera, has this to say of the allegory of the giant Adamastor (Canto V) who menaces the navigators as they try to round the Cape of Good Hope:

> Adamastor represents Mahomet and his followers, who opposed the discovery and conquest of the Indies by the Portuguese with all their might. The Moors and the Turks were masters of the sea route, and carefully kept all knowledge of it from the peoples of Europe. When

Clove: engraving from Chenu's *Encyclopédie d'histoire naturelle* of 1873

they saw that their secrets were about to be revealed they resorted to
arms, to cunning, and to every means that might close the gates of the
East to us.

Marco Polo, speaking for the Italian merchants who would also have liked to
dispense with intermediaries, questioned the Chinese. However, we cannot be quite
sure that he himself is telling the truth about the replies they gave him. He says
that cloves come from the country of the Ghindous in the south of Tibet (Gaindu),
from Java, 'a very rich island', and from other islands called Nocaran and
Gavenispola (the Nicobar Islands off the coast of Sumatra). Two hundred years
later a compatriot of his, Nicolo Conti, who travelled the archipelagos for 25 years,
discovered that the cloves in the Java warehouses came from other and even more
easterly lands, perhaps the Celebes.

In 1497 Vasco da Gama rounded the Cape of Good Hope, despite all Adamastor
could do, and set up Portuguese trading posts in Mozambique. He reached Mombasa
in Kenya, where the local petty king told him, 'If you are going to the East for
the merchandise it produces, if you want cinnamon, cloves, and those various
aromatics which encourage lust by feeding pleasure ... none of those things shall
be wanting in our island, you shall find them in such abundance that you need
only content yourself here and go no farther.' Such, at least, was the gist of what
he said as Camoëns reports it in elegant terms.[25] Da Gama did not trust the king
of Mombasa and, besides, he had to go on to India. But there does seem to have
been a deliberate attempt to keep Europeans out of the Indian Ocean. Thanks to

505

his spies and a renegade Italian monk-cum-adventurer, da Gama's successor Albuquerque finally received confirmation that cloves came from the Moluccas or Spice Islands.

> The Moluccas haunted Albuquerque's mind. They were there, present but still unknown beyond the Strait of Malacca, growing on shores fragrant with their spices. They were within reach, like a fruit guessed at but unseen within thick foliage. That fruit had to be plucked.[26]

The fruit was found by chance. One of Albuquerque's ships was wrecked, and its captain, Serraó, was picked up by a Malay *prao* on its way to Amboina in the Moluccas for cloves. Serraó eventually became viceroy of the island and died there nine years later, in the arms of his native wife.

His friend Magellan, a former officer of Albuquerque's who was unjustly treated by King Manuel of Portugal, offered his services to the Spanish King Charles I, later to be Emperor Charles V. He suggested sailing west to those clove-bearing lands of which he knew from Serraó. He did indeed circumnavigate the globe, checkmating the Pope's plan for sharing out the world, but died on the voyage, and as the Emperor had other matters on his mind the Portuguese remained masters of the Spice Islands and their clove trees.

In his account of Magellan's voyage, his Italian supercargo, Pigafetta, describes such wonderful islands as Zzubu, Babar, Miaou, and their dangers. The navigators had intended to win over the natives with presents of cheap trinkets, and Pigafetta carefully notes in his mini-glossaries that, whereas the 'Gentiles', as he terms the pagans of the Moluccas, called the clove *chiande*, the people of Babar and Miaou in particular called small handbells *colon-colon*, and little round bells *girin-girin*; unfortunately, this currency was of little use in obtaining cloves. 'Some 50 years ago the Moors lived in the Moluccas, and before them the Gentiles who set no price on the cloves. There are still some left, but they are in the mountains where the cloves came from.' The Moorish traders had only to provide little bells in exchange for the cloves grown by their slaves, and the Spanish arrived on the scene too late in too old a world. That in itself was proof of the conspiracy of silence towards the Western world master-minded by the Arabs.

In 1619 some Englishmen managed to procure a few clove seedlings for their own estates in Amboina and Miaou. The young trees grew very well. But the Dutch, now owners of the Moluccas and their clove trees, massacred or expelled all the English in the archipelago. They then forced the natives whom they ruled to destroy all the clove trees except for those growing on the islands of Ternate and Amboina, where they kept as jealous a watch on the plantations as if they were a state secret.

The third episode in the saga of cloves begins in the boardroom of the French East India Company in the year 1748. For over a century the French had not been making as much use as before of most of the spices so lavishly included in medieval recipes. In fact, this was one of the distinguishing marks of French cooking compared with that of other European countries, in particular Spain, Germany and Poland. Italian cooking followed the French, slightly later, in adopting the wise policy of moderation. Only cloves and pepper had avoided banishment, and indeed, as they were now almost the only standard spices, their use was on the increase: they feature in 40 per cent of the recipes in the Sieur de La Varenne's *Cuisinier françois* of 1651, compared with 4 to 16 per cent of recipes in the fourteenth and fifteenth centuries, as calculated by Jean-Louis Flandrin.[27] Nutmeg was showing a recovery too (we shall come to nutmeg in a moment), but cinnamon and ginger were used only to flavour sweet dishes. Meanwhile the native aromatics beloved of the Gallo-Romans and rather despised in the Middle Ages were coming to the fore again. As gardening became fashionable, they were grown in greater quantity and variety.

In the seventeenth and eighteenth centuries, the age of the Enlightenment,

> one senses that, at a time when the aristocracy was refining its taste, culture and habits, all of which were increasingly different from the tastes and habits of popular culture, the grand cuisine of France paradoxically abandoned the feature that had previously distinguished it from ordinary cookery – its use of spices – and drew new inspiration at least in part from regional cooking, i.e., the cookery of the middle and lower classes. But the paradox is only apparent. For one thing, the use of spices such as pepper and cloves which were the hallmark of dishes for the aristocracy in the Middle Ages gradually became more widespread as first the Portuguese and then the Dutch, despite their monopoly and their Malthusian policy, brought them within the reach of middle-class tables.'[28]

Even in such exotic exceptions as the recipe for *pasté de jambon à la turque* in *Le cuisinier françois*, refinements were added; in this case the meat was studded with cloves. So were onions in the *pot-au-feu* which had to wait for the French Revolution to receive its culinary certificate of respectability: it is not found in Menon's *Cuisinière bourgeoise* of 1773, but two generations later Dumas specifies that *pot-au-feu* should contain 'three big onions, two with a clove stuck in each of them, the third with a clove of garlic.'

However, to return to the boardroom of the French East India Company: among the many problems it had to tackle was the importing of cloves. Lavoisier tells us that France was consuming 9000 pounds a year of them at the end of the *ancien régime*. Importing in such quantity was bad for the kingdom's balance of trade.

A young man of about 30, of engaging and enthusiastic disposition although he has unfortunately lost one arm, stands before the chief officials of the company, explaining his project. An artist, a scholar and a naturalist, he has travelled widely in the Far East and knows it very well. The project appeals to the board, for in spite of the success of Dupleix, its representative in India, the company is making a poor recovery from a series of ludicrous and ill-fated operations. The proposition now under discussion may seem ludicrous too, but the directors of the company have faith in it. The engaging young adventurer who has put his idea to them is called Pierre Poivre, a particularly propitious name for one about to engage in the grocery trade, for the French for 'grocer' is *épicier* and originally meant a spice merchant, like the English 'pepperer' mentioned above (whereas 'grocer' comes from Old French *grossier*, a dealer selling in the gross, i.e., wholesale).

The Great Trading Companies

In 1587 the future English admiral Francis Drake was cruising off Cadiz, where a fleet of galleys lay. He was to annihilate it in the same way as he had just devastated the Spanish territories on the west coast of America in the course of his second voyage round the world. Drake's luck was in: he next seized a Portuguese carrack which incautiously crossed his path, confiscated its rich cargo, and laid hands on the ship's papers, which contained valuable information about the East Indian trade.

When he brought the documents back to London they interested the merchants of the City, who decided to form a company to trade in the East Indies, hitherto the province of the Portuguese. However, they had to wait another 13 years. Finally, on 31 December 1600, Queen Elizabeth I incorporated the East India Company by royal charter as 'The Governor and Company of Merchants of London, trading into the East Indies'. It also had the right to trade with Africa and America, and was granted the authority to use a personal seal, to take administrative decisions, and to elect its own governor and 20 directors. A very large capital sum was immediately raised, enabling the company to fit out and arm five vessels of 150 to 600 tons. Each ship's captain was commissioned and empowered to conclude trading agreements in the name of Her Gracious Majesty, particularly with the sultans of the Sunda Islands and the governors of Indian cities.

England's intervention occasioned bitter military rivalry with the Portuguese and the Dutch. As André Maurois put it: 'The system of great trading companies which aroused both commercial greed and a desire for conquest was, of all forms of colonization, the most threatening to the natives and the hardest for the national government to control.' The commercial spice-trading empires ran with blood. The great nineteenth-century economist James Rogers, professor of political economy at Oxford, remarked that more blood had been spilt over cloves than over dynastic struggles.

The company made a good profit from the start. It set up a factory at Surale, the first such English station on the Indian subcontinent. This did not suit the Portuguese and Dutch, who were already busy trying to edge each other out, especially as the latter were in a mood of patriotic pride in the recent constitution of their nation. Hoping to retain the spices monopoly, and judging the English method a good one, they founded their own Dutch East India company on 2 March 1602, governed by a remarkable merchant, Cornelius Houtman, who had served a long apprenticeship in trade in Lisbon and Java. The Dutch East India Company was a very modern concept for its time: it did not, like its English rival and forerunner, consist of a group of large merchants, but of a great many small local associations which were able, acting all together, to raise considerable capital. From little acorns mighty oaks do grow.

The Dutch East India Company swiftly gained control of the Moluccas or Spice Islands and their cloves, and, although democratic by definition, it proved the most totalitarian of all the colonial powers. Having concentrated spice-growing in places that could easily be guarded, and forbidding any competition from the natives on pain of death, the Dutch built a dozen prison fortresses to hold uncooperative native princelings. They then imported fierce animals and let them loose in lands where they had never been known before, a new and very efficacious kind of Praetorian guard. Unfortunates suspected of surreptitiously selling a few nutmegs or cloves to foreigners were cruelly tortured.

For its own part, and from lack of interest rather than grim determination, the English East India Company clung to India, particularly Madras and Hooghly, leaving the Dutch, who had the best sailors of their time and the best accountants in the world, to conquer the seas and the European trading stations elsewhere in the East Indies. So great was Dutch naval domination that one of their admirals ventured into the Thames itself followed by a fleet, with a broom tied to the prow of his flagship. The message was obvious: Holland had swept the seas before her.

While the Netherlands were the greatest naval power of the time, the Dutch East India Company feared no one. It was entirely autonomous, and was run with all the gravity of a parish council. It took over Java, Malacca, Ceylon, the Celebes, and certain ports on the Malabar coast where the Arabs and Italians had previously had everything their own way. Ploughing the seas with the pride of its 200 ships, which were hardly enough for all the business it did, it made an exclusive trade treaty with Japan under the noses of the Spanish Jesuits who were well established in the country and operating in great secrecy.

It took Cromwell's armed fist to strike a blow that enabled England to raise her head again: the Protector forced the Dutch to pay huge damages for the massacre of Amboina. In 1657 the charter of the English East India Company was renewed by Charles II. It soon became a state within the state. A second company was formed in 1698, and after some years of rivalry and fierce quarrelling the two merged under the name of the United East India Company, which acquired vast tracts of land, made a great deal of money from tea, and provided careers and wealth for many younger sons of noblemen who were not qualified, by the laws of primogeniture, to inherit the family titles and revenues.

The Dutch and the English seemed to be seated in the scales of the international spice trade: when one went up the other went down. As England grew rich, the fortunes of Holland began to decline. The year 1697 was disastrous for the Dutch. Absorbed in their rivalry, the merchants of England and Holland took no notice of another company, founded in 1664 by Colbert, Louis XIV's minister, after two abortive attempts to colonize Madagascar. The French East India Company wanted its own share of the riches of the spice trade. Admittedly those first two attempts, under Henri IV and Louis XIII respectively, had been dismal failures. Colbert granted his company a 50-year charter and a subsidy of four million *livres* a year. Unfortunately, instead of merchants, administrators and people with experience of the physical and psychological conditions of the tropics, the colonists who actually went out were the idle sprigs of the aristocracy, empty-headed youths who thought more of their embroidered coats than keeping proper accounts or maintaining good relations with the natives.

In 1714, errors and foolishness, ill-judged operations and clumsy initiatives, negligence and irresponsibility left the company facing a debt of 50 million *livres*. The Edinburgh-born French banker Law and his Company of Louisiana or the Occident took it over in 1719. The East Indies and China companies were merged, and the whole body became the Perpetual Company of the Indies. Encouraged by this optimistic title, the Regent, Philippe of Orléans, granted Law a charter to deal in tobacco and run a lottery. But the company soon declined into a mere collection of tax-farmers who were less inclined than ever to distinguish between company property and their personal expenses.

With the ruin of Law and the failure of his system, the company, ceasing to be 'perpetual', was reorganized on a purely commercial basis. In 1731 it abandoned the exploitation of the American colonies to devote itself to the East Indies, where there was still much to be done. Cardinal Fleury provided as large a new injection of funds as he could and, most important of all, he finally appointed competent agents. In line with this policy, when Mahe, Karikal and Yanam had been added to the existing French possessions of Pondicherry and Chandernagore, a very able man, Mahé de La Bourdonnais, was appointed governor of the Île de France (Mauritius), an important staging post on the way to India. La Bourdonnais fitted out a fleet at his own expense, seized Madras – and was then recalled to France on vague accusations of prevarication. He was consigned to the Bastille and replaced by Dupleix, who turned Chandernagore into a major trading station, made friends with the Indian rulers who were anxious to be rid of the English, and interfered with internal Indian affairs perhaps rather more than was necessary.

In any event, the authorities in Paris decided that his policy of making great acquisitions for France was completely unrealistic, and he too was recalled. The French East India company lost its monopoly in 1769 and its charter in 1791, and the revolutionary Convention suppressed it.

Seven years later, the Dutch East India Company too ceased to exist. The war between Holland and England finished it. The English company was virtually nationalized by Pitt's India Act of 1784 because of the intrigue and wastefulness which always seemed to plague colonial enterprises run by younger sons of the nobility, and Lord Liverpool abolished its trade monopoly in 1813. After the Indian Mutiny of 1857, the administration of India passed from the company to the Crown, in which India became known as the jewel.

Pierre Poivre succeeded in his mission to Indochina. He then went on to the Philippines to be closer to the Moluccas, where no one might land, on pain of death, without special permission from the Dutch authorities. They never gave such permission. Poivre made his way into the good books of the Spanish who had settled in the Philippines, and was instrumental in obtaining the freedom of a Moluccan petty king imprisoned there. The grateful king helped him with his plan. They set sail for the Moluccas, and after many vicissitudes reached Timor, with the complicity of the natives. Poivre managed to persuade the authorities that he was only a crippled and insignificant traveller who had lost his way. By dint of great effort and cunning, he managed to acquire several nutmeg and clove plants. Stuffing them into the big pockets of his coat, he made haste to reach the Île de France, arriving there at the end of 1753.

A few of the colonists of the island, now Mauritius, were willing to accept the young plants, but there were not really enough of them for an orchard. The French East India Company, caught up in difficulties as usual, had forgotten all about its clove-hunter. Disillusioned, Poivre returned to France and retired into seclusion for nine years, pursuing scientific research.

In 1767, however, the duc de Praslin, who was naval minister at the time, sent him out to the Mascarene Islands as governor. And he was forgotten again. Though he was an excellent administrator, he was still obsessed by his clove trees, and this time he sent two ships to the Moluccas. Local chiefs who had not forgotten the extraordinary little Frenchman helped his commando unit to bring back a complete range of the spice plants so closely guarded by the Dutch. Five clove trees were left in the care of a Creole, the Sieur Hubert, who lived on the island of La Réunion. They were sabotaged by the jealous director of the trial garden, but one survived and produced an excellent crop. It was to be the ancestor of all the clove trees on La Réunion and Sainte-Marie in Madagascar. Descendants of that tree were sent to Cayenne, San Domingo and Martinique.

Plants from the Île de Bourbon were taken to Zanzibar, and did so well there that the island became one of the major world centres of clove-growing. In the days of sea travel by the great shipping lines, passengers used to tell, marvelling, how the breeze blowing off the land carried the wonderful scent of cloves, telling them they were approaching the island even while they were still far out to sea.

Pleased with the success of his clove trees, but yet again discouraged by the apathy of the French administration, Pierre Poivre retired to Dijon in 1773 and died there 13 years later. His widow married the economist and politician Dupont de Nemours. The present clove trees on Madagascar, the Comores and the Seychelles are all descended from the trees transplanted to Mauritius and La

Réunion. There are almost no clove trees left on the Moluccas at all. A chapter of history had finally been closed.

Nutmeg and Mace

Myristica fragrans, of the Myristicaceae family, the nutmeg, is a large tropical tree with small yellow flowers and large, very fragrant leaves. Only the flowers of female trees will produce fruit, and they must be fertilized by pollen from the flowers of male trees. The nutmegs are the seeds inside these fruits. They are surrounded by a kind of fleshy network, red when fresh, which is mace, and has a slightly different aroma. When the fruits are harvested, several times a·year, the nutmegs are separated from the mace and both are dried. In its natural state nutmeg is a dark red-brown colour. The Dutch used to dip nutmegs in lime to prevent them from germinating, and even when their monopoly was no more they continued the habit, which also protected the nutmegs from insects and weevils.

The dried mace is flattened into 'blades'. The nutmeg itself is grated as it is needed; mace is broken into pieces. Both contain a highly volatile essential oil. They should therefore be kept in air-tight containers, in small quantities. Mace is stronger and more pungent in flavour than nutmeg itself.

'Do you like nutmeg? It is put into everything', said Boileau. How long had this passion for nutmeg been nurtured? Nutmeg is thought to be the last but one of the exotic spices to become known in Europe, although it has been identified among the spices and aromatics stuffed inside Egyptian mummies (L. Guyot). There is still controversy as to whether the Greeks and Romans of classical times were really familiar with nutmeg and the mace that surrounds it. Was the latter the *macis* mentioned by Plautus or the *macis* of Pliny? Was nutmeg the *kaumacon* described by Theophrastus? Plautus the comic dramatist was speaking of the bark of a tree, Pliny the naturalist of a large root and Theophrastus of cubeb, a large and very bitter pepper.

The first really authenticated nutmegs are thought to have arrived at the Byzantine court in the sixth century, coming by way of the Bedouins; the Greeks translated the Arab word *mesk*, from Persian *muchk*, as *moskhos*. The modern French *muscade* is said to come from Provençal *muscado*, and thus, like Italian *moscada* and German *Muskat*, derives from Low Latin *muschatus*, perfumed. These words are all related to 'musk, musky', and the muscat grape, notable for its perfumed flavour, takes its name from the same idea. Old French, however, had *mug* for 'musk', and called the spice *la nois mugade* (*Le roman de la Rose*, 1343), which became *noix muguette* in the *Ménagier*, the same word as modern French *muguet* for the highly scented lily of the valley. The English word nutmeg derives from that Old French version; similarly, we find *nuez moscada* as well as *nuez de especia* in Spanish and *noce moscada* in Italian. Mace is *macis* in both French and Italian, and *macias* in Spanish; German has no separate word for it as a spice, using *Muskat* for both mace and nutmeg, but does have *Macisöl* for oil of mace or nutmeg.

Around the year 1000 the Persian physician Ibn Sina or Avicenna, the most remarkable man of his time, described the *muchk* as *jansi ban*, nut of Banda. This is the first known mention west of the Euphrates of the Banda Islands, a group in the Moluccan archipelago.

In accordance with the usual pattern in the history of spices, and following the Arab example, nutmeg and mace were initially used as perfumes or medicinally in the Western world. However, although apothecaries were usually enthusiastic in their praise of most other such spices, which ended up in the kitchen, they approached nutmeg with more caution. In the incorrect dosage it acted like a drug in the modern sense of the word.[29] There was great suspicion of such mind-changing drugs in general, a lucky state of affairs for humanity and one which lasted centuries. Nutmeg was used only in making hypnotic and soothing remedies, for instance in Nicolai's *requies* (a soporific) and Sylvius's theriac (an antidote to the bites of poisonous creatures) and carminative spirit (to relieve flatulence). The Salerno School decreed sagely that 'one nut is good for you, the second will do you harm, the third will kill you'.

In fact a whole nut represented a considerable quantity of spice, far more than a whole peppercorn or a single clove, which are both small items. Mace was the spice most used in cooking, since it was more easily broken up. In the middle of his recipes the *Ménagier*, bearing in mind the precepts of the Salerno School, mentions: 'Note, that nutmegs, mace and garingal make the head ache.' Garingal or *galanga* was a kind of ginger. Mace, less expensive than nutmegs and a good seller on the retail market, cost four *francs-or* a pound in France when Jeanne d'Évreux's inventory was drawn up at the end of the fourteenth century – but in England that amount was worth half the price of a cow, as we learn from the list of Jean le Bon's spices mentioned above.

Once they had seized the Moluccas, therefore, the Portuguese ruined the lucrative Arab-Italian nutmeg trade which had centred on Acre. Lisbon profited by that fact until the Dutch East India Company came to the Banda Islands in 1656. Anxious to have a monopoly, of nutmeg as well as the other spices which brought them such fabulous wealth, the Dutch forbade the export of nutmeg trees and did all they could to keep everyone, even the botanists of their own country, from knowing anything about them. We have seen how Pierre Poivre, by dint of determination, cunning and courage, managed to make his way into the archipelago in the course of one of the most interesting chapters in the history of spices. He brought out nutmegs and young nutmeg trees as well as clove seedlings, and a few years later his emissaries were even luckier, for birds, stealing nutmegs from under the noses of first the Portuguese and then the Dutch, had dispersed the trees over quite a large area around the Moluccas.

Then, in tune to the rhythm of the wars and diplomatic agreements of the late eighteenth and early nineteenth centuries, the English and Dutch succeeded one another several times in dominating the archipelago. Eventually the English decided the most practical thing to do was to take nutmeg trees to the safety of the island of Penang in Malaysia, and thence to Singapore. The plantations flourished until a fungus disease killed them all in 1865.

Today nutmegs are grown throughout the tropics, not only in their country of origin, the Moluccas (unlike the clove, which no longer grows there), but also in Sumatra, Java, Bengal, the West Indies, Brazil, Colombia, Central America, the Mascarenes and Madagascar, anywhere the climate is hot and humid and there is plenty of shade. But the Banda archipelago remains the most important producer of nutmegs, a 'nutmeg park' as it has been described, although the West Indian island of Grenada is a strong contender for the title of island of nutmegs, since it supplies almost 40 per cent of world consumption.

Nutmeg: engraving from Chenu's *Encyclopédie d'histoire naturelle* of 1873

The nutmeg is a tree which is usually either male or female; in botanical terminology, it is dioecious. Joseph Hubert of La Réunion, who was given the first nutmeg tree to come from the Moluccas by Pierre Poivre, had the idea of grafting some male branches on female trees to save the space which would otherwise be occupied by trees which bore no crop. Another method is to plant one male tree for every 20 female trees, taking care to place it where the prevailing wind will carry the pollen of these arboreal sultans to every tree in their harems. Some trees will yield over 20,000 nutmegs every season, and they often live to the age of 100.

A great many nutmegs were required when the passion for the spice reached its peak at the end of the seventeenth century, as witness Boileau. At dinner parties, the *précieux* and *précieuses* of the period in France would bring a little case containing a grater and a nutmeg with them, in case they needed it. An engraving of the

514

period shows these fashionable and greedy intellectuals sitting at dinner on one side of the picture, while the other side shows natives decked with feathers beating a tree to bring the fruits down. A caption says:

> Vous aimez la muscade, et savez en quels lieux
> On cultive, on recueille un fruit si précieux.

[You love nutmeg, and know where so precious a fruit is grown and gathered.']

A double meaning of *précieux* is involved, referring to the affectations of the fashionable diners.

Then French cooking calmed down, as works such as Menon's *Cuisinière bourgeoise* show.[30] Nutmeg was no longer automatically added except to white sauces, and mace was rarely used at all. It is a spice typical of Tuscan gastronomy, however, especially in spinach *à la florentine* and ravioli with herbs. Dutch cooking, which tends to be rich, is more easily digested when it includes nutmeg, as it often does. The same is true of Quebec, where, as we have seen, many seventeenth-century French culinary habits linger on. Curiously, Indian cookery uses very little nutmeg, unlike the cuisines of Lebanon, Egypt and North Africa. Mace, with its attractive orange colour, is used to colour and impart a delicate flavour to sauces, rice and curry, and the Indians like it.

Finally, as I mentioned above, the Dutch were in the habit of dipping their nutmegs into lime before exporting them, to prevent germination and preserve their monopoly of the spice. It was not in fact an efficient method, but it became so usual to see nutmegs bleached in this way that the practice was continued to please the consumer, who would not have bought them in their natural state.

Chillies and Sweet Peppers

Capsicum frutescens, of the Solanaceae family, is a perennial shrub in tropical regions, and is grown under glass in temperate climates. Hot chilli peppers are long or rounded fruits which vary from the size of a fingernail to the size of a hand. They turn red as they ripen but never become mild, unlike the fruits of *Capsicum annuum*, the sweet pepper, an annual with larger leaves and fruits. As the sweet pepper ripens it turns from green to yellow and then red, and becomes fleshy and segmented. Dried chillies keep well, but sweet peppers are always eaten fresh, as a vegetable; if they are kept too long they will wither or rot. Paprika, a variety of semi-sweet pepper, is used as a spice after it has been dried and powdered.

The journal of Christopher Columbus provides our first mention of the chilli, a 'better spice than our pepper (*mejor que pimienta nuestra*)'. Columbus is describing the island of Hispaniola (subsequently Haiti and the Dominican Republic) in his entry dated 15 January 1493. The Spaniards looked no further for a name for the local spice, but christened it *pimiento*, as being better and stronger than *pimienta*, and therefore grammatically masculine.

The Caribbean islanders themselves called this fiery vegetable a name something like *ahi*, transcribed in Castilian Spanish as *aji* or *axi* (one must remember the aspirated Spanish pronunciation of *j* and *x*). *Ahi* or *axi* under some such name was found among most of the American Indians, which may show that the West Indies was the area of origin of all chilli varieties, and that they diversified after the colonization of the American continent. In Mexico, however, the pepper is *chili* or *tchili*, and was already being grown by the Toltecs and the Aztecs. In Brazil, it became *quixa*. Lucien Guyot mentions that travellers of the seventeenth century noted the 'very usual employment' of a chilli pepper in the Sunda Islands; it cannot have been a native plant, being as unknown here as elsewhere in the wild state. The mention seems to confirm the theory, discussed above, that certain Central American vegetables were spread by people going east across the Pacific.

Long red chilli, long yellow chilli, and Cayenne pepper: engraving
from Vilmorin and Andrieux's catalogue *Les plantes potagères*, 1883

The Spanish and Portuguese soon introduced the chilli to the Old World, but while the sensitive palates of Europeans remained wary of so hot a flavour, it was a revelation to the peoples of Africa, Arabia and Asia. They took to using it lavishly, and were imitated by the island-dwellers of the Indian and Pacific Oceans, to such an extent that in the sixteenth century, when the spice had spread like the wildfire its fierce flavour suggests, no one was quite sure if 'Calcutta pepper', a chilli which quickly became naturalized in India and was immediately added to the catalogues of traders in Oriental spices, actually came from the East or the West Indies. The Bavarian naturalist Leonhard Fuchs[31] (1501–1566) describes this *siliquastrum* in his *Historia Stirpium* as originating in Calcutta in all its four forms: small, large, pointed and broad. The Germans and northern French used it in small quantities to give body to their beer and help it to keep. The English put it into pickles.

Not all these New World peppers turned out so ferocious, though. In the eighteenth century a large and much milder variety, known in French as *poivron*, from Provençal *pébroun*,[32] began to make its way into the cookery of southern Europe, eaten as a vegetable either cooked or raw. The Abbé J.-F. Rozier's *Cours complet d'agriculture*, published on the eve of the French Revolution, distinguishes it from 'India pepper' (the Indies, East and West, were still being confused); he says, rather boldly, that it was the usual breakfast of the people of Provence, and is not afraid to add that, 'I may say it is the only plant, besides broad beans, which the peasants of Provence and Languedoc do not grudge growing.' But the Abbé was from Lyons and thus a foreigner! Until after the Second World War, in fact, cookery books scarcely ever condescended to mention sweet peppers except as a condiment, pickled in vinegar, a method of preparation which brings it into the scope of this chapter.

Paprika, mild or strong, is also a sweet pepper. Its original name is Polish, *pierprzyca*, but the Hungarians adopted it as their national spice when they made it a basic ingredient of goulash. Mild paprika is made from the seeds only; strong paprika, darker in colour, is made from the whole fruit, dried and ground. Spain produces chillies, paprika and sweet peppers in abundance, particularly in the Estremadura and Murcia areas. Chorizo, Catalan and Basque sausages or *sobressadas* all owe their colour and spicy flavour to paprika. Fifteen hundred tons of sweet peppers a year are grown in the South of France. Green peppers are simply unripe sweet peppers; they turn yellow when half-ripe, and red when fully ripe. As they ripen they become progressively milder, unlike their relatives paprika and chilli.

As their Linnaean scientific name of *Capsicum annuum* suggests (*Capsicum* indicating that they are capsules or seed cases), sweet peppers and paprika are annual plants, a natural adaptation to temperate climates. True, pungent chillies come from shrubs which may grow to two metres and are perennials in tropical or well-sheltered sub-tropical countries. To grow them in Europe permanent artificial heat under glass must be provided. Chillies grown from hothouse plants put out in the garden will last only one summer, unless they are taken under cover again. The large varieties of sweet peppers and paprika are always mild; the medium-sized kinds vary in pungency; and the smaller chillies are, the fiercer their heat. The African *pili-pili* and West Indian *z'ozio*, no bigger than birds' tongues, are extremely strong. Chillies are not always long and thin; some African varieties in particular are round like tomatoes, and there have been some painful misunderstandings on the part of incautious or short-sighted European visitors. In the West Indies one variety is known as *bouda à Man Jacques*, 'Madame Jacques's bum', a graphic description of its stout and rounded form.

Chillies and sweet peppers contain a great deal of vitamins C and A. The chilli still helps American Indians to compensate for the poor vitamin content of their diet. Because of the ferocity of chillies the Incas, Mayas and Aztecs used them in their techniques of torture. They also provided a poison in which arrows were dipped, and the same substance was used to poison reservoirs of water for fishing: fish which died of it were well spiced even before they were cooked. The chilli also has antiseptic qualities, and its powder might be dusted over suspect food, or even used to fumigate a room. In Africa it is considered a panacea for use against intestinal infections, parasites and diarrhoea, an astringent, an aid to the formation of scar tissue, and even a remedy for piles, a use endorsed by a number of 'alternative' European doctors. It is a drastic remedy, though, and unless you have been accustomed to it for generations the cure may be worse than the disease – although it is a fact that the natives of the tropics, who roast chillies to make them even stronger, suffer far less from digestive troubles than the cautious Europeans.

Finally, chilli peppers have become typical of all exotic gastronomy, and one wonders what those culinary traditions would have done without it. It is as if Italian cooking were to be deprived of that other American fruit, the tomato. To mention only a few uses at random: it is the essential ingredient of the *harissa* used in Arab couscous, originally a sauce made of the chillies of Orissa, in the *achards* of La Réunion, in Indian chutney and curry, in Chinese fruit *kung pro* and in *tsiao-yeou* 'red' oil, in Moroccan and Brazilian fruit salads, and in any number of Mexican *mole* sauces.

The last spice to be revealed to the world at large, chilli has in a way become the superlative among spices.

Aromatics and the Imagination

... Tout un monde lointain, absent presque défunt
Vit dans tes profondeurs, forêt aromatique ...

['An entire, distant world, absent, almost dead, dwells in your depths, O aromatic forest ...']

The forest Baudelaire meant was a woman's perfumed hair, but nothing speaks more tellingly to the unconscious mind than an aroma. 'Perfume also symbolizes memory, which may be one reason for its use in funeral rites', says Pierre Prigent.[33] It also denotes light. 'All plants are lamps, and their light is perfume', wrote Victor Hugo.

Saffron

Crocus sativus, a member of the Iridaceae family, is a bulbous plant which resembles its cousin the garden crocus. What we call saffron is the branching stigmas of the flowers. The three stigmas of the wild saffron crocus growing on hillsides from Italy to Kurdistan are much smaller than those of the cultivated flower, which grow above the level of the petals and droop over. Saffron is grown by division of the bulbs in autumn; if the plant is sown from seed it is three years before any flowers appear. Every cultivated saffron crocus has three stigmas which must be gathered by hand. It takes between 70,000 and 80,000 stigmas to produce a pound of saffron.

Saffron is grown in soil worked to a good tilth, well drained and sheltered. Valencia in Spain has the best reputation for modern saffron. In medieval England, so much was grown in Essex that the town of Saffron Walden was actually named after the aromatic.

To use Victor Hugo's terms, saffron is perhaps 'light' rather than perfume. Its colour is brilliant, its aroma deep. Its name, from Persian *safra* and ultimately from Arabic *za'faran*, means 'yellow'. The golden colour signifies enlightenment, illumination, wisdom. Its ritual uses derived from the symbolism of wisdom revealed. It was once used to dye the robes of Buddhist monks (turmeric, cheaper and more readily available, is now used instead), and to mark the breasts and arms of Indian married women, i.e., those who had truly become women in the full sense. In Tyre the veils of new brides were dyed with saffron.

Since it takes 100,000 flowers of *Crocus sativus* to obtain a kilo of dried stigmas, which must be plucked by hand, saffron has always been almost literally worth its weight in gold. It is hardly surprising, therefore, that in Greek mythology Zeus, the king of the gods, had a bed of saffron. The legend attributes the plant's creation to Hermes the messenger and inventor, who is also credited with kindling fire. Hermes accidentally gave his friend Crocos a mortal wound; blood flowed from his head and was sprinkled on the ground, where the god at once changed it into the little flowers with their precious pistils. Hermes was also the father of Daphnis, named for the laurel or bay, and these aromatics, so profitable in trade and warming to both the palate and the imagination, were obviously suitable items for his divine patronage.

That Greek legend of the origin of saffron derives from the traditions of Asia Minor, and here we are dealing with one of the few aromatic products which did not originate in India or the East Indies. *Crocus sativus* comes from the west of Asia, and grew naturally from Palestine to Kashmir. The wind, blowing from the east whence light itself comes, carried it to Italy, where it is still found in the wild state. The beautiful coloured frescos of the palace of Knossos in Crete show a man gathering saffron, still absorbed in his task after 4000 years.

Crocus sativus does not grow in Egypt, or not naturally. The *Papyrus Eber* mentions the saffron crocuses grown in the sacred gardens of Luxor because they were an ingredient in a wonderful remedy known as *kuphi*, mixed with other aromatics and that other edible gold, honey. Saffron was regularly grown in Mesopotamia, but was earmarked for certain special uses: as a dye, a medicine, and an aromatic or a condiment also reputed to be an aphrodisiac. (Perhaps that was at the back of Zeus' mind when he made his bed of it.)

It was for this last quality as well as its colour that the Romans valued saffron.

It was sprinkled on the marriage beds of young couples in high society, and on the couches where fashionable guests reclined at feasts. Trimalchio has saffron at his banquet in the *Satyricon*. It was thrown before the feet of Roman emperors, who would fling it lavishly about the banqueting room after supper in the luxurious manner of the Sybarites, who themselves claimed that drinking an infusion of saffron before indulging in the pleasures of wine delayed intoxication. Dumas tells us that 'the Romans made an alcoholic tincture of it, which they used to perfume their theatres'. This was perhaps an infusion, or a flavoured wine, since the art of distilling the spirits usually employed in a tincture had not yet been discovered. In any case, the effect must have been largely in the mind, for the true saffron which, according to Pliny, came from Cilicia or Phrygia, fetched such prices that bastard saffron or safflower, *Carthamus tinctorius*, was used when display was the object; safflower has little aroma but produces a very yellow colouring. It was to remain in use until the Renaissance, as we shall see below.

Saffron-growing in Europe goes back to the occupation of Spain by the Moors between the eighth and tenth centuries, and Spain was to remain the centre of saffron production. It still provides almost all the saffron sold throughout the world. Spanish cooking has always been brightened by its yellow colour.

The medical authorities of the Salerno School unreservedly recommended the use of saffron.

> Saffron arouses joy in every breast,
> Settles the stomach, gives the liver rest.

Roger Bacon, the *doctor mirabilis*, claimed that saffron delayed ageing. When the French began growing it in the Comtat Venaissin during the fourteenth century, it contributed a good deal to the region's prosperity, and guaranteed it after the Popes, to whom the territory had been ceded, ceased to hold it as a papal possession. At the Papal court at Avignon, where people were as anxious to stay young as anyone else, saffron was added to many dishes.

The saffron cake or saffron bread, such as the Lebanese plait, found almost everywhere in the Mediterranean, dates from Roman times – although it is likely that the Romans themselves made it with safflower. Like aniseed bread, it was a gift given by Provençal bakers to their best customers at Christmas and Easter.

By the same token Provençal cookery was able to use the local saffron without going to ruinous expense, for the people of Provence, even those in comfortable circumstances, have never liked throwing their money away. A very old recipe going back to the time of Queen Jeanne was popular among the more prosperous classes of Aix and Marseilles: it consisted of tripe and offal with saffron simmered long and slowly in copper moulds, and was served on every high day and holiday.

Saffron spread up the Rhône valley by way of Vienne, crossed the Loiret, was widely grown in the Gâtinais area until the beginning of this century, and went on into Angoulême. But according to Olivier de Serres this 'sombre contagion', as Bruyerin-Champier called it, originated in the South of France, spreading 'from the saffron plantation of Albi, where such fruit has a place among the best revenues of the country.'

A recipe given by the *Ménagier* for making 'composte' uses saffron: 'Note, that it must be begun on St John's Day, which is the twenty-fourth day of June ... ' This compote, to which more fruit is added as crop after crop is gathered, going on until St Andrew's Day on 30th November, sounds rather like a modern German *Rumtopf*, though there is no alcohol in it. Among the many spices mentioned, including almost everything then on the market, the *Ménagier de Paris* prescribes 'half an ounce[34] of saffron of Orte dried and pounded.' In a note, his editor Pichon mentions that a saying in the sixteenth-century *Dicts des pais* still held that 'good saffron comes from Orte'. The climate of Orthez and indeed the whole well-sheltered Pau region is mild and must have been just right for saffron, although references are still found to Gâtinais and Albigensian saffron.

Lucien Guyot mentions a study written by one C. Grégoire and published in 1804, an *Essai historique sur l'état de l'agriculture en Europe au XVIe siècle*. This work mentions a 'very rare' document concerning saffron:

> Its cultivation in the Gâtinais was so successful that it has long been preferred to the saffron of other countries. ... It was the subject of a very rare work, ignored by almost all who have written of saffron and entitled *Le safran de La Rochefoucaut*, Portiers, 1567, in quarto. ... Before the year 1520 little saffron was grown; the eagerness of purchasers aroused interest, and soon the plant covered the countryside of Angoulême, to such an extent that it produced more than enough to satisfy Gaul, Germania and many another country. La Rochefoucaut was the main market and when the exhausted soil around that town would produce no more saffron, and wheat was grown instead, it retained its reputation as the centre of the saffron trade, and buyers and sellers flocked there from every point of the compass.

In the sixteenth century, the saffron grown in France meant that Spain had lost her customers from Toulouse. Until now they had had the monopoly of distributing Spanish saffron 'in Gaul and in Germania'. Spanish saffron therefore had to go along the spice road in the opposite direction, and was exchanged in Alexandria and Damascus for cinnamon and ginger, to the great vexation of the Portuguese and Italians.

Where did the saffron used by Master Helye for the wedding mentioned in the *Ménagier de Paris* come from? If saffron was not yet being grown in Angoulême, was it from Orthez, Carpentras in the Comtat Venaissin, Albi, or Spain by way of Toulouse? All we know is its price, which was high and suggests a foreign product: three silver sous an ounce, more than the cost of two pounds of 'beaten rice' (polished). Despite such prices, saffron was widely used in the Middle Ages. It went not only into *jaunette*, i.e., yellow, sauce for eggs, as mentioned in the *Viandier*, but into all kinds of recipes for ragoûts and sweet dishes. The *Ménagier* adds it to the herbs in a salad of *fraze* (strawberries), and Rabelais' girdle cakes still contained it in the sixteenth century.

Early in the fourteenth century Marianne Mulon finds *safranum* used 41 times and *crocum* used 29 times in the 172 recipes of the *Liber coquina*. In her glossary and index, she seems to think, although she gives no reasons, that *safranum* actually meant the bastard saffron or safflower already being used in Roman times, while *crocum* was genuine saffron. It is a fact that the recipes using *safranum* need colour more than they need an additional aromatic. As we saw above, throughout the Middle Ages and at the beginning of the Renaissance it was thought very elegant, particularly in Italy, to gild the roasts displayed at banquets (and 'displayed' is a better term than 'eaten' in the context). If the host was a very wealthy man, gold leaf was used, but the recipes indicate that if you wanted to imitate gold leaf you brushed a slack paste of flour, egg and 'saffron' over the meat. The saffron itself was probably an imitation, i.e., safflower, which was perfectly suitable for the purpose, and cheaper than the real thing. The *Viandier*'s 'stuffed chicken' served at the French court included in its stuffing 'a fair amount' of saffron. First the fowls were boiled in a court-bouillon of beef broth 'and great plenty of saffron', and then they were roasted.

> And to gild them ... take great plenty of the yolks of eggs and beat them well, and put a little saffron to them, and put this gilding in a dish or some other vessel. ... And when your fowls are cooked, and your apples[35] too, take the spit to the vessel where your gilding is, and cast your gilding all along it, and put it back over the fire and turn it two or three times so that your gilding shall take, and make sure that your gilding does not go over too hot a flame, and does not burn.

I suspect that the 'fair amount' and 'great plenty' of saffron in the stuffing and the court-bouillon were the real thing, and the substance added to the gilding was actually safflower. Imagination would have done the rest, even at the French courts, which in fact practised a good deal of economy. But the honour of a master cook would have required him to say the ingredient was always saffron.

By the eighteenth century the use of saffron had been in decline for several generations, at least in French cooking for the upper classes. In his preface to *Le cuisinier françois*, Jean-Louis Flandrin mentions the distaste of several French noblemen on their travels when confronted with the saffron and spices which German, Polish and Spanish cooking still used in abundance, thus refuting Maria Gonzaga and Mme d'Aulnoy, to mention only those two ladies. The fact was that, from the sixteenth century onwards, saffron, now that it was grown in France, had become an affordable luxury for people in modest circumstances: 'A luxury that even reached the villages, where people wanted seasonings of pepper, saffron, spices, etc.' (Champier). In short, by the end of the eighteenth century saffron had become quite vulgar. Alexandre Dumas echoes the sentiments of his time. Although he says that the smell 'suggests death', he recognizes that the flavour 'has nothing disagreeable about it ... there are several countries where this flower is used as a seasoning, or to colour cakes, vermicelli, butter, etc. It is used today only in making babas, pilau, rice à l'africaine, and scubac.'

Was the scubac Dumas mentions shish-kebabs? He was partly correct, in any case, for saffron is now used in France only in some regional recipes such as bouillabaisse, Provençal fish soups and rice dishes incorporating various seafoods, and the *mourtayrol* of the south-east of the country. It lingers on in such dishes, a memento of the saffron-growing that was once so prosperous a business in the South of France. It is also still typical of other Mediterranean dishes such as Spanish *paella*, Moroccan *tajine*, Oriental *shish-kebabs*, Iranian and Indian yoghurt sauces, and in particular various Middle Eastern fried egg dishes.

Vanilla

Vanilla planifolia is a kind of tropical orchid, a climbing plant with greenish white flowers, and in its natural state it clambers over the jungle trees of Central America and the northern part of South America. The fruit is a hard green pod 10 to 15 centimetres long, containing a great many tiny seeds. Because of the way the flowers are formed, with a kind of thin film like a hymen over them, pods are borne only when they have been artificially pollinated.

The pods are picked when barely ripe, plunged into boiling water or exposed to the sun, with a protective cover over them. Their natural liquids seep out and they ferment, turning very dark in colour. They are finally dried, and at this stage they are seen to be covered with a fine frosting of crystals of vanillin, or aromatic aldehyde.

If some exquisite little goddess of gluttony were to exist, her name would surely be Vanilla, and she would be a delicate, slim, dark creature in a dress sparkling with tiny perfumed crystals. Vanilla was unknown in the Old World until the beginning of the sixteenth century.

The Aztecs gave us the smooth flavour of vanilla, and we also owe them chocolate, to which I shall come in chapter 18. Vanilla pods were first harvested from wild plants in the jungle of the hot regions to the south-west of Mexico. Someone may have noticed that when the long, thin pods of certain orchids, pods which rather resembled the tresses of Indian women's hair, fell to the ground before they were fully ripe they fermented under their covering of humus, giving off a delicious aroma – and an unexpected one, since the slender white flowers are almost scentless.

These remarkable pods were of course reserved for great dignitaries, to add an even more delicious flavour to their favourite drink of cocoa sweetened with honey,

Drying vanilla on the island of Bora-Bora

that other marvel of the forest. In spite of their reputation for cruelty, the Aztecs were very keen on botany and gardening, beauty and perfume:

> And so I sing my perfumed song
>   Like a polished jewel,
> like a shining turquoise, like a glittering emerald,
>   a flowery hymn to spring ...

says an Aztec poem as given by Jacques Soustelle.[36] The immediate concern of the first Aztec emperor Moctezuma around 1450, when he had conquered Haxtepec, the capital of the Tierras Calientes ('the hot countries'), was to lay out a trial garden into which tropical plants, both ornamental and useful, were transplanted from the surrounding jungle and even farther away. It is possible that vanilla was one of these plants, since vanilla vines had long been cultivated by the time the Spanish arrived in 1520.

In fact the conquistadores found that it was grown not only in Mexico, but all over the isthmus and as far afield as Venezuela, Colombia and Guiana. The small scented pod, which they called *vainilla*, delighted them, and they brought it back to Spain along with cocoa. It was together with cocoa, surely its natural companion, that *vainilla* conquered the court of the Sun King, where it received its French

524

name of *vanille*, expressed similarly in other European languages: English vanilla, German *Vanille*, Italian *vaniglia*.

In fact there are several kinds of vanilla. The tropical forests of Central America contain a great many plants of *Vanilla inodora* which, as the name indicates, has no aroma. An absent-minded botanist collected a quantity of these in Guiana around 1820 and proudly bore them off to La Réunion, where he learned his mistake. Another species, *Vanilla pompona* or vanillon, grew so well in the West Indies that it invaded the forests and returned to the wild. However, the slightly nutmeg-like aroma of the short pods is not the same as that of classic vanilla. True, fragrant vanilla is indigenous to Central America and to the Greater Antilles, the West Indian islands to which it may have been carried by birds or the wind.

Growing *Vanilla planifolia* or *fragrans* away from its birthplace seemed very difficult at first, even impossible. The vine obligingly clung to the supporting stakes or trees provided for it and produced elegant flowers, but no pods, or a very few which seemed to have appeared by chance. Moreover, it did not reproduce itself. Was it homesick? What did it need to make it happy? It actually needed its friends of the American forest, those curious stingless but voracious bees which we encountered in the chapter on honey. These *Meliponae* provided the honey which sweetened the Aztecs' vanilla-flavoured cocoa, and they also, by an ingenious quirk of nature, fertilized the vanilla flowers by entering the calyx, penetrating the thin film covering it. Since Aztec times the plantations had been perpetuated by cuttings, but only the bees could fertilize the flowers. Without them vanilla remained virgin and sterile.

Not until around 1830 did a brilliant gardener called Neumann perfect a technique of artificial pollination in the glasshouses of the Museum of Paris. A vanilla cutting from the plants collected there had been taken to La Réunion, and became the ancestor of all the vanilla plants of the Mascarene and Comoros Islands and Madagascar. Other plants, from various places, were sent to Tahiti, where they flourished.

Most of the vanilla grown in Mexico is destined for the North American market. The needs of France are supplied by the islands of the Indian Ocean and Tahiti. Madagascar supplies almost three-quarters of world consumption, about 1000 tons a year.

The scent of vanilla is so intoxicating that in large doses, for instance inhaled by workers who handle large quantities daily, it sometimes has an effect like a drug. This phenomenon is known as vanillism: it induces headache, lassitude and allergic skin reactions of the face, neck and hands. Unlikely as it may seem that one can be drugged by vanilla, there is no treatment except a change of job.

The small amount of annual world consumption of vanilla – 1600 tons in a good year – may seem surprising when the entire planet is so obviously fond of its flavour, particularly since the advent of ice-cream production on an industrial scale. But vanilla and vanilla flavour are not necessarily the same thing. Natural vanilla goes into the most expensive luxury products. Other, cheaper products are merely vanilla-flavoured; they use a synthetic product, ethylvanillin, which is a very good imitation of the real thing. Indeed, it is probably the most important of all artificial flavourings, supplying a very high demand in perfumery as well as in foods. The high price of vanilla naturally led chemists to look for industrial ways of manufacturing the frosted crystals that are the aromatic aldehyde of vanilla, or vanillin, the substance which gives the pods their aroma after fermentation. You have to study labels carefully to be sure whether a product owes its vanilla flavour to genuine vanillin or to artificial ethylvanillin, which is a by-product of wood pulp.

Although evasive labelling is always annoying and seems designed to confuse the consumer, there is not really anything to worry about, since after all the aroma of even the most natural foods is the result of a spontaneous chemical process due to the mixture of certain molecules and the changes that occur in them, as perceived by the receptive cells of the nose, the palate and the hypothalamus. The rest is simply imagination.

Everyday Condiments and Herbs

James Joyce remarked in *Ulysses* that God made food and the Devil made seasoning. If so, the Devil has as much imagination as his adversary. The list of condiments used since the days of classical antiquity is so long that it would become wearisome if I were to enumerate them all here. Isidore of Seville mentions 133 aromatic and condimentary herbs, and a dozen fruits *de arboribus aromaticis*. In passing, one notices on his list not only thyme, saffron, fennel, cardamom and marjoram, but some plants which do not sound much like condiments to us today: nettles (bitter, although good in soup when very young and tender), asphodel, cyclamen, tares, pyrethrum, and herbs now used in tisanes or lotions such as celandine,[37] centaury and hyssop, as well as seaweeds and agaric mushrooms. I shall return to these curious and now outdated condiments, but first let us look at one which has proved a perennial favourite, mustard.

Mustard is a typical condiment in the sense in which we understand the word today: its piquant, aromatic flavour has made it popular for thousands of years. It is made from the crushed seeds of the plant. At first they were mixed with vinegar, which was replaced in the Middle Ages by grape must, whence the name, very much the same in most European languages: *moutarde* in French, mustard in English, *Mostrich* in north German dialect, *mostarda* in Italian, *mostaza* in Spanish. The botanical name of *Sinapis* gives the French name for the actual plant, *sénevé*, and standard German *Senf*, like the carrot, *Sinapis* is a member of the Cruciferae family. Its yellow flowers produce pods full of small seeds, and the mustard flour that results from crushing them can be bought for mixing at home. There are also many kinds of ready-mixed mustard on the market, with various other aromatic substances added to taste.

Originally a weed growing among cereal crops, mustard has been cultivated for its own sake since classical Greek times, and Athenaeus, quoting Antiphanes, makes special mention of Cyprus mustard (*napu kuprion*). However, most of the classical authors used the term which inspired the botanists who eventually gave the plant its scientific Latin name, and called it *sinapi* or *senepi*. *Senapis* occurs in Plautus and *sinapi* in Pliny.

The preparation of Roman mustard, according to Columella, was not a simple matter. However, the recipe given by Palladius is merely a mixture of the seeds crushed with honey, oil and strong vinegar; modern mustard is made in much the same way, with sugar replacing the honey. Diocletian's edict of 301 defined mustard as a food and not a condiment, and may possibly refer not to the seeds but to the stalks and leaves of the plant itself, since it was also eaten as a vegetable or a salad. This may have been the way in which the Jews ate it, too; there is no mention of mustard as a condiment in the Bible, but the parable of the grain of mustard seed is a famous one. In it (Mark 4, xxx-xxxii) Jesus compares the Kingdom of God to a grain of mustard seed, 'which, when it is sown in the earth, is less than all the seeds that be in the earth: But when it is sown, it groweth up, and becometh greater than all herbs, and shooteth out great branches; so that the fowls of the air may lodge under the shadow of it.' Not that mustard actually grows more than a metre high.

Athenaeus mentions mustard along with lettuce in his chapter on salads: 'and Theophrastus lists, as plants which sprout a second growth, beet, lettuce, rocket, mustard, spinach dock, coriander, dill and cress.' Mustard is an annual.

Speaking of salads, the Byzantines liked to put mustard in vinaigrette sauces, and would not have dreamt of flavouring them in any other way. In passing, we may notice the antiquity of vinaigrette. Other Byzantine sauces also used mustard, but in conjunction with oxymel (a drink flavoured with vinegar and honey) or *oenogarum* (see the section on garum above), which must have made more of a difference to the flavour of the final mixture.

There are two kinds of mustard. One is the white mustard (*Sinapis alba*) of Southern Europe, North Africa and the Middle East, still found growing wild or as a weed in fields of cereal crops. It is not so robust as black mustard, *Sinapis nigra*, which grows in the same places but will also stand up to colder northern climates. White mustard seeds were the first to be used for the table. They made the classic Dijon mustard which from the twelfth to the fifteenth century was sold dry, compressed into slabs which were then diluted in sauces or with vinegar. Some ways of preparing mustard, such as Meaux mustard or mustard *á l'ancienne*, ('old-fashioned mustard'), mixed the seeds of coarsely ground black and white mustard. Black mustard, which is very strong, is liked by those who are very fond of the flavour, but its main use is therapeutic, for mustard plasters, etc.

The French word appeared as *mostarde* in the thirteenth century, and the 's' is preserved in English, as in so many words taken from Norman French (such as 'forest, castle, master') where modern French has lost the consonant. The *Viandier*, 100 years later, describes a 'mustard soup', a broth of wine and water added to the oil in which eggs have been fried, and flavoured 'with a little spiced mustard'. An *aillée* (*ailloli*) flavoured with mustard, ginger and verjuice is described as 'a good sauce for fried hake and other fish'.

In the Middle Ages, mustard, a fixture on every table, made it possible to eat the eternal salt meat – salt pork, of course, and also salt beef, goat and mutton – with more relish than would otherwise have been possible. It was made at home, at least until the seventeenth century, just as vinaigrette and mayonnaise sauces are still made at home now, but slabs of dried mustard to be mixed with liquid could also be bought. The recipe given by the *Ménagier* for an 'unboiled sauce' is very simple, and unlike many medieval recipes contains no ingredients which seem far-fetched to our taste; it can easily be made today.

When grape must was not available, people mixed mustard with vinegar and compensated for its sharpness by adding honey or sugar, like the Romans. Mustard made with grape must was red. Verjuice was another good alternative; initially, verjuice was the acid juice of sorrel, then the juice of unripe plums. It was not until the sixteenth century that anyone thought of using the juice of unripe grapes, crushed and strained, for condimentary purposes. This was much more economical than using the juice of lemons or oranges, which were often unobtainable, and, most important of all, it was a way of using up grapes which had not had a chance to ripen in bad summers. Outside vine-growing areas the juice of unripe apples or crab apples served the same purpose. These juices also made a kind of vinegar. Cider vinegar, although in fact a contradiction in terms (since vinegar means literally *vin aigre*, sour wine), is still made, and is supposed to be good for rheumatism.

Mustard followed the general evolution of popular taste. It was spiced in the Middle Ages and had chillies added at the end of the Renaissance. Vanilla was added in the late seventeenth century, when floral fragrances also appeared on the dinner table, and mustard might be made with orange-flower water or violet water. The eighteenth century saw the advent of mustard with capers, with anchovies, even with champagne – 'for the ladies' (champagne mustard is still made). Today there are many kinds of mustard to be found in luxury foodstuff departments, and they are delicious in small quantities, but they sometimes tend to disguise the characteristic aroma of the main ingredient, the mustard itself. Now as in the past, however, mustard gives body and flavour to foods that may lack it in themselves, and its acidity helps the digestion of fatty food, as people instinctively knew in the Middle Ages. Moderation is the golden rule with all condiments: *uti non abuti*, as the Epicureans said – they should be used, not abused.

Socrates would eat no condiments at all, and seems to have been something of a pioneer of the practice of jogging, which is beneficial to those with sluggish digestive systems. He regarded exercise as the best stimulant for the stomach; a man seeing the philosopher exercising vigorously asked why he was exhausting himself in such a manner. 'Can't you see that I am seasoning my dinner?' replied Socrates. However, he did not make many instant converts to this branch of his philosophy.

And while I am telling anecdotes, it is quite amusing to recall the origin of the French expression 'Il se prend pour le moutardier du pape', 'he thinks himself the Pope's mustard maker', applied to persons who are vain and self-important. Pope Clement VII, a member of the Medici family, was passionately fond of mustard, and ate it at every meal. Naturally the Roman court made haste to imitate the Pontiff, and mustard appeared at every banquet. People went to great pains to prepare mustard, add refinements of their own, and present the results to the Pope in person. The Pope would taste it, meditate gravely, and if he liked it would never refuse a favour asked by the happy man who had tickled his palate and stimulated his appetite. Thereafter the jealous would call one of these successful intriguers 'the Pope's mustard-maker', particularly if the person concerned seemed very vain of his new honours. Another story goes that Pope John XXII had a nephew who was no good at anything, not even bright enough to qualify for a cardinal's hat – which in those days meant that you were very dim indeed. Casting around for some suitable office for the young man, therefore, the Pope appointed him mustard-maker. However, this anecdote seems rather contrived.

Among other classic condiments were capers, used by the ancient Greeks and included by Athenaeus as *capparion* in his list of seasonings. The caper bush, *Caperes spinosa*, is a prickly shrub which grows naturally around the Mediterranean basin and in the Middle East, and was a wild plant for a long time. Capers are its flower buds pickled in seasoned vinegar. The English word 'capers' is from French *câpres*, found as *caspres* in the fifteenth-century Chartes Bible. In the Renaissance the surgeon Ambroise Paré found the condiment so agreeable that he wrote: 'Capers are good, in that they sharpen the appetite and relieve bile.' Olivier de Serres and the Abbé Rozier, in the sixteenth and eighteenth centuries respectively, gave the peasants of southern France advice on growing a plant which might bring some revenues to those poverty-stricken Mediterranean regions.

The first written mention of gherkins is not found until 1549, when it occurs in the work of Robert Estienne, although cucumbers (and gherkins are only a small variety of rough-skinned cucumber) had been very popular in Europe in classical times. Gherkins, picked before they ripen, have been eaten in India for more than 30 centuries, with salt or lemon juice; we use vinegar instead. Few of us realize how exotic the gherkin once was. Gherkins came to Europe during the Renaissance. The English 'gherkin', like the related German *Gurke* (for cucumbers and gherkins alike), comes ultimately from Greek *aggourion*.

Finally, as well as such condiments and seasonings as I have already mentioned, native aromatic European plants have been used for thousands of years to flavour food. They often grow wild, and have been in almost constant use because they were economical, and people sensed that they were a good addition to the diet. The wise and thrifty Gauls ate a great many herbs. In the Renaissance, when the tidal wave of spices had receded, the herbs that had never been abandoned by the peasants came back into fashion. In modern France it is sometimes supposed that herbs are confined to Provençal cuisine, which is a complete misconception, although it is true that the cookery of Provence, where people were too poor for a long time to buy exotic spices, can make the most simple, rustic dishes a symphony of aromas blending grace-notes from all the plants of the Mediterranean. The miraculous effect of these herbs is due to the precision with which they are used. A legend has it that King Balthazar, one of the Magi, sowed the herbs of Provence as he passed through.

The herbs of the Provençal hillsides are wiry and vigorous plants, but they grow in such profusion that there is an art, or perhaps a science, in using them with judicious moderation. A famous doctor called Critias illustrated the principles of that science in the days when Massilia was a Roman colony. Although the housewife may not know it, her choice of the right aromatics to flavour certain foods arises from a kind of collective memory. Does anyone today, enjoying a lamb chop flavoured with thyme or a red mullet with fennel, stop to think that the use of aromatics in the culinary ritual echoes an ancient practice in sacrificial offerings, or that every meal is a kind of sacrifice? Herbs stimulate the palate, and their aroma instantly puts one into the right frame of mind to enjoy food, but they also carry messages from the beginning of time, messages which convey one to a state of grace. The mere scent of a handful of herbs, even a list of their names, can conjure up the sound of cicadas under plane trees, the fragrance of sun-baked hillsides basking in the sun, a vision of yourself bending, scissors in hand, over some corner of the garden pearled with morning dew. Herbs, the very essences of the natural world, rich in mineral salts, do not need complicated recipes. They respect food, complement it, and bring out its flavour. We should respect them in turn, or we shall find that the spirit of regional cookery has been lost.

These delicious herbs, particularly fragrant when they have been gathered fresh or properly dried, and which do so much for a modest court-bouillon or an otherwise ordinary dish, are as rich in aroma as in therapeutic value. The virtue of the liqueurs which were the glory of French monasteries lay in the addition of a judiciously assessed amount of herbs. Every monastery had a herb garden within its thick walls, and the monks went out into the countryside to pick herbs too, with sacks slung over their shoulders.

The people of antiquity were right: these herbs and aromatics do not just elevate a humble cuisine to the sublime. Their aromatic essences (or alkaloids, in chemical terminology), and their high content of mineral salts and, when they are fresh, vitamins, aid digestion and thus make any dish containing them, however frugal, more nourishing and so appetizing that the mouth waters as it is brought to the table.

There are many more aromatic plants not found in Western Europe, but which are an integral part of the cuisine of other countries. Some of the herbs used as favourite condiments in classical and medieval times would not appeal to us now at all if we tried using them in the 'authentic' manner, as Mme Dacier and Mme Vigée-Lebrun did in their famous Greek dinners.[38]

One such is malobathrum, a native of China. It was a great success on the patrician tables of Rome and Roman Gaul, and was praised by Ausonius himself. It was in fact patchouli, the strongly scented Eastern plant used in scents, and a patchouli-flavoured ragoût sounds far from appetizing. *Autres temps, autres moeurs.* At the other end of the aromatic spectrum from the highly scented was asafoetida, the sap of a large umbelliferous plant, which is extremely bitter, more pungent than garlic, and has a stench like carrion. It was rubbed over plates before the food was put on them – perhaps to make the food taste better by comparison, just as aloes (which were also used in the kitchen) make the water you drink taste particularly sweet after you have inflicted something so bitter on your palate. Asafoetida remained in use for a long time. Maurizio tells us that Catherine the Great's lover, Stanislas Augustus Poniatowski (1732–1798), who became king of Poland, liked it. Rue is another strong-smelling herb which was once a favourite condiment. Its main use now is as an insect-repellent, like the pyrethrum, mentioned above, which the Romans enjoyed eating. The Romans also liked nard, an Indian plant related to valerian, for its strong odour of decay. It is mentioned as late as the sixteenth century in the *Thrésor de santé*, and if the *Ménagier de Paris* is to be believed it was very popular 200 years before. Finally, and for the record, there was silphium, a kind of wild carrot which has disappeared so completely that we cannot now account for its amazing popularity. If the Devil made aromatics as well as other seasonings, perhaps he could tell us.

However, we need not hold up our hands in horror at the tastes of the past. Our own customs will be criticized in the same way tomorrow or the day after, and other dietary habits will prevail. Perhaps scientifically calculated, flavourless survival rations will replace the pleasures of the table. As the French essayist Suarès said, 'There is no heresy in a dead religion.'

Herbs

Basil (*Ocymum basilicum*), meaning 'royal', from Greek *basilikos*, a plant dear to the Provençals and Italians, was once a sacred herb. Women were not allowed to pick it, and the gathering process was a ritual. The officiating priest had to purify his right hand with water from three different springs, sprinkled with an oak branch. He had to be dressed in new garments, without anything made of metal about his person, and he usually had to keep well away from women in a state of impurity, i.e., menstruating. Basil is still a sensitive herb. It must be used fresh; it loses most of its character when dried, whatever the food manufacturers may say. It is a very fragile plant, and must be used with care. Cooking spoils it, so it is best used raw, either whole, chopped or crushed. Basil is called *pistou* in Provence because it is

531

the principal flavour in *soupe au pistou* (*pistou* means pounded). It is very good with salads, pâtés and tomatoes.

Chervil (*Anthriscus cerefolium*). This umbelliferous plant, related to parsley, comes from Western Asia and the Balkans. It was popular with the Romans. It is a herb to be eaten fresh, and loses all its aroma when dried. Chervil, long valued for its medical uses as a cleanser of the blood, an anti-spasmodic, and in skin lotions, is an easily grown annual and will seed itself. It is eaten in omelettes, soups and salads, not alone but as part of a *fines herbes* mixture with parsley, tarragon and chives. The wild plant which resembles it, hemlock, is poisonous and should be avoided.

Chives (*Allium schoenoprasum*). The long, thin leaves of chives, a member of the Alliaceae family, have been enjoyed fresh since the time of the ancient Greeks. Chives go well with eggs and cream sauces, and are part of the *fines herbes* mixture for salads and omelettes.

Coriander (*Coriandrum sativum*). The leaves of this umbelliferous plant are now thought of as typical of Arab, Chinese or Indian cookery; people have forgotten that it was also a favourite herb among the Hebrew, Greek and Roman peoples of antiquity. Fresh, its leaves (said to have a faint odour of bugs by those who dislike it) are used like parsley or chervil in oriental, Chinese and Dutch cuisine. The seeds are an ingredient in many Scandinavian and Greek marinades. The leaves are also used in making liqueurs, and the writers of antiquity claimed that they made wine stronger and more exhilarating. Coriander has many medicinal virtues, as a stimulant, a digestive, a carminative and a bactericide. Its dried leaves have no flavour; they are just dead leaves.

Dill (*Anethum graveolens*). Dill comes from Central Asia, and is more strongly aromatic than its cousin fennel. It is very popular with the Scandinavians, who use both its feathery leaves and its seeds in small quantities. The Romans were very fond of it, crediting it with especially fortifying qualities. They covered the food given to gladiators with the herb. Dill, which grows wild in the Mediterranean regions, became semi-naturalized in Great Britain after the Romans left, and subsequently reached Scandinavia, where it has to be cultivated. Dried, the leaves lose all their scent, so they are used fresh as a flavouring, chiefly for fish, cheese and yoghurt.

Fennel (*Foeniculum vulgare*). Fennel is another umbellifer used in Provence as a common accompaniment to fish. It is picked wild on the hillsides, and the hotter the weather the stronger its aroma. Its stems and seeds are used dried but, as with dill, its leaves are pleasant to eat only when they are fresh. It also grows in Brittany, but the Bretons, having forgotten how and why the Romans brought it there, use it only to dose rabbits with colic. The plant has always been known as the best herb to encourage a cow's milk yield. Its seeds are among the 'four hot seeds' used as stimulants, stomachics, digestives, carminatives and aperients. The bulbous Florence fennel is eaten as a vegetable.

Mint (*Mentha*). There are several kinds of mint, and five at least of them grow

532

wild. Cultivated mint is usually 'peppermint' (for pharmacy and food flavourings) or spearmint (also known as green mint and garden mint), which is milder; it is used in cooking, and is delicious with salad, green peas or lamb. It is a favourite herb of both the English and the Arabs. The mints are stimulating tonics, good for the stomach and anti-spasmodic. A leaf of mint in milk prevents it from curdling or turning, and it would be almost impossible to make cheese from the milk of a cow who had been grazing the herb. In the past, wet-nurses were forbidden to drink mint tisanes. Dried mint remains very aromatic.

Parsley (*Petroselinum crispum* or *hortense*). The best known of all herbs, parsley, a biennial, has been grown all over the world for thousands of years, although Sardinia claims to be its native place (as it also claims basil). When Sardinia was still independent, parsley featured on its coinage. The herb had a high reputation among the Greeks: parsley crowns were worn at banquets, whereas nowadays it is seen garnishing meat in butchers' shops. It was thought to stimulate the appetite and promote good humour. The Romans used parsley freely in their cooking. It is a plant particularly rich in vitamins A and C, calcium, iron and manganese. A spoonful of chopped parsley a day provides the necessary ration of these. It is a diuretic, encourages the menstrual flow, reduces fever and has many external uses (for scrofulous swellings, conjunctivitis and freckles). It is also an excellent antiscorbutic for sailors. There are two kinds of parsley in culinary use: flat-leaved parsley, which has a stronger flavour, and the more common curled parsley. Parsley was involved in the ritual of casting lots, and in many popular superstitions. Dried parsley is rather disappointing.

Rosemary (*Rosmarinus officinalis*). Rosemary was a favourite plant in the Middle Ages, not only for its medicinal virtues but as a symbol of the declaration of love. The famous Queen of Hungary's Water, or Hungary Water, made of rosemary flowers infused in spirits of wine, was used plain as a toilet water; if sweetened it was a liqueur, and Queen Isabella claimed to have been given the recipe by an angel. This elixir, which was regarded as a panacea for all ills, had a remarkably long life, and was fashionable from the sixteenth century to the eighteenth. Rosemary does have therapeutic qualities, particularly for disorders of the digestive system and the liver. The Provençals make a rosemary tisane and drink it after a good meal. They use it to flavour roast meat, especially lamb, and fish and game. The Italians associate it with rice, and the famous honey of Narbonne known in Roman times owed its unique flavour to rosemary. Many superstitions are attached to the herb, and in some countries it is usual to put a rosemary branch in the hand of the dead. The connotations of death and love are combined in Ophelia's remark, as she distributes her herbs: 'There's rosemary, that's for remembrance – pray you, love, remember.' If rosemary is picked before it flowers, then dried and crumbled, it keeps well; fresh, it can be unpleasantly bitter.

Sage (*Salvia officinalis*). The Salerno School called sage *Salvia salviatrix*, an indication of the virtues ascribed to this herb, which was very popular in Provence too. It should be picked on the dawn of Midsummer Day when the first ray of sunlight strikes the highest mountain. The Spanish call sage *ierba buena*, another tribute to its virtues. Like the people of Provence and Languedoc, they use it to flavour fatty dishes, particularly pork, which is more easily digested accompanied by sage. Arnaud de Villeneuve was recommending it as early as the thirteenth century. A Provençal proverb assures us that 'he who has sage in his garden needs no doctor'. The Chinese of the eighteenth century liked it so much when they encountered it that, according to Valmon de Bomare, they would exchange two crates of best tea for a crate of sage. Sage dried and kept in a closed jar is better than fresh sage, which can be bitter.

Tarragon (*Artemisia dracunculus*) is related to wormwood. It is a perennial native to northern Asia, and does not grow wild in Western Europe. The only parts used are the leaves. It has had many uses since the Middle Ages: in vinegar, with pickled gherkins, in piquant or white sauces. It is part of the classic *fines herbes* mixture. Dried tarragon is not particularly good.

Thyme (*Thymus vulgaris*). Thyme is known as *farigoule* in the south of France, and rabbits like it; any who have been eating thyme taste and smell delicious when cooked, and so in the South of France it is fed to domestic rabbits on purpose before they are killed. The Greeks thought thyme a symbol of vigour. They had observed that it is a stimulating plant, and had a beneficial effect on the mental powers of old people who drank a tisane of the herb. In the Middle Ages, ladies often embroidered a branch of thyme surrounded by bees on the scarves worn by their knights. The fragrant thyme of Hymettus made the reputation of Hymettus honey in classical times. Virgil said of thyme and the honey the bees make from it, 'Redolentque thymo fragrantia mella' – 'the honey smells of thyme'. Cultivated thyme is not nearly as fragrant as the wild sort, but cultivated or not it should never be watered; rainfall provides all the moisture it needs. Thyme is used to flavour grilled meats and game, and as part of a bouquet garni together with parsley, bay and sometimes rosemary for casserole dishes and ragoûts. Regarded as a panacea in the South of France, thyme has earned its reputation as a digestive, an antiseptic and a healer of wounds. When gathered wild in Mediterranean climates it is already almost dried by the sun, and will keep very well in a closed jar. Like rosemary, fresh green thyme may taste bitter.

The Proper Use of Spices, Aromatics and Condiments

Like Alfred Franklin,[39] writing on the cookery of the past at the end of the nineteenth century, we may regard the list of spices required by most of the Roman and medieval recipes for 'those dreadful dishes our fathers ate' with some alarm.

However, one may take the part of devil's advocate – since James Joyce regarded the Devil as the inventor of seasonings, and in any case every trial must have a defending counsel – and point out that as an almost general rule these ancient recipes give no indication of the proportions in which spices were to be used, and the amounts may have been quite modest. In fact the *Viandier* and even the *Ménagier de Paris* – despite the artifice whereby the latter purports to be addressing his young wife – to mention only those two works, assume that their reader is a competent specialist and not an apprentice. This is literature for professionals able to judge for themselves when advised to use 'a fair amount' of something, or when told: 'Take cinnamon, ginger, small spices and plenty of cloves' for an *arboulaste* or *arbleste* of fish. After all, most modern *cordon bleu* cooks use the 'guestimate' method as much as they use the scales. The other argument in my plea shall be borrowed from Odile Redon and Jean-Louis Flandrin, who remind us, *à propos* Italian cookery books of the fourteenth and fifteenth centuries, that even books written for the cook of a household were kept on the shelves of the master's library, and it was the master's taste that the cook had to consider in preparing food.

The 'mania for specifying quantities' in cookery books, as Revel describes it, did not set in until the nineteenth century, for instance in the works of Carême. Menon, in the generation before the French Revolution, was relatively sparing in his use of spices other than nutmeg, pepper and ginger, in line with the taste of the times, and he did give a minimum of indications, a feature which makes his book remarkably modern in tone.

All the same – and we will let counsel for the prosecution speak here – even if only a very small quantity of each of these spices was used, there was such a variety of them, in lists that are always identical, that we must conclude they amounted to a large quantity of spice in all, and there was no preference for any single flavour. Chicken with ginger, and no other spice than ginger, is not a dish that would ever have been cooked in the Middle Ages, or indeed in Roman times. We may therefore wonder if the final result of this mixture of many flavours was not a strong but vague pungency, each spice killing the subtlety of the others and leaving only their general ferocity. Many modern authors have tried cooking such recipes and have not liked them at all. When we consider that in Roman times other ingredients, added separately or all at once, included garum, nard and asafoetida, we cannot help feeling that such flavours would have completely obliterated the spices, and that those spices played a purely figurative part.

So the question is: why so many spices all at once when their flavours could not have been identified separately, and were thus wasted? Was it just for the principle of the thing? And if so, what exactly was the principle?

The main preoccupation of the medieval cook seems to have been to concoct a highly flavoured dish; the sheer strength of the flavour was the important point. The *Ménagier de Paris* explains carefully, and twice in the course of the work, that spices, scrupulously pounded, should not be sifted afterwards (*coullées*). For soups, where they would be drowned in the broth, 'add the spices as late as you may, for

535

they will lose their savour the more the earlier they go in.' As a general rule spices were added at the end of the preparation of any dish. In India, where cooks are expert in the use of spices, they roast or fry their pounded spices; they are then simmered as long as is necessary for the alchemy of a skilled cooking process to transform them into something sublime.

There is another puzzle about the use of spices in medieval cookery: absolutely identical sauces might be served with foods that were completely different, or of an opposite nature (such as fish and game). Only the consumers of the Middle Ages themselves could answer our question. 'The cooking of a society is a language into which it unconsciously translates its structure unless, also unconsciously, it resigns itself to showing its contradictions.'[40]

As it is obvious that medieval people did not know all the whys and wherefores of spices, we may look to the way of life of medieval society itself for an explanation. Like its classical forerunner, it consisted not so much of contradictions as of contrasts, notably between the rich and the poor. There were a great many poor people. The rich were the exception. Exceptional people eat exceptional food. Spices, as social symbols, were intended to mark a dichotomy necessary to the functioning of the established order, and in the gradation of their abundance they also marked the hierarchy of a nuclear social system. This explains why there is such a profusion of spices in the medieval books of recipes I have taken as my examples, one describing the cuisine of a court (*Le Viandier*) and the other the cookery of a prosperous middle-class household to some extent striving to emulate the court (*Le Ménagier*). Spices were reserved for a certain caste which did not constitute the majority of European people of the time; seasonings used by the majority would have been limited to wild herbs and salt, and as little of the latter as possible, because of the salt tax.

'I find it quite painful to think of so accomplished a king as Charles V condemned to such cooking as this', remarked Alfred Franklin. How could he, a man of the nineteenth century, judge the quality of dishes he took care not to taste, and to which, if he had in fact tasted them, he would have applied the standards of the nineteenth century? We may simply note that this lavish use of spices was sheer waste, perhaps with no end in view but that of conspicuous consumption in the name of appearances. When we study the attitudes of past (or foreign) societies, says Marc Bloch, we should avoid 'perpetual and constant anachronisms, unconsciously perpetrated by historians who project themselves into the past as they are, with their own feelings, ideas, intellectual and moral prejudices.'[41] We should observe, but not judge. In the absence of criteria proper to our own age, let us look at the collective psychology expressed in such daily practices as the use of spices, practices which may be described, depending on our viewpoint, as tradition, habit, routine or even fashion.

It seems that this excessive use of spices, raised to the level of mythology, was not so much a demonstration of the height of human folly as a manifestation of concepts worked out in the social psychology of a time of change, a period of transition – even though quite a long one – appropriately called the Middle Ages. The concepts were those of identification, compensation and simulation.

We saw above, in discussing meat, the message delivered by the medieval diet – more of a coded message than was the case at other periods which had, so to speak, come of age and were no longer in search of an identity. Although collective psychology is not the sum of all personal psychologies in a society, everyone knows that the choice or rejection of this or that food is one of the elements in our 'mental equipment' (Lucien Faure). All dietary codes reveal the cohesion of a social (or religious) group. Such a diet, strictly reserved for the privileged and making lavish use of foods which in themselves were very rare, thus constituted the symbol of their own superiority for the favoured few in the ruling classes. It was a symbol of caste such as was also expressed in clothing: the privileged wore layers of rich garments and ornaments, while the villein wore a simple tunic and went barefoot. By dint of the power of their flavour and their abundance, spices, as an ornament or garnish to food, allowed people who could afford them to assert their identity, simulating a superiority of which they were not in fact perfectly confident because they were so few. The fact that they could afford spices was also a reassurance in a period of great anxiety dominated by an essentially repressive religious system which was designed to inculcate guilt feelings. The great medieval popular festivals were attempts to escape from that collective anxiety, or even to defy it.

If eating one's fill was a double pleasure because of the two advantages it procured – physical strength and social power – the addition of spices conferred both physiological and mental excitement. Later, in a return to the example of ancient Rome, the unrestrained gluttony of libertines was allied to the aristocratic or élitist desire for extravagant expense to gratify both the stomach and the genitals.

Perhaps Brillat-Savarin had the key to the enigma of spices when he remarked in his twenty-seventh Meditation that

> in their search for new methods of seasoning they [the Romans] tried anything which could stimulate the palate, and employed many substances the use of which is beyond our understanding, such as asafoetida, rue, etc.... Nor was this all. In obedience to that instinct for improvement which we have already mentioned, ways were sought of increasing the bouquet and the flavour of wines; floral essences, spices, and drugs of various kinds were infused into them, and the preparations which contemporary writers have handed down to us under the name of *condita* must have burnt the mouth and had a profoundly irritating effect on the stomach. Thus already, at that period, the Romans dreamed of alcohol, which was not discovered until more than fifteen centuries later.[42]

Roman wines did of course contain alcohol, although its nature was not fully understood. While waiting for fashionable alcoholism to make its appearance, people sought extremes of sensation in fashionable food. François de Sales, at the time of the Counter-Reformation, did not fail to point out the resemblance between the sensual pleasures of sex and of food. Later on the Jansenists denounced sauces and spices as instruments of perversity. In fact perversity is a mild word to describe the coprophagy of two emperors, the Roman Commodus and the aptly nicknamed Byzantine Constantine Copronymous; they easily outdid the Emperor Vitellius, whose own gluttony went only to the lengths of eating food made disgusting by its advanced state of decay. The coprophagy and disgusting behaviour of the three emperors were those of brute beasts (although Constantine proved himself a shrewd monarch in other respects), while the conduct of the Marquis de Sade's heroes in *Les cent vingt journées de Sodome* arose from a kind of circuitous refinement of feeling taken to excess. However, rather than regarding the behaviour of these people as a dietary sin or a kind of counter-nutrition, we should probably see in it the pleasure of disobeying a fundamental taboo with complete impunity, taking the shameful pleasure of eating to its utmost limits. The members of the convulsionary sect which grew up around the tomb of the dead Jansenist François de Pâris in the early eighteenth century were impelled by the opposite desire, for mortification of the flesh. They ate disgusting foods with nothing but the fire of faith to spice them.

Apart from such extreme examples of perversions of taste, in fact, it is difficult to say that a particular food is good or bad. Even rue and asafoetida are good to those who like them, 'perverse' as we may suspect such tastes to be. Most Europeans like *pâté de foie gras*, but some people are revolted by it. The Bushmen of Africa, hungry for protein, eat termites, and a Buddhist can live quite well without any protein, on nothing but a bowl of rice. In all humility, therefore, we might as well admit that the most cultivated and prosperous of our forebears really did enjoy the German broth which was flavoured with five different spices, had almond milk added to mollify it, and then had fried onions put in and was acidulated with mustard.

The sense of taste, as everyone knows, is aroused by the excitement of the papillae of the tongue in direct contact with food. Taste is the only sense which needs to be accompanied by the four others to function fully. The sense of smell brings us the aroma of the food even before we raise it to our mouths ('an advance sentry, crying: "who goes there?"', as Brillat-Savarin puts it). The sense of touch (involving lips, tongue and palate) tells us whether the food is soft or crisp, and what its temperature is. The colour, form or presentation of the food appeal to the sense of sight. Even hearing comes into it, for the cord of the tympanum contains fibres conveying the sense of taste to the brain, the cortex, thalamus and hypothalamus; if it is removed, sensation at the front of the tongue, where we taste sweetness, is suppressed. Taste is thus a matter of physical sensation, but it also involves consciousness, analysis, and is thus an intellectual act. To the five senses, Brillat-Savarin (again, but he is, after all, the authority on taste) suggests adding a sixth, 'the sense of physical desire, which brings the two sexes together, and whose aim is the reproduction of the species.' And we may indeed say that a person has a 'taste' for a certain kind of partner.

However, I will leave aside the senses of hearing, which acts as a vector, and touch, which is chiefly concerned with the material aspect of food – and indeed physical desire, which may well follow a good meal but does not concern us here. We are left with the three functions of spices: their aroma, appealing to the sense of smell, their flavour, appealing to the sense of taste, and their colour, appealing to the sense of sight.

The sensations of taste are aroused by four basic flavours: bitterness (to which we are most sensitive), sweetness, acidity and salinity. But before we have tasted a dish, and even if it is out of sight, it will set off the most primitive reaction of all, appetite, if it smells good. Appetite is also the state of being hungry; one might almost call it a state of grace.

Spices were first valued for their antiseptic qualities as well as their aromas. Consequently it has been thought that they were used so lavishly by the Romans, and in the medieval cookery to which the Romans left many legacies, in meat and fish dishes and particularly combined with acid elements such as verjuice, vinegar and unripe fruit because those foods were of suspect quality. The idea was that the spices acted both as a preservative and to mask unpleasant flavours. In that case the necessity of using them should have persisted until the invention of refrigeration, whereas from the Renaissance onwards the mania for spices declined, and excessive use of them was considered extremely vulgar.

We should beware of regarding our ancestors as primitive. Seafood might be of dubious quality in summer, despite the swift transport of the fish-carts, but you could get perfectly good freshwater fish at all seasons, even in inland towns, taken from rivers or fishponds. The regulations, as we have seen, were very strict. Meat, also subject to strict controls, was sold on the day of slaughter, or at the latest two days afterwards in winter. Poultry came live from the market or the farmyard, or ready roasted from the 'poulterers' of towns.

Of course keeping food wholesome was always an anxiety in an age which, contrary to popular opinion, was much preoccupied with hygiene (there were more bath-houses in medieval Paris than public baths in the nineteenth century or even the beginning of the twentieth). Not only salt but sugar was used for its preserving qualities; there was an adage to the effect that 'sugar never spoiled food'. The sweet-sour mixture which is in fashion again today never really fell completely out of sight after its vogue in antiquity. The recipes of Apicius contained honey (if only to mollify the bitter fieriness of all the other condiments used), and at the height of the spice mania a change to its use is again apparent, rising from 3 per cent of recipes in the *Viandier* to 31 per cent in the *Livre fort excellent de cuysine*, which appeared in the second half of the sixteenth century. The Renaissance prepared the way for the commercial advent of sugar and the decline of the use of spices other than pepper, cloves and nutmeg. Those survivors went well with a certain sweetness, already evident in the *épices de chambre* or 'chamber spices' we shall come to in a moment. Sugar began to be a mark of social distinction.

The perpetual search for a balance between the four basic flavours – bitter, sweet, acid, salty – is one of the major concerns in Aldebrandin of Sienna's *Régime des corps*.[43] A thirteenth-century contemporary of St Louis, Aldebrandin wrote his treatise on hygiene in French; most of it is in fact a translation of Arabic medical texts.

To the medieval doctors, as to the theologians (they were often one and the same), cookery was chiefly a matter of dietetics, with the object of preserving the physical and mental health of a body kindly provided by God. In the old universal subconscious, sickness was a punishment for sin or transgression; Mary Baker Eddy was not the first to devise the precepts of Christian Science. Keeping body and soul healthy was one of the reasons for fasting, and one of the causes of the Church's swift reaction to the nutritional severity of the Counter-Reformation. The best state, obviously, is one of equilibrium.

The ideal expressed in the therapy of the time, as inspired by the Greeks and the Arabs, was to maintain the balance of the four humours of the human frame: 'quattuor humores in humano corpores constant', as Arnaud de Villeneuve said, 'there are always four humours in the human body.' These four humours were essentially the products of heat, cold, dryness and humidity (man was hot and dry, woman cold and damp).

By means of a judicious diet, you could correct bad outside influences, climatic or even cosmic. Aldebrandin of Sienna, like the Salerno School, classified food under four headings: cold, hot, dry and wet, descriptions which had nothing to do with the actual consistency or temperature of the dishes served. Illness was an error, a mistake in functioning owing to a surplus of humours. To prevent it or combat it, you had to correct the excess and re-establish equilibrium, eating 'cold' foods if you had an excess of hot humours and vice versa, taking dry foods to correct humid humours or the other way around.

Accordingly, it was advisable to eat spices, 'hot' substances *par excellence*, in cold winter weather. 'And note that in winter, one puts in more ginger, to make the spices stronger, for in winter all sauces must be stronger than in summer', says the *Ménagier de Paris*. For instance, according to Arnaud de Villeneuve, 'sauces proper for winter' contain ginger, cinnamon, pepper and cloves. These spices heightened the beneficial effects of the 'hot' and 'humid' meat of chicken, suitable winter food[44] – for you could never get warm enough in a medieval winter. Even more spices were added to goose, 'cold' and 'dry' by nature, to make it more digestible. Good digestion meant good health. The one spice permissible in summer, according to medical doctrines, was saffron, which was more of a colouring than a spice, particularly when safflower was used instead. It did not have an unduly 'heating' effect on beef, regarded as cold and dry. (Today we imitate, perhaps mistakenly, the culinary habits of hot climates, spicing food in summer with a variety of flavours to stimulate the salivary and digestive functions.) Lenten fasting, which claimed to elevate the soul and calm bodily ardour, rejected stimulating spices in favour of cinnamon, which was milder and 'humid', or sugar. One of the chief functions of humidity was thought to be to encourage the elimination of harmful humours – *peccantes*, as Molière called them, since sin was involved. 'Humid' substances acted as a psychological and physiological diuretic and purge. 'Sugar cleanses the loins and the bladder well and soothes the entrails.'

The purifying spices of sacrificial offerings thus developed, by way of the magic of medicine, into an indispensable accessory to food, divesting themselves quite naturally of sacred ritual to become an ordinary, everyday part of the diet.

The 'accoutrements of the gullet', as Rabelais called them – luxury products for the pleasure and nutritional privilege of the rich – were often given as presents, as we have seen, and they were much appreciated for both their luxury and their utility.

Etiquette demanded that spices were offered as the company rose from table; their heat was meant to aid the digestion of the copious menu, which in medieval times was itself highly spiced. If the meal had included fish, as it almost always did, as well as a variety of meat dishes, the coldness and humidity of the fish required immediate correction. Dried fruits and seeds were regarded as 'styptic' foods, astringent and drying. The 'many spices delitable, To eten whan men rise fro table',[45] were therefore offered in the form of whole seeds, for instance of coriander, fennel or aniseed. Another advantage was that they deodorized the breath. When means allowed, the seeds were cooked in sugar, providing a sort of sweetmeat along the lines of the sugared almonds and pralines of a later period. Preserved fruits cooked with many aromatics or strong spices fulfilled the same function. So did medieval jams, which were more like fruit pastes.

Wealthy people offered their guests these spices in pretty little boxes; you took them away with you to eat the contents at home, or in your bedroom if you were staying at your host's house. These were known as *épices de chambre*, bedroom or chamber spices, and eating them was a bedtime ritual much like cleaning the teeth today.

When you went visiting, moreover, meetings with your friends generally took place in bedrooms; privacy was of only relative value in the Middle Ages, and the drawing or 'withdrawing' room was an innovation of the late seventeenth century. Meanwhile the common rooms of great houses were not very comfortable, and with members of the household, family or servants, passing in and out all the time they did not always provide the privacy and quiet that was sometimes desirable. Just as you might offer a cigarette or a drink today, good manners required you to offer spices in your bedroom, for people to nibble as they talked. 'After washing, the lady had wine poured and afterwards offered spices', wrote Du Cange in the seventeenth century.

In France the *épices des juges*, 'spices for judges', were presents sent to magistrates as thanks for the happy outcome of a legal case. But since you could never be too careful, particularly if the case appeared a difficult one, the spices ceased to be thanks and became bribes. As soon as a trial was about to begin and before it even came up in court, the two parties concerned sent the judges their sugared almonds or their preserves. These attempts at corruption, of course, cancelled each other out, leaving the honour of the courts relatively unscathed. Having received sweeteners from both sides, the authorities felt free to make their own decision.

The whole procedure soon became an obligatory tax imposed on any legal transaction, however minor, and contributed a good deal to reducing the backlog of legal cases. Gifts in kind, which the lawyers no doubt sold, were finally replaced by sums of money. 'Those taxes usually called spices, amounting to great and excessive sums in deniers' was the price that great and genuine spice merchant Jacques Coeur paid for his trial. The French expression *payer en espèces*, to pay in cash (cf. the etymology of 'spice' and 'species' above), is said to be a play on words, but there was nothing very funny about it for those who had to pay up.

The 'spices' kept their name, although they had changed their nature, and such sums continued to be demanded from unfortunate plaintiffs by the magistrates until the end of the *ancien régime*. Racine's comedy *Les plaideurs* contains the character of Petit-Jean, who pretends not to understand the custom, describing how:

> Il me redemandait sans cesse ses épices;
> Et j'ai tout bonnement couru dans les offices
> Chercher la boîte au poivre ...

[He kept asking me for his spices, so I went straight off to the kitchen to look for the pepperpot.]

One of the first acts of the French Revolution was to abolish these legal 'spices' by the law of 24 August 1790 and make the judges civil servants. There was to be no more cooking of the legal books.

The Grocer's Trade

Particularly in the last century, members of the upper classes would call someone a 'grocer' as an insult; perhaps because young idlers whose families provided or sometimes did not provide them with funds did not always find grocers sympathetic. Grocers might get tired of allowing credit and have recourse to the law to get their bills paid.

In this era of supermarkets with their multiple branches there will soon be nothing left of the traditional grocer except in literature or in Daumier's engravings, where he figures either as a modest figure in an apron or presiding majestically behind his counter like Jupiter in the clouds, more preoccupied with the ringing of the till than passing fashions. America owes much to her aristocracy of trade, which was probably worth more than the older sort of aristocracy, being founded on hard work and method, if also on a certain rigour of the mind. That kind of tradition made Margaret Thatcher, a grocer's daughter, the first woman prime minister of the United Kingdom, which for so long regarded itself as the most important trading power in the world.

A Parisian grocer among the wonders of his stock in trade (1975)

Before the late eighteenth century, in fact, the grocer's shop did not exist as we think of it today: an emporium stocked not only with foodstuffs including spices, salt and salt fish, but also with soap, candles and, in the time of our great-grandparents, oil and wicks for lamps, besides a range of household cleansing products.

In the Middle Ages the grocer sold only spices, as the French term *épicier* (see above) denotes, like the original English 'pepperer'. But because of the therapeutic virtues of spices those who dealt in them were also apothecaries of a kind. An edict of Louis XII tries to draw the dividing line. 'He who is an *épicier* is not an apothecary, but he who is an apothecary is an *épicier*.' Apothecaries could therefore sell spices, but grocers were not allowed to prepare and sell pharmaceutical products. The distinction between the two remained very hazy and occasioned many quarrels, as we shall see when discussing sugar.

The trade of *épicier* occupied second place in the hierarchy of all the trades of Paris in the Middle Ages. Similarly, the 'Mistery [Guild] of Grossers, Pepperers and Apothecaries' was one of the largest of the trade associations of London. The word 'corporation', introduced into France from England, did not come into use there until the reign of Henri II. Until 1585, just seven trades were recognized in Paris: drapers, grocers, furriers, mercers, money changers, goldsmiths and dyers. These made up the aristocracy of the crafts. Grocers ranked well above goldsmiths not only because of the enormous value of the products they sold, but also on account of their therapeutic and cultural connotations. The apothecaries branched off from the grocers later. Today people complain that pharmacists are turning back into grocers, selling diet foods. The French Revolutionary law of 21 Germinal of the year XI, still in force, perpetuated the medieval edicts by forbidding grocers to make and sell any pharmaceutical products.

To become a master grocer you served a long apprenticeship, spent some time as a journeyman, and then had to pass examinations before your master's peers. You paid your dues and finally made your masterpiece, an ornate concoction of confectionery and spices, jams and crystallized fruits; since sugar was regarded as a spice, grocery included confectionery until the confectioners formed a separate body. Grocers were also chandlers, a very profitable speciality in view of the many religious festivals requiring candles, and all the others needed for domestic lighting. They also sold wax and honey.

After the fourteenth century the King of France and the great lords of the realm had an *Épicier* among the officers of their household. This was a very honourable position, and a lucrative and responsible one too. At most courts and great households, however, as in the thirteenth-century household of Philippe the Bold, the master cook[46] kept the spices and dispensed them to the *saucier* or sauce-maker at their discretion and in the necessary quantities, tasting the dishes before and after they were seasoned.

Dealing in mustard and vinegar remained the province of a small subsection of the association of sauce-makers and master cooks, the vinegar and mustard-makers. They became distillers under King Francois I when he withdrew that privilege from the apothecaries. *Fines herbes*, shallots, gherkins and lemons were sold by the fruiterers, who also dealt in the unripe fruit and fruit products used for seasoning. In 1782, Maille, 'vinegar distiller to the King and to their Majesties the Emperors of Russia and Austria', published a catalogue listing 175 vinegars of different composition and 24 different mustards.

With the French Revolution the trade corporations disappeared. Today, there are only trade associations. The motto of the trade association of French grocers is that of the Three Musketeers: all for one and one for all. Its history, peaceful until the introduction of VAT, was troubled only once, in December 1905, by a strike of grocers' boys.

And finally, I will mention a forgotten man: the grocer Cortey who, with the civil servant Michois and the Baron de Batz, tried to rescue Louis XVI on the morning of his execution. Despite his failure he and the Chevalier de Maison-Rouge then attempted to save Marie Antoinette and her children. Their plans were discovered, and Cortey the grocer went to the guillotine in his turn.

PART VII

With the Renaissance, the import and export of foods from the colonies changed the face of the world, bringing . . .

NEW NEEDS

SUGAR
CHOCOLATE
COFFEE
TEA

Gluttony and Greed for Gain

In 1453 the Turkish troops of Mahomet II had just taken Constantinople. The curtain had fallen on that act in the history of the world which was later designated the Middle Ages.

The period that followed was the only one in human history to give itself a name at once: the Renaissance. Fifteenth-century Italian humanists did not hesitate to proclaim that they were of the *Rinescitá*. They had been the first to scent renewal in the air of the Italian peninsula. The Renaissance was purely a cultural revolution. Injured morally rather than physically by the fact that the Muslims were at her gates, possibly for good, Europe needed to prove that she existed. Her pride, as Delumeau puts it, took the form of 'promoting Western values at a time when the civilization of Europe was clearly ahead of parallel cultures'. In seizing the ancient imperial city the Turks may after all have done Christianity a service, forcing the West to look in another direction.

The Renaissance, therefore, was not just a movement of aesthetic progress in the spheres of art and ideas, but an economic revival too. Unconsciously repeating the actions of their distant ancestors thousands of years before, Europeans henceforward sought acquisitions beyond the western horizon, and could do so with less and less fear of the unknown as time went on.

For more food had to be found, and better ways of preserving and preparing it. The Renaissance was a period of great demographic growth, from the end of the fifteenth century onwards. After the catastrophic decades that had preceded it, there were now new mouths to be fed daily, and fewer starving people. The better fed you were, the more likely you were to have children; famine and disease did not kill them off so fast, and they had time to live long enough and well enough to procreate in their own turn.

Analysis of the oxygen isotopes 016 and 018 contained in the Greenland ice has shown that the cold period of the Middle Ages came to a sudden end around 1450; between 1480 and 1525, however, the average temperature fell again by several degrees. The plankton which fed the shoals of fish in the North Atlantic thus moved twice, preferring the more northerly Danish fishing grounds once the temperature rose again.

As we have seen, the Dutch had built their fortunes on herring. In the absence of the herring shoals they had to make money some other way, and to compete in trade, or failing that in industry, with the Venetians, Genoese and Provençals, all better placed than they were around the navel of the world of their time, the Mediterranean, which was regarded by its people as their personal property. For some time, moreover, the Portuguese had been successfully sailing along the Atlantic coasts of the known world, showing their teeth. If someone did not soon go farther afield, the sea was going to be too small.

In a parallel development, the subsistence economy was also in transition. Whereas a mild climate had favoured stock-breeding and agriculture, the sudden but brief cooling which sent country people, suddenly unable to make a living, into the towns coincided with a period of industrial progress in Northern and Central Europe, and the competitive trading, in terms of both status and the economy, of the great fairs.

As usual, a lower crop yield and a change in life-style brought with it dietary change: the higher consumption of animal protein typical of urban areas meant a demand for the products of stock-breeding and fishing. Not only more salt but also more spices were needed to preserve and prepare meat and fish. One of the spices which were also regarded as medicaments was sugar, and the noticeable rise in purchasing power allowed people to satisfy their increased appetite for that fabulous food, once an Arab monopoly. Europeans now wanted to bypass the Arabs and get it for themselves.

The moving forces behind the great voyages of discovery may be said to have been sugar and spices in Southern Europe, herrings and whale-oil in Northern Europe. Economic competition with Islam (the only battlefield on which there was any hope of victory) also played its part. There came a time when the great discoveries allowed the discovery and enjoyment of other exotic marvels. Together, gluttony and the greed for gain it engendered pushed the frontiers of curiosity, appetite and cupidity farther and farther out. The shrewdest operators were those who sat in their offices in the seaports making money out of both demand and supply.

The Portuguese were the first to organize this vast potential market to their own profit. They were lucky in being governed by shrewd sovereigns and in having intrepid seamen at their disposal, in this case Basque mercenaries. The King of Portugal was soon 'the first grocer of Europe'. His cousins and neighbours in Spain followed his example, imitated by those other countries capable of doing so, with varying degrees of success.

By 1442 the Castilian court had almost entirely shaken off the Arabs. Castile had leisure to turn to a new world which a Genoese explorer, even shrewder than the Portuguese, offered it on a silver dish – or rather a dish of solid gold: the gold of the Americas, or rather the West 'Indies'.

Christopher Columbus proved not only a skilful navigator but also a knowledgeable scholar and a thorough-going careerist. He has left a copy of Marco Polo's *Book* and one of Pliny the Elder's *Geography*, annotated in the margin with 366 comments of his own in which the words 'gold' and 'spices' constantly recur, used almost synonymously. We know the manner in which he shared his dreams with the Spanish crown, and the letter he sent to the Grand Treasurer of His Most Catholic Majesty after discovering the West Indies is a cry of triumph:

> I found very many islands thickly peopled ... the mountains are all most
> beautiful ... and covered with trees of a thousand kinds ... the number

and size and wholesomeness of the rivers, most of them bearing gold, surpass anything that would be believed by one who had not seen them. ... In this island there are many spices and extensive mines of gold and other metals. ... Finally, their Highnesses may see that I shall give them all the gold they require ... spices also, and cotton, mastic, and aloes. ... I think also I have found rhubarb and cinnamon.... Done on board the caravel, off the Canary Islands, on the fifteenth of February, fourteen hundred and ninety-three.

The Admiral Cristoforo Colombo

The gold which haunted the dreams of the navigator and his rivals did exist, but not in such phenomenal quantities as would have satisfied their greed and that of their sleeping partners. Gold does not grow on trees, even 'trees of a thousand kinds'. But ways would soon be found of turning anything that really could be gathered in those latitudes into gold.

By the same token, the whole world was about to change, not only this new half of it, for the Dutch and the English, staking their own fortunes on the Indian Ocean, ensured that trading in the produce of those lands would become a matter of rivalry too.

In his Papal Bull of 3 May 1493, Pope Alexander VI, sharing the new lands discovered and those yet to be discovered between the Spanish and the Portuguese, specified that this seizure of new territories, colonization (meaning 'the establishment of colonists or cultivators on lands of which they shall pay the rent in kind') was to be seen as a Christian duty 'so that the Catholic faith and religion may be exalted and spread everywhere.'

This duty provided moral and theological justification for the practise of *encomendia* or 'commandery', whereby the native was handed over to the colonists, who might use him as slave labour in return for teaching him the Christian religion. In fact, when it came to the intensive exploitation of those colonial foods which were more abundant than spices and were destined for the European market, teaching the catechism was far from being in the forefront of the colonial mind, and the serial baptisms that took place were pure farce. The urgent requirement was for a workforce as numerous and as cheap as possible – in fact free.

Colonization, born solely of the desire to get rich and always only too obviously accompanied by violence, did not encumber itself with any wish to 'civilize' the natives. The American Indian populations were swiftly decimated. Black Africa was plundered of its human wealth to replace them. In the name of civilization and the cause of those new dietary habits involving foreign foodstuffs which were not strictly necessary but now seemed indispensable – sugar, chocolate, coffee, tea and many other delicacies – a true adventure story began, a story in as many chapters as there are shelves in a grocer's shop, full of colour, flavour, pleasures and pains. The preface to that story, however, had been written centuries before.

Chapter 16

The Lure of Sugar

Although medieval Europe called the crystallized sap of sugar cane 'white salt' (as opposed to sea or rock salt, grey because it was not refined at the time) or 'Indian salt', the Chinese claim to have been the first to make cane sugar, among their many other inventions. The craft may have been practised from very ancient times in the region of Kouang-tong (Canton), but it seems more likely and more logical that they learned it from the Indians. In fact there is a clear statement to that effect in the *Natural History* of Su-kung, of the seventh century AD: 'The Emperor Tai-Hung sent workmen to learn the art of making sugar in Lyu [India] and more particularly in Mo-Ki-To [Bengal].'

Sugar cane, a giant grass, is native to India and in particular the Ganges delta. According to Humboldt's theory, most plants related to it are still found there in the wild state. However, the classic species of sugar cane, *Saccharum officinarum*, which was probably the result of a mutation, is not found anywhere, even in India, except in its cultivated form.

Indian tradition – and tradition often bears out scientific theories – places the origin of sugar cane a very long way back. According to legend, the ancestors of Buddha came from the land of sugar, or Gur, a name then given to Bengal. The Sanskrit epic of the *Ramayana* (*c.* 1200 BC) describes a banquet 'with tables laid with sweet things, syrup, canes to chew ...'

Seven centuries later, when Darius made his foray into the valley of the Indus, the Persians in their turn discovered 'a reed that gives honey without the aid of bees' and brought it home with them. It seems that at first they guarded their monopolies of growing it and exporting its sugar as jealously as if they were state secrets. Eventually invasions, conquests and trading caravans, most notably those of the Assyrians, spread sugar cane all through the Middle East, from the Indus to the Black Sea, from the Sahara to the Persian Gulf.

The 'sweet reed' which may be the 'sweet calamus' of the Bible, was brought to the Mediterranean by caravans in the very earliest days of the history of the import–export business. Its syrup, considered a spice even rarer and more expensive than any other, was used in medicine by the Egyptians and Phoenicians even before the Greeks and Romans; it is this pharmaceutical use that gives sugar cane its species name of *officinarum*.

Theophrastus, who succeeded Aristotle as head of the Lyceum, was going only on hearsay when he noted in one of his botanical treatises, in 371 BC, that: 'There are three kinds of honey, that of the flowers, that of the dew, and that which flows from a reed.'

During Alexander's campaigns his admiral, Nearchus, learned as he went down the Indus that this 'honey' was actually the juice of the cane, evaporated by boiling. Because of the climate and the time spent in transit, the resulting syrup appeared like a thick liquid, which crystallized by desiccation, and also fermented.

Several of the great medical authors of antiquity mentioned this 'Indian salt'. Dioscorides, a Greek contemporary of Augustus, remarks that: 'There is a kind of solid honey called *saccharon*, which is found in the reeds of India and Arabia the fortunate. It resembles salt in consistency, and crunches in the mouth.' The classical Greek and Roman naturalists Pliny, Strabo, Seneca, Lucan and Galen all agree with Dioscorides in using the word *saccharon* or *saccharum*, a Graeco-Latin distortion of the Sanskrit word *sarkara*, another indication of the Indian origin of sugar cane. In his *Natural History*, Pliny does not say just how sugar is made from the cane, but he does add: 'It is used solely in medicine' – a medicine, according to Dioscorides and Galen, that was worth its weight in silver.

Varro (116–27 BC), not the consul but the naturalist, was the first to describe the plant in his *De re rustica*. Moreover, he was the first to explain at last just how the Persians in particular made *saccharum*.

For a very long period, the label 'Indian' rendered sugar even more valuable in Western eyes: sugar was Indian, and the dwellers on the banks of the Ganges were described by Lucan in a famous line: 'Quique bibunt tenera dulces ab arrundine succos' ('they who drink the sweet juice from a weak reed').[1]

Until modern times, then, sugar was an expensive medicine to Europeans, or a luxury reserved for the rich and powerful, a fabulous food brought from beyond the deserts by caravans that ended their journeys in the ports of the eastern Mediterranean.

In 966 the newly created republic of Venice was already building a warehouse from which sugar was exported to Central Europe, the Black Sea and the Slav countries. The fate and fortune of Venice were founded on sugar and the trade in silks and spices.

The Arabs installed the first 'industrial' sugar refinery on the island of Candia or Crete – its Arabic name, *Qandi*, meant 'crystallized sugar' – around the year 1000. The aroma wafting from that refinery attracted Crusaders to the Near East like flies to honey. Having conquered Persia, the Arabs had reorganized its ancient sugar-making industry, and as they expanded they established plantations and sugar refineries in the other countries that fell under their rule. Sugar was a gold mine, and contributed greatly to Arab wealth.

The Arabs also invented caramel. Perfecting the process of the decantation of sugar, they obtained a new product, dark brown, sticky and highly fragrant: *kurat al milh*, or 'ball of sweet salt'. One of the first uses of caramel was as a depilatory for harem ladies.

The whole Near East was fragrant with sugar. Joinville, who had followed King Louis IX to the Crusade, sniffed its enchanting perfume in passing, and mentions in his memoirs 'very fair canes, from which they obtain that which makes sugar'.

After Acre and the loss of Syria in 1291, the Christians who had withdrawn to Cyprus probably had time to bring some suckers of the cane in their baggage. Sugar soon became synonymous with prosperity in the island, which exported several thousand 'lightweight' quintals (50 kilos) of it in the fifteenth century. We may note in passing that the last queen of Cyprus, the beautiful Catherine, wife of the last Lusignan king, was also an heiress of the patrician Cornaro family of Venice; the Cornaros were the sugar kings of their time, and much richer than any king who ruled merely by divine right.

As we have seen, spices, of which sugar represented the largest tonnage, were the basis of the economic power of the great Mediterranean ports. Despite the high price of these foods, which were not very heavy and were easy to transport, demand was increasing so much that cargo after cargo could be landed without any fear of failing to find a buyer.

When sugar or spices passed through the towns of Provence or Languedoc on their way by land to Northern Europe and England, the price of the merchandise, high enough already when it began its journey, was greatly increased by the many levies that had to be paid as it came to the toll barriers. The towns or feudal lords who owned the tolls had every intention of profiting by the manna as it passed by. It was partly for this reason that the sea route by way of the Atlantic was developed. Its three poles were Venice, Genoa and the Hanseatic ports, and although it was longer there was no need for constant unloading or for the payment of successive tolls. This route made Bruges the centre of the sugar and spice trade, and it was soon visited by the Portuguese, anxious to maintain their domination of the western coasts, particularly when they were able to offer sugar from Madeira.

Around the twelfth century taxes paid on sugar made their first official appearance in the records of the South of France. The civic archives of Narbonne tell us that in 1153 a toll on sugar was introduced, called the *lende*: eight deniers per quintal if the goods arrived by sea, 14 deniers if they arrived by land. Marseilles instituted the *lesde* in 1228, and the Count of Provence added sugar to his toll tariff 25 years later. A distinction was drawn between sugar-loaves and powdered sugar.

We do not know which sort the countess of Savoie preferred in 1273, but the accounts of her household mention the sum of two gold sous and five silver deniers for a pound of sugar. The countess of Burgundy, Mahaut d'Artois, a peeress of

France and the formidable mother-in-law of Philippe V and Charles IV, may perhaps have drawn her proverbial energy from sugar; although she was constantly pleading poverty to her sons-in-law and her peers, the good lady did not hesitate to buy 15 sugar-loaves at the fair of Lagny in 1299. A sugar-loaf could weigh anything between one pound and 20 pounds, but whatever it weighed it was worth that weight in silver.

As we have seen already, there is no need to feel too sorry for King Jean Le Bon of France in his prison in London; he too was always complaining of his sad plight, and his kingdom bled itself dry for him, but his captivity must have had its sweet consolations: besides consuming a great many spices he also had plenty of sugar, bought for about 20 deniers 'esterlins' [sterling] the pound.

In the next century the pharmacy of the Hôtel-Dieu bought five and a half pounds of sugar at the famous Lendit fair at Saint-Denis, near Paris. Sieur Hughes Du Jardin paid a gold *écu* for the medicine, 'worth XXV sous and VIII deniers in Paris money'. Queen Marguerite of Navarre tells us in her *Heptameron* that around 1515 a sugar-loaf the size of a little finger was enough to pay for a lavish dinner served in an Alençon tavern to a lawyer of that town and a gentleman who was a friend of his.

The handsome gift of a quintal of sugar was made by the 'Sultan' of Egypt to the king of France, Charles VII. By then, of course, that monarch had become known as 'the Victorious' (in the Hundred Years' War), and he was a friend of Jacques Coeur, the greatest grocer of them all.

Loaf sugar, also called rock sugar, was refined sugar, hard and very white, moulded into a conical shape. But the apothecaries gave other charming names to a whole range of products.

Caffetin or *caften* sugar owed its name both to its origin and its presentation: the Genoese town of Caffa in the Crimea (a port of transit between Europe and Central Asia) and the plaited leaves of the palm, or 'caffas', which were used for the loaves. (A basket made of the same material was a *caffin* or *couffin*; the word is related to English 'coffer' and 'coffin'.)

Casson, a fragile sugar, broke easily. It became *cassonade* in the sixteenth century, and was also called *crac* in French, 'cracked sugar'. It was the ancestor of caster sugar. Sugar of this kind from Cyprus, Rhodes and Babylon was the best. There was a *crac* of Montréal – not in Canada, which had yet to be discovered, but a Syrian town on the borders of the Dead Sea on the site of an old Crusader fort.

Muscarrat was not scented with musk, but was the best of all the sugars, almost a mythical product, since it was said to have been made in Egypt for the exclusive use of the Sultan of Babylon. Its Italian name *mucchera*, according to the Venetians who claimed to have smuggled it in, denoted that it had been twice refined.

Cypre, *chypre*, or red sugar was made from recovered waste sugar or sugar that had not been much refined, and was mainly used for enemas. But unscrupulous apothecaries would put it in their potions because its low price left them with a better profit margin.

Candy, originally from Candia, had very large crystals. There were five kinds of candy in pharmacists' stocks: plain candy, or candy flavoured with rose, violet, lemon or currant. All these were natural flavours, of course, extracts of fruit and flower syrups.

Finally, *Barbary* sugar, a Bruges speciality, came from the Berber country of North Africa. And there was also *panelle*, the finest of the powdered sugars.

The white sugar described in French records as *blanc officinal* was not often used for the medical purposes its name suggests, but remains a part of the standard French pharmacopoeia, a last witness to the fabulous era of sugar and spices.

Henry the Navigator, prince regent of Portugal, calculated in 1420 that exporting sugar cane from his own territories made him a better profit than importing it from the Levant. However, experimental attempts actually to grow sugar cane in Southern Europe (in Spain, Provence, Sicily and Italy) all failed. Only the Balearic Islands could boast a few cane-fields abandoned by the Arabs. Sugar cane needed not only rich, moist soil, but also great heat combined with good and regular ventilation, such as the trade winds provide. The recently discovered Madeira Islands were highly suitable. Henry the Navigator was very successful in the archipelago, and cane from Madeira was taken to the Spanish Canary Islands and the island of São Tomé.

Then Christopher Columbus reached the New World, and in 1506 one Pedro d'Arranca took sugar cane to Hispaniola, now the Dominican Republic. It grew there so profusely that by 1518 the island had eight sugar plantations, and it was said that the magnificent royal palaces of Madrid and Toledo, built by the Emperor Charles V, were paid for entirely with the profits from sugar.

Soon, however, taking sugar cane across the Atlantic to a Europe which was closer to sources of sugar production in the Middle East than in the West Indies was perceived to be a wasteful business. The bundles of cut cane did not travel well. Not only did they turn bitter and rot, but the cargoes took up a great deal of space in the holds of relatively small ships.

The Venetians too had studied the market, and had just, with a considerable fanfare of publicity, inaugurated the first true industrial refinery. They had looked at the primitive Turkish factories already in existence, and had improved on the system. The yield they obtained, and the prices their Muslim suppliers allowed them with a view to breaking the monopoly of the Catholic and American market, ushered in less prosperous times for the Spanish and Portuguese colonists. Soon they were setting up their own refineries in the West Indies, the Canaries and Madeira to extract raw sugar or 'syrup' by crushing the cane.

The Dutch, anxious not to be outdone, increased cane production in their own domains in the East Indies and in those few parts of the West Indies they had managed to acquire. They also exported sugar from South China and Formosa. Dutch sugar, sold on the quayside in loaves weighing 18 to 20 pounds and at remarkably low prices, was called 'palm sugar' because of the palm leaves used to wrap the sugar-loaves, like the old *caften* sugar. It was of excellent quality, with a

Taking freshly cut sugar cane to the mill in Colombia (1979)

delicious flavour of violets.

In the end, with so much production and undercutting of competitors, sugar became cheaper, and sugar consumption was constantly growing. As early as 1572 the geographer Ortelius was writing, in his *Theatrum orbis terrarum*, that 'instead of being obtainable only in the shops of apothecaries, who kept it for the sick, as before, sugar is now eaten for appetite alone. That which was once a remedy now serves us as food.'

In 1640, when he took command of the French West Indies, Jean Aubert introduced sugar-cane growing there. It is often said that the French are one war behind the rest of the world, and they were late in the day with sugar, but at least they were able to benefit by other nations' experiments. Twenty-five years later Colbert noted, with satisfaction: 'The quantities of sugar sent home to France are increasing, refineries are multiplying, and the kingdom, once obliged to buy its sugar from foreigners, can now sell it to them.'

The sugar refineries now proliferating near French ports were encouraged. More and more 'syrup' came from the mills of the West Indies. It is interesting to note that in Brazil, where sugar preceded coffee, the owners of the *fazendas* were called 'masters of the mills', a nickname which remained with them.

557

Sugar mills in the West Indies are almost always worked by wind, less frequently by water, very occasionally indeed by steam. It is difficult for mechanical methods and modern industrial processes to be adopted in countries which still lag far behind the civilization of the American continent. Although some modern machinery has recently been introduced into colonial sugar mills, the vast majority still use the old type of equipment described below.

Three large metal cylinders placed above a stone receptacle are set in motion by the sails of a windmill connected to them by a system of gear-wheels. The middle cylinder, the only one to receive the impulsive force direct, sets the other two in motion turning in the opposite direction. A negro takes a handful of canes and feeds them between two of the cylinders. The motion carries them through, crushing them, and the juice flows out. Another slave receives the crushed canes and feeds them back between the central cylinder and the cylinder on the other side of it: the canes thus go through the mill a second time and are crushed again to extract more juice.

The residue is called bagasse or cane-trash, and is used as fuel in the sugar mills. Firewood is so difficult to transport in the West Indies that the crushed canes have to be used, although it is realized that they still contain a considerable amount of sugar because the extraction methods used are so inadequate. Cane-trash from ordinary mills still contains 28 to 30 per cent of its weight in sugar. It is a fact that the boilers are heated by sugar in the colonies: sad proof of the backward state of the industry today.

Louis Figuier, Les merveilles de l'industrie. 1868

Making sugar in the West Indies in the nineteenth century: above, sugar mill with vertical cylinders; below, the boilers

On the eve of the French Revolution one-fifth of European consumption was supplied by the refineries of Bordeaux, where there were no fewer than 26 factories. Marseilles, Rouen, La Rochelle and Nantes did not lag far behind. A busy traffic between Europe and the New World had developed under the influence of the great trading companies formed by the various nations. The royal courts set an example, and every family in first the aristocracy and then the newly prosperous bourgeoisie felt it was a matter of pride to own stocks in those companies, in the same way as it was fashionable to consume exotic products.

In fact the fashion for coffee and chocolate had caused sugar consumption to treble in the courts of the eighteenth century. Like manners and society in general, those delicacies were becoming democratic. But beet sugar came to the fore with the great changes of the nineteenth century. The inevitable effect was a drop in the price of cane sugar, and the whole economic system of the West Indies and the French Atlantic ports eventually had to be reconsidered.

The era of the 'sugar standard' lasted only 200 years, two centuries in which millions of human beings were sacrificed in its cause, far more of them, and more spectacularly, than those who died in the cause of the gold standard. For, together with leaf tobacco, cane sugar syrup had become an international currency. European merchandise was paid for in the West Indies with *boucans* (casks deriving their name from their origin as goatskin buckets) of either tobacco or syrup. Paris paid its colonial administrators on a similar scale, with rates varying according to the harvest.

Everything, indeed, was sacrificed to sugar, so great was the greed for gain displayed by the planters and sugar dealers. Prosperity became a double-edged sword, and the vats in which the syrup boiled were magic cauldrons over which myopic sorcerers' apprentices bent until they felt dizzy.

Intensive syrup-processing on the plantations of the New World had quickly posed a major problem: the labour force. If it was to be profitable, such an industry could not afford to pay wages. Native Indian workers were pressed into service until it became illegal – by which time they had almost died out. They were much regretted, for the few colonists who could bring themselves to do manual work in such heat expected wages that would compensate for their exile from the home country, particularly if it was voluntary. While the emigrants were mostly sturdy peasants from the Vendée or Saintonge in the case of the French possessions, or Andalusian peasants in the Spanish territories, there were other expatriates, convicts and rogues, who soon infected the volunteers. Gangs of them would be found breaking their contracts in the slums of the ports.

The less cunning stayed on the plantations, but never made old bones there: working conditions, the climate, epidemic disease, malnutrition, alcoholism and brawls all took their toll.

Reduced to their own resources, the colonists who had been granted land were no longer able to produce the wealth that had been hoped for, indeed demanded, by their home countries, which were anxious to see some return on their investments. The situation was the same everywhere in the New World, in the French, Spanish,

559

Portuguese, English and Dutch colonies. By the same token, the colonists had no labour available to grow food or raise livestock (the original imported animals had taken to the wild at the same time as the few Indian survivors), and a good deal of the sugar and tobacco produced had to be exchanged for provisions from Europe at shamelessly high prices. The colonies made the fortune of many a ship's captain, and in 1775 the Abbé Raynal, author of an *Histoire philosophique et politique de la colonisation et du commerce des Européens dans les deux Indes*, was complaining that 'to feed an American colony you must cultivate a whole province in Europe'.

If the colonies were to yield a profit, therefore, the island planters and their backers had to compensate for the labour shortage in a way which seemed only sensible at the time, although the idea sends a shiver down the spine today: they needed slaves. Otherwise they could write off the whole New World. They took those slaves in their millions from the coasts of Africa. As Werner Sombart has said: 'We grew rich because whole races died for us. For us, continents were depopulated.' He is echoing the comments of Bernardin de Saint-Pierre which reached the ears of millions who, however, were more moved by the loves of his Paul and Virginie: 'I do not know whether coffee and sugar are necessary to the happiness of Europe, but I know very well that those two plants have brought misfortune on both parts of the world.' And indeed, the wish for sugar and other exotic foodstuffs changed the planet more than many centuries of history and conquests. For very many people, nothing would ever be the same again. So many tears were shed for sugar that by rights it ought to have lost its sweetness.

In 1575 Olivier de Serres pointed out that beet had a high sugar content: 'A kind of root which came to us from Italy not long since ... the juice of which, yielded in the cooking, resembles sugar syrup, and its vermilion colour is very handsome to behold.' But no one was particularly interested.

In 1745 the German chemist Marggraf had reported to the Berlin Academy of Sciences on 'chemical experiments with a view to deriving true sugar from various plants which grow in our own latitudes.' He was the first to succeed in extracting and isolating beet sugar. In 1786 his disciple Achard, a French émigré of Huguenot origin, built an industrial refinery in Silesia which took the fancy of the King of Prussia. The English, remembering at this point that they lived on an island, tried to induce the chemist to come to them to make this foodstuff, which would be so useful in case of any blockade. They offered him large sums, but he refused.

Another French chemist, however, the famous Liebig, said that making European sugar was 'if not nonsense, at least extremely impolitic' (with regard to the West Indian colonists and in particular their backers).

Finally, during the Continental Blockade Napoleon ordered 32,000 hectares of land to be put down to sugar-beet growing, to free the French economy from dependence on colonial imports. When the first beet sugar refinery was built at Passy in 1813 any manufacturer producing ten tons of sugar was exempt from taxes for four years.

A chapter in the history of sugar had just closed. Beet was to strike a heavy blow at the economies of the West Indies, Brazil and Réunion, based on the cane sugar which was now more expensive than sugar from beet.

Maple sugar and fruit sugars are of only incidental importance. The maple tree is the emblem of Canada, and the syrup obtained by cooking its sap has much folklore attached to it. In appearance it is rather like the 'sugar' of antiquity.

Sugar can also be extracted from many other plants rich in starch or fructose. Dates and figs were long used as a source of such fruit sugars. In 1808 Parmentier, famous in connection with the potato and greatly honoured at the time, recommmended the extraction of grape sugar, which became the object of great enthusiasm for a while and was then forgotten until the Second World War, when it was made again as a matter of expediency.

Irrigating sugar-cane fields near Piraciacaba, São Paulo, Brazil: once cultivated by black slaves, sugar cane is now grown on an industrial scale, and is still the main source of sugar production.

Since 1979 the world has made more sugar than can be sold. Transformation of the surplus into alcohol is attended by other problems, the least of them being a slump in sugar prices. The petrol shortage saw a new era open with the conversion of sugar into fuel. Cars in the Latin-American countries have begun to run on cane alcohol, promoted by a huge publicity campaign. The limousine of one president bears a banner saying: 'I run on alcohol, don't you?'

The future will show whether sugar-beet growing, a perpetual source of controversy in the Common Market, will come to the aid of the fuel stations. The Arab oil magnates are great consumers of sugar but will not touch alcohol, forbidden by the Koran: all the more reason, perhaps, for them to feel some anxiety.

Rum, A Sugar Spirit

Many centuries before the birth of Christ, an old man told Croesus to beware of attacking the Persians, 'those men who drink no wine but only water, and have nothing well-flavoured to eat, not even figs'. Presumably, then, it was the Macedonian conquerors who came after Croesus, or those Indian kings who were vassals of the Achaemenid dynasty, who taught the ancestors of today's piously sober Iranians how to make rum from the fermented juice of the sugar cane. They seem to have been among the first to do so, for long after the old man had offered Croesus his wise advice Marco Polo, dictating his memoirs in his Genoese prison to his editor Rusticiano of Pisa, mentioned among the many marvels of his book a beverage calculated to displease today's ayatollahs. 'They make very good wine of sugar, and many become drunk with it.' This was in the fourteenth century, and is the first recorded mention of rum.

It should be remembered that alcohol and alembic are words of Arabic origin, although the Koran forbade alcohol and all fermented drinks. The alembic was a still, and was already known to the author of the first part of the *Roman de la Rose*, Guillaume de Lorris, around 1236.

'Sugar wine' was not called rum until after 1688, and the word seems to have been an abbreviation of 'rumbullion' or 'rumbustion'. The word may have been a term from the new pidgin English of Barbados and possibly derived from the distortion of a term in the dialect of Seville, combining Low Latin *rheu*, 'stem', and bullion or *bouillon*, 'boiling'. Rumbullion was made from the boiling of sugar-cane stems. (Similarly, 'rhubarb' is a plant with edible stems originating from somewhere foreign, i.e., 'barbarous'.)

Foods seldom get their names by chance, and the trail left by those names, from table to table, can help us to trace them back to their origins.

The Legend of Sugar

Li-schi Tchin, the most famous of Chinese naturalists, recounts a Chinese legend of the eighth century:

Our ancestors drank the juice of the cane raw, then it was cooked to a syrup, then it was hardened and dried to make white sugar. This was in the time of the T'ang dynasty [AD 766 to 790]. A bonze called Tsen lived on the Plan-shan mountain in the district of Sui-mung. No one knew where he came from. One day his donkey came down the mountain and destroyed the cane plantation of a man named Noang-chi. As compensation, the bonze taught him how to make sugar.

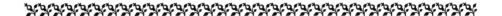

You must also know that in these parts, before the Great Khan subjected them to his lordship [in 1720], the people did not know how to prepare and refine sugar so well as it is done at Babylon. They did not let it congeal, and solidify it in moulds, but merely boiled and skimmed it, so that it hardened into a kind of paste, and was black in colour. But after the country had been acquired by the Great Khan, there came into these regions some men of Babylon, who had been at the court of the Great Khan, and who taught them how to refine it with the ashes of certain trees.

The Travels of Marco Polo

The process was reproduced and perfected by Pierre Figuier, in 1810, at Montpellier, using charcoal or bone black:

In Cochin China, around the twelfth century, a company of the royal guard, magnificent specimens of manhood, received high pay for the sugar and the cane that they were obliged by law to eat daily, in order to preserve their stout figures.

Louis Figuier, *Les merveilles de l'industrie*

Chapter 17

Confectionery and
Preserves

All the peoples of antiquity made sweetmeats of honey before they had sugar: the Chinese, the Indians, the people of the Middle East, the Egyptians and then the Greeks and Romans used it to coat fruits, flowers, and the seeds or stems of plants, to preserve them or for use as an ingredient in the kind of confectionery still made in those countries today.

Confectionery and preserves featured in the most sumptuous of Athenian banquets, and were an ornament to Roman feasts at the time of the *Satyricon*, but it seems that after the barbarian invasions Europe forgot them for a while, except at certain wealthy courts where Eastern products were eaten. Thus we find mention of preserves and jellies of quince, citron, rose, apple, plum and pear in the *Book of Ceremonies* of the Byzantine emperor Constantine VII Porphyrogenetes ('born to the purple'), a book which is not only a treatise on the etiquette of imperial banqueting in the ninth century but a catalogue of the foods available and the dishes made of them.

At the height of the Middle Ages sweetmeats reappeared, on the tables of the wealthy at first. The rest of Europe imitated Italy, which led the way in culinary splendour, and it should be remembered that Venice and Genoa were among the first exporters of Eastern sugar.

In fact the confectionery of the time began as a marriage of spices and sugar, and was intended to have a therapeutic or at least preventative function, as an aid to digestive troubles due to the excessive intake of food which was neither very fresh nor very well balanced. As we saw above, guests were in the habit of carrying these sweetmeats to their rooms to be taken at night. They were contained in little comfit-boxes or *drageoirs* (according to some etymologists, the word *dragée*, sugared almond or comfit, which had a now obsolete English version 'dredge', derives from

Latin *tragemata* or sweetmeat). The host would sometimes distribute such comfit-boxes as presents; this was done, for instance, in 1468 at the marriage of Charles the Bold of Burgundy to Margaret of York, sister of Edward IV of England.

These sugared spices became the 'chamber spices' discussed above, and for a long time they had a reputation for 'dispelling wind and encouraging the seed', as Savary was still putting it in the seventeenth century. They were the ancestors of modern sweets (the French word *bonbon* did not appear until early in the reign of Henri IV). Cloves, ginger, aniseed, juniper berries, almonds and pine kernels were dipped in melted sugar and well cooked in a pan over a flame. The pan was stirred so that the mixture would not stick to the bottom, and more melted sugar was added as necessary before it caramelized. The result was a kind of *dragée* or *praline* mixture, although the latter term did not appear until later. The kind of preserve known as 'dry', a fruit paste strongly flavoured with aromatics and even perfume (which cooks did not hesitate to add to sauces too), was a frequent companion of the 'chamber spices'.

Arnaud de Villeneuve, the famous travelling physician of Languedoc, in a long list of fruit pastes and sugar-coated seeds, recommends violet-flavoured sugar for its digestive virtues. He also makes particular mention of *pignolat*, a caramel containing pine kernels, the ancestor of nougat. Pine kernels were thought to aid conception.

A dessert of confectionery and preserves is recorded on the menu of the amazing banquet given at Avignon in 1344 for the coronation of Pope Clement VI. The generous host was Cardinal di Ciccario. The eighth and last course, a final delicious titbit, comprised 'candied fruits of many colours'. However, a treatise on etiquette of the same period, by Jehan de Brasseuse, condemned nuts candied with honey and sticky dragées 'which cannot be eaten in a cleanly fashion' ('quae non potuerunt munde capi').

The romance *Petit Jehan de Saintré*, published by Anthoine de La Salle in 1400, gives an account of a meal for a lady which includes 'Lenten figs roasted with sugar', served as an aperitif with 'toasts' dipped in white hippocras. The menu concluded with 'peeled and sugared almonds'.

The magnificent supper given by the no less magnificent Gaston Phébus de Foix to the ambassadors of Ladislas of Austria, who came on his behalf to ask for the hand in marriage of King Charles VII of France's daughter, featured a profusion of candied spices, preserves and crystallized fruits along with the wafers served in the fifth course.

However, the palm of gastronomic magnificence went to the Italian courts, particularly that of the Visconti-Sforza family, *magni comestatores* according to Ortenso Landi, author of the *Commentario delle piu notabili e monstruose cose d'Italia*, which appeared in 1550. The Milanese are said to have invented marzipan, almond paste and meringue, which began as egg whites beaten with Messina sugar and mixed with water-melon seeds. This is not really any odder than the melon candied with sugar, again from Messina, which concludes the verse menu written by the court poet Antonio Cammeli for a wealthy Milanese.

What does seem odd, or at least surprising, is a 'collation' served in Venice when Beatrice d'Este, the wife of Ludovico Moro, was visiting the city. The Venetian Republic set out to rival the menus of the Sforza court. The meal served to the duchess of Milan in the Doges' palace consisted of 'divers items all made of gilded sugar, to the number of three hundred.'

Another Venetian 'collation', this time given for Henri III of France, was another and particularly extravagant fantasy of the same kind. Everything on the table had been made of spun sugar: bread, plates, knives, forks (in themselves a novelty at the time, and still provided with only two prongs), the tablecloth, the napkins, and countless decorations, groups, centre-pieces, statues and allegorical figures – in short, 1286 masterpieces had been created by the famous Nicolo delle Cavalliera, copying models designed by the goldsmith Sansovino.

Like many artists, sculptors, and goldsmiths, the master confectioners of Venice were in touch with Florence, the mother of the arts, when they were not Florentines themselves.

The Medici queens of France, first the gluttonous Catherine, then Marie, who was also fond of her food, brought with them to their new country not only embroidery maids, goldsmiths, glovemakers and astrologers, but Italian virtuosi who had a great influence on French cooking, particularly in the art of concocting desserts and working with sugar.

Of course confectionery, like cakes, is not always of Italian origin, although sugared almonds, one of the oldest sweetmeats in history, do perhaps come from ancient Rome.

Metz, Nancy, Paris, Verdun and Toulouse are among the cities and towns of France famous for their sugared almonds. Earlier still, however, the Romans of classical times distributed them at public and private ceremonies. Sugared almonds are mentioned among the gifts given to great men in accounts of receptions. The origin of the word 'dragée' itself is controversial. If it is not from that Roman delicacy *tragemata*, was it perhaps invented by one Julius Dragatus, of the illustrious family of the Fabii, who had *dragata* distributed to the Roman people on the occasion of births and marriages? Or was the name that of a slave, subsequently freed, who invented the sweetmeats for his master? Theories abound. Another is that the word comes from *diadragum*, an almond sweetmeat made in the early years of the present era in Montpellier, a town famous for its remedies.

Dragées are mentioned not only by Froissart, Rabelais and Guillaume de Provins, but also in the archives of the town of Verdun; from 1200 onwards sugared almonds were presented to the powerful bishops of that city. Dragées of Verdun were distributed at the baptism of all the royal princes of France. On St Valentine's Day Charles IV, Duke of Lorraine, gave sugared almonds to a young girl of Verdun chosen by lot. In the time of Turgot, the eighteenth-century economist and administrator, the city sold 60,000 pounds a year of them, as the minister's records a little while before the French Revolution tell us.

In fifteenth-century Cambrai, Marguerite of Burgundy, at her wedding to Guillaume IV of Hainault, wished to have sugared almonds given 'to the common people by her comfit-maker Pierre Host, but as the latter had drunk much ale and mead, he sank into a heavy slumber, and the children seized their chance to lay hold of the basket of sugared almonds.' Marguerite had the poor man paraded through the town in disgrace, 'clothed in white, with a herald crying his misdeed and his punishment'. The event has subsequently been celebrated on 4th August every year in the carnival of Pierre Host, whose name gradually became distorted to Pierre Bimberlot (a *bimberlot* is a toy or bauble). A puppet dressed in pierrot costume is paraded amid a hail of sweets in this summer carnival procession.

Crystallized fruits, familiar in the East, in Rome and throughout medieval Europe, have always been a speciality of the South of France with its many orchards. At Nice in 1680 the governor of the city, Prince Antoine of Savoy, gave them to his brother Duke Gabriel as a sign of welcome. The municipal accounts mention 'six boxes of fine *frutti confetti*'. Such gifts became traditional for ceremonies of welcome. Flowers, also found in abundance on the Côte d'Azur, were crystallized as well.

Nougat: engraving from the *Livre de cuisine* by Jules Gouffé, 1881

Nougat, dark or white, hard or soft, has been known as *torron* or *tourron* in Spain since the Arab occupation. But Montélimar, the chief town of France's almond-growing country, also had every reason to use its produce in this delicious confection, which is related to the *pignoulats* of Arnaud de Villeneuve. It appears that one M. de Nougarède, of a great Provençal family, perhaps inspired by the happy accident of his surname, spent no less than 55 years of his life writing a book of 8721 pages all about nougat. In spite of his industry he did not solve the riddle of its name, which may derive either from Latin *nux* (nut) and *nucatum* (nutty), or from a Provençal term. Nougat is *torrone* in Italy, but that term comes from the Spanish name. The people of Cremona made a model of the tallest tower of their city out of a paste of sugar, honey, egg white and almonds on the occasion of the marriage of Francesco Sforza, future duke of Milan, with Bianca Maria Visconti, daughter of the reigning duke. The masterpiece was presented to the king of France, Charles VII.

Pastilles took their name from Giovanni Pastilla, a skilled Italian confectioner patronized by the Medicis. When Marie de Medici went to Paris to marry Henri IV, Pastilla accompanied his mistress to court, and his sweetmeats became very fashionable. It was from this time that we date the term *bonbon*, literally 'good-good', used by the royal children to describe these delicious confections with their many flavours. Pastilla accompanied his queen into exile in Cologne, where he too died.

Praline was invented at about the time of Pastilla's death. We owe it to Lassagne, officer of the table to Maréchal du Plessis, who was duke of Choiseul-Praslin. One day, in the servants' quarters of his residence at Montargis, Lassagne found his children caramelizing almonds stolen from the kitchens. The wonderful odour emanating from the spot where the little cooks were at work gave away their guilty secret and its delicious results. His mouth watering, Lassagne promised to keep quiet in exchange for some of the sweetmeats. He perfected the recipe and took it to the court of Louis XIII, where the confection became known as *prasline*, not that the duke himself had anything to do with inventing it. Another story holds that the recipe was the result of clumsiness on the part of an apprentice, who dropped some almonds into caramel made with Gâtinais honey. Whatever the truth of the matter was, Lassagne retired to Montargis and opened a confectioner's shop there, the Maison de la prasline, which still exists and is as good as a museum. Praline is made and sold at modern fairs in France, but the cheap sort contains peanuts instead of the authentic almonds.

Calissons, the famous sweets of Aix-en-Provence, *must* be made with almonds. They consist of marzipan and crystallized fruits mixed with orange-flower water, all the ingredients being Provençal, and worthy of a sweetmeat which is the pride of Aix. Olivier de Serres, in his *Théâtre d'agriculture et mesnage des champs*, describes a confection very much like *calissons d'Aix*. Mme de Sévigné was delighted with a big box of them that her daughter gave her. The word *calisson* may be from Latin. At Christmas festivities in Aix-en-Provence rich families and confectioners had them distributed by priests at Mass instead of the consecrated bread. In fact *calissons* do contain a wafer substance like the wafers of the Host. The priest distributing the sweets chanted 'Venite ad calicem' – 'Come to the chalice' – translated by the good folk into Provençal as 'Venes toui à calisoum', whence *calisson*.

Marrons glacés, familiar to us for centuries, began to be made on an industrial scale in the Ardèche at the end of the nineteenth century. The rather surprising reason was that the invention of artificial silk put the workers in the silkworm-breeding houses of the Cévennes and Ardèche areas out of work. The locality had to fall back on its forests of sweet chestnut trees as its only asset. In 1882 Clément Faugier of Privas boldly embarked upon the large-scale manufacturing of *marrons glacés* to aid his fellow-countrymen. Since he wanted to send them all round the world, he decided to wrap them in metallic 'paper' made of tinfoil and called silver paper, a method soon adopted by chocolate manufacturers who faced the same problem of getting the goods to keep. Before long the Ardèche area could not produce enough sweet chestnuts to supply Faugier, and he imported them from Italy, particularly Calabria. The confectioners of Turin in their own turn then took to manufacturing a delicacy without which Christmas would hardly be Christmas.

Chewing-gum, contrary to tales told by mothers to put their children off it, is not made from old rubber tyres. The true story of this American speciality which has conquered the postwar world and has one of the largest turnovers of any confectionery industry is as follows: 100 years ago the famous general Antonio de Santa Anna, exiled in New York after the revolution in Mexico, had providently brought 250 kilos of *chicle* with him. Chicle is a gum extracted from the sapodilla, a tree which grows abundantly in the Yucatan desert. He hoped to make money out of selling it as a substitute for rubber. Like his fellow Mexicans, he was always chewing little pieces of this gum. His American partner, one Thomas Adams, was charged with negotiating its sale. Adams, a photographer by trade, failed in the gum business, and was left with the stock on his hands, for by this time Santa Anna had been granted an amnesty and had returned to Mexico, leaving the gum behind. One day Adams saw a pharmacist's little girl chewing some paraffin wax, remembered the general's habit, and offered his gum for sale at a price of one cent for a narrow strip the length of the little finger. He invested 55 dollars out of his total profits in more stock, and set up to manufacture chewing-gum with the assistance of his son Horatio, who died in 1956 at the age of 102. One of his competitors thought of adding glucose and mint to the gum. Another, Wrigley, used some of the enormous profits of his sales for a vast advertising campaign. Soon all America was chewing, greatly to the surprise of the Europeans in the First World War when American troops arrived on the other side of the Atlantic in 1917.

Sugar and sweetmeats were once valuable gifts, appreciated even by monarchs (confectionery always formed part of the traditional presents made to them, and such gifts were regarded as a delicate attention). According to the chronicler Commines, when Charlotte of Savoy, the wife of Louis XI, visited Paris for the first time in 1467, the municipal dignitaries, magistrates and consuls gave her 'a hart made of preserves [the dry, paste-like sort, obviously!] with the arms of that noble queen hanging from its neck, and there were also several comfit-boxes all full of chamber spices and of fine preserves.'

Like the expensive chamber spices, gifts of preserves were among the expenses incurred by all who had anything to do with the law (and they were legion in the litigious Middle Ages). The formula *non deliberetur donec salvanture species* is found in the records of the *parlement*, the high court of Paris. A satirical quatrain went around the city after the fire which destroyed part of the Palais de Justice in the seventeenth century. It ran:

> Certes ce fut un triste jeu
> Quant à Paris, Dame Justice
> Pour avoir mangé trop d'épices
> Se mit tout le palais en feu.

['It was indeed a sad thing in Paris when Dame Justice, having eaten too many spices, set the whole palace on fire.']

The Revolution, by a law reforming the organization of the judiciary passed on 24 August 1790, put an end to such practices. Although they were of very dubious morality, they must have contributed a great deal to the prosperity of the confectionery trade.

The confectioners of Paris were part of the grocers' corporation, the second of the six merchant associations. Its statutes, dating back to 1311, covered both grocers and apothecaries, who were not always on friendly terms and mutually forbade each other to sell certain products. An edict of 1353 directed apothecaries to sell honey to ordinary citizens and reserve sugar, that rare and noble food which they had been granted the concession to sell, for their aristocratic customers. But sugar, in its various different forms, fed the quarrels between the two trades for centuries. In fact the grocers could sell preserves, chamber spices, sugared almonds, conserves, and even all kinds of sugared drugs, but they were forbidden to make them. So high did tempers run that when they went to the Augustinian church where the confraternities met, one set took precedence over the other for exactly half the year each. A decree of the *parlement* of 1 September 1689 ended two centuries of squabbling and disputes.

At the great annual fairs such as the fair of Saint-Germain-des-Prés in Paris, all kinds of sweet things might be found on the stalls, but the master confectioners were persons of substance and prominent citizens. To acquire the title of 'master' you had to have sold no less than 800 pounds of merchandise, a fact which shows how rich the community was.

After the fourteenth century most of the confectioners of Paris settled around Les Halles and made their fortunes. The area had previously been the quarter of the Italian moneylenders known as Lombards, and an air of wealth seemed to linger in the streets, judging by shop signs such as 'Le Pilon d'or' or 'La Barbe d'or', and various 'Mortars' and 'Pestles', always golden.

In the seventeenth century Abraham du Pradel, the Sieur de Blégny, a physician and a shrewd businessman, published a book called the *Livre commode des adresses de Paris pour 1692* which indicates that a great many confectioners continued to do business in that quarter. The fashion magazines of the next century were still publishing advertisements from the tradesmen of the rue des Lombards. Labels, prospectuses and catalogues have also been found which allow us to compile a directory of the confectioners of Paris at the period and a list of famous shops which had been trading for over a century, such as 'Le Fidèle Berger' and 'Le Grand Monarque'. These confectionery shops were part of the attraction of life in Paris, places where the best people met, for they were thought superior to the cafés then in the course of expansion. Chocolate was often served in them too.

Under the Valois monarchs there was a passion for preserves, and a host who gave his guests something particularly good or original could ensure the renown of his table by his jams, pastes and jellies as much as by the contents of his cellar. King François I had a great liking for *cotignac*, quince paste, and is said to have eaten it with tears in his eyes. One day he paid a surprise visit to his current mistress, Mme d'Étampes, to feast on the delicacy with her. He realized that another lover had dived into hiding as he entered the room, and as he left he slipped the dish of quince preserve under the bed, remarking, 'Here you are, Brissac, everyone has to live!'

In 1555 there appeared an *Excellent et moult utile opuscule à tous nécessaire*. This 'excellent and most useful little work' was actually a treatise on the art of making preserves, and its author, the Provençal magus Michel de Notre-Dame or Nostradamus, is better known for his remarkable prophecies.[1] Catherine de Medici was very fond of prophets and preserves alike. And in fact Nostradamus showed as much talent as an author of recipes as he did for predictions. He was good at adapting Eastern recipes which had come through Italy and Moorish Spain to the taste of France and the fruits available there. Merely reading him still makes one want to make the 'jelly of black cherries which is as clear a vermilion as a fine ruby', or the green ginger conserve mentioned above. As sugar was a great luxury, and the Provençals are economical folk, he recommends proportions of seven pounds of fruit to only two pounds of sugar.

Under Henri IV, Olivier de Serres too dispensed advice on the making of household preserves: pastes of peaches or apricots 'of which the recipe comes from Genoa', a paste of raspberries 'much liked for its pleasant odour', candied lemon peel preserved 'dry, in an oven', pears so small that, tied together and preserved as a bunch, 'you may put all seven in your mouth at once', whence the name of that delicacy, *sept-en-gueule*, 'seven in the mouth'.

It is not surprising that the great lords of the time, even the sovereigns themselves, were tempted to lend a hand. It was in the kitchen, making his own preserves, that Louis XIII heard news of the execution of Cinq-Mars, who had plotted against him. His funeral oration was brief and to the point: 'Cinq-Mars had a soul as black as the bottom of this pan.'

Not content with the many fruits of French orchards, which had been flourishing since the beginning of the Renaissance, the master confectioners of the sixteenth, seventeenth and eighteenth centuries, professional or amateur, used flowers from their gardens and vegetables from their kitchen plots. There was a preserve of roses which remained a classic, a marmalade of violets, ribs of lettuce leaves in syrup (very like preserved angelica, and perhaps called *bouches d'ange*, 'angel's mouths', for that reason), and sweet preserves of celery, a popular vegetable because it was thought to be an aphrodisiac.

The chroniclers describe at length the magnificent royal feasts of the era of Louis XIV, which always ended with marmalades and jellies served in silver dishes. The princes no longer made them personally, but every one of the delicacies served at Versailles was made with fruit from the King's own gardens and glasshouses, which even grew pineapples to be candied like the less exotic fruits.

Chapter 18

Chocolate and Divinity

That witty letter-writer the Marquise de Sévigné had strong feelings about the exotic foodstuff chocolate. On 11 February 1671 she was obviously madly in love with it. She writes to her daughter, Mme de Grignan: 'If you are not feeling well, if you have not slept, chocolate will revive you. But you have no chocolate pot! I think of that again and again. How will you manage?' By 15th April disillusion has set in: 'I can tell you, my dear child, chocolate is not what it was to me. I was carried away by the fashion, as usual. All who used to praise chocolate to me now condemn it. It is scorned. It is accused of causing every evil under the sun.' On 13th May she is in a state of great anxiety, for her daughter is pregnant: 'My dear, my beautiful child, I do beg you not to drink chocolate. In your present condition it would prove fatal to you.' By 23rd October she is quite paranoid on the subject: 'The Marquise de Coëtlogon drank so much chocolate when she was expecting last year that she was brought to bed of a little boy as black as the devil, who died.' (There were rumours at court that, the year before that birth, Mme de Coëtlogon's chocolate had been brought to her every morning and evening by a young and very affectionate African slave.)

At the end of the nineteenth century a chocolate maker of Royat who had literary leanings took the outspoken Marquise as the emblem of his brand, and made a fortune.

But long before the good lady ever raised a cup of chocolate to her lips cocoa had existed – or rather *cacahuaquchtl*, a tree four to ten metres tall growing in the virgin forests of Yucatan and Guatemala. *Cacahuaquchtl* means not only cocoa tree but simply, and principally, just 'tree'. It was *the* Tree, the tree of the Mayan gods.

The gods, whoever they are and wherever they come from, do not eat the food of ordinary mortals. In Greece, they fed on ambrosia. In Mexico and Guatemala they favoured a decoction of the seeds of the fruit of the Tree, and it was not made like any ordinary tisane. You took the seeds (later described by the unim-aginative Spanish as 'beans') of the cocoa pods, called *cabosses* in French, from Spanish *cabeza* 'head', a word perhaps suggested by the long, narrow heads of the Amerindians. You roasted them in an earthenware pot. You crushed them between two stones. You then mixed the powder you had obtained with boiling water and whisked it with little twigs – chac-chac, choc-choc, went the twigs as they whisked up little bubbles. You could add other things to this boiling liquid (*tchacahoua*, as it was called in Mayan, or *tchocoatl*, in Aztec): either chilli, musk and honey, or ground maize when you were going to war and needed additional calories. Then you drank it.

You drank it because the gods were good and in certain very specific circumstances allowed mortals to taste their sacred food. This is one of the usual features of a sacrifice; there can be no question of the actual physical matter of the foods involved being lost to human consumption, it is the religious intention that counts. The Mayas, like other peoples, took that attitude.

Who exactly were the Mayas? Towards the beginning of the fourth century AD the Maya people, who had come down from Alaska in the course of the millennia, occupied Yucatan, an enormous peninsula situated between Mexico and Guatemala. Around the year 900 their remarkable but bloodthirsty civilization was suddenly extinguished. We still do not know why. Their cities, some still being built, were abandoned, with temples, pyramids, paved roads and all. The Mayas went into the all-concealing virgin forest and never came out again. It was in this forest that the Tree grew. When the Spanish penetrated Central America for the first time in 1523 there was nothing left of the Mayas but a few primitive tribes, as if they had forgotten everything they once knew.

Meanwhile first the Toltecs and then the Aztecs of Mexico, who had come down from North America in their turn, had occupied the territory, sending expeditions not always of a peaceful nature into the forest to get various provisions which included stocks of the beans of the Tree. The Aztecs loved *tchocoatl* as much as the Mayas had liked *tchacahoua*.

Now Quetzalcoatl, the great bearded god of the forest, was also the gardener of Paradise. It was to him that mankind owed the Tree, *cacahuaquchtl*, giving both fortune and strength, for he even allowed the seeds of his tree to be used as money. However, in time the Aztecs found themselves in great and lasting distress, and it was all his fault.

One day, no one knew just when – perhaps at the time of the decline of the Mayas? – the god had boarded a raft and gone east across the ocean, towards the rising of the sun. Ever since then his people had been impatiently awaiting his return. It would be a day of great rejoicing. Everyone would whisk *tchocoatl* to a froth and drink it till they could drink no more.

Accordingly when the conquistador Cortez, bearded and clad in iron, arrived on a strange creature which was also iron-clad, coming from the east across the sea, the Emperor Moctezuma and his subjects, delirious with joy, hailed him as the god. Cortez took advantage of this warm welcome to ask at once where the treasures were kept. The treasures? 'Come, great god!' was the reply – as if the god did not know! Still, they led him to the royal plantation of Maniapeltec where the Tree had been greatly improved over the years, and offered him mountains of cocoa. After a fit of rather discourteous mirth, the bearded newcomer managed to explain that he had come for gold, not cocoa beans. He wanted mountains of gold. Eventually, he realized that possession of the cocoa was the way to get possession of the precious yellow metal.

The ceremonial attending the growing and harvesting of cocoa impressed the visitors, who were less world-weary than they liked to appear: it included human sacrifice, masked dancing, propitiatory rites (13 days of abstinence by the workers, followed by orgiastic erotic games on the day of the harvest itself). This final ritual particularly interested the soldiers, and they no longer felt like laughing during the community cocoa-parties when the Emperor, behind a screen, and the court dressed in their best and seated on the palace esplanade, religiously enjoyed the frothing drink served in 2000 fine golden cups by delightfully unclad virgins.

When the Emperor explained, therefore, that he never entered his harem without drinking this dark brown brew first, the Spanish held out their cups with one accord. Whether because of the chilli, ambergris and musk added to it or not, no one liked his first mouthful of chocolate. Then they became used to the drink, either for its aphrodisiac virtues or as a substitute for the wine they missed. After Cortez had gone home in 1527 he always kept a full chocolate-pot on his desk.

The first concern of the missionary nuns in Central America was to use their culinary gifts to convert chocolate to Christianity. They thought, correctly, that it was diabolical only because of the spices and flavourings added to it. They replaced them with vanilla, sugar and cream, and the result was delicious.

In 1585 the fame of Moctezuma's brew had spread so far through Europe that the first cargo to reach land from Vera Cruz was snapped up at once, despite the high price.

Although he had been among the first to be informed of the discovery, Pope Clement VII, formerly Giulio de Medici, could not actually drink chocolate at his coronation in 1523, for all he had was the enthusiastic description in Latin of Father Petrus de Angleria, who said it made the mouth water and soothed the soul: 'It is not only a delicious drink, but a useful form of money which permits no speculation, since it cannot be kept very long.'

Pope Clement VIII did drink a cup of cocoa in 1594; it was given him by the Florentine Father Francesco Carlati, just back from America, but he was the eleventh Pope in line from Giulio de Medici, and it was his task to resolve the grave question of whether or not drinking chocolate broke the fast. Not only did Spanish ladies of both the colonies and the mother country have such a passion for cocoa flavoured with cinnamon that they drank it all day long, they even had it served to them in church. The Jesuit Father Escobar, renowned for his casuistry, and Cardinal François-Marie Brancacio could hardly suppress the fashion unless they wanted to see the Communion table deserted, so they appeared to go along with it and reiterated, on behalf of their lady penitents, the old adage *liquidum non frangit jejunum*, 'liquid does not break the fast' – in this case chocolate made with water. The Sorbonne fulminated; Pius V, who had not drunk chocolate any more than Clement VII, expressed his own doubts and let it be known that he differed from the cardinal and the reverend father.

In the year 1636 the problem loomed large. A priest of Madrid discussed it at length in a quarto entitled *Question moral si el chocolate quebrante el ayuno ecclesiastico*. Was it mortal sin for a priest to drink chocolate before celebrating Mass? Mme de Sévigné, still an enthusiast at this point, wrote to her daughter that she drank chocolate before going to bed to nourish her at night, and on getting up in the morning so that she could fast better: 'The agreeable part of it all is that what counts is the intention.' (She was referring to the opinion held by such priests as Escobar that purity of intention justifies otherwise immoral actions.)

A certain Bachot, in a medical thesis published on 20 March 1685, maintained that cocoa and not ambrosia must have been the food of the gods. This opinion aroused a certain amount of interest, and 50 years later, when Carl von Linné published his *Systema Naturae* in 1737, he classed the cocoa tree in 'the eighteenth polyadelphy of Candire' as the genus *Theobroma*, meaning 'divine food'. Theobromine, a medicament extracted from cocoa, is an alkaloid similar to caffeine, and its diuretic qualities also make it a cardiovascular analeptic.

During the first half of the seventeenth century exorbitant taxes prevented ordinary mortals from serving the drink of the gods on their own tables. The scientist Johann Georg Volkmer brought it from Naples to Germany in 1641 and then to the Netherlands, where it was a huge success in high society. England, perhaps for economic or political (anti-Spanish) reasons, politely turned its nose up at cocoa in 1657. It is true that the Londoners tried making it with Madeira.

France had received chocolate in two stages, with the successive marriages of two of its kings to Spanish Infantas: Louis XIII to Anne of Austria, Louis XIV to Maria Theresa of Spain. The maid who brewed Maria Theresa's chocolate must have been better at it than her mother-in-law's maid, for 'the Queen's one passion' ('after the King', the modest wife used to remind people, eyes cast down) soon spread spontaneously to the whole court. However, Fagon, the Queen's doctor, was accused of making a brew of it which hastened her demise at the eleventh hour, much to the satisfaction of Mme de Maintenon.

Louis XIV, with his habitual distrust, did not develop a taste for chocolate until he developed one for Mme de Maintenon, another enthusiastic lover of chocolate who made her favourite drink for herself. It was the safer course. However, in 1682 the *Mercure de France* published an account of a party at Versailles where the popular drink of cocoa was served.

A former page of the queen mother Anne of Austria, one David Chaillon (or possibly Chalion), obtained from the Sun King, who still preferred Burgundy wine to the Aztec brew, the 'sole privilege for 23 years of making, retailing and selling in all towns of the Kingdom a certain composition known as chocolate, in liquid form or as pastilles or in any other form that he may please.' By now a way of evaporating the liquid chocolate and moulding it into solid shapes had been discovered.

David Chaillon (or Chalion) therefore set up shop at the sign of 'La Croix du Tiroir' (or 'Trahoir') at the corner of the rue Saint-Honoré and the rue de l'Arbre-Sec, in the confectioners' quarter. His establishment was opened on 20 May 1659. In 1690 chocolate reached the Left Bank when the Sieur Rère and the Sieur Renaud, new licence-holders, both occupied premises in the rue Dauphine. Then the great grocer François Dumaine extended his catalogue, which already listed coffee beans at four francs the pound and tea at 100 francs, to include cocoa at four francs and chocolate at six francs the pound.

You could drink a cup of cocoa for eight sous, expensive in view of the fact that even in the most fashionable establishments tea or coffee cost three sous six deniers at the most. But the cocoa prices were of the black market variety, because of the licence held by Chaillon and his successors. Finally, in 1693, the sale of cocoa and chocolate was thrown open to all, much to the annoyance of the religious communities, who had been dreaming for years of obtaining a monopoly of the drink of the gods.

In 1770 the first industrial chocolate-manufacturing firm was set up: Chocolats et Thés Pelletier & Compagnie. Van Houten & Bvloker opened in Amsterdam in 1815. Cailler was set up at Vevey in Switzerland in 1819, and Suchard occupied Neuchâtel. The first true chocolate factories, however, were those of Menier in the Paris region, first opened in 1824.

In 1826, Brillat-Savarin, the pundit of gastronomy, was still advocating 'ambered chocolate', which he described as 'the chocolate of the afflicted'. He recommended it to 'any man who has drunk too deeply of the cup of pleasure ... who finds his wit temporarily losing its edge, the atmosphere humid, time dragging ... or who is tortured by a fixed idea.' Alexandre Dumas mentions Brillat-Savarin's endorsement of 'chocolate with ambergris as a sovereign remedy for those fatigued by any sort of labour', which obviously means a great many people.

Le confiseur royal ou art du confiseur, published in Paris in 1818, however, mentions only confectionery or chocolate such as pistachios with *chocolat de santé*, *diablotins au chocolat*, and a pastille or dragée stuffed with chocolate paste 'identical to that so greatly liked by the unfortunate Queen Marie-Antoinette'.

Finally, in 1875, a Swiss from Vevey called Daniel Peter had the distinction of inventing milk chocolate. He then went into partnership with his competitors Cailler and Kohler. The three brands merged with Nestlé in 1929, and thereafter Switzerland was one of the world's great shrines to chocolate.

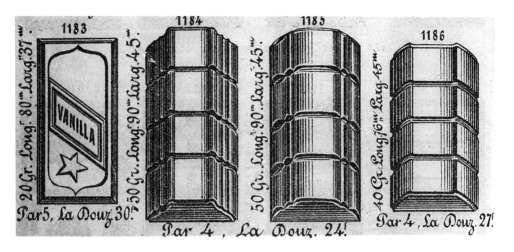

Moulds for chocolate slabs: engraving from Letang's catalogue of 1893

Definitions of Chocolate

Cocoa beans. The cultivated cocoa tree (*Theobroma cacao*), a member of the Malvaceae family, grows only in tropical regions, particularly America and Africa. It produces large fruits or 'pods', which contain 20 to 50 seeds, the 'beans'. The Maya Indians used them as money. They are surrounded by a sweet-sour, whitish pulp. Once picked, cocoa beans are left where they are for four to six days to ferment and develop the cocoa aroma; they are then dried and put into sacks to be sent to the chocolate-manufacturing countries.

Cocoa paste. The beans are roasted to release and enhance their aroma. They are then shelled and crushed to extract the kernels, themselves ground to a bitter paste, the basic material of all chocolate products.

Powdered chocolate. 'Cocoa' or 'cocoa powder' is made by grinding the residue of cocoa beans left after the cocoa paste has been pressed to extract some of the 'cocoa butter'. The fat content of the powder depends on the extraction rate, at least 20 per cent being the regulation amount, a proportion calculated from the weight of dry matter. 'Chocolate powder' or 'sweet cocoa' is a mixture of cocoa powder and sugar in such proportions that the product contains at least 32 per cent of dry cocoa matter. 'Chocolate vermicelli' or 'chocolate flakes', flakes or granules, must contain at least 32 per cent of dry cocoa matter and 12 per cent of cocoa butter. Powders flavoured with 'chocolate' or 'cocoa' contain varying proportions of cocoa, starch, sugar and milk. They are suitable for making drinks but not for flavouring puddings.

Chocolate bars. A mixture of cocoa paste, added cocoa butter and sugar, with other optional additions such as milk, dried fruits, coffee, liqueurs, etc. These ingredients are ground, strained and mixed while hot to give chocolate its characteristic smooth and mellow consistency. It may be moulded, or filled with various other confectionery products such as fondant, caramel, praline or liqueurs, in a proportion of at least 25 per cent of its weight.

'Cooking chocolate' must contain at least 30 per cent of total dry cocoa matter, i.e., at least 14 per cent of de-fatted dry cocoa and 18 per cent of cocoa butter. 'Couverture chocolate' is enriched with cocoa butter (at least 31 per cent). It is the basic ingredient used by chocolate manufacturers for sweets or moulded chocolate. However, it can also be bought from specialist shops and used for icing home-made chocolate cakes.

'Milk chocolate' contains at most 55 per cent sugar, at least 25 per cent of total dry cocoa matter, 14 per cent of dry matter of lactic origin, and must have at least 25 per cent of fatty matter in all.

The cocoa content of chocolate should be indicated on the wrapping. If the chocolate contains at least 43 per cent of total dry cocoa matter and at least 26 per cent cocoa butter the main description of 'chocolate' or 'milk chocolate' may be complemented by mention of the quality, e.g. superior, extra fine, bitter, etc.

Chocolates. 'Chocolates' are individual sweets consisting of either chocolate with a filling, or various kinds of chocolate mixed with other edible matter, the chocolate content representing at least 25 per cent of their weight.

Chapter 19

Coffee and Politics

According to Louis Figuier,[1] coffee seems to have been drunk in Persia since the ninth century. The great doctor Abu ibn Sina, known in the West as Avicenna, the prince of physicians, was already acquainted with coffee around the year 1000, and called it not *kahwa* but *bunc*, the name by which it is still known in Abyssinia.

At the time it was still a very rare drink, a decoction of seeds brought by caravans from Upper Egypt and Libya from an even more distant country, Abyssinia. Only very high Arab dignitaries drank it, as a tonic. The first European to mention coffee is Prospero Alpino of Padua. In 1580 he went to Egypt, then under Ottoman rule, with a consul of the Venetian Republic. The work in which he mentions coffee is written in Latin and addressed to one Gianni Morazini: 'The Turks have a brew, the colour of which is black. It is drunk in long draughts, and not during the meal, but afterwards ... as a delicacy and in mouthfuls, while taking one's ease in the company of friends, and there is hardly any gathering among them where it is not drunk.' Alexandre Dumas too, in his *Dictionnaire de cuisine*, says that 'the taste for coffee went so far in Constantinople that the imams complained their mosques were empty while the coffee houses were always full.'

Not just in Constantinople but in Medina, Mecca, Cairo, Damascus, Baghdad, and all the capitals of the Islamic world, coffee houses were opened and customers flocked to them to enjoy the brown brew while discussing their affairs – and affairs of state.

Discussing affairs of state was as dangerous then as it still is now in countries with a totalitarian régime. Sultan Amurat III, after celebrating his accession by assassinating his five elder brothers, thought there was too much talk about the matter in the coffee houses. With a view to closing talkative mouths he had the coffee houses of Constantinople closed and their proprietors tortured. Coffee was proclaimed *mekreet*, undesirable.

Gradually people plucked up courage, and under Mahomet IV there were many coffee houses again. Mahomet IV, admittedly, proved to be one of those sovereigns who indulged themselves in pleasures and left the business of running the state to their favourites. The man who governed in his name was old Mahomet Kolpili, a vizier who could neither read nor write and did not care for the liberty of the press, or in this case of the tongue, for tongues wagged freely in the coffee houses of the Ottoman Empire. He answered criticism with the bastinado, conscientiously applied to all coffee consumers taken *in flagrante delicto*. When the bastinado proved ineffective he ordered *all* public establishments to be closed this time. People came in through the back yards. He had the walls razed to the ground, condemning the proprietors and their more conspicuous customers to be thrown into the Bosphorus, sewn into leather sacks.

> ... Ce sont des sacs pesants d'où partent des sanglots.
> On verrait, en sondant la mer qui les promène,
> Se mouvoir en leurs flancs comme une force humaine.
> La lune était sereine et jouait sur les flots.

[They were heavy sacks, whence came sobs. Scanning the sea that carried them away, one might see something like human strength moving within them. The moon was serene, playing on the waves.]

These cruel measures did not discourage coffee drinkers, and indeed later sultans had officers solely concerned with coffee in their seraglios, called *kahwaghis*. They supervised *battaghis*, slaves especially charged with preparing coffee for their master and his armies.

An English tourist who visited those parts in 1617 tasted a beverage which he said was called *kahoua*; he described it as being made of a blackish bean boiled in water 'to which it imparts almost no flavour'. Later on the English were to take a warm, coloured water of a different flavour to their hearts and make it their national brew. One wonders whether this seventeenth-century Englishman had thought of grinding his coffee bean. The two circumstances might not be unconnected.

In the eighteenth century the city of Marseilles was already the gateway to the Orient, and its merchants were on very good terms, as trade demanded, with their foreign colleagues. The people of Marseilles, true descendants of the Massalian merchants of classical times, had trading stations or agents in all the main Mediterranean ports ruled by the Sublime Porte. A Turco-Algerian family living not far from the Vieux Port acted as a consular office for the Grand Turk and were also import-export agents. Naturally there was fraternization between colleagues (and in the course of time the Samat family became genuine Marseillais, baptised and speaking with the local accent). It was at the house of these merchants that the Sieur La Roque was offered a cup of the Turkish brew around 1643. Legend has it that La Roque liked everything Turkish. Thanks to his friends, and taking advantage of his voyages, he had furnished a room in his house as an Eastern divan, with sofas, hookah pipes and low tables. He liked the drink called *cahoua* as much as he liked Eastern furniture, and invited his friends to taste it at the first opportunity. It was the first European coffee party.

Some years later Jean de Thévenot, a relation of Melchisédech de Thévenot, founder of the Academy of Sciences and the author, like Jean, of travel writings, also mentioned the drink *caoué* or *caffé*, which he could no longer do without. The manuscript of his *Relations d'un voyage fait au Levant* (1664) was sold in January 1981, the auctioneers inaccurately claiming that he was the inventor of coffee.

Subligny, a lawyer who also wrote poetry, put in a plea for the black liquid in verse in the number of *La muse de la cour* of 2 December 1666. He had it acquitted on the principle of the benefit of the doubt. From the literary viewpoint the work was relatively successful, but the public at large did not take to its subject.

At last, three years later in 1669, Soleiman Aga, the Grand Panjandrum in person, really launched coffee in the Western world. The diamond jewellery and kohl-rimmed eyes of this turbaned ambassador to Louis XIV had the duchesses of the courts swooning in raptures. He offered his visitors tiny cups filled with the oriental brew. Whether because of the dark, hot liquid, or because of the impressive muscles of his equally dark slaves, the ladies' hearts beat faster. 'Caffé' became tremendously fashionable. As we would say today, Soleiman Aga's embassy was lobbying for coffee, and his promotion of the product was a huge success. Everyone wanted coffee; few could get it. You needed relations in Marseilles, the only port through which it might pass, and the importers were agents of the Sultan.

In Paris a person described as a 'Levantine' soon set up a sales outlet at the sign of the 'Cahuet' in the alley leading to the Petit Châtelet. His shop offered for sale 'German boxes, lined with lead and closed with screws'. They contained small, hard, black objects rather resembling droppings, which were roasted coffee beans. He also sold stone-ground coffee in leather bags greased to preserve the aroma (the manual coffee mill was not available until after 1687). Unfortunately these 'boxes' and the cost of handling them raised yet further the price of a foodstuff which already cost the equivalent of about a thousand pounds a pound in modern money. Such prices obviously put a brake on the spread of coffee.

The Levantine, or his suppliers, tried a promotional sale to bring the price down, mixing the 'caffé' powder with a certain proportion of ground broad beans, cornel stones, acorns or barley. The barley was roasted in a manner revived, as historical events sometimes do recur, after the 1940 armistice in France. It tasted no better in the seventeenth century than it would during the Occupation, and there were not even patriotic reasons for pretending to like it. Customers would have nothing to do with the 'German boxes' and their adulterated contents.

Then a little hunchback had an idea. He was said by some to be Turkish and others to be Greek, but in any case came from Candia, the Greek island of Crete then occupied by the Turks, and so he was called 'the Candiot'. His idea was to take the drink to its potential customers: he would wave the irresistible aroma of

'A history of coffee in pictures': lithograph by Develly, 1831. Well known in the Islamic world, and popular in Turkey, coffee did not appear at the court of Louis XIV until 1669, when Soleiman Aga came there as ambassador. Captain Des Clieux took it across the Atlantic and planted it successfully in the West Indies.

a cup of 'caffé' under their noses. It was an even better idea in that he had no money with which to open a shop and pay for a licence. Tea was already being sold in this way in London.

The little cripple Candiot, a white napkin tied round his waist doing duty for an apron, announced his arrival at door after door by singing, at the top of his voice, a Greek song, which he was happy to translate:

> O drink that I adore
> You rule the universe!
> O drink that I adore,
> You rule the universe!
> You wean the faithful from the vine
> You're more delectable than wine.

He held his cap in one hand and in the other a miniature stove with a pot on it, the kind used for making tisanes. How could anyone resist the aroma escaping from the coffee pot, and the charming smile of the little singing hunchback? For two sous – two gold sous – you could hardly do better than offer coffee to your guests, for the Candiot had advance notice from the servants of any parties in the offing, and they of course obtained a commission on his sales. The master of the house would try to appear delighted to see him rather than look miserly.

Moreover, even if you could afford coffee beans (and the price finally came down), making a cup of the brew was no light matter; you could see why the Grand Turk had required a body of slaves to do it. Louis XV and Mme Du Barry (who had her portrait painted in Eastern dress, drinking coffee) discussed the subject for evenings on end.

First you had to get hold of 'coffee cherries' through a complicated commercial circuit (Louis XV actually grew them in his glasshouses at Versailles). You dried the 'cherries', which were sold fresh so that they would weigh heavier, then skinned them, roasted the berries without burning them too much, crushed or pounded them, and make the decoction in the Turkish manner, boiling it as many as ten times. 'Boiled coffee' was not thought to be spoiled coffee in those days.

He who invented the cafetière in two sections was therefore a real benefactor of humanity. Cardinal du Belloy mendaciously claimed responsibility for that brilliant little utensil.

The sale of ready-to-drink coffee from door to door had a long innings. There was also an Armenian called Pascal (or in some accounts an American called Pascall) who had a booth at the Saint-Germain fair where, for the first time, a cup of the decoction was sold in a public place. The price was just a little cheaper than that of coffee sold door to door, but it must have suited the customers, since Pascal (or Pascall) soon moved to the quai de l'École and made a fortune there, enough to employ a waiter – the first café waiter in history, an Italian called Procope.

Procope was not just any Italian; he came from Palermo and he was of noble birth, a double misfortune in that the aristocrats of Sicily were the most impecunious of all European noblemen. Short of money but not ideas, Francisco Procopio dei Coltelli (literally, 'of the knives') did not intend to stay in Sicily waiting for some miracle to save him from starvation. He left for the Continent when very young, rolled up his sleeves and set out in search of a job with prospects. It was thus that he came to make his mark around 1672 serving in the establishment of the famous Armenian or American purveyor of 'caffè', Pascal or Pascall.

In 1683 Procope did not know that his eleventh year as a paid employee would be his last, though he was already looking around for a new situation. Several thousand kilometres away, however, something happened which was to affect his subsequent fate: the Turks were soundly beaten by the king of Poland, Jan Sobieski, at the siege of Vienna. The Turkish general Kara Mustapha had no faith at all in the valour of his armies and fled – leaving behind him a vast quantity of coffee which, had it been drunk before the battle, certainly ought to have given the soldiers of the Crescent the strength they needed.

Opening up the mountains of sacks left in their city, the people of Vienna thought at first that they had found the cavalry's stocks of 'Turkish corn', i.e., maize, for their horses. But a compatriot of Sobieski's, formerly a prisoner of war of the Turks and now liberated, told the general in command how lucky he was. This man, Franz Kolschitsky, had been a *battaghi*, one of the slaves employed in the making of coffee, and he brought back with him from captivity a great talent for the art of making mocha. Perhaps Sobieski gave him some of the sacks as a reward? In any case, he soon opened a genuine coffee house in Vienna, in a style of oriental magnificence which made it a dazzling success. Within a few years he was at the head of a whole chain of establishments in Central Europe, and Vienna was its coffee-making capital. Viennese coffee, first with whipped cream and then made into an ice, was all the rage.

Iced coffee had been drunk since the middle of the century, with such enthusiasm that Boileau mentions the craze for it in his *Repas ridicule*. But ice cream, actually a Venetian invention and descended from the ancient Roman sorbets, seemed the very last word in luxury.

There was much talk in Paris of these delicious Viennese specialities, and Francisco Procopio dei Coltelli told himself that he could hardly continue to make his fortune, as they say, by selling cups of coffee out of doors at a sou each (the price had fallen steeply). Paris needed a *salon de café* along the lines of the Viennese *Kaffeehäuser* – an attractive place, even more attractive than the customer's own home, where people could enjoy an atmosphere of luxury at a reasonable price, where they would come in order to meet each other, and where they could find a menu of specialities not confined solely to coffee.

The Viennese ices made by Procope attracted as many people as the mirrors on the walls and the crystal chandeliers hanging from the ceilings of the establishment he opened in the rue des Fossés-Saint-Germain, opposite the Comédie-Française (you could even go there after the play). Then he moved to the rue de Tournon, and finally to the rue de l'Ancienne-Comédie, where the Café Procope still stands.

People met at a spot where, as its advertisements boasted, 'the luxury guarantees the fine quality of articles consumed', not just to drink coffee and enjoy other delicacies, but for amusement, to play chess, to read the journals and the news of the day pinned up by the astute Procope on the stovepipes, and to discuss current events and fashionable ideas. At this period the newsmongers, who were simultaneously informers, philosophers, agitators, secret or double agents, both discreet and glib of tongue, were everywhere in salons, ante-rooms and 'ruelles' – the alcoves where ladies received guests – to give and receive information, retailing all the rumours of Paris and Versailles. Procope had been shrewd enough to attract some of these people, who in their turn attracted customers as much as the lampoons and satires on the stovepipes.

Many others imitated Procope, just as they imitated but could not equal his menu, which offered the very best of coffees and also sweetmeats, sorbets, syrups, liqueurs, apéritif wines and other delicious drinks. In 1721 there were 300 cafés in Paris. There were to be 2000 at the time of the Revolution and 4000 at the beginning of the Empire. Montesquieu wrote in his *Lettres persanes*: 'Were I the King, I would close the cafés, for the people who frequent those places heat their brains in a very tiresome manner. I would rather see them get drunk in taverns. Then, at least, they would harm only themselves, while the intoxication which coffee arouses in them causes them to endanger the country's future.'

Such too was the opinion of the King's police, whose raids were announced in the smoke-filled cafés by boys posted at strategic spots. (The fashion for tobacco had become associated with that for coffee.) There was too much talk in cafés, as had been the case in the coffee houses of Turkey two centuries earlier, and the police were severely overworked. 'If all who criticize the government were arrested, one would have to arrest everyone', commented d'Argenson.

At the dawn of the French Revolution, therefore, the cafés had become clubs of a kind, with meetings parallel to those of the National Assembly. Camille Desmoulins perched on a gable in the Café du Foy in the Palais-Royal, shouting, 'Let us wear a cockade!' and pinning a leaf to his hat. Desmoulins, Danton and Marat built the Republic in such cafés, particularly Procope's, which was now run by a man called Zoppi. Robespierre preferred a café called La Régence (rather inappropriately, for the resort of a Republican) but came to Procope's to drink its still incomparable mocha and suck oranges.

At the end of the seventeenth century in England, Charles II, like the Turks, had begun by fulminating against both the coffee houses (one of the first of which was opened by the Armenian Pascal, who had gone bankrupt in Paris after Procope left him) and their rivals the alehouses, on the very reasonable grounds that such places were hotbeds of sedition and a breeding ground for subversive movements. But the young Cavaliers resorted in great numbers to those malodorous caverns, where more brandy was drunk than coffee or tea. They were the scene of duels, cock-fighting and dog-fighting, horrifying the Puritans as much as the seditious propositions and scandalous anecdotes which were the staple of conversation in them. Coffee houses not open to the general public eventually became such famous London clubs as the Kit-Kat Club, the Beefsteak Club and the October Club, where a man could get drunk among others of his own background. And it was in the back room of a coffee house opened in 1689 by one Edward Lloyd that merchandise bound for the East and West Indies could be insured, in a kind of wager against misadventure and shipwreck. This was the origin of the greatest insurance company in the world.

Doctors had appropriated coffee, as they did everywhere else, at least for the purposes of dissertation. Pocock, Sloane and Radcliffe declared it a panacea for all ills, a remedy for consumption, ophthalmic catarrh, dropsy, gout, scurvy and smallpox – although taken mixed with milk it might give you leprosy.

Unfortunately coffee as a beverage aroused the ire of the brewers who regarded England as their personal property. They protested loudly, denouncing the Levantine café proprietors 'as being no free men', i.e., having no right to compete with the vendors of ale in particular, that honest national product. Moreover, so the brewers said, coffee houses disturbed the neighbours with their bad smells and put the whole vicinity in great and constant danger day and night (because of the fires kept alight under the coffee pots).

Like the British Navy, however, coffee and the coffee houses held out against wind and weather. Finally, permission was definitively given for the drinking of coffee in public. Pope praises it in *The Rape of the Lock*:

> Coffee (which makes the politician wise,
> And see through all things with his half-shut eyes).

At the time far more coffee than tea was drunk in England, and without the coffee houses seventeenth-century English literature might not have flourished so well. England came late to neoclassicism, and provided fewer of its original ideas than other European countries, but writers came into contact with the thinking of the century in the coffee houses. Perhaps they also nurtured the English sense of humour. It was in the coffee houses where they met that the style of such writers as Pope, Addison, Steele, Philips, Johnson, Defoe, Sterne and Dryden was formed. Dryden, according to Dr Johnson in the *Lives of the English Poets*, frequented Will's Coffee House, where he sat in an 'armed chair, which in the winter had a settled and prescriptive place by the fire' and 'was in the summer placed in the balcony.' The tale goes that he was thrashed there by men hired by the Earl of Rochester. However, the vogue for coffee was overtaken in England around 1730 by the vogue for tea.

In Germany too, coffee had a strong traditional rival in beer, generally regarded as a better drink even if it did leave you with a nasty hangover. The Prince-Bishop of Paderborn imposed a thrashing as well as a fine on coffee drinkers, and only in the second half of the eighteenth century did middle-class snobbery, emulating the courts (Frederick the Great practically lived on coffee), call coffee houses into being *en masse*. The first recorded German coffee house was at Hamburg in 1690, but it was opened for the benefit of British sailors.

Leipzig, a rich commercial city, proud of its fairs and its men of letters (it was the European capital of printing), had to open coffee houses for the rich merchants passing through and the whole subversive body of intellectuals wanting to get their works published. The baroque German literary style with its use of the hexameter was born here, and so later was Romanticism, a movement hatched out at student meetings in the warmth of those smoke-filled rooms.

Although both coffee and cafés, the drink and the places where it was drunk, enjoyed a parallel vogue they did not always make for a quiet life, to the way of thinking of many honest citizens as well as the police. The Princess Palatine, the German wife of Monsieur, Louis XIV's brother, compared the odour of coffee to the Archbishop of Paris's breath. Malebranche, at the same period, would have nothing to do with coffee except as an enema, although he did think it answered that purpose very well. Saint-Simon was scandalized by the amazing number of cups of coffee drunk by the Regent – 'mud which is good for nothing but the very dregs of the people', he called it. Doctors continued to condemn coffee as a 'dangerous poison' and warn that it might prevent conception. If so, retorted Voltaire and Fontenelle, who both enjoyed coffee, it was a slow poison, and indeed the former lived to 85 and the latter to the age of 100.

The Prince de Ligne tells us that an experiment was made 'in some northern country, I know not which' to judge the relative violence of those two poisons, tea and coffee. Two criminals condemned to death, men in their prime, had their sentences commuted to imprisonment on condition that one of them drank a cup of tea and the other a cup of coffee three times a day. 'As a result, he who took tea died at 79, and the other at 80.'

Frederick the Great of Prussia, bowing to the advice of his physicians who were alarmed by his excessive coffee consumption, cut down on it. 'I take only seven or eight cups in the morning, and a pot of coffee in the afternoon.' Frederick's coffee, incidentally, was made with champagne, and as a further refinement flavoured with a good spoonful of mustard.

Mme de Sévigné, after an initial enthusiasm for coffee, took violently against it, just as she had taken against chocolate. After recommending sweet white coffee as a consolation in Lent, the versatile and inexhaustible letter-writer stated confidently that the fashion for coffee would pass, like the fashion for the works of Racine. Her reputation for foresight has never quite lived it down.

The first coffee plant was introduced to Brazil from Guiana in 1727. The history of that vast country was to revolve around coffee thenceforward. Unlike rubber, coffee has managed to survive a number of economic crises, being inimitable and irreplaceable. In our own day it accounts for half the revenues of Brazil. Up to the end of the nineteenth century the coffee-growing economy was inextricably linked to slavery, and it shaped a society, almost a culture, unlike any other. The *fazendeiros* (farmers) soon chose to grow coffee rather than sugar, since it needed only rudimentary industrial plant and far less capital than the sugar mills. The main requirement was a large labour force. The acquisition of large stocks of slaves eventually led the large *fazendas* into a state of heavy and permanent debt, but it was worth it in view of the profits that also accrued and a policy of marriages and alliances between *fazendeiros* which encouraged the concentration of properties and their businesses. Credit, constantly renewed, was in the hands of the banks until 1850, the date of the abolition of the slave trade.

For ten more years coffee production and the surface area under cultivation continued to expand. Then signs of fatigue set in. The human livestock of the *fazendas* was getting old and the soil was becoming exhausted. The small farmers or *sitientes*, having no new slaves, became tenants or *agregados* of the large *fazendas*. This development was the death blow for any other food crops. There followed a steep rise in prices, until the time when disease, pests and drought ravaged the plantations one after another.

The price of coffee rose spectacularly because of its scarcity and the enfranchisement of the slaves, now wage-earning labourers. Feverish progress was made with the building of railroads to facilitate the transport of convoys; that had previously been the job of one-third of the slaves, who transported the coffee over appalling roads. Unfortunately the European depression of 1870–71 saw prices fall again. Severe unemployment was the result, and was at the root of the primitive urbanization of the notorious suburbs of Rio, São Paulo and Belo Horizonte. During the great periods of prosperity of the coffee and sugar trades, the southeast of the country had already seen a vast influx of European immigrants who were now demanding work.

Those *fazendeiros* who managed to survive the crises, either because they had reserves to fall back on or because they changed to growing rubber, developed for themselves a smart society which was entirely up to date with the fashions of Paris and London. Offenbach immortalized the stock figure of the Brazilian millionaire in *La vie parisienne*.

At the beginning of the twentieth century, the coffee consumption of the industrialized countries of Europe and the United States increased spectacularly, practically doubling. The first international syndicate to control coffee had been set up at Frankfurt am Main in Germany after the 1873 crisis. An organization controlling import and sales was set up in New York in 1880. In 1906, the yield from São Paulo represented 64 per cent of world production, almost 22 million sacks. This record harvest obviously caused prices to collapse.

Various further cyclical crises, in 1912 and 1929, were also heavy blows, and the *favellas* of Rio and other large Brazilian cities saw a new influx of the unemployed. In 1931 the Coffee Institute was set up to regulate over-production. Each new coffee tree planted was to be taxed, and whenever capitalists became anxious about the amount of their profits the precious beans were to be burned in locomotive engines.

Even at the best of times coffee is a major field for speculation, and a kind of war is conducted between the coffee-growing states, manipulating stocks to cause artificial rises or falls in the price. The great planter families have become formidable speculators, while small tenant farmers are in debt to the real estate companies, who may distrain upon their land and treat them very badly indeed if the interest of the moment seems to require it.

Finally, the huge influx of slaves to the sugar and coffee plantations in the eighteenth and nineteenth centuries has made the population of Brazil today an extraordinary spectrum of half-castes, mulattos, blacks, whites, Asians and Indians, a mixture of races unique in the world.

Coffee from the Islands

Coffee originally grew best in the kingdom of Yemen in the Aden and Moka areas; it was from there that the Dutchman Van Hom had plants taken to the Dutch colony of Batavia in Indonesia in 1690. The coffee plants grown in the Botanical Gardens of Leyden did so well that specimens were generously given to several other European capitals. Louis XIV was presented with one at the Peace of Utrecht, and had it grown in the Jardin des Plantes in Paris. Cuttings were taken, and produced many more coffee trees.

Captain Gabriel des Clieux obtained permission from the naturalist Jussieu to naturalize coffee in the French colonies of America. Jussieu was initially horrified at the idea of mutilating the tree for which he was responsible, and the King's physician had to plead for des Clieux to get him his cutting. The crossing to the West Indies was a long and difficult one. Fresh water on the ship began to run short, and had to be carefully rationed out to the crew and passengers. They quenched their thirst with a few drops of the precious liquid a day. There was also a Dutchman on board – perhaps a secret agent, but in any case he tried to destroy the coffee plant which might injure the Batavian trade.

Not content with mounting guard on his cutting day and night, des Clieux deprived himself entirely of drinking water. 'Stronger than Tantalus', he tells us in his memoirs, 'I stifled and repressed my desires, so that every day I could sprinkle a spoonful of water on the soil containing my treasure, even though it would evaporate in a few moments because of the temperature of those latitudes.' The vessel was also attacked and damaged by Spanish pirates, which prolonged the voyage yet further. By the time it touched land both the coffee plant and its guardian were very unwell. Planted in suitable soil and caressed by the trade winds, however, the plant revived. Des Clieux continued,

> At the end of eighteen months, I had a very abundant crop. The beans were distributed to the religious communities and to various inhabitants who knew the price of the product, and guessed how it would enrich them. The coffee plantation grew by degrees; I continued distributing

591

fruits of the young plants that grew in the shade of the father of them all. Guadeloupe and San Domingo were soon well provided with the plants. ... They spread the more rapidly in Martinique because of the disease which had struck down all the cocoa trees without exception, a disaster attributed by some to the eruption of a volcano on the island, which had opened a new crater, by others to abundant and continual rains lasting over two months. However that may be, the inhabitants of the place, to the number of five or six thousand, completely deprived of the food crop they had grown, which was almost the only thing they had to exchange for foods from France, had no resource but coffee-growing, to which they devoted themselves exclusively, with success which went far beyond their hopes and soon repaired their losses. Within three years the island was covered with as many coffee trees as there had been cocoa trees before.

As the Creole poet Esmenars wrote:

> Heureuse Martinique, ô bords hospitaliers
> Dans un monde nouveau, vous avez les premiers
> Recueilli, fécondé ce doux fruit de l'Asie
> Et dans un sol français mûri son ambroisie!

['Happy Martinique, O hospitable shores, in a new world you were the first to receive and fertilize this sweet fruit of Asia, and ripen its ambrosia on French soil!]

The story of this miraculous plant rather suggests that of the breadfruit trees which were the cause of the mutiny of the *Bounty*. Des Clieux's cutting was the ancestor of all the coffee trees of Martinique, the West Indies, Brazil and Colombia, and some of them went back across the Atlantic to become a source of income to the African colonies that have now gained their independence, in particular the Ivory Coast and Cameroon. In gratitude to des Clieux, the French colonists of the West Indies awarded him a well-deserved pension. However, after the peace of 1763 over-production ruined a number of planters, and for the first time coffee was burnt on the quaysides. (There were no steam engines yet to make use of this new kind of fuel, as happened in Brazil at the time of the great Depression.)

Only the French colonists of the American acquisitions grew coffee at this period. It did grow in the wild state in the Île de Bourbon, now La Réunion, but no one thought much of it. Not until a schooner arrived from Moka in Arabia with a branch of a coffee tree in flower fixed to her mast, to announce what cargo she carried, did the planters of the island think of growing it as an alternative to the sugar cane which was so subject to disease.

When Pierre Poivre was governor of the French colonies in the Indian Ocean, he imported coffee plants to be grafted on native stocks; they took so well that 50 years later the island of Réunion had almost a million trees. Its volcanic soil grew one of the best coffees of all. Madagascan coffee was also very highly esteemed.

Coffee in Legend

Once upon a time, perched on the hillsides of the coast of South Yemen in Arabia, there was a monastery of devout Muslims which derived its main resources from a flock of goats. The goats gave them milk and meat, and provided leather which they took to town to sell.

One day the goatherd complained to the Imam that sometimes, and against their usual nature, his beasts remained awake and lively all night. The Imam suspected that this wakefulness was the result of whatever the goats were grazing. He visited the flock to investigate, and saw some shrubs with firm, glossy leaves, which the goats had ravaged. They had also eaten the fruits: small, red berries like cherries with not much flesh and a large kernel. The holy man cut a branch still bearing berries, and back in the monastery he searched his library for a treatise on botany, for the members of these Arab religious communities were very learned men. He found no reference to the berry, but on reflection it occurred to him that the shrubs seemed to have been growing in regular rows, as if they had once been planted by the hand of man. They must have reverted to the wild long ago, although it could be seen that they had once been aligned in an orchard. But how could an orchard have been planted in this remote spot?

It turned out, however, that a colony of black people said to have come from the country of Kaffa in Abyssinia had once lived in those parts. Islamic tradition gave their greatest queen the name of Balkis. The Imam read that:

> This queen, having heard tell of the Jewish king Soliman (Solomon), left her country of Sheba, the old name of that region, to visit him. When she came home she bore a son, called Menelik, who later returned to Abyssinia to introduce Judaism there, and that cult became Coptic Christianity. The Sabaeans, because of their geographical position at the entrance to the Red Sea, long had a monopoly of trade in spices, gold, and also the copper necessary to make brass, for they had fabulous mines somewhere. They vanished from history two centuries before the Prophet Mohammed, may his name be praised, revealed the truth to the faithful.

It seemed likely that the Sabaeans had brought some of the plants they most valued from Kaffa, their native land in Africa. What, then, was the use of the trees which had so excited the goats, always supposing the subjects of the Queen of Sheba really had planted them or their descendants? To find out, the Imam decided to try eating them. The red berries, eaten raw with their kernels crushed, tasted unpleasant to any palate but a goat's. So he boiled the crushed fruits, which did

593

'A history of coffee in pictures': lithograph by Develly, 1836. The ten vignettes depict the story of coffee, from its first discovery by goats, who found the shrub stimulating (see p. 593), to its planting in the West Indies.

not bulk very large, apart from their kernels, and bravely drank the purée-like infusion. It was nothing special.

Suddenly remembering that cereals were sometimes roasted to make them more appetizing, he put some of the kernels in the embers. They gave off an exquisite aroma, even though they now looked like goat droppings. He crushed them with a stone and made a liquid gruel of them; it looked like tar, and as it was still bitter he sweetened it with a little honey.

A few moments after tasting this mixture, his heart began beating so fast that he had to lie down, but instead of falling asleep he felt extraordinarily lucid. His brain, becoming as active as in his youth, was teeming with brilliant ideas. The Imam, a man of considerable intellectual powers in any case, became even more knowing. He watched through the night, feeling as if he could embrace the universe, and did not even feel tired next morning. At the midnight hour of prayer he was the only man in the monastery to be truly wide awake; as usual, the other members of the community dragged themselves wearily to their devotions, muttering. But when the Imam gave them some of his decoction the same miracle happened to them all.

It was subsequently discovered that the tree from Kaffa also had therapeutic qualities against fevers. In their gratitude the monks gave the brew the name of *kawah*, a triple play on words, meaning 'that which excites and causes the spirits to rise', and also referring to the name of Kawus Kai, a great Persian king who, according to legend, had been able to free himself from his terrestrial weight and fly to the heavens by the mere power of thought.

This story was told around 1670 by Antonio Fausto Nairone, a Maronite scholar who taught Syriac at the University of Rome. He wrote the first book on coffee. In the next century the French encyclopedists, Diderot and d'Alembert, who were also very fond of coffee, rediscovered a passage in the *Odyssey* which they thought might refer to it. 'An Egyptian lady, Polydamna', has given Helen of Troy some seeds. 'Into the bowl in which their wine was mixed, she slipped a drug that had the power of robbing grief and anger of their sting and banishing all painful memories. No one that swallowed this dissolved in wine could shed a single tear that day ...' (*Odyssey*, Book IV). Helen used it to calm the grief of Telemachus and his companions at the failure of Odysseus to return home. It has since been scientifically proved that a dose of caffeine is not only cheering but dries up the secretions of the lachrymal glands.

It seems quite possible that Helen of Troy might have encountered coffee, since the Achaeans traded with Pharaonic Egypt, and some foods came to them from Nubia along the land routes taken by the caravans and in the trading vessels of the 'peoples of the sea'. However, some scholars think Helen's berries might equally well have been the cola nut, of which the Africans are extremely fond; it is even richer in caffeine. Be that as it may, a flight of fancy or so is surely permissible by way of a daydream: the Turks themselves say that the first cup of coffee in history was given by the archangel Gabriel to the prophet Mohammed when he was weary with his pious watching.

Chapter 20

Tea and Philosophy

Chinese texts of the first century BC describe tea as the elixir of immortality, referring to Lao-tsze, the founder of Taoism. The first philosophical and technical treatise devoted to the subject, the *Cha-sing* or *Classic Art of Tea*, appeared during the magnificent period of the T'ang dynasty, around the eighth century AD. It was by the Taoist poet Lu-yu. Lu-yu himself was even immortalized by the beverage, for after his death he was supposed to have become Chazu, the genie of tea, and his effigy is still honoured by all tea merchants from Hong Kong to Singapore.

Tea did not become a popular drink in China until about the sixth century. At first it was chewed, as cakes of pressed leaves. Later on decoctions were made of it. Around the year 1000 a powder of dried, ground leaves was mixed with boiling water, and beaten with a thin bamboo stick until it frothed, in just the same way as the Aztecs whisked their chocolate. (The Tibetans still make tea with blocks of leaves which they crumble into water. It is boiled and reboiled, mixed with rancid yak butter, and is eaten rather than drunk, for the resulting mixture is a nourishing and invigorating paste, very useful at such altitudes.)

The way of making tea we now know, as an infusion, soon became the usual one in China, and under the Ming dynasty it developed into a positive ritual, involving an intellectual discipline and symbolizing poetry and beauty, strength and determination. A cup of tea became the mirror of the soul.

Towards the beginning of the ninth century tea-drinking spread to Japan, where it soon became the ritual and sacramental drink of a kind of cult of aesthetics which sought the beautiful in the mundanity of everyday life. The Japanese tea ritual has its code, even its laws. The 'drink of immortality' has to be brewed in accordance with a very precise ceremonial, making each gesture and each mouthful both an initiation and a poetic ecstasy. The tea ceremony, although a domestic affair, is more than just a matter of enjoying a cup of tea: it is an ethic, a philosophy, it expressed the art of living. It illustrates one of the paths of Zen – 'accomplishing perfectly something possible in that dimension which it is impossible to evaluate, and which we know to be life.'

In China, however, tea houses, with a history going back to the thirteenth century, are still places of great importance for the general public. Like cafés in Turkey, France and Great Britain, they have played a large part in the political life of the country, and the first revolution, of 1911, was planned in the back room of a Shanghai tea house.

Marco Polo, of course, mentions both tea and tea houses in his *Book*, but Western civilization did not encounter the drink until the beginning of the seventeenth century. Around the time of the death of Henri IV of France, a Dutch ship – some accounts say Portuguese, but in any case it came from Macao – brought Europe the first bale of fragrant tea-leaves.

A great many kinds of infusion were already known in the West. They had specific uses, and it did not at once seem obvious what this new one was for. A doctor of Corsican origin, Simon Paoli, tasted it and said in print that it should be banned because it was intoxicating. Other medical men such as the Dutchman Tulpius in 1641 and the Frenchman Jouques in 1657 also pronounced upon the tisane. Jouques, who was very enthusiastic, praised it highly, not hesitating to compare it to ambrosia and calling it the 'divine herb'; cocoa, after all, had just staked its claim to the name of the 'drink of the gods'.

But anything from overseas was bound to become popular sooner or later. Curiously, tea had a dual career. While coffee became the favourite drink of rich and poor alike in the Latin countries of France, Italy and Spain, tea there was a privilege of the upper classes. In England and the Netherlands, however, tea was the favourite drink of everyone, from the gentry to the poorest labourers. While tea swiftly became a democratic beverage – Thomas Garaway opened the first tea house in England in 1640 – Cromwell, scenting profit for the state, decided to put a special tax on it. But in this case he had misjudged his countrymen. They did not cut back on their consumption of tea (Cromwell's judgement was accurate there), far from it. But tea, now a contraband item, benefited from the publicity attached to smuggling, particularly as clergymen were among the best agents in the business: the militia did not like to raid church crypts in which tombs, emptied of the human remains that had lain there for centuries, now concealed fragrant bales of tea. Drinking untaxed tea became a way of opposing Cromwell, and when his chapter in history was over the habit was well established. There is nothing like prohibition for creating appetites, particularly as coffee did not have a very high reputation in England.

Tea, accordingly, became a passion with the English, one to be indulged the moment you got out of bed to make a pot of early morning tea and sharpen your appetite for the lavish breakfast which followed – in prosperous Victorian house-holds, anyway – comprising smoked fish, porridge, eggs and bacon, and so on. During the day any social call, any happy or unhappy occasion, called for 'a nice cup of tea', to keep you going until the time for either afternoon tea, around four o' clock, with cakes, buns, sandwiches, muffins, scones, jam, etc., or high tea, a main meal eaten rather later, and including a cooked dish as well as the items on the afternoon tea menu. The sweet things eaten at either meal used a lot of sugar, much to the advantage of the colonial sugar planters in America.

The French firmly believe that the English like their tea cold and their beer warm. The English tea ritual has nothing in common with the Sino-Japanese ceremony, but runs a very traditional course all the same: milk in the cup first (or very occasionally lemon instead), then the tea, then sugar, the resulting brew to be not so much drunk as delicately sipped. Between every refilling of cups, the dregs are poured into a slop basin. Another French legend has it that even at the height of battle British armies used to observe a cease-fire on the stroke of five o'clock (believed on the Continent to be the traditional English tea-time), and that during the two World Wars their German opponents were gentlemen enough to respect the truce.

Tea was the occasion of the first long-distance races between transatlantic sailing ships. By around 1770 the English were importing six million pounds of tea-leaves a year, and the Dutch and Danish four and a half million pounds each. This involved what amounted to a special tea fleet, for profitability depended to a great extent on the ships' times of arrival. Another argument in favour of short voyages and speedy ships was that tea quickly went stale during a long journey. In the nineteenth century the shipbuilders created that marvel of the seas, the clipper with her superb set of sails, skimming the crests of the waves in a rapid furrow as she raced across them at a fast 'clip'. The blue ribbon of the tea race, and a handsome reward, were solemnly awarded to the captain of the winning vessel every year.

The race was enthusiastically followed in all ports of the world, and improbable bets were placed on it. Life on board the tea clippers must have been somewhere between hysteria and hell. But the crew of the winning clipper could be sure of free drinks everywhere, at least until next year.

The tea trade became almost all profit for Great Britain after 1834, when tea began to be grown systematically in the Indian Empire, to the dismay of the Chinese. In the time of the Empress Tzu-hsi of China, the Chinese also saw Ceylon take to growing tea after a disease had ravaged the coffee trees of the island. Thereafter China tea lost its pre-eminence on all markets but those of Russia and the Arab countries, which still prefer it.

In France, tea, like politics, was always to divide the country in two. As I mentioned above, there was a kind of class consciousness attached to it from the first, and after the time of Louis XIV it remained, in the popular mind, a drink for those who did not work (i.e., did no manual labour): intellectuals, idlers or fashionable folk, and above all the ladies. It was associated with silverware, lace tablecloths, elegant slices of cake, and the crooking of the little finger as you drank it.

Louis XIV, who religiously took tea 'to prevent vertigo and the vapours', had it

Packing tea in the presence of the Chinese merchant and the European buyer: eighteenth-century water-colour on fabric, from the series *Récolte et fabrication du thé*

made in a golden teapot given him by the Siamese ambassador. Mme de Sablé, according to the Marquise de Sévigné, thought of adding a drop of milk even before the English.

At Procope's, tea was served in a carafe, sweetened with herbal syrup, and called 'Bavaroise' in honour of the princes of Bavaria who accompanied their princess to her wedding when she became the second wife of Philippe d'Orléans. However, the Princess Palatine, as she was known, continued to prefer choucroute, herrings and Munich fricassees; she thought tea horrible – 'good for nothing but to empty the bladder' – and enjoyed mulled beer spiced with nutmeg instead.

It has been said that 'a few tea-leaves made the Atlantic Ocean overflow', and tea is indeed involved in the origin of the United States of America, officially at any rate, since almost any other pretext would have served the purpose just as well. The '13 plantations' that had become the English colonies of America had three million inhabitants by the 1760s. They were prosperous people, jealous of their independence, proud of their idiosyncrasies, and they had gradually managed to wrest genuine local power from the government at home. It was as much on their own behalf as on Britain's that they had fought the French Canadians during the Seven Years' War, although they were happy enough to let the mother country bear the cost of the campaign.

As it seemed necessary, after the war, to keep a standing army of 10,000 men on guard at the St Lawrence border, Grenville, George III's prime minister, suggested that the colonists might defray the expenses of the armed peace. Grenville, who had succeeded the popular Pitt, had a reputation for looking for money for the war everywhere. Songs about him were sung in the coffee-houses, and the journals lampooned the man nicknamed 'gentle shepherd' by Pitt.

The reply of the shepherdess, or rather the colonies, to the gentle shepherd was brief and to the point. They said no. To the characteristics mentioned above, the colonies added another: they hated taxes, particularly taxes imposed by London. In a sense they were right, since a British principle had always been 'no taxation without representation', and the benches of the Mother of Parliaments contained no Americans at all.

This was particularly unjust because English trade depended on America, as it did on India. It did well out of the colonies, especially as, in line with the principles of mercantilist doctrine, no one was making the colonists any presents: all merchandise, whichever way it was going, had to travel on vessels fitted out in England, or belonging to English shipowners. The English ports had the exclusive right to trade with the colonies, and sold their goods on at a profit to the Dutch and the French. Without the mother country as an intermediary, the Americans could have made that profit themselves. Finally, they were forbidden to build factories overseas for processing or manufacturing items which were necessities of life.

A tax on molasses, Benjamin Franklin pointed out to the aged Pitt, was already arousing protest from the distillers of rum, and a timber duty would light the tinder.

Pitt, in his old age, succeeded in getting the project emended, but his second successor, Lord North, was intent on preserving at least its principles. With one voice, Parliament voted to tax glass and to tax tea. It had brewed a glass of tea that was to burn English hands, and when she dropped it she lost America.

The colonists announced that they would drink no more tea, and would take their beverages from tin mugs or cups. It seemed inconceivable in London that anyone of Anglo-Saxon origin could do without the sacred brew, especially as it would mean lost profits for the East India Company. The company's balance sheets had always assumed that large quantities would be delivered annually to Boston. To make up for those lost profits the company decided to send over a ship with a full cargo of tea, to be sold direct by the captain to the consumers without the intermediary of dealers, thus recovering the tax which would be tacitly included in the price, bringing it up to that of goods sold retail. This poorly kept secret infuriated Boston, and some very distinguished citizens of a town which still has a reputation for high-mindedness disguised themselves as Indians, raided the ship and threw its cargo overboard. This was the famous Boston Tea-Party. Lord North retaliated with the Boston Bill: no vessels were to put in to its harbour. All the other ports of the colony stood by Boston, and when Benjamin Franklin came home the American War of Independence had begun.

In Russia, tea had been known for generations, but the first surviving accounts to mention it date from 1618 and concern a caravan coming from China. The Russians are still very fond of tea, which they drink in their own manner, slowly and at length. They make a strong black China tea with a special aroma, called Russian tea, in a teapot. Everyone then dilutes it to taste with the water constantly simmering in the samovar, which has a small lamp always burning under it. You add lemon and sugar, or rose petal jam.

In the old days the way in which the Russians sweetened their tea expressed the order of the social hierarchy. The poorest of the *moujiks* contented themselves with hanging a lump of sugar from a string above the table, where everyone could look at it while sipping tea as bitter as injustice. Small free farmers would take turns to suck the piece of sugar before drinking their brew. The rich *baryni* could actually put one or two pieces of sugar in their cups. However, such luxury was as nothing compared with that enjoyed by the Tsar, Little Father of All the Russias, who was said to use a hollowed-out sugar loaf as a cup; his tea was poured into it.

In his *Dictionnaire de cuisine*, Alexandre Dumas claims that

> the best of teas is drunk at Petersburg, and all over Russia in general: as China shares a border with Siberia, the tea does not need to cross the sea to reach Moscow or Petersburg, and sea voyages do tea a good deal of harm. ... A custom peculiar to Russia, and one which always surprises foreigners when they first encounter it, is that men drink their tea from glasses and women from china cups.

It is a fact that tea-drinkers fall into two camps here. The Arabs, like the Russians, prefer tea in glasses. Perhaps they seem more virile and less delicate than porcelain (another Chinese invention), which according to other tea-lovers is the only material that suits the taste and beauty of the amber liquid. What could be better than porcelain, especially genuine Chinese porcelain, for a Chinese drink? Chinese cups are actually bowls, without handles or saucers, very small, and with a lid, because the chosen mixture (black or green tea and jasmine flowers) is infused directly in them.

Speaking of teacups, Dumas also tells a tale of Brashov, in the Dracula country of Romanian Transylvania, when the city was still a German colony called Cronstadt:

> The first tea cups were made at Cronstadt. It often happened that, for reasons of economy, the café proprietors put less tea than they should have done into a pot. The bottoms of the cups showed a view of Cronstadt, and if the watery nature of the liquid allowed one to see too clearly, the customer would call the proprietor and show him the bottom of the cup, saying, 'I can see Cronstadt.' As the proprietor could not deny it, and as it would not have been possible to see Cronstadt had the tea been strong enough, he was caught in the act of fraud. Consequently, the proprietors decided to use glasses, where you could see nothing at the bottom, instead of the cups in which you could see Cronstadt.

Offering tea is a delicate expression of Arab hospitality. It is given to all visitors in the most primitive of tents or the most wretched of shacks in the shanty-towns, just as it is in the most fabulous of palaces complete with ornate marble-work and mosaic-patterned walls. In every Arab household, tea is drunk as you sit cross-legged on the floor, on a rug or on cushions, gravely and in silence. The tea tastes all the hotter because of the heat beating down on the countryside.

In Morocco three glasses of boiling hot and very sweet tea are traditionally drunk after meals. They help to digest the sumptuous series of fat, spicy dishes on which guests are feasted. The head of the family or his eldest son always makes the tea: never a servant, and still less – Allah forfend! – a woman. Sometimes the host may wish to honour his chief guest by asking him to make the tea.

The officiating priest – it is really the only way to describe him – first places a large pinch of green tea in the metal teapot, preferably of finely chased silver. He immediately pours a little boiling water on it to remove its bitterness. A handful of fresh mint leaves are added, and a large piece of loaf sugar broken off with a copper hammer as the sugar-loaf is held above the tea-pot. The mixture is then covered with more boiling water, and the pot is wrapped in a hot napkin or a cover. A few moments of meditation follow, and smiles of complicity are exchanged. The officiating priest then stirs the mixture, tastes the tea in a tumbler, nods his head, adds a little bit more of this or a little bit more of that. Then he serves each of his companions, pouring the tea from a great height so that the crystalline sound of the aromatic liquid falling into the glasses shall echo in the ears of Allah, a true libation offered in thanks for the happiness of the diners.

In the baggage (often just a knotted bundle) of every Arab traveller, pilgrim or dealer, there will be a string of prayer beads and a prayer mat, and the teapot which also, filled with fresh water, serves for the ritual ablutions performed before the traveller's devotions.

Punch does not necessarily contain rum, but must have some kind of spirit in its ingredients; grog does not necessarily contain tea, but may be made with hot water. Those are the only differences between them.

The word 'punch' and the preparation of the drink – a mixture of tea, lemon, sugar and alcohol – appeared in France first as *bolleponche* ('bowl of punch') in 1653. Punch seems to come from Hindustani *panch*, meaning five. It does in fact have five ingredients in it if you count the hot water and tea-leaves in the tea as two.

The Dutch also made punch, and in both Rotterdam and London it was served in cafés or at stag parties; ladies disliked the odour it left on the breath. Procope, yet again, had a good idea: he served punch iced to reduce the alcoholic aroma, and called it Roman punch. At the end of the eighteenth century, the fashion for anything exotic did the rest.

Grog, a mixture of rum and water, is said to take its name from the nickname of 'Old Grog' given to Admiral Vernon by his sailors; much like Mountbatten later, he was in the habit of wearing a kind of heavy coat of grogram, a coarse weatherproof fabric (the word comes from French *gros-grain*). Around 1740 he made his crews dilute their rum ration with water. It was discovered that if the water was hot it improved the drink, bringing out the flavour of the modest standard measure of rum. Thanks to the diuretic qualities of tea, tea grog soon proved a good precaution against fever and one of the best remedies for a nasty cold. You put your hat at the end of your bed and drink grog until you see two hats there. You are then cured.

Fourteen thousand cups of tea a second are drunk in the world today, although some countries drink more of it than others; in France the average is a cup and a half per month per inhabitant. According to statistics, the Italians drink only three cups a year each (and for all we know those may be drunk by English tourists passing through). The people of the Latin countries – and this may explain their low tea-drinking figures – have the deplorable habit of buying any kind of cheap tea, making it in a slapdash way, and even, sacrilegiously, using teabags containing the dusty ends of stocks. I will not linger over soluble instant tea for fear of bringing the poet Lu-yu who became the immortal Chazu, spirit of tea, down from his seventh heaven.

But like wine, which the Mediterranean peoples respect so much, tea has its *crus*, poetically called 'gardens', with their different flavours, the various ways of relishing them, and their traditions. Tea has its blends too, and every tea merchant or tea expert has his own secret.

603

Although tea-leaves look brown, they are classified as either black tea or green tea, depending on whether they have been fermented or not.

Green teas, almost exclusively from China, Japan and Formosa, are the most popular with the Japanese and Arabs (the Koran forbids all fermented drinks). The Japanese and Chinese do not sweeten their tea at all; the Arabs drink theirs very sweet. The best known kinds are gunpowder tea, in which the leaves have been rolled up like beads, and imperial tea, with flat leaves.

After the tea-leaves of black tea have wilted they too are rolled and then fermented, roasted or smoked, and finally dried to just the right stage. A semi-black Formosa tea called *koolong* is the basis of many blends. It has a natural aroma of ripe peaches. But in general the provenance of black tea is varied. As with wine, the soil that grows it, the climate that nurses it and the altitude at which it breathes are the factors that contribute to its *cru* and its special flavour.

China teas are always the finest. They need no sugar or lemon, and they certainly do not need milk. They include pekoe, (a Chinese word meaning 'white down' from the fact that the leaves are picked while young with the down on them), the full-bodied Yunnan (which some say has an aroma of chocolate), the smoky Lapsang Souchong, with its very pronounced flavour, and Earl Grey, named after a British diplomat. Earl Grey, a true aristocrat among teas and flavoured with bergamot, is worth its price. Experts will make a special blend at the last moment with China teas and Indian Darjeeling.

Ceylon tea is the classic kind drunk by the not particularly imaginative. Chosen with care, however, its straightforward, simple taste can be excellent. It goes well with milk, lemon or rum, none of which disturb the flavour too much. It is divided into pekoe, orange pekoe and flowery. Orange pekoe Ceylon tea is a subtle blend from 15 plantations in 15 different geographical and climatic areas.

The teas of Assam or Darjeeling, on the slopes of the Himalayas, are the best Indian teas. They are ideal for afternoon tea, and good to drink in the morning too. Assam is fuller-bodied; Darjeeling is the champagne of teas, with an aftertaste of honeyed fruit. It will accept a slice of lemon, and goes very well in partnership with its only equal, Earl Grey.

There are also teas from Indochina, Africa (Tanzania), Brazil and Iran.

Whatever kind it is, tea should be drunk soon after it is sold, kept in a tightly closed tin, and bought in date-stamped packets. A month and a half will already have passed in any case between its preparation in its country of origin, its handling in London, and its setting out on the commercial circuit all over Europe.

Today there are also all kinds of perfumed teas, flavoured with rose, mint, lotus, jasmine, orange or bergamot peel, cherry, lychee – something for every taste. The art lies in making tea (like coffee) with pure spring water, demineralized and not chlorinated. The Queen of England always takes supplies of pure spring water when she travels.

In general tea is grown, like coffee, in the shade of tall trees. Altitude improves its flavour. The tea shrub is pruned back to remain at a height of about a metre, since the leaves are picked by the small hands of women and children. In the time of the emperors of China, the pickers were supposed to be virgins aged less than 14, and were to wear a new dress and new gloves daily; these garments were perfumed, and so was their breath. They had to preserve complete silence as they worked.

Every 10 to 15 days the terminal shoots of the stems are cut. The fresh tea, once gathered, is spread on wicker trays to wilt for 24 hours. Then the leaves are crushed and bruised to release the aroma, a process now carried out mechanically. They are then fermented for several hours in a hot, humid place. To stop the fermentation the leaves then go into a drying room. They are sifted, graded, selected, and sent off to London, the world centre of the tea trade, where the tea is blended, packed, distributed – and quoted on the stock exchange.

'Tea-leaves', said the Chinese poet Lu-yu, 'should have folds like the leather boots of Tartar horsemen and curls like the dewlaps of a mighty ox, they should be moist and soft to the touch, like the earth freshly swept by rain.'

Tea in Legend

In China there is a legend that the Emperor Chen-nung invented tea in the year 2374 BC by accident. One summer's day he stopped in the shade of a shrub and put water to boil to refresh himself (hot water is more refreshing than iced water). A slight breeze plucked several leaves from the tree. They fell into the boiling water. Cheng-nung did not notice until he breathed in the subtle aroma of the miraculous brew as he raised it to his mouth to drink.

In India, however, a legend goes as follows:

Long, long ago there lived a prince called Darma. After a wild youth, he embraced the way of asceticism, became a begging monk called Bodhi Dharma and went to China as a Buddhist missionary, vowing never to sleep again in penance for his wild nights of debauchery. For years his faith helped him to keep his vow, but one day, when he was meditating on the slopes of the Himalayas, the sleep so long postponed overcame him. On waking, overwhelmed by remorse for breaking his word, he cut off his eyelids, buried them and set off again, tears mingling with the blood on his face. Years later, passing the place of his sacrifice once more, he saw an unknown bush on the spot. He picked the leaves and steeped them in the hot water which was his only nourishment. After the first mouthful, his weariness was gone and his spirit, suddenly stimulated, attained the greatest heights of knowledge and beauty.

Continuing on his way, he distributed seeds of the miraculous tree as he passed. Ever since, monks have drunk tea to aid their meditation.

The Symbolism of Tea

In Japan, only five persons may join in the tea ceremony at once – 'more than the Graces and fewer than the Muses', it has been said, five being the symbol of union, like the fingers of the hand, of harmony and equilibrium, the figure of hierogamy, the marriage of the celestial principle (signified by the number 3) with the terrestrial principle (signified by the number 2), and also the symbol of yin and yang. The five qualities of knowledge are those of Buddha: perfection integrated into a whole.

'Tea is not only the antidote to drowsiness', said Lu-yu, over 13 centuries ago, 'but one of the ways whereby man may return to his source.'

> The first tea ceremony, according to the Taoists, was held when Yin-hi offered Lao-tsze the cup of immortality [in the sixth century BC]. Lao-tsze was about to give him the Tao-te-king, the Book of the Way and of Virtue. The tea ceremony has all the appearance of a religious rite, which it probably once was – it is claimed that the object was to calm rough manners, master the passions, overcome antagonism and establish peace. It is chiefly marked by sobriety; the relinquishing of action is intended to encourage the relinquishing of individuality. As in all the Zen arts, the end to be attained is for the action to be carried out not by the ego, but by a person's essential nature or emptiness. Tea, finally, is the symbol of the essence in which the self participates, but the 'emptiness' involved is not the oblivion of slumber; it is intense watchfulness in contemplative silence.
>
> Pierre Grison, *Dictionnaire des symboles*,
> Seghers, Paris

PART VIII

The late seventeenth century and the Age of Enlightenment were the period of the 'government' of the garden

ORCHARDS AND KITCHEN GARDENS

To Monique Mosser, a fairy of the eighteenth-century garden

Instructions for the Garden

As we fill our baskets with the produce of the royal kitchen garden created for Louis XIV by his gardener La Quintinie, it appears that we shall be ending our journey through the history of food where we began it: with gathering. Not, however, indiscriminate gathering of leaves, berries or roots from any available shrub, to be instantly snapped up by hungry mouths, but careful selection of the perfectly ripened produce of 'a garden as delightful and useful as has ever been seen', as Bernard Palissy (1510–1589) put it in the sixteenth century.

Following Voltaire, whose reputation is founded on reason but who was not necessarily always right, academic studies have tended to ridicule Palissy, 'a natural philosopher and a man of a wonderfully quick and acute mind',[1] as a mere potter, a member of the Illuminati and a pyromaniac. People have forgotten what an excellent naturalist this brilliant self-educated scientist, alchemist and man of many talents actually was. Louis Figuier described him as 'one of those sixteenth-century figures who did most to dispel the darkness into which scholasticism had plunged the human mind.'[2] A hundred years later that darkness was to give way to the dazzling brightness of the Age of the Enlightenment.

> He had no book at first from which to teach himself but the heavens and the earth, a book in which all may read. But he had no Latin or Greek, and he would have liked to know whether the philosophers of antiquity explained the book of nature in the same way as he understood it himself, or whether they had some other interpretation of it. It was with such ends in view that he decided to give a series of lectures in Paris (Louis Figuier).

In 1580 Bernard Palissy published an octavo volume comprising the following treatises:

> Admirable discourses of the nature of waters and founts both natural and artificial; of metals, salts and salt springs; of stones, soils, fire and enamels; with many other excellent secrets of natural things. With a treatise on marling, very useful and necessary to those employed in agriculture. The whole set out as dialogues which introduce the theory and the practice. By Monsieur B. Palissy, inventor of rustic *figulines* to the King and the Queen Mother.

Rather long as titles go, but explicit. The King was Henri III and the Queen Mother Catherine de Medici, and their *figulines* were artificial grottos made of earthenware and decorated with pottery animals, particularly reptiles and batrachians,

609

life-size and in their natural colours. They stood in the gardens of the Louvre on the present site of the Tuileries. In spite of the *figulines*, the royal couple did not hesitate to have the 80-year-old Palissy thrown into prison for his Protestant faith, and he died there.

'Pomona, or the fair gardener': enamelled faïence dish by Bernard Palissy (*c.* 1510–1589). Although the great potter often decorated his dishes with careful reproductions of fish, reptiles and shellfish, depictions of plants and gardens are less common in his work.

In 1583 another work by Palissy was published at La Rochelle. It had an even longer title, and mentioned 'the design of a garden both pleasant and useful' by 'Maître Bernard Palissy, potter and inventor of the King's rustic *figulines*.'

The theories 'set out as dialogues' were among the first genuinely modern approaches to the science of agronomy. Palissy was also the first person to comprehend the role of mineral salts, and we owe to him both the discovery of chemical fertilizers and an understanding of the ammoniac products which make manure work. He was able to show that farmers had been mistaken in not spreading their soiled straw in the fields until it had been washed by the rain, when it produced poor results: 'If the soil were tilled as it should be, it would bear twice as much', he pronounced, very much in line with that combination of reflection and knowledge which was to usher in the Enlightenment.

There is no art in the world to which a grand philosophy is more necessary than to agriculture, and to approach agriculture without philosophy is to degrade the land and its produce, and indeed I marvel that the land and its natural products do not cry out for vengeance against those ignorant and ungrateful folk who do nothing but spoil and squander trees and plants without any consideration ... the acts of ignorance I see daily in agriculture frequently torment my mind ...

He was right: with due respect to that town-dweller Voltaire, agriculture is indeed an art and a philosophy. Palissy's 'treatise on marling' sets out the basics of both hydrology and geology, in the same way as his treatise on stones prefigures paleontology.

Palissy, of course, was a product of his times. At around the same period, as people gradually became aware of changes in the environment, others too set out to show their contemporaries that proper use of the land could provide more nourishment for an expanding population. The deviser of the *figulines* was not the only one to hold that if the soil were properly cultivated it would produce twice as much. This was not a new idea, but it was now to be explained in the vernacular so that farm workers could understand it, rather than simply being given orders, the way in which Charlemagne had approached the matter in his time ('Let there be apple trees, pear trees, service trees, plum trees, cherry trees, walnut trees and chestnut trees'). Methods were explained and demonstrated; the countryman, no longer treated as an idiot, regained confidence.

It was only in England, where the agricultural revolution of the eighteenth century was preached by example, that the miraculous doubling of production actually came about. Swift echoed Palissy in remarking that 'whoever could make two ears of corn or two blades of grass to grow upon a spot of ground where only one grew before, would deserve better of mankind ... than the whole race of politicians put together', a theme taken up by agriculturalists such as Arthur Young. Their empiricism was combined with a genuine understanding of the soil, the rotation of crops, and the advent of farm machinery.

But the way for the agricultural revolution had been prepared by the inquiring minds of the Renaissance. Palissy had been preceded by Charles Estienne, the youngest of a family of great scholars, who did not feel it was beneath him to publish a treatise on *L'agriculture et la maison rustique* in 1504. This work contained much useful gardening advice, and so did Symphorien Champier's *Le jardin françois*, published in 1532. In 1553 that other inquiring mind, Pierre Belon the botanist and traveller, who was murdered by footpads while botanizing in the Bois de Boulogne, produced *Les remontrances sur les défauts de labour et de la culture des plantes*. Belon suggested the idea, entirely new at the time, of acclimatizing exotic plants which might prove useful in nurseries. The great University of Padua took up the project. A little later, Richer de Belleval ruined himself to acquire 5000 plant species and found the Botanic Garden of Montpellier under the auspices of the Faculty of Medicine, and Paris subsequently followed this example. In 1633 a doctor, Guy de La Brosse, with the aid of Jean Robin, 'apothecary-herbalist' to King Louis XIII, took the royal gardens in hand. They covered an area of some 24 acres in the faubourg Saint-Victor, which was to become the Jardin des Plantes. A series of notable scholars succeeded La Brosse as its director, including Duverney, Jussieu, Buffon, Daubenton, Bernardin de Saint-Pierre, Lakanal, Geoffroy Saint-Hilaire, Linnaeus and Cuvier, to mention only the best-known names. It is to such men that we owe many vegetables which are an everyday part of our present diet (and many flowers too).

In 1571 the French public was offered Belleforest's *Secrets de la vray agriculture*. Claude Gauchet's *Les plaisirs des champs* followed in 1583, the *Sommaire traité des melons* of Jacques de Pons in 1586, and the very important *Histoire générale des plantes*, by Jacques Daleschamps, in 1587. Élie Vinet's *La maison champêtre* was published in 1607. These delightfully evocative titles are evidence of a genuine, unaffected love of the countryside, and brought a very welcome breath of fresh air into the atmosphere of a period that stank of blood shed in the many massacres perpetrated in the name of religion.

Notable names of sixteenth-century gardening literature in England included Leonard Mascall, *The Booke of Arte and Maner, howe to Plant and Graffe all Sortes of Trees*, first published in 1572, Thomas Tusser, with passages in the *Hundreth Good Points of Husbandrie*, and John Gerard, with his *Catalogue of Plantes* and *Herball*.

Olivier de Serres' *Théâtre d'agriculture et mesnage des champs*, published in 1606 and commissioned by Sully, was extremely successful for over a century. A Protestant from the Ardèches area, de Serres had been commissioned by Henri IV's minister to show that 'tilling the land and tending the flocks are the two breasts from which France is fed', a remark which makes much more sense than its frequent (and rather startling) misquotation to the effect that 'tilling the soil and tending the flocks are the two breasts of France'.

Olivier de Serres had introduced silkworm culture to France, and it remained the major resource of the Gard until the twentieth century. The silkworms, and the silk-weaving of Lyons, halted a severe drain of French currency to Italy, and moreover considerable prestige attached to the silk industry. Olivier de Serres was not just a theoretician: he put his theories into practice on his own not very large estate of Pradel, which he made into a model farm. He was practising rotation of crops and advocating root crops as part of the process well before the Dutch and the English, he was a pioneer in dressing vines with copper sulphate, and he naturalized maize and rice in France. He was also the first to indicate the potential of sugar beet and the importance of the potato. The *Théâtre d'agriculture* summed up 40 years of experience, and its social, technical and scientific significance was immense.

The agronomical books of the sixteenth and seventeenth centuries, following the shock delivered to the social system by the religious wars, show that in this field as in others people were ceasing to believe that all wisdom might be found in the literature of antiquity. Cato, Columella, Varro, Pliny and even Virgil were no longer regarded as Holy Writ. The face of the world had changed, and the Roman Empire had declined once again. Voltaire mocked the proliferation of technical works in his time[3] (including Quesnay's *L'essai physique sur l'économie animale* of 1736 and Mirabeau senior's *Philosophie rurale ou économie générale et politique de l'agriculture* of 1763), calling them 'works that everyone reads except the labourers themselves', and commenting on the fact that 'the nation, surfeited with poetry, plays and novels, sets itself to musing on wheat', but his mockery itself can be seen as clear proof that the seeds sown by Palissy and the others had taken root. Curiously, whether by chance or not, almost all these pioneers were Protestants.

Henri IV, that dubious convert from Protestantism, had been greatly in favour of this return to the land, and had turned his attention to such agricultural projects as rice-growing in the Camargue before his assassin Ravaillac put an end to him (and them). Henri had a long memory, and hoped that once the wars of religion were over the nobility would leave him to work in peace and go back to their estates.

> Vivez donc aux champs, gentilshommes
> Vivez sains et joyeux, cent ans ...

[Live in the fields, then, gentlemen. Live happy and healthy a hundred years ...]

Fifty years after the time of Henri IV, however, the French landed gentry of the seventeenth century were still more interested in fashion than agriculture, and those rustic squires who did cultivate their own estates were mocked as boors by the wits who cultivated only the sterile flowers of rhetoric. But the majority of French people, always more rural than urban,[4] and the educated élite, as yet untroubled by the intellectual cares of the Enlightenment, both showed genuine feeling for nature, and enjoyed reading works on agriculture written some time before.

It should not be forgotten that the phenomenon of the seventeenth century in France was the advance of the bourgeoisie, either ennobled or about to be ennobled, which put its talents at the service of the administration. These shrewd men took an interest in estates which might now be theirs, 'setting the seal on their rapid rise'.[5] They took pains to improve the cultivation and yield of such lands. The acquisition of a town house was succeeded by the satisfaction – and perhaps the vanity – of owning a manor in the country, in much the same way as a 'second home' is today's sign of worldly success.

If the wits who could not afford estates affected to despise the country, the great men of the world of Louis XIV, steeped in the same traditions as their sovereign – traditions to which we shall return – proudly competed with the financiers in tending their gardens for pleasure or profit. More than 2000 châteaux were built in the seventeenth century, by self-made men as well as wealthy aristocrats, and their gardens were managed by educated and competent gardeners.

The agronomical books of the previous century, constantly reissued, were now joined in the libraries of country gentlemen by the *Catalogue des arbres fruitiers* drawn up by the King's attorney at Orléans, M. Le Lectier, a distinguished grower who possessed specimens of all the fruit trees he mentioned. Louis XIII's gardener, Boyceau de La Baraudière, published a remarkable treatise on gardening in 1638, and above all, in 1652, Antoine Le Gendre, the curé of Hénonville and formerly gardener to the Prince de Condé at Chantilly, wrote a little masterpiece which was frequently reprinted, *La manière de cultiver les arbres fruitiers*. It was translated into English by the diarist John Evelyn as *The Manner of Ordering Fruit Trees*. There followed the important *Jardinier françois* of the 'pomologist' Bonnefons, and in 1674 another successful book, *Nouvelles instructions pour connaître les bons fruits selon les mois de l'année*, by Dom Claude de Saint-Etienne. The monks had not lost their horticultural touch, and even the recluses of Port-Royal-des-Champs followed Arnaud d'Andilly in gardening as efficiently as they prayed fervently. The Abbot of Ponchateau went to the nearby market himself to sell his fruit and vegetables.

Similarly, the seventeenth century in England saw the publication of horticultural works by the nurseryman Ralph Austen (*A Treatise of Fruit Trees*, 1653), John Parkinson (*Paradisi in Sole*, 1629), and Evelyn, both as writer and translator; his English version of La Quintinie's *Instructions pour les jardins fruitiers et potagers* appeared as *The Compleat Gard'ner* in 1693. The first edition of this work appeared in 1690. Its author, Jean-Baptiste de La Quintinie, King Louis XIV's gardener, had died two years before, and his book represented the intellectual testament of 'the man more skilled in the knowledge of these things than any other in France'.[6]

The Jardin du Roy at Versailles, with its kitchen garden and orchard, the greatest of La Quintinie's achievements, was a favourite resort of Louis XIV, like the park of the palace itself. When La Quintinie died the monarch said that he had lost a friend. They shared a love of gardens. La Quintinie approved of the intelligent attention with which the King listened to his principles on the pruning of trees, which he claimed were entirely new. We can imagine the greatest sovereign in Europe, who gravely put 'a hundred questions' to Cardinal Mazarin, taking gardening lessons with equal gravity from an honest fellow in brown breeches and shirtsleeves, sniffing the soil of Versailles (which La Quintinie deplored, because it was cold and wet). The French royal family was traditionally inclined to lend as attentive an ear to the 'government' of the garden as to affairs of state.

The enclosed medieval garden contained fruit and vegetables, and always had a corner for medicinal herbs. Umberto Eco's fine novel *The Name of the Rose*[7] shows us Remigio de Varaghi, cellarer of the monastery in which the action takes place, lovingly tending his herb garden. Flowers were introduced after the Crusades, a move inspired by the great Arab gardens; they were cut to strew the threshold of church doorways. Almost all the intrigues of such tales of chivalry as the *Romaunt of the Rose* take place in gardens. Charles V's garden at the Hôtel Saint-Pol could have come straight out of a manuscript illuminated by Jean Fouquet. King René had designed the plans of his own gardens, first at Angers and then at Aix. Even the sombre Louis XI relaxed by walking in his garden, and we shall see below how carefully he watched over the ripening of fruit at Plessis-lez-Tours.

Charles VIII brought a taste for fresh young vegetables back from his Italian wars, together with Italians to grow them and organize an efficient system of irrigation. In the Loire valley, the garden of France, another Italian, Leonardo da Vinci, studied botany at Clos-Lucé. His sketchbooks combine remarkably precise drawings with acute observation.

Henri IV and Sully had found a man very well equipped to serve their own tastes and ideas in Olivier de Serres, and the King put his precepts into practice, not just at Blois, where the kitchen garden attained considerable proportions, but also at Fontainebleau; the orchard here grew every kind of peach and plum, brought from the South of France and well acclimatized.

Henri's mother-in-law Catherine de Medici had much to do with French consumption of fruit, raw or in those preserves which Nostradamus made so well. However, she left Palissy to die in prison, for although he had advised her in laying out the park of Chenonceaux he would not pray in Latin. Richelieu was another great lover of fruit. His orchards at Rueil and on his lands at Richelieu in the Loire country were famous.

When architects turned their attention to landscape gardening the orchard and the kitchen garden (often containing beehives) were separated from the pleasure garden 'in the French style', although they might still exist side by side. But the design of the parks was an inspiration to the great gardeners of 'useful' gardens (not that a park is ever precisely useless), and the aim was that in the kitchen garden too all should be order, calm and beauty.

The 'French garden' of the classical age can be defined or explained in terms of the profession of faith made by a contemporary, Nicolas Poussin: 'My nature urged me to seek well-ordered things.' The same spirit is found in La Fontaine, whose bent was for the truth well formed by work, research and calculation. 'Nature and Truth are the same everywhere, and Reason shows them everywhere alike', said Alexander Pope at the same period. André Le Nôtre, creator of the parks of Vaux-le-Vicomte and Versailles, embroidered with plants, not in any timid or artificially academic spirit but with a coherent harmony of design that shows man's will and creativity applied to Nature with respect. As Poussin said: 'The constant link between Nature and Man is a lesson taught by the former to the latter.'

It was at this period, in fact, that the two meanings of the word 'culture' came together. A Latin saying ran: *cultura animi philosophia est*, philosophy is the cultivation of the mind.[8] This was the natural philosophy to which the unfortunate Palissy aspired. With its design and its symmetrical harmony the formal 'French garden' bore witness, in its own not inconsiderable way, to the geometrical spirit of Spinoza's philosophy. It was a spirit in the air of the time, even the fresh air of the countryside.

'The eighteenth century needed Nature to form its idea of the world', says Chaunu of the crisis of conscience which was 'the prelude to the Enlightenment'. But the need for a universal natural order presiding over the plans of the Maker, that Great Architect now beginning to win recognition on the continent of Europe, was now inspiring landscape gardeners as well as philosophers.

As we never quite forget the foundations of our civilization, it was natural enough, in going back to the source, for gardeners to call on the *Ars topiaria* of that other classical age now finally ending, that of the Romans: the art of the rational and useful manipulation of the landscape.

This taming of nature to make it a calculated work of art, the garden as embroidery, tapestry or mosaic, had its first and imaginary description (if a dream can be called imaginary) in the Italian Francesco Colonna's *Dream of Poliphilo* in 1496. It was a prophetic dream. The garden in question was the garden of Venus in the isle of Cytherea. It was translated into real terms at the end of the Renaissance, first by Bramante in the Belvedere of the Vatican, then by Ligorio at the Villa d'Este. However, the rigorous geometrical order which the French contributed brought it to perfection.

Order in the garden was very much to the taste of the *grande bourgeoisie*, the friends of law and order. Now that they had risen in the social scale, the higher civil servants began to cultivate their leisure pursuits. Their tastes, dictated by studies generally more serious than those of the gentry and expressed to the people they employed to create the setting for those leisure pursuits, and their money, judiciously spent, were the leaven of neoclassical Europe.

Their gardens, like those of Fouquet at Vaux, Tambonneau in the faubourg Saint-Germain, or Colbert on his estate at Sceaux, were perfect studies for the final perfection of Versailles: works of collaboration, with buildings designed by architects such as Le Vau, Perrault and Le Brun, pleasure gardens laid out by Le Nôtre, and kitchen gardens by La Quintinie. The last-named wrote, in his *Instructions*, of having laid out one of the best kitchen gardens imaginable for a 'great minister'. He had been able to choose a site which was just what he wanted, and what he wished everyone interested in gardening might have. He praised his kitchen garden for its excellence, neatness and order, the vigour of its trees, the fine quality of its fruit, and the delicious and beautiful vegetables that grew in it.

In the seventeenth century a place as lavish with the provision of good things to eat as the kitchen garden was not an unattractive eyesore. It was the twin brother of the pleasure garden, well conceived, well laid out and of pleasing appearance, and the owners of such gardens were so proud of them and their produce that they liked to walk with friends there.

The great minister mentioned by La Quintinie, Colbert, had asked Perrault, architect of the Louvre colonnade, to build him a pavilion in the middle of the kitchen garden. 'The admirable Pavilion of Aurora in the finest garden in the world'[9] was a place where the prime minister of France held private receptions, and to which he resorted for cultural relaxation and informal meetings of the Academy. Louis XIV was served a collation here after admiring the fruits and vegetables; Colbert was as proud of them as La Quintinie himself. When La Quintinie, once a lawyer, later gardener first to farmers-general and then to princes, moved on to serve his sovereign, the King himself did the honours of the kitchen garden of Versailles, showing off its lettuces, cabbages, strawberries and peaches to the Doge of Venice and the Siamese ambassadors, who tasted and enjoyed everything. Colbert had previously lured La Quintinie away from the Prince de Condé, who himself had snapped him up from under the nose of La Grande Mademoiselle, not to mention all the other great lords and ministers who would have liked to have his services.

There was already a kitchen garden at Versailles when it was Louis XIII's hunting lodge. In the first 15 years after the palace was built this garden provided all the fruit and vegetables necessary to supply it. La Quintinie had increased and improved its yield. New plants arrived daily from the provinces, from other European countries, even from overseas, and did very well, thanks to forcing, the clever management of aspects, and the glasshouses supervised by the *Intendant en Chef des Maisons Royales* – such was La Quintinie's official title.

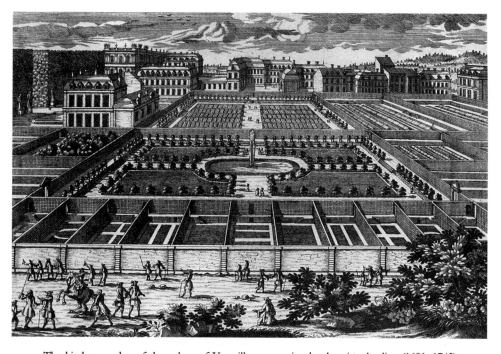

The kitchen garden of the palace of Versailles: engraving by Antoine Aveline (1691–1743)

The kitchen garden, 260 by 126 metres, lay next to the Orangery, and when that site was needed for government departments the garden had to be moved. In 1678 La Quintinie was given eight hectares to cultivate in a very bad situation, a marshy stretch of land near the place pinpointed for the Suisses ornamental pool. This damp spot was filled in with sandy soil taken from the nearby pool, and then by an actual hill, the 'mount' of Satory, the soil of which remained resistant to water in its new position.

La Quintinie had an aqueduct built from La Bièvre, with water pipes and pumps as good as those of Marly, and contrived to coax the best possible yield from this unpromising site by means of soil improvement, judicious irrigation with a slope separately calculated for each of the rectangular divisions of the garden, and in particular by the technique of building small banked-up beds against the walls with good aspects, called *ados*, where he forced vegetables. Although it has been under cultivation for three centuries, the soil of La Quintinie's garden is not yet exhausted, a fact appreciated by the students of the École Nationale d'Horticulture who use it in their studies, and the people of Versailles who buy its produce.

The plan of the kitchen garden which illustrates La Quintinie's *Instructions* could be the design for a handsome and geometrically symmetrical tapestry. There is a central garden of three hectares around a pool of water with a fountain that has played for 300 years. This central garden is surrounded in turn by 31 enclosures. On the plan their external dimensions look similar, but none is just the same inside as any of the others, in layout or in the plants they contain. Small walls, breaking the wind and providing support for espaliers, mark off these enclosures, and the whole thing is put to such good use that a basket need never be brought back from the garden empty at any time of the year. In the day of the Sun King, the garden had to provide fruit and vegetables for thousands of people. The magic of La Quintinie's frames and cloches provided baskets full of fruit, and the assortment was always different. He insisted to the court officers of the table that the fruit piled into pyramids or arranged in the fine porcelain dishes that always stood on the tables was actually for eating, not an ornament to be left untouched and so lead to sumptuous and perishable waste.[10] He knew how much labour and money the fruit had cost, and meant it to be eaten and enjoyed. Great silver vases were filled with flowers and branches laden with fruit in season. Sometimes they held the orange trees of which the King was very fond.

If we wonder, as we well may, at the sheer organization involved in all this, the list La Quintinie wrote to go with the plan of the kitchen garden illustrates the man's gifts and his delightful sentiments; it is given here in John Evelyn's English translation of 1693:

The King's Kitchen Garden at Versailles

1. 2. 3. and 4. Gardens design'd for Strawberrys.

5. 6. 7. 8. Gardens slop'd, and situated for the benefit of the Sun, in the four different expositions.

9 to 19. Eleven small Gardens all enclos'd with walls, full of different Fruits, and Legumes.

20. Asparagus to be kept warm.

21. The Plum Garden, for all sorts of Plums, both dwarfs, and espaliers.

22. The City Garden, where asparagus are also kept warm.

23. Fig trees, in Dwarfs and Espaliers.

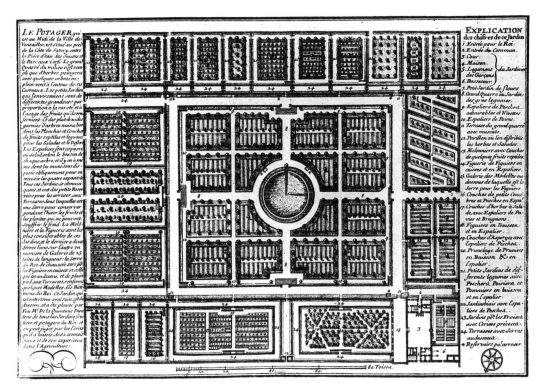

Plan of the kitchen garden at Versailles: engraving by Nicolas Parelle (1631–95). The text accompanying the engraving does not correspond exactly to La Quintinie's account of it.

24 and 25. Gardens design'd to make Beds in, for Cucumbers and small Sallads.

26. A Mellonry, and all sorts of Beds.

27. The Publick Entrance, where they distribute the Herbs, and legumes ...

30. The Stove-house for the Fig-trees are incas'd.

31. The House built by the King for my self ...

39. A Vault where to keep Roots, Artichokes, Colly-flowers, etc., in the Winter.

The Espaliers of the Great Garden are filled with Admirables, and Nivitz.[11]

All the Walls of the Terrass of the Great Garden are planted with Grapes.

The Northerne Expositions of all the gardens are planted with Pear trees ...

There wants in this Plane only the Garden of Novelties, which is next adjoining the garden marked 23, that being at other times the Yard for Dunghills.

It is pleasant to imagine La Quintinie standing at the window of 'the House built by the King for my self', looking out at his kitchen garden the moment he rose from bed, to make sure all was in order, and the view still what it had been the evening before, providing 'a continual successive supply of Fruits throughout all the Seasons', and that without artificial aids, but simply as a result of the gardener's skill and his pleasure in exercising it.

> ... The most Considerable of those Pleasures, is not only to be able to obtain what may be produced by Earth, that shall have been well ordered, and a Ground well improv'd with Trees that perhaps shall have been Graffed, Planted, Prun'd, Cultivated, etc., by ourselves, though really the Ideas of such Injoyments are powerful Charms to engage us to the Study of them ...[12]

The word 'paradise' comes from Persian *paradyi*, signifying 'garden'. Jean-Baptiste de La Quintinie must surely have felt very much at home when he arrived there. And when it rains, perhaps we are standing under his watering can, for no doubt he found means of employing his talents in that great Garden of Delights, the celestial Paradise.

Chapter 21

The Tradition of Fruits

'God Almighty first planted a garden. And indeed it is the purest of human pleasures.' That first garden to which Bacon referred[1] was the legendary setting for the first act of a tragedy which has not yet reached its close.

Although Eve is often said to have been cast out of the Earthly Paradise forever because she ate an apple, this widespread European tradition goes back only to the fifth century. The Bible merely speaks of a fruit, without specifying what kind. 'And when the woman saw that the tree was good for food, and that it was pleasant to the eyes, and a tree to be desired to make one wise, she took of the fruit thereof, and did eat, and gave also unto her husband with her; and he did eat. And the eyes of them both were opened ...' (Genesis 3, vi).

The Latin for 'fruit' is *pomum* (*karpos* in Greek). The first translators of the Old Testament into Latin thought that if there was only one fruit in Paradise it had to be the apple, a fruit found even in the most modest orchard, and the Latin for apple was *malum* (*melon* in Greek). The apple therefore, ceasing to be *malum*, took on the identity of *the* fruit, the fruit of fruits, *pomum*, whence modern French *pomme*, apple. All the fruits of the orchard were under the protection of Pomona, goddess of abundance.

The Symbolism of the Apple

In esoteric cults and white magic the apple is the feminine symbol *par excellence*, associated with Venus. If you cut an apple vertically into two exact halves you can in fact see some resemblance to the female genital system. Alternatively, if you cut it in half horizontally you could, like the Pythagoreans, see it as a perfect five-pointed star, the pentagram, a key to the occult sciences, in that it reveals the secret

621

of the knowledge of good and evil (and here the Eve legend surfaces again). No doubt it is merely coincidence – or is it? – that the Latin for apple, *malum*, is a homonym of the Latin for evil. Magicians used the pentagram for casting spells or in such enchantments as the apple given to Snow White. The apple of the *Song of Songs* was supposed to represent the Divine Word, perhaps because of the pentagram it contained. Apples were eaten in Brittany before prophecies were made, and the enchanter Merlin sat under an apple tree to teach.

Frequently associated with the colour yellow or gold, the apple, already bearing an ambiguous weight of symbolism, took on the powers of that colour, which may be either beneficent or maleficent, as with sulphur; either celestial or Satanic. It was the alchemists' Golden Apple. The golden apples of the Garden of the Hesperides (which were not apples, but some other fruit) conferred immortality. Sulphur, transmuting mercury, makes it into cinnabar, red mercuric sulphide, also a symbol of eternal life.

The apples of the Hesperides continued their career in Celtic tradition. In Irish legend they were given by a woman of the Other World to the hero Candle to nourish him for a month, never growing any less, and to confer immortality on him in that time. Similarly, they made the gods of the Scandinavian pantheon immortal. The search for the fruits of eternal life was one of the tasks imposed by the Gaulish blacksmith god Lug on the three sons of Tuleran as penance for the murder of their father. In the Elysian Fields of the Isle of Avalon (the word means 'apple orchard' in Celtic), where King Arthur waited among the dead heroes for his time to come, a woman of the Other World plucked a branch of an apple tree for Bran before taking him to the eternal kingdom beyond the seas. It is interesting to recall, in this connection, that mistletoe grows on apple trees; it was cut by druids on the night of Samhain, 1st November, the day of the dead preceding the Celtic New Year (causing the New Year to begin on 1st January is a Christian pseudo-tradition).

Apples were credited with procuring longevity, a power which interested Alexander the Great. On the expedition which also sought the Water of Life,[2] he found apples allegedly capable of prolonging the lives of the priests who fed on them and nothing else to as much as 400 years. Alexander cannot have eaten enough of them, for he died of malaria at the age of 33.

Finally, there is that darker side of the symbol which I mentioned above. The golden apple awarded by Paris in the beauty contest which began the Trojan War became the apple of discord. The golden apples thrown down by Hippomenes were harmful to the nymph Atalanta in that she broke her vow of chastity, but beneficial in revealing love to her. The myth is a familiar one: the virgin huntress wagered that she could win a race against any of her suitors, who would pay for her victory with his life. As Hippomenes ran he threw the wonderful fruits over his shoulder. Letting him outstrip her in her desire to pick them up, and finally won over by the gifts, Atalanta lost the race, her athletic reputation, and then her virginity.

However, leaving aside the mental manipulations practised by the patriarchal society which invented the sin of Eve, the apple has been regarded as either beneficent or magical since the dawn of time. The ancient story of Snow White's enchanted apple is simply the ever-present obverse of the magic. The narrator in the *Song of Songs* begs, 'Stay me with flagons, comfort me with apples, for I am sick of love.' In the time of Rameses II the Egyptians gave apples 'laid on wattles' to the highest of the priests, the guardians of knowledge.

It has been claimed that the apple of Eden was actually an apricot. The theory is based on the fact that apricots grew in the Near East before apples did. In fact the apricot did not reach Armenia from China and cross the Fertile Crescent towards the south-east of the Mediterranean until caravans made contact with the Semites living in northern Assyria around the third millennium. The apple had already invaded the Middle East by that time, and thus it reached Europe, moving from the east with the human waves coming down from Central Asia. It made its conquest as the hordes made theirs, a stowaway hidden in their provisions. Apple pips, spat out all along the way, gave rise to wild South Caucasian and European apple trees with small, sour fruits, *Malus silvestris* and *M. pumila*, clumps of which still mark out the great emigration routes. These in turn probably gave rise to *Malus paradisiaca*, the French Paradise apple, much used as a rootstock later.

Sown by chance, or even sown intentionally, apple trees almost always revert to the wild form instead of breeding true to the mother tree. Similarly, a cherry stone does not grow a cherry tree identical with the tree from which the fruit was picked, but a wild cherry. Mutations to improve the fruit are obtained first by hybridization, then by grafting a budding branch of a tree that has already developed well on a rootstock. Like many fruit trees, the apple will not bear unless it is fertilized with the pollen of another variety by birds or insects. It could be described as naturally adulterous, for unfertilized flowers will be sterile or abort their fruits. The apple is a love-child, and the tree likes nothing better than company. Several different apple trees growing together will all give more fruit than if they were grown separately. The more apple orchards a region has the more they will produce, with the aid of the wind and the bees.

It has sometimes been claimed that the Romans brought apple trees to Gaul. The Neolithic lake-dwellers of Switzerland and northern Italy were already eating apples from trees that had been dispersed in the course of the great invasions. Traces have been found in their villages of fruits which cannot have been particularly nice, but were apples rather than crabs. When the Romans brought their own apples to Gaul, the country's existing inhabitants, learning from their conquerors, were able to improve their fruit further.

And moving now out of the realm of those legends that the apple seems to attract, it has long been recognized that the Etruscans knew about grafting before the Romans did. No one is absolutely sure where the industrious Etruscans came from when they arrived to colonize central Italy; their civilization appeared there around 750 BC. They may have been a mixed group of Greek or Mycenean refugees, the last survivors of the Homeric wars. At any rate, there is good evidence, in Hesiod's *Works and Days*, that the art of grafting apples was known in ninth-century Greece. Sappho and Theophrastus both wrote of the numerous varieties of apples of their time. Today there are 7000 of them worldwide, and they can be divided into four races. The Pomme d'Api, for instance, the first improvement on the red crab, was brought from the Peloponnese to Rome by Claudius Appius in the third century BC.

Grafting

Young orchard trees are created by grafting branches that will bear fruit on a rootstock which need not necessarily be of the same species, but is of the same family. Etymologically the word 'graft' is from Greek *graphion*, a stylus. When the base of a small branch bearing buds – the scion or slip – has been trimmed to a shape like a stylus or quill, it is inserted into the stock, a branch or the trunk of another tree or bush slit to receive it.

Grafting allows the gardener to combine a robust stock with the finer qualities of the tree or bush from which the scion comes. The same method can be used to make a sterile plant fertile, to bring fruiting on earlier or delay it, or to grow a plant in a soil which does not suit it, but which is tolerated by the stock, especially if it is wild. For instance, a pear can be grafted on a hawthorn. However, there must be an affinity between scion and stock, and in principle they should be of the same botanical genus, although pears do well on a quince stock.

Once the scion is inserted in the wound made in the stock the two are bound tightly together by means of a ligature or a special mastic, so that the generative parts of the two plants merge as scar tissue forms, and the sap of the stock feeds the scion. There are several methods of grafting. The most common make use of a detached twig, either by introducing it into the rind of the stock, the top of which has been cut off and split, or by the budding or shield grafting method, when it is introduced on the side of the stock where the bark has been slit in a T-shape.

There are several criteria for the choice of a stock for apple trees. Though modern kinds with various useful qualities have now been developed, the traditional choice was between 'Free' or seedling, Doucin or sweeting, and Paradise. The roots are the vital point: the tree which provides the scion has been brought so far from the wild state for the sake of good fruit that it is usually very fragile, while the robust, rustic stock has strong roots to give the new tree health and long life.

In a sandy or arid soil, Free stock grows deep roots that can go down in search of water. A tree grown as a standard will also stand up to bad weather better on such a stock.

In damp soil, or if a tree with restricted growth is wanted to form an espalier after being pruned in various ways (for instance, as a goblet or fan), Doucin or Paradise stock with roots remaining near the surface is best.

If windfalls from a fruit tree produce a new seedling, and you would like to grow it to bear fruit itself, it should be used as a stock for a scion from the mother tree, or another variety if you want a change. Otherwise the tree you grow will be a throwback to the wild.

The golden apples of the Garden of the Hesperides which Hercules went to the Canaries to fetch were not really apples at all, of any variety. If the fruits (*poma*) really existed, they were probably citrus fruits of some kind, more likely citron than orange.

The Etruscans may not actually have invented grafting, but they did prove themselves shrewd fruit growers. Varro said proudly that Italy was one vast orchard, so well had the Romans profited by the lessons they learned from the Etruscans and then passed on to the Gauls. According to Pliny, they could create a tree bearing different fruits on every branch: apples, pears, cherries, grapes, walnuts and pomegranates. The naturalist assures us that he saw this marvel with his own eyes at Tibur (Tivoli), a famous leisure resort where grand parties were held at the time of the Roman Empire. Perhaps a sense of euphoria after a good meal explains Pliny's tall story, for the last three fruits in particular have nothing whatsoever in common.

The Romans were very fond of fruit, even wild fruit, which grew profusely all over the Italian peninsula, as Cato points out when discussing crab apples around the first half of the second century BC.[3] They soon became enthusiastic nurserymen, doing research and making experiments with a view to satisfying their greed. This liking for fruit remained an Italian tradition, and spread from Italy during the Renaissance. Just as the Romans had invested a good deal of money and effort in fish-farming and viticulture, they turned what had initially been an important dietary supplement into the *raison d'être* of an increasingly demanding luxury trade. Early fruits were wanted, enormously large fruits, rare fruits, even monstrous hybrids: Pliny cites the apple-plum, *Prunum malinum*, to be obtained by grafting a plum on an apple tree.[4] (The tree he claimed to have seen at Tibur bore distinct known fruits.) That particular experiment cannot have got very far! But many new apple varieties – 32 by the end of the Empire – were established, bearing the names of their breeders, and they still have descendants today. These varieties had their own various standards of size, taste, fruiting season, hardiness and keeping quality.

Dessert Apples

The apple tree is a member of the Rosaceae family. New trees are obtained by sowing, layering or grafting, the last-named procedure being the most common. Much care is required to obtain good quality fruits: the trees have to be manured, sprayed against pests and disease, pruned, thinned, and so on. The average life for a wall-trained apple is 20 to 25 years, and for a standard 30 to 35 years. The apple will naturalize anywhere, and grows spontaneously all over Europe.

Of the six classic tree fruits – apricot, cherry, peach, plum, pear and apple – the apple is easily the most widely grown. In 1977 one-third of the entire fruit-growing area of France was devoted to apples, some 94,135 hectares. Both old and new varieties of apples are now grown, and it is a good idea to know about the differences between them. In France in 1977, 84 per cent of total apple orchard area was occupied by 11 varieties, with Golden Delicious predominating; 34,695 hectares were grown, 60 per cent of the entire area devoted to apples. The other main varieties each occupied an area of between 1000 and 3000 hectares. The area producing the Granny Smith has recently been expanding; it was 3200 hectares when these figures were drawn up. At the same time the Reinette Blanche or Grise du Canada occupied 2420 hectares, and the Reine des Reinettes 2500 hectares. In the 'Red American' group, the Spur Delicious was grown on 2835 hectares, while the Starking Delicious, Richared Delicious and Cardinal each occupied an area of about 1000 hectares.

The traditional European varieties, which are not so robust but are very well flavoured, represent only about 20 per cent of the market in France. They include the Calville, the best of all, appreciated by La Quintinie in the seventeenth century (it matures in October), the Reine des Reinettes, the earliest (ready to eat in September and October), the Reinette du Canada (ready to eat in December), the Reinette Clochard (ready to eat in December to March), the Reinette du Mans, the latest of the group (for eating at the end of winter), and the Belle de Boskoop, the most robust (ready to eat in September and October). Traditional English varieties include the very popular Cox's Orange Pippin, raised in the early nineteenth century.

American varieties now account for over 80 per cent of the world market. Picking of these apples begins in the second half of August, and most of it is done between 8th September and 20th October. The picking season ends at the beginning of November. Early varieties can be cold-stored until March, and later varieties until April.

The Golden Delicious is the most widely eaten variety, by itself accounting for over 65 per cent of the market. It grew by chance from a seed in West Virginia in the United States around the end of the nineteenth century. It is a fruit of medium to large size, and tends to be smaller as the tree grows older. When ripe it is yellow. Its skin is thin and sometimes rough, its flesh white and tender, sweet, and in the best specimens should be melting, but it is not strongly flavoured, and is often floury at the end of the season. It is sold freshly picked from the end of August to the end of December, and stored apples are available until June.

The handsome red American apples are picked from mid-August. They are sold fresh until the end of the year, and can be kept in cold store until April. They comprise Red Delicious (the best), Starking and Richared, and Winesap.

The Starking, large to medium in size, has a thick, shiny skin, very red, streaked, sprinkled with pale freckles. Its fine, white, crunchy, perfumed flesh may become floury when it is over-ripe. It is ready for eating from the end of September.

The Richared has a red skin with pale freckles, and white, juicy, sweet flesh, but it too may become floury. It is picked in September and October.

The Starkimson, like the Starking, is a mutation of a group of Red Delicious varieties. The trees are of the 'spur' type, i.e., small in size with a great many small spurs on which the fruit is borne. They fruit early in their comparatively short life. The apples are medium to large, with a very red skin, not streaked, and elongated in shape. The creamy white, firm, fine and juicy flesh is slightly acid and can be eaten until March.

The Granny Smith originated in New South Wales in Australia. One Mrs Smith, a grandmother, was the first to grow it, in 1868, and gave it her name. The apple has been known in France since 1952. It is one of the main apple varieties grown in the southern hemisphere. The tree is quite vigorous, but prone to mildew and scab. The elongated fruit, of medium and homogeneous size, is green with large pale spots; its skin is waxy. The flesh is firm, very juicy, crisp, very acid, with little sweetness or scent. It is picked late. As it is very robust and very much in fashion, it is a popular variety for export. Chile provides the European market with Granny Smiths in winter.

To supply commercial demand, apples are kept in cold store in rooms where ozone is circulated to create an artificial storm-like atmosphere, which destroys bacteria and moulds and keeps the apples from rotting or withering.

The apple is the most widely grown and eaten fruit in the world, with total world production of 35,707,000 tonnes in 1979, but the figures vary according to the weather in any given year. For instance, in 1981–2 European apple production rose to 7,138,000 tonnes, and then in 1982–3 fell to 5,212,000 tonnes.

In 1977 four fruits represented 88 per cent of total production in France: apples topped the list with 1,242,520 tonnes, then came peaches (328,790 tonnes), pears (289,810 tonnes) and dessert grapes (209,220 tonnes). In spite of the fruit used in

Table 21.1   Production of Apples in EC Countries, 1982–3 (in thousands of tonnes)

Italy	1773
France	1700
West Germany	1000
The Netherlands	285
The United Kingdom	280
Belgium	116
Denmark	49
Ireland	5
Luxembourg	4
Total	5212

the food-manufacturing industry, the question of surpluses arises, and there are cases every year of stocks having to be destroyed and demonstrations by farmers.

There are three main apple-growing areas in France, the south-east, the south-west, and the Loire valley. Out of these, eight main regions are famous for their apples: Provence, the Loire, central Aquitaine, Languedoc-Roussillon, the South Pyrenees, the Rhône Alps, the Île-de-France and the North.

France does import some apples, though not very many, to supply a demand for varieties not grown at home. These come from Italy – the Italian varieties Abondanza and Imperatore and Canada – and Boskoop and Cox's Orange Pippin come from Belgium and the Netherlands. Britain imports French Golden Delicious, South African or Chilean Granny Smiths, red American apples, and New Zealand Coxes. The difference in the seasons of the southern hemisphere brings apples from Argentina, South Africa, Chile and New Zealand to European supermarkets in late winter.

Apple consumption in the countries of the European Community is not necessarily in line with their own production. Without mentioning particular orchards, and going on commercial data, we may say that an average 17 kilos of apples per inhabitant per year are eaten in France (about 140 fruits per head), mainly in autumn and winter. Most apples are eaten in the Parisian region, particularly the Paris basin; next come the Mediterranean area, the north, the east, the central east, the south-west and the west. The areas where most apples are consumed are apple-producing regions where dessert apples are a part of the local gastronomic tradition. Most Golden Delicious are eaten in areas of high apple consumption, while the other apple varieties are eaten in areas of lower apple consumption.

According to various surveys, 16 per cent of households eat apples for breakfast and 80 per cent eat them in between meals.

The food-manufacturing industry uses a comparatively small proportion of apples, mainly as canned apple compote, apple jelly, in jam with other fruits, for making apple juice and other fruit drinks, and as fruit-pie fillings. Cider is made with special cider apple varieties which are not very good eating, and conversely dessert apples do not make good cider.

Apples, like all fruits, should not be picked too early. Picked green, even if they are left to ripen, they will never have the same nutritional qualities or flavour as if they are picked perfectly ripe.

Fruits should be chosen according to their degree of ripeness, which can be judged by their colour. Another way is to tap the apple lightly near the stem end; if the sound is dull, the fruit is just right, but if it sounds hollow the fruit is over-ripe and will not keep well. The various methods of using apples in cooking make them a wonderful standby for the family menu, for they go well in both sweet and savoury dishes.

Most of the Roman writers on agriculture and domestic economy also mentioned ways of keeping fresh fruit. It might be stored in a cool room (walled with marble in a rich household) in the Greek manner. This storeroom, *oporotheca*, became *pomarium* to Pliny in the first century AD. But the simplest method was to put the fruit in a hermetically sealed container and bury it in a trench or in sand. The container might be an amphora, a vessel coated with pitch on the inside and sealed with wax, but apples in particular, according to Pliny and Columella, were kept in boxes of beech or lime wood. These fruits were left on the tree as late as possible, and then picked with a gentle twist of the stem. There were more elaborate techniques of dipping the apples in wax or clay, or scalding them in sea water (because of its salt and the regenerating magical power of the sea) before they were hung up in the open air. Methods of keeping apples in honey or wine, cooked to strengthen and sweeten it (or in vinegar or garum!) sound as if the end product was more like jam.

As with all fruits, even exotic fruits, the average Roman citizen without a garden of his own could buy apples from the stalls of the fruiterers (*pomarii*) in the market or in the streets; there were plenty of pedlars selling fruit.

These fruits were mainly eaten raw, but seldom as a dessert course, an idea that hardly existed at the time. The fifth course of Trimalchio's banquet included fruits and cakes, perhaps to allow a breathing space before the poultry, game and oysters were served. But a great many recipes included fruit: in dishes sweetened with honey, as preserves, or in savoury recipes and their accompaniments. However, the recipes of Apicius do not mention any vegetable accompaniments to savoury dishes. Instead, there is garum with everything – not an attractive notion to our modern taste. Apicius' recipe for *minutal matianum*,[5] a ragoût of pork, contains apples and, without the fishy seasoning and superfluity of spices, this is a kind of dish still made and eaten, particularly in Northern and Central Europe. The acidity of apples helps the digestion of fat meat such as pork:

> Put into a pan oil, garum, stock, chopped leek and coriander and small quenelles. Cut a leg of pork cooked with its crackling into dice. Cook all together. When the dish is half done add Matian apples cored and cut into pieces. While the ragoût is cooking, pound pepper, cumin, green coriander or coriander seeds, mint and wild carrot root. Moisten this mixture with vinegar, honey, garum, a little cooked wine and stock from the meat in the pan, and work all together with a little vinegar. Bring it to the boil. When it has boiled, thicken it with crumbled pastry, sprinkle with pepper and serve.

Matius, a friend of Caesar, was the author of some famous cookery books, and this may have been one of his recipes. He grew trees as a hobby and had raised a scented golden apple which bore his name. In the Latin text of Apicius which we have, the word for apples is not *mala* but *matiana*, much as we might specify the use of Reinettes, Coxes, Calvilles or Granny Smiths in a recipe. The *matiana* was so highly regarded and so popular that it soon outstripped all other varieties and came to be synonymous with the word 'apple' itself, as might well happen in modern France with the Golden Delicious, even though the variety does not have the outstanding flavour that would account for its huge popularity. The *matiana* may possibly have been the variety later called Court-Pendu. Spanish *manzana* and Portuguese *masa* are evidence of the Iberian pronunciation of *matiana*; the French translator of Apicius, Jacques André, has remarked of the recipe quoted above that the use of the term *matiana* is probably the result of a late revision of the text. It is in studying the whys and wherefores of words that we discover the hows and whens of their recorded use.

The Celts called the apple *aballo*, a word found in the French place-name Avallon, a town of the Yonne area, where there are a great many apple trees, and in the legend of the sacred island of Avalon or Abalon (Ynis Afallach in Welsh), in other words, 'apple orchard'. All European languages other than the Romance languages, i.e., the great majority of Indo-European idioms, including the Celtic tongues, use a word with a root *ap*, *ab*, *af* or *av* for apples and apple trees. They include German *Apfel* and English 'apple', from Old English *aeppel*, Irish *abhal*, Icelandic *epli* and Welsh *afal*. Clearly the common ancestors of all these peoples were familiar with the apple, which had a place of origin and a name in common to them all. The name has lasted, with slight modifications, for thousands of years. In the Slavonic languages, the Russians call it *iablokaa*, the Poles *jablko* and the Hungarians *almaa*. The French, however, forgot the original name of the apple, adopted the word used by their Roman conquerors, and called it *pomme*.

It may be some consolation to French national pride to remember that the Romans were particularly fond of the pale, dappled Reinettes they obtained from Gaul – from Champagne, to be precise – although of course they did not know them by that name; Reinette, as the description of a type of apple, is a word of medieval origin.

With the coming of Christianity and the decline of the Roman Empire, apple trees, like other orchard trees, were preserved as far as possible in the gardens of monasteries. The monks tended them well, and despite the supposed Biblical guilt of the apple, which the religious professionals did not take too seriously, it became and remained part of the celebration of the great festivals of the calendar such as Christmas and All Saints' Day.

It had always in fact been part of such festivities, but now it had the blessing of the Church. In England apples used to be part of the celebrations of Hallowe'en, the old Celtic festival of Samhain. They were picked, eaten, and pressed to make new cider, and what remained of the previous year's cider was drunk, a practice recommended by those good Irishmen St Patrick, St Columba and their missionaries. But rooted as it was in pagan tradition, such revelry came to seem unsuitable to the eve of All Souls' Day, also an invention of the Irish clergy, and the festivities once held on Hallowe'en were moved to 1st August, Lammas Day. The summer was short of occasions for relaxation anyway in those industrious centuries when no one ever had a holiday with pay. Lammastide became the festival of the firstfruits, including corn (the grains of which are its fruit), and was observed as a kind of harvest festival. The word 'Lammas' comes from Old English *hlafmaesse*, and is made up of *hlaf*, loaf, and *maesse*, a festival, as in the religious term 'Mass' for the Eucharist. Nationalist and devolutionist feeling in the Celtic parts of the British Isles has recently tried restoring apples to their old position, and there have been celebrations of Lammas on 1st November for their benefit.

Cider and Calvados

Cider may be said to have existed before it became the drink made from fermented apple juice we know today. *Shekar* in Hebrew meant any intoxicating drink other than wine (which is always specified by name) made by the fermentation of any kind of fruit juice. When the angel announced the conception of John the Baptist to Zacharias, prophesying that 'He shall be great in the sight of the Lord, and shall drink neither wine nor strong drink', the word for 'strong drink' was *shekar*.[6]

The prehistoric lake-dwellers of Switzerland left remains of stored apples that had been cut in half and dried, a method still in use in Central Europe and North America. Did they also crush fresh apples in the same way as they crushed certain berries, filtering the juice through the strainers that have sometimes been taken for cheese drainers? There is no actual evidence to say so.

In any case, crushed fruit must contain sufficient quantities of sugar and water if its juice is to ferment. The fermentation first transforms, then preserves the juice by the action of yeasts; preservation, rather than the making of an intoxicating drink, was its first purpose. When vines spread around the Mediterranean basin, and abundant sweet grape juice was available, wine became the most usual manufactured drink, along with beer. The 'fruit wines' mentioned by Pliny and Dioscorides were fruit macerated in grape juice, and were for medicinal rather than table use. To compensate for the lack of sugar in apple juice, a form of mead was made at the beginning of the period of the Roman Empire, sweetened with honey and using the best apple variety, the *matiana*, but it was nothing like as popular as wine. Pears were an easier proposition: pear juice flows more freely and is sweeter than apple juice, and gives good results without needing any additives. The *sikera* of the Greeks – today the word is used for a genuine cider which has its aficionados – meant the same as Hebrew *shekar* in antiquity, judging by the translation of the books of the Old Testament.

There are no grounds for the theory that the Basques learned to make their *sizra* from Greek colonists, since it was on the east coast of Spain that the Greeks settled. Apples were already plentiful in the north-west of the Iberian peninsula, and the Basques would hardly have needed foreign advice on the use to be made of them. But there does seem to be some truth in the tradition that Basque sailors and fishermen spread the art of cider-making around the sixth century, when they came into contact with the people of that region of Gaul which was to become Normandy, a great apple-growing area.

The Merovingian king Thierry II served *sidre* early in the seventh century at a banquet to which St Columba was invited. *Sidre* was Queen Radegonde's usual drink. We have no way of knowing where it came from, and whether it was made in northern France or exported from Biscay. But in any case, when Normandy obtained its name after it was settled by the Vikings or Northmen, *sydre* was its staple drink. Charlemagne's *Capitularies* mentioned the trade of *sicerator*, cider-maker, among the 'ordinary trades'. William the Conqueror took casks of cider to England with him, and it was to remain a strong competitor to beer in an island poor in vines but rich in apple trees.

After the ninth century, *sidre* began to feature in the dues owed to monasteries and feudal estates north of the Loire and in central France; it is entered among the provisions mentioned in accounts. Peasants drank full-strength cider only on high days and holidays, contenting themselves usually with a *menu bère* ('small drink'), made of the residue of the pressed cider apples steeped in water.

In the thirteenth century cider had a poet, Olivier Basselin, to sing its praises:

> Le bon sidre, en dit-on rien?
> Il vaut bien
> Que quelque chose on en die.
> Et certes qui m'en croiroit.
> On n'auroit
> Autre boire en Normandie ...
>
> ... S'il y a sidre excellent,
> Bien souvent
> On l'aime sur tout breuvage
> Tu es, bon sidre orangé,
> Tout songé,
> Un bon meuble de mesnage.

[Does no one speak of good cider? It is worthy of mention, and indeed you may believe me; they would drink nothing else in Normandy. ... If there is good cider, it is very often preferred to any other drink; good orange-tinted cider, all things considered, you are a good addition to the household.]

In 1589 the Sieur Le Paulmier published in Caen *Le traité du vin et du sidre*, listing the different varieties of apples that gave different flavours to cider. He thought the best was the Cotentin apple. At the end of the last century Truelle's *L'art de reconnaître les fruits du pressoir* listed 360 varieties, including *Peau de Vache* ('cow's skin'), *Rat d'Or* ('golden rat'), *Gros Matois* ('fat slyboots'), *Argile Nouvelle* ('new clay') and *Moulin à Vent*, ('windmill'). In England at the same period, old varieties were being revived, and cider apple varieties now grown include such names as Brown Snout, Taylor's Bitter Sweet and Yarlington Mill.

Contrary to popular belief, cider cannot be made with any kind of apple. A fine dessert apple will produce only an insipid drink which does not keep well. Cider apples, although bitter, contain plenty of sugar, which is masked by the necessary tannin. However, the sugar is essential for a good fermentation. The best varieties have a russet skin. Red cider apples have the strongest scent, and the juiciest can be recognized by their smooth peel. The art of cider-making consists in blending very mellow, very acid and very bitter apples; good cider is never made from one variety alone.

There are six operations involved in making cider:

The apples, after picking, are piled up to ripen further; they are classified according to the time they were picked. The latest, December cider apples, give a cider with a high alcohol content which keeps well. Each kind of apple is roughly broken up in a grinder with blades which extract the pips without crushing them. If crushed they would exude an oil (which can be extracted, and is sometimes to be found in health food shops).

The pulp goes into the press between layers of canvas; straw was formerly used. Each hundredweight of apple pulp gives some 30 litres of juice, which can be sold as plain apple juice, either just as it comes from the press, or filtered and pasteurized.

The pulp is steeped in very pure water for 48 hours to produce a residue which is then pressed again. The operation may be repeated a third time.

The juice from the second pressing is added to the first to get a strong cider which is put into sulphurated barrels. A weaker cider is made if the juice from the third pressing is added.

Fermentation begins in casks with the bung-holes left open. A white froth, the head, shows that fermentation is in progress. At the end of a week the bung is put in. If the cask is left open any longer the cider will turn sour and become cider vinegar.

It is left to rest all winter, and racked periodically. Then it is clarified in the same way as wine.

Cider-making is usually a small-scale business; that is its charm. Early in the twentieth century it was thought a good idea to replace the granite trough and wooden vats by metal, which gave the cider an unpleasant flavour. Today plastic or stainless steel are used, as with wine-making. Cider-lovers will tell you it is not the same thing.

Sparkling cider has been made in the Pays d'Auge since the thirteenth century. Sugar is added to the best of the strong cider, well clarified after long fermentation and with an alcohol content of six to eight degrees. Density rises from 1010 to 1018 after the sugar is added (the density of water being 1000). The cider is put into thick bottles, capped and kept upright. The *champenoise* method can also be applied to cider, although it loses its original fruit flavour in the process. Poorer quality sparkling cider has had carbon dioxide added to it under pressure. The label should say so. In Normandy, natural still cider is preferred, and most lovers of English cider would agree.

France is the biggest cider maker in the world, with most production centred on Normandy and Brittany, although production fell from 2,590,000 tonnes in 1970 to 1,460,000 tonnes at the beginning of the 1980s, showing the effect of a certain slump in sales. (Obviously it is hard to assess the quantities of cider made at home.) Next comes Germany with some excellent *Apfelwein* products, very well made and packaged. Third comes England, with Somerset the traditional cider-making area, famous for its strong, rough cider or 'scrumpy'. Ireland is proud of its own very strong and alcoholic cider. North America, Switzerland, Austria and Luxembourg also produce cider, but the best of all, after 15 centuries, is still the Spanish cider of Asturias, which costs a good deal more than wine and has the delicious perfume of apple blossom.

Calvados is not distilled from the residue of cider apple pulp, which goes back to feed the apple trees; forked in around their feet, it makes an excellent fertilizer, a kind of magical promise of future good harvests. Calvados is made from cider distilled in two stages. The first product, called *petite eau*, is not yet distilled to a very high degree, and goes through the still again to produce a spirit called *blanche* in Normandy. The best of the *blanches*, the *coeur* ('heart'), is aged in oak casks. Almost every Norman landowner makes his own spirit, or has it made by the itinerant distiller, paying the taxes on it – exemption from taxation on Calvados, once hereditary, was abolished on 29 November 1960 'from the death of each of the beneficiaries or their surviving spouses'. The old privilege of making ten litres free of tax was suppressed at the time of the Revolution, re-established under Napoleon by popular demand, and then extended to an amount of 35 litres (of 100-degree-proof spirit!) in 1923. It was largely responsible for the scourge of alcoholism in the west of France, as gin is responsible in the north and schnapps in the east; alcoholism is much less common in wine-growing areas. Consumed in moderation, however, Calvados is an excellent digestive. A glass drunk between the courses of a meal is the famous *trou normand*.

Apples were very popular in the Middle Ages; they were abundant and cheap everywhere. Continuing in the Roman tradition, they were eaten as a 'vegetable', and even in soups, for they adapt easily to either sweet or savoury dishes.

Marianne Mulon has published fourteenth-century apple recipes in her edition of the *Tractatus de modo preparandi et condiendi omnia cibaria* (the *Liber de coquina*). Chapter V, No. 16, is a recipe for a soup of apples cut up small, cooked in meat stock, then pounded and flavoured with saffron and powdered spices before being thickened with flour and enriched with butter or some other fat. The mention of butter is unusual for the period, and indeed extremely surprising if the manuscript really did derive from the Angevin court of Italy. To my mind, however, the combination of butter and apples, which go so well together, suggests that the recipe actually comes from Angers; Anjou is a great apple-growing district.

Another apple-growing centre is Catalonia, where both apples and pears have always featured prominently in the diet. The century of the *Tractatus de modo* was one in which many cookery books were written, including the manuscript of the *Libre del coch*. This work, which Éliane Comelade has studied at the Bibliotheca Torres Amat in Barcelona, was written not in Latin but in medieval Catalan. Under the heading *De pomada* there is a recipe very similar to the one quoted above, this time to be served as a sauce, with a base of apple pulp, ground almonds, chicken broth and such spices as cinnamon, ginger and cloves. We may note in passing that Catalan, disassociating itself from Spanish, says *pome* and not *manzana*.

Apples were also used in medieval Catalonia as an accompaniment, or as a basis for stuffings of meat, poultry and oily fish, to which they make a very good nutritional companion because of their acidity. Modern ideas of 'nouvelle cuisine' are not so new as all that, or not in Catalonia and the Roussillon, where these recipes came from.

Another advantage of apples recognized in the Middle Ages was that an apple eaten after a meal cleaned the teeth. There is still a tradition to that effect, partly true.

The medieval pharmacopoeia made much use of the apple. Its pulp was the vehicle for medicaments applied externally, and for beauty products. It was the origin of the word *pomade*.

When the *Mayflower* landed in America, the first British governor of Massachusetts planted apple trees in an orchard which stretched to the foot of Boston lighthouse. The famous hybrid Canada apples were raised when Norman colonists from Lisieux came to America; they had no intention of doing without their cider. Since then American and Canadian apples have claimed to dictate the world market, for they travel well, although in Western Europe there is a certain swing of opinion back to the old apples with their fine flavours, such as Reinettes and Calvilles in France, while the nineteenth-century Cox's Orange Pippin has never lost its great popularity in the United Kingdom.

In downtown New York the old and notorious but picturesque Bowery occupies the site of the farm (*bouwerie* in Dutch) of Peter Stuyvesant, the last Dutch governor of what was still Nieuw Amsterdam at the time. There was an orchard, planted on land confiscated from the Indians, between Broadway and the East River, on the perimeter marked out by East 15th and 17th streets and First and Third avenues. Stuyvesant boasted that he grafted the first truly American tree here in 1647. No doubt he had wild American stocks available. That historic tree, which was still bearing fruit, was knocked down by the derailed carriage of a train in 1866.

Democratic as they were, apples had a place in King Louis XIV's orchard, and La Quintinie recommends some: 'Among the apples that are good to Eat Raw, or Baked ... I count seven principal sorts ... the Gray-Pippin, the White, or Frank-Pippin, the Autumn Calville, the Fennelles, or Fennell-Apple, the Court-Pendu, or Short-hung, or Short-stalked Apple, the Api and the Violet-Apple.'

'An excellent syrup may be made of Reinette or Court-Pendu apples', wrote

Ambroise Paré. The Reinette type of apple was known in Gaul as early as the first century AD, and returned to favour in the early sixteenth century. Many people believe, with the Littré dictionary, that it should be spelt with an 'a', Rainette, meaning a kind of frog blotched in the same way as the apple. But twentieth-century research has finally settled the question. This delicious apple seems to derive its name from the game of Reinette, a sort of chess played during the Renaissance in which the most important piece was the 'Reinette', literally 'little queen'. Of that other venerable apple the Pomme d'Api, the etymology of whose name we know, La Quintinie remarks:

> The Api, which is in truth, a Right Lady's-apple, and good Company, is known by all the World, as being remarkable for an extraordinary piercing and lively colour. It begins to be good to eat as soon as it has no green left ... which happens pretty often in the Month of December, and then, if I may be permitted so to speak, it requires to be Eaten greedily, at a chop, with its coat all on.

Had there really been an apple in Paradise, La Quintinie would obviously have been the man to describe it.

It would be a shame to think of cooking the pretty Pomme d'Api, and although jams and jellies had continued in favour since the Renaissance in spite of the price of sugar, it is not likely that Mme de Maintenon, who knew as much about household management, that of the royal household included, as La Quintinie did about the government of the garden, had that variety in mind when she wrote to her brother: 'One does not need a quarter for a compote; for the rest, one may arrange a dish of apples and pears which will last a week if a few of the wilted leaves underneath are renewed.'[7] Conspicuous waste was a thing of the past in the closing years of the Sun King's court. The winter of 1709 was a terrible one, reminding people of the famine of 1663, when the starving peasants of the Dauphiné 'were driven to eat the grass of the meadows and the barks of trees', and the winter of January 1692 when 'nearly 70,000 persons in Limousin were reduced to begging and eating half-rotten chestnuts', in Vauban's indignant words. The weather in 1709 was so cold that it even killed the grass. 'I never saw so sad a time in my life', lamented the Princess Palatine. But by then, luckily for La Quintinie, he was no longer there to mourn his beloved espaliers, which froze where they grew despite the care his successors lavished on them.

Pears

La Quintinie had a weakness for pears, and so did his King. The gardener speaks of them lovingly. Pears had been popular with gourmets for a very long time. 'Graft thy pears, Daphnis; thy children's children shall gather fruits of thine', sang

Virgil.[8] The Romans tended their pear trees with particular care. The pear grew in all their gardens, and they liked to see:

> Le poirier en buisson, courbé sous son trésor
> Sur le gazon jauni roule des globes d'or . . .

[The bush pear tree, bending under its treasure, cast its golden globes on the yellowing turf . . .]

Another native of the Middle East and the sub-Alpine zones of Kashmir, the pear tree grows wild in all the temperate regions of Europe and of western and central Asia. But the fruits of the wild pear are so tiny and so few, for it does not blossom profusely, that you need to look very hard for them. Taken in hand by man, however, improved by forcing and successive grafts, it produced many different varieties, distinguished from each other by the size, shape and succulence of the fruit.

The Greeks, Hebrews and Egyptians do not seem to have been familiar with the pear, but Cato the Elder enumerated six varieties. Under the Roman Empire the number rose to the 40 or so listed by Pliny and then to 60. In his list Pliny mentioned the *pirum libralium* which weighed a pound (in the seventeenth century La Quintinie was to grow pears weighing a kilo). The Roman pound was under 500 grams, but all the same this must have been a magnificent fruit, for patrician tables only. The Romans ate pears, like apples, both raw and cooked. The less exquisite fruits were made into perry, or into pear vinegar, for which Pliny, Varro, Columella and the other Roman authors on such subjects all had their own recipes. The Byzantines feasted on pears in jelly, pear preserves, pears cooked in wine or in oxymel (a syrup of vinegar and honey).

The Romans spread the cultivation of the pear. As evidence of that fact, all languages have retained the Latin name, with the usual distortions caused by different accents. At this point I should mention that in the Low Latin of the fifth century the plural of *pirum*, pear, which was *pira*, pears, turned into a feminine singular noun, *pira*. The same thing had happened to the apple when it became *the* fruit (*pomum* becoming *poma*) and the plum, which turned from *prunum* to *pruna*.

The Middle Ages seem to have been content with half a dozen pears descended from the most widely grown of the many Roman varieties. The Caillou pear of Burgundy, although a hard fruit which had to be cooked, was popular in England, where King Henry III's gardener planted a number. Another hard pear was the Poire d'Angoisse, mentioned figuratively by Rabelais, originally a very nasty instrument of torture. Semantic confusion was involved when it also became the name of a hard, sharp-tasting pear. *Angoisse*, 'anguish', meant a constriction of the throat, from Latin *angustus*, narrow, before its meaning became more general as one of the signs of extreme apprehension. But Angoisse is also the name of a village in the Dordogne where a grower succeeded, if that is the word, in raising a pear as hard as a stone (the literal meaning of the name of the Caillou), which could only be eaten well cooked; it was said to resemble a turnip.

The best medieval pears were the Hastibeau (an early pear), the Saint-Rieul, and above all the famous Bon Chrétien, ancestor of today's Williams, which Louis XI was extremely anxious to eat, although he did not live long enough to do so.

Some people, like La Quintinie, who thought the winter Bon Chrétien was 'justly preferred before all others', claimed that it dated back to Roman times, and was supposed to have been part of the tribute paid to the masters of the world. Others say that the Bon Chrétien dates from the times of the barbarian invasions and was brought to Poitou from Hungary by St Martin. But in fact the 'Good Christian' was St Francis of Paola, who was summoned by Louis XI to his royal residence of Plessis-lez-Tours; the King had been urging Pope Sixtus IV for years to persuade the Calabrian hermit to leave the retreat near Naples where he spent his life in quiet meditation, surrounded by those other good Christians his disciples.[9]

The King suffered from eczema and internal disorders, all of them stubbornly resistant to any treatment his doctor, Maître Cottier, could offer. Louis, in pursuit of the divine mercy, hoped that the 'Bon Chrétien', who was credited with many miracles, could cure him. When Francis of Paola eventually arrived at Plessis-lez-Tours in the summer of 1482, the story goes that he gave the King a small pear tree brought from Italy, and advised him to tend it until it bore fruit. He had seen that the King's mind above all was sick (and much later, research has confirmed that if a sick person has a plant or an animal to care for, it can help him to shake off certain mental disorders).

There was a tale that Louis XI had described the gibbets used for hanging men convicted under the royal laws as his garden, but in fact he was something of a thwarted countryman, and had a real and very fine orchard in a corner of the park not far from his menagerie, which he supervised with care. Delighted with the present, he waited impatiently for a whole year for the Good Christian's tree, having taken root in its new home, to produce the pears which, if picked on St Martin's Day, would make a compote to work wonders for digestive disorders, particularly if they were gently cooked in an earthenware pot plunged in the embers, with rosewater, honey and spices, the method recommended by Taillevent.

Hope is a stimulant, and the King managed to bear his troubles until autumn was approaching. Then, one morning, his inspection of the orchard ended in drama. There were only eight left of the ten pears, still green, that the little tree was bearing. The thief was none other than the Dauphin, for the daily diet of the royal family was so meagre that the poor lad was hungry. No doubt the future Charles VIII was soundly thrashed. But King Louis XI never did taste his pears gently cooked with rosewater and honey. 'He died on the last Saturday but one of August 1483, at eight o'clock in the evening, at the said Plessis where his sickness had overcome him the previous Monday. May our Lord receive him in his kingdom of paradise. Amen', wrote Philippe de Commines.

Such is the story of the Bon Chrétien pear, and since the apple has so many stories attached to it, the pear surely deserves at least one.

Other pears very popular in the sixteenth century, when they were thought the best fruit of all, were the Louise-Bonne, 'from the land of the Essarts, the lady of which was named Louise', the Muscat, the Colmar, the Bergamotte or Martin-Sec, the Frangipane, the Cuisse-Madame and the Virgouleuse or Virgoulé of Limousin, the most widely grown in all the gardens of Europe according to La Quintinie, who recorded the names of a hundred in a list which sings like a nursery rhyme. A very famous English cooking pear was the Warden, first mentioned by Alexander Neckham in the twelfth century, from which the popular dishes of baked Wardens and Warden pies were made.

There are even more varieties today, but commercial requirements have selected only a dozen or so to be grown for the market. The others are hidden away in old orchards or vicarage gardens. There is in fact a pear called the Poire du Curé, but it will not be found for sale in the markets or shops.

The earliest of the summer pears, the small Saint-Jean, is seldom seen now, and then only in country areas. However, the Guyot and Williams are picked in August, and are sweet and juicy. The big golden, melting Williams was raised in Great Britain around 1796 from the Bon Chrétien, which is a winter pear. It is the only variety commercially grown on a large scale in France (occupying 23 per cent of pear orchard area), and it is suitable for preserving and distilling (it makes a delicious fruit spirit, Williamine). The Americans, who call it the Bartlett pear, grow millions for the canning industry.

Autumn brings the Beurré Hardy, with a season lasting until mid-November, and the ever-faithful, mellow Louise-Bonne. The Doyenné du Comice, formerly La Quintinie's Doyenné, keeps well and can still be bought in early January.

Winter pears, picked in late autumn, are kept in cold store today, in an ozone-laden atmosphere. The most widely distributed are the Conference, with its pretty pink flesh, and the Passe-Crassane, which is white and melting – unless it has been picked too green and turned grainy. It was raised in Rouen in 1845, and was first grown in the Rhône valley and in Italy. The curious intricacies of foreign trade mean that the French now export about the same amount of these pears to the Benelux countries as they import from the Italian peninsula.

The Passe-Crassane, known as Passacrassana when it comes from Italy, is a fine example of arboricultural success, for it is grafted on quince stocks. In France the stocks used are either Angers quinces, which were brought into use by the nurserymen of Angers in the first half of the nineteenth century, or Provence quinces, which came into use around 1930 and come from the region of Mount Ventoux and the right bank of the Rhône. They are hardier than the Angers quince stocks.

It takes some time for the Passe-Crassane pear to begin fruiting well; it bears regularly and abundantly after eight to ten years. The tree is of medium vigour, and needs a soil which will keep cool in summer. It tolerates lime quite well, and is not too susceptible to spring frosts. The pollination of an orchard of Passe-Crassane pears is encouraged by planting a row of a pollinating variety such as Williams, Beurré Hardy or Conference to every five rows of Passe-Crassanes. These varieties encourage fertilization. Rich, deep soils are necessary for good fruit, and the pear will not tolerate drought-induced disruptions of its vegetative cycle. The fruits are large or very large, with a thick, rough and not very waxy skin. They are yellowish green in colour, and by the time they are picked they sometimes have a bronzed look derived from the quince stocks on which they are grafted. When the pear is fully ripe it turns yellow.

Plums

In the middle of the nineteenth century, the ideal of beauty was to have a heart-shaped mouth, as a glance at the engravings of the period will confirm. Even Chateaubriand is not spared! Young ladies learning deportment were taught a little rhyme intended to compress the lips in youth and prevent wrinkles later. It went 'Pomme, poire, prune, pêche, pomme, poire, prune, pêche ...', repeated several dozen times.

Having tasted apples and pears, the first two fruits of the rhyme, we now come to plums, and peaches will follow. Not all plums are called 'plums' when you buy them: they may go simply by their variety names, like the Czar or the Victoria, both raised in the nineteenth century. Greengages are called after the eighteenth-century Sir William Gage, who brought the French Reine-Claude over to England, where it acquired a new English name. There is also the small yellow Mirabelle plum, and the dark Quetsche. Dried plums, of course, are available all the year round, and in England go by the French word for a fresh plum, *prune*, whereas the French for prune is *pruneau*.

Plum trees are always obtained by grafting. Raising plum trees from stones gives nothing but stocks reverting to the wild, prickly blackthorn with its sour sloes, which has grown wild in the forests of western Asia for thousands of years and is a familiar hedgerow plant in Britain.

Plums were known in Egypt; prunes have been found among the provisions for the afterlife stored in the tomb of Kha, the architect of Thebes. The trees spread through most of Europe, perhaps during the ancient invasions of the twenty-second century BC (judging by the dating of the first fossil plumstones showing signs of improvement), or perhaps they were spread by birds. The wild plum was known to the Etruscans. Following Cato, Pliny speaks of the cultivation of the *ingens turba prunorum*, the 'great crowd of plums' which was the glory of Roman orchards. According to Jacques André's dictionary of botanical terms in Latin,[10] the 'great crowd' could actually be reduced to a dozen varieties, and of that number – taking from Caesar the things which are not Caesar's – Syria or more precisely Damascus must be credited with the *Prunum damascenum*, the damask plum or damson, which

Dioscorides thought was so good for the stomach dried.[11] The laxative virtues of prunes have long been celebrated. The poet Martial, not always given to symbolism, agreed: 'Frigida sunt, laxant, multum prosunt tibi pruna' ('Plums are cold, relaxing to the stomach, and very good for you').

According to Galen, Spanish prunes were even better, and we may wonder whether the Iberians of Catalonia, where many fruit trees are still grown, had not improved the wild plums of the Phoenician and Greek colonies without waiting for enlightenment from the Romans. Although most of Western Europe remembers the Latin name of *prunum*, later *pruna*, in the names of the fruit – English plum, German *Pflaume*, Italian *prugna* – Spain is the odd one out with *ciruela*, which suggests *cereza*, the cherry, *kerasion* to the Greeks. (I shall come to the false etymology for the cherry provided by the Romans below.) Curiously the Slavs remember the wild plum or the sloe of the woods, the literal meaning of its Greek name, in their terms for the plum: the Russians call it *sliva*, the Poles *sliwka*, and the Hungarians *szilva*.

It used to be claimed that of the highly regarded plums of France in the Middle Ages the dark-skinned 'damask plums' of Tours and Brignoles, the kind now used for making prunes, were brought back from Syria by the Angevin counts; as we have seen, they were already known in Europe. But perhaps the Angevins did bring some back to regenerate the variety.

When the Renaissance came, plums had a part to play in the history of France. One famous variety keeps alive the memory of poor Queen Claude, wife of the magnificent François I, a 'humble flower beside the royal oak', in the words of André Castelot,[12] who also tells us that she was 'far from pretty, but so good, kind and sweet that the naturalist François Belon thought of her at once when he needed a name for the plum he had brought back from the East to be naturalised in Touraine'. Belon, whose name was really Pierre and not François, was a great traveller, but this is no way to write history, even the history of plums. We should do better to believe Merlet,[13] writing in the seventeenth century and describing the Reine-Claude as 'a kind of white damascus plum, round, somewhat flattened and squarish in shape, with a very firm, thick flesh coming clean away from the stone, and one of the sweetest and best of plums; it is highly regarded and much sought after.'

Cooked, the purple plum of Brignoles in the Var was also 'highly regarded' by the French royal family; it was therefore called the *prune de Monsieur*, perpetuating the name of Gaston d'Orléans, the Sun King's brother, who was particularly fond of it. Blois, the town to which that gentleman was exiled when he over-stepped the mark, had already given the plum a walk-on part in a tragedy.

It took place early on the morning of Christmas Eve 1588, when the Duc de Guise came to the meeting-place appointed by Henri III, who planned to have him assassinated. De Guise had not had time to dine. Waiting to be shown into the 'Cabinet Vieux', de Guise felt faint, and told his secretary to go and find a comfit-box containing crystallized grapes, the kind of 'chamber spice' which became a sweetmeat, as described in chapter 15. The secretary was intercepted by the

King's men and failed to return, removed by Fate from the side of his master, who could soon have done with his aid. Feeling extremely uneasy and apprehensive, the Duke then insisted that the King's valet, whose unexpected presence seemed strange, should go and fetch some of the preserved Brignoles plums that Henri III always kept beside his bed in the royal apartments next door. When they had at last been brought to him, he made his way unsteadily towards the King's own bedroom, which Henri had left, and down a small passage leading to the 'Cabinet Vieux'. The preserved plums had not had time to restore de Guise's strength (he must actually have been suffering from hypoglycaemia) by the time he walked straight into a trap and was killed by the assassins posted there. Having thus settled accounts with the head of the Ligue (formed to promote the Roman Catholic religion), Henri went to his mother and announced, 'I am King of France now; I have killed the King of Paris!'

If Henri de Guise had not been literally dying for those plums, but had eaten them at his leisure, he might have been able to put up a better defence.

The plums used for drying, having come from Damascus to Tours and Brignoles, ended up in Agen: Agen prunes are the very best sort. For a while the plum was called in French 'robe de sergent', sergeant's coat, its colour being that of the uniform worn by police officers before 1789. Fittingly enough, since its oval shape is very like that of a rugby ball, it chose as its new home the south-west of France, where a great deal of rugby football is played. It is not very juicy, but has a high sugar content. It was initially grown in Aquitaine solely to be dried and make prunes.

The Agen plum grown all over western France is not picked; the trees have to be shaken. The fallen fruits are then sorted on the cloths that have been spread under the trees. Before they ripen the plums have already been thinned on the tree to give really large fruits. The comparatively few plums left can then use all the sap of the tree for themselves. Once the plums are gathered they are put to dry on wattles for several days, and are turned frequently. They are then taken to an oven – it used to be the local baker's oven; they were put in after the bread had finished baking and when the heat had fallen to 90 degrees, and left overnight (today, special ovens are used). Next day they are turned and put into a kiln at a higher temperature to sterilize them. The operation is repeated a second time. In the past these very superior prunes used to be arranged between two rows of bay leaves in their wooden boxes. Stoned Agen prunes, stuffed with prune paste flavoured with plum spirit, are a great delicacy.

After the Algerian war many of the former French colonials who returned to France started growing plums for prunes, and the south-west of France became their new home; they brought their North African agricultural knowledge and expertise with them. However, at the end of the 1970s French prunes found themselves in competition with the enormous prunes of California, much less expensive and always available in large quantities.

The Quetsche, the pride of Alsace, is a delicious plum. Elongated, like the Agen plum, it is juicier and fragrant. The true Alsatian Quetsche, when bought in France, should have its place of origin specified on its packaging. If it is anonymous, it may well come from Italy, where the variety has much less flavour, scent and sugar. It was raised after the war from an American hybrid, like the first early yellow or purple plums now obtainable, and is now pouring into the European market from the orchards of Romagna and Sicily. There is also a false Quetsche, the Anna Spath of Romania.

The word Quetsche, from German *Zwetsche* or dialect *Quetsche*, was included in French dictionaries only on the eve of the 1870 Franco-Prussian war, in which France lost Alsace.

It is not far from Alsace to Lorraine (which the French also lost to Prussia for a while), and the Mirabelles of Nancy. The name is from 'myrobolan', ultimately deriving from Greek *muron*, unguent, and *balanos*, acorn. The tree bears a large crop of small, deep golden plums with a fine perfume which should be savoured before they are actually eaten. They impart that perfume to the spirit made from them, which has been known since the sixteenth century. Mirabelles make a softer and more full-bodied liqueur than the spirit made from the Quetsche. In Alsace, Lorraine and West Germany it is usual to put the fallen plums into a cask, for the ripest of them (which the wasps like too if they can get them) also make a kind of schnapps which can be given body by the addition of other orchard fruits, and is very good indeed.

To avoid disappointment, all plums should be carefully chosen. They should be covered with a faint dusting of white, the bloom. And if you pass your hand above a heap of plums without touching them (for if you touch them the bloom will disappear), they should give off a certain coolness as they transpire, even in hot weather, for they are still alive. If they have to wait too long they will give up the ghost and become soft and insipid.

Peaches

'The vermilion peach proudly displays its downy crimson to my delighted eye', announces the caption to an Edwardian postcard, where a peach and a pretty girl are shown cheek to cheek, inviting admiration. The Chinese, the first to know the peach in the third millennium, venerated it and still do. The peach tree is regarded as magical, and its blossom is the symbol of virginity.

Before it arrived in Europe and then, much later, went on to America, the peach had crossed Persia, spending quite a long time there acquiring new qualities and a new name. When it reached the Romans in the time of Augustus, they called it *malum persicum*, Persian apple. The *persicum* then became *pessicum*, *pessica* and *pesca*. In modern Russian, it is still *piersika*. The Italians have retained the term *pesca*, and it has become 'peach' in English, *pêche* in French, and *Pfirsich* in German. Yet again the Spanish differ from the rest of Europe with *melocoton*, suggesting a downy-skinned apple.

In the first years of the present era Pliny mentions several varieties, complaining that they have more juice than flavour. A fresco from Herculaneum of this period, now in the Museum of Naples, shows peaches. One of them has just had a bite taken out of it, and is showing its crimson kernel, with a glass carafe half full of water beside it. Pliny said that although it was very watery, the peach induced thirst. Archeological excavations have shown that peaches were being cultivated in southern Germany at about the same period.

The delicate fruit was a rarity for quite a long time, judging by the poetry of a curious sixth-century character, the Italian priest Venantius Fortunatus, who gives the lie to the saying about digging one's grave with one's teeth, for he died, replete, at 80, which was a great age for his time. His verse, although mediocre, provides valuable information about Frankish gastronomy. An accredited sponger on the courts of Chilperic and Clotaire, Fortunatus was chaplain to Queen Radegonde, and clearly thought it advisable to know what he was talking about when he spoke of the sin of gluttony; he devoted himself to its study so zealously that he may be considered one of the greatest gluttons of all time. The meals to which he was invited and the gastronomic gifts he received inspired his grateful pen, but unlike the Muse of the kindly and fastidious Ausonius, his must surely have been named Indigestion, in tune with the barbarous times.

The dessert at a sumptuous banquet given at Soissons by one Mummolenus made an unforgettable impression on Fortunatus.

> First I was given those sweet fruits the common people call peaches; they never tired of serving them to me, and I never tired of eating them; soon my stomach was distended like that of a woman about to give birth; I wondered how it was that I could stretch so far. Thunder growled and rolled within me, wandering in my entrails. There was great wind.

Peach trees, mentioned in Charlemagne's *Capitularies*, were grown as standards until the ancient Chinese espalier method was rediscovered in the Renaissance. The Chinese claimed to have invented it especially for the peach tree. They had also noticed that the fruits thus grown were even better if the wall against which the trees stood was painted white to cast back the warmth and light of the sun.

The contemporaries of François I grew at least 40 different kinds of peach with delightful names that often had connotations of femininity: Téton de Vénus (nipple of Venus), Admirable, Belle de Chevreuse, Belle de Vitry, to name but a few.

The gardens of the Île-de-France produced outstanding peaches; in those days Paris was the shrine of gastronomy. There were peaches of Fontainebleau and Bagnolet, of Chevreuse and Vitry. Legend has it that a retired musketeer, who had taken up farming in Bagnolet early in the reign of Louis XIV, thought of growing peaches as espaliers against a white wall because there was not enough space for the trees in his garden. The 'Girardot walls', as they were called, enabled the old soldier to pick his peaches earlier than anyone else – magnificent peaches which fetched a very high price. In the time of Louis XV, however, without reference to the Chinese precedent discovered later, the people of Montreuil and their parish priest the Abbé Schabol began protesting loudly that the growing of peaches as espaliers was their own invention, and the method had long been a professional secret of theirs. Of course there *are* no secrets in agriculture; such things will always be rediscovered.

La Quintinie certainly knew about growing espaliers, and although he wanted his orchards to be productive he also insisted on

> the Idea of Beauty which Wall-Trees require. ... To advance our Wall-Trees to that perfection of Beauty which best becomes them, I am of Opinion, that it must be our particular Care, that all the Branches of each Tree, in spreading over the sides of that part of the Wall which they are to garnish, must be so well stretch'd, and so equally plac'd, both on the right and left; that in their whole extent, taking them from the place, whence they severally proceed, as far as all the extremities of their height and roundness, no part of the Tree may appear thinner or fuller than another; in so much, that at first sight, one may distinctly see all the Branches that compose it, so far as to be able, to tell them with ease, if so minded.

La Quintinie wanted the many peaches from his beautifully trained espaliers, and indeed all his other fruits, to be properly appreciated:

> This Excellence further appears when we cut a Peach with the Knife, which is, in my Opinion the first thing to be done to them at Table, by any one that would eat them delightfully, and with a true relish, and then we may see all along where the Knife has past, as 'twere an infinite number of little Springs, which are methinks, the prettiest things in the World to look upon.

La Quintinie, like the Japanese, great growers and eaters of peaches, liked the pleasure of the eye to supplement the pleasures of the table, and indeed intellectual pleasure too. There can be real poetry in a fruit, as Andrew Marvell knew in writing of 'the nectarine and curious peach'.

The peach is a tree which is best grafted on almond or plum stock grown from seed; it is a member of the Rosaceae family. But one variety of clingstone peach, the *pêche de vigne*, reproduces true to type. The peach tree lives 15 to 18 years, and is never very hardy. Yield varies considerably depending on the age of the trees. They usually bear best from 4 to 12 years old.

The peach is the typical fruit of summer. In July and August peaches account for over one-third of all the fresh fruit eaten. Up to the end of the last century, however, before the advent of refrigerated rail transport, southern Mediterranean fruits as perishable as peaches seldom travelled either far or well. This explains the importance of the old peach orchards of the Paris region. The orchards have mostly been built over now, but in any case they could no longer compete with peaches from the South of France, Spain or Italy, where there is enough sun to ripen the fruit two months earlier. For all the espaliers and the skill of the nurserymen, peaches used not to be available in Paris and Versailles until the end of summer. La Quintinie classes them among September fruits.

> It is the true Month for good Peaches, there being every where such an extream Abundance of them, that they are served up in no lesser Quantities than by great Pyramids at every Meal ... every one Ripening, regularly, according to the Order of Maturity that Nature has establish'd among them, and that, without doubt, with a particular intent that they should be able to furnish with a sufficient and successive store, all the parts of the whole Month.

There are two main groups of peach varieties: white-fleshed peaches, which account for about 30 per cent of production, and yellow-fleshed peaches, accounting for the other 70 per cent. Peach production as a whole has now stabilized after a period of rapid growth.

The white-fleshed varieties are earlier, and most of them ripen in June. They make up only 10 to 15 per cent of sales in July and August. They are thin-skinned, juicy and succulent, but they do not travel well; they do not like refrigeration, and still less does the heat of the market-place suit them.

The yellow-fleshed varieties, of American origin, yield a bigger crop than the white-fleshed kinds, and are less fragile to transport and market. In fact they now tend to flood the market, and flavour is increasingly sacrificed to resilience and good looks.

There are several hundred peach varieties at present. They are usually classified according to the colour of their flesh, the nature of their kernels (clingstone or freestone), the appearance of their skin and their time of ripening.

The downy-skinned peaches, either white or yellow-fleshed, and the smooth-skinned nectarines are both very good eaten fresh. Nectarines are not grown quite as widely as peaches, but production is increasing, for the fruit seems to be in fashion – a fashion stimulated by supply. Nectarines may be clingstone or freestone, like peaches, and have smooth, shiny, prettily coloured skin. There are both white-fleshed and yellow-fleshed nectarines, the latter in a clear majority.

Until 1964 all peaches used for canning were dual-purpose (for eating fresh or preserving in cans), and they were always yellow-fleshed freestone varieties. Today clingstone peaches of the variety called Pavie, with a firm yellow flesh, are used.

Pavie is a very old peach, for La Quintinie mentions it, and it has now been revived for the food manufacturing industry. Pavie peaches of Spanish origin predominate.

In France, unlike Italy, Spain and in particular the United States, the market for canned peaches is quite small, absorbing hardly more than 5 per cent of the fresh crop, all the Pavie peaches grown in the country. It is difficult, therefore, for the market to absorb any surplus. Peach jam, except as home-made peach and apple jam, has never been very successful. The other possible outlets for peaches in food manufacturing are as bottled fruit in syrup or natural juice, and as peach pulp to make sorbets.

The Peach in Legend

China and Japan still celebrate the blossoming of the peach tree as a sign and symbol of spring, the season of renewal and growth. Brides in those countries wear wreaths of peach blossom as Western brides wear orange blossom; it still symbolizes virginity and fertility.

Growing from so beneficent a flower, the peach is supposed to provide protection from lightning, and most important of all from evil spirits. The royal sceptre was made of peach wood, and was a magic wand that could be used in exorcisms.

Even better than any terrestrial peach tree, however, was the wonderful tree belonging to Siwang Mou, the Royal Mother, which was said to grow west of western China. It bore fruit only once in 3000 years, and its sap made the body of anyone who touched it luminous. In contemplating its flowers, upon which the immortals fed once in every 30 centuries, the monk Ling Yun received enlightenment, which was even better. This tree was none other than the Tree of Life, carrying those who reached the centre of the Great Whole back to the origin of Knowledge. For this reason the ki-pi, a double stylus lacquered red and used to trace the characters of oracles, is made entirely of peach wood.

The peach tree of the Garden of Immortality is vast. It takes a thousand men holding hands to encircle it. At the first fork in its branches an invisible gate opens, and the spirits of the dead can slip out. The guardians of this gate let only souls of good-will pass them. The others are seized and thrown to the tigers. However, it sometimes happens that ill-disposed ghosts, swifter or more cunning than their fellows, manage to get past and descend to human habitations, where they enter to torment people. The Emperor Huang-ti, tired of hearing complaints, finally ordered the shapes of the guardians be painted or carved on door lintels of peach wood. Since then the importunate ghosts have turned back, tongues hanging out, forced to return to their own place where they tirelessly await a chance to try again, hoping someone will forget to take precautions.

Apricots

The apricot is a delicious fruit, but one with surprises in store. The fruit is as temperamental as its tree, and still answers to a false name. It was thought for so long that apricots were a kind of plum and came from Armenia that botanists continue to follow Linnaeus in calling it *Prunus armeniaca*. It is a member of the Rosaceae family.

The apricot really comes from China, like the peach, and it too has a history going back 5000 years there. Five thousand years of domestication, however, have not entirely tamed it. It spread from China to northern India, the Punjab and Tibet, where it will ripen perfectly on sunny slopes up to altitudes of 3000 metres. Why, then, is it such an unreliable cropper in our temperate regions, to the despair of nurserymen? In principle, a fruit tree should bear well at least one year out of two, but this ancient mountain-dweller is coy, and a late frost or a strong wind can destroy all hope of the blossom which, admittedly, is very early. However, the apricot quite likes the Mediterranean climate, particularly in the Roussillon area.

Another enemy of the apricot tree, which likes limy and even stony soil, is drought, which can undo the grafting of the tree in a single night, giving it a fatal seizure which shrivels it up within a few days. It will not accept any ordinary fertilizer or manure either. The volume of fertilizer must be carefully adjusted, and it has to be right for the nature of the soil, determined after chemical analysis which may show different results from year to year.

Even the name of the apricot, which in French was *aubercot* until the fifteenth century, has not just one simple etymology but is a combination of several, involving considerable juxtaposition of ideas. On the one hand we have Portuguese *albricoque*, Spanish *albaricoque* and Italian *albicocca*, all from Arabic *al barqouq* or *al birqûq*, for the Iberian peninsula owed much to the Arab gardeners of Andalusia. The Arabic word means 'early-ripe', and itself derives from Latin *praecox* or *praecoquum malum* (in Greek, *praecoxon*), an early-ripening fruit, the name the Romans gave the apricot when it was brought back by legionaries returning from the Near East in the first century. Being easy to eat, it was also called *aperitum* (fruit which opens easily), and there is an association with Greek *abros*, delicate, for it does not travel well and ripens very fast. The idea that there was a connection with Latin *apricus*, ripe, may have given rise to the 'p' in English 'apricot', which combines with the French *-cot* ending. The fruit is *Aprikose* to the Germans and *abrikos* to the Russians. But all these roads lead to Rome, whence the apricot spread through Europe.

The apricot thus gives trouble to linguists and growers alike. But in 1978 the growers of the Roussillon area decided to take it on, and they seem to be winning, at least in the market for fresh fruits. They decided, after a number of miscalculations, that disappointment was the result of growing sophisticated varieties from over-developed grafts, poorly adapted to regional soils and climates and showing too little affinity with the almond, peach or plum stocks on which they were grown.

In the past, when a faultless appearance was not so essential, brightly coloured, juicy little Bulida apricots were abundant in France from Midsummer to Assumption Day. The Roussillon growers decided that such apricots must be replanted if they hoped to reconquer and above all maintain a market, and went ahead with the project.

The huge apricots found in the shops in June, weighing up to 70 grams each, are exactly the same whether they come from Spain, Italy or California: floury and pale yellow. At the end of July the Gros Rouge apricot of Rivesaltes comes on the market; despite its name, it is not very red, and nor is it juicy. It is better to buy the Polonais or Bergeron apricots of Provence, a rosy orange in colour, well perfumed and juicy.

By common consent, however, the best of all are the enormous Turkish and Greek apricots, muscat-flavoured and very dark in colour, called *malatya* or *urgub*. They are to be found fresh only in very exclusive luxury shops, and at such steep prices that they have helped to boost the market for the best of the French apricots. These oriental apricots are destined mainly to make dried or crystallized apricots for their home markets, and Middle Eastern grocers' shops sell them from the crate; they are so sweet that they seem to have been crystallized when they are merely dried. They are much used by confectioners. The pale yellow dried apricots of Iran, Australia and California are cheaper, but still expensive. Their size accounts for a price not justified by their insipid and rather acid flavour.

Unfortunately all dried apricots (there are none from France, since French apricots are unsuitable for processing) contain a great deal of sulphur dioxide. They have been treated with sulphur as a precaution against insects before being dried in the sun. The label will say that preservative E22 is added. If you were to eat too many you could get headaches and digestive troubles, and they would certainly be bad for your figure: 100 grams (two Turkish apricots) contain 250 calories which are not usually a necessary addition to the diet.

The Dietetics of Apricots

The writer Fontenelle, a nephew of Corneille and a member of the Royal Society of London as well as the Académie Française, lived to be 100. He ascribed his longevity to certain precepts passed on by his grandmother, 'a woman of an orderly mind who never confused reality with mere show'. One of these precepts was to eat plenty of apricots, fresh, dried or as a preserve: 'a royal fruit, she called it, saying that the scatter-brained folk of our days ought to make more use of it.'

The golden fruit is indeed good for the intellect, since it is rich in mineral salts including phosphorus and magnesium. Professor Delbet has published studies showing that the apricot can develop the faculty of memory efficiently and indeed in quite a spectacular manner, and it also rapidly increases the red blood corpuscle count.

The apricot is richer than any other fruit in carotene, or provitamin A, which gives it its beautiful orange colour. The carotene content is especially high when the fruit is ripe, fresh, and of a dark-coloured variety; 100 grams of apricots contain 2790 IU, almost half the daily ration an adult needs. In other words, it is good for growth (babies seldom eat enough apricots), hastens the formation of scar tissue, counters anaemia just as efficiently as calves' liver (and without any risk that one is also absorbing hormones or sulphamides), and improves vision. The vitamin C it contains (5 to 10 milligrams per 100 grams) provides energy and helps to fight off infections. It is a surprising fact that more of the vitamin is present in canned apricots made with fresh fruit picked ripe than in raw fruit which has been picked unripe and too long before it is eaten, and has often been kept in cold store.

Professor Delbet also points out that apricots contain valuable mineral salts and trace elements, including magnesium, phosphorus, calcium, potassium, sodium, sulphur, manganese – and fluoride, for healthy teeth.

Cherries

The wild cherry is a cousin of the plum. *Prunus avium*, also known as mazzard or gean, is a native of Europe as well as of the Middle East. Our Neolithic ancestors knew it, and pressed its fruits to extract their juice before the invention of wine made from grapes.

Athenaeus, in Book II of the *Deipnosophistai*, quotes an extract from Theophrastus' treatise on plants. In the fourth century BC, Theophrastus had said:

> The *kerasos* [cherry] is a tree of peculiar character and large growth; it even attains a height of 24 cubits.[14] Its leaf is similar to that of the medlar, but is tough and broader; its bark is like the linden's, the blossom is white, resembling the pear and the medlar, composed of tiny flowers, and waxy.[15] The fruit is red ... in size like a bean ... but the stone of the cherry is brittle.

In the discussion of these literary references around the table which serves as the pretext for Athenaeus' book, a Roman called Larensis[16] intervenes.

> There are many things which you Greeks have appropriated, as if you had given them names or were the first to discover them; but you are unaware that Lucullus, the Roman general who conquered Mithridates and Tigranes,[17] was the first to import into Italy this tree from Cerasus, a city in Pontus.[18] And he is the one who called the fruit *cerasus* from the name of the city, as our Roman historians record.
>
> But a certain Daphnos[19] contradicted him: Why! Many years before Lucullus, a man of note, Diphilos of Siphnos,[20] who flourished in the time of King Lysimachus, one of Alexander's successors, mentioned cherries in these words: 'Cherries are wholesome, juicy, but afford little

650

nourishment; they are especially wholesome when eaten uncooked. The red Milesian varieties are superior, being diuretic.'

The argument has continued ever since. Pliny, like a good Roman, backed Lucullus, a famous epicure as well as a general. And there is much to be said for his compatriots: beginning with Pliny's grandfather, they improved existing varieties of cherry, and soon had kinds producing red, black and parti-coloured fruits. Modern botanists have finally distinguished the origins of the cherry. The wild sweet cherry, *Prunus avium*, was the ancestor of today's sweet cherries, which fall into two groups. One, the Bigarreau group, has firm, crisp fruits with colourless juice, and includes the Burlat, the Marmotte and the Napoleon, the last-named raised in the nineteenth century. The other is the Guignes or Geans, with soft flesh and dark juice, and includes the Hâtif de Céret and the Early Rivers, the best of the June cherries. However, sour cherries, the dark Morellos and the red Amarelles or Griottes, which make the best cherry jam, are descended from *Prunus cerasus*.

At the end of the Middle Ages, when cherries became very popular in France, Germany and England alike, growers in the region of Montmorency, where many cherry orchards had been planted, tried bringing the fruit on early by painting the foot of the tree with whitewash and watering with warm water. According to Marlet, however, genuinely early varieties were created at the very beginning of the seventeenth century by grafting dwarf cherries and growing cherry trees as espaliers. These early varieties included the Nanterre, 'with a small fruit and not much juice, but as it is the first of our fruits, everyone wants it.'

The Dietetics of Cherries

Because of the cherry's high potassium content (250 milligrams per 100 grams) it has always been recommended as a diuretic. The Salerno School said of it:

> Cherry, good fruit, what blessings you procure!
> Sweet to the taste, you make our humours pure
> Sending new blood to run through every vein,
> Relieving gallstone sufferers of their pain.

There is a cleansing diet which consists entirely of cherries, at least a kilo a day. The idea is that the cellulose in the flesh of the fruits will eliminate toxins and clean the intestine. However, no one should embark on it without medical advice; its drawback is that it causes digestive fermentations, and if you drink liquid at the same time it makes the pulp in the stomach and the small intestine swell.

Cherries are not very nourishing, having about 60 calories per 100 grams, provided by the 12 to 17 grams of sugar (fructose) that amount contains. They are easily assimilated, and can be eaten by diabetics. Like all red fruits they contain vitamins A and C, and they also contain B vitamins. The mineral salts in them comprise the potassium mentioned above, sodium, magnesium and calcium.

Cherry stalks are used as an astringent and diuretic, and cherry bark is a febrifuge. The black cherry is fermented and distilled to make kirsch. The cheaper sort, labelled *kirsch fantaisie*, is a poor-quality spirit, flavoured with the prussic acid contained in the kernel of the stone.

Apart from their use in cherry tarts and pie fillings, cherries are made into jam, crystallized, and bottled in eau-de-vie, kirsch or cherry syrup. Cherry leaves steeped in good white wine make an aperitif.

Strawberries

'Voici les fraises du bois joli! En voici, mon panier est tout rempli', little French girls sing, dancing in a circle: 'Here are the strawberries of the pretty wood! My basket is full.'

For centuries the only strawberries were wild or wood strawberries, a deliciously scented miracle scrambling over the moss on the outskirts of woods, growing wild in temperate climates, and with a preference for sub-mountainous areas. The fruit's name differs in the various European languages, although those names deriving from Latin still suggest the exquisite fragrance that caused the small, scented berry to be termed *Fragaria vesca*. The Italians call it *fragola*, the Spanish *fresa* and the French *fraise*. The English 'strawberry' refers to the layer of straw placed around the plants to keep the fruits off the soil, a particularly good idea in damp climates; the Germans call it *Erdbeere*, 'earth berry', and in Hungarian it is *eper*.

It was not cultivated until quite late, around the fifteenth century. Jacques André, referring to E. Schremann's *Entstehung der Kulturpflanzen*, suggests that the reason was the quantity of surface area in a garden that strawberries occupy permanently, while they produce only a small crop in one month of the year, for the strawberry is a perennial. It also exhausts the soil, so strawberry beds need to be moved to a new site every two or three years.

The strawberry propagates itself by runners straggling over the surface of the soil, and putting down roots here and there. People began cultivating the plant in medieval gardens, when runners of wood strawberries were transplanted, improved by manuring, and kept from spreading unchecked. Perhaps because of their scent, strawberries had a reputation as a love potion. In any case they were always considered very delicious.

La Quintinie's plan of his kitchen garden shows rectangles 1, 2, 3 and 4 reserved for strawberries, of which that great lover the Sun King was very fond. The ingenious use of windbreaks, frames and glasshouses made it possible to start picking strawberries in early spring. Similarly, the 'wood strawberries' that may sometimes be seen for sale today in tiny punnets at very high prices have never seen any real woodland. They are cultivated in polythene tunnels, and are twice as big as their genuinely wild sisters – a couple of centimetres long. They have also lost half their perfume, although they do retain enough to put up a reasonable show. To find the real thing nowadays, you have to make your way into the depths of what woods are left.

The seventeenth-century strawberries grown by such gardeners as La Quintinie were of only four varieties, according to Nicolas de Bonnefons (*Le jardinier françois*): red, white and yellow wood strawberries, and Hautbois. Merlet thought that 'the white strawberry, which is the male berry, usually grows larger than the red, but its flavour is less pronounced ... the strawberry plant called Hautbois does not give such good fruits as the others, being insipid, but it is very large, and suitable for decorating the border of a dish of strawberries.'

No one knows just why Louis XIV's doctor Fagon forbade his royal patient to eat strawberries in 1709, but the monarch, who was unable to practise moderation when he really liked something, gave himself serious indigestion. He took no notice of Fagon's advice for at least a year, and went on eating strawberries in wine – strawberries and cream were for the supposedly weaker sex. Louis XIV even held a literary competition on the subject of his favourite fruit. First prize went to the following verse:

> Quand de juin, s'éveille le mois
> Allez voir les fraises des bois
> Qui rougissent dans la verdure,
> Plus rouge que le vif corail,
> Balançant comme un éventail
> Leurs feuilles à triple découpure.

[When the month of June comes in, go and see the wood strawberries blushing red among the greenery, redder than bright coral, their three-lobed leaves spreading like a fan.]

The following lines came second:

> Là, de l'oeillet sauvage éclatent les boutons
> Et la fraise vermeille embaume le gazon ...

[There the buds of the wild pink flower, and the vermilion strawberry scents the sward ...]

None of the major poets of the time, such as Boileau, Racine and La Fontaine, took part in the competition.

In the time of Louis XV, who was as fond of strawberries as his great-grandfather, there were ten strawberry varieties and, thanks to glasshouses heated by a process invented in Germany, they could now be served at the royal table all the year round.[21] Although neither La Varenne's *Le cuisinier françois*, published in 1652, nor *Le jardinier françois* by Nicolas de Bonnefons, published the year before, mentions strawberries in its recipes for preserves, both include raspberries. But *La cuisine bourgeoise* of 1774 gives a recipe for strawberry 'compote' which can be criticized from the modern standpoint only because it does not specify the quantity of strawberries meant to go with 'a quarter of sugar'. Another dish well worth making is the same book's 'strawberry cream', which can also be produced with a mixture of strawberries and raspberries, using egg yolks instead of rennet.

The English, who invented the strawing of the berries, had greatly improved the Alpine strawberry, which was further improved by the Dutch, using heated frames. The Trianon gardens grew thousands of plants for the French court. At Montreuil, obviously a place favourable to horticultural innovation, the Sieur Fressant gave his name to a variety which became very popular.

In 1713 a Breton naval officer by the name of Frézier, which is wonderfully suggestive of the *fraisier* or strawberry plant, brought some plants of a large native species back from Chile. They were to be the ancestors of the dozens of varieties subsequently grown in Europe. Some of his plants went to the region of Plougastel, which is still a great French strawberry-growing area. Other French centres of strawberry-growing are the Périgord (particularly since many colonials returned to France from Algeria) and the Vaucluse and Orléanais areas. It was not until after 1820, however, that really large-scale strawberry-growing began. The idea was to satisfy demand in Paris now that rail transport meant the berries could arrive in the capital fresh and in good condition. Plougastel's great strawberry fair is still held on the third Sunday in June.

Carpentras strawberries used to be the first to arrive in Paris. These berries, grown in Provence, were sold in the nineteenth century 'in pots of pink earthenware under a covering of brown paper with a frill of gold esparto', as Charles Maurras tells us. The Aubagne strawberry pots made to hold these Carpentras strawberries have become valuable museum pieces.

The strawberry is a member of the Rosaceae family. It will grow in almost any soil; however, it crops especially well in soils where clay and siliceous elements predominate. It also likes slightly acid soils, and needs a temperate climate where there is no fear of excessive humidity or drought. Today nurserymen are even beginning to raise climbing strawberries, with fruits borne high above ground level, out of reach of their mortal enemies the slugs.

Spring frosts can damage strawberry blossom severely, and the plant is very prone to disease; its yield is unpredictable and the fruit itself fragile. For all these reasons the selection of varieties has to be very careful. Strawberry-growing is an expanding business, for although the berries have a short season (from May to the end of July in France) their price is relatively high even at the height of the season. A large labour force is needed to tend the strawberry fields and pick the fruit by hand. Strawberries cannot be mechanically picked.

Italy is the biggest strawberry-growing country in the EC, with France in second place; in 1982 they produced 205,000 tonnes and 87,445 tonnes respectively. The main French strawberry-growing regions, in order of importance, are the south-west of the country (particularly in the Dordogne and Lot-et-Garonne departments, where the area devoted to strawberries is increasing), the south-east, and the valley of the Rhône, with the departments of Vaucluse, the Drôme and the Rhône concentrating on early-fruiting varieties. The valley of the Loire, Brittany and the Moselle area grow only between 2 to 4 per cent of the French strawberry crop each, usually for local markets, or in the case of the Moselle for the food processing industry. There are some 9300 hectares of strawberries under cultivation in fields or market gardens. It is very difficult to get precise figures for strawberry production and consumption. Strawberry consumption before the fruit ever reaches the market is impossible to check, and so large that figures differ from year to year. It may be as much as 15 to 20 per cent of production. Self-pick strawberry farms are proliferating everywhere.

The average French person buys a little above one kilo of strawberries a year but eats about 1.8 kilos. On average, consumption of other fruits per head appears to be considerably greater (16.18 kilos of apples, 4.44 kilos of peaches; 4.44 kilos of pears, 4.08 kilos of dessert grapes). The reason is that the strawberry is a very seasonal fruit and retails, as mentioned above, at a relatively high price. In Europe the French consumer comes fourth, after the Dutch (2.4 kilos a year), the Belgian (2.3 kilos) and the Swiss (1.650 kilos).

However, although consumption of strawberries as fresh fruit is dropping in France, more and more of the berries are being eaten annually in manufactured food products: jams, syrups, ice creams and sorbets, cakes and biscuits. Jams account for most of these processed strawberries, although the relatively recent frozen strawberry market is an important outlet for producers.

Freezing, which regulates the market by making it possible to stock surplus products, also allows food manufacturers to spread their operations over several months. However, as the quantity of French strawberries supplied to industry is only about 10,000 tonnes, most strawberries for manufactured foods (rather over 10,000 tonnes, according to 1982 statistics) are imported either fresh or frozen. The principal suppliers of strawberries to France are Poland and Romania (where the fruit was almost entirely withdrawn from the home market to earn much-needed currency). They have ousted Italy and Spain, only the third and fourth largest suppliers to France since the early 1980s. These imported strawberries are of inferior quality and most of them are not good to eat as they are; even if they are sold as 'fresh' strawberries, the imported fruit has travelled in container lorries, surrounded with ice and covered by plastic.

Although freezing means strawberries will keep, it has to be said that frozen strawberries are not a great success from the consumer's point of view. The large amount of water they contain seeps out when they are defrosted, turning them into a soggy mess without much flavour which soon turns sour at room temperature. Frozen strawberries are no use in a fruit salad, and turn a pastry case soggy. Quebec has an annual glut of strawberries in July: old ladies and little girls may be seen all along the ring road of the Ile d'Orléans in the middle of the St Lawrence, wearing old-fashioned costumes and the traditional head-dress of the Berry area, offering baskets full of huge, fragrant fruit at a low price. The Canadians, wishing to have the fruits that ripen in their short summer available to eat during the long winter, have developed a method of home freezing which may not be perfect, but produces results much better than commercial frozen strawberries: they roll the fruit, washed and still slightly damp, in fine caster sugar and freeze the berries separately on trays before putting them in containers. The strawberries are spread out in a single layer again for defrosting. They will stay whole, look attractive and taste good, but they must be eaten quickly.

Most imported dessert strawberries eaten in France come from Spain (6000 tonnes), Italy (1500 tonnes) and Romania (1400 tonnes). In the United Kingdom, where the season does not begin until mid-June, imports from Spain and France precede home-grown strawberries. France also exports to West Germany and to Belgium and Luxembourg. Outside the European strawberry season, imported strawberries arrive from Israel, Kenya and some other African countries.

Italy has increased strawberry production in recent years, selling a great many abroad from mid-April to the end of July, especially in Germany and Switzerland, at quite low prices. Over half of Italian strawberries grown are the variety Gorella. Morocco, Belgium and the Netherlands also export considerable quantities of strawberries to Germany and Denmark. Hoping to compete with these other European countries, French producers have organized themselves into a number of groups to market over 20,000 tonnes of strawberries.

Some of the older varieties are still grown in private gardens, including in France the Surprise des Halles, the Première, the small and delicious Sans Rivale, and the large Madame Montot; in the United Kingdom the highly esteemed variety Royal Sovereign, bred in 1892, is still cultivated. However, there is not a great range of commercially grown strawberries; the main variety in the United Kingdom is Cambridge Favourite. Varieties widely grown in Europe are Gorella and Red Gauntlet, often cultivated under polythene tunnels.

Gorella is the most important of the early varieties. It has a large berry, elongated and conical in shape, and firm, juicy, sweet and quite well-coloured flesh. Its high yield (each stalk of a plant bears an average 166 grams of fruit) and its ability to travel well counterbalance a flavour which is only average. It ripens in the Mediterranean countries at the beginning of April, so the South of France can produce a large quantity of these early strawberries.

Red Gauntlet, the most important of the main season varieties, is grown both under cover and in the open. The fruit is medium in size, a clear, bright red, and the flesh is firm and sharp-flavoured. It has a good yield (on average 122 grams per stalk). It ripens from the end of April to the end of June in the south-east of France, and from the end of April to the middle of July in the south-west. It is a remontant strawberry, which flowers successively through the season, and in the United Kingdom, where the season begins and ends later than in the warmer parts of Europe, may fruit until October. The fruits at the end of the season have the best flavour.

Another variety, Sengana, is round and highly flavoured, and is grown mainly for jam.

Melons

Les amis de l'heure présente ont le naturel du melon.
Il faut en essayer cinquante avant d'en trouver un de bon.

[Friends of the present day are like the melon. You must try 50 before you find a good one.]

So said a versifying philosopher.

It took the melons we know today centuries to become really succulent, and they must still be chosen carefully: a melon should be heavy in relation to its size, with a stem that comes away easily. The skin opposite the stem end should be slightly recessed, but not brownish; the smell should be pleasant but not of ether, a sign that it is rather over-ripe. The best may have absorbed so much rain that they split slightly while they are growing. These cracks are not large, but they can be a breeding-ground for mould as the fruit comes to the end of its travels on the commercial circuit. The melon is a summer fruit, in season from July to September; early melons fetch a price which is not justified by their flavour.

The melon is the fruit not of a tree, like the exotic papaya which resembles it, but of an annual trailing plant of the large Cucurbitaceae family, which includes pumpkins, gourds, marrows and courgettes, and squashes, all of American origin, and the cucumber, an old inhabitant of Europe. Both the melon and its big sister the water melon come from Africa. There is also a Chinese melon, to which I shall come in a moment.

Melons and water melons not much larger than apples still grow in the wild state around watering-holes in the sub-Saharan savannas, and in desert oases in the southern part of the African continent. Even if the spring feeding them is invisible, the Bushmen can tell there is one below the ground from the presence of the fruits, which makes them doubly welcome and refreshing. The explorer Livingstone saw them and marvelled at them in central Africa.

For a long time it was thought that the paintings of the first Pharaonic tombs showed melons, but the fruits were actually water melons, which are still more common from Mauritania to Nubia, and inclined to grow spontaneously. The melon came afterwards. Around the fifth century BC, the Egyptians succeeded in growing larger and less bitter melons and water melons. At this point the fruits crossed the Mediterranean as shipboard provisions and reached Greece. The melon arrived in Campania around the first century AD, but Dioscorides for one still seems to have preferred the water melon. So did Pliny, who saw it as a kind of round cucumber the size of a quince.[22] Perhaps they had to taste 50 melons before they found a good one.

657

Like the cucumber, the melon, which was probably not much sweeter, was usually eaten at this period as a kind of salad, with pepper and vinegar, well seasoned with garum and silphium. But its mere novelty caused the prices asked to reach fantastic heights, so much so that Diocletian's edict fixed the price of melons at two denarii apiece for the largest, which weighed about 200 grams. They were an imperial luxury. Tiberius ate melons at almost every meal, and Albinus had ten as an hors-d'oeuvre. Given the weight of a melon of Roman times, its rind removed, the ten melons would have weighed not much more than four pounds in all.

Under the patient care of Mediterranean gardeners through the centuries, the melon increased in size, flavour and sweetness, and was no longer thought of as a green vegetable. During the Renaissance monks grew it for the popes at their summer residence of Cantalupo near Rome. The cantaloupe melon gradually became the marvellous orange-fleshed fruit we know today. The darker-skinned variety grown by another order of monks was known as the Black Cantaloupe of the Carmelites. In France the name is sometimes misspelt Cantalou by people who think it has something to do with the Cantal department.

The cantaloupe melon arrived in Avignon long after the popes had left, and flourished in the fertile soil among the cypresses of the Comtat Venaissin. Cavaillon became a major producing area, and hybridization raised the netted Cavaillon melon, which has bright orange, almost red flesh, and is much in demand for making crystallized melon. It is already extremely sweet naturally. Its skin, netted with yellow and green, makes it look like some kind of swollen rustic earthenware creation.

Alexandre Dumas, when working on *The Count of Monte Cristo*, passed through Marseilles while cholera was raging there. He enjoyed Cavaillon melons so much that he ate more than was wise. (At the time it was thought that melons predisposed you to infection in times of epidemic disease.) One of his friends in Marseilles warned him against possible indigestion. 'I know', replied the writer, 'but no one is eating them just now, they are almost being given away, so I am taking my chance!' Another of his friends, Castel-Blaze, a native of Cavaillon, asked for a present of Dumas' books to be given to the town library. 'By all means ... on condition Cavaillon will give me an annuity of 12 melons a year!'

Today people will tell you that Cavaillon melons are not what they were now that they are forced, fed with a lot of fertilizer, and picked green so that they will be easier to transport. Even physically they have changed. Jules Belleudy[23] wrote, in 1929:

> The Cavaillon melon used to be elongated, with a greenish skin and pale green flesh. The skin was neither smooth nor warty, but looked as if it were covered by Arabic or Chinese characters, and so it was described as *escrich*, 'written'. The flavour was very sweet, and the melon was as juicy as a sorbet. It was possible to taste melons before buying if you paid five centimes above the regular price, and the melons that

had been cut into for tasting were sold to street urchins for a sou a slice.

Where, one may ask, are the melons of yesteryear?

The cantaloupe also emigrated to Charente. Other segmented melons are grown at Tours and in the market gardens around Paris. North Africa, where this refreshing fruit is widely eaten, learned to grow the early cantaloupe of Algiers during the French colonial period. And ever since the great days of Carthage, people around the whole Mediterranean coast have always been very fond of water melons. In Provence, the water melon is known as *meravilho*, the marvel.

The Spanish melons called *verdaù* in Provence ripen at the end of autumn and will keep until Epiphany. They are always part of the 'Thirteen Desserts' of the traditional Christmas supper. Oval, with a lightly patterned skin, their flesh is ivory or pale green and delicately rose-scented.

The Chinese have always grown a large winter melon with a very floury flesh which they eat as a vegetable. Cooked in chicken broth with good mushrooms and diced ham it makes the traditional soup called *Dong gua tang*, served and sometimes cooked in the rind of the melon itself, which artistic cooks decorate with the point of a knife, carving fabulous animals or strange flowers into it.

Melons contain few calories (about 31 per 100 grams), and a great deal of water (they are 92 per cent water). They are very rich in potassium (2.60 per cent) and have diuretic and laxative qualities when over-ripe or under-ripe. They contain vitamins C (0.33 per cent) and above all A (3240 IU), as their colour suggests.

There is a piece of country lore that warns against growing melons anywhere near pumpkins or squashes, in case the pollen of their close relations harms the quality of the fruit. People in the South of France eat melon for dessert, and in the North as an hors-d'oeuvre (sometimes with port poured into it, which does nothing at all for the flavour). The Italians eat melon with *prosciutto*, curls of very thinly sliced Parma ham; its strong flavour enhances the sweetness of the melon.

Oranges

In the nineteenth century poor children dreamed all the year round of getting the precious, scented present of an orange for Christmas. Most of them did not know what an orange tasted like, or even if they would dare to eat that golden, almost magical fruit.

At an earlier date, William of Orange's anti-Catholic laws made him so unpopular in Ireland that the people of the Emerald Isle declared no orange tree should ever grow on Irish soil. The House of Orange, from which King William was descended, took its name from the principality and town of Orange in south-east France.

Oranges were taken to prisoners in La Santé prison in France, where many of the inmates were lunatics; coincidentally, since the name of the prison means 'health' (it was originally a charitable hospital), oranges are indeed good for the health. They contain vitamin C and mineral salts; an orange provides a day's ration of them.

Woman selling oranges: early nineteenth-century
engraving from the *Cris de Paris*

In certain traditions the orange, not the apple, is the fruit responsible for original sin. Malaysia, where the orange first grew, knew nothing about the Old Testament, but Malay tradition did link the orange with the sin of gluttony. The culprit in this case was an elephant. The word 'orange' is explained by a legend of days long before the empire of Srivijaya (the seventh to eleventh centuries), in very distant times indeed, when the animals could talk. One of those animals, the elephant, ate so much that he had grown enormous. Passing through the forest, he found a tree unknown to him in a clearing, bowed under its weight of beautiful, tempting golden fruit. The elephant ate so many that he burst.

Much later another traveller came to the same place: a human traveller this time, for mankind had been invented since the elephant suffered his unfortunate accident.

660

The fossilized remains of the elephant were still lying in the clearing, and a cluster of trees bearing a thousand golden fruits grew from what had been its stomach. 'Amazing!' said the man. 'What a fine *nagā rangā*' Which meant, in the Sanskrit of the time, 'fatal indigestion for elephants'. He picked some of the fruit, knotted them into a bundle made with his loincloth and went home to feast on them with his family. Thereafter the name for the tree that bore the golden fruit was *nagā rangā*, as we find it in the writings of Panini, the Indian grammarian of the fourth century BC who helped to fix the literary language of Sanskrit. The name does not seem to be originally an Indo-European word. As for the elephants themselves, they had learnt by experience and never ate oranges again.

Another legend concerning oranges is the tale of the golden apples of the Hesperides. Scholars have never been able to decide what fruit they actually were, but I would say the most generally accepted thesis is that the fabulous fruits were citrons. The Earth Mother Gaia gave them to the goddess Hera for her garden, possibly situated in the north of Mauritania, but in any case cared for by the shepherd Atlas and his daughters, the Hesperides. As La Fontaine says:

> Vos fruits aux écorces solides sont un véritable trésor.
> Et le jardin des Hespérides n'avait point d'autres pommes d'or.
>
> (*Psyché*, Act I)

[Your fruits, with their firm rinds, are a true treasure, and the Garden of the Hesperides grew no golden apples but these.]

Now *melon*, fruit in Greek, has a precise archaic Greek homonym, denoting sheep or goats with russet-coloured fleece (*Odyssey*, Book 12, 301, and Book 14, 105), before coming to mean specifically citrus fruits (orange, lemon or citron) in Sophocles, Hesiod and Plutarch, an apricot in Dioscorides when qualified by the description 'Armenian', even a quince in Galen, and a peach when described as Persian. The 'golden apples' recovered by Heracles as the twelfth of his labours could thus in very ancient times have been simply sheep, since Atlas was a shepherd. This hypothesis, which neither questions nor disproves the possibility that there was some historical or toponymic basis for the legend of Heracles, simply raises the question of just when citrus fruits first appeared in the Mediterranean basin.

The Italians use the word *agrumi*, connected with Latin *acer*, bitter,[24] for the whole family of citrus fruits, which contains a great many of the brothers, sisters and cousins of the orange such as citrons, pomelos and grapefruits, mandarins, etc. It is a prolific family, royal and even divine if legends are to be believed, and like the Egyptian royal dynasties it has allowed all kinds of close, incestuous marriages which have turned out very successful, as indeed they should have done in the favourable climates where they grew. The world was large enough for each to have its own kingdom; citrus fruits have cohabited on the planet for a very long time, each originally in its own sphere of influence.

The citron set out on its travels before the orange. I mention it first because of its great age; the Chinese knew it in the fourth millennium. It was cultivated at Nipour, the religious capital of the Sumerians, as a sacred fruit dedicated to Enlil, god of the earth and the air. Simon Maccabeus, the first king of independent Judaea, chose it to feature on his coinage in 142 BC. It was mentioned by the Egyptians, singled out by Alexander, and highly regarded by Pliny[25] and Virgil[26] for its virtues as an antidote. According to Theophrastus' account of what was still an exotic fruit, it was not cultivated in southern Italy, Sicily and Corsica until the fourth century BC. Corsica is now almost the only place where citrons are still grown for crystallized peel, preserves, and essential oils for perfume.

The citron, which resembles a large, thick-skinned lemon and is very bitter, was used only medicinally and in perfumery in classical times: hence its use in religious ceremonies. The citron, and indeed the whole *Citrus* genus, takes its name from its scent; the Romans also called the thuja, with its bitter leaves, *citrus*. Diocletian's edict, limiting the exorbitant price of citron to 24 denarii, calls it *citrus maximus*.

The lemon, *Citrus limon*, owes its name entirely to the botanists, for it was unknown to classical writers. However, it was widely used from the Middle Ages onwards. It was regarded as an essential in the seventeenth century; Boileau, presenting it in much the same light as nutmeg, inquired in his *Repas ridicule*, 'Sentez-vous le citron dont on a mis le jus?' ('Do you smell the lemon juice that has been put in?') Originally from the foothills of Kashmir, the lemon did not reach China by way of the province of Kuang-tong (Canton) until around 1900 BC. In China, it was given the name of *limung*, which it retained almost unchanged when it moved on to Persia and Media. From the tenth century AD onwards the Arabs, who called it *li mûm* (*Medical Treatise of Ebembitar*, 1187), took it all around the Mediterranean basin, eastwards to Greece by way of Constantinople, westwards to Spain by way of the Maghreb and Fezzan. The Spanish and Russians retained the name *limon*, which becomes 'lemon' in English, while the old Latin name of the citron was used for the lemon in Germany (*Zitrone*), France (*citron*), Poland (*cytryna*) and Hungary (*citron*). The lime, a small green lemon, was introduced into the West Indies by the Spanish in the sixteenth century.

The orange itself, *Citrus aurentium*, crossing India like Buddha, reached China around 2200 BC. The Chinese liked it very much, even in its primitive and still extremely bitter form. The larger pomelo was its companion: both of them, 'wrapped in an embroidered silk scarf at the bottom of a basket', were among the tributes offered to the Emperor Tayun who reigned from 2205 to 2197 BC, or so we are told in the *Yu Kung* manuscript where the orange and pomelo make their first appearances in literature.

The pomelo was the ancestor of the grapefruit. It grew wild in the Indo-Chinese peninsula and Indonesia, and seems to have come to Asia from the East Indian Sunda Islands, particularly Fiji, where the jungles are full of it. However, there is an alternative place of origin for the pomelo and grapefruit in the West Indies. But for the Central American isthmus one might suppose it had crossed the Pacific in one direction or the other, like some of the other food plants mentioned already.

The botanical name of the grapefruit is *Citrus paradisi*. It may be either a sport of the pomelo or a cross between it and the sweet orange, and was recognized as a distinct species in the early nineteenth century.

The mandarin, which came from Cochin-China and naturalized itself in China, may take its name from the yellow robes of the Chinese civil servants called 'mandarins'. The orange and pomelo both took the Silk Road and the path trodden by Chinese medicine to Europe through the East, each going at its own pace. The orange had an easy passage, especially as it had gastronomic as well as medicinal qualities (although it was still bitter and had not yet acquired all its delicious flavour). In China the *Thousand Prescriptions of Great Price* and the *Remedies of Immortality*, like the *Charaka-Sambuta*, the Sanskrit pharmacopoeia, made much of the restorative principles of its juice and essential oil. One fruit which is related to the bitter orange and originated in China stayed there, being too small to travel; this was the kumquat. It is best known in Europe in preserves, although fresh kumquats have been imported in recent years.

At the banquets given by Roman patricians of the second century AD, oranges finally began to appear. They were imported from Palestine, like the faith of the first Christians imported themselves to tempt the appetites of the lions in the Coliseum. At this point the great landowners of North Africa decided to make a profit by planting well-tended orange groves. A whole system of earthenware irrigation pipes still exists outside Tunis, at a place on the Carthage road called Soukra, because the air there is so sweet with the scent of orange blossom. The system is still in working order after nearly 2000 years, supplying copious amounts of brackish water to the greedy trees.

St Augustine of Hippo, a child of North Africa, denounced the refined veg-etarianism of the Manichaeans who drank orange juice instead of tipping the thick, harsh Algerian wine down their throats. But when the barbarians thought they had destroyed the last Roman orangeries of the declining Empire, there were still enough oranges left in Sicily and Calabria for St François of Paola, centuries later, to take some to Louis XI along with the pear tree mentioned above. By now the oranges were sweet, and delicious to eat. They must have done the King some good as he waited for the Bon Chrétien pears he would never taste to ripen.

South of the Pyrenees oranges, now very much a Spanish fruit, had also grown in fame and excellence. Nothing could stop them.

At Pamplona, Eleanor of Castille grew an orange in a tub so that it could be brought indoors on winter nights. In 1523 the tub and its contents were first acquired and then lost by the Duke of Bourbon, Constable of France, whose possessions were confiscated by the Queen Mother Louise of Savoy. The Valois kings built an orangery at Fontainebleau around this tree. Mme de Sévigné saw the tree at Versailles: lovingly pruned, it ended its days in 1858, still a virgin, for it had never produced a single fruit.

Orangeries were for orange trees rather than fruit.

Orangers, arbres que j'adore
Vos fleurs ont embaumé tout l'air que je respire.

[Orange trees, trees that I love, your flowers have scented all the air I breathe.]

These lines by La Fontaine might be conveying his king's delight in the trees that were the pride of the gardeners of Versailles, and a source of concern to Louis XIV himself. During the Franche-Comté campaign he wrote to Colbert, expressing his anxiety about new planting. 'Tell me what the orange trees look like.' The first orange trees in France had been grown in open ground by Paolo di Mercoglierio, an Italian gardener who worked for Charles VIII at Château-Gaillard, and although the Fontainebleau orangery continued to harbour sterile specimens on which imitation fruits were hung, Louis XIV was very proud of those which bore blossom to perfume his apartments. In silver containers, they also decorated the Gallery of Mirrors and the rooms of state on festive occasions.

Some orange trees were brought at great expense from San Domingo and Algeria, some were supplied to the palace by those great lords and prosperous members of the *grande bourgeoisie* who could afford orangeries and skilled gardeners. (The accounts of the secretariat, for instance, record a payment 'to M. de Fienbert for 33 orange trees from his house at Beauregard.') When the Petite Orangerie, managed by Le Trumel and naturally requiring orange trees, was replaced by the Grande Orangerie, La Quintinie, who was in charge this time (a very important post), appealed to Henri Dupuis, the best specialist orange-tree grower of the time, to supply more.

Louis XV, 'le Bien-Aimé', continued the tradition, but his minister Choiseul cannot have felt much liking for the royal fruit. The tale goes that Mme Du Barry brought about the fall of the 'coachman of Europe', as he was nicknamed, in 1770 while playing ball with an orange. Every time the orange was thrown in the air she chanted, 'Jump, Choiseul! Fall, Choiseul!' until the King could no longer resist the persuasions of his mistress – or the Catholic faction, which for once was in agreement. Choiseul fell.

Even when these indoor orange trees were cared for like princes and grown for princes, they might be courteous enough to flower but they produced hardly any oranges, and those they did produce were not much good. The orange does not like captivity. It needs the brightness of the sun, insects to visit it, the scent of the wind, the humidity of the sea near by, and the loving care of a whole agricultural army to treat it lovingly and gather its fruits with respect. It gets that loving care and those climates, enhancing its beauty, delicious flavour and opulence, in the most delightful parts of the world. After invading Israel, Greece, Cyprus, Turkey, Morocco, Spain and Portugal, it left Lisbon to discover America with Christopher Columbus on his second voyage. He planted the first orange tree in the New World on 22 November 1493, in Haiti, then called Hispaniola.

Oranges of Portuguese stock, pampered like some star or astronaut of the twentieth century, also made their mark – so successfully that from Persia to the Fezzan the Arab world no longer called the fruit *naranj* but termed it *bortugal* (or *porteghal* in Iran), the name it still bears in Arab countries today (and in Romania, once colonized by the Turks), although in literary Arabic *tchina* is the term preferred, reminding us that sweet oranges were originally known as China oranges.

From Haiti, oranges spread from island to island in the West Indies until they reached the American continent, in the footsteps of Miguel Diaz. The American branch of the orange family was to become extremely distinguished.

The first American orange plantation was Spanish, in Florida. It flourished in Saint-Augustin from 1579 onwards. Indians stole the fruits, ate them, and spat out the pips in the forest, where specimens were soon found which some people believe were of native origin. As with West Indian grapefruit, the question remains open.

While the orange groves of Florida gradually became the marvels of good management and high yield they are today, a Spanish missionary reached the West, and in 1707 he planted the ancestor of the orange trees of California. However, it was not until 1848 that planting on a large scale really began, on a site which is now a railway station in the middle of Los Angeles. In that year California was overtaken by the tidal wave of the Gold Rush. While adventurers of every kind gave themselves up to the frenzied search for gold, wiser pioneers – growers of citrus fruits – realized that the beautiful, bright oranges were better gold than the metal mined from the ground. Scurvy was rife among the prospectors, who were exhausted, often alcoholic, and badly nourished on canned food. The effects of scurvy had often been observed in sailors deprived of fresh food, particularly red and yellow fruits.[27]

As the few local orange trees were insufficient to supply demand, shrewd doctors all over the West Coast made a fortune out of orange or lemon juice, imported with some difficulty from Florida, selling it by the spoonful. Prospectors, horrified to find their teeth suddenly dropping out, could be seen offering a sardine can stuffed with gold dust for a consultation – equivalent to more than 200 dollars of the time. Imagine what that would be in modern money!

A man called Duck came to an agreement with Queen Pomare of Tahiti on the far side of the Pacific to buy Papeete oranges, which he then sold at a fabulous price. The son of John Sutter, who had begun the entire Gold Rush, went in search of oranges in Mexico, where growers had begun planting what would become one of the country's major sources of income.

At this point a wonderful orange was grown at Bahia in Brazil, at the other end of the American continent. It is said that there are men for the times: perhaps there are oranges for the times too. A tree – a very fine one – one day produced a miraculous fruit: a perfect orange, sweeter and juicier than the usual sort, even more beautiful, and without a single pip. It turned out later that it also contained more vitamins. Even more extraordinary, this new orange had a navel at the end opposite the stem. Whether Adam and Eve had navels and the question of the sex of the angels were great subjects of medieval discussion, never to be settled, but this seedless orange – a kind of angel among oranges – certainly had a navel. From what was it born, and to what would it give birth?

The question deserved investigation. A missionary called Schneider, working in Brazil, thought Washington should be informed. He took a cutting of the tree and sent it to Horace Capon at the American Ministry of Agriculture, explaining the situation. Horace Capon planted the cutting and took several more from it, which he gave to his friends Luther and Eliza Thibet, who were setting off by covered wagon for the West. Luther and Eliza suffered from thirst and attacks by Indians on their long and arduous journey, but when they finally arrived in California the cuttings were intact, and had never gone without water. They were planted out. Some years later, they bore more fruit. As its name suggests, the Washington Navel became central to the world of oranges.

Meanwhile, in Africa, the orange and its companions had been developing too. North Africa, one of the places where they grow best, produced two new kinds at the end of the nineteenth century. One was a pure-bred orange with such sweet, scented flesh and so fine a skin that when the Bey of Tunis tasted it he was delighted, and embraced his gardeners. The orange, he said, should be called the Maltese, because it reminded him of his beloved Maltese mistress.

At Messerghine in Algeria a priest, Father Clément, succeeded in marrying an orange to a mandarin (to the pure of heart all things are pure). They had a beautiful child, the clementine, to which the good priest naturally stood godfather. (In the 1970s the mandarin family also had a Spanish daughter, conceived in Japan: the satsuma, with patches of green on its skin and with coral-coloured, acid and very juicy flesh.)

South Africa, another country where citrus fruits grow well, had yet to be explored. Here we must go back on our tracks to the seventeenth century, when the orange, making its way around Africa from one island trading post to another, reached St Helena, not as an exile like Napoleon but on a kind of mission. The ships which put in there took stocks of food and fresh water aboard, and when the first Dutch governor, Hans Van Riebeeck, was installed at the Cape, he decided to plant the fruit he had thought so delicious when he stopped at the island; he had kept some of the pips.

The South African pioneers – Boers, Dutch, French Huguenots, Irish and English – profiting by the example of the navigators before them, took oranges among the provisions in their covered carts. At nightfall the emigrants set up camp in the middle of a circle of carts, from which the oxen had been unharnessed so that they could graze. In Dutch, this procedure was described as *uitspan*, unharnessing. The name came to be applied to the camp inside the circle, and then became *outspan*, which in turn became a synonym for the orange. What could be more refreshing and relaxing than to eat an orange? In our European summer such oranges now bring us the cool refreshment of the southern winter. After going all round the world, the fabulous orange is carefully tended, a source of health and fortune.

Moreover, every orange has its personality. Oranges with the qualities of the sunny countries where they grew can be bought all the year round. The most popular are the Moroccan orange, royal and pure, an Arab princess; the Spanish orange, an enchanting and proud señorita; the Tunisian orange, a seductive and fascinating favourite; the Israeli orange, a marvel of Paradise lost and regained; and the South African orange, a fine, handsome traveller. And then there are the American oranges, who are definitely beauty queens: the opulent, generous Florida orange, and the California orange, a millionairess pin-up girl. Nor must the head of the dynasty, the Portuguese orange, be forgotten; or the Italian orange, the oranges of Algeria, Cyprus, Greece and Brazil, or the orange of black Africa which is green outside, has pink flesh, and a great many pips.

To eat an orange is to travel in imagination to countries where the climate is heavenly, the sun kind, water abundant and pure, the breeze caressing, the soil light, the nights cool and restful, and man skilful, patient, careful and well organized.

Growing and Selling Oranges

At first sight the orange looks a very robust fruit. In itself, it is nothing like as perishable as the strawberry or the grape. However, beneath its sturdy appearance, the orange is a fruit which requires particularly delicate treatment between picking and its arrival at its destination.

All along its way, the orange fears rough treatment. A small scratch, a rough jolt, and the fruit will be spoilt. Moreover, it may well contaminate its travelling companions, and oranges travel much and far. More and more are exported from North Africa and Spain every year to go all over Europe, to France, Belgium, Germany and Switzerland, and farther afield to the United Kingdom, the Netherlands, Denmark, Sweden, Norway and even Finland. The distance is even greater for fruits from America, South Africa and Israel, although a Spanish orange may have been picked only a couple of days before it is eaten. If an orange is to travel well it must be in perfect health. That is the all-important factor from the moment the fruit is picked.

Oranges are picked as soon as they reach the right degree of maturity to be sent on their way. Judging their readiness is a delicate business, and is mainly a matter of experience. Every exporting country has its own legal standards regulating citrus fruits. The importing countries have their own requirements too, which the growers must know, and must obviously fulfil. Spanish and Moroccan oranges are picked when perfectly ripe, unlike the oranges of America, Brazil and South Africa, picked earlier on.

The first stage of the journey, from tree to packing station, is made in crates. The picking process itself requires many precautions, for at this point the orange is full of water and easily damaged. Any injury to the skin of the fruit must be carefully avoided. Spanish and Moroccan pickers have to show their hands for inspection before they start work, like children sitting down to a meal. In America the pickers wear gloves, a measure that cannot be insisted on everywhere, but at least pickers must have their nails cut short. The golden rule is to handle the fruit gently.

When the oranges arrive at the packing station they meet with mechanization. Various operations prepare them for packing. These operations are now performed by machinery with a minimum output of a tonne and a half an hour. But the oranges still have to have a beauty treatment. They are fed into a tub of warm, soapy water, where they spend several minutes, and then take a second bath to disinfect them. Now comes the drying process, which takes several hours. Drying is carried out in an aerated room; its purpose is to firm up the skin of the fruit by evaporating moisture from it.

The beauty treatment is not over yet. Nicely dried, as if at the hairdresser's, by powerful hot-air ventilation, the fruits are polished with soft brushes and finally lightly waxed to give them an attractive shiny appearance and help them and their vitamins to keep: vitamin C will evaporate.

Before they are graded for size, the oranges are sorted for the last time to pick out fruit that will not stand the journey. The conveyor belt for the sorting process is very strict: injured fruits, insufficiently ripe fruits, the flabby-skinned and those that look overblown or tainted in any way do not leave for export. Some go to local markets, others are used in the food-manufacturing industry.

The oranges are automatically graded into lots in order of size, each corresponding to a scale of official standards. The grading is done by rubber rollers on which the fruits roll about, falling when the graduated opening of the rollers will let them through. But this is simply the visible part of the operation. They are then given their passports, stamped with the name of their place of provenance.

Before the final packing the oranges are sometimes wrapped in tissue paper, especially in Spain and Israel. To protect the fruit, the tissue paper is usually impregnated with diphenyl, in such a tiny proportion and so carefully measured and checked that it cannot harm the consumer. All you need do is rinse the orange in warm water and wipe it dry if you are going to eat the zest. The wrapping operation, performed either mechanically or by hand, has the great advantage of preventing contamination should a fruit spoil on the journey. The oranges are then at last packed by expert packers.

And now the journey begins, in crates or loose in containers, or in divided packing cases containing one to three kilos of fruit in supermarket plastic nets. Each pack contains the same quantity of homogeneous fruits of the same variety and nature, uniform in appearance, without any parasites or flaws.

A dessert fruit of outstandingly high vitamin content, the orange is also the basic material of a thriving industry. The fallen or damaged fruit sorted out is not thrown away. It is made into fruit juice, liqueurs, aperitifs, marmalade, or the essences and essential oils used in pharmacy, cosmetics, patisserie, confectionery and chemicals. In the United States, over 600 different products are made from oranges – even including anti-freeze!

A Who's Who of Oranges

The Thomson orange is the earliest on Western European markets. Usually of good size, it has smooth, thick skin and divides easily into segments, to be eaten as it is or in salads.

The navel orange, as its name tells us, has a navel. Its skin is rough. It is scented, sweet and juicy, and seedless.

The Hamlin is of medium size. It is very juicy and sharp under its grainy skin.

The melting Maltese is well flavoured, with a very fine skin. The blood orange variety is even juicier, with skin that comes away easily from the segments.

The Portuguese blood orange is oval, and red in colour. Its thin, smooth skin sticks to the segments. It is strongly scented, with few pips.

The late Valencia orange is round and pale in colour. It is very juicy, and has a great many pips under a smooth skin.

The late Vernia orange is very sweet, and has brightly coloured flesh.

Jaffa is not a variety of orange, but an indication of the fruit's Israeli place of origin.

Outspan is not a variety but a South African brand name.

Sunkist is not a variety either, but the brand name of a syndicate of Californian growers.

It is said that the skin of oranges grown in sandy soil, such as Israeli oranges, is thicker than that of the oranges of Morocco or Spain, grown on clay.

The colour of oranges is due to the difference between the daytime and the night-time temperature. When they are the same, as in black Africa, too much chlorophyll is manufactured during the night. The orange turns green and loses some of its carotene and provitamin A, which are obviously present in yellow fruits.

The aroma of orange peel comes from certain essential oils contained in the little vessels that can be seen under the skin, and are freed when the peel is scraped, grated or crushed. But the pulp of oranges also contains other aromatic principles which contribute to making the fruits more appetizing by mingling the closely linked senses of smell and taste.

Tests have been made which show that orange-coloured fruits seem more appetizing than fruits of any other colour.

The orange is *naranja* in Spanish and Hungarian. The Germans have several words for the fruit: *Orange*, *Apfelsine* (especially in north Germany), and *Pomeranze* for the bitter Seville orange. In Polish the fruit is *pomarancz* and in Russian *apielcine*. In Italian it is *arancia*, and *orange* is the word in both French and English.

Grapefruit

The pomelo lingered around the Indian Ocean for some time before deciding, much later, to travel to the Middle East, an area no more stable then than it is today. The French word is *pamplemousse*, and the name at least began to be known in France at the end of the seventeenth century. It is mentioned by the traveller Melchisédek Thévenot, related to one of the men who introduced coffee to the West, and himself one of the founder members of the Académie des Sciences. In his *Recueils de voyages* of 1681, he speaks of *pompelmous*, a French version of Dutch *pompelmoes*, the Dutch having made the north-east of the Indian Ocean their own. But the improved version of pomelo now known as grapefruit, much grown in modern Greece, did not become really familiar in Europe until after the Second World War, when it was popularized as a breakfast fruit by the Americans.

Around 1800, fruits called 'shaddocks' arrived in America. They were only pomelos or grapefruits, but it was claimed that they had been discovered on the Fiji islands by a sea captain who gave them his name. They did indeed grow in Fiji, but they had been almost forgotten for 150 years. Their other possible place of origin, in the West Indies, has been suggested only recently; some people think the West Indian trees may have been descended from cultivated ones that reverted to the wild. Be that as it may, when Napoleon was invading Europe, shaddocks were invading Florida from their base in Pinella County. Since life seldom proceeds in a straight line, they reverted to the name of pomelo and then, after hybridization with orange pollen to make them sweeter, to grapefruit.

Figs

Cato the Elder hated two things, and it is hard to say which of them he loathed more: the lax morals of his compatriots, or the proud city of Carthage. He ended every speech he made in the Roman Senate, whatever the subject, by adding 'Carthago delenda est' – 'Carthage must be destroyed'. At last, tired of getting no positive decision from his colleagues, he produced a fresh fig from the folds of his toga, held it up and cried, 'Do you see this fig? It was still growing on a Carthaginian fig tree three days ago. See how close the enemy is.' The Romans took arms, and Carthage was duly destroyed. Thanks to a fig, Rome now had no rival.

Except in the Mediterranean, figs are thought of as a luxury fruit because of their high price. Around the Mediterranean basin, however, every wall has its fig tree, sometimes more visited by wasps and birds than by humans, so that the ground around the tree when the fruits are ripe and dropping seems to be covered with fig jam.

For thousands of years figs have played a very important part in the diet and the economy of the Mediterranean countries, from the days of the hunters and gatherers to the exchange economies of today. While there was no sugar, or very little, they were used for the preservation of cooked fruits. Preserves of figs are still made in Provence. A handful of fresh or dried figs made a very nourishing meal, perhaps with milk clotted with the sap of the fig tree, or with flat cakes of bread. Plato called figs a food for athletes. The Greeks were well aware of the fig's value, and, as we saw above, forbade its export in order to protect Attica's main resource, 'more precious than gold'. Figs were never picked before the priests, known as 'sycophants' (see chapter 1), declared that they were ripe and the crop could be gathered. The name 'sycophant' was subsequently given, ironically, to those who denounced the contraband fig trade, and then to all informers.

Cultivated fig: engraving from Chenu's
Encyclopédie d'histoire naturelle of 1873

The fig is the first tree to be mentioned in the Bible. When Adam and Eve had eaten the forbidden fruit, 'the eyes of them both were opened, and they knew that they were naked; and they sewed fig leaves together, and made themselves aprons.'[28] Given the abundance of the tree in the presumed region of Eden, one might think that the fruit of knowledge itself was plucked from its branches, rather than from the apple, apricot or even orange tree, depending on your theory. It would be a logical conclusion and put a stop to argument! Moreover, the fig and the fig tree, sacred in all ancient religions, are important symbols and are linked to knowledge in particular.

Having just mentioned the 'aprons' of fig leaves made by Eve, obviously a needlewoman from the first, I might as well add that it is only since the Middle

671

Ages that vine leaves have hidden the private parts in pictures of Adam and Eve and statues of athletes whose nudity offended Christian morality. ('Gymnast' means naked in Greek.) The artists of northern Gaul, not knowing the Mediterranean fig tree, failed to identify the fig leaves placed in the crucial spot by Byzantine mosaic artists and illuminators, from whose work they drew their inspiration at the time of Charlemagne. They took them for vine leaves instead.

If one wants to be scientifically precise, then the fig could not possibly be the fruit of knowledge, since it is not properly speaking a fruit at all. It is actually an involucre or hollow flowerhead formed by the globular receptacle containing the inflorescence, open at the end opposite the stem, where a small navel-shaped aperture bears male flowers at the entrance and female flowers farther inside. After fertilization inside the receptacle, it swells, enclosing a great many small monospermal drupes, which are the real fruits produced by the ovaries of the fertilized female flowers, and which we call seeds.

Some kinds of fig cannot be fertilized without help from the fig wasp. The fig tree that concerns us here, *Ficus carica*, which grew wild all around the Mediterranean basin at first and is now cultivated, is only one species of a family that has 600 members, including the banyan of India with its aerial roots, the climbing fig of the jungles, a parasite which strangles large trees, and the philodendron and rubber plant, which grow to a huge size in the tropics, but are ordinary green house plants in the West.

Dried or roasted for consumption, figs were part of the diet of all the ancient peoples of the Mediterranean, and might even replace bread. The Romans and the people of southern Gaul followed the example of Greeks in fattening dormice and in particular geese on figs. As we saw, the liver (*jecur*) of those geese, swollen to vast size after such a diet, was called *jecur ficatum* and then simply *ficatum*. There was also a kind of fig wine which was very popular.

The country around Paris, as the writings of the Emperor Julian show, had been well planted with figs in the most favourable and sheltered places to satisfy the tastes of Roman functionaries who found themselves posted to Gaul, and indeed of the native Gauls who wanted to emulate their masters. But the climate did not suit a tree which lives on sunlight. The declining Roman Empire preferred to devote its attention to other plants, better adapted to the climate, and fig trees north of the Loire became unusual. However, figs were still widely eaten in both the Middle Ages and the Renaissance, and most of those consumed in France came from Provence, as the *Ménagier de Paris* points out, mentioning that they were served roasted with bay leaves over them at such choice meals as the Lenten banquet of 1379 for eight settings, i.e., 16 guests sharing food two to a dish, given by the Abbé de Lagny, when sitting in the *parlement*.

A kind of dried fruit pudding is mentioned in Taillevent's *Viandier*. It sounds rather like an ancestor of Swiss muesli, using a kind of crumbled wafer as we would use cereals, and it hardly needed the expensive ingredient sugar, although sugar is indicated. The figs, dates and 'raysins de Daigne' (Digne, in the Lower

672

Alps) all chopped, would have made it quite sweet enough for modern tastes without added sugar.

Hoping to provide Louis XIV with fresh figs whenever he wanted, La Quintinie allotted them rectangle 27 in his orchard and kitchen garden, growing the trees as dwarfs and espaliers. He also grew figs in moveable tubs, like orange trees, to outwit the seasons. He particularly praises the local varieties of the round white fig of Versailles and the long white fig of Argenteuil, very good if well protected and grown in a sheltered spot.

White figs, which are thin-skinned, are juicier than the thick-skinned purple sort which the public tends to prefer, simply because colour influences choice. As with other fruits (and despite what I have said above, we must call the fig a fruit), French figs from the south of the country have a better flavour than Italian figs. This is because the Italian figs are forced. The growers of Provence prefer to leave nature to her own devices. At the beginning of the season, in June and July, there is the very large dark purple Dottato; the Solliès fig, which travels very well, comes from the Var and is on sale from mid-August. It is not very juicy, but has a good flavour when it is really ripe. However, real lovers of figs prefer the small fruits of late summer, which are extremely sweet, especially when they are oozing slightly. The green or purple pear-shaped Caromb is one of these, and so is the exquisite Marseillaise, which is both firm and melting. These figs, served at the beginning of a meal in Provence so that everyone can help himself at will between courses, really call for a Frédéric Mistral to sing their praises.

Peasants going to work in the fields of the fifteenth century, like the great lords and ladies of Paris whose palates were tempted by Taillevent, knew only the figs of Provence, dried by the sun and the mistral, one of the few modest exports of an economically poor part of France. Eaten as a local titbit for thousands of years, dried figs also feature among the traditional 'Thirteen Desserts' of Christmas. With walnuts or hazelnuts, raisins and almonds, they were one of what were called the *quatre mendiants*, the four orders of begging friars (so called because the different colours of the nuts and dried fruits suggested the colours of their habits). A treat for children was a 'Capuchin nougat' – a dried fig split open and stuffed with a green walnut.

Hardly anyone in Provence now goes to the trouble of drying the local figs, which may taste delicious but look puny beside those on sale in supermarkets. Like apricots, today's dried figs almost all come from Turkey, and are magnificent specimens. They are white figs dried on the ground in the sun, washed with sea water, then treated against insects and dried in hot air before they are packed. They come from Turkey to France by way of Marseilles, and the best, because they are the freshest, are on sale in the shops in October. After Christmas they tend to harden as the sugar in them makes its way to the exterior, producing a white marbled effect. Shrewd importers who have not packed all their figs at once sometimes treat the remaining stocks with steam and then roll them in flour. It is best not to buy these figs, whether or not the packet mentions flour as an additive:

the statement, though honest, does not make the fruit any better.

The best dried figs are sold strung on raffia loops. They are selected for size and picked when ripe. Unless those in packets or boat-shaped punnets say that they are of Turkish origin (for only the importer is bound to mention the source), they will be thick-skinned, hard Greek or Italian fruits. Their quality is defined in 'crowns', a method which can confuse purchasers. The seven- and nine-crown kinds are the fleshiest, the five- and six-crown kinds the least well flavoured. People who really know about figs, however, buy dried figs by weight, sold straight from the crates in which they were imported and which bear the mark of the Turkish grower. Such are the mysteries of international trade.

There are other ways of serving dried figs than as a dessert, as there were in the time of the Romans, whose culinary notions were not so bad as we sometimes think. Soaked in a mixture of warm water and port, and then cooked separately, they make an excellent accompaniment to game or pork.

Most delicious of all are dried figs gently poached and then steeped in whisky. Purists who shudder at the idea are missing a great delicacy. This marriage of Mediterranean sun and Irish mist was apparently invented by Sir William Bonaparte Wyse (1826–1892), grandson of Lucien Bonaparte. On visiting Avignon he fell in love with the place, became a *félibriste* and wrote some very fine poems in Provençal.

Another poet, this time of Languedoc, Paul Valéry, claimed, 'You may deprive me of anything you like except coffee, cigarettes and figs.'

The Symbolism of Figs and The Fig Tree

The symbolic meanings of figs preceded those of the fig tree: figs have connotations of abundance and initiation. Ancient Egyptian priests ate them at the moment of their consecration ceremonies, and the first desert hermits ate them too (their nutritional value is also obvious). The many seeds in the fig are supposed to signify unity and the universality of true understanding, knowledge and sometimes faith. The same idea is found in the symbolism of the pomegranate.

The white sap of the fig tree, which also runs from the stem of the cut fruit, is a kind of latex and was symbolically associated with both milk and sperm. Feminine and masculine at once, it conveyed universal energy. African women use it in ointments against sterility and to encourage lactation.

The Indians consecrated the fig tree to Vishnu, the second god in the Brahman trinity, saviour of the world, and the ancient Greeks to Dionysos, god of renewal. It sheltered Romulus and Remus at their birth. I have already mentioned the importance of the 'sycophant' priests in ancient Athens, charged with announcing that the figs were ripe; a proof of the regeneration of nature, the news was celebrated by ritual copulation.

The fig trees of East Asian tradition are sacred. One of them was Buddha's famous banyan. Power and life, the axis of the world, inhabited by genies, they stood for knowledge acquired by meditation.

In North Africa the fig is still a fertility symbol, and more particularly a blessing of the earth, itself fertilized by the dead. This gift from the invisible world is restored to it again in offerings of figs left on the rocks at ploughing time, a Berber custom severely criticized by orthodox Muslims. The Berbers have retained many of the ancestral animist beliefs of their race, going back to the dawn of time.

There is some ambiguity in the Arab attitude to the fig, which is nutritionally valuable, and beneficent in its symbolic association with fertility, but also suggestive in shape. Its similarity to the male genitals has led to their being called 'figs', and the word is not now applied to the fruits themselves in polite usage. They are called *khrif*, autumn, after the season that brings them.

Dates

The date, the fruit of *Phoenix dactylifera*, one of the many species of palm trees and described by Linnaeus as 'the prince of plants', was the first exotic fruit Europe knew. As Cato had pointed out to the Senate, Italy was close enough to Africa for African produce to have only a short journey to reach the Forum. Dates eaten in Athens and Rome came easily enough from the other side of the Mediterranean, where people had been eating these fruits, which keep well, since the dawn of time. European palm trees produce nothing edible.

Dates take their name from the fingers, *daktylos*, to which Aristotle compared them, although a bunch of dates really looks more like a clenched fist. The Greeks and Romans knew several varieties of these imported dates; vendors walked around the theatres selling them, wrapped in gilded paper, much as choc ices are sold in the theatre today.

The natural sugar of dates – which contain as much of it as figs – was and still is used to sweeten not only *dulcia*, sweet dishes, but vegetable, meat and fish dishes as well. The Arabs of the Machrek use dates in their *sik badja*, sauté of veal, and the Arabs of the Maghreb include them in a dish of stuffed shad, *sahamak mahchi bittamr*. Apicius also mentions dates as making a *conditum paradoxium*,[29] a 'marvellous' wine, and in confectionery. Dates were used in similar ways in the Middle Ages, and they appear in the seventeenth century in Pierre de Lune's *Cuisinier*, in a recipe for *pâté à la portugaise*.

The fact that dates are so rich in energy-giving sugar was providential for the peoples of the Near East and North Africa, even before they settled down. Dates were eaten fresh, naturally preserved, or dried and ground into meal to make cakes of the kind with which the Persian worshippers of Mazda celebrated the death and resurrection of Zarathustra. The Hebrews pressed them in vessels pierced with holes to make a syrup or *debas* to please the Lord. Even the stones were used as fuel, or in feed for camels and sheep after being soaked in hot water.

Dates may be said to have contributed to the flowering of Sumerian and Babylonian civilization. In gratitude, the Sumerians and Babylonians made the date palm their sacred tree, while the Hebrews saw it as a symbol of justice showered with divine blessings. 'The righteous shall flourish like the palm tree!' said the Psalmist (Psalms 92, xii). It was a model for the columns of the Egyptians, who called it the 'tree of life, the stay and prosperity of the world'. Date-sellers still sing the praises of the Aubret variety in the streets of Cairo: 'O thou, thou red, thou date! Neither the fig nor the grape can compare with thee. Thy blessed flesh is like the flesh of lamb!'

The date had medicinal uses too. Its emollient and sweetening properties (for sugar was regarded as a medicine) were used in the Near East in the same way as in medieval Europe. The 'Diaphoenix Electuary', for instance, was to purge 'the pituitary of the serosities of the brain' – in other words, it was good for a cold. The paste made of dates for chest complaints had no equal for a long time. The Arabs listed 365 culinary and pharmaceutical uses of the date. To them, it was the symbol of the year. The three hundred and sixty-fifth use was as date *shekar*, an alcoholic drink made by the fermentation of date juice, condemned by the Hebrews and their priests. John the Baptist, before his birth, was described as one who would drink no *shekar*. However, the Egyptians had been drinking it since the Second Dynasty.

Cultivation of the date palm goes back over 7000 years, as carved pictures and texts bear witness. It was increased by cuttings or from seed in the oases, although trees grown from seed are either sterile males or females which bear mediocre fruit by parthenogenesis. The female flowers can be fertilized by having male flowers hung among their bunches.

The 500,000 tonnes of dates which now come on the international market represent barely 20 per cent of total production. Most dates are eaten where they are grown. The honey-flavoured *halawi* of Mesopotamia and the *kalesh* of the Persian Gulf are considered the best. In Western Europe, however, the *deglet en nour*, the date of light, is preferred. It is a spicily flavoured date from Algeria. True connoisseurs of dates will hardly even glance at those glove-boxes lined with lacy paper in which they are neatly packed, and prefer whole bunches, which may be less juicy but are absolutely fresh and natural.

Pineapples

When Columbus landed in Guadeloupe in 1493 he found pineapples, which probably came from Brazil. The word *nana* (perfumed), part of the native name retained in French and German *ananas*, is a Brazilian Guarani vocable. As Father de Acosta observed as early as 1589, the Spanish thought this new fruit resembled a pine cone, whence the Spanish name of *piña*, and the English pineapple (the fruit was often just called a 'pine' when it was first introduced into Britain). The

Portuguese set about naturalizing the pineapple in India, Indonesia, Madagascar and Java, and it settled down very well.

Pineapples were also brought to Europe, of course, to give the Old World a taste of their succulence, but the Emperor Charles V, the first monarch to try one, thought it very nasty. The long voyage had completely spoilt the decorative fruit. It was grown in Holland a century later, when hot-houses were first invented, by a French Huguenot who had taken refuge in Leyden. Around 1642 a pineapple was grown in the Duchess of Cleveland's hot-house. It was presented to King Charles II, and immortalized by the court painter. Louis XIV is said to have asked La Quintinie to grow this exotic marvel for him in the frames of the Versailles vegetable garden, but it seems more likely that his successor Louis XV was the only one to benefit. In any case, pineapples became extremely fashionable in the second half of the eighteenth century. Market gardeners asked very high prices because of the great cost of growing them. As yet there could be no question of importing the fruit from the West Indies, for transport was not much faster than in the days of the Emperor Charles V.

The outstanding characteristic of the hot-house pineapple was its acidity. One can see why Alexandre Dumas, who was not a lover of the fruit, recommended soaking it in water and then serving it in wine and sugar. With the advent of steamships voyages became much shorter, but the pineapple was expensive until the end of the Second World War, except as juice or in cans from the United States.

Pineapples have become more democratic since air transport has made it possible to deliver them almost perfectly ripe, a miracle which today's consumer takes for granted. We now get pineapples from Hawaii (one of the major centres of the industry, providing three-quarters of world pineapple consumption), the West Indies, Florida, Kenya, South Africa, Cameroon and the Ivory Coast. Pineapples are the Ivory Coast's main export. They can be found in any market at a reasonable price. The French were eating nearly 50,000 tonnes a year at the beginning of the 1980s: 42,000 tonnes from the Ivory Coast and 5000 from Cameroon. The people of Martinique, who consider themselves very French, protest at trade agreements favouring former colonies that have won their independence, while all they can manage to export themselves are a few thousand tonnes. Small pineapples are better flavoured. The unfortunate people of Benin, formerly Dahomey, laboured to produce an enormous variety at Bohicon and then found they could not market it.

The taste for pineapple can of course be explained by its delicious flavour and its freshness – and nowadays we can be sure it is perfectly fresh – and by its high vitamin and mineral salt content, which make it very welcome in European winters, but it also has digestive properties. Many 'slimming' diets praise it to the skies. It is even claimed that it can make you thin. It does in fact contain an enzyme, bromelin (the pineapple is a bromeliad) which can digest a thousand times its own weight in protein. Some specialists in obesity have promoted a diet consisting solely

677

of pineapple. The idea is that the bromelin, once ingested and finding nothing in the stomach, will set about devouring extra unwanted fat. A kilo of fresh pineapple a day as a 48-hour diet once a week was expected to work wonders. Dieticians of the old school, like Apfelbaum, are sceptical if not actually hostile. There is another method: you drink a decoction of pineapple peel, well rinsed to remove insecticides sprayed on the fruit while it is growing. Three litres a day of this infusion is supposed to melt away as many pounds of fat. However, some people find the drink has a very purgative effect.

Fresh pineapple, whether for a diet or as a delicious food, should be prepared just as it is in its native countries; peeled thickly and cut into slices lengthwise, like melon. It is also an ingredient in many sweet-sour or spicy dishes of more or less authentic exotic cookery, Indian, Sri Lankan and Chinese. Duck with pineapple, from South China, is a very famous recipe.

Although I have been describing the pineapple as a fruit, that is not quite accurate. It is really a collection of berries, the 'eyes', which have fused together. A herbaceous plant of the Bromeliaceae family, with stiff, slender leaves that are prickly at the tips, the pineapple grows to a maximum height of one metre, bearing a central stem which swells into a compact inflorescence and has a plume of similar leaves on top. The flowers produce the multiple fruit. Plants are obtained from cuttings, or very often by replanting the top cut off the fruit, which will produce a new inflorescence in a year's time.

Bananas

The banana tree is not actually a tree at all but a herb, a giant herb, and even more extraordinary than the pineapple. It sprouts from a rhizome and can reach a height of nine metres, growing very rapidly, and the process takes only a year. The leaves emerge one above another, passing up through the tube formed by the older leaf stems. When the last has grown, an inflorescence forms at the base of the banana and mounts the stem too, eventually emerging at the axis and drooping towards the ground. Each group of flowers, borne like a crown around the stem, becomes a bunch or 'hand' of bananas. No fertilization takes place, and the flowers are sterile.

For this reason Buddha made the banana plant the symbol of the futility of earthly possessions. Classic Chinese iconography shows him meditating on this key to wisdom at the foot of a banana tree.

A banana plant produces only one bunch or 'hand' in its life, but that bunch may comprise from 100 to 400 bananas. Then it dies. You cannot grow a new banana plant from banana seeds, although a new plant may grow spontaneously beside its dead brother, for the good reason that bananas, not being true fruits, have no seeds, any more than the 'flowers' had any sexual organs. The banana plant which comes up next time grows from the rhizome, and when you are starting a banana plantation you plant pieces of rhizomes or cuttings of spontaneous shoots.

The banana looks as if it had landed on earth from another world: a tree which is really a herb, 'flowers' and 'fruits' which are so called for lack of any real way to define them by normal terrestrial standards. Nor are these all the surprises the banana has in store: at the dawn of time it produced neither inflorescence nor bananas, as those naturalized in Europe still do not. No one knows when, why or how the miracle occurred, but it was in South-East Asia. Although they do not actually invoke the Holy Ghost, ancient traditions of those regions made the banana a kind of original fruit, or at any rate a gift of the gods. The first botanists of the Renaissance followed the lead of the Arabs and called the plant *Musa paradisiaca*.

The mystery of the banana becomes even stranger when you reflect that it is found on the other side of the world too, in Central America and the Caribbean, not in its wild state (*Musa acumiata*) but in the cultivated mutation which produces bananas. Moreover, it has done so for so long that it has a name in all the local languages. Even before Father de Acosta gave us a description of it, Garcilaso, grandson of the last Incas, spoke of it as a tree native not to Peru but to the Atlantic seaboard. Again, this looks like evidence for social contacts in very ancient times occurring across the Pacific and the Central American isthmus, for propagation of the banana by such natural means as dispersal by birds seems impossible. Some people have wondered whether it was carried by marine currents, but that does not explain how it crossed the isthmus. Others have taken their chance to propound the theory that we owe bananas to benevolent extra-terrestrials, making the unlikely more unlikely yet.

The enormous bunch of grapes, *esh kol*, which the Hebrew emissaries of Moses cut in a valley near Hebron (in Jordan, south of Jerusalem) may actually have been a bunch of bananas. ('And they came unto the brook of Eshcol, and cut down from thence a branch with one cluster of grapes, and they bare it between two upon a staff ... the place was called the brook Eshcol, because of the cluster of grapes which the children of Israel cut down from thence ...' [Numbers 13, xxiii-xxiv].) The banana can grow and bear fruit in such climates quite well if it has water available. It passed through Arabia, crossed the Red Sea in the opposite direction from the Children of Israel (how, though?) and invaded Ethiopia in the sixth century AD. Earlier, the ancient Egyptians did not know it. By the fourteenth century it had colonized the whole of Africa. An Arab traveller mentions it as existing in the south of Morocco. In the fifteenth century the Portuguese called it by its Arab name of *al vaneyra*. The islanders of São Tomé called the fruit *abana*, and Pigafetta mentions seeing it in the Congo at the end of the sixteenth century, where it has long been grown.

Another oddity is the name given to the banana plant by the Spanish when they arrived in the New World. Father de Acosta himself wondered at it. Why *platano* or *plantano*, which normally meant plane tree? As he realized, there was a vast amount of difference between the branches of the plane in which the Emperor Caligula had picnicked magnificently with 11 guests and banana leaves, if only because the banana has no branches at all. The size of the leaves is quite different too. One of them, as he reported, could almost cover a man. Perhaps the name was originally a joke, based on the idea that bananas are as common in the West Indies as plane trees in Castile.

Banana fritters with honey sweetened Napoleon's last days on St Helena, but the cookery writers of the sixteenth to nineteenth centuries ignore the fruit entirely. Dumas is alone in referring briefly to it. Admittedly exporting bananas was difficult because transport was so slow. ('Yes! We have no bananas!' ran an Edwardian music-hall song.) Bananas ripen very quickly above a temperature of 12 degrees, and freeze below it. They had to wait to come to Europe in any quantity until the 1920s, when they were brought by specially equipped banana boats with air-conditioned holds. The banana ports of France are Le Havre, for American bananas, and Marseilles, for African bananas. The fruit then became very popular. Some years later they had another good advertisement in variety, when Josephine Baker, clad only in a girdle of bananas, sang a song with a refrain to the effect that she liked bananas because they had no bones.

The banana is a staple of the diet of tropical countries. Large kinds such as the 'plantain' (from *plantano*), to which the Creoles of the West Indies and La Réunion have given a number of picturesque names such as 'Oh! là là maman!' accompany savoury dishes in the same way as starchy roots. In West Africa they are pounded to make a kind of bread called *foutou* or *foufou*, which is served with spicy sauces, meat or fish, and such dishes have taken on that generic name. In the West Indies, South America, Africa and Asia, whether large or small, they are spiced and fried. In India they are stuffed and baked. The smaller the banana, the sweeter it is; the little red-skinned varieties, known as 'figs' in Martinique, are hard to find in Europe except in luxury food shops. Canary bananas, small and thin-skinned, are thought to have a particularly good flavour.

The banana contains a lot of starch (21 per cent), especially when it is unripe. It is hard to digest in that state. As it ripens the starch turns to glucose. The fruit provides a great deal of energy (90 calories per 100 grams). It is also rich in potassium (380 milligrams), so that a banana a day would provide more than an adult's daily requirement. In hot countries where people lose a lot of moisture by perspiration this makes it very valuable. If bananas are at all unripe it is a good idea to poach them in their skins, especially for small children and old people, but they must be well washed first, because while the bunches are still on the tree they are frequently powdered with thiobenzadole, a very toxic fungicide. A banana beer is made in Kenya from a fermented decoction of the fruit.

The natural aroma of the banana is extremely volatile, and proves disappointing in cooked dishes, creams, milk products, ices and even liqueurs. For such purposes, therefore, the flavour is provided by amyl acetate, which is very like ripe bananas.

Avocados

As Father de Acosta said feelingly, it would be 'impossible to intreate' of all the exotic fruits, so I will complete my basketful with the avocado pear, *Persea americana*, also sometimes known as the alligator pear. This handsome fruit, with its large stone, grows on a tree of the laurel family.

Although the Americans had cultivated it in Florida and California since the United States came into existence, the avocado remained almost unknown to Europeans in the Old World until after the Second World War. It is a native of Central America, and was found in Colombia by Hernandez de Oviredo in 1526. It was highly esteemed by the Mayas and Aztecs. The Spanish turned its native name of *awa gualt* into *avocado*.

The colonists appreciated its nutritional value – it has a high fat content and a nutty flavour – and they planted its large stone in any of the tropical regions they came to. Eventually, local varieties developed.

In American culinary tradition, from the southern United States to South America, the buttery pulp is served as an appetizer with chilli or spices, like the famous Mexican purée called guacamole. The French-speaking Creoles of the Indian Ocean traditionally serve it as a dessert, with sugar and lemon. Bernardin de Saint-Pierre, posted to Mauritius, thought it quite good. Both chilli or lemon aid the digestion of the very rich pulp. Today the American manner seems to be in the ascendant. The many tonnes of avocados for sale on market stalls and in supermarkets are rather unimaginatively eaten, with vinaigrette or a mayonnaise, which may have ketchup added to it or crabmeat or prawns mixed in.

We certainly eat nothing like as many avocados as the Mexicans (in Mexico consumption is 15 kilos per head a year), but advertising has brought them to all parts of Western Europe, and like oranges they are a good source of income to Israel, which provides some 70 per cent of imports. The Israeli avocado sold under the Carmel brand name, originally the kind with a purplish skin, has had competition in the shape of the *lulla* from Martinique, which can be enormous and is not too expensive. In its native land it is made into a salad with shredded raw salt cod. The small African avocadoes from the Ivory Coast, Senegal and Kenya are much fattier than those from the West Indies, containing 22 per cent lipids instead of 8 per cent.

Avocado oil, used in cosmetics, is extracted from the pulp, and the people of Zaire brew a beer called *babine* from avocado leaves. An Avocado grown as a house plant from a stone soaked in a yoghurt pot full of water until it germinates will not fruit, as they discovered at the Jardin des Plantes when they obtained an avocado plant from a stone early in the nineteenth century. In any case the avocado has a curious method of fertilization. The female organ, or pistil, comes to maturity first. Next day the male organs or stamens unfold ... who says that punctuality is a specifically masculine virtue?

681

FRUITS OF THE MONTH OF AUGUST

When we are once in August, we are arrived, as I may say, to the great Magazin of an infinite number of good Fruits. For in the beginning of this Month there continues still as great a Plenty as can be desired, both of Figs and backward Cherries, of bigarros and Apricocks … and above all, this is the illustrious and happy Month for the Fruits that charm me most, that is to say, for certain plums … the two sorts of Perdrigons, white and violet; the Prune Royal, the Cloath of Gold Plum, the Queen Claude, etc. … likewise all those … that bear the title of Damask, and are of Five or Six Fashions very different from one another, either in Bigness, Colour, Figure, or more or less early Maturity; there being of them the White, Black, Red, Violet, Grey, etc. …

Jean-Baptiste de La Quintinie (1626–1688) *The Compleat Gard'ner*
(translated by John Evelyn)

STRAWBERRY CREAM

Take about half a setier of hulled, washed and drained strawberries, and crush them in a mortar; boil three half-setiers of cream with half a setier of milk, and some sugar; let them boil and reduce by half; let them cool a little, and then add your strawberries, and mix all together; add rennet, about as much as the size of a coffee bean, and put it in when the cream is just luke-warm; then put all through a strainer and place it in a pot which may go over the hot embers without breaking; put your pot over the hot embers, cover with a lid, and place a little of the hot embers on the lid; when the cream is set, put it in a cool place, or on ice, until you serve it.

Menon, *La cuisinière bourgeoise* (1774)

FROM GRIGNAN, 9 SEPTEMBER 1694, TO M

DE COULANGES

... and as for melons, figs and muscat grapes, it is a curious thing, but if for some strange fantastical reasons we wanted to find a bad melon, we would have to send to Paris for it. There are no such fruits here.

The Marquise de Sévigné

PINES

The Pines, or Pine-aples, are of the same fashion and forme outwardly to those of Castille, but within they wholly differ, for that they have neither apples, nor scales, but are all one flesh, which may be eaten when the skinne is off. It is a fruit that hath an excellent smell, and is very pleasant and delightfull in taste, it is full of iuyce, and of a sweete and sharpe taste, they eate it being cut in morcells, and steeped a while in water and salt. Some say that this breedes choler, and that the use thereof is not very healthfull. But I have not seen any experience thereof, that might breede beleefe. They grow one by one like a cane or stalke, which riseth among many leaves, like to the lilly, but somewhat bigger. The apple is on the toppe of every cane, it growes in hote and moist grounde, and the best are those of the Ilands of Barlovente. It growes not in Peru, but they carry them from the Andes, the which are neither good nor ripe. One presented one of these Pine-apples to the Emperour Charles the fift, which must have cost much paine and care to bring it so farre, with the plant from the Indies, yet would he not trie the taste. I have seene in New Spaine, conserves of these pines, which was very good.

Father Joseph de Acosta (1539–1600)
The Natural and Moral History of the Indies
(Translated by Edward Grimston, 1604)

THE PLANTAIN [banana]

It is a plant that makes a stock within the earth, out of the which springs many and sundrie sprigges, divided and not ioyned together. These sprigges growe bigge, every one making a small tree apart, and in growing they cast forth these leaves, which are of a fine greene, smooth, and great, as I have said. When it is grown to the height of an estado *and a halfe, or two, it puttes forth one only bough of fruite, whereon sometimes there are great numbers of this fruite, and sometimes lesse. I have tolde upon some of these boughs three hundred, whereof every one was a spanne long, more or lesse, and two or three fingers bigge; yet is there much difference heerin betwixt some and others. They take away the rinde, and all the rest is a firme kernell and tender, good to eate, and nourishing. This fruite inclines more to cold then heate.*

Father Joseph de Acosta (1539–1600)
The Natural and Moral History of the Indies
(Translated by Edward Grimston, 1604)

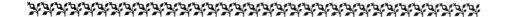

THE PALTAS *[avocados]* ARE HOTE AND DELICATE

... *The Palta is a great tree, and carries a faire leafe, which hath a fruit like to great peares; within it hath a great stone, and all the rest is soft meate, so as when they are full ripe, they are, as it were, butter, and have a delicate taste. In Peru the Paltas are great, and have a very hard skale, which may be taken off whole. This fruit is most vsuall in Mexico, having a thinne skinne, which may be pilled like an apple: they hold it for a very holesome meate, and, as I have said, it declines a little from heat. These Mamayes, Guayavos, and Paltas, be the Indians peaches, apples and peares; and yet would I rather choose them of Europe. But some others by vse, or it may be by affection, doe more esteem those of the Indies. I doubt not but such as have not seene nor tasted of these fruites, will take small pleasure to read this discourse, yea, they will grow wearie to heare it, as I have done in writing it, which makes me to abridge it, speaking of some other sortes of fruites, for it were impossible to intreate of them all.*

Father Joseph de Acosta (1539–1600)
The Natural and Moral History of the Indies
(Translated by Edward Grimston, 1604)

687

Chapter 22

The Evolution of Vegetables

Around the year 400 BC Hippocrates wrote:

> I hold that not even the mode of living and nourishment enjoyed at the present time by men in health would have been discovered, had a man been satisfied with the same food and drink as satisfy an ox, a horse, and every animal save man, for example the products of the earth – fruits, wood and grass ... our present ways of living have, I think, been discovered and elaborated during a long period of time ... so from what, after steeping it, winnowing, grinding and sifting, kneading, baking, they produced bread. ... Experimenting with food they boiled or baked, after mixing, many other things, combining the strong and uncompounded with the weaker components so as to adapt all to the constitution and power of man.

Over the centuries science has confirmed the old Greek doctor's theories.

As we saw in part I, in the early days of hunter-gatherer societies the vegetable foods eaten were mainly those small fruits or large seeds and grains which grew within easy reach. With roots and bulbs, they made up a substantial part of the diet. Such foods were rich in starch that satisfied the stomach for some time. But leaves were not scorned, although you had to eat a great deal more of them before your hunger was satisfied. They have their own virtues, and are unlikely ever to be dropped from the diet. The same applies to certain fruits with flesh that is not sweet, or only slightly sweet, but still have a good flavour.

In French, it was not until the sixteenth century that the term *légumes* was used for vegetables in the English sense of the word: edible plants of which the leaves, stems, roots or fruits (other than sweet fruits) are eaten. Before that people spoke of herbs, roots or fruits, whichever was appropriate, and *légumes* was used in the present English sense of 'legumes', the edible seeds of leguminous plants such as peas, broad beans and, later on, haricot beans. Similarly, the writers of classical antiquity used the term 'asparagus' for 'any long green stem like that of asparagus',[1] and lettuces and cabbages were allowed to bolt on purpose. Today we take care not to let them go to seed, and sometimes hold the influence of the moon and Fridays responsible when they do. As we consign the bolted lettuce we consider unfit to eat to the compost heap, we might remember the wise words of La Quintinie, who did not credit the moon or Fridays with any such influence at all.

> Sow or set any sort of Seeds or Plants, in all the several Quarters of the Moon, and I will promise you the same success in all, provided your Earth be good and well prepared; that there be no Fault in your Seeds or Plants, and that the Season be Favourable.... 'Twould be a rare Secret indeed, if the Moone should hold an Intelligence with the Gard'ner, causing some of his Plants to Spring up apace, and hindering the growth of others, just as he would have them.

The discussion is not yet closed.

I have discussed legumes, roots and bulbs above; in the kitchen garden which is the scene of this chapter, therefore, I shall look first at green vegetables. But not all vegetables are green: there are blanched salad plants, and colourful vegetable fruits such as the red tomato and the purple aubergine.

The kitchen garden, known in France as a *potager* from the sixteenth century onwards, was the place where plants grew and were gathered for the pot, to be boiled and made into *potage* or pottage.[2] A sop of bread dipped into this liquid dish made it a 'soup', almost a complete meal. As we have seen, early pottages of this kind began to be made as soon as mankind devised some means of balancing a hollow vessel of fireproof material over a flame.

Many former food plants are no longer part of our diet. Some of those once cultivated have reverted to the wild, including orache and spinach dock, now a weed in grassland; mallow, used only in herbal remedies today; nettles, although they are delicious young and tender; plantains, which people stopped eating in the eighteenth century; cardoons, related to the globe artichoke but not as good; marsh-samphire, which now grows only among the dunes; and mustard as a vegetable, though it is still grown for its seeds. In all, more than 50 edible plant species disappeared from European tables at the beginning of the nineteenth century, although one new one, chicory, came into existence.

'The greengrocer's shop': painting by Pieter Aertz or Aertsen (*c.* 1508–1575). Vegetables and other foodstuffs were not always thought of as decorative motifs; Aertsen, of Amsterdam, is famous for the leading part he played in developing still life and genre paintings, depicting heaps of vegetables, fruit and other foods with great and indeed sometimes excessive realism.

Cabbages

The cabbage is the oldest of the edible varieties of vegetables which provided inspiration for the gatherers in their plant-hunting and their culinary creativity. The wild cabbage, *Brassica oleracea*, was a small plant but had firm, fleshy leaves. It grew in all European coastal areas, absorbing fortifying mineral salts, and can still be found on the coasts of the English Channel. The magic of cultivation has now created some 400 varieties: there are green cabbages, red cabbages, white cabbages, pointed or wrinkle-leaved Italian cabbages, round, frost-resistant North European cabbages, kohl-rabi with its edible roots, oilseed rape, broccoli grown for its spears of flower-heads, Brussels sprouts grown ever since the seventeenth century for the little buds sprouting from the stem, and the cauliflowers that resemble a bridal bouquet and were popular in ancient Greece and known to the Romans, but then fell out of favour until La Quintinie reintroduced them at Versailles. The elongated Chinese cabbage and the swede are also brassicas. The latter, believed to be a cross between the cabbage and the turnip, was a great standby in the diet during the Second World War.

The Neolithic Near Eastern peoples, the Hebrews and the Egyptians did not eat cabbage; the plant is an old inhabitant of Europe. The first recorded mention of it is in a treatise on plants allegedly written by Eudemus of Athens, which distinguishes between three kinds of cultivated cabbage. The Greeks and Romans believed that if you ate cabbage during a banquet it would keep you from getting drunk. A legend attributes its origin to the sworn enemy of Dionysus, King Lycurgus of the Edones, a Thracian people. He did not invent it on purpose. Dionysus, sweeping triumphantly through Europe with his train, reached Thrace with his gifts of wine and found Lycurgus opposing him. Armed only with an ox goad, the king captured the entire intoxicated army except for Dionysus himself. The god dived into the sea and took refuge in the cave of Thetis. Rhea, goddess of the Earth, sent Lycurgus mad, and he cut his son Dryas to pieces, thinking he was a vine stock. The Edones overpowered him, tortured him and had him torn apart. Cabbages grew from the sand where the tears of Lycurgus had fallen.

The B vitamins contained in cabbage leaves do seem to have soothing and oxygenating qualities, very welcome when the mind is clouded by the fumes of alcohol. Research at a Texan university has extracted a substance from cabbage which is useful in the treatment of alcoholism.

Like Lycurgus, the cabbage remains hostile to the vine. Mediterranean farmers never plant it near vineyards in case bees transfer its odour to the bunches of grapes. Nor is it grown near beehives, because it might taint the flavour of the honey.

From classical times to the present day, cabbage has not been regarded as a sophisticated vegetable. Horace liked it, but he ate it with plenty of pickled pork, and in any case he affected a taste for all things rustic.[3] The genuine countrymen of his time who ate cabbage daily had nothing but salt and thyme to go with it. The cabbage is inclined to cause wind, and the smell while it cooks is unpleasant. Lucullus said it had no place on a gentleman's table.

As everyone knows, Diogenes, famous for his philosophy and his boorish manners, lived in a tub and had low standards of personal hygiene. For reasons of economy and idealism combined he ate nothing but cabbage and drank only water, cupped in his hands. Cabbage had been recommended by Pythagoras. But another philosopher, Aristippus of Cyrene, a pupil of Socrates and founder of the Hedonist school, was tireless in his search after subtle and refined pleasures, and was entirely opposed to the ideas of Diogenes. Cabbage, he claimed, was a melancholy food which dulled sensations and so cut life itself short; Diogenes was mad, but would never be an old madman. To this Diogenes replied that if Aristippus ate more

691

cabbage he would not fawn on the great (for the hedonist was a 'parasite' at the court of Dionysius, tyrant of Syracuse). In fact Diogenes lived to the good old age of 90, while Aristippus was only just over 40 when he died.

Is the cabbage really a panacea and the secret of long life? Cato, another classical writer attracted by the idea of the simple life, said so, and he lived to be over 80. He particularly recommended it raw, dressed with vinegar.[4] He also recommended a diet containing cabbage to prevent disease, and claimed to owe the existence of his 28 sons to it: like himself, he said, they had never eaten anything else! He must have been exaggerating slightly, since his youngest child was not yet weaned at the time of writing, but it was still an impressive family for a period when infant mortality was so high. The French have it that babies are found in the cabbage patch (the equivalent of the British gooseberry bush), but this 'tradition' is a late, nineteenth-century fabrication and can hardly have been in Cato's mind, although the stalk of the cut cabbage does exude a milky liquid, like the fig tree, which could be seen as a symbol of fertility. Although the tradition of cabbage-patch babies is not an authentic piece of country lore, it was an old custom in many parts of France to bring newly married couples cabbage soup first thing in the morning after their bridal night.

Cabbages were at first eaten for their stems, like broccoli. The heads became more rounded in Caesar's time. The Romans liked their vegetables large, and according to Pliny cultivation enlarged the cabbage to the point where it was too big for the tables of the poor. The Emperor Tiberius, who did have a large enough table, had to be stern before his son Drusus would eat it, but one should remember that Drusus was a friend of Apicius who – according to Pliny again – preferred *cauliculi*, cabbage shoots. He gives six recipes for them,[5] highly seasoned with aromatics, one including leeks and another green olives. The latter seems to have been a kind of pudding made with semolina, pine kernels and dried raisins, seasoned with pepper. *Cauliculi*, called *krambosparagos* (cabbage asparagus) by the Greeks, were sold in bunches at market, conforming to Diocletian's sixth edict.

In commenting on the personal tastes of Apicius, Pliny does not fail to mention the healing properties of cabbage leaves and cabbage juice applied externally. We know now that cabbage is rich in sulphur, which accounts for its unattractive smell as it cooks.[6] In the Middle Ages a cabbage plaster was used as a remedy for sciatica and varicose ulcers (it still is in some country districts), and there was a cough syrup made with cabbage. An open fracture suffered by the Emperor Maximilian in 1569 closed spectacularly under a dressing of cabbage which the Emperor's doctor Rembert Dodens insisted on applying despite his patient's protests.

At the end of the eighteenth century ships setting out on long voyages included many crates of cabbages among their provisions for the anti-scorbutic virtues of the vitamin C cabbage contains. During Captain Cook's first expedition in 1769 a violent storm injured some 40 members of the *Adventurer*'s crew. The ship's doctor saved the victims from gangrene by applying compresses of cabbage leaves to their wounds. We are assured by the ship's log that the idea came into his mind as he sat down to eat a dish of cabbage and bacon.

Choucroute or sauerkraut, cabbage preserved in brine, has been known since very ancient times. Preserving food from decay by acid fermentation was a very old culinary discovery. Dr Maurizio claims that it was as useful to humanity as drying and smoking. Lactic fermentation, as we saw in connection with beer and bread, destroys microbes.

Choucroute had its forerunners in the shape of acid soups made from the young shoots, buds and leaves of birch eaten by the people of Northern Europe in Neolithic times, and those made of nettles, cardoons and sorrel in the Central European manner and eaten until the sixteenth century. Choucroute made with cabbage goes back to the Germanic invasions. Germanic tribes from the steppes brought the recipe in their baggage, or at least applied their own procedures to the native cabbages they found.

At first choucroute was always made at home, but in the seventeenth century it became one of the first foods produced by the manufacturing industry, then just developing from such small-scale activities as oil and wine pressing, salting and pickling. Choucroute was a source of great profit to Magdeburg in Germany and Strasbourg in Alsace.

Rich in phosphorus, potassium and vitamins preserved by fermentation, choucroute was regarded by Captain Cook as one of the secrets of the success of his expeditions, and he included it among his shipboard provisions.[7] As we have just seen, he also had fresh cabbage available for the ship's doctor. The British Navy's suppliers soon installed sauerkraut magazines where pursers could stock up before sailing.

Cooked or raw, choucroute is perfectly digestible by most people, particularly if it contains juniper berries. It is commonly thought to cause flatulence, but the real culprits are the fat meats often eaten with it, or quite frequently the white wine used in cooking such dishes or the beer drunk with them. It has been made in the same way for centuries, although the process is mechanized now: the cabbage is chopped into thin strips, put in brine with spices, and then fermented in casks.

There are about 400 cabbage species. The most common can be divided into five categories:

Round cabbages with smooth leaves, including white, green and red cabbages; cabbages with wrinkled leaves, such as the Savoy.

Pointed cabbages, including European spring cabbages and Chinese cabbage.

Green, curly brassicas such as kale, particularly useful for animal fodder or for decorative purposes.

Cabbages with hypertrophied, budding stems, i.e., Brussels sprouts.

Cabbages with dense inflorescences, such as cauliflower, or inflorescences borne in spears, such as broccoli.

Cauliflowers

In the time of Henri IV, Oliver de Serres mentioned the cauliflower reintroduced into France by the Genoese at the end of the Renaissance, but the vegetable did not become popular until the time of Louis XIV, who liked it cooked in stock, seasoned with nutmeg, and served with fresh butter. If the cauliflower is blanched first, this recipe still tastes very good.

The cauliflower is principally a summer vegetable in all European countries. In the EC, Italy is the major producer of cauliflowers, with France second. Third comes the United Kingdom, where the cauliflower is the most widely grown of all vegetables. Out of total production, summer and autumn cauliflowers predominate (65 per cent), while winter cauliflowers account for only about 35 per cent of the crop. Belgium and Germany grow only summer cauliflowers, and a few for picking in autumn.

The French cauliflower season begins in June and ends in May of the following year, so there are cauliflowers on the market all the year round. They are cheapest in June, at the beginning of the new summer season. Summer cauliflowers are grown mainly in the north of the country, Burgundy, Aquitaine and the Loire valley; autumn, winter and spring cauliflowers in Provence, Brittany and Lower Normandy. Brittany, where two-thirds of all French cauliflowers are grown, has air links exporting them to the United Kingdom in the months when no British cauliflowers are available.

The French eat an average 3.55 kilos of cauliflowers per head a year. The Paris area consumes most – 4.05 kilos a head – while the people of the southern Mediterranean areas eat only just over 3 kilos each. West Germany, the Netherlands and the United Kingdom are the main export outlets for French cauliflowers. France imports more cauliflowers from Italy than anywhere else.

The cauliflower has about 36 calories per 100 grams. It contains from 4 to 6 per cent glucids and from 1 to 5 per cent protids. It is rich in vitamins C, B and K (which helps blood to clot), and its vitamin C content (50 to 100 milligrams) is greater than that of orange juice. It contains a number of mineral salts, calcium, magnesium and potassium, and is good for the bones, the skin, the hair and the nails.

Cauliflowers with a fine, compact, regular flower-head or curd are the best. The green leaves surrounding the curd should be bright and exude moisture when they are broken. The cauliflower should be heavy, and is best eaten really fresh, although it will keep for two or three days in the vegetable drawer of the refrigerator. Cooked with two dessert-spoons of flour and the juice of half a lemon, it will keep its colour and give off almost no odour.

People sometimes forget that cauliflowers are good eaten raw, when all their vitamins are retained, divided into small sprigs and dipped into various kinds of sauces, or vinaigrette or mayonnaise.

Salad

The name of *zelada*, 'salad', was first applied to a dish which often appeared on festive tables in fifteenth-century Milan.[8] It was actually a kind of ragoût, very liquid and very salty (whence its name), and it was flavoured with preserves, mustard and lemon and decorated with marzipan. It was served in individual cups – a novelty at the time. This 'salad' became so famous as a local delicacy that it had a place of honour at the magnificent celebrations in Innsbruck of the wedding of Bianca Sforza, the younger daughter of Duke Galeazzo, to the Emperor Maximilian. On that occasion the dish was a 'salad' of pike, surrounded by marzipan figures representing the great personages of both courts, each announced and accompanied by a fanfare as it was borne in.

The sauce for this soup-like dish, originally a hot one, came to include various kinds of green stuff which had usually been pickled in vinegar or salt, and then fresh cooked greens, or raw greens in the Roman manner.[9] In the fourteenth century, *Le Viandier* (in the Bibliothèque Nationale manuscript) recommends serving watercress as a *porée* (a dish of vegetables chopped or of a soupy consistency) mixed with white beet, no doubt to alleviate the strong flavour. The *Ménagier de Paris*, his contemporary, specifies no use for lettuce except in ragoûts and pies. It was always chopped. In the next century, raw vegetables were sprinkled with oil and vinegar in the Roman manner instead of being served with sauces. Rabelais gives a long list of 'salads', including cress, hops, wild cress, asparagus and chervil. Platina adds lettuce, bugloss, purslane, mallow, chicory, pimpernel, sorrel, dandelion, boiled leek, etc. As Montaigne says, 'any variety of herb in existence may go by the name of salad.' Ronsard, who was very fond of salads, turned the recipe of his time into a poem. At the beginning of the eighteenth century, the French word *salade* came to be used for the salad plants themselves, and began to have its secondary, disparaging sense of a hotchpotch or mess in modern French.

According to Saint-Simon, Louis XIV always had a weakness for salads. 'He ate a prodigious quantity of salad all the year round.' The hygienic precepts of the time held that salads were 'moistening and refreshing, liberate the stomach, promote sleep and appetite, temper the ardours of Venus and quench thirst', all of which is true enough, although modern dieticians seldom concern themselves with the ardours of Venus. In Brillat-Savarin's anecdote of the curé's omelette, he remarks: 'Next came the salad. (I commend salad to all those that have faith in me; it refreshes without weakening, and soothes without irritating: I often call it the rejuvenator).'

But Fagon, Louis XIV's stern medical mentor, did not approve of La Quintinie's fresh, healthy salad stuff, any more than he approved of green peas, which he regarded as his personal enemies; he would not even have them added to the King's soup. There was some reason for his distrust of salads. It is now considered that the cellulose in vegetable fibres, particularly eaten raw, makes them inadvisable in the diet of people with digestive disorders such as those from which his august patient suffered as a result of his prodigious Bourbon appetite. Towards the end of his life, Louis XIV was forbidden to eat salads in general, and more particularly salads of lettuce and cucumber (which are certainly hard to digest) flavoured with *fines herbes*, pepper, salt and vinegar, which was lavishly and indiscriminately added. The famous saying that a good dressing demands 'a miser for the vinegar, a spendthrift for the oil, and a wise man for the salt' postdates the seventeenth century, and so does the precept cited by Le Roux de Lincy: 'Salad well washed and salted, a little vinegar and plenty of oil'.[10]

Late in life, the Sun King was obliged to follow the Spartan diet which Mme de Maintenon supervised, but he compensated for its austerity by a grandeur which astonished the crowds who came to watch their king at dinner. In his more carefree youth his table manners had been less dignified, and he used to amuse himself by throwing bread pellets or even fruit at the ladies (to the despair of La Quintinie, who did not like to see his precious produce treated with such disrespect). The Duc de Luynes tells us that one day a lady in waiting of the Princesse de Conti was struck in the face by an apple. Without more ado, the young lady picked up a salad bowl containing lettuce in vinaigrette and emptied it over her sovereign's head. Thirty years later, when Fagon had banished salad from his table, she would not have had such a weapon at hand.

Despite appearances, there is considerable gastronomic art involved in mixing a salad. Like the royal person, indeed, it deserves respect, for there is an element of sacred ceremonial about it, especially when it is really simple, and must therefore be perfect. You do not just make a salad, you dress it, in the same way as altars are dressed for particular liturgical occasions. This usage, like the most usual sense of the verb 'to dress', meaning to clothe oneself, comes ultimately from Latin *directus*, the past participle of the verb *dirigere*, meaning 'to put straight', and a garment which falls in a straight line is elegant and perfect, just as a good salad should be.

Dressing a salad is not simply a matter of putting leaves and other ingredients in a salad bowl; it embraces a whole ritual, which should begin first thing in the morning in the vegetable garden. You choose the crispest, freshest and best lettuce, still quivering with dew as it wakes from its sleep. The next part of the ritual is picking it over. The less perfect leaves must be firmly rejected and over-large ones torn; they should never be left so large that they have to be cut on the plate. The lettuce must be scrupulously and delicately washed and drained, so as not to bruise the tender leaves. Finally, if the dressing itself is to be the familiar, simple and excellent vinaigrette, the French custom is to put it in the bottom of the salad bowl, with the large salad servers crossed above it (they should never be of metal, even silver) and the leaves lightly laid over them, to be mixed in just before the salad is served. If this is done they will not wilt. There was an old saying that politeness was at the bottom of the salad bowl: it was good manners to help yourself first, since the best of the salad would be at the bottom.

The classic French way of making a salad is usually considered the best, particularly in the English-speaking countries, where vinaigrette is known as French dressing. Paul Newman has lent his name to the promotion of a ready-bottled vinaigrette sold to benefit young drug addicts.

According to Brillat-Savarin, the art of salad-making in the French style was introduced to England by a French émigré who had fled to London from the Revolution. He tells us 'the story of a Frenchman who made his fortune in London through his skill in mixing salad'. This man, d'Albignac by name, was approached in a tavern by some fashionable young men who asked 'politely: "Mr Frenchman, your countrymen are said to excel in the art of salad-making; would you do my friends and myself the favour of mixing one for us?"' The salad was 'the required masterpiece' and d'Albignac, having become known in London as 'the fashionable salad-maker', used to go from house to house to prepare his dressings.

> He soon had a carriage to convey him more quickly to the various places where he was summoned, and a servant carrying in a mahogany case all the ingredients he had added to his repertory, such as different sorts of vinegar, oils with or without fruity flavour, soy, caviare, truffles, anchovies, ketchup, meat extracts, and even yolks of egg, which are the distinguishing feature of mayonnaise. Later, he had similar cases manufactured, which he fitted out completely and sold by the hundred.

Having made his fortune, d'Albignac returned to France 'when times had improved'. If he had lived to be 100, the 'fashionable salad-maker' would have been sad to see the introduction of so-called Russian salad set with mayonnaise mixed with gelatine, a gastronomic sin of the Second Empire.

The ancient Greeks had a taste for lettuce, the best of all salad plants. It was originally picked in its spindly wild state. When people first began cultivating it they ate it when it had bolted, in the same way as they let cabbage bolt. Its botanical name, *Lactuca sativa*, reminds us that its sap resembles milk. The plant was popularized by the Romans, and many European languages have names for it deriving from Latin: English 'lettuce', French *laitue*, Spanish *lechuga*, Italian *lattuca* and German *Lattich* (although lettuce is very often called simply *Salat* in German).

A legend about the origin of lettuce implies some connection between the plant and amatory prowess, no doubt suggested by the way its shoots come up again when they have been cut. The prowess in the story was that of a young boatman, Phaon of Mitylene, who ferried Venus from the island of Lesbos to the mainland one day and would accept no payment. The goddess gave him a flask of perfume which made him handsome and irresistible to women when he sniffed it. His reputation inspired violent love in the breast of the poetess Sappho, and when he scorned her she threw herself off the cliff of Leucas into the sea. Holding Phaon responsible for her death, Venus turned him into a lettuce.

The legend fails to take account of the fact that Sappho was a real woman who lived in the sixth century BC. However, it is sometimes thought that the legend of the rustic Lothario's punishment was a way of explaining the soothing properties of a plant which Galen called the herb of the wise. He advised a decoction of lettuce before going to bed, as an aid to slumber. According to another story, Venus slept on a bed of lettuce to forget her lost Adonis. It may have been because of its soothing qualities that the Romans, who at first ate lettuce at the beginning of a meal, under the Empire, when banquets required a certain amount of stamina, moved it to the end. Thereafter, the more sophisticated Romans came to despise it, regarding herbs as food for the common people. They forgot that Aristoxenus of Tarentum, a philosopher, voluptuary and musicologist, had sprinkled the lettuces in his garden with wine and honey and then picked them next day at dawn; he called them the 'green cakes' given him by the earth. Apicius, like Dr Fagon later, held that the lettuce was indigestible, and if it is not very tender it may indeed be hard for some people to digest.

The lettuce owes its soothing properties to magnesium, one of the mineral salts in which it is rich, so long as it has grown in a garden or an open field. Lettuces grown under glass have something artificial about them, and can boast only of their price. These lettuces used to be raised in compost enriched with artificial fertilizers, but today they are increasingly grown in fine grit impregnated with various chemical, nutritive and fungicidal products. They owe their green colour to carbonic gas blown into the hot-houses to activate chlorophyll assimilation under neon lighting. These fragile, featherweight lettuces are packed in plastic bags. Is this the salad of the year 2000?

However, large round lettuces of a more robust kind are available all winter. They include the Trocadero variety from the Eastern Pyrenees, which has a good flavour and is grown under retractable frames. The frames cover the lettuces in bad weather, but they get the benefit of the Catalonian sun most of the time. Once spring comes we get the golden, curly-leaved Batavia lettuce with its nutty flavour. The Cos lettuce, firm, very large and elongated, is a crisp salad plant for May to July. It is very juicy, and is sometimes said to have 'green blood'. The story that Rabelais brought Cos lettuce seed from Italy to France is inaccurate; we know it was grown in the Comtat Venaissin, where the papal gardeners acclimatized it, from the fourteenth century onwards.

Chicory and Endive

Clumps of perennial-rooted wild chicory starred with blue flowers can still be seen growing on sloping ground. *Cichorium intybus* was the 'endive' of the ancient Greeks and Romans before the salad plant which was to take the name even existed. Wild chicory is the ancestor of the Batavian endive or scarole, the curly endive or *frisée*, the variety of chicory called *barbe de capucin*, friar's beard, and cultivated chicory itself, which is known in French as *endive*. The cultivated scarole may have originated in either India or the Mediterranean basin. The Egyptians grew it, and the Romans discovered it around the time of Cleopatra's exile in Rome with her son Cesarion. As a salad plant, it is still bitter and crisp, and if the gardener has remembered to tie the leaves together two weeks before it is picked it will have a large, pale yellow, slightly curly heart. The curly green endive dear to the Provençals, who add croutons rubbed with garlic to it (bacon is the usual accompaniment elsewhere), can be blanched in the same way. However, blanching these salad plants decreases their vitamin content.

On the Continent of Europe the old term 'endive' was applied from the thirteenth century onwards to chicory (as the term is used in English) tied up very tightly, and so blanched, but it did not mean the chicory we know now until around 1850. Modern chicory is of Belgian origin, and should really be called by its Flemish name of *witloof*, white leaf. The market gardeners of Montreuil, who still specialize in chicory, grew it in cellars in dim light, aiming to get the long, ivory, lacy-edged leaves of the *barbe de capucin* variety which was very popular in the early nineteenth century because of its diuretic qualities. Its leaves became elongated as they sought the light. A gardener of the Botanical Gardens of Brussels had drawn up a small mound of earth around some plants of wild chicory (the roots of wild chicory are dried to make a coffee substitute) and was surprised to find he had grown a plant consisting of broad, tightly wrapped white leaves. The *witloof* was introduced into France in 1873; it had only to make a short journey across the border to settle in the Pas-de-Calais, where it became very popular. But it remained extremely bitter until after the Second World War, when selection and improvement made the flavour milder. Today northern France is the main producing region in the world for chicory for winter salads, ahead of Belgium and Holland.

At the end of the last century, when advertising frequently took poetic form, there was an 'advertisement' which ran:

> Ainsi, loin du soleil, dans nos celliers captive
> Pâlit la chicorée et se blanchit l'endive.

[Thus, far from the sun, imprisoned in our cellars, the endive turns pale, and chicory is blanched.]

However, growing chicory is rather more complicated than that. Seed is sown in the open ground in spring. Plants with large roots grow, and their leaves are cut off near the ground. In August the roots are lifted and replanted under a layer of 35 centimetres of peat or soil covered with straw and a sheet of plastic, while a system of heated pipes keeps the plants in a constant temperature of 20 degrees centigrade. The French Institut National de la Recherche Agronomique has now developed a method of forcing chicory in dry material, in crates piled on top of each other, which is faster and cleaner. The laboratory encroaches on the kitchen garden more and more these days!

Before they are sent off to be sold the chicons undergo a beauty treatment.

Their bitter roots and outer leaves are trimmed off, and then the hearts are washed and centrifugally dried. The chicons are sorted and graded. The most expensive have very tight hearts and are very white, barely edged with yellow. The small chicons grown by farmers around Paris and in the east of France are not so tight and have a few green leaves; people who really like chicory prefer their extra bitterness.

Watercress

Watercress has been known since the time of Artaxerxes, who apparently had a passion for it. So did the ancient Greeks and Romans. Its botanical name of *Nasturtium officinale* reminds us that this cruciferous plant has the kind of flavour that wrinkles the nose. With its mustardy bite, it is an aromatic plant, said to expel worms. It used to be eaten to give strength, courage and character, as recommended by Aristophanes in *The Wasps*. Its richness in iodine, sulphur, iron and vitamin C may explain its reputation. Very popular in the Middle Ages, when it was called *kresse* in France and *cresse* in English (from a West Germanic word), watercress was also used to make remedies for external use, as the Salerno School advises:

> If you will rub your head with juice of watercress
> Baldness you may avoid, or else you may repair.
> Its juices cure far more than loss of hair.
> It soothes; relief from toothache it will win,
> And mixed with honey clarifies the skin.

Wild watercress grew, as it still does, in the beds of small streams. Then people began growing it in special pools diverted from watercourses – where the stagnant water enriched it with bacteria and parasites. The *Ménagier de Paris* and the *Viandier*, to mention only those two medieval culinary treatises, give recipes for cooking watercress; it was usually eaten cooked at the time. The *Viandier*'s recipe, mentioned above, has the merit of being relatively simple: '*Porée* of cress: parboil a handful of beets with it, then turn it and chop it and fry all in oil; then put in milk of almonds, and serve with meat on meat days, or with butter, or with cheese; when it is seasoned with salt, this cress will be much liked.'

Today watercress is grown in running water, and there are strict hygienic controls on watercress farms. However, some people with sensitive kidneys and bladders may find that its exceptional richness in oxalic acid and potassium causes a reaction which can also be set off by sorrel.

Asparagus

The Greeks soon discovered that wild asparagus, *Asparagus officinalis*, was delicious. They ate the young shoots of the plants that still grow wild in the Mediterranean undergrowth, the asparagus fern used by florists today. The Egyptians seem to have offered bundles of asparagus to their gods.

Curiously, for the Romans usually preferred large fruits and vegetables, they shared the Greek taste for wild asparagus, although the Ravenna area, according to Pliny, was famous for the growing of asparagus shoots some of which weighed a third of a pound. It would have been a Roman pound, of course, but this does seem to have been asparagus of a remarkable size, although the naturalist did not think much of it. 'Nature ordained that asparagus should grow wild, so that everyone may go and pick it, and now we see cultivated asparagus!' The best of the wild asparagus grew on mountain-sides, such as the asparagus of the volcanic island of Nisida in the Gulf of Pozzuoli. The asparagus served by Juvenal to his guest[11] probably came from the Apennines: 'some wild asparagus, gathered by the bailiff's wife'. Today the hillsides of Provence and Corsica grow splendid asparagus which would fill many baskets, but is largely ignored. The Sardinians of today still know only wild asparagus: perhaps this is a case of a Paradise not lost after all.

We cannot be sure whether the asparagus for which Apicius gives recipes was cultivated or not. His French translator, Jacques André, seems to doubt it. In any case, his advice to boil it in two changes of water to firm it up is interesting. Apicius then used it to make *patinae*, a kind of purée with egg, seasoned with garum and aromatics. The sheer quantity of these seasonings must have overpowered the delicate flavour of asparagus, wild or not. He served the dish as a gratin to accompany the little birds called *beccafici*.

The barbarian invasions do not seem to have encouraged asparagus-growing. Whether or not people gathered it wild from the woods to improve their daily diet, it is not mentioned again until around 1300, when it began to be grown around Paris (always a centre for gourmets, of course), in Argenteuil, which was to become famous for it, in Bezons and in Épinay. Neither the *Ménagier de Paris* nor the *Viandier* mentions it at the end of the century. The Arabs seem to have introduced it into Spain, whence it spread to France. However, its name in the vernacular of most European languages recalls its Greek and Latin past: in Spanish it is *espárrago*, in German it is *Spargel*, in Italian *sparagio* and in French *asperge*, while in English it retains its Latin name, has a dialectal version 'sparrowgrass', and had a now obsolete form 'sperage'.

During the Renaissance asparagus finally found the niche it was to continue to occupy, as a food for special occasions. The first colonists of North America took asparagus crowns with them to be planted out. It has remained 'the aristocrat of vegetables', as they call it in Quebec.[12]

Its diuretic qualities, due to a substance called asparagine discovered by Broussais in 1829, were of empirical interest to doctors for a long period, as its botanical

701

name *officinalis* suggests. Platina alludes to it: 'Asparagus alleviates inflammations of the stomach, excites lechery, is good for the sight and pain in the eyes, soothes the stomach gently, causes pissing, and is good for pain in the kidneys, stomach and intestines'.

I have already mentioned the alleged aphrodisiac properties of the various edible stems and shoots which were all grouped together as 'asparagus' in classical antiquity. They may have acquired their reputation from the fact that asparagus is particularly rich in phosphorus and vitamin A, as well as oxalic acid. The belief is a tenacious one, and that witty nineteenth-century gastronomic writer Stanislas Martin claims that husbands who had strayed could be caught out by their wives in this way, 'for asparagus has the drawback of giving the urine an unpleasant odour, which has more than once betrayed an illicit dinner.'

It may have been for its reputation that Louis XIV liked asparagus so much. He even asked La Quintinie to provide it in the month of December. Nothing was beyond the great gardener, and many plots in his garden were permanently occupied by 'hot-beds' for asparagus crowns. They were forced from September onwards.

Jean-Paul Aron comments on the prestige enjoyed by asparagus.[13] It featured regularly on the menus of grand nineteenth-century dinners, sharing the honours with roast lamb or chicken, and proving more popular than green peas and only a little less popular than the finest green beans. Once Nicolas Appert had invented his method of preserving vegetables in 'little bottles', so that they were 'more delicious this winter than in the preceding year',[14] asparagus could be had in winter and summer alike. (I shall come to the little bottles in the next chapter.) Of course fresh asparagus could always be bought from Alsace, at a price: it was 40 francs a bundle at 'the shop of Mme Chevet, the most famous provision-merchant in Paris, who has always been extremely kind to me', says Brillat-Savarin.[15] He was horrified by the cost of it, though, at a time when a workman earned about 2.50 francs a day, always supposing he had any work at all.

> 'They are certainly very fine, but at such a price no one but the King or some prince will be able to eat them.' 'You are mistaken; such luxuries never find their way into palaces; what kings and princes want is goodness, not magnificence but for all that, my bundle of asparagus will sell, and this is how it will happen ...' As she was talking, two fat Englishmen, who were strolling by arm in arm, stopped in front of us, and immediately their faces lit up with admiration. One of them had the miraculous bundle wrapped up without so much as asking the price, paid for it, tucked it under his arm, and carried it off, whistling 'God Save the King'.

Though not an Englishman (the modern equivalent would perhaps be an oil-rich Arab), Auguste Comte, whose household accounts Aron has studied, paid a more reasonable price of 1.10 francs a kilo in season (May 1843) for asparagus for two, himself and his maid. The three pounds of beef bought the same day cost 1.60 francs. Asparagus was therefore still an expensive item on a food budget of 3.55 francs a day, but it was affordable if the budget was for only two people. By comparison the meat seems very cheap; the proportions would be the other way around today. But in any case asparagus and roast meat were food for the privileged. Few country people ever tasted either, and even in towns only a very small minority, of course including the 'gastrolaters' of the nineteenth century, could eat such things.

> It was this privileged minority from the Chaussée d'Antin, the Faubourgs Saint-Germain and Saint-Honoré, who took an eager interest in the alimentary world unveiled to us by appetizing window displays, names to be conjured with, and delicious recipes. Between 60, 80 and 100,000 people at the most, depending on the period, took part in the great gastronomic affair which was the pride of Paris. It was to them that Baron Brisse, who formed the taste of the time, addressed himself; he did not know how influential his work would be, but he was a conscientious interpreter of the bourgeois appetite.[16]

Growing Asparagus

The asparagus plant consists of an underground 'crown' of roots and buds. In spring the buds grow upwards and pierce the surface of the soil. They are then called 'spears', and these spears are picked and eaten. If the spears grow on they will turn green and produce a stem above the ground bearing fine, feathery leaves, the asparagus fern used by florists as greenery in bouquets.

To get good long spears which will make a neat bundle, the rows of crowns are earthed up so that the spears will grow longer and remain white until the terminal bud comes through the surface. The Italians prefer long-stemmed green asparagus.

Asparagus likes a light soil. Crowns which are a year to 18 months old, raised from seed or bought from growers, are planted in February to April, in trenches 25 to 35 centimetres deep by 30 to 40 centimetres wide. The crowns are placed at the bottom of the trench, roots well spread, and covered with four to five centimetres of light soil. They are covered again in the second year with 10 to 15 more centimetres of soil. The distance between rows varies from 1.80 to 3 metres, and the crowns are set 25 to 60 centimetres apart along the rows.

An asparagus bed needs to be conscientiously maintained: fed with manure or compost, earthed up, weeded and mulched. Mulching with plastic film brings crops on earlier, in neater groups, and with a better yield.

Spears must not be cut from an asparagus bed until three years after you have planted the crowns. Cutting may then go on for two or three weeks. The bed will continue to be productive for a maximum 10 or 11 years.

Asparagus: anonymous engraving of the first half of the nineteenth
century

Asparagus spears are cut daily in France for about two or three months, from
March until the beginning of June, first in some regions and then in others. Daily
cropping is necessary during the season, for as soon as they emerge above ground
the spears which are not cut will begin turning green and putting out leaves. They
look less attractive then, although they taste just as good, and many connoisseurs
like green asparagus, which is grown in a slightly different way. The rows are not

704

earthed up so high as for white asparagus, and the spears are cut when they have emerged above ground and one-third of their length shows green. The maximum length for green asparagus is 27 centimetres, and for white and purple asparagus 22 centimetres. Thin spears of asparagus are called sprue.

Asparagus has to be cut by hand, with a special asparagus knife. The operation calls for skill if the underground part of the plant is not to be injured. It takes an hour to cut two kilos of asparagus, and you walk almost four kilometres in that time. Yield varies from three to six tonnes a hectare, depending on the age of the bed and the nature of the soil.

After the crop has been harvested it is cut to length and sorted into bundles for the market. As the stem is cut in the middle of its growth period, asparagus is delicate and fragile. Cutting does not arrest development, and if it is not put into a cold, damp atmosphere at once it will soon become fibrous, losing a good deal of the flavour which is its main attraction. Really fresh asparagus should exude a little juice when you press the base of the spear in your fingers.

France is easily the largest asparagus-producing country in the EEC, with a surface area of 17,600 hectares producing 48,600 tonnes. Three departments produce 44 per cent of the crop: the Gard (8000 tonnes), the Loir-et-Cher (6800 tonnes) and the Vaucluse (4500 tonnes). Four other departments, producing 2000 to 2500 tonnes each, account for 20 per cent of production: the Maine-et-Loire, the Loiret, the Hérault and the Bouches-du-Rhône. Five further departments account for 15 per cent of production with 1000 to 2000 tonnes each.

The most important asparagus-growing zones of France include the south-east, which provides 50 per cent of national production of forced and early asparagus, from 15th February onwards. The label on the bundle should specify the place of origin. If it does not, the asparagus comes from North Africa. The Loire valley provides 25 per cent of all national production. Its early asparagus is on the market at the beginning of April, and the season is at its height in May. The purple sort is the best. Other zones, such as the Landes, the Garonne and Lot valleys, and Alsace, are increasing their growing of asparagus.

The Île-de-France, which with Argenteuil was once the most famous asparagus-growing area of France, was still providing the Paris region with some 210 tonnes in 1982. Two years earlier, the figure had been 400 tonnes, but urban sprawl has inexorably destroyed the asparagus fields, and soon Argenteuil will be only a memory on menus denoting asparagus soup. It is also the name of the late variety from which all the others have been developed by hybridization. The finest asparagus in France is the green Lauris kind, which comes from the sandy soil of the Camargue.

Most asparagus is eaten fresh. Official consumption figures in 1982 were 600 to 650 grams per head per year in France (a survey in 1977 produced a figure of 560 grams per head). The consumption figure had been over a kilo a head ten years earlier. The fall in consumption is probably because asparagus is not so readily available, not because the consumer has tired of it. However, the drop in consumption of fresh asparagus is compensated for by an increase in consumption of the canned and frozen spears, which is rather surprising in view of their price.

France exports a little more than 10,000 tonnes a year, a quantity which brings in considerable revenue (175 million francs in 1979). The main importers of French asparagus are West Germany, Switzerland and the Benelux countries.

France imports little fresh asparagus: from 100 to 200 tonnes a year, mainly from Spain and Italy. Early asparagus comes from North Africa in March; it has little flavour, although the spears are very large. However, a lot of canned asparagus is imported: about 15,000 tonnes a year at the beginning of the 1980s.

So far asparagus does not seem to respond well to freezing; even when the best and biggest spears are used, the result is disappointing. The best way to cook it is to steam it.

Artichokes

Globe artichokes entered the byways of history thanks to Catherine de Medici. The chronicler Pierre de L'Estoile, who is not usually guilty of exaggeration, is probably fairly accurate in his account of her vast appetite. In his *Journal* for 19 June 1576, he tells us that, on the occasion of the wedding of the Marquis de Loménie and Mlle de Martigues, 'the Queen Mother ate so much she thought she would die, and was very ill with diarrhoea. They said it was from eating too many artichoke bottoms and the combs and kidneys of cockerels, of which she was very fond.'

The artichoke had made its first appearance in history some 50 years before, and was still a novelty, particularly in France, to which the Queen had brought it along with many other Italian gastronomic innovations.

Cynara scolymus, a member of the very large Compositae family, is a kind of thistle with finely chiselled leaves of the kind which inspired much Gothic and later on Modernist ornamentation. The artichoke is the scaly-looking flower bud, of which we eat the fine, delicate flesh. If the bud is left it will become a large flower with handsome, plumy, purple petals.

Known to the Romans as *carduus*, the plant of the time was a slight improvement by the Greeks on the *kaktos*, the wild thistle of Sicily. In antiquity, its bitter leaves as well as its flower-heads were eaten. The plant seems to have reached Sicily from North Africa, where it is still found in the wild state. Poor people there pick the thistle they call *korchef* to enrich the sauce for their couscous. This kind of thistle was also the ancestor of the cardoon, a speciality of Provence and part of the traditional Christmas supper there. Cardoons deserve to be eaten more often. Their nutritional value is in the large ribs of the leaves.

The Italians make an aperitif from artichokes which is good for bile, but the principal use resides in the bitter leaves, from which a medicament is also extracted. The globe artichoke can be a little tricky to deal with. Once cooked, it will not keep more than 24 hours, and develops a toxic mould the colour of verdigris called *bremia*.

Tomatoes

In spite of the excellence of its pasta, Italian cookery would never have found its full expression had America not entered the picture. In the saucepan as in many other spheres of life, nothing was ever quite the same again once Christopher Columbus had returned. One wonders how on earth the Italian peninsula managed to do without the tomato for thousands of years.

Lycopersicon esculentum, belonging to the same family as its compatriots the potato and tobacco plants, grew in Mexico and the countries of Central America. A small and unspectacular although pleasant-smelling plant, it produced round marble-sized fruits, resembling the cherry tomato we know today, but it was much less prolific. The Indians explained to the first Andalusian colonists, the Moriscos, who had been market gardeners for generations, that the *tomatl* made good sauces flavoured with *ahi*, that chilli pepper which Father de Acosta described as being 'extreamly sharpe and biting'.

It was by way of Naples, a Spanish possession, that the tomato, initially regarded in the usual way as a medicinal plant, entered Italian cuisine in the sixteenth century, with or without chilli, but more usually without, for the Italians are not so keen on its very hot flavour as the Spanish. The lyrical Italians called it *pomodoro*, golden apple, and it reached Provence by way of Genoa and Nice. The Provençals gave it the name of *pomme d'amour*, love-apple. They thought the red berries which deterred ants and mosquitos by their odour were pretty, but it was not until the next generation that they made up their minds to eat them – cautiously at first and then with enthusiasm. British colonists also encountered the tomato in North America, but they distrusted it for even longer. It was known in English too as 'love-apple'.

In the very early years of the nineteenth century Brillat-Savarin,[17] like other Parisians, had known the tomato for only a few years, and seldom in the form of sauces. He writes:

> This vegetable or fruit, as one may call it, was almost wholly unknown in Paris 15 years ago. We owe its introduction to the great influx of those southerners brought by the Revolution to the capital, where most of them made their fortunes. Very expensive at first, it then became very common, and might be seen in great baskets-full in La Halle last year, while before it used to be sold by the half-dozen ... be that as it may, tomatoes are a great blessing to good cookery. They make excellent sauces which go well with every kind of meat.

Brillat-Savarin's slightly condescending mention of 'southerners' no doubt referred in particular to the *Trois frères provençaux*, actually brothers-in-law and not brothers, who opened their famous restaurant in the rue Sainte-Anne in 1786, before the fall of the Bastille and the rise of the tomato. They prospered until the July Revolution. A fellow-countryman of theirs, from Marseilles, opened his restaurant the *Boeuf à la mode* in the rue de Valois in 1792, when blood was flowing in the streets – the real stuff, not the tomato ketchup of later stage use. However, when life returned to normal, perhaps one of them may have mentioned the old Provençal saying that 'poumo d'amour qu'es bono viando' – 'it is the tomato [sauce] that makes good meat'. In fact this was a newly invented 'old saying', and comments such as Brillat-Savarin's should not be taken too seriously. They produced spurious legends fabricated by the advertising industry of the time, such as the tale of the people of Marseilles who came up to Paris to celebrate the first anniversary of the fall of the Bastille in 1790, and loudly demanded tomatoes to eat.

However, the tomato left those Provençal window-sills where it had grown as a house-plant for such places as the garden of Maître Roumanille, an army veteran of the Empire who became a gardener and father of the noted Provençal writer Joseph Roumanille. Well watered and tended, it became plump, juicy and tasty, like its sisters back in Italy. French tomato-growing began in Barbentane, Châteaurenard (now a great tomato-growing centre), Mallemort (where much canned tomato purée is now made), Marseilles and Perpignan.

The tomato came just in time, for the traditional produce of the South of France (vines, madder, olives) was going through a serious crisis. Madder for dye was being ousted by industrially produced dyes, and the misfortunes of the vine, attacked by phylloxera, have been described above. Later on the mulberry tree too suffered from the advent of rayon, artificial silk, but by then the tomato had taken over. The development of irrigation networks, rail transport, and the invention of canning and pasteurization meant a spectacular rise in the consumption of tomatoes, first as salad, then as sauces. By a happy coincidence, it was around the time when the Provençal writers Frédéric Mistral and Alphonse Daudet were born that Provençal gastronomy had really become accepted, partly because of the tomato.

With Roumanille and Mistral, and the *Félibrige* movement, the Provençal language 'became not a rustic dialect, but a classic idiom with images and harmonies to delight the imagination and the ear'. However, that is another story. We may wonder seriously, all the same, whether the fashion for Provençal writers, like that of the restaurateurs from Provence, did not count for something in the revelation of the virtues of the tomato and Provençal cooking in general. Naturally enough, the people of the North of France and the English-speaking countries despised these sun-filled dishes at first and thought them common. Later they realized that given a little cheerfulness and sunlight you could feel you were already on holiday.

From being an ingredient in a sauce the tomato became a dish in itself: as a salad, a cooked vegetable, juice and even jam. But the best way of all to cook it, the recipe for which it was surely expressly created, is *tomates à la provençale*, prepared exactly as tomatoes should be.

Tomates à la provençale are never worthy of that name if the ritual of the recipe is not observed *precisely*. First you take tomatoes which are not over-ripe; they should be fleshy, not watery. You cut them in half downwards, from top to bottom (this is the first secret!) so that the two halves are exactly the same; you do not want to end up with top and bottom halves. You remove the seeds with a pointed knife, season the tomatoes with a little salt, and put them cut side down on a plate while you heat some olive oil in an iron frying pan. Shake the tomatoes to drain them, and then put them *cut side down* in the smoking oil. When they begin to sizzle, and the skin lifts at the cut edges, turn them over with a wooden spatula (so as not to bruise them) and cook the rounded sides. If they stick, shake the pan. Add more oil if necessary. Now for the second secret: when just cooked, the tomatoes are delicately placed in a gratin dish, seasoned with a little salt and with pepper, and kept hot. In the hot oil of the pan where the tomatoes had begun to caramelize, fry some garlic, chopped parsley, and dried, crushed breadcrumbs. Sprinkle this mixture over the tomatoes, and put the dish in a hot oven for a few minutes, taking care not to let the tomatoes dry out.

Today more tomatoes are grown in France than any other vegetable – even potatoes.

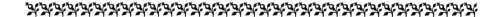

ODE TO JAMYN

First wash your hands, that they be clean and fair,
Then follow after me; a napkin bear.
Let us go gathering fresh young plants, and take
Them home, a salad for our friends to make.
I shall go one way, wandering at will
From bank to ditch, from ditch again to rill,
Searching those lonely places at my ease;
Eyes wandering hither, thither, as they please,
And straying on into the fallow field
Which, left untended, of itself does yield
Herbs of all kinds for plucking every day.
And do you, Jamyn, go another way.
Search for the daisy with its little leaf,
Seek out lamb's lettuce, and for the relief
Of blood disorders, pick the burnet green
Which also cures the aching side and spleen.
Meanwhile I'll look among the moss for shoots
Of rampion with its sweet, delicious roots,
And pick the tender currant buds which bring
Promise, its heralds, of the coming Spring.
Then, reading Ovid, that ingenious guide
To works of Love, let us walk side by side
Back to our lodging, there roll up our sleeves
And wash our herbs and roots and fresh young leaves
In sacred, springing water from my fount.
To set the salad off to best account
We'll season it with salt and, as a foil,
Dress it with rosé vinegar and oil:
With olive oil, which must be of Provence.
The oil that comes from olive groves of France
Harsh to the stomach, is no use as food.
And this, Jamyn, all this will do me good.
Such country pastimes are my sovereign art
Until the quartan fever shall depart
That rages in my veins the livelong day
Wasting my languid limbs and heart away.

Pierre de Ronsard (1524–1585)

Chapter 23

The Potato Revolution

In 1600, Olivier de Serres published his *Théâtre d'agriculture et mesnage des champs*. On p. 516 he comments: 'This plant, called *cartoufle*, bears fruits of the same name resembling truffles, and so called by some. It came to the Dauphiné from Switzerland not long since.' Such is the baptismal certificate of the potato, to be filed along with its portrait painted some ten years earlier by the Franco-Viennese botanist Pierre de l'Écluse or Clusius, an excellent but seldom reproduced watercolour.

This 'inestimable gift to the numerous class of the needy, which was to have the greatest influence on Man, his liberty and his happiness', as the dramatist and critic Mercier[1] put it in the eighteenth century, was to take its important place in the diet when it was realized that hunger causes popular unrest, and the Enlightenment illuminated the stage upon which the drama of the Revolution was played out. Women mobbed Versailles, demanding bread.

In fact 'bread' was only the metonymic response to the problem of starvation. Since the dawn of human civilization, as we have seen, the daily 'bread' of the majority had been a kind of mush or porridge, and among the poor it was almost never made with wheat. Anything that could be ground and would fill the stomach economically and for some time was used: cereals coarser than wheat, broad beans, acorns, and above all chestnuts, Virgil's *castaneae molles*.[2] In classical antiquity, curiously, chestnuts were reserved for women.

For thousands of years, the chestnut was a standby in those mountainous Mediterranean areas where the humblest cereals would not grow. It was a local resource and an object that could be used in barter, sometimes the only one. Even before the Spartans, the Thracians were making chestnut bread, which was more of a flat cake of the kind still eaten in the Balkans, central Italy, Sardinia, Sicily, Corsica and the eastern Pyrenees. The traditional Corsican economy depended for so long on the resources of the island's forest that the large and appropriately

711

named Castagniccia region in the heart of Corsica,[3] between Corte and Bastia, might be called the seat of a chestnut civilization.

All over the island, where so many traditions have been preserved, chestnuts prepared in innumerable different ways were the main and sometimes the only part of the diet that provided energy, over a very long period. They were often eaten raw, as they had been long ago in the days before fire, fresh at the beginning of the season, later on dried and skinned (*castagne bianche*), and slowly and thoroughly masticated to impregnate them with saliva. Shepherds – or bandits in hot pursuit of the blood feud – would fill their knapsacks with chestnuts before leaving for the maquis.

At home, *pulenta* – a not unfamiliar word – took the place of daily bread. It was a solid porridge shaped in a napkin to form it into a round loaf. The West Africans make their *foutout* or *foufou* of cassava or banana in just the same way. The distribution of *pulenta* among the family was a remarkable sight. The mother would divided the big, solid loaf into four quarters, the *barone*. Then the head of the clan, father or grandfather, dealt with each quarter in turn. He held the end of a wire between his teeth, pulling it taut in his left hand; with his other hand, he passed each *barone* over the wire to cut regular slices or *fetta* which fell into a dish.

Dried white chestnuts were also made into a goat's milk soup which was then thickened with vermicelli or short lengths of macaroni until you could cut it with a knife. The idea was that a spoon put into it should stand upright. It was called *suppa a cuchjara ritta*.

The chestnut was also one of the principal resources of the Cevennes, where it was systematically and properly cultivated. The first chestnut growers were the Roman colonists of the Vivarais area, who planted grafted trees from northern Italy there, for the chestnut tree does not grow naturally in the region. Then came the monks, very often of Italian origin themselves, who took new land into cultivation and brought seedlings from the mother house of their order in Italy. From the eighth century onwards they founded settlements in the valleys of the Cevennes, starting by building a monastery and a church around which an increasingly large population gathered. Then they gradually moved on to those parts of the countryside that lay higher up, leaving behind them well-organized parishes and valleys under cultivation. The seedlings and scions for grafting were given to the peasants; in return they were bound to pay a certain percentage of their harvests to the abbey. These dues became known as the *censive*.

Feudal laws, which favoured the cultivation of several kinds of crops a year, contributed to the increase in chestnut growing. But at the beginning of the seventeenth century the process came to an abrupt halt, and much of the forest became copse. The *dragonnades* of the Wars of Religion, which sent heads of households into hiding from persecution, were partly responsible.

With the demographic rise of the eighteenth and nineteenth centuries, however, there was an unprecedented increase in the growing of chestnut trees. By around

'Chestnuts': miniature from the *Tacuinum sanitatis in medicina*, a fourteenth-century translation of a medical treatise by Albucacis, an Arab doctor of the twelfth century

1850 whole mountains were under cultivation to as high above sea level as the trees would grow.

On the plains, chestnut woods were usually near human houses (the *mas*). These *masières* often grew a subsidiary crop of potatoes or cereals too. The trees benefited from the cultivation of the soil and the successive manuring, and sometimes grew to enormous size. Terraced chestnut groves, called *traversiers, faisses* or *bancels* depending on the region, were supported by dry-stone walling to prevent erosion of the soil and the leaching of its nutritional elements, and to encourage leaves to accumulate and provide precious humus. Whole areas of mountain-side were built up in this way, each small wall propping up a row of trees or a single superb specimen. Chestnut groves on gentler slopes and valley floors grew in fields that were regularly maintained, and were in no danger of being washed away.

Wherever chestnuts grew, the soil was always kept clean, and suckers were trimmed away every three years. The people of the Cevennes say that the chestnut tree 'is fertilized with the axe'; if this cleansing operation is neglected the top of the tree will die and the foot be encumbered with useless competing suckers. The best chestnut groves were ploughed and manured, and the less flourishing ones were at least cleansed of brushwood and chestnut husks. The careful grower would collect all this material and dig it lightly into small arable areas to enrich them. Other growers burned it away in small, carefully watched fires. Most of the chestnut crop was harvested, and livestock ate what little was left where it fell.

The family labour force was supplemented by seasonal workers, men and women who hired themselves out for one to three months. They were of local origin, and had often just returned from gathering in the grapes of the wine-growing plains of the Gard and Hérault.

The chestnut harvest, which lasted from the end of September to Christmas, was used in different ways according to the kind of chestnuts gathered. In general, every property grew several varieties for different purposes. Early chestnuts in particular went to be sold fresh in the markets of Saint-Jean-du-Gard, Anduze, Alès, Les Vans, Nîmes, and as far afield as Lyons. Others were dried over wood fires and kept for family consumption in winter and for sale. These dried chestnuts made soup or broth. The recipe, which goes back to Roman times, has not changed. The chestnuts are put to soak some hours before they are wanted, and then gently simmered over a low flame, and eaten with goat's milk to drink. This soup was called *badjana*. The origin of the word is from the Italian town of Baiae, a health resort for rich Romans who had been indulging in too much good living; they took a cure at Baiae to settle the damage done to their stomachs by the banquets mentioned above. They were served vegetables cooked in water, called 'Baian vegetables', as one might say 'Vichy carrots' today, and in the *langue d'oc* dialect the term became *badjana*.

Chestnut-growing was the mainstay of the economy of the Cevennes for a long time. It called for a large labour force, and the component parts of that economy were so independent that it remained a precarious business, involving as it did the

714

density of population necessary to provide the labour force, and the occupation of maximum space for intensive cultivation of a not very profitable crop.

At the beginning of the twentieth century the market economy came to the mountains: along with new criteria of profitability, the appeal of town life, a massive exodus, wars, the aging of the population and above all a change in dietary habits, it finally led to the abandonment of some of the chestnut woods of the Cevennes.

Since the late 1960s, however, the native-born inhabitants of the Cevennes have been joined by a number of newcomers, idealists who were not particularly bothered about agricultural profitability. Quite a number of people seeking an alternative way of life wanted to live in the country. Today, after a good many years of apprenticeship, these 'new peasants' are well integrated with the original population.

Whether old-established residents or newcomers, the people of the Cevennes are interested in the chestnut tree. Its cultivation is seen as involving their culture too. The older inhabitants are perpetuating the authentic tradition of their grandparents. The latter are making that tradition their own, drawing from it all the symbolic values of permanence, continuity, even immortality that trees represent to people who have been uprooted.

The tree lets them experiment with the survival economy. It stands for a feasible application of theories of individual salvation, a libertarian ecology breaking with a model of society in which mass organization is felt to be dehumanizing, dispossessing the human being of his or her true self. Accordingly, it symbolizes the chance of a life founded on family intimacy and friendship in the community. Furthermore, when chestnut-growing was abandoned as modern agriculture including the use of various chemicals developed, the chestnut returned to the sphere of natural agriculture. The organic farming of these small-holdings has won the approval of those who dislike the accelerated economic growth of the last 30 years.

This was one consequence of the European student unrest of 1968 which no one expected at the time! *Les événements*, as the riots were known in France, felt like a minor revolution – and may have restored the chestnut to a little of its lost favour. For from the chronological viewpoint, its consumption decreased most when the potato revolution came, at much the same time as the French Revolution itself.

Sweet Chestnuts

The chestnut tree grows in France in areas of old geological origin where the soil is acid. The native chestnut, *Castanea sativa*, likes light soils with a basis of siliceous sand and granite gravel, volcanic soils and mountain-sides. It grows in several different climates: the maritime climates of the Breton Atlantic coast; the Pyrenees, with their relatively mild winters and wet summers; hot, dry Mediterranean climates; and continental climates with severe winters and hot summers.

At the end of the nineteenth century two other species of chestnut were used as rootstocks in order to counter the death of chestnut trees from two serious forms of canker. They were the Japanese chestnut (*Castanea crenata*) and the Chinese chestnut (*Castanea mollissima*).

The type of sweet chestnut known as a *marron* in France (and used for *marrons glacés*) is a fruit with a single seed, which if sown will produce a single seedling. The ordinary sweet chestnut known as *châtaigne* is a fruit containing several normally formed seeds within one pericarp or husk; if they are sown they can produce a seedling each. The number of seeds within the husk may be from two to five. If you cut across a *marron* you will see that the kernel is whole: in botanical terms, the fruit is not septate. The kernel of the *châtaigne* is divided into several partitions, and the fruit is described as septate. Both kinds of sweet chestnut can be eaten fresh, when they need not conform to any particular size. Small chestnuts are used in the food preserving industry. Whole *marrons* of a size giving 70 to 85 fruits to the kilo are canned, and large *marrons* providing 40 to 65 fruits to the pound are used in confectionery.

The largest chestnut-producing countries of Europe are Italy, Spain, Portugal and France, in that order. French production has been falling steadily for the last 100 years. In less than a century, total production has fallen from 510,000 tonnes to a little over 40,000 tonnes.

The main chestnut-growing regions of France are Corsica, the Rhône Alps, Languedoc-Roussillon, the southern French Pyrenees, and the Provençal Alps and Côte d'Azur regions. The Ardèche department accounts for one-quarter of the crop and 33 per cent of all French chestnuts marketed. In general, 40 per cent of French chestnuts are eaten at home, a considerable amount of that quantity being fed to livestock. The rest is sold commercially.

Sweet chestnuts of the *marron* type used in the food-manufacturing industry undergo two preliminary operations, one to preserve them and one to skin them. To preserve them, they are soaked in water for six to nine days and then dried out again. This process eliminates wormy chestnuts, improves quality and appearance, and means they will keep for some months. Less frequently the sterilization method is used: they are plunged in hot water for 45 minutes and then in cold water for 3 to 15 minutes. The skinning process is done by either roasting or steaming.

At present most of the chestnuts used by the French food industry are imported fruits, and imports are rising annually because of falling home production and growing demand. The main items manufactured from chestnuts are sweetened chestnut cream, unsweetened chestnut purée and whole canned chestnuts, not forgetting *marrons glacés* for special occasions. Those used in confectionery are the handsome Italian kind; Spanish chestnuts are used for other purposes.

French chestnut-growing is not nearly enough for home demand, so very few chestnuts are exported. Those that do leave the country are usually bound for West Germany, the United Kingdom and Belgium.

716

Potatoes

In 1789 the Bastille fell. At the same time, people became aware of the usefulness of the potato. Parmentier's treatise on growing and cooking potatoes was in all good Republican bookshops. It is likely that those providential tubers might have had to wait even longer to get into the recipe books but for war and famine, themselves a recipe for disaster.

Parmentier, an army pharmacist, had long been doing his best to explain to the nation that there was nothing like the potato for lining the stomach. Since returning from captivity in 1763, after the Seven Years' War, he had devoted his energies to promoting it. Antoine-Auguste Parmentier had eaten the strange tuber in his Westphalian prisoner-of-war camp. The Germans of Westphalia called it *Kartoffel*, and regarded it as good only for pigs and therefore, *a fortiori*, for French prisoners.

People on both sides of the Rhine tended to believe that you caught leprosy from eating potatoes. Parmentier certainly seemed to be visible proof that you did not, but, as a decree issued by the Besançon *parlement* in 1748 had forbidden the growing of potatoes for fear of the disease, well-informed persons looked at him askance whenever he mentioned the subject, particularly as his motives were philanthropic. In a century when speculation ruled as supreme as the Bourbon kings, if not more so, no one knew what to make of that.

However, since the Besançon decree other scientists had come to share Parmentier's views in an increasingly disastrous economic situation. Their memos got nowhere; the peasants, as Voltaire pointed out, were illiterate, and the landowners had other things on their minds. The idea of an experiment was broached – but the experiment was to be conducted as far as possible from the capital, to be on the safe side. The Bishop of Castres was detailed to organize this new crusade. He ordered the parish priests of his diocese to encourage people to eat potatoes, now declared to be miraculous. If the good priests survived the consumption of potatoes themselves, however, they were in some danger of being stoned by their parishioners.

In 1769 the parish priest of Saint-Roch in Paris decided to give his starving flock an economical potato soup. The recipe was published in Dijon in 1772, in the *Cuisine des pauvres*, a philanthropical work by Varenne de Béost ('to remedy the unforeseen effects of the grain famine'). The soup, euphemistically called 'economy rice' soup, was said to be 'greatly superior to the usual food of the common people', and Mirabeau senior, a bad father and husband but a good 'rural philosopher' said in a letter of 26 February 1769 that potato purée was 'comparable to the best of soups'.

But the experiment led no further until, as it was still urgently necessary to find a way of countering the growing threat of famine (and the marriage of the Dauphin Louis to Princess Marie Antoinette of Austria did not look like much of a guarantee of lasting peace in Europe), the Académie of Besançon launched a competition for a 'study of alimentary substances which may alleviate the disaster of famine'.

717

Parmentier, now employed as a pharmacist at Les Invalides, was a determined man; once again he suggested the potato he had eaten in Germany. He won the competition. The local *parlement* forgot its denunciation of the potato, and the medical faculty of Paris took Parmentier under its wing. He went through his explanations again. Unfortunately people were no keener than before to eat potato bread. Either they were not hungry enough, or it was not a very good recipe.

The fact is that the potato will not make bread because it lacks gluten, as Parmentier was well aware. The great *Encyclopédie*, which was many years in the writing and editing, had published a short article on the potato in 1767, more or less *in memoriam*, but the 1772 supplement included a report by the Swiss naturalist Samuel Engel. He suggested making bread from potatoes and described plans for an industrial mill to crush large quantities. However, the potato could not appear in the light of miraculous manna until the hopeless idea of making potato bread was abandoned. It had to be given its own dignity and personality.

Louis XVI and Marie Antoinette, in their enthusiasm for the rustic life, had potatoes grown experimentally at Les Sablons in Neuilly, on 50 acres of fallow land where Louis XV used to review his troops. The growing plants were ostentatiously guarded by soldiers with fixed bayonets, and naturally attracted intrigued spectators every Sunday. The general opinion was that if the King sent his army to guard a plant previously considered fit only for animal fodder it could not be so bad after all, so why should the people of France not have it too? At night the mock guard was apparently relaxed, and the thieves upon whom the authorities were counting stocked up with potatoes and thereby advertised them.

Visiting the fields on his name-day, the King was given a bunch of potato flowers which he put in his hat. The court thought them charming; there was quite a fashion for wearing potato flowers. The makers of fabrics and ceramics were urged to use the flowers in decorative patterns, with the idea of encouraging people to eat the nutritious tubers. This primitive advertising campaign was behind the potato-flower patterns on the famous china of Moustiers and Marseilles and *toiles de Jouy* of the period.

But the events of 1789 and the consequences of the French Revolution were much more persuasive. Under the Convention and the Directory, people were so hungry that potatoes no longer needed advertising. Although it was no use for bread-making, the vegetable became egalitarian. Its promoter nearly ended on the scaffold for enlisting the aid of the King in his plan to feed the people.

By a decree of 21 Ventôse (late February to late March) of Year III of the Republic, the Paris Commune ordered the Tuileries gardens to be turned into potato fields. Germain Chevet, florist to Marie Antoinette and accordingly regarded as a sworn enemy of the Republic, but then freed for the sake of his large family, still had to dig up his unrepublican roses and replant the beds with patriotic potatoes. (After the Consulate he became a luxury grocer, as it were the Fauchon or the Fortnum and Mason's of his time. We have seen his wife selling asparagus to the English under the eye of Brillat-Savarin.)

'Poster issued by the Minister of Agriculture to the provinces concerning the Colorado Beetle, a threat to the potato': from the *Journal illustré*, drawn by Jules Claverie (1859–1932)

One of the reasons why potatoes were shunned at first was that they belong to the botanical family of Solanaceae which contains a number of poisonous plants. *Solanum tuberosum*, the potato, has now become the most widespread member of the family on this planet, and is so versatile in cookery that it is a staple item on the menu of millions of families. It is also popular with the food industry, in various dried, frozen and dehydrated forms, and it is used to make spirits and as animal feed.

Despite its difficulty in finding a place in the market, there were already 40 different potato varieties in the late eighteenth century. By the end of the Empire period in France there were more than 100, and at the beginning of the twentieth century 1000. A German institute has listed 3000 varieties in existence today. For reasons of convenience, however, only 100 or so of those varieties suitable for human consumption are entered on the register of cultivated varieties officially recognized by the French Ministry of Agriculture. The criteria employed involve agronomical and culinary factors (dry matter content, blackening, yield, etc). New varieties are added every year, and others are deleted to make room for them.

Classification is related to the use made of potatoes: they fall into firm-fleshed varieties which will not disintegrate when boiled, and the ordinary varieties used for purées, soups and the industrial extraction of starch. It is nothing to do with whether the potatoes are early or late: there are early and late varieties in both categories.

The firm-fleshed, more expensive varieties most popular with the French consumer are Belle de Fontenay, BF 15, the pink Rosa, Roseval, Stella and Viola. Among the ordinary varieties, which are two to three times cheaper than the firm-fleshed kinds, the most popular are Bintje (with 90 per cent of the market), Esterling and Institut de Beauvais.

New potatoes grown in France must correspond to their legal definition: a new potato has been dug before it is completely mature, and its skin will come off easily. To the consumer, it has the virtues of being genuinely new, the first potato of the year, and fresh, i.e., not processed in any way. New potatoes, which are particularly perishable, have to be sold soon after they are dug. The main new potato varieties sold in France are Ostara (with about 50 per cent of the area grown with new potatoes), Sirtema, Jaerla, Bea and Resy.

The perishability of the product, and the fact that it needs to be eaten soon after purchase, account for its marketing problems. Unpredictable weather conditions also affect it. Exporting new potatoes would help the market to avoid the risk of stagnating, so long as export outlets are available, but international competition is particularly lively in the new potato market. Over the last 20 years or so, mechanisms have been set up among groups of growers to establish a sensible marketing strategy, avoiding excessive variations in price and available quantities, and thus ensuring that the grower can make a profit and the market can be adequately supplied. Variations in French potato exports are quite considerable, and show that more effort needs to be made to adapt the French supply, both in quantity and in quality, to restricted and ephemeral foreign markets.

New potatoes are dug over a period of about two months. In France, the earliest are dug in early May in the Loire valley, and the latest begin their season at the end of June or the beginning of July in the north and the Paris region. The height of the season is the first fortnight in June.

French production has developed in recent years in line with the economic situation and a fairly general drop in potato consumption. Growers have had difficulty in covering their costs, and the area given over to new potatoes is getting smaller every year. The main producing regions, in order of importance, are Brittany, Provence, the north, Languedoc-Roussillon, and Aquitaine. The commercial balance in France is thus regularly in deficit in the new potato market; home demand comes in the first months of the year, two or three months before home production is in full swing. New potatoes are therefore bought from abroad.

In order of importance, foreign suppliers to France are Spain, Italy and Morocco (a total 74,405 tonnes in 1982, for instance). However, a progressive drop is being seen in the quantity imported from Morocco, which used to head the table of countries supplying France. In fact there is a progressive drop in French imports of new potatoes in general; they cost too much.

Exports too have been limited by the same economic factors (high transport costs for a fragile product which is not always of great value at its point of departure), and by competition from some of the Mediterranean countries, notably Italy and Cyprus. The figures for exports are about equal to those of imports (76,900 tonnes in 1982).

The two main traditional outlets for French new potatoes are the United Kingdom and West Germany. Of recent years the British market has been the better one, because of its proximity to the potato-growing area of Brittany and efficient transport by transporter ferries.

Maincrop potatoes make up three-quarters of French production. Dug fully mature from August to October, when their skins are well developed and strong, they will keep until the middle of the next year, supplying consumers and the manufacturing industry as they are needed until the next potato crop.

The quantities grown in France are usually enough both to satisfy home demand and to supply the foreign market. From 5 to 10 per cent of French maincrop potatoes are exported; the precise amount varies from year to year. However, supplies sometimes have to be imported from abroad. Manufacturers in particular sometimes need large potatoes which give a better yield when processed. Research has been done in France to improve the growing, lifting, packaging and storing of potatoes in the main growing regions. The aim is to achieve complete and permanent self-sufficiency, providing industry (particularly the chip factories) with better quantity and quality.

When there is a poor crop, as happened in 1983, the high level of potato prices in the home market may justify less expensive purchases from abroad. Manufacturers of potato products resort to importing potatoes now and then. The development of a policy on contracts may offer price guarantees to both growers and manufacturers, besides limiting imports or making them unnecessary.

The present tendency towards eating fewer calorie-rich foods and the difficulties experienced by the maincrop potato market may account for the regular decrease in consumption between 1977 and 1983 (a drop from 6353 tonnes to 3944 tonnes). Failing to get an adequate and stable income, growers have been reducing the area under cultivation every year. The drop in production is sometimes aggravated by a drop in yield, something that cannot be predicted in advance. This happened in 1983. Growers cannot count on bad weather to make prices rise to profitable levels again, but we may expect that prices pinned to production will stabilize or slightly increase potato cultivation. The present economic situation might also send consumers back to the potato, still one of the cheapest of foods.

Maincrop potatoes are still the subject of speculation, but as they store well the market can be controlled. Manufacturing and export are two indispensable outlets.

Potato consumption in France seems to be related to the climate and dietary customs of the various regions. In the north of the country, people eat 123 kilos a head per year; in the east, 80 kilos; in the south-west, 61 kilos; in the centre of the country and the south, 59 kilos; in the west, 56 kilos; in the French Alps 53 kilos, and in the Paris region 45 kilos.

But how did the potato turn up in the Prussian prison camps of the eighteenth century, and where had it come from? From America, of course, along with maize, another food that was long regarded as animal fodder, with the tomato, still regarded with suspicion at this time, and with chocolate and turkeys, which made their mark more easily. Pedro Cieça, an adjutant of Pizarro, sent some tubers to the Spanish sovereigns in 1588. They gave them to the Pope, who had them examined by the botanist Clusius. Clusius planted the curious little items in land lent to him by the Papal Nuncio Bonomi at Verceil-les-Champs, and depicted the plants that came up – the first ever grown in European soil – in some magnificent botanical plates, for he was a fine artist. Not knowing what Latin name to give his work, in order to catalogue it fittingly, he called the tuber *taratufli*, little truffle.

The Italian Pope read this as *tartufoli*, the Germans called the tuber *Kartoffel*, the Russians *kartopfel* and the French *tartouste* or *cartoufle* (Olivier de Serres' spelling). Similar tubers brought back from Virginia by Sir Walter Raleigh do not seem to have aroused more than the passing attention of British botanists at the time. The soldiers of the expeditionary British and Spanish forces to the Americas confused them with the sweet potato, from the Peruvian word *papas* or *bappa*,[4] and although they were not very keen on what they called an 'edible stone', even when they were cut off from their base supplies, they gave it the attractive name of little *bappa*, *bappatas*, which then became *patatas* in Spanish and 'potato' in English.

Spanish missionaries brought these *patatas* back to Andalusia, and managed to get the starving locals to eat some as a purée. Then Castilian mercenaries fighting in Germany during the Thirty Years' War began carrying potatoes with them as provisions – for their horses in case of need, and in case of very dire need for themselves. The commissariat was not always in attendance, and the economic situation of Saxony and Westphalia was a nightmare. Those peasants who were given potatoes by the armies of occupation, or managed to steal them, seized upon this strange and foreign manna and ate the potatoes raw, unpeeled. Not surprisingly, they had severe indigestion, which was easily confused with epidemic disease in those plague-ridden times. It was a long time before anyone thought of peeling potatoes (even to supply a task for military fatigues).

In 1780, when Parmentier had just published his *Traité de la châtaigne* and the Paris Commune was declaring the potato Republican and compulsory, people did not always think much of its bland 'non-taste' even after it had been peeled. It became really popular once it got together with frying oil. Alexandre Dumas, a gastronome of distinction, mentions only *maître d'hôtel* potatoes fried in butter. However, the recipes for potatoes in the first cookery book published in France for ordinary people sound modern, appetizing and economical. This work, *La cuisine républicaine*, came out in 1793, and was the first French cookery book written by a woman, Mme Méridiot. It was entirely devoted to the potato.

Not content with nourishing very large numbers of people for 150 years or so, the potato may be said to have changed the face of the world, for America owes many of her most notable families of Irish descent to it, including the Kennedys. The potato was not much liked in eighteenth-century England; the seedsman and garden designer Stephen Switzer described it in 1733 as 'That which was heretofore reckon'd a food fit only for Irishmen and clowns'. As his comment shows, it had been welcomed at a considerably earlier period to Ireland, where famine was endemic. It continued to feed the Irish until the great potato blight of the mid-nineteenth century, which decimated both the potato crop and the starving population. Many of the survivors emigrated, mostly to America.

As well as its direct culinary applications, the potato has long been a raw material in food manufacturing, although it was neglected for a while after the failure of eighteenth-century attempts to make potato bread. Potatoes are now industrially processed on a vast scale, but the mountain-dwellers of the Andes must be credited with getting the idea first. As Dr Maurizio writes: 'It is certain that potatoes have been dried as long as they have been known.'

The Neolithic farmers of the highlands of Bolivia invented a kind of freeze-drying, a process they also applied to other plants or parts of plants which contained a great deal of water, including certain bulbs. At altitudes of 3000 to 3500 metres the cold is very severe. To make their *chumo* or *chuño*, the Andeans dipped the tubers in water and left them to freeze. They were then defrosted by the fire before being crushed and pressed. The pulp obtained was exposed to the cold again: a very dry cold in full sunlight. The *chumo* turned black as coal, and was called *chumo negro*; to make *chumo blanco*, the pulp was dried out in a place from which all light was excluded.

Father de Acosta had encountered potatoes, or rather *papas*, and knew *chuño*.

There is another extreame contrary to this, which hinders the growing of mais or wheate in some parts of the Indies, as on the heights of the Sierra of Peru, and the provinces which they call the Collao, which is the greatest part of this Realme, where the climate is so cold and drie, as it will not suffer any of these seedes to grow: in steede thereof the Indians vse an other kind of roote, which they call Papas. These rootes are like to grownd nuttes, they are small rootes, which cast out many leaves. They gather this Papas, and dry it well in the Sunne, then beating it they make that which they call *Chuño*, which keeps many daies, and serves for bread. In this realme there is great trafficke of *Chuñu*, the which they carry to the mines of Potosi.

By the end of the eighteenth century the peasants of north Germany, having decided the potato was fit for human consumption after all, were making it into potato noodles, *Erdäpfelgrütze*, pressing the pulp through a mill. The noodles were put in front of the stove to dry, either for use as they were, or to be crushed and added to cereal flour and made into a kind of bread; potato flour has to be mixed with some other kind of bread-making flour if it is to rise at all.

The extraction of starch from potatoes goes back to the second half of the nineteenth century, but it was during the Second World War that the Americans really started large-scale industrial manufacturing of potatoes into the ready-to-use products demanded by the army commissariats. Wars act as a spur to practical inventions. The results were pre-cooked chips, potato crisps and instant mashed potato. (Potato crisps had already been made in Great Britain in the 1930s, and Nazi Germany resuscitated the old peasant tradition of potato noodles.)

In 1977 over half the American potato crop went to the factories. The best known of their products today is dehydrated potato flakes for instant mashed potato. It takes 6.5 kilos of potatoes to make a kilo of dehydrated flakes. The variety used is Bintje, the flouriest and most widely grown. The potatoes are washed, brushed and steamed until the skins can be removed by jets of water. They are then sliced, rinsed and boiled in the ordinary way, but on a vast scale. A huge pressing machine makes them into a purée. The purée passes over a heated cylinder so as to form a very thin film which is removed and broken up into flakes. 0.8 per cent of emulsifier (E 471 or glycerol monostearate) is added, to fix the starch and prevent the purée from being too sticky, as well as anti-oxygens to prevent rancidity (E 450 or sodium disphosphate and ascorbic acid).[5] It is vacuum-packed. Mixtures of dehydrated potato with carrots, spinach or celeriac are also made; the principle remains the same.

The Bintje variety is widely used for making crisps too. The potatoes are graded, peeled by abrasion between emery rollers, then put to soak in several changes of water to remove excess starch. They are fried in vegetable oil, drained, salted and vacuum-packed. Potato crisps contain no chemicals at all, which is unusual in food manufacturing today. Potato wafers and potato straws are made in a similar way, and there are many different flavours of crisps – bacon, onion, even pizza.

The traditional potato chip is also manufactured on a large scale. The chips are pre-cooked and need only to be briefly deep-fried in very hot oil, which saves the boring job of peeling. They are frozen or chilled; the chilled kind will be described as 'fresh'.

Dauphine or croquette potatoes are manufactured from mashed potato, eggs, milk, etc. They are briefly fried to give them a pale gold colour and then frozen.

Small potatoes pre-cooked in water or steam used to be preserved by the bottling method, and were sold in jars. Now they are sold in sachets, frozen in a vacuum or a controlled atmosphere. The double pasteurization technique has made it possible to keep the sachets at room temperature without adding any chemicals to their contents. Small new potatoes are also canned.

As the twentieth century draws to a close, these industrially prepared potatoes, used by thousands of restaurants and institutions and bought from supermarkets by millions of consumers the world over, are evidence of all the research being done to make food more practical and quicker to prepare, and of the dynamism of the food manufacturing industry which first began to develop in the nineteenth century.

Soufflé Potatoes

Soufflé potatoes, Courtine has written, are 'the poetry of the potato'. He adds that 'They are nothing and everything, for they will not tolerate mediocrity, so they either go limp, collapse and return to nothing, or else they are marvellous.'

These slices of fried potato transformed into little puffed-up balloons by a double cooking, first at moderate and then at very high heat, were discovered by chance. Great inventions such as the steam engine, radioactivity, penicillin – and soufflé potatoes – usually *are* the result of chance.

On 26 August 1837 the first railway line from Paris to Saint-Germain, constructed by Flachat, was opened. King Louis Philippe and Queen Amélie were on board the train, and a banquet was to be served when they arrived. The menu, as comfortably bourgeois as the royal couple themselves, included roast fillet of beef with fried potato. The chef began to cook his potatoes according to the timetable that had been drawn up, but the train did not arrive, so he took them out of the oil before they were fully cooked, intending to put them back as soon as the guests began on the hors-d'oeuvre.

Once drained, however, the potatoes looked shrivelled, and the chef thought briefly of repeating Vatel's heroic gesture of suicide. But perhaps Vatel himself was keeping watch from Paradise, for when the chef not very hopefully put the limp slices back in the oil, while his assistants blew up the fire with touching zeal, a miracle happened. The slices puffed up into golden bubbles, and when the soufflé potatoes were served they were a triumph. As Voltaire put it, 'time and happy chance have perfected the arts and the sciences.'

A TREATISE ON THE CHESTNUT

By M. PARMENTIER, *pensioner of the Hôtel des Invalides, Royal Censor, Member of the Paris College of Pharmacy and the Academies of Sciences of Rouen and Lyons. Honorary Member of the Economic Society of Berne, Demonstrator of Natural History, and Apothecary-Major to the King's Army.*
Published at Bastia
and to be bought
in Paris
from Monory, Bookseller to His Serene Highness
Monseigneur the Prince de Condé
opposite the old Comédie Française
M. DCC. LXXX

... When the chestnuts are dry, they are taken from the hurdle, and beaten to remove their skins from them: a very strong bench is necessary for this operation, which is done directly after the chestnuts have been removed from the hurdle. The upper surface of the bench must be all in one piece, and its width in proportion to the quantity of chestnuts to be beaten. Twenty setiers of chestnuts are usually beaten at once, and the work takes two men. A bag is made of stout grey cloth to hold the dried chestnuts, and left open at both ends; before the chestnuts are put in, the bag is dipped in water in which bran has been boiled, to make the cloth more supple.

One of the two men holds the end of the bag while the other fills it with a measure of dry chestnuts; both ends are tied, and after it is placed on the bench they both beat it with sticks, 50 to 60 times; this breaks the outer shell and removes the inner skin, disclosing the floury substance of the chestnut. One of the men opens the sack, removes the beaten chestnuts and puts them in a winnowing basket held by the other; he shakes them and winnows them, and by that operation separates out those which have not yet shed their skin at all along with those which retain most of it; the first are put back in the sack to be beaten again. It is necessary to dip the sack in water from time to time, for otherwise it would be torn by the beating.

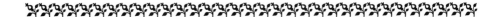

THE POTATO BLIGHT

... They both followed the old man. He had already got his spade from the barn and he had begun to run across the fields towards the far garden by the river bank. The ground was so sodden with rain that the water splashed from his feet as he ran.

'Great God!' he yelled back at them. 'The river is flooded.'

The river had at this point overflowed its banks and the swirling water was half-way up the potato garden. The pit, however, was still beyond the flood. The old man at once dug into its end with the spade and laid bare the covering of ferns. These he hurriedly pulled aside with his hands. Then he slowly raised himself to his full height, some rotting ferns still in his hands. He stared, speechless, at the mass of corruption into which the potatoes had turned.

Then he drew back a pace and looked sideways up at the sky, his face wrinkled into a foolish grin, as if asking God for an explanation of this awful mischief ... He got on his knees beside the hole he had made in the pit and plunging his arms up to the elbows into the heap, he groped about among the mass of corruption, to find out if the centre also had rotted.

Thomsy arrived while the old man was groping in this way. He gaped and cried out:

'In the name of God, what is it?'

The old man started, drew back, rose slowly to his feet, turned about and held out his arms towards Thomsy.

'That's all that's left of them,' he stammered, holding out his arms, from which the corruption dripped to the ground.

'God have mercy on us,' said Thomsy, taking off his hat and crossing himself.

The old man walked out of the garden, stooping, his arms hanging limply by his sides. He seemed suddenly old and decrepit ...

'It's a curse that has fallen on the land,' muttered the old man, as he continued towards the house.

Liam O'Flaherty, *Famine*

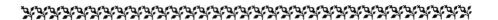

PART IX

On the threshold of the twenty-first century, as the door opens on a new millennium, our concern is with

SCIENCE AND CONSCIENCE IN THE DIET

The Hows and Whys of Quality

The French Revolution shook the structure of European society for ever. It also brought with it a profound change in domestic and social habits, including diet and table manners. But when 'times had improved', in Brillat-Savarin's tactful phrase, the new nobility of the Empire took up the élitist traditions of the old aristocrats who were now in exile or dead, and perhaps they took themselves a little too seriously as the reincarnation of the Roman patriciate. Meanwhile the bourgeoisie, emerging from its probationary period as fresh as Venus rising from the waves, seized upon all the signs of prestige that go with conviviality, both to reassure itself and to ensure that it won proper recognition. Its members had not received many invitations to grand houses in the old days, when the aristocracy looked down on them.

All at once the last generation of chefs in noble households found themselves out of a job. Some of them, who might be politically suspect, kept a low profile and opened food shops, including Clause and Doyen, who claimed to be the first to make Strasbourg *pâté de foie gras*. Others set up in the restaurant business on their own account, and contributed to the flourishing state of such establishments under the Consulate.

Others again, wishing to put their skills to good use as salaried employees, used their former reputations to get themselves posts as major-domos in the households of prosperous self-made men. The latter thus inherited and profited by the renown of men who had been trusted and highly esteemed in their previous positions in noble households.

Beauvilliers, formerly steward to the Count of Provence, escaped the Terror and opened the first great modern restaurant of Paris at no. 26 rue de Richelieu. Boucher, who had presided over the Prince de Condé's kitchens, entered Talleyrand's service as 'controller' of his household, where he was to influence the future career of Marie-Antoine (or Antonin) Carême.

Carême was 20 at this time. He was not one of that generation which had to make a new start in life. His entry into the world of cooking in the grand style coincided with the discovery of Gastronomy with a capital G. Determinism, social determinism included, is only the response to a need brought about by change.

Even Carême's surname seems a wonderfully appropriate stroke of fate. Napoleon re-established the observance of 'carême', Lenten fasting, along with a number of other customs, and so gave Carême the man the chance to exercise his talents and express his philosophy. He developed a sophisticated and refined form of menu for fast days, a very long way from the grim penance or hypocritical pretence of the past. 'What could be more ridiculous and absurd', he wrote, 'than seeing served Pikes and Carp à la Chambord, the garnitures of which were composed of larded sweetbreads, young pigeons, coxcombs and kidneys, whilst it was so easy to alter

731

this ancient usage by the infinite variety that presents itself of the fillets of fish, such as soles, trouts, whitings, salmon, etc., serving them in *escalopes, attereaux, conti*, with truffles, quenelles with truffles, or with mushrooms …'

The culinary art of the whole nineteenth century bore the imprint of the most famous chef in French gastronomy. The Académie Culinaire de France (a project of which he dreamed) would take him for its emblem. A legendary figure in the world of cuisine, Antonin Carême was the archetype of the great modern chef. Of the role he saw cookery fulfilling in society, he wrote: 'When there is no more good cooking in the world, there will be no more keen and elevated intelligence, no more pleasing relationships, no more social unity.' These ideas, which were extraordinarily new at the time, are part of his culinary testament, *Le cuisinier parisien ou l'art de la cuisine au XIXe siècle.*

Carême proved himself philosopher as well as chef, and Jean-François Revel[1] calls him as prolific a writer as Chateaubriand, adding, 'He wrote about everything he cooked.' He was always taking notes. ('It was my custom every evening, on returning home, to note down the changes I made to my work as a result of my daily experience. That detailed account was the cause of the progress I made.') We need not read vanity into the statement so much as a proper awareness of his worth; as an innovator, he urges other chefs to follow his example and further the good cause themselves. 'My colleagues now see the clear evidence of the progress I have made in the French cuisine of the nineteenth century. I do not claim that this new work of mine will fix the culinary art for ever: other practitioners with the gifts and skill for it will doubtless create new things, but my work will have inspired them.'[2]

A bold innovator and an iconoclast, Carême broke with old culinary routines by inventing new methods and utensils. As a great theoretician and a fine virtuoso, he longed to see a true academy of the culinary arts set up. As head of this new school of cuisine he made presentation and arrangement a priority, while still preserving the fine gastronomic quality of the dishes served at the best tables. Above all, he was passionate in his pursuit of freshness and quality. The *de luxe* style of hotel cookery derived from his ideas, and soon, as if in answer to his demands, freshness could be guaranteed by the new methods of preserving foods by heat or by cold.

Up to the time of the Second World War, Carême's work was perpetuated by chefs such as Jules Gouffé, who was head chef of the Jockey Club; Escoffier, César Ritz's partner in London; Urbain Dubois, chef to Count Uruski; and Édouard Nignon, proprietor of the famous Larue restaurant. The worldwide supremacy of French cuisine is their doing. In its classic form, it may not quite respond to the tastes and needs of today, but it is still the model to which we must refer.

Gastronomy – the word had only recently been invented by Joseph Berchoux, author of a poem entitled *La gastronomie et l'homme des champs à table* – became a religion in the early nineteenth century, with its Pope and its anti-Pope: it is hard

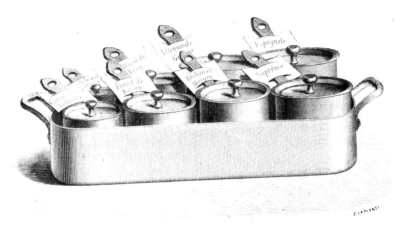

Bain-marie container: engraving from the *Livre de cuisine* by Jules Gouffé, 1881

to choose between Grimod de La Reynière and Brillat-Savarin, the one so assured, the other so engaging.

The genesis of Gastronomy (let us allow it a capital), like the original Genesis, began with the Word. The utterances of its prophets soon became dogma, codifying not the Tables of the Law but the Laws of the Table. Soon gastronomic literature became truly democratic and took the Word to the middle classes, who were waiting enthusiastically to receive it. As with the rites of the Church, Gastronomy had a mythology made to measure, with its heroes such as Antonin Carême obviously predestined for that role (he had even started life in poor and needy circumstances and carried out secret espionage missions, spying on the Tsar under cover of his profession as chef).

Without exaggeration (for once), Grimod de La Reynière could write of Paris, now the Mecca of gastronomy:

> It is indubitably the best place in the world to eat, and the only one able to provide every civilized nation of the world with excellent chefs. Although Paris in itself produces nothing, for not a grain of corn grows there, not a lamb is born or a cauliflower picked, it is a centre to which all things are brought from every corner of the globe. It is the place where the particular qualities of all that serves for human nourishment are best appreciated, and where there is most knowledge of the way to prepare it for the pleasure of our senses.[3]

The appreciation of good food still reigned, as it had since Valois times, in the middle-class Paris of the nineteenth century. The most striking phenomenon associated with gastronomy, as I have indicated above, was the advent of restaurants. Taking over from the inns to which people resorted simply to satisfy hunger, they satisfied a taste for good food. Famous names, as well as those I have already mentioned, included La Maison Dorée, Magny, Le Café Anglais, Les Frères Provençaux, Les Frères Véry, and Le Rocher de Cancale with its chef Baleine. Jean-François Revel[4] points out, accurately, that the success of these restaurants did not depend on the patronage of the great but on the approval of a new and vociferous body of men, the gastronomic critics, headed by Grimod de La Reynière: 'Like the politician, the writer, the musician and the sculptor, the cook of the nineteenth century depended on the three mainsprings of the liberal society: the law of supply and demand, universal suffrage, and the freedom of the press.'

We may add to that presiding trinity a beneficent and generous ally in the shape of science. The labours of a remarkable body of chemists and physicists were about to give food not its letters patent of nobility – it had authentic specimens of those already, as old as the human race for which it had unfailingly provided – but its guarantee documents. The nineteenth century saw the advent of the science of nutrition.

Brillat-Savarin had foreseen it:

APHORISMS

By the Professor to serve as a prologue to his work and an eternal foundation for his Science.

I. The world is nothing without life, and all that lives takes nourishment.

II. Animals feed: man eats: only the man of intellect knows how to eat.

III. The fate of nations depends on the way they eat.

IV. Tell me what you eat: I will tell you what you are.

V. The Creator, who made man such that he must eat to live, incites him to eat by means of appetite, and rewards him with pleasure.

VI. Gourmandism is an act of judgement, by which we give preference to things which are agreeable to our taste over those which are not.[5]

Henceforth, people would understand the hows and whys of quality.

Chapter 24

Preserving by Heat

'It was the need to cook which taught man to use fire, and it was by using fire that man conquered Nature', wrote Brillat-Savarin.[1]

Ensuring that food will keep well, obviously, has been a major preoccupation of mankind. At a very early stage people understood (though they did not yet know why) that one of the secrets was to keep foods away from contact with air, light and damp by coating or enclosing them in impermeable substances such as clay and honey, and later on oil, wine or vinegar, and fat. Other substances used in this way, such as ashes and salt, also modified appearance and flavour. It was realized later that these antiseptic and dehydrating substances helped to prevent oxidization and the proliferation of the bacteria that cause decay. Smoking or simply drying protected food, particularly meat and fish, and modified the chemical and biological processes which encourage decomposition. The Sumerians were the first to combine the smoking and drying processes, but all peoples have empirically discovered various methods of drying meat.

One such method is the *tasajo* of South America, a kind of ball of very fine strips of dried meat. It provides the meat in the daily diet of the poor, and it has been made since time immemorial. The strips of meat are dipped in maize flour before being exposed to the wind. Then they are tightly rolled up. The North American Indians reduced dried meat of this kind to powder so that they could mix it with hot water, just like the Celts of Armorica and the nomads of Asia Minor in the account given by the historian Dio Cassius in the second century AD. Under Louis XIV and Louis XV of France, there were several attempts to feed the French troops a nourishing decoction of powdered meat called Martin broth, after the man who invented it in 1680. However, in 1779 the soldiers threatened to go on strike if the authorities persisted in their intention, and the broth was withdrawn from their rations for good.

735

Simple dehydration of meat is practised mainly in regions where salt is difficult to obtain, or expensive. One example still made today is the dried meat of the Grisons, now a luxury food more expensive than the best ham. Ham itself, dry-cured or smoked, is a preserved food that has been made since the dawn of time. The buccaneers of the Caribbean were not originally pirates but purveyors of leather, hunting the cattle of San Domingo that had reverted to the wild. They also dried and smoked the meat of the animals, as provisions for ships' crews. However, their bad reputation (which was well earned) led to their expulsion from Spanish territory, and they turned to piracy. Making smoked meat was an old practice in the Caribbean islands. The original word *mukem* or *bukem* comes from the extinct Tupi language.

As soon as people learned to use fire they realized that meat and fish kept better cooked than raw. Cooking involves a chemical change in substances and the temporary destruction of germs. One could say that cakes of flat bread baked on the hearthstone were the first foods intended for keeping. Another important stage was the fermentation of dough and of fruit juices. Unlike the fruits themselves, fermented drinks made from them did not spoil. I have mentioned the fermentation caused by the lactic bacteria of chopped vegetable matter above.

When sugar became more common at the end of the Middle Ages, those crystallized fruits, jams and sweet confections which could once be made only with honey became progressively more available too. This was the beginning of a genuine if initially small-scale food-preserving industry.

One of the keys to making preserves successfully, as everyone knows, is cooking at high heat. The prolonged effects of heat on the preservation of fruit, and its similar but more transitory effect on meat, were observed, but until people really understood what happened during putrefaction that was all.

As we have seen, the people of classical times believed in spontaneous generation. For instance, they thought that bees were magically born from the carcases of oxen. 'All dry bodies that become damp, or all damp bodies which become dry, will produce animalcules so long as they are able to feed them', Aristotle had said. By animalcules he meant small living creatures, particularly invertebrates. Lucretius, taking up the same idea, remarked that 'living worms may emerge from foul earth when it is wet after rain and begins to putrefy',[2] an observation rather than an explanation. In classical antiquity it was believed that this was how mushrooms grew.

Homer himself, however, gave the Tuscan naturalist and poet Francesco Redi (1626–1698) an insight into the enigma: when poet meets poet, the result may be a sudden flash of inspiration. In the *Iliad* (Book XIX, 27), Achilles asks his mother Thetis to care for the body of Patroclus. 'Yet am I sore afraid lest meantime flies enter the wounds that the bronze hath dealt on the corpse of the valiant son of Menoetius, and work shame upon his corpse ... and so all his flesh shall rot.'

Flies, of course, lay eggs on carrion, and their larvae then hatch out as wriggling maggots. Redi tried an experiment. He placed fish and meat (being an Italian, he

736

chose veal) in small flasks. He sealed some of these flasks hermetically and left others open but covered them carefully with fine linen so that air but no insects could get through. Those flasks which were not hermetically sealed were soon swarming with maggots, but the others remained free of them. Anton van Leeuwenhoeck (1632–1723), the inventor of the microscope, confirmed Redi's theory by carrying out a similar experiment and observing the actual hatching of the eggs. He even announced the existence of microbes.[3]

In 1748 an English Catholic priest who had taken refuge in Belgium, John Needham, observed some test-tubes containing meat juices diluted in hot water. He had thought it hot enough to kill any potential animal life, but decomposition still set in. A little later another Italian, the priest Lazaro Spallanzani (1729–1799), observed that the water, which was already polluted, had not been boiled hard enough to kill 'those small organic bodies which I will call by the name of *germs*. These germs will resist the strength of fire for a certain time, but will eventually succumb to it.' He also suggested that the corks Needham used could have been contaminated, and pointed out that in any case they did not provide a hermetic seal.

With the new climate of thought of the nineteenth century there was a revolution, not political but technological, in the history of food. It was as important in its way as the discovery of fire, and was the sequel, coming thousands of years later, to that first victory over hunger. The secret was preservation by sterilization, and it meant safety in food never before achieved. No man is a prophet in his own country, and so the Americans were the first to call the process 'appertizing', after its inventor Nicolas Appert (1749–1841), a native of Châlons-sur-Marne. He was officially declared a 'benefactor of humanity' in 1822 by the Société d'Encouragement pour l'Industrie Nationale, but nonetheless died in poverty and was buried in a communal grave, like Molière before him.

Nicolas Appert was not a scientist, but a former brewer who became steward to the duke of Zweibrücken, Christian IV, then to the Duchess of Forbach, and thereafter became a confectioner. As he made the sweets that were preserved with sugar, he became obsessed with an idea which was echoed in the preoccupations of the Directory: research into the keeping of foods hitherto considered highly perishable, such as milk, meat and green vegetables.

Napoleon was leading the French Army to victory after victory in Italy at this time, but the army commissariat was less efficient, and there was waste on a huge scale. The government therefore offered a prize of 12,000 francs to anyone who could find a means of preserving the victuals of soldiers and sailors. This was in 1795, a year of many stirring events. The ten-year-old son of Louis XVI and Marie Antoinette had just died in prison, a stunned Europe was signing treaties and ceasefires with French generals in their early twenties, Poland was partitioned, the metric system was adopted in France, and the washing machine was invented in England. The British Navy made the distribution of lemon juice to its crews as an antidote to scurvy compulsory, which did not prevent the fiasco of the Quiberon landing. And Nicolas Appert had just sold his shop to retire to Ivry-sur-Seine and immerse himself in his mysterious labours. In spite of the mystery about them, he was highly esteemed locally, and held the post of village mayor until he finally found what he had been after for so many years, when he resigned.

He then bought a market garden at Massy, and soon built a four-roomed structure among his rows of beans and peas. In one of the rooms he set up an enormous cauldron with a capacity of over 200 litres; milk and fresh cream were prepared in another. The third room was for bottling, and the fourth contained three copper boilers in which the bottles of milk, peas or beans were brought to the boil. The project was under the patronage of Grimod de La Reynière, Pope of the new religion of gastronomy, which shows how seriously Appert's 'little bottles' were being taken.

Alexandre Balthasar Laurent Grimod de La Reynière (1758–1838) had been a lawyer under the *ancien régime* and now did occasional journalism, but his principal calling, in J.-F. Revel's words, was that of 'the first modern gourmand and well-organized parasite'. He had made a good thing out of his weaknesses. He ate at the expense of restaurateurs, food manufacturers and pâtissiers, all of whom wanted him to endorse their products. The process was almost official: a jury of tasters consisting of his best friends met at the famous restaurant Le Rocher de Cancale or at Grimod de La Reynière's home, where the larder was always full of delicacies proffered for his approval. In 1803 Grimod began publishing the *Almanach des gourmands*, a kind of forerunner of the Michelin guide, listing the good eating houses of the period, and keeping the restaurants of Paris in a state of fear and trembling. The food products were discussed in the same author's *Guide nutritif*. A considerable number of lawsuits followed.

However, there was no doubt about the achievement of Nicolas Appert, who must certainly have helped to feed his patron. The milk and vegetables in his little bottles turned out to keep remarkably well. They were wholesome, and they tasted good.

Appert's establishment soon became a considerable industry, employing 25 to 40 women during the summer to prepare and bottle the vegetables, while a shop at no. 28 rue Boucher in Paris sold them. Appert, a dynamic and jovial little man despite his bald head and Mephistophelian eyebrows, could provide good references for his business. Official shipboard experiments from 1804 onwards had proved the value of his preserved food, and in 1809 the process was approved by a committee on which Parmentier sat, and then by another in 1810 which included Gay-Lussac. The Bureau Consultatif des Arts et Manufactures awarded Appert a 12,000-franc prize. The public and the press were loud in their praises. The *Courrier de l'Europe* of 10 February 1809 wrote that: 'M. Appert has found a way to fix the seasons; at his establishment, spring, summer and autumn live in bottles, like those delicate plants protected by the gardener under glass domes against the intemperate seasons.'

The next year Appert published *L'art de conserver pendant plusieurs années toutes les substances animales et végétales.* He made his methods common knowledge so that everyone could preserve food at home, and never bothered to take out a patent (which the Americans and English did not scruple to do on their own accounts). Preserving was basically a very simple business, once you had the idea. All you had to do, said Appert, was

> First, enclose the substances you wish to preserve in bottles or jars; second, close the openings of your vessels with the greatest care, for success depends principally on the seal; third, submit the substances, thus enclosed, to the action of boiling water in a bain-marie for a period of longer or shorter duration, depending on their nature and the manner I shall indicate for each kind of foodstuff; fourth, remove the bottles from the bain-marie at the appropriate time.

This method was to be the basis for all the preserved food produced on the planet, from industrial conveyor-belt lines to housewives bottling jars of garden produce in a home sterilizer. The drawback to glass was its fragility, and it was soon replaced by cans of welded tin-plate, used first by the Dutch for fish and then by the British for fruits preserved in syrup.

In 1814 Appert went to London and became interested in steam, which worked much better than boiling water. Back in France, however, he had an unpleasant surprise: his factory at Massy had been requisitioned for use as a hospital. He took refuge in Paris and found small premises in the rue Cassette, but without his full range of equipment he had great difficulty in experimenting with new refinements. Moreover, the restored monarchy did not seem inclined to patronize a Republican. But at last, having been declared a benefactor of humanity all the same in 1822, he acquired bigger and better equipped premises, devoted himself to many other works of research on the food industry and published his results. His small grant of 12,000 francs financed his experiments, but left him hardly anything to live on. His wife left him, and he died, abandoned by almost everyone, on 1 June 1841. He was given a pauper's funeral and buried in a communal grave.

In America the first big canneries for fish, meat and fruits began to expand in a way that would turn the world economy upside down. But it was a long time before perfectly efficacious sterilization could be guaranteed. Appert's nephew, Raymond Chevallier-Appert, carrying on where his uncle had left off, invented and patented a sterilizer using high-pressure steam in 1851, and the chemist Favre discovered that boiling water could reach a temperature of over 100 degrees centigrade if it was salted. In 1853 the American Winslow finally achieved perfect sterilization at high temperatures. Success at last! Corned beef sterilized in this way figured prominently in the commissariats of the War of Secession, and contributed to the fortunes of the West.

In his *L'art de conserver*, Appert, who was not a scientist but an empiricist, explained the phenomenon: 'The action of fire destroys or at least neutralizes all the fermentations which, in the ordinary way of nature, produce modifications that change the characteristics of animal substances in changing their constituent parts.'

This 'theory', foreshadowing Pasteur's discoveries, most notably pasteurization itself, is expressed in the cautiously imprecise language of the period. 'Fermentation', known since antiquity, meant any alteration of organic material which led to the production of alcoholic or acid substances, such as wine and choucroute – but the nature of the forces at work remained mysterious. In 1810 Gay-Lussac thought that when such substances were exposed 'to the temperature of boiling water, in well closed vessels, the oxygen absorbed produces a new combination which is no longer favourable to fermentation or putrefaction.'[4]

Since Spallanzani's time it had been known that air was necessary for one form of fermentation, but there were also 'fermentations' which appeared to take place even when air was excluded. Pasteur solved this problem when he revealed the importance of the world of microbes. His brilliant discoveries, bringing Appert's premonitions to fulfilment, were the incentive for a new approach to all concepts of chemistry, physics and physiology.

Louis Pasteur was born in Dole in 1822, to the family of a humble tanner. He was a gifted draughtsman, but only just passed his Baccalauréat examination, with a mark of 'mediocre' for chemistry. However, he went to the École Normale Supérieure in Paris to study science. His first discoveries, made while he was a laboratory assistant, took him to a post as lecturer in chemistry at Lille, and he became dean of the faculty there in 1854.

While the most eminent scientists of his time kept coming back to the theory of the spontaneous generation of fermentation, for want of any other way to explain it, Pasteur carried out some remarkable work on crystallization. His studies of tartaric acid led him to examine the problems of fermentation. Some industrialists of Lille asked for his help: they had suffered severe losses because the table wine they exported to Great Britain regularly went 'off'. Being from the Arbois region, Pasteur was interested in wine, and in any case the problem was a fascinating one. Examining a slide holding a drop of wine under the microscope, he had already seen microbes making their way to the edges of the glass as if in search of oxygen there. But on another occasion, when he was studying a fermented solution produced by the action of butyric acid (an organic acid which exists in certain fatty substances), he had seen the opposite movement: microbes fleeing from oxygen and assembling in the middle of the drop. Even more interesting, when the slide was placed in a strong current of air fermentation stopped: the microbes responsible therefore lived only in the absence of air. This was contrary to all received opinion. Air was not essential to life after all. Pasteur called the germs that needed to 'breathe' the oxygen of the atmosphere 'aerobic organisms', and those destroyed or inhibited by oxygen 'anaerobic organisms'. The latter extracted oxygen from their nutritive medium and not from the air around them. Some fermentations or processes of decomposition occurred in mediums exposed to air, but others developed only when the germs were sufficiently deprived of oxygen.

To return to the spoilt wine and the dismay of its exporters, one must remember that new wine is thick, cloudy and harsh in flavour. As it ages it clarifies and develops its bouquet and pleasant flavour. This is the result of fermentations feeding on organic matter suspended in the grape juice.

In ageing, however, wine sometimes deteriorates as if by the action of new fermentations. Pasteur put various samples under the microscope: young wine, sour wine, wine that had gone off, spoilt wine. He found that, in the process of souring, the micro-organisms changed and a new kind began to act. If he saw that micro-organisms of this kind were present in apparently good wine, he could actually predict the change. It was obvious that the process of contamination had to be halted: the flora must be destroyed before they reproduced, but after they had made the yeasts in the mycoderma of the grapes turn grape sugar into alcohol. As we saw in the chapter on wine, these yeasts are carried to the grapes by the dust in the air.

The new, unwanted fermentations were carried on the hands of the grape-pickers (not to mention the feet of the grape-crushers), and contaminated the must at a later stage. Pasteur reasoned that it would be easier to try destroying those fermentations after vinification than to prevent their appearance. Wine-growers, however, continued to believe that only exposure to the air was responsible for spoiled wine. If the new wine were bottled and hermetically sealed, it would not continue to age and would remain cloudy. The air passing through the cork was indispensable to wine-making, and excluding it would ruin the whole process.

Using very newly made wine, and checking through the microscope to make sure it was perfectly wholesome, Pasteur half-filled bottles, leaving plenty of air in them before corking but not sealing them so that aeration could continue. The wine cleared and developed a good colour and bouquet, but did not spoil. So air was not responsible for the damage.

Next, taking samples of the contaminated wine, Pasteur experimented with several ways of disinfecting it, but if any of the chemical products he tried did kill off unwanted micro-organisms, the wine was still ruined. There remained the possibility of sterilization by heat, Appert's method. What was the ideal temperature which would kill the germs without harming the product itself? Not boiling point, obviously; cooked wine is no longer natural wine. Several experiments eventually showed that heating to a temperature of 53 degrees centigrade, followed by immediate and swift cooling, neutralized the unwanted pathogenic germs and did not spoil the flavour of the wine. It was also necessary for a certain amount of air to be left in the vessels containing the new wine that had been treated in this way, so that it could continue its subsequent development.

Predictably, the gourmets were outraged: this was just cooked wine. A jury of experts was invited to a tasting. Not one of them could tell the difference between pasteurized and natural wine. However, pasteurization obviously does halt the development and slow improvement of the very best wines. Great *crus* and fine wines, therefore, are never pasteurized (and today, in any case, considerable progress

741

has been made in hygiene and handling during vinification itself). However, pasteurization of table wines is neither illegal nor to be deplored; indeed, it is a guarantee to both the wine merchant and the consumer.

Pasteurization was subsequently to be a means of protection applied to milk, butter, cheese, beer, fruit juice and many other food products as well as wine.

Canned Sardines

More sardines are eaten canned in oil than fresh. This is not a new state of affairs, although canning in metal containers dates only from the middle of the nineteenth century.

Caught in large quantities on the Atlantic seaboard of the west coasts of France, Spain and Portugal, the sardine has long been one of the main resources of Brittany and the maritime provinces of the Iberian peninsula. The sardine is also found in abundance in the Mediterranean, where it gave its name to Sardinia. The Romans called the fish *sardae sine sardinae*; *sarda* was their word for a kind of Atlantic tunny fish. It was considered a coarse, second-rate fish, and remained quite cheap.

The Mediterranean sardine is really an Atlantic winter sardine. It comes to the Mediterranean to spawn from December to February, and is not at its best for eating then. Exhausted after spawning, pale and flabby, it has hardly any flavour, and is despised by people who really like sardines. But from March to November it revives and sees the world with a clear, lively, bright and protuberant eye. There are two main sardine fishing seasons in the Gulf of Lions, in November and February. More of the fish have been caught there since temperature variations in the Atlantic and the English Channel after 1960 sent it emigrating either to Morocco and West Africa or meant that it stayed in the Mediterranean. Former French colonials back from Algeria have made Sète and Marseilles great sardine-fishing ports. It is sometimes said that the mistral chases the sardine away from its usual fishing grounds, but in fact the wind merely prevents the boats from going out, and market prices rise accordingly.

From ancient times the sardine was salted and pressed to be sold inland. Columella cites it in his list of preserved fish, salted either by itself or among the small fry left to decompose to make garum and its nutritious residue *allec*. The fish did not always keep, but at least they were then fed to the higher-class fish in the fishponds. Columella and Juvenal both recommend feeding the latter on rotten sardines.[5]

In the Middle Ages, the Nantes area was famous for its sardines preserved in vinegar, in the local melted butter, or in imported olive oil. They were packed in the large jars of Berry earthenware called *oules* and sent off to the rest of France.

In 1822 a confectioner of Nantes called Joseph Moulin decided to apply his ex-colleague Nicolas Appert's sterilization method to sardines. He used the tin cans perfected by the Dutch and the British, and in 1824 he opened the first French fish cannery. Again following Appert's example, and hoping to find a good long-term market as a supplier to the French Navy, he had solicited the approval of an expert, one Captain Freycinet. Freycinet endorsed his product, and the *Journal de Nantes et de la Loire-Inférieure* of 8 June 1822 published an interview with the captain, pointing out that, 'At Colin's, in the rue du Moulin, a complete range of all preserved foods may be bought, including items which cannot be found in Paris, such as sardines in butter and in oil. They have come through all the tests to which I have subjected them in 38 months of navigation.'

However, if we are to believe another article, published in *Sciences et nature* in 1884, sardines in oil were invented by a Lorient magistrate who had them prepared by an old lady he knew, Mlle Le Guillon. They were so successful that the magistrate opened a factory, the first of the kind, in Lorient.

Throughout the nineteenth century and the first half of the twentieth, the canning industry expanded in Brittany and the Basque country. Breton sardines of a good average size which fits the cans nicely were caught offshore, and arrived at the factories very fresh. Here they were beheaded and gutted by hand, then lightly fried and packed in cans which were subsequently welded and sterilized.

Today, as we have seen, the sardines seem to have deserted the Breton coast, and Mediterranean sardines are used. However, they have farther to travel to the Breton canneries and are not as good as Atlantic sardines. Alternatively, the factories can Moroccan sardines delivered in brine or frozen. Their flesh is harder and does not absorb as much oil. They can be recognized by a red line running down the backbone. Sardines canned on the spot in Morocco from freshly caught fish are much better than exported Moroccan sardines canned elsewhere.

Canned sardines are no longer fried in oil, but steamed or baked. The fish have already been slightly salted as soon as they come ashore, to firm up their flesh and make them less fragile. They are sorted and graded, beheaded and gutted. All these operations are carried out manually on a conveyor belt, although machinery is used in the process. Successful attempts have been made in America to gut pilchards by suction, but the method will not work on sardines. The Norwegians do not gut the fish at all, but instead leave it to fast in reservoirs before canning.

The sardines are then washed in running water, and steeped in brine for half an hour to blanch them and clean them of blood and bacteria. They are showered, dried in hot air, and then cooked in a tunnel oven from which they emerge in neat rows, dropping into a line of cans which then passes under a device filling them with oil at a temperature of 90 degrees centigrade. Finally the cans are closed and sterilized.

In 1880 the temperature of the Atlantic suddenly turned colder, and the sardines emigrated from Brittany to the Portuguese coast. The French canners moved part of their plant to Cezinha. Ten years later the fish tired of Portuguese waters and moved back to France. So did the canners.

Portuguese sardines have their aficionados. The oil in which the best quality sardines are canned, wherever they come from, must be olive oil. If the can does not actually specify olive oil then it is some other kind. Sardines are also canned in tomato sauce added after they have been baked. Lemon or piquant spices may be included with the sauce in the can to make the fish more digestible. Boneless sardines are more expensive but no better in flavour; the same applies to all filleted ready-prepared fish. If the bones are left in they also add calcium, dissolved into the sauce.

The sardine is regarded as a fatty food in itself, containing a little more than 2 per cent lipids; the proportion rises to 17 per cent once it has been canned in oil, giving around 70 milligrams of cholesterol per 17 grams. All its other constituent elements are augmented in the canning process too. It is very nourishing, if a little difficult to digest. Sardines should be regarded as a main dish rather than an hors d'oeuvre.

People who really like sardines in oil say they improve with age, like wine, and are delicious after three or four years. They should be kept in a cupboard, not the refrigerator, where the oil would solidify and the flesh dry out.

The Technique of Canning

Cans are made of tin-plate, which today is a mild steel consisting of 0.005 to 0.10 per cent carbon, with a layer of tin on both sides. It has been cold-laminated to a thickness of 0.25 millimetres. The purpose of the tinning is to prevent corrosion either from inside, by the action of the contents, which could even dissolve the metal, or from the outside. For added protection, the insides of the cans are now coated with synthetic resins (natural resins were used in the past), and baked at 170 degrees centigrade or fixed by electrolysis.

Cans were made by hand in the nineteenth century. Today machinery cuts the sheets of tin-plate into strips, which are then bent into the required shape – cylindrical, rectangular or oval. One of the narrower edges of the strip is notched and then clamped to the other before they are hammered or welded together. The larger edges are folded to form a kind of hem to which the ends of the can will be welded or crimped.

The ends are cut out of more strips of tin-plate, and to withstand internal pressure they are stamped with a circular outline surrounded by concentric channels. When gases inside the can push the end of the can out into a concave shape, a process facilitated by the central circle and the channelling, it means that the contents are unfit for consumption and should not be eaten. The ends, which sometimes have a plastic joint, are crimped or welded into place. Sardine and mackerel cans have a metal tongue instead, which can be rolled back with a key to open them.

Products to be canned are prepared in the various ways appropriate to them. Green vegetables are not usually cooked but only blanched, plunged in boiling water for two or three minutes. The cans, previously sterilized and cooled, are filled to the top, and then liquid is added.

The lids are crimped on at the same time as a jet of steam is forced into the can, so that there will be a vacuum when the can cools. All this is done automatically, at a rate of 250 cans a minute. The cans move along a conveyor belt towards the sterilizer. Sterilization at 115 degrees centigrade takes 40 minutes for large cans to reach the requisite temperature. The sterilizer is controlled by a manometer, and the operation of the machinery is often recorded so that checks can be kept on it. Cooling is by immersion in very cold water, to stop the cooking process fast.

Very likely the twenty-first century will see sterilization by steam pressure replaced by high frequencies, by radiation which will ionize without heat, or by induction, as in a microwave oven, where heat methods are retained for certain types of food. In that case the container will no longer be metal. Other ways of preserving food, by methods involving a very brief period in intense cold, or by antibiotics, are envisaged as real possibilities for the future.

When the cans have been closed they are labelled, but it is increasingly usual to have indelible indications stamped directly on the metal.

The ordinary French citizen does not eat much canned food, only 17 or 18 kilos a year, unlike the average American, who eats 50 kilos, i.e., a can a day. The French dislike of canned food is based on the belief that it lacks flavour and vitamins.

I will not dilate upon the canned *pâtés de foie gras*, the excellent cooked French provincial dishes, exotic fruits, crab, and out-of-season vegetables that canning makes available; I will mention only the nutritional and hygienic value of canned foods. Common sense requires a varied diet to contain fresh and even raw elements whenever foods are fresh or tender enough, but a certain proportion of canned food is perfectly healthy. There is a vast amount of literature describing the results of studies on the nutritional value of canned food by very eminent specialists. Comparisons of the vitamin content of fresh and canned foods show that apparently fresh foods are not always the best. Time spent in prolonged storage, on the shop shelves or at home, cooking for too long and in too much water or fat, all decrease the amount of vitamins and mineral salts contained in fresh foods. In good canned foods the content is equal or even superior. Canned vegetables are processed the moment they are picked and never over-cooked, so that the vitamins are preserved. Fish too are canned as soon as they are caught.

If you want to be sure the contents of a can are safe to eat you need only check that it looks perfect, and reject any that seem to be bulging, broken or rusty. To satisfy consumer organizations, dates of manufacture and eat-by dates are now clearly and indelibly printed on French cans. The EC too will have to standardize regulations in its member countries. The coded indications on cans up to now have been useless, never understood by the consumer even if he or she goes to the trouble of reading them.

Food Preservation

To understand the various different ways of preserving it, we need to know why food goes bad after a certain time.

For a long time, it was thought that foods spontaneously produced invisible elements which caused decomposition, but, as we have seen, Louis Pasteur's work in the middle of the nineteenth century relegated spontaneous generation to the sphere of mythology. The micro-organisms present everywhere – in air, water and matter – are of three kinds, all belonging to the vegetable kingdom.

Moulds and yeasts, which are tiny fungi, and the bacteria related to seaweeds, reproduce either by dividing or by spores, innumerable particles like very fine dust which germinate in suitable surroundings.

Moulds can be seen at work on fruits, which they very soon destroy. They also attack cheese. Certain useful and beneficial moulds develop on curdled milk (*Penicillium album*) and turn it into cheese. Moulds like sweetness.

Yeasts, like those on grape skins, also feed on sugar and start a fermentation; the sweeter the product, the faster the fermentation. Yeasts reproduce by cell division.

The most common bacteria are *bacilli*, which are very dangerous if ingested, because the temperature of the human body, at 37 degrees centigrade, encourages them to reproduce by division. Higher or lower temperatures do not destroy them, but plunge them into a kind of lethargy from which they revive in more favourable conditions. The germs of some other bacteria, which are extremely hardy, do not mind the cold at all (some of them can live at temperatures as low as minus 191° centigrade) but production stops at plus 3 degrees of heat (up to 130°) although they are no longer seen to be reproducing at 42 degrees. They like humidity, but if conditions are too dry they can perfectly well sleep in their outer casings. Bacteria include *cocci* and *vibrii*.

The tough resistance such germs put up led to the invention by an Irishman, John Tyndall (1820–1893), of a process perfecting pasteurization. It entails heating the food several times, for periods of three-quarters of an hour to an hour, alternating with chilling for periods of 24 hours. Although the mother bacteria are destroyed by the first heating, any germs which may already have been emitted will be reactivated in the cold, but they are now more fragile and cannot stand up to the following sterilizations. This method, called tyndallization, also preserves the flavour and vitamins of the food.

Microbes are living creatures, and need the following essentials to survive comfortably:

Food: the protids, glucids and mineral salts contained in food. They do not like lipids. An old, rustic way of preserving food, therefore, was in oil or fat. Moulds and yeasts, greedy for sugar and mineral salts, are uninvited guests which consume vegetable foods rich in carbohydrates. Bacteria, which like protids, prefer meat foods.

Humidity: after a while bacteria will die as they dehydrate with the food where they are sheltering. Drying is one of the oldest ways of preserving foods. Salt speeds up the process of dehydration, and so does smoking. Freeze-drying entails the dehydration of foods after freezing.

Oxygen: bacteria in particular are aerobic organisms and need air to live. When food is coated with a substance that excludes air, or enclosed as it often is now in hermetically sealed plastic, it will keep fresh longer. But since Pasteur's discovery it has been realized that other microbes, those anaerobic organisms that cannot tolerate air, manufacture oxygen themselves as they decompose the food harbouring them.

Moderate warmth (an optimum 37° centigrade): pasteurization, like ordinary sterilization and tyndallization, as we have seen, destroys microbes and yeasts by raising this temperature, but if care is taken to keep food cool the germs will reproduce more slowly. The cold temperatures of refrigerators also help food to keep, and quick-freezing protects it perfectly.

A certain degree of alkalinity: foods are acid to different extents, described in terms of their pH figures. Microbes do not like acidity and prefer an alkaline medium. Acid foods such as vinegar, lemon and most fruits with a very low pH factor (that of lemon is 1.9) do not change as quickly as others, and long before people could explain it they realized that the presence of such foods offered some protection. Thus alkaline foods such as potatoes, asparagus and meat (pH 5 to 6.5) have to be sterilized for longer than others. Acid fermentation, as in choucroute, creates a medium hostile to decomposition.

Since microbes make the foods in which they proliferate toxic, we may wonder why, when they are still present after being killed by sterilization, they are now harmless. The explanation is that microbes in themselves *are* harmless, but they secrete poisons or toxins, such as the one which causes botulism and is secreted by the bacillus *Botulinus*, particularly common in minced meat which has not been cooked at once and in ham (especially sliced ham kept in plastic bags at temperatures above 3 degrees centigrade); the bacillus of typhoid fever is secreted by the typhus bacillus found in shellfish from waters that are not perfectly clean, ice cubes made from polluted water, or vegetables contaminated by manure.

Canned foods, salt fish and meat, and frozen food cannot be guaranteed harmless once the can is opened, the salt meat soaked to remove salt or humidified, and the frozen food defrosted; they can be contaminated again by the atmosphere around them, or by handling and packing. They must be eaten as soon as they are prepared. Strict hygiene is still one of the best methods of avoiding accidents, and it has to be observed both before and after food is preserved.

747

Pasteurized Milk

The pasteurization of milk consists of heating raw milk for some minutes to between 63 and 95 degrees centigrade and then cooling it to 4 degrees. This destroys the harmful germs it may contain and reduces the number of those micro-organisms which are no threat to health but can impair the keeping qualities of the product, and finally preserves it in good condition.

Great progress has been made in the field of nutrition and dietetics over the last 60 years or so, and has contributed to modern methods of pasteurization. Milk can now be treated without any noticeable effect on its composition, and pasteurization makes no difference at all to its nutritional value.

With new technology and much stricter legislation, the quality of milk as a whole has improved considerably during the last 20 years, from the point of view of flavour as well as freedom from bacteria. Pasteurized fresh milk is now very like raw milk, particularly in flavour. As it has been pasteurized it is not necessary to boil it.

Pasteurized milk is fresh, live milk. Milk is subject to strict legislation. Until the moment it goes on sale, pasteurized milk must be clean, free of pathogenic germs, contain no more than ten coliform bacteria per millilitre and no more than 30,000 living microbic germs per cubic centimetre, be kept at a temperature of 10 degrees centigrade or below, be packed where its last treatment took place, have a negative phosphatase reaction (which shows that pasteurization has been efficient), have a minimum protein content of 28 grams per litre, and a minimum fat matter content of 35 grams per litre for pasteurized full-cream milk, 15.45 grams for pasteurized half-cream milk, and 3.09 grams for pasteurized skim milk. All milk is entirely skimmed so that it can then have added to it the standard amount of fat matter for its commercial description, which may be full-cream, half-cream, skim or UHT.

In France, a high-quality fresh pasteurized milk is now sold as a luxury product, and may be full-cream or half-cream. Its selection, the checks it must undergo and its special treatment give it above-average flavour.

Sterilized UHT milk is also available; the initials are for Ultra High Temperature, indicating the sterilization method employed. The milk is first homogenized and then heated by a blast of steam at 140/150 degrees centigrade for only a few seconds before it is packed. It is usually sold in waxed cartons.

Pasteurized milk is sold as 'fresh pasteurized milk', despite the French ruling that the word 'fresh' should not be used for pre-packed products. Its sell-by date is fixed at three days from 13 hours after packing. All milk may be kept for two to four days in closed containers in the refrigerator, at a temperature below 6 degrees centigrade. When opened it will keep for between one to three days in the refrigerator.

Chapter 25

Preserving by Cold

Very long ago indeed it was realized that cold keeps dead flesh from decomposing and vegetable products from rotting for a certain time. Remains of provisions have been found at the backs of caves where people of the distant Paleolithic lived, and there are even indications that once dwellings had been constructed perishable foods were stored in the cold either in natural caverns or in holes dug in the ground, a practice still current in tropical and equatorial zones. Wells have made excellent larders. Northern races, well served by their environment, used ice to store food they had caught by fishing and hunting. This method was and still is used by mountain dwellers, as we saw above with the Peruvian freeze-drying of potatoes.

Fish from the Rhine, the North Sea and the Baltic were surrounded with ice as soon as they were caught and sent off to the markets of ancient Rome, still packed round with ice under layers of insulating furs. Convoys brought blocks of ice or compacted snow to Rome even in winter, and they were buried so that they would keep. Nero gave his guests a mixture of fruits crushed with snow and honey, the first recorded sorbet. Seneca was always reproaching his fellow citizens for the expense and trouble they went to for iced desserts, even though Hippocrates had disapproved of chilled drinks, which he thought 'generate fluxes of the stomach'.

However, the Chinese may be credited with inventing a device to make sorbets and ice cream. They poured a mixture of snow and saltpetre over the exteriors of containers filled with syrup, for, in the same way as salt raises the boiling-point of water, it lowers the freezing-point to below zero. It is said that Marco Polo observed the practice and brought it home to Italy, traditionally a country that specializes in making ices. But all manner of things are said of Marco Polo. Alexandre Dumas, in his *Dictionnaire de cuisine*, tells us that during the meetings at Nice between François I, the Emperor Charles V and Pope Paul III (formerly Alessandro

Farnese, the married Pope) the King of France's doctor was 'much surprised to see the wine cooled with ice from the mountains near that town'.

François I's daughter-in-law, Catherine de Medici, brought the fashion for sorbets to France. It soon spread from privileged tables to the middle classes when coffee houses became popular in the eighteenth century, and the ingenious Italian Procope made ice cream one of his café's specialities. Others followed his example. The word *sorbet* is from Italian *sorbetto*, itself borrowed from Turkish *chorbêt* which is from Arabic *charâb*, properly speaking a fruit drink, or sherbet; 'syrup' is derived from the same word. At the end of the eighteenth century ice cream was made at home, in those households that owned an ice-cream maker, and Menon gives some recipes which are still very good.

Until the end of the nineteenth century ice sent down from the mountains during winter was stored in ice houses, and there was a large ice depot in Paris which gave its name to the rue de la Glacière just beyond the Maine gate. The ice stored in this way was natural ice until, eventually, industrial civilization provided ice that could be made at will.

The refrigerator, a machine which works by absorption or compression and creates a cold temperature in totally insulated areas where perishable foods such as milk and meat will keep in perfect condition for some time, had two fathers. Both Ferdinand Carré (1824–1900) and Charles Tellier (1828–1913) were engineers. Carré was the first to develop a machine which could make ice cubes. He showed it at the Great Exhibition in London in 1859 (an event which set a fashion for large exhibitions, which were extremely useful in encouraging technological progress).

Less than 20 years later, in 1876, Charles Tellier wagered that he could send a leg of mutton across the Atlantic Ocean. At this time the crossing still took three and a half months. He fitted out a ship, renamed it the *Frigorifique*, a word newly coined for the occasion (and now the French for 'refrigerator'), filled it with meat frozen by his new method, and sent it off to Buenos Aires. The meat arrived in perfect condition. The Argentines, whose pampas were thick with herds of cattle, saw this as their chance to do what they anticipated would be a thriving trade with Europe. But it was Tellier's rival, Carré, who obtained Argentine aid to fit out another ship, the *Paraguay*. It crossed the Atlantic in the other direction and landed at Le Havre with 80 tonnes of meat frozen at −30 degrees centigrade. Argentina's fortune was made, and so were Tellier's and Carré's.

It was another 50 years, however, before the technique of freezing was completely mastered. Freezing vegetable foods 'cooked' them in the same way as naturally frozen vegetable matter, which decays when it thaws out. The freezing of the time was not the deep-freezing or quick-freezing of today, and the problem seemed insuperable. The flavour and appearance of frozen foods, even meat, were not entirely satisfactory. They seemed flabby, as if they had been dehydrated, and collapsed as soon as they returned to normal temperatures; their cells had burst under the pressure of the water in them which expanded as it froze. Thawed meat had a spongy texture, and was no good for roasting.

This drawback did nothing for the gastronomic reputation of frozen food in France (and every true Frenchman considers himself a gastronome). It was not until 1929 that an American, Clarence Birdseye, found the answer. Birdseye knew that the Eskimos of Labrador exposed fish and meat to the severe temperatures of their long winter, and it was in perfect condition when they thawed it out. He went to Labrador and found that the secret was in the speed with which the food froze when exposed to intense cold. Accordingly, he made a very powerful freezer which acted very fast. Quick-freezing had been invented. The United States and Sweden, always in the ván of progress, adopted the method with enthusiasm before the Second World War, the States for meat, Sweden for fish. This method of freezing meat and fish was known in France, but left people – well, cold. Suspicion lasted rather longer than it might have done but for the war: war-time has never provided a favourable climate for progress in Europe.

By the end of the 1950s life had returned to normal, and Europeans too could benefit by the improvements in freezing that had been made in America. Forty years later, when almost all families owned a refrigerator, freezers too became standard household equipment, and indispensable to food shops and restaurants.

The present boom in eating out, with school and works canteens, fast-food chains, snack bars at airports and railway stations, meals served on trains and planes, has created a whole frozen food industry providing pre-packed ready-to-cook and complete frozen meals. All this in turn means great savings on time and labour.

Freezer centres selling a wide range of frozen foods in and out of season are in every high street today. Those who have no time, talent or inclination to cook elaborate dishes can buy them frozen. There are everyday frozen dishes of reasonable price, and *de luxe* frozen dishes, often backed by some famous name in the world of cuisine, more expensive but still good value. A vast range of iced desserts and exotic dishes is also available. In France, people can often choose at home from a catalogue and have the foods delivered to their homes to go in the family freezer, which has taken over from the larder of the past.

Home freezing has become common. Country families, people with second homes in the country or relations there, and those who go to wholesale markets for bargains all freeze fruits and vegetables in season, as well as poultry, game, freshly caught fish, part-carcases of meat, and cooked dishes they have made in advance. If La Fontaine were alive now he would surely give the ant in his fable a freezer for storing earthworms.

No doubt the ant would also follow the modern trend and use a microwave oven, which works by induction and will defrost, reheat or cook food almost instantaneously and just before it is served. With all the leisure now available, perhaps the industrious ant would even learn to sing like the grasshopper.

Autres temps, autres moeurs. In the section on *Privations* at the end of his *Physiologie du goût*, Brillat-Savarin says: 'Roman financiers, who bled the known world white, your famous halls never saw those tasty jellies which delight the idle, nor those varied ices which would brave the torrid zone. How I pity you!'

Quick-Freezing

Below a certain temperature, around −2 or −5 degrees centigrade, the development and reproduction of micro-organisms slow down, whether they reproduce by division or germs. At −20 degrees the enzyme action of yeasts and moulds stops, and there is a halt to the chemical phenomenon of oxidation which causes rancidity. The progress towards a state of decomposition which, we should remember, begins at the moment of slaughter or gathering is entirely arrested, but the micro-organisms have only gone into a kind of coma and may be reactivated when the temperature rises again. Freezing is not sterilization.

Frozen foods, then, have a limited storage period, even at a temperature of −20. The period can be extended if the freezer is very powerful and functions at −30 degrees the whole time.

Storage periods depend on the particular freezer or refrigerator used:

> in the ice compartment of a one-star refrigerator (−6 degrees): 2 to 7 days;
>
> in the ice compartment of a two-star refrigerator (−12 degrees): 1 to 3 weeks.
>
> in the three or four-star frozen food compartment of a refrigerator (−18 degrees): 3 to 4 months.

Even in a domestic freezer, food cannot be kept for ever. The maximum recommended storage times for various foods are:

Blanched vegetables	12 months
Raw fruits	10 to 12 months
Joints of beef, veal and lamb	6 to 12 months
Minced beef, veal and lamb	6 to 9 months
Pork and charcuterie	4 months
Offal	4 to 6 months
Poultry	6 to 12 months
Game	12 months
White fish	4 to 6 months
Oily fish	1 to 2 months
Shellfish, molluscs and crustaceans	4 to 6 months
Cooked dishes	2 to 3 months
Baked pâtisserie	2 months
Unbaked pâtisserie	2 to 4 months
Butter and cheese	6 to 8 months
Ice cream and sorbets	1 to 2 months

These storage periods are for industrial quick-freezing, and should be decreased for ordinary domestic freezing. Freezers have zones of particularly intense cold, specified by the manufacturer.

Foods should not go into the freezer wrapped in paper or cardboard, which would insulate them, or in glass, which is breakable. There is always some evaporation, as the frost which accumulates inside the freezer shows. Food should always be wrapped in special freezer plastic or light aluminium foil.

Until 1964, in France, products preserved by the negative action of cold were legally described as *congelé*. The description *surgelé* was imposed by a law of 9 September 1964 to denote quality standards: a clean, wholesome product containing no dust or pathogenic germs, quick-frozen at −40 degrees immediately after the food has been slaughtered, caught, picked or manufactured, and kept in freezer cabinets at a permanent temperature of −14 degrees from freezing to the point of sale.

French law maintains the description *congelé* for large items such as whole quarters of animal carcases or very large fish, when freezing takes several hours for the item to reach a temperature of −18 degrees at the centre. France is the only country to operate this distinction. In other countries, including other member countries of the EC, there is only one description, 'frozen', in current use for both quick-frozen products and those which cannot freeze quite so fast.

Storage times of fresh products in the refrigerator will obviously vary with the quality and freshness of food when it goes in. They also depend on the refrigerator's being properly adjusted.

Foods of both vegetable and animal origin consist of cell tissues containing water. This water makes up the greater part of their weight and volume. A beefsteak is 74 per cent water; a salad is 90 per cent water.

If foods are exposed to a freezing temperature of between −1 and −5 degrees the water in them freezes, but only on the surface. If the food is to freeze all the way through the temperature must drop to −18 degrees. The first 'frozen' meats produced by Carré and Tellier were frozen at only −8 degrees.

However, if that threshold temperature of −18 degrees is progressively reached, the water in foods freezes slowly, forming large crystals which expand and break up the cell structure. When the food is defrosted the damage cannot be undone: serum or sap and mineral salts all drain out of it.

However, in quick-freezing (also called deep-freezing) the food is plunged into a temperature of −40 to −50 degrees which freezes it instantly, before there is time for the cellular water to form large ice crystals. The crystals remain small and the cells themselves do not lose their shape or burst. After defrosting the undamaged tissues regain their normal appearance. As the serum or sap is still inside the cells the food may be roasted or fried without loss of its substance, or hardly any more loss than if it were fresh.

Quick-freezing, which does not alter the physical structure or the flavour of food, also has the great advantage of preserving all its nutritional quality. Indeed, food quick-frozen the moment it has been picked, slaughtered or taken from the sea is considerably fresher than most of the food you will find in the market place. The purine content of frozen meat or fish is almost nil (purines are nitrogenous products of decomposition and cause allergies). Bacteria have had no time to develop. Above all, the vitamin content remains similar to the vitamin content of fresh food. Even the highly perishable vitamin C is retained. Of course the food must be eaten as soon as it is defrosted, or the whole situation has to be re-assessed.

Chapter 26

The Reassurance of Dietetics

Several times in this book, I have mentioned the principles of the School of Salerno,[1] which believed that 'Health consists in the moderate use of the air we breathe, of food and drink, activity and repose, sleep and waking, and of the passions of the soul, that use being called the diet.' The word 'diet' itself derives from Greek *diaita*, meaning 'way of life'.

The science of dietetics has existed since Hippocrates. It was basically a form of preventative medicine – 'the second part of medicine is called dietetics, which helps the sick by good health in life', said Ambroise Paré. Maunders's encyclopedia of 1848 defined dietetics as 'the science or philosophy of the diet'. In Europe today dietetics is often not so much a science as a religion, espoused with all the more fervour because it is not fully understood. It has become a fashion too, with everyone counting calories, proteins, vitamins and carbohydrates. Molière would have enjoyed the inflated terminology of the subject. Now that fasting in Lent is nothing but a historical curiosity, cholesterol and cellulite have replaced our fear of the Last Judgement.

Medieval cookery books combined recipes with dietary advice, since health depended on the proper use of food. That food, as we have seen, was divided into kinds according to the teachings of Hippocrates, most notably into 'hot' and 'cold' foods, much like the Chinese principles of *yin* and *yang*. The idea was to counter the effects of the climate by opposites, so that a diet of 'hot' foods for cold weather was high in calories and a diet of 'cold' foods for hot weather low in calories, or to correct the ill effects of the 'humours', heating anaemic temperaments or cooling plethoric dispositions, warming and cheering the melancholy, refreshing the passionate.

A French law of 25 March 1966 defined diet foods as: 'All food products not of the nature of medicinal drugs, with particular qualities relevant to human health or conforming to certain diets, or to the feeding of infants. ... These products must be clearly differentiated from ordinary foodstuffs of the same category either in their composition or in the special preparation they have undergone.' The clearest difference is usually their price. The description 'biological' sometimes given to such foods means nothing, either legally or scientifically; it is simply designed to be reassuring.

The science of nutrition did not get much attention from either scientists or the general public until the beginning of the twentieth century. The attitude of the medical profession was one of mild and amused good-will.

Even before the nineteenth century there had been research into the criteria determining life. Scientists attempted to explain the difference between inert matter and living matter, and gradually worked out the chemical composition of organic and mineral substances. It was discovered that proteins, glucids and lipids are 'alimentary principles', foods able to give us the physical and mental energy we need in order to live. The essential part played by proteins in the formation and renewal of organic tissue was established. The first scientific studies of nutrition, incidentally, were almost entirely from the physiological viewpoint. It was not until the end of the century – in France, perhaps as a result of the famine during the siege of Paris in 1870–71 – that anyone took the importance of nutrition to health seriously, or understood that inadequate diet plays a part in causing disease. Art and literature had drawn new inspiration from medieval and Gothic sources, but no one thought anything of ancient medicine, thereby dismissing the only part of it which really was still of value, its dietetics.

It was in the nineteenth century that people tried calculating human requirements in terms of calories. What exactly is a calorie? In 1842 the German physician Julius Robert von Mayer (1814–1878) set out to determine the mechanical equivalent of heat by calculating the amount of heat produced by the compression of gases. He was the first to formulate the principle of the conservation of energy, in the same way as Lavoisier had demonstrated the conservation of matter. His work was continued by such scientists as Joule, Helmotz, Sadi Carnot, and Clapeyron.

Liebig divided foods into two categories: nitrogenous substances, those 'plastic foods' he thought necessary to replace muscular tissue worn down by work; and non-nitrogenous substances, those 'respiratory foods' (carbohydrates and fats) which were turned into heat by oxidation. Following on from his work and that of Marcellin Berthelot (1827–1907), scientists discovered that ingested substances gave off heat progressively within the organism. A quantitative appraisal of the calorific value of foods could now be made.

Metabolism means the process whereby food is broken down and transformed within the organism into nutriments or simple elements which the cells can assimilate directly. It is accompanied, therefore, by liberation of the energy necessary to the automatic functioning of our bodies: the heartbeat, respiration, circulation of the blood, contractions of the stomach, peristaltic movements of the intestines, cell renewal and muscle tone. This basic metabolism (worked out on a basis of calories per square metre of cutaneous body surface per hour) varies with age, sex, climate, occupation, health and hormonal balance, including the effects of the functioning of the thyroid gland.

A calorie is the amount of heat necessary to raise the temperature of a kilo of water one degree centigrade at normal atmospheric pressure. One gram of glucids ingested liberates four calories; one gram of lipids nine calories; one gram of protids four calories. Thus a food provides more or less energy according to its richness in glucids, protids or lipids. Calories are usually worked out per 100 grams of foodstuffs to facilitate calculation.

Enzymes, or diastases, also enter into the process of metabolism. Enzymes are natural catalysts secreted by certain cells of the organism such as the salivary glands, and they are also found in a natural state in foods of animal and vegetable origin. The papaya, for instance, contains an enzyme which will pre-digest raw meat. The Africans, who have to eat meat directly it is slaughtered because of the risk of rapid putrefaction in a hot climate, wrap it in papaya leaves before they cook it. Such extremely fresh meat would normally be very tough, but wrapped in the leaves it is as tender and succulent as if it had been hung to perfection. Papain, the juice of the fruit or the leaves, is also used for gastric disorders. The mere presence of these enzymes makes them active in the breaking down of food and its assimilation in the digestive and cellular systems.

Providing energy, however, is not the only purpose of food. Early twentieth-century laboratory experiments, particularly those of T. B. Osborne and C. B. Mendel in 1909 in the United States, demonstrated that life – even in small forms of animal life – could not be maintained if the experimental subjects were given not food but only nutrients in a chemically pure state: proteins, lipids, glucids and mineral salts. Purification, like sterilization, destroys what might be described as the life principle.

Even earlier, in Java in 1901, a Dutch doctor called Ejkmann who kept chickens happened to notice some of them showing the fatal symptoms of polyneuritis seen in beri-beri, a deficiency disease found among peoples who eat only polished rice. He realized what the cause of the symptoms was, and cured his chickens by adding rice bran to their feed. What had been considered an impurity, therefore, contained a substance necessary to life. Our ancestors, who lived mainly on coarsely bolted cereals (wheat, maize and rice), had been right, although as they had no choice in the matter perhaps they did not know it.

In 1914 the Polish doctor C. Fink proved that the substance of life existed in cereal husks, although he was unable to isolate it chemically. Because of the chemically carbonaceous nature of bran, *amine* (which in fact has nothing to do with it), he suggested the name of *vitamin*.

Worldwide scientific study of the subject was unable to continue until after the end of the First World War. From 1920 onwards, work on the identification, isolation and synthesization of vitamins was a major part of nutritional physiology and biochemistry, particularly as a result of the studies of the Swiss scientist P. Karrer.

However, vitamin or protein deficiencies are not the only causes of deficiency diseases which may attack whole populations, particularly in the Third World. Between the wars people learned to recognize and combat certain diseases caused by a deficiency of inorganic nutrients: endemic goitre and anaemia, to name but two, associated respectively with iodine and iron deficiency.

In modern times intensive research on deficiency diseases has extended to other fields. Besides its increasing influence on medicine, hygiene, the economy and the social sciences (through better understanding of public health), the science of nutrition has become important in the breeding technology of agriculture, and most of all in the food industry, upon which the question of hunger in tomorrow's world largely depends.

Vitamins

Vitamins are organic substances indispensable to the functioning and regulation of the organism. The body cannot manufacture them, and has to find them in food or synthesize them from certain foods (in the case, for instance, of vitamin A or retinol). Only very small doses are required, of the order of a milligram. The same vitamin may occur in a number of foods, and the improvement in living conditions since the Second World War has caused such major deficiency diseases as scurvy and beri-beri to disappear from industrialized countries.

However, alcoholism, nicotine poisoning, peculiar diets undertaken without medical supervision, anorexia in old age and serious diseases all cause deficiencies that only a doctor can correct, after analysis or examination of the patient. The fashion for vitamin pills simply makes money for the laboratories that manufacture them. In cases of hypervitaminosis, the organism can usually eliminate the excess easily enough, but too much vitamin A may cause hypertension and too much vitamin D upsets the metabolism.

A balanced diet guarantees the necessary quantities of vitamins, although it should be remembered that vitamins are altered or destroyed by prolonged storage and by cooking, particularly the very perishable vitamin C. Twenty per cent of vitamin B1 is lost in cooking, but vitamin B2 is not affected.

Vitamins are classified as hydrosoluble (soluble in water) or liposoluble (soluble in fatty matter). The former are therefore impaired by boiling in water, in which they will dissolve, and the latter by cooking in fat.

Chronology of Dietary Progress
(first occurrences known from dated archeological evidence)

Epoch	Date	Acquisitions	Place
Lower Paleolithic			
1) Australopithicus	–2,000,000	Small game hunted; small fish caught; gathering	Africa
		Stone tools for hunting and food preparation	Africa
2) *Homo erectus* (pre-Neanderthal)	–800,000	Use of fire	Africa
	–750,000	Use of fire; cannibalism	China, Europe
	–500,000	Forest elephants hunted (traps)	Europe
		Big and medium-sized game hunted	everywhere
3) *Homo sapiens*	–430,000	An almost entirely carnivorous diet (Tautavel man)	Europe
Middle Paleolithic			
Neanderthal man	–50,000	Woolly mammoth hunted	Europe
Upper Paleolithic			
Cro-Magnon man	–40,000	Woolly mammoth hunted	North America
	–30,000	Oven (hole with hot stones)	Europe
	–27,000	Clay oven	Czechoslovakia
	–21,000	Gazelle and deer exploited	Sinai
		Sheep exploited	Maghreb
	–15,000	Bison hunted	North America
		(Extinct) horse hunted	North America
	–12,000	Selective exploitation of reindeer	France (Dordogne)
		Domestication of the dog	Switzerland, Ukraine, Turkey
	–11,000	First mills to grind grain, first baskets	North America
		Sheep reared	Iran
		Sunflowers	North America
		Millet gathered	North America
	–10,000	Hunting with bows	Europe
		Root vegetables grown	New Guinea
		Earthenware vessels	Japan

Epoch	Date	Acquisitions	Place
		Wild grapes gathered	Southern Europe
		First non-brittle wheat	Jericho (Near East)
Mesolithic			
	−9000	Domestication of the goat	Persia
	−8000	Stone sickle (cereals harvested)	France (Dordogne)
		Representations of the mother goddess; decline of hunting (masculine)	Middle East Europe
		Maize grown	Mexico
		Haricot beans grown	Mexico
		Gourds grown	Mexico
	−7800	Proto-culture of cereals (barley, wheat)	Near East and Mas-d'Azil
	−7500	Broad beans grown	Central America, Thailand
	−7000	Domestication of the aurochs	Greece, Near East
		Settlement in areas where wild cereals grew	Near East
		The date palm cultivated	Sumeria
		Proto-culture of barley, peas and lentils	Far East, Europe
		Appearance of the hoe	Middle East
	−6000	Olives exploited, oil pressed	Near East
		Domestication of the dog, goat and sheep	Mediterranean Europe
		Fruit-juice strainers used in lake-dwellers' villages	Switzerland
		Gradual change from gathering to farming	Northern hemisphere
		Gradual change from hunting to stock-breeding	Northern hemisphere
		Cherries, cherry wine	Turkey
		Beer brewed	Turkey
		Pottery made	Turkey
		Shellfish gathered	North America
Neolithic			
	−5000	Farms established, wheat grown	Europe
		Cereal-thickened beer made	Babylonia
		Domestication of the wild boar (pig)	Italy

Epoch	Date	Acquisitions	Place
		Mills to grind grain	Mexico
		Domestication of the ox	Middle East, Maghreb, Near East
		Selective methods of stock-breeding	Sumeria
	−4500	Viticulture, wine-making	Near East, Sumeria, Egypt
		Dairy produce, butter, cheese	Near East
	−4000	Millet grown	China
		Quinces grown	Babylon, Near East
		Maize grown	Peru
		Beer brewed	Egypt
		Chickens reared	India, Pakistan
		Rye eaten	France (Provence)
		Decoys used in catching fowl	North America
		Wild 'rice' gathered	North America
		Pine kernels eaten (oil and pulp)	North America
		Wild hyacinth bulbs eaten	North America
		Domestication of the horse	Central Asia
	−3500	Potatoes grown	Peru
		First farm accounts	Near East
		Rice grown	Thailand
		First maritime trading	Mediterranean
		Llamas bred	Peru
	−3000	Donkeys bred	Egypt, Palestine
		Figs grown	Egypt
		Paddy fields flooded	South China
		Mead	Egypt
		Irrigated fields	Egypt, Near East
		Apricots grown	China
		Domestication of the camel	Central Asia
		Deep-sea fishing	Crete
		Draught animals used in ploughing	Egypt
		Vines cultivated	Crete, Greece
		Metal ploughshare	Near East
		Bees kept in hives	Egypt
		Domestication of the buffalo	Thailand
	−2500	First agricultural legislation	Sumeria

761

Epoch	Date	Acquisitions	Place
		Onions grown	Chaldea
		Gourds grown	Peru
		Streams dammed for fish	Canada
		Domestication of the duck and goose	Egypt, Near East
		Domestication of the yak	Tibet
		Melons grown	Sudan, East Africa
	−2000	Millet grown	Mauritania
		Barley grown	Central Europe
		Whales hunted	North America
	−1500	Vegetable gardens on drained marshes	Mexico
		Potatoes grown	Mexico, Central America
		Domestication of the goose	Germany
		Domestication of the pigeon	Greece
		Soya beans grown	North China
	−1200	Sugar mentioned in the *Ramayana*	India
		Method of deep-frying	Egypt
		Maize, haricot beans and gourds grown	North America
		Citrus fruit grown	India
	−1000	Domestication of the reindeer	Europe, North Asia
		Cassava grown	Colombia, Central America
	−800	Lucerne grown	Babylonia, the Middle East
	−600	Melons grown	Egypt, Greece, Persia
		Chickens reared	Greece
	−400	Sugar cane grown	Mesopotamia
		Soft wheat grown	North China
		Rice grown	Japan
		Use of chervil	Rome
		Elks bred	Rome
		Vines cultivated	France (Provence)
	−100	Use of tea	China
		Bread raised with beer yeast	Gaul
		Oyster farming	Gaul

Epoch	Date	Acquisitions	Place
Christian Era			
	1st century	Invention of the barrel	Gaul
		Invention of the mill with vanes	Britain
		Cider commonly drunk	Gaul
	7th century	Spirits distilled	Iran
	13th century	Buckwheat grown	Europe
	1276	First official whiskey distillery	Ireland
	14th century	Rice mill	Italy (Lombardy)
	1500	Spinach grown	Europe
		Oil palm grown	Guinea
	1520	First wheat	North America
		First vineyard	North America
	1523	First maize	The Basque country, Europe
	1528	Haricot beans grown	Italy
	1550	Pumpkins grown	Europe
	1570	Turkeys reared	Europe
	1603	Jerusalem artichoke mentioned	Quebec
		Arrival of sweet peppers	The Basque country, Europe
	1610	Arrival of tea	Europe
	1660	Green peas grown	Holland, France
	1664	Arrival of coffee	France (Provence)
	1678	Champagne	France
	1750	Tomatoes grown in gardens	France, Italy
	1772	New Zealand spinach grown	Austria, England
	1776	Rabbit-catching allowed to the common people	France
	1801	Beet sugar refinery	France
	1804	Food preservation by sterilization (the Appert method)	France
	1842	Discovery of calories	Germany
	1830	Chicory developed from the endive	Belgium
	1912	Discovery of vitamins	Poland

Notes

Part I   Collecting, Gathering, Hunting

Introduction   From fire to the pot

1 The words *soup* and *supper* both in fact derive from *sop* or *sup*, the bread which mopped up the liquid in which the food was cooked. *Pottage* or *potage* – the latter spelling is still one of the French words for soup – denotes that the dish was made in a pot.

CHAPTER 1   Collecting honey

1 Claude Lévi-Strauss, *Du miel aux cendres*, Plon, Paris, 1960; English edition, *From Honey to Ashes*, trans. J. and D. Weightman, Cape, London, 1973.
2 Claude Lévi-Strauss, *Les origines des manières de table*, Plon, Paris, 1968; English edition, *The Origin of Table Manners*, trans. J. and D. Weightman, Cape, London, 1978.
3 Philippe Marcheray, *L'homme et l'abeille*, Berger-Levrault, Paris, 1979. I owe this work a great deal in these paragraphs. To quote Montaigne: 'Bees raid the flowers here and there, but the honey they make is all their own.'
4 The must of grapes was also used. Olivier de Serres recommends it for making 'very excellent preserves'.
5 Cf. Jean-Louis Flandrin and Odile Redon, in *Les livres de cuisine italiens des XIVe et XVe siècles*, Archéologia Médiévale VIII, 1981, CLUSF, Sienna. This fluctuation has been noticed, particularly in new editions of *Le viandier*, a fourteenth-century cookery book; the figures were first 3 per cent and then 18 per cent of dishes. It was to be 31 per cent in the *Livre fort excellent de cuysine* of 1555. Flandrin and Redon add: 'We must also emphasize that, if a liking for sweetness in meat dishes and sauces had been traditional, the Tuscans and the French, who had less sugar to hand than the Venetians, would have imitated the Romans of antiquity who had none at all; they would have sweetened their dishes with honey and grape sugar, both being native products of France and Italy. However, honey is seldom used in the Tuscan book and almost never in the other collections. And it is often indicated that the addition of a sweet element is optional.

From all this we get the impression that a taste for sweetness in savoury dishes did not continue unbroken from antiquity to the late Middle Ages, but was revived.'

6 Jean-Louis Flandrin, *Le goût et la nécessité ...*, Annales 2, March-April 1983, Armand Colin, Paris.

7 Petronius playfully described poetry as *mellitos verborum glovulus* (a spoken sweetmeat). *Globula* were small, puffed-up honey-cakes, a kind of little choux pastry. The image is even more comical in Latin, particularly when applied to pretentious and puffed-up bad verse.

8 Virgil, *Georgics*, Book IV, trans. C. Day Lewis.

9 Philippe Marcheray, op. cit.

10 Mexican honey is made by bees of European stock. It is cheap because labour is cheap in Mexico. Like all honey from tropical countries, it is very strong.

11 This varnish was one of the secrets of the violin makers of Cremona.

12 Martine Chauney, *Le pain d'épice de Dijon*, Christiane Benneton Éditions, 1978.

13 Op. cit.

14 Claude Lévi-Strauss, op. cit.

15 Adopted into the Christian calendar as All Saints' Day, or Hallowe'en.

16 A. Maurizio, *Die Geschiechte unserer Pflanzennahrung von den Urzeiten bis zur Gegenwart*, Berlin, 1927; French edition, *Histoire de l'alimentation végétale*, Payot, Paris, 1932.

CHAPTER 2   The history of gathering

1 In *La comédie humaine*, Balzac echoed the belief that food influenced procreation. 'Seafood makes girls, butcher's meat makes boys.' As we shall see, fish was long regarded as a 'cold' food suitable for fast days, like plant foods.

2 Claude Meillassoux, *Fermes, greniers et capiteaux*, F. M. Fondation, Paris, 1982.

3 See M. Détienne, 'La Cuisine de Pythagore', *Archives de sociologie des religions*, No. 29, 1970.

4 The poet Horace recommends broad beans with pickled pork: 'O quando faba, Pythagorae cognata, simulque / Uncta satis pingui possentur oluscula lardo!'

5 The Greek and Roman jars brought up from shipwrecks by divers along the coasts of the Aegean Sea are usually filled with lentils, broad beans or peas. Jars found in the Gulf of Lions were filled with wine, and those found off Spain with oil, thus showing us the tendencies of trade.

6 Audiger, *La maison réglée*, Paris, 1692.

7 K. C. Balderston, *The Collected Letters of Oliver Goldsmith*, Cambridge, 1928.

8 Cf. Jean Servier, *L'homme et l'invisible*, Robert Laffont, Paris, 1964.

9 Taillevent, *Le viandier*, 1393.

10 The colorado beetle, the scourge of the potato, is thus of American origin. However, it was American vines that allowed European vineyards to recover after they had been ravaged by phylloxera. The phylloxera louse did not recognize them.

11 Maize.

12 A kind of *nuoc man* analogous to Graeco-Roman *garum*, and made at the same period as that condiment. See below, in the chapter on fish.

13 Gemelli Careri, *Giro del monde*, 1693–9.

14 Josette Lyon, *Les aliments*, Ramsay, Paris, 1978.

15 World production of mushrooms in 1970 was 131 million tonnes.

16 He also wrote a *Georgics*, now lost, upon which Virgil may have drawn.

17 'The Chinese dislike carrots because of their lack of flavour, but may sometimes add them to a dish for the sake of their attractive colour', according to Françoise Sabban in *La cuisine en Chine*, Annales No. 2, Colin, Paris, 1983.

18 In 1983 a Yugoslav newspaper, *Politika*, published a posthumous manuscript by a former sailor, Aristide Vinceti, setting out to prove that Odysseus, driven off course, came not to the Tunisian coast but the Yugoslav islands of the Adriatic. Thus the country of the Lotophagi 'who eat a flowery food' would be around Dubrovnik, where the lotus *Lotus ziziphus* grows in abundance. Its edible fruit used to be considered a delicacy in that locality.

19 As we shall see, there is no evidence that maize was unknown in the Old World before Columbus.

20 The recipe was brought to the Caribbean by slaves from that part of Africa, along with the Dahomeyan cult of voodoo.

21 The wild, bitter cassava is thought to be indigenous.

22 Jacques Barrau, *Les hommes et leurs aliments*, Temps actuels, 1983.

23 Cf. Guy Thuillier, *La vie quotidiene dans les ministères au XIXe siècle*, Hachette, Paris, 1976: 'There is the office of the Alsatians, which smells of sauerkraut, and the office of the Provençals, which smells of garlic.'

CHAPTER 3   Hunting

1 As literature and the press in communist countries used the word 'worker'.

2 *Elephas antiquus* left Europe after the last, Würmian, Ice Age, to settle in India, where it has lived ever since.

3 Sigmund Freud, *Totem and Taboo*, Collected Works, Vol. XIII, trans. and ed. J. Strachey, London, 1953, pp. 140–6.

4 Erich Hobusch, *Histoire de la chasse*, Pygmalion, Paris, 1980.

5 Caesar, *The Gallic War*, trans. H. J. Edwards, Book VI, 28.

6 Pliny, *Natural History*, Book VIII.

7 Alfred Gottschalk, *Histoire de l'alimentation et de la gastronomie*, Hippocrate, Paris, 1948.

Part II   Stock-breeding, Arable Farming: Meat, Milk, Cereals

Introduction   The evidence of occupied sites

1 From Greek *pleistos*, most, and *kainos*, new, and much that was new was indeed seen on the planet during this period, the longest division of the Quaternary era in which we are still living. The Pleistocene period corresponds to the Stone Age, or Paleolithic.

2 From Greek *holos*, all, and *kainos*, new. Everything is new. Everthing has changed.

CHAPTER 4   The history of meat

1 As opposed to woman.
2 F. Zenner, *The History of Domesticated Animals*, Hutchinson, 1963.
3 Once homage had been paid, those officiating at the ceremony feasted. This first cooking method may be seen as the ancestor of the barbecue, a word derived from Spanish *barbacoa*, which itself comes from Haitian *barbacòa*, a wooden frame on posts.
4 Uno Harva, *Les représentations religieuses des peuples altaïques*, Paris, 1959.
5 A fast also had to be observed on the eve of the other great festivals of the Church which entailed carousing: there was fasting in Advent, and in Provence the festive Christmas Eve supper is still a meal at which fish, fruit and vegetables are eaten. During the 30 days (one lunar month) of Ramadan, Muslims observe a complete fast from sunrise to sunset.
6 Juvenal, *Extravagance and Simplicity of Living*, Satire XI.
7 F. Sacchetti, *Il trecento novelle* (No. 107); French translation by several hands, ed. O. Redon and J. Brunet, Presses Universitaires de Saint-Denis, 1984.
8 As a French rhyme has it: 'S'il me fallait les vendre, j'aimerais mieux me pendre' (If I had to sell them, I'd rather hang myself).
9 Only the master butcher and perhaps his son or son-in-law, those most likely to succeed him, had the right to wear the *devanteau*, an apron with a purse in the front of it.
10 Roger Chartier and Hugues Neveu, 'La Ville dominante et soumise', in *Histoire de la France urbaine*, Vol. 3, Editions du Seuil, Paris, 1981.
11 R. Chartier and H. Neveu, *op. cit*. In the Aude and Quercy regions, prominent personages were called *ventres d'or*, 'bellies of gold', because of the gold watch-chains they wore across their ample paunches.
12 The modern Frenchman requires 90 kilos of meat a year, to the despair of dieticians. The 1900 figures, 58.5 kilos, of which 31.2 were pork and 27.3 were beef, would be a healthier amount.
13 Emmanuel Le Roy Ladurie, 'Baroques et Lumières', in *Histoire de la France urbaine*, Vol. 3, Editions du Seuil, Paris, 1981.
14 Robert Faivreau, 'La boucherie au Poitou, à la fin du Moyen Âge', in *Bulletin philologique et historique*, 1968. Transactions of the 93rd Congress of Tours, Bibliothèque Nationale, Paris, 1971.
15 Honoré Roux, Seigneur de Lamanon and d'Aurons, was certainly the biggest stock-breeder in Provence in 1494.

CHAPTER 5   The history of dairy produce

1 Jean-Louis Flandrin and Odile Redon (op. cit.) have noted a chapter relating to curds in the *Platine en fransoys*, a French translation of Platina's *De honesta voluptate*. The 1475 French version was the first printed cookery book. 'In spring or in summer curds should be eaten at the first table, and before any other dish, so that they be not harmful, as at other times ... for they corrupt and putrefy easily, or draw down to themselves such meat as they find to be badly cooked.'
2 Pierre Charbonnier, 'L'alimentation d'un seigneur auvergnat au début du XVe siècle', in

Bulletin philologique et historique. Proceedings of the Congress of Tours, 1968, Bibliothèque National, Paris, 1971.

3 In Italy, 'if you had to eat old, strong cheese, you were advised to do so at the end of your meal, not just because of the heat engendered by the cheese but because it was believed to "seal the stomach, compress and restrain food as by a press, bring the food low down to mature and curb those fumes which rise to the brain". Today, salty and strong-smelling cheese is served towards the end of the meal, and the English even eat it after sweet dishes and desserts.' (J.-L. Flandrin and Odile Redon, op. cit.)

4 Marc Bloch, 'Les aliments des Français', in *Encyclopédie française*, Vol. XIV, 45–7.

5 Jean-Louis Flandrin, 'Le goût et la nécessité: sur l'usage des graisses dans les cuisines d'Europe occidentale (XIVe et XVIIe siècle)', in *Annales No. 2*, Armand Colin, Paris, March-April 1983.

6 We may note that in Spanish lard and all such rendered fats are termed *manteca*, whereas butter is *mantequilla*, 'little fat'.

7 Op. cit.

8 Jean Bruyerin Champier, doctor to King François I of France, recalls that since the days of antiquity 'the fact is that butter is almost absent from the food of Narbonese Gaul, since oil is so abundant there' (*De re cibaria*, Nuremberg, 1659).

9 Butter is a valuable source of vitamins, containing vitamin A for growth, vitamin D which combats rickets, and vitamin E, necessary for fertility.

CHAPTER 6   The history of cereals

1 Abbé Guillaume Raynal (1713–96), *Historie philosophique et politique des établissements et du commerce des Européens dans les deux Indes*, Paris, 1770. The Abbé was a curious character who attacked the colonizers who brought 'civilization', the missionaries, the Inquisition and the clergy in general all alike.

2 Cf. A. Aaronsohn, 'Contributions à l'historie des céréales', in *Bulletin de la société bontanique*, 1909.

3 N. I. Vavilov, 'The Origin, Variation, Immunity and Breeding of Cultivated Plants', in *Chronica botanica*, Vol. 13, 1949–50.

4 D. Zohary, 'The Progenitors of Wheat and Barley in Relation to Domestication and Agricultural Dispersal in the Old World', in *The Domestication and Exploitation of Plants and Animals*, ed. Ucko and Dimbleby, London, 1960, pp. 47–67.

5 Plato, *The Republic*, II, 372 b.

6 Ceres to the Romans. Other Latin equivalents to the Greek names of these deities are: Cronos – Saturn; Poseidon – Neptune; Zeus – Jupiter; Persephone – Proserpina; Dionysos – Bacchus; Hades – Pluto; Hermes – Mercury.

7 Hippolyte Taine, *Origines de la France contemporaine*, Paris, 1875–93.

8 Olivier de Serres, op. cit.

9 Claude Hohl, 'Alimentation à l'Hôtel-Dieu de Paris', in *Bulletin philologique et historique*, 1968: 'Pour une histoire de l'alimentations', Vol. I, p. 187, Paris, 1971.

10 *Chapeler* meant to cut bread in large slices or 'trenchers', used as plates on which other food was served.

11 Op. cit.

12 Hubert Collin, 'Ressources alimentaires en Lorraine', in *Bulletin philologique et historique*, op. cit., pp. 33–6.

13 *Le ménagier de Paris*, op. cit.

14 Marc Block, 'Les aliments de l'Ancienne France', in *Bulletin philologique et historique*, op. cit., pp. 232–3.

15 Piero Camporesi, *Le pain sauvage*, Éditions Le Chemin Vert, Paris, 1981.

16 Fernand Braudel, *La Méditerranée et le monde méditerranéen à l'époque de Philippe II*, Paris, 1966, pp. 532–50.

17 Andrea Metra, 'Il mentore perfette de negozianti', 1797, p. 75, quoted by F. Braudel in *Civilisation matérielle, économie et capitalisme (XVe–XVIIIe siècle)*, Armand Colin, Paris, 1979.

18 Op. cit.

19 *Almanach historique de Marseille pour l'année de grâce 1782*, published by Jean Mossy, Marseilles, 1782.

20 Cf. André Maurois, *Histoire d'Angleterre*, Fayard, Paris, 1937.

21 One bushel = 8 gallons = 36.35 litres, i.e., about 3 bushels to the hectolitre.

22 Bernard Assinwi, *Recettes typiques des Indiens*, Éditions Le Meac, Ottawa, 1972.

23 Fernand Braudel, *Civilisation matérielle, économie et capitalisme (XVe–XVIIIe siècle)*, vol. 1: *Les structures du quotidien*, Armand Colin CNL, Paris, 1979, English version; *Civilization and Capitalism 15–18th Century*, vol. 1: *The Structures of Everyday Life*, translation revised by Sîan Reynolds, Collins, London, 1981.

24 Régis Huc, *L'empire chinois*, 2 vols., Paris 1854. English version, *The Chinese Empire*, 2 vols., London 1855.

25 Op. cit.

26 *Le chant du riz pilé*, collection of writings by Vietnamese authors, Éditeurs français réunis, Paris, 1974.

27 The *Cronica* (from 1168 to 1288) of Fra Ognibene de Guido d'Adamo Salimbene (1221–1300) is a most valuable source for thirteenth-century Italian history.

28 Quiqueran de Beaujeu, *De laudibus Provinciae*, Paris, 1555. French version: *La Provence louée*, Lyons, 1614.

29 Modern Canadian maize is the result of hybridization which allows the plant to survive in the harsh Canadian climate.

30 Miguel Angel Asturias, *Les hommes de maïs*, André Martel, Paris, 1953.

31 Cf. Carl Ortwin Sauer, *Agricultural Origins and Dispersal*.

32 Possibly from Spanish *pella agra*, 'rough skin'.

33 Iowa, Illinois, Indiana, Ohio, Missouri, Nebraska, Kansas, South Dakota and Minnesota.

34 Ping Ti-Ho, 'The Introduction of American Food Plants into China', in *American Anthropologist*, 1955, No. 37.

35 'Gilgamesh', in *Myths from Mesopotamia*, translated with an Introduction and Notes by Stephanie Dally, Oxford, 1989.

36 Op. cit.

37 Léo Moulin, 'Bière et cervoise', *Bulletin de l'Académie royale de la langue et de la littérature françaises*, Vol. LIX, pp. 111–48.

38 Léo Moulin, *La vie quotidienne des religieux au Moyen Âge (Xe-XVe siècle)*, Hachette, Paris, 1978.

39 Luc Ullus, *Coutumes culinaires du pays de Liège*, Nathan Labor, Liège, 1981.

40 Philiber Schmitz, *Histoire de l'ordre de Saint-Benoît*, Éditions de Maredsons, 1942. Quoted by Léo Moulin.

41 The Abbé Tichon, in *Revue Wallonia*, Liège.

42 There is also the Southern French word *fougasse*, which applies to a similar cake.

43 Le Grand d'Aussy, *La vie privée des François*, Paris, 1783.

44 Ortensio Landi, *Delle piu notabili e monstruose cose d'Italia*, printed at Piacenza in 1553.

45 Quoted by Dr Gottschalk, op. cit.

46 Fernand Lequenne, *Le livre des boissons*, Robert Morel, Forcalquier, 1970.

Part III   The Three Sacramental Foods: Oil, Bread, Wine
Introduction   The fundamental trinity

1 'Let your table be healthy, let luxury be banished from it', says No. XIX of the *Golden Verses* ascribed to Pythagoras.

2 Jean-François Revel, *Festins en paroles*, Pauvert, Paris, 1979.

3 Jean-François Revel, op. cit.

CHAPTER 7   The history of oil

1 Guy Fourquin, *Histoire économique de l'Occident médiéval*, Armand Colin, Collection U, Paris, 1979.

2 Hugues Neveu, *Histoire de la France rurale*, Vol. I, Part 1, Éditions du Seuil, Paris, 1975.

3 Frédéric Mistral, *Trésor du félibrige*, Édition du centenaire, Flammarion, Paris, 1932.

4 Louis Stouffe, *Ravitaillement et alimentation aux XIVe et XVe siècles*, Éditions Mouton, Paris, 1970.

5 The temple raised to Erechtheus, the mythical first king of Athens and father of Cecrops. It contains the famous porch of the Caryatids. Erysichthon, the grandson of Erechtheus, offended Demeter and was punished with insatiable hunger. He died from eating himself, and so surely deserves a place in a history of food.

6 Frédéric Mistral, *Calendal*, Chant I, Alphonse Lemerre, Paris, 1887.

7 Anselme Mathieu, *La farandoulo*, Roumanille, Avignon, 1868; also in *Anthologie du félibrige provençal*, Delagrave, Paris, 1920.

8 Different olive varieties.

9 Also contained in egg yolk.

CHAPTER 8   The history of bread and cakes

1 Gregory of Tours, *Historia Francorum*, III, 15.

2 Josette Lyon, *Les aliments*, Ramsay, Paris, 1978.

3 Hubert Collin, 'Ressources alimentaires en Loraine', in *Bulletin philologique et historique*, 1968, vol. 1.

4 Hubert Collin, op. cit.

5 Bruyerin-Champier, *Le recibaria*, Lyons, 1560.

6 Quoted in Jeannine Grinbert, *Je veux savoir ce que je mange*, Le Pavillon, Paris.

CHAPTER 9   The history of wine

1 Charles Baudelaire, 'Le vin des amants', in *Le vin*, La Taille douce éditions, Paris, 1947.

2 Maurice Constantin-Weyer, *L'âme du vin*, Rieder, Paris, 1932.

3 Plato, *Laws*, II.

4 Aristotle, *Meteorologica*, I, 14.

5 Lorenzo de Medici, 'the Magnificent', *Simposio*, Olschki, Florence, 1966.

6 Plato, *The Symposium*, trans. W. Hamilton, Penguin Classics, Harmondsworth, 1951.

7 Now in the Museo degli Argenti in Florence.

8 Jérôme Carcopino, *La vie quotidienne à Rome sous l'Empire*, Hachette, Paris, 1939. English version, *Daily Life in Ancient Rome*, Penguin, Harmondsworth, 1978.

9 Horace, *Odes*, Book I, 37.

10 Ovid, *Ars Amatoria*, Part I.

11 Pliny, *Natural History*, XIV, 137.

12 Cicero, *De republica*, II.

13 Claude Royer, *Les vignerons*, Berger-Levrault, Paris, 1980.

14 Jean Watelet, *Histoire du compagnonnage*, Éditions Famot, Geneva, 1982.

15 La Varenne, *Le cuisinier françois*, 1651, new edition in the Bibliothèque bleue, ed. J.-L. Flandrin and M. and P. Hyman, Montalba, Paris, 1983.

16 Op. cit.

17 Desmond Seward, *Monks and Wine*, Mitchell Beazley, London, 1979.

18 Desmond Seward, op. cit.

19 Maurice Constantin-Weyer, op. cit.

20 Charles Parain, 'Voies et formes de la différenciation dans les vignobles du nord-est de la France', in *Arts et traditions populaires*, 1968, 3–4.

21 Guy Fourquin, 'Le temps de la connaissance', in *Histoire de la France rurale*, ed. Georges Duby, Éditions du Seuil, Paris, 1975.

Part IV   The Economy of the Markets
Introduction   The centre of the city

1 Martial, *Epigrams*, XII, 8: 'Rome, goddess of the earth and of nations, that has no peer and no second.'

2 Petronius, *Satyricon*, 119.

CHAPTER 10   The history of fish

1 Rabelais speaks of 'Master Belly, first master of arts in the world' (*Pantagruel*, Book IV, Chapter LVII).

2 Apuleius, *Apologia*.

3 The present writer owns the exclusive right to catch salmon in the Dronne, a small French river which flows near Brantôme in Périgord; the right is attached to the possession of a fief now reduced to a few hectares of heathland and a ruined manor house. But anyway it is a long time since there were any salmon to be caught in the Dronne.

4 Leviticus, 11.

5 Paul Charbonnier, 'Alimentation d'un seigneur auvergnat', in *Bulletin philologique et historique*, 1968, Vol. 1.

6 Quoted by Hubert Collin, 'Ressources alimentaires en Lorraine', in *Bulletin philologique et historique*, 1968, Vol. 1.

7 Massimo Montanari, 'Valeurs, symboles, messages alimentaires durant le haut Moyen Âge', in *Médiévales*, No. 5 (*Nourritures*), PUV, Saint Denis, 1983.

8 Jean-François Bergier, *Une histoire du sel*, Office du Livre, Fribourg, 1982.

9 In Taillevent's *Viandier* (the Vatican manuscript) the *'balaine'* features among sea fish – in fact among flat fish, with the plaice and the sole.

10 In *Moby Dick* Herman Melville mentions cheese made with whale's milk found in the whaling ports of America, but I have found no definite confirmation of this. If true, the milk must have come from harpooned whales. Melville also reminds us that Benjamin Franklin was related through his maternal line to a famous family of English harpooners, the Folgers.

11 Cf. J.-F. Bergier, op. cit.

12 Éditions Masson, Paris, 1981.

13 Scottish salmon is slightly sweetened before being smoked.

14 Françoise Sabban, 'Cuisine à la cour de l'empereur de Chine au XIVᵉ siècle', *Médiévales*, No. 5, Saint-Denis, 1983.

CHAPTER 11   The history of poultry

1 The Bibliothèque Mazarine manuscript of the *Thrésor de santé* says that 'Chickens are castrated at two and a half or three months old, at full moon, when they are beginning to approach the size of hens, throughout the summer until autumn, and if the winter is very hard until the end of December.'

2 Abbé Jacques Delille (1738–1813), *Paradis perdu*, VII.

3 Because of the high value as fertilizer of the droppings from the dovecotes.

4 Jean Favier, *Philippe le Bel*, Fayard, Paris, 1978.

5 Charles Estienne, *L'agriculture et la maison rustique*, Paris, 1564.

6 Françoise Sabban, 'La cuisine en Chine', *Annales*, No. 2, Colin, Paris, 1982.

7 Alain Chapel, *La cuisine, c'est beaucoup plus que des recettes*, Laffont, Paris, 1980.

8 Charles Dickens, *A Christmas Carol*, London, 1843.

9 Alphonse Daudet, *Les lettres de mon moulin*, Bibliothèque Charpentier-Fasquelle, new edition.

10 Vitus Dröscher, *Le sens mystérieux des animaux*, Laffont, Paris, 1965.

11 Arnold Van Gennep, *Manuel de folklore français*, Vol. I, VI, Picard, Paris, 1949.

12 Horace, *Satires*, Book II, iv.

13 J. Babinski, psuedonym Ali-Bab, *La gastronomie pratique*, Paris, 1907.

Part V   Luxury Foods
Introduction   The revels of the Gauls

1 Ausonius, *Parentalia*, IV.
2 Régine Pernoud, *Les Gaulois*, Seuil, 1961.
3 Ausonius, *Cento Nuptialis*, II.
4 Ausonius, *Ephemeris*, VI.
5 Henri Queffélec, *Saint Antoine du désert*, Hachette, Paris, 1950.
6 Not St Anthony himself, but another monk; Anthony was Aeduan.

CHAPTER 12   Treasures from the sea

1 Jean Markale, *Les Celtes et la civilisation celtique*, Payot, Paris, 1967. English version, *Celtic Civilization*, London, 1978.
2 Jean-François Revel, *Un festin en paroles*, Pauvert, Paris, 1979.
3 Jean-François Revel, op. cit.
4 Albert Cohen, *Belle du Seigneur*, Gallimard, Paris, 1968.
5 Rabelais, *Gargantua*, Book 1.
6 Quiqueran de Beaujeu, *De laudibus Provinciae*, Paris, 1555. French version: *La Provence Louée*, Lyons, 1614.
7 Diplomatic relations were restored in 1925.
8 Simone de Beauvoir, *Pour une morale de l'ambiguïté*, Gallimard, Paris, 1947. English version, *The Ethics of Ambiguity*, tr. B. Frechman, New York, 1967.
9 Strabo, *Geography*, IV, 1–8.
10 Pliny, *De Muciane*, 32–62.
11 Ausonius, *Epistolae* V and XV.
12 Bordeaux.
13 Sidonius Appollinaris, *Epitrae* VIII, 12 and 7, texts collected by Dom Bouquet, *Rerum gallicarum et franciarum Scriptores*, 1869.
14 Charles de Marguetec de Saint-Denys de Saint-Evremont, 1614–1703, polemicist, essayist and historian, a wit and a Frondist, author among other works of *La comédie des académistes*. Exiled by Louis XIV.

CHAPTER 13   The treasure of the forests

1 Joseph Bédier, *Le roman de Tristan et Iseult*, Paris, 1958.
2 The Celtic word for a clearing, *ialos*, is found in the names of modern French towns ending in -euil: Argenteuil, Nanteuil, Mareuil. The villages from which these towns arose were situated in such clearings.
3 Camille Jullian, *Historie de la Gaule*, Hachette, Paris, 1907.
4 Caesar, *The Gallic War*, Book V, XIX.
5 Camille Jullian, op. cit.
6 Buffon, *Oeuvres complètes*, Vol. 3, Dufour, Mulet et Boulanger, Paris, 1856.
7 Henriette Dussourt, *Les secrets des fermes au coeur de la France*, Berger-Levrault, Paris, 1982.

8 Annette Pourrat, *Traditions d'Auvergne*, Marabout, Verviers, 1976.

9 The *blanc* of Paris was a silver coin of the time of Philippe de Valois.

10 Georges Chaudieu, *De la gigue d'ours au hamburger*, La Corpo, Paris, 1980.

11 Pharaohs of the Fifth Dynasty. The Pyramids, both royal tombs and storehouses of vast treasures, were managed by a high officer of state, while a priest saw to their religious upkeep.

12 Cf. M. Viandier, *Manuel d'archéologie égyptienne*, T.V. 2, Paris, 1969.

13 Cato, *De agri cultura*, Ch. LXXXIX.

14 Columella, *De re rustica*, Book III, Ch. XIII.

15 Palladius, *De re rustica*, Book I, Ch. XXX.

16 Pliny the Elder, *De natura rerum*, Book X, Ch. XXVI.

17 Juvenal, *Satire V*.

18 Horace, *Satire VII*.

19 The quinces of the period were about the size of a modern apricot.

20 *Bulletin de la Société historique et archéologique du Périgord*, 1916, Vol. 43, p. 199.

21 Eustache Deschamps fought the English fiercely both on the battlefield and with his pen. He died *c.* 1406.

22 Diviners have also been called in, with remarkably encouraging results.

Part VI   The Era of the Merchants
Introduction   Making a good profit

1 Anon., *Blandin de Cornouailles*, Turin MS, from the modern French translation by P. Meyer in *Romania* II–170–202.

2 Cf. Le Goff, 'The Town as Agent of Civilization', in *The Fontana Economic History of Europe*, ed. C. Cipolla, Collins, London & Glasgow, 1972.

3 Robert Delors, *La vie au Moyen Âge*, Points-Historie, Éditions du Seuil, Paris, 1982.

4 The *hanses*, which were really guilds, were initially groups intended to operate abroad, limiting the number of participants in commerce on the large scale so as to obtain a kind of monopoly and run a system of financial assistance similar to a cooperative.

The Paris *hanse*, which became very powerful, met from 1289 onwards in an *hôtel* near Saint-Pol, the 'Parloir aux bourgeois'. Besides operating a closed shop, the organization was also a parallel high court, an informal city council, a commodities exchange, and an intermediary between the people of Paris and the king. In fact the *hanse* may be regarded as an early form of Mafia. It succeeded in reducing or even abolishing tolls and improving navigational conditions, but with its associates (brokers and agents, inspectors and other trade officials) it received commissions on many transactions, most notably on deals involving the wine trade, and these went into a bribery fund.

The German Hanseatic League, on the other hand, which dated from the thirteenth century, was more of a political and economic association of several cities in the region of Hamburg. Hamburg still proudly proclaims itself to be a Hanseatic port, and cars registered in the city bear the initials HH, for Hansestadt Hamburg, on their number-plates.

5 Cf. Achille Luchaire, 'Philippe Auguste et son temps', in *L'historie de France*, ed. Ernest Laune, Vol. III, Taillandier-Hachette, 1982 (reprint).

6 Carrack derives from Arab. *karakir*, meaning a light ship.

CHAPTER 14   An essential food

1 We should not forget the practice of preserving vegetables in brine either; it goes back to very ancient times. Choucroute or *Sauerkraut*, chopped cabbage preserved in casks of brine, was a basic part of the diet of the Germanic and Central European peoples very long ago. Salted 'herbs' enabled the first American colonists to eat greens all through the winter. Even today the cookery of French-speaking Canada, which has many practices surviving from old French methods, makes much use of herbs, cabbage, cucumbers and green beans preserved between layers of salt in large earthenware pots (Melvin Galland and Marielle Bondreau, *Le guide de la cuisine traditionnelle acadienne*, Stanké, Montreal).

2 It is sometimes thought, incorrectly, that sea salt is not available in the Arctic. There is a reasonably thick film of salt on the surface of the pack ice, which of course consists of frozen sea water; physical phenomena have brought this salt to the top. Moreover, in the long run sleigh dogs get the pads of their paws rubbed sore and then wounded by the salt. It has been observed that when they lick this salty crust on the ice it is not because they are thirsty and want refreshment, but to replace salt they have lost through the expenditure of energy. The Eskimos – those of Baffin Island, for instance – scrape this salt up to provide themselves with a supply for the summer, when hunting and fishing are easy. They can thus salt flesh which will freeze naturally in winter temperatures.

3 Jean-François Bergier, *Une historie du sel*, Office du livre, Fribourg, 1982.

4 The Dead Sea contains almost ten times more salt than the oceans: 275 grams per litre.

5 Sea salt treated with sulphuric acid (vitriol) gives off hydrochloric acid, which is saturated with water, for which it has a great affinity. The first chlorine factories were at Javel near Paris, whence the name of the disinfectant bleach *eau de Javel*.

6 The process consisted of heating sea salt treated by sulphuric acid with ground chalk and charcoal. Then the Belgian scientist Solvay found an easier way to make soda from a reaction of ammonia with salt mixed with limestone.

7 Julius Ceasar, *The Gallic War*, Book 1, 31.

8 Cf. J.-F. Bergier, op. cit.

9 Guy Fourquin, *Historie économique de l'Occident médiéval*, Armand Colin, collection U., Paris, 1979.

CHAPTER 15   Spice at any price

1 And not of Fort-de-France in Martinique, as stated in *Le grand livre des produits exotiques* (Jean Suyeux), Sycomore, Paris, 1980.

2 Édit. Migne PL, Vol. 82, col. 620.

3 Apicius, *Ars Magirica*, text copied at the end of the fifth century, ed. J. André, Les Belles-Lettres, Budé, Paris, 1974.

4 Shallots, wrongly said to have been brought to Europe by the Crusaders.

5 Aldebrandin of Sienna, *Régime des corps*, Landouzy, R. Pépin, Paris, 1911.

6 Françoise Sabban, *Cuisine à la cour de l'empereur de Chine au XIVe siècle*, in *Médiévales*, C.R.U. Paris VII, Saint-Denis, 1983.

7 Marianne Mulon, 'Deux traités d'art culinaire médiéval', in *Bulletin philologique et historique*, 1968.

8 Pliny, *Natural History*.

9 Dioscorides, *Materia medica*. A copy of his manuscript, the Codex Vindobonensis of AD 512, was illustrated with excellent watercolours. It is in the Bildarchiv der Österreichischen Nationalbibliothek, Vienna.

10 Giotto Dainelli, *Marco Polo*, Denoël, Paris, 1946.

11 Bruno Laurioux, 'De l'usage des épices dans l'alimentation médiévale', in *Médiévales*, C.R.U. Paris VIII, Saint-Denis, 1983.

12 Éliane Comelade, *La cuisine catalane*, Lanore, Paris, 1983.

13 At the beginning of his reign the Sultan Soleiman the Magnificent had been persuaded by the Venetians, who of course were Christians but were furious to see the spice trade of the Mediterranean escape them, to mount an expedition against their Portuguese rivals. It proved disastrous. Turkish caravans transported the exotic merchandise from ports in the south of Arabia, and Soleiman abandoned his naïve hopes of a monopoly of the seas.

14 The Sultan of Malacca, Baabullah of Timor, dispossessed by the Portuguese in the sixteenth century, had appealed to the Dutch for aid, hoping to be restored to his lands. (Thierry Alberny, *Les origines du conflit post-colonial; la guerre à Timor*, memoir of the D.E.A., Paris I, Sorbonne, 1977.

15 Philippe and Mary Hyman, 'Connaissez-vous le poivre long?' *L'histoire*, No. 24, 6/80.

16 Jérôme Carcopino, *À Rome à l'apogée de l'Empire*, Hachette, Paris, 1939.

17 The *denarius* was worth four *sestertii* in the time of Caesar. Cf. Pierre Grimal, *La civilisation romaine*, Arthaud, Paris, 1960.

18 Pliny, *Natural History*, Book XII.

19 Pegolotti, *Pratica della mercatura* (1340), Evans, Cambridge (Mass.), 1936.

20 *De observatore ciborum*, ed. E. Liechtenhan, in *Corpus medicorum latinorum*, VIII, I, Berlin, 1928.

21 Nostradamus, *Des confitures*, 1555, re-issued Olivier Orban, Paris, 1981.

22 Lucien Guyot, *Les épices*, P.U.F., Paris, 1972.

23 Athenaeus, *Deipnosophistai*, Book II, 68, ed. A. M. Desrousseaux, Les Belles-Lettres, Paris, 1956.

24 In the case of France, in 15.55 per cent of recipes in the *Viandier* and 14.79 per cent of those in the *Ménagier*; in the case of England, in 7.21 per cent of recipes in the *Form of cury* and 22.11 per cent of those in *Ancient Cookery* (B. Laurioux's figures).

25 Camoens, *La Lusiade*, trans. Duperron de Castera, Paris, 1735.

26 Léonce Peillard (rendering in modern French, with notes), *Premier voyage autour du monde* (of Magellan), by Antonio Pigafetta, 10/18, Paris, 1964.

27 Jean-Louis Flandrin, preface to the *Cuisinier françois*, op. cit.

28 Ibid.

29 Today nutmeg is used in the 'ecstasy' pill, a hallucinatory drug which also contains amphetamines and sassafras oil.

30 Menon, *La cuisinière bourgeoise*, op. cit.

31 Fuchs gave his name to the fuchsia, a flower native to America.

32 A Provençal proverb says, 'Red as a November *pébroun*'.

33 Pierre Prigent, *Dictionnaire des symboles*, Seghers, Paris, 1973.

34 15 grams.

35 Large stuffing balls cooked on the spit with the fowls.

36 Jacques Soustelle, *La vie quotidienne des Aztèques*, Hachette, 1955.

37 Celandine is very efficacious applied to warts, and was also a remedy for liver troubles because of its yellow juice. The followers of Paracelcus used it in a curious way. Placed on the head of a sick person, it made him weep if he was going to get better and sing if he was going to die, or so at least they said. In any case, celandine is poisonous ingested in large dosages.

38 Monique Mosser, 'Le souper grec de Mme Vigée-Lebrun', in *Le dix-huitième siècle. Aliments et cuisine*, Éditions Garnier, 1983.

39 Alfred Franklin, *La vie privée d'autrefois, du XIIe au XVIIIe siècle*, Vol. III, 'La cuisine' and Vol. VI, 'Les repas', Paris, 1888 and 1889.

40 Claude Lévi-Strauss, *The Origin of Table Manners*, trans. J. and D. Weightman, Cape, London, 1978.

41 Marc Bloch, 'Aspects de la mentalité médiévale', in *Mélanges historiques*, Vol. II, Paris, 1963.

42 Brillat-Savarin, *La physiologie du goût*, reissued Champs-Flammarion, Paris, 1982. English edition, *The Philosopher in the Kitchen*, trans. Anne Drayton, Penguin Books, Harmondsworth, 1970.

43 Aldebrandin of Sienna, op. cit., and new edition, Slatkin, Geneva, 1978.

44 By a fortunate coincidence poultry born in spring or early summer is just right for eating in winter.

45 *Le roman de la Rose*, English quotation from translation attributed to Chaucer, *The Romaunt of the Rose*.

46 Legrand d'Aussy, *Histoire de la vie privée des Français*, Paris, 1825, Vol. III, p. 353.

Part VII   New Needs: Sugar, Chocolate, Coffee, Tea

CHAPTER 16   The lure of sugar

1 Lucan, *Pharsalia*.

CHAPTER 17   Confectionery and preserves

1 Cf. Nostradamus, *Des confitures*, Olivier Orban, Paris, 1981.

CHAPTER 19   Coffee and politics

1 Louis Figuier, *Le savant au foyer*, Hachette, Paris, 1867.

Part VIII   Orchards and Kitchen Gardens
Introduction   Instructions for the garden

1 François Lacroix du Maine (1552–1592), a bibliographer killed for his Protestant convictions.
2 Louis Figuier, *Vie des savants illustres de la Renaissance*, Librairie Internationale, Paris, 1868.
3 26 titles in the seventeenth century, 1200 in the eighteenth.
4 The proportion of the active population working in the fields was 80 to 90 per cent, laboriously providing the nation's diet and the larger part of its taxes. Most of the peasants were still using the techniques of the year 1000, such as the wooden plough, and barely 50 per cent of arable soil was under cultivation.
5 Pierre Chaunu, *La civilisation de l'Europe classique*, Arthaud, Paris, 1970.
6 Dedication to La Quintinie of *L'abrégé de la culture des arbres nains*, by Maître Laurent, a notary of Caen (1673).
7 Umberto Eco, *The Name of the Rose*, Secker and Warburg, London, 1983.
8 Bacon spoke of 'the Georgics of the mind' (*The Advancement of Learning*, Book II, 1605), comparing the mind to land that had to be transformed by learning and truth into a fertile garden. Bacon, who had asked Elizabeth I, in vain, to set up a botanic garden, thus using a good collection of plants to promote scientific research into nature ('Solomon's House', in *The New Atlantis*, 1627), was a forerunner of Diderot and his *Interpretation de la nature* of 1753. Diderot dedicated the great undertaking of the *Encyclopédie* to Bacon.
9 Dezallier d'Argenville, *Voyage pittoresque des environs de Paris*, 1770.
10 In grand houses, fruit was peeled in the kitchens before it was served at table with its own skin neatly put back in place. These fruits, nibbled to stimulate appetite, were 'the *hors-d'oeuvre* at the King's court', La Quintinie explains.
11 The 'Admirables' were pears; the 'Nivitz' (*nivettes*) a variety of peach.
12 Jean-Baptiste de La Quintinie, *Instructions pour les jardins fruitiers et potagers*, 1690, English translation by John Evelyn, 1693, entitled *The Compleat Gard'ner*. From the chapter on 'How necessary it is for a Gentleman, who designs to have Fruit and Kitchen-Gardens, to be at least reasonably Instructed in what relates to those kind of Gardens.'

CHAPTER 21   The tradition of fruits

1 Francis Bacon, *Essays*, 1597.
2 No doubt an elixir of youth or a potion promising immortality.
3 Cato, *De agricultura*, 143, 3.
4 Pliny, *Natural History*, 15–42. He also speaks of a *prunum amygdalum*, a plum-almond, which is difficult to imagine, and must have been a chimera in the true sense of the word.
5 Apicius, *Ars Magirica*, IV, 4, this recipe from the French translation by Jacques André, Les Belles-Lettres, Paris, 1974.

NOTES

6 Luke 1, xv.

7 It was usual to present fruits on a bed of vine leaves, to set off their colour, and itinerant fruiterers or *regrattières* offered them arranged in this way on a wicker tray, the *noquet*, wrapped in a knotted napkin and hanging from their shoulders by straps.

8 Virgil, *Eclogues*, Ninth Eclogue.

9 Maguelonne Toussaint-Samat, *Récits des châteaux de la Loire*, Nathan, Paris, 1971.

10 Jacques André, *Lexique des termes botaniques en Latin*, Klinksiek, Paris, 1949.

11 In Book II (50) of the *Deipnosophistai*, Athenaeus tells us:

> *Damsons*: many old writers mention the great and famous city of Damascus. Now in the territory of the Damascenes there is a very large quantity of the so-called cuckoo-apples (*kokkumelon*), cultivated with great skill. Hence this fruit gets the special name of 'damson', excelling the same kind grown in other countries. These, then, are plums, mentioned, among others, by Hipponax: 'They wore a chaplet of plums and mint.'

> He adds that the Sicilians, like Theocritus of Syracuse, called plums *brabilon*, finding that apples were sweeter. In his *Glossary*, Seleucus describes them as laxative fruits which 'expel food'.

12 André Castelot, *Les grandes heures des cités et châteaux de la Loire*, Librarie académique Perrin, Paris, 1962.

13 Merlet, *L'abrégé des bons fruits*, 1665.

14 A little more than eight metres.

15 This was the corymb. The description of cherrystones is slightly surprising.

16 P. Livius Larensis was a great landowner of the time (the third century AD) who employed Athenaeus as his librarian. He stands for the Roman gentleman of the time.

17 In 73 BC.

18 The Black Sea.

19 A Greek, a citizen of Ephesus.

20 A well-known writer on hygiene.

21 Duchesne, *Histoire naturelle du fraisier*, 1760.

22 Pliny, *Natural History*, 19–67.

23 Quoted by René Jouveau, *La cuisine provençale de tradition populaire*, Béné, Nîmes and Aix-en-Provence, 1976.

24 The medieval sellers of *aigrun*, vinegary substances of any kind, sold lemons and other sharp-flavoured juicy fruits.

25 Pliny, *Natural History*.

26 Virgil, *Georgics*, II, 126.

27 In 1747 one Dr Lend, a ship's doctor, was the first to discover the efficacy of orange juice in preventing scurvy. He gave half of the affected sailors two oranges a day, cured them, and compared this success with the serious condition of the rest of the crew.

28 Genesis 3, vii.

29 Apicius, *Ars Magirica* I, 1, and III, 3: 'Ad digestionem et inflationem et ne laetucae laedant.' (An aid to digestion and a preventative of flatulence, so that lettuce will not harm you.)

CHAPTER 22   The evolution of vegetables

1 Pliny, *Natural History*, XXI, 91.
2 Nicolas de Bonnefons comments, in his *Délices de la campagne*: 'A cabbage soup should taste of nothing but cabbage, a leek soup of leeks, and so on.'
3 Horace, *Satires*, II, ii, 117.
4 Cato, *De agricultura*, CLVI, CLVII.
5 Apicius, *Ars Magirica*, Book III, 9.
6 The smell is considerably less if one takes the precaution of cooking the cabbage in two changes of water, and putting a piece of bread in the second water.
7 J.-L. Poiret, *Histoire philosophique, littéraire et économique des plantes d'Europe*, Paris, 1829.
8 Maguelonne Toussaint-Samat, *Gastronomie et fastes culinaires à la cour sforzesque et chez les bourgeois de Milan, au milieu du xvᵉ siècle* (Proceedings of the Nice Conference, 'Boire et manger au Moyen Âge', 1982, Bulletin du Centre d'études médiévales de la faculté des lettres et sciences humaines, Nice, 1984). Cf. Reggirato: *Cicaloto in lode dell' insolata*.
9 Pliny (*Natural History*, XIX, 58) tells us that 'those products of the garden were most in favour which needed no fire for cooking and saved fuel, and which were a resource in store and always ready, whence their name of *acetaria*.' *Acetaria*, 'vinegared' plants, were the ancestors of our salads. They were also seasoned with garum and oil, cumin and lentisk berries, according to Apicius (Book III, 16, on 'herbs raw and cooled').
10 Le Roux de Lincy, *Proverbes*, Vol. II, p. 126.
11 Juvenal, *Satires*, XI, 68.
12 Jehane Benoît, *Ma cuisine maison*, Éditions de l'Homme, Montreal, 1979.
13 Jean-Paul Aron, *Essai sur la sensibilité alimentaire à Paris au XIXᵉ siècle*, Annales, Armand Colin, Paris, 1967, and *Le mangeur du XIXᵉ siècle*, Laffont, Paris, 1973.
14 Grimond de La Reynière, *Almanach des gourmands*, Paris, 1810.
15 Op. cit., *Miscellanea*, 15.
16 J.-P. Aron, op. cit.
17 Brillat-Savarin, *Almanach des gourmands*, Paris, 1803.

CHAPTER 23   The potato revolution

1 Mercier, *Tableau de Paris*, Vol. IV, Amsterdam, 1782–8.
2 Virgil, *Eclogues*, I, 81.
3 F. Pomponi and F. Ettori, *Corse*, Christiane Bonneton, 1981.
4 The Peruvian calendar for 1580 now in the Museum of the University of Pennsylvania calls December the month of potato-planting (*labrador des papas*). They were lifted in June.
5 The extra ascorbic acid means that ready-to-use potato purées are sometimes inadvisable for very small children because of its stimulating effect.

Part IX   Science and Conscience in the Diet
Introduction   The hows and whys of quality

1 Jean-François Revel, *Un festin en paroles*, Pauvert, Paris, 1981.
2 Antonin Carême, *L'art de la cuisine française*, 3 vols, 1847. New edition Kerangué et Pollès, Paris, 1981.
3 Grimod de La Reynière, *Écrits gastronomiques. Almanach des gourmands*, Paris, 1803.
4 J.-F. Revel, op. cit.
5 Brillat-Savarin, *The Philosopher in the Kitchen*, trans. Anne Drayton, Penguin Books, Harmondsworth, 1970.

CHAPTER 24   Preserving by heat

1 Op. cit. (Meditation 27: Philosophical history of cooking).
2 Lucretius (98–55 BC), *De natura rerum*.
3 Anton van Leeuwenhoeck, *Opera omnia seu arcana naturae*, 1722.
4 Gay-Lussac, memorandum to the Institut of 3 December 1810.
5 Columella, *De re rustica*, 8, 17, 12; Juvenal, *Satires*, 14, 132.

CHAPTER 26   The assurance of dietetics

1 Dr Martin, *L'école de Salerne mise en vers burlesques*, Herrault, Paris, 1694.

Bibliography

I have given references to or quotations from various works in the course of this book, and for reasons of space I think those sources need not be listed again here.

A really exhaustive bibliography, which could never be complete, might daunt the reader, so I give only a list of works of real quality where anyone who is interested may find plenty of information on the fascinating subject of food. I recommend them for their clear presentation of general and particular data. I have omitted from my list publications now so old that they have become obsolete. The absence of references to German, Spanish, Dutch and Russian works is no reflection on their content or quality, but an admission of my lack of proficiency in the languages concerned.

However, I will mention the excellent Italian monthly journal *La Gola*, published in Milan. It contains extremely interesting articles on food, and publishes a highly relevant Italian bibliography every month.

Books or special issues of journals

M. Apfelbaum, L. Perlemuter, P. Niclos, C. Forat and M. Begon, *Dictionnaire pratique de la nutrition*, Masson, Paris, 1981.

J. André, *L'alimentation et la cuisine à Rome*, Les Belles-Lettres, Paris, 1981.

P. Androuet, *Un fromage pour chaque jour*, Éd. de Verfèvre, Paris, 1981.

M. Arnott, *Gastronomy: the Anthropology of Food Habits*, Mouton, La Haye, 1976.

J.-P. Aron, *Essai sur la sensibilité alimentaire à Paris au XIXe siècle*, Cahier des Annales, A. Colin, Paris, 1967.

BIBLIOGRAPHY

J.-P. Aron, *Le mangeur du XIXᵉ siècle*, Denoël-Gonthier, Paris, 1976.

J.-F. Bergier, *Une histoire du sel*, Office du Livre, Lausanne, 1984.

K. Birket-Smith, *The Origin of Maize Cultivation*, Munksgaard, Copenhagen, 1943.

G. and G. Blond, *Histoire pittoresque de notre alimentation*, Fayard, Paris, 1960.

D. Bois, *Les plantes alimentaires chez tous les peuples et à travers les âges*, 2 vols, Lechevalier, Paris, 1927–28.

A. Bourgaux, *Quatre siècles d'histoire du cacao et du chocolat*, Office international du cacao et du chocolat, Brussels, 1935.

F. Braudel, *Civilisation matérielle, économie et capitalisme XVᵉ-XVIIIᵉ siècle*, Vol. 1, *Les structures du quotidien, le possible et l'impossible*, A. Colin, Paris, 1979.

E. Briffault, *Paris à table*, J. Hetzel, Paris, 1846

G. Chaudieu, *De la gigue d'ours au hamburger*, La Corpo, Paris, 1971.

M. Chauney, *Une tradition, le pain d'épice de Dijon*, C. Bonneton, Paris, 1978.

C. and L. Clergeaud, *Mystères et secrets du soja*, La Vie claire, CEVIC, Paris, 1964.

C. and J. Craplet, *Dictionnaire des aliments et de la nutrition*, Le Hameau, Paris, 1979.

R. Dion, *Histoire de la vigne et du vin en France, des origines au XIXᵉ siècle*, R. Dion, Paris, 1959.

G. Duby, *Guerriers et paysans*, Bibliothèque des histoires, Gallimard, Paris, 1973.

G. Duby, *Le Moyen Âge*, Skira, Geneva, 1984.

G. Duby and A. Wallan (eds), *Histoire de la France rurale*, Éd. du Seuil, Paris, 1978.

G. Duby and A. Wallan (eds), *Histoire de la France urbaine*, Éd. du Seuil, Paris, 1981.

H. Dupin, *L'alimentation des Français*, ESF, Paris, 1978.

P. Farb and G. Armelagos, *Anthropologie des coutumes alimentaires*, Denoël, Paris, 1980.

A. Farge, *Le vol d'aliments à Paris au XVIIIᵉ siècle*, Plon, Paris, 1975.

B. Faÿ, *L'aventure coloniale*, Librairie académique Perrin, Paris, 1962.

D. M. Forrest, *Tea for the British: a Social and Economic History of a Famous Trade*, Chatto & Windus, London, 1967.

F. Forster and O. Ranum, *Food and Drink in History*, Johns Hopkins University Press, Baltimore, 1979 [selection of articles from *Annales: économies, sociétés et civilisations*].

T. B. Franklin, *A History of Agriculture*, G. Bell, London, 1948.

J. Goody, *Cuisine, cuisines et classes*, Centre de création industrielle (Beaubourg), Paris, 1984.

A.-G. Haudricourt and L. Hédin, *L'homme et les plantes cultivées*, Gallimard, Paris, 1943.

J.-J. Hémardinquer, *Pour une histoire de l'alimentation* (Cahier des Annales, 28), A. Colin, Paris, 1970.

L'Histoire (journal). Collective issue: *5,000 ans de gastrononomie*, No. 86, Paris, 1986.

Hobusch, *Histoire de la chasse*, Pygmalion, Paris, 1984.

H.-E. Jacob, *Six Thousand Years of Bread: its Holy and Unholy History*, Doubleday, Garden City, NY, 1944.

H.-E. Jacob, *L'épopée du café*, Éd. du Seuil, Paris, 1953.

B. Ketcham-Wheaton, *L'office et la bouche*, Calmann-Lévy, Paris, 1985.

F. Lequenne, *Le livre des salades*, Morel, Forcalquier, 1968.

BIBLIOGRAPHY

F. Lequenne, *Le livre des boissons*, Morel, Forcalquier, 1970.

J. Lyon, *Les aliments*, Encyclopédie des connaissances, Paris, 1979.

Manger et boire au Moyen Âge, proceedings of the Nice conference of 15–17 October 1982, Nos. 27 and 28, vols 1 and 2. Centre d'études médiévales de la faculté des lettres et sciences humaines de Nice, Les Belles-Lettres, Nice, 1984.

G. Martin, *Négriers et bois d'ébène*, Arthaud, Grenoble, 1934.

G. Martin, *Histoire de l'esclavage dans les colonies françaises*, PUF, Paris, 1948.

Médiévales, Nourritures, journal of the PUV, Saint-Denis, 1983.

M. Miquel, *Quand le bon roi René était en Provence*, Fayard, Paris, 1979.

M. Mollat, *Le rôle du sel dans l'histoire*, Recherches, PUF, Paris, 1968.

H. A. Monckton, *A History of English Ale and Beer*, Bodley Head, London, 1966.

L. Moulin, *Bière, houblon et cervoise*, Académie royale de langue et de littérature françaises, Vol. LIX, No. 2, Brussels.

L. Moulin, *La vie quotidienne des religieux au Moyen Âge*, Hachette, Paris, 1978.

L. Moulin, *L'Europe à table*, Elsevier-Séquoia, Paris, 1975.

M. Mourre, *Dictionnaire encyclopédique d'histoire* (8 vols), Bordas, Paris, 1978, revised edition 1986.

M. Parisse, *Les nonnes au Moyen Âge*, C. Bonneton, Paris 1978.

A. Pigafetta, *Premier voyage autour du monde par Magellan*, 10/18, Paris, 1964.

J. A. Reeds, *The Grocery Trade: its History and Romance* (2 vols), Duckworth, London, 1910.

Y. Renouard, *Les hommes d'affaires italiens du Moyen Âge*, A. Colin, Paris, 1970.

J.-F. Revel, *Un festin en paroles: histoire littéraire de la sensibilité gastronomique de l'Antiquité à nos jours*, Pauvert, Paris, 1979.

J.-P. Roux, *Les Barbares*, Bordas, Paris, 1983.

C. Royer, *Les vignerons*, Berger-Levrault, Paris, 1983.

M. Sahlin, *Âge de pierre, âge d'abondance*, Bibliothèque des sciences humaines, Gallimard, Paris, 1976.

J. Saillenpest, *Le soja, sa culture et sa civilisation*, Montsouris-Rustica, Paris, 1944.

R. N. Salaman, *The History and Social Influence of the Potato*, Cambridge University Press, Cambridge, 1949.

L. Stouff, *Ravitaillement et alimentation en Provence aux XIVe et XVe siècles*, Mouton, Paris, 1970.

J. Suyeux, *Le grand livre des produits et de la cuisine exotiques*, Le Sycomore, Paris, 1980.

R. Tannahill, *Food in History*, Eyre Methuen, London, 1973.

F.-J. Temple, *Célébration du maïs*, Morel, Forcalquier, 1963.

A. Van Gennep, *Manuel du folklore français. Cérémonies périodiques cycliques*, Vol. 1, III, Picard, Paris, 1947.

C. A. Wilson, *Food and Drink in Britain*, Constable, London, 1973.

J. Wynne-Tyson, *Food for a Future: the Ecological Priority of a Human Diet*, Davis-Pointer, London, 1975.

F. E. Zeuner, *A History of Domesticated Animals*, Hutchinson, London, 1963.

Articles

J.-P. Aron, 'Biologie et alimentation au XVIIIe siècle et au début du XIXe siècle', *Annales ESC* 16 (1961), pp. 971–7.

M. Aymard, 'Pour l'histoire de l'alimentation: quelques remarques de méthode', *Annales ESC* 30 (1975), pp. 431–44.

R. Barthes, 'Pour une psycho-sociologie de l'alimentation contemporaine', *Annales ESC* 16 (1961, pp. 977–86.

B. B. Bennassar and J. Goy, 'Contribution à l'histoire de la consommation alimentaire du XIVe au XIXe siècle', *Annales ESC* 30 (1975), pp. 402–30.

J.-C. Bonnet, 'Le réseau culinaire dans l'*Encyclopédie*', *Annales ESC* 31 (1976), pp. 891–914.

F. Braudel, 'Alimentation et catégories de l'histoire', *Annales ESC* 16 (1961), pp. 723–8.

F. Braudel, 'Vie matérielle et comportement biologique', *Annales ESC* 16 (1961), pp. 545–9.

K. H. Connell, 'The potato in Ireland', *Past and Present* 23 (1962), pp. 57–71.

P. Courie, 'L'alimentation au XVIIe siècle: les marchés de pourvoirie', *Annales ESC* 19 (1964), pp. 467–79.

H. Dennis-Jones, 'Zones of cuisine', *Geographical Magazine* 45 (Oct 1972), p. 19.

R. Doehord, 'Un paradoxe géographique: Laon, capitale du vin au XIIe siècle', *Annales ESC* 5 (1950), pp. 145–65.

H. Enjalbert, 'Comment naissent les grands crus', *Annales ESC* 8 (1953), pp. 315–28, 457–74.

L. Febvre, 'Vignes, vins et vignerons', *Annales ESC* 2 (1947), pp. 281–7.

A. Girard, 'Le triomphe de *La cuisine bourgeoise*, livres culinaires, cuisines et société en France aux XVIIe et XVIIIe siècles', *Revue d'histoire moderne et contemporaine* 24 (1977), pp. 497–523.

V. M. Godinho, 'Le Portugal, les flottes du sucre et les flottes de l'or', *Annales ESC* 5 (1950), pp. 184–97.

J.-J. Hémardinquer, 'Essai de cartes des graisses de cuisine en France', *Annales ESC* 16 (1961), pp. 747–71.

J.-J. Hémardinquer, 'À propos de l'alimentation des marins', *Annales ESC* 18 (1963), pp. 1141–50.

J.-J. Hémardinquer, 'Faut-il *démythifier* le porc familial de l'Ancien Régime?', *Annales ESC* 25 (1970), pp. 1745–66.

E. S. Higgs, 'Les origines de la domestication', *La Recherche* 16 (April 1976), pp. 308–15.

P. Hurtubise, 'La table d'un cardinal de la Renaissance ...', *Mélanges de l'école française de Rome*, 92/1 (1980), pp. 249–82.

A. Lebigre, 'La grande boucherie (XIIe–XIXe siècle)', *L'Histoire* 17 (Nov 1979), pp. 41–9.

J. Leclant, 'Le café et les cafés à Paris (1644–1693)', *Annales ESC* 6 (1951), pp. 1–14.

H. A. Monckton, 'English ale and beer in Shakespeare's time', *History Today* 17 (1967), pp. 828–34.

M. Morineau, 'La pomme de terre au XVIIIe siècle', *Annales ESC* 25 (1970), pp. 1767–84.

H. Neveux, 'L'alimentation du XIVe siècle au XVIIIe: essai d'une mise au point', *Revue d'histoire économique et sociale* 51 (1973), pp. 336–79.

M. Rouche, 'La faim à l'époque carolingienne: essai sur quelques types de rations alimentaires', *Revue historique* 250 (1973), pp. 295–320.

M. Rodinson, 'Recherches sur les documents arabes relatifs à la cuisine', *Études islamiques* (1949 and 1950), pp. 116–60.

D. Sinclair, 'How France saved its vineyards from the destroyer', *The Times* (26 July 1975), p. 12.

M. Sorro, 'La géographie de l'alimentation', *Annales de géographie* 61 (1952), pp. 184–99.

T. Stoianovitch, 'Le maïs', *Annales ESC* 6 (1951), pp. 190–3.

T. Stoianovitch, 'Le maïs dans les Balkans', *Annales ESC* 21 (1966), pp. 1026–40.

L. Stouff, 'La viande: ravitaillement et consommation à Carpentras au XVe siècle', *Annales ESC* 24 (1969), pp. 1431–48.

Y. Verdier, 'Pour une ethnologie culinaire', *L'Homme* 9 (1969), pp. 49–59.

Index

Note: Numerals in bold type indicate a main entry.

INDEX

INDEX

INDEX

INDEX